HUMAN RIGHTS LAW

In this completely revised and updated second edition of *Human Rights Law*, the judicial interpretation and application of the United Kingdom's Human Rights Act 1998 is comprehensively examined and analysed. Part I concerns key procedural issues including: the background to the Act; the relationship between UK courts and the European Court of Human Rights; the definition of victim and public authority; determining incompatibility including deference and proportionality; the impact of the Act on primary legislation; and damages and other remedies for the violation of Convention rights.

In Part II of the book, the Convention rights as interpreted and applied by UK courts, are discussed in detail. All important Convention rights are included with a new chapter on freedom of thought, conscience and religion. Other Convention rights considered in the national context include: the right to life; freedom from torture; the right to liberty; fair trial; the right to private life, family life and home; the right to peaceful enjoyment of possessions; and the right to freedom from discrimination in the enjoyment of Convention rights.

The second edition of *Human Rights Law* will be invaluable for those teaching, studying and practising in the areas of United Kingdom human rights law, constitutional law and administrative law.

Human Rights Law

Second Edition

Merris Amos

·HART·
PUBLISHING

OXFORD AND PORTLAND, OREGON
2014

Published in the United Kingdom by Hart Publishing Ltd
16C Worcester Place, Oxford, OX1 2JW
Telephone: +44 (0)1865 517530
Fax: +44 (0)1865 510710
E-mail: mail@hartpub.co.uk
Website: http://www.hartpub.co.uk

Published in North America (US and Canada) by
Hart Publishing
c/o International Specialized Book Services
920 NE 58th Avenue, Suite 300
Portland, OR 97213-3786
USA
Tel: +1 503 287 3093 or toll-free: (1) 800 944 6190
Fax: +1 503 280 8832
E-mail: orders@isbs.com
Website: http://www.isbs.com

British Library Cataloguing in Publication Data

Data Available

ISBN: 978-1-84946-380-5

Typeset by Forewords, Oxon
Printed and bound in Great Britain by
CPI Group (UK) Ltd, Croydon CR0 4YY

Contents

Table of Cases   xxv
Table of National Legislation   lxxv
Table of International and European Instruments   lxxxv

PART I: THE HUMAN RIGHTS ACT   **1**

1   Background and Interpretation   3

2   The Benefit and Burden of the Human Rights Act   31

3   The 'Acts' to which the Human Rights Act Applies   59

4   Determining Incompatibility   83

5   The Defence of Primary Legislation   113

6   Remedies   147

PART II THE CONVENTION RIGHTS   **179**

7   Article 2: The Right to Life   181

8   Article 3: Prohibition of Torture and Inhuman or Degrading Treatment or Punishment   227

9   Article 5: The Right to Liberty and Security   269

10   Article 6: The Right to a Fair Trial   319

11   Article 8: The Right to Respect for Private Life   409

12   Article 8: The Right to Respect for Family Life   465

13   Article 8: The Right to Respect for Home   503

14   Article 9: Freedom of Thought, Conscience and Religion   527

15   Article 10: The Right to Freedom of Expression   549

16   Article 14: Prohibition of Discrimination   605

17   Article 1 Protocol No 1: Protection of Property   639

Index   679

Contents

Table of Cases   xxv
Table of National Legislation   lxxv
Table of International and European Instruments   lxxxv

PART I: THE HUMAN RIGHTS ACT   1

1   Background and Interpretation   3
    1. The Protection of Human Rights Prior to the Human Rights Act   3
    2. Background to the Human Rights Act   4
        2.1   The Incorporation Debate   4
        2.2   The Human Rights Bill   7
    3. Purpose of the Human Rights Act   8
    4. Structure of the Human Rights Act   10
    5. Convention Rights Given Further Effect   11
        5.1   The Nature and Scope of the Convention Rights   11
        5.2   The Impact of Other International Conventions   12
        5.3   The Convention as a 'Living Instrument'   13
        5.4   The Non-absolute Nature of the Majority of the Convention Rights   14
        5.5   Derogations and Reservations   15
    6. Principles of Interpretation   17
    7. The Relationship between UK Courts and the European Court of Human
        Rights   19
        7.1   The Current Approach   19
        7.2   Exceptions to the Current Approach   20
        7.3   Assessment of the Current Approach   23
    8. Other Aids to Interpretation   26
        8.1   Judgments in Devolution Cases   26
        8.2   Case Law and Instruments from Other Jurisdictions   27
        8.3   Reports of the Joint Committee on Human Rights   28
    9. Reform of the Human Rights Act   29

2   The Benefit and Burden of the Human Rights Act   31
    1. Introduction   31
    2. The Benefit of Convention Rights: Victims   31
        2.1   Section 7 Human Rights Act   31
        2.2   Categories of Victim   33
              2.2.1 Core Public Authorities   33
              2.2.2 Potential Victims   34
              2.2.3 Indirect Victims   34
              2.2.4 Non-nationals and Those Living Outside the United Kingdom   34
              2.2.5 Representative Bodies   35
        2.3   Loss of Victim Status   36

2.4　An *actio popularis*?　37
3.　The Burden of Convention Rights: Public Authorities　39
4.　Core Public Authorities　40
　4.1　Definition　40
　4.2　Courts and Tribunals　42
　4.3　Parliament　42
　4.4　Which Core Public Authority is Responsible?　43
　4.5　Application: Core Public Authorities　44
5.　Hybrid Public Authorities　45
　5.1　Definition　45
　5.2　Ensuring HRA Protection when Contracting Out　48
　5.3　Application: Hybrid Public Authorities　49
　　5.3.1 Enforcement of Chancel Repairs　49
　　5.3.2 Seeking Possession of a Property　50
　　5.3.3 Provision of Care and Accommodation　51
　　5.3.4 Denying Application to Participate in a Farmers' Market　53
　　5.3.5 Regulation of Membership　53
　　5.3.6 Approving Minority Buy-outs　54
6.　Private Bodies　54
　6.1　Interpreting Primary Legislation in Accordance with Section 3
　of the HRA　55
　6.2　The Development of the Common Law　56

3　The 'Acts' to which the Human Rights Act Applies　59
1.　Introduction　59
2.　Limitation Period　59
3.　Retrospective Effect　60
　3.1　Generally　60
　3.2　Criminal Proceedings　61
　3.3　Civil Proceedings　64
　3.4　The Application of Sections 3 and 4 of the Human Rights Act　65
　3.5　Section 22(4) of the Human Rights Act　67
　3.6　Getting Around the Problem of Retrospective Effect　68
　　3.6.1 Ongoing Violation of Convention Rights　68
　　3.6.2 Investigations into Deaths Occurring before 2 October 2000　69
　　3.6.3 The 'Act' Is Not Yet Complete　70
　　3.6.4 Utilising the Pre-HRA Position　70
　　3.6.5 Modified Common Law　71
4.　Acts which Occur Outside of the United Kingdom: Extra-territorial Effect　72
　4.1　Acts of Non-UK Actors　72
　4.2　Acts of UK Public Authorities　73
　　4.2.1 Jurisdiction as Defined by the European Court of Human
　　Rights　74
　　4.2.2 Exceptions to Territorial Jurisdiction　74
　　4.2.3. State Agent Authority and Control　75
　　4.2.4 Effective Control over an Area　75
　4.3　Extra-territorial Effect in Practice　76

	4.3.1	Entry Clearance	76
	4.3.2	British Diplomatic and Consular Agents	76
	4.3.3	British Armed Forces	77
4.4		The Channel Islands and the Isle of Man	78
4.5		British Overseas Territories	79
5.		Failure to Act: Positive Duties	79
6.		Satellite Litigation	80
6.1		Criminal Proceedings	80
6.2		Civil Proceedings	81

4   Determining Incompatibility   83

1.		Introduction	83
2.		Prescribed by Law	84
2.1		Generally	84
2.2		A Legal Basis in Domestic Law	85
2.3		Sufficiently Accessible and Precise	85
	2.3.1	Generally	85
	2.3.2	Retrospective Effect	87
	2.3.3	The Common Law	87
	2.3.4	Codes and Guidelines	89
2.4		Applied in a Way which is Not Arbitrary	89
3.		Necessary	90
4.		Proportionality	90
4.1		Definition	90
4.2		The Shift from *Wednesbury*	92
4.3		Merits Review?	93
5.		Deference	96
5.1		Definition	96
5.2		Expertise Rather than Democratic Credentials	98
5.3		When to Defer?	102
6.		Deference in Practice	104
6.1		Criminal Justice	104
	6.1.1	Prevention of Terrorism	104
	6.1.2	Road Traffic Offences	105
	6.1.3	Rape Complainant's Prior Sexual History	106
	6.1.4	Policing	106
	6.1.5	Sentencing	107
6.2		National Security	107
6.3		Social and Economic Policy	109
	6.3.1	State Support	109
	6.3.2	Pensions	109
	6.3.3	Housing	110
	6.3.4	Family Law	110
	6.3.5	Social Justice	111
	6.3.6	Cruelty to Animals	111
6.4		Political Decisions	112

5   The Defence of Primary Legislation   113
    1. Introduction   113
    2. Section 6(2) Human Rights Act   114
        2.1   Introduction   114
        2.2   Section 6(2)(a) Human Rights Act   115
        2.3   Section 6(2)(b) Human Rights Act   116
    3. Section 3 Human Rights Act   119
        3.1   Introduction   119
        3.2   The Nature of Section 3   120
        3.3   What Is Not Possible   121
        3.4   What Is Possible   122
        3.5   The Application of Section 3 in Hypothetical Cases   123
        3.6   The Application of Section 3 in Practice   124
              3.6.1 Criminal Justice   125
              3.6.2 Anti-terrorism Measures   126
              3.6.3 Sentencing   127
              3.6.4 Parole Board   127
              3.6.5 Coroner's Inquests   128
              3.6.6 Family Law   128
              3.6.7 Housing   129
              3.6.8 Civil Procedure   130
              3.6.9 Other   131
    4. Section 4 Human Rights Act   132
        4.1   Interpretation   132
        4.2   A Reasonable Period within which to Amend Domestic Law   134
        4.3   A Declaration where the Government already Has Plans to
              Legislate   135
        4.4   Failure to Legislate   135
        4.5   The Use of Section 4 in Hypothetical Cases   136
        4.6   Problems with the Declaration of Incompatibility   137
        4.7   The Application of Section 4 in Practice   138
              4.7.1 Criminal Justice   139
              4.7.2 Gender Reassignment   139
              4.7.3 Prevention of Terrorism   140
              4.7.4 Care Standards   140
              4.7.5 Mental Health   140
              4.7.6 Immigration   141
    5. The Use of Hansard and Other Materials in Compatibility Cases   141
    6. Section 19 Human Rights Act: Statements of Compatibility   144

6   Remedies   147
    1. Introduction   147
    2. Just and Appropriate   148
    3. Effective   149
    4. The Power to Award Damages   150
    5. Court Must Have the Power to Award Damages   152
    6. Just Satisfaction   152

6.1   Any Other Relief or Remedy Granted   153
6.2   The Consequences of Any Decision   154
6.3   Other Circumstances   155
7.   The Principles Applied by the European Court of Human Rights   156
7.1   Introduction   156
7.2   Pecuniary Damage   158
7.3   Non-pecuniary Damage   160
7.4   Exemplary Damages   162
8.   The Level of Damages   163
9.   Application: Article 2   164
10. Application: Article 3   166
11. Application: Article 5   166
11.1   Section 9(3) Human Rights Act and Article 5(5)   166
11.2   Article 5(4): Delay   167
11.3   Article 5(4): Independence and Impartiality   168
12. Application: Article 6   169
12.1   Article 6(1) Reasonable Time: Post Conviction   169
12.2   Article 6(1) Reasonable Time: Pre Conviction   170
12.3   Article 6(1): Independence and Impartiality   171
13. Application: Article 8   173
13.1   Introduction   173
13.2   Private Life—Breaches by Public Authorities   174
13.3   Private Life—Breaches by the Private Sector   176
13.4   Family Life   177
14. Application: Article 14   178

PART II: THE CONVENTION RIGHTS   **179**

7   Article 2: The Right to Life   181
1.   Introduction   181
2.   Scope   183
3.   Definition of 'Life'   184
4.   Intentional Deprivation of Life   186
5.   Positive Duty to Safeguard Life   188
5.1   Nature of the Duty   188
5.2   State Responsibility   189
5.3   Justiciability   190
5.4   Knew or Ought to Have Known   190
5.5   Real and Immediate Risk to Life   191
5.6   Reasonable Measures   193
5.7   Application   194
5.7.1 Protection of Those Whose Lives Are at Risk from the Acts
of Another   194
5.7.2 Protection of Witness Identity   195
5.7.3 Protection of Identity Generally   197
5.7.4 Protection of Those in the Care of the State   197
5.7.5 Protection of Members of the Armed Forces   200

5.8   The Relationship between Article 2 and Common Law Negligence 202
6. Duty to Investigate 204
    6.1   Nature of the Duty 204
    6.2   When Does the Duty Arise? 205
        6.2.1 Death or Life-threatening Injuries post 2 October 2000 205
        6.2.2 Link to the Substantive Obligations Imposed by Article 2 206
        6.2.3 Justiciability 208
        6.2.4 Intentional or Non-intentional Killing by an Agent of the State 209
        6.2.5 Intentional or Non-intentional Killing by a Non-state Agent 210
        6.2.6 Exculpating Factors 211
    6.3   Form of the Investigation 211
        6.3.1 Authorities Must Act of their Own Motion 212
        6.3.2 Investigation Must Be Effective 212
        6.3.3 Independence 214
        6.3.4 Public Scrutiny 215
        6.3.5 Involvement of Next of Kin 216
        6.3.6 Outcome of the Investigation 217
    6.4   Application 219
        6.4.1 Deaths in Custody 219
        6.4.2 Near Deaths in Custody 221
        6.4.3 Deaths in Hospital 222
        6.4.4 Death Involving the Police 223
        6.4.5 Death Involving the Armed Forces 223
        6.4.6 Death of Member of the Armed Forces 224
        6.4.7 Death of Vulnerable Adult 224
7. Exceptions 225

8 Article 3: Prohibition of Torture and Inhuman or Degrading Treatment or Punishment 227
1. Introduction 227
2. Severity of Ill-treatment 228
3. Negative and Positive Duties 230
    3.1   Distinguishing Negative from Positive 230
    3.2   Positive Duty 232
        3.2.1 When Does the Duty Arise? 232
        3.2.2 Knew or Ought to Have Known 233
        3.2.3 Reasonable Measures 233
        3.2.4 Application 234
4. Illness and Medical Treatment 235
    4.1   State Responsibility 236
    4.2   The Right to Die and the Right to Die with Dignity 236
    4.3   Medical Treatment 237
5. Conditions of Detention 239
    5.1   Conditions of Detention Generally 239
    5.2   Vulnerable Detainees 239
    5.3   Detention for Treatment of a Mental Disorder 240
    5.4   Prisoners with Medical Conditions 240

	5.5	Handcuffing Outside of Prison	241
	5.6	Physical Restraint in Detention	242
	5.7	Seclusion and Segregation	242
	5.8	Slopping Out	242
6.		Violence and Threatening Behaviour	243
7.		Sentencing	244
	7.1	Taking into Account Ill-health	245
	7.2	Automatic Life Sentence	245
	7.3	Mandatory Life Sentence	246
	7.4	Whole Life Tariff	246
8.		Criminal Law	248
9.		State Support	248
10.		Deportation and Extradition	250
	10.1	The Nature of the Duty	250
		10.1.1 Real Risk Test	250
		10.1.2 Evidential Issues	251
		10.1.3 Article 3 in an Extradition Context	252
		10.1.4 Assurances from the Destination State	253
		10.1.5 Safe List of Countries	254
		10.1.6 Contracting States to the ECHR	255
		10.1.7 Member States of the European Union	255
	10.2	Application	256
		10.2.1 Exacerbation of Illness and Risk of Suicide	256
		10.2.2 Medical Treatment in Destination State	258
		10.2.3 Punishment and Sentencing	259
		10.2.4 Conditions of Detention	260
		10.2.5 Legal Restrictions on Homosexuality	262
		10.2.6 Ill-treatment by Non-state Actors: Sufficiency of State Protection	262
11.		Duty to Investigate	263
	11.1	The Nature of the Duty	263
	11.2	The Content of the Duty to Investigate	264
	11.3	The Duty to Investigate in Practice	266
		11.3.1 Detention	266
		11.3.2 Policing	266
		11.3.3 Armed forces	267
9		**Article 5: The Right to Liberty and Security**	**269**
1.		Introduction	269
2.		What Constitutes a Deprivation of Liberty?	270
	2.1	Restrictions on Liberty of Movement	272
	2.2	Control Orders	272
	2.3	Provision of Care	274
	2.4	Parents and Children	275
	2.5	Crowd Control	275
	2.6	Stop and Search	276

3. Article 5(1) — 277
   3.1 Procedure Prescribed by Law — 278
   3.2 Lawful — 278
      3.2.1 Lawful under Domestic Law — 279
      3.2.2 Prescribed by Law — 279
      3.2.3 Not Arbitrary — 280
      3.2.4 Extradition and Deportation — 280
   3.3 Article 5(1)(a): Conviction by a Competent Court — 280
      3.3.1 Causal Link — 280
      3.3.2 Disproportionate Period of Detention — 282
   3.4 Article 5(1)(b): Non-compliance with the Lawful Order of a Court or to Secure the Fulfilment of any Obligation Prescribed by Law — 284
   3.5 Article 5(1)(c): Reasonable Suspicion of Having Committed an Offence — 284
   3.6 Article 5(1)(d): Minors — 285
   3.7 Article 5(1)(e): Persons of Unsound Mind — 286
      3.7.1 Minimum Conditions — 286
      3.7.2 Public Safety — 289
      3.7.3 Treatment — 289
   3.8 Article 5(1)(f): Unauthorised Entry, Action Taken with a View to Deportation or Extradition — 290
      3.8.1 Unauthorised Entry: Detention of Asylum Seekers — 290
      3.8.2 Deportation: Detention of Deportees — 291
      3.8.3 Deportation: Length of Detention — 292
      3.8.4 Extradition: Meaning of Lawfulness — 293
4. Article 5(2): Reasons for Arrest — 293
5. Article 5(3) — 295
   5.1 The Right to Be Released on Bail — 295
   5.2 The Right to Be Tried within a Reasonable Time — 296
6. Article 5(4) — 297
   6.1 Introduction — 297
   6.2 Access to Court — 298
   6.3 Review of Lawfulness — 299
      6.3.1 Introduction — 299
      6.3.2 Unsound Mind — 299
      6.3.3 Determinate Sentences — 299
      6.3.4 Indeterminate Sentences — 301
   6.4 Attributes of a Court — 302
   6.5 Independence and Impartiality — 303
      6.5.1 Home Secretary — 303
      6.5.2 Medical Member, Mental Health Tribunal — 304
      6.5.3 Parole Board — 305
   6.6 Fairness — 306
      6.6.1 Introduction — 306
      6.6.2 Burden of Proof and Evidence — 307
      6.6.3 Oral Hearing — 308
      6.6.4 Equality of Arms — 309

6.7	Decided Speedily	310
	6.7.1 Principles	310
	6.7.2 Mental Health Detainees	311
	6.7.3 Life Sentence Prisoners	313
	6.7.4 Prisoners Serving Indeterminate Sentences	314
	6.7.5 Prisoners Serving Determinate Sentences	315
7.	Article 5(5): Enforceable Right to Compensation	316

10 Article 6: The Right to a Fair Trial 319

1.	Introduction	319
2.	Deportation and Extradition	322
3.	Article 6(1) Application: Determination of Civil Rights and Obligations	323
3.1	Civil Rights and Obligations	324
	3.1.1 Generally	324
	3.1.2 Public Law Rights	325
	3.1.3 Public Sector Workers	326
3.2	Determination	327
3.3	Administrative Decisions: The Two-stage Process	329
3.4	Examples: Determination of Civil Rights and Obligations	331
4.	Article 6(1) Application: Determination of Any Criminal Charge	333
4.1	Determination	333
	4.1.1 Pre-trial Decisions	334
	4.1.2 Sentencing	335
4.2	Criminal Charge	335
	4.2.1 Domestic Classification	335
	4.2.2 Nature of the Offence	337
	4.2.3 Severity of the Potential Penalty	338
4.3	Examples	339
5.	Access to Court	340
5.1	Generally	340
5.2	Substantive and Procedural Bars	341
5.3	Limitation Periods	342
5.4	Security for Costs	344
5.5	Vexatious Litigants	344
5.6	Immunity from Suit	345
5.7	Prisoners	346
5.8	Absence of Legal Representation	347
5.9	Striking Out	347
6.	Fair Hearing	348
6.1	Equality of Arms	349
	6.1.1 Generally	349
	6.1.2 Legal Representation	350
	6.1.3 Disclosure	350
	6.1.4 Public Interest Immunity	352
	6.1.5 National Security: Control Order Cases	353
	6.1.6 National Security: Other Types of Case	355
	6.1.7 Child Witnesses	357

	6.2	Self-incrimination	358
	6.3	Right to Silence	360
	6.4	Presumption of Innocence	361
	6.5	Representation	362
	6.6	Oral Hearing	363
	6.7	Conducting a Proper Examination	364
	6.8	Evidence	364
		6.8.1 Generally	364
		6.8.2 Evidence Obtained by Entrapment	364
		6.8.3 Illegally Obtained Evidence	365
		6.8.4 Evidence Procured by Torture	366
		6.8.5 Hearsay Evidence	366
		6.8.6 Dock Identification Evidence	367
		6.8.7 Exclusionary Rules	367
		6.8.8 Trial in Absentia	368
	6.9	Reasons	370
7.	Public Hearing and Public Pronouncement		371
8.	Reasonable Time		372
	8.1	Generally	372
	8.2	Criminal Proceedings	373
		8.2.1 Start of the Time Period	373
		8.2.2 Determining a Reasonable Time	374
		8.2.3 Application	375
	8.3	Civil Proceedings	376
		8.3.1 Start of the Time Period	376
		8.3.2 Determining a Reasonable Time	376
	8.4	Remedy	376
		8.4.1 Criminal Proceedings: Pre-conviction	377
		8.4.2 Criminal Proceedings: Post-conviction	378
9.	Independent and Impartial Tribunal		379
	9.1	Generally	379
	9.2	Test for Independence and Impartiality	380
		9.2.1 Subjective Test	380
		9.2.2 Objective Test	380
		9.2.3 Rehearing: Generally	381
		9.2.4 Rehearing: Administrative Decisions	382
	9.3	Separation of Powers	383
	9.4	Waiver	384
	9.5	Application	385
		9.5.1 Judiciary	385
		9.5.2 Juries	388
		9.5.3 Courts Martial	388
		9.5.4 Government Ministers	389
		9.5.5 Local Authorities	390
		9.5.6 Professional Bodies	390
10.	Tribunal Established by Law		391
11.	Article 6(2): Presumption of Innocence		392

11.1   Generally   392
11.2   Burden of Proof   393
11.3   Application   395
       11.3.1 Confiscation Orders   395
       11.3.2 Drugs Offences   396
       11.3.3 Road Traffic Offences   397
       11.3.4 Trade Marks Offences   397
       11.3.5 Terrorism Offences   398
12. Article 6(3)(a): Informed of the Nature and Cause of the Accusation   399
13. Article 6(3)(b): Adequate Time and Facilities for Preparation of Defence 400
14. Article 6(3)(c): Legal Assistance   400
    14.1 Waiver of the Right   401
    14.2 Process of Investigation   402
    14.3 Effective Representation   403
    14.4 Legal Assistance   404
15. Article 6(3)(d): Witnesses   405
16. Article 6(3)(e): Interpreter   408

11   Article 8: The Right to Respect for Private Life   409
1.   Introduction   409
2.   Private Life   410
     2.1   Generally   410
     2.2   Information   413
           2.2.1 Generally   413
           2.2.2 Is the Information Private?   413
           2.2.3 Public Figures and Private Life   415
           2.2.4 Relationships   416
           2.2.5 Photographs in Public Places   417
           2.2.6 Filming in Public Places   419
           2.2.7 Convictions and Other Information Retained by Police   419
           2.2.8 Corporate Information   420
     2.3   Identity   421
     2.4   Physical and Psychological Integrity   422
           2.4.1 Generally   422
           2.4.2 Medical Treatment   423
           2.4.3 Policing   423
           2.4.4 Prison and Prison Conditions   424
           2.4.5 State Support   425
           2.4.6 Environmental Pollution   425
           2.4.7 Deportation and Extradition   425
     2.5   Autonomy (Self-determination)   426
     2.6   Social Life and Working Life   427
     2.7   Correspondence   429
3.   Positive Duties   430
     3.1   Generally   430
     3.2   The Test to Establish a Breach of the Positive Duty   431
     3.3   State Support   431

3.4	Policing and Criminal Justice	433
4.	Who Has a Private Life?	434
5.	Who Must Respect Private Life?	435
6.	Permitted Interferences	436
6.1	In Accordance with the Law	436
6.2	General Factors Affecting the Proportionality Analysis	437
6.3	Deference to the Primary Decision Maker	438
7.	National Security	440
8.	Economic Well-being of the Country	440
8.1	Deportation and Extradition: Foreign cases	441
8.1.1	Generally	441
8.1.2	Medical Treatment	441
8.1.3	Homosexuality	442
8.2	Deportation and Extradition: 'Domestic' Cases	442
8.3	Other	444
9.	Prevention of Disorder or Crime	445
9.1	Evidence Obtained by Secret Filming or Recording	445
9.2	Fingerprints, DNA Samples and Other Personal Information—Taking and Retention	446
9.3	Police Photography	447
9.4	Stop and Search	448
9.5	Disclosure of Police Information	449
9.5.1	Enhanced Criminal Record Certificates	449
9.5.2	Convictions and Cautions	451
9.5.3	Notification and Licence Requirements	451
9.6	Offender Naming Schemes	452
9.7	Prisoners	453
9.8	Control orders	454
10.	Protection of Health	455
11.	Protection of Morals	456
12.	Protection of Rights and Freedoms of Others	456
12.1	Fair Trial and Open Justice	457
12.1.1	Generally	457
12.1.2	Access to Court	457
12.1.3	Applications for Anonymity	458
12.2	Right to Life	458
12.3	Private Life	459
12.4	Freedom of Expression	460
12.5	Children and Vulnerable Adults	462
12	Article 8: The Right to Respect for Family Life	465
1.	Introduction	465
2.	Family Life	465
2.1	Definition	465
2.2	Parents and Children	466
2.3	Adoptive Relationships	468
2.4	Same-sex Relationships	469

3. Interference   470
    3.1   Children   471
          3.1.1 Generally   471
          3.1.2 Procedural Rights   472
          3.1.3 Positive Duties   473
    3.2   State Support   475
    3.3   Deportation and Extradition   476
    3.4   Deportation and Extradition—Foreign Cases   477
    3.5   Entry Clearance and Visas   478
4. Permitted Interferences   480
5. Economic Well-being of the Country   480
    5.1   Deportation and Removal   480
          5.1.1 Generally   480
          5.1.2 Assessing Proportionality—The Task of an Appellate
                Immigration Authority   482
          5.1.3 Impact on Other Family Members   484
          5.1.4 Children   484
          5.1.5 Delay   485
    5.2   Entry Clearance and Visas   486
          5.2.1 Leaving the UK to Apply for Entry Clearance   486
          5.2.2 Fees and Other Barriers   486
          5.2.3 Historic Injustice   487
    5.3   Dispersal of Asylum Seekers   487
6. Prevention of Disorder or Crime   488
    6.1   Deportation and Removal   488
    6.2   Extradition   488
          6.2.1 Generally   488
          6.2.2 Impact on Children   489
    6.3   Prisoners   491
    6.4   Parenting Orders   493
    6.5   Compellable Witnesses   493
7. Protection of the Rights and Freedoms of Others   494
    7.1   Children: Care Orders   494
    7.2   Children: Contact Orders   496
    7.3   Children: Adoption   497
          7.3.1 Generally   497
          7.3.2 Adoption without Consent   497
          7.3.3 Adoption with Consent   498
          7.3.4 Contacting Relatives Prior to Adoption   498
          7.3.5 Time Limits   499
    7.4   Children: Removing a Child from the Jurisdiction   499
    7.5   Children: Abduction   500
    7.6   Children and Parents: Paternity   501
    7.7   Children and Parents: Health   501
    7.8   Vulnerable People: Entry Clearance   502

13 Article 8: The Right to Respect for Home   503
    1. Introduction   503
    2. Home   504
    3. Interference   505
        3.1   Planning   505
        3.2   Proceedings for Possession   506
        3.3   Care Homes   507
        3.4   Environmental Pollution   508
        3.5   Criminal Justice   509
    4. Positive Duties   509
    5. Permitted Interferences   510
    6. For the Prevention of Disorder or Crime   511
    7. Economic Well-being of the Country   512
        7.1   Care Home Closures   512
        7.2   Standards of Public Housing   513
        7.3   Management of Sewage and Drainage   513
    8. Protection of the Rights and Freedoms of Others   514
        8.1   Generally   514
        8.2   Bankruptcy—The Rights of Creditors   515
        8.3   Public Interest in Preserving the Environment   515
        8.4   Compulsory Purchase   517
        8.5   Proceedings for Possession   518
               8.5.1 Generally—Conflicting Jurisprudence   518
               8.5.2 The Current Approach to Proceedings for Possession:
                     Pinnock and *Powell*   520
               8.5.3 Lower Courts post *Pinnock*   524

14 Article 9: Freedom of Thought, Conscience and Religion   527
    1. Introduction   527
    2. The Right to Believe   529
    3. The Right to Manifest   530
        3.1   Recognising a Manifestation of Belief   530
        3.2   Manifestations within the Protection of Article 9   532
        3.3   Manifestations Outside of the Protection of Article 9 534
        3.4   Conscientious Objection   535
    4. Interference with Manifestation of Belief   536
        4.1   Difficulties in Establishing an Interference with Manifestation of
               Belief   536
        4.2   Examples of No Interference with Manifestation of Belief   538
        4.3   Examples of Interferences with Manifestation of Belief   541
        4.4   A Change in Approach   542
        4.5   Deportation and Extradition   542
    5. Permitted Interference with the Right to Manifest   543
        5.1   Health or Morals   543
        5.2   Protection of the Rights and Freedoms of Others   544
               5.2.1 Respect for the Homosexual Community   544

	5.2.2 Vulnerable People	545
	5.2.3 Children	545
	5.2.4 Employers	547
	5.2.5 Prisons and Prisoners	547
	5.2.6 Fair Administration of Justice	548

15   Article 10: The Right to Freedom of Expression   549

1. Introduction   549
2. Expression   551
3. Medium, Manner and Timing of Communication   553
4. Freedom to Receive and Impart Information and Ideas   555
5. Interference   557
6. Positive Duties   559
7. Permitted Interferences   560
8. General Principles   561
   8.1   Section 12 HRA   561
   8.2   Importance of Freedom of Expression   562
   8.3   Importance of Freedom of the Press   563
   8.4   The Public Interest   564
      8.4.1 Defining the Public Interest   565
      8.4.2 Political Information   566
      8.4.3 Public Figures   567
      8.4.4 Commercial Expression   570
9. National Security   570
10. Prevention of Disorder or Crime   572
11. Protection of Health or Morals   573
12. Protection of the Reputation of Others   574
   12.1   Qualified Privilege   575
      12.1.1 The Nature of Reynolds Privilege   576
      12.1.2 Public Interest   577
      12.1.3 Responsible Journalism   577
   12.2   The Impact of Article 10 on Other Aspects of Defamation Law   579
13. Protection of the Rights of Others   580
   13.1   Articles 2 and 3   581
   13.2   Article 8   581
      13.2.1 Private Lives of Public Figures   581
      13.2.2 Anonymity Orders in Legal Proceedings   583
      13.2.3 Super-injunctions   585
      13.2.4 Protection of Identity   586
      13.2.5 Restrictions on Reporting Legal Proceedings   587
      13.2.6 Private Lives of Private Figures   588
   13.3   Article 9   588
   13.4   Article 1 Protocol No 1   588
   13.5   Right Not to Be Insulted and Distressed   590
      13.5.1 Protest   590
      13.5.2 Extreme Protest   593

	13.5.3 Pre-emptive Policing and Protest	593
	13.5.4 Taste Decency and Causing Offence	594
13.6	Democratic Rights	595
14.	Preventing the Disclosure of Information Received in Confidence	597
14.1	Generally	597
14.2	Disclosure of a Journalist's Source	598
15.	Maintaining the Authority and Impartiality of the Judiciary	601

16	Article 14: Prohibition of Discrimination	605
1.	Introduction	605
2.	Application: No Independent Existence	607
2.1	Within the Ambit of One or More Convention Rights	607
2.2	Article 3	608
2.3	Article 5	609
2.4	Article 8: Private Life	609
2.5	Article 8: Family Life	610
2.6	Article 8: Respect for Home	611
2.7	Article 9	612
2.8	Article 1 Protocol No 1	613
2.9	Article 2 Protocol 1: Education	613
3.	Without Discrimination	614
3.1	Difference in Treatment: Direct Discrimination	614
3.2	No Difference in Treatment: Indirect Discrimination	615
	3.2.1 Gypsies and Travellers	615
	3.2.2 Nationality	616
	3.2.3 Disability	616
	3.2.4 Sex	617
4.	Positive Duty	618
5.	Grounds	618
5.1	Introduction	618
5.2	'Other Status'	619
5.3	Included within 'Other Status'	619
5.4	Not Included within 'Other Status'	620
5.5	Suspect Grounds of Discrimination	621
6.	Analogous Position	623
6.1	Determining Analogous Situations	623
6.2	Examples of Analogous Situations	624
6.3	Examples of Non-analogous Situations	625
7.	Objective and Reasonable Justification	626
7.1	Determining Justification	626
7.2	Reasonable Time for Change	628
7.3	Social and Economic Factors	629
	7.3.1 Generally	629
	7.3.2 Welfare Benefits	629
	7.3.3 Taxation	631
	7.3.4 Immigration Control	632

	7.4	Protection of the Environment	634
	7.5	Health	634
	7.6	Protection of the Traditional Family Unit	635
	7.7	Crime and Sentencing	636
	7.8	Protection against Terrorist Acts	637
8.	Remedy for Breach		638

17   Article 1 Protocol No 1: Protection of Property   639
  1.   Introduction   639
  2.   Possessions   640
       2.1   Generally   640
       2.2   Personal Possessions   642
       2.3   Business Possessions   643
       2.4   Licences   644
  3.   Interferences with the Peaceful Enjoyment of Possessions   646
       3.1   Generally   646
       3.2   Deprivation   647
             3.2.1 Incident of Ownership   648
             3.2.2 Future Deprivation   650
       3.3   Control   651
  4.   Justifying Interferences   652
       4.1   Generally   652
       4.2   Lawfulness of Interference   655
       4.3   Legitimate Aim   656
       4.4   Proportionality   657
             4.4.1 Generally   657
             4.4.2 Deference   657
             4.4.3 Compensation   658
             4.4.4 Procedural Rights   659
  5.   Consumer Protection   660
  6.   Planning and the Environment   662
  7.   The Rights of Others   663
       7.1   Freedom of Expression   663
       7.2   Article 1 Protocol 1   664
             7.2.1 Generally   664
             7.2.2 Adverse Possession   666
       7.3   Vulnerable People   667
  8.   Social Justice   667
  9.   Protection of Morals   668
 10.   Prevention of Crime and Illegality   669
       10.1   Confiscation Orders   669
       10.2   Anti-terror Measures   672
       10.3   Illegality   672
 11.   Economic Well-being of the Country   672
       11.1   Taxes   672
       11.2   Duties   674

11.3 Penalties—Clandestine Entrants 676
11.4 Child Support 677
11.5 Nationalisation in the Public Interest 677
11.6 Reduction of the National Budget Deficit 678
11.7 Recovery of Overpaid Welfare Benefit 678

Index 679

Table of Cases

A (Afghanistan) v Secretary of State for the Home Department [2009] EWCA Civ 825 466

A v Denmark (1996) 22 EHRR 458 162

A v Hounslow London Borough Council, Employment Appeal Tribunal, 11 July 2001 643

A v Hungary [2013] EWHC 3132 (Admin) 491

A v Independent News & Media Ltd [2010] EWCA Civ 343 .... 458, 587

[2010] 1 WLR 2262 458

A v P [2011] EWHC 1738 (Fam), [2012] 3 WLR 369 471

A v Secretary of State for the Home Department (No 1) [2004] UKHL 56, [2005] 2 AC
68 .... 15–16, 34, 99, 102–4, 108, 140, 151, 227, 263, 269, 279, 606, 609, 615, 620, 623, 637

A v Secretary of State for the Home Department [2002] EWCA Civ 1502, [2004] QB
335 .... 332, 340

A v Secretary of State for the Home Department [2003] EWCA Civ 175 227

A v Secretary of State for the Home Department [2005] UKHL 71, [2006] 2 AC 221 ..... 13, 28, 366

A v United Kingdom (1998) 3 FCR 597 231

A v United Kingdom (1998) 27 EHRR 611 262

A v United Kingdom (2009) 49 EHRR 29 354

A v United Kingdom, ECtHR, Grand Chamber, 19 February 2009 150–1

A v X [2004] EWHC (QB) 447 457

AAA v Associated Newspapers Ltd [2012] EWHC 2103 (QB), [2012] HRLR 31 461

AAA v Associated Newspapers Ltd [2013] EWCA Civ 554 461

AAM v Secretary of State for the Home Department [2012] EWHC 2567 (QB) 290

Abdul v Director of Public Prosecutions [2011] EWHC 247 (Admin), [2011] Crim LR 553 591

Abdulaziz v United Kingdom (1985) 7 EHRR 471 .... 35, 466, 479

Achmant v Greece [2012] EWHC 3470 (Admin) 261

Ackroyd v Mersey Care NHS Trust [2003] EWCA Civ 663, [2003] EMLR 36 .... 567, 599

Adams and Benn v United Kingdom (1997) 88A D&R 137 .... 35, 558

Adan v Newham London Borough Council [2001] EWCA Civ 1916, [2002] 1 WLR
2120 ....130, 325, 383, 390

Al-Adsani v United Kingdom (2001) 34 EHRR 273 346

AG (Eritrea) v Secretary of State for the Home Department [2007] EWCA Civ 801,
[2008] 2 All ER 483

Agee v United Kingdom (1976) 7 D&R 164 .... 35, 558

Agius v the Court of Magistrates, Malta [2011] EWHC 759 (Admin) 255

AH v Secretary of State for the Home Department [2011] EWCA Civ 787 274

Ahmad v United States [2006] EWHC 2927 (Admin), [2007] HRLR 8 254

Ahmed v Revenue & Customs Commissioners [2013] EWHC 2241 (Admin) 671

Ahmed v United Kingdom (1995) 20 EHRR CD 72 36

Airedale NHS Trust v Bland [1993] AC 789 .... 183–4, 187–8

Airey v Ireland (1979) 2 EHRR 305 347

AJ (Liberia) v Secretary of State for the Home Department [2006] EWCA Civ 1736 257

Akdivar v Turkey, Judgment of 1 April 1998 159

Akram v Adam [2005] 1 All ER 741 343

Aksoy v Turkey (1997) 23 EHRR 553...162

AL (Serbia) v Secretary of State for the Home Department [2008] UKHL 42, [2008] 1
WLR 1434...609, 620, 622–3, 633

Al Fayed v Commissioner of Police of the Metropolis [2004] EWCA Civ 1579......................285

Al Khawaja and Tahery v United Kingdom (2009) 49 EHRR 1 ....21, 407

Al Nashif v Bulgaria (2003) 36 EHRR 37..488

Al Rawi v Security Service [2011] UKSC 34, [2012] 1 AC 531 ....3, 356

Al Sadoon v United Kingdom (2010) 51 EHRR 9...74–5

Al Skeini v United Kingdom (2011) 53 EHRR 18...74–5, 77–8

Albert and Le Compte v Belgium (1983) 5 EHRR 533...330, 382, 388

Aldhouse v Thailand [2012] EWHC 3385 (Admin)...261

Ali and Begum v Customs & Excise Commissioners V&DTr 30 May 2002 340

Ali v Birmingham City Council [2010] UKSC 8 23

Allenet de Ribemont v France (1996) 22 EHRR 582...158

Allgemeine Gold-und Silverscheideanstalt v United Kingdom (1986) 9 EHRR 1.....................675

Alliance Spring Co Ltd v First Secretary of State [2005] EWHC (Admin) 18.........................663

Allison v HM Advocate [2010] UKSC 6, [2010] HRLR 16...352

Alliss v Legal Services Commission [2002] EWHC (Admin) 2079..347

AM (Somalia) v Entry Clearance Officer [2009] EWCA Civ 634, [2009] UKHRR 1073.........611,
615, 617, 620, 622, 627, 632

AM v Secretary of State for the Home Department [2011] EWCA Civ 710 354

Amare v Secretary of State for the Home Department [2005] EWCA Civ 1600, [2006]
Imm AR 217...262

Ambrose v Harris [2011] UKSC 43, [2011] 1 WLR 2435...403

AMM v HXW [2010] EWHC 2457 (QB)..585

AMP v Persons Unknown [2011] EWHC 3454...414, 561, 588

Amuur v France (1996) 22 EHRR 533 277

Anderson v Scottish Ministers [2001] UKPC D5, [2003] 2 AC 602.............278–9, 286, 289, 291,
299, 309

Anderton v Clwyd County Council [2002] EWCA Civ 933, [2002] 1 WLR 3174 343

Andreou v Lord Chancellor's Department [2002] EWCA Civ 1192, [2002] IRLR 728.............370

Andrews v Reading Borough Council [2005] EWHC (QB) 256 ....425, 508

Anufrijeva v Southwark LBC [2003] EWCA Civ 1406, [2004] QB 1124...............80, 147–8, 151,
153–4, 157–8, 161–4, 173, 249, 409, 431–2, 470, 475, 478

AP v Crown Prosecution Service [2007] EWCA Crim 3128...671

Archer v Williams [2003] EWHC (QB) 1670, [2003] EMLR 38................. 57, 435, 568, 586, 603

Arscott v The Coal Authority [2004] EWCA Civ 892, [2005] Env LR 6.............57, 508, 514, 665

Arthur J S Hall & Co (a firm) v Simons [2000] 2 FCR 673 345

Artico v Italy (1980) 3 EHRR 1..403–4

Arundel Corporation v Khokher [2003] EWCA Civ 491 371

AS (Libya) v Secretary of State for the Home Department [2008] EWCA Civ 289,
[2008] HRLR 28 ....251, 254

AS (Somalia) v Secretary of State for the Home Department [2009] UKHL 32, [2009]
1 WLR 1385...478, 480, 486

Ash v McKennitt [2006] EWCA Civ 1714, [2007] 3 WLR 194 ....413, 416, 568, 581

Ashdown v Telegraph Group Ltd [2001] EWCA Civ 1142, [2001] 3 WLR 1368............. 550, 555,
557–8, 561–4, 566, 588, 642, 647, 663

Ashingdane v United Kingdom (1983) 6 EHRR 69 341

Ashingdane v United Kingdom (1985) 7 EHRR 528 ....272, 289, 344, 392

Ashworth Hospital Authority v MGN Ltd [2002] UKHL 29, [2002] 1 WLR 2033 .... 557, 564, 598–600

Assistant Deputy Coroner for Inner West London v Channel 4 Television Corporation
[2007] EWHC 2513 (QB), [2008] 1 WLR 945 600–1

Associated Newspapers Group Ltd v Wade [1979] 1 WLR 697..5, 549

Association of British Civilian Internees—Far East Region, v Secretary of State for
Defence [2003] EWCA Civ 473, [2003] QB 1397..613, 640

Association X v United Kingdom (1978) 14 D&R 31 .... 187, 200

Aston Cantlow and Wilmcote with Billesley Parochial Church Council v Wallbank
[2003] UKHL 37, [2004] 1 AC 546..............27, 32–3, 40–1, 44, 46–9, 68, 70, 118, 639, 648–9

Aswat v United Kingdom 34 BHRC 656..256

Atkinson v Secretary of State for the Home Department [2004] EWCA Civ 846, [2004]
ACD 71 262–3

Attorney-General of The Gambia v Momodou Jobe [1984] AC 689 17

Attorney General v BBC [1980] 3 WLR 109 .... 5, 549

Attorney General v Covey [2001] EWCA Civ 254 344–5

Attorney General v MGN Ltd [2011] EWHC 2074 (Admin), [2012] 1 Cr App R 1.................601

Attorney General v Punch Ltd [2002] UKHL 50, [2003] 1 AC 1046.............555, 557, 571, 601–2

Attorney General v Scotcher [2005] UKHL 36, [2005] 1 WLR 1867................................ 557, 603

Attorney General v Times Newspapers Ltd [1992] 1 AC 191 601

Attorney General v Times Newspapers Ltd [2001] EWCA Civ 97, [2001] 1 WLR 885 557

Attorney General v Wheen [2001] IRLR 91..345

Attorney General's Reference No 1 of 2004 [2004] EWCA Crim 1025, [2004] 1 WLR
2111.. 126, 395

Attorney General's Reference No 2 of 2001 [2003] UKHL 68, [2004] 2 AC 72........9, 26, 148–9,
170, 319, 348, 372–3, 377–9

Attorney General's Reference No 3 of 1999 [2001] 2 AC 91......................................414, 423, 446

Attorney General's Reference No 3 of 1999 [2009] UKHL 34, [2010] 1 AC 145....415, 563, 567,
586

Attorney General's Reference No 3 of 2000 [2001] UKHL 53, [2001] 1 WLR 2060.................364

Attorney General's Reference No 4 of 2002 [2004] UKHL 43, [2005] 1 AC 264............ 120, 126,
134, 392–5, 398, 557

Attorney General's Reference No 7 of 2000 [2001] EWCA Crim 888, [2001] 1 WLR 1879 359

Attorney General's Reference No 82a of 2000 [2002] EWCA Crim 215 350

Ausiello v Italy (1996) 24 EHRR 568...376

Austin Hall Building Ltd v Buckland Securities Ltd [2001] BLR 272 45

Austin v Commissioner of Police of the Metropolis [2009] UKHL 5, [2009] 1 AC 564........22–3,
271, 275–7

Australian Broadcasting Corporation v Lenah Game Meats Pty Ltd (2001) 185 ALR 1 413

Author of a Blog v Times Newspapers Ltd [2009] EWHC 1358 (QB), [2009] EMLR 22 415, 586

Axa General Insurance Ltd v Lord Advocate [2011] UKSC 46, [2012] 1 AC 868........34, 39, 87,
111, 639, 643, 646, 650, 654–7, 667

Aydin v Turkey (1998) 25 EHRR 251 161–2

Ayuntamiento de Mula v Spain, Court, 1 February 2001...41

AZ v Secretary of State for Communities & Local Government [2012] EWHC 3660
(Admin) 516

B & C v A [2002] EWCA Civ 337, [2002] 3 WLR 542........416, 435–6, 438, 461, 551, 563, 565, 568, 582

B R & C (Children) [2002] EWCA Civ 1825 457

B v Chief Constable of Avon and Somerset Constabulary [2001] 1 WLR 340 336

B v France (1992) 16 EHRR 1...374

B v G [2012] UKSC 21, [2012] Fam LR 56...475

B v Secretary of State [2011] EWCA Civ 828 245

B v Secretary of State for Work and Pensions [2005] EWCA Civ 929 .... 620, 642

B v United Kingdom [2000] 1 FLR 1..468

Badu v BBC [2010] EWHC 616 (QB)..580

Baker v Secretary of State for the Home Department [2001] UKHRR 1275 ....87, 131, 413, 440

Balmer-Schafroth v Switzerland (1997) 25 EHRR 598..327

Bangs v Connex South Eastern Ltd [2005] EWCA Civ 14, [2005] 2 All ER 316 377

Bank Mellat v HM Treasury [2011] EWCA Civ 1, [2011] 3 WLR 714 .... 651, 659–60

Bank Mellat v HM Treasury [2013] UKSC 38..356

Bankovic v Belgium (2007) 44 EHRR SE5..74

Bannatyne v Secretary of State for the Home Department [2004] EWHC (Admin) 1912.........372

Baragiola v Switzerland (1993) 75 DR 76...379

Barca v Mears [2004] EWHC (Ch) 2170, [2005] 2 FLR 1 .... 132, 515

Barclays Bank v Guardian [2009] EWHC 591 (QB) 598

Barnette v United States [2004] UKHL 35, [2004] 1 WLR 2241 73

Barrett v Enfield London Borough Council [2001] 2 AC 550...348

Batayav v The Secretary of State for the Home Department [2003] EWCA Civ 1489.. 252, 260–1

Bath & North East Somerset Council v Connors [2006] EWHC 1595 (QB)............................516

Battista v Bassano [2007] EWCA Civ 370 370

Baturina v Times Newspapers Ltd [2011] EWCA Civ 308, [2011] 1 WLR 1526 579

Bayatyan v Armenia (2012) 54 EHRR 15..535–6

BB v France, 9 March 1998, Commission..258

BBC v Secretary of State for Justice [2012] EWHC 13 (Admin), [2012] 2 All ER 1089 553

B&C v A [2002] EWCA Civ 337, [2002] 3 WLR 542 ....57, 416, 565

Beaulane Properties Limited v Palmer [2005] HRLR 19..642, 649, 659

Beck v Norway, Judgment of 26 June 2001 .... 171, 378–9

Beckles v United Kingdom (2002) 13 BHRC 522 360

Bedford v Bedfordshire County Council [2013] EWHC 1717 (QB), [2013] HRLR 33....... 60, 431

Beghal v Director of Public Prosecutions [2013] EWHC 2573 (Admin)...................................449

Begum (Runa) v Tower Hamlets London Borough Council [2003] UKHL 5, [2003] 2
  AC 430 ....322, 325, 382, 390

Begum v Anam [2004] EWCA Civ 578..404

Begum v The Commissioners of Customs and Excise, VADT, 30 May 2002 332

Belfast City Council v Miss Behavin' Ltd [2007] UKHL 19, [2007] 1 WLR 1420......96, 98, 101,
  550–1, 557, 570, 573, 646, 651–3, 668

Bellinger v Bellinger [2003] UKHL 21, [2003] 2 AC 467 ......13, 64, 68, 103, 134–5, 139, 421–2,
  430, 439

Benjamin and Wilson v United Kingdom, Judgment of 26 September 2002............................304

Bensaid v United Kingdom (2001) 33 EHRR 205 ....236, 238, 425

Bento v Chief Constable of Bedfordshire [2012] EWHC 1525 (QB)......................................579

Beoku-Betts v Secretary of State for the Home Department [2008] UKHL 39, [2009] 1
  AC 115...477, 484

Berezovsky v Forbes [2001] EWCA Civ 1251, [2001] EMLR 45 579
Bernard v London Borough of Enfield [2002] EWHC (Admin) 2282, [2003] HRLR 4 475–6
Berrehab v Netherlands (1988) 11 EHRR 322..466
Berry Trade Ltd v Moussavi [2002] WLR 1910..339, 400
Bezicheri v Italy (1989) 12 EHRR 210..311
BH v Lord Advocate [2012] UKSC 24, [2012] 3 WLR 151 491
Bhamjee v Forsdick (No 2) [2003] EWCA Civ 1113..344–5
Birmingham City Council v Beech [2013] EWHC 518 (QB)..526
Birmingham City Council v Clue [2010] EWCA Civ 460, [2011] 1 WLR 99 ....429, 433
Birmingham City Council v James [2013] EWCA Civ 552..455
Birmingham City Council v Lloyd [2012] EWCA Civ 969, [2012] HLR 44 524
Birmingham City Council v Yardley [2004] EWCA Civ 1756..387
BKM Ltd v British Broadcasting Corporation [2009] EWHC 3151 (Ch)..........413, 427, 438, 567
Black v Wilkinson [2013] EWCA Civ 820...111, 530, 532, 542, 544
BLCT (13096) Limited v J Sainsbury plc [2003] EWCA Civ 884, [2004] 2 P&CR 32.... 340, 363
Blečić v Croatia (2004) 41 EHRR 185 520
Blunkett v Quinn [2004] EWHC (Fam) 2816, [2005] 1 FLR 648...584
Boehringer Ingelheim Ltd v Vetplus Ltd [2007] EWCA Civ 583, [2007] HRLR 33 590
Boner v United Kingdom (1994) 19 EHRR 246 404
Botta v Italy (1998) 26 EHRR 341 431
Bouamar v Belgium (1989) 11 EHRR 1 285–6
Bow Spring, the and the Manzanillo II [2004] EWCA Civ 1007, [2005] 1 Lloyd's Rep 1 372
Bowden v Secretary of State for the Environment and Others, Divisional Court, 17
    December 1997 156
Bowman v United Kingdom (1996) 21 EHRR CD 79..36
Boyd v The Army Prosecuting Authority [2002] UKHL 31, [2003] 1 AC 734 ....21, 380, 388
Boyle v United Kingdom [1994] 2 FCR 822..466
Bozano v France (1986) 9 EHRR 297 277
Braithwaite v Secretary of State for Communities & Local Government [2012] EWHC
    2835 (Admin), [2013] JPL 312 517
Brasserie du Pecheur SA v Germany and R v Secretary of State for Transport ex parte
    Factortame [1996] ECR I–1029..155
Brazil v Secretary of State for Transport, Local Government and the Regions [2001]
    EWHC (Admin) 991 516
Briffett v DPP [2001] EWHC Admin 841, [2002] EMLR 12..87, 557
British Steel Corp v Granada Television Ltd [1981] AC 1096 599
Britton v Secretary of State for the Home Department [2003] EWCA Civ 227 263
Broadland District Council v Brightwell [2010] EWCA Civ 1516..516
Brogan v United Kingdom (1988) 11 EHRR 117..285
Brookes v Secretary of State for Work and Pensions [2010] EWCA Civ 420, [2010] 1
    WLR 2448 471
Brown v Stott [2003] 1 AC 681 .... 11, 14, 21, 81, 91, 97, 105, 319–20, 334, 348, 358–9, 392
Brown v United Kingdom, Judgment of 26 October 2004 338
Brumfitt v Ministry of Defence [2005] IRLR 4..422
Bryan v United Kingdom (1995) 21 EHRR 342 ....330, 381–2, 388
Buckley v United Kingdom (1996) 23 EHRR 101..504–5
Bui van Thanh v United Kingdom, 12 March 1990..79
Bull v Hall [2012] EWCA Civ 83, [2012] 2 All ER 1017..532, 544

Bunkate v Netherlands (1995) 19 EHRR 477 .... 171, 378–9

BUQ v HRE [2012] EWHC 774 (QB), [2012] IRLR 653 415

Burden and Burden v United Kingdom (dec), Application No 13378/05 (12 December 2006) .. 138

Burnip v Birmingham City Council [2012] EWCA Civ 629 .... 613, 616, 620, 631

Burns v HM Advocate [2008] UKPC 63, [2009] 1 AC 720 373

Butler v Derby City Council [2005] EWHC 2835 (Admin), [2006] 1 WLR 1346 .... 558, 591

BX v Secretary of State for the Home Department [2010] EWCA Civ 481, [2010] 1
  WLR 2463 355

BX v Secretary of State for the Home Department [2010] EWHC 990 (Admin) 471

Bysermaw Properties Ltd v Revenue & Customs Commissioners [2008] STC (SCD) 322 673

C (A Child) v XYZ County Council [2007] EWCA Civ 1206, [2008] 3 WLR 445 ..... 421, 466–7,
                                                                                                                      474

C (Zimbabwe) v Secretary of State for the Home Department [2008] UKHL 40, [2008]
  1 WLR 1420 .... 478, 486

C MBA v London Borough of Merton EAT 13/12/2012, [2013] Eq LR 209 527

C v Bury Metropolitan Borough Council [2002] EWHC (Fam) 1438, [2003] 2 FLR 868 472

C v Secretary of State for the Home Department [2004] EWCA Civ 234 619

Cachia v Faluyi [2001] EWCA Civ 998, [2001] 1 WLR 1966 130

Cadder v HM Advocate [2010] UKSC 43 .... 20, 117, 148, 401–3

Cameron v Network Rail Infrastructure Ltd [2006] EWHC 1133 (QB), [2007] 1 WLR 163 46, 60

Campbell and Fell v United Kingdom (1985) 7 EHRR 165 372

Campbell v MGN Ltd [2004] UKHL 22, [2004] 2 AC 457 .... 27, 56–7, 409, 413–14, 416, 435,
                                                                         437–8, 460–1, 562–3, 566, 568, 581–2, 597

Campbell v South Northamptonshire District Council [2004] EWCA Civ 409, [2004] 3
  All ER 387 .... 618, 642

Caroll Vikius v Lithuania, 7 April 2005 260

Carr v News Group Newspapers, Divisional Court, 24 February 2005 586

Carson v United Kingdom (2010) 51 EHRR 13 630

Cassell & Co v Broome [1972] 2 WLR 645 .... 5, 549

Castorina v Chief Constable of Surrey [1996] LG Rev Rep 241 284–5

Catholic Care (Diocese of Leeds) v Charity Commission for England & Wales [2010]
  EWHC 520 (Ch), [2010] 4 All ER 1041 622

Cazenave de la Roche v France, Judgment of 9 June 1998 161

CC v AB [2006] EWHC 3083 (QB), [2007] 2 FLR 301 .... 417, 568, 583

CD (Democratic Republic of Congo) v Secretary of State for the Home Department
  [2011] EWCA Civ 1425 387

Chahal v United Kingdom (1996) 23 EHRR 413 .... 291, 293

Champion v Chief Constable of the Gwent Constabulary [1990] 1 WLR 1 93

Chancellor, Masters and Scholars of the University of Oxford v Broughton [2004]
  EWHC (QB) 2543 586

Chapman v United Kingdom (2001) 33 EHRR 399 .... 330, 505

Chappell v United Kingdom (1989) 12 EHRR 1 444

Chase v Newsgroup Newspapers Ltd [2002] EWCA Civ 1772, [2003] EMLR 11 579

Cheshire West v P [2011] EWCA Civ 1257, [2012] 1 FLR 693 .... 271, 274, 277

Chichester District Council v The First Secretary of State [2004] EWCA Civ 1248,
  [2005] 1 WLR 279 .... 510, 517

Chief Constable of Greater Manchester Police v McNally [2002] EWCA Civ 14, [2002]
  Cr LR 832 353

Chief Constable of Hertfordshire v Van Colle [2008] UKHL 50, [2009] 1 AC 225 ....
    34, 57, 163, 189, 191, 193–4, 202–3
Chief Constable of West Yorkshire Police v A [2004] UKHL 21, [2005] 1 AC 51....................421
Chief Constable of Wiltshire v McDonagh [2008] EWHC 654 (QB) 504, 509, 512
Chiltern District Council v Webb [2007] EWHC 1686 (QB), [2008] JPL 1323........................516
Christian Federation of Jehovah's Witnesses in France v France, Application no
    53430/99, 6 November 2001, ECtHR 34
City of London v Samede [2012] EWCA Civ 160, [2012] 2 All ER 1039................................592
Claire F v Secretary of State for the Home Department [2004] EWHC (Fam) 111,
    [2004] 2 FLR 517 .... 472, 492
Clark (Procurator Fiscal) v Kelly [2003] UKPC D1, [2004] 1 AC 681 ....349, 372, 381
Clarke v Secretary of State for Transport, Local Government and the Regions [2002]
    EWCA Civ 819 ....516, 612, 615, 620
Clayton v Clayton [2006] EWCA Civ 878, [2006] 3 WLR 599... 461, 588
Clayton v HM Coroner for South Yorkshire (East District) [2005] EWHC (Admin) 1196........205
Clift v Slough Borough Council [2010] EWCA Civ 1484, [2011] 1 WLR 1774 .... 422, 453
Clift v United Kingdom 13 July 2010.. 619, 621
Coates v South Bucks DC [2004] EWCA Civ 1378, [2005] BLGR 626 516
Codona v Mid-Bedfordshire District Council [2004] EWCA Civ 925, [2005] HLR 1....... 510, 615
Colozza v Italy (1985) 7 EHRR 516...171
Commissioner of Police for the Metropolis v Hurst [2005] EWCA Civ 890.............................119
Condron v United Kingdom (2002) 31 EHRR 1 360
Conka v Belgium (2002) 11 BHRC 555 291
Connolly v Director of Public Prosecutions [2007] EWHC 237 (Admin), [2007] 2 All
    ER 1012...532, 551, 594
Connors v United Kingdom (2004) 40 EHRR 189.. 110, 520
Connors v United Kingdom (2005) 40 EHRR 9..518
Consumer Credit Act 1974...66, 115, 649, 660–1
Coppard v HM Customs and Excise [2003] EWCA Civ 511, [2003] QB 1428 391
Copsey v WWB Devon Clays Ltd [2005] EWCA Civ 932, [2005] HRLR 32 ....24, 56, 527,
                                                                                                                        539–40, 547
Corby Borough Council v Scott [2012] EWCA Civ 276, [2012] HLR 23................................524
Core Issues Trust v Transport for London [2013] EWHC 651 (Admin), [2013] HRLR
    22 ....32, 86, 89, 549, 551, 560, 595
Cornwall Waste Forum St Dennis Branch v Secretary of State for Communities and
    Local Government [2011] EWHC 2761 (Admin)..38
Corton Caravans and Chalets Limited v Anglian Water Services Limited [2003] RVR 323.......658
Ćosić v Croatia 15 January 2009...520
Costello-Roberts v United Kingdom (1993) 19 EHRR 112 244
Coyne v United Kingdom, Judgment of 24 September 1997..159
Cranage Parish Council v First Secretary of State [2004] EWHC (Admin) 2949 506
Crawford v Crown Prosecution Service [2008] EWHC 854 (Admin).......................................587
Crawford v Department of Agriculture and Rural Development [2012] NICA 53 362
Cream Holdings Ltd v Banerjee [2004] UKHL 44, [2005] 1 AC 253.......................................561
Crilly v the Commissioners of Customs and Excise, VADT 28 July 2003 676
Crime and Disorder Act 1988, s 66...340
Croissant v Germany (1992) 16 EHRR 135 404
Crompton v Department of Transport North Western Area [2003] EWCA Civ 64.....................643

Crown Prosecution Service v Eastenders Group [2012] EWCA Crim 2436, [2013] 1 Cr
App R 24 .... 655, 671
Cruz Varas v Sweden (1991) 14 EHRR 1 250
CTB v News Group Newspapers Ltd [2011] EWHC 1232 (QB) 417, 568, 583
Culnane v Morris [2005] EWHC 2438 (QB), [2006] 1 WLR 2880 579
Cumming v Chief Constable of Northumbria Police [2003] EWCA Civ 1844, [2004]
ACD 42 284–5
Cusack v Harrow London Borough Council [2013] UKSC 40, [2013] 1 WLR 2022 651,
659, 662
Customs and Excise Commissioners v Han [2001] EWCA Civ 1040, [2001] 1 WLR 2253 .. 336–9
Customs and Excise Commissioners v Newbury [2003] EWHC (Admin) 702, [2003] 2
All ER 964 675
CVB v MGN Ltd [2012] EWHC 1148 (QB) 458
CW (Jamaica) v Secretary of State for the Home Department [2013] EWCA Civ 915 485
D v Commissioner of Police of the Metropolis [2012] EWHC 309 (QB) 60
D v East Berkshire Community NHS Trust [2003] EWCA Civ 1151, [2004] QB 558 ...... 345, 348
D v Secretary of State for the Home Department [2002] EWHC (Admin) 2805, [2003]
1 WLR 1315 .... 141, 303, 314
D v United Kingdom (1997) 24 EHRR 423 .... 236, 238, 258
Dacorum Borough Council v Purcell [2009] EWHC 742 (QB) 516
Daltel Europe Ltd v Makki [2006] EWCA Civ 94, [2006] 1 WLR 2704 339
Darker v Chief Constable of the West Midlands Police [2000] 3 WLR 747 345
Davidson v Scottish Ministers [2004] UKHL 34, [2004] HRLR 34 .... 379–80, 383, 386–7
Davies v Crawley Borough Council [2001] EWHC (Admin) 854 .... 640, 644, 652, 658, 662
Davies v Health and Safety Executive [2002] EWCA Crim 2949 395
Davis v Tonbridge & Malling Borough Council [2004] EWCA Civ 194 .... 504, 516
De Cubber v Belgium (1984) 7 EHRR 236 381–2
De Freitas v Permanent Secretary of Ministry of Agriculture, Fisheries, Lands and
Housing [1999] 1 AC 69 91
De Haes and Gijsels v Belgium (1997) 24 EHRR 1 349
De Keyser Ltd v Wilson [2001] IRLR 324 457
De Wilde, Ooms and Versyp v Belgium (No 1) (1971) 1 EHRR 373 301
Delta v France (1990) 16 EHRR 574 171
Democoli v Malta (1991) 14 EHRR 47 338
Denkavit Internationaal v Bundesamt fur Finanzen [1996] ECR I–5063 156
Dennis v Ministry of Defence [2003] EWHC (QB) 793, [2003] 19 EG 118 (CS) 164, 508, 514,
648, 659
Derbyshire County Council v Times Newspapers Ltd [1993] AC 534 574
Deripaska v Cherney [2012] EWCA Civ 1235, [2013] CP Rep 1 197
Devlin v United Kingdom (2002) EHRR 43 326
Deweer v Belgium (1980) 2 EHRR 439 .... 336–7, 384
Dhillon v Asiedu [2012] EWCA Civ 1020 370
Dickson v United Kingdom, Application no 44362/04, 18 April 2006 100
Dillenkofer and others v Federal Republic of Germany [1996] ECR I–4845 156
Director General of Fair Trading v Proprietary Association of Great Britain [2001]
EWCA Civ 1217, [2002] 1 WLR 269 .... 36, 155, 380
Djali v Immigration Appeal Tribunal [2003] EWCA Civ 1371 .... 425, 444
DM (Zambia) v Secretary of State for the Home Department [2009] EWCA Civ 474 ...... 425, 444

DN v Switzerland, Judgment of 29 March 2001 305

Dobson v Thames Water Utilities [2009] EWCA Civ 28, [2009] 3 All ER 319.........................153

Dobson v Thames Water Utilities [2011] EWHC 3253 (TCC).. 60, 153

Doherty v Birmingham City Council [2008] UKHL 57, [2008] 3 WLR 636 21, 25, 117, 519, 521

Dombo Beheer v The Netherlands (1993) 18 EHRR 213 .... 333, 349

Doncaster Metropolitan Borough Council v AC [2013] EWHC 45 (QB)....................................516

Doorson v The Netherlands (1996) 22 EHRR 330.. 308, 374

Douglas v Hello! Ltd [2001] QB 967 ....18, 57, 88, 120, 413–14, 427, 435, 437, 461, 551, 557, 561–2, 582, 613, 620, 630

Dougoz v Greece (2001) 34 EHRR 1480 260

Doustaly v France, Judgment of 23 April 1998 161

DPP v Ellery, Divisional Court, 14 July 2005 397

DPP v Sheldrake [2004] UKHL 43, [2005] 1 AC 264...397

Dramatico Entertainment Ltd v British Sky Broadcasting Ltd [2012] EWHC 1152 (Ch)..........590

Draon v France (2005) 42 EHRR 807...656

Draper v United Kingdom (1980) 24 DR 72 493

DS (India) v Secretary of State for the Home Department [2009] EWCA Civ 544,
    [2010] Imm AR 81...488

DS v HM Advocate [2007] UKPC D1, [2007] HRLR 28...368

D'Souza v Lambeth London Borough [2001] EWCA Civ 794 342

Dulieu v White & Sons [1901] 2 KB 669 154

Dunn v Parole Board [2008] EWCA Civ 374, [2009] 1 WLR 728...................................... 60, 282

Duport Steels Ltd v Sirs (1980) 1 WLR 142...384

Dyer v Watson [2002] UKPC D1, [2002] 1 AC 379..311

E (by her litigation friend the Official Solicitor) v Channel Four [2005] EWHC (Fam)
    1144, [2005] EMLR 30..427, 461, 586

E v DPP [2005] EWHC 197 (Admin)... 422, 427

E v Norway (1990) 17 EHRR 30 310

Eagerpath Ltd v Edwards (Inspector of Taxes) [2001] STC 26...332

Earl Spencer v United Kingdom (1998) 25 EHRR CD 105 436

East African Asians v United Kingdom (1973) 3 EHRR 76..229

Eastaway v Secretary of State for Trade and Industry [2007] EWCA Civ 425 32

Eastenders Cash & Carry plc v Revenue & Customs Commissioners [2012] EWCA Civ
    689, [2012] STC 2036 342

EB (Kosovo) v Secretary of State for the Home Department [2008] UKHL 41, [2008] 3
    WLR 178..485

Ebert v Official Receiver [2001] EWCA Civ 340, [2002] 1 WLR 320......................................344

Eckle v Germany (1982) 5 EHRR 1 .... 171, 378–9

Edwards v United Kingdom (2002) 35 EHRR 19 .... 209, 212, 217

ELH v United Kingdom (1997) 91A DR 61...493

EM (Eritrea) v Secretary of State for the Home Department [2012] EWCA Civ 1336,
    [2013] HRLR 1 .... 4, 255

EM (Lebanon) v Secretary of State for the Home Department [2008] UKHL 64, [2008]
    3 WLR 931...466, 477, 484

Emerson Developments Ltd v Avery [2004] EWHC (QB) 194 552

Engel v Netherlands (No 1) (1976) 1 EHRR 647....................................... 277, 279, 291, 335, 338

English v Emery Reimbold & Strick Ltd [2002] EWCA Civ 605..370

Equality and Human Rights Commission v Prime Minister [2011] EWHC 2401 (Admin) 33

Ergi v Turkey (2001) 32 EHRR 18 .... 197, 211

Esfandiari v Secretary of State for Work and Pensions [2006] EWCA Civ 282, [2006]
HRLR 26 ....610, 614, 616, 631

Estate Acquisition and Development Ltd v Wiltshire [2006] EWCA Civ 533 370

Estevez v Spain 10 May 2001 469

Estima Jorge v Portugal, Judgment of 21 April 1998...161

ETK v News Group Newspapers Ltd [2011] EWCA Civ 439, [2011] 1 WLR 1827 ....
417, 563, 568, 588

Evans v Amicus Healthcare Ltd [2004] EWCA Civ 727, [2005] Fam 1 ....
143, 183, 427, 439, 459, 467

Evans v United Kingdom (2008) 46 EHRR 34 183

Eweida v United Kingdom [2013] IRLR 231 542

Ezeh and Connors v United Kingdom Judgments of 15 July 2002, 9 October 2003 .... 338, 372

F v G UKEAT/0042/11/DA 21 September 2011 458

F v M [2004] EWHC (Fam) 727...474

Family T v Austria (1990) 64 DR 176..275

Fareham Borough Council v Miller [2013] EWCA Civ 159, [2013] HLR 22 525

Farrer v Secretary of State [2002] EWHC (Admin) 1917...414

Fayed v United Kingdom (1994) 18 EHRR 393 341

Federal Bank of the Middle East v Hadkinson, Court of Appeal, 5 November 1999......... 342, 344

Federation of Tour Operators v HM Treasury [2008] EWCA Civ 752, [2008] STC 2524.........673

Ferdinand v MGN Ltd [2011] EWHC 2454 (QB)..................................... 417, 461, 564, 569, 583

FGP v Serco plc [2012] EWHC 1804 (Admin)...241

Financial Services Authority v Amro International [2010] EWCA Civ 123, [2010] 3 All
ER 723 421

Financial Times v Interbrew [2002] EWCA Civ 274, [2002] EMLR 446.........................
131, 563–4, 598–600, 661

Financial Times v United Kingdom (2010) 50 EHRR 46 600

Findlay v United Kingdom (1997) 24 EHRR 221 .... 159, 379–81

Fitzpatrick v Sterling Housing Association Ltd [2001] 1 AC 27 .... 3, 55

Flynn v HM Advocate [2004] UKPC D1, [2004] HRLR 17 .... 277, 280

FM (Zimbabwe) v Secretary of State for the Home Department [2011] EWCA Civ 168...........259

Fogarty v United Kingdom (2002) 34 EHRR 13...341

Ford v Alexander [2012] EWHC 266 (Ch)..515

Fox, Campbell and Hartley v United Kingdom (1990) 13 EHRR 157.............................. 284, 294

Fox v HM Customs and Excise [2002] EWHC (Admin) 1244, [2003] 1 WLR 1331 .... 131, 675

FP (Iran) v Secretary of State for the Home Department [2007] EWCA Civ 13, [2007]
Imm AR 450..370

Francis v Secretary of State for Work and Pensions [2005] EWCA Civ 1303, [2006] 1
WLR 3202 ....610, 620, 624, 631

Francovich and Bonifaci v Italy [1991] ECR I–5357...155

Fraser v HM Advocate [2011] UKSC 24, [2011] HRLR 28 352

Friend v Lord Advocate [2007] UKHL 53, [2008] HRLR 11..
9, 111, 412, 428, 439, 456, 530, 537, 553, 608, 621

Funke v France (1993) 16 EHRR 297..444

Furness v Environment Agency [2002] Env LR 26...425

G v E (by his litigation friend the Official Solicitor) [2010] EWCA Civ 822, [2011] 3
WLR 652 286

Gale v Serious Organised Crime Agency [2011] UKSC 49, [2011] 1 WLR 2760 362
Gallagher v Church of Jesus Christ of Latter-Day Saints [2008] UKHL 56, [2008] 1
    WLR 1852 .... 612, 631
Galloway v Telegraph Group Ltd [2006] EWCA Civ 17, [2006] HRLR 13 579
Ganusaukas v Lithuania, Application No 47922/99 338
Gas & Electricity Markets Authority v Infinis plc [2013] EWCA Civ 70, [2013] JPL
    1037 .... 160, 641
Gascoyne v HM Customs and Excise [2004] EWCA Civ 1162, [2005] Ch 215 676
Gaskin v United Kingdom (1989) 12 EHRR 36 .... 463, 556
Gasus Dosier-und Fordertecknik GmbH v The Netherlands (1995) 20 EHRR 403 652
Gaughran [2012] NIQB 88 447
Gezer v Secretary of State for the Home Department [2004] EWCA Civ 1730, [2005]
    HRLR 7 .... 232–4, 243
Ghai v Newcastle City Council [2009] EWHC 978 (Admin) 532
Ghaidan v Godin-Mendoza [2004] UKHL 30, [2004] 2 AC 557 ....
    55, 66, 97, 103, 111, 118–23, 129, 134, 605–7, 612, 614, 616, 620, 622–3, 626, 628–9, 634–5
Gibson v Revenue & Customs Prosecution Office [2008] EWCA Civ 645, [2009] 2 WLR 471655
Gillan v United Kingdom (2010) 50 EHRR 45 ....86, 89, 277, 424
Gillick v West Norfolk and Wisbech Area Health Authority [1986] 1 AC 112 502
Gillow v United Kingdom (1986) 11 EHRR 335 .... 79, 504
Girling v Parole Board [2005] EWHC (Admin) 5469 304
Global Knafaim Leasing Ltd v Civil Aviation Authority [2010] EWHC 1348 (Admin),
    [2011] 1 Lloyd's Rep 324 651
Goddi v Italy (1984) 6 EHRR 457 .... 171, 403
Golder v United Kingdom (1975) 1 EHRR 524 ....5, 323, 330, 341, 344, 390
Golobiewska v The Commissioners of Customs and Excise [2005] EWCA Civ 607 676
Goode v Martin [2001] EWCA Civ 1899, [2002] 1 WLR 1828 .... 130, 343
Goodwin v NGN Ltd [2011] EWHC 1437 (QB) 417, 566, 570, 583
Goodwin v United Kingdom (1996) 22 EHRR 123 599
Goodwin v United Kingdom (2002) 35 EHRR 18 ....14, 134–5, 421, 438
Gora v Customs and Excise Commissioners [2003] EWCA Civ 525, [2004] QB 93 339
Gough v Chief Constable of the Derbyshire Constabulary [2002] EWCA Civ 351,
    [2002] QB 459 .... 336–7, 339
Gouriet v Union of Post Office Workers [1978] AC 435 384
Granger v United Kingdom (1990) 12 EHRR 469 404
Grant v Ministry of Justice [2011] EWHC 3379 (QB) 228–30, 239, 242, 424
Grape Bay Ltd v AG of Bermuda [2000] 1 WLR 574 658
Gray v UVW [2010] EWHC 2367 (QB) 458
Greenfield v Irwin [2001] EWCA Civ 113, [2001] 1 WLR 1279 476
Greengate Furniture Ltd v The Commissioners of Customs and Excise, VAT and Duties
    Tribunals, 11 August 2003 673
Gregory v United Kingdom (1997) 25 EHRR 577 603
Griffiths (n 300 348
Guerra v Italy (1998) 26 EHRR 357 ....423, 425, 556
Guleç v Turkey (1998) 28 EHRR 121 211
Gunn-Russo v Nugent Care Society [2001] EWHC (Admin) 566, [2002] 1 FLR 1 468
Gunter v South Western Staffordshire Primary Care Trust [2005] EWHC 1894 (Admin),
    (2006) 9 CCL Rep 121 471

Guyer v Walton (Inspector of Taxes) [2001] STC (SCD) 75 .... 420, 444

Guzzardi v Italy (1980) 3 EHRR 333 .... 271–2, 289, 337

H (A Healthcare Worker) v Associated Newspapers Ltd [2002] EWCA Civ 195, [2002]
    EMLR 23 ....414, 557, 567, 598

H v A City Council [2011] EWCA Civ 403, [2011] UKHRR 599 463

H v France (1989) 12 EHRR 74.. 323, 372

H v Tomlinson [2008] EWCA Civ 1258, [2009] ELR 14..415

H v United Kingdom (1985) 45 DR 281 344

Hadiova v Secretary of State for the Home Department [2003] EWCA Civ 701 .... 430, 442

Haikel v The General Medical Council [2002] UKPC 37, [2002] Lloyd's Rep 415 376

Halford v United Kingdom (1997) 24 EHRR 523..160

Hall v First Secretary of State [2007] EWCA Civ 612 663

Hall v Mayor of London [2010] EWCA Civ 817... 554, 592

Halsey v Milton Keynes General NHS Trust [2004] EWCA Civ 576, [2004] 1 WLR 3002 340

Hamer v United Kingdom (1979) 4 EHRR 139 493

Hamilton v Al Fayed [2002] EWCA Civ 665, [2003] QB 1175...557

Hammerton v Hammerton [2007] EWCA Civ 248, [2007] 2 FLR 1133 362

Hammond v Director of Public Prosecutions [2004] EWHC (Admin) 69 .... 552, 591

Hampshire County Council v Beer [2003] EWCA Civ 1056, [2004] 1 WLR 233 .... 41, 53

Handyside v United Kingdom (1979–80) 1 EHRR 737..86

Harding v The Commissioners of Customs and Excise, VADT, 4 August 2003 676

Harlan Laboratories UK Ltd v Stop Huntingdon Animal Cruelty [2012] EWHC 3408 (QB).....593

Harman v Secretary of State for the Home Department [1982] 2 WLR 338 .... 5, 549

Harrison (Jamaica) v Secretary of State for the Home Department [2012] EWCA Civ
    1736, [2013] 2 CMLR 23 4

Harrison v Secretary of State for the Home Department [2003] EWCA Civ 432 .... 328, 332

Harrow London Borough Council v Qazi [2003] UKHL 43, [2004] 1 AC 983 .... 11, 14, 503–4,
                                                                            506, 518, 521

Hassan v Secretary of State for Justice [2011] EWHC 1359 (Admin)......................................242

Hautanemi v Sweden (1996) 22 EHRR CD 156 41

Head v Social Security Commissioner [2009] EWHC 950 (Admin), [2009] Pens LR 207 643

Heald v Brent London Borough Council [2009] EWCA Civ 930, [2010] 1 WLR 990..............390

A Health Authority v X [2001] EWCA Civ 2014, [2002] 2 All ER 780 .... 455, 457

Heath v Commissioner of Police for the Metropolis [2004] EWCA Civ 943, [2005]
    ICR 329 .... 326–7, 345

Heathrow Airport Ltd v Garman [2007] EWHC 1957 (QB)..593

Helle v Finland (1997) 26 EHRR 159...370

Helman v Commissioners of Customs and Excise, Administrative Court, 18 October 2002 676

Henderson v Chief Constable of Cleveland Constabulary [2001] EWCA Civ 335 284

Henra v France, Judgment of 29 April 1998..161

Herczegfalvy v Austria (1992) 15 EHRR 437 .... 89, 237

HH (Iran) v Secretary of State for the Home Department [2008] EWCA Civ 504 332

HH v Italy [2012] UKSC 25, [2012] 3 WLR 90..490

Hickling v Baker [2007] EWCA Civ 287, [2007] 1 WLR 2386.................................... 284, 294–5

Hill v Chief Constable of West Yorkshire [1989] AC 53 203

Hillingdon London Borough Council v Neary [2011] EWHC 413 (Fam); [2011] CP Rep 32....587

Hillingdon London Borough Council v Neary [2011] EWHC 1377 (Fam), [2011] 4 All
    ER 584.. 275, 471

Hiro Balani v Spain (1995) 19 EHRR 566 370
Hirst v Parole Board, Court of Appeal, 25 September 2002 307
Hirst v Secretary of State for the Home Department [2002] EWHC (Admin) 602,
    [2002] 1 WLR 2929 .... 553, 572
Hirst v Secretary of State for the Home Department [2006] EWCA Civ 945, [2006] 1
    WLR 3083 282
Hirst v United Kingdom, Application no 74025/01, 6 October 2005, Grand Chamber 100
Hirst v United Kingdom 24 October 2001 314
HM Advocate v Murtagh [2009] UKPC 36, [2010] 3 WLR 814 ....351, 419, 457
HM Advocate v P [2011] UKSC 44, [2011] 1 WLR 2497 402
HM Advocate v R [2002] UKPC D3, [2004] 1 AC 462 ....26, 81, 157, 373, 375, 379
HM Treasury v Ahmed [2010] UKSC 1, [2010] 2 AC 697 584
HM Treasury v Ahmed [2010] UKSC 2, [2010] 2 AC 534 ....3, 13, 340
HM v Switzerland, Judgment of 26 February 2002 272
Hoare v United Kingdom [1997] EHRLR 678 86
Hodgson v United Kingdom (1987) 10 EHRR 503 36
Holder v Law Society [2000] EWHC (Admin) 2023 391
Holder v Law Society [2003] EWCA Civ 39, [2003] 1 WLR 1059 661
Holland (executor of Holland, deceased) v Inland Revenue Commissioners [2003] STC
    (SCD) 43 66
Holland v HM Advocate [2005] HRLR 25 ....351, 359, 364, 367
Holland v Lampen-Wolfe [2000] 1 WLR 1573 .... 340, 346
Holmes v Royal College of Veterinary Surgeons [2011] UKPC 48 391
Holmes v Westminster City Council [2011] EWHC 2857 (QB) 526
Holy Monasteries v Greece (1995) 20 EHRR 1 .... 41, 658
Hopkins v Parole Board [2008] EWHC 2312 (Admin), [2009] Prison LR 223 309
Horgan v Horgan [2002] EWCA Civ 1371 .... 278, 284
Horncastle [2009] UKSC 14, [2010] 2 AC 373 .... 21, 407
Horsham Properties Group Ltd v Clark [2008] EWHC 2327 (Ch); [2009] 1 WLR 1255 642,
                                                                                                                             650, 665
Hounslow London Borough Council v Powell [2011] UKSC 8, [2011] 2 WLR 287.132, 504, 522
Howard v United Kingdom, 16 July 1987 330
Howarth v Commissioner of Police of the Metropolis [2011] EWHC 2818 (Admin)........ 423, 448
HRH Prince of Wales v Associated Newspapers Ltd [2006] EWCA Civ 1776, [2007] 3
    WLR 222 ....415–16, 569, 582, 603
Huang v Secretary of State for the Home Department [2007] UKHL 11, [2007] 2 AC
    167 .... 91, 93–9, 102–3, 442–3, 481–3
Hughes v Customs and Excise Commissioners [2002] EWCA Civ 670, [2002] 4 All ER
    633 .... 396, 671
Hughes v Paxman [2006] EWCA Civ 818, [2007] RPC 2 650
Humberclyde Finance Group Limited v Hicks, Chancery Division, 14 November 2001 57
Humphreys v Revenue & Customs Commissioners [2012] UKSC 18, [2012] 1 WLR
    1545 .... 613, 617, 620, 627, 632
Hunt v Times Newspapers Ltd [2012] EWHC 110 (QB) 564
Hussein v Chong Fook Kam [1970] AC 942 285
Hussein v Secretary of State for Defence [2013] EWHC 95 (Admin) 229
Hutcheson v News Group Newspapers Ltd [2011] EWCA Civ 808 .... 565, 583
Hutchinson v Newbury Magistrates Court, Divisional Court, 9 October 2000 554

HXA v Home Office [2010] EWHC 1177 (QB)..290
HXT v Secretary of State for the Home Department [2013] 1962 (QB)....................................290
Hyde Park Residence Ltd v Yelland [2001] Ch 143..589
I v Secretary of State for the Home Department [2005] EWCA Civ 886..................................251
Ibrahim v Secretary of State for the Home Department [2005] EWCA Civ 1816.................258–9
Igroup Ltd v Ocwen [2003] EWHC (Ch) 2431, [2004] 1 WLR 451 421
Imutran Ltd v Uncaged Campaigns Ltd [2001] 2 All ER 385...................................558, 561, 598
In Re British Broadcasting Corporation [2009] UKHL 34, [2009] 3 WLR 142......................462
In Re Crawley Green Road Cemetery, Luton [2001] 2 WLR 1175..532
In Re Durrington Cemetery [2000] 3 WLR 1322...532
In Re McClean [2005] UKHL 46...301, 307, 310
In Re Medicaments and Related Classes of Goods (No 2) [2001] 1 WLR 700........................214
In Re P [2008] UKHL 38, [2008] 3 WLR 76...............................22, 110, 606, 610–11, 620, 635
In the Matter of an Application by Brewster for Judicial Review [2012] NIQB 85...................631
In the Matter of an Application by Brigid McCaughey for Judicial Review [2011]
  UKSC 20, [2011] 2 WLR 1279...206
In the Matter of C (A Child) [2011] EWCA Civ 521, [2011] 2 FLR 912.................................496
In the Matter of D (Interim Receiver Order: Proceeds of Crime Act 2002),
  Administrative Court, 7 December 2004 671
In the Matter of FI Call Ltd [2013] EWCA Civ 819, [2013] 1 WLR 2993.............................457
In the Matter of G (A Child) v D [2013] EWHC 134 (Fam), [2013] 1 FLR 1334 ....470, 496
In the Matter of General Dental Council [2011] EWHC 3011 (Admin) 455
In the Matter of Guardian News and Media [2010] UKSC 1, [2010] 2 AC 697.......422, 431, 462,
                                                                                                             567, 575, 584
In the Matter of K (children) [2002] EWCA Crim 1071, [2002] 1 WLR 2833.......................404
In the Matter of Kirk Session of Sandown Free Presbyterian Church's Application
  [2011] NIQB 26 ....551, 595
In the Matter of M (A Child) [2012] EWCA Civ 1905..350
In the Matter of S (A Child) [2012] UKSC 10, [2012] 2 AC 257...500
In the Matter of Saggar, Court of Appeal [2005] EWCA Civ 174 377
In the Matter of the Trusts of the X Charity [2003] EWHC (Ch) 1462, [2003] 1 WLR 2751 ...372
In the Matter of X, Family Division, 21 February 2001 463
Incal v Turkey, Judgment of 9 June 1998 .... 159, 161
International Transport Roth GmbH v Secretary of State for the Home Department
  [2002] EWCA Civ 158, [2002] 3 WLR 344...102, 141, 339, 676
Inzunza v United States [2011] EWHC 920 (Admin) [2011] ACD 68......................................260
IR (Sri Lanka) v Secretary of State for the Home Department [2011] EWCA Civ 704,
  [2011] 4 All ER 908 .... 332, 488
ISKCON v United Kingdom, 8 March 1994 330
Islington Borough Council v Jones [2012] EWHC 1537 (QB)..593
Issa v Turkey (2005) 41 EHRR 27..75
J & PM Dockeray (a firm) v Secretary of State for the Environment, Food & Rural
  Affairs [2002] EWHC (Admin) 420, [2002] HLR 27...343
J Council v GU [2012] EWHC 3531 (COP)..436
J v London Borough of Enfield [2002] EWHC (Admin) 735, [2002] 2 FLR 1.........................475
J v Secretary of State for the Home Department [2005] EWCA Civ 629..................................256
J1 v Secretary of State for the Home Department [2013] EWCA Civ 279................................254
JA Pye (Oxford) Ltd v Graham [2002] UKHL 30, [2002] 3 WLR 221 .... 64, 666

Jain v Trent Strategic Health Authority [2009] UKHL 4, [2009] 1 AC 853 ....64, 328, 644, 649, 653, 659, 667

Jameel v Wall Street Journal Europe SPRL [2006] UKHL 44, [2006] 3 WLR 642 ..... 550, 576–80

James, Wells and Lee v United Kingdom (2013) 56 EHRR 12.. 281, 315

James v United Kingdom (1986) 8 EHRR 123 ....324, 341, 639, 649, 653, 656

Jasarevic v Secretary of State for the Home Department [2005] EWCA Civ 1784....................429

JB (India) v Entry Clearance Officer [2009] EWCA Civ 234...467

JD v East Berkshire Community Health NHS Trust [2005] 2 AC 373 475

Jersild v Denmark (1994) 19 EHRR 1 552

JIH v News Group Newspapers Ltd [2011] EWCA Civ 42, [2011] 2 All ER 324......... 458, 585–6

JM v United Kingdom (2011) 53 EHRR 6 611

JO (Uganda) v Secretary of State for the Home Department [2010] EWCA Civ 10 .... 481, 488

Johansen v Norway (1996) 23 EHRR 33.. 494, 499

Johnson v Havering London Borough Council [2007] UKHL 27, [2008] 1 AC 95 .... 504, 508

Johnson v United Kingdom (1997) 27 EHRR 296.. 161, 286

Johnston v Chief Constable of the Royal Ulster Constabulary [1986] ECR 1651.......................41

Jokelala v Finland (2003) 37 EHRR 26 659

Jomah v Attar [2004] EWCA Civ 417 73

Jones v Ministry of the Interior [2004] EWCA Civ 1394, [2005] QB 699................................131

Jones v Saudi Arabia [2006] UKHL 26, [2007] 1 AC 270 ....20, 28, 346

Jones v University of Warwick [2003] EWCA Civ 151, [2003] 1 WLR 954 .... 413, 445–6

Jordan v United Kingdom (2003) 37 EHRR 2 ....204–5, 209, 211–12, 214–17

JSC BTA Bank v Ablyazov [2012] EWCA Civ 1551, [2013] 1 WLR 1845...................... 384, 387

Jude v HM Advocate [2011] UKSC 55, [2012] HRLR 8 401

Junior Books Ltd v Veitchi Ltd [1983] 1 AC 520 154

K v LBX [2012] EWCA Civ 79, [2012] 1 FCR 441 471

K v United Kingdom (1987) 50 D&R 199 468

Kafkaris v Cyprus, Application No 21906/04, 12 February 2008....................................... 246, 259

Kalashnikov v Russia (2002) 36 EHRR 587..261

Kansal v United Kingdom, 10 November 2004..63

Kaplan v United Kingdom (1982) 4 EHRR 64...330

Kapri v Lord Advocate [2013] UKSC 48, [2013] 1 WLR 2324...323

Kay v Lambeth London Borough Council [2006] UKHL 10, [2006] 2 AC 465 ...20, 22, 95–6, 98, 510, 518

Kay v London Borough of Lambeth [2004] EWCA Civ 926, [2004] 3 WLR 1396...................649

Kay v United Kingdom (2012) 54 EHRR 30 .... 110, 520

Kaya v Turkey (1998) 28 EHRR 1.. 160, 211

KD v Chief Constable of Hampshire [2005] EWHC 2550 (QB) [2005] Po LR 253 .... 410, 414

Kearney v HM Advocate [2006] UKPC D 1, [2006] HRLR 15...385

Keazor v Law Society [2009] EWHC 267 (Admin)...661

Keegan v Ireland (1994) 18 EHRR 342.. 161, 468

Keenan v United Kingdom (2001) 33 EHRR 913...217

Kennedy v Charity Commission [2012] EWCA Civ 317, [2012] EMLR 20 556

Kent v Griffiths [2001] QB 36 347

Kerr v Northern Ireland Housing Executive Lands Tr NI 10/1/2013 663

Keyu v Secretary of State for Foreign & Commonwealth Affairs [2012] EWHC 2445
   (Admin) 206

KH (Afghanistan) v Secretary of State for the Home Department [2009] EWCA Civ 1354......258

Khan v Revenue & Customs [2006] EWCA Civ 89, [2006] STC 1167.....................................395

Khan v Royal Air Force Summary Appeal Court [2004] EWHC 2230 (Admin), [2004]
 HRLR 40 .... 89, 535

Khan v Secretary of State for the Home Department [2003] EWCA Civ 530..........................227

Khan v United Kingdom (2000) 8 BHRC 310 365

Khemiri v Court of Milan Italy [2008] EWHC 1988 (Admin)..250

King v Secretary of State for the Home Department [2003] EWHC (Admin) 2831,
 [2004] HRLR 9 314

Kingsalton Ltd v Thames Water Developments Ltd [2001] EWCA Civ 20........642, 647, 658, 662

Kingsley v United Kingdom (2001) 33 EHRR 288.. 155, 381

Kinloch v HM Advocate [2012] UKSC 62, [2013] 2 WLR 141 419

Al-Kishtaini v Shanshal [2001] EWCA Civ 264, [2001] 2 All ER (Comm) 601 .... 655, 672

Klass v Germany (1978) 2 EHRR 214..32

Kleyn v The Netherlands, Judgment of 6 May 2003..383

Koendjbiharie v The Netherlands (1990) 13 EHRR 820...311–12

Kolanis v United Kingdom, 21 June 2005..63

Koniarska v United Kingdom 12 October 2000 .... 275, 285–6

König v Germany (1978) 2 EHRR 170.. 323, 376

KR (Iraq) v Secretary of State for the Home Department [2007] EWCA Civ 514,
 [2007] INLR 373... 426, 443–4

Kraska v Switzerland (1993) 18 EHRR 188 364

Krasner v Dennison [2000] 3 WLR 720 ....642, 647, 655, 664

Krolik v Poland [2012] EWHC 2357 (Admin), [2012] 1 WLR 490 261

Kroon v The Netherlands (1994) 17 EHRR 263 468

KRS v United Kingdom, 2 December 2008..255

Kugathas v Secretary of State for the Home Department [2003] EWCA Civ 31 467

Kulkarni v Milton Keynes Hospital NHS Trust [2009] EWCA Civ 789, [2009] IRLR
 829 .... 331, 362

L v Finland [2000] 3 FCR 219..499

L v Human Fertilisation & Embryology Authority [2008] EWHC 2149 (Fam), [2008] 2
 FLR 1999..427

L v Reading Borough Council [2001] 1 WLR 1575 345

Ladele v Islington London Borough Council [2009] EWCA Civ 1357, [2010] 1 WLR
 955 .... 527, 544

Lai v Commissioners of Customs & Excise, VADT, 1 July 2002 334

Lancashire County Council v Barlow [2002] 2 AC 147 .... 471, 495

Lancashire County Council v Taylor [2005] EWCA Civ 284, [2005] HRLR 17.....38, 137, 142–3,
 621

Lane v Kensington & Chelsea Royal London Borough [2013] EWHC 1320 (QB) 505

Langley v Liverpool City Council [2005] EWCA Civ 1173.. 471, 495

Laporte v Chief Constable of Gloucestershire [2006] UKHL 55, [2007] 2 AC 105...................276

Lauko v Slovakia (1998) 33 EHRR 994 .... 335, 337

Law Society v Sritharan [2005] EWCA Civ 476..661

Lawal v Northern Spirit Ltd [2003] UKHL 35, [2004] 1 All ER 187..................71, 214, 380, 386

Lawless v Ireland (No 3) (1979–80) 1 EHRR 15...16

Lawntown Ltd v Camenzuli [2007] EWCA Civ 949 662

Lawrence v Pembrokeshire County Council [2007] EWCA Civ 446................................. 57, 475

Laws v Society of Lloyd's [2003] EWCA Civ 1887 .... 66, 342

Le Compte, Van Leuven and De Meyere v Belgium (1981) 4 EHRR 1 .... 323, 327, 330

Leander v Sweden (1987) 9 EHRR 433 556

Lechner and Hess v Austria (1987) 9 EHRR 490 171

Lee v Leeds City Council [2002] EWCA Civ 6, [2002] 1 WLR 1488 .... 510, 513

Leeds Teaching Hospital NHS Trust v A [2003] EWHC (QB) 259 .... 467, 474, 501

Legal Services Commission v Loomba [2012] EWHC 29 (QB), [2012] 2 All ER 977 650

Lehideux and Isorni v France (1998) 5 BHRC 540 552

Lendvai v Veszprem City Court of Hungary [2009] EWHC 3431 (Admin) 441

Levi Strauss & Co v Tesco Stores Ltd [2002] EWHC (Ch) 1556, [2003] RPC 18 .... 558, 590,
                                                                                                                                    643, 664

Lindsay v Customs and Excise Commissioners [2002] EWCA Civ 267, [2002] 1 WLR
    1766 ....647, 657, 674–5

Lion Laboratories [1985] QB 526 589

Lithgow v United Kingdom (1986) EHRR 329 658

Lithuania v Campbell [2013] NIQB 19 261

Livingstone v Adjudication Panel for England [2006] EWHC 2533 (Admin), [2006]
    HRLR 45 .... 551, 594

Livingstone v Rawyards Coal Co (1880) 5 App Cas 25 158

Lloyds UDT Finance Ltd v Chartered Finance Trust Holdings plc [2002] EWCA Civ
    806, [2002] STC 956 .... 66, 613

LNS v Persons Unknown [2010] EWHC 119 (QB), [2010] EMLR 16 ....417, 461, 569, 583

Locabail (UK) Ltd v Bayfield Properties Ltd [2000] 1 All ER 65 387

Local Authorities Mutual Investment Trust v Customs and Excise Commissioners
    [2003] EWHC (Ch) 2766, [2004] STC 246 .... 643, 649

A Local Authority v A Health Authority [2003] EWHC (Fam) 2746, [2004] Fam 96 584

London Borough of Bexley v Secretary of State for the Environment, Transport and the
    Regions [2001] EWHC (Admin) 323 .... 647, 662

London Regional Transport v The Mayor of London, Divisional Court, 31 July 2001 ...... 567, 597

London Regional Transport v The Mayor of London [2001] EWCA Civ 1491, [2003]
    EMLR 4 567

Lopez Ostra v Spain (1994) 20 EHRR 277 423

Lorsé v Netherlands (2003) 37 EHRR 3 229

Lough v First Secretary of State [2004] EWCA Civ 905, [2004] 1 WLR 2557 ....506, 514, 648

Loutchansky v Times Newspapers Ltd (No 2) [2001] EWCA Civ 1805, [2002] 2 WLR
    640 ....551, 576, 579

Luberti v Italy (1984) 6 EHRR 440 286

Lukaszewski v Poland [2012] UKSC 20, [2012] 1 WLR 1604 .... 130, 324, 327, 332, 340, 343

Lustig-Prean and Beckett v United Kingdom; Smith and Grady v United Kingdom
    (1999) 29 EHRR 493 96

Lutsyuk v Ukraine [2013] 189 (Admin) 261

Lutz v Germany (1987) 10 EHRR 182 .... 333, 338

Lydiashourne Ltd v The Commissioners of Customs & Excise, Court of Appeal, 1
    November 2000 .... 647, 673

M (A Minor) v Newham London Borough Council [1995] 2 AC 633 154

M v F [2011] EWCA Civ 273, [2011] 2 FLR 123 474

M v Home Office [1994] 1 AC 377 384

M v Italy (1991) 70 DR 59 337

M v Netherlands (1993) 74 D&R 120 467

M v United Kingdom (1983) 6 EHRR 345...404
MA (Somalia) v Secretary of State for the Home Department [2010] UKSC 49, [2011]
 2 All ER 65 251
Mabon v Mabon [2005] EWCA Civ 634, [2004] 3 WLR 460 472
Macdonald v Advocate General for Scotland [2003] UKHL 34, [2004] 1 All ER 339.................64
MacMahon [2012] NIQB 93...412
MacNeill v Parole Board [2001] EWCA Civ 448 314
Maddock v Devon County Council, Divisional Court, 13 August 2003............................ 450, 464
Mahajan v Department of Constitutional Affairs [2004] EWCA Civ 946..............................345
Mahan Air v Blue Sky One Ltd [2011] EWCA Civ 544 344
Malcolm v Mackenzie [2004] EWCA Civ 1748, [2005] 1 WLR 1238..................................71
Malcolm v Ministry of Justice [2011] EWCA Civ 1538.. 424, 436
Maley v Secretary of State for Communities & Local Government [2008] EWHC 2652
 (Admin) 517
Malik v Fassenfelt [2013] EWCA Civ 798.. 504, 526
Malik v Manchester Crown Court [2008] EWHC 1362 (Admin), [2008] 4 All ER 403.... 557, 601
Malik v United Kingdom 13 March 2012...646
Manchester City Council v Pinnock [2010] UKSC 45, [2011] 2 AC 104......20, 25, 101, 110, 115,
 117, 132, 507, 520–1, 523–4
Mangera v Ministry of Defence [2003] EWCA Civ 801 326
Marcic v Thames Water Utilities Ltd [2003] UKHL 66, [2004] 2 AC 42..........510, 513, 642, 648,
 652, 659, 664
Marckx v Belgium (1979) 2 EHRR 330 .... 466, 503
Mark v Mark [2005] UKHL 42, [2005] 3 WLR 111..341
Marleasing SA v La Commercial Internacional de Alimentación SA Case C-106/890
 [1990] ECR I-4135...120
Marmont v Secretary of State for Culture, Media and Sport [2003] EWHC (QB) 2300 555
Martins Moreira v Portugal, Judgment of 26 October 1988 159
Mason v Ministry of Justice [2008] EWHC 1787 (QB)..300
Massey v United Kingdom, 16 November 2004...63
Massingham v Secretary of State for Transport, Local Government and the Regions
 [2002] EWHC (Admin) 1578 506
Mastromatteo v Italy, 24 October 2002...217
Matthews v Ministry of Defence [2003] UKHL 4, [2003] 1 AC 1163..................... 14, 238, 341–2
Mattu v University Hospitals of Coventry and Warwickshire NHS Trust [2012] EWCA
 Civ 641, [2012] 4 All ER 359.. 328, 333
Mayor and Burgesses of the London Borough of Lambeth v Howard [2001] EWCA Civ 468..506
Mayor of London (On behalf of the Greater London Authority) v Haw [2011] EWHC
 585 (QB)..592
Mazurkiewicz v Poland [2011] EWHC 659 (Admin)...257
McCann v United Kingdom (1996) 21 EHRR 97 ....162, 204–5, 209, 217
McCann v United Kingdom (2008) 47 EHRR 40 519
McCann v United Kingdom (2008) 47 EHRR 913 .... 110, 520
McCartan Turkington Breen v Times Newspapers Ltd [2001] 2 AC 277 .... 17, 84
McClaren v News Group Newspapers Ltd [2012] EWHC 2466 (QB)....................................461
McDonald v HM Advocate [2008] UKPC 46, [2009] HRLR 3..350
McFarlane v Relate Avon Ltd [2010] EWCA Civ 880, [2010] IRLR 872...........................531–2
McGonnell v United Kingdom (2000) 30 EHRR 289...379–80, 384

McGowan (Procurator Fiscal) v B [2011] UKSC 54, [2011] 1 WLR 3121 401

McGowan v Scottish Water [2005] IRLR 167..446

McGrath v Secretary of State for Work & Pensions [2012] EWHC 1042 (Admin)........... 643, 678

McInnes v HM Advocate [2010] UKSC 7, [2010] HRLR 17...352

McIntosh v Lord Advocate [2001] 1 AC 1078 .... 26, 91, 320, 331, 335–6, 339, 361, 392, 394–6

McKellar v Mayor & Burgesses of the London Borough of Hounslow [2003] EWHC
   (QB) 3145...199, 508, 512

McKerr v United Kingdom (2002) 34 EHRR 20 37

McKerry v Teesdale & Wear Valley Justices [2001] EMLR 5..557

McLean v Ireland [2008] EWHC 547 (Admin)..263

McLean v Procurator Fiscal, Fort William [2001] 1 WLR 2425 ....81, 349–50, 400, 403–4

McLoughlin v O'Brian [1983] 1 AC 410...154

McMichael v United Kingdom (1995) 20 EHRR 205..468

McPherson v Secretary of State for the Home Department [2001] EWCA Civ 1955 .... 251, 262

Medhurst v Secretary of State for Communities & Local Government [2011] EWHC
   3576 (Admin)...516

Medvedyev v France (2010) 51 EHRR 39..75

Medway Council v BBC [2002] 1 FLR 104..567

Mengesha v Commissioner of Police of the Metropolis [2013] EWHC 1695 (Admin),
   [2013] ACD 120... 437, 447

Menson v United Kingdom (2003) 37 EHRR CD 220 .... 205, 210

Merchant International Co Ltd v Natsionalna Aktsionerna Kompaniia Naftogaz
   [2012] EWCA Civ 196, [2012] 1 WLR 3036...323

Mersey Care NHS Trust v Ackroyd [2007] EWCA Civ 101, [2007] HRLR 19........................600

MGN Limited v United Kingdom (2011) 53 EHRR 5...582

MH v United Kingdom 22 October 2013 298

Michael v Chief Constable of South Wales [2012] EWCA Civ 981, [2012] HRLR 30..... 195, 203

Millar v Dickson [2002] 1 WLR 1615...319

Millar v Procurator Fiscal, Elgin [2001] 1 WLR 1615....................................14, 81, 379–81, 383–5

Mills v HM Advocate (No 2) [2002] UKPC D2, [2004] 1 AC 441 .....26, 169, 319, 372–3, 376, 378

Mills v MI Developments (UK) Ltd [2002] EWCA Civ 1576 649

Mills v News Group Newspapers Ltd [2001] EMLR 41 414

Minister of Home Affairs v Fisher [1980] AC 319 17

Minto and Cuthbert v Police (1990–92) NZBORR 208...62

Mitchell v Glasgow City Council [2009] UKHL 11, [2009] 1 AC 874 .... 191, 194–5, 203

ML v ANS [2012] UKSC 30, [2012] HRLR 27.. 85, 120, 471, 480, 497

MM (Lebanon) v Secretary of State for the Home Department [2013] EWHC 1900 (Admin).....487

MM (Zimbabwe) v Secretary of State for the Home Department [2012] EWCA Civ 279 442

MN (India) v Secretary of State for the Home Department [2008] EWCA Civ 38,
   [2008] 2 FLR 87 469

Mohammed Adam v Secretary of State for the Home Department [2003] EWCA Civ 265.......261

Monnell & Morris v United Kingdom (1987) 10 EHRR 205..404

Montgomery v HM Advocate [2003] 1 AC 641 .... 81, 334, 349, 379–80, 388

Moreira de Azevedo v Portugal (1990) 13 EHRR 721...327

Morris v United Kingdom (2002) 34 EHRR 1253 .... 21, 389

Morrison v Buckinghamshire CC [2011] EWHC 3444 (QB) 422

Mosley v News Group Newspapers [2008] EWHC 1777 (QB), [2008] EMLR
   20 .... 176, 415–16, 438, 564–6, 569, 582–3

A Mother v A Father [2009] EWCA Civ 1057, [2010] 2 FLR 1757..457
Mouisel v France (2004) 38 EHRR 34 241
Mountney v Treharne [2002] 2 FLR 406...515
MS (Algeria) v Secretary of State for the Home Department [2011] EWCA Civ 306................254
MS [2007] EWCA Civ 133, [2007] Im AR 538...482
MSS v Belgium and Greece, 21 January 2011 255
MT (Zimbabwe) v Secretary of State for the Home Department [2007] EWCA Civ 455 483
Mudarikwa v Secretary of State for the Home Department [2003] EWCA Civ 583..................262
Muller v Switzerland (1991) 13 EHRR 212 .... 86, 573
Murbarak v Murbarak [2001] 1 FCR 193...339
Murray v Big Pictures (UK) Ltd [2008] EWCA Civ 446, [2008] 3 WLR 1360...413–14, 417, 582
Murray v Parole Board [2003] EWCA Civ 1561 314
Murray v United Kingdom (1994) 19 EHRR 193 ....105, 285, 320
Murray v United Kingdom (1996) 22 EHRR 29 360
Murungaru v Secretary of State for the Home Department [2008] EWCA Civ 1015,
    [2009] INLR 180..642
Muse v Entry Clearance Officer [2012] EWCA Civ 10, [2012] Imm AR 476 479
Musial v Poland (2001) 31 EHRR 29 311
N v Governor of HM Prison Dartmoor, Administrative Court, 13 February 2001 .... 420, 463
N v Secretary of State for the Home Department [2005] UKHL 31, [2005] 2 AC 296...............72,
    250–1, 258
N v SSHD [2005] UKHL 31; [2005] 2 AC 296...24
N v United Kingdom (2008) 47 EHRR 39 258
Nadarajah v Secretary of State for the Home Department [2003] EWCA Civ 1768 .... 85, 279,
    291–2
Nasser v United Bank of Kuwait [2001] EWCA Civ 556, [2002] 1 WLR 1868.......................344
Nasser v United Bank of Kuwait [2001] EWCA Civ 1454...608, 620, 624
National and Provincial Building Society v United Kingdom (1997) 25 EHRR 127.................309
National Health Service Trust v D [2000] 2 FCR 577...183, 188, 200
National Health Service Trust v D [2000] 2 FLR 677...185, 237
Neil Martin Ltd v Revenue & Customs Commissioners [2007] EWCA Civ 1041.............. 65, 647
Neuback v Germany (1983) 41 DR 13 ....171, 378
Neulinger and Shuruk v Switzerland [2011] 1 FLR 122..500
New Testament Church of God v Stewart [2007] EWCA Civ 1004, [2008] HRLR 2528, 530, 533
Newcastle City Council v Z [2005] EWHC 1490 (Fam), [2007] 1 FLR 861 .... 532, 546
Newman (Inspector of Taxes) v Hatt [2002] 04 EG 175 420
Newman v Modern Bookbinders Ltd [2000] 2 All ER 814...399, 404
Ngene v Secretary of State for the Home Department [2002] EWCA Civ 185..........................261
NHS Trust A v H [2001] 2 FLR 501...200
NHS Trust A v Mrs M [2001] 2 WLR 942.................. 103, 182–4, 186–8, 200, 238, 422–3
NHS Trust v DJ [2012] EWHC 3524 (COP)..184
NHS Trust v P, Family Division, 19 December 2000...103, 182, 200
Nicholds v Security Industry Authority [2006] EWHC 1792 (Admin), [2007] 1 WLR
    2067 ....644, 657, 661
Nielsen v Denmark (1988) EHRR 175... 272, 275
Norris v United States [2010] UKSC 9, [2010] 2 AC 487.. 477, 488–90
North Range Shipping Ltd v Seatrans Shipping Corporation [2002] EWHC Civ 405,
    [2002] 1 WLR 2397..370–1

Norwich Pharmacal Co v Customs and Excise Commissioners [1973] 2 All ER 943 .... 4, 564, 598–9

Norwood v Director of Public Prosecutions [2003] EWHC (Admin) 1564, [2003] Crim LR 888 .... 552, 591

Novartis Pharmaceuticals UK Ltd v Stop Huntingdon Animal Cruelty [2009] EWHC 2716 (QB), [2010] HRLR 8 593

NS v United Kingdom [2011] EUECJ C-411/10 and C-493/10 255

Ntuli v Donald [2010] EWCA Civ 1276, [2011] 1 WLR 294 .... 562, 586

O v Harrow Crown Court [2006] UKHL 42, [2007] 1 AC 249 295–7

O v United Kingdom (1988) 13 EHRR 578 171

OA (Nigeria) v Secretary of State for the Home Department [2008] EWCA Civ 82, [2008] HRLR 24 429

Obermeier v Austria (1990) 13 EHRR 290 374

Öcalan v Turkey (2005) 41 EHRR 45 75

O'Connell v Parole Board [2009] EWCA Civ 575, [2009] 1 WLR 2539 300

Odawey v Entry Clearance Officer [2011] EWCA Civ 840 479

Office of Fair Trading v X [2003] EWHC (Comm) 1042, [2004] ICR 105 505

Ofulue v Bossert [2008] EWCA Civ 7, [2008] 3 WLR 1253 .... 651, 666

Oldham v United Kingdom, Judgment of 26 September 2000 314

Olympic Delivery Authority [2012] EWHC 1012 (Ch) 590

OOO v Commissioner of Police of the Metropolis [2011] EWHC 1246 (QB), [2011] HRLR 29 .... 166, 267

OPQ v BJM [2011] EWHC 1059 (QB), [2011] EMLR 23 588

Orejudos v Royal Borough of Kensington and Chelsea [2003] EWCA Civ 1967 .... 410, 412

O'Riordan v Director of Public Prosecutions [2005] EWHC (Admin) 1240 584

O'Shea v MGN Ltd [2001] EMLR 40 .... 551, 580

Osman v United Kingdom (1997) 29 EHRR 245 ....
    88, 189, 191, 193–4, 197–8, 203, 232–4, 244, 262, 341–2, 347, 431, 476

Othman v United Kingdom, Judgment of 17 January 2012 322–3

Outram v Academy Plastics [2000] IRLR 499 347

Özkan v Turkey, Judgment of 6 April 2004 211

Ozturk v Germany 6 EHRR 409 335

P, a barrister v The General Council of the Bar [2005] 1 WLR 3019 391

P and Q (by their litigation friend the Official Solicitor) v Surrey County Council [2011] EWCA Civ 190, [2012] 2 WLR 1056 .... 270, 274

P v Nottinghamshire Healthcare NHS Trust [2003] EWHC (Admin) 1782, [2003] ACD 403 269

P v Secretary of State for the Home Department [2004] EWCA Civ 1640 263

Pabla Ky v Finland, 22 June 2004 384

Pakelli v Germany (1983) 6 EHRR 1 .... 400, 404

Papachelas v Greece Judgment, 25 March 1999 658

Papageorgiou v Greece, Judgment of 22 October 1997 [1998] HRCD 24 161

Papamichalopoulos v Greece (1996) 21 EHRR 439 .... 158, 161

Parkins v Westminster City Council, Court of Appeal, 20 March 2000 345

Pascoe v First Secretary of State [2006] EWHC 2356 (Admin), [2007] 1 WLR 885 517

Patel v Entry Clearance Officer, Mumbai [2010] EWCA Civ 17 467

Paton v United Kingdom (1980) 3 EHRR 408 225

Paulić v Croatia 22 October 2009 520

Pay v Lancashire Probation Service [2004] ICR 187 .... 551, 558, 574

Payne v Payne [2001] EWCA Civ 166, [2001] 2 WLR 1826...........................465, 471, 494, 499

Peck v United Kingdom (2003) 13 BHRC 669...436

Peers v Greece (2001) 33 EHRR 1192...260

Pellegrin v France (1999) 31 EHRR 651...327

Pelling v Bruce-Williams [2004] EWCA Civ 845, [2004] Fam 155.........................372, 461, 584

Pennycook v Shaws (EAL) Ltd [2004] EWCA Civ 100, [2004] Ch 296.........................342, 649

Percy v DPP [2001] EWHC (Admin) 1125, [2002] Crim LR 835.....................551, 554, 557, 591

Perotti v Collyer-Bristow (a firm) [2003] EWCA Civ 1521, [2004] 2 All ER 189...........347, 362

Perry v Nursing & Midwifery Council [2013] EWCA Civ 145, [2013] 1 WLR 3423..............328

Persey v Secretary of State for Environment, Food and Rural Affairs [2002] EWHC
    (Admin) 371, [2003] QB 794...555, 559, 660

Petrovic v Austria (2001) 33 EHRR 307...607

Pfeifer and Plankl v Austria (1992) 14 EHRR 692...384

PG and JH v United Kingdom, Judgment of 25 September 2001......................................85

Phillips v DPP [2002] EWHC (Admin) 2903, [2003] RTR 8.......................................651, 662

Phillips v United Kingdom [2001] Crim LR 817...671

Piermont v France (1995) 20 EHRR 301...35, 558

Pinder v United Kingdom (1984) 7 EHRR 464...341

Pine v Solicitors' Disciplinary Tribunal [2001] EWCA Crim 1574, [2002] UKHRR 81..........362,
                                                                                        370, 391

Pine Valley Developments v Ireland (1993) 16 EHRR 379.......................................159, 161

Pisarek v Regional Court in Elblag 11 [2010] EWHC 877 (Admin)..................................261

PM v United Kingdom, 19 July 2005..63

Poland v Wolkowicz [2013] EWHC 102 (Admin), [2013] 1 WLR 2402...............................257

Polanski v Condé Nast Publications [2005] UKHL 10, [2005] 1 WLR 637.....................324, 341

Poplar Housing and Regeneration Community Association v Donoghue [2001] EWCA
    Civ 595, [2001] QB 48.........................17, 41, 45–8, 50, 52, 103, 119, 129, 506

Porter v Magill [2001] UKHL 67, [2002] 2 WLR 37........64, 71, 214, 319, 331, 336–9, 348, 373,
                                                                                        376, 380–1

Potocky v Slovakia [2013] EWHC 2052 (Admin)...489

Powell and Rayner v United Kingdom (1990) 12 EHRR 355...341

Preiss v General Dental Council [2001] UKPC 36, [2001] 1 WLR 1926............67, 324, 331, 379,
                                                                                        381, 390

Pressos Compania Naviera SA v Belgium, Judgment of 3 July 1997..................................159

Pretty v United Kingdom (2002) 35 EHRR 1.........................25, 229, 236–7, 422, 426, 459, 534

Price v United Kingdom (2001) 34 EHRR 128...236, 238

Principal Reporter v K [2010] UKSC 56, [2011] 1 WLR 18..............129, 324, 467–8, 471–3, 620

Probstmeier v Germany, Judgment of 1 July 1997...159

Procurator Fiscal, Linlithgow v Watson [2002] UKPC D1, [2004] 1 AC 379.....11, 13, 26–7, 296,
                                                                                    319, 348, 372–4, 376–7

Psychology Press Limited v Flanagan [2002] EWHC (QB) 1205......................................590

Public & Commercial Services Union v Minister for the Civil Service [2011] EWHC
    2041 (Admin), [2012] 1 All ER 985.......................................110, 643, 647, 657, 678

Pullar v United Kingdom (1996) 22 EHRR 391...379, 381

PW & Co v Milton Gate Investments Ltd [2003] EWHC (Ch) 1994...........................66, 132, 641

QB v Secretary of State for the Home Department [2010] EWHC 483 (Admin).....................479

Quila v Secretary of State for the Home Department [2011] UKSC 45, [2012] 1 AC
    621...21, 91–2, 466, 479, 502

R (A) v B [2009] UKSC 12, [2010] 2 AC 1 .... 32, 371

R (A) v Chief Constable of Kent [2013] EWHC 424 (Admin) 450

R (A) v Harrow Crown Court [2003] EWHC (Admin) 2020 278

R (A) v Hertfordshire CC [2001] EWHC (Admin) 211, [2001] ACD 469 462

R (A) v London Borough of Croydon [2009] UKSC 8, [2009] 1 WLR 2557 .... 325, 329

R (A) v Lord Saville of Newdigate [2001] EWCA Civ 2048, [2002] 1 WLR 1249 .... 189, 196

R (A) v Lowestoft Magistrates' Court [2013] EWHC 659 (Admin) 461

R (A) v National Asylum Support Service [2003] EWCA Civ 1473, [2004] 1 WLR 752 479

R (A) v National Probation Service [2003] EWHC (Admin) 2910 420

R (A) v North West Lancashire Health Authority [2000] 1 WLR 977 423

R (A) v Partnerships in Care Limited [2002] 1 WLR 2610 52

R (A) v Secretary of State for the Home Department [2003] EWHC (Admin) 2846,
    [2004] HRLR 12 .... 558, 571–2

R (A) v Secretary of State for the Home Department [2007] EWCA Civ 655,
    [2007] Imm AR 817 485

R (A) v Secretary of State for the Home Department [2008] EWHC 2844 (Admin),
    [2009] 1 FLR 531 .... 609, 620, 633

R (AA) v Secretary of State for the Home Department [2013] UKSC 49 290

R (AB) v Secretary of State for Justice [2009] EWHC 2220 (Admin) [2010] 2 All
    ER 151 .... 422, 445

R (Abbasi) v Secretary of State for Foreign and Commonwealth Affairs [2002] EWCA
    Civ 1598, [2003] UKHRR 76 73

R (Abdelaziz) v London Borough of Haringey [2001] EWCA Civ 803, [2001] 1 WLR 1485 67

R (Adesina) v Nursing & Midwifery Council [2013] EWCA Civ 818, [2013] 1 WLR 3156 343

R (Adlard) v Secretary of State for Environment, Transport & Regions [2002] EWCA
    Civ 735, [2002] 1 WLR 2515 331

R (Ahmadi) v Secretary of State for the Home Department [2002] EWHC (Admin) 1897 426

R (Aina) v London Borough of Hackney, Court of Appeal, 24 November 2000 647

R (Al-Ali) v Secretary of State for the Home Department [2012] EWHC 3638 (Admin) 255

R (Al-Jedda) v Secretary of State for Defence [2007] UKHL 58, [2008] 1 AC
    332 ....12, 18, 43, 270

R (Al Rawi) v Secretary of State for Foreign and Commonwealth Affairs
    [2006] EWCA Civ 1279, [2007] 2 WLR 1219 .... 73, 108, 234, 424, 431, 611, 625

R (Al-Sadoon) v Secretary of State for Defence [2009] EWCA Civ 7,
    [2009] 3 WLR 957 .... 74, 188

R (Al-Skeini) v Secretary of State for Defence [2004] EWHC (Admin) 2911, [2005]
    2 WLR 1401 .... 18, 72, 210–11, 221, 263–4

R (Al-Skeini) v Secretary of State for Defence [2007] UKHL 26 .... 12, 20–1, 35, 74

R (Al-Sweady) v Secretary of State for Defence [2009] EWHC 2387 (Admin) 228

R (Ali) v Minister for the Cabinet Office [2012] EWHC 1943 (Admin) 436

R (Ali) v Secretary of State for the Home Department, Administrative Court,
    21 January 2005 426

R (Allen) v HM Coroner for Inner North London [2009] EWCA Civ 623 .... 208, 219

R (AM) v Secretary of State for the Home Department [2009] EWCA Civ 219,
    [2009] Prison LR 133 264

R (Amin (Imtiaz)) v Secretary of State for the Home Department [2003] UKHL 51,
    [2004] 1 AC 653 .... 80, 181, 205, 209–12, 214–16, 219–20, 266

R (Amvac Chemicals UK Ltd) v Secretary of State for the Environment, Food and
    Rural Affairs [2001] EWHC (Admin) 1011, [2002] ACD 219 .... 644, 657

R (AN) v Mental Health Review Tribunal [2005] EWCA Civ 1605, [2006] QB 468................287
R (AN) v Secretary of State for Justice [2009] EWHC 1921 (Admin).............................. 242, 424
R (Anderson) v Secretary of State for the Home Department [2002] UKHL 46,
    [2003] 1 AC 837 .... 283, 303
R (Animal Defenders International) v Secretary of State for Culture, Media & Sport
    [2008] UKHL 15, [2008] 2 WLR 781, [2008] 1 AC 1312 ....
    12, 21, 112, 136, 145, 550–1, 553, 557, 563, 566, 595–6
R (AP) v HM Coroner for Worcestershire [2011] EWHC 1453 (Admin),
    [2011] BLGR 952 .... 191, 206
R (Argos Ltd) v Birmingham City Council [2011] EWHC 2639 (Admin)..................................663
R (Aru) v Chief Constable of Merseyside [2004] EWCA Civ 199, [2004] 1 WLR 1697..........340
R (Atapattu) v Secretary of State for the Home Department [2011] EWHC 1388
    (Admin) 428, 641, 643
R (Axon) v Secretary of State for Health [2006] EWHC 37 (Admin),
    [2006] QB 539 ....27, 475, 501
R (Ay) v Secretary of State for the Home Department [2003] EWCA Civ 1012 444
R (B) v Director of Public Prosecutions [2009] EWHC 106 (Admin), [2009] 1 WLR
    2072 .... 166, 235
R (B) v Haddock [2005] EWHC (Admin) 921...430
R (B) v Responsible Medical Officer, Broadmoor Hospital [2005] EWHC (Admin)
    1936 ....44, 227, 423
R (B) v Secretary of State for the Foreign and Commonwealth Office [2004] EWCA
    Civ 1344, [2005] QB 643 .... 17, 76–7
R (B) v SS (Responsible Medical Officer) [2006] EWCA Civ 28, [2006] 1 WLR 810..............238
R (Bagdanavicius) v Secretary of State for the Home Department [2003] EWCA Civ
    1605, [2004] 1 WLR 1207, [2005] UKHL 38, [2005] 2 WLR 1359 .... 233, 262–3
R (Bahrami) v Secretary of State for the Home Department, Administrative Court, 22
    June 2003...261
R (Bardiqi) v Secretary of State for the Home Department [2003] EWHC (Admin) 1788 425
R (Bary) v Secretary of State for the Home Department [2009] EWHC 2068 (Admin).... 253, 260
R (Bashir) v Independent Adjudicator [2011] EWHC 1108 (Admin), [2011]
    HRLR 30 ....530, 532, 542, 547
R (Bazdoaca) v Secretary of State for the Home Department [2004] EWHC Admin 2054........263
R (BB) v Special Immigration Appeals Commission [2011] EWC 336 (Admin), [2011]
    3 WLR 958...310
R (BB) v Special Immigration Appeals Commission [2012] EWCA Civ 1499, [2013] 2
    All ER 419 .... 328, 332
R (BBC) v Secretary of State for Justice [2012] EWHC 13 (Admin), [2012] 2 All ER 1089....567
R (Beeson) v Secretary of State for Health [2002] EWCA Civ 1812, [2003]
    HRLR 345 .... 323, 325, 330, 383, 390
R (Begum) v Denbigh High School [2005] 2 WLR 3372, [2006] UKHL 15, [2007] 1
    AC 100 ....24, 96, 530, 532, 537–8, 546
R (Bernard) v London Borough of Enfield [2002] EWHC (Admin) 2282, [2003] HRLR
    4 .... 148, 154–5, 158, 164, 174, 425
R (Bibi) v Secretary of State for the Home Department [2013] EWCA Civ 322, [2013]
    3 All ER 778 ....104, 479, 487, 626
R (Black) v Secretary of State for Justice [2009] UKHL 1, [2009] 1 AC 949 300
R (Blackett) v The Nursing and Midwifery Council [2004] EWHC (Admin) 1494...................343
R (Blackwood) v Secretary of State for the Home Department [2003] EWHC (Admin)
    98, [2003] HLR 638..426

R (Bloggs 61) v Secretary of State for the Home Department [2003] EWCA Civ 686,
[2003] 1 WLR 2724..181, 189, 192, 196
R (BN) v Secretary of State for the Home Department [2011] EWHC 2367 (Admin)..............485
R (Borak) v Secretary of State for the Home Department [2005] EWCA Civ 110....................256
R (Bozkurt) v South Thames Magistrates Court [2001] EWHC (Admin) 400 408
R (Brehony) v Chief Constable of Greater Manchester Police [2005] EWHC (Admin) 640......551
R (British Aggregates Associates) v Her Majesty's Treasury [2002] EWHC (Admin) 926 662
R (British American Tobacco UK Ltd) v The Secretary of State for Health [2004]
EWHC (Admin) 2493 ....27, 551, 557, 570, 574
R (British Gurkha Welfare Society) v Ministry of Defence [2010] EWCA Civ 1098........ 607, 626
R (British Sky Broadcasting) v Chelmsford Crown Court [2012] EWHC 1295 (Admin),
[2012] 2 Cr App R 33..573
R (Brooke) v Parole Board [2008] EWCA Civ 29, [2008] 1 WLR 1950 305
R (Brooke) v Secretary of State for Justice [2009] EWHC 1396 (Admin)..................................626
R (Bryant) v Commissioner of Police of the Metropolis [2011] EWHC 1314 (Admin).............433
R (Buglife: The Invertebrate Conservation Trust) v Medway Council [2011] EWHC
746 (Admin)...38
R (Burke) v The General Medical Council [2005] EWCA Civ 1003...33, 187, 200, 237, 423, 431
R (C) v Brent, Kensinton, Chelsea and Westminster Mental Health NHS Trust [2002]
EWHC (Admin) 181, [2002] Lloyd's Med Rep 321 ....505, 507, 510, 512
R (C) v Mental Health Review Tribunal London and South West Region [2001] EWCA
Civ 1110, [2002] 1 WLR 176..310–11
R (C) v Ministry of Justice [2009] EWHC 2671 (Admin)...452
R (C) v Secretary of State for Justice [2008] EWCA Civ 882, [2009] QB 657 .... 239, 242
R (C) v Secretary of State for the Home Department [2002] EWCA Civ 647............................303
R (C) v Secretary of State for the Home Department [2012] EWHC 801 (Admin)....................257
R (Calver) v Adjudication Panel for Wales [2012] EWHC 1172 (Admin)..................550, 566, 594
R (Carson) v Secretary of State for Work and Pensions [2003] EWCA Civ 797,
[2003] 3 All ER 577 .... 606, 621–2
R (Carson) v Secretary of State for Work and Pensions [2005] UKHL 37, [2005]
2 WLR 1369...109, 606–7, 613–14, 620, 622–4, 630, 642
R (Cart) v Upper Tribunal [2009] EWHC 3052, [2010] 2 WLR 1012..297
R (Cash) v HM Coroner for Northamptonshire [2007] EWHC 1354 (Admin), [2007] 4
All
ER 903...218–19
R (Catt) v Association of Chief Police Officers [2013] EWCA Civ 192, [2013] 3 All
ER 583..420, 427, 447
R (Cawser) v Secretary of State for the Home Department [2003] EWHC Civ 1522,
[2004] UKHRR 101.. 270, 281
R (Challender) v Legal Services Commission [2004] EWHC (Admin) 925, [2004]
ACD 57 .... 210, 216
R (Chen) v Secretary of State for the Home Department [2012] EWHC 2531 (Admin),
2012] HRLR 33...432, 610, 621, 626
R (Clays Lane Housing Co-Operative Limited) v The Housing Corporation [2004]
EWCA Civ 1658, [2005] 1 WLR 2229.. 653, 663
R (Clift) v Secretary of State for the Home Department [2006] UKHL 54, [2007]
2 WLR 24... 139, 608–9, 614, 619–21, 636
R (Clough) v Secretary of State for the Home Department [2003] EWHC (Admin) 597..........314
R (CN) v Lewisham LBC [2013] EWCA Civ 804...525
R (Cockburn) v Secretary of State for Health [2011] EWHC 2095 (Admin) 60, 630

R (Condliff) v North Staffordshire Primary Care Trust [2011] EWCA Civ 910, [2012]
1 All
ER 689.. 430, 433

R (Countryside Alliance) v Attorney General [2007] UKHL 52, [2007] 3 WLR
922 .... 10, 22, 24, 111, 410–11, 437, 439, 456, 505, 553, 621, 652–3, 655, 669

R (Cowl) v Plymouth City Council [2001] EWCA Civ 1935, [2002] 1 WLR 803 512

R (Craven) v Secretary of State for the Home Department [2001] EWHC (Admin) 813 494

R (Crown Prosecution Service) v Chorley Justices [2002] EWHC (Admin) 2163 .....284, 509, 512

R (D) v Secretary of State for the Home Department [2006] EWCA Civ 143, [2006]
3 All ER 946... 206, 208, 212, 215, 217, 221–2

R (D) v Secretary of State for the Home Department [2012] EWHC 2501 (Admin)................240

R (da Silva) v The Director of Public Prosecutions [2006] EWHC 3204 (Admin),
[2006] Inquest LR 224...219

R (Data Broadcasting International Ltd) v Office of Communications [2010] EWHC
1243 (Admin), [2010] ACD 77 .... 643, 650

R (Davies) v Birmingham Deputy Coroner [2003] EWCA Civ 1739, [2004] HRLR 13 ..
209, 218, 220

R (Davies) v Secretary of State for the Home Department [2004] EWHC (Admin) 1512 509

R (Davies) v Secretary of State for the Home Department [2010] EWHC 2656 (Admin) 290, 292

R (Davies) v South Devon Magistrates' Court, Divisional Court, 21 December 2004................272

R (Day) v Secretary of State for the Home Department [2004] EWHC (Admin) 1742,
[2004] ACD 78... 304, 314

R (De Almeida) v Kensington & Chelsea Royal London Borough Council [2012]
EWHC 1082 (Admin)...259

R (Denson) v Child Support Agency [2002] EWHC (Admin) 154, [2002] 1 FLR 938....
422, 471, 642, 651, 677

R (Director of Public Prosecutions) v Havering Magistrates' Court [2001] 1 WLR 805 131

R (Doka) v Immigration Appeal Tribunal [2004] EWHC (Admin) 3072, [2005] 1 FCR 180 467

R (Downing) v Parole Board [2008] EWHC 3198 (Admin), [2009] Prison LR 327..................317

R (Dowsett) v Secretary of State for Justice [2013] EWHC 687 (Admin) 424

R (Dudley) v East Sussex County Council [2003] EWHC (Admin) 1093, [2003] ACD
353 .... 199, 512

R (Dudson) v Secretary of State for the Home Department [2005] UKHL 52...........................363

R (E) v Ashworth Hospital Authority [2001] EWHC (Admin) 1089, [2002] ACD 149....... 89, 439

R (EH) v Secretary of State for the Home Department [2012] EWHC 2569 (Admin)...............240

R (Eidarous) v Governor of Brixton Prison [2001] UKHL 69, [2002] 2 WLR 101 308

R (Elayathamby) v Secretary of State for the Home Department [2011] EWHC 2182 (Admin)254

R (Ellis) v Chief Constable of Essex Police [2003] EWHC (Admin) 1321, [2003] 2
FLR 566.. 420, 452

R (Erskine) v London Borough of Lambeth [2003] EWHC (Admin) 2479....................... 608, 612

R (European Roma Rights Centre) v Immigration Officer, Prague Airport [2004] UKHL
55, [2005] 2 AC 1...76

R (Evans) v First Secretary of State [2005] EWHC (Admin) 149 517

R (Evans) v Secretary of State for Defence [2010] EWHC 1445 (Admin)................38, 252, 260

R (EW) v Secretary of State for the Home Department [2009] EWHC 2957
(Admin) 249, 254–5

R (F) v Secretary of State for Justice [2012] EWHC 2689 (Admin) 244

R (F) v Secretary of State for the Home Department [2010] UKSC 17, [2010] 2 WLR
992 .... 92, 139, 451–2

R (Faizovas) v Secretary of State for Justice [2009] EWCA Civ 373, [2009] UKHRR
1093 .... 229, 241

R (Farrakhan) v Secretary of State for the Home Department [2001] EWHC (Admin)
781, [2002] 3 WLR 481 ....34–5, 483, 550, 552, 554–5, 558–9, 572

R (Faulkner) v Secretary of State for Justice [2013] UKSC 23, [2013] 2 WLR 1157 ......
157–8, 160, 167, 315–16

R (Fisher) v English Nature [2004] EWCA Civ 663, [2005] 1 WLR 147 .... 651, 662

R (Fleurose) v Securities and Futures Authority Ltd [2002] EWCA Civ 2015, [2002]
IRLR 297 .... 332, 339

R (Foley) v Parole Board for England & Wales [2012] EWHC 2184 (Admin)................. 621, 637

R (Ford) v The Press Complaints Commission [2001] EWHC (Admin) 683, [2002]
EMLR 5 .... 55, 417, 427

R (Foster) v Governor of High Down Prison [2010] EWHC 2224 (Admin) 229, 412

R (Foster) v Secretary of State for Justice [2013] EWHC 1951 (Admin).............................308

R (Francis) v West Midlands Probation Board [2010] EWCA Civ 1470 .... 470, 493

R (Fuller) v Chief Constable of Dorset Police [2001] EWHC (Admin) 1057, [2003] QB
480 .... 229, 504–5, 513, 651, 664

R (G) v Immigration Appeal Tribunal [2004] EWCA Civ 173, [2005] 1 WLR 1445 .... 620, 625

R (G) v Mental Health Review Tribunal [2004] EWHC (Admin) 2193 272

R (G) v X School Governors [2011] UKSC 30, [2011] 3 WLR 237 328

R (Gallastegui) v Westminster City Council [2013] EWCA Civ 28, [2013] HRLR 15 ...... 555, 592

R (Gardner) v Parole Board [2006] EWCA Civ 1222, [2007] Prison LR 78.....................310

R (Gaunt) v Office of Communications [2011] EWCA Civ 692, [2011] 1 WLR 2355 .....
551, 557, 560, 563, 594

R (GC) v Commissioner of Police for the Metropolis [2011] UKSC 21, [2011] 1 WLR
1230 ....25, 117, 119, 423, 446

R (Gedara) v Secretary of State for the Home Department [2006] EWHC 1690 (Admin).........262

R (Gentle) v Prime Minister [2008] UKHL 20, [2008] 1 AC 1356....................................
19, 23, 74, 190, 204, 206–8, 212

R (Ghai) v Newcastle City Council [2010] EWCA Civ 59, [2010] 3 WLR 737 .... 528, 533

R (Gibson) v Winchester Crown Court [2004] EWHC (Admin) 361, [2004] 1 WLR 1623 297

R (Giles) v Parole Board [2003] UKHL 42, [2004] AC 1 .... 297, 301

R (Gillan) v Commissioner of Police for the Metropolis [2006] UKHL 12, [2006] 2 AC
307 .... 84, 86, 89, 276, 423, 448

R (Green) v City of Westminster Magistrates' Court [2007] EWHC 2785 (Admin),
[2008] HRLR 12 .... 551, 588

R (Green) v Police Complaints Authority [2004] UKHL 6, [2004] 1 WLR 725 ....205, 263–4, 266

R (Gunn) v Secretary of State for Justice [2009] EWHC 1812 (Admin)......................... 428, 452

R (Guntrip) v Secretary of State for Justice [2010] EWHC 3188 (Admin) 297, 317

R (Gurung) v Ministry of Defence [2008] EWHC 1496 (Admin)......................................626

R (Gurung) v Secretary of State for the Home Department [2013] EWCA Civ 8 .... 467, 487

R (H) v Ashworth Hospital Authority [2001] EWHC (Admin) 872, [2002] 1 FCR 206...
103, 181, 200, 423

R (H) v Ashworth Hospital Authority [2002] EWCA Civ 923 302

R (H) v Kingston Upon Hull City Council [2013] EWHC 388 (Admin), [2013]
Fam Law 804 494

R (H) v Mental Health Review Tribunal, North & East London Region [2001] EWCA
Civ 415, [2002] QB 1 .... 140, 287–8, 307

R (H) v Mental Health Review Tribunal [2007] EWHC 884 (Admin) 423

R (Haase) v Independent Adjudicator [2008] EWCA Civ 1089, [2009] QB 550 379

R (Hafner) v Westminster Magistrates Court [2008] EWHC 524 (Admin) [2009] Bus LR 489 421

R (Haggerty) v St Helens Council [2003] EWHC (Admin) 803, [2003] ACD 304..........
49, 182, 194, 199–200, 229, 508, 512

R (Hair) v Her Majesty's Coroner for Staffordshire (South) [2010] EWHC 2580
(Admin), [2010] Inquest LR 197...213

R (Hall) v University College Hospitals NHS Foundation Trust [2013] EWHC 198 (Admin)......241

R (Hamilton) v United Kingdom Central Council for Nursing, Midwifery and Health
Visiting [2003] EWCA Civ 1600, [2004] 79 BMLR 30...653, 661

R (Hammond) v Secretary of State for the Home Department [2005] UKHL 69, [2006]
1 AC 603 ....122, 132, 363

R (Harrison) v Secretary of State for Health [2009] EWHC 574 (Admin).........607, 609, 620, 635

R (Harrow Community Support Ltd) v Secretary of State for Defence [2012] EWHC
1921 (Admin)...108, 508

R (Hasan) v Secretary of State for Trade and Industry [2007] EWHC 2630 (Admin).................38

R (HC) v Secretary of State for the Home Department [2013] EWHC 982 (Admin),
[2013] Crim LR 918 424

R (Heather) v Leonard Cheshire Foundation [2002] EWCA Civ 366, [2002] ACD 271 ..
41, 47–8, 52, 510

R (Hester) v Secretary of State for Justice [2011] EWHC 3926 (Admin) 317

R (Hicks) v Commissioner of Police of the Metropolis [2012] EWHC 1947 (Admin),
[2012] ACD 102..285, 594

R (Hooper) v Secretary of State for Work and Pensions [2005] UKHL 29, [2005] 1
WLR 1681 ....68, 103, 109, 114–15, 117–18, 134, 608, 613, 620–1, 624, 628–9, 642

R (Hounslow London Borough Council) v Schools Admissions Appeal Panel for
Hounslow [2002] EWCA Civ 900...613

R (Hoverspeed Ltd) v Customs and Excise Commissioners [2002] EWCA Civ 1804,
[2003] QB 1041 675

R (Howard) v Secretary of State for Health [2002] EWHC (Admin), [2003] QB 830 556

R (Huitson) v Revenue & Customs Commissioners [2011] EWCA Civ 893, [2012] 2
WLR 490 ....641–2, 673

R (Humberstone) v Legal Services Commission [2010] EWCA Civ 1479, [2011] 1
WLR 1460..212, 216, 223

R (Hurst) v Commissioner of Police of the Metropolis [2007] UKHL 13, [2007] 2 AC
189 ....3, 67, 71, 206

R (I) v Secretary of State for the Home Department [2002] EWCA Civ 888 292–3

R (IA) v Secretary of State for Communities & Local Government [2011] EWCA Civ
1253, [2012] JPL 579..517

R (Irfan) v Secretary of State for the Home Department [2012] EWCA Civ 1471,
[2013] 2 WLR 1340...452

R (J) (Somalia) v Secretary of State for the Home Department [2009] EWHC 1281 (Admin)..250

R (J) v Chief Constable of Devon & Cornwall [2012] EWHC 2996 (Admin)..........................450

R (J) v Enfield London Borough Council [2002] EWHC (Admin) 432, [2002] 2 FLR 1.. 131, 509

R (J) v Southend Borough Council, Administrative Court, 5 August 2005................................428

R (Jarvis) v The Parole Board [2004] EWHC (Admin) 872...307

R (JB) v Haddock [2006] EWCA Civ 961, [2006] HRLR 40 237–8

R (JL) v Secretary of State for Defence [2013] EWCA Civ 449 507

R (JL) v Secretary of State for Justice [2008] UKHL 68, [2009] 1 AC 588 ....
205, 208, 210–12, 214–16, 221

R (JL) v Secretary of State for Justice [2009] EWHC 2416 (Admin), [2010] HRLR 4 222

R (Johns) v Derby City Council [2011] EWHC 375 (Admin), [2011] 1 FLR 2094........... 528, 543

R (Johnson) v Secretary of State for Health [2006] EWHC 288 (Admin)....................................32

R (Johnson) v Secretary of State for the Home Department [2007] EWCA Civ 427,
[2007] 1 WLR 1990...315

R (K) v Camden and Islington Health Authority [2001] EWCA Civ 240, [2002] QB
198 ....43, 288, 302

R (K) v HM Treasury [2009] EWHC 1643 (Admin).. 647, 672

R (K) v Lambeth London Borough Council [2003] EWCA Civ 1150, [2004] 1 WLR 272232, 478

R (K) v Mental Health Review Tribunal [2002] EWHC (Admin) 639 .... 44, 310–12

R (Kambadzi) v SSHD [2011] 1 WLR 1299... 279, 290

R (Kashamu) v Governor of Brixton Prison [2001] EWHC (Admin) 980, [2002] 2
WLR 907..293, 299, 303

R (Kastrati) v Special Adjudicator [2002] EWHC (Admin) 415 425

R (KB) v Mental Health Review Tribunal [2003] EWHC (Admin) 193, [2004] QB 936.
156, 159, 161–2, 164, 167–8, 317

R (KB) v Secretary of State for Justice [2010] EWHC 15 (Admin).....................................428

R (Kehoe) v Secretary of State for Work and Pensions [2005] UKHL 48, [2005] 3 WLR 252.324

R (Kelsall) v Secretary of State for the Environment, Food and Rural Affairs [2003]
EWHC (Admin) 459 .... 643, 658

R (Kent County Council) v HM Coroner for Kent [2012] EWHC 2768 (Admin).....................225

R (Khan) v Oxfordshire County Council [2004] EWCA Civ 309, [2004] BLGR 257................432

R (Khan) v Secretary of State for Foreign & Commonwealth Affairs [2012] EWHC
3728 (Admin)..190

R (Khan) v Secretary of State for Health [2003] EWCA Civ 1129, [2004] 1 WLR 971..
182, 209, 211, 216, 222

R (King) v Secretary of State for Justice [2012] EWCA Civ 376, [2012] 4 All ER 44....
324, 330, 333

R (Klimas) v Lithuania [2010] EWHC 2076 (Admin)..255

R (Knowles) v Secretary of State for Work & Pensions [2013] EWHC 19 (Admin).616, 620, 631

R (Kpandang) v Secretary of State for the Home Department [2004] EWHC (Admin) 2130....493

R (Kurtolli) v Secretary of State for the Home Department [2003] EWHC (Admin) 2744........257

R (L) v Chief Constable of Cumbria Constabulary [2013] EWHC 869 (Admin).......................450

R (L) v Commissioner of Police of the Metropolis [2009] UKSC 3, [2010] 1 AC 410 ...
132, 410, 419–20, 428, 450

R (L) v Manchester City Council [2001] EWHC (Admin) 707, [2002] FLR 43........618, 620, 630

R (L) v Secretary of State for Health [2001] 1 FLR 406..466, 472, 493

R (L) v Secretary of State for the Home Department [2003] EWCA Civ 25, [2003] 1
All ER 1062 477

R (Lamanovs) v Secretary of State for the Home Department [2001] EWCA Civ 1239...........256

R (Laporte) v Chief Constable of Gloucestershire [2006] UKHL 55, [2007] 2 AC 105...
558, 560, 590

R (Leary) v Chief Constable of West Midlands [2012] EWHC 639 (Admin), [2012]
ACD 67 .... 509, 511

R (Lepage) v HM Assistant Deputy Coroner for Inner South London [2012] EWHC
1485 (Admin)..213

R (Lewis) v HM Coroner for the Mid and North Division of the County of Shropshire
[2009] EWCA Civ 1403, [2010] 1 WLR 1836... 218, 220

R (Limbu) v Secretary of State for the Home Department [2008] EWHC 2261
(Admin), [2008] HRLR 48 ....605, 609, 626

R (Limbuela) v Secretary of State for the Home Department [2004] EWCA Civ 540,
[2004] QB 1440 ....227–8, 231–2, 234, 243

R (Limbuela) v Secretary of State for the Home Department [2005] UKHL 66, [2006]
1 AC 396 ....229, 231–2, 249

R (Loch) v Secretary of State for Justice [2008] EWHC 2278 (Admin), [2009] Prison
LR 212 314

R (London and Continental Stations and Property Ltd) v Rail Regulator [2003] EWHC
(Admin) 2607 659

R (London Christian Radio) v Radio Advertising Clearance Centre [2012] EWHC 1043
(Admin), [2012] HRLR 19 596

R (Lord Carlile of Berriew) v Secretary of State for the Home Department [2013]
EWCA Civ 199 ....108, 550, 559

R (Lumba) v SSHD [2011] 2 WLR 671 292

R (Luthra) v General Dental Council [2004] EWHC (Admin) 458.................................371

R (M) v Immigration Appeal Tribunal [2005] EWHC (Admin) 251 442

R (M) v Inner London Crown Court [2003] EWHC (Admin) 301, [2003] 1 FLR 994 493

R (M) v Merseyside Police [2003] EWHC (Admin) 1121...229

R (M) v Parole Board [2013] EWHC 1360 (Admin), [2013] EMLR 23 .... 197, 581

R (M) v Secretary of State for Constitutional Affairs and Lord Chancellor [2004]
EWCA Civ 312, [2004] 1 WLR 2298...328

R (M) v Secretary of State for Health [2003] EWHC (Admin) 1094, [2003] ACD 389...
135, 141, 427

R (M) v Secretary of State for the Home Department [2010] EWHC 3541 (Admin).................230

R (M) v Secretary of State for the Home Department [2011] EWHC 3667 (Admin).................148

R (MA) v National Probation Service [2011] EWHC 1332 (Admin)............................274

R (MA) v Secretary of State for Work & Pensions [2013] EWHC 2213 (QB)................ 109, 610,
615–17, 627, 629, 631

R (Mackenzie) v Governor of Wakefield Prison [2006] EWHC 1746 (Admin)................. 239, 424

R (Madden) v Bury Metropolitan Borough Council [2002] EWHC (Admin) 1882 .... 507, 512

R (Mahfouz) v Professional Conduct Committee of the General Medical Council
[2004] EWCA Civ 233, [2004] Lloyd's Rep Med 389 391

R (Main) v Minister for Legal Aid [2007] EWCA Civ 1147, [2008] HRLR 8.........................217

R (Malik) v Waltham Forest NHS Primary Care Trust [2007] EWCA Civ 265, [2007] 1
WLR 2092 ....640, 645

R (Massey) v Secretary of State for Justice [2013] EWHC 1950 (Admin) 626

R (Matthias Rath BV) v The Advertising Standards Authority Ltd [2001] EMLR 22 89

R (Mbanjabahizi) v Immigration Appeal Tribunal, Administrative Court, 10 June 2004 261

R (McCann) v Crown Court at Manchester [2002] UKHL 39, [2003] 1 AC 787 .... 15, 68, 324,
331, 333, 335–9, 366, 392

R (McDonald) v Kensington & Chelsea Royal London Borough Council [2011] UKSC
33, [2011] 4 All ER 881 431–2

R (McDougal) v Liverpool City Council [2009] EWHC 1821 (Admin)................................613

R (McKeown) v Wirral Borough Magistrates' Court [2001] 1 WLR 805......................... 295, 306–7

R (McKinnon) v Secretary of State for the Home Department [2009] EWHC 2021
(Admin), [2010] Crim LR 421 253

R (McLellan) v Bracknell Forest Borough Council [2001] EWCA Civ 1510, [2002] QB
1129 ....383, 507

R (McLellan) v Bracknell Forest Borough Council [2002] 1 All ER 899 325

R (MD (Angola)) v Secretary of State for the Home Department [2011] EWCA Civ 1238.......241

R (MD) v Secretary of State for the Home Department [2011] EWCA Civ 121 254

R (Medihani) v HM Coroner for Inner South District of Greater London [2012] EWHC
1104 (Admin) 209, 223

R (Mehmeti) v Secretary of State for the Home Department [2004] EWHC (Admin)
2999 .... 425–6, 444

R (Mellor) v Secretary of State for the Home Department [2001] 3 WLR 533 100

R (Mersey Care Trust) v Mental Health Review Tribunal [2004] EWHC (Admin) 1749,
[2005] 1 WLR 2469 371

R (MH) v Secretary of State for Health [2004] EWCA Civ 1609, [2005] 1 WLR 1209 ... 135, 140

R (Middlebrook Mushrooms Ltd) v The Agricultural Wages Board of England & Wales
[2004] EWHC (Admin) 1447 ....613, 620, 624, 647

R (Middleton) v HM Coroner for Western Somerset [2004] UKHL 10, [2004] 2 AC
182 .... 128, 181, 205, 209–10, 217

R (Middleton) v Secretary of State for the Home Department [2003] EWHC (Admin) 315 279

R (Miller Gardner Solicitors) v Minshull Street Crown Court [2002] EWHC (Admin)
3077 .... 505, 511

R (Minter) v Chief Constable of Hampshire [2011] EWHC 1610 (Admin) 457

R (Minter) v Chief Constable of Hampshire [2013] EWCA Civ 697 .... 619, 621

R (MK (Iran)) v Secretary of State for the Home Department [2010] EWCA Civ 115,
[2010] 1 WLR 2059 332

R (MK) v Secretary of State for the Home Department [2010] EWHC 1002 (Admin) 476

R (MM) v Secretary of State for the Home Department [2012] EWCA Civ 668 265–6

R (Modaresi) v Secretary of State for Health [2013] UKSC 53 298

R (Mohamed) v Secretary of State for the Home Department [2010] EWHC 1227
Admin) 486

R (Mohammed) v Chief Constable of West Midlands [2010] EWHC 1228 (Admin) 175

R (Montana) v Secretary of State for the Home Department [2001] 1 WLR 552 .... 70, 479, 625

R (Moor) v Financial Ombudsman Service [2008] EWCA Civ 642 .... 332, 372

R (Morales) v Parole Board [2011] EWHC 28 (Admin), [2011] 1 WLR 1095 303

R (Morgan Grenfell & Co Ltd) v Special Commissioners of Income Tax [2002] UKHL
21, [2003] 1 AC 563 .... 414, 444

R (Morgan) v Secretary of State for Transport, Local Government and the Regions
[2002] EWHC (Admin) 2652 506

R (Morley) v Nottinghamshire Health Care NHS Trust [2002] EWCA Civ 1728, [2003]
1 All ER 784 453

R (Morris) v Westminster City Council [2004] EWHC (Admin) 2191, [2005] 1 WLR 865 141

R (Morris) v Westminster City Council [2004] EWHC Admin 2191, [2005] 1 WLR 865 610

R (Mortell) v Secretary of State for Communities & Local Government [2009] EWCA
Civ 1274 .... 506, 517

R (Mousa) v Secretary of State for Defence [2011] EWCA Civ 1334, [2012] HRLR 6 267

R (Mousa) v Secretary of State for Defence [2013] EWHC 1412 (Admin) 224

R (Mousa) v Secretary of State for Defence No 2 [2013] EWHC 2941 (Admin) 224

R (MP) v Secretary of State for Justice [2012] EWHC 214 (Admin) 492

R (Mudie) v Kent Magistrates' Court [2003] EWCA Civ 237, [2003] 2 WLR 1344 337–9

R (Munjaz) v Mersey Care NHS Trust [2003] EWCA Civ 1036, [2004] QB 395, [2005]
UKHL 58, [2006] 2 AC 148 .... 84, 89, 233–4, 242, 269, 297, 424, 454

R (Muqtaar) v SSHD [2012] EWCA Civ 1270, [2013] 1 WLR 649 .... 290, 293

R (Murad) v SSHD [2012] EWHC 1112 (Admin) 293

R (Muwangusi) v Secretary of State for the Home Department [2003] EWHC (Admin) 813 426

R (MV) v Secretary of State for the Home Department [2013] EWHC 1017 (Admin) 254

R (MWH & H Ward Estates Ltd) v Monmouthshire CC [2002] EWCA Civ 1915,
[2003] ACD 115 ....651, 658, 664

R (N) v Ashworth Special Hospital Authority [2001] EWHC (Admin) 339, [2001] 1
WLR 25 ....414, 439, 454

R (N) v M [2002] EWCA Civ 1789, [2003] 1 WLR 562 227

R (N) v Secretary of State for Health [2009] EWCA Civ 795, [2009] HRLR 31 .... 112, 412,
455, 610, 620, 627, 634

R (Nagre) v Secretary of State for the Home Department [2013] EWHC 720 (Admin) 482

R (Naik) v Secretary of State for the Home Department [2011] EWCA Civ 1546,
[2012] Imm AR 381 ....554–5, 559, 571

R (Napier) v Secretary of State for the Home Department [2004] EWHC (Admin) 936,
[2004] 1 WLR 3056 338–9

R (National Farmers Union) v Secretary of State for the Environment, Food and Rural
Affairs, Administrative Court, 6 March 2003 640–1

R (National Secular Society) v Bideford Town Council [2012] EWHC 175 (Admin),
[2012] 2 All ER 1175 528

R (Negassi) v Secretary of State for the Home Department [2013] EWCA Civ 151 429

R (New London College Ltd) v Secretary of State for the Home Department [2012]
EWCA Civ 51, [2012] Imm AR 563 646

R (Newhaven Port & Properties Ltd) v Secretary of State for the Environment [2013]
EWCA Civ 673, [2013] 3 All ER 719 667

R (Nicklinson) v Ministry of Justice [2013] EWCA Civ 961, (2013) 16 CCL Rep 413 ...... 86, 436

R (NM) v Secretary of State for Justice [2012] EWCA Civ 1182 266

R (Noorkoiv) v Secretary of State for the Home Department [2002] EWCA Civ 770,
[2002] 1 WLR 3284 .... 43, 103, 270, 280, 310–11, 313

R (Nunn) v First Secretary of State [2005] EWCA Civ 101, [2005] 2 All ER 987 172

R (O) v Hammersmith & Fulham London Borough Council [2011] EWCA Civ 925,
[2012] 1 WLR 1057 432

R (Omar) v Secretary of State for the Home Department [2012] EWHC 3348 (Admin),
[2013] Imm AR 601 132

R (Orange Personal Communications Ltd) v Secretary of State for Trade and Industry,
Administrative Court, 25 October 2000 .... 643, 660

R (P & Q) v Secretary of State for the Home Department [2001] EWCA Civ 1151 .470, 472, 491

R (P) v HM Coroner for the District of Avon [2009] EWCA Civ 1367, [2010] 112
BMLR 77 218

R (P) v Secretary of State for Justice [2009] EWCA Civ 701, [2010] QB 317 .... 206, 264–5

R (P) v Secretary of State for the Home Department [2003] EWHC (Admin) 1963 424

R (P) v Secretary of State for the Home Department [2003] EWHC (Admin) 2953 298–9

R (Painter) v Carmarthenshire County Council Housing Benefit Review Board [2001]
EWHC (Admin) 308 510

R (Panjawani) v Royal Pharmaceutical Society of Great Britain [2002] EWHC (Admin)
1127 391

R (Parratt) v Secretary of State for Justice [2013] EWHC 17 (Admin) 314

R (PD) v West Midlands and North West Mental Health Review Tribunal [2004]
EWCA Civ 311 385–6

R (Pearson) v Driving & Vehicle Licensing Agency [2002] EWHC (Admin) 2482,
[2003] Crim LR 199 .... 414, 420

R (Peart) v The Secretary of State for Transport, Local Government and the Regions
[2002] EWHC (Admin) 2964 647

R (Pekkelo) v HM Coroner for Central & South East Kent [2006] EWHC 1265
(Admin), [2006] Inquest LR 119 218–19
R (Petsafe Ltd) v Welsh Ministers [2010] EWHC 2908 (Admin), [2011] EuLR 270 640, 644, 669
R (Phillips) v Walsall Metropolitan Borough Council [2001] EWHC (Admin) 789 ..504, 507, 512
R (Playfoot) v Millais School Governing Body [2007] EWHC 1698 (Admin), [2007]
HRLR 34 ....534, 539, 547
R (Plumb) v Secretary of State for Work and Pensions [2002] EWHC (Admin) 1125 471
R (Ponting) v Governor of HMP Whitemoor [2002] EWCA Civ 224 .... 341, 346, 349, 430, 454
R (Pounder) v HM Coroner for North & South Districts of Durham & Darlington
[2009] EWHC 76 (Admin), [2009] 3 All ER 150 ....212, 219
R (Pow Trust) v The Chief Executive and Registrar of Companies [2002] EWHC
(Admin) 2783, [2004] BCC 268 661
R (Pretty) v Director of Public Prosecutions [2001] UKHL 61, [2001] 3 WLR 1598, [2002]
1 AC 800 .... 13, 18, 25, 27, 81, 97, 182–4, 227–8, 234–6, 426,439, 458–9, 529, 534, 545, 620
R (Primrose) v Secretary of State for Justice [2008] EWHC 1625 (Admin), [2009]
Prison LR 165 ....609, 620, 626
R (Prolife Alliance) v British Broadcasting Corporation [2003] UKHL 23, [2004] 1 AC
185 ....559, 566, 595
R (Prothero) v Secretary of State for the Home Department [2013] EWHC 2830 (Admin) 452
R (Purdy) v Director of Public Prosecutions [2009] UKHL 45, [2009] 3 WLR 403 ....
25, 86, 426, 436, 459
R (Purja) v Ministry of Defence [2003] EWCA Civ 1345, [2004] 1 WLR 289 .607, 613, 623, 625
R (Q) v Secretary of State for the Home Department [2003] EWCA Civ 364, [2004]
QB 36 .... 228–9, 325, 331, 425, 476
R (Qazi) v Secretary of State for Work and Pensions [2004] EWHC (Admin) 1331 677
R (Quark Fishing Ltd) v Secretary of State for Foreign and Commonwealth Affairs
[2004] EWCA Civ 527, [2005] QB 93 79
R (R) v Chief Constable [2013] EWHC 2864 (Admin) 423, 446
R (R) v Child & Family Court Advisory & Support Service [2012] EWCA Civ 853,
[2012] 2 FLR 1432 473
R (R) v Durham Constabulary [2005] UKHL 21, [2005] 1 WLR 1184 ....28, 334, 340
R (R) v Leeds City Council [2005] EWHC 2495 (Admin) 537
R (R) v Shetty (Responsible Medical Officer) [2003] EWHC (Admin) 3022 .... 44, 239–40
R (RA) v Secretary of State for the Home Department [2002] EWHC (Admin) 1618 .... 43, 303
R (Razgar) v Secretary of State for the Home Department [2004] UKHL 27, [2004] 2
AC 368 .... 72, 91, 410, 422, 425, 441, 443–4, 480–1
R (RD) v Secretary of State for Work and Pensions [2010] EWCA Civ 18, [2010]
HRLR 19 ....613, 620, 631
R (Reynolds) v Independent Police Complaints Commission [2008] EWCA Civ 1160,
[2009] 3 All ER 237 213–14
R (Reynolds) v Secretary of State for Work and Pensions [2005] UKHL 37, [2005] 2
WLR 1369 ....620, 630
R (Richards) v Secretary of State for the Home Department [2004] EWHC (Admin) 93,
[2004] ACD 69... 159–60, 162, 168
R (RJM) v Secretary of State for Work and Pensions [2008] UKHL 63, [2009] 1 AC
311 .... 20, 613, 619–20, 627, 630
R (RMC) v Commissioner of Police of the Metropolis [2012] EWHC 1681 (Admin),
[2012] 4 All ER 510 ....419, 427, 448
R (Roberts) v Commissioner of Police of the Metropolis [2012] EWHC 1977 (Admin),
[2012] HRLR 28 ....86, 277, 423, 449

R (Robertson) v Wakefield Metropolitan District Council [2001] EWHC (Admin) 915,
[2002] 2 WLR 889 .... 414, 444

R (Rogers) v Swindon NHS Primary Care Trust [2006] EWHC 171 (Admin), [2006] 88
BMLR 177 .... 200, 229, 433

R (Rose) v Secretary of State for Health [2002] EWHC (Admin) 1593, [2002] 3 FCR
731 .... 136, 421, 428, 430, 474

R (Rostami) v Secretary of State for the Home Department [2013] EWHC 1494 (Admin) 429

R (Rottman) v Commissioner of Police of the Metropolis [2002] UKHL 20, [2002] 2
WLR 1315 .... 84, 87–8, 92, 509, 511

R (Rusbridger) v Attorney General [2003] UKHL 38, [2004] 1 AC 357 .... 34, 121, 123, 134,
137, 557, 566

R (S and Marper) v Chief Constable of South Yorkshire [2004] UKHL 39, [2004] 4 All
ER 193 25

R (S) v Chief Constable of South Yorkshire [2004] UKHL 39, [2004] 1 WLR 2196 .... 83, 423,
439, 446, 606, 609, 615, 619, 621, 625, 636, 657, 668

R (S) v Mental Health Review Tribunal [2002] EWHC (Admin) 2522 304

R (S) v Plymouth City Council [2002] EWCA Civ 388, [2002] 1 WLR 2583 .... 414, 457, 472

R (S) v Secretary of State for Justice [2012] EWHC 1810 (Admin), [2013] 1 All
ER 66 .... 111, 617, 642

R (S) v Secretary of State for the Home Department [2003] EWHC (Admin) 352 .... 262, 442

R (S) v Secretary of State for the Home Department [2007] EWCA Civ 546 429

R (S) v Secretary of State for the Home Department [2010] EWHC 705 (Admin) 4, 249, 255

R (S) v Secretary of State for the Home Department [2011] EWHC 2120 (Admin) 240, 290

R (Saadi) v Secretary of State for the Home Department [2002] UKHL 41, [2002] 1
WLR 3131 .... 270, 290–1

R (Sacker) v HM Coroner for the County of West Yorkshire [2004] UKHL 11, [2004] 1
WLR 796 .... 128, 209, 218, 220

R (Samaroo) v Secretary of State for the Home Department [2001] EWCA Civ
1139 .... 477, 481, 483

R (Sandhu) v Secretary of State for the Home Department [2003] EWHC (Admin) 2152 477

R (Sandiford) v Secretary of State for Foreign & Commonwealth Affairs [2013] EWCA
Civ 581, [2013] 1 WLR 2938 76

R (Scholes) v Secretary of State for the Home Department [2006] EWCA Civ 1343,
[2006] HRLR 44 .... 208, 215, 222

R (Secretary of State for the Home Department) v Mental Health Review Tribunal
[2004] EWHC (Admin) 2194 272

R (Serrano) v Secretary of State for Justice [2012] EWHC 3216 (Admin) 609

R (Sessay) v South London & Maudsley NHS Foundation Trust [2011] EWHC 2617
(QB), [2012] 2 WLR 1071 278

R (Shaheen) v Secretary of State for Justice [2008] EWHC 1195 (Admin), [2009]
Prison LR 91 491

R (Sheikh) v Secretary of State for the Home Department [2011] EWHC 3390 (Admin) 486

R (Shiner) v Revenue & Customs Commissioners [2011] EWCA Civ 892, [2011]
STC 1878 640

R (Sim) v Parole Board [2003] EWCA Civ 1845, [2004] QB 1288 .... 127, 297, 301, 307

R (Sinclair Collis Ltd) v Secretary of State for Health [2011] EWCA Civ 437,
[2012] 2 WLR 304 .... 112, 639, 651–2, 657

R (Singh) v Aberdare Girls' High School Governors [2008] EWHC 1865 (Admin),
[2008] 3 FCR 203 541

R (Singh) v Chief Constable of West Midlands [2006] EWCA Civ 1118, [2006] 1 WLR
3374 ....86, 551, 558, 593
R (Singh) v Immigration Appeal Tribunal [2002] EWHC (Admin) 2096 478
R (Sino) v SSHD [2011] EWHC 2249 (Admin) 292
R (SM) v Secretary of State for the Home Department [2013] EWHC 1144 (Admin)...............482
R (Smeaton on behalf of the Society for the Protection of Unborn Children) v The
Secretary of State for Health [2002] EWHC (Admin) 886, [2002] 2 FLR 146....................559
R (Smith) v Parole Board [2005] UKHL 1, [2005] 1 WLR 350 .... 280, 299, 308, 323, 327, 332,
337, 339
R (Smith) v Secretary of State for Defence [2010] UKSC 29, [2011] 1 AC 1.........74, 206–7, 224
R (Smith) v Secretary of State for Defence and Secretary of State for Work and
Pensions [2004] EWHC (Admin) 1797, [2005] 1 FLR 97 642
R (Smith) v Secretary of State for the Home Department [2005] UKHL 51..............................390
R (Spence) v Secretary of State for the Home Department [2003] EWCA Civ 732...................314
R (Spinks) v Secretary of State for the Home Department [2005] EWCA Civ 275....... 241, 263–4
R (SR) v Mental Health Review Tribunal [2005] EWHC 2923 (Admin) 272
R (Stanley, Marshall and Kelly) v Metropolitan Police Commissioner [2004] EWHC
(Admin) 2229, [2005] EMLR 3 453
R (Stokes) v Gwent Magistrates' Court [2001] EWHC (Admin) 569 470
R (Suresh) v Secretary of State for the Home Department [2001] EWHC (Admin) 1028... 73, 478
R (Suryananda) v Welsh Ministers [2007] EWCA Civ 893 .... 533, 544
R (Szuluk) v The Governor of HMP Full Sutton [2004] EWCA Civ 1426 .... 430, 454
R (T) (Sri Lanka) v Secretary of State for the Home Department [2013] EWHC 1093
(Admin) 257
R (T) v Chief Constable of Greater Manchester [2013] EWCA Civ 25, [2013] 2 All ER
813 .... 139, 451
R (T) v Secretary of State for Health, Court of Appeal, 29 July 2002.......................................609
R (T) v Secretary of State for Justice [2013] EWHC 1119 (Admin)..424
R (T) v Secretary of State for the Home Department [2003] EWCA Civ 1285 .... 103, 227–9
R (Tabbakh) v Staffordshire & West Midlands Probation Trust [2013] EWHC 2492
(Admin) 452
R (Takoushis) v HM Coroner for Inner North London [2005] EWCA Civ 1440, [2006]
1 WLR 461..223
R (Tataw) v Immigration Appeal Tribunal [2003] EWCA Civ 925...263
R (Taylor) v The Governor of Her Majesty's Prison Risley, Administrative Court, 20
October 2004...454
R (TD) v Commissioner of the Police of the Metropolis [2013] EWHC 2231 (Admin) 447
R (Thompson) v Law Society [2004] EWCA Civ 167, [2004] 1 WLR 2522.............324, 328, 332
R (Thomson) v Secretary of State for Education and Skills [2005] EWHC (Admin) 1378........468
R (Toovey) v The Law Society [2002] EWHC (Admin) 391 641
R (Tozlukaya) v Secretary of State for the Home Department [2006] EWCA Civ 379,
[2006] Imm AR 417... 256, 444
R (Trailer & Marina (Leven) Ltd) v Secretary of State for the Environment, Food &
Rural Affairs [2004] EWCA Civ 1580, [2005] 1 WLR 1267 .... 137, 648, 651, 659, 662
R (Trinity Mirror Plc) v Croydon Crown Court [2008] EWCA Crim 50, [2008] QB 770.........461
R (Ullah) v Special Adjudicator [2004] UKHL 26, [2004] 2 AC 323....... 12, 20, 22–5, 72–3, 228,
250, 332, 441, 477, 542
R (V) v Independent Appeal Panel for Tom Hood School [2010] EWCA Civ 142,
[2010] HRLR 21 .... 324–5, 332

R (Van Hoogstraten) v Governor of Belmarsh Prison [2002] EWHC (Admin) 1965,
[2003] 4 All ER 309 400

R (Vickers) v West London Magistrates' Court [2003] EWHC (Admin) 1809, [2004]
Crim LR 63 296

R (W) v Chief Constable of Warwickshire [2012] EWHC 406 (Admin)....................................450

R (W) v Lambeth London Borough Council [2002] EWCA Civ 613, [2002] 2 All ER 901 509

R (Wagstaff) v Secretary of State for Health [2001] 1 WLR 292 555–6

R (Warnborough College Ltd) v Secretary of State for the Home Department [2013]
EWHC 1510 (Admin)...646

R (Watts) v Bedford Primary Care Trust [2003] EWHC (Admin) 2228, [2004] Lloyd's
Rep Med 113...423

R (Watts) v Bedford Primary Care Trust [2003] EWHC Admin 2401 ....229, 235, 238

R (Waxman) v Crown Prosecution Service [2012] EWHC 133 (Admin) 176, 434

R (Weaver) v London & Quadrant Housing Trust [2009] EWCA Civ 587, [2010] 1
WLR 363 ....46, 50

R (Wellington) v Secretary of State for the Home Department [2008] UKHL 72, [2009]
1 AC 335 ....247, 252–3, 259–60

R (West) v Lloyd's of London [2004] EWCA Civ 506, [2004] 3 All ER 251 54

R (West) v Parole Board [2005] UKHL 1, [2005] 1 WLR 350...282

R (Westminster City Council) v Mayor of London [2002] EWHC (Admin) 2440......33, 508, 515,
648

R (Whiston) v SS Justice [2012] EWCA Civ 1374, [2013] 2 WLR 1080 ....272, 282

R (Whitmey) v The Commons Commissioners [2004] EWCA Civ 951, [2005] QB 282...........331

R (Wilkinson) v Inland Revenue Commissioners [2005] UKHL 30, [2005] 1 WLR
1718 ....115, 131, 163, 178, 613, 620, 624, 638

R (Wilkinson) v The Responsible Medical Officer, Broadmoor Hospital [2001] EWCA
Civ 1545, [2002] 1 WLR 419 ....93, 103, 182, 192, 227, 237, 332, 423

R (Willcox) v Secretary of State for Justice [2009] EWHC 1483 (Admin)......................244, 280

R (Williams) v Secretary of State for the Home Department [2002] EWCA Civ 498,
[2002] 1 WLR 2264..309

R (Williamson) v Secretary of State for Education and Employment [2005] UKHL 15,
[2005] 2 AC 246 ....527, 529–32, 534, 537, 541, 543, 545

R (Wilson) v Coventry City Council [2008] EWHC 2300 (Admin) 200

R (Wilson) v Wychavon District Council [2007] EWCA Civ 52, [2007] 2 WLR 798 ...... 143, 616,
627, 634

R (Wooder) v Feggetter [2002] EWCA Civ 554, [2003] QB 219 ....131, 237, 423, 430

R (Woolas) v Parliamentary Election Court [2010] EWHC 3169 (Admin), [2011] 2
WLR 1362.. 552, 597

R (Wright) v Secretary of State for Health [2009] UKHL 3, [2009] 1 AC 739 ....140, 324, 328,
331–2, 349, 464

R (Wright) v Secretary of State for the Home Department [2001] EWHC (Admin) 520,
(2001) 62 BMR 16... 263–4, 266

R (Wright) v Secretary of State for the Home Department [2006] EWCA Civ 67,
[2006] HRLR 23 .... 168, 316

R (X) v Chief Constable of West Midlands Police [2004] EWCA Civ 1068, [2005] 1
WLR 65.. 420, 449

R (X) v Headteachers and Governors of Y School [2007] EWHC 298 (Admin), [2008]
1 All ER 249 ....89, 532, 538, 546

R (X) v Tower Hamlets [2013] EWHC 480 (Admin) 620, 631

R (Y) v Ayelsbury Crown Court [2012] EWHC 1140 (Admin), [2012] Crim LR 893 586

R (Yakoub) v SSHD [2012] EWHC 3109 (Admin) 293
R (Z) v Secretary of State for the Home Department [2013] EWHC 498 (Admin)...................242
R (Zagorski) v Secretary of State for Business, Innovation & Skills [2010] EWHC
    3110 (Admin), [2011] HRLR 6 4
R (Zhang) v Secretary of State for the Home Department [2013] EWHC 891 (Admin)............486
R v A [2001] UKHL 25, [2002] 1 AC 45 .....81, 90, 97, 102, 106, 120–2, 125, 134, 144, 320, 367
R v A Local Authority in the Midlands, ex p LM [2000] 1 FCR 736.................. 420, 462–3
R v Ahmed [2004] EWCA Crim 2599, [2005] 1 WLR 122 509
R v Al-Khawaja [2005] EWCA Crim 2697, [2006] 1 WLR 1078..407
R v Allen [2001] UKHL 45, [2001] 4 All ER 768.. 64, 68
R v Allsopp [2005] EWCA Crim 703 445
R v Altham [2006] EWCA Crim 7, [2006] 1 WLR 3287 236
R v An Immigration Officer, ex p Xuereb [2000] 56 BMLR 180 299
R v Antoine [2000] 2 All ER 208 338
R v Avery [2009] EWCA Crim 2670, [2010] 2 Cr App R (S) 33 593
R v Axworthy [2012] EWCA Crim 2889...671
R v Bailey [2001] EWCA Crim 733 366
R v Ballinger [2005] EWCA Crim 1060..343
R v Bamber [2009] EWCA Crime 962, [2010] 1 Prison LR 297.....................................247
R v Barnham [2005] EWCA Crim 1049..362
R v BBC ex p Prolife Alliance [2003] UKHL 23, [2004] 1 AC 185 192
R v Benjafield [2002] UKHL 2, [2003] 1 AC 1099 .... 26, 64, 68, 362, 642, 647, 657, 671
R v Betts; R v Hall [2001] 2 Cr App R 257..360–1
R v Bieber [2008] EWCA Crim 1601, [2009] 1 WLR 223 246
R v Bishop, Court of Appeal, 10 November 2003 350
R v Botmeh [2001] EWCA Crim 2226, [2002] 1 WLR 531 353
R v Briggs-Price [2009] UKHL 19, [2009] 1 AC 1026 ....337, 339, 362
R v Broadcasting Standards Commission, ex p British Broadcasting Corporation [2001]
    QB 885 ....3, 410, 427, 434–5
R v Brown [2001] EWCA Crim 1771...404
R v Brushett [2001] Crim LR 471...353
R v Button [2005] EWCA Crim 516...366
R v Camberwell Green Youth Court, ex p D [2005] UKHL 4, [2005] 1 WLR 393...................357
R v Chenia [2002] EWCA Crim 2345, [2004] 1 All ER 543 360–1
R v Chief Constable of Norfolk Police, ex p F [2002] EWHC 1738 (Admin)...........................192
R v Chief Constable of North Wales, ex p AB [1998] 3 FCR 371 462
R v Coates [2004] EWCA Crim 3049...375
R v Compton [2002] EWCA Crim 2835..361
R v Connor; R v Mirza [2004] UKHL 2, [2004] 1 AC 118 368
R v Crown Court at Leeds, ex p Wardle [2001] UKHL 12, [2001] 2 WLR 865..............
    120, 277, 279, 295–6
R v D, Crown Court, 16/9/2013 ....530, 543, 548
R v Daniel [2002] EWCA Crim 959, [2003] 1 Cr App R 6 126
R v Davis [2001] 1 Cr App Rep 115..349
R v Debnath [2005] EWCA Crim 3472, [2006] Crim LR 451.....................................558
R v Deyemi [2007] EWCA Crim 2060, [2008] Crim LR 327......................................393
R v Dimsey; R v Allen [2001] UKHL 46, [2001] 3 WLR 843 .... 83, 359, 642, 647, 652, 673

R v Director of Public Prosecutions
ex p Kebilene [2000] 2 AC 326 ..... 17–18, 61, 63, 80, 90, 97, 102–4, 114, 120, 192, 320, 334, 392–3, 398
ex p Manning [2001] QB 330 .... 181–2, 218–19
R v DM [2011] EWCA Crim 2752 557
R v Drew [2003] UKHL 25, [2003] 1 WLR 1213 ....228, 240, 246, 283
R v Drummond [2002] EWCA Crim 527, [2002] 2 Cr App R 25 397
R v Dudley [2005] EWCA Crim 719..389
R v Dundon [2004] EWCA Crim 621, [2004] UKHRR 717 389
R v Dunn [2010] EWCA Crim 1823, [2010] 2 Cr App R 30..340, 387
R v E [2004] EWCA Crim 1234, [2004] 1 WLR 3279...445
R v East London and the City Mental Health NHS Trust, ex p von Brandenburg [2003]
UKHL 58, [2004] 2 AC 280...269, 289, 303
R v English Nature ex p Aggregate Industries UK Ltd [2002] EWHC (Admin) 908,
[2003] Env LR 3 332
R v Everson [2001] EWCA Crim 896..366
R v Forbes [2001] UKHL 40, [2001] 3 WLR 428 349
R v Francom [2001] 1 Cr App Rep 237 360–1
R v G [2008] UKHL 37, [2009] 1 AC 92... 393, 412
R v Galfetti [2002] EWCA Crim 1916 .... 152, 169
R v Goldstein [2003] EWCA Crim 3450, [2004] WLR 2878..558
R v Goodenough [2004] EWCA Crim 2260, [2005] 1 Cr App R (S) 88 ....396, 509, 671
R v Goring [2004] EWCA Crim 969 377
R v Gorman, 2 April 2004 377
R v Gough [1993] AC 646 380
R v Governor of Brockhill Prison, ex p Evans (No 2) [2001] 2 AC 19.......277, 279–80, 282, 291, 316
R v Governor of Pentonville Prison, ex p Osman [1989] 3 All ER 701 88
R v Grant 1 [2001] EWCA Crim 2611, [2002] 2 WLR 1409..338
R v Grant [2001] EWCA Crim 2611, [2002] 2 WLR 1409...288–9
R v H [2001] EWCA Crim 1024, [2002] 1 Cr App R 7... 71, 248
R v H [2004] UKHL 3, [2004] 2 AC 134...336, 338–9, 352
R v H [2006] EWCA Crim 853...357
R v H [2007] EWCA Crim 2622...452
R v Hall [2013] EWCA Crim 82...245
R v Hamadi [2007] EWCA Crim 3048...368
R v Handley (1874) 13 Cox CC 79...183
R v Hardy [2003] EWCA Crim 3092..505
R v Harrison [2006] EWCA Crim 18..400
R v Harvey [2013] EWCA Crim 1104...671
R v Hasan [2005] UKHL 22, [2005] 2 WLR 709 120
R v Haslam [2003] EWCA Crim 3444 400
R v Hayward; R v Jones [2001] EWCA Crim 168, [2001] 3 WLR 125............................. 369, 404
R v Hertfordshire County Council, ex p Green Environmental Industries Ltd [2000] 2
AC 483 358
R v HM Treasury ex parte British Telecommunications plc [1996] ECR I–1631......................156
R v Holding [2005] EWCA Crim 3185, [2006] 1 WLR 1040...................................132, 557, 596
R v Home Office, ex p Wright [2001] EWHC (Admin) 520, [2002] HRLR 1.................. 182, 220

R v Home Secretary ex p Launder [1997] 1 WLR 839 70
R v Horncastle [2009] UKSC 14, [2010] 2 AC 373..21
R v Howell [2003] EWCA Crim 01, [2005] 1 Cr App Rep 1 360
R v Hundal; R v Dhaliwal [2004] EWCA Crim 389...359
R v Hursthouse [2013] EWCA Crim 517 671
R v Ibrahim [2012] EWCA Crim 837, [2012] 4 All ER 225..407
R v Inland Revenue Commissioners, ex p Banque Internationale à Luxembourg SA
    [2000] STC 708...420, 434, 444
R v ITN News [2013] EWCA Crim 773, [2013] EMLR 22...588
R v James [1988] 1 SCR 669 62
R v James [2002] EWCA Crim 119 ....373, 375
R v Jawad [2013] EWCA Crim 644, [2013] Crim LR 698 670–1
R v Johnstone [2003] UKHL 28, [2003] 1 WLR 1736...394, 397
R v Jones [2002] UKHL 5, [2002] 2 WLR 524 369
R v K [2009] EWCA Crim 1640, [2010] 2 WLR 905 359
R v Kansal [2001] EWCA Crim 1260, [2001] 3 WLR 751...63
R v Kansal [2001] UKHL 62, [2001] 3 WLR 1562 ....63, 149
R v Kearns [2002] EWCA Crim 748, [2002] WLR 2815...358–9
R v Kelly [2001] EWCA Crim 1030, [2002] 1 Cr App 11 246
R v Kelly [2001] EWCA Crim 1751, [2001] Crim LR 836..283
R v Keogh [2007] EWCA Crim 528, [2007] 1 WLR 1500 ....126, 395
R v Kirk [2002] EWCA Crim 1580, [2002] Crim LR 756 625
R v Lambert [2001] UKHL 37, [2002] 2 AC 545 .... 9, 17–18, 27, 61–4, 67–8, 121, 123, 125,
                                                       134, 149, 349, 392, 394, 396, 398
R v Lemon [1979] 2 WLR 281 ....5, 549
R v Lewis [2005] EWCA Crim 859...349
R v Lichniak [2002] UKHL 47, [2003] 1 AC 903 ....107, 244, 246, 270, 280, 282–3
R v Loosley [2001] UKHL 53, [2001] 1 WLR 2060 365
R v Lord Chancellor
    ex p Lightfoot [1999] 4 All ER 583..332, 340, 344
    ex p Lightfoot [2000] QB 597..327
    ex p Witham [1997] 2 All ER 779 340
R v Loveridge [2001] 2 Cr App R 591 ....366, 445
R v Loveridge [2001] EWCA Crim 1034, [2001] 2 Cr App R 29 427
R v Lyons [2002] UKHL 44, [2003] 1 AC 976.. 11, 19, 21, 64, 536
R v Mason [2002] 2 Cr App R 628..366, 445
R v Mason [2002] EWCA Crim 385, [2002] 2 Cr App R 38..85, 414
R v Matthews [2003] EWCA Crim 813, [2004] QB 690..395
R v May [2005] EWCA Crim 97, [2005] 1 WLR 2902..671
R v Ministry of Agriculture Fisheries and Food ex parte Lay, Divisional Court, 15 May 1998....156
R v Ministry of Defence, ex p Smith [1996] QB 517..94
R v Morgan [2013] EWCA Crim 1307 671
R v Mushtaq [2005] UKHL 25, [2005] 1 WLR 1513..42, 360, 391
R v Navabi [2005] EWCA Crim 2865 395
R v North and East Devon Health Authority, ex p Coughlan [2001] QB 213 ....504, 507, 512
R v Oakes [1986] 1 SCR 103..91
R v Oakes [2012] EWCA Crim 2435...247

R v Oates, Court of Appeal, 25 April 2002 404
R v Offen [2001] 1 WLR 253 ....65, 127, 245, 283
R v P [2001] 2 WLR 463..365–6, 414, 445
R v Parchment [2003] EWCA Crim 2428... 246, 283
R v Pearce [2001] EWCA Crim 2834, [2002] 1 WLR 1553 493
R v Pedley [2009] EWCA Crim 840, [2009] 1 WLR 2517...280
R v Perrin [2002] EWCA Crim 747..86, 551, 557, 573
R v Porter [2001] EWCA Crim 2699..400
R v Poulton (1832) 5 C&P 329 183
R v Qazi [2010] EWCA Crim 2579, [2011] HRLR 4 .... 240, 245
R v Rezvi; R v Benjafield [2002] UKHL 1, [2003] 1 AC 1099................................26, 331, 361
R v Richards [1999] Crim LR 764...371
R v Robinson [2003] EWCA Crim 2219 361
R v Rosenberg [2006] EWCA Crim 6, [2006] Crim LR 540 366
R v Secretary of State, ex p World Development Movement [1995] 1 WLR 386........................38
R v Secretary of State for Health
    ex p C [2000] 1 FCR 471...327
    ex p Eastside Cheese Co [1999] 3 CMLR 12 ....639, 646–7, 651–2, 657–8
R v Secretary of State for Home Affairs, ex p O'Brien [1923] 2 KB 361.....................................549
R v Secretary of State for the Environment, Transport and the Regions, ex p Alconbury
    Developments Ltd [2001] UKHL 23, [2001] 2 WLR 1389.................. 14, 19–21, 82, 97, 321,
                                                                      323–5, 327, 329–31, 382, 390
R v Secretary of State for the Home Department
    ex p Al-Hasan [2005] UKHL 13, [2005] 1 WLR 688..71, 387
    ex p Amin [2003] UKHL 51, [2004] 1 AC 653 34
    ex p Anderson [2002] UKHL 46, [2003] 1 AC 837........ 14, 121, 134, 139, 335, 339, 383, 389
    ex p Daly [2001] UKHL 26, [2001] 2 AC 532 ....3, 91–4, 96, 430, 453, 560, 653
    ex p Fire Brigades Union [1995] 2 AC 513 384
    ex p Gallagher [1996] 2 CMLR 951...156
    ex p Greenfield [2005] UKHL 14, [2005] 1 WLR 673..... 151, 153, 158, 160, 163–4, 171–3, 175
    ex p IH [2003] UKHL 59, [2004] 2 AC 253 ....288, 302–3, 316
    ex p Isiko [2001] 1 FLR 930...91, 477, 481
    ex p Mahmood [2001] 1 WLR 840... 69, 91, 93, 477, 481
    ex p Mellor [2001] EWCA Civ 472, [2002] QB 13.. 472, 492
    ex p Samaroo, Administrative Court, 20 December 2000...91
    ex p Sezek [2001] EWCA Civ 795, [2002] 1 WLR 348 .... 290, 292
    ex p Simms [1999] 3 WLR 328..563
    ex p Simms [2000] 2 AC 115... 84, 113, 550
    ex p Turgut [2001] 1 All ER 719...227
R v Secretary of State for Transport ex parte Factortame (No 5) (1998) The Times, 28 April......156
R v Shabir [2008] EWCA Crim 1809, [2009] 1 Cr App R (S) 84 671
R v Shannon [2001] 1 WLR 51...364
R v Shaw [2011] EWCA Crim 98...378
R v Shayler [2002] UKHL 11, [2002] 2 WLR 754......... 84, 90, 92, 107, 550, 557, 560, 564, 567,
                                                                      571, 602
R v Sherwood, ex p The Telegraph Group plc [2001] EWCA Crim 1075, [2001] 1
    WLR 1983 ....555, 563, 602

R v Singh [2003] EWCA Crim 3712 369

R v Smethurst [2001] EWCA Crim 772, [2002] 1 Cr App R 6..463, 557

R v Smith (No 2) [2005] UKHL 12, [2005] 1 WLR..388

R v Smith [2002] EWCA Crim 2561 353

R v Soroya [2006] EWCA Crim 1884, [2007] Crim LR 181 368

R v Stevens [1988] 1 SCR 1153..62

R v Stow [2005] EWCA Crim 1157...389

R v T; R v H [2001] EWCA Crim 1877, [2001] 1 WLR 632 368

R v Taylor [2001] EWCA Crim 2263, [2002] 1 Cr App R 37......................................543

R v Teeside Crown Court, ex p Gazette Media Co Ltd [2005] EWCA Crim 1983...........461, 584

R v Templar [2003] EWCA Crim 3186 353

R v Thakrar [2001] EWCA Crim 1096..362

R v Thoron [2001] EWCA Crim 1797 388

R v Togher [2001] 3 All ER 463...349

R v Ungvari [2003] EWCA Crim 2346..408

R v Waya [2012] UKSC 51, [2013] 1 AC 294.....................................126, 647, 670–1

R v Weaver [2001] EWCA Crim 2768..218

R v Webster [2010] EWCA Crim 2819, [2011] 1 Cr App R 16 ....126, 395

R v Weir [2001] 1 WLR 421...319

R v Wheeler [2004] EWCA Crim 572 .... 170, 377

R v Witchell [2005] EWCA Crim 2900 636

Rabone v Pennine Care NHS Foundation Trust [2012] UKSC 2, [2012] 2 AC 72.....34, 36–7, 60,
157, 165, 189, 191, 198, 204

Rafferty v Secretary of State for Communities & Local Government [2009] EWCA Civ
809, [2010] JPL 485..506

Raimondo v Italy (1994) 18 EHRR 237 .... 337, 671

Raja v van Hoogstraten [2004] EWCA Civ 968, [2004] 4 All ER 793.......................400

Ram v Ram [2004] EWCA Civ 1452, [2004] 3 FCR 425 640

Rampal v Rampal (No 2) [2001] EWCA Civ 989, [2001] 3 WLR 795........................347

Ramsahai v The Netherlands, 15 May 2007, ECtHR..213

Rance v Mid-Downs Health Authority [1991] 1 QB 587...183

Rantsev v Cyprus and Russia [2010] 51 EHRR 1 267

Ratcliffe v Secretary of State for Defence [2009] EWCA Civ 39, [2009] ICR 762.......613, 624, 628

RB (Algeria) v Secretary of State for the Home Department [2009] UKHL 10, [2010] 2
AC 110.. 72, 95, 150, 250–4, 322, 332

Re A (A Child: Disclosure of Third Party Information) [2012] UKSC 60, [2012] 3
WLR 1484 .... 358, 457

Re A (A Child) [2012] UKSC 60, [2012] 3 WLR 1484...230

Re A (A Child) [2013] EWCA Civ 1104, [2013] 3 FCR 257 .... 473, 496

Re A (A Minor) [1992] 3 Med L Rev 303..183

Re A (Children) (Conjoined Twins: Surgical Separation) [2001] Fam 147.102, 182–3, 185–7, 225

Re A (Children) v X London Borough Council [2010] EWCA Civ 344, [2010] 2 FLR 661 495

Re A (permission to remove child from jurisdiction:
human rights) [2000] 2 FLR 225 471
human rights) [2001] 1 FCR 43 499

Re A [2002] 2 FCR 481 .... 640, 673

Re A [2002] EWHC (Admin/Fam) 611, [2002] 2 FCR 481 .... 509, 511

Re a Solicitor No 11 of 2001 [2001] EWCA Civ 153801 229

Re an application to vary the undertakings of A [2005] STC (SCD) 103 641
Re B (a child) (adoption order) [2001] EWCA Civ 347, [2001] 2 FCR 89 .... 471, 497
Re B (a child) (sole adoption by unmarried father) [2001] UKHL 70, [2002] 1 WLR
    258 ....471, 497
Re B (a child) [2013] UKSC 33, [2013] 1 WLR 1911 ....95, 471, 497–8
Re B and T (care proceedings: legal representation) [2001] 1 FCR 512....................................362
Re B-S (Children) [2013] EWCA Civ 1146...497
Re C (care proceedings: disclosure of local authority's decision making process) [2002]
    EWHC (Fam) 1379, [2002] 2 FCR 673...472
Re C and B (children) (care order: future harm) [2002] 2 FCR 614............................. 471, 495–6
Re Christian Institute Application for Judicial Review [2007] NIQB 66, [2008] IRLR
    36 ....32, 533, 541
Re D (Children) (care order) [2003] EWCA Civ 1592 472
Re E (A Child) [2008] UKHL 66, [2009] 1 AC 536..32, 34, 106, 230
Re E (Children) [2011] UKSC 27, [2011] 2 WLR 1326...500
Re E [2008] UKHL 66, [2009] 1 AC 536..233–4, 244, 608, 614
Re F (A Child) v East Sussex CC [2008] EWCA Civ 439, [2008] 2 FLR 550.........................499
Re F (in utero) [1988] 2 All ER 193...183
Re G (a child: residential assessment) [2004] EWCA Civ 24, [2004] 1 FCR 317......................332
Re G (a child) [2013] EWCA Civ 965, [2013] 3 FCR 293 497
Re G (adult incompetent: withdrawal of treatment) [2002] 65 BMLR 6 185
Re H (a child) (interim care order) [2002] EWCA Civ 1932, [2003] 1 FLR 350 495
Re H; Re G (adoption: consultation of unmarried fathers) [2001] 1 FLR 646 ....467–8, 473, 499
Re Hardial Singh [1984] 1 All ER 983..292
Re J (a minor) (wardship: medical treatment) [1991] FCR 370 .... 183, 185
Re J (Adoption: Contacting Father) [2003] EWHC (Fam) 199, [2003] 1 FLR 933 ...467, 471, 476
Re K (a child) (secure accommodation order: right to liberty) [2001] 2 All ER 719........ 275, 277,
                                                                                                                    285–6
Re K (children) [2010] EWCA Civ 1365, [2011] 1 FLR 1592...370
Re L (a child) [2013] EWCA Civ 489, [2013] 3 FCR 90..492
Re L (care proceedings: human rights claims) [2003] EWHC (Fam) 665, [2004] 1 FCR 289 495
Re LM [2007] EWHC 1902 (Fam), [2008] 1 FLR 1360 585
Re M (a child) (adoption) [2003] EWCA Civ 1874, [2004] 1 FCR 157.....................................497
Re M (a child) (secure accommodation) [2001] EWCA Civ 458, [2001] 1 FCR 692.... 331, 338–9
Re M (adoption: rights of natural father) [2001] 1 FLR 745.. 468, 473
Re M [2001] FLR 745 498
Re MB (an adult: medical treatment) [1997] 2 FCR 541...183
Re McCaughey [2011] UKSC 20, [2012] 1 AC 725...14, 20, 69
Re McE [2009] UKHL 15, [2009] 1 AC 908 ....85, 414, 446
Re McKerr [2004] UKHL 12, [2004] 1 WLR 807............................. 12, 23, 37, 69, 181, 206
Re O (children) (representation: McKenzie friend) [2005] EWCA Civ 759 350
Re Officer L [2007] UKHL 36, [2007] 1 WLR 2135... 189, 191–3, 196
Re P (care proceedings: father's application to be joined as a party) [2001] FLR 781 473
Re P [2007] EWCA Civ 2, [2007] 1 FLR 1957.. 156, 177
Re P [2008] EWCA Civ 535, [2008] 2 FLR 625 498
Re P-S (children) [2013] EWCA Civ 223, [2013] 2 FCR 299 357
Re R (a child) [2003] EWCA Civ 182, [2003] Fam 129 467

Re Roddy (a child) (identification: restriction on publication) [2003] EWHC (Fam)
2927, [2004] FCR 481 .... 427, 435, 459, 552, 554, 586
Re S (a child) (adoption: order made in father's absence) [2001] 2 FCR 148 370
Re S (a child) (adoption proceedings: joinder of father) [2001] 1 FCR 158 473
Re S (a child) (contact) [2004] EWCA Civ 18, [2004] 1 FLR 1279 .... 494, 496
Re S (a child) (identification: restrictions on publication) [2004] UKHL 47, [2005] 1
AC 593 .... 57, 435, 438, 460–1, 563, 582, 584
Re S (a child) (residence order: condition) (No 2) [2002] EWCA Civ 1795, [2003] 1
FCR 138 500
Re S [2001] EWHC (Admin) 334, [2001] FLR 776 463
Re S [2002] UKHL 10, [2002] 2 WLR 72033, 43, 120–3, 128, 134–5, 149, 324, 331, 471–4, 495
Re Scriven, Court of Appeal, 22 April 2004 299
Re T (a child) (DNA tests:
paternity) [2001] 2 FLR 1190 ....468, 474, 501
paternity) [2001] 3 FCR 577 421
Re V (a child) (care proceedings: human rights claims) [2004] EWCA Civ 54, [2004] 1
All ER 997 .... 331, 494
Re W (children) [2010] UKSC 12, [2010] 1 WLR 701 358
Re Webster (a child) v Webster [2006] EWHC 2733 (Fam), [2007] 1 FLR 1146 .... 567, 587
Re West Norwood Cemetery [2005] 1 WLR 2176 641
Re Westminster Property Management Ltd [2001] 1 WLR 2230 .... 340, 359
Re X & Y (children) [2012] EWCA Civ 1500, [2013] 2 FLR 628 461
Re X [2001] 1 FCR 541 .... 567, 587
Redmond-Bate v Director of Public Prosecutions [2000] HRLR 249 550
Rees v United Kingdom (1986) 9 EHRR 56 234
Remli v France (1996) 22 EHRR 252 368
Revenue & Customs Commissioners v Banerjee [2009] EWHC 1229 (Ch), [2009] 3 All
ER 930 .... 414, 458
Revenue & Customs Commissioners v Berriman [2007] EWHC 1183 (Admin), [2007]
4 All ER 925 676
Revenue & Customs Commissioners v Total Technology (Engineering) Ltd [2012]
UKUT 418 (TCC) 640, 674
Revenue & Customs v Smith [2007] EWHC 488 (Ch), [2008] STC 1941 673
Reynolds v Times Newspapers Ltd [1999] 4 All ER 609 .... 550–1, 557, 564, 575, 600
Reynolds v United Kingdom (2012) 55 EHRR 35 193
Richards v Ghana [2013] EWHC 1254 (Admin) 261
Rimmer v HM Advocate, 23 May 2001 379–80
Ringeisen v Austria (No 1) (1971) 1 EHRR 455 323
Roberts v Parole Board [2005] UKHL 45, [2005] 3 WLR 152 .... 297, 307, 309, 353
Roberts v Secretary of State for the Home Department [2005] EWCA Civ 1663, [2006]
1 WLR 843 282
Rocknroll v News Group Newspapers Ltd [2013] EWHC 24 (Ch) 461
Roose v Parole Board [2010] EWHC 1780 (Admin) 308
Rothenthurm Commune v Switzerland, Commission, 14 December 1988 41
Rowe v Kingtson-Upon-Hull City Council and Essex County Council [2003] EWCA
Civ 1281 343
Rowland v Environment Agency [2003] EWCA Civ 1885, [2005] Ch 1 .... 641, 662
Royal Borough of Kensington and Chelsea v O'Sullivan [2003] EWCA Civ 371 ......68, 504, 509,
612, 614, 618

RP v Nottingham City Council [2008] EWCA Civ 462, [2008] 2 FLR 1516 .... 350, 473

RSPCA v Attorney General [2001] 3 All ER 530 53

RU (Bangladesh) v Secretary of State for the Home Department [2011] EWCA Civ
  651, [2011] Imm AR 662 488

RU (Sri Lanka) v Secretary of State for the Home Department [2008] EWCA Civ 753 ....429, 443

Rugby Football Union v Consolidated Information Services Limited [2012] UKSC 55,
  [2012] 1 WLR 3333 4

S & M v United Kingdom (1993) 18 EHRR CD 172 404

S and Marper v United Kingdom (2009) 48 EHRR 50 .... 415, 423, 446–7

S T and P v London Borough of Brent [2002] EWCA Civ 693, [2002] ACD 90 325

S v B (a child) (abduction: objections to return) [2005] EWHC 733 500

S v France (1990) 65 D&R 250 .... 648, 659

S v Miller [2001] UKSC 977 335

S v Secretary of State for the Home Department [2012] EWHC 1939 (Admin) 290

S v Switzerland (1991) 14 EHRR 670 404

Saadi v United Kingdom (2008) 47 EHRR 17 291

Saha v General Medical Council [2009] EWHC 1907 (Admin) 455

St Brice v London Borough of Southwark [2001] EWCA Civ 1138, [2002] 1 WLR
  1537 ....328, 506, 606, 612, 614, 621

Salduz v Turkey (2008) 49 EHRR 421 402–3

Salesi v Italy (1993) 26 EHRR 187 325

Salisbury District Council v Le Roi [2001] EWCA Civ 1490 505

Salman v Turkey (2002) 34 EHRR 17 .... 204, 209–10

Salvesen v Riddell & Lord Advocate [2013] UKSC 22, [2013] HRLR 23 .... 651, 656–7, 668

Sanchez-Reiss v Switzerland (1986) 9 EHRR 71 310

Saskatchewan Human Rights Commission v Kodellas (1989) 60 DLR (4th) 143 148

Saunders v The Independent Police Complaints Commission [2008] EWHC 2372
  (Admin), [2009] 1 All ER 379 213

Saunders v United Kingdom (1997) 23 EHRR 313 .... 159, 359

Savage v South Essex Partnership Foundation [2010] EWHC 865 (QB), [2010] HRLR
  24 .... 165, 198

Savage v South Essex Partnership NHS Foundation Trust [2008] UKHL 74, [2009] 1
  AC 681 .... 198, 204

Savage v United States [2012] EWHC 3317 (Admin) 426

Scanfuture UK Ltd v Secretary of State for Trade and Industry [2001] IRLR 416 386

Schenk v Switzerland (1988) 13 EHRR 242 365

Schering Chemicals Ltd v Falkman Ltd [1981] 2 WLR 848 .... 5, 549

Schmautzer v Austria (1996) 21 EHRR 511 159

Scott v United Kingdom [2000] 2 FCR 560 499

Seal v Chief Constable of South Wales [2007] UKHL 31, [2007] 1 WLR 1910 345

Secretary of State for Defence v Guardian Newspapers Ltd [1984] 3 WLR 986 .... 5, 549

Secretary of State for Defence v Times Newspapers Ltd, Divisional Court, 28 March
  2001 .... 197, 571

Secretary of State for Justice v James [2009] UKHL 22, [2010] 1 AC 553 .... 116, 280, 297, 314

Secretary of State for Justice v Rayner [2008] EWCA Civ 176, [2009] 1 WLR 310 .... 298, 313

Secretary of State for Social Security v Tunnicliffe [1991] 2 All ER 712 65–6

Secretary of State for the Department of Health v MH [2005] UKHL 60, [2006] 1 AC
  441 .... 298, 312

Secretary of State for the Foreign and Commonwealth Office v Maftah [2011] EWCA
Civ 350, [2012] 2 WLR 251 333

Secretary of State for the Home Department v AF [2009] UKHL 28, [2009] 3 WLR 74
20, 127, 354

Secretary of State for the Home Department v AHK [2009] EWCA Civ 287, [2009] 1
WLR 2049 355

Secretary of State for the Home Department v AP [2010] UKSC 24, [2010] 3 WLR 51 273

Secretary of State for the Home Department v AP [2010] UKSC 26, [2010] 1 WLR
1652 ....235, 458, 581, 585

Secretary of State for the Home Department v CD [2011] EWHC 2087 (Admin).....................454

Secretary of State for the Home Department v CE [2011] EWHC 3159 (Admin).....................455

Secretary of State for the Home Department v E [2007] UKHL 47, [2008] 1 AC 499 273

Secretary of State for the Home Department v Hayat [2012] EWCA Civ 1054, [2013]
Imm AR 15... 478, 486

Secretary of State for the Home Department v JJ [2007] UKHL 45, [2008] 1 AC 385. 270–1, 273

Secretary of State for the Home Department v MB [2007] UKHL 46, [2007] 3 WLR
681 ....126, 332–3, 340, 353

Secretary of State for the Home Department v Mental Health Review Tribunal 'PH'
[2002] EWCA Civ 1868 272

Secretary of State for the Home Department v Nasseri [2009] UKHL 23, [2010] 1 AC
1 .... 101, 136, 254

Secretary of State for the Home Department v Z [2002] EWCA Civ 952 ....228, 262, 442

Secretary of State for Work and Pensions v M [2004] EWCA Civ 1343, [2005] 2 WLR
740 ....109, 131, 651

Secretary of State for Work and Pensions v M [2006] UKHL 11, [2006] 2 AC 91 ....
22, 469, 607, 610, 614, 620, 628

Selçuk and Asker v Turkey, Judgment of 24 April 1998.. 159, 162

Selwood v Durham County Council [2012] EWCA Civ 979... 195, 204

Senthuran v Secretary of State for the Home Department [2004] EWCA Civ 950,
[2004] 4 All ER 365 466

Sepet v Secretary of State for the Home Department [2003] UKHL 15, [2003] 1 WLR 856 535

SH (Palestinian Territories) v Secretary of State for Home Department [2008] EWCA
Civ 1150, [2009] Imm AR 306..229

SH v United Kingdom (2012) 54 EHRR 4 256

Shaw (Inspector of Taxes) v Vicky Construction Ltd [2002] EWHC (Ch) 5659, [2002]
STC 1544..641, 643, 673

Sheffield City Council v Hopkins [2001] EWCA Civ 1023, [2001] 26 EG 163 (CS)................506

Sheffield City Council v Personal Representative of Wall [2010] EWCA Civ 922,
[2010] HRLR 35 ....612, 620, 631

Sheffield City Council v Smart [2002] EWCA Civ 4, [2002] ACD 56......................................332

Shrimpton v The General Council of the Bar, The Visitors to the Inns of Court, 6 May 2005 391

Šilih v Slovenia (2009) 49 EHRR 996... 69, 206

Silkin v Beaverbrook Newspapers Ltd [1958] 2 All ER 516..549

Silva Pontes v Portugal (1994) Series A No 286-A...159

Silverton v Gravett, Divisional Court, 19 October 2001 552

Sims v Dacorum Borough Council [2013] EWCA Civ 12, [2013] HLR 14...................... 504, 650

Sinclair Garden Investments (Kensington) Ltd v Lands Tribunal [2005] EWCA Civ
1305, [2006] 3 All ER 650 340

Sinclair v Glatt [2009] EWCA Civ 176, [2009] 1 WLR 1845...671

Sinclair v HM Advocate [2005] HRLR 26 350–1
Singh v Entry Clearance Officer New Delhi [2004] EWCA Civ 1075, [2005] QB 608 ...
    35, 76, 466, 468, 478
SKA v Persons Unknown [2012] EWHC 766 (QB)..417
Smith & Ors v Ministry of Defence [2013] UKSC 41, [2013] 3 WLR 69......................19, 74, 78
Smith and Ellis v Ministry of Defence [2013] UKSC 41, [2013] 3 WLR 69.186, 190, 200–1, 204
Smith v Secretary of State for Trade & Industry [2007] EWHC 1013 (Admin), [2008] 1
    WLR 394...517
Smith v United Kingdom (1999) 29 EHRR 493..540
Smithkline Beecham plc v Advertising Standards Authority [2001] EWHC (Admin) 6,
    [2001] EMLR 23..551
SN v Secretary of State for the Home Department [2005] EWCA Civ 1683, [2006] INLR 273441
Soering v United Kingdom (1989) 11 EHRR 439.. 72, 250, 252, 259, 374
Sole v Secretary of State for Trade & Industry [2007] EWHC 1527 (Admin)...........................517
Sorokins v Latvia [2010] EWHC 1962 (Admin)..260
Soteriou v Ultrachem Ltd [2004] EWHC (QB) 983, [2004] IRLR 870......................................649
South Buckinghamshire District Council v Cooper [2004] EWHC (QB) 155...........................516
South Buckinghamshire District Council v Porter [2003] UKHL 26, [2003] 2 AC 558 ...
    42, 504–5, 515–16
South Cambridgeshire District Council v Flynn [2006] EWHC 1320 (QB), [2007] JPL 440.....516
South Cambridgeshire District Council v Price [2008] EWHC 1234 (Admin)...........................516
South Somerset District Council v Hughes [2009] EWCA Civ 1245.......................................516
Southend-On-Sea Borough Council v Armour [2012] EWHC 3361 (QB)..................................526
SP v Secretary of State for Justice [2009] EWHC 13 (Admin), [2009] ACD 59 .212, 214–15, 222
Spelman v Express Newspapers [2012] EWHC 355 (QB)...588
Spicer v Tuli [2012] EWCA Civ 845, [2012] 1 WLR 3088 342
Spiers v Ruddy [2007] UKPC D2, [2008] 1 AC 873.. 26, 378
Sporrong and Lönnroth v Sweden (1982) 5 EHRR 35...374, 639, 646
SRM Global Master Fund LP v Treasury Commissioners [2009] EWCA Civ 788,
    [2009] UKHRR 1219...642, 647, 656, 658, 660, 677
SS (India) v Secretary of State for the Home Department [2010] EWCA Civ 388....................488
SS (Malaysia) v Secretary of State for the Home Department [2013] EWCA Civ 888..............543
SS (Nigeria) v Secretary of State for the Home Department [2013] EWCA Civ 550........ 104, 485
Stafford v United Kingdom (2002) 35 EHRR 1121 .... 168–9, 383
Stan Greek Refineries and Stratis Andreadis v Greece, Judgment of 9 December 1994.............159
Stanley v London Borough of Ealing, Court of Appeal, 16 April 2003............................... 651, 657
Stansbury v Datapulse plc [2003] EWCA Civ 1951, [2004] ICR 523 .... 324, 364
Starrs v Ruxton [2000] JC 208... 381, 385
Stec v United Kingdom (2005) 41 EHRR SE 295 .... 613, 627
Stedman v United Kingdom (1997) 23 EHRR CD 168 540
Stellato v Ministry of Justice [2010] EWCA Civ 1435, [2011] 2 WLR 936 284
Stewart v Secretary of State for Work and Pensions [2011] EWCA Civ 907 .....617, 620, 622, 631
Stögmuller v Austria (1969) 1 EHRR 155 .... 372, 374
Stone v South East Coast Strategic Health Authority [2006] EWHC 1668 (Admin) 567, 588
Storck v Germany (2005) 43 EHRR 96 271
Stovin v Wise [1996] AC 923...154
Strbac v Secretary of State for the Home Department [2005] EWCA Civ 848..........................252
Stretford v Football Association Ltd [2007] EWCA Civ 238, [2007] All ER (Comm) 1...........320

Stubbings v United Kingdom (1996) 23 EHRR 213 341
Sufiand Elmi v United Kingdom (2012) 54 EHRR 9..256
Sugar (deceased) v BBC [2012] UKSC 4, [2012] 1 WLR 439 556
Sullivan v United States [2012] EWHC 1680 (Admin) 277
Summers v Fairclough Homes Ltd [2012] UKSC 26, [2012] 1 WLR 2004 .... 642, 647, 665
Sunday Times v United Kingdom (1979–80) 2 EHRR 245 .... 5, 84, 279, 291, 549
Swami Omkarananda and the Divine Light Zentrum v Switzerland (1997) 25 D&R 105 ....35, 558
Swift v Secretary of State for Justice [2013] EWCA Civ 193.. 627, 631
SXH v Crown Prosecution Service [2013] EWHC 71 (QB)..412
T v British Broadcasting Corporation [2007] EWHC 1683 (QB), [2008] 1 FLR 281................587
Tabernacle v Secretary of State for Defence [2009] EWCA Civ 23...........................554, 558, 591
Tagci and Sargin v Turkey (1995) 20 EHRR 505..296
Tangney v The Governor of HMP Elmley [2005] EWCA Civ 1009 .... 137, 338–9
Tariq v Home Office [2011] UKSC 35, [2011] 3 WLR 322...355–6
Taylor v Chief Constable of Thames Valley Police [2004] EWCA Civ 858, [2004] 1
   WLR 3155 294
Taylor v Lawrence [2001] EWCA Civ 119, [2002] EWCA Civ 90, [2003] QB 528 387
Taylor v United Kingdom (1994) 18 EHRR CD 215..556
Teinaz v London Borough of Wandsworth [2002] EWHC Civ 1040, [2002] ICR 1471 369
Teixeira de Castro v Portugal (1998) 28 EHRR 101 .... 159, 365
Tekin v Turkey, Judgment of 9 June 1998 162
Tekle v Secretary of State for the Home Department [2008] EWHC 3064 (Admin)
   [2009] 2 All ER 193 .... 428–9, 444
Telchadder v Wickland (Holdings) Ltd [2012] EWCA Civ 635, [2012] HLR 35.......................524
Terry v Hoyer (UK) Limited [2001] EWCA Civ 678 347
Tewkesbury Borough Council v Brown [2006] EWHC 2697 (QB) 516
TH v Crown Court Wood Green [2006] EWHC 2683 (Admin), [2007] 1 WLR 1670 284
Thaw v United Kingdom (1996) 22 EHRR CD 100 404
Theakston v MGN Ltd [2002] EWHC (QB) 137, [2002] EMLR 22...............................
   57, 417, 435–6, 438, 461, 562, 568, 582
Thlimmenos v Greece (2001) 31 EHRR 15...535
Thomas v Bridgend County Borough Council [2011] EWCA Civ 862, [2012] 2 WLR
   624 ....132, 648, 658, 663
Thomas v News Group Newspapers [2001] EWCA Civ 1233, [2002] EMLR 4.......................552
Threlfall v General Optical Council [2004] EWHC (Admin) 2683, [2005] Lloyd's Rep
   Med 250..371
Thurrock Borough Council v West [2012] EWCA Civ 1435, [2013] HLR 5 525
Tillery Valley Foods v Channel Four Television [2004] EWHC (Ch) 1075.............................598
Times Newspapers Ltd v Flood [2012] UKSC 11, [2012] 2 WLR 760 576–8
Times Newspapers Ltd v R [2008] EWCA Crim 2559, [2009] Crim LR 114 197
Times Newspapers Ltd v Secretary of State for the Home Department [2008] EWHC
   2455 (Admin)..458
Tinnelly & Sons Ltd v United Kingdom (1998) 27 EHRR 249 341
Tomlinson v Birmingham City Council [2010] UKSC 8, [2010] 2 AC 39 .... 326, 330
Torija v Spain (1994) 19 EHRR 553..370
TP and KM v United Kingdom (2001) 34 EHRR 42..348
Trimingham v Associated Newspapers Ltd [2012] EWHC 1296 (QB), [2012] 4 All ER
   717 ....414, 461

Trust A v H (An Adult Patient) [2006] EWHC 1230, [2006] FLR 958 200
Tsirlis and Kouloumpas v Greece [1997] 25 EHRR 198 ....161, 279, 291
Tuba v Hungary [2013] EWHC 1767 (Admin) 257
Tucker v Secretary of State for Social Security [2001] EWCA Civ 1646..............................612
Turcu v News Group Newspapers Ltd [2005] EWHC (QB) 799 563
Turner v East Midlands Trains Ltd [2012] EWCA Civ 1470, [2013] 3 All ER 375 428
Tweed v Parades Commission for Northern Ireland [2006] UKHL 53, [2007] 2 All ER
    273, [2007] 1 AC 650..92, 551
Twentieth Century Fox Film Corp v British Telecommunications plc [2011] EWHC
    1981 (Ch), [2012] 1 All ER 806 ....588, 590
UE (Nigeria) v Secretary of State for the Home Department [2010] EWCA Civ 975,
    [2011] 2 All ER 352 443
UK Association of Fish Producer Organisations v Secretary of State for Environment,
    Food & Rural Affairs [2013] EWHC 1959..643, 648
United States v Shlesinger [2013] EWHC 2671 (Admin)..489
Uyan v Turkey Application No 7496/03, 8 January 2009..241
V v United Kingdom (1999) 30 EHRR 121 ....246, 283
Vacher v France (1997) 24 EHRR 482 158–9
Vallen International Limited v Secretary of State for Transport, Local Government and
    the Regions [2002] EWHC (Admin) 1107, [2002] 21 EG 145 (CS)......................................506
Van Colle v United Kingdom (2013) 56 EHRR 23..194
Van de Hurk v The Netherlands (1994) 18 EHRR 481..370
Van der Ven v The Netherlands (50901/99) 4 February 2003..242
Van Droogenbroek v Belgium (1982) 4 EHRR 443..282
Van Raalte v Netherlands (1997) 24 EHRR 503 178
Varey v United Kingdom, 27 October 1999..330
Vasilescu v Romania, Judgment of 22 May 1998..161
Venables v News Group Newspapers Ltd [2001] 2 WLR 1038 ...... 88, 181, 189, 191, 197, 550, 581
Veolia ES Nottinghamshire Limited v Nottinghamshire County Council [2010] EWCA
    Civ 1214, [2011] Eu LR 172..421
Veolia ES Nottinghamshire Ltd v Nottinghamshire CC [2010] EWCA Civ 1214, [2010]
    UKHRR 1317..643
Vilvarajah v United Kingdom (1991) 14 EHRR 248 250
Vinter v United Kingdom 34 BHRC 605..247
Volkswagen Aktiengesellschaft v Garcia [2013] EWHC 1832 (Ch)..598
VW (Uganda) v Secretary of State for the Home Department [2009] EWCA Civ 5,
    [2009] Imm AR 436...481
W (Algeria) v Secretary of State for the Home Department [2012] UKSC 8, [2012] 2
    AC 115...254
W v Doncaster Metropolitan Borough Council [2004] EWCA Civ 378, [2004] LGR 743........288
W v M [2011] EWHC 2443 (Fam), [2012] 1 FCR 1 ....183–5, 423
W v United Kingdom (1987) 10 EHRR 29 472
W v W [2001] 2 WLR 674..421
W v Westminster City Council [2005] EWHC (QB) 102 ....155, 175, 413
Wainwright v Home Office [2003] UKHL 53, [2004] 2 AC 406 ....155, 409, 435
Waite and Kennedy v Germany (1999) 30 EHRR 261 341
Waite v London Borough of Hammersmith & Fulham [2002] EWCA Civ 482 .... 612–13, 619,
                                                                                   621, 625
Walden v Liechtenstein, Judgment of 16 March 2000 135

Waltham Forest London Borough Council v Secretary of State for Transport, Local
  Government and the Regions [2002] EWCA Civ 330, [2002] 13 EG 99 (CS) 651, 662
Walumba Lumba (Congo) v SSHD [2011] UKSC 12 .... 279, 290, 292–3
Wandsworth LBC v Michalak [2002] EWCA Civ 271, [2003] 1 WLR 617 .... 509, 606, 612,
                                                                                          619–21, 625, 629–30
Watkins v Woolas [2010] EWHC 2702 (QB) 558, 597
Webb v Times Publishing Co Ltd [1960] 2 QB 535 549
Weeks v United Kingdom (1987) 10 EHRR 293.. 159, 244
Weeks v United Kingdom (1988) 13 EHRR 435..171
Weir v Secretary of State for Transport [2005] EWHC 2192 (Ch)..................................... 32, 642
Wemhoff v Germany (1968) 1 EHRR 55.. 296, 372
Westminster City Council v Morris [2005] EWCA Civ 1184, [2006] 1 WLR 505 .... 610, 620,
                                                                                                              622, 633
Whitefield v General Medical Council [2002] UKPC 62, [2003] HRLR 243.....423, 428, 455, 651
Whittaker v P&D Watson [2002] ICR 1244 133
Widmer v Switzerland Application 20527/92 (1993)... 187, 200
Wife and Children of Othman v English National Resistance QBD Admin 25/2/2013...............593
Wilkinson v S [2003] EWCA Civ 95, [2003] 1 WLR 1254 387
Wilson v First County Trust [2003] UKHL 40, [2003] 3 WLR 568 .... 10, 649, 657, 660
Wilson v Secretary of State for Trade and Industry [2003] UKHL 40, [2003] 3 WLR
  568, [2004] 1 AC 816...42, 65, 91–2, 103, 115, 142–3, 340–2
Wilson v The Chief Constable of Lancashire Constabulary [2001] 2 WLR 302 294
Windisch v Austria, Judgment of 28 June 1993..159
Wingrove v United Kingdom (1997) 24 EHRR 1 .... 86, 573
Winterwerp v The Netherlands (1979) 2 EHRR 387................................278, 286–9, 299, 310
Witold Litwa v Poland (2000) 33 EHRR 1267..289
WM v Denmark, 15 EHRR CD 28 77
Wood v Commissioner of Police of the Metropolis [2009] EWCA Civ 414, [2010] 1
  WLR 123 ....418, 427, 447
Woolgar v Chief Constable of Sussex Police [1999] 3 All ER 604...455
Woolgar v Chief Constable of Sussex Police [2000] 1 WLR 25 .... 420, 439
Woolmington v Director of Public Prosecutions [1935] AC 462...392
Worcestershire County Council v HM Coroner for Worcestershire [2013] EWHC 1711 (QB)......225
Wright v Commissioner of the Metropolitan Police [2012] EWHC 669 (QB) 261
Wright v Law Society, Chancery Division, 4 September 2002...661
Wrobel v Poland [2011] EWHC 374 (Admin)...257
X (a woman formerly known as Mary Bell) v O'Brien [2003] EWHC (QB) 1101,
  [2003] 2 FCR 686 ....438, 461, 562
X (South Yorkshire) v Secretary of State for the Home Department [2012] EWHC 2954
  (Admin), [2013] 1 WLR 2638..464
X and Y v Netherlands (1985) EHRR 235...262
X and Y v Persons Unknown [2006] EWHC 2783 (QB), [2007] EMLR 10 .... 414–15, 583
X and Z v Federal Republic of Germany, Application no 3897/68, 5 February 1970,
  ECommHR 34
X v Bedfordshire County Council [1995] 2 AC 633.. 154, 340
X v Germany (1980) 25 DR 142.. 171, 378
X v Secretary of State for the Home Department [2001] 1 WLR 740..................69, 103, 228, 256
X v Switzerland (1978) 13 D&R 241 493

X v United Kingdom (1979) 17 DR 122 335

X v United Kingdom (1998) 28 D&R 177 323

X v United Kingdom 4 EHRR 188 286

X v Y [2004] EWCA Civ 662 ....54–6, 120, 420, 609

XX (Ethiopia) v Secretary of State for the Home Department [2012] EWCA Civ 742,
[2013] 2 WLR 178 .... 254, 323

Y (Sri Lanka) v Secretary of State for the Home Department [2009] EWCA Civ 362,
[2009] HRLR 22 257

Yasa v Turkey (1998) 28 EHRR 408 .... 204, 209

YL v Birmingham City Council [2007] UKHL 27, [2008] 1 AC 95 ....46, 48, 51

Yonghong v Portugal, Reports of Judgments and Decisions 1999—XI, 385 79

Young, James and Webster v United Kingdom (1982) 4 EHRR 38 159

Young v First Secretary of State [2004] EWHC (Admin) 2167 662

Young v Western Power Distribution (South West) plc [2003] EWCA Civ 1034.......................343

Yumsak v London Borough of Enfield [2002] EWHC (Admin) 280 .... 471, 487

Z County Council v R [2001] 1 FLR 365 .... 473, 498

Z v Finland (1998) 25 EHRR 371 599

Z v News Group Newspapers [2013] EWHC 1371 (Fam) 588

Z v The Secretary of State for the Home Department [2004] EWCA Civ 1578 442

Z v United Kingdom (2001) 34 EHRR 97 348

Z v United Kingdom (2002) 34 EHRR 3 341

Zakharov v White [2003] EWHC (Ch) 2463 278

Zamir v United Kingdom (1985) 40 DR 42 .... 279, 291

ZB (Pakistan) v Secretary of State for the Home Department [2009] EWCA Civ 834,
[2010] INLR 195 466

Zehentner v Austria 16 July 2009 520

ZH (Tanzania) v Secretary of State for the Home Department [2011] UKSC 4, [2011] 2
WLR 148 .... 28, 484, 490

ZH v Commissioner of Police of the Metropolis [2013] EWCA Civ 69, [2013] 3 All ER 113.....230

Zielinski v France (2001) 31 EHRR 532 309

ZT (Kosovo) v Secretary of State for the Home Department [2009] UKHL 6, [2009] 1
WLR 348 150

ZT v Secretary of State for the Home Department [2005] EWCA Civ 1421, [2006]
Imm AR 84 .... 258, 441–2

Table of National Legislation

Note that, as the entire book deals with the Human Rights Act 1998, only references to specific provisions of that Act are cited in this Table.

United Kingdom
Anti-social Behaviour Act 2003..511, 558, 593
Anti-terrorism, Crime and Security Act 2001 ....15, 150, 366, 609
  s 21 ....101, 108, 573
  s 23 ....101, 108, 140, 637
  s 25(2)(b)...16
  s 30 16
Arbitration Act 1996..371
Bail Act 1976...295
  s 7(3)...131
Borders, Citizenship and Immigration Act 2009, s 55...484
British Nationality Act 1981
  s 2 625
  s 3 625
Broadcasting Act 1996 .... 427, 434
Capital Allowances Act 1990, s 35(2) 66
Care Standards Act 2000...140
  s 82(4)(b)...140
Chancel Repairs Act 1932.. 49, 70, 118
Child Support Act 1991... 324, 677
Child Support (Maintenance Assessments and Special Cases) Regulations 1992, reg 1(2).........131
Children Act 1989 ....43, 128, 149, 275, 286, 331, 457, 461–2, 474, 494–6
  Pt IV 331, 494
  s 1(1).. 494, 587
  s 1(3)..494
  s 17 131
  s 20(1)..325–6
  s 25 339
  s 31(2)...471
  s 38(6)...332
Children and Young Persons Act 1933, s 39...87
Children (Scotland) Act 1995
  Pt II.. 473, 636
  s 93(2)(b)(c)..129

Civil Partnerships Act 2004 628
Civil Procedure Rules..666
  6.7 343
    17.4(1) and (2)..130
    17.4(2)..343
Commons Act 2006, s 15(4) 667
Communications Act 2003 566
  s 319 595–6
  s 321 595–6
  s 321(2)..112
Company Directors Disqualification Act 1986....................................340
Constitution of Antigua and Barbuda 91
Constitutional Reform Act 2005, s 40(2) 357
Consumer Credit Act 1974, s 127(3).. 342, 649
Contempt of Court Act 1981.. 557, 601–2
  s 4(2)...602–3
  s 8 603
  s 10 .... 131, 564, 599
Copyright, Designs and Patents Act 1988
  s 30(2)..589
  s 171 589
  s 171(3)...589
Coroners Act 1988...67, 128, 217
  s 11(5)(b)(ii) 128, 206
Coroners and Justice Act 2009 218
Coroners Rules 1984 (SI 1984/553) 128, 217
  r 36(1)(b) 128
  r 43...218
Counter Terrorism Act 2008...452, 647, 672
Crime and Disorder Act 1988...334
  s 65 340
Crime and Disorder Act 1998.....................................15, 328, 336, 366
  s 1 .... 324, 331
  s 8 493
Crime (Sentences) Act 1997
  s 2 ....65, 127, 283
  s 28 304
  s 29 139
Criminal Appeal Act 1968, s 2 349
Criminal Justice Act 1988 ....64, 396
  s 72AA...671
  s 139(4) and (5)..395
Criminal Justice Act 1991 139
  s 32(6)..304
  s 34(5)..141
  s 44A(4).. 127, 307
Criminal Justice Act 2003 407

Sch 22, para 11(1) 132
Criminal Justice and Public Order Act 1994
   s 25 296
   s 34 360
   s 35 360
   s 36 361
   s 51(7) 395
   s 60 277
   s 61 ....651, 664
Criminal Legal Aid (Fixed Payments) (Scotland) Regulations 1999 405
Criminal Procedure (Insanity) Act 1964 338–9
   s 4(5) 288
   s 4A 336
Crown Proceedings Act 1947 342
   s 2(5) 167
   s 21 386–7
Customs and Excise Management Act 1979 339
   s 49 674
   s 139 339
   s 141 674
   s 141(1)(b) 131
   Sch 3 339
Data Protection Act 1998 ....4, 131, 410
   Pt II 440
Debtors Act 1869 339
Defamation Act 1952, s 10 579
Drug Trafficking Act 1994 ....64, 396, 640, 647
   s 4 671
Education Act 1996 ....286, 541
Employment Equality (Religion or Belief) Regulations 2003 ....527, 530
Employment Rights Act 1996
   Pt X 56
   s 98 56
Equality Act 2006 ....9, 544
   s 30(1) 32
   s 30(3) 33
Equality Act (Sexual Orientation) Regulations (Northern Ireland) 2006 541
Extradition Act 1989
   s 8 ....87, 511
   s 8(1)(b) 88
Extradition Act 2003 ....130, 327, 343
Fatal Accidents Act 1976 631
   s 2(3) 130
Finance Act 1994 339
   s 8(1) 339
Financial Restrictions (Iran) Order 2009 356
Firearms Act 1968 395

Food Safety Act 1990, s 13 651
Football Spectators Act 1989 339
Freedom of Information Act 2000 556
Gender Recognition Act 2004 422
Health and Safety at Work Act 1974, s 40 395
Health and Social Care Act 2008 51
   s 145 47
   s 145(1) 47
Homicide Act 1957, s 4(2) 395
Housing Act 1980, s 89 523
Housing Act 1985 ....625, 630
   Pt IV 649
   s 189 612
Housing Act 1988
   ss 19A-21 524
   s 21(4) 129
Housing Act 1996 ....330, 390, 520, 526, 610, 633, 663
   Pt VII 326, 526
   ss 124-130 524
   s 127(2) 132, 523
   s 143D 522
   s 143D(2) 132
   s 188 526
   s 190(2) 526
   s 193(5) 326
   s 204(1) 130
Housing Grants Construction and Regeneration Act 1996 45
Human Fertilisation and Embryology Act 1990 ....439, 459, 501
   s 8(d) 136
   s 31(4)(a) 136
Human Fertilisation and Embryology Act 2008 471
Human Rights Act 1998
   s 1 10
   s 1(1) 150
   s 1(2) 15
   s 2 ....10, 27, 102
   s 2(1) 156, 237
   s 3 .... 10, 18, 20, 34, 49, 54–6, 65–7, 102, 106, 113, 117, 119–32, 139–40, 217, 245, 283,
          296, 307, 343–4, 354–5, 368, 397, 399, 494, 522–3, 663, 671
   s 3(1) 66, 114, 119–20, 123, 139
   s 3(2) 120
   s 3(2)(a) 119
   s 3(2)(b) 119
   s 3(2)(c) 119
   s 4 .... 10, 20, 34, 65, 113, 120, 123–5, 132–41, 151
   s 4(1) 132
   s 4(2) 132

s 4(3)..133
s 4(4)..133
s 4(5)..133
s 4(6)..102, 133, 137
s 5(1)..133
s 6 .... 10, 17, 39–40, 42, 49, 54, 61, 63, 67, 69, 74, 149
s 6(1)... 32, 34, 39–41, 66–8, 113–17
s 6(2)... 113–19, 522
s 6(2)(a)..59, 66, 114–16, 638
s 6(2)(b)...59, 114–19
s 6(3)...39, 42
s 6(3)(a)..42
s 6(3)(b)...39, 45–8, 51, 508
s 6(4)..39
s 6(5)..39, 54
s 6(6)...42, 59, 79, 135–6
s 7 .... 3, 10, 31–4, 36, 74, 79, 124, 137, 474
ss 7-9 3
s 7(1)..31, 36, 68, 117
s 7(1)(5)..59
s 7(1)(a)..32, 67
s 7(1)(b).. 60, 63, 67, 70, 495, 522
s 7(3)..32, 67
s 7(6)..63
s 7(6)(a)..70
s 7(7)..32
s 7(9)..32
s 8 .... 147, 149, 155, 163, 316–17
s 8(1)..148–9, 151
s 8(2)..151–2
s 8(3)..151–2
s 8(3)(a)..153
s 8(3)(b)..154
s 8(4)..151, 156, 163
s 8(5)..150
s 9 ....59, 151
s 9(3)..166–7
s 10 28
s 10(1)(b)..133
s 10(2)..133, 137
s 11..3, 550
s 12 ....18, 120, 529, 561–2
s 12(2)..561
s 12(3)..561–2
s 12(4)..460, 561–2
s 13 529
s 13(1)..528

ss 14–17 15

s 18 60

s 19 ....112, 114, 144–7

s 19(1)(b) 112, 144–5, 596

s 20 60

s 21(1) 113

s 21(5) 60

s 22 60

s 22(4) 60–4, 67–8, 70

Sch 2 ....10, 28

Human Rights Act 1998 (Designated Derogation) Order 2001 (SI 2001/3644) 16

Hunting Act 2004 ....111, 411, 456, 652, 669

Immigration and Asylum Act 1999 339

Pt II 676

s 32 141

s 65 ....93, 482

Sch 4 93

Immigration Nationality (Fees) Regulations 2010

reg 6 132

reg 30 132

Income and Corporation Taxes Act 1988

Pt VII 131

s 262 115

s 561 641

ss 739-746 673

Inheritance Tax Act 1984, s 18 66

Insolvency Act 1986 ....284, 332, 344, 359

s 310 664

s 335 515

s 335A 132

s 352 395

s 364 294

s 364(2) 294

Land Compensation Act 1973, Pt I 132

Land Registration Act 1925, s 75 ....650, 666

Landlord and Tenant Act 1954 649

Law of Property Act 1925

s 101 665

ss 141 and 142 ....66, 131

Legal Aid (Scotland) Act 1986, s 24 405

Limitation Act 1980

s 17 ....650, 666

s 33(3) 60

Lloyd's Act, s 14(3) 66

Local Government Act 1982 339

Local Government Finance Act 1982 337

s 20 331

Magna Carta 1215, ch 39..269
Malicious Communications Act 1988...594
Matrimonial Causes Act 1973..421, 439, 640
  s 11(c)...68, 134, 139, 430
Mental Health Act 1983.................52, 89, 141, 199, 287, 298–9, 303–4, 332, 345, 427, 457, 473
  s 2...135–6, 140, 298
  s 26...141
  s 29...141
  s 29(4)...136, 141, 312
  s 37...169
  s 58(3)(b)...238
  s 66...298
  s 67...298
  s 72...287
  s 73...140, 287
  s 74...141
  s 75(1)..313
  s 132...131
Mental Health Act 1983 (Remedial) Order 2001...287
Misuse of Drugs Act 1971...61, 543
  s 28...125–6
  s 28(3)..396
  s 28(3)(b)(i)...396
Murder (Abolition of Death Penalty) Act 1965, s 1(1).............................107, 246, 282
National Assistance Act 1948...48, 508
  s 21...48, 52, 131, 331
  s 26...48–9, 52
National Health Service Act 1977..52
Northern Ireland Act 1998, s 71(2B)(c)..33
Northern Ireland (Emergency Provisions) Acts 1973, 1978, 1991 and 1996...............301
Nursing Homes and Mental Nursing Homes Regulations 1984....................................52
Obscene Publications Act 1959...86, 557, 573
  s 1(3)...551
Official Secrets Act 1989...107, 557
  s 1(1)(a)...571
  ss 2 and 3..395
  s 4(1)...571
  s 4(3)(a)...571
  s 9(1)...571
Petition of Right 1628..269
Police Act 1997...139
  s 115...419, 449
  s 115(7)(b)...132
Police and Criminal Evidence Act 1984..293, 365, 512
  s 8...509
  s 28(3)..294
  s 64(1A)..119

s 76(2)..360
s 78 ....364–6, 402, 445–6
s 80(1)...493
Powers of Criminal Courts (Sentencing) Act 2000
  s 85 301–2
  s 109 245
Prevention of Terrorism Act 2005 .... 15, 99, 127, 273–4, 332, 340, 353–4, 471
  s 1(4)..273
  s 3 126
Prevention of Terrorism (Temporary Provisions) Act 1989.............................. 80, 104
  s 16A..398
Proceeds of Crime Act 2002.. 647, 671
  Pt 2..126
  s 6(5)(b)...670
  s 41(4)...671
Proceeds of Crime (Scotland) Act 1995
  s 3 395
  s 3(2)..336
Protection from Eviction Act 1977, s 1(2) 395
Protection from Harassment Act 1997..410, 552, 558, 586
Protection of Children Act 1978..557
Protection of Children Act 1999..140
Protection of Wild Mammals (Scotland) Act 2002.. 412, 608
Public Bodies Corrupt Practices Act 1889 395
Public Order Act 1986..552, 557, 572, 591
  s 5 591
Race Relations Act 1976... 327, 541
Registered Homes Act 1984..660
  Pt II...52, 644, 667
Regulation of Investigatory Powers Act 2000... 85, 446
Rehabilitation of Offenders Act 1974.. 420, 463
Rent Act 1977... 3, 129, 612, 614, 623
  Sch 1
    para 2..55–6
    paras 2 and 3..129
    para 2(2)..55
Representation of the People Act 1983 557
  s 75 596
  s 106 ....558, 597
Road Traffic Act 1988..334
  s 5(2)..397
  s 172(2)...105
  s 172(2)(a) 105, 359
Road Traffic Offenders Act 1988, s 15...397
Scotland Act 1998 ....26, 81, 334, 336, 350, 359, 381
  s 57 26
  s 57(2)..26, 385

Sexual Offences Act 2003...451
   s 82...139
Sexual Offences (Amendment) Act 1982...584
Sexual Offences (Procedure and Evidence) (Scotland) Act 2002 368
Social Security Contributions and Benefits Act 1992..116
   s 36...116, 118
   s 37...116, 118
State Immunity Act 1978 .... 131, 346
Suicide Act 1961 ....25, 182, 426
   s 2(1)... 25, 81, 86, 426, 458–9
   s 2(4).. 81, 458
Supreme Court Act 1981
   s 31 153
   s 31(3)...38
   s 31(4)...152
   s 42...344
Terrorism Act 2000... 89, 276–7, 449, 557, 601
   s 11(1)...399
   s 11(2)...399
   s 44 86
   Sch 5 601
Terrorism (United Nations Measures) Order 2006........................... 422, 567, 584
Town and Country Planning Act 1990
   s 187B.. 42, 515
   s 226(1)...662
Trade Marks Act 1994
   s 92 397
   s 92(5)..397
Treason Act 1848, s 3 ....34, 123, 557
Value Added Tax Act 1994, s 60(1)...339
Wildlife and Countryside Act 1981 651
   s 28 332
Youth Justice and Criminal Evidence Act 1999............................... 144, 368, 588
   s 41 ....81, 106, 125, 367

Canada
Charter of Rights and Freedoms...27, 62, 148
   s 7 27

India
Constitution...27

New Zealand
Bill of Rights Act 1990.. 27, 62

South Africa
Constitution...27

United States
Constitution...27
   1st Amendment.. 27, 552
   14th Amendment 622

Table of International and European Instruments

Note that, as the entire book deals with the European Convention on Human Rights, only references to specific provisions of that instrument are cited in this Table.

Convention on the Elimination of Racial Discrimination...28
EU
   Brussels II revised Regulation...500
   Charter of Fundamental Rights.. 4, 11
      Art 8 4
   Equal Treatment Directive 1976..421
   Treaty on the Functioning of the European Union
      Art 34 640
      Art 36 640
   VAT Directive 2006...640
European Convention on Human Rights (ECHR)
   Art 1..35, 74–8, 141, 204
   Art 2..
     16, 34, 36–7, 49, 67, 69, 71, 77–8, 80, 128, 157, 160, 164–6, 181–225, 231–4,
     237, 264, 266, 276, 310, 431, 581, 609
   Arts 2-12..11
   Art 2(1)...181, 187–9, 204, 207
   Art 2(2).. 181, 186
   Art 3..
     14, 16, 38, 49, 77, 80, 103, 106–7, 127, 155, 162, 166, 182, 200, 205, 227–67,
     310, 324, 387, 425, 432, 534, 581, 608
   Art 4..166, 267, 535
   Art 4(1)..16
   Art 5.......... 13, 15, 44, 103, 107, 127, 139–40, 166–9, 245, 269–317, 332, 454, 511, 609, 614
   Art 5(1)..13, 22, 140, 164, 269–70, 276–93, 315–16
   Art 5(1)(a) 280–3, 301, 322
   Art 5(1)(b) 284, 295
   Art 5(1)(c) 284–5, 295
   Art 5(1)(d) 285–6
   Art 5(1)(e) 286–9
   Art 5(1)(f)..290–3
   Art 5(2).. 291, 293–4

Art 5(3).. 295–7, 373
Art 5(4)..43–4, 135, 140–1, 159, 167–9, 270, 297–317
Art 5(5)..161, 166–7, 316–17
Art 5(7)..396
Art 6....13, 21, 26, 36, 42–3, 64, 73, 80–2, 106, 125–6, 130, 132, 139–41, 148, 150, 155, 159, 169–73, 248, 306–7, 310, 319–408, 446, 454, 457–8, 464, 472, 496, 603, 660, 671, 677
Art 6(1)............43, 80, 97, 105, 150, 161, 169–73, 296, 319, 323–40, 347–8, 350–1, 353, 358, 361, 367, 372, 379, 381–4, 386, 388, 391–2, 402–3
Art 6(2)......................................61, 90, 105, 126, 319, 333–4, 336, 349, 358, 361, 392–9
Art 6(3)..319, 333, 399
Art 6(3)(a) 399
Art 6(3)(b) 400
Art 6(3)(c) 171, 400–5
Art 6(3)(d) 366, 405–7
Art 6(3)(e) 408
Art 7..16, 87, 248
Art 8..........................3, 14, 22, 25, 35, 43, 48–9, 55–7, 73, 80, 83, 88, 93–5, 99–100, 111, 129, 131–2, 134, 139–41, 150, 155, 162, 173–7, 182, 200, 235, 248, 257, 262, 324, 332, 366, 409–526, 534, 545, 561, 575, 580–8, 597, 608–12, 615, 653
Art 8(1).....25, 86, 409, 413, 418–19, 423, 426–7, 429–30, 434, 441, 457, 468, 470, 503, 506, 509
Art 8(2)............... 85–6, 94–5, 98, 418, 423, 436, 441, 443, 447, 456, 459, 462, 465, 475, 478, 480–2, 484, 492, 494–5, 503, 506, 512, 518–19, 523, 653
Art 9..73, 83, 409, 527–48, 588, 612, 631
Art 9(2)..529, 543, 545, 653
Art 10.......5, 35, 55, 57, 83, 88, 107, 112, 145, 176–7, 197, 276, 324, 409, 435, 460, 549–603
Art 10(1)..555–6
Art 10(2)..549, 560–2, 570, 572, 590, 592, 594, 597, 603, 653
Art 11.. 83, 111, 155, 276, 324, 409, 553, 592–3, 653
Art 11(2)..653
Art 12.. 14, 100, 134, 139, 430, 492
Art 13..18, 40, 64, 116, 149–50, 160, 162, 251
Art 14.......11, 22, 56, 73, 83, 110–11, 116, 129, 139–40, 161, 178–81, 344, 469, 478, 605–38, 642, 651, 656
Art 15.. 15–16, 101, 103, 108, 181, 227
Art 15(1)..16
Art 15(1)(f)..16
Art 15(2)..16
Arts 16-18..11
Art 34..32, 36, 40–1
Art 35..138
Art 41..67, 147, 151, 153, 156, 158, 160, 163, 171–2
Art 46..64
Art 56..79
Art 57..15–16
Protocol No 1 .... 11, 13, 79, 100, 132, 141, 159, 164, 511, 588, 590, 611–12, 626, 629
Art 1....... 15, 26, 111, 116, 126, 131–2, 160–2, 178, 342, 503, 511, 588–90, 610–11, 613, 626, 639–78

Arts 1-3 11
Art 2 ....534, 613, 639
Art 3 ....100, 597, 639
Art 4 79
Protocol No 4, Art 2 272
Protocol No 6
  Art 1 181
  Arts 1-2 11
  Art 2 181
Protocol No 12, Art 1 605
Hague Convention on the Civil Aspects of International Child Abduction 1980........................500
  Art 12...500
International Covenant on Civil and Political Rights 4, 27
UN
  Charter
    Art 25 13
    Art 103 13
    Ch VII 13
  Convention against Illicit Traffic in Narcotic Drugs and Psychotropic Substances 1998.......395
  Convention on the Rights of the Child 234, 239, 244, 290, 375, 484, 492
    Art 3 ....28, 290, 484
  Security Council Resolution 1546...13
Universal Declaration of Human Rights...27, 428
Vienna Convention on the Law of Treaties, Art 31(3)(c)...13

PART I

THE HUMAN RIGHTS ACT

1

Background and Interpretation

1. The Protection of Human Rights Prior to the Human Rights Act

Interest in the promotion and protection of human rights in the countries of the United Kingdom did not start on 2 October 2000 with the coming into force of the Human Rights Act 1998 (HRA). For many years the common law, primary and secondary legislation, and European Union (EU) law have provided legal protection for human rights whilst international human rights law, although not directly enforceable in national courts,[1] has provided an important benchmark for the courts, executive and legislature. With the coming into force of the HRA, these other mechanisms of protection have not disappeared but operate alongside the HRA, in some instances filling the gaps[2] and in others providing equivalent[3] or even stronger legal protection for human rights.[4] Section 11 of the HRA provides that a person's reliance on a Convention right does not restrict 'any other right or freedom conferred on him by or under any law having effect in any part of the United Kingdom' or restrict 'his right to make any claim or bring any proceedings which he could make or bring apart from sections 7 to 9' of the HRA.[5]

---

[1] See eg *R (Hurst) v Commissioner of Police of the Metropolis* [2007] UKHL 13, [2007] 2 AC 189, where it was confirmed by the House of Lords that decision-makers are under no obligation to exercise discretionary powers conferred upon them so as to comply with unincorporated international obligations.

[2] In some instances the HRA may not apply. For example, if the act occurred before 2 October 2000 or the claimant does not fall within the definition of victim in s 7 of the HRA.

[3] For example, in *R v Secretary of State for the Home Department, ex p Daly* [2001] UKHL 26, [2001] 2 AC 532 the House of Lords reached the conclusion that the Secretary of State's policy governing the searching of prisoners' cells was unlawful on an 'orthodox application of common law principles derived from the authorities and an orthodox domestic approach to judicial review even though the same result was achieved by reliance upon Art 8 of the Convention. See also *HM Treasury v Ahmed* [2010] UKSC 2, [2010] 2 AC 534 and *Al Rawi v Security Service* [2011] UKSC 34, [2012] 1 AC 531.

[4] For example, in *Fitzpatrick v Sterling Housing Association Ltd* [2001] 1 AC 27, in deciding that the meaning of family in the Rent Act 1977 encompassed a same sex partner, a majority of the House of Lords was not influenced by the fact that the European Court of Human Rights had not so far accepted claims by same sex partners to family rights.

[5] It is clear that legislation can be compatible with Convention rights if it actually provides greater protection. See the comments of Lord Woolf in *R v Broadcasting Standards Commission, ex p British Broadcasting Corporation* [2001] QB 885, [17].

Whilst the common law has remained fairly static in relation to the protection of human rights following the coming into force of the HRA, over the last ten years the national protection of human rights through EU law has grown and there are now some judgments where human rights law is clearly given effect to in this way. For example, in the *Rugby Football Union* case[6] the Supreme Court considered and applied the EU Charter of Fundamental Rights where the Rugby Football Union sought, under *Norwich Pharmacal* principles, the identity of those who had advertised for sale or sold tickets for the autumn international and 'six nations' rugby matches. It was argued by the respondent that to make such an order would breach Article 8 of the EU Charter which guaranteed the protection of personal data. The Supreme Court accepted that in making the order it could be regarded as implementing EU law, namely the Data Protection Act 1998, which gave effect to the EU data protection directive. The EU Charter therefore had to be considered but no breach of Article 8 was established.[7]

Much has been written about these other important mechanisms for the promotion and protection of human rights and the essential features of this machinery will not be repeated here.[8] The focus of this book is the HRA, which, whilst not the only means for the legal protection of human rights domestically, is at present clearly the most effective.

2. Background to the Human Rights Act

2.1 The Incorporation Debate

Constitutional tradition, in particular the principle of the sovereignty of Parliament and the protection for human rights provided by common law and statute, meant that for a long time there was very little interest in adopting a modern form of a Bill of Rights. But by the late 1970s this had changed, with bodies such as the National Council for

---

[6] *The Rugby Football Union v Consolidated Information Services Limited* [2012] UKSC 55, [2012] 1 WLR 3333.

[7] See also *R (S) v Secretary of State for the Home Department* [2010] EWHC 705 (Admin); *R (Zagorski) v Secretary of State for Business, Innovation & Skills* [2010] EWHC 3110 (Admin), [2011] HRLR 6; and *Harrison (Jamaica) v Secretary of State for the Home Department* [2012] EWCA Civ 1736, [2013] 2 CMLR 23. It is possible for different interpretations of human rights law to be reached in the two jurisdictions. See eg *EM (Eritrea) v Secretary of State for the Home Department* [2012] EWCA Civ 1336, [2013] HRLR 1.

[8] See further C McCrudden and G Chambers (eds), *Individual Rights and the Law in Britain* (Oxford, Oxford University Press, 1994) ch 1; F Klug, K Starmer and S Weir, 'The British Way of Doing Things: The United Kingdom and the International Covenant on Civil and Political Rights, 1976–94' [1995] *Public Law* 504; B Dickson (ed), *Human Rights and the European Convention* (London, Sweet & Maxwell, 1997); M Hunt, *Using Human Rights Law in English Courts* (Oxford, Hart Publishing, 1998); D Feldman, *Civil Liberties and Human Rights in England and Wales*, 2nd edn (Oxford, Oxford University Press, 2002) ch 2; D Fottrell, 'Reinforcing the Human Rights Act—The Role of the International Covenant on Civil and Political Rights' [2002] *Public Law* 485; MA Dauses, *The Protection of Fundamental Rights in the Legal Order of the European Union* (Bern, Peter Lang, 2010); R Schütze, *European Constitutional Law* (Cambridge, Cambridge University Press, 2012) ch 12; P Craig, 'The Charter, the ECJ and National Courts' in D Ashiagbor, N Countouris and I Lianos (eds), *The European Union after the Treaty of Lisbon* (Cambridge, Cambridge University Press, 2012) ch 3.

Civil Liberties (now Liberty) campaigning for just such a bill. Agitation for a Bill of Rights soon transformed into calls for 'incorporation' of the European Convention on Human Rights (ECHR) into domestic law as the first—or only—step in the process of improving the legal protection of human rights.[9] Many non-governmental organisations (NGOs) joined the campaign, including JUSTICE, the Runnymede Trust, the Constitutional Reform Centre, the Institute for Public Policy Research, the British Institute of Human Rights and Charter 88. The shared view was that the traditional freedom of the individual 'under an unwritten constitution to do himself that which is not prohibited by law' gave no protection from misuse of power by the state, nor any protection from acts or omissions of public bodies which harmed individuals in a way that was incompatible with their human rights.[10]

Around this time judicial interest in human rights was also stirred. For example, in their decisions judges began referring to the 'right to freedom of expression', sometimes the 'constitutional right to freedom of expression'.[11] In many cases, Article 10 of the ECHR was also mentioned.[12] It is likely that this development was in some part driven by the finding in 1979 of a violation of Article 10 by the European Court of Human Rights (ECtHR) in *Sunday Times v UK*.[13] In many quarters, the finding had shattered the illusion that acceptance of the Convention would have 'few implications for the United Kingdom' and the assumption that the United Kingdom 'as a democracy would have nothing to be concerned about'.[14]

The judicial interest in human rights continued, and by the 1990s many judges, writing and speaking extra-judicially, had entered the rights debate. For example, in the 1993 Denning Lecture, Lord Bingham, then the Master of the Rolls, stated that:

> [T]he ability of English judges to protect human rights in this country and reconcile conflicting rights in the manner indicated is inhibited by the failure of successive governments over many years to incorporate into United Kingdom law the European Convention on Human Rights.[15]

He saw the European Convention as an instrument which lay ready to hand which, if not providing an ideal solution, nonetheless offered a clear improvement on the present position.[16] In the 1994 FA Mann Lecture Lord Woolf considered that it was unaccep-

---

[9] Whilst the prospect of a UK Bill of Rights and Responsibilities was mentioned in the Labour Party consultation paper by Jack Straw MP and Paul Boateng MP, 'Bringing Rights Home: Labour's Plans to Incorporate the European Convention on Human Rights into UK Law' (London, Labour Party, 1996) 14, there was no mention of such an instrument in the Home Office White Paper *Rights Brought Home: The Human Rights Bill* (Cm 3782) (London, TSO, 1997), published once Labour assumed office.

[10] HL Deb, vol 582, col 1228 (3 November 1997), Lord Chancellor. On the campaign for incorporation, see KD Ewing, 'The Futility of the Human Rights Act' [2004] *Public Law* 829.

[11] See eg *Cassell & Co v Broome* [1972] 2 WLR 645 per Lord Kilbrandon at 726; *Harman v Secretary of State for the Home Department* [1982] 2 WLR 338 per Lord Scarman at 351; *Secretary of State for Defence v Guardian Newspapers Ltd* [1984] 3 WLR 986 per Lord Fraser at 1001.

[12] See eg *R v Lemon* [1979] 2 WLR 281 per Lord Scarman at 315; *Associated Newspapers Group Ltd v Wade* [1979] 1 WLR 697 at 708–09 per Lord Denning; *A-G v BBC* [1980] 3 WLR 109 per Lord Scarman at 130; *Schering Chemicals Ltd v Falkman Ltd* [1981] 2 WLR 848 per Lord Denning at 862, 864.

[13] *Sunday Times v UK* (1979) 2 EHRR 245. See the comments of Lord Scarman in *A-G v BBC* [1980] 3 WLR 109, 130.

[14] E Wicks, 'The United Kingdom Government's Perceptions of the European Convention on Human Rights at the Time of Entry' [2000] *Public Law* 438, 441. This was not the first finding of a violation on the part of the United Kingdom which had occurred in *Golder v UK* (1975) 1 EHRR 524.

[15] See TH Bingham, 'The European Convention on Human Rights: Time to Incorporate' (1993) 109 *Law Quarterly Review* 390, 390.

[16] Ibid, 393.

table 'that our citizens should be able to obtain a remedy which the Government will honour in the European Court of Human Rights, which they cannot obtain from the courts in this country'.

In his view, a 'British Bill of Rights would avoid the difficulty which exists at present in protecting some of our basic rights. It would enable us to play our part in the development of human rights jurisprudence internationally.'[17]

Various attempts were also made via private members' bills in Parliament to achieve some measure of statutory human rights protection.[18] However, all suffered from the fact that although there was considerable interest and enthusiasm for such a measure elsewhere, there was very little interest in the Conservative government. In 1994, in its Fourth Periodic Report to the UN Human Rights Committee under the Covenant on Civil and Political Rights,[19] the government of the day maintained that the rights and freedoms recognised in international instruments and in the constitutions of those countries that had enacted a comprehensive Bill of Rights were inherent in the United Kingdom's legal system and were protected by it and by Parliament unless they were removed or restricted by statute.

> The Government does not consider that it is properly the role of the legislature to confer rights and freedoms which are naturally possessed by all members of society. It also believes that Parliament should retain the supreme responsibility for enacting or changing the law, including that affecting individual rights and freedoms, while it is properly the role of the judiciary to interpret specific legislation.[20]

Furthermore, it stated its belief that the incorporation of an international human rights instrument into domestic law was not necessary to ensure that the United Kingdom's obligations under such instruments was reflected in the deliberations of government and of the courts.

> The United Kingdom's human rights obligations are routinely considered by Ministers and their officials in the formulation and application of Government policy, while judgments of the House of Lords have made clear that such obligations are part of the legal context in which the judges consider themselves to operate.[21]

It was clear that only a change in government would make any chance of incorporation possible.[22]

---

[17] The Rt Hon Lord Woolf of Barnes, 'Droit Public—English Style' [1995] *Public Law* 57, 70. See also Sir Nicolas Browne-Wilkinson, 'The Infiltration of a Bill of Rights' [1992] *Public Law* 405; The Hon Sir John Laws, 'Is the High Court the Guardian of Fundamental Constitutional Rights?' [1993] *Public Law* 59 and id, 'Law and Democracy' [1995] *Public Law* 72; The Hon Sir Stephen Sedley, 'Human Rights: A Twenty-First Century Agenda' [1995] *Public Law* 386.

[18] See eg the Human Rights Bill 1994 presented and First Reading HL Deb, vol 559, col 150 (22 November 1994). See further M Zander, *A Bill of Rights?* (London, Sweet & Maxwell, 1985).

[19] CCPR/C/95/Add.3, 19 December 1994.

[20] Ibid, [4].

[21] Ibid, [5].

[22] For a background to the Human Rights Act generally, see F Klug, *Values for a Godless Age: The Story of the UK's New Bill of Rights* (London, Penguin, 2000); and H Fenwick, *Civil Liberties and Human Rights* (London, Cavendish, 2002) 117–32.

2.2 The Human Rights Bill

In March 1993, 'incorporation' of the ECHR was adopted as Labour Party policy. In December 1996 the Labour Party published 'Bringing Rights Home',[23] outlining its plans to incorporate the Convention into UK law and thereby enable British people 'to bring grievances against the state covered by the Convention to a British court whilst still retaining a right of ultimate recourse to the Strasbourg court'.[24] The Labour Party saw incorporation as a way to 'change the relationship between the state and the citizen, and to redress the dilution of individual rights by an over-centralising government'. It also saw incorporation as a way to encourage citizens to better fulfil their responsibilities and to improve awareness of human rights thus nurturing a culture of understanding of rights and responsibilities at all levels in our society.[25]

With 'incorporation' a key manifesto commitment, Labour won the General Election in May 1997 with a majority of 179 seats. In October 1997 the Home Office published the White Paper *Rights Brought Home*,[26] which accompanied a draft Bill. The Bill was an important part of the new government's commitment to a comprehensive policy of constitutional reform, including the establishment of a Scottish Parliament and a Welsh Assembly, reform of the House of Lords, freedom of information, an elected Mayor for London and a referendum on the voting system for the House of Commons.[27] It was seen as a 'key component' of the government's

> drive to modernise our society and refresh our democracy. It is part of a blueprint for changing the relationship between the Government and people of the United Kingdom to bring about a better balance between rights and responsibilities, between the powers of the state and the freedom of the individual.[28]

In *Rights Brought Home* the case for change comprised a number of points. First, the rights and freedoms guaranteed under the Convention were ones with which the people of this country were plainly comfortable.[29] Secondly, the growing awareness that it was not sufficient to rely on the common law and that incorporation was necessary.[30] Thirdly, the fact that the rights were no longer seen as British rights, and enforcing them took too long and cost too much.[31] Fourthly, the approach which the UK adopted towards the Convention did not sufficiently reflect its importance and had not stood the test of time—the most obvious proof lying in the number of cases in which violations had been found by the Commission and the Court.[32] The key argument was put as follows:

---

[23] Straw and Boateng, 'Bringing Rights Home' (n 9).
[24] Ibid, 4.
[25] Ibid, 14. For a discussion of possible models for incorporation, see B Emmerson, 'Opinion: This Year's Model—The Options for Incorporation' [1997] *European Human Rights Law Review* 313. On the motivations for incorporation, see M Amos, 'Transplanting Human Rights Norms: The Case of the United Kingdom's Human Rights Act' (2013) 35 *Human Rights Quarterly* 386.
[26] Home Office, *Rights Brought Home* (n 9).
[27] Ibid, 1.
[28] HC Deb, vol 306, col 783 (16 February 1998), Secretary of State for the Home Department, Mr Jack Straw.
[29] Home Office, *Rights Brought Home* (n 9), [1.3].
[30] Ibid, [1.4].
[31] Ibid, [1.14].
[32] Ibid, [1.15]–[1.16].

Bringing these rights home will mean that the British people will be able to argue for their rights in the British courts—without this inordinate delay and cost. It will also mean that the rights will be brought much more fully into the jurisprudence of the courts throughout the United Kingdom, and their interpretation will thus be far more subtly and powerfully woven into our law. And there will be another distinct benefit. British judges will be enabled to make a distinctly British contribution to the development of the jurisprudence of human rights in Europe.[33]

Following lengthy parliamentary debates,[34] the Human Rights Bill was passed by both Houses and received the Royal Assent on 9 November 1998. However, it was not brought fully into force until 2 October 2000.

---

3. Purpose of the Human Rights Act

The purpose of the HRA is not obvious from the Act itself. In the Long Title it is described as 'An Act to give further effect to rights and freedoms guaranteed under the European Convention on Human Rights'. The reason the word 'further' was used was that prior to the HRA the courts already applied the Convention in many different circumstances.[35] More information is contained in the White Paper *Rights Brought Home*,[36] where the purpose of the Act is stated succinctly as 'to make more directly accessible the rights which the British people already enjoy under the Convention ... to bring those rights home'.[37]

The longer version provides as follows:

> [T]he time has come to enable people to enforce their Convention rights against the State in the British courts, rather than having to incur the delays and expense which are involved in taking a case to the European Human Rights Commission and Court in Strasbourg and which may altogether deter some people from pursuing their rights. Enabling courts in the United Kingdom to rule on the application of the Convention will also help to influence the development of case law on the Convention by the European Court of Human Rights on the basis of familiarity with our laws and customs and of sensitivity to practices and procedures in the United Kingdom. ...Enabling the Convention rights to be judged by British courts will also lead to closer scrutiny of the human rights implications of new legislation and new policies.[38]

The further purposes of nurturing a culture of understanding of rights and responsibilities at all levels in society and assisting public discussion of what might be the character of any future UK 'Bill of Rights and Responsibilities', originally present in

---

[33] Ibid, [1.14].
[34] See generally F Klug, 'The Human Rights Act 1998, *Pepper v Hart* and All That' [1999] *Public Law* 246.
[35] HL Deb, vol 583, col 478 (18 November 1997).
[36] Home Office, *Rights Brought Home* (n 9).
[37] Ibid, [1.19].
[38] Ibid, [1.18]; see also [2.4].

the consultation paper 'Bringing Rights Home',[39] were not included, although it was noted that the Act would 'enhance the awareness of human rights in our society' and stand alongside the decision to put the promotion of human rights at the forefront of foreign policy.[40] In the Parliamentary debates the Lord Chancellor also noted that our 'courts will develop human rights throughout society. A culture of awareness of human rights will develop.'[41] Lord Williams expanded on this, stating that every public authority 'will know that its behaviour, its structures, its conclusions and its executive actions will be subject to this culture,'[42] and in the House of Commons the Home Secretary noted that, over time, 'the Bill will bring about the creation of a human rights culture in Britain.'[43] Furthermore, in evidence to the Parliamentary Joint Committee on Human Rights, the Home Secretary stated that the HRA was intended, over time, to help bring about the development of a culture of rights and responsibilities.[44]

Early judicial comment on the purpose of the HRA was reflective of the observations in *Rights Brought Home*. For example, in *Lambert*[45] Lord Clyde stated that the HRA did not incorporate the rights set out in the Convention into the domestic laws of the United Kingdom:

> The purpose of the Act, as set out in its preamble, was 'to give further effect to rights and freedoms' guaranteed under that Convention. The Convention rights have not become part of the constitution so as to obtain any superiority over the powers of Parliament or the validity of primary legislation … One principle achievement of the Act is to enable the Convention rights to be directly invoked in the domestic courts. In that respect the Act is important as a procedural measure which has opened a further means of access to justice for the citizen, more immediate and more familiar than a recourse to the Court in Strasbourg.

Lord Rodger emphasised in *Attorney General's Reference No 2 of 2001*[46] that these rights were to have effect in a way that had not previously been possible in domestic law in that the national courts were to have power to grant victims remedies in terms of the Act for violations of their rights.[47] However in more recent years, judges have found purposes beyond that of simply bringing rights home. Baroness Hale has observed that the HRA 'is for the benefit of ordinary people who lead ordinary lives'. In her view:

> [The HRA] is to protect them inter alia against arbitrary interceptions of their mail, email and telephone conversations, searches of their homes and persons, arrest, prolonged imprisonment without charge or trial, enforced separation from their children and families, trials in secret before military tribunals, inhuman and degrading treatment in hospital and care homes. … It may well be that, in practice, the people who have had the most need of its protection are rather out of the ordinary; but that does not alter the fact that it is there to protect us all as we go about our everyday lives.[48]

---

[39] Straw and Boateng, 'Bringing Rights Home' (n 9), 14.
[40] Home Office, *Rights Brought Home* (n 9), 1.
[41] HL Deb, vol 582, col 1228 (3 November 1997).
[42] Ibid, col 1308.
[43] HC Deb, vol 317, col 1358 (21 October 1998).
[44] Minutes of evidence taken on Wednesday 14 March (2000–01 HL 66 HC 332). Building a culture of respect for human rights law is now seen to be primarily the responsibility of the Equality and Human Rights Commission created by the Equality Act 2006.
[45] *R v Lambert* [2001] UKHL 37, [2002] 2 AC 545.
[46] *Attorney General's Reference No 2 of 2001* [2003] UKHL 68, [2004] 2 AC 72.
[47] Ibid, [173].
[48] *Friend v Lord Advocate* [2007] UKHL 53, [2008] HRLR 11, [38].

Baroness Hale has also observed that the HRA is a limit upon what a democratically elected parliament may do in order to 'protect the rights and freedoms of individuals and minorities against the will of those who are taken to represent the majority'.[49]

4. Structure of the Human Rights Act

The structure of the HRA has been described as unique[50] in that it addresses each of the three aspects of government.

> The Act ... follows a scheme which recognises that the role of the judiciary is to apply and enforce the 'Convention rights' municipally, treats the executive branch of government, in the form of any public authority, as being civilly liable for any breach of the 'Convention rights' on its part and makes their offending conduct unlawful, and recognises that laws passed by the Legislature may be incompatible with a 'Convention right'.[51]

Section 1 defines the Convention rights given further effect by the HRA. Section 2 provides that a court or tribunal determining a question which has arisen in connection with a Convention right must take into account, inter alia, any judgment, decision, declaration or advisory opinion of the ECtHR or opinion of the Commission. Section 6, a key provision, provides that it is unlawful for a public authority to act in a way which is incompatible with a Convention right. However, this section also provides a defence to a public authority if, as a result of primary legislation, it could not have acted differently. The HRA clearly preserves the sovereignty of Parliament and this part of section 6 is an important part of that objective. Where primary legislation is itself incompatible with a Convention right, the courts have only two alternatives. First, they must apply section 3 of the Act and read and give effect to the legislation in a way which is compatible with Convention rights, so far as it is possible to do so. If this is not possible, the court may make a declaration of incompatibility under section 4 of the Act. However, such a declaration does not affect the validity, continuing operation or enforcement of the provision. Once a declaration is made, section 10 of the Act applies, empowering a minister to make such amendments to the legislation as he considers necessary to remove the incompatibility. Schedule 2 of the Act makes further provision about such remedial orders. Section 7 provides that only the victims of the unlawful acts of public authorities as defined in section 6 may bring proceedings under the HRA or rely on the Convention rights in any legal proceedings. Finally, section 8 sets out the remedies that may be granted for the acts of public authorities incompatible with Convention rights.

As Lord Rodger commented in *Wilson*,[52] the HRA applies across the board:

---

[49] *R (Countryside Alliance) v Attorney General* [2007] UKHL 52, [2007] 3 WLR 922, [114].
[50] See eg the comments of Lord Hobhouse in *Wilson v First County Trust* [2003] UKHL 40, [2003] 3 WLR 568.
[51] Ibid, [126].
[52] Ibid.

While most statutes apply to one particular topic or area of law, the 1998 Act works as a catalyst across the board, wherever a Convention right is engaged. It may affect matters of substance in such areas as the law of property, the law of marriage and the law of torts. Or else it may affect civil and criminal procedure, or the procedure of administrative tribunals.[53]

5. Convention Rights Given Further Effect

5.1 The Nature and Scope of the Convention Rights

The HRA gives further effect to the 'Convention rights', and in section 1 these are defined as Articles 2–12 and 14 of the ECHR, Articles 1–3 of Protocol No 1 to the ECHR and Articles 1–2 of Protocol No 6 to the ECHR. All must be read with Articles 16 to 18 of the ECHR and have effect subject to any designated derogation or reservation.

These rights are predominantly what are known as civil and political rights and, given that the ECHR was drafted in 1950 and Protocol No 1 in 1952, are obviously not the most modern list of rights that could be given effect in domestic law.[54] However, it is often observed that these are the most fundamental and important rights.

> Those who negotiated and first signed the convention were not seeking to provide a blueprint for the ideal society. They were formulating a statement of very basic rights and freedoms which, it was believed, were very largely observed by the contracting states and which it was desired to preserve and protect both in the light of recent experience and in view of developments in Eastern Europe. The convention was seen more as a statement of good existing practice than as an instrument setting targets or standards which contracting states were to strive to achieve. … Thus the rights guaranteed by the convention were minimum rights.[55]

In addition, it is clear that the rights and freedoms guaranteed under the Convention are ones with which the people of the United Kingdom are plainly comfortable.[56]

There remains a divergence of views over whether the Convention rights are a part of domestic law or remain international law. The question was first addressed by Lord Hoffmann in his speech in *R v Lyons*[57] where he stated as follows:

> Parliament may pass a law which mirrors the terms of the treaty and in that sense incorporates

---

[53] Ibid, [182].

[54] Compare eg the EU Charter of Fundamental Rights. See further G Van Bueren, 'Including the Excluded: The Case for an Economic, Social and Cultural Human Rights Act' [2002] *Public Law* 456 and id, 'Socio-economic Rights and a Bill of Rights—An Overlooked British Tradition' [2013] *Public Law* 821.

[55] *Procurator Fiscal, Linlithgow v Watson* [2002] UKPC D1, [2004] 1 AC 379, [48]–[49] per Lord Bingham. See also the comments of Lord Bingham in *Brown v Stott* [2003] 1 AC 681 and in *Harrow London Borough Council v Qazi* [2003] UKHL 43, [2004] 1 AC 983, [8]. As to the background to the rights included in the EHCR, see generally D Nicol, 'Original Intent and the European Convention on Human Rights' [2005] *Public Law* 152.

[56] Home Office, *Rights Brought Home* (n 9), [1.3].

[57] *R v Lyons* [2002] UKHL 44, [2003] 1 AC 976.

the treaty into English law. But even then, the metaphor of incorporation may be misleading. It is not the treaty but the statute which forms part of English law. And English courts will not (unless the statute expressly so provides) be bound to give effect to interpretations of the treaty by an international court, even though the United Kingdom is bound by international law to do so.[58]

Returning to the topic in *McKerr*[59] his Lordship stated that the HRA had created domestic rights expressed in the same terms as those contained in the Convention. However, he saw these as domestic rights, not international rights: 'Their source is the statute, not the Convention. They are available against specific public authorities, not the United Kingdom as a state. And their meaning and application is a matter for domestic courts, not the court in Strasbourg.'[60] As he later summarised, '[t]he Act did not transmute international law obligations into domestic ones. It created new domestic human rights.'[61] In the same case Lord Nicholls explained that 'by enacting the 1998 Act Parliament created domestic law rights corresponding to rights under the convention'.[62] Picking up on these observations in his judgment in *Al-Skeini*,[63] Lord Bingham noted that there was a distinction between (1) rights arising under the Convention and (2) rights created by the 1998 Act by reference to the Convention.[64] However, in *Animal Defenders*[65] his Lordship expressly disagreed with the comment of Lord Scott that the articles were a part of domestic law and the House of Lords was the final court of appeal on the interpretation and application of the Convention rights.[66] As discussed below, the prevailing view remains that expressed by Lord Bingham in *Ullah*[67] that it is not possible for UK courts to adopt an interpretation of Convention rights more generous to a claimant than that adopted by the ECtHR. Most judges see the Convention rights as part of an international instrument, the interpretation of which can only be authoritatively expounded by the ECtHR.[68]

5.2 The Impact of Other International Conventions

The interpretation of the Convention rights in this way has in practice meant that where another international convention is relevant to a HRA claim, as a matter of international law this may displace the ECHR and alter the application of the Convention right at the national level.[69] This was the position in *Al-Jedda*[70] where the claimant, a national of the UK and Iraq, was held in custody by British troops at a detention facility in Iraq. He

---

[58] Ibid, [27]. See also [40].

[59] *In re McKerr* [2004] UKHL 12, [2004] 1 WLR 807.

[60] Ibid, [65]. See also Lord Nicholls at [26], Lord Steyn at [50], Lord Rodger at [77].

[61] Ibid, [68].

[62] Ibid [34].

[63] *R (Al-Skeini) v Secretary of State for Defence* [2007] UKHL 26.

[64] Ibid, [10].

[65] *R (Animal Defenders) v Secretary of State for Culture, Media and Sport* [2008] UKHL 15, [2008] 1 AC 1312.

[66] Ibid, [44].

[67] *R v Special Adjudicator, ex p Ullah* [2004] UKHL 26, [2004] 2 AC 323.

[68] Ibid, [20].

[69] See further C Eckes and S Hollenberg, 'Reconciling Different Legal Spheres in Theory and Practice' [2013] *Maastricht Journal of European and Comparative Law* 220.

[70] *R (Al-Jedda) v Secretary of State for Defence* [2007] UKHL 58, [2008] 1 AC 332.

claimed under the HRA that his detention was in breach of Article 5 of the ECHR. The question before the House of Lords was whether Article 5(1) of the ECHR was quali-fied by the legal regime established pursuant to UN Security Council Resolution 1546, and subsequent resolutions, by reason of the operation of Articles 25 and 103 of the UN Charter such that his detention was not actually in violation of Article 5(1). The House of Lords concluded that a binding Security Council decision taken under Chapter VII of the Charter of the United Nations superseded all other treaty commitments.[71] Lord Bingham stated as follows:

> I do not think that the European Court, if the appellant's article 5(1) claim were before it as an application, would ignore the significance of article 103 of the Charter in international law. The court has on repeated occasions taken account of provisions of international law, invoking the interpretative principle laid down in article 31(3)(c) of the Vienna Convention on the Law of Treaties, acknowledging that the Convention cannot be interpreted and applied in a vacuum and recognising that the responsibility of states must be determined in conformity and harmony with the governing principles of international law.[72]

The House of Lords held that where there was a clash between a power or duty to detain exercisable on the express authority of the UN Security Council and a funda-mental right which the UK had undertaken to secure to those within its jurisdiction, this could only be reconciled by ruling that the UK may lawfully, where it was necessary for imperative reasons of security, exercise the power to detain authorised by the UN Security Council Resolutions but must ensure that the detainee's rights under Article 5 are not infringed to any greater extent than is inherent in such detention.[73]

5.3 The Convention as a 'Living Instrument'

The ECtHR regards the ECHR as a 'living instrument'. The language in which the Convention rights are written is open textured and permits adaptation to modern conditions.[74] The House of Lords has also held that: 'As an important constitutional instrument the convention is to be seen as a "living tree capable of growth and expan-sion within its natural limits".'[75]

As will become apparent in Part II of this book, what is written down in the ECHR and Protocol No 1 to the ECHR is only the starting point for determining the scope of the Convention rights. For example, the right not to incriminate oneself, the right of access to a court and the right to equality of arms are all rights that have been implied into Article 6, the right to a fair trial. The concept of living instrument also means that the scope of a Convention right may change over time. For example, in *Bellinger*[76] the House of Lords took account of the fact that although previously the ECtHR had

---

[71] Ibid, per Lord Bingham at [35].

[72] Ibid, [36].

[73] Ibid, per Lord Bingham at [39]. See also *A v Secretary of State for the Home Department* [2005] UKHL 71, [2006] 2 AC 221; *HM Treasury v Ahmed* [2010] UKSC 2, [2010] 2 AC 534.

[74] *R (on the application of Pretty) v Director of Public Prosecutions* [2001] UKHL 61, [2001] 3 WLR 1598 per Lord Steyn at [56].

[75] *Brown* (n 55). See also the comments of Lord Clyde and the observations of Lord Bingham in *Procurator Fiscal, Linlithgow v Watson* [2002] UKPC D1, [2004] 1 AC 379, [48]–[49].

[76] *Bellinger v Bellinger* [2003] UKHL 21, [2003] 2 AC 467.

determined that non-recognition of a change of gender by a post-operative transsexual person did not constitute a violation of either Article 8 or Article 12, it had recently changed this view in *Goodwin v UK*,[77] finding that non-recognition by the state of a sex change constituted a violation of Articles 8 and 12.[78]

Under the HRA the higher courts have made clear that there are limits to the living instrument approach. In *Brown*[79] Lord Clyde stated that the Convention is dealing with the realities of life and it is not to be applied in ways which run counter to reason and common sense. In his Lordship's view, if the Convention rights were to be applied by the courts in ways which would seem absurd to ordinary people then the courts would be doing a disservice to the aims and purposes of the Convention, and the result would simply be to prejudice public respect for an international treaty which seeks to express the basic rights and freedoms of a democratic society. Similarly in *Matthews*[80] Lord Bingham observed that

> the exact limits of such rights are debatable and, although there is not much trace of economic rights in the 50-year-old Convention, I think it is well arguable that human rights include the right to a minimum standard of living, without which many of the other rights would be a mockery. But they certainly do not include the right to a fair distribution of resources or fair treatment in economic terms—in other words, distributive justice. Of course distributive justice is a good thing. But it is not a fundamental human right.[81]

Nevertheless, as discussed below, in the relationship between UK courts and the ECtHR, there is considerable willingness on the part of UK courts to follow the jurisprudence of the ECtHR regardless of the path that it has taken.

5.4 The Non-absolute Nature of the Majority of the Convention Rights

As discussed in detail in Part II of this book, very few of the Convention rights are expressed in absolute terms. The majority are subject to exceptions, and it is the determination of the limits of these exceptions which forms the bulk of judicial decision making under the HRA. In relation to absolute rights, such Article 3, it has been held that such rights should not be capable in any circumstances of being overridden by the majority, even if it is thought that the public interest so requires.[82] This belief was of considerable importance in the case of *Millar*,[83] where the absolute right to an independent and impartial tribunal was upheld notwithstanding the prediction that the Scottish legal system would be 'plunged into chaos' as a result.[84]

With respect to the non-absolute rights, as Lord Steyn noted in *Brown*,[85] the framers

---

[77] *Goodwin v UK* (2002) 35 EHRR 18.
[78] See also *R v Secretary of State for the Home Department, ex p Anderson* [2002] UKHL 46, [2003] 1 AC 837 and *Re McCaughey* [2011] UKSC 20, [2012] 1 AC 725 concerning the extension of the ambit of Art 2.
[79] *Brown* (n 55).
[80] *Matthews v Ministry of Defence* [2003] UKHL 4, [2003] 1 AC 1163.
[81] Ibid, [26]. See also the comments of Lord Scott in *Harrow London Borough Council v Qazi* [2003] UKHL 43, [2004] 1 AC 983, [123].
[82] *R v Secretary of State for the Environment, Transport and the Regions, ex p Alconbury Developments Ltd* [2001] UKHL 23, [2001] 2 WLR 1389 per Lord Hoffmann.
[83] *Millar v Procurator Fiscal* [2002] 1 WLR 1615.
[84] See eg J Oldham and A Jamieson, 'Law Lords Rule Against Sheriffs', *The Scotsman*, 26 July 2001, 2.
[85] *Brown* (n 55).

of the Convention realised that from time to time the fundamental right of one individual may conflict with the human right of another.

> They also realised only too well that a single-minded concentration on the pursuit of fundamental rights of individuals to the exclusion of the interests of the wider public might be subversive of the ideal of tolerant European liberal democracies. The fundamental rights of individuals are of supreme importance but those rights are not unlimited: we live in communities of individuals who also have rights.

Such an interpretation was of particular importance in *McCann*,[86] which concerned a challenge to the making of anti-social behaviour orders. Lord Steyn pointed out that in Parliament the view was taken that proceedings for an antisocial behaviour order would be civil and would not 'attract the rigour of the inflexible and sometimes absurdly technical hearsay rule which applies in criminal cases'. In his view, if this supposition was wrong 'it would inevitably follow that the procedure for obtaining anti-social behaviour orders is completely or virtually unworkable and useless'. His starting point was 'an initial scepticism of an outcome which would deprive communities of their fundamental rights'.[87] Similarly Lord Hope stated that 'respect for the rights of others is a price that we all must pay for the rights and freedoms that it guarantees.'[88] He noted that if the proceedings were classified as criminal

> much of the benefit which the legislation was designed to achieve would be lost ... It would greatly disturb the balance which section 1 of the Crime and Disorder Act 1998 seeks to strike between the interests of the individual and those of society.[89]

5.5 Derogations and Reservations

Section 1(2) of the HRA provides that the Convention rights given further effect are subject to any designated derogation or reservation. Derogations may be made pursuant to Article 15 of the ECHR and reservations pursuant to Article 57.[90] Following the withdrawal of a derogation to Article 5 in April 2005,[91] the United Kingdom currently maintains no derogations and only one reservation to Article 2 of Protocol No 1 accepting the second principle of Article 2 'only so far as it is compatible with the provision of efficient instruction and training, and the avoidance of unreasonable public expenditure'.

Although the HRA refers to derogations and reservations in sections 14–17, neither Article 15 nor Article 57 of the ECHR is included in the Convention rights given

---

[86] *R (McCann) v Crown Court at Manchester* [2002] UKHL 39, [2003] 1 AC 787.

[87] Ibid, [18].

[88] Ibid, [41].

[89] Ibid, [43]. See also Lord Hutton at [85] and [113].

[90] On derogations, see A Mokhtar, 'Human Rights Obligations v Derogations: Art 15 of the European Convention on Human Rights' (2004) 8 *International Journal of Human Rights* 65 and J Allain, 'Derogation from the European Convention of Human Rights in the Light of "Other Obligations" under International Law' [2005] *European Human Rights Law Review* 480.

[91] This followed the declaration of incompatibility by the House of Lords in *A v Secretary of State for the Home Department* [2004] UKHL 56, [2005] 2 AC 68, the repeal of the detention provisions in the Anti-Terrorism Crime and Security Act 2001 and their replacement with control orders under the Prevention of Terrorism Act 2005.

further effect by the HRA. Whilst few rules attach to the making of a reservation under Article 57, there are a number of requirements specified in relation to derogations under Article 15. Article 15(1) provides that

> in time of war or other public emergency threatening the life of the nation any High Contracting Party may take measures derogating from its obligations under this Convention to the extent strictly required by the exigencies of the situation, provided that such measures are not inconsistent with its other obligations under international law.

Pursuant to Article 15(2), no derogation from Article 2, except in respect of deaths resulting from lawful acts of war, or from Articles 3, 4(1) and 7 is possible under this provision. As Article 15 is not given further effect by the HRA, it is not clear how challenges to derogation orders can be brought domestically. Even in *A v Secretary of State*,[92] where a derogation order was successfully challenged, it was not made clear exactly how this was possible.[93]

Despite the questions surrounding the power to quash the derogation order in this case, it is important to examine the reasoning of their Lordships. The Order subject to challenge provided for a derogation from Article 5(1)(f) to allow legislation to detain a person against whom no action was being taken with a view to deportation.[94] The first argument of the claimants was that there was no public emergency threatening the life of the nation within the meaning of Article 15. A majority of their Lordships rejected this claim. Lord Bingham held that it had not been shown that the Special Immigration Appeals Commission or the Court of Appeal had misdirected themselves on this issue. He also found support in the conclusion of the ECtHR in *Lawless v Ireland (No 3)*[95] and stated that great weight should be given to the judgment of the Home Secretary, his colleagues, and Parliament on this question, because they were called upon to exercise a 'pre-eminently political judgment'.[96]

However, Article 15 also requires that the derogating measures must not go beyond what is 'strictly required by the exigencies of the situation'. 'Thus the Convention imposes a test of strict necessity or, in Convention terminology, proportionality.'[97] A majority of their Lordships found that this test was not satisfied in the present case and that the Order was disproportionate. Lord Bingham noted that the courts were not effectively precluded by any doctrine of deference from scrutinising the issues raised.[98] His Lordship concluded that the choice of an immigration measure to address a security problem had the inevitable result of failing adequately to address that problem (by allowing non-UK suspected terrorists to leave the country with impunity and leaving British suspected terrorists at large) while imposing a severe penalty of indefinite detention on persons who, even if reasonably suspected of having links with Al-Qaeda,

---

[92] [2004] UKHL 56, [2005] 2 AC 68.

[93] It is likely that it was possible due to provisions of the Anti-terrorism, Crime and Security Act 2001, notably ss 30 and 25(2)(b), which provide that the Special Immigration Appeals Commission must cancel a certificate (certifying an individual as a terrorist) if it considers 'for some other reason the certificate should not have been issued'. It appears that the Secretary of State conceded that if the derogation order was not compatible with Art 15, this would constitute 'some other reason' within the meaning of s 25(2)(b).

[94] Human Rights Act 1998 (Designated Derogation) Order 2001 (SI 2001/3644).

[95] *Lawless v Ireland (No 3)* (1979–80) 1 EHRR 15.

[96] Ibid, [27]–[29]. See also Lord Hope at [116], Lord Scott at [154], Lord Rodger at [166], Lord Walker at [208], Baroness Hale at [226].

[97] Ibid, per Lord Bingham at [30].

[98] Ibid, [42].

may harbour no hostile intentions towards the United Kingdom.[99] A quashing order was made in respect of the Derogation Order.[100]

6. Principles of Interpretation

As discussed above, a number of principles of interpretation relate to the Convention rights themselves, including the view that the rights given further effect are the most important and fundamental; the concept of the Convention as a living instrument, within limits; and the non-absolute nature of the majority of Convention rights. Other principles of interpretation of Convention rights, such as the principles of legality and proportionality and the practice of judicial deference, are discussed in Chapter 4, which concerns the process of determining incompatibility. There are also some principles of interpretation relating to the HRA itself. First, it has been held that a generous and purposive construction is to be given to that part of a constitution which protects and entrenches fundamental rights and freedoms, and that such an approach should be applied to the HRA.[101] It has also been held that the HRA 'must be given its full import' and that 'long or well entrenched ideas may have to be put aside, sacred cows culled'.[102]

However, the utilisation of a strong purposive approach to the construction of the HRA does not yet appear widespread, as evidenced by the approach of the courts to the issue of retrospective effect. As already discussed, it is clear that one purpose of the HRA is to allow claims of violations of Convention rights to be heard in domestic courts rather than in the ECtHR. However, in *Lambert*,[103] only Lord Steyn interpreted section 6 of the HRA in the 'broader framework of an Act which was undoubtedly intended "to bring home" the adjudication on fundamental rights'[104] and thereby found that it could apply to a trial which took place before the Act came into force.[105] A strong purposive approach was far more evident in the case of *B*,[106] where the Court

---

[99] Ibid, [43]. See also Lord Hope at [131]–[132], Lord Scott at [155]–[156], Lord Rodger at [189], Baroness Hale at [231].

[100] See further TR Hickman, 'Between Human Rights and the Rule of Law: Indefinite Detention and the Derogation Model of Constitutionalism' (2005) 68 *Modern Law Review* 655; S Tierney, 'Determining the State of Exception: What Role for Parliament and the Courts?' (2005) 68 *Modern Law Review* 668; A Tomkins, 'Readings of *A v Secretary of State for the Home Department*' [2005] *Public Law* 259.

[101] *R v Director of Public Prosecutions ex p Kebilene* [2000] 2 AC 326 per Lord Hope endorsing the observations of Lord Wilberforce in *Minister of Home Affairs v Fisher* [1980] AC 319, 328 and Lord Diplock in *Attorney-General of The Gambia v Momodou Jobe* [1984] AC 689, 700. See also the speeches of Lord Steyn in *McCartan Turkington Breen v Times Newspapers Ltd* [2001] 2 AC 277 and *Brown* (n 55).

[102] *Lambert* (n 45), per Lord Slynn. See also *Poplar Housing and Regeneration Community Association Ltd v Donoghue* [2001] EWCA Civ 595, [2000] QB 48 per Lord Woolf CJ at [58]. See further RA Edwards, 'Generosity and the Human Rights Act: The Right Interpretation?' [1999] *Public Law* 400; D Pannick, 'Principles of Interpretation of Convention Rights under the Human Rights Act and the Discretionary Area of Judgment' [1998] *Public Law* 545.

[103] Ibid.

[104] Ibid, [29]. See also the speech of Lord Clyde at [135].

[105] See also Lord Steyn's speech in *Kebilene* (n 101).

[106] *R (on the application of B) v Secretary of State for the Foreign and Commonwealth Office* [2004] EWCA Civ 1344, [2005] QB 643.

of Appeal held that, in determining whether the HRA could be applied to acts of UK public authorities outside of the territory of the United Kingdom, the approach taken to the interpretation of the Convention in such circumstances by the ECtHR should be followed.[107]

Second, it has also been held that, in accordance with section 3 of the HRA, the HRA itself must be read and given effect in a way that is compatible with Convention rights.[108] Whilst this has had some impact on the interpretation of section 12 of the HRA, which concerns freedom of expression,[109] as Article 13 of the ECHR, the right to an effective remedy, is not a Convention right given further effect by the HRA, the potential for radical reinterpretation of the key provisions of the HRA using section 3 is limited. Indeed, it is likely that one of the fears prompting the non-inclusion of Article 13 was the possibility that a court would declare the HRA itself incompatible with Article 13 in that it failed to provide an effective remedy to those who had been subject to a violation of Convention rights perpetrated by primary legislation.

Third, satellite litigation within the criminal justice system utilising the HRA has been discouraged. For example, in *Kebilene*[110] prior to trial it was argued that the enactment of the HRA gave rise to an enforceable legitimate expectation that the Director of Public Prosecutions would exercise his prosecutorial discretion in accordance with the ECHR. Lord Steyn, with whom Lords Slynn and Cooke agreed, held that once the HRA was fully in force it would not be possible to apply for judicial review on the ground that a decision to prosecute was in breach of a Convention right and the only available remedies would be in the trial process or on appeal.

> If the Divisional Court's present ruling is correct, it will be possible in other cases, which do not involve reverse legal burden provisions, to challenge decisions to prosecute in judicial review proceedings. The potential for undermining the proper and fair management of our criminal justice system may be considerable.[111]

His Lordship continued:

> While the passing of the Human Rights Act 1998 marked a great advance for our criminal justice system it is in my view vitally important that, so far as the courts are concerned, its application in our law should take place in an orderly manner which recognises the desirability of all challenges taking place in the criminal trial or on appeal. The effect of the judgment of the Divisional Court was to open the door too widely to delay in the conduct of criminal proceedings. Such satellite litigation should rarely be permitted in our criminal justice system.[112]

---

[107] Ibid, [75]–[79]. See also *R (on the application of Al-Skeini) v Secretary of State for Defence* [2004] EWHC (Admin) 2911, [2005] 2 WLR 1401; and *Al-Jedda* (n 70).

[108] See the speeches of Lords Hope and Clyde in *Lambert* (n 45).

[109] See *Douglas v Hello! Ltd* [2001] QB 967.

[110] *Kebilene* (n 101).

[111] Ibid, per Lord Steyn.

[112] Lord Hope commented that he could see no reason why, in a clear case where the facts of the case were of no importance, a decision that a provision was incompatible should not be capable of being taken at a very early stage. However, he agreed that, absent dishonesty, bad faith or some other exceptional circumstance, the DPP's decisions to consent or not to consent to a prosecution were not amenable to judicial review. In *Pretty* (n 74) Lord Steyn at [67] stood by this rule as did Lord Hobhouse at [119], [121] and [123]. Lord Hope at [78] held that in these exceptional circumstances it was open to Mrs Pretty to raise the issue by judicial review. In *R v Hertfordshire CC ex p Green Environmental Industries Ltd* [2000] 2 AC 483 Lord Cooke stated that the comments in *Kebilene* (n 101) concerning satellite litigation in the criminal justice system had nothing to say about the general ability by a citizen to challenge by appropriate civil proceedings

Finally, although the coming into force of the HRA has meant that many areas formerly regarded as non-justiciable by the courts have come under scrutiny, there are still limits to how far a court is prepared to go. For example, in *Gentle*[113] the House of Lords was reluctant to find that Article 2 imposed upon the government a duty to establish an independent public inquiry into all the circumstances surrounding the invasion of Iraq by British forces in 2003. Lord Bingham observed that if the claimants had a legal right it was justiciable in the courts, but in deciding whether a right existed, it was relevant to consider what exercise of the right would entail:

> Thus the restraint traditionally shown by the courts in ruling on what has been called high policy—peace and war, the making of treaties, the conduct of foreign relations—does tend to militate against the existence of the right.[114]

7. The Relationship between UK Courts and the European Court of Human Rights

7.1 The Current Approach

Of all the principles of interpretation developed in relation to the HRA, it is those which concern the relationship between UK courts and the ECtHR that are the most important. This relationship is governed by the HRA itself and many years of judicial development and interpretation. The starting point is section 2 of the HRA, which provides that a court or tribunal determining a question which has arisen in connection with a Convention right, must take into account, inter alia, any judgment, decision, declaration or advisory opinion of the ECtHR, whenever made or given, so far as, in the opinion of the court or tribunal, it is relevant to the proceedings in which that question has arisen. It has been confirmed by the House of Lords that section 2(1) does not make these decisions directly binding as a matter of domestic law on the courts.[115] However, this jurisprudence has been very warmly received by UK courts. In his speech in *Alconbury*[116] Lord Slynn observed:

> Although the Human Rights Act 1998 does not provide that a national court is bound by these decisions it is obliged to take account of them so far as they are relevant. In the absence of some special circumstances it seems to me that the court should follow any clear and constant jurisprudence of the ECtHR. If it does not do so, there is at least a possibility that

the validity of a requisition issued against him or her by a public authority—here a request for information under the Environmental Protection Act 1990. Lord Hobhouse agreed. See further *Alconbury* (n 82).

[113] *R (Gentle) v Prime Minister* [2008] UKHL 20, [2008] 1 AC 1356.
[114] Ibid, [8]. Contrast the approach of the majority of the Supreme Court in *Smith v Ministry of Defence* [2013] UKSC 41, [2013] 3 WLR 69. See further R Moosavian, 'Judges and High Prerogative: The Enduring Influence of Expertise and Legal Purity' [2012] *Public Law* 724.
[115] *R v Lyons* (n 57), per Lord Millet at [105].
[116] *Alconbury* (n 82).

the case will go to that court, which is likely in the ordinary case to follow its own constant jurisprudence.[117]

A few years later Lord Bingham held in *Ullah*[118] that it was not possible for UK courts to adopt an interpretation of Convention rights more generous to a claimant than that adopted by the ECtHR. In his opinion, the ECHR was an international instrument, the correct interpretation of which could be authoritatively expounded only by the ECtHR:

> From this it follows that a national court subject to a duty such as that imposed by s 2 should not without strong reason dilute or weaken the effect of the Strasbourg case law. It is indeed unlawful under s 6 of the 1998 Act for a public authority, including a court, to act in a way which is incompatible with a convention right. It is of course open to member states to provide for rights more generous than those guaranteed by the convention, but such provision should not be the product of interpretation of the convention by national courts, since the meaning of the convention should be uniform throughout the states party to it. The duty of national courts is to keep pace with the Strasbourg jurisprudence as it evolves over time: no more, but certainly no less.[119]

Similarly in *Al-Skeini*[120] Baroness Hale stated that if Parliament wished to go further, or if the courts wished to develop the common law further, this was possible. 'But that is because they choose to do so, not because the Convention requires it of them.'[121]

7.2 Exceptions to the Current Approach

The current approach of the UK courts to ECtHR jurisprudence, as outlined above, is subject to exceptions which have been employed in a small number of cases. Clearly, a judgment of the ECtHR cannot prevail if it conflicts with primary legislation and it is not possible for the court to utilise the interpretative power contained in section 3 of the HRA. All that a court may do in such instances is issue a declaration of incompatibility pursuant to section 4 of the HRA. It is also not possible for a UK court to follow a judgment of the ECtHR which conflicts with a binding domestic precedent. It has been held that a court below the level of the Supreme Court faced with this dilemma can only express its views and give leave to appeal.[122]

There are also two further exceptions that are more complex. Firstly, a judgment of the ECtHR might not be followed if a UK court considers that it is wrong. In *Alcon-bury*[123] Lord Hoffmann stated that the House of Lords was not bound by decisions of the ECtHR which compelled a conclusion fundamentally at odds with the distribution

---

[117] Ibid, [26].

[118] *Ullah* (n 67).

[119] Ibid, [20].

[120] *Al-Skeini* (n 63).

[121] Ibid, [90]. See also *Jones v Saudi Arabia* [2006] UKHL 26, [2007] 1 AC 270; *Secretary of State for the Home Department v AF* [2009] UKHL 28, [2009] 3 WLR 74; *Cadder v HM Advocate* [2010] UKSC 43 where the SC noted that a unanimous decision of the Grand Chamber was a formidable reason for following it at [46]; *Manchester City Council v Pinnock* [2010] UKSC 45, [2011] 2 AC 104; and *Re McCaughey* [2011] UKSC 20, [2012] 1 AC 725.

[122] *Kay v Lambeth London Borough Council* [2006] UKHL 10, [2006] 2 AC 465, per Lord Bingham at [44] with whom the others agreed. See also *R (RJM) v Secretary of State for Work and Pensions* [2008] UKHL 63, [2009] 1 AC 311 per Lord Neuberger at [59]–[67].

[123] *Alconbury* (n 82).

of powers under the British constitution.[124] In *R v Lyons*[125] again Lord Hoffmann stated that if an English court considered that the ECtHR had misunderstood or been misinformed about some aspect of English law, it may wish to give a judgment which invited the ECtHR to reconsider the question. 'There is room for dialogue on such matters.'[126]

It is not usual for UK courts to question ECtHR jurisprudence in this manner and there are not many examples of this exception being applied in practice. Almost all concern Article 6 of the ECHR where UK judges obviously feel more comfortable questioning the jurisprudence of the ECtHR than they do in relation to other Convention rights. One example is *Boyd*.[127] In determining whether the appointment of junior officer members to courts martial and the role of the reviewing authority were compatible with Article 6 of the ECHR, the House of Lords did not follow the judgment of the ECtHR in *Morris*[128] which concerned the same issue and where the ECtHR had found a violation. Lord Bingham explained that there were a large number of points in issue in *Morris* and it seemed clear that on this particular aspect the European Court did not receive all the help which was needed to form a conclusion.[129]

The clearest example to date of this exception in operation is the judgment of the Supreme Court in *Horncastle*.[130] The appeal of each of the appellants was based on the fact that there was placed before the jury the statement of a witness who had not been called to give evidence and it was argued that this was in breach of Article 6. The appellants based their appeal on the judgment of the ECtHR in *Al-Khawaja*[131] where a breach of Article 6 had been found when statements had been admitted in evidence in a criminal trial of a witness who was not called to give evidence. The Supreme Court accepted that the requirement to 'take into account' would normally result in the court applying the principles that were clearly established by the ECtHR. However, it concluded that in this case, *Al-Khawaja* would not be followed, noting that there would be

> rare occasions where this court has concerns as to whether a decision of the Strasbourg Court sufficiently appreciates or accommodates particular aspects of our domestic process. In such circumstances it is open to this court to decline to follow the Strasbourg decision, giving reasons for adopting this course. This is likely to give the Strasbourg Court the opportunity to reconsider the particular aspect of the decision that is in issue, so that there takes place what may prove to be a valuable dialogue between this court and the Strasbourg Court. This is such a case.[132]

It is also possible that rather than finding the decision of the ECtHR wrong, a court may conclude that a particular decision is not in keeping with the 'clear and constant jurisprudence' requirement set out in *Alconbury*. For example, in *Quila*[133] the Supreme Court declined to follow a judgment of the ECtHR given in 1985. Its reasons were that

---

[124] Ibid, [76].
[125] *R v Lyons* (n 57).
[126] Ibid, [46].
[127] *Boyd v The Army Prosecuting Authority* [2002] UKHL 31, [2003] 1 AC 734.
[128] *Morris v UK* (2002) 34 EHRR 1253.
[129] *Boyd* (n 127), [12]–[13]. See also *Brown* (n 55); *Al-Skeini* (n 63); *Doherty v Birmingham City Council* [2008] UKHL 57, [2008] 3 WLR 636 per Lord Hope at [20]; *R (Animal Defenders International) v Secretary of State for Culture, Media & Sport* [2008] UKHL 15, [2008] 2 WLR 781 per Lord Bingham at [29].
[130] *R v Horncastle* [2009] UKSC 14, [2010] 2 AC 373.
[131] *Al-Khawaja and Tahery v United Kingdom* (2009) 49 EHRR 1.
[132] *R v Horncastle* (n 130), [11].
[133] *Quila v Secretary of State for the Home Department* [2011] UKSC 45, [2012] 1 AC 621.

it was an old decision, there was dissent from it at the time and more recent decisions of the ECtHR were inconsistent with it—it found no clear and constant jurisprudence to follow.[134]

Secondly, a judgment of the ECtHR may also not be followed if the UK court considers that the subject matter of the claim engages the UK's margin of appreciation. This is the principle employed by the ECtHR to allow a degree of latitude to states as to how they protect the individual rights set out in the Convention. It is 'especially important in areas where there is said to be an absence of consensus or common practice across Europe'.[135] Again this exception is very rarely employed and early case law indicated that the possibility was subject to much doubt.[136] However, in its judgment in *In re P*[137] the House of Lords confirmed and applied this exception. The question was whether or not it was compatible with Articles 8 and 14 for a couple to be excluded from consideration as the adoptive parents of a child on the ground only that they were not married to each other. Having considered the judgments of the ECtHR, Lord Hoffmann found support for the conclusion that there was a violation of Article 14, although he was concerned that in reaching this conclusion, the House of Lords may have been going further than the ECtHR. He considered that Lord Bingham's observations in *Ullah* had no application here as the remarks were not made in the context of a case where the ECtHR had declared a question to be within the national margin of appreciation. In his view this meant that the question was one for the national authorities to decide for themselves and it followed that different Member States may well give different answers.[138] The House of Lords concluded here that the question was within the national margin of appreciation and it could reach its own judgment:

> [I]t is for the court in the United Kingdom to interpret articles 8 and 14 and to apply the division between the decision-making powers of courts and Parliament in the way which appears appropriate for the United Kingdom . . . It follows that the House is free to give, in the interpretation of the 1998 Act, what it considers to be a principled and rational interpretation to the concept of discrimination on the ground of marital status.[139]

Finally, it is also important to note that there may be the rare occasion where there is actually no relevant ECtHR jurisprudence for a UK court to follow. In such instances, the UK courts are free to interpret and apply the particular Convention right for themselves. For example, in *Austin*[140] the House of Lords recognised that the application of Article 5(1) to measures of crowd control was something the ECtHR had not considered. As Lord Hope stated, there was no direct guidance as to whether Article 5(1) was engaged where the police imposed restrictions on movement for the sole purpose of protecting people from injury or avoiding serious damage to property.[141] The House of

---

[134] Ibid, per Lord Wilson at [43] with whom the majority agreed.

[135] T Lewis, 'What Not to Wear: Religious Rights, the European Court, and the Margin of Appreciation' (2007) 56 *International and Comparative Law Quarterly* 395, 397.

[136] See *Kay v Lambeth London Borough Council* [2006] UKHL 10, [2006] 2 AC 465 per Lord Bingham at [44]; *Secretary of State for Work and Pensions v M* [2006] UKHL 11, [2006] AC 91 per Lord Nicholls at [30] and per Lord Mance at [136]; *R (Countryside Alliance) v Her Majesty's Attorney General* [2007] UKHL 52 per Baroness Hale at [124]–[132] and Lord Brown at [141].

[137] *In re P* [2008] UKHL 38, [2008] 3 WLR 76.

[138] Ibid, [31].

[139] See also Lord Hope at [50], Baroness Hale at [120], Lord Mance at [129].

[140] *Austin v Commissioner of Police of the Metropolis* [2009] UKHL 5, [2009] 1 AC 564.

[141] Ibid, [23].

Lords' conclusion that the police cordon restricting the claimant's liberty was not the kind of arbitrary deprivation of liberty proscribed by the Convention was eventually approved by the ECtHR itself, demonstrating the contribution which can be made by UK judges to the jurisprudence of the court where the opportunity is taken.[142]

7.3 Assessment of the Current Approach

The approach adopted by UK courts to section 2 of the HRA and the jurisprudence of the ECtHR has generated considerable academic interest.[143] Many question why the UK courts have chosen this path when there is no strict legal basis for it in common law, statute law or international law. It is also clear that the drafters of the HRA never intended to make ECtHR jurisprudence binding. During the parliamentary debates the Lord Chancellor stated that there may be occasions when it would be right for UK courts to depart from ECtHR decisions.[144] The reasons put forward by UK courts themselves do not stand up to scrutiny. Lord Bingham's observations in *Ullah* applied to Convention rights, but not the jurisprudence of the ECtHR. A UK court adopting an interpretation of Convention rights different to that adopted in the ECtHR might be acting incompatibly with international law but not with the obligations imposed by the HRA.

In *Ullah* Lord Bingham also explained that only the ECtHR could correctly interpret the ECHR and that the meaning of the ECHR should be uniform throughout the states party to it.[145] It is clear that a more narrow interpretation of Convention rights by a state may undermine the effectiveness of the ECHR system and make a mockery of that state's international obligations. However, it is difficult to see how a national court adopting a more generous interpretation of Convention rights could impact on the effectiveness of the ECHR system. Furthermore, to see the ECtHR as the only institution capable of correctly interpreting the ECHR leaves the Convention rights as creatures of international law when these are very clearly considered by many judges as part of UK law. As noted above, in *McKerr*[146] Lord Hoffmann held that the HRA had created domestic rights expressed in the same terms as those contained in the Convention:

> But they are domestic rights, not international rights. Their source is the statute, not the Convention. They are available against specific public authorities, not the United Kingdom as a state. And their meaning and application is a matter for domestic courts, not the court in Strasbourg.[147]

---

[142] *Austin v United Kingdom* ECtHR Grand Chamber 15 March 2012. See also *Ali v Birmingham City Council* [2010] UKSC 8.

[143] See eg R Clayton, 'Smoke and Mirrors: The Human Rights Act and the Impact of Strasbourg Case Law' [2012] *Public Law* 639; Lord Irvine, 'A British Interpretation of Convention Rights' [2012] *Public Law* 237; P Sales, 'Strasbourg Jurisprudence and the Human Rights Act: A Response to Lord Irvine' [2012] *Public Law* 253; A Kavanagh, 'Strasbourg, the House of Lords or Elected Politicians: Who Decides about Rights after Re P?' [2009] *Modern Law Review* 828; J Wright, "Interpreting Section 2 of the Human Rights Act 1998: Towards an Indigenous Jurisprudence of Human Rights' [2009] *Public Law* 595.

[144] HL Deb vol. 584, col. 1271 (19 January 1998).

[145] *Ullah* (n 67), [20]. This was repeated by the House of Lords in its judgment in *R (Gentle) v Prime Minister* [2008] UKHL 20, [2008] 1 AC 1356.

[146] *In re McKerr* [2004] UKHL 12, [2004] 1 WLR 807.

[147] Ibid, [65] See also Lord Nicholls at [26], Lord Steyn at [50] and Lord Rodger at [77].

It is also questionable for UK courts to be driven by the notion that the meaning of the Convention should be uniform throughout the states party to it and that an enlargement of the scope of the Convention in one Contracting State was an enlargement for them all. Forty-seven states have ratified the ECHR and accepted the jurisdiction of the ECtHR. It is difficult to imagine a German court, for example, considering itself bound by a particularly generous interpretation of Convention rights by the UK Supreme Court although this might provide strong persuasive authority. More convincing are concerns about what might happen in the instant case if a UK court adopts an interpretation of Convention rights which is too narrow or too generous. A narrow construction may result in a successful claim to the ECtHR. A more generous interpretation is also problematic. Contracting States have no standing to bring the matter before the ECtHR to have the issues considered again.[148]

Whilst it remains on shaky foundations, it is important to appreciate that the present approach to the jurisprudence of the ECtHR has some advantages for the protection of human rights. The reception of this jurisprudence into the law of the UK has been, on the whole, a positive development and has enabled the judiciary to take many decisions which they might not have been prepared to take without it.[149] There are also considerations of legal certainty. Many of the Convention rights are of little or no meaning without the backing of the jurisprudence of the ECtHR and public authorities in the UK clearly rely upon the meaning of the Convention rights as these have been interpreted and applied by the ECtHR. However, there is also a downside to UK courts adhering so closely to this jurisprudence. In instances where a more generous interpretation of Convention rights may have been preferred, this has been prevented by a particular judgment or series of judgments from the ECtHR. For example, in *N v SSHD*[150] the House of Lords had to determine a difficult political issue: should an individual be able to lawfully resist deportation from the UK to Uganda on Article 3 grounds because she had advanced HIV/AIDS. All of their Lordships were careful to point out that they were only applying the Strasbourg case law and would not be diverted by their sympathy for the appellant.[151] Baroness Hale indicated that she would prefer not to follow Strasbourg but felt compelled to do so:

> [W]e would be implying far more into our obligations under article 3 than is warranted by the Strasbourg jurisprudence, if we were to allow the appeal in this case, much though I would like to be able to do so.[152]

Close adherence to Strasbourg jurisprudence also means that the UK judges are not making a full contribution to the interpretation and development of Convention standards. The ECtHR is not formally bound to follow its previous judgments and is willing to respond to changing conditions and any emerging consensus discernible within the domestic legal order.[153] Legal certainty at the domestic level can also suffer from the

---

[148] See the observations of Lord Brown in *Al-Skeini* (n 63), [106].

[149] See eg *Ullah* (n 67).

[150] *N v SSHD* [2005] UKHL 31; [2005] 2 AC 296.

[151] Ibid, Lord Nicholls at [18], Lord Hope at [25].

[152] Ibid, [71]. See also the observations of Lord Brown in the *Countryside Alliance* case [2007] UKHL 52, [139] and [141]; *R (Begum) v Denbigh High School* [2006] UKHL 15, [2007] 1 AC 100; and *Copsey v WWB Devon Clays Ltd* [2005] EWCA Civ 932, [2005] ICR 1789.

[153] See further M Amos, 'The Dialogue between United Kingdom Courts and the European Court of Human Rights' (2012) 61 *International and Comparative Law Quarterly* 557.

ECtHR's view of the ECHR as a living instrument, the meaning of which may change over time. UK courts closely following the ECtHR's judgments often means that domestic law has effectively changed and a new avenue for redress has opened up.[154] This can lead to previously litigated issues being litigated once again at the national level. One example is *Purdy*[155] where the House of Lords, following the judgment of the ECtHR in *Pretty v UK*,[156] reversed its own conclusion in its judgment in *Pretty*[157] and accepted that section 2(1) of the Assisted Suicide Act 1961 constituted an interference with the right to respect for private life as protected by Article 8(1). Lord Hope confirmed that the House was free to depart from its earlier decisions and follow that of the ECtHR:[158]

> [T]he interests of human rights law would not be well served if the House were to regard itself as bound by a previous decision as to the meaning or effect of a Convention right which was shown to be inconsistent with a subsequent decision in Strasbourg. Otherwise the House would be at risk of endorsing decisions which are incompatible with Convention rights.[159]

Furthermore, ECtHR case law itself can be unclear, confusing and admitting of many possible interpretations. It is not uncommon for a UK court to place its own interpretation upon a confusing area of Strasbourg case law and then treat this as binding.[160] Finally, it is important to appreciate that UK judges relying on and following the jurisprudence of the ECtHR in this way contributes to the perception that the HRA is 'European' and imposed upon the UK by supranational institutions rather than something interpreted and applied by the country's own judiciary.

Fundamental change of the position adopted by UK courts towards section 2 of the HRA is not likely. The best way forward would be for the exceptions to the principle, in particular the margin of appreciation exception, to continue to develop. A margin of appreciation exception allows UK courts to reach their own more generous interpretations of Convention rights. Whilst this may result in replacing one set of problems with another, as disagreements over the width of the margin of appreciation would be likely, at least national courts would have a little more freedom to develop a UK interpretation of the Convention rights.[161]

---

[154] This has been a particular problem where claimants have argued that Art 8 of the ECHR applies to an order for possession. See *Doherty v Birmingham City Council* [2008] UKHL 57, [2008] 3 WLR 636 and *Manchester City Council v Pinnock* [2010] UKSC 45, [2011] 2 AC 104.

[155] *R (Purdy) v Director of Public Prosecutions* [2009] UKHL 45, [2009] 3 WLR 403.

[156] *Pretty v United Kingdom* (2002) 35 EHRR 1.

[157] *R (Pretty) v Director of Public Prosecutions* [2002] 1 AC 800.

[158] Ibid, [34].

[159] Ibid. See also *R (GC) v Commissioner of Police for the Metropolis* [2011] UKSC 21, [2011] 1 WLR 1230.

[160] See eg *Ullah* (n 67) and *R (S and Marper) v Chief Constable of South Yorkshire* [2004] UKHL 39, [2004] 4 All ER 193.

[161] See further M Amos, 'The Principle of Comity and the Relationship between British Courts and the European Court of Human Rights' (2009) 28 *Yearbook of European Law* 503; Amos (n 153).

8. Other Aids to Interpretation

8.1 Judgments in Devolution Cases

Whilst human rights judgments in devolution claims[162] are not binding on courts determining HRA claims, and judgments in HRA claims are not binding on courts determining devolution claims, both types of judgment are routinely taken into account across both types of claim. For example, in *Rezvi*[163] the House of Lords considered the compatibility of confiscation orders under drugs legislation with Article 6 and Article 1 Protocol No 1. Lord Steyn, with whom the others agreed, noted that the point had recently been considered by the Privy Council in relation to confiscation proceedings in drugs legislation in Scotland.[164] As it had been considered in depth in the context of the law of Scotland and European jurisprudence, it was held to be unnecessary to cover all the same ground again.[165] His Lordship adopted the Privy Council's categorisation of the confiscation order as a penalty imposed for the offence of which he had been convicted but involving no accusation of any other offence.[166] A number of Privy Council and Supreme Court[167] human rights judgments in devolution cases under the Scotland Act 1998 are referred to in this book.[168]

In theory, divergences between human rights law in Scotland and England and Wales are possible. In *Watson*[169] Lord Hope warned that there may be room for the view that there is a fundamental difference of approach between the Scotland Act and the HRA in relation to the reasonable time guarantee in Article 6. Referring to a recent article,[170] he noted that the HRA does not impose a vires control upon UK Ministers—section 57(2) of the Scotland Act provides that a member of the Scottish Executive has no power to perform any act so far as it is incompatible with any of the Convention rights.[171] However, whilst such a division did eventually open up between the two jurisdictions in relation to the reasonable time guarantee,[172] it closed shortly after with the English position adopted in relation to both.[173]

---

[162] Primarily claims made under the human rights provisions of the Scotland Act 1998 s 57.

[163] *R v Rezvi; R v Benjafield* [2002] UKHL 1, [2003] 1 AC 1099.

[164] *McIntosh v Lord Advocate* [2003] 1 AC 1078.

[165] Ibid, [10].

[166] See also the judgment of the Privy Council in *Mills v HM Advocate (No 2)* [2002] UKPC D2, [2004] 1 AC 441, where much reference was made to judgments of the House of Lords.

[167] Since October 2009 the Supreme Court has had jurisdiction in devolution claims.

[168] On human rights law in Scotland, see generally R Reed and J Murdoch, *A Guide to Human Rights Law in Scotland* (Edinburgh, Butterworths, 2001).

[169] *Procurator Fiscal, Linlithgow v Watson* [2002] UKPC D1, [2004] 1 AC 379.

[170] I Jamieson, 'Relationship between the Scotland Act and the Human Rights Act' [2001] *SLT (News)* 43.

[171] *Watson* (n 169), [111].

[172] *HM Advocate v R* [2002] UKPC D3, [2004] 1 AC 462 in Scotland and *Attorney General's Reference No.2 of 2001* [2003] UKHL 68, [2004] 2 AC 72 in England.

[173] In *Spiers v Ruddy* [2007] UKPC D2, [2008] 1 AC 873 the Privy Council held that the law in Scotland was the same as in England.

8.2 Case Law and Instruments from Other Jurisdictions

In interpreting both the HRA and the Convention rights, case law from other jurisdictions is often referred to. For example, in *Brown*[174] Lord Bingham, in discussing the right not to incriminate oneself, referred to the Constitution of the United States, the Indian Constitution, the Canadian Charter of Rights and Freedoms, the New Zealand Bill of Rights Act 1990, the Constitution of South Africa, the International Covenant on Civil and Political Rights and the Universal Declaration of Human Rights.[175] In *Pretty*[176] his Lordship referred to section 7 of the Canadian Charter of Rights and Freedoms and associated judgments, but noted that the judgments were directed to a provision with no close analogy in the ECHR.[177] In *R v D*[178] the Crown Court relied extensively upon Canadian jurisprudence when determining whether a criminal defendant should be permitted to wear a *burqa* or *niqaab* during her trial.

However, it still appreciated that, given section 2 of the HRA, Strasbourg jurisprudence is to be preferred.[179] The dangers of transplanting other human rights jurisprudence without question have also been appreciated. For example, in *British American Tobacco*[180] it was pointed out that US First Amendment jurisprudence should be treated with care:

> While it is instructive, in general terms, to see how another respected jurisdiction has dealt with a related but confined problem, the balance between State legislation and federal legislation in the United States is a subject of renowned complexity. Decisions on such matters can have limited effect on our consideration of the balance to be struck in considering a restriction of a limited Convention right and the measure of a discretion to be afforded to Parliament and ministers under our own rather different constitutional system.[181]

Increasing reference is also being made in judgments under the HRA to international human rights instruments and bodies in addition to the ECHR and the Council of Europe. For example, in *A v Secretary of State for the Home Department*[182] considerable reference was made to the Universal Declaration of Human Rights, the International Covenant on Civil and Political Rights, General Comments of the UN Human Rights Committee, Opinions of the Council of Europe Commissioner for Human Rights, Resolutions of the Parliamentary Assembly of the Council of Europe, Recommendations of the European Commission against Racism and Intolerance, Resolutions of the Security Council of

---

[174] *Brown* (n 55).
[175] See also the speech of Lord Steyn in *Lambert* (n 45), where he referred to judgments of the Canadian Supreme Court and South African Constitutional Court; *Aston Cantlow and Wilmcote with Billesley Parochial Church Council v Wallbank* [2003] UKHL 37, [2004] 1 AC 546, where reference was made to German constitutional law; and *Campbell v MGN Ltd* [2004] UKHL 22, [2004] 2 AC 457, where reference was made to privacy cases from Australia and New Zealand.
[176] *Pretty* (n 74).
[177] Ibid, [23]. See generally C McCrudden, 'A Common Law of Human Rights? Transnational Judicial Conversations on Constitutional Rights' (2000) 20 *Oxford Journal of Legal Studies* 499.
[178] Crown Court 16 September 2013, unreported.
[179] See the comments of Lord Hope in *Procurator Fiscal, Linlithgow v Watson* [2002] UKPC D1, [2004] 1 AC 379.
[180] *R (on the application of British American Tobacco UK Ltd) v The Secretary of State for Health* [2004] EWHC (Admin) 2493.
[181] Ibid, [36]. See also *R (Axon) v Secretary of State for Health* [2006] EWHC 37 (Admin), [2006] QB 539 where similar observations were made concerning US jurisprudence on abortion.
[182] Above n 73.

the United Nations and the Convention on the Elimination of Racial Discrimination.[183] In some instances the use of international law by the ECtHR has influenced the way a decision is made at the UK level. In *ZH*[184] the Supreme Court adopted the approach of the ECtHR, holding that a where a child was subject to deportation with his or her family, the best interests of the child were the primary consideration in accordance with Article 3 of the UN Convention on the Rights of the Child.

8.3 Reports of the Joint Committee on Human Rights

The establishment of the Joint Committee on Human Rights was suggested in *Rights Brought Home*, where it was stated that

> [t]he new committee might conduct enquiries on a range of human rights issues relating to the Convention, and produce reports so as to assist the Government and Parliament in deciding what action to take. It might also want to range more widely, and examine issues relating to the other international obligations of the United Kingdom such as proposals to accept new rights under other human rights treaties.[185]

The Committee was established during the 2000–01 parliamentary session to consider matters relating to human rights in the United Kingdom, and proposals for remedial orders, draft remedial orders and remedial orders made under section 10 of and laid under Schedule 2 to the Human Rights Act 1988. All government Bills are examined by the Committee for human rights compliance and its reports on such Bills are often referred to in HRA judgments.[186] It has also enquired into a number of general human rights issues and published some detailed and useful reports.[187]

---

[183] For a similar scale of reference, see also *Jones v Saudi Arabia* [2006] UKHL 26, [2007] 1 AC 270. See generally R Singh, 'The Use of International Law in the Domestic Courts of the United Kingdom' (2005) 56 *Northern Ireland Legal Quarterly* 119.

[184] *ZH (Tanzania) v Secretary of State for the Home Department* [2011] UKSC 4, [2011] 2 WLR 148.

[185] Home Office, *Rights Brought Home* (n 9), [3.7].

[186] See eg *A v Secretary of State for the Home Department* (n 73); *R (on the application of R) v Durham Constabulary* [2005] UKHL 21, [2005] 1 WLR 1184. On the work of the Committee generally, see A Lester, 'Parliamentary Scrutiny of Legislation under the Human Rights Act 1998' [2002] *European Human Rights Law Review* 432; D Feldman, 'Parliamentary Scrutiny of Legislation and Human Rights' [2002] *Public Law* 323; D Feldman, 'Can and Should Parliament Protect Human Rights?' (2004) 10 *European Public Law* 635; JL Hiebert, 'Parliamentary Review of Terrorism Measures' (2005) 68 *Modern Law Review* 676; F Klug and H Wildbore, 'Breaking New Ground: The Joint Committee on Human Rights and the Role of Parliament in Human Rights Compliance' [2007] *European Human Rights Law Review* 231; and the Joint Committee's own report, *The Work of the Committee in the 2001–2005 Parliament*, Nineteenth Report (2004–05 HL 112, HC 552).

[187] See eg *The Making of Remedial Orders*, Seventh Report (2001–02 HL 58, HC 473); *The Case for a Human Rights Commission*, Sixth Report (2002–03 HL 67, HC 489); *Work of the Northern Ireland Human Rights Commission*, Fourteenth Report (2002–03 HL 132, HC 142); *The Meaning of Public Authority Under the Human Rights Act*, Sixth Report (2003–04 HL 39, HC 382); *A Bill of Rights for the UK?*, Twenty-ninth Report (2007-08 HL 165-I, HC 150-I); *Enhancing Parliament's role in relation to human rights judgments*, Fifteenth Report (2009-10 HL 85, HC 455); *Facilitating Peaceful Protest*, Tenth Report (2010-12 HL 123, HC 684).

9. Reform of the Human Rights Act

Finally, in this introductory chapter it is important to note that since coming into force on 2 October 2000, the HRA has been subject to some fairly harsh criticism from a variety of sources including government ministers, opposition leaders, and prominent newspapers and journalists.[188] Unsurprisingly, these criticisms are often accompanied by promises to reform the HRA or indeed to repeal it and replace it with a Bill of Rights, but very few serious and comprehensive proposals for reform have actually been made. In March 2009, the then Labour government published *Rights and Responsibilities: Developing our Constitutional Framework*.[189] This built upon the work already done on the possibility of a bill of rights by human rights organisation JUSTICE[190] and the Joint Committee on Human Rights.[191] However, any possible move towards reform was ended by a change in government following the general election in May 2010.

In a new coalition government, the Conservative Party and Liberal Democrats undertook to establish a Commission to investigate the creation of a British Bill of Rights that incorporated and built upon obligations under the ECHR, ensured that these rights continued to be enshrined in British law, and protected and extended British liberties.[192] Members of the Commission were appointed and it reported in December 2012.[193] A majority of members of the Commission believed that, on balance, there was a strong argument in favour of a UK Bill of Rights. This view was primarily based on the present lack of ownership of the HRA amongst the general public and a perceived opportunity to provide greater protection against the possible abuse of power by the state.[194] A minority of the Commission's members were not in favour as they believed that the majority has failed to identify or declare any shortcomings in the HRA or its application by UK courts.[195] However, comprehensive reform of the HRA is probably still a long way off and it is not likely that the report of the Commission will be acted upon until after the next general election in 2015.

---

[188] See further M Amos, 'Problems with the Human Rights Act 1998 and How to Remedy Them: Is a Bill of Rights the Answer?' (2009) 72 *Modern Law Review* 883.

[189] *Rights and Responsibilities: Developing our Constitutional Framework*, Cm 7577 (2009).

[190] *A British Bill of Rights: Informing the Debate* (London, JUSTICE, 2007).

[191] *A Bill of Rights for the UK?* HL 165 (2008), HC 150 (2008).

[192] The Coalition, *Our Programme for Government* (London, TSO, 2010) 11.

[193] The Commission on a Bill of Rights, *A UK Bill of Rights?—The Choice Before Us*, vol I (London, Commission on a Bill of Rights, 2012).

[194] Ibid, 176–77.

[195] Ibid, 177. See further F Klug and A Williams, 'The Choice before Us? The Report of the Commission on a Bill of Rights' [2013] *Public Law* 459; M Elliott, 'A Damp Squib in the Long Grass: The Report of the Commission on a Bill of Rights' [2013] EHRLR 137; H Fenwick, 'The Human Rights Act or a British Bill of Rights: Creating a Down-grading Recalibration of Rights against the Counter-terror Backdrop? [2012] *Public Law* 468.

2

The Benefit and Burden
of the Human Rights Act

1. Introduction

Not every person may bring a claim under the HRA and not every decision-maker is obliged by the HRA to act compatibly with the Convention rights. The HRA contains a number of provisions controlling who may bring a claim under the Act or rely on Convention rights in legal proceedings (the benefit of the HRA) and which bodies must act compatibly with Convention rights (the burden of the HRA). These provisions have been carefully designed to mirror those employed in the international system for enforcement of the ECHR. The objective was to ensure that it would be possible to bring any claim that could be brought before the ECtHR under the HRA before the domestic courts.

> The purpose of the Bill is to give greater effect in our domestic law to the convention rights. It is in keeping with this approach that persons should be able to rely on the convention rights before our domestic courts in precisely the same circumstances as they can rely upon them before the Strasbourg institutions.[1]

In practice, the effect is also to ensure that claims which could not be brought in Strasbourg also cannot be brought under the HRA.

2. The Benefit of Convention Rights: Victims

2.1 Section 7 Human Rights Act

Section 7(1) of the HRA provides that a person who claims that a public authority has

---

[1] HL Deb, Vol 583, col 831, Lord Chancellor.

acted (or proposes to act) in a way which is made unlawful by section 6(1) may: (a) bring proceedings against the authority under the HRA in the appropriate court or tribunal;[2] or (b) rely on the Convention right or rights concerned in any legal proceedings,[3] but only if he is (or would be) a victim of the unlawful act.

The definition of 'victim' is given by reference to Article 34 of the ECHR. Section 7(7) provides that, for the purposes of the section, a person is a victim of an unlawful act only if he would be a victim for the purposes of Article 34 of the ECHR if proceedings were brought in the ECtHR in respect of that act. Article 34 provides that the Court 'may receive applications from any person, non-governmental organisation or group of individuals claiming to be the victim of a violation be one of the High Contracting Parties of the rights set forth in the Convention or the protocols thereto'. Therefore, in order to bring a claim under the HRA, the claimant must be able to demonstrate that he or she has been directly affected. There is no 'scope for proceedings to be brought by a person who has not himself been affected by the alleged violation'.[4]

It has been held that, skilfully drawn though these provisions are, they leave a great deal of open ground. There is room for doubt and for argument. 'It has been left to the courts to resolve these issues when they arise.'[5] A few matters are plain. The victim test is narrower than the test of standing to bring an application for judicial review. This is reflected in section 7(3) of the HRA, which provides that if the proceedings 'are brought on an application for judicial review, the applicant is to be taken to have a sufficient interest in relation to the unlawful act only if he is, or would be, a victim of that act'.

Interest groups are able to bring claims under the HRA only if they themselves are victims of an unlawful act,[6] although it is still possible for them to provide support to victims who bring cases, intervene in the proceedings[7] or provide amicus written briefs.[8] The only exception is that which has been made for the Equality and Human Rights Commission. The Commission may institute proceedings under the HRA without being a victim or a potential victim. However, it may only act 'if there is or would be one or more victims of the unlawful act' and no award of damages may be made to it.[9]

---

[2] S 7(1)(a) jurisdiction has been conferred by rules made under s 7(9) on the Special Immigration Appeals Commission and the Proscribed Organisations Appeal Commission.

[3] This is not subject to the time limit on proceedings in s 7(1)(a). It has been held that the purpose is to enable persons against whom proceedings have been brought by a public authority to rely on the Convention rights for their protection. See R (A) v B [2009] UKSC 12, [2010] 2 AC 1 per Lord Hope at [45].

[4] Eastaway v Secretary of State for Trade and Industry [2007] EWCA Civ 425 per Arden LJ at [49] in reliance upon Klass v Germany (1978) 2 EHRR 214. See also R (Johnson) v Secretary of State for Health [2006] EWHC 288 (Admin) and Core Issues Trust v Transport for London [2013] EWHC 651 (Admin), [2013] HRLR 22. In Weir v Secretary of State for Transport [2005] EWHC 2192 (Ch) it was confirmed that shareholders were not victims.

[5] Aston Cantlow and Wilmcote with Billesley Parochial Church Council v Wallbank [2003] UKHL 37, [2004] 1 AC 546 per Lord Hope at [36].

[6] See eg R (Johnson) v Secretary of State for Health [2006] EWHC 288 (Admin). Religious groups often have victim status where other groups may not. See Re Christian Institute Application for Judicial Review [2007] NIQB 66, [2008] IRLR 36.

[7] In Re E (A Child) [2008] UKHL 66, [2009] 1 AC 536 Lord Hoffmann observed [3] that an intervention was of no assistance if it merely repeated points which the appellant or respondent had already made.

[8] HL Deb, vol 583, col 833, Lord Chancellor. See further M Arshi and C O'Cinneide, 'Third-party Interventions: The Public Interest Reaffirmed' [2004] Public Law 69; S Hannett, 'Third Party Intervention: In the Public Interest?' [2003] Public Law 128.

[9] S 30(1) of the Equality Act 2006 provides that the Commission shall have the capacity to institute or intervene in legal proceedings, whether for judicial review or otherwise, if it appears to the Commission that the proceedings are relevant to a matter in connection with which the Commission has a function. See

Furthermore, although it has been held that section 7 must be given a generous interpretation as befits its human rights purpose,[10] this does not extend to affording remedies under the HRA where the authority has not acted or proposed to act unlawfully. For example, in *Re S*[11] the House of Lords considered the Court of Appeal's proposed starring system in relation to care orders. In brief, if a starred milestone had not been achieved within a reasonable time after the date set at trial, the local authority was obliged to reactivate the process that had contributed to the creation of the care plan, and the child's guardian or the local authority had the right to apply to the court for further directions. Their Lordships concluded that the starring system would impose obligations on local authorities in circumstances where there had been no finding that the authority had acted unlawfully or was proposing to do so.[12]

Courts are wary of determining hypothetical problems. For example, in *Burke*[13] the Court of Appeal explained the dangers of adjudicating upon claims where these were divorced from a factual context that required their determination.

> [T]he court should not be used as a general advice centre. The danger is that the court will enunciate propositions of principle without full appreciation of the implications that these will have in practice, throwing into confusion those who feel obliged to attempt to apply those principles in practice. This danger is particularly acute where the issues raised involve ethical questions that any court should be reluctant to address, unless driven to do so by the need to resolve a practical problem that requires the court's intervention.[14]

2.2 Categories of Victim

2.2.1 Core Public Authorities

Core public authorities do not enjoy Convention rights and cannot be victims under the HRA.[15] For example, in *Westminster City Council*[16] it was confirmed that a local authority could not bring a claim under the HRA as it was not a victim within the meaning of section 7. However, hybrid public authorities, those which exercise both public and private functions, can be victims under the HRA.[17]

---

also s 30(3). To date the Commission has brought only one claim under the HRA: *Equality and Human Rights Commission v Prime Minister* [2011] EWHC 2401 (Admin). The Northern Ireland Human Rights Commission also has standing under s 71(2B)(c) of the Northern Ireland Act 1998.

[10] *Re S* [2002] UKHL 10, [2002] 2 WLR 720 per Lord Nicholls at [48].

[11] Ibid.

[12] Ibid, per Lord Nicholls at [49].

[13] *R (on the application of Burke) v The General Medical Council* [2005] EWCA Civ 1003.

[14] Ibid, [21]. On the victim test generally, see J Miles, 'Standing under the Human Rights Act 1998: Theories of Rights Enforcement and the Nature of Public Adjudication' (2000) 59 *Cambridge Law Journal* 133; J Marriott and D Nicol, 'The Human Rights Act, Representative Standing and the Victim Culture' [1998] *European Human Rights Law Review* 730.

[15] *Aston Cantlow* (n 5). However, there has been criticism of this conclusion. See H Davis, 'Public Authorities as "Victims" under the Human Rights Act' (2005) 64 *Cambridge Law Journal* 315.

[16] *R (on the application of Westminster City Council) v Mayor of London* [2002] EWHC (Admin) 2440, [96]. See further, Davis (n 15).

[17] *Aston Cantlow* (n 5).

2.2.2 Potential Victims

Potential victims are those who can produce reasonable and convincing evidence of the likelihood that a violation affecting him or her personally will occur.[18] Whilst this type of victim is also recognised in section 7 (those who claim that a public authority has acted, or proposes to act, in a way which is made unlawful by section 6(1)), claims under the HRA from potential victims are very rare. The most high-profile example to date has been the claim brought by the editor of *The Guardian* newspaper, and a well-known journalist, for a declaration that section 3 of the Treason Act 1848, when read in light of the HRA, did not apply to those advocating republicanism.[19] Articles had been published in *The Guardian* and copies sent to the Attorney General but no prosecution took place.

The House of Lords concluded that the claimants were victims, for the purposes of section 7, but that this claim was at the upper limit of what was possible. Lord Walker observed that sections 3 and 4 of the HRA were 'intended to promote and protect human rights in a practical way, not to be an instrument by which the courts can chivvy Parliament into spring-cleaning the statute book, perhaps to the detriment of more important legislation'.[20]

2.2.3 Indirect Victims

Indirect victims, usually close relatives of the direct victim, have victim status as they have either suffered damage as a result of violation of the rights of the direct victim or they have a valid personal interest in securing cessation of such violations.[21] In claims under the HRA, indirect victims have played an important role where the direct victim has died and a remedy is sought under Article 2 of the ECHR.[22]

2.2.4 Non-nationals and Those Living Outside the United Kingdom

Non-UK nationals living in the United Kingdom can be victims,[23] as can non-nationals living outside the UK.[24] In *Farrkhan*[25] it was conceded by the Secretary of State that the fact that an individual was neither a citizen of a Contracting State nor within the

---

[18] *The Christian Federation of Jehovah's Witnesses in France v France*, Application no 53430/99, 6 November 2001, ECtHR.

[19] *R (Rusbridger) v Attorney General* [2003] UKHL 38, [2004] 1 AC 357.

[20] Ibid, [61]. See also *Axa General Insurance Limited v The Lord Advocate* [2011] UKSC 46.

[21] *X and Z v Federal Republic of Germany*, Application no 3897/68, 5 February 1970, ECommHR.

[22] See eg *Chief Constable of Hertfordshire Police v Van Colle* [2008] UKHL 50, [2009] 1 AC 225; *R v Secretary of State for the Home Department, ex p Amin* [2003] UKHL 51, [2004] 1 AC 653; and *Rabone v Pennine Care NHS Foundation Trust* [2012] UKSC 2, [2012] 2 AC 72. In *Re E (A Child)* [2008] UKHL 66, [2009] 1 AC 536 the House of Lords observed that it would have been preferable if the child was also a claimant rather than her mother acting as the victim. See further J Varuhas, 'Liability under the Human Rights Act 1998: The Duty to Protect Life, Indirect Victims and Damages' (2012) 71 *Cambridge Law Journal* 263.

[23] *A v Secretary of State for the Home Department* [2004] UKHL 56, [2005] 2 AC 68.

[24] *R (on the application of Farrakhan) v Secretary of State for the Home Department* [2001] EWHC (Admin) 781, [2002] 3 WLR 481.

[25] Ibid.

territory of a Contracting State did not, of itself, preclude the application of the Convention. This was also accepted by the court without an examination of whether or not the concession was correctly made.[26] Similarly in *Singh*[27] the court proceeded on the assumption that the HRA applied even though the claimant was not a UK citizen and lived in India. The claimant had been refused entry clearance to join his adoptive parents in the United Kingdom. Chadwick LJ commented that the court had not been invited to consider the question of whether the Convention or the Act should be treated as having extra-territorial reach and 'should not be taken to have reached any conclusion on that question'.[28]

It is well established in ECtHR jurisprudence that the exclusion of a person from a State where members of his family are living might raise an issue under Article 8.[29] In relation to other Convention rights, the Court of Appeal accepted in *Farrakhan* that Strasbourg jurisprudence established that where the authorities of a State refuse entry to, or expel an alien from, its territory solely for the purpose of preventing the alien from exercising a Convention right within the territory, or by way of sanction for the exercise of a Convention right, the Convention would be directly engaged.[30] The Court went on actually to modify the Strasbourg test in this case, concluding that even though only one object of the exclusion of Mr Farrakhan was to prevent him exercising the right to freedom of expression, Article 10 was engaged.[31]

Outside of the immigration context, in *Al-Skeini*[32] the Divisional Court found it was no obstacle to a claim under the HRA that the son, who had died in a British military prison in Iraq, and his father, who had brought the claim, had no connection with the United Kingdom 'other than as residents of a province in a foreign country where the United Kingdom is an occupying power … and other than, in the case of the son, as a prisoner in a British military prison'.[33] The court continued:

> It is hard to say that the Act was designed to bring rights home in their case, for the United Kingdom is in no way their home: in their case, it is not their rights which are brought home, but the United Kingdom's responsibilities. Even so, we would be reluctant to distinguish their case from that of a British resident or national where Convention rights are interfered with in a narrow extra-territorial context interpreted by Strasbourg jurisprudence (itself founded in concepts of international law) to be within a state party's essentially territorial jurisdiction under Art 1.[34]

2.2.5 Representative Bodies

Trade unions or other representative bodies which have an interest on behalf of their

---

[26] Ibid, [34].

[27] *Singh v Entry Clearance Officer New Delhi* [2004] EWCA Civ 1975, [2005] QB 608.

[28] Ibid, [94].

[29] *Abdulaziz v United Kingdom* (1985) 7 EHRR 471 as cited in *Farrakhan* (n 24), [35].

[30] *Farrakhan* (n 24), [55] in reliance upon *Agee v United Kingdom* (1976) 7 D&R 164; *Swami Omkarananda and the Divine Light Zentrum v Switzerland* (1997) 25 D&R 105; *Piermont v France* (1995) 20 EHRR 301; *Adams and Benn v United Kingdom* (1997) 88A D&R 137.

[31] Ibid, [62].

[32] *R (Al-Skeini) v Secretary of State for Defence* [2007] UKHL 26, [2008] 1 AC 153.

[33] Ibid, [302].

[34] Ibid, [302].

members in general or are otherwise interested in the point at issue in the case but are not themselves directly affected are not 'victims' within the meaning of section 7 of the HRA.[35] For example, in *Director General of Fair Trading*[36] the Proprietary Association of Great Britain (PAGB) sought compensation for the costs it wasted when a trial was vacated as a result of an Article 6 independence and impartiality breach on the part of one member of a court and proceedings were begun again before a reconstituted court. The PAGB was an association of manufacturers, importers and suppliers of branded 'pharmacy only' and 'general sales list' medicines, vitamins and mineral supplements sold over the counter (without the need for a prescription) in the United Kingdom. It was alleged that the majority of PAGB members established and maintained a system of resale price maintenance in relation to the sale of such branded goods in the United Kingdom.

The Court of Appeal noted that it was possible under the Rules of the Restrictive Practices Court for the Court on application to order that some or all of the suppliers, retailers or trade associations who were before the Court be represented by such a representative respondent as the Court may direct.[37] It concluded that

> the rules provided a route by which the individual parties could have been formally represented by PAGB, but they chose not to follow that route. In those circumstances PAGB cannot be properly regarded as a victim for the purposes of making a claim under s 7(1) of the 1998 Act.[38]

However, a different conclusion was reached in relation to the Proprietary Articles Trade Association as it adduced evidence which showed that the proceedings in the Restrictive Practices Court were indeed determinative of its own civil rights and obligations because the outcome sought by the Director General rendered illegal an activity which constituted one of its constitutional objects and its primary practical objective.[39]

2.3 Loss of Victim Status

A person ceases to be a victim within the meaning of Article 34 of the ECHR if the respondent public authority has provided adequate redress and 'acknowledged, either expressly or in substance, the breach of the Convention'.[40] In *Rabone* it was argued that the parents of a young woman who had committed suicide whilst in the care of a hospital had lost their victim status in relation to their claim under Article 2 as they had settled a negligence claim with the NHS Trust concerned. The Supreme Court did not agree that acceptance of compensation in settlement of a domestic law cause of action arising from a death necessarily meant that the individual could no longer be regarded as victim for the purposes of an Article 2 claim arising from the same death.[41] Lord Dyson explained:

---

[35] *Director General of Fair Trading v Proprietary Association of Great Britain* [2001] EWCA Civ 1217, [2002] 1 WLR 269 in reliance upon *Hodgson v UK* (1987) 10 EHRR 503; *Ahmed v UK* (1995) 20 EHRR CD 72; *Bowman v UK* (1996) 21 EHRR CD 79.

[36] Ibid.

[37] Ibid, [12].

[38] Ibid, [19].

[39] Ibid, [9].

[40] *Rabone* [2012] UKSC 2, [2012] 2 AC 72 per Lord Dyson at [49].

[41] Ibid, [54].

[I]f (i) the domestic law claim that is settled was made by the same person as seeks to make an article 2 claim and (ii) the head of loss embraced by the settlement broadly covers the same ground as the loss which is the subject of the article 2 claim, then I would expect the ECtHR to say that, by settling the former, the claimant is to be taken to have renounced any claim to the latter.[42]

In the present case the Supreme Court concluded that in settling the negligence claim, the parents did not renounce an Article 2 claim as no such claim was available in English law, but could only be made under the HRA. Furthermore, it considered that adequate redress had not been made as no compensation had been made for the non-pecuniary damage suffered:

No decision of the ECtHR has been cited to us which supports the surprising proposition that the compensation that has been paid in respect of the estate's losses would be considered by the court to be adequate redress in respect of the personal losses of Mr and Mrs Rabone.[43]

Whilst it was not necessary to do so, the question of acknowledgement was also considered. The Supreme Court found that there was no express acknowledgement of a breach of Article 2 but it did find an acknowledgement in substance: '[T]he trust admitted that they had negligently caused Melanie's death and they paid compensation to reflect that admission. There is a considerable degree of overlap between the claim in negligence and the article 2 claim.'[44]

An individual may remain a victim within the meaning of the HRA even if he or she has succeeded in proceedings before the ECtHR and received compensation. In *McKerr*[45] a son brought proceedings in the ECtHR in 1993 questioning why his father had been killed by agents of the state. The Court made an award of compensation on the basis that, due to the violation of the procedural obligation, the son suffered feelings of frustration, distress and anxiety.[46] In 2002 he commenced proceedings under the HRA seeking an order to compel the Secretary of State for Northern Ireland to hold an effective investigation into the circumstances of his father's death. A majority of their Lordships rejected the government's argument that he lacked standing as a victim because he had already received 'just satisfaction' from the ECtHR. Lord Steyn noted that the procedural obligation remained unfulfilled as the state had never conducted a proper investigation: 'The compensation was plainly not intended by the ECtHR to be the price which, if paid, relieved the Government of its unfulfilled procedural obligation even in circumstances where such an obligation was still capable of being fulfilled.'[47]

2.4 An *actio popularis*?

Apart from the exception made for the Equality and Human Rights Commission, the HRA *actio popularis*, or 'action of the people in the public interest', remains impossible

---

[42] Ibid, [57].
[43] Ibid, [59].
[44] Ibid, [72].
[45] *McKerr v United Kingdom* (2002) 34 EHRR 20.
[46] Ibid.
[47] *In re McKerr* [2004] UKHL 12, [2004] 1 WLR 807, [43]. See also the comments of Lord Nicholls at [27].

and those who have tried have not succeeded. For example, the claimant in *Taylor*[48] argued that legislation, which had no effect on him, was incompatible with Convention rights. This was rejected by the Court of Appeal which held that it was not 'the intention of the HRA or the Convention' that members of the public should use these provisions if they are not adversely affected by them to change legislation 'because they consider that the legislation is incompatible with the Convention'. The only claimant to succeed with this type of claim has been Maya Evans, a peace activist, who claimed that the UK policy and practice in relation to the transfer to the Afghan authorities of suspected insurgents detained by UK armed forces in the course of operations in Afghanistan was incompatible with Article 3 of the ECHR.[49] However, her lack of victim status was not an issue only because the respondent Secretary of State for Defence did not contest it. The Court of Appeal observed:

> [T]he claim itself is brought in the public interest, with the benefit of public funding. It raises issues of real substance concerning the risk to transferees and, although the claimant's standing to bring it was at one time in issue, the point has not been pursued by the Secretary of State.[50]

By contrast, a judicial review claimant must only demonstrate a 'sufficient interest' in the matter to which the application relates.[51] Over the years this test has been liberalised by the courts to such an extent that a judicial review *actio popularis* is now effectively possible. As Beloff has observed:

> [T]he factors which the court now takes into account in deciding whether an applicant has standing are: (i) the merits of the application; (ii) the importance of maintaining the rule of law; (iii) the importance of the issue raised; (iv) the likely absence of any other responsible challenger; (v) the nature of the breach of duty against which relief is sought; and (vi) the expertise and experience of the applicant body.[52]

Claims for judicial review can be brought by organisations[53] or individuals. An example where human rights were at stake is the decision of the Administrative Court in *Hasan*.[54] Here the claimant, a Palestinian who lived in a village near Bethlehem, brought a claim for judicial review of the decision by the Secretary of State for Trade and Industry, to grant export licences for military items to be exported to Israel. The claimant argued that whilst he was not directly affected by any of the items exported during the two quarters in question, he could be affected by any items of military equipment exported to Israel, particularly if they were used for repression of Palestinians such as him. The Administrative Court concluded that the claimant:

---

[48] *Lancashire County Council v Taylor* [2005] EWCA Civ 284, [2005] HRLR 17.

[49] *R (Evans) v Secretary of State for Defence* [2010] EWHC 1445 (Admin).

[50] Ibid, [2].

[51] Supreme Court Act 1981 s 31(3).

[52] M Beloff, "Who—Whom? Unresolved Issues in Judicial Review" [2008] 20 *Denning Law Journal* 35, 38.

[53] The most cited example of an organisation successfully seeking judicial review is *R v Secretary of State, ex p World Development Movement* [1995] 1 WLR 386. More recent examples include *Cornwall Waste Forum St Dennis Branch v Secretary of State for Communities and Local Government* [2011] EWHC 2761 (Admin) and *R (Buglife: The Invertebrate Conservation Trust) v Medway Council* [2011] EWHC 746 (Admin).

[54] *R (Hasan) v Secretary of State for Trade and Industry* [2007] EWHC 2630 (Admin).

as a Palestinian living in a part of the occupied territories affected by Israel's attempts to contain attacks upon its citizens and so indirectly affected by any trade in military equipment to Israel is not a busybody and has ... sufficient interest to pursue this claim.[55]

To match developments in England and Wales, there has also been a liberalisation of the rules of standing to seek judicial review in Scotland. Claimants have to show that they are 'directly affected' and, until recently, this had been interpreted narrowly.[56] In its judgment in *Axa*,[57] the Supreme Court broadened the test, noting that standing could not be 'based on the concept of rights, but must be based on the concept of interests'.[58] Whilst Lord Hope still made a distinction between the mere busybody and those affected or having a reasonable concern, he also held that a 'personal interest need not be shown if the individual is acting in the public interest and can genuinely say that the issue directly affects the section of the public that he seeks to represent'.[59] Similarly, Lord Reed opened the way to the Scottish *actio popularis* by holding that the test was now one of sufficient interest and what was to be regarded as a sufficient interest depended upon the context and 'what will best serve the purposes of judicial review in that context'.[60]

---

3. The Burden of Convention Rights: Public Authorities

Similar to the benefit of Convention rights, the burden of Convention rights closely reflects the position before the ECtHR. Section 6(1) provides that it is unlawful for a 'public authority' to act in a way that is incompatible with a Convention right. No comprehensive definition of public authority is provided in the HRA, although section 6(3) provides that 'public authority' includes: (a) a court or tribunal, and (b) any person certain of whose functions are functions of a public nature. It also provides that 'public authority' does not include either House of Parliament or a person exercising functions in connection with proceedings in Parliament although Parliament does not include the House of Lords in its judicial capacity.[61] Furthermore, in relation to those exercising public functions, section 6(5) makes clear that a person is not a public authority by virtue only of subsection (3)(b) if the nature of the act is private.[62]

Section 6 of the HRA has in practice created three classes of respondent that are obliged to act compatibly with Convention rights in different ways. The first are known as 'core

---

[55] Ibid, [8]. His claim eventually failed.
[56] Rule 58.8.(2) Rules of the Court of Session 1994 and *D & J Nicol v Dundee Harbour Trustee* 1915 SC (HL) 7.
[57] *Axa General Insurance Limited v The Lord Advocate* [2011] UKSC 46, [2012] 1 AC 868.
[58] Ibid, [62] per Lord Hope.
[59] Ibid, [63].
[60] Ibid, [170]. See further J Miles, 'Standing under the Human Rights Act 1998: Theories of Rights Enforcement and the Nature of Public Law Adjudication' (2000) 59 *Cambridge Law Journal* 133; Marriott and Nicol (n 14).
[61] S 6(4).
[62] See generally D Oliver, 'The Frontiers of the State: Public Authorities and Functions under the Human Rights Act' [2000] *Public Law* 476.

public authorities'. All of the functions exercised by such bodies are public functions and they are bound by section 6 to act compatibly with Convention rights in respect of all of their acts. The second are usually known as 'hybrid public authorities'. These exercise both public and private functions, but are only bound by section 6 to act compatibly with Convention rights in respect of their public functions. The third type of body are private bodies which are indirectly bound to act compatibly with Convention rights essentially via the obligation of the courts, as public authorities, under section 6. All three types of respondent are discussed in the following paragraphs.

4. Core Public Authorities

4.1 Definition

A core public authority is required to act compatibly with Convention rights in every-thing it does regardless of whether it is an act of a private or public nature.[63] However, the expression 'public authority' is not defined in the HRA in any detail, nor is it an expression in English law with a specific recognised meaning.[64] In determining the meaning of 'public authority', it has been held that the broad purpose to be achieved by the HRA is key.

> The purpose is that those bodies for whose acts the state is answerable before the European Court of Human Rights shall in future be subject to a domestic law obligation not to act incompatibly with Convention rights. If they act in breach of this legal obligation victims may henceforth obtain redress from the courts of this country.[65]

In other words, a purposive construction of section 6 indicates that 'the essential char-acteristic of a public authority is that it carries out a function of government which would engage the responsibility of the United Kingdom before the Strasbourg organs'.[66]

It has also been held that the reference to non-governmental organisations in Article 34 of the ECHR provides an important guide as to the nature of those persons who, for the purposes of section 6(1) of the Act and the remedial scheme which flows from it, are to be taken to be public authorities.

> Non-governmental organisations have the right of individual application to the European Court of Human Rights as victims if their Convention rights have been violated. If the scheme to give effect to Art 13 is to be followed through, they must be entitled to obtain a remedy for a violation of their Convention rights under s 7 in respect of acts made unlawful by s 6.[67]

To this end it has been held that a distinction should be drawn between those persons

---

[63] *Aston Cantlow* (n 5), per Lord Nicholls at [7] and per Lord Hobhouse at [85].
[64] Ibid per Lord Nicholls at [6].
[65] Ibid. See also the comments of Lord Hope at [44].
[66] Ibid per Lord Rodger at [160].
[67] Ibid per Lord Hope at [46].

who, in Convention terms, are governmental organisations on the one hand and those who are non-governmental organisations on the other.

> A person who would be regarded as a non-governmental organisation within the meaning of Art 34 ought not to be regarded as a 'core' public authority for the purposes of s 6. That would deprive it of the rights enjoyed by the victims of acts which are incompatible with Convention rights that are made unlawful by s 6(1).[68]

As the House of Lords pointed out in *Aston Cantlow*,[69] the Convention institutions have developed their own jurisprudence as to the meaning which is to be given to the expression 'non-governmental organisation' in Article 34.[70] Indeed, in the opinion of their Lordships, this jurisprudence was far more relevant than the decided cases on the amenability of bodies to judicial review. Such cases

> have been made for purposes which have nothing to do with the liability of the state in international law. They cannot be regarded as determinative of a body's membership of the class of 'core' public authorities ... [n]or can they be regarded as determinative of whether a body falls within the 'hybrid' class.[71]

Similar observations were made by Lord Hope in relation to the concept of 'emanation of the state' in EU law.[72] However, in some instances it is possible that the judicial review and EU case law may provide some assistance in determining what does and does not constitute a function of a public nature as discussed in the paragraphs below. Indeed, in *Beer*,[73] which was decided after *Aston Cantlow*, the Court of Appeal held that the test for a functional public authority and for amenability to judicial review were, for practical purposes, the same.[74]

Beyond this, some criteria have been specified to assist in identification, such as: the possession of special powers; democratic accountability; public funding in whole or in part; an obligation to act only in the public interest; a statutory constitution;[75] association with the process of either central or local government; statutory powers exercisable against the general public or a class or group; and surrender or delegation of state powers to it.[76]

---

[68] Ibid, [47].

[69] Ibid.

[70] See eg *Rothenthurm Commune v Switzerland, Commission*, 14 December 1988; *Ayuntamiento de Mula v Spain*, Court, 1 February 2001; *Holy Monasteries v Greece* (1995) 20 EHRR 1; *Hautanemi v Sweden* (1996) 22 EHRR CD 156. All cited by Lord Hope in *Aston Cantlow* (n 5).

[71] *Aston Cantlow* (n 5), per Lord Hope at [52] and per Lord Hobhouse at [87]. Lord Scott agreed with Lord Hope. Lords Nicholls and Rodger did not mention judicial review cases, indicating that they regarded these as irrelevant to resolving the question. See also *R (on the application of Heather) v Leonard Cheshire Foundation* [2002] EWCA Civ 366, [2002] ACD 271, [36]. But *cf Donoghue v Poplar Housing & Regeneration Community Association Ltd & Anor* [2001] EWCA Civ 595, [65] and *Hampshire County Council v Beer* [2003] EWCA Civ 1056, [2004] 1 WLR 233, [29].

[72] *Aston Cantlow* (n 5), [53]–[55] per Lord Hope, citing *Johnston v Chief Constable of the Royal Ulster Constabulary* [1986] ECR 1651. See also the comments of Lord Hobhouse at [86].

[73] *Hampshire County Council v Beer* [2003] EWCA Civ 1056, [2004] 1 WLR 233.

[74] Ibid, [14].

[75] The previous five criteria were cited by Lord Nicholls in *Aston Cantlow* (n 5), [7].

[76] The previous two criteria were cited by Lord Hope in *Aston Cantlow* (n 5), [59] and [61].

4.2 Courts and Tribunals

Section 6(3)(a) includes courts and tribunals within the definition of public authority, reflecting the fact that if, in complying with and applying the municipal law, the judiciary

> do not provide an outcome which is compliant with the rights of victims under the Convention, for example, by failing to recognise a right or grant an adequate remedy, the State is in breach of its Convention obligations and should change its municipal law.[77]

In criminal trials, it has been confirmed that it is appropriate to treat the court made up of both judge and jury as the public authority for the purposes of Article 6, and it is not possible to treat the jury as a separate entity.[78]

Requiring courts and tribunals to act compatibly with Convention rights has had a number of unforeseen consequences, and has given courts and tribunals a role where previously they had none. For example, in *Porter*[79] the House of Lords concluded that in exercising its discretion and determining whether an injunction for breach of planning control should be granted under section 187B of the Town and Country Planning Act 1990, the court was bound by section 6 of the HRA to act compatibly with Convention rights: '[W]hen asked to grant injunctive relief under s 187B the court must consider whether, on the facts of the case, such relief is proportionate in the Convention sense, and grant relief only if it judges it to be so.'[80]

Their Lordships appreciated that the new landscape of the HRA required a different perspective.[81]

> [I]t is not for the court to act merely as a rubber stamp to endorse the decision of the local planning authority to stop the user by a particular defendant in breach of planning control. Moreover the court is as well placed as the local planning authority to decide whether the considerations relating to the human factor outweigh purely planning considerations; the weight to be attached to the personal circumstances of a defendant in deciding whether a coercive order should be made against him is a task which is constantly performed by the courts.[82]

4.3 Parliament

As outlined above, section 6(3) also provides that either House of Parliament or a person exercising functions in connection with proceedings in Parliament is not a public authority within the meaning of the HRA. It is therefore not possible to bring proceedings under the HRA for a failure to legislate or for a failure to introduce legislation. This is also made clear in section 6(6), which provides that whilst an 'act' includes a failure to act, it does not include a failure to introduce in or lay before Parliament a proposal for legislation, or a failure to make any primary legislation or remedial order.

---

[77] *Wilson v Secretary of State for Trade and Industry* [2003] UKHL 40, [2003] 3 WLR 568 per Lord Hobhouse at [131].
[78] *R v Mushtaq* [2005] UKHL 25, [2005] 1 WLR 1513.
[79] *South Buckinghamshire District Council v Porter* [2003] UKHL 26, [2003] 2 AC 558.
[80] Ibid per Lord Bingham at [37].
[81] Ibid per Lord Steyn at [58].
[82] Ibid per Lord Clyde at [86].

The question arose in *Re S*,[83] where the principle contention was that the incompatibility with Articles 8 and 6 lay in the absence from the Children Act 1989 of an adequate remedy if a local authority failed to discharge its parental responsibilities properly and, as a direct result, the rights of the child or his parents were violated. The House of Lords concluded that the failure to provide a young child with an effective remedy in this situation did not mean that the Children Act was incompatible with Article 8: '[F]ailure to provide a remedy for a breach of Article 8 is not itself a breach of Article 8.'[84]

With respect to Article 6, their Lordships continued this line of reasoning, noting that the alleged Convention violation consisted of a failure to provide access to a court.

> The absence of such provision means that English law may be incompatible with Article 6(1). The United Kingdom may be in breach of its treaty obligations regarding this article. But the absence of such provision from a particular statute does not, in itself, mean that the statute is incompatible with Article 6(1). Rather, this signifies at most the existence of a lacuna in the statute.[85]

4.4 Which Core Public Authority is Responsible?

An issue which has arisen in a number of cases where more than one public authority is involved is the question of which particular core public authority should take responsibility for the violation of Convention rights. For example, *Noorkoiv*[86] concerned an individual serving an automatic life sentence. Although his tariff period expired on 21 April 2001, it was not until 22 June 2001 that the Parole Board held a hearing. This was due to the Secretary of State's policy, and a shortage of judicially qualified chairmen and psychiatrists. The Secretary of State argued that the Parole Board lacked resources in terms of judges and psychiatrists because they had not been made available to it by other government departments. The Court of Appeal pointed out that if this matter were proceeding in Strasbourg, this argument would not avail the Secretary of State.[87] It concluded that, being a complaint about detention, it should be directed at the organ of the state actually responsible for the detention.

> Mr Noorkoiv was detained by the Secretary of State, who was implementing arrangements made by the state, including the slowness of consideration by the Board forced on it by the limited resources made available to it by the state. The Secretary of State cannot therefore excuse any failing under art 5(4) by pointing to policies adopted by other departments.[88]

---

[83] *Re S* [2002] UKHL 10, [2002] 2 WLR 720.

[84] Ibid per Lord Nicholls at [64].

[85] Ibid per Lord Nicholls at [85]. It was noted that the matter may be different regarding the inability of parents and children to challenge in court care decisions made by a local authority while a care order was in force. See [87].

[86] *R (on the application of Noorkoiv) v Secretary of State for the Home Department* [2002] EWCA Civ 770, [2002] 1 WLR 3284.

[87] Ibid, [28].

[88] Ibid, [30]. See also *R (K) v Camden and Islington Health Authority* [2001] EWCA Civ 240, [2002] QB 198. In *RA v Secretary of State for the Home Department,* Administrative Court, 30 July 2002, a similar case, the court held that damages were not therefore payable by the Secretary of State. In *R (Al-Jedda) v Secretary of State for Defence* [2007] UKHL 58, [2008] 1 AC 332 the House of Lords determined that the detention of the claimant was not attributable to the United Nations.

Similarly in K,[89] also an Article 5(4) case, the Administrative Court held that it was for the state to ensure speedy hearings of detained patients' applications: 'It is therefore irrelevant to question whether there has been an infringement of art 5.4 which government department or other public authority was at fault.'[90] However, the court did make clear the respective responsibilities of central government and the tribunals themselves, concluding that the responsibility for the delays was that of central government rather than of the regional chairmen or their staff.[91]

It may also be the case that one of the decision-makers cannot be challenged on Convention grounds. For example, in *Shetty*[92] proceedings were brought against the responsible medical officer (RMO) at a clinic and the Secretary of State in order to prevent the claimant being returned to prison. The Administrative Court found that the RMO's function and responsibility was to notify the Secretary of State if his patient no longer required treatment for a mental disorder. The court concluded that his duty was to exercise a clinical judgment and come to a clinical opinion. 'And assuming he has done it fairly and rationally he cannot be challenged on the grounds that the recommendation, if implemented by the Secretary of State, will or may involve a violation of his patient's Convention rights.'[93]

4.5 Application: Core Public Authorities

It is rare for questions about whether or not a body is a core public authority to arise in HRA litigation as usually the answer is obvious. It has been assumed that the meaning of core public authority includes bodies such as government ministers, coroners, NHS Trusts, police, prisons, local authorities, Legal Services Commission, General Medical Council, Police Complaints Authority, Parole Board, Commissioners of Customs and Excise, Securities and Futures Authority, Nursing and Midwifery Council, General Optical Council, General Dental Council, Child Support Agency and the Broadcasting Standards Commission.

Nevertheless, there have been a few claims where classification as a core public authority is not so obvious. In *Aston Cantlow*[94] the House of Lords concluded unanimously that parochial church councils were not core public authorities. Although the Church of England was found still to have special links with central government, it was found to be essentially a religious organisation.[95] 'It has regulatory functions within its own sphere, but it cannot be said to be part of government. The state has not surrendered or delegated any of its functions or powers to the Church.'[96] Furthermore, the constitution and functions of parochial church councils lent no support to the view that they should be characterised as governmental.

---

[89] *R (on the application of K) v Mental Health Review Tribunal* [2002] EWHC (Admin) 639.
[90] Ibid, [112].
[91] Ibid, [113].
[92] *R (on the application of R) v Shetty (Responsible Medical Officer)* [2003] EWHC (Admin) 3022.
[93] Ibid, [40]. *Cf R (on the application of B) v Responsible Medical Officer, Broadmoor Hospital* [2005] EWHC (Admin) 1936.
[94] *Aston Cantlow* (n 5).
[95] Ibid per Lord Nicholls at [13].
[96] Ibid per Lord Hope at [61].

The essential role of a parochial church council is to provide a formal means, prescribed by the Church of England, whereby ex officio and elected members of the local church promote the mission of the Church and discharge financial responsibilities in respect of their own parish church, including responsibilities regarding the maintenance of the fabric of the building. This smacks of a church body engaged in self-governance and promotion of its affairs. This is far removed from the type of body whose acts engage the responsibility of the state under the European Convention.[97]

It has also been held that housing associations, as a class, are not core public authorities[98] and that arbitrators are not public authorities as their jurisdiction springs from a private agreement.[99] However, if arbitration is compulsory, the nature of the arbitrator is more likely to be that of a public authority.[100] Adjudicators under the Housing Grants Construction and Regeneration Act 1996 have been held not to be public authorities[101] despite the fact that any construction agreement that does not contain adequate provision for adjudication is subjected to compulsory contract terms imposed by statute. The court reached its conclusion as it did not regard an adjudicator as a person before whom legal proceedings may be brought, and noted that his or her decision was not enforceable.[102] Furthermore, the adjudicator did not look like a tribunal to the court as he might be appointed once only and never appointed again:[103] 'Proceedings before an adjudicator are not legal proceedings. They are a process designed to avoid the need for legal proceedings.'[104]

---

5. Hybrid Public Authorities

5.1 Definition

Section 6(3)(b) provides that the obligations imposed by the HRA also extend to any person certain of whose functions are 'functions of a public nature'.[105] However, the extension only applies in respect of *public* functions, not if the nature of the act is private. This reflects the fact that there are many bodies which exercise both public and private functions.

In a modern developed state governmental functions extend far beyond maintenance of law and order and defence of the realm. Further, the manner in which wide ranging governmental

---

[97] Ibid, [14]. See also the comments of Lord Rodger at [152]–[157] and [166].
[98] *Donoghue* (n 71).
[99] *Austin Hall Building Ltd v Buckland Securities Ltd* [2001] BLR 272, [27].
[100] Ibid, [28].
[101] Ibid, [40].
[102] Ibid, [35].
[103] Ibid, [39].
[104] Ibid, [40].
[105] See, generally: Joint Committee on Human Rights, Seventh Report, 'The Meaning of Public Authority under the Human Rights Act' (2003–04 HL 39, HC 382); M Sunkin, 'Pushing Forward the Frontiers of Human Rights Protection: The Meaning of Public Authority under the Human Rights Act' [2004] *Public Law* 643; D Oliver, 'Functions of a Public Nature under the Human Rights Act' [2004] *Public Law* 329.

functions are discharged varies considerably. In the interests of efficiency and economy, and for other reasons, functions of a governmental nature are frequently discharged by non-governmental bodies.[106]

During the parliamentary debates, the Lord Chancellor gave the following examples:

Railtrack would fall into that category because it exercises public functions in its role as a safety regulator, but it is acting privately in its role as a property developer. A private security company would be exercising public functions in relation to the management or a contracted-out prison but would be acting privately when, for example, guarding commercial premises. Doctors in general practice would be public authorities in relation to their National Health Service functions, but not in relation to their private patients.[107]

In relation to such bodies, there must be a twofold assessment, first of the body's functions and secondly of the particular act in question,[108] and it is important to focus on the context in which the act occurs.[109] No further definition is given in the HRA as to the meaning of 'function of a public nature'. As for core public authorities, it has been suggested that the contrast being drawn is essentially between functions of a governmental nature and functions, or acts, which are not of that nature.[110] And, furthermore, that giving a generously wide scope to the expression 'public function' 'will further the statutory aim of promoting the observance of human rights values without depriving the bodies in question of the ability themselves to rely on Convention rights when necessary'.[111]

In YL[112] a majority of the House of Lords held that while authorities on judicial review can be helpful, section 6(3)(b) has a different rationale linked to the 'scope of State responsibility in Strasbourg'.[113] Relying on the judgment in Aston Cantlow, it confirmed that a broad test was appropriate as well as a factor-based approach.[114] In relation to the relevant factors, Lord Mance held that typical governmental functions included powers conferred and duties imposed or undertaken in the general public interest, 'in addition to special powers, democratic accountability, public funding in whole or in part, an obligation to act only in the public interest and a statutory constitution.'[115]

In the present case, the majority concluded that a private company providing care and accommodation, and then terminating that relationship with the resident in its home, was not exercising a function of a public nature. This decision was later reversed, in so

---

[106] Aston Cantlow (n 5), per Lord Nicholls at [9].

[107] HL Deb, vol 583, col 811 (24 November, 1997). In Cameron v Network Rail Infrastructure Ltd [2006] EWHC 1133, [2007] 1 WLR 163 the High Court held that Railtrack was not responsible for an accident as the responsibility for the maintenance of points and track on the railway network was not a public function.

[108] Aston Cantlow (n 5), per Lord Hobhouse at [85].

[109] R (Weaver) v London & Quadrant Housing Trust [2009] EWCA Civ 587, [2010] 1 WLR 363 per Elias LJ at [66].

[110] Ibid per Lord Nicholls at [10].

[111] Ibid, [11].

[112] YL v Birmingham City Council [2007] UKHL 27, [2008] 1 AC 95.

[113] Ibid per Lord Mance at [87].

[114] Ibid, [91]. See also Donoghue (n 71), [65]–[66].

[115] Ibid, per Lord Mance at [103]. This judgment has been the subject of considerable academic comment. See further: A Williams, 'A Fresh Perspective on Hybrid Public Authorities under the Human Rights Act 1998: Private Contractors, Rights-Stripping and "Chameleonic" Horizontal Effect' [2011] Public Law 139; S Choudhry, 'Children in "Care" after YL—The Ineffectiveness of Contract as a Means of Protecting the Vulnerable' [2013] Public Law 519; S Palmer, 'Public, Private and the Human Rights Act 1998: An Ideological Divide' (2007) 66 Cambridge Law Journal 559; J Landau, 'Functional Public Authorities after YL' [2007] Public Law 630.

far as it related to the provision of social care, by section 145 of the Health and Social Care Act 2008. Section 145(1) provides that a person who provides accommodation, together with nursing or personal care, in a care home for an individual under the relevant statutory provisions, is to be taken for the purposes of section 6(3)(b) to be exercising a function of a public nature when doing so.[116]

In other judgments criteria suggested to assist in deciding whether or not a function is public have included the extent to which, in carrying out the relevant function, the body is publicly funded;[117] is exercising statutory powers;[118] is taking the place of central government or local authorities; or is providing a public service.[119] Other factors include statutory authority for what is done and the extent of control over the function exercised by another body which is a public authority. The more closely the acts that could be of a private nature are enmeshed in the activities of a public body, the more likely they are to be public. However, it has also been held that the fact that the acts are supervised by a public regulatory body does not necessarily indicate that they are of a public nature.[120]

After considering the most important factors, it is desirable to step back and look at the situation as a whole.[121] Taking one factor as determinative appears problematic. For example, in *Donoghue*[122] the Court of Appeal held that the fact that a body performs an activity which otherwise a public body would be under a duty to perform cannot mean that such performance is necessarily a public function.

> A public body in order to perform its public duties can use the services of a private body. Section 6 should not be applied so that if a private body provides such services, the nature of the functions are inevitably public. If this were to be the position, then when a small hotel provides bed and breakfast accommodation as a temporary measure, at the request of a housing authority that is under a duty to provide that accommodation, the small hotel would be performing public functions and required to comply with the Human Rights Act 1998.[123]

In the view of the court, this was not what the HRA intended.

> The purpose of section 6(3)(b) is to deal with hybrid bodies which have both public and private functions. It is not to make a body, which does not have responsibilities to the public, a public body merely because it performs acts on behalf of a public body which would constitute public functions were such acts to be performed by the public body itself. An act can remain of a private nature even though it is performed because another body is under a public duty to ensure that that act is performed.[124]

Similarly in *Heather*[125] the Court of Appeal held that whilst the degree of public funding of the activities of an otherwise private body was certainly relevant as to the nature of the functions performed, by itself it was not determinative of whether the functions

---

[116] For an application of s 145, see *R (Chatting) v Viridian Housing* [2012] EWHC 3595 (Admin), [2013] HRLR 12 where it was held that s 145 does not apply if only accommodation, rather than 'care and accommodation' is being provided.

[117] *Heather* (n 71), [35].

[118] Ibid.

[119] The latter four were suggested by Lord Nicholls in *Aston Cantlow* (n 5), [12].

[120] The latter two were suggested in *Donoghue* (n 71), [65].

[121] Ibid, [66].

[122] Ibid.

[123] Ibid, [58].

[124] Ibid, [59].

[125] *Heather* (n 71).

were public or private.[126] It has also been held that the fact that a body is a charity or is conducted not for profit means that it is likely to be motivated in performing its activities by what it perceives to be in the public interest. However, this does not point to the body being a public authority. In addition, even if such a body performs functions that would be considered to be of a public nature if performed by a public body, nevertheless such acts may remain of a private nature.[127]

Finally, it is important to note that unlike a core public authority, hybrid public authorities are not absolutely disabled from having Convention rights.[128]

5.2 Ensuring HRA Protection when Contracting Out

The provision of accommodation in a care home pursuant to section 21 of the National Assistance Act 1948 by a local authority is a public function. Making arrangements for the accommodation to be provided by a private sector provider is also a public function of the local authority. However, if a body which is a charity provides accommodation to those to whom the authority owes a duty under section 21 in accordance with an arrangement under section 26 of the National Assistance Act 1948, it does not follow that the charity is performing a public function.[129] Nevertheless, the courts have been careful to ensure that this does not thereby leave potential victims of Convention rights breaches in a vacuum.

> If this were a situation where a local authority could divest itself of its art 8 obligations by contracting out to a voluntary sector provider its obligations under s 21 of the 1948 Act, then there would be a responsibility on the court to approach the interpretation of s 6(3)(b) in a way which ensures, so far as this is possible, that the rights under art 8 of persons in the position of the appellants are protected.[130]

So far as protection is concerned, the Court of Appeal pointed out in *Heather*[131] that the local authority contracting out its care obligations under section 21 of the National Assistance Act 1948 remained under an obligation under section 21 and retained an obligation under Article 8 to those being cared for. In addition, residents of the care home had contractual rights against the private sector provider.[132] It also pointed out that if the arrangements which the local authorities had made with the private sector provider had been made after the HRA came into force, then it would arguably be possible for a resident to require the local authority to enter into a contract with its provider which fully protected the residents' Article 8 rights, and if this was done it would provide additional protection.

---

[126] Ibid, [35]. See further P Craig, 'Contracting Out, the Human Rights Act, and the Scope of Judicial Review' (2002) 118 *Law Quarterly Review* 551; M McDermont, 'The Elusive Nature of the "Public Function": Poplar Housing and Regeneration Community Association v Donoghue' (2003) 66 *Modern Law Review* 113; J Morgan, 'The Alchemists' Search for the Philosophers' Stone: The Status of Registered Social Landlords under the Human Rights Act' (2003) 66 *Modern Law Review* 700.

[127] *Donoghue* (n 71), [65].

[128] *Aston Cantlow* (n 5), per Lord Nicholls at [11].

[129] *Heather* (n 71), [15] and *YL* (n 112).

[130] *Heather* (n 71), [33].

[131] Ibid.

[132] Ibid.

Local authorities who rely on s 26 to make new arrangements should bear this in mind in the contract which they make with the providers. Then not only could the local authority rely on the contract, but possibly the resident could do so as a person for whose benefit the contract was made.[133]

In *Haggerty*,[134] obviously following this advice, the claimant residents of a private nursing home sought to argue that the decision by St Helens Council not to enter into a revised and more onerous arrangement with the company which operated the home led to the company deciding to close the home. The Administrative Court agreed that there were two ways which the Council's actions in relation to the contract with the company could be impugned on ECHR grounds. First, pursuant to section 3 of the HRA, to read and give effect to the Council's obligations under section 26 of the National Assistance Act 1948 so that the claimant's Convention rights were taken into account by the Council in performing its section 26 obligations.[135] Secondly, the Council was potentially liable under section 6 of the HRA, which made it unlawful for it to act incompatibly with a Convention right.[136] The court assumed, without deciding, that commercial dealings by a local authority with a provider of residential care were public in nature.[137] However, the court found no breach of Articles 2, 3 or 8 on the part of the Council and the application was dismissed.[138]

5.3 Application: Hybrid Public Authorities

The question of the meaning of 'function of a public nature' has arisen more often in HRA litigation than the meaning of core public authority. However, there are still very few cases. Those that have been decided are examined in the following paragraphs.

5.3.1 Enforcement of Chancel Repairs

Having determined in *Aston Cantlow*[139] that parochial church councils were not core public authorities, the House of Lords also considered whether such bodies were hybrid public authorities within the meaning of the HRA. The impugned act was the enforcement by the council of Mr and Mrs Wallbank's liability, as lay rectors, for the repair of the chancel of the church of St John the Baptist at Aston Cantlow. A majority of their Lordships concluded that the nature of the impugned act was private.

> If a parochial church council enters into a contract with a builder for the repair of the chancel arch, that could hardly be described as a public act. Likewise when a parochial church council enforces, in accordance with the provisions of the Chancel Repairs Act 1932, a burdensome incident attached to the ownership of certain pieces of land: there is nothing particularly 'public' about this. This is no more a public act than is the enforcement of a restrictive covenant of which church land has the benefit.[140]

---

[133] Ibid, [34].
[134] *R (on the application of Haggerty) v St Helens Council* [2003] EWHC (Admin) 803, [2003] ACD 304.
[135] Ibid, [23].
[136] Ibid, [24].
[137] Ibid, [25].
[138] See further Craig (n 126).
[139] *Aston Cantlow* (n 5).
[140] Ibid, per Lord Nicholls at [16]. See also the comments of Lord Hobhouse at [90] and Lord Rodger at

5.3.2 Seeking Possession of a Property

In *Donoghue*[141] the Court of Appeal considered whether Poplar Housing and Regeneration Community Association Ltd was exercising a public function in seeking possession on the expiry of an assured shorthold tenancy. The Association had been created as a housing association by the London Borough of Tower Hamlets in order to transfer to it a substantial proportion of the Council's housing stock. The Court took into account a number of factors, as outlined in the paragraphs above. However, it was particularly influenced by the closeness of the relationship between Tower Hamlets and Poplar. Poplar was created by Tower Hamlets to take a transfer of local authority housing stock; five of its board members were also members of Tower Hamlets; Poplar was subject to the guidance of Tower Hamlets as to the manner in which it acted towards the tenant. Furthermore, the tenant at the time of the transfer was a sitting tenant of Poplar and it was intended that she would be treated no better and no worse than if she remained a tenant of Tower Hamlets: 'While she remained a tenant, Poplar therefore stood in relation to her in very much the position previously occupied by Tower Hamlets.'[142]

The court concluded that while activities of housing associations need not involve the performance of public functions, in this case, in providing accommodation for the defendant and then seeking possession, the role of Poplar was so closely assimilated to that of Tower Hamlets that it was performing public and not private functions. Poplar was therefore a functional public authority although the court was careful to point out that this did not mean that all of its functions were public.[143]

Similarly in *Weaver*[144] the principle question before the Court of Appeal was whether, when terminating the tenancy of someone in social housing, the housing trust, a registered social landlord, was exercising a public function. A majority of the Court of Appeal concluded that it was. Elias LJ pointed out that there was significant reliance on public finance; a substantial public subsidy; the trust was operating in close harmony with local government; the provision of subsidised housing was governmental and could be described as providing a public service; it was acting in the public interest and had charitable objectives; it was subject to regulation 'to ensure that the objectives of government policy with respect to this vulnerable group in society are achieved'.[145] He concluded as follows:

> [T]he act of termination is so bound up with the provision of social housing that once the latter is seen, in the context of this particular body, as the exercise of a public function, then acts which are necessarily involved in the regulation of the function must also be public acts. The grant of a tenancy and its subsequent termination are part and parcel of determining who should be allowed to take advantage of this public benefit. This is not an act which is purely incidental or supplementary to the principal function'.[146]

---

[171]. Lord Rodger did note that when, in the course of his pastoral duties, a minister marries a couple in the parish church, he may be carrying out a governmental function in a broad sense and so may be regarded as a public authority for the purposes of the HRA. See [170].

[141] *Donoghue* (n 71).

[142] Ibid, [65].

[143] Ibid, [66]. It stated, at [65], that the act of providing accommodation for rent was not, without more, a public function.

[144] *R (Weaver) v London & Quadrant Housing Trust* [2009] EWCA Civ 587, [2010] 1 WLR 363.

[145] Ibid, [68]–[72].

[146] Ibid, [77].

5.3.3 Provision of Care and Accommodation

As discussed above, in a controversial judgment, a majority of the House of Lords determined in YL[147] that in providing care and accommodation for a resident of one of its care homes, and then terminating its agreement with the resident, a private company was not exercising a public function for the purposes of section 6(3)(b) of the HRA. Lord Scott held as follows:

> Southern Cross is a company carrying on a socially useful business for profit. It is neither a charity nor a philanthropist. It enters into private law contracts with the residents in its care homes and with the local authorities with whom it does business. It receives no public funding, enjoys no special statutory powers, and is at liberty to accept or reject residents as it chooses (subject, of course, to anti-discrimination legislation which affects everyone who offers a service to the public) and to charge whatever fees in its commercial judgment it thinks suitable. It is operating in a commercial market with commercial competitors.[148]

In his view, and that of the majority, the fees charged by the company and paid by local authorities or health authorities were for a service and there was no element of subsidy from public funds. 'It is simply carrying on its private business with a customer who happens to be a public authority.'[149] There were not special statutory powers over residents.[150] And the activities were not carried out pursuant to statutory duties and responsibilities imposed by public law.[151] Lord Mance did not regard the actual provision of care and accommodation for those unable to arrange it themselves as an inherently governmental function.[152] He held as follows:

> In providing care and accommodation, Southern Cross acts as a private, profit earning company. It is subject to close statutory regulation in the public interest. But so are many private occupations and businesses, with operations which may impact on members of the public in matters as diverse for example as life, health, privacy or financial well-being. Regulation by the State is no real pointer towards the person regulated being a state or governmental body or a person with a function of a public nature, if anything perhaps even the contrary. The private and commercial motivation behind Southern Cross's operations does in contrast point against treating Southern Cross as a person with a function of a public nature.[153]

In the minority, Lord Bingham and Baroness Hale concluded that the private company was exercising a public function. Taking into account the assumption of state responsibility for seeing the task performed; the public interest in having the task undertaken; public funding; the use of statutory coercive powers; and the risk of violation of Convention rights, Baroness Hale concluded that the company, in providing accommodation, health and social care for the claimant, was performing a function of a public nature.[154] The decision of the majority, in so far as it related to the provision of social care, was reversed by section 145 of the Health and Social Care Act 2008.

Nevertheless, a similar approach to the provision of care has been taken in the lower

---

[147] YL (n 112).
[148] Ibid, [26].
[149] Ibid, [27].
[150] Ibid, [28].
[151] Ibid, [30].
[152] Ibid, [115].
[153] Ibid, [116]. See also the judgment of Lord Neuberger at [147]–[153].
[154] Ibid, [66]–[73].

courts. In *Heather*[155] the Court of Appeal considered whether the Leonard Cheshire Foundation was exercising a public function in providing accommodation at one its care homes. The Foundation was the United Kingdom's leading voluntary sector provider of care and support services for the disabled. The majority of the residents at the home had been placed there by the social services departments of their local authority or by their health authority. In making the placements and providing the funding which the placements required, the authorities were exercising statutory powers. The court held that if a body like the Foundation provided accommodation to those to whom the authority owed a duty under section 21 of the National Assistance Act 1948, in accordance with an arrangement under section 26, it did not necessarily follow that the charity was performing a public function. Concluding that it was clearly not performing any public function, it took into account the fact that the degree of public funding was not determinative; that it was not standing in the shoes of the local authorities; and that, whilst there was statutory authority for the actions of the local authorities, the Foundation was not provided with any powers and was not exercising statutory powers in performing functions for the appellants.[156]

A different conclusion was reached in the *Partnerships in Care* case,[157] which concerned the decision of the managers of a private psychiatric hospital to change the focus of one of its wards. The claimant alleged that as a result she was denied the care and treatment appropriate to her condition. The Administrative Court held that the starting point was the statutory framework. In the present case the claimant came to be cared for by the private hospital as a result of her health authority making a contractual arrangement with the hospital pursuant to the National Health Service Act 1977. The hospital was registered as a mental nursing home under the provisions of Part II of the Registered Homes Act 1984 and it was subject to the Nursing Homes and Mental Nursing Homes Regulations 1984. Admission to the hospital, and the detention and treatment there of patients suffering from mental disorders, was governed by the Mental Health Act 1983.

The court found that the relationship between the managers of the hospital and the health authorities who had arranged for the hospital to provide care and treatment to patients with mental disorders was different from the relationship between the housing association and local authority in *Donoghue*.

> Accordingly, it may be that the statutory obligations of the Health Authorities ended when they arranged for the Defendant to provide care and treatment to patients with mental disorders, and that those statutory obligations, i.e. those of the Health Authorities, were not assumed by the defendant.[158]

However, in the view of the court, the question remained whether there were any other obligations imposed on the managers of the hospital which made the decision complained of an act of a public nature.[159] It observed that the decision to change the focus of the ward was an act of a public nature:

---

[155] *Heather* (n 71).
[156] Ibid, [35].
[157] *R (on the application of A) v Partnerships in Care Limited* [2002] 1 WLR 2610.
[158] Ibid, [23].
[159] Ibid.

But whether facilities can and should be provided, and adequate staff made available, to enable the treatment which the psychiatrists say should take place is another matter entirely. That is the subject of specific statutory underpinning directed at the hospital.[160]

And further concluded: '[T]he need for the hospital's patients to receive care and treatment which may result in their living in the community again is a matter of public concern and interest.'[161]

5.3.4 Denying Application to Participate in a Farmers' Market

In Beer[162] the Court of Appeal considered whether Hampshire Farmers' Markets Ltd was exercising a public function when it rejected an application by Mr Beer to be allowed to participate in the 2002 Farmers' Markets Programme. The Court of Appeal took into account a number of factors, including the fact that the power was being exercised in order to control the right of access to a public market;[163] the markets were held on town centre sites all owned by other local authorities;[164] the company owed its existence to Hampshire County Council and was set up using the Council's statutory powers;[165] the company stepped into the shoes of the Council in relation to these markets;[166] and from the date of incorporation of the company until the time when the company started operating the markets, the Council assisted the company in a number of respects.[167] The court concluded that the combined effect of these three features was sufficient to justify the conclusion that the decision was an exercise of a public function.

> HFML was not simply another private company that was established to run markets for profit. It was established by a local authority to take over on a non-profit basis the running of the markets that the authority had previously been running in the exercise of its statutory powers in what it considered to be the public interest.[168]

5.3.5 Regulation of Membership

RSPCA v Attorney General[169] concerned the RSPCA, a well-known charity devoted to the prevention of cruelty to animals. The case arose when the governing body of the charity, its council, adopted a policy which would enable it to exclude from membership those who had joined or were seeking to join the Society with the ulterior purpose of changing its policy against hunting with dogs. The Society brought charity proceedings seeking guidance. Some who had joined or were seeking to join for this ulterior purpose brought arguments under the HRA, in particular Article 11, freedom of association.

Lightman J in the Chancery Court concluded that the RSPCA was not a public

---

[160] Ibid, [24].
[161] Ibid, [25].
[162] Hampshire County Council v Beer [2003] EWCA Civ 1056, [2004] 1 WLR 233.
[163] Ibid, [30].
[164] Ibid, [32].
[165] Ibid, [36].
[166] Ibid, [37].
[167] Ibid, [38].
[168] Ibid, [40]. See further B Hough, 'Public Law Regulation of Markets and Fairs' [2005] Public Law 586.
[169] RSPCA v Attorney General [2001] 3 All ER 530.

authority and had no public functions within the meaning of section 6 of the HRA. Furthermore, it was noted that, in any event, the acts in question were private acts relating to its regulation of membership. Therefore, pursuant to section 6(5), even if it was possible to argue that the RSPCA was a functional public authority, these acts were private and therefore section 6(5) meant that the Society was not subject to the HRA in this instance.[170] Whilst Lightman J's conclusions are undoubtedly correct in this case, it should not be concluded that a charity can never be a public authority within the meaning of section 6 of the HRA. Many charities, eg the National Trust, perform what can only be described as public functions, and should be required to act compatibly with Convention rights when doing so.

5.3.6 Approving Minority Buy-outs

In *West*[171] the Court of Appeal concluded that decisions of the Business Conduct Committee of Lloyd's approving minority buy-outs in four syndicates in which the claimant was a member were not the exercise of a public function.

> The objectives of Lloyd's are wholly commercial. The nature of Lloyd's is not governmental, even in the broad sense of that expression. If any question arises as to the performance of any obligation on the part of the state to protect investors, it is the FSA which is the governmental organisation which will be answerable to the Strasbourg court, and not Lloyd's.[172]

It also referred to the observation of Lord Woolf in *Donoghue* that the fact that the acts were supervised by a public regulatory body did not necessarily indicate that they were of a public nature.[173]

---

6. Private Bodies

The HRA does not directly oblige private bodies to act compatibly with Convention rights. Section 6 of the HRA does not

> give the applicant any cause of action under the HRA against a respondent which is not a public authority. In that sense the HRA does not have the same full horizontal effect as between private individuals as it has between individuals and public authorities.[174]

However, an obligation to act compatibly with Convention rights can arise indirectly via the courts. There are two main routes by which the rights of private parties may be affected: (i) through the interpretation of primary legislation pursuant to section 3 of the HRA; and (ii) via the development of the common law.

---

[170] Ibid, [37].
[171] *R (on the application of West) v Lloyd's of London* [2004] EWCA Civ 506, [2004] 3 All ER 251.
[172] Ibid, [38].
[173] Ibid.
[174] *X v Y* [2004] EWCA Civ 662, [58].

It is also possible for the rights of private bodies to be affected by the activities of regulatory bodies which, whilst not considered to be courts or tribunals, are nevertheless public authorities within the meaning of the HRA. For example, in *Ford*[175] the claimant sought permission to quash a decision of the Press Complaints Commission. With no argument the Commission accepted that it was a public authority within the meaning of the HRA. In making its determinations it was therefore obliged to act compatibly with Articles 8 and 10. '[T]he sensitive task of the Commission is to consider not only the right to privacy but also the freedom of expression of the newspapers and then seek to balance them before reaching its conclusion.'[176]

6.1 Interpreting Primary Legislation in Accordance with Section 3 of the HRA

It is clear that the section 3 obligation to interpret primary legislation, so far as it is possible to do so, in a way which is compatible with Convention rights, applies in cases between private parties, thereby indirectly imposing an obligation to comply with Convention rights on private parties.

> [T]he interpretative duty imposed by s 3 applies to the same degree in legislation applying between private parties as it does in legislation which applies between public authorities and individuals. There is nothing in the HRA which, either expressly or by necessary implication, indicates a contrary intention. If the position were otherwise, the same statutory provision would require different interpretations depending on whether the defendant was a public authority or a private individual.[177]

Whilst the significance of extending the duty to act compatibly with Convention rights to private parties was not commented upon directly, the judgment of the House of Lords in *Ghaidan v Godin-Mendoza*[178] is an example of this development. Pursuant to paragraph 2 of Schedule 1 to the Rent Act 1977, on the death of a protected tenant of a dwelling-house, his or her surviving spouse, if then living in the house, became a statutory tenant by succession. Marriage was not essential for this purpose,[179] but this provision did not include persons in a same-sex relationship.[180] In the present case, in 1983 Wallwyn-James was granted an oral residential tenancy of a flat where he lived until his death in 2001 in a stable and monogamous homosexual relationship with Godin-Mendoza. The landlord brought proceedings claiming possession of the flat and

---

[175] *R (on the application of Ford) v The Press Complaints Commission* [2001] EWHC (Admin) 683, [2002] EMLR 5.

[176] Ibid, [23]. On the horizontal effect see generally: R Buxton, 'The Human Rights Act and Private Law' (2000) 116 *Law Quarterly Review* 48; HWR Wade, 'Horizons of Horizontality' (2000) 116 *Law Quarterly Review* 217; A Lester and D Pannick, 'The Impact of the Human Rights Act on Private Law: The Knight's Move' (2000) *Law Quarterly Review LQR* 380; N Bamforth, 'The True "Horizontal Effect" of the Human Rights Act 1998' (2001) 117 *Law Quarterly Review* 34; D Beyleveld and SD Pattinson, 'Horizontal Applicability and Horizontal Effect' (2002) 118 *Law Quarterly Review* 623; J Morgan, 'Questioning the "True Effect" of the Human Rights Act' (2002) 22 *Legal Studies* 259; I Hare, 'Verticality Challenged: Private Parties, Privacy and the Human Rights Act' [2001] *European Human Rights Law Review* 526; M Hunt, 'The "Horizontal Effect" of the Human Rights Act' [1998] *Public Law* 423.

[177] *X v Y* [2004] EWCA Civ 662.

[178] *Ghaidan v Godin-Mendoza* [2004] UKHL 30, [2004] 2 AC 557.

[179] Rent Act 1977 Sch 1, para 2(2).

[180] *Fitzpatrick v Sterling Housing Association Ltd* [2001] 1 AC 27.

the question was whether, subject to the HRA, Godin-Mendoza could succeed to the tenancy of the flat as the surviving spouse of Wallwyn-James within the meaning of paragraph 2 of Schedule 1 to the Rent Act 1977. A majority of their Lordships concluded that paragraph 2 of Schedule 1, construed without reference to section 3 of the HRA, violated Godin-Mendoza's Convention rights under Article 14 taken together with Article 8. Utilising section 3, the majority concluded that paragraph 2 should be read and given effect to as though the survivor of such a homosexual couple were the surviving spouse of the original tenant.

By contrast, in *X v Y*[181] the fact that section 3 of the HRA was being utilised in a case between private parties was of considerable comment. The Court of Appeal held that in the case of private employers under section 3, an employment tribunal, so far as it is possible to do so, must read and give effect to section 98 and the other relevant provisions in Part X of the Employment Rights Act 1996 in a way which is compatible with Articles 14 and 8.[182]

> In many cases if would be difficult to draw, let alone justify, a distinction between public authority and private employers. In the case of such a basic employment right there would normally be no sensible grounds for treating public and private employees differently in respect of unfair dismissal, especially in these times of widespread contracting out by public authorities to private contractors.[183]

In the present case the Court of Appeal noted that it was not immediately obvious how section 98 of the Employment Rights Act could be incompatible with or applied so as to violate Articles 8 and 14 and so attract the application of section 3.

> Considerations of fairness, the reasonable response of a reasonable employer, equity and substantial merits ought, when taken together, to be sufficiently flexible, without even minimum interpretative modification under s 3, to enable the employment tribunal to give effect to applicable Convention rights.[184]

It did, however, appreciate that there may be cases where the HRA point could make a difference to the reasoning of the tribunal and even to the final outcome of the claim for unfair dismissal.[185] Here there was no need to apply section 3 as the facts did not engage either Articles 8 or 14.[186]

6.2 The Development of the Common Law

Whilst the HRA does not create any new cause of action between private parties, 'if there is a relevant cause of action applicable, the court as a public authority must act compatibly with both parties' Convention rights'.[187] This is particularly the case with respect to the development of the common law, although it has been observed that the common law will only relatively rarely not be Convention-compliant.

---

[181] *X v Y* [2004] EWCA Civ 662.
[182] Ibid, [57].
[183] Ibid.
[184] Ibid, [59].
[185] Ibid.
[186] Ibid. See also *Copsey v WWB Devon Clays Ltd* [2005] EWCA Civ 932.
[187] *Campbell v MGN Ltd* [2004] UKHL 22, [2004] 2 AC 457 per Baroness Hale at [132].

One would normally expect the established common law to be consistent with the spirit of the Convention, and, given that the common law is always developing, one would expect it to develop along the same general lines as the Convention in any event.[188]

There have been a number of examples of the courts using Convention rights to develop the common law in cases between private parties. Most occur in the area of respect for private life in particular with respect to the tort of breach of confidence. It has been held that the

values embodied in Arts 8 and 10 are as much applicable in disputes between individuals or between an individual and a non-governmental body such as a newspaper as they are in disputes between individuals and a public authority.[189]

The impact of the respective Convention rights is clear:

Instead of the cause of action being based upon the duty of good faith applicable to confidential personal information and trade secrets alike, it focuses upon the protection of human autonomy and dignity—the right to control the dissemination of information about one's private life and the right to the esteem and respect of other people.[190]

In *Campbell*[191] a majority of the House of Lords concluded that, in relation to the fact that the claimant was receiving treatment at Narcotics Anonymous, the details of the treatment and the visual portrayal (photograph) of her leaving a specific meeting, the modified tort of breach of confidence had been made out and she was entitled to damages.[192]

The impact of the HRA has also been felt on the inherent jurisdiction of the High Court to restrain publicity. In *Re S*[193] the House of Lords considered the application for an injunction restraining the publication by newspapers of the identity of a defendant in a murder trial which had been intended to protect the privacy of her son who was not involved in the criminal proceedings. Their Lordships observed that the foundation of the jurisdiction to restrain publicity in such a case was now derived from Convention rights.[194] Balancing Articles 8 and 10, they concluded that the injunction should not be granted.[195]

---

[188] *Humberclyde Finance Group Limited v Hicks,* Chancery Division, 14 November 2001, [44].

[189] *Campbell v MGN Ltd* [2004] UKHL 22, [2004] 2 AC 457 per Lord Nicholls at [17].

[190] Ibid, per Lord Hoffmann at [51].

[191] Ibid.

[192] See also *Douglas v Hello! Ltd* [2001] QB 967; *Theakston v MGN Limited* [2002] EWHC (QB) 137; *B&C v A* [2002] EWCA Civ 337, [2002] 3 WLR 542; *Archer v Williams* [2003] EWHC (QB) 1670, [2003] EMLR 38. See further, A Young, 'Remedial and Substantive Horizontality: The Common Law and Douglas v Hello! Ltd' [2002] *Public Law* 232.

[193] *Re S (A Child) (Identification: Restrictions on Publication)* [2004] UKHL 47, [2005] 1 AC 593.

[194] Ibid, per Lord Steyn at [23].

[195] See also *Arscott v The Coal Authority* [2004] EWCA Civ 892, [2005] Env LR 6 concerning the impact of the HRA on the tort of nuisance. In *Lawrence v Pembrokeshire County Council* [2007] EWCA Civ 446, the Court of Appeal declined to modify the duty of care owed by investigating professionals to parents suspected of child abuse. Similarly in *Chief Constable of Hertfordshire v Van Colle* [2008] UKHL 50, [2009] 1 AC 225 the principle that police owed no common law duty of care, in the absence of special circumstances, was not modified as a result of the impact of the Convention rights. There is obviously much further scope for the common law to develop in the light of the HRA. See generally: R English and P Havers (eds), *An Introduction to Human Rights and the Common Law* (Oxford, Hart Publishing, 2000); C McIvor, 'Getting defensive about Police Negligence: The Hill Principle, the Human Rights Act 1998 and the House of Lords' (2010) 69 *Cambridge Law Journal* 133; G Phillipson and A Williams, 'Horizontal Effect and the Constitutional Constraint' (2011) 74 *Modern Law Review* 878; G Anthony, 'Article 6, Civil Rights and the Enduring Role of the Common Law' (2013) 19 *European Public Law* 75.

3

The 'Acts' to which the Human Rights Act Applies

1. Introduction

The HRA applies to the acts of public authorities[1] incompatible with Convention rights as well as their proposed acts[2] and failures to act.[3] However, whilst it may be possible for a victim to identify an act, proposed act or failure to act of a public authority which is incompatible with a Convention right, it may not be possible to bring a claim under the HRA. First, as discussed below, there is a limitation period. Second, section 6(2)(a) provides a defence for a public authority if, as the result of one or more provisions of primary legislation, it could not have acted differently. This section and section 6(2)(b) are considered in more detail in Chapter 5, which concerns primary legislation. Third, section 9 of the HRA provides that proceedings in respect of a judicial act may be brought only by appeal or judicial review.[4] In addition to these constraints, others have been developed by the courts covering: retrospective effect; extra-territorial effect; the application of the HRA to failures to act; and the inability of victims to use the HRA to pursue 'satellite litigation'. These restrictions on the type of act incompatible with Convention rights a claimant under the HRA can bring to court are the subject of this chapter.

2. Limitation Period

Section 7(1)(5) provides that proceedings must be brought within one year from the

---

[1] Section 6(1).
[2] Section 7(1).
[3] Section 6(6).
[4] See further, *Forresters Ketley v Brent* [2012] EWCA Civ 324.

date on which the act complained of took place. This can be extended if the court considers it equitable having regard to all the circumstances.[5] The court has a wide discretion in this respect and it has been held that it is appropriate to take into account factors of the type listed in section 33(3) of the Limitation Act 1980.

> These may include the length of and reasons for the delay in issuing the proceedings; the extent to which, having regard to the delay, the evidence in the case is or is likely to be less cogent than it would have been if the proceedings had been issued within the one year period; and the conduct of the public authority after the right of claim arose, including the extent (if any) to which it responded to requests reasonably made by the claimant for information for the purpose of ascertaining facts which are or might be relevant.[6]

One particular factor does not have a greater weight than others. A court should look at the matter broadly and attach such weight as is appropriate in each given case.[7]

3. Retrospective Effect

3.1 Generally

The HRA was passed on 9 November 1998 but did not come fully into force until 2 October 2000.[8] The only reference in the HRA to any possible retrospective effect it may have is contained in section 22(4), which provides as follows:

> [S]ection 7(1)(b) applies to proceedings brought by or at the instigation of a public authority whenever the act in question took place; but otherwise that subsection does not apply to an act taking place before the coming into force of that section.

Section 7(1)(b) allows a person who has claimed that a public authority has acted incompatibly with Convention rights to rely on the Convention rights in any legal proceedings.

With little guidance it has therefore been up to the courts to determine whether or not the HRA could apply to acts incompatible with Convention rights which took place before 2 October 2000. In the early days, this was an important question, particularly in criminal cases if an act allegedly incompatible with Convention rights had occurred at a trial prior to the HRA coming into force. However, as the years pass, the issue is

---

[5] However, this is subject to any rule imposing a stricter time limit in relation to the procedure in question. Therefore, if proceedings are brought by way of an application for judicial review, the time limit is three months.

[6] *Rabone v Pennine Care NHS Foundation Trust* [2012] UKSC 2, [2012] 2 AC 72, [75].

[7] The time limit was not extended in *Cameron v Network Rail Infrastructure Ltd* [2006] EWHC 1133 (QB), [2007] 1 WLR 163; *Dunn v Parole Board* [2008] EWCA Civ 374, [2009] 1 WLR 728; or *Bedford v Bedfordshire County Council* [2013] EWHC 1717 (QB), [2013] HRLR 33. The time limit was extended in *R (Cockburn) v Secretary of State for Health* [2011] EWHC 2095 (Admin); *Rabone v Pennine Care NHS Foundation Trust* [2012] UKSC 2, [2012] 2 AC 72; *Dobson v Thames Water Utilities* [2011] EWHC 3253 (TCC); and *D v Commissioner of Police of the Metropolis* [2012] EWHC 309 (QB).

[8] Only ss 18, 20, 21(5) and 22 came into force on the passing of the Act.

declining in importance. It has now been established that, apart from the exception created by section 22(4), the HRA does not apply to the acts of courts, tribunals or public authorities which took place prior to 2 October 2000.[9]

3.2 Criminal Proceedings

The House of Lords first considered the retrospective effect of the HRA in *Lambert*.[10] Lambert had been convicted of possession of a controlled drug with intent to supply contrary to the Misuse of Drugs Act 1971 in April 1999. The judge had directed the jury that in order to establish possession of a controlled drug, the prosecution merely had to prove that he had the bag in his possession and that the bag in fact contained a controlled drug. Thereafter, under section 28 of the Act, the burden was on the defendant to prove, on the balance of probabilities, that he did not know that the bag contained a controlled drug. This was a legal rather than an evidential burden of proof. Lambert appealed, relying on Article 6(2), and the Court of Appeal heard his appeal as if the HRA was in force. On appeal to the House of Lords, one certified question was whether a defendant whose trial took place before the coming into force of the HRA could rely, in the course of an appeal, on an alleged breach of his Convention rights by the trial court or an investigating or prosecuting authority.

Lords Slynn, Hope, Clyde and Hutton approached the question as one concerning the effect of section 22(4) of the HRA. By contrast, Lord Steyn based his dissenting judgment on the effect of section 6 of the HRA, stating that the effect of section 22(4) was 'obscure'.[11] To come within the exception provided by section 22(4) the victim must show that the proceedings where he wishes to rely on the Convention right are 'proceedings brought by or at the instigation of a public authority.' Lords Slynn, Clyde and Hutton concluded that 'proceedings brought by or at the instigation of a public authority' did not include an appeal from the decision of a court by an unsuccessful defendant.[12] Therefore, Lambert was not able to rely on Convention rights in respect of a conviction before the HRA came into force.

By contrast, Lord Hope concluded that proceedings brought by or at the instigation of a public authority included appeals:

> The appeal is treated by the Act as if it were part of the same legal proceedings as those brought by or at the instance of the public authority, irrespective of the person at whose instance the appeal is brought.[13]

---

[9] *R v Lambert* [2001] UKHL 37, [2002] 2 AC 545. See generally, A Rodger, 'A Time for Everything under the Law: Some Reflections on Retrospectivity' (2005) 121 *Law Quarterly Review* 57.

[10] Ibid. The issue actually first arose before their Lordships in *R v Director of Public Prosecutions, ex p Kebilene* [1999] 3 WLR 972. The HRA was not in force at the time of the trial or when the appeal went to the House of Lords. However, only Lord Steyn commented *obiter* on the question of retrospective effect, noting that the trial and appeal should be treated as part of the same process and, even if at the time of the trial the Act was not in force, the applicants on appeal would be entitled to rely on the HRA. Lords Slynn and Cooke agreed with this view.

[11] *Lambert* (n 9), [28].

[12] Their Lordships were bolstered in reaching this conclusion by the distinction made in s 7(6) between 'proceedings brought by or at the instigation of a public authority' and 'an appeal against the decision of a court or tribunal'.

[13] *Lambert* (n 9), [104]. See further the speech of Lord Steyn in *Kebilene* (n 10), with whom Lord Slynn and Lord Cooke agreed.

However, Lord Hope introduced a further stumbling block. In order for section 22(4) to apply, not only must the public authority have brought the proceedings, it must also have committed the act incompatible with Convention rights. Lord Hope therefore concluded that if the appellant's complaint had been that the prosecuting authority had breached the Convention, he would have been entitled to rely on the Convention right in his appeal. But the complaint here concerned not an act of the prosecuting authority but an act of the court, therefore the appellant was not so entitled.

Discovering the intention of Parliament in including section 22(4) in the HRA is difficult given that no comment was made on the section during the parliamentary debates on the Bill and no mention was made of it in *Rights Brought Home*. In *Lambert* Lord Hope suggested that section 22(4) was included to prevent a public authority seeking to rely on acts of its own which were lawful under the domestic law at the time when they were done but were incompatible with a Convention right. His Lordship saw it as a deliberate choice by Parliament in order to provide a person whose Convention rights had been violated with an effective remedy. Lord Clyde came closer to solving the mystery by pointing out the positions in New Zealand and Canada. In both jurisdictions it is not possible to appeal against a conviction occurring before the coming into force of the Bill of Rights or Charter on Bill of Rights[14] or Charter[15] grounds. Furthermore, it has also been established in Canada that no remedy under the Charter can be sought at trial in relation to an action of an executive or administrative kind, such as search, seizure, arrest or detention, which was taken before the date the Charter came into force.[16]

It is possible therefore that, taking into account the experience in other jurisdictions, in particular Canada, section 22(4) was inserted in order to clarify the position in this jurisdiction at the start and avoid a plethora of litigation over the issue of retrospective effect. Section 22(4) addresses two issues. First, as the majority of the House of Lords concluded in *Lambert*, it is not possible to use the HRA to challenge on appeal a conviction or adverse judgment obtained before 2 October 2000. As the majority pointed out, if it had been intended that section 22(4) did extend to an appeal, this would have been made clear in section 22(4), given that the distinction is made between proceedings brought by a public authority and an appeal in section 7(6). Secondly, in contrast to the position in Canada, under the HRA it *is* possible at trial to rely on a violation of a Convention right whenever it took place but only if the proceedings are brought by or at the instigation of a public authority. As the prime beneficiaries of section 22(4), the drafters would have had in mind criminal defendants facing trial after 2 October 2000 where it is sought to lead against them evidence obtained in violation of the HRA but prior to 2 October 2000.

If these assumptions concerning the intentions surrounding section 22(4) are correct, the majority of the House of Lords in *Lambert* reached the correct decision. But even though technically correct, there remains the question of whether it furthered the purpose for which the HRA was passed and afforded an effective remedy for a violation of a Convention right. The experiences of New Zealand and Canada are a little different to that of the United Kingdom. The HRA gives further effect to certain Convention rights contained in the ECHR—an international instrument which has imposed obligations in

---

[14] New Zealand Bill of Rights Act 1990. *Minto and Cuthbert v Police* (1990–92) NZBORR 208.
[15] Canadian Charter of Rights and Freedoms 1982. *R v Stevens* [1988] 1 SCR 1153.
[16] *R v James* [1988] 1 SCR 669. See further, Hogg, *Constitutional Law of Canada* (Toronto, Carswell, 1998) 663.

international law on the United Kingdom since 1953. Furthermore, it has been open to individuals in the United Kingdom to take their complaints concerning breach of the Convention to the ECtHR since 1966. Despite the House of Lords' conclusion that Mr Lambert could not have recourse to the HRA in his appeal, it remained open to Mr Lambert to take his case to the ECtHR. All of those in a similar position to Mr Lambert have this avenue for redress, and many who have been denied a remedy under the HRA due to problems of retrospective effect have already taken it.[17]

Concerns about giving the HRA retrospective effect are misplaced when it is considered that public authorities, including courts, in the United Kingdom have been bound in international law since 1953 to ensure that Convention rights are not breached. Similarly, concerns about 'great confusion and uncertainty'[18] or increasing the workload of the Court of Appeal and Criminal Cases Review Commission[19] are also misplaced when the HRA is perceived not as a change in the law but as an instrument which gives 'further effect' to the Convention rights which have been operative in the UK national legal system since 1953. In short, if international human rights law were afforded appropriate respect in the UK legal system prior to the HRA coming into force, none of these concerns should arise. From the perspective of a purposive construction, far preferable was the dissenting judgment of Lord Steyn, who considered the HRA in the broader framework of an Act which was undoubtedly intended 'to bring home' the adjudication of fundamental rights.[20] Finding the meaning of section 22(4) obscure, Lord Steyn based his decision on section 6 of the HRA, concluding simply that it is unlawful for an appellate court to uphold a conviction obtained in breach of a Convention right.[21]

The difficulties with the judgment of the majority in *Lambert* were highlighted when the House of Lords considered the question again almost five months later in *R v Kansal*.[22] Here a majority of their Lordships, including Lord Hope, held that *Lambert* was wrongly decided but should nevertheless be followed and could not be distinguished by reason of the fact that *Lambert* concerned the act of the trial judge whilst *Kansal* concerned the act of the prosecuting authority. Lord Lloyd concluded that the language of section 7(6) was not sufficiently clear to exclude by implication appeals in proceedings brought by or at the instigation of a public authority from the retrospective operation of section 22(4).[23] Similarly Lord Steyn held that the word 'proceedings' in section 22(4) covers both trials and appeals.[24] He also noted that the rationale of section 22(4) was recognition of the United Kingdom's international obligations under the ECHR. Finally, Lord Hope concluded that a defendant whose trial took place before the date of the coming into force of section 7(1)(b) was entitled to rely in an appeal after that date on an alleged breach of his Convention rights at the trial by the prosecutor.[25] He based his conclusion on a number of factors, including the judgment in *Kebilene*;[26]

---

[17] See eg *Kansal v United Kingdom*, 10 November 2004; *Massey v United Kingdom*, 16 November 2004; *Kolanis v United Kingdom*, 21 June 2005; *PM v United Kingdom*, 19 July 2005.
[18] *Lambert* (n 9), per Lord Slynn at [10].
[19] *R v Kansal* [2001] EWCA Crim 1260, [2001] 3 WLR 751.
[20] *Lambert* (n 9), [29].
[21] Ibid, [28].
[22] *R v Kansal* [2001] UKHL 62, [2001] 3 WLR 1562.
[23] Ibid, [15].
[24] Ibid, [26].
[25] Ibid, [75].
[26] Ibid, [52].

Articles 13 and 46 of the Convention, finding that these obligations have been binding on the United Kingdom in international law since ratification in 1951;[27] and the underlying policy that the state should no longer be able to take advantage in proceedings brought by or at the instigation of a public authority of its breach of its obligation not to act incompatibly with the Convention rights.[28]

But despite the doubts, *Lambert* has been followed, and in subsequent litigation its effects have been felt. For example, in *R v Allen*[29] the House of Lords held that as the trial and conviction took place before 2 October 2000, it was not possible to consider the argument under Article 6.[30] Nevertheless, as often occurs in such instances, given that the point was one of general importance, opinions were expressed on it. Similarly in *R v Benjafield*,[31] when determining the compatibility of confiscation orders made under the Criminal Justice Act 1988 and Drug Trafficking Act 1994, the House of Lords accepted that the HRA was not applicable as the trial had been held prior to 2 October 2000. Nevertheless, bearing in mind the importance of the points raised, consideration was given to the impact of the Convention.[32]

3.3 Civil Proceedings

It was suggested by Lord Hope in *Porter v Magill*[33] that the conclusion of the majority in *Lambert* did not apply to civil proceedings and he approached the respondent's Article 6 submissions on the assumption that they were entitled to rely on their Convention rights in the appeal irrespective of the fact that all the acts in question took place before 2 October 2000.[34] However, in *JA Pye (Oxford) Ltd*,[35] also a civil case, it was conceded that the HRA did not affect the appeal as the original decision was made before 2 October 2000. And in *Bellinger*,[36] another civil case, Lord Hope held that section 3 of the HRA was not retrospective and could not be applied to a marriage celebrated in 1981.[37]

Any remaining doubt that there was the prospect of retrospective effect in civil cases was put to rest by the House of Lords in *Macdonald*,[38] which concerned discriminatory treatment well before the HRA came into force. Lord Nicholls held in relation to section 22(4) that

---

[27] Ibid, [55].

[28] Ibid, [74]. See further D Beyleveld, R Kirkham and D Towndend, 'Which Presumption? A Critique of the House of Lords' Reasoning on Retrospectivity and the Human Rights Act' (2002) 22 *Legal Studies* 185.

[29] *R v Allen* [2001] UKHL 45, [2001] 4 All ER 768.

[30] Ibid, [23].

[31] *R v Benjafield* [2002] UKHL 2, [2003] 1 AC 1099.

[32] Ibid, per Lord Steyn at [5]. In *R v Lyons* [2002] UKHL 44, [2003] 1 AC 976 it was held that it made no difference that the ECtHR had found that the use made at the trial before 2 October 2000 rendered the trial unfair and in breach of Art 6. The Crown was entitled to rely after 2 October 2000 on the evidence in order to support the safety of the conviction and the court was entitled to hold the conviction safe in reliance on such evidence.

[33] *Porter v Magill* [2001] UKHL 67, [2002] 2 WLR 37.

[34] Lords Bingham, Steyn, Hobhouse and Scott agreed with Lord Hope on issues of fairness but did not comment on the issue of retrospective effect.

[35] *JA Pye (Oxford) Ltd v Graham* [2002] UKHL 30, [2002] 3 WLR 221.

[36] *Bellinger v Bellinger* [2003] UKHL 21, [2003] 2 AC 467.

[37] Ibid, [65]. See also *Jain v Trent Strategic Health Authority* [2009] UKHL 4, [2009] 1 AC 853.

[38] *Macdonald v Advocate General for Scotland* [2003] UKHL 34, [2004] 1 All ER 339.

[s]ubsequent steps in the proceedings, including an appeal, are all part of the proceedings. In the ordinary course they are not themselves separate proceedings for the purpose of s 22(4). To treat them as separate proceedings would lead to irrational and capricious results. It would mean that the law falling to be applied to a single set of proceedings would vary depending on the adventitious circumstance of which party was the appellant.[39]

3.4 The Application of Sections 3 and 4 of the Human Rights Act

In both criminal and civil proceedings, as discussed in the paragraphs above, it has been established that the HRA has no application to the acts of courts, tribunals or public authorities which took place prior to 2 October 2000 unless section 22(4) applies. However, the argument has also been made that the rules as to retrospective effect do not apply where sections 3 or 4 of the HRA are being applied. In *Offen*,[40] a very early HRA case, the question of retrospective effect did not even arise and the Court of Appeal concluded that section 3 of the HRA should be utilised to construe section 2 of the Crime (Sentences) Act 1997 in relation to sentences imposed well before 2 October 2000. '[S] 2 will not contravene convention rights if courts apply the section so that it does not result in offenders being sentenced to life imprisonment when they do not constitute a significant risk to the public.'[41]

However, a couple of years later in *Wilson*[42] the House of Lords held that, in general, the principle of interpretation in section 3 does not apply to causes of action accruing before the section came into force.

> The principle does not apply because to apply it in such cases, and thereby change the interpretation and effect of existing legislation, might well produce an unfair result for one party or the other. The Human Rights Act was not intended to have this effect.[43]

It is important to note that their Lordships held that section 3 does not apply 'in general'—meaning that in certain circumstances section 3 can apply to acts which took place prior to 2 October 2000. It was held by Lord Nicholls that the application of section 3 to pre-Act events depended upon the application of the principle identified by Staughton LJ in *Tunnicliffe*,[44] which is as follows:

> [T]he true principle is that Parliament is presumed not to have intended to alter the law applicable to past events and transactions in a manner which is unfair to those concerned in them, unless a contrary intention appears. It is not simply a question of classifying an enactment as retrospective or not retrospective. Rather it may well be a matter of degree—the greater the unfairness, the more it is to be expected that Parliament will make it clear if that is intended.

An example Lord Nicholls gave of where section 3 might apply was a post-Act criminal trial in respect of pre-Act happenings. 'The prosecution does not have an accrued or

---

[39] Ibid, [23]. See also *Wilson v Secretary of State for Trade and Industry* [2003] UKHL 40, [2003] 3 WLR 568.

[40] *R v Offen* [2001] 1 WLR 253.

[41] Ibid, [97].

[42] *Wilson* (n 39).

[43] Ibid, per Lord Nicholls at [20]. See also *Neil Martin Ltd v Revenue & Customs Commissioners* [2007] EWCA Civ 1041.

[44] *Secretary of State for Social Security v Tunnicliffe* [1991] 2 All ER 712, 724.

vested right in any relevant sense.'[45] Similarly Lord Hope held that accrued rights and the legal effects of past acts should not be altered by subsequent legislation.

[T]here is an important distinction to be made between legislation which affects transactions that have created rights and obligations which the parties seek to enforce against each other and legislation which affects transactions that have resulted in the bringing of proceedings in the public interest by a public authority.'[46]

In the present case it was concluded that Parliament could not have intended that application of section 3 should have the effect of altering the parties' existing rights and obligations under the Consumer Credit Act.

The case was held to be a 'typical example' of the situation where the legislation in question affects transactions that have 'created rights and obligations which the parties to it seek to enforce against each other'.[47] Furthermore, for the same reasons, no declaration of incompatibility could be made.

[I]t is only when a court is called upon to interpret legislation in accordance with s 3(1) that the court may proceed, where appropriate, to make a declaration of incompatibility. The court can make a declaration of incompatibility only where s 3 is available as an interpretative tool. That is not this case.[48]

It was also held that it was not possible to get around this conclusion by regarding the court as a public authority obliged to act compatibly with Convention rights.

The court's decision in these proceedings gives effect to the mandatory provisions of the Consumer Credit Act. An order giving effect to these provisions of primary legislation is excluded from the scope of s 6(1) by s 6(2)(a). Thus, reference to s 6(1) takes the matter no further forward.[49]

Applying these principles in *Milton Gate Investments Ltd*[50] the Chancery Division held that section 3 could be applied to sections 141 and 142 of the Law of Property Act 1925, even though the headleases and underleases had been entered into before 2 October 2000. This was because, in the view of the court, the earliest that any vested rights could be said to have arisen under clause 5(6) of the lease was the date of the service of the Notice. It was argued that the underleases were determined on 24 June 2002 as a result of the service of the Notice. The response was that clause 5(6) meant that unless the headlease came to an end as a result of the notice, the underleases continued.

[45] Ibid, per Lord Nicholls at [21].
[46] Ibid, [98]. See further D Mead, 'Rights, Relationships and Retrospectivity: The Impact of Convention Rights on Pre-existing Private Relationships Following *Wilson* and *Ghaidan*' [2005] *Public Law* 459.
[47] *Tunnicliffe* (n 44), per Lord Hope at [101].
[48] Ibid, per Lord Nicholls at [23].
[49] Ibid, per Lord Nicholls at [25]. See also the comments of Lord Hope at [88]–[102]; Lord Hobhouse at [126]–[135]; Lord Scott at [152]–[162]; Lord Rodger at [186]–[220]. In *Lloyds UDT Finance Ltd v Chartered Finance Trust Holdings plc* [2002] EWCA Civ 806, [2002] STC 956 the court concluded that s 3 of the HRA did not apply to the construction of s 35(2) of the Capital Allowances Act 1990 since the events took place in 1999; in *Laws v Society of Lloyd's* [2003] EWCA Civ 1887 the court concluded that s 3 had no application to s 14(3) of the Lloyd's Act, which would allow for a claim in damages for negligent misrepresentation, especially in litigation between the parties which had commenced before the HRA came into force; in *Holland (executor of Holland, deceased) v Inland Revenue Commissioners* [2003] STC (SCD) 43 it was held that s 3 did not apply to s 18 of the Inheritance Tax Act 1984 where the death occurred before 2 October 2000.
[50] *PW & Co v Milton Gate Investments Ltd* [2003] EWHC (Ch) 1994.

Unless and until clause 5(6) was operated, the rights and obligations of any of the parties as a result of the exercise were merely contingent, and not vested. ... If one approaches the question by reference to fairness, it does not appear to me to be unfair that the 1998 Act should be capable of being invoked to produce a result which the parties clearly intended at the time when they entered into their contracts, and was intended by the person who exercised the unilateral right which gives rise to the relevant issue.[51]

However, in *Hurst*[52] the House of Lords held that it was not possible to apply Article 2 of the ECHR using section 3 of the Human Rights Act to the Coroners Act 1988 as the death the subject of the inquest had occurred prior to 2 October 2000. Lord Brown held as follows:

The plain object of section 3 was to avoid where possible action by a public authority which would otherwise be unlawful under section 6. It applies only where there would otherwise be a breach of a Convention right under domestic law.[53]

3.5 Section 22(4) of the Human Rights Act

As already discussed, section 22(4) is the only section in the HRA in which reference is made to acts which took place before the coming into force of the HRA. It provides that section 7(1)(b) applies to proceedings brought by or at the instigation of a public authority whenever the act in question took place.

[I]t was appreciated that victims of a violation by the state of their Convention rights were already entitled to obtain a remedy in the European Court of Human Rights under Art 41 of the Convention. In that context it made sense for the provisions of s 6(1) to be made available for use defensively where proceedings are brought against the victim by or at the instigation of a public authority, whenever the violation took place.[54]

However, recourse to the section is rare and a number of limits have been placed on its use. It was established in *Lambert*[55] that the section did not apply to allow a claimant to raise on appeal a breach of a Convention right occurring at his trial prior to the date of the HRA coming into force. It has also been held that judicial review proceedings are not proceedings brought 'by or at the instigation of a public authority' within the meaning of the section nor is the holding of an inquest.[56]

When the provisions of s 7(3) are considered, they make it quite plain that, where a claim is brought in judicial review proceedings, it is the applicant for judicial review who is considered to be bringing the claim under s 7(1)(a).[57]

In *Preiss*[58] the section was used to allow an appeal against the Professional Conduct Committee (PCC) of the General Dental Council to take place. On 28 September 2000,

---

[51] Ibid, [114]–[115].
[52] *R (Hurst) v Commissioner of Police of the Metropolis* [2007] UKHL 13, [2007] 2 AC 189.
[53] Ibid, [44].
[54] *Wilson* (n 39), per Lord Hope at [90].
[55] *Lambert* (n 9).
[56] *Hurst* (n 52).
[57] *R (on the application of Abdelaziz) v London Borough of Haringey* [2001] EWCA Civ 803, [2001] 1 WLR 1485, [31].
[58] *Preiss v General Dental Council* [2001] UKPC 36, [2001] 1 WLR 1926.

before the HRA came into force, the PCC suspended the appellant's registration as a dentist for 12 months in consequence of a finding by them that he had been guilty of serious professional misconduct. In response to the argument that the HRA had no application, the Privy Council distinguished *Lambert* as here the appellant had the benefit of section 22(4).

> The General Dental Council is a public authority within the meaning of ss 6(1) and 7(1). It is the action of the council, in bringing disciplinary proceedings under a system allegedly not complying with Article 6.1, of which he complains. In Lambert there was no question of the prosecuting authority having acted unlawfully.[59]

It has also been held that proceedings for possession brought by a local authority qualify as proceedings brought by or at the instigation of a public authority, enabling the appellant in *O'Sullivan*[60] to rely on alleged Convention breaches by the local authority between 1983 and 1991.

3.6 Getting Around the Problem of Retrospective Effect

In many cases, although the HRA has not in law applied to the facts as the act in question occurred before 2 October 2000, the court has given consideration to the impact of the Convention.[61] It is also possible for counsel to invite the court to deal with the matter as if the HRA were applicable.[62] Beyond these options, considered in the following paragraphs are a few other techniques used to get the Convention rights issue before the court.

3.6.1 Ongoing Violation of Convention Rights

If the violation of Convention rights first occurred before 2 October 2000 but continued after that date, it may be considered an 'ongoing' violation and therefore within the scope of the HRA. For example, in *Bellinger*[63] the couple actually married in 1981 but, pursuant to section 11(c) of the Matrimonial Causes Act 1973, the marriage was void as the parties were not respectively male and female at the time. The House of Lords accepted that it could deal with the claim for a declaration of incompatibility as the non-recognition of their ability to marry continued to have adverse practical effects—the statute continued to prevent them from marrying each other.[64] Similarly in *Hooper*,[65] which concerned the denial to widowers of benefits that would have been payable to widows, the House of Lords held that in respect of acts or omissions before 2 October 2000 they could make no complaint. However, the submission that, in denying them the

---

[59] Ibid, per Lord Cooke.
[60] *Royal Borough of Kensington and Chelsea v O'Sullivan* [2003] EWCA Civ 371.
[61] See eg *Allen* (n 29) and *Benjafield* (n 31).
[62] See eg *R (McCann) v Crown Court at Manchester* [2002] UKHL 39, [2003] 1 AC 787; *Aston Cantlow and Wilmcote with Billesley Parochial Church Council v Wallbank* [2003] UKHL 37, [2004] 1 AC 546.
[63] *Bellinger* (n 36).
[64] Ibid, per Lord Nicholls at [50].
[65] *R (on the application of Hooper) v Secretary of State for Work and Pensions* [2005] UKHL 29, [2005] 1 WLR 1681.

benefits after that date, the Secretary of State had acted incompatibly with Convention rights was considered.[66]

It may also be the case in an immigration context that a decision to deport adhered to after the HRA came into force engages the operation of Act.[67] However, in *Mahmood*,[68] the court rejected the submission that the HRA applied as, although the decision to deport was made before 2 October 2000, his actual removal would be after 2 October 2000.

> [T]he court is required to review the legality of an administrative decision already made it is generally no part of its duty to go further and review also (as a distinct exercise) the legality of the decision-maker's carrying the decision into effect at some future date. ... It cannot be for the court, faced with a judicial review only of the earlier decision, in some way to police the considerations which might or might not impel the decision-maker to give effect to his decision.[69]

3.6.2 Investigations into Deaths Occurring before 2 October 2000

There are limits to the notion of an ongoing violation. In *McKerr*[70] the son of a man fatally shot in Northern Ireland in 1982 sought an order compelling the Secretary of State for Northern Ireland to hold an effective investigation into the circumstances of his father's death. The House of Lords concluded that the obligation to hold an investigation was an obligation triggered by the occurrence of a violent death and was consequential upon the death.

> If the death itself is not within the reach of s 6, because it occurred before the Act came into force, it would be surprising if s 6 applied to an obligation consequential upon the death. ... The event giving rise to the Art 2 obligation to investigate must have occurred post-Act.[71]

However, if a decision is made after 2 October 2000 to inquire into a death which occurred prior to that date, that inquiry must comply with the procedural obligations of Article 2. The procedural duty to investigate is now considered to be a freestanding duty, detachable from the substantive obligation. Taking into account the judgment of the ECtHR in *Šilih v Slovenia*,[72] in his judgment in *McCaughey*[73] Lord Phillips held as follows:

> The spectre that the House of Lords confronted in *McKerr* is shown to be a chimera. Just because there has been an historic failure to comply with the procedural obligation imposed by article 2 it does not follow that there is an obligation to satisfy that obligation now. Insofar as article 2 imposes any obligation, this is a new, free standing obligation that arises by reason of current events. The relevant event in these appeals is the fact that the Coroner is to hold an inquest into Martin McCaughey's and Dessie Grew's deaths. *Šilih* establishes that this event gives rise to a free standing obligation to ensure that the inquest satisfies the procedural requirements of article 2. That obligation is not premised on the need to explore

---

[66] Ibid, per Lord Hoffmann at [10].
[67] See eg *X v Secretary of State for the Home Department* [2001] 1 WLR 740, [9].
[68] *R v Secretary of State for the Home Department, ex p Mahmood* [2001] 1 WLR 840.
[69] Ibid, per Laws LJ at [29], with whom May LJ agreed.
[70] *In re McKerr* [2004] UKHL 12, [2004] 1 WLR 807.
[71] Ibid, per Lord Bingham at [22].
[72] *Šilih v Slovenia* (2009) 49 EHRR 996.
[73] *Re McCaughey* [2011] UKSC 20, [2012] 1 AC 725.

the possibility of unlawful state involvement in the death. The development of the law by the Strasbourg Court has accorded to the procedural obligation a more general objective than this, albeit that in the circumstances of these appeals state involvement is likely to be a critical area of investigation.[74]

3.6.3 The 'Act' Is Not Yet Complete

In *Aston Cantlow*[75] Lord Hope suggested that the HRA may be applicable as the unlawful act was the enforcement by the PCC of the liability for the cost of the repairs to the chancel. He considered the service of the notice to repair to be just the first step in the taking of proceedings under the Chancel Repairs Act 1932 to enforce the liability to repair. The final step in the process was the giving by the court of judgment for the responsible authority for 'such sums as appears to it to represent the cost of putting the chancel in proper repair'.[76] In Lord Hope's view, the proceedings to give effect to the notice were still on foot and in this situation there was no issue of retrospectivity.

> Mr and Mrs Wallbank do not need to rely on s 22(4). It is sufficient for their purpose to say that they wish to rely on their Convention right in the proceedings which the PCC are still taking against them with a view to having the notice enforced. This is something they are entitled to do under s 7(1)(b).[77]

Lord Hope also considered that the appeal here related to a preliminary issue only—the court had yet to reach the stage in the proceedings when effect could be given to the notice which the PCC had served.

> Section 7(6)(a) states that the expression 'legal proceedings' in s 7(1)(b) includes 'proceedings brought by or at the instigation of a public authority.' The preliminary issue has been examined as part of these proceedings.[78]

3.6.4 Utilising the Pre-HRA Position

Even if the HRA does not apply, if a decision-maker has indicated that he or she has taken the Convention into account, the correctness of the Convention conclusion can be examined by the court. For example, in *Montana*[79] the Court of Appeal held that as the Secretary of State had contended that his decision on registering a child as a British citizen complied with the Convention, it would be unrealistic for the court to determine the appeal on any other basis.[80]

> If the applicant is to have an effective remedy against the decision which is flawed because the decision maker has misdirected himself on the Convention which he himself says he took into account, it must surely be right to examine the substance of the argument.[81]

---

[74] Ibid, [61]. See also the observations of Lord Hope at [77] and Lord Brown at [101]. See further M Requa, 'Keeping Up with Strasbourg: Article 2 Obligations and Northern Ireland's Pending Inquests' [2012] *Public Law* 610.

[75] *Aston Cantlow* (n 62).

[76] Ibid, [31].

[77] Ibid, [31].

[78] Ibid, [32]. However, the eventual conclusion was that the PCC was not a public authority.

[79] *R (on the application of Montana) v Secretary of State for the Home Department* [2001] 1 WLR 552.

[80] Ibid, [14].

[81] *R v Home Secretary ex p Launder* [1997] 1 WLR 839, per Lord Hope at 867.

There is also the possibility that the court may adopt the pre-HRA position and use the Convention as an interpretative tool.

> [W]ords in a domestic statute should be construed in a manner which is consistent with Parliament's assumed intention to give effect to the UK's obligations under an international treaty or convention. ...But that is subject to the qualification that the words must be reasonably capable of bearing the meaning which it is sought to put upon them.[82]

In *Hurst*[83] Lord Brown held that even if a coroner had felt able to satisfy the international law obligations of the United Kingdom under Article 2 of the ECHR by reopening an inquest, his refusal to do so was not irrational or otherwise unlawful.[84] By contrast Lord Mance, agreeing with Baroness Hale, held that it was not entirely a matter for a discretionary decision-maker whether or not the 'values engaged by this country's international obligations' have any 'relevance or operate as any sort of guide'.[85] He held as follows:

> This country's international obligations in relation to a death potentially involving state responsibility appear to me to merit equivalent recognition at least as a relevant factor, even if the decision-maker were in the event to regard them as outweighed by other considerations.[86]

3.6.5 Modified Common Law

Finally, in *Al-Hasan*[87] the House of Lords applied the common law test for bias to prison disciplinary proceedings held in 1998 and 1999. What was not commented upon in the judgments given was that the test that was applied had been modified as a result of the HRA: 'The question is whether the fair-minded and informed observer, having considered the relevant facts, would concluded that there was a real possibility that the tribunal was biased.'[88]

Modifications to the common law as a result of the HRA appear to have escaped the problem of retrospective effect. Similarly in *R v H*[89] the defendant faced trial in 2001 for an offence contrary to section 47 of the Offences Against the Person Act 1861. His defence was that he was exercising his right as a parent to chastise his son. The issue was whether the trial judge and jury could take into account the Convention when determining the limits of this defence. The Court of Appeal concluded that this was possible.

> The common law is evolutionary, as was indicated in the case of *R v R*. The directions which it is proposed the judge should give to the jury ... seem to us to be an appropriate and accurate reflection of the current state of the common law in the light of the Strasbourg jurisprudence to which the English courts, by virtue of the Human Rights Act 1998, must now have regard.[90]

---

[82] *Malcolm v Mackenzie* [2004] EWCA Civ 1748, [2005] 1 WLR 1238, [26].
[83] *Hurst* (n 52).
[84] Ibid, [59].
[85] Ibid, [78].
[86] Ibid, [79].
[87] *R v Secretary of State for the Home Department, ex p Al-Hasan* [2005] UKHL 13, [2005] 1 WLR 688.
[88] Ibid, [30] per Lord Brown citing *Porter v Magill* (n 33) and *Lawal v Northern Spirit Ltd* [2003] UKHL 35, [2004] 1 All ER 187.
[89] *R v H* [2001] EWCA Crim 1024, [2002] 1 Cr App R 7.
[90] Ibid, [35].

4. Acts which Occur Outside of the United Kingdom: Extra-territorial Effect

There are two categories of acts which take place outside the territorial jurisdiction of the United Kingdom to which the HRA can apply. First, acts incompatible with Convention rights perpetrated by non-UK actors. Second, acts incompatible with Convention rights perpetrated by UK public authorities. There are also particular considerations affecting acts committed in dependencies of the Crown and British Overseas Territories.

4.1 Acts of Non-UK Actors

The label 'foreign cases' has been attached to cases in which it is not claimed that the state complained of has violated or will violate the applicant's Convention rights within its own territory but in which it is claimed that the conduct of a state in removing a person from its territory to another territory will lead to a violation of the person's Convention rights in that other territory.[91] Such cases represent an exception to the general rule that a state is only responsible for what goes on within its own territory or control. 'The Strasbourg court clearly regards them as exceptional.'[92] It is a little misleading to place this category of acts under the heading of extra-territorial effect as in addition to the act in breach of Convention rights taking place outside of UK territory, there is an act within UK territory consisting of the decision to deport or extradite an individual. Such a case involves 'an exercise of power by the state affecting a person physically present within its territory'.[93]

It has been established in both HRA and Strasbourg jurisprudence that whenever substantial grounds have been shown for believing that an individual would face a real risk of being subjected to treatment contrary to Article 3 if removed to another state, the responsibility of the contracting state to safeguard him or her against such treatment is engaged in the event of expulsion.[94] In *Ullah*[95] the House of Lords held that, in such cases, reliance may be placed on any Article of the Convention but it must be shown that there would be a flagrant denial or gross violation of the right whereby the right would be completely denied or nullified in the destination country.[96]

---

[91] See the explanation of Lord Bingham in *R (on the application of Ullah) v Special Adjudicator* [2004] UKHL 26, [2004] 2 AC 323, [9].

[92] *R (on the application of Razgar) v Secretary of State for the Home Department* [2004] UKHL 27, [2004] 2 AC 368, per Baroness Hale at [42].

[93] *Ullah* (n 91), per Lord Bingham at [9]. In *R (on the application of Al-Skeini) v Secretary of State for Defence* [2004] EWHC (Admin) 2911, [2005] 2 WLR 1401 the court noted that this exception to territorial limitation was not a true exception because the victim and act of the respondent state were located in the home territory; see [246].

[94] See eg *Soering v United Kingdom* (1989) 11 EHRR 439; *N v Secretary of State for the Home Department* [2005] UKHL 31, [2005] 2 AC 296.

[95] *Ullah* (n 91).

[96] Ibid, per Lord Bingham at [24]. See also *RB (Algeria) v Secretary of State for the Home Department* [2009] UKHL 10, [2010] 2 AC 110.

This principle has not just been applied in cases of deportation and extradition. In *Barnette*[97] the House of Lords concluded that Article 6 was capable of being applied to the enforcement in a Convention state of a judgment obtained in another state, whether or not the latter was an adherent to the Convention. However, such a jurisdiction was exceptional and a flagrant breach of the applicant's rights was required to trigger it. In the present case it concluded that the fugitive disentitlement doctrine under which the US Court of Appeals dismissed the appeal on the ground that the applicant was a fugitive from justice was not an arbitrary deprivation of a party's right to a hearing but was intended to be a means of securing proper obedience to the orders of the court. It could not be described as a flagrant denial of the applicant's Article 6 rights or a fundamental breach of Article 6.[98]

If the victim of the violation of Convention rights by non-UK actors is not within the territory of the United Kingdom, it has been held that no duty under the HRA is owed to him or her, although it is possible that a duty may be owed under the HRA to close relatives of the victim who are resident in the United Kingdom.[99] In *Abbasi*[100] the Court of Appeal held that the HRA did not afford any support to the contention that the Foreign Secretary owed Mr Abbasi, who was being held by US forces in Guantanamo Bay, Cuba, a duty to exercise diplomacy on his behalf.[101] Nevertheless, the court did conclude that judicial review may be available.

[T]he Foreign Office has discretion whether to exercise the right, which it undoubtedly has, to protect British citizens. It has indicated in the ways explained what a British citizen may expect of it. The expectations are limited and the discretion is a very wide one but there is no reason why its decision or inaction should not be reviewable if it can be shown that the same were irrational or contrary to legitimate expectation; but the court cannot enter the forbidden areas, including decisions affecting foreign policy.[102]

4.2 Acts of UK Public Authorities

The assumption that the HRA would have a limited impact on the activities of UK public authorities outside of the territorial jurisdiction of the United Kingdom has been proved false and increasingly this type of claim is being brought under the HRA. Taking account of the jurisprudence of the ECtHR, national courts have expanded the reach of the HRA to acts of UK public authorities abroad, in particular activities of the British

---

[97] *Barnette v United States* [2004] UKHL 35, [2004] 1 WLR 2241.

[98] Ibid, per Lord Carswell at [29]. See further A Briggs, 'Foreign Judgments and Human Rights' (2005) 121 *Law Quarterly Review* 185. It is also possible that the HRA applies to the return of a child to a foreign jurisdiction although in *Jomah v Attar* [2004] EWCA Civ 417 (pre the House of Lords' judgment in *Ullah*) the court rejected the argument that it would be in breach of Arts 6, 8 and 14 of the mother to return the child to Saudi Arabia. In any event, the court concluded that it would be open to an English judge to refuse to return the child if the evidence was that his welfare was likely to be compromised. 'Welfare is paramount: the fact that a return may or may not breach the art 6, 8, 9 or 14 rights of the abducting parent is secondary' [58].

[99] *R (on the application of Suresh) v Secretary of State for the Home Department* [2001] EWHC (Admin) 1028. See also *R (on the application of Abbasi) v Secretary of State for Foreign and Commonwealth Affairs* [2002] EWCA Civ 1598, [2003] UKHRR 76.

[100] *Abbasi*, Ibid.

[101] Ibid, [79].

[102] Ibid, [106]. See also *R (Al Rawi) v Secretary of State for Foreign and Commonwealth Affairs* [2006] EWCA Civ 1279, [2007] 2 WLR 1219.

armed forces. This is an area where there has been disagreement between UK courts and the ECtHR on the territorial reach of the ECHR which has a direct impact on the territorial reach of the HRA. The position before both courts is now the same, meaning that most claims under the HRA determined prior to the judgment of the ECtHR in *Al-Skeini v United Kingdom*[103] are no longer good authority in so far as they concern the extra-territorial effect of the HRA.[104] Those which remain relevant are discussed below.

4.2.1 Jurisdiction as Defined by the European Court of Human Rights

A majority of the House of Lords in *Al-Skeini*[105] held that the territorial scope of the obligations and rights created by sections 6 and 7 of the HRA was intended to be 'co-extensive' with the territorial scope of the obligations of the United Kingdom and the rights of victims under the ECHR. Therefore, in order to identify the territorial scope of a Convention right, it is necessary to consider how the ECtHR would consider the territorial scope of that particular Convention right.[106] Lord Rodger observed as follows:

> [S]ection 6 should be interpreted as applying not only when a public authority acts within the United Kingdom but also when it acts within the jurisdiction of the United Kingdom for purposes of article 1 of the Convention, but outside the territory of the United Kingdom.[107]

4.2.2 Exceptions to Territorial Jurisdiction

Although the House of Lords held in *Al-Skeini* that the jurisprudence of the ECtHR concerning extra-territorial effect had to be followed, it then faced the problem that at this point the jurisprudence of the ECtHR on this question was not clear. The majority held that the case law indicated that liability for acts taking effect or taking place outside the territory of a Contracting State was exceptional and required 'special justification'.[108] Basing its judgment on *Bankovic v Belgium*,[109] the majority determined that Article 1 of the Convention reflected an essentially territorial notion of jurisdiction, but there were other bases of jurisdiction which were exceptional.

In its later judgment in *Smith v Ministry of Defence*,[110] adopting the judgment of the ECtHR in *Al-Skeini v UK*, the Supreme Court confirmed that the ECtHR has recognised extra-territorial jurisdiction in instances of state agent authority and control and where there was effective control over an area. The ECtHR also specified that these excep-

---

[103] *Al-Skeini v United Kingdom* (2011) 53 EHRR 18. See also *Al-Saadoon v United Kingdom* (2010) 51 EHRR 9.

[104] See eg *R (Al-Skeini) v Secretary of State for Defence* [2007] UKHL 26, [2008] 1 AC 153; *R (Gentle) v Prime Minister* [2008] UKHL 20, [2008] 1 AC 1356; *R (Smith) v Secretary of State for Defence* [2010] UKSC 29, [2011] 1 AC 1; *R (Al-Sadoon) v Secretary of State for Defence* [2009] EWCA 7, [2009] 3 WLR 957.

[105] *Al-Skeini*, Ibid.

[106] Ibid, per Lord Rodger at [58].

[107] Ibid, [59]. It was also held in *Smith & Ors v Ministry of Defence* [2013] UKSC 41, [2013] 3 WLR 69 that the approach of the ECtHR to Art 1 jurisdiction was the approach which must be adopted under the HRA.

[108] *Al-Skeini* (n 104), per Baroness Hale at [91].

[109] *Bankovic v Belgium* (2007) 44 EHRR SE5.

[110] *Smith* (n 107).

tions were not limited to the legal space of the ECHR and the jurisdiction under Article 1 could exist outside the territory covered by the Council of Europe Member States.[111] In the following paragraphs, the meaning of these two exceptions is examined.[112]

4.2.3. State Agent Authority and Control

In *Al-Skeini v UK* the ECtHR held that state agent authority and control included the acts of diplomatic and consular agents, who were present on foreign territory in accordance with provisions of international law.[113] There may also be state agent authority and control by a Contracting State where, 'through the consent, invitation or acquiescence of the Government of that territory', it exercises all or some of the public powers normally to be exercised by that government.[114] In addition, it held that in certain circumstances, the use of force by a state's agents operating outside its territory may bring individuals under the control of state authorities and into that State's Article 1 jurisdiction. This principle has been applied where an individual is taken into the custody of state agents abroad.[115] The ECtHR held as follows:

> It is clear that, whenever the State through its agents exercises control and authority over an individual, and thus jurisdiction, the State is under an obligation under Article 1 to secure to that individual the rights and freedoms under Section 1 of the Convention that are relevant to the situation of that individual. In this sense, therefore, the Convention rights can be 'divided and tailored'.[116]

4.2.4 Effective Control over an Area

In *Al-Skeini v UK* the ECtHR explained that extra-territorial jurisdiction under Article 1 also applied when, as a consequence of lawful or unlawful military action, a Contracting State exercises effective control of an area outside that national territory:

> Where the fact of such domination over the territory is established, it is not necessary to determine whether the Contracting State exercises detailed control over the policies and actions of the subordinate local administration. The fact that the local administration survives as a result of the Contracting State's military and other support entails that State's responsibility for its policies and actions. The controlling State has the responsibility under Article 1 to secure, within the area under its control, the entire range of substantive rights set out in the Convention and those additional Protocols which it has ratified. It will be liable for any violations of those rights.[117]

---

[111] Ibid, [142].

[112] See further: J Farrant, 'Is the Extra-territorial Application of the Human Rights Act Really Justified?' (2009) 9 *International Criminal Law Review* 833; M Andenas and E Bjorge, 'Human Rights and Acts by Troops Abroad: Rights and Jurisdictional Restrictions' (2012) 18 *European Public Law* 473; M Duttwiler, 'Authority, Control and Jurisdiction in the Extraterritorial Application of the European Convention on Human Rights' (2012) 30 *Netherlands Quarterly of Human Rights* 137; M Schaefer, 'Al-Skeini and the Elusive Parameters of Extraterritorial Jurisdiction' [2011] *European Human Rights Law Review* 566.

[113] *Al-Skeini* (n 103), [134].

[114] Ibid, [135].

[115] Ibid, [136]. Cited as examples were *Öcalan v Turkey* (2005) 41 EHRR 45; *Issa v Turkey* (2005) 41 EHRR 27; *Al-Sadoon v United Kingdom* (2010) 51 EHRR 9; *Medvedyev v France* (2010) 51 EHRR 39.

[116] *Al-Skeini* (n 103), [137].

[117] Ibid, [138].

The ECtHR confirmed that it was a question of fact whether effective control was exercised and it would primarily have reference to the strength of the state's military presence in the area. Other indicators included the extent to which the state's military, economic and political support for the local subordinate administration provided it with influence and control over the region.[118]

4.3 Extra-territorial Effect in Practice

4.3.1 Entry Clearance

The application of the HRA to the entry clearance function abroad is not clear. In *European Roma Rights Centre*[119] Lord Bingham had the very greatest doubt that the functions performed by British immigration officers in Prague, even though they were formally treated as consular officials, could possibly be said to be an exercise of jurisdiction in any relevant sense over non-UK nationals.[120] However, in *Singh*[121] the Court of Appeal proceeded on the assumption that the HRA applied to a decision of a British entry clearance officer in New Delhi, although Chadwick LJ commented that the court was not invited to consider the question of whether the Convention or the Act should be treated as having extra-territorial reach in this case; 'and we have not done so. We should not be taken to have reached any conclusion on that question.'[122]

4.3.2 British Diplomatic and Consular Agents

The activities of diplomatic and consular agents may so affect an individual as to bring the individual within the jurisdiction of the UK for the purposes of Article 1. However, the acts or omissions of which complaint is made come within the scope of an exercise of control and authority by the state in question.[123] The mere involvement of these agents is not sufficient, what they do must amount to the exercise of authority and control and this is a fact-sensitive question.[124] In *Sandiford* the Court of Appeal concluded that at all points the claimant was completely under the control of and detained by a foreign state and the necessary degree of authority and control was not exercised by diplomatic and consular agents to bring her within the jurisdiction of the HRA.[125]

The activities of British embassies abroad were given detailed consideration in the case of *B*,[126] which concerned two boys, claiming to be of Afghan origin, who, having escaped from an asylum-seeker detention centre, sought asylum in the British Con-

---

[118] Ibid, [139].

[119] *R (on the application of European Roma Rights Centre) v Immigration Officer, Prague Airport* [2004] UKHL 55, [2005] 2 AC 1.

[120] Ibid, [21].

[121] *Singh v Entry Clearance Officer New Delhi* [2004] EWCA Civ 1075, [2005] QB 608.

[122] Ibid, [94].

[123] *R (Sandiford) v Secretary of State for Foreign & Commonwealth Affairs* [2013] EWCA Civ 581, [2013] 1 WLR 2938, [44].

[124] Ibid. [45].

[125] Ibid, [47].

[126] *R (on the application of B) v Secretary of State for the Foreign and Commonwealth Office* [2004] EWCA Civ 1344, [2005] QB 643.

sulate in Melbourne, Australia. Having reviewed Strasbourg authority, the Court of Appeal found that the authority closest to the situation here was *WM v Denmark*,[127] although there was a distinction in that the embassy officials in *WM* appear to have conducted negotiations with the authorities on behalf of the applicant and 'may be said to have assumed some responsibility (or exercised some authority) in respect of the applicant'.[128] Taking into consideration that the applicants were told that while they were in the Consulate they would be kept safe, and that they were given some protection by being brought from the reception area into the office area, the court was content to assume, without reaching a positive conclusion on the point, that while in the Consulate the applicants were sufficiently within the authority of the consular staff to be subject to the jurisdiction of the United Kingdom for the purpose of Article 1.[129]

Assuming the HRA applied, the court then turned to whether there had been a breach here. It held that the UK officials could not be required by the Convention and the HRA to decline to hand over the applicants unless this was clearly necessary in order to protect them from the immediate likelihood of experiencing serious injury.[130] It found that this was not the case.

> The applicants were not subject to the type and degree of threat that, under international law, would have justified granting them diplomatic asylum. To have given the applicants refuge from the demands of the Australian authorities for their return would have been an abuse of the privileged inviolability accorded to diplomatic premises. It would have infringed the obligations of the United Kingdom under public international law.[131]

4.3.3 British Armed Forces

In *Al-Skeini*[132] the claimant relatives of deceased Iraqi civilians who had been killed by or in the course of action taken by British soldiers in the period following completion of major combat operations in Iraq, and prior to the assumption of authority by the Iraqi Interim Government, brought proceedings under the HRA against the Secretary of State for Defence, alleging violations of Articles 2 and 3. A majority of the House of Lords concluded that the 'effective control of an area' exception to the principle of territoriality did not apply here as Iraq was not a party to the ECHR.[133] However, in relation to the second exception to the principle of territoriality resulting from the extra-territorial activity of state agents, the court reached a different conclusion. In relation to the first five claimants, it held that this exception did not apply because the deaths occurred as a result of military operations in the field. In relation to the sixth claimant, the court found that the circumstances were different. This claimant had been arrested by British forces and taken into custody in a British military base, where he met his death. Finding the HRA applicable to this case, it later concluded that the procedural obligations arising under Articles 2 and 3 in relation this claimant's death had not been satisfied.

---

[127] *WM v Denmark*, 15 EHRR CD 28.
[128] *B* (n 126), [66].
[129] Ibid.
[130] Ibid, [89].
[131] Ibid, [96].
[132] *Al-Skeini* (n 104).
[133] This was held to be incorrect in *Al-Skeini v UK* (n 103).

In *Al-Skeni v UK* the ECtHR held that the effective control exception applied anywhere in the world and was not limited to Contracting States to the ECHR. It concluded that during the period when the claimants' deaths occurred the United States and United Kingdom were exercising powers of government for the provisional administration of Iraq, including the maintenance of civil law and order. Therefore, the UK, through its soldiers, exercised authority and control over individuals killed in the course of such security operations. Jurisdiction was found in relation to all six claimants.

In *Smith*[134] the Supreme Court held that the ECtHR did not specify in *Al-Skeini v UK* which of the general principles led to its conclusion that there was a jurisdictional link between the deceased and the United Kingdom, but it was most likely the general principle of state authority and control:

> The United Kingdom was not exercising public powers through the consent, invitation or acquiescence of the government of Iraq as during the relevant period no such government was in existence. But it was exercising powers normally to be exercised by that government had it existed. The case thus fell within the general principle of state authority and control.[135]

The extra-territorial effect of the HRA can also have an impact on the treatment of the British armed forces themselves. In *Smith*[136] the Supreme Court considered an application to strike out Article 2 claims arising from the deaths of members of the armed forces while serving in the British Army in Iraq. It held that the UK had authority and control over its armed forces when serving abroad.

> It has just as much authority and control over them anywhere as it has when they are serving within the territory of the United Kingdom ... the legal and administrative structure of the control is, necessarily, non-territorial in character.[137]

Therefore, the category of extra-territorial effect relevant to this claim was state agent authority and control. Lord Hope stated as follows:

> [T]he jurisdiction of the United Kingdom under article 1 of the Convention extends to securing the protection of article 2 to members of the armed forces when they are serving outside its territory and that at the time of their deaths Pte Hewett and Pte Ellis were within the jurisdiction of the United Kingdom for the purposes of that article. To do so would not be inconsistent with the general principles of international law, as no other state is claiming jurisdiction over them.[138]

4.4 The Channel Islands and the Isle of Man

The Channel Islands and the Isle of Man are dependencies of the Crown. Pursuant to Article 1 of the European Convention on Human Rights the United Kingdom is obliged to ensure that these dependencies comply with the ECHR. However, pursuant to the wishes of the appropriate Island governments, the HRA has not been extended to them.[139]

---

[134] *Smith* (n 107).
[135] Ibid, per Lord Hope at [40].
[136] *Smith* (n 107).
[137] Ibid, per Lord Hope at [28].
[138] Ibid, [55].
[139] See further, HL Deb, Vol 584, cols 1303–11 (19 January 1998).

4.5 British Overseas Territories

Unless the Convention and Protocol No 1 have been extended to the particular British Overseas Territory, it is not possible to found a claim under section 7 of the HRA. For example, in *Quark Fishing Ltd*[140] the Court of Appeal concluded that as the First Protocol had not been extended to South Georgia, there was no breach of Convention rights capable of founding an HRA claim.

> However complete the control exercised by the Convention state over the dependent territory, the Convention applies to the territory only if there has been a notification under article 56 and, in the case of the Protocol, only if there has been a notification under its article 4.[141]

However, it was also established in this case that it is possible for UK powers to be exercised in an overseas territory where Her Majesty is queen and where there are competent local authorities.[142]

> The fact that Her Majesty the Queen is Head of State in the United Kingdom does not stand in the way of governmental actions in other territories where Her Majesty is Head of State from being treated as actions of the entities concerned, whether the territories are independent, self-governing or dependencies.[143]

Here it concluded that the instruction was given by the Secretary of State in right of the UK government.[144] He had directed the Commissioner for South Georgia, who in turn directed the Director of Fisheries for that territory, not to grant the fishing licence sought. If the First Protocol had been extended, this would have been an act to which the HRA would apply.

---

5. Failure to Act: Positive Duties

Section 6(6) provides that an 'act' incompatible with Convention rights includes a failure to act. However, it is also provided in this section that a failure to act does not include a failure to (a) introduce in, or lay before, Parliament a proposal for legislation; or (b) make any primary legislation or remedial order.

Expressly including failures to act within the meaning of acts which may be incompatible with Convention rights reflects the principle of positive obligations which has been a long-standing principle of Strasbourg jurisprudence.[145] As discussed in Part II of this book concerning the interpretation and application of the Convention rights under

---

[140] *R (Quark Fishing Ltd) v Secretary of State for Foreign and Commonwealth Affairs* [2004] EWCA Civ 527, [2005] QB 93.
[141] Ibid, [56], in reliance upon *Bui van Thanh v United Kingdom*, 12 March 1990; *Yonghong v Portugal*, Reports of Judgments and Decisions 1999—XI, 385; and *Gillow v United Kingdom* (1986) 11 EHRR 335.
[142] *Quark Fishing Ltd* (n 140), [44].
[143] Ibid, [45].
[144] Ibid, [50].
[145] See further A Mowbray, *The Development of Positive Obligations under the European Convention on Human Rights by the European Court of Human Rights* (Oxford, Hart Publishing, 2004).

the HRA, almost every right either expressly or impliedly requires public authorities not only to refrain from infringing rights, but also to take action to prevent rights from being breached. For example, Article 2, the right to life, imposes not only a duty not to take life but, in some circumstances, to take steps to prevent life being taken and, as part of that duty, an obligation to investigate the circumstances surrounding the death, should it occur.[146] Article 6(1) obliges public authorities to ensure that in the determination of civil rights and obligations, or any criminal charge, everyone has a fair and public hearing within a reasonable time by an independent and impartial tribunal established by law. There is also an implied duty attached to the right to respect for private life protected by Article 8 obliging public authorities to take reasonable measures so as to avoid an interference with private life.[147]

As outlined in Part II of this book, proceedings under the HRA for a failure to act which is incompatible with Convention rights can be more controversial than proceedings for an act incompatible with Convention rights. This is generally because requiring a public authority to take action requires the expenditure of more resources than would otherwise be the case. Resources arguments have been a particular issue in claims which have arisen under Articles 3 and 8 in the context of welfare support.[148] Nevertheless, generally the courts have not failed to apply the HRA and determine incompatibility in such instances.

6. Satellite Litigation

6.1 Criminal Proceedings

An issue which has arisen in some criminal claims is the inappropriateness of what has been labelled 'satellite' litigation within the criminal justice system. Whilst it has not yet occurred, it is possible that a court will decline to exercise its jurisdiction under the HRA if it feels that the matter could have been more appropriately raised in the trial or on appeal. For example, in *Kebilene*,[149] at the close of the prosecution case at trial, the three defendants sought a ruling from the trial judge that section 16A of the Prevention of Terrorism (Temporary Provisions) Act 1989 reversed the burden of proof and was therefore in breach of Article 6. The jury was later discharged and a new trial date set. Meanwhile, the defendants applied for judicial review, arguing that the continuing decision of the Director of Public Prosecutions to give his consent to the prosecution under section 16A was incompatible with Article 6.

A majority of their Lordships held that, once the HRA was fully in force, it would

---

[146] *R (on the application of Amin (Imtiaz) v Secretary of State for the Home Department* [2003] UKHL 51, [2004] 1 AC 653 per Lord Slynn at [40].

[147] For a discussion of the meaning of 'reasonableness' in this context, see TR Hickman, 'The Reasonableness Principle: Reassessing its Place in the Public Sphere', (2004) 63 *Cambridge Law Journal* 166.

[148] See eg *Anufrijeva v Southwark LBC* [2003] EWCA Civ 1406, [2004] QB 1124.

[149] *Kebilene* (n 10).

not be possible to make such an application as the remedy would be in the trial process or on appeal. They concluded in the present case that, absent dishonesty or mala fides or an exceptional circumstance, the decision of the Director of Public Prosecutions to consent to the prosecution was not amenable to judicial review. Lord Steyn commented that while the passing of the HRA

> marked a great advance for our criminal justice system it is in my view vitally important that, so far as the courts are concerned, its application in our law should take place in an orderly manner which recognises the desirability of all challenges taking place in the criminal trial or on appeal. ... Such satellite litigation should rarely be permitted in our criminal justice system.[150]

A similar dilemma arose in *R v A*.[151] At a preparatory hearing, counsel for the defendant applied for leave to cross-examine the complainant about the alleged previous sexual relationship between the complainant and the defendant and to lead evidence about it. Relying on section 41 of the Youth Justice and Criminal Evidence Act 1999, the judge ruled that the complainant could not be cross-examined, nor could evidence be led about her alleged sexual relationship with the defendant and that the prepared statement could not be put in evidence. The defendant appealed. Only three members of the House of Lords commented on the timing of the challenge, although the silence of Lords Slynn and Hutton could be taken to mean that they also considered it important to resolve the issue at this stage. Lord Steyn noted that the same issue arose in 13 other criminal cases, and it was therefore a matter of some urgency.[152] Lord Clyde also found that there were strong practical reasons for determining a matter of compliance with the Convention in advance of the trial even though it could only be answered on a very preliminary basis.[153]

Only Lord Hope held that the question of whether or not section 41 was incompatible with Article 6 could not be finally determined at this stage. '[I]t will only be in rare and isolated cases, that the question of fairness will be capable of being determined before the trial.'[154]

6.2 Civil Proceedings

It is also possible, although less common, for satellite litigation to arise in civil claims.

---

[150] See also *R (on the application of Pretty) v Director of Public Prosecutions* [2001] UKHL 61, [2001] 3 WLR 1598, where it was sought to challenge the refusal of the DPP to give an undertaking that he would not, under s 2(4) of the Suicide Act 1961, consent to the prosecution of Mr Pretty under s 2(1) if he were to assist his wife to commit suicide. Lord Hobhouse, at [123], commented that 'the procedure of seeking to by-pass the ordinary operation of our system of criminal justice by raising questions of law and applying for the judicial review of "decisions" of the Director cannot be approved and should be firmly discouraged. It undermines the proper and fair management of our criminal justice system.'

[151] *R v A* [2001] UKHL 25, [2002] 1 AC 45.

[152] Ibid, [26].

[153] Ibid, [120].

[154] Ibid, [106], [107]. Under the Scotland Act 1998, satellite human rights litigation has been common. See eg *Montgomery v HM Advocate* [2003] 1 AC 641; *Brown v Stott* [2001] 1 AC 681; *McLean v Procurator Fiscal, Fort William* [2001] 1 WLR 2425; *Millar v Procurator Fiscal, Elgin* [2001] 1 WLR 1615; and *HM Advocate v R* [2002] UKPC D3, [2004] 1 AC 462.

For example, in *Alconbury*[155] the claimants sought clarification as to whether or not the role of the Secretary of State in planning matters was compatible with Article 6. The matters were by no means concluded but were merely at the stage where the Secretary of State had exercised his powers to intervene by referring a planning application to himself and appointing inspectors to hold public inquiries. Lord Clyde commented that their Lordships had been asked to form a view at a preliminary stage and it was not yet known what the decisions would be. 'Far less is it known what grounds, if any, will emerge for dissatisfaction with the decision.' However, in his Lordship's view the practical advantages of testing the issue at the early stage were obvious: 'A very considerable expenditure of effort, time and money would have been spent in vain if the decision of the Divisional Court was correct.'[156]

---

[155] *R v Secretary of State for the Environment, Transport and the Regions, ex p Alconbury Developments Ltd* [2001] UKHL 23, [2001] 2 WLR 1389.
[156] Ibid, [171].

4

Determining Incompatibility

1. Introduction

Once it has been established that the HRA applies, the next step is to determine whether or not the act is incompatible with a Convention right. The majority of the Convention rights are discussed in detail in Part II of this book. Very few are absolute rights, for example, the Convention right to freedom of expression, as protected by Article 10

> may be subject to such formalities, conditions, restrictions or penalties as are prescribed by law and are necessary in a democratic society, in the interests of national security, territorial integrity or public safety, for the prevention of disorder or crime, for the protection of health or morals, for the protection of the reputation or rights of others, for preventing the disclosure of information received in confidence, or for maintaining the authority and impartiality of the judiciary.

Articles 8 (private life, family life, home and correspondence), 9 (freedom of thought, conscience and religion) and 11 (freedom of assembly and association) are drafted in a similar manner. In addition, some rights which appear absolute from the text of the Convention are also subject to exceptions. For example, differences in treatment contrary to Article 14 (prohibition of discrimination) may be subject to an interference which has a legitimate aim and bears a reasonable relationship of proportionality to that aim.[1] Any interference with the right to peaceful enjoyment of possessions is lawful as long as a fair balance is struck between the demands of the general interest of the community and the requirement of the protection of the individual's fundamental rights. Again, there must be a reasonable relationship of proportionality between the means employed and the aim pursued.[2]

Although there are different considerations attached to the interpretation of each Convention right (as discussed more fully in Part II), certain concepts are key to determining incompatibility whatever Convention right is in play. First, the requirement of 'prescribed by law'; second, the test of proportionality; and third as a part of the test of proportionality, the practice of judicial deference to the primary decision-maker. Indis-

---

[1] *R (on the application of S) v Chief Constable of South Yorkshire* [2004] UKHL 39, [2001] 1 WLR 2196 per Lord Steyn at [42].

[2] *R v Dimsey; R v Allen* [2001] UKHL 46, [2001] 3 WLR 843.

pensable to the process of determining incompatibility, and the subject of considerable HRA jurisprudence, these three concepts are the subject of this chapter.

2. Prescribed by Law

2.1 Generally

The lawfulness requirement addresses 'supremely important features of the rule of law'.[3] In *Gillan*, Lord Bingham explained as follows:

> The exercise of power by public officials, as it affects members of the public, must be governed by clear and publicly-accessible rules of law. The public must not be vulnerable to interference by public officials acting on any personal whim, caprice, malice, predilection or purpose other than that for which the power was conferred.[4]

In determining whether or not an interference with a Convention right is prescribed by law, a court must address three distinct questions.

> The first is whether there is a legal basis in domestic law for the restriction. The second is whether the law or rule in question is sufficiently accessible to the individual who is affected by the interference, and sufficiently precise to enable him to understand its scope and foresee the consequences of his actions so that he can regulate his conduct without breaking the law. The third is whether, assuming that these two requirements are satisfied, it is nevertheless open to the criticism on the convention ground that it was applied in a way that was arbitrary because, for example, it has been resorted to in bad faith or in a way that is not proportionate.[5]

The principle of prescribed by law is reflective of the principle of legality at common law which means that

> Parliament must squarely confront what it is doing and accept the political cost. Fundamental rights cannot be overridden by general or ambiguous words. ... In the absence of express language or necessary implication to the contrary, the courts therefore presume that even the most general words were intended to be subject to the basic rights of the individual.[6]

Applying this principle in the case of *Simms*,[7] the House of Lords concluded that paragraphs 37 and 37A of the Prison Service Standing Order 5A left untouched the fundamental and basic right of the prisoners to freedom of expression and were therefore not ultra vires.[8]

---

[3] *R (on the application of Gillan) v Commissioner of Police for the Metropolis* [2006] UKHL 12, [2006] 2 AC 307 per Lord Bingham at [34].

[4] Ibid.

[5] *R (on the application of Rottman) v Commissioner of Police of the Metropolis* [2002] UKHL 20, [2002] 2 WLR 1315 per Lord Hope at [35] in reliance upon *Sunday Times v United Kingdom* (1979) 2 EHRR 245, 271; *R v Shayler* [2002] UKHL 11, [2002] 2 WLR 754, [56]. See also the observations of Lord Bingham in *R (Munjaz) v Ashworth Hospital Authority* [2005] UKHL 58, [2006] 2 AC 148.

[6] *R v Secretary of State for the Home Department, ex p Simms* [2000] 2 AC 115 per Lord Hoffmann.

[7] Ibid.

[8] See also *McCartan Turkington Breen (A Firm) v Times Newspapers Ltd* [2000] 3 WLR 1670.

Although a fundamental part of human rights jurisprudence, the principle of prescribed by law has actually given rise to very few claims under the HRA and it is rare for primary legislation to be found lacking in this respect. Those issues which have arisen are examined in the following paragraphs.

2.2 A Legal Basis in Domestic Law

Where a breach of the requirement of lawfulness is alleged, the first task of the court is to identify the legal basis for the restriction. If the interference is not in accordance with the domestic law, this requirement is not met and a breach of the Convention right is established with no need to consider the proportionality of the interference. This can raise difficult questions of legal interpretation. For example, in *McE*[9] the House of Lords was divided over the question of whether or not the Regulation of Investigatory Powers Act 2000 authorised the covert surveillance by police of consultations between solicitors and clients ordinarily protected by professional privilege. A majority concluded that it did authorise such surveillance.[10]

A breach of guidelines can result in a finding that an interference is not prescribed by law. For example, in *R v Mason*[11] the police had covertly taped the conversations of a number of suspects detained in the custody suite of a police station. These tapes played a fundamental role in the case for the prosecution against the defendants. The Chief Constable thought that he was applying the Home Office Guidelines on the Use of Equipment in Police Surveillance (1984), but his decision was not in accordance with a strict interpretation of the Guidelines. The Court of Appeal concluded that the prosecution could not rely on Article 8(2) to justify what took place because the surveillance was not conducted according to law. '[T]his is because of the lack of any legal structure to which the public have access authorising the infringement. If there had been such authorisation there would have been no breach.'[12]

2.3 Sufficiently Accessible and Precise

2.3.1 Generally

Of the three requirements in order to be 'prescribed by law', it is the second, relating to accessibility and precision, which has given rise to the most claims under the HRA. For example, in *Nadarajah*[13] the Court of Appeal was required to consider whether or not the detention of an asylum seeker, who was to be deported, was lawful. The policy of the immigration service was not to detain those to be imminently removed where proceedings challenging the right to remove had been instituted. However, it was also the policy to disregard information from those acting for asylum seekers that proceedings were about to be initiated. The latter aspect of the policy was not known

---

[9] *Re McE* [2009] UKHL 15, [2009] 1 AC 908.
[10] See also *ML v ANS* [2012] UKSC 30, [2012] HRLR 27.
[11] *R v Mason* [2002] EWCA Crim 385, [2002] 2 Cr App R 38.
[12] Ibid, [65], in reliance upon *PG and JH v United Kingdom* Judgment of 25 September 2001.
[13] *Nadarajah v Secretary of State for the Home Department* [2003] EWCA Civ 1768.

or accessible, and the Court of Appeal therefore concluded on this ground that the detention was not lawful.[14]

In *Purdy*[15] it was argued that there was no publicly accessible information concerning the policy of the Director of Public Prosecutions on decisions to prosecute those who had allegedly assisted a person commit suicide contrary to section 2(1) of the Suicide Act 1961. The House of Lords agreed that Article 8(1) was engaged and that the important issue was the Convention principle of legality. It held that the current guidance for Crown Prosecutors was not sufficient:

> [F]or anyone seeking to identify the factors that are likely to be taken into account in the case of a person with a severe and incurable disability who is likely to need assistance in travelling to a country where assisted suicide is lawful, these developments fall short of what is needed to satisfy the Convention tests of accessibility and foreseeability. The Director's own analysis shows that, in a highly unusual and extremely sensitive case of this kind, the Code offers almost no guidance at all.[16]

It concluded that the Director of Public Prosecutions was under an obligation to clarify what his position was as to the factors that he regards as relevant for and against prosecution in this 'very special and carefully defined class of case'.[17]

By contrast, in *Gillan*[18] the police had carried out their stop and search in reliance upon an authorisation made under section 44 of the Terrorism Act 2000 by the Assistant Commissioner of the Metropolitan Police and its subsequent confirmation by the Secretary of State. It was claimed that the law in this context meant not only the Act but also the authorisation and confirmation and that these were not accessible. The House of Lords did not agree, holding that the stop and search regime met the test of lawfulness given the Act informed the public that the powers were, if duly authorised, available. Lord Bingham observed that there were strong reasons for not publishing the authorisations as these would reveal locations where the measures were in place.[19]

With respect to the requirement of precision, it is often argued that interferences on the grounds of obscenity, taste or decency are not prescribed by law. For example, it was argued in *R v Perrin*[20] that there was a lack of clarity in the statutory definition of obscenity under the Obscene Publications Act 1959. Relying on Strasbourg jurisprudence, the Court of Appeal concluded that the offence was prescribed by law.[21] It has

---

[14] Ibid, [66]–[67].

[15] *R (on the application of Purdy) v Director of Public Prosecutions* [2009] UKHL 45, [2009] 3 WLR 403.

[16] Ibid, per Lord Hope at [53].

[17] Ibid, [55]. See also *R (Nicklinson) v Ministry of Justice* [2013] EWCA Civ 961, (2013) 16 CCL Rep 413, where it was held that the policy was still not sufficiently clear to satisfy the requirements of Art 8(2) in relation to healthcare professionals. See further J Montgomery, 'Guarding the Gates of St Peter: Life, Death and Law Making" (2011) 31 *Legal Studies* 644; P Lewis, 'Informal Legal Change on Assisted Suicide: The Policy for Prosecutors" (2011) 31 *Legal Studies* 119; J Rogers, 'Prosecutorial Policies, Prosecutorial Systems and the Purdy Litigation' [2010] *Criminal Law Review* 543.

[18] *Gillan* (n 3).

[19] Ibid, [33]. The ECtHR disagreed in *Gillan v United Kingdom* (2010) 50 EHRR 45. See also *R (Singh) v Chief Constable of West Midlands* [2006] EWCA Civ 1118, [2006] 1 WLR 3374 and *R (Roberts) v Commissioner of Police of the Metropolis* [2012] EWHC 1977 (Admin), [2012] HRLR 28.

[20] *R v Perrin* [2002] EWCA Crim 747.

[21] Ibid, [46], in reliance upon *Muller v Switzerland* (1991) 13 EHRR 212; *Handyside v United Kingdom* (1979–80) 1 EHRR 737; *Wingrove v United Kingdom* (1997) 24 EHRR 1; *Hoare v United Kingdom* [1997] EHRLR 678. See also *Core Issues Trust v Transport for London* [2013] EWHC 651 (Admin), [2013] HRLR 22.

also been argued that the phrase 'national security' lacks clarity. However, in *Baker*[22] the Information Tribunal did not agree, holding that where the Strasbourg organs had considered the phrase it had never been suggested that the concept was so vacuous as to fail the test of clarity. 'The phrase itself is found in the 1981 Convention, in the Directive, and in the statutes and codes of Member States. The fact that it is incapable of comprehensive definition does not mean that it lacks adequate definition.'[23]

One example of where the principle of precision was not met is *Briffett v DPP*,[24] where the Divisional Court held that the order imposing reporting restrictions under section 39 of the Children and Young Persons Act 1933 was insufficiently clear and unambiguous. It was held that to be sufficiently clear and unambiguous, the order must leave no doubt, in the mind of a reasonable reader or recipient, as to precisely what it is that is prohibited.[25]

2.3.2 Retrospective Effect

In the criminal sphere, there is limited scope for legislation which has a retrospective effect, and this is also reflected in Article 7 of the ECHR. However, it has been held that the position is different in the civil sphere.[26]

> Changes in family law, for example, are not applicable only to families which subsequently come into existence, but affect existing families, even although the changes may not have been foreseeable at the time when individuals married or had children. Similarly, a person who buys a house, or a company that employs staff, cannot expect the law governing the rights and responsibilities of homeowners or employers to remain unchanged throughout the period of ownership or employment.[27]

In *Axa*[28] the Supreme Court held that retrospective legislation which restores the position to what it was previously understood to be may not be incompatible with legal certainty or the rule of law.[29] It may be that the retroactive effect is considered in the assessment of proportionality rather than the requirement of lawfulness.

2.3.3 The Common Law

Questions have often arisen in HRA cases as to whether or not the common law meets the test of prescribed by law. For example, in *Rottman*[30] the House of Lords considered whether under common law a police officer executing a warrant of arrest issued pursuant to section 8 of the Extradition Act 1989 had power to search for and seize any goods or documents which he reasonably believed to be material evidence in relation to the extradition crime in respect of which the warrant was issued. A majority of their

---

[22] *Baker v Secretary of State for the Home Department*, Information Tribunal, 1 October 2001.
[23] Ibid, [68].
[24] *Briffett v DPP* [2001] EWHC Admin 841, [2002] EMLR 12.
[25] Ibid, [13].
[26] *Axa General Insurance Ltd v Lord Advocate* [2011] UKSC 46, [2012] 1 AC 868 per Lord Reed at [120].
[27] Ibid.
[28] Ibid.
[29] Ibid, per Lord Reed at [121].
[30] *Rottman* (n 5).

Lordships concluded that the police had power under the common law, after arresting a person in his house or in the grounds of his house pursuant to section 8(1)(b) of the 1989 Act, to search the house and seize articles which they reasonably believed to be material evidence in relation to the crime for which they had arrested that person.[31] It also concluded that the search and seizure was in accordance with law as required by Article 8.[32] However, Lord Hope dissented, holding that the common law powers which were available to a police officer when effecting an arrest did not extend to a search of the premises where the person was arrested for the purpose of obtaining evidence.[33] Here he concluded that the search was unlawful because it was undertaken without the respondent's consent and because the police had not obtained a search warrant. He found there was no settled basis in domestic law for the carrying out by the police of a search of the respondent's house for evidence of an extradition crime without his consent and without having first obtained a search warrant. Even if there was an undoubted power of search at common law, his Lordships found that the second and third requirements relating to accessibility, precision and lack of arbitrariness were not satisfied.[34] Given that the common law continues to develop, it is conceivable that this could give rise to problems with the principle of prescribed by law. For example, in *Venables*[35] the court concluded that the law of confidence could extend to cover the injunctions sought to protect identities in the case and therefore the restriction imposed on freedom of expression was in accordance with the law. 'The common law continues to evolve, as it has done for centuries, and it is being given considerable impetus to do so by the implementation of the convention into our domestic law.'

In light of such rapid development, the argument was made in *Douglas v Hello! Ltd*[36] that when Hello! took the decision to publish the unauthorised photographs the relevant law was so uncertain that it was not possible to predict that publication would be held to be unlawful. The Court of Appeal concluded that, given the interlocutory proceedings, it was reasonably foreseeable to Hello! when it decided to proceed with the publication that this developing area of English law might result in it being held to have infringed the Douglases' rights of privacy or confidence.[37]

> If one postulates that, at the time of the publication by Hello! of the unauthorised photographs, English law was insufficiently clear to satisfy the requirements of providing protection to privacy in a manner 'prescribed by law', the court was on the horns of a dilemma. If it gave a decision which developed the law so as to provide a protection to respect for privacy 'prescribed by law', it risked infringing Hello!'s Article 10 rights. If, however, it ruled that the law was insufficiently clear to provide a remedy, it perpetuated the infringement of the Douglases' Article 8 rights. It seems to us that in this situation the proper course was for the court to attempt to bring English law into compliance with the Convention, even if this was at the cost of a restriction, in the instant case, of Hello!'s Article 10 rights by findings which, up to that moment, could not be said to have been 'prescribed by law'.[38]

[31] Ibid, per Lord Hutton at [63].

[32] Ibid, [80]. Lord Hutton noted that the law was clearly stated by Lloyd LJ in *R v Governor of Pentonville Prison, ex p Osman* [1989] 3 All ER 701 and clearly set out at p 175 of the well-known textbook on extradition, A Jones, *Jones on Extradition* (London, Sweet & Maxwell, 1995).

[33] *Rottman* (n 5), [32].

[34] Ibid, [36].

[35] *Venables v News Group Newspapers Ltd* [2001] 2 WLR 1038, [80].

[36] *Douglas v Hello! Ltd* [2005] EWCA Civ 595.

[37] Ibid, [147].

[38] Ibid, [150].

2.3.4 Codes and Guidelines

Codes and guidelines can satisfy the requirement of prescribed by law although there must be some legislative underpinning. For example, in *Matthias Rath*[39] it was held that the British Codes of Advertising and Sales Promotion, which have an underpinning of subordinate legislation and which are readily accessible, were prescribed by law.[40] In *E*[41] the Administrative Court held that the restrictions placed on a patient in a secure mental hospital to dress as a woman had a basis in the Mental Health Act 1983 and that this was accessible.

> [T]he requirement of forseeability is also met. Although the statutory provision itself is in very general terms, greater precision has been given to it by the case law. ... The limits on the exercise of the power, which are subject to the supervision of the court by way of judicial review, are sufficiently defined to provide the requisite protection against arbitrary interference with a patient's right to dress as a woman.[42]

The court also noted that the degree of precision required depended on the particular subject matter and that the subject matter here was not particularly important. Furthermore, the claimant knew in practice precisely what he was and was not permitted to do since the arrangements had been set out in a written plan.[43]

2.4 Applied in a Way which is Not Arbitrary

The question of arbitrary application of the law was also considered by the House of Lords in *Gillan* as it was argued that police had used their power to stop and search without reasonable suspicion, in a way which was arbitrary. The House of Lords also rejected this argument. Lord Bingham held that a police officer was not free to exercise the power arbitrarily.

> It is true that he need have no suspicion before stopping and searching a member of the public. This cannot, realistically, be interpreted as a warrant to stop and search people who are obviously not terrorist suspects, which would be futile and time-wasting. It is to ensure that a constable is not deterred from stopping and searching a person whom he does suspect as a potential terrorist by the fear that he could not show reasonable grounds for his suspicion.[44]

However, in *Gillan v United Kingdom*[45] the ECtHR concluded that the interference was

---

[39] *R (on the application of Matthias Rath BV) v The Advertising Standards Authority Ltd* [2001] EMLR 22.

[40] Ibid, [26]. See also *Core Issues Trust v Transport for London* [2013] EWHC 651 (Admin), [2013] HRLR 22.

[41] *R (on the application of E) v Ashworth Hospital Authority* [2001] EWHC (Admin) 1089, [2002] ACD 149.

[42] *Herczegfalvy v Austria* (1992) 15 EHRR 437 followed.

[43] Ibid, [43]. See also *R (Munjaz) v Ashworth Hospital Authority* [2005] UKHL 58, [2006] 2 AC 148 (code of practice on seclusion in high-security mental hospitals); *Khan v Royal Air Force Summary Appeal Court* [2004] EWHC 2230 (Admin), [2004] HRLR 40 (Queen's Regulations on the subject of conscientious objection); and *R (X) v Headteacher and Governors of Y School* [2007] EWHC 298 (Admin), [2008] 1 All ER 249 (school uniform policy).

[44] *Gillan* (n 3), [35]. See further D Moeckli, 'Stop and Search under the Terrorism Act 2000' (2007) 70 *Modern Law Review* 659.

[45] *Gillan v United Kingdom* (2010) 50 EHRR 45.

not in accordance with the law. In particular, it was concerned at the breadth of discretion conferred upon the individual police officer involving a clear risk of arbitrariness. It concluded that the powers of authorisation and confirmation as well as those of stop and search were 'neither sufficiently circumscribed nor subject to adequate legal safeguards against abuse'.[46]

3. Necessary

Whilst the phrase 'necessary in a democratic society' is the phrase which appears in the wording of a number of Convention rights, the meaning of 'necessary' has received very little attention in the courts, with most attention being focused on the meaning of proportionality. It has been held that to be necessary, relevant and sufficient reasons must be given by the national authority to justify the restriction; the restriction on disclosure must correspond to a pressing social need; and the restriction must be proportionate to the legitimate aim pursued.[47]

4. Proportionality

4.1 Definition

In determining whether an interference with a Convention rights is necessary, a key element is the question of whether or not the interference is proportionate to the legitimate aim pursued.[48] Until the HRA, the principle of proportionality was only known in UK law via the medium of EU law and it still does not constitute a ground for judicial review. Given the relative lack of experience in domestic courts with the concept, when it was first applied under the HRA, slight divergences in approach were evident. For example, in *Kebilene*,[49] when determining whether an interference with the presumption of innocence protected by Article 6(2) was justified, Lord Hope referred to striking a fair balance between the general interest of the community and the fundamental rights of the individual. However, in *R v A*[50] Lord Steyn set out the essence of the test as whether the means used to impair a right or freedom were no more than was necessary

---

[46] Ibid, [87].

[47] *Shayler* (n 5), per Lord Hope at [58]. See also Lord Bingham at [23].

[48] On the 'legitimate aim' test, see R Gordon, 'Legitimate Aim: A Dimly Lit Road' [2002] *European Human Rights Law Review* 421.

[49] *R v Director of Public Prosecutions, ex p Kebilene* [1999] 3 WLR 972.

[50] *R v A* [2001] UKHL 25, [2002] 1 AC 45.

to accomplish the objective,[51] a slightly more difficult test to meet; meanwhile, Lord Hope continued to refer to striking a fair balance between the general interest of the community and the protection of the individual.[52]

Shortly after, in *Daly*,[53] the House of Lords unanimously addressed the meaning of proportionality in an attempt to clarify confusion which had arisen from judgments of the Court of Appeal.[54] Lord Steyn, with whom the others agreed, held that there was a material difference between the *Wednesbury* and *Smith* grounds of review and the approach of proportionality applicable in respect of review where Convention rights are at stake.[55] Adopting a recent decision of the Privy Council concerning the Constitution of Antigua and Barbuda,[56] his Lordship set out the contours of the principle of proportionality. In determining whether a limitation (by act, rule or decision) is arbitrary or excessive, the court should ask itself whether:

(i)   the legislative objective is sufficiently important to justify limiting a fundamental right;
(ii) the measures designed to meet the legislative objective are rationally connected to it; and
(iii) the means used to impair the right or freedom are no more than is necessary to accomplish the objective.[57]

In *Huang*[58] the House of Lords established that the 'fair balance' and 'no more than is necessary' tests were both correct and must be used together. Their Lordships confirmed the *Daly* formulation of the questions as set out above. To this was added an overriding requirement drawn from the judgment of Dickson CJ in *R v Oakes*[59] 'from which this approach to proportionality derives'. The overriding requirement was 'the need to balance the interests of society with those of individuals and groups'.[60] In the opinion of the House of Lords, this was an 'aspect which should never be overlooked or discounted' and was also recognised in *Razgar*.[61] Summing up, Lord Bingham held that there were four questions when determining proportionality:

(a)   is the legislative objective sufficiently important to justify limiting a fundamental right?
(b)   are the measures which have been designed to meet it rationally connected to it?
(c)   are they no more than are necessary to accomplish it?
(d)   do they strike a fair balance between the rights of the individual and the interests of the community?[62]

---

[51] Ibid, [38].

[52] Ibid, [91]. See also *Brown v Stott (Procurator Fiscal, Dunfermline)* [2001] 1 AC 681 and *McIntosh v Lord Advocate* [2001] 1 AC 1078.

[53] *R v Secretary of State for the Home Department, ex p Daly* [2001] UKHL 26, [2001] 2 AC 532.

[54] The cases leading to the confusion were *R (Mahmood) v Secretary of State for the Home Department* [2001] 1 WLR 840; *R v Secretary of State for the Home Department, ex p Isiko* [2001] 1 FLR 930; and *R v Secretary of State for the Home Department, ex p Samaroo*, Administrative Court, 20 December 2000.

[55] *Daly* (n 53), [26].

[56] *De Freitas v Permanent Secretary of Ministry of Agriculture, Fisheries, Lands and Housing* [1999] 1 AC 69.

[57] Ibid, [27].

[58] *Huang v Secretary of State for the Home Department and Kashmiri v Secretary of State for the Home Department* [2007] UKHL 11, [2007] 2 WLR 581.

[59] *R v Oakes* [1986] 1 SCR 103.

[60] At [19].

[61] *R (Razgar) v Secretary of State for the Home Department* [2004] UKHL 27, [2004] 2 AC 368, [20].

[62] At [19]. Questions of proportionality have to be answered by reference to the time the events took place. If primary legislation is involved, it is not correct to merely examine the situation at the time the Act in question was passed. See *Wilson v Secretary of State for Trade and Industry* [2003] UKHL 40, [2003] 3 WLR 568 per Lord Hobhouse at [144]. See also *Quila v Secretary of State for the Home Department*

4.2 The Shift from *Wednesbury*

The criteria outlined by Lord Steyn in *Daly*[63] are more precise and more sophisticated than the traditional grounds of judicial review, and his Lordship suggested three concrete differences:

> First, the doctrine of proportionality may require the reviewing court to assess the balance which the decision maker has struck, not merely whether it is within the range of rational or reasonable decisions. Secondly, the proportionality test may go further than the traditional grounds of review inasmuch as it may require attention to be directed to the relative weight accorded to interests and considerations. Thirdly, even the heightened scrutiny test developed in ... *Smith* ... is not necessarily appropriate to the protection of human rights.[64]

In any application for judicial review alleging a violation of a Convention right, the court will now conduct a much more rigorous and intrusive review than was once sought to be permissible.[65] It is no longer enough to assert that the decision that was taken was a reasonable one. 'A close and penetrating examination of the factual justification for the restriction is needed if the fundamental rights enshrined in the Convention are to remain practical and effective for everyone who wishes to exercise them.'[66]

In order to make an assessment of proportionality, sometimes a court will need additional background information showing likely impact. Such information may be provided in the course of Parliamentary debate, and it is 'legitimate to have recourse to Hansard in the search for it'.[67] Furthermore the procedure of judicial review is constantly evolving to meet the new challenges presented by the HRA. For example, in *Tweed v Parades Commission for Northern Ireland*[68] the House of Lords ordered the disclosure of five documents on an application for judicial review although in the past the general rules governing disclosure had not been applied to applications for judicial review. Lord Bingham noted that such applications for disclosure are likely to increase in frequency, since human rights decisions under the Convention tend to be very fact-

---

[2011] UKSC 45, [2012] 1 AC 621 On the meaning of proportionality, see generally: Lord Justice Arden, 'Proportionality: The Way Ahead?' [2013] *Public Law* 498; A Brady, *Proportionality and Deference under the UK Human Rights Act: An Institutionally Sensitive Approach* (Cambridge, Cambridge University Press, 2012); C Chan, 'Proportionality and Invariable Baseline Intensity of Review' (2013) 33 *Legal Studies* 1; T Hickman, 'The Substance and Structure of Proportionality' [2008] *Public Law* 694.

[63] *Daly* (n 53). On the meaning of proportionality in Convention law, see generally P Sales and B Hooper, 'Proportionality and the Form of Law' (2003) 119 *Law Quarterly Review* 426; D Feldman, 'Proportionality and the Human Rights Act 1998' in E Ellis (ed), *The Principle of Proportionality in the Laws of Europe* (Oxford, Hart Publishing, 1999).

[64] *Daly* (n 53), [27].

[65] *Shayler* (n 5), per Lord Bingham at [33] and per Lord Hope at [75].

[66] Ibid, per Lord Hope at [61]. See also Lord Hutton's comments at [111] and Lord Hope's comments in *Rottman* (n 5), at [37]. See further T Hickman, 'The Reasonableness Principle: Reassessing its Place in the Public Sphere' (2004) 63 *Cambridge Law Journal* 166; J Jowell, 'Beyond the Rule of Law: Towards Constitutional Judicial Review' [2000] *Public Law* 671; P Craig, 'The Courts, the Human Rights Act and Judicial Review' (2001) 117 *Law Quarterly Review* 589; M Elliott, 'The Human Rights Act 1998 and the Standard of Substantive Review' [2001] *Cambridge Law Journal* 301; A Le Sueur, 'The Rise and Ruin of Unreasonableness' (2005) 10 *Judicial Review* 32.

[67] *R (F) v Secretary of State for the Home Department* [2010] UKSC 17, [2011] 1 AC 331, [18]; *Wilson v Secretary of State for Trade and Industry* [2003] UKHL 40, [2004] 1 AC 816. See, for example, the level of evidence considered by the Supreme Court in *Quila* (n 62). Questions of justiciability are discussed further in Chapter 1 and the process for determining the incompatibility of primary legislation is discussed further in Chapter 5.

[68] *Tweed v Parades Commission for Northern Ireland* [2006] UKHL 53, [2007] 2 All ER 273.

specific and any judgment on the proportionality of a public authority's interference with a protected convention right is likely to call for 'careful evaluation of the facts'.[69]

4.3 Merits Review?

In *Daly*,[70] noting that the differences in approach between traditional grounds of review and the proportionality approach may yield different results, Lord Steyn held that it was important that cases involving Convention rights must be analysed in the correct way. However, he was careful to point out that this did not mean that there had been a shift to merits review:

> [T]he respective roles of judges and administrators are fundamentally distinct and will remain so. To this extent the general tenor of the observations in *Mahmood* ... are correct. And Laws LJ rightly emphasised in *Mahmood* ... 'that the intensity of review in a public law case will depend on the subject matter in hand'. That is so even in cases involving Convention rights. In law, context is everything.[71]

When exercising their powers of judicial review, courts are extremely reluctant to be seen to be engaging in merits review by operating as a court of appeal, analysing the evidence and reaching their own conclusion as to the correct decision.[72] However, as the majority of cases brought under the HRA have reached the courts via the judicial review route, judges have been faced with a dilemma. Are they exercising judicial review and therefore unable to essentially retake the decision? Or are they exercising a new power of human rights adjudication by which they are not exercising merits review but ensuring that public authorities do not act incompatibly with Convention rights?[73]

In *Huang*[74] the House of Lords was called upon essentially to answer this question. The appeal concerned the proper approach to be taken by an immigration adjudicator when determining, on appeal, whether or not the Secretary of State's decision to remove an individual from the United Kingdom was a disproportionate interference with his or her right to respect for family life, as protected by Article 8 of the ECHR. The issue which separated the applicants and the Secretary of State was whether or not the adjudicator should decide for himself, on the merits, whether the removal was proportionate or not. The Secretary of State argued that the adjudicator's assessment of proportionality should be limited to a review of his decision, and only ask whether or not it was within the range of reasonable assessments of proportionality.

With reference to section 65 and Schedule 4 of the Immigration and Asylum Act 1999, their Lordships stated as follows:

> These provisions, read purposively and in context, make it plain that the task of the appellate immigration authority, on an appeal on a Convention ground against a decision of the primary official decision-maker refusing leave to enter or remain in this country, is to decide whether

---

[69] Ibid, [3]. See also *R (Wilkinson) v The Responsible Medical Officer Broadmoor Hospital* [2001] EWCA Civ 1545, [2001] 1 WLR 419.

[70] *Daly* (n 53).

[71] Ibid, [28].

[72] *Champion v Chief Constable of the Gwent Constabulary* [1990] 1 WLR 1.

[73] See further I Leigh, 'Taking Rights Proportionately: Judicial Review, the Human Rights Act and Strasbourg', [2002] *Public Law* 265.

[74] *Huang* (n 58).

the challenged decision is unlawful as incompatible with a Convention right or compatible and so lawful. It is not a secondary, reviewing function dependent on establishing that the primary decision-maker misdirected himself or acted irrationally or was guilty of procedural impropriety. The appellate immigration authority must decide for itself whether the impugned decision is lawful and, if not, but only if not, reverse it.[75]

In explaining its conclusion, the House of Lords' first point of discussion was the comment of Lord Steyn in *Daly*[76] that although there was a material difference between the *Wednesbury* and the *Smith*[77] approach and the proportionality approach, this 'does not mean that there has been a shift to merits review'.[78] Their Lordships observed that this statement had 'given rise to some misunderstanding'[79] and they endeavoured to provide some much-needed clarity. First a distinction was made between the ultra vires challenge in *Daly* and the irrationality challenge in *Smith*. Their Lordships stated that whilst the judgment in *Daly* depended on the application of 'pure legal principle',[80] in *Smith* a rationality challenge had been made to the recruitment policy adopted by the Ministry of Defence. The point they understood that Lord Steyn wished to make was that although the Convention calls for a more exacting standard of review, it remains the case that the judge is not the primary decision-maker. It is not for him to decide what the recruitment policy for the armed forces should be.[81]

Their Lordships then turned to the question of deference and the task of the appellate immigration authority. Observing that much argument had been directed towards the issue of due deference, discretionary areas of judgment, the margin of appreciation, democratic accountability and relative institutional competence,[82] they gave a pithy summation of the last seven or so years of confusion in the lower courts:

> We think, with respect, that there has been a tendency, both in the arguments addressed to the courts and in the judgments of the courts, to complicate and mystify what is not, in principle, a hard task to define, however difficult the task is, in practice, to perform.[83]

Their Lordships then defined the task of the appellate immigration authority, assuming that the applicant did not qualify for leave to enter or remain under the Rules and reliance was placed on the right to respect for family life as protected by Article 8 of the ECHR. The first task was seen as establishing the relevant facts.[84] The next task was described in detail:

> The authority will wish to consider and weigh all that tells in favour of the refusal of leave which is challenged, with particular reference to justification under article 8(2). There will, in almost any case, be certain general considerations to bear in mind: the general administrative desirability of applying known rules if a system of immigration control is to be workable, predictable, consistent and fair as between one applicant and another; the damage to good administration and effective control if a system is perceived by applicants internationally to be unduly porous, unpredictable or perfunctory; the need to discourage non-nationals

---

[75] Ibid, [11].
[76] *Daly* (n 53).
[77] *R v Ministry of Defence, ex p Smith* [1996] QB 517.
[78] *Huang* (n 58), [28].
[79] Ibid, [13].
[80] Ibid.
[81] Ibid.
[82] Ibid, [14].
[83] Ibid.
[84] Ibid, [15].

admitted to the country temporarily from believing that they can commit serious crimes and yet be allowed to remain; the need to discourage fraud, deception and deliberate breaches of the law; and so on.[85]

Their Lordships then tackled the question of deference, noting that to give weight to factors such as these was not aptly described as deference but as 'performance of the ordinary judicial task' of weighing up the competing considerations on each side and according 'appropriate weight to the judgment of a person with responsibility for a given subject matter and access to special sources of knowledge and advice'.[86] Their Lordships saw this as how any rational judicial decision-maker was likely to proceed.[87]

Providing further clarification, the House of Lords also responded to the Secretary of State's argument that by analogy with its judgment in *Kay v Lambeth London Borough Council*,[88] the appellate immigration authorities should assume that the Immigration Rules and supplementary instructions, made by the responsible Minister and laid before Parliament, had the imprimatur of 'democratic approval' and should be taken to strike the right balance between the interests of the individual and those of the community.[89] Their Lordships found the analogy unpersuasive, stating that domestic housing policy had been a continuing subject of discussion and debate in Parliament over many years and the outcome could therefore be said to represent a considered democratic compromise. 'This cannot be said in the same way of the Immigration Rules and supplementary instructions, which are not the product of active debate in Parliament, where non-nationals seeking leave to enter or remain are not in any event represented'.[90] Furthermore, it is a 'premise of the statutory scheme enacted by Parliament that an applicant may fail to qualify under the Rules and yet may have a valid claim by virtue of article 8'.[91]

The House of Lords concluded by setting out the ultimate question for the appellate immigration authority:

> In an article 8 case where this question is reached, the ultimate question for the appellate immigration authority is whether the refusal of leave to enter or remain, in circumstances where the life of the family cannot reasonably be expected to be enjoyed elsewhere, taking full account of all the considerations weighing in favour of the refusal, prejudices the family life of the applicant in a manner sufficiently serious to amount to a breach of the fundamental right protected by article 8. If the answer to this question is affirmative, the refusal is unlawful and the authority must so decide. It is not necessary that the appellate immigration authority directing itself along the lines indicated in this opinion, need ask in addition whether the case meets a test of exceptionality.[92]

The judgment of the Secretary of State was not specifically referred to in the process described although arguably, given the preceding comments, it would be included in

---

[85] Ibid, [16]. It is interesting to note that none of these justifications appears in the text of Art 8(2).
[86] Ibid.
[87] Ibid.
[88] *Kay v Lambeth London Borough Council* [2006] UKHL 10, [2006] 2 AC 465.
[89] *Huang* (n 58), [17].
[90] Ibid.
[91] Ibid.
[92] Ibid, [20]. The task of an appellate court reviewing the conclusion of a lower court is different. See *RB (Algeria) v Secretary of State for the Home Department* [2009] UKHL 10, [2010] 2 AC 110. In *Re B (A Child)* [2013] UKSC 33, [2013] 1 WLR 1911 the Supreme Court held that the task of an appellate court was to ask whether the determination of the lower court was wrong.

'all the considerations weighing in favour of the refusal'. In the appeals at issue, both were remitted to be heard by a properly directed Asylum and Immigration Tribunal.

The judgment of the House of Lords, although short, contains two very important clarifications to the law. The first is the conclusion that the task of an appellate immigration authority, on an appeal on a Convention ground against a decision of the Secretary of State refusing leave to enter or remain in this country, is to decide for itself whether the challenged decision is unlawful as incompatible with a Convention right or compatible and so lawful. It is not a secondary, reviewing function dependent on establishing that the primary decision-maker misdirected himself or acted 'irrationally or was guilty of procedural impropriety'.[93] However, this is not merits review. As their Lordships explained, the point they understood Lord Steyn to be making in *Daly* was that it remained the case that the judge was not the primary decision-maker.[94] This is undoubtedly correct. On a human rights challenge the court is not deciding the recruitment policy of the armed forces (*Smith*) or the policy governing the searching of prisoner's cells (*Daly*). What it is deciding is whether or not the application of a policy to a particular individual is incompatible with that person's Convention rights, and it is only concerned with that aspect of the primary decision-maker's decision which engages Convention rights.[95] It might be the case that it is no longer possible to maintain the policy following a finding of incompatibility in the case of an individual, as was the situation in *Smith* following the judgment of the ECtHR.[96] However, in some instances it is possible to maintain the policy if exceptions are made for particular individuals to ensure compatibility with their Convention rights, as was the situation in *Daly*. In the appeals before the House of Lords the policy reflected in the Immigration Rules remained in place; all the adjudicator was deciding was whether or not the application of the Rules, in the case of a particular individual, was compatible with their Convention rights.[97]

The second important clarification was in relation to the practice of deference and is this is discussed in the following section.

---

5. Deference

5.1 Definition

Prior to the HRA coming into force there was much discussion about what role the margin of appreciation would play in the domestic context.[98] Most commentators

---

[93] *Kay* (n 88), [11].
[94] *Huang* (n 58), [13].
[95] See further Jowell (n 66).
[96] *Lustig-Prean and Beckett v United Kingdom; Smith and Grady v United Kingdom* (1999) 29 EHRR 493.
[97] See also *R (Begum) v Headteacher and Governors of Denbigh High School* [2006] UKHL 15 and *Belfast City Council v Miss Behavin' Limited* [2007] UKHL 19.
[98] See eg D Pannick, 'Principles of Interpretation of Convention Rights under the Human Rights Act and the Discretionary Area of Judgment' [1998] *Public Law* 545; R Singh, M Hunt and M Demetriou, 'Current

accepted that the doctrine of the margin of appreciation does not apply when a national court is considering the HRA. However, it was generally recommended that a similar doctrine should be recognised by national courts.[99] This recommendation was soon reflected in the case law. In *Kebilene*[100] Lord Hope held that the doctrine of margin of appreciation, exercised by the ECtHR, was not available to the national courts when they were considering Convention issues. However, his Lordship also stated that in this area

> difficult choices may have to be made by the executive or the legislature between the rights of the individual and the needs of society. In some circumstances it will be appropriate for the courts to recognise that there is an area of judgment within which the judiciary will defer, on democratic grounds, to the considered opinion of the elected body or the person whose act or decision is said to be incompatible with the Convention.

In the early years of the HRA the courts rarely defined what exactly was meant by deference—apart from indicating that it involved affording 'weight' to the decisions of the legislature or executive.[101] In practice, deference usually only arises in the context of a decision on proportionality,[102] and it is important not to confuse deference when making a proportionality judgment with determining the limits of what is 'possible' under section 3 of the HRA.[103]

In its judgment in *Huang* the House of Lords provided some much-needed clarity. As noted above, their Lordships held that giving weight to the judgment of the primary decision-maker was not aptly described as deference but as performance of the ordinary judicial task of weighing up the competing considerations on each side and according appropriate weight to the judgment of a person with responsibility for a given subject matter and access to special sources of knowledge and advice.[104] However, as their Lordships also make clear, according appropriate weight to the judgment of the primary decision-maker does not absolve the court, or immigration adjudicator, from determining whether or not the interference with Convention rights is proportionate.[105] In order for the primary decision-maker to have his or her judgment taken into account in this process, they need to have responsibility for a given subject matter, access to special sources of knowledge and advice, and arguably have also given effective consideration to whether or not there is a disproportionate interference with the individual's Convention rights. This is undoubtedly correct and supports the opinion of those who

---

Topic: Is there a Role for the "Margin of Appreciation" in National Law after the Human Rights Act?' [1999] *European Human Rights Law Review* 15.

[99] Pannick, ibid, 545, 549.

[100] *Kebilene* (n 49).

[101] See *Brown* (n 52), per Lord Bingham and *R v A* (n 50), per Lord Steyn at [37].

[102] Although it can also arise when a court is determining the scope of a Convention right. For example, in *R v Secretary of State for the Environment, Transport and the Regions, ex p Alconbury Developments Ltd* [2001] UKHL 23, [2001] 2 WLR 1389 deference to the executive was apparent in their Lordships' conclusion that a breach by the executive of the guarantee of independence and impartiality in Art 6(1) could be overcome by the existence of a sufficient opportunity for appeal or review. See also *R v Director of Public Prosecutions, ex p Pretty* [2001] UKHL 61, [2001] 3 WLR 1598. See further S Atrill, 'Keeping the Executive in the Picture: A Reply to Professor Leigh' [2003] *Public Law* 41; Leigh (n 73); Craig (n 66.

[103] See further A Young, 'Ghaidan v Godin-Mendoza: Avoiding the Deference Trap' [2005] *Public Law* 23.

[104] *Huang* (n 58), [16].

[105] Ibid, [16] and [20].

have argued that deference should be rooted in institutional competence rather than respect for democratic credentials.[106]

5.2 Expertise Rather than Democratic Credentials

The judgment in *Huang* establishes that what is important is no longer democratic credentials but the expertise of the primary decision-maker—in particular, if he or she has already used such expertise to carry out an assessment of the proportionality of the interference with Convention rights. However, from their Lordships' subsequent discussion of their earlier judgment in *Kay*[107] the impression could arise that the link between deference and democracy has not yet been completely severed. As their Lordships explained, in *Kay* it had been held that the right of a public authority landlord to enforce a claim for possession under domestic law against an occupier whose right to occupy (if any) had ended, and who was entitled to no protection in domestic law, would in most cases automatically supply the justification required by Article 8(2) 'and the courts would assume that domestic law struck the proper balance, at any rate unless the contrary were shown'.[108] By analogy in the present appeals, the Secretary of State argued that the Immigration Rules, made by the Minister and laid before Parliament, also had the imprimatur of democratic approval and should be taken to strike the right balance. Their Lordships did not accept this submission, finding the analogy unpersuasive:

> Domestic housing policy has been a continuing subject of discussion and debate in Parliament over many years, with the competing interests of landlords and tenants fully represented, as also the public interest in securing accommodation for the indigent, averting homelessness and making the best use of finite resources. The outcome, changed from time to time, may truly be said to represent a considered democratic compromise. This cannot be said in the same way of the Immigration Rules and supplementary instructions, which are not the product of active debate in Parliament, where non-nationals seeking leave to enter or remain are not in any event represented.[109]

What their Lordships did not say, although it is implicit from their earlier comments, was that weight, or deference, was given to the judgment of Parliament in *Kay* because here Parliament was the 'person with responsibility for a given subject matter and access to special sources of knowledge and advice',[110] and although Convention rights or any assessment of proportionality did not feature in the Parliamentary debates, the debate was such that these issues had effectively been considered and that careful judgment deserved to be given respect, not because it possessed the democratic imprimatur,

---

[106] See further: A Young, 'Deference, Dialogue and the Search for Legitimacy' (2010) 30 *Oxford Journal of Legal Studies* 815; A Kavanagh, 'Defending Deference in Public Law and Constitutional Theory' (2010) 126 *Law Quarterly Review* 222; A Young, 'In Defence of Due Deference' (2009) 72 *Modern Law Review* 554; A Kavanagh, "Judging the Judges under the Human Rights Act: Deference, Disillusionment and the "War on Terror"' [2009] *Public Law* 287.

[107] *Kay* (n 88).

[108] Ibid, [17].

[109] Ibid. See also the comments of Baroness Hale concerning this judgment in *Miss Behavin' Limited* (n 97), [36]–[37].

[110] *Kay* (n 88), [16].

but because the primary decision-maker had done its job properly with respect to Convention rights.

Understanding the judgment of their Lordships in this way is important. Deferring to the judgment of a primary decision-maker simply because of the presence of 'democratic credentials' has always been fraught with difficulties.[111] The HRA itself carries with it its own democratic mandate,[112] and its very structure, by only allowing a declaration of incompatibility in the face of inconsistent primary legislation, preserves the sovereignty of Parliament.[113] This is well illustrated by the response of Parliament to the declaration of incompatibility issued in *A v Secretary of State for the Home Department (No 1)*,[114] the 'Belmarsh detainees' case: Parliament immediately designed a new system of 'control orders' enshrined in the Prevention of Terrorism Act 2005.[115]

It is important for the courts not to abandon the role they have been assigned by the HRA in the face of an argument from democracy. As Phillipson notes, '[W]hat then happens when democracy turns on certain individuals or certain groups, not strong enough, because they are individuals or small groups, to protect themselves only through democracy?'[116] A better example could not be provided than that the situation of an individual immigrant seeking to remain in this country on human rights grounds. Deferring too readily to a 'democratic' decision-maker also leads to anomalies with relatively similar fact situations being dealt with differently by the courts. An example is provided by the approach of the Court of Appeal in *Huang*. Seeking to take a 'principled' approach to deference, it determined that what was important was respect for democratic powers.[117] It explained that considerable deference had been afforded to the judgment of the Secretary of State in *Samaroo* because this required the court to pass judgment upon an aspect of government policy. However, it was not necessary for the adjudicator in *Huang* and *Kashmiri* to defer, as although the question was the same, ie whether or not the interference with Article 8 was proportionate, they were not required to pass judgment on any aspect of government policy.[118] A far simpler, and fairer, approach would be for the court, or adjudicator, to accept in both applications that the Secretary of State, the primary decision-maker with the expertise, had already made a careful judgment on proportionality, and afford this weight when coming to its own conclusion.

If a court defers too readily to a democratic decision-maker, and as a result no effective consideration of the proportionality of an interference is undertaken by any domestic institution, this may also have implications at the international level by hampering the ability of the United Kingdom to argue before the ECtHR that an inter-

---

[111] See generally Lord Justice Dyson, 'Some Thoughts on Judicial Deference' [2006] *Judicial Review* 103; Lord Steyn, 'Deference: A Tangled Story' [2005] *Public Law* 346.

[112] *A v Secretary of State for the Home Department (No 1)* [2004] UKHL 56, [2005] 2 AC 68 per Lord Bingham at [42].

[113] See further D Nicol, 'Law and Politics After the Human Rights Act' [2006] *Public Law* 722 and K Economides, W Twining, G Phillipson, S Chakrabarti and C Gearty, 'Can Human Rights Survive? A Symposium on the 2005 Hamlyn Lectures' [2007] *Public Law* 209.

[114] *A v Secretary of State* (n 112).

[115] See further T Poole, 'Tilting and Windmills? Truth and Illusion in "The Political Constitution"' [2007] 70 *Modern Law Review* 250. However, it must be noted that aspects of this system have also been declared incompatible with Convention rights and appeals are pending in the House of Lords.

[116] Above n 113 at [222]. See also S Fredman, 'From Deference to Democracy: The Role of Equality under the Human Rights Act 1998' (2006) 122 *Law Quarterly Review* 53.

[117] [2005] EWCA Civ 105, [2006] QB 1, [51].

[118] Ibid, [50]–[60].

ference with Convention rights comes within its margin of appreciation. For example, in *Hirst v United Kingdom*[119] the Grand Chamber of the ECtHR considered the blanket ban on convicted prisoners voting in elections. The Divisional Court had considered the question under the HRA and, affording considerable deference to Parliament, found no violation of Article 3 of Protocol No 1 (free elections). Although the Grand Chamber held that Contracting States must be afforded a wide margin of appreciation in this sphere,[120] it was not impressed with the approach of the UK institutions, finding that there was no evidence that Parliament had 'ever sought to weigh the competing interests or to assess the proportionality of a blanket ban'[121] and that the Divisional Court, as it saw this as a matter for Parliament and not the national courts, also did not undertake any assessment of the proportionality of the measure itself.[122] The Grand Chamber concluded that the restriction fell outside any acceptable margin of appreciation and was incompatible with Article 3 of Protocol No 1.

By contrast, in *Dickson*[123] the applicants wished to have access to facilities for artificial insemination even though the first applicant was in prison. Their application for judicial review had been dismissed as a result of the judgment of the Court of Appeal in *Mellor*[124] where the Court had found that the policy of the Secretary of State was compatible with Article 8. The ECtHR concluded that the state had a wide margin of appreciation[125] and it drew upon the judgment in *Mellor*, noting that 'two principal aims underlie the policy: the maintenance of public confidence in the penal system and the welfare of any child conceived as a result of artificial insemination and, therefore, the general interests of society as a whole'.[126] Concluding by four votes to three that there was no violation of Articles 8 or 12, it observed that the

> decision of the Secretary of State was examined by the High Court and the Court of Appeal which found not only that the policy was rational and lawful but that, in applying the policy in the circumstances of the present case, the decision of the Secretary of State to refuse the facilities was neither unreasonable nor disproportionate.[127]

Finally, the suggestion that what is important is the expertise of the primary decision-maker, and the fact that it has already carried out its own careful assessment of proportionality, rather than its democratic credentials, also finds support in other judgments. In *Begum*, the House of Lords gave considerable weight, when assessing the proportionality of the interference, to the judgment of the school. Lord Bingham stated that it would be 'irresponsible of any court, lacking the experience, background and detailed knowledge of the head teacher, staff and governors, to overrule their judgment on a matter as sensitive as this'.[128] In his view, if a decision-maker had conscientiously paid attention to all human rights considerations, 'a challenger's task will be the harder'.[129] Whilst the school had not given express consideration to Article 9 in

---

[119] *Hirst v United Kingdom*, Application no 74025/01, 6 October 2005, Grand Chamber.
[120] Ibid, [60].
[121] Ibid, [79].
[122] Ibid, [80].
[123] *Dickson v United Kingdom*, Application no 44362/04, 18 April 2006.
[124] *R (Mellor) v Secretary of State for the Home Department* [2001] 3 WLR 533.
[125] Ibid, [31].
[126] Ibid, [33].
[127] Ibid, [38].
[128] Ibid, [34].
[129] Above n 97, [31]. See also the comments of Lord Hoffmann at [68].

its decision-making, the process followed, and matters taken into account, effectively amounted to an assessment of the proportionality of the uniform policy and its application to the claimant:

> It had taken immense pains to devise a uniform policy which respected Muslim beliefs but did so in an inclusive, unthreatening and uncompetitive way. The rules laid down were as far from being mindless as uniform rules could ever be. The school had enjoyed a period of harmony and success to which the uniform policy was thought to contribute. On further enquiry it still appeared that the rules were acceptable to mainstream Muslim opinion. It was feared that acceding to the respondent's request would or might have significant adverse repercussions.[130]

The same principle was applied in *Miss Behavin' Limited* although, by contrast to the school in *Begum*, the Council had not actually given any detailed consideration, explicit or implicit, to the proportionality of its interference with Convention rights. As Baroness Hale explained, this meant that it was for the court to determine the proportionality of the interference, without the assistance of the judgment of the Council:

> [T]he court has to decide whether the authority has violated the convention rights. In doing so, it is bound to acknowledge that the local authority is much better placed than the court to decide whether the right of sex shop owners to sell pornographic literature and images should be restricted—for the prevention of disorder or crime, for the protection of health or morals, of for the protection of the rights of others. But the views of the local authority are bound to carry less weight where the local authority has made no attempt to address that question. Had the Belfast City Council expressly set itself the task of balancing the rights of individuals to sell and buy pornographic literature and images against the interests of the wider community, a court would find it hard to upset the balance which the local authority had struck. But where there is no indication that this has been done, the court has no alternative but to strike the balance for itself, giving due weight to the judgments made by those who are in much closer touch with the people and the places involved that the court could ever be.[131]

The most strident assertion of the role of the judiciary under the HRA was contained in *A v Secretary of State for the Home Department*.[132] The appellants had been certified under section 21 of the Anti-terrorism Crime and Security Act 2001 and detained under section 23 of that Act. All were foreign nationals. None had been the subject of a criminal charge and in none of their cases was a criminal trial in prospect. It was for their Lordships to determine whether there was a public emergency threatening the life of the nation within the meaning of Article 15. And, if there was, whether the measures taken went beyond what was strictly required by the exigencies of the situation.

Answering the second question, Lord Bingham did not accept the distinction drawn by the Attorney General between democratic institutions and the courts.

> [T]he function of independent judges charged to interpret and apply the law is universally recognised as a cardinal feature of the modern democratic state, a cornerstone of the rule of law itself. The Attorney-General is fully entitled to insist on the proper limits of judicial

---

[130] Ibid, per Lord Bingham at [34]. See further D Mead, 'Outcomes Aren't All: Defending Process-Based Review of Public Authority Decisions under the Human Rights Act' [2012] *Public Law* 61.

[131] Above n 97 at [37]. See also the comments of Lord Hoffmann at [16], Lord Rodger at [26]–[27], Lord Mance at [46], and Lord Neuberger at [91]. See also *Secretary of State for the Home Department v Nasseri* [2009] UKHL 23, [2010] 1 AC 1 and *Manchester City Council v Pinnock* [2010] UKSC 45, [2011] 2 AC 104.

[132] Above n 112.

authority, but he is wrong to stigmatise judicial decision-making as in some way undemocratic. It is particularly inappropriate in a case such as the present in which Parliament has expressly legislated in s 6 of the 1998 Act to render unlawful any act of a public authority, including a court, incompatible with a Convention right, has required courts (in s 2) to take account of relevant Strasbourg jurisprudence, has (in s 3) required courts, so far as possible, to give effect to Convention rights and has conferred a right of appeal on derogation issues. The effect is not, of course, to override the sovereign legislative authority of the Queen in Parliament, since if primary legislation is declared to be incompatible the validity of the legislation is unaffected (s 4(6)) and the remedy lies with the appropriate minister (s 10), who is answerable to Parliament. The 1998 Act gives the courts a very specific, wholly democratic, mandate.[133]

5.3 When to Defer?

The first edition of this book pre-dated the judgment of the House of Lords in *Huang*, and at that point in time there was considerable confusion in the courts concerning proportionality and deference. Many of the claims decided prior to *Huang* can no longer be regarded as authoritative although some important principles remain in place. In judgments pre-dating and post-dating *Huang*, it remains the position that there may be scope for deference to the expertise of primary decision-maker taking into account: first, the nature of the Convention right or rights at issue; and second, the subject matter of the legislation or act.

> The latitude will vary according to the subject matter under consideration, the importance of the human right in question, and the extent of the encroachment upon that right. The courts will intervene only when it is apparent that, in balancing the various considerations involved, the primary decision-maker must have given insufficient weight to the human rights factor.[134]

It has been held that deference should be afforded where a Convention right is qualified rather than absolute, and not of such high constitutional importance that the court is especially well placed to assess the need for protection.[135] For example, in *R v A*[136] Lord Steyn held that when a question arose whether, in the criminal statute in question, Parliament adopted a legislative scheme which made an excessive inroad into the right to a fair trial, the court was qualified to make its own judgment and must do so.[137] Given the fundamental nature of the right to life and the importance with which it is regarded, deference is rarely shown by the courts to primary decision-makers in Article 2 cases. In *Re A*[138] Ward LJ commented that deciding matters of disputed life and death was 'surely and pre-eminently a matter for a court of law to judge. That is what

---

[133] *Ibid*, at [42]. See also the comments of Lord Nicholls at [80], Lord Hope at [114], [116] and [131], Lord Rodger at [176], Lord Scott at [145] and [154], Lord Walker at [192 and [196], and Baroness Hale at [226]. See also *International Transport Roth GmbH v Secretary of State for the Home Department* [2002] EWCA Civ 158, [2002] 3 WLR 344 at [27], [29] and [54] per Simon Brown LJ and [139] per Jonathan Parker LJ. See further Hickman, above n 62; A Tomkins, 'Readings of A v Secretary of State for the Home Department' [2005] *PL* 259; and M Arden, 'Human Rights in the Age of Terrorism' (2005) 121 *LQR* 604.

[134] *A v Secretary of State* (n 112), per Lord Nicholls at [80]. See also the observations of Laws LJ in *International Transport Roth*, ibid, [83]–[87].

[135] *Kebilene* (n 49), per Lord Hope.

[136] *R v A* (n 50).

[137] Ibid, [37].

[138] *Re A (Children) (Conjoined Twins: Surgical Separation)* [2001] Fam 147.

courts are here for.'[139] Similarly, deference is rarely mentioned in the context of Article 5, reflecting the importance with which the right is regarded, its narrow construction and the fact that many of its protections are absolute.[140] However, deference is not uncommon when adjudicating on the right to respect for private life.[141]

In relation to subject matter, it has been held that deference to the expertise of the primary decision-maker may be appropriate where the issues involve questions of social or economic policy.[142] Examples of policy-making have included the payment of welfare benefits,[143] housing matters[144] and the protection of consumers.[145] It has also been held that political judgments call for some deference on the part of the court.

> The more purely political (in a broad or narrow sense) a question is, the more appropriate it will be for political resolution and the less likely it is to be an appropriate matter for judicial decision—and therefore the smaller the potential role of the court. It is the function of political and not judicial bodies to resolve political questions. Conversely, the greater the legal content of any issue, the greater the potential role of the court, because under our constitution and subject to the sovereign power of Parliament it is the function of the courts and not of political bodies to resolve legal questions.[146]

An example of a political matter was the judgment of the Secretary of State in *A v Secretary of State*[147] that there was a public emergency threatening the life of the nation within the meaning of Article 15 of the ECHR.

Whilst the judgment in *Huang* has resulted in less willingness on the part of the courts to defer unless the primary decision-maker has relevant expertise, it remains important for courts to keep in mind the dangers of too much deference which can lead to inconsistency in decision-making, the categorisation of some groups as less deserving of the protection of the HRA—a violation of Article 13 of the ECHR[148]—and the abdication of judicial responsibility under the HRA. As Lord Steyn has noted extra-judicially:

> If the judges of today teach a new generation of lawyers, and judges, that complaisance by the judiciary to the view of the legislature and the executive in policy areas is the best way forward, one of the pillars of our democracy will have been weakened.[149]

---

[139] See also the comments of Dame Butler-Sloss in *NHS Trust A v Mrs M* [2001] 2 WLR 942, [38] and *NHS Trust v P*, Family Division, 19 December 2000; *R (on the application of Wilkinson) v The Responsible Medical Officer Broadmoor Hospital* [2001] EWCA Civ 1545, [2002] 1 WLR 419; *R (on the application of H) v Ashworth Hospital Authority* [2001] EWHC (Admin) 872, [2002] 1 FCR 206. A similar approach has been taken to Art 3. See eg *X v Secretary of State for the Home Department* [2001] 1 WLR 740 and *R (on the application of T) v Secretary of State for the Home Department* [2003] EWCA Civ 1285, [19].

[140] See eg *R v Secretary of State for the Home Department, ex p Noorkoiv* [2002] EWCA Civ 770, [2002] 1 WLR 3284, [44].

[141] See eg *Bellinger v Bellinger* [2003] UKHL 21, [2003] 2 AC 467 per Lord Nicholls at [37].

[142] *Kebilene* (n 49), per Lord Hope; *Wilson* (n 67), per Lord Nicholls at [70]; *Ghaidan v Godin-Mendoza* [2004] UKHL 30, [2004] 2 AC 557 per Lord Nicholls at [19].

[143] *R (Hooper) v Secretary of State for Work and Pensions* [2005] UKHL 29, [2005] 1 WLR 1681.

[144] *Poplar Housing and Regeneration Community Association v Donoghue* [2001] EWCA Civ 595, [2001] QB 48.

[145] *Wilson* (n 67).

[146] *A v Secretary of State* (n 112), per Lord Bingham at [29].

[147] Ibid.

[148] See further Leigh (n 73).

[149] Lord Steyn, 'Deference: A Tangled Story' [2005] *Public Law* 346. For further critique of the practice of deference see KD Ewing, 'The Futility of the Human Rights Act' [2004] *Public Law* 829; R Clayton, 'Judicial Deference and "Democratic Dialogue": The Legitimacy of Judicial Intervention under the Human Rights Act 1998' [2004] *Public Law* 33; J Jowell, 'Judicial Deference: Servility, Civility or Institutional

As Lord Bingham observed in *A v Secretary of State*,[150] the Convention regime for the international protection of human rights requires national authorities, including national courts, to exercise their authority to afford effective protection,[151] and domestic courts must themselves form a judgment as to whether a Convention right has been breached.[152] Similarly Lord Hope observed that the margin of appreciation afforded by the European Court of Human Rights could not be equated to the role of the domestic courts.

> [T]he fact that the European Court will accord a large margin of appreciation to the contracting states on the question whether the measures taken to interfere with the right to liberty do not exceed those strictly required by the exigencies of the situation cannot be taken as the last word on the matter so far as the domestic courts are concerned. Final responsibility for determining whether they do exceed these limits must lie with the courts, if the test which Art 15(1) lays down is to be applied within the domestic system with all the rigour that its wording indicates.[153]

6. Deference in Practice

To gain further insight into the practice of deference, it is useful to consider some of the judgments divided by reference to subject matter, although it is important to note that the level of deference will vary according to: the Convention right; the subject matter; the expertise of the primary decision-maker; and whether or not a thorough proportionality analysis has already been undertaken. Proportionality and deference are also considered in Part II of the book in the context of each of the Convention rights.[154]

6.1 Criminal Justice

6.1.1 Prevention of Terrorism

In *Kebilene*[155] the House of Lords considered section 16A of the Prevention of Terrorism (Temporary Provisions) Act 1989, which reversed the legal burden of proof and

---

Capacity?' [2003] *Public Law* 592; Leigh (n 73); RA Edwards, 'Judicial Deference under the Human Rights Act' [2002] 65 *Modern Law Review* 859.

[150] *A v Secretary of State* (n 112).

[151] Ibid, [40].

[152] Ibid.

[153] Ibid, [114]. See also [116] and [131], Lord Rodger at [176], Lord Scott at [145] and [154], Lord Walker at [192] and [196], and Baroness Hale at [226].

[154] The current approach to proportionality and deference in the context of immigration is discussed in the preceding section concerning the judgment of the House of Lords in *Huang*. See also *R (Bibi) v Secretary of State for the Home Department* [2013] EWCA Civ 322, [2013] 3 All ER 778 and *SS (Nigeria) v Secretary of State for the Home Department* [2013] EWCA Civ 550.

[155] *Kebilene* (n 49).

was therefore alleged to be incompatible with Article 6(2). Although agreeing with the majority that the decision of the Director of Public Prosecutions to consent to the prosecution was not amenable to judicial review, Lord Hope alone went on to consider the compatibility of the provision with Article 6(2). His Lordship commented that it was necessary to bear in mind the jurisprudence of the ECtHR which recognised that due account should be taken of the special nature of terrorist crime and the threat which it posed to a democratic society.[156] In striking a fair balance between the demands of the general interest of the community and the protection of the fundamental rights of the individual, his Lordship also took into account

> the nature of the threat which terrorism poses to a free and democratic society. It seeks to achieve its ends by violence and intimidation. It is often indiscriminate in its effects, and sophisticated methods are used to avoid detection both before and after the event. Society has a strong interest in preventing acts of terrorism before they are perpetrated—to spare the lives of innocent people and to avoid the massive damage and dislocation to ordinary life which may follow from explosions which destroy or damage property. Section 16A is designed to achieve that end.

However, his Lordship reached no final conclusion, holding that the problem of compatibility would have to await a decision after trial.

6.1.2 Road Traffic Offences

In *Brown*[157] the Privy Council considered the compatibility of section 172(2)(a) of the Road Traffic Act 1988 with the right not to incriminate oneself, as protected by Articles 6(1) and 6(2). At this trial for driving a car after consuming excessive alcohol, the prosecutor sought to rely on the claimant's admission that she was driving the car which had been obtained compulsorily under this section. Lord Bingham, having already commented that the judiciary would give weight to the decisions of a representative legislature, noted that the high incidence of death and injury on the roads caused by the misuse of motor vehicles was a very serious problem and the need to address it in an effective way, for the benefit of the public, could not be doubted. He concluded that the section was not incompatible with Article 6. Lord Steyn also found deference to be of some relevance in the present case.

> Here s 172(2) addresses a pressing social problem, namely the difficulty of law enforcement in the face of statistics revealing a high accident rate resulting in death and serious injuries. The legislature was entitled to regard the figures of serious accidents as unacceptably high. It would also have been entitled to take into account that it was necessary to protect other convention rights, viz the right to life of members of the public exposed to the danger of accidents. ... On this aspect the legislature was in as good a position as a court to assess the gravity of the problem and the public interest in addressing it.

---

[156] In reliance upon *Murray v United Kingdom* (1994) 19 EHRR 193.
[157] *Brown* (n 52).

6.1.3 Rape Complainant's Prior Sexual History

In *R v A*[158] the House of Lords considered the compatibility with Article 6 of section 41 of the Youth Justice and Criminal Evidence Act 1999 following the trial judge's ruling that the complainant could not be cross-examined, nor could evidence be led, about her alleged sexual relationship with the defendant. Lord Steyn noted that weight must be given to the decision of Parliament, yet concluded that

> when the question arises whether in the criminal statute in question Parliament adopted a legislative scheme which makes an excessive inroad into the right to a fair trial the court is qualified to make its own judgment and must do so.[159]

He further concluded that whilst the statute pursued desirable goals, the methods adopted amounted to legislative overkill.[160]

By contrast, Lord Hope held that there were areas of law which lay within the discretionary area of judgment which the court ought to accord to the legislature and that prima facie section 41 was in that category.[161]

> The area is one where Parliament was better equipped than the judges are to decide where the balance lay. The judges are well able to assess the extent to which the restrictions will inhibit questioning or the leading of evidence. But it seems to me that in this highly sensitive and carefully researched field an assessment of the prejudice to the wider interests of the community if the restrictions were not to take that form was more appropriate for Parliament. An important factor for Parliament to consider was the extent to which restrictions were needed in order to restore and maintain public confidence.[162]

However, using section 3 of the HRA, their Lordships concluded that the test of admissibility was whether the evidence was nevertheless so relevant to the issue of consent that to exclude it would endanger the fairness of the trial under Article 6.

6.1.4 Policing

In *Re E*[163] the House of Lords considered deference to the police not in the context of a qualified right but in the context of the positive duty imposed by Article 3. The claim concerned the policing of a lengthy protest in Belfast. The claimant argued that police had failed to take appropriate steps to discharge their positive obligation under Article 3 to protect her and her daughter from inhuman and degrading treatment. The key question before the House of Lords was whether the police, in the circumstances, did all that could reasonably be expected of them to avoid a breach of Article 3. Finding no breach of Article 3, deference was afforded to the expertise and actions of police here:

> The police had such responsibility and were uniquely placed through their experience and intelligence to make a judgment on the wisest course to take in all the circumstances. They

---

[158] *R v A* (n 50).
[159] Ibid, [36].
[160] Ibid, [43].
[161] Ibid, [58].
[162] Ibid, [99].
[163] *Re E (A Child)* [2008] UKHL 66, [2009] 1 AC 536.

had long and hard experience of the problems encountered in dealing with riotous situations in urban areas in Northern Ireland.[164]

6.1.5 Sentencing

In *Lichniak*[165] the House of Lords considered the compatibility of the mandatory life sentence for murder, pursuant to section 1(1) of the Murder (Abolition of Death Penalty) Act 1965, with Articles 3 and 5. Their Lordships noted that section 1(1) represented the settled will of Parliament.

> Criticism of the subsection has been voiced in many expert and authoritative quarters over the years, and there have been numerous occasions on which Parliament could have amended it had it wished, but there has never been a majority of both Houses in favour of amendment. The fact that section 1(1) represents the settled will of a democratic assembly is not a conclusive reason for upholding it, but a degree of deference is due to the judgment of a democratic assembly on how a particular social problem is best tackled. ... It may be accepted that the mandatory life penalty for murder has a denunciatory value, expressing society's view of a crime which has long been regarded with peculiar abhorrence.[166]

6.2 National Security

In *Shayler*[167] the appellant argued that his prosecution under the Official Secrets Act 1989 was incompatible with Article 10. Lord Bingham, with whom Lords Scott and Hobhouse agreed, in response to the submission that the courts were reluctant to intervene in matters concerning national security, held that the court's willingness to intervene would very much depend upon the nature of the material which it was sought to disclose.

> If the issue concerns the disclosure of documents bearing a high security classification and there is apparently credible unchallenged evidence that disclosure is liable to lead to the identification of agents or the compromise of informers, the court may very well be unwilling to intervene. If, at the other end of the spectrum, it appears that while disclosure of the material may cause embarrassment or arouse criticism, it will not damage any security or intelligence interest, the court's reaction is likely to be very different.[168]

In the present case it was concluded that the sections of the Act were compatible with Article 10, essentially because the safeguards built into the Act were sufficient to ensure that unlawfulness and irregularity could be reported to those with the power and duty to take effective action.[169] By contrast, Lord Hope simply held that a wide margin of discretion was to be accorded to the legislature in matters relating to national security especially where the Convention rights of others, such as the right to life, may be put

---

[164] Ibid, [58].
[165] *R v Lichniak* [2002] UKHL 47, [2003] 1 AC 903.
[166] Ibid, per Lord Bingham at [14].
[167] *Shayler* (n 5).
[168] Ibid, [33].
[169] Ibid, per Lord Bingham at [36].

in jeopardy.[170] However, he also concluded that the choice of a system which favoured official authorisation before disclosure subject to judicial review on grounds of proportionality was within this margin of discretion.[171]

The issue of national security arose again in *A v Secretary of State for the Home Department*.[172] As discussed in the paragraphs above, the appellants had been certified under section 21 of the Anti-terrorism Crime and Security Act 2001 and detained under section 23 of that Act. All were foreign nationals. None had been the subject of a criminal charge and in none of their cases was a criminal trial in prospect. It was for their Lordships to determine whether there was a public emergency threatening the life of the nation within the meaning of Article 15. And, if there was, whether the measures taken went beyond what was strictly required by the exigencies of the situation.

A majority of their Lordships concluded that there was a public emergency threatening the life of the nation and that this was an issue where great weight should be given to the judgment of the Home Secretary, his colleagues and Parliament, 'because they were called on to exercise a pre-eminently political judgment'.[173] However, on the second question not as much deference was shown, a majority of their Lordships concluding that the measures taken were not strictly required. Lord Nicholls observed that

> Parliament must be regarded as having attached insufficient weight to the human rights of non-nationals. The subject matter of the legislation is the needs of national security. This subject matter dictates that, in the ordinary course, substantial latitude should be accorded to the legislature. But the human right in question, the right to individual liberty, is one of the most fundamental of human rights.[174]

Lord Hope noted that whilst the executive and legislature were to be afforded a wide margin of discretion in matters relating to national security, the width of the margin depended on the context.

> We are not dealing here with matters of social or economic policy, where opinions may reasonably differ in a democratic society and where choices on behalf of the country as a whole are properly left to government and to the legislature. We are dealing with actions taken on behalf of society as a whole which affect the rights and freedoms of the individual. This is where the courts may legitimately intervene, to ensure that the actions taken are proportionate. It is an essential safeguard, if individual rights and freedoms are to be protected in a democratic society which respects the principle that minorities, however unpopular, have the same rights as the majority.[175]

---

[170] Ibid, [80].

[171] Ibid, [83].

[172] *A v Secretary of State* (n 112).

[173] Ibid, per Lord Bingham at [29].

[174] Ibid, [81].

[175] Ibid, [108]. See also Lord Rodger at [176]–[178]. See also *R (Lord Carlile of Berriew) v Secretary of State for the Home Department* [2013] EWCA Civ 199 and *R (Harrow Community Support Ltd) v Secretary of State for Defence* [2012] EWHC 1921 (Admin). The Court of Appeal held in *R (Al Rawi) v Secretary of State for Foreign and Commonwealth Affairs* [2006] EWCA Civ 1279 that where issues of national security were combined with the conduct of foreign relations, the court should afford an especially broad margin of discretion.

6.3 Social and Economic Policy

6.3.1 State Support

In *Hooper*[176] the House of Lords made clear its view that it regarded the payment of welfare benefits, such as widow's benefit, a matter of social and economic policy.

> In a domestic system which (unlike the Strasbourg court) is concerned with the separation of powers, such decisions are ordinarily recognised by the courts to be matters for the judgment of the elected representatives of the people. The fact that the complaint concerns discrimination on grounds of sex is not in itself a reason for a court to impose its own judgment. Once it is accepted that older widows were historically an economically disadvantaged class which merited special treatment but were gradually becoming less disadvantaged, the question of the precise moment at which such special treatment is no longer justified becomes a social and political question within the competence of Parliament.[177]

It was concluded that the preservation of a widow's pension for those bereaved before 9 April 2001 was objectively justified and involved no breach of Convention rights.[178]

6.3.2 Pensions

Shortly after, in *Carson*,[179] the House of Lords considered the compatibility with the Convention rights of the non-payment of the annual pension increment to certain UK pensioners living abroad and the difference in rates of Jobseeker's Allowance and Income Support based on age. Lord Hoffmann noted that whilst certain grounds of discrimination (race, caste, noble birth, membership of a political party, gender) required careful examination by the courts, other differences in treatment (such as grounds of ability, education, wealth, occupation and age) usually depended upon considerations of the general public interest and were very much a matter for the democratically elected branches of government.[180] With respect to the differences in pensions, he noted that this was very much a case in which Parliament was entitled to decide whether the differences justified a difference in treatment.

> [I]n deciding what expatriate pensioners should be paid, Parliament must be entitled to take into account competing claims on public funds. ... Once it is conceded ... that people resident outside the UK are relevantly different and could be denied any pension at all, Parliament does not have to justify to the courts the reasons why they are paid one sum rather than another. Generosity does not have to have a logical explanation. It is enough for the Secretary of State to say that, all things considered, Parliament considered the present system of payments to be a fair allocation of available resources.[181]

---

[176] *Hooper* (n 143).
[177] Ibid, per Lord Hoffmann at [32].
[178] *Cf Secretary of State for Work and Pensions v M* [2004] EWCA Civ 1343, [2005] 2 WLR 740. See also *R (MA) v Secretary of State for Work & Pensions* [2013] EWHC 2213 (QB).
[179] *R (on the application of Carson) v Secretary of State for Work and Pensions* [2005] UKHL 37, [2005] 2 WLR 1369.
[180] Ibid, [16].
[181] Ibid, [25]–[26].

Similarly in relation to the levels of Income Support and Jobseeker's Allowance, his Lordship held that

> once it is accepted that the necessary expenses of young people, as a class, are lower than those of older people, they can properly be treated differently for the purpose of social security payments. No doubt there are different ways of given effect to the distinction, but that is a matter for Parliament to choose.[182]

A majority concluded that there was no breach of Convention in relation to the increase in pension, and it was unanimously concluded that there was no breach in relation to Jobseeker's Allowance and Income Support.[183]

6.3.3 Housing

The allocation of social housing has traditionally been considered an area where in interpreting and applying the Article 8 right to respect for home, the courts will show deference to the legislature. However, as has been pointed out by the ECtHR in a number of decisions,[184] there are limits to how deferential the courts can be whilst still carrying out the task assigned to them by the HRA. In *Pinnock*[185] the Supreme Court held that where a court was asked to make an order for possession of a person's home, the court must have the power to assess the proportionality of making the order, and in making that assessment, to resolve any relevant disputes of fact.[186] However, it was still prepared to give some weight to the legislative scheme, albeit not as overtly as previously:

> [I]n virtually every case where a residential occupier has no contractual or statutory protection, and the local authority is entitled to possession as a matter of domestic law, there will be a very strong case for saying that making an order for possession would be proportionate.[187]

6.3.4 Family Law

In *Re P*[188] the House of Lords considered a Northern Ireland Order prohibiting unmarried couples from adopting. The claim was made under Article 14 in conjunction with Article 8. Lord Hoffmann observed that this was a question of social policy and ordinarily, where these questions admitted of more than one rational choice, that would be a matter for Parliament. However, in his view, the choice of the legislature here was not worthy of respect and a violation of Article 14 was found.

> But that does not mean that Parliament is entitled to discriminate in any case which can be described as social policy. The discrimination must at least have a rational basis. In this case,

---

[182] Ibid, [40]. See also Lord Rodger at [45] and Lord Walker at [80] and [91]. *Cf* Lord Carswell at [99].
[183] See also *Public & Commercial Services Union v Minister for the Civil Service* [2011] EWHC 2041 (Admin), [2012] 1 All ER 985.
[184] See eg *Connors v United Kingdom* (2004) 40 EHRR 189; *McCann v United Kingdom* (2008) 47 EHRR 913; *Kay v United Kingdom* (2012) 54 EHRR 30.
[185] *Manchester City Council v Pinnock* (n 131).
[186] Ibid, [49].
[187] Ibid, [54],
[188] *In Re P* [2008] UKHL 38, [2008] 3 WLR 76.

it seems to me to be based upon a straightforward fallacy, namely, that a reasonable generalisation can be turned into an irrebuttable presumption for individual cases.[189]

6.3.5 Social Justice

Axa[190] concerned a claim by insurance companies under Article 1 of Protocol No 1 against an Act of the Scottish Parliament which reversed a decision of the House of Lords and made particular conditions actionable harm for the purposes of an action of damages for personal injury. The Supreme Court, first determining whether or not the objective sought to be addressed was 'without reasonable foundation or manifestly unreasonable' held that this was a matter where respect for the considered opinion of the elected body by which these choices were made was necessary.[191] It then considered proportionality and also afforded a measure of deference to the legislature:

> I am prepared, given the wide margin of appreciation properly accorded to a democratically elected body determining the public interest by reference, as here, to political, economic and social considerations, to regard this legislation (ill-judged though many might regard it to be) as legitimate and proportionate and so immune from challenge under A1P1.[192]

6.3.6 Cruelty to Animals

A strong theme of the judgments in the *Countryside Alliance*[193] case, which concerned a challenge to the Hunting Act 2004, was that prevention of cruelty to animals was something which fell within the constitutional responsibility of the legislature, and there had been considerable discussion in Parliament about the aim of the legislation and whether or not it was proportionate. This was held to command respect when considering if any interference with Convention rights[194] was justified; as Lord Bingham observed:

> Here we are dealing with a law which is very recent and must (unless and until reversed) be taken to reflect the conscience of a majority of the nation. The degree of respect to be shown to the considered judgment of a democratic assembly will vary according to the subject matter and the circumstances. But the present case seems to me pre-eminently one in which respect should be shown to what the House of Commons decided. The democratic process is liable to be subverted if, on a question of moral and political judgment, opponents of the Act achieve through the courts what they could not achieve in Parliament.[195]

---

[189] Ibid, [20]. See also Lord Hope at [48], Baroness Hale at [122], Lord Mance at [144]. See also *Mendoza v Ghaidan* [2004] UKHL 30, [2004] 2 AC 557 and *Black v Wilkinson* [2013] EWCA Civ 820.

[190] *Axa General Insurance Ltd v Lord Advocate* [2011] UKSC 46, [2012] 1 AC 868.

[191] Ibid, per Lord Hope at [32].

[192] Ibid, per Lord Brown at [83]. See also *R (S) v Secretary of State for Justice* [2012] EWHC 1810 (Admin), [2013] 1 All ER 66 where it was held that it was appropriate to defer when assessing the proportionality of the imposition of a special tax upon prisoners in receipt of enhanced earnings to support the victims of crime.

[193] *R (Countryside Alliance) v Attorney General* [2007] UKHL 52, [2007] 3 WLR 922.

[194] Arguments were made in relation to Arts 8, 11, 14 and Art 1 of Protocol No 1.

[195] *Countryside Alliance* (n 193), [45]. See also *Friend v Lord Advocate* [2007] UKHL 53, [2008] HRLR 11.

6.4 Political Decisions

Whilst not labelled as such, the legislation the subject of the claim in the *Animal Defenders* case[196] had a political objective. Section 321(2) of the Communications Act 2003, the subject of the claim, prevented political advertising. The Bill had been the subject of lengthy debate in Parliament and the Minister was unable to make a statement under section 19 of the HRA that the provisions of the Bill were compatible with the Convention rights. The Bill was also considered by the Joint Committee on Human Rights and questions of the proportionality of the interference with Article 10 rights were considered at length. The House of Lords concluded that this section of the Act was compatible with Article 10. It was decided that great weight should be given to the decision of Parliament here, as Lord Bingham explained:

> First, it is reasonable to expect that our democratically-elected politicians will be peculiarly sensitive to the measures necessary to safeguard the integrity of our democracy. It cannot be supposed that others, including judges, will be more so. Secondly, Parliament has resolved, uniquely since the 1998 Act came into force in October 2000, that the prohibition of political advertising on television and radio may possibly, although improbably, infringe article 10 but has nonetheless resolved to proceed under section 19(1)(b) of the Act. It has done so, while properly recognising the interpretative supremacy of the European Court, because of the importance which it attaches to maintenance of this prohibition. The judgment of Parliament on such an issue should not be lightly overridden. Thirdly, legislation cannot be framed so as to address particular cases. It must lay down general rules.[197]

---

[196] *R (Animal Defenders) v Secretary of State for Culture, Media and Sport* [2008] UKHL 15, [2008] 2 WLR 781. The area of protection of health also usually attracts some deference from the courts, see eg *R (Sinclair Collis Ltd) v Secretary of State for Health* [2011] EWCA Civ 437, [2012] 2 WLR 304 (ban on cigarette vending machines); and *R (N) v Secretary of State for Health* [2009] EWCA Civ 795, [2009] HRLR 31 (ban on smoking in secure hospitals).
[197] *Animal Defenders*, ibid, [33].

5

The Defence of Primary Legislation

1. Introduction

The HRA has been carefully drafted to preserve the sovereignty of Parliament.

> Parliamentary sovereignty means that Parliament can, if it chooses, legislate contrary to fundamental principles of human rights. The Human Rights Act 1998 will not detract from this power. The constraints upon its exercise by Parliament are ultimately political, not legal.[1]

Although section 6(1) provides that it is unlawful for a public authority to act in a way which is incompatible with a Convention right, section 6(2) provides that section 6(1) does not apply to an act if: (a) as the result of one of more provisions of primary legislation,[2] the authority could not have acted differently; or (b) in the case of one or more provisions of, or made under, primary legislation which cannot be read or given effect in a way which is compatible with the Convention rights, the authority was acting so as to give effect to or enforce those provisions.

Whilst section 6(2) appears to provide a fairly robust defence for public authorities bound by or relying on primary legislation in their decision making, sections 3 and 4 of the HRA must also be considered. Section 3 provides that, so far as it is possible to do so, primary legislation and subordinate legislation must be read and given effect in a way which is compatible with the Convention rights. Therefore, if an act is justified by reference to primary legislation incompatible with Convention rights, following the guidance in section 3, it may be possible for the court to construe the legislation so that it is compatible. If it is not possible to apply section 3, section 4 allows a court to make a declaration of incompatibility. Although this does not affect the validity, continuing operation or enforcement of the provision, it does set in process a mechanism by which the offending provision may be quickly amended by Parliament.[3]

---

[1] *R v Secretary of Sate for the Home Department, ex p Simms* [2000] 2 AC 115 per Lord Hoffmann.

[2] 'Primary legislation' is defined in s 21(1), the definition including Orders in Council made pursuant to Her Majesty's Royal Prerogative. See further P Billings and B Pontin, 'Prerogative Powers and the Human Rights Act: Elevating the Status of Orders in Council' [2001] *PL* 21.

[3] See s 10 and Sch 2.

It is crystal clear that the carefully and subtly drafted Human Rights Act 1998 preserves the principle of Parliamentary sovereignty. In a case of incompatibility, which cannot be avoided by interpretation under section 3(1), the courts may not disapply the legislation. The court may merely issue a declaration of incompatibility which then gives rise to a power to take remedial action.[4]

The final section of the HRA relating to primary legislation is section 19, which provides that a minister in charge of a Bill in either House of Parliament must, before the Second Reading of the Bill, make a statement to the effect that in his view the provisions of the Bill are compatible with the Convention rights (a 'statement of compatibility'). If this is not possible, he must make a statement to the effect that, although he is unable to make a statement of compatibility, the government nevertheless wishes the House to proceed with the Bill. This section and the others relating to primary legislation are the subject of this chapter.

---

2. Section 6(2) Human Rights Act

2.1 Introduction

Both sections 6(2)(a) and 6(2)(b) provide a public authority with a defence based on primary legislation.

> Paragraphs (a) and (b) both qualify the basic principle in section 6(1) that it is unlawful for a public authority to act in a way that is incompatible with the Convention rights. The purpose of these paragraphs is to prevent section 6(1) being used to undermine another of the Act's basic principles. This is that in the final analysis, if primary legislation cannot be interpreted in way that is compatible with them, Parliamentary sovereignty takes precedence over the Convention rights.[5]

However, it is not always clear which section applies. Further confusion has been caused by the judgment of the House of Lords in *Hooper*,[6] where Lords Hoffmann and Hope held that the appropriate defence was section 6(2)(b), Lords Scott and Brown held that it was section 6(2)(a), and Lord Nicholls held that it was not necessary to decide as section 6(2) clearly applied and the point was better left for a decision on another occasion. The respective views of their Lordships are discussed in the following paragraphs.[7]

---

[4] *R v Director of Public Prosecutions, ex p Kebilene* [1999] 3 WLR 972 per Lord Steyn. On the relationship between the judiciary, legislature and executive under the HRA, see generally TR Hickman, 'Constitutional Dialogue, Constitutional Theories and the Human Rights Act 1998' [2005] *Public Law* 306; CA Gearty, *Principles of Human Rights Adjudication* (Oxford, Oxford University Press, 2004).

[5] *R (on the application of Hooper) v Secretary of State for Work and Pensions* [2005] UKHL 29, [2005] 1 WLR 1681 per Lord Hope at [70].

[6] Ibid.

[7] See further P Cane, 'Church, State and Human Rights: Are Parish Councils Public Authorities?' (2004) 120 *Law Quarterly Review* 41.

2.2 Section 6(2)(a) Human Rights Act

Section 6(2)(a) provides that section 6(1), which makes it unlawful for a public authority to act in a way which is incompatible with a Convention right, does not apply to an act if, as the result of one or more provisions of primary legislation, the authority could not have acted differently. It applies where the legislation imposes a duty to act.[8] In *Hooper*[9] Lord Hope held that the situation to which the paragraph was addressed arose where the effect of the primary legislation was that the authority had no alternative but to do what the legislation told it to do.

> The language of the paragraph tells us that this may be the result of one provision taken by itself, or that it may be the result of two or more provisions taken together. Where more than one provision is involved, they may be part of one enactment or they may be found in several different enactments. The key to its application lies in the fact that the effect of the legislation, wherever it is found, is that a duty is imposed on the authority. If the legislation imposes a duty to act, the authority is obliged to act in the manner which the legislation lays down even if the legislation requires it to act in a way which is incompatible with a Convention right. The authority has no discretion to do otherwise. As it is a duty which has been imposed on the authority by or as a result of primary legislation, Parliamentary sovereignty prevails over the Convention right. The defence is provided to prevent the legislation from being rendered unenforceable.[10]

Assuming section 6 applied, Lord Nicholls held in *Wilson*[11] that the court's decision in the proceedings gave effect to the mandatory provisions of the Consumer Credit Act 1974. 'An order giving effect to these provisions of primary legislation is excluded from the scope of s 6(1) by s 6(2)(a).'[12] Section 6(2)(a) was also held to apply in *Wilkinson*.[13] Here a widower alleged discrimination in that he was not entitled to a widow's bereavement allowance by way of deduction from his liability for income tax under section 262 of the Income and Corporation Taxes Act 1988. Whilst there was a discretion which enabled the commissioners to formulate policy in the interstices of the tax legislation, it was held to not justify construing the power so widely as to enable the commissioners to concede, by extra-statutory concession, an allowance which Parliament could have granted but did not grant.[14] Their Lordships concluded that as the legislation gave the commissioners no power to act otherwise than to disallow claims for allowances by widows, they were therefore protected by section 6(2)(a).[15] Lord Hoffmann, with whom Lords Nicholls and Hope agreed, also noted that if the powers of the commissioners had been wider, they would have been protected by section 6(2)(b),[16] although Lord Brown expressly disagreed with this reasoning.[17]

In *Hooper*[18] only Lords Scott and Brown concluded that section 6(2)(a) was the

---

[8] *Manchester City Council v Pinnock* [2010] UKSC 45, [2011] 2 AC 104, [98].
[9] *Hooper* (n 5).
[10] Ibid, per Lord Hope at [71].
[11] *Wilson v Secretary of State for Trade and Industry* [2003] UKHL 40, [2003] 3 WLR 568.
[12] Ibid, [25].
[13] *R (on the application of Wilkinson) v Inland Revenue Commissioners* [2005] UKHL 30, [2005] 1 WLR 1718.
[14] Ibid, per Lord Hoffmann at [21]. See also Lord Scott at [36] and [39]–[40].
[15] Ibid, per Lord Hoffmann at [22].
[16] Ibid, [23].
[17] Ibid, [43].
[18] *Hooper* (n 5).

appropriate defence. It had been claimed by widowers that the non-payment of payments corresponding to widow's payment and widowed mother's allowance under sections 36 and 37 of the Social Security Contributions and Benefits Act 1992 violated their Convention rights under Article 14 read with Article 1 of Protocol No 1. The Secretary of State claimed a defence under section 6(2). Lord Nicholls explained the problem in choosing 6(2)(a) or 6(2)(b) lay in the view taken of the Secretary of State's common law powers. In Lord Nicholls's view, if the effect of the statutory provision was that he could not lawfully have made corresponding payments to widowers in exercise of the Crown's common law powers, the case would fall within section 6(2)(a).[19] However, if, in the exercise of his common law powers, he could have lawfully made the payments, in Lord Nicholls's view the case fell within section 6(2)(b).

> Clearly, in making payments to widows the Secretary of State was giving effect to sections 36 and 37 of the Social Security Contributions and Benefits Act 1992. Likewise in not making corresponding payments to widowers the Secretary of State was giving effect to those statutory provisions. ... The fact that the Secretary of State could lawfully have made corresponding payments to widowers does not detract from the crucial fact that in declining to pay widowers he was 'giving effect' to the statute.[20]

Either way, Lord Nicholls held that section 6(2) provided a defence.

Both Lord Scott and Lord Brown concluded that the Secretary of State could not lawfully have made corresponding payments to widowers in exercise of the Crown's common law powers, and therefore section 6(2)(a) was the appropriate defence. Lord Scott stated that the widowers, and the widows who did not satisfy the statutory conditions were not entitled to the statutory benefits. Hence, the Secretary of State could not authorise the payment to them of the statutory benefits.[21] Similarly, Lord Brown held that the Secretary of State could not be required to act in such a way as to subvert the intention of Parliament.[22] 'Given Parliament's unambiguous intention in the matter it would seem to me an obvious abuse of power for the Secretary of State to have introduced a scheme to make matching extra-statutory payments to widowers.'[23] He concluded that section 6(2)(a) was appropriate on the basis that, as a result of sections 36 and 37, the Secretary of State could not have acted differently: he had to pay the widows and could not lawfully have made matching payments to widowers.[24]

2.3 Section 6(2)(b) Human Rights Act

Section 6(2)(b) provides that section 6(1), which makes it unlawful for a public authority to act in a way which is incompatible with a Convention right, does not apply if, in the case of one or more provisions of, or made under, primary legislation which cannot

---

[19] Ibid, [4].
[20] Ibid, [6].
[21] Ibid, [93]. However, similarly to Lord Nicholls, although preferring the s 6(2)(a) route, he also noted that the difference between (a) and (b) when applied to a case such as the present was immaterial. See [95].
[22] Ibid, [122].
[23] Ibid, [123].
[24] Ibid, [124]. His Lordship also noted that, the wider the ambit given to s 6(2), the more often the United Kingdom will be acting incompatibly with Art 13 of the ECHR. See [120]. See also *Secretary of State for Justice v James* [2009] UKHL 22, [2010] 1 AC 553.

be read or given effect in a way which is compatible with the Convention rights, the authority was acting so as to give effect to or enforce those provisions. The section makes the link with section 3 of the HRA explicit.[25]

In *Doherty*[26] Lord Hope held that three distinct situations may arise. First, where a decision to exercise or not to exercise a power that is given by primary legislation 'would inevitably give rise to an incompatibility'. The second is where the act or omission of the public authority which is incompatible with the Convention right is not 'touched by one or more provisions of primary legislation in any way at all'. In this instance the act or omission is unlawful under section 6(1) as section 6(2)(b) does not apply to it. The third is where the act or omission takes place within the context of a scheme which primary legislation had laid down 'that gives general powers, such as powers of management, to a public authority'.[27] In this latter situation, the answer to whether or not section 6(2)(b) applies will depend on the extent to which the act or omission 'can be said to be giving effect to any of the provisions of the scheme that is to be found in the statutes'.[28]

> [S]ection 6(2)(b) assumes that the public authority could have acted differently but excludes liability if it was giving effect to a statutory provision which could not be read in a way that was compatible with the Convention rights. It protects a decision to exercise or not to exercise a discretion that is available to it under the statute.[29]

Where it is possible to give effect to Convention rights in giving effect to primary legislation, a public authority must do so.[30] Similarly in his judgment in *Hooper*[31] Lord Hope held that the situation to which paragraph (b) was addressed arose where the authority had a discretion

> which it has the power to exercise or not to exercise as it chooses, to give effect to or enforce provisions of or made under primary legislation which cannot be read or given effect to in a way which is compatible with the Convention rights. The source of that discretion may be in a single statutory provision which confers a power on the authority which it may or may not choose to exercise … the source of the discretion that is given to the authority may also be found in several statutory provisions which taken together have that effect. Or, as there is nothing in the language of the paragraph to indicate the contrary, it may be found in the common law.[32]

In Lord Hope's view, the source of the discretion did not matter. What mattered was that the provision conferring the discretion could not be read or given effect compatibly with the Convention rights and that the authority had decided to exercise or not to exercise its discretion so as to give effect to those provisions or to enforce them.

> If it does this, this paragraph affords it a defence to a claim under section 7(1) that by acting or failing to act in this way it has acted unlawfully. In this way it enables the primary legisla-

---

[25] *R (GC) v Commissioner of Police of the Metropolis* [2011] UKSC 21, [2011] 1 WLR 1230 per Baroness Hale at [68].
[26] *Doherty v Birmingham City Council* [2008] UKHL 57, [2008] 3 WLR 636.
[27] Ibid, [39].
[28] Ibid, [39].
[29] Ibid, [40].
[30] *Manchester City Council v Pinnock* [2010] UKSC 45, [2011] 2 AC 104, [101]. See also *Cadder v HM Advocate* [2010] UKSC 43, [2010] 1 WLR 2601.
[31] *Hooper* (n 5).
[32] Ibid, per Lord Hope at [72].

tion to remain effective in the way Parliament intended. If the defence was not there the authority would have no alternative but to exercise its discretion in a way that was compatible with the Convention rights. The power would be a duty to act compatibly with the Convention, even if to do so was plainly in conflict with the intention of Parliament.[33]

In *Aston Cantlow*[34] Lord Nicholls held that, even assuming section 6 was applicable and the Act was incompatible with Convention rights, the Parochial Church Council would not be acting unlawfully in enforcing liability. Here the Chancel Repairs Act 1932 provided that if the defendant would have been liable to be admonished to repair the chancel by the appropriate ecclesiastical court, the court shall give judgment for the cost of putting the chancel in repair. Lord Nicholls found that when a Council acted pursuant to that provision, it was acting within the scope of the exception set out in section 6(2)(b).[35]

In *Hooper*[36] only Lords Hoffmann and Hope held that section 6(2)(b) was the appropriate defence as they had concluded that, in the exercise of his common law powers, the Secretary of State could have lawfully made the payments to the widowers. Lord Hoffmann noted that section 6(2)(b) assumed that the public authority could have acted differently but nevertheless excluded liability if it was giving effect to a statutory provision which could not be read as Convention-compliant in accordance with section 3.It followed that section 6(1) did not apply if the Secretary of State was acting incompatibly with Convention rights because he was giving effect to sections 36 and 37 of the 1992 Act.[37]

Lord Hope concluded that the Secretary of State's act in not exercising his common law power by making payment to widowers was not unlawful pursuant to section 6(2)(b).

> A common law power to make payments for which the statutes do not provide is only a power. By declining to exercise it, the Secretary of State was simply doing what the 1992 and 1999 Acts told him to do. He was giving effect to their provisions, as they obliged him to make payments to widows only and not to both widows and widowers.[38]

His Lordship found that it made no difference that the power the Secretary of State was declining to exercise was a common law power as section 6(2)(b) said nothing about the origin of the act or failure to act which gave effect to or enforced the provisions of primary legislation which cannot be read or given effect in a way which was compatible with Convention rights. In his view the failure to act which was incompatible with Convention rights could consist of a refusal to exercise a power which had its origins elsewhere because to exercise it in a way that was compatible with the Convention would conflict with the intention of Parliament.[39]

> There is no indication in section 6(2)(b) or elsewhere that public authorities whose powers are not derived from statute or whose powers are derived in part from the common law are in a less favourable position for the purposes of the defence which it provides than those which

---

[33] Ibid, [73]. See also *Aston Cantlow and Wilmcote with Billesley Parochial Church Council v Wallbank* [2003] UKHL 37, [2004] 1 AC 546 per Lord Hobhouse at [93] and *Ghaidan v Godin-Mendoza* [2004] UKHL 30, [2004] 2 AC 557 per Lord Rodger at [108].

[34] *Aston Cantlow*, Ibid.

[35] Ibid. See also Lord Hobhouse at [93], Lord Scott at [137] and Lord Rodger at [172].

[36] *Hooper* (n 5).

[37] Ibid, [49].

[38] Ibid, [81].

[39] Ibid, [82].

are entirely the creatures of statute. The primacy that is given to the sovereignty of Parliament requires that they be treated in the same way, irrespective of the source of the power.[40]

---

3. Section 3 Human Rights Act

3.1 Introduction

Section 3(1) provides that so far as it is possible to do so, primary legislation and subordinate legislation must be read and given effect in a way which is compatible with the Convention rights.[41] It applies to primary and subordinate legislation whenever enacted.[42] However, it does not affect the validity, continuing operation or enforcement of any incompatible primary legislation; nor does it affect the validity, continuing operation or enforcement of any incompatible subordinate legislation if (disregarding any possibility of revocation) primary legislation prevents removal of the incompatibility.[43]

Section 3 requires the court to 'interpret legislation in a manner which it would not have done before.' When it applies,

> the courts have to adjust their traditional role in relation to interpretation so as to give effect to the direction contained in section 3. It is as though legislation which predates the Human Rights Act 1998 and conflicts with the Convention has to be treated as being subsequently amended to incorporate the language of section 3.[44]

However, it is important to note that in some instances the traditional approach to statutory interpretation will suffice to achieve an interpretation compatible with the Convention rights. For example, in *GC*[45] a majority of the Supreme Court concluded that section 64(1A) of the Police and Criminal Evidence Act 1984, which provided for the retention of fingerprints and biometric data, could be read and given effect in a way which was compatible with Article 8. In the opinion of the majority, this was not a case where the HRA required the court to accord a statutory meaning which it did not naturally bear.[46]

Section 3 is often described as a key section of the HRA and one of the primary means by which Convention rights have been brought into the law.[47] The section is undoubtedly

---

[40] Ibid, [83].

[41] In *The Commissioner of Police for the Metropolis v Hurst* [2005] EWCA Civ 890 the Court of Appeal held that the 'Convention rights' referred to in s 3 were the international obligations of the United Kingdom as opposed to the obligations created by the HRA. See [44] and [58].

[42] Section 3(2)(a). It thereby removes the doctrine of implied repeal in that the HRA does not impliedly repeal inconsistent legislation.

[43] Sections 3(2)(b) and 3(2)(c).

[44] *Donoghue v Poplar Housing* [2001] EWCA Civ 595, [2000] QB 48 per Lord Woolf CJ. See further F Bennion, 'What Interpretation is "Possible" under Section 3(1) of the Human Rights Act 1998?' [2000] *Public Law* 77.

[45] *R (GC) v Commissioner of Police of the Metropolis* [2011] UKSC 21, [2011] 1 WLR 1230.

[46] Ibid, per Lord Phillips at [55].

[47] *Ghaidan* (n 33), per Lord Nicholls at [26].

crucial to the working of the 1998 Act. It is the means by which Parliament intends that people should be afforded the benefit of their Convention rights—'so far as it is possible', without the need for any further intervention by Parliament.[48]

It has been held that section 3 can apply to the interpretation of the HRA itself. For example, in *Douglas*[49] it was held that section 3 had to be applied to the interpretation of section 12 of the HRA. Therefore, consistently with other Convention rights, it was not possible to give the right of freedom of expression presumptive priority over other rights.[50] Furthermore, the interpretative duty imposed by section 3 applies to the same degree in legislation affecting private parties as it does to legislation affecting public authorities and individuals.[51]

When applying section 3, the first step is to determine, using ordinary principles of statutory construction (both literal and purposive), whether or not the primary legislation is incompatible with a Convention right. Only if there is an incompatibility is it necessary to consider section 3.[52] Whilst there may be some judicial deference afforded at this stage, it is important that this is not confused with the determination of what is possible under section 3 if an incompatibility is found.[53]

3.2 The Nature of Section 3

Section 3 is often described as a 'strong interpretative obligation'[54] and as a 'powerful tool', not an 'optional cannon of construction'.[55] The section requires a broad approach 'concentrating, amongst other things, in a purposive way on the importance of the fundamental right involved'.[56] Full weight must be given to the will of Parliament as expressed in the HRA[57] and if Parliament disagrees with an interpretation by the courts under section 3 it is free to override it by amending the legislation and expressly reinstating the incompatibility.[58] Section 3 is regarded by the courts as the prime remedial remedy under the HRA whilst resort to a declaration of incompatibility under section 4 is regarded as an exceptional course.[59] Comparisons have been drawn with EC law as to the lengths to which a court may go.[60]However, there are limits.

The difficulty lies in the word 'possible'. Section 3(1), read in conjunction with ss 3(2) and 4, makes one matter clear: Parliament expressly envisaged that not all legislation would be

---

[48] Ibid, per Lord Rodger at [106]. See also Lord Steyn at [39] and [46].
[49] *Douglas v Hello! Limited* [2001] QB 967.
[50] Ibid, per Sedley LJ at [137] and per Keene LJ at [149].
[51] *X v Y* [2004] EWCA Civ 662, [2004] ICR 1634, [66].
[52] *R v A* [2001] UKHL 25, [2002] 1 AC 45, per Lord Hope at [58]. See also *R v Crown Court at Leeds, ex p Wardle* [2001] UKHL 12, [2001] 2 WLR 865; and *R v Hasan* [2005] UKHL 22, [2005] 2 WLR 709, per Lord Steyn at [62]; and *ML v ANS* [2012] UKSC 30, [2012] HRLR 27, per Lord Reed at [15]–[17].
[53] See further A Young, 'Ghaidan v Godin-Mendoza: Avoiding the Deference Trap' [2005] *Public Law* 23.
[54] See eg *Kebilene* (n 4), per Lord Steyn and Lord Cooke; *Attorney General's Reference No 4 of 2002* [2004] UKHL 43, [2005] 1 AC 264, per Lord Bingham at [28].
[55] *Re S* [2002] UKHL 10, [2002] 2 WLR 720, per Lord Nicholls at [37].
[56] *Ghaidan* (n 33), per Lord Steyn at [41].
[57] Ibid, [40].
[58] Ibid, [43].
[59] Ibid, [50].
[60] Ibid, [45] per Lord Steyn, citing *Marleasing SA v La Commercial Internacional de Alimentación SA* Case C-106/890 [1990] ECR I-4135, 4159. See also Lord Rodger at [118].

capable of being made Convention-compliant by application of s 3. Sometimes it would be possible, sometimes not. What is not clear is the test to be applied in separating the sheep from the goats.[61]

The limits beyond which a Convention-compliant interpretation is not possible are examined in the following paragraphs.[62]

3.3 What Is Not Possible

When adjudicating on section 3, the courts have warned that the section does not entitle judges to act as legislators.[63]

> Section 3 is concerned with interpretation. ... In applying section 3 courts must be ever mindful of this outer limit. The Human Rights Act reserves the amendment of primary legislation to Parliament. By this means the Act seeks to preserve parliamentary sovereignty. The Act maintains the constitutional boundary. Interpretation of statutes is a matter for the courts; the enactment of statutes and the amendment of statutes, are matters for Parliament.[64]

It is not possible to use section 3 if the legislation contains provisions which expressly contradict the meaning which the enactment would have to be given to make it compatible, or provisions which do so by necessary implication.[65] Furthermore, it is not possible to do 'violence' to the language or to the objective of the provision[66] so as to make it unintelligible or unworkable,[67] or to commit 'judicial vandalism' by giving the provision an effect quite different from that which Parliament intended.[68] In short, it is not possible to use section 3 if it would involve adopting a meaning which was inconsistent with a fundamental feature of the legislation.[69] It does not allow courts to change the substance of a provision completely.[70]

> That would be to cross the constitutional boundary s 3 seeks to demarcate and preserve. Parliament has retained the right to enact legislation in terms which are not Convention-compliant. The meaning imported by application of s 3 must be compatible with the under-

---

[61] Ibid, per Lord Nicholls at [27].

[62] There has been considerable academic comment on s 3. See further: R Bellamy, 'Political Constitutionalism and the Human Rights Act" (2011) 9 *International Journal of Constitutional Law* 86; id, 'Rights-consistent Interpretation and the Human Rights Act 1998" (2011) 127 *Law Quarterly Review* 217; P Sales, 'A Comparison of the Principle of Legality and Section 3 of the Human Rights Act 1998' (2009) 125 *Law Quarterly Review* 598; J Van Zyl Smit, 'The New Purposive Interpretation of Statutes: HRA Section 3 after Ghaidan v Godin-Mendoza' (2007) 70 *Modern Law Review* 294; A Kavanagh *Constitutional Review under the UK Human Rights Act* (Cambridge, Cambridge University Press, 2009).

[63] *R v A* (n 52), per Lord Hope at [108].

[64] *Re S* (n 55), per Lord Nicholls at [39].

[65] *R v A* (n 52), per Lord Hope at [108]; *R v Lambert* [2001] UKHL 37, [2002] 2 AC 545, per Lord Hope at [79]; *Re S* (n 55), per Lord Nicholls at [40]; *R v Secretary of State for the Home Department, ex p Anderson* [2002] UKHL 46, [2003] 1 AC 837, per Lord Steyn at [59]; *R (on the application of Rusbridger) v Attorney General* [2003] UKHL 38, [2004] 1 AC 357, per Lord Steyn at [8]; *Ghaidan* (n 33), per Lord Rodger at [117].

[66] *Lambert*, Ibid, per Lord Slynn at [17].

[67] Ibid, per Lord Hope at [80].

[68] *Anderson* (n 65), per Lord Bingham at [70].

[69] *Re S* (n 55), per Lord Nicholls at [40].

[70] *Ghaidan* (n 33), per Lord Rodger at [110].

lying thrust of the legislation being construed. Words implied must ... 'go with the grain of the legislation'.[71]

Lord Rodger in *Ghaidan*[72] stated that the key lay in a careful consideration of the essential principles and scope of the legislation being interpreted.

> If the insertion of one word contradicts those principles or goes beyond the scope of the legislation, it amounts to impermissible amendment. On the other hand, if the implication of a dozen words leaves the essential principles and scope of the legislation intact but allows it to be read in a way which is compatible with Convention rights, the implication is a legitimate exercise of the powers conferred by s 3(1).[73]

It has also been held that the courts should not use section 3 to make decisions for which they are not equipped. 'There may be several ways of making a provision Convention-compliant, and the choice may involve issues calling for legislative deliberation.'[74]

Even if the proposed interpretation does not run counter to any underlying principle of the legislation, it may involve reading into the statute powers or duties with far-reaching practical repercussions of that kind.

> In effect these powers or duties, if sufficiently far-reaching, would be beyond the scope of the legislation enacted by Parliament. If that is right, the answer to such questions cannot be clear-cut and will involve matters of degree which cannot be determined in the abstract but only by considering the particular legislation in issue. In any given case, however, there may come a point where, standing back, the only proper conclusion is that the scale of what is proposed would go beyond any implication that could possibly be derived from reading the existing legislation in a way that was compatible with the Convention right in question.[75]

3.4 What Is Possible

It is important not to approach section 3 in a too literal and technical way with too much emphasis on linguistic features.[76] Staying within the provisos outlined above, certain guidelines have developed. Section 3 can be applied even if there is no ambiguity in the language in the sense of the language being capable of two different meanings.[77] 'Even if, construed according to the ordinary principles of interpretation, the meaning of the legislation admits of no doubt, s 3 may nonetheless require the legislation to be given a different meaning.'[78]

An interpretation which linguistically may appear strained can be adopted.[79] It is possible to read in words[80] to the legislation and to read down words.[81] It may be possible to

---

[71] Ibid, per Lord Nicholls at [33].
[72] Ibid.
[73] Ibid, [122].
[74] Ibid, [33].
[75] Ibid, per Lord Rodger at [115]. See also *Re S* (n 55), per Lord Nicholls at [40].
[76] Ibid, per Lord Steyn at [49].
[77] *R v A* (n 52), per Lord Steyn at [44]; *Re S* (n 55), per Lord Nicholls at [37].
[78] *Ghaidan* (n 33), per Lord Nicholls at [29] citing *R v A* (n 52), as an example. See also Lord Steyn at [44].
[79] *R v A* (n 52) at [44] per Lord Steyn.
[80] See eg *R (Hammond) v Secretary of State for the Home Department* [2005] UKHL 69, [2006] 1 AC 603.
[81] *R v A* (n 52), per Lord Steyn at [44].

isolate a particular phrase which causes the difficulty and to read in words that modify it so as to remove the incompatibility. Or else the court may read in words that qualify the provision as a whole. At other times the appropriate solution may be to read down the provision so that it falls to be given effect in a way that is compatible with the Convention rights in question.[82]

It also may be enough for the court to simply state what the effect of the provision is without altering the ordinary meaning of the words used.[83] It may be necessary for the words used to be expressed in different language in order to explain how they are to be read in a way that is compatible.[84]

Using these techniques, it is possible for a court to modify the meaning, and hence the effect, of primary and secondary legislation.[85] A court may be required to depart from the intention of the enacting Parliament.[86]

> Once the 1998 Act came into force, whenever, by virtue of s 3(1), a provision could be read in a way which was compatible with Convention rights, that was the meaning which Parliament intended that it should bear. For all purposes, that meaning, and no other, is the 'true' meaning of the provision in our law.[87]

However, that is not to say that the limit outlined in the paragraphs above may be overstepped. It remains not possible to use section 3 if doing so would involve adopting a meaning which is inconsistent with a fundamental feature of the legislation.[88]

Observations have also been made by the courts concerning the correct procedure to be followed when applying section 3. It has been held that it is important to identify precisely the word or phrase which, if given its ordinary meaning, would otherwise be incompatible.

> So far as possible judges should seek to achieve the same attention to detail in their use of language to express the effect of applying s 3(1) as the parliamentary draftsman would have done if he had been amending the statute. It ought to be possible for any words that need to be substituted to be fitted in to the statute as if they had been inserted there by amendment.[89]

3.5 The Application of Section 3 in Hypothetical Cases

Although to date it has only occurred on one occasion, it appears that it is possible for a court to apply section 3 in a hypothetical case. In *Rusbridger*[90] the House of Lords had to determine whether or not to grant a declaration as to the construction of section 3 of the Treason Act 1848 in light of section 3 of the HRA and Article 10 (the right to freedom of expression). This was an application not for a declaration of incompatibility pursuant to section 4 of the HRA but for a declaration that certain proposed conduct was lawful. The proceedings were brought by the editor and a well-known journalist

---

[82] *Ghaidan* (n 33), per Lord Rodger at [124].
[83] *Lambert* (n 65), per Lord Hope at [81]; *Ghaidan* (n 33), per Lord Rodger at [107].
[84] *Lambert* (n 65), per Lord Hope at [81]; *Ghaidan* (n 33), per Lord Rodger at [124].
[85] *Ghaidan* (n 33), per Lord Nicholls at [32].
[86] Ibid, [30].
[87] Ibid, per Lord Steyn at [106].
[88] *Re S* (n 55), per Lord Nicholls at [40].
[89] *Lambert* (n 65), per Lord Hope at [80]; *Re S* (n 55), per Lord Nicholls at [41].
[90] *Rusbridger* (n 65).

of *The Guardian* newspaper, which had published articles urging the abolition of the monarchy.

Their Lordships made clear that, save in exceptional circumstances, it was not appropriate for a member of the public to bring proceedings against the Crown for a declaration that certain proposed conduct was lawful and name the Attorney-General as the formal defendant to the claim. However, there was jurisdiction for a civil court to make such a declaration.[91] It had been conceded that it was not necessary for *The Guardian* to demonstrate that they were victims under section 7 of the HRA and Lord Steyn held that this was obvious on a proper view of the place of section 3 in the scheme of the HRA. 'For present purposes it is sufficient that The Guardian has an interest and standing. That is the threshold requirement.'[92] His Lordship, with whom Lords Scott and Walker agreed, considered that *The Guardian* may be entitled to seek certainty;[93] that the case was not fact-sensitive;[94] and that the issue may be a matter of constitutional importance.[95] He concluded that the case may fall within the exceptional category.[96] However, he also concluded that the case did not have to be heard again by the Administrative Court.

> The idea that s 3 could survive scrutiny under the Human Rights Act is unreal. The fears of the editor of *The Guardian* were more than a trifle alarmist. In my view the courts ought not to be troubled further with this unnecessary litigation.[97]

Therefore, it may be possible, in an exceptional case, to seek a declaration as to the correct interpretation of a section of primary legislation in the light of section 3 of the HRA and a Convention right. However, the meaning of exceptional is not clear from the judgment of the majority. Lord Steyn referred to three factors: the need for a genuine dispute about the subject matter, although noting that this could not by itself conclude the matter or be a weighty criterion if there were otherwise good reasons to allow the claim for a declaration to go forward;[98] whether the case was fact-sensitive or not, 'it has always been recognised that a question of pure law may more readily be made the subject matter of a declaration';[99] and finally the question of whether there was a cogent public or individual interest which could be advanced by the grant of a declaration noting that the jurisdiction was in no way limited to life and death issues.[100]

3.6 The Application of Section 3 in Practice

A far better understanding of what is actually possible for a court to achieve by using

---

[91] Ibid, [16].
[92] Ibid, [21].
[93] Ibid, [22].
[94] Ibid, [24].
[95] Ibid, [24].
[96] Ibid, [25].
[97] Ibid, [28]. Lord Hutton did not agree that this was an exceptional case and held that it was not a function of the courts to decide hypothetical questions which did not impact on the parties before them or to keep the statute book up to date using ss 3 and 4 of the HRA; see [33]–[36]. Lord Rodger reached a similar conclusion, see [57]–[58].
[98] Ibid, [22].
[99] Ibid, [23].
[100] Ibid, [24].

section 3 can be gained by an examination of the cases in which it has been applied. In accordance with the view that this is the primary remedial measure, section 4 being a measure of last resort, section 3 has been applied in numerous cases. Many of these examples are examined in the following paragraphs.

3.6.1 Criminal Justice

(a) Admission of Evidence

$R \ v \ A$[101] concerned a trial for rape. During the trial the defendant alleged that, approximately three weeks prior to the date of the alleged rape, he and the complainant had a sexual relationship. His defence was that sexual intercourse took place with the complainant's consent or, alternatively, that he believed she consented. At a preparatory hearing, counsel for the defendant applied for leave to cross-examine the complainant about the alleged previous sexual relationship and to lead evidence about it. Relying on section 41 of the Youth Justice and Criminal Evidence Act 1999, the trial judge ruled that the complainant could not be cross-examined, nor could evidence be led, about her alleged sexual relationship with the defendant.

On appeal, the Court of Appeal held that questioning and evidence in relation to the alleged prior sexual activity was admissible in relation to the defendant's belief in her consent but inadmissible on the issue of consent. The Crown appealed and the appeal in the House of Lords turned predominantly on the meaning of section 3. On ordinary principles of construction, a majority concluded that section 41 was prima facie capable of preventing an accused person from putting forward evidence critical to his defence and, thus construed, was incompatible with Article 6.[102] Remitting the case to the Crown Court, the majority held that, applying section 3, the test of admissibility should be whether the evidence was so relevant to the issue of consent that to exclude it would endanger the fairness of the trial.[103]

(b) Burden of Proof

In *Lambert*[104] the claimant had been convicted of possession of a controlled drug with intent to supply contrary to the Misuse of Drugs Act 1971. The judge had directed the jury that in order to establish possession of a controlled drug, the prosecution merely had to prove that he had the bag in his possession and that the bag in fact contained a controlled drug. Thereafter, under section 28 of the Act, the burden was on the defendant to prove, on the balance of probabilities, that he did not know that the bag contained a controlled drug. This was a legal rather than a merely evidential burden of proof. One of the questions for their Lordships was whether, using section 3, section 28 could be interpreted so as to impose a merely evidential burden.

Having determined that the HRA did not actually apply here as it did not have ret-

---

[101] $R \ v \ A$ (n 52).

[102] Although Lord Hope concluded it was not necessary or appropriate to resort to s 3, he agreed with the test set out by Lord Steyn for the trial judge which entailed reading s 41 of the Youth Justice and Criminal Evidence Act 1999 compatibly with Art 6.

[103] $R \ v \ A$ (n 52), per Lord Steyn at [46]. See further P Mirfield, 'Human Wrongs?' (2002) 118 *Law Quarterly Review* 20.

[104] *Lambert* (n 65).

rospective effect, their Lordships did not have to consider this question, although most did. Lord Slynn held that it was possible, 'without doing violence to the language or to the objective of that section, to read the words as imposing only the evidential burden of proof'.[105] Lords Steyn, Hope and Clyde also held that, applying section 3, section 28 could be read as creating an evidential burden only.[106]

(c) Post-conviction Confiscation Orders

In *Waya*[107] the Supreme Court held that Part 2 of the Proceeds of Crime Act 2002, dealing with post-conviction confiscation, might in some circumstances give rise to an order which was incompatible with Article 1 of Protocol No 1 to the ECHR. However, it was also concluded that any violation could be avoided by using section 3 to give effect to the relevant sections in a manner which was compliant with the Convention right: 'The judge should, if confronted by an application for an order which would be disproportionate, refuse to make it but accede only to an application for such sums as would be appropriate.'[108]

3.6.2 Anti-terrorism Measures

In *MB*[109] the House of Lords concluded that the procedures provided for by section 3 of the Prevention of Terrorism Act 2005, resulting in the case made against the claimant for a control order being entirely undisclosed to him, were incompatible with Article 6. A majority concluded that the relevant provision could be read down using section 3 of the HRA so that they would take effect 'only when it was consistent with fairness for them to do so'.[110] Baroness Hale set out why, in her view, this was possible:

> First, when Parliament passed the 2005 Act, it must have thought that the provisions with which we are concerned were compatible with the convention rights. In interpreting the Act compatibly we are doing our best to make it work. This gives the greatest possible incentive to all parties to the case, and to the judge, to conduct the proceedings in such a way as to afford a sufficient and substantial measure of procedural justice. This includes the Secretary of State, who will, of course, be anxious that the control order be upheld. A declaration of incompatibility, on the other hand, would allow all of them to conduct the proceedings in a way which they knew to be incompatible. Secondly, there is good reason to think that Strasbourg would find proceedings conducted in accordance with the Act and rules compatible in the majority of cases. ... Thirdly, and above all, there are powerful policy reasons in support of procedures which enable cases to be proven through the evidence of infiltrators and informers rather than upon evidence which may have been obtained through the use of torture.[111]

---

[105] Ibid, [17].

[106] Ibid, per Lord Steyn at [42], per Lord Hope at [94] and per Lord Clyde at [157]. Lord Hutton found that s 28 as drafted was not actually incompatible with Art 6(2). See also *Attorney General's Reference No 4 of 2002* (n 54); *R v Daniel* [2002] EWCA Crim 959, [2003] 1 Cr Ap R 6; *Attorney-General's Reference No 1 of 2004* [2004] EWCA Crim 1025, [2004] 1 WLR 2111; *R v Keogh* [2007] EWCA Crim 528, [2007] 1 WLR 1500; *R v Webster* [2010] EWCA Crim 2819, [2011] 1 Cr App R 16.

[107] *R v Waya* [2012] UKSC 51, [2013] 1 AC 294.

[108] Ibid, [16].

[109] *Secretary of State for the Home Department v MB* [2007] UKHL 46, [2007] 3 WLR 681.

[110] Ibid, per Lord Bingham at [44].

[111] Ibid, [73].

In its later judgment in *AF*[112] it was also determined by the Supreme Court that the Prevention of Terrorism Act 2005 could be read down in control order proceedings so that the judge would have to consider not merely the allegations that have to be disclosed but whether there was any other matter whose disclosure was essential to the fairness of the trial. Lord Phillips observed that this departure from the apparently absolute requirements of the primary legislation was even more marked than it was in *MB*, but that no party had suggested a declaration of incompatibility was more appropriate.[113]

3.6.3 Sentencing

In *Offen*[114] the Court of Appeal determined that it was clear that there were circumstances where section 2 of the Crime (Sentences) Act 1997, imposing the automatic life sentence, could violate Articles 3 and 5. However, there was no need to impose such a sentence under the section if there were exceptional circumstances. Using section 3, the court concluded that 'exceptional circumstances' should be interpreted in such a way that offenders would not be sentenced to life imprisonment where they did not constitute a significant risk to the public.[115] It was held that this would still give effect to the intention of Parliament but in a more just, less arbitrary and more proportionate manner.[116]

> The objective of the legislature ... will be achieved, because it will be mandatory to impose a life sentence in situations where the offender constitutes a significant risk to the public. Section 2 of the 1997 Act therefore provides a good example of how the 1998 Act can have a beneficial effect on the administration of justice, without defeating the policy which Parliament was seeking to implement.[117]

3.6.4 Parole Board

Section 3 has also had an impact on the role of the Parole Board. In *Sim*[118] the Court of Appeal held that it was necessary to apply section 3 to section 44A(4) of the Criminal Justice Act 1991, which provided that the Board shall direct the prisoner's release if satisfied that it is no longer necessary for the protection of the public that he should be confined. It was held that this gave rise to a presumption that the prisoner would be detained unless the Board was satisfied to the contrary and that this was incompatible with Article 5. However, applying section 3, section 44A could be interpreted in a such a way that the Board was obliged to conclude that detention was no longer necessary for the protection of the public unless it was positively satisfied that detention was necessary in the public interest.[119]

---

[112] *Secretary of State for the Home Department v AF* [2009] UKHL 28, [2009] 3 WLR 74.
[113] Ibid, [67].
[114] *R v Offen* [2001] 1 WLR 253.
[115] Ibid, [97].
[116] Ibid, [99].
[117] Ibid, [100].
[118] *R (on the application of Sim) v Parole Board* [2003] EWCA Civ 1845, [2004] QB 1288.
[119] Ibid, [51].

3.6.5 Coroner's Inquests

In *Middleton*[120] the House of Lords held that the regime for holding inquests established by the Coroners Act 1988 and the Coroners Rules 1984 (SI 1984/553) as hitherto understood and followed in England and Wales did not meet the requirements of the Convention under Article 2. However, it was concluded that only one change was needed using section 3. 'How' in section 11(5)(b)(ii) of the Act and rule 36(1)(b) of the Rules was to be interpreted in the broader sense to mean not simply by what means someone died but to include also 'by what means and in what circumstances'.[121]

> This will not require a change of approach in some cases, where a traditional short form verdict will be quite satisfactory, but it will call for a change of approach in others. … In the latter class of case it must be for the coroner, in the exercise of his discretion, to decide how best, in the particular case, to elicit the jury's conclusion on the central issue or issues.[122]

The same conclusion was reached by their Lordships in *Sacker*.[123]

3.6.6 Family Law

In *Re S*[124] the House of Lords commented in detail on what it considered to be an inappropriate use of section 3 by the Court of Appeal. In short, the Court of Appeal, using section 3 to interpret the Children Act 1989, propounded a new procedure by which the essential milestones of a care plan would be identified at the trial and elevated to a starred status. If a starred milestone was not achieved within a reasonable time after the date set at trial, the local authority was obliged to reactivate the interdisciplinary process that contributed to the creation of the care plan. At the least, the local authority must inform the child's guardian of the position. Either the guardian or the local authority would then have the right to apply to the court for further directions.

Their Lordships concluded unanimously that the starring system could not be justified as a legitimate exercise in interpretation of the Children Act in accordance with section 3.[125] It was found that a cardinal principle of the Children Act was that the courts were not empowered to intervene in the way local authorities discharge their parental responsibilities under final care orders.

> Parliament entrusted to local authorities, not the courts, the responsibility for looking after children who are the subject of care orders. To my mind the new starring system would depart substantially from this principle. … In short, under the starring system the court will exercise a newly-created supervisory function.[126]

Their Lordships considered that this judicial innovation passed well beyond the boundary of interpretation and would constitute amendment of the Children Act, not

---

[120] *R (on the application of Middleton) v HM Coroner for Western Somerset* [2004] UKHL 10, [2004] 2 AC 182.

[121] Ibid, per Lord Bingham at [35].

[122] Ibid, [36].

[123] *R (on the application of Sacker) v HM Coroner for the County of West Yorkshire* [2004] UKHL 11, [2004] 1 WLR 796.

[124] *Re S* (n 55).

[125] Ibid, per Lord Nicholls at [36].

[126] Ibid, [42].

its interpretation. It would have far-reaching practical ramifications for local authorities and their care of children.[127] It concluded that these were matters for decision by Parliament, not the courts as it was 'impossible for a court to attempt to evaluate' these ramifications or assess what would be the views of Parliament if changes are needed.[128]

By contrast, in *Principal Reporter v K*[129] the Supreme Court utilised section 3 to read into section 93(2)(b)(c) of the Children (Scotland) Act 1995 a provision so that those who had established family life with a child, and would be affected by a children's hearing in relation to that child, would be able to participate in the children's hearing as a relevant person. It was held that this went with, rather than against, the grain of the legislation: 'This is simply widening the range of such people who have an established relationship with the child and thus something important to contribute to the hearing. Mostly, these will be unmarried fathers, but occasionally it might include others.'[130]

3.6.7 Housing

In *Ghaidan*[131] the question was whether section 3 could be applied to paragraphs 2 and 3 of Schedule 1 to the Rent Act 1977 so that it embraced couples living together in a close and stable homosexual relationship as much as couples living together in a close and stable heterosexual relationship so that the surviving spouse of a homosexual couple could succeed to the statutory tenancy. A majority of their Lordships concluded that section 3 could be so applied, finding that the provisions construed without reference to section 3 violated Article 14 taken together with Article 8.

> [T]he social policy underlying the 1988 extension of security of tenure under para 2 to the survivor of couples living together as husband and wife is equally applicable to the survivor of homosexual couples living together in a close and stable relationship. ... I see no reason to doubt that application of s 3 to para 2 has the effect that para 2 should be read and given effect to as though the survivor of such a homosexual couple were the surviving spouse of the original tenant. Reading para 2 in this way would have the result that cohabiting homosexual couples and cohabiting heterosexual couples would be treated alike for the purposes of succession as a statutory tenant. This would eliminate the discriminatory effect of para 2 and would do so consistently with the social policy underlying para 2.[132]

Lord Rodger simply saw this result as a modest development of the extension of the concept of spouse which Parliament itself made in 1988 when it provided that the couple did not have to be married. Therefore, it did not contradict any cardinal principle of the Rent Act, nor did it entail far-reaching practical repercussions which the House was not in a position to evaluate.[133]

In *Poplar Housing*[134] it was argued that section 21(4) of the Housing Act 1988 should be interpreted so that an order for possession was only to be made by a court

---

[127] Ibid, [43].
[128] Ibid, [44]. See further J Herring, 'The Human Rights of Children in Care' (2002) 118 *Law Quarterly Review* 534.
[129] *Principal Reporter v K* [2010] UKSC 56, [2011] 1 WLR 18.
[130] Ibid, [69].
[131] *Ghaidan* (n 33).
[132] Ibid, per Lord Nicholls at [35].
[133] Ibid, [128].
[134] *Poplar Housing* (n 44).

if it was reasonable to do so. The Court of Appeal concluded that the effect of this amendment would be very wide indeed and would significantly reduce the ability of landlords to recover possession and defeat Parliament's original objective of providing certainty. Section 3 was not employed.[135] In *Adan*,[136] also a housing case, a majority of the Court of Appeal did not think it possible to interpret section 204(1) of the Housing Act 1996 in such a way as to allow the County Court to allocate to itself jurisdiction to entertain an appeal on issues of fact so as to comply with Article 6.

3.6.8 Civil Procedure

In *Lukaszewski*[137] the short time limits for lodging appeals against extradition contained in the Extradition Act 2003 were found in some instances to be incompatible with Article 6. The Supreme Court used section 3 to give the High Court power in any individual case to determine whether the operation of time limits would conflict with the right of access to an appeal process and if so, to the extent that it would do so, 'permit and hear an out of time appeal which a litigant personally had done all he could to bring and notify timeously'.[138]

In *Cachia v Faluyi*[139] the Court of Appeal used section 3 to interpret the word 'action' in section 2(3) of the Fatal Accidents Act 1976 as meaning 'served process' in order to give effect to rights under Article 6 of the children whose mother had died.[140] The Act provided that no more than one action shall lie for and in respect of the same subject matter of complaint. The problem was that a writ had been issued but never served—it was argued that this precluded the bringing of a new action. Similarly, in *Goode v Martin*[141] the Court of Appeal had to construe CPR 17.4(1) and (2), which precluded the amendment of a statement of case unless the new claim arose out of the same facts or substantially the same facts as a claim in respect of which the party applying for permission had already claimed a remedy in the proceedings. Finding that Article 6 altered the position, the court held that there was no sound policy reason why the claimant should not add to her claim the alternative plea.

> No new facts are being introduced: she merely wants to say that if the defendant succeeds in establishing his version of the facts, she will still win because those facts, too, show that he was negligent and should pay her compensation.[142]

It concluded that the Rule should be interpreted as if it contained the additional words 'are already in issue on', therefore reading:

> if the new claim arises out of the same facts or substantially the same facts as are already in issue on a claim in respect of which the party applying for permission has already claimed a remedy in the proceedings.[143]

---

[135] Ibid, [77].
[136] *Adan v Newham London Borough Council* [2001] EWCA Civ 1916, [2002] 1 WLR 2120.
[137] *Lukaszewski v Poland* [2012] UKSC 20, [2012] 1 WLR 1604.
[138] Ibid, [39].
[139] *Cachia v Faluyi* [2001] EWCA Civ 998, [2001] 1 WLR 1966.
[140] Ibid, [20].
[141] *Goode v Martin* [2001] EWCA Civ 1899, [2002] 1 WLR 1828.
[142] Ibid, [42].
[143] Ibid, [46].

3.6.9 Other

It has been argued in a number of HRA claims that section 3 should be employed to provide an effective remedy to the claimant. In some instances, this has not been possible given the limits imposed on its use. For example, in *Wilkinson*[144] the House of Lords held that it was not possible to use section 3 to understand the word 'widow' as referring to the more general concept of a surviving spouse as the contrary indications in the language of Part VII of the Income and Corporations Taxes Act 1988 were too strong.[145] However, in many other instances section 3 has been successfully employed to provide an interpretation of primary legislation compatible with Convention rights. Some further examples of the use of section 3 by the courts are listed below:

- Section 10 of the Contempt of Court Act 1981—disclosure of a journalist's source must meet a pressing social need, must be the only practical way of doing so, must be accompanied by safeguards against abuse and must not be such as to destroy the essence of the primary right;[146]
- Section 132 of the Mental Health Act 1983—the patient must be informed of the reasons for treatment without consent in order to ensure compatibility with Article 8;[147]
- State Immunity Act 1978—it was not appropriate to give a blanket effect to a foreign state's claim to state immunity ratione materiae in respect of a state official alleged to have committed acts of systemic torture;[148]
- Bail Act 1976—a court was not entitled to deny a defendant bail simply on the basis that he has been arrested under section 7(3) of the Act;[149]
- Data Protection Act 1998—it was not possible for the Security Service to benefit from a blanket exemption relieving it of any obligation to give a considered answer to individual requests;[150]
- Section 21 National Assistance Act 1948 and section 17 of the Children Act 1989— to enable a local authority to provide financial assistance compatibly with Article 8;[151]
- Section 141(1)(b) of the Customs and Excise Management Act 1979—to make it compatible with Article 1 Protocol No 1;[152]
- Sections 141 and 142 of the Law of Property Act 1925—to ensure compatibly with

---

[144] *R (on the application of Wilkinson) v Inland Revenue Commissioners* [2005] UKHL 30, [2005] 1 WLR 1718.

[145] Ibid, per Lord Hoffmann at [19]. See also *Secretary of State for Work and Pensions v M* [2004] EWCA Civ 1343, [2005] 2 WLR 740, where a majority of the court held that discrimination against absent parents living in same-sex relationships could be remedied by deleting the definition of unmarried couple in Reg 1(2) of the Child Support (Maintenance Assessments and Special Cases) Regulations 1992 so as to leave the meaning of married couple intact at the same time as liberating the meanings of family and partner, where there was no marriage, from the requirement of heterosexuality.

[146] *Financial Times Ltd v Interbrew SA* [2002] EWCA Civ 274, [2002] EMLR 24.

[147] *R (Wooder) v Feggetter* [2002] EWCA Civ 554, [2002] 3 WLR 591.

[148] *Jones v Ministry of the Interior* [2004] EWCA Civ 1394, [2005] QB 699 at [91]–[92], [96].

[149] *R (on the application of the Director of Public Prosecutions) v Havering Magistrates' Court* [2001] 1 WLR 805.

[150] *Baker v Secretary of State for the Home Department* [2001] UKHRR 1275.

[151] *R (on the application of J) v Enfield London Borough Council* [2002] EWHC (Admin) 432, [2002] 2 FLR 1.

[152] *Fox v HM Customs and Excise* [2002] EWHC (Admin) 1244, [2003] 1 WLR 1331.

Article 1 Protocol No 1 and thereby enable a landlord, under a head tenancy which had been determined by a break notice, to enforce the lessee's covenants as contained in the subtenancy;[153]

- Section 335A of the Insolvency Act 1986—to ensure that the immediate sale of a property would not violate a family's rights under Article 8;[154]
- Paragraph 11(1) of Schedule 22 to the Criminal Justice Act 2003—to imply a provision that when setting a term of imprisonment, where it was necessary to comply with a prisoner's rights under Article 6, an oral hearing would be held;[155]
- Section 115(7)(b) of the Police Act 1997—so that information which ought to be included on an enhanced criminal record certificate was read and given effect in a way which was compatible with Article 8;[156]
- Section 143D(2) of the Housing Act 1996—so that it allowed a court to exercise the powers which were necessary to consider, and where appropriate, to give effect to, any article 8 defence which the defendant raised in possession proceedings;[157]
- Section 127(2) of the Housing Act 1996—so a tenant was permitted to raise his Article 8 right by way of a defence to the proceedings in the county court and enable the judge to address the issue of proportionality;[158]
- Part I of the Land Compensation Act 1973—to give effect to the intention that those adversely affected by noise from new roads should be adequately compensated in accordance with Article 1 of Protocol No 1.[159]
- Regulations 6 and 30 of the Immigration Nationality (Fees) Regulations 2010—made subject to the qualification that no fee was due for an application for an extension of discretionary leave to remain where to require it to be paid would be incompatible with a person's Convention rights.[160]

---

4. Section 4 Human Rights Act

4.1 Interpretation

Section 4 gives a court the power to make a declaration of incompatibility where a provision of primary legislation is incompatible with a Convention right[161] and where a provision of subordinate legislation is incompatible with a Convention right but the

---

[153] *PW & Co v Milton Gate Investments Ltd* [2003] EWHC (Ch) 1994, [2004] 2 WLR 443, [130].
[154] *Barca v Mears* [2004] EWHC (Ch) 2170, [2005] 2 FLR 1.
[155] *Hammond* (n 80).
[156] *R (L) v Commissioner of Police of the Metropolis* [2009] UKSC 3, [2010] 1 AC 410.
[157] *Manchester City Council v Pinnock* [2010] UKSC 45, [2011] 2 AC 104.
[158] *Hounslow London Borough Council v Powell* [2011] UKSC 8, [2011] 2 WLR 287. See also *R v Holding* [2005] EWCA Crim 3185, [2006] 1 WLR 1040.
[159] *Thomas v Bridgend County Borough Council* [2011] EWCA Civ 862, [2012] 2 WLR 624.
[160] *R (Omar) v Secretary of State for the Home Department* [2012] EWHC 3348 (Admin), [2013] Imm AR 601.
[161] Sections 4(1) and 4(2).

primary legislation prevents removal of the incompatibility.[162] It is only open to certain courts to make a declaration of incompatibility;[163] such a declaration does not affect 'the validity, continuing operation or enforcement of the provision in respect of which it is given' and is not binding on the parties to the proceedings in which it is made.[164] Furthermore, where a court is considering whether to make a declaration of incompatibility, the Crown is entitled to notice in accordance with the rules of court.[165] In *Rights Brought Home*[166] it was stated that whilst a declaration would not of itself change the law, 'it will almost certainly prompt the Government and Parliament to change the law'.[167] It was decided not to give the courts the power to set aside primary legislation due to the importance attached to Parliamentary sovereignty.

> To make a provision in the Bill for the courts to set aside Acts of Parliament would confer on the judiciary a general power over the decisions of Parliament which under our present constitutional arrangements they do not possess, and would be likely on occasions to draw the judiciary into serious conflict with Parliament. There is no evidence to suggest that they desire this power, nor that the public wish them to have it. Certainly, this Government has no mandate for any such change.[168]

Once a provision of legislation has been declared to be incompatible, a minister, if he considers that there are compelling reasons, may by order make such amendments to the legislation as he considers necessary to remove the incompatibility.[169] Again this power is discretionary, and the decision whether to seek a remedial order is a matter for the government to decide on a case-by-case basis. It was thought that it would be wrong for a declaration to automatically lead to a remedial order as this would in effect 'be tantamount to giving the courts power to strike down Acts of Parliament'.[170] The procedure for making such a remedial order is set out in Schedule 2 to the HRA. In brief, the procedure which must be followed is the affirmative procedure, and a draft of the order must be approved by a resolution of each House of Parliament. However, in urgent cases it is possible to make the order without the draft being so approved.[171] It is important to note that the victim of the incompatible act resulting in the declaration may actually have no other enforceable remedy although it may be possible for a remedial order affecting the legislation to take effect from a date earlier than that on which the order was made or for ex gratia compensation to be sought.[172]

As to the circumstances where a declaration may be made, these encompass the

---

[162] Sections 4(3) and 4(4).

[163] Section 4(5) lists the House of Lords; Judicial Committee of the Privy Council; Courts-Martial Appeal Court; in Scotland, the High Court of Justiciary sitting otherwise than as a trial court or the Court of Session; in England and Wales or Northern Ireland, the High Court or the Court of Appeal. It is therefore not open to the Employment Appeal Tribunal to make a declaration, although occasionally the opportunity arises. See eg *Whittaker v P&D Watson* [2002] ICR 1244.

[164] Section 4(6).

[165] Section 5(1).

[166] Home Office, *Rights Brought Home: The Human Rights Bill* (Cm 3782) (London, TSO, 1997).

[167] Ibid, [2.11].

[168] Ibid, [2.13].

[169] Section 10(2). This section also allows amendment where, having regard to a finding of the ECtHR in proceedings against the United Kingdom, a provision of legislation is incompatible with an obligation of the United Kingdom arising from the Convention. See s 10(1)(b).

[170] HL Deb, Vol 583, col 1139 (27 November 1997), Lord Chancellor.

[171] See paras 2(b) and 4 Sch 2. See further Joint Committee on Human Rights, *Seventh Report* (2001–02 HL 58, HC 473).

[172] HL Deb, Vol 583, col 1108 (27 November 1997), Lord Chancellor.

instances where it is not possible to use section 3 as discussed in the paragraphs above. It may be that the legislation contains provisions which expressly contradict the meaning which the enactment would have to be given to make it compatible or provisions which do so by necessary implication.[173] It may also arise that the use of section 3 would involve adopting a meaning inconsistent with a fundamental feature of the legislation[174] or involve the court in making a decision for which it was not equipped.[175] In keeping with the view that a declaration of incompatibility is a measure of last resort[176] and an exceptional course to take,[177] very few declarations of incompatibility have actually been made by the courts. During the parliamentary debates, the Lord Chancellor commented that in 99% of the cases that will arise, there will be no need for judicial declarations of incompatibility.[178]

4.2 A Reasonable Period within which to Amend Domestic Law

It has been accepted by the courts that there may be circumstances where maintaining an offending law in operation for a reasonable period pending enactment of corrective legislation is justifiable and that, during the transitional period, an individual would not be able to claim that his or her rights had been violated.[179] Therefore, where a declaration of incompatibility is likely to be made, it is not uncommon for the defendant Secretary of State to resist such a declaration on the ground that the government should be entitled to a reasonable period in which to amend domestic law. For example, in *Bellinger*[180] the Secretary of State submitted that the House of Lords should not make a declaration of incompatibility as the European Court of Human Rights in *Goodwin v United Kingdom*[181] envisaged that the government should have a reasonable period in which to amend domestic law on a principled and coherent basis.

However, this was not accepted by their Lordships. Lord Nicholls held that this was not a situation where legal acts or situations which antedated the judgment in *Goodwin* were being reopened. Section 11(c) of the Matrimonial Causes Act 1973 remained a continuing obstacle to Mr and Mrs Bellinger marrying each other[182] and was clearly not compatible with Articles 8 and 12.

> The European Court of Human Rights so found in July 2002 in *Goodwin*, and the government has so accepted. What was held to be incompatible in July 2002 has not now, for the purposes of s 4, become compatible. The government's announcement of forthcoming legislation has not had that effect, nor could it. That would make no sense.[183]

---

[173] *R v A* (n 52), per Lord Hope at [108]; *Lambert* (n 65), per Lord Hope at [79]; *Re S* (n 55), per Lord Nicholls at [40]; *Anderson* (n 65), per Lord Steyn at [59]; *Rusbridger* (n 65), per Lord Steyn at [8]; *Ghaidan* (n 33), per Lord Rodger at [117].

[174] *Re S* (n 55), per Lord Nicholls at [40].

[175] *Ghaidan* (n 33), per Lord Nicholls at [33].

[176] *R v A* (n 52), per Lord Steyn at [44].

[177] *Ghaidan* (n 33), per Lord Steyn at [50]. See also *Attorney General's Reference No 4 of 2002* (n 54), per Lord Bingham at [28].

[178] HL Deb, Vol 585, col 840 (5 February 1998). See further R Buxton, 'The Future of Declarations of Incompatibility' [2010] *Public Law* 213.

[179] *Bellinger v Bellinger* [2003] UKHL 21, [2003] 2 AC 467 per Lord Nicholls at [53].

[180] Ibid.

[181] *Goodwin v United Kingdom* (2002) 35 EHRR 18.

[182] Ibid, [52].

[183] Ibid, [53]. It was also held in *Hooper* (n 5) that if a form of discrimination which was historically

4.3 A Declaration where the Government already Has Plans to Legislate

It has also been submitted by respondent Secretaries of State that there is no need to make a declaration where the government already has plans to legislate in the area. However, such arguments are generally not successful. For example, it was also submitted in *Bellinger*[184] that a declaration would serve no useful purpose as the government had already announced its intention to bring forward primary legislation on this subject. Lord Nicholls was not persuaded.

> [W]hen proceedings are already before the House, it is desirable that in a case of such sensitivity this House, as the court of final appeal in this country, should formally record that the present state of statute law is incompatible with the Convention.[185]

Similarly, in *M*[186] it was submitted that the Mental Health Bill would resolve the problem. The Administrative Court rejected this argument, holding that it would be wrong to make assumptions about the form in which a Bill may be enacted or about the timing of its coming into force.

> If I make a declaration, it is for the Government to decide what, if anything, to do about it. It is not for me to express or imply any view as to what it, through Parliament, ought to do about it. If I make a declaration, the door is opened to a remedial order under s 10, but it remains a matter for the Secretary of State as to whether he wishes to walk through that door.[187]

4.4 Failure to Legislate

It is not possible to issue a declaration of incompatibility in relation to a failure to legislate. The absence of a particular provision from a statute does not, in itself, mean that the statute is incompatible with a Convention right. '[T]his signifies at most the existence of a lacuna in the statute.'[188] It is also stated in section 6(6) that an act includes a failure to act but does not include a failure to introduce in, or lay before, Parliament a proposal for legislation, or make any primary legislation or remedial order.

Nevertheless, there have been deviations from this rule. In *MH*[189] the Court of Appeal declared that there was lacking from the scheme of the Mental Health Act 1983 provisions that were necessary to make that scheme compliant with the Convention rights. Section 2 was declared incompatible with Article 5(4) in that it was not attended

---

justified but, with changes in society, has gradually lost its justification, a period of consultation, drafting and debate must be included in the time which the legislature may reasonable consider appropriate for making a change and up to the point at which that time is exceeded, there is no violation of a Convention right. However, this did not apply in the present case. See *Goodwin*, per Lord Hoffmann [62]–[63] in reliance upon *Walden v Liechtenstein*, Judgment of 16 March 2000.

[184] *Bellinger* (n 179).
[185] Ibid, [55].
[186] *R (on the application of M) v Secretary of State for Health* [2003] EWHC (Admin) 1094, [2003] ACD 389.
[187] Ibid, [17]. See also [14]–[22].
[188] *Re S* (n 55), [85].
[189] *R (on the application of MH) v Secretary of State for Health* [2004] EWCA Civ 1609, [2005] 1 WLR 1209.

by adequate provision for the reference to a court of the case of a patient detained pursuant to section 2 in circumstances where a patient had a right to make application to a Mental Health Review Tribunal but the patient was incapable of exercising that right on his own initiative.[190]

Furthermore, in *Rose*[191] the Administrative Court made a distinction between regulations falling with the affirmative resolution procedure and regulations falling within the negative resolution procedure. The claimants sought access to non-identifying information and, where possible, identifying information in respect of an anonymous sperm donor. The Administrative Court confirmed that section 6(6)(a) prevented the claimants from complaining of any failure to enact primary legislation or of any failure to make regulations under section 31(4)(a) of the Human Fertilisation and Embryology Act 1990. 'Any regulations under this subsection require the positive approval of both Houses of Parliament.'[192] However, the court pointed out that the claimants were not debarred from claiming that the Secretary of State had acted unlawfully in failing to make regulations under section 8(d) of the 1990 Act because such regulations would fall within the negative resolution procedure.[193] In the opinion of the court, where the primary legislation provides that a statutory instrument shall be subject to annulment by resolution of either House after being made, it would not be a proposal for legislation within the meaning of section 6(6)(a) of the HRA. It contrasted the position where the primary legislation provided that a statutory instrument may not be made unless authorised by affirmative resolution as there the instrument would be a proposal for legislation for the purposes of section 6(6)(a).[194]

4.5 The Use of Section 4 in Hypothetical Cases

The possibility that section 4 may be applied in a hypothetical case has not been ruled out. In his judgment in *Nasseri*[195] Lord Hoffmann, taking into account the discretionary nature of the remedy, held as follows:

> I would not ... wish to exclude the possibility that in a case in which a public authority was not, on the facts, acting incompatibly with a Convention right, the court might consider it convenient to make a declaration that if he had been so acting, a provision of primary legislation which made it lawful for him to do so would have been incompatible with Convention rights. But such cases, in which the declaration is, so to speak, an obiter dictum not necessary for the decision of the case, will in my opinion be rare.[196]

It has also been held that the requirement for a claimant to be a victim within the meaning of section 7 of the HRA does not apply where a declaration of incompatibility

---

[190] Ibid, [29]. Section 29(4) was also declared incompatible.

[191] *R (on the application of Rose) v Secretary of State for Health* [2002] EWHC (Admin) 1593, [2002] 3 FCR 731.

[192] Ibid, [50].

[193] Ibid.

[194] Ibid, [51].

[195] *Secretary of State for the Home Department v Nasseri* [2009] UKHL 23, [2010] 1 AC 1.

[196] Ibid, [20]. In the present case it was determined that a declaration was unnecessary. See also the observations of Lord Scott in *R (Animal Defenders International) v Secretary of State for Culture Media & Sport* [2008] UKHL 15, [2008] 2 WLR 781, [42].

is sought.[197] However, in *Taylor*[198] the issue was whether a litigant could obtain a declaration of incompatibility on a ground from which he could not benefit. The Court of Appeal held that it was not the intention of the HRA or the Convention that members of the public should use these provisions if they were not adversely affected by them to change legislation because they considered that the legislation was incompatible with the Convention. In the view of the court, this was made clear by the language of section 7, and the claimant here was not a victim.[199] In addition, it pointed out that the grant of a declaration of incompatibility was discretionary.

> It is doubtful in the extreme that a court would exercise its discretion in favour of Mr Taylor if he could not be affected by the breach of the Convention on which he was attempting to rely.[200]

Taking into account the judgment of the House of Lords in *Rusbridger*,[201] the court pointed out that the desirably flexible approach to the grant of declarations could not be applied in the present circumstances where the claimant has not been and could not be personally adversely affected by the repealed legislation on which he seeks to rely. 'To allow him to do so would be to ignore section 7 of the HRA.'[202]

4.6 Problems with the Declaration of Incompatibility

As already discussed, under section 4 all that a court may do is issue a 'declaration of incompatibility' which does not affect the validity, continuing operation or enforcement of the provision in respect of which it is given, and is not binding on the parties to the proceedings in which it is made.[203] It remains for a government minister, if he or she considers there are compelling reasons, to make by order such amendments to the legislation as considered necessary to remove the incompatibility.[204] From the start, this solution was seen to be the only viable option:

> To make a provision in the Bill for the courts to set aside Acts of Parliament would confer on the judiciary a general power over the decisions of Parliament which under our present constitutional arrangements they do not possess, and would be likely on occasions to draw the judiciary into serious conflict with Parliament. There is no evidence to suggest that they desire this power, nor that the public wish them to have it. Certainly this Government has no mandate for any such change.[205]

However, whilst parliamentarians, members of the executive, courts and pragmatic commentators on the HRA have almost universally not questioned the declaration of incompatibility, the remedy has been the subject of comment by external institutions. Particularly serious is the opinion of the ECtHR. In a number of applications, the

---

[197] *R (on the application of Trailer & Marina (Leven) Ltd) v Secretary of State for the Environment, Food & Rural Affairs* [2004] EWCA Civ 1580, [2005] 1 WLR 1267.
[198] *Lancashire County Council v Taylor* [2005] EWCA Civ 284, [2005] HRLR 17.
[199] Ibid, [38]–[41].
[200] Ibid, [42].
[201] *Rusbridger* (n 65).
[202] Ibid, [44]. See also *Tangney v The Governor of HMP Elmley* [2005] EWCA Civ 1009.
[203] Human Rights Act 1998, s 4(6).
[204] Ibid, s 10(2).
[205] *Rights Brought Home* (n 166), [2.13].

Court has held that the declaration of incompatibility is not an effective remedy firstly 'because a declaration was not binding on the parties to the proceedings in which it was made'; and secondly, 'because a declaration provided the appropriate minister with a power, not a duty, to amend the offending legislation by order so as to make it compatible with the Convention'.[206] As the declaration of incompatibility is not considered to be an effective remedy, it is not a domestic remedy which must be exhausted in accordance with Article 35 of the ECHR prior to an application being brought to the ECtHR. Therefore, where the incompatibility lies in an Act of Parliament, and the only realistic remedy at the domestic level is a declaration of incompatibility, in the view of the ECtHR there is no need for the applicant to air his or her complaint at the domestic level first, thereby defeating one of the main purposes of the HRA, to bring rights home, and adding to the number of applications against the UK declared admissible.[207]

The Joint Committee on Human Rights has drawn attention to additional problems. In a small number of cases 'the time taken to consider a response to the relevant declaration of incompatibility has been significantly longer than six months'.[208] And it does not consider that the guidance in the DCA publication *Human Rights: Human Lives* provides enough 'detailed guidance on the application of the HRA and the Convention in order to allow departmental officials to respond effectively to declarations of incompatibility'. In its view 'much more specific guidance is required to guide departments in responding promptly and adequately to declarations of incompatibility.'[209]

However, in the absence of a new constitutional settlement resulting in a limitation on the sovereignty of Parliament in relation to Convention rights as well as directly effective EC law, it is difficult to imagine a better mechanism for dealing with the relationship between Convention rights and Acts of Parliament. However, improvements could be made. The ECtHR has signalled that it is possible that at some future date, 'evidence of a long-standing and established practice of ministers giving effect to the courts' declarations of incompatibility might be sufficient to persuade the Court of the effectiveness of the procedure'.[210] The Government could also give consideration to the observations of the Joint Committee and respond to declarations of incompatibility more promptly whilst providing more detailed guidance to departmental officials to equip them to respond effectively.[211]

4.7 The Application of Section 4 in Practice

Given that there have been so few declarations of incompatibility to date, the majority of those that have been made are examined in the following paragraphs.

---

[206] *Burden and Burden v United Kingdom* (dec), Application No 13378/05 (12 December 2006), [37].

[207] See further Joint Committee on Human Rights, *Monitoring the Government's Response to Court Judgments Finding Breaches of Human Rights* HC 728 (2007), HL 128 (2007), [110]–[111] and M Amos 'The Impact of the Human Rights Act on the United Kingdom's Performance before the European Court of Human Rights' [2007] *Public Law* 655.

[208] Joint Committee on Human Rights, Ibid, [114].

[209] Ibid, [121].

[210] *Burden* (n 206), [59].

[211] See further Joint Committee on Human Rights, *A Bill of Rights for the UK?* HL 165 (2008), HC 150 (2008), [224]–[229].

4.7.1 Criminal Justice

In *Anderson*[212] the House of Lords found unanimously that it was not possible to apply section 3 to section 29 of the the Crime (Sentences) Act 1997.

> Since, therefore, the section leaves it to the Home Secretary to decide whether or when to refer a case to the [Parole] board, and he is free to ignore its recommendation if it is favourable to the prisoner, the decision on how long the convicted murderer should remain in prison for punitive purposes is his alone. It cannot be doubted that Parliament intended this result when enacting section 29 and its predecessor sections. … To read section 29 as precluding participation by the Home Secretary, if it were possible to do so, would not be judicial interpretation but judicial vandalism: it would give the section an effect quite different from that which Parliament intended and would go well beyond any interpretative process sanctioned by section 3 of the 1998 Act.[213]

Their Lordships therefore issued their first declaration of incompatibility, declaring section 29 incompatible with the right under Article 6 to have a sentence imposed by an independent and impartial tribunal.[214]

A declaration of incompatibility was also made by the Supreme Court in F[215] in relation to section 82 of the Sexual Offences Act 2003 which subjected sex offenders, sentenced to 30 months or more, to notification requirements for the rest of their lives.[216]

4.7.2 Gender Reassignment

In *Bellinger*[217] the House of Lords unanimously declared section 11(c) of the Matrimonial Causes Act 1973 incompatible with Articles 8 and 12 as it made no provision for the recognition of gender reassignment. This step was taken even though it had no effect on the validity or otherwise of the marriage ceremony celebrated in 1981. Lord Hope recognised that

> problems of great complexity would be involved if recognition were to be given to same sex marriages. They must be left to Parliament. I do not think that your Lordships can solve the problem judicially by means of the interpretative obligation in s 3(1) of the 1998 Act.[218]

Similarly, Lord Hobhouse found a declaration appropriate, as to use section 3 to read section 11(c) so as to include additional words such as 'two people of the same sex' would be a legislative exercise of amendment.[219]

---

[212] *Anderson* (n 65).

[213] Ibid, per Lord Bingham at [30]. See also Lord Steyn at [59] and Lord Hutton at [81].

[214] See also *R (Clift) v Secretary of State for the Home Department* [2006] UKHL 54, [2007] 1 AC 484 where the House of Lords declared the early release provisions contained in the Criminal Justice Act 1991 incompatible with Art 14 in conjunction with Art 5.

[215] *R (F) v Secretary of State for the Home Department* [2010] UKSC 17, [2011] 1 AC 331.

[216] See also *R (T) v Chief Constable of Greater Manchester* [2013] EWCA Civ 25, [2013] 2 All ER 813 where the Court of Appeal declared the Police Act 1997, which allowed for the blanket disclosure of police warnings, cautions and convictions, incompatible with Art 8.

[217] *Bellinger* (n 179).

[218] Ibid, [69].

[219] Ibid, [78]. See further D Nicol, 'Gender Reassignment and the Transformation of the Human Rights Act' (2004) 120 *Law Quarterly Review* 194.

4.7.3 Prevention of Terrorism

In *A v Secretary of State for the Home Department*[220] the question of using section 3 to interpret section 23 of the Anti-Terrorism Crime and Security Act 2001 was not even discussed, it having been found incompatible with Article 14 taken together with Article 5. A majority of their Lordships simply made a declaration of incompatibility, declaring that the section was incompatible with Articles 5 and 14 insofar as it was disproportionate and permitted detention of suspected international terrorists in a way that discriminated on the ground of nationality or immigration status.[221]

4.7.4 Care Standards

In *Wright*[222] the House of Lords found that section 82(4)(b) of the Care Standards Act 2000 was incompatible with Articles 6 and 8. In short the Act established a scheme whereby those considered unsuitable to work with vulnerable adults were placed on a list which would thereby prevent him or her from gaining employment as a care worker. Finding the scheme too complex for a section 3 solution, the House of Lords decided to make a declaration of incompatibility. It hesitated to make any suggestions as to how the scheme could be made compatible. Baroness Hale explained as follows:

> First, the incompatibility arises from the interaction between the three elements of the scheme—the procedure, the criterion and the consequences. It is not for us to attempt to rewrite the legislation. There is, as I have already said, a delicate balance to be struck between protecting the rights of the care workers and protecting the welfare, as well as the rights, of the vulnerable people with whom they work. It is right that that balance be struck in the first instance by the legislature. Secondly, both the Care Standards Act 2000 and the Protection of Children Act 1999 will in due course be replaced by a completely different scheme.[223]

4.7.5 Mental Health

In *H*[224] the Court of Appeal concluded that section 73 of the Mental Health Act 1983 was incompatible with Articles 5(1) and 5(4) of the Convention in that the burden of proof was placed on the patient. The patient had to prove that the criteria for admission were not satisfied, whereas, in the opinion of the court, he should be entitled to be discharged if it could not be demonstrated that the criteria were satisfied. Section 3 was not considered and a declaration of incompatibility was made under section 4. As discussed above, in *MH*[225] the Court of Appeal declared section 2 of the Mental Health Act 1983 incompatible with Article 5(4) in that it was not attended by adequate provision for the reference to a court of the case of a patient detained pursuant to section 2 in circumstances where a patient had a right to make application to a Mental

---

[220] *A v Secretary of State for the Home Department* [2004] UKHL 56, [2005] 2 AC 68.
[221] Ibid, per Lord Bingham at [73].
[222] *R (Wright) v Secretary of State for Health* [2009] UKHL 3, [2009] 1 AC 739.
[223] Ibid, [39].
[224] *R (on the application of H) v Mental Health Review Tribunal, North & East London Region* [2001] EWCA Civ 415, [2002] QB 1.
[225] *MH* (n 189).

Health Review Tribunal but the patient was incapable of exercising that right on his own initiative.[226]

A declaration of incompatibility was also made in *D*,[227] where the Administrative Court found that the fact that a discretionary life prisoner who had served the minimum period of his detention but who remained also compulsorily detained under the Mental Health Act 1983 had no statutory right to apply to the Parole Board or to require the Secretary of State to refer his case to the Board under section 34(5) of the Criminal Justice Act 1991 in order for it to review the lawfulness of his detention was incompatible with Article 5(4). Section 74 of the Mental Health Act 1983 was declared incompatible. Sections 26 and 29 of the Mental Health Act 1983 were declared incompatible with Article 8 in *M*,[228] the Administrative Court finding that the absence of any possibility to apply to the court to change the claimant's nearest relative was incompatible with Article 8.

4.7.6 Immigration

In *International Transport Roth*[229] a majority of the Court of Appeal found that a penalty scheme created pursuant to section 32 of the Immigration and Asylum Act 1999 making carriers liable to a fixed penalty for every clandestine entrant found concealed in a vehicle was inconsistent with Article 6 and Article 1 of Protocol No 1. It was held that it was impossible to recreate the scheme by any interpretative process as one compatible with Convention rights. 'We cannot create a wholly different scheme … so as to provide an acceptable alternative means of immigration control. That must be for Parliament itself.'[230] Section 32 was declared incompatible with the Convention rights.[231]

---

5. The Use of Hansard and Other Materials in Compatibility Cases

It has been appreciated by the courts that the HRA requires them to exercise a new role in respect of primary legislation.

> This new role is fundamentally different from interpreting and applying legislation. The courts are now required to evaluate the effect of primary legislation in terms of Convention

---

[226] Ibid, [29]. Section 29(4) was also declared incompatible.

[227] *D v Secretary of State for the Home Department* [2002] EHC (Admin) 2805, [2003] 1 WLR 1315.

[228] *M* (n 186).

[229] *International Transport Roth GmbH v Secretary of State for the Home Department* [2002] EWCA Civ 158, [2003] QB 728.

[230] Ibid, per Simon Brown LJ at [66].

[231] See also Ibid, per Jonathan Parker LJ at [184], [186]. A declaration of incompatibility was also made in *R (on the application of Morris) v Westminster City Council* [2004] EWHC (Admin) 2191, [2005] 1 WLR 865.

rights and, where appropriate, make a formal declaration of incompatibility. In carrying out this evaluation the court has to compare the effect of the legislation with the Convention right. If the legislation impinges upon a Convention right the court must then compare the policy objective of the legislation with the policy objective which under the Convention may justify a prima facie infringement of the Convention right.[232]

When making these comparisons, it has been held that the court will look primarily at the legislation.

The first question is whether the policy justification for the distinction which is in issue is apparent from the legislation, whether read by itself or with its antecedents and the cases decided on the provisions. Only if the policy is not apparent from these materials should it become necessary to look wider.[233]

However, it is also possible for a court to look outside the statute in order to see the complete picture.[234]

[S]ometimes the court may need additional background information tending to show, for instance, the likely practical impact of the statutory measure and why the course adopted by the legislature is not appropriate. Moreover, as when interpreting a statute, so when identifying the policy objective of a statutory provision or assessing the 'proportionality' of a statutory provision, the court may need enlightenment on the nature and extent of the social problem (the 'mischief') at which the legislation is aimed. This may throw light on the rationale underlying the legislation.[235]

Such background information may include published documents, such as a White Paper, or explanatory notes prepared by the relevant government department and published with the Bill.[236] It may also include information gleaned from the parliamentary debates on the Bill.

By having regard to such material the court would not be 'questioning' proceedings in Parliament or intruding improperly into the legislative process or ascribing to Parliament the views expressed by a minister. The court would merely be placing itself in a better position to understand the legislation.[237]

However, it has been noted that such occasions when resort to Hansard is necessary will seldom arise and, if it did, the court must be careful

not to treat the ministerial or other statement as indicative of the objective intention of Parliament. Nor should the courts give a ministerial statement, whether made inside or outside Parliament, determinative weight. It should not be supposed that members necessarily agreed with the minister's reasoning or his conclusions.[238]

Furthermore, it is clear that Hansard may only be used as a source of background information.

The proportionality of a statutory measure is not to be judged by the quality of the reasons advanced in support of it in the course of parliamentary debate, or by the subjective state of

---

[232] *Wilson* (n 11), per Lord Nicholls at [61].
[233] *Taylor* (n 198).
[234] *Wilson* (n 11).
[235] Ibid, [63].
[236] Ibid, [64].
[237] Ibid.
[238] Ibid, [66]. See also *Taylor* (n 198), [58].

mind of individual ministers or other members. ... The court is called upon to evaluate the proportionality of the legislation, not the adequacy of the minister's exploration of the policy options or his explanations to Parliament.[239]

In addition to concerns about the use of Hansard, particular issues have arisen surrounding the submission of witness statements by government ministers in compatibility cases. For example, in *Evans*[240] the Secretary of State filed a 19-page witness statement containing evidence as to the legislative history of the provision, the policy justification for the regime of the Act and relevant legal practice in other Council of Europe states. A majority of the Court of Appeal was concerned about its admissibility, commenting that they were not persuaded that the speeches in *Wilson* would accommodate the full ambit of the witness statement.

> If it is open to a minister whose predecessor was administratively responsible for a Bill to give evidence for s 4 purposes of the departmental policy and intent behind the measure, it is not immediately obvious why a minister may not give evidence—potentially conclusive evidence—of what he or his predecessor intended in making a statutory instrument of which the meaning is being debated in court.[241]

However, the majority did no more than record its concerns.[242]

The issue returned in *Taylor*,[243] where the Secretary of State submitted a witness statement containing: a summary of the history of legislative reform; substantial extracts from the reports of the Parliamentary debates on what became the predecessor Acts; a cutting from *Farmers' Weekly*; extracts from the drafter's Notes on Clauses on the 1976 Bill; correspondence dating from 1951 between the National Farmer's Union and the Ministry of Agriculture; some extracts from the 1947 Act; a comment on and gloss on the Hansard extracts; and an account of current government policy. The court pointed out that, insofar as this represented argument, its proper source was counsel, not a witness. Insofar as it recounted history, it was relevant and helpful. However, the use of drafter's Notes on Clauses was found to be problematic as they were not available to members of either House. 'To the extent that ministers used them in debate, they will feature in Hansard. It is therefore to Hansard that one needs principally to turn.'[244] It also concluded that, had it been necessary to go beyond the text and the legislative and judicial history of the 1986 Act, it would have admitted little if any of the parliamentary materials admitted in the court below, including contributions of members to the debates and ministerial statements which said no more than could be readily seen from the legislation itself.[245]

---

239 *Wilson* (n 11), [67]. Lord Hope reached a similar conclusion at [110]–[118], as did Lord Hobhouse at [139]–[144]. Lord Scott agreed with Lord Nicholls, and Lord Rodger made no comment on the issue. See further A Kavanagh, 'Pepper v Hart and Matters of Constitutional Principle', (2005) 121 *Law Quarterly Review* 98.
240 *Evans v Amicus Healthcare Ltd* [2004] EWCA Civ 727, [2004] 3 WLR 681.
241 Ibid, [53].
242 Ibid, [56].
243 *Taylor* (n 198).
244 Ibid, [55].
245 Ibid, [59]. See also *R (Wilson) v Wychavon District Council* [2007] EWCA Civ 52, [2007] 2 WLR 798.

6. Section 19 Human Rights Act: Statements of Compatibility

The final provision of the HRA concerning primary legislation is section 19 which provides that a Minister of the Crown in charge of a Bill in either House of Parliament must, before Second Reading of the Bill: (a) make a statement to the effect that in his view the provisions of the Bill are compatible with the Convention rights; or (b) make a statement to the effect that although he in unable to make a statement of compatibility the government nevertheless wishes the House to proceed with the Bill. The statement must be in writing and be published in such manner as the Minister making it considers appropriate.[246] It was suggested by the Lord Chancellor during the Parliamentary debates that this section was a very large gesture, as well as a point of substance, 'in favour of the development of a culture of awareness of what the convention requires in relation to domestic legislation'.[247]

The Home Office has stated that in considering whether to make a statement of compatibility the basic test applied is whether, on the balance of probabilities, the provisions of the Bill would be found compatible with the Convention rights if challenged in court or tribunal. However, it is appreciated that

> the Minister's view is reached only after very careful consideration but is not legally binding. Ultimately, only a court can determine the Convention rights and give a definitive view as to whether a particular provision complies with those rights or not.[248]

Whilst a useful addition to mechanisms for the protection and promotion of human rights in the legislative process, section 19 statements have had little impact in HRA jurisprudence and such statements carry very little weight. Lord Hope in *R v A*[249] pointed out that the Secretary of State did not seek to rely on the statement of compatibility attached to the Youth Justice and Criminal Evidence Act 1999 in the course of his argument.

> I consider that he was right not to do so. These statements may serve a useful purpose in Parliament. They may also be seen as part of the parliamentary history, indicating that it was not Parliament's intention to cut across a Convention right. ... No doubt they are based on the best advice that is available. But they are no more than expressions of opinion by the minister. They are not binding on the court, nor do they have any persuasive authority.[250]

To date the courts have only considered one statement made under section 19(1) (b). On the introduction of the Communications Bill 2003 to Parliament, the Secretary of State felt unable to make a statement pursuant to section 19(1)(b) but nevertheless

---

[246] More specific information on the human rights aspect of a Bill is provided in the Explanatory Notes which accompany the Bill.

[247] HL Deb, Vol 583, col 1163 (27 November 1997).

[248] Memo by Home Office to the Joint Committee on Human Rights, minutes of evidence taken on Wednesday 14 March 2001 (2000–01 HL 66, HC 332) at [15].

[249] *R v A* (n 52).

[250] Ibid, [69].

wished the House of Commons to proceed with the Bill. The government's position was that it believed and had been advised the ban on political advertising in the Bill was compatible with Article 10, but given recent ECtHR authority, it could not be sure.

In concluding that the interference with Article 10 was proportionate, the House of Lords considered the section 19(1)(b) statement as an indication of how carefully Parliament had considered the potential violation of Article 10 contained in the Bill, therefore, its judgment should be given some weight in the balancing process to be carried out by the court. Lord Bingham observed as follows:

> Parliament has resolved, uniquely since the 1998 Act came into force in October 2000, that the prohibition of political advertising on television and radio may possibly, although improbably, infringe article 10 but has nonetheless resolved to proceed under section 19(1)(b) of the Act. It has done so, while properly recognising the interpretative supremacy of the European Court, because of the importance which it attaches to maintenance of this prohibition. The judgment of Parliament on such an issue should not be lightly overridden.[251]

---

[251] *R (Animal Defenders International) v Secretary of State for Culture, Media & Sport* [2008] UKHL 15, [2008] 2 WLR 781, [33].

6

Remedies

1. Introduction

In relation to any act of a public authority which a court finds unlawful, section 8(1) of the HRA provides that the court may grant such relief or remedy, or make such order, within its powers as it considers just and appropriate. As with other key features of the HRA, the remedies available closely mirror those which would be available to a claimant before the ECtHR under Article 41 of the ECHR,[1] which enables the Court to award 'just satisfaction to the injured party' for Convention violations. It has been held that the approach of the UK courts should be no less liberal than that applied at Strasbourg or one of the purposes of the HRA will be defeated and claimants will still be put to the expense of having to go to Strasbourg to obtain just satisfaction.[2]

Where an infringement of a person's human rights has occurred, the concern will usually be to bring the infringement to an end. Any question of compensation is often considered to be of secondary importance.[3] The remedies most frequently sought for an act incompatible with Convention rights are the 'orders which are the descendants of the historic prerogative orders or declaratory judgments'. These enable the court to order a public body to refrain from or to take action, or to quash an offending administrative decision. 'Declaratory judgments usually resolve disputes as to what is the correct answer in law to a dispute.'[4] Whilst in practice this is the position, the focus of section 8, and HRA jurisprudence in this area, is primarily on the award of damages for a breach of Convention rights.

---

[1] 'If the Court finds that there has been a violation of the Convention or the protocols thereto, and if the internal law of the High Contracting Party concerned allows only partial reparation to be made, the Court shall, if necessary, afford just satisfaction to the injured party.'

[2] *Anufrijeva v Southwark LBC* [2003] EWCA Civ 1406, [2004] QB 1124, [57]. On remedies under the HRA generally, see D Feldman, 'Remedies for Violations of Convention Rights under the Human Rights Act', [1998] *European Human Rights Law Review* 691.

[3] *Anufrijeva*, Ibid, [53]. However, it is important to note that, whilst a number of observations concerning the award of remedies, specifically damages, were made in this case, these were *obiter* given that the court actually found no violation of a Convention right.

[4] Ibid.

2. Just and Appropriate

A court's discretionary power under section 8(1) to grant a remedy extends to such remedy as it considers 'just and appropriate'. There has been very little consideration of this phrase in HRA case law apart from the observation that just and appropriate in Convention terms really means 'effective, just and proportionate'.[5]

The notion of a remedy being a 'just' remedy implies that it must be fair to all who are affected by it, including persons other than the person whose right was violated.[6] For example, in *Anufrijeva*[7] the Court of Appeal held that in considering whether to award compensation, and, if so, how much, there was a balance to be drawn between the interests of the victim and those of the public as a whole.[8] In *Cadder*[9] the Supreme Court determined that the leading and relying on the evidence of the appellant's interview by the police was a violation of his rights under Article 6 as he had not had access to legal advice before the interview. The case was remitted to the trial court but the Supreme Court made clear that its decision had no direct effect on proceedings that had been completed, as to hold otherwise would be to create uncertainty and 'cause widespread injustices'.[10]

Appropriateness suggests that the remedy, from the standpoint of the person whose Convention right was violated, will effectively address the grievance brought about by the violation.[11] For example, in relation to the reasonable time guarantee in Article 6, it has been held that if the breach is established before the hearing, the appropriate remedy may be a public acknowledgement of the breach, action to expedite the hearing to the greatest extent practicable and perhaps, if the defendant is in custody, his release on bail.[12] In the case of *M*[13] the Administrative Court determined that the appropriate remedy was the return of a family to the United Kingdom so as to restore them to the position they would have been in but for their unlawful deportation in breach of their Convention rights. An order was made, directed at the Secretary of State, for their return.

---

[5] *Attorney General's Reference No 2 of 2001* [2003] UKHL 68, [2004] 2 AC 72, per Lord Bingham at [24].

[6] *Saskatchewan Human Rights Commission v Kodellas* (1989) 60 DLR (4th) 143, per Bayda CJS at 162. This interpretation was of the remedies clause in the Canadian Charter of Rights and Freedoms, which is in very similar terms to s 8(1) empowering the court to award appropriate and just remedies for the infringement of rights.

[7] Above n 2.

[8] *Attorney General's Reference No 2 of 2001* (n 5), [56]. See also *R (on the application of Bernard) v London Borough of Enfield* [2002] EWHC (Admin) 2282, [2003] HRLR 4, [58]–[59].

[9] *Cadder v HM Advocate* [2010] UKSC 43, [2010] 1 WLR 2601.

[10] Ibid, per Lord Rodger at [102].

[11] *Attorney General's Reference No 2 of 2001* (n 5).

[12] Ibid, [24] per Lord Bingham, with whom Lords Nicholls, Steyn, Hoffmann, Hobhouse and Scott all agreed.

[13] *R (M) v Secretary of State for the Home Department* [2011] EWHC 3667 (Admin).

3. Effective

It has been suggested that, whilst it is not expressly referred to in section 8(1), any remedy awarded for an act incompatible with Convention rights should also be effective.

> Since the aim of the Act is that the domestic courts, rather than the Strasbourg court, should be able to remedy violations of the convention, it can readily be inferred that a remedy will be just and appropriate if it constitutes the kind of effective remedy required by art 13 of the convention.[14]

The obligation to ensure that remedies are effective, as well as just and appropriate, could have a significant impact. Arguably an effective remedy under the HRA would adequately compensate those who have suffered damage as a result of the act of a public authority incompatible with a Convention right and, secondly, emphasise the importance of the Convention rights and deter future violations by public authorities.

However, the difficulty with obliging courts to ensure that remedies are also effective is that, despite parliamentary pressure, Article 13 of the Convention (the right to an effective remedy)[15] was deliberately omitted from the HRA. The Lord Chancellor explained that it was not necessary to include it as section 8 already 'provides effective remedies before our courts'.[16] Nevertheless, although courts as public authorities are not obliged to act in a way which is compatible with Article 13,[17] the Lord Chancellor during the parliamentary debates did state that the courts may have regard to Article 13 when considering the provisions of section 8.[18]

Despite this encouragement, there has been little evidence of the impact of Article 13 or the notion of an effective remedy in the case law. In the majority of instances where it has been referred to by the courts, it has been to lament its non-inclusion as a Convention right given further effect by the HRA. For example, in *Lambert*[19] Lord Hope suggested his conclusion that the HRA did not have retrospective effect in the circumstances of the case may have been different if Article 13 had been one of the Convention rights given further effect by the HRA.[20] In *Re S*[21] it had been argued that the absence from the Children Act 1989 of an adequate remedy if a local authority failed to discharge its parental responsibilities properly was a violation of Article 8.

---

[14] *Attorney General's Reference No 2 of 2001* (n 5), per Lord Rodger at [175].

[15] Art 13: 'Everyone whose rights and freedoms as set forth in this Convention are violated shall have an effective remedy before a national authority notwithstanding that the violation was committed by persons acting in an official capacity.'

[16] Lord Chancellor, HL Deb, Vol 583, col 475 (18 November 1997). See also the observations of the House of Lords in *Re S* [2002] UKHL 10, [2002] 2 WLR 720, per Lord Nicholls at [61].

[17] Section 6, Human Rights Act 1998.

[18] HL Deb, Vol 583, col 477 (18 November 1997).

[19] *R v Lambert* [2001] UKHL 37, [2002] 2 AC 545.

[20] Ibid, [111]. See also the comments of Lord Clyde at [142]. However, in *R v Kansal* [2001] UKHL 62, [2001] 3 WLR 1562 Lord Hope indicated that it was the influence of Art 13 which lead to his conclusion that the HRA did have retrospective effect.

[21] *Re S* [2002] UKHL 10, [2002] 2 WLR 720.

The House of Lords disagreed, holding that failure by the state to provide an effective remedy for a violation of Article 8 was not itself a violation of Article 8.[22]

> Article 13 is not a Convention right as defined in section 1(1) of the Human Rights Act. So legislation which fails to provide an effective remedy for infringement of Article 8 is not, for that reason, incompatible with a Convention right within the meaning of the Human Rights Act.[23]

Similarly, in relation to Article 6 it has been held that Article 13 was the guarantee of an effective remedy for breach of a Convention right, not Article 6(1).[24] In some instances, it is not clear what real difference being able to utilise Article 13 would make to claimants. For example, in *RB*[25] it was argued by deportees before the House of Lords that a closed material procedure employed by the Special Immigration Appeals Commission was in breach of Article 13. When Article 13 was applied to the facts, most of their Lordships were satisfied that the claimant's right under Article 13 to an effective remedy was actually afforded by the procedure.[26]

In theory, there are a variety of instances where an Article 13 claim could be made. For example, in *ZT*[27] the House of Lords considered the ability of the Secretary of State to certify human rights immigration claims as clearly unfounded, thereby preventing a court's consideration of the human rights argument. Article 13 was not raised in argument but there were clear issues concerning the inability of deportees to have an effective consideration of their human rights claim. Furthermore, as discussed in chapter 5, the declaration of incompatibility pursuant to section 4 of the HRA could be vulnerable to an Article 13 challenge although this would have to take place in the ECtHR. It was actually argued before the ECtHR in *A v UK*[28] that the HRA remedies available to those detained under the Anti-Terrorism Crime and Security Act 2001 were not compatible with the requirements of Article 13. This was rejected by the Grand Chamber, however, which confirmed that Article 13 did not guarantee a remedy allowing a challenge to primary legislation before a national authority on the ground of being contrary to the Convention rights.[29]

---

4. The Power to Award Damages

It is not specifically stated in section 8 that a court may award damages, although 'damages' is defined in subsection 8(5) as 'damages for the unlawful act of a public authority'[30] and the remaining subsections of section 8 concern limitations on any

---

[22] Ibid, [59].
[23] Ibid, per Lord Nicholls at [60].
[24] Ibid, per Lord Nicholls at [70].
[25] *RB (Algeria) v Secretary of State for the Home Department* [2009] UKHL 10, [2010] 2 AC 110.
[26] Ibid, eg Lord Hoffmann at [177] and Lord Hope at [234].
[27] *ZT (Kosovo) v Secretary of State for the Home Department* [2009] UKHL 6, [2009] 1 WLR 348.
[28] *A v UK*, ECtHR, Grand Chamber, 19 February 2009.
[29] Ibid, [135].
[30] 'Unlawful act' is defined in subs 8(5) as 'unlawful under section 6(1)'.

award of damages indicating that such an award is possible.[31] There is also consider-able extra-statutory evidence that this is the case, the Lord Chancellor commenting during the Parliamentary debates that the aim was that people should receive damages equivalent to what they would have obtained had they taken their case to Strasbourg.[32]

It is clear that there is no right to damages for the violation of a Convention right,[33] and a number of preconditions relate to such an award.[34] First, there must be a finding of unlawfulness or prospective unlawfulness based on breach or prospective breach by a public authority of a Convention right.[35] Damages are not available where a dec-laration of incompatibility has been made under section 4 of the HRA. A victim of a breach of Convention rights contained in primary legislation can only hope that he or she receives an ex gratia payment from the state, compensating for any loss or damage suffered. The only alternative is to bring proceedings in the ECtHR and hope eventu-ally to receive a damages award there. The claimants in *A v Secretary of State*,[36] who were eventually released from over three years in detention after a change in the law following a declaration of incompatibility made by the House of Lords, received no compensation from UK public authorities. The ECtHR eventually awarded them their costs and expenses in bringing the proceedings to the ECtHR and amounts ranging from €1,700 to €3,900.[37]

Secondly, the court must have the power to award damages, or to order the payment of compensation, in civil proceedings.[38] Thirdly, the court should consider an award of damages to be just and appropriate.[39] Fourthly, the court should be satisfied, taking account of all the circumstances of the particular case, that an award of damages is necessary to afford just satisfaction to the person in whose favour it is made.[40] Finally, in deciding whether to award damages, and if so how much, the court is not strictly bound by the principles applied by the European Court in awarding compensation under Article 41 of the Convention, but it must take those principles into account.[41] These various constraints on the award of damages are considered in the following paragraphs.[42]

---

[31] See also s 9 of the Act, which concerns damages that may be awarded in respect of judicial acts, also indicating that such an award is possible.

[32] Lord Chancellor, HL Deb, Vol 582, col 1232 (3 November 1997).

[33] *Anufrijeva* (n 2), [55].

[34] See generally *R v Secretary of State for the Home Department, ex p Greenfield* [2005] UKHL 14, [2005] 1 WLR 673.

[35] Section 8(1).

[36] *A v Secretary of State* [2004] UKHL 56, [2005] 2 AC 68.

[37] *A v UK* (n 28).

[38] Section 8(2).

[39] Section 8(1).

[40] Section 8(3).

[41] Section 8(4).

[42] On damages under the HRA, see generally: Law Commission, Report No 266, *Damages under the Human Rights Act 1998*, Cm 4853 (2000); ME Amos, 'Damages for Breach of the Human Rights Act 1998' [1999] *European Human Rights Law Review* 178; D Fairgrieve, 'The Human Rights Act 1998, Damages and Tort Law' [2001] *Public Law* 695; J Hartshorne, 'The Human Rights Act 1998 and Damages for Non-pecuniary Loss' [2004] *European Human Rights Law Review* 660; and R. Clayton, 'Damage Limitation: The Courts and Human Rights Act Damages' [2005] *Public Law* 429.

5. Court Must Have the Power to Award Damages

Section 8(2) of the HRA provides that damages may be awarded only by a court which has power to award damages, or to order the payment of compensation in civil proceedings. It is therefore not possible for a criminal court to award damages.[43] In making this limitation, it was thought

> appropriate for an individual who considers that his rights have been infringed in such a case to pursue any matter of damages through the civil courts where this type of issue is normally dealt with; in other words, to pursue the matter in the courts that are accustomed to determining whether it is necessary and appropriate to award damages and what the proper amount should be.[44]

However, damages may be awarded by the High Court on an application for judicial review. The Supreme Court Act 1981 provides that on an application for judicial review, the High Court may award damages to the applicant if (a) he has joined with his application a claim for damages arising from any matter to which the application relates; and (b) the court is satisfied that, if the claim had been made in an action begun by the applicant at the time of making his application, he would have been awarded damages.[45] Obviously, the claim for damages joined would be a claim for damages for breach of the Act by the public authority. It is therefore quite possible for an applicant to bring judicial review proceedings against a public authority purely on Convention grounds, seeking, for example, certiorari and damages for the unlawful act of the public authority.[46]

6. Just Satisfaction

Section 8(3) of the HRA provides that no award of damages is to be made unless, taking account of all the circumstances of the case, including (a) any other relief or remedy granted, or order made, in relation to the act in question (by that or any other court) and (b) the consequences of any decision (of that or any other court) in respect of that act, the court is satisfied that the award is necessary to afford just satisfaction to the person in whose favour it is made.

It has been observed that the language of 'just satisfaction' is distinct from the approach in common law, where a claimant is invariably entitled, so far as money can achieve this, to be restored to the position he would have been in had he not suffered

---

[43] See eg *R v Galfetti* [2002] EWCA Crim 1916.
[44] Lord Chancellor, HL Deb, Vol 583, cols 854–55 (24 November 1997).
[45] Subsection 31(4). See also RSC O53 r 7. Contrast the position under the old Order 53.
[46] HL Deb Vol 582, col 1232 (3 November 1997).

the injury of which the complaint is made.[47] 'Just satisfaction' is obviously a Convention concept, reflecting the wording of Article 41, and relevant judgments of the Court will be key to its interpretation. Nevertheless, two important circumstances are already referred to in the section.

6.1 Any Other Relief or Remedy Granted

In deciding whether an award is necessary to afford just satisfaction, pursuant to subsection 8(3)(a) the court must take into account 'any other relief or remedy granted, or order made, in relation to the act in question.' Only those remedies that have already been granted are relevant, not the prospect of future alternative remedies. It is likely that when a violation of a Convention right occurs, the victim will have a number of alternative remedies available to him or her in addition to damages for breach of the Act. For example, on an application for judicial review, such remedies will include those available under section 31 of the Supreme Court Act—certiorari, prohibition, mandamus, injunction, declaration and damages for a private law wrong[48] or breach of EU law. Section 8(3)(a) is designed to avoid double recovery. Clearly no further compensation would be required under the HRA if the victim had already received just satisfaction via an alternative route.

In *Dobson*[49] the Court of Appeal considered whether just satisfaction demanded that compensation be awarded to a claimant under the HRA where common law damages had already been awarded to his parents, the property owners, with whom he lived. The claim was that he was affected by odours and mosquitoes caused by the negligent operation of a sewage treatment works. The court did not reach a final conclusion on the issue, noting that it would depend on the trial judge's findings in relation to his parents.[50] At trial it was eventually concluded that an award of damages under section 8 was not necessary to afford just satisfaction to such a claimant with no proprietary interest in the property taking into account the remedies already made available to his parents.[51]

What is not clear from the case law is whether a victim would receive a higher or similar level of compensation under the HRA than he or she would from a claim in tort. In *Anufrijeva*[52] the Court of Appeal warned against drawing too close an analogy between a claim for damages under the HRA and a claim against a public authority in tort.[53] And in *Greenfield*[54] the House of Lords held that, in awarding damages under the HRA, courts should not follow the domestic scale but that of the European Court.

> They are not inflexibly bound by Strasbourg awards in what may be different cases. But they should not aim to be significantly more or less generous than the Court might be expected to be, in a case where it was willing to make an award at all.[55]

---

[47] *Anufrijeva* (n 2), [55].
[48] Eg negligence, false imprisonment, nuisance, misfeasance in public office and breach of contract.
[49] *Dobson v Thames Water Utilities* [2009] EWCA Civ 28, [2009] 3 All ER 319.
[50] Ibid, [54].
[51] *Dobson v Thames Water Utilities* [2011] EWHC 3253 (TCC).
[52] *Anufrijeva* (n 2).
[53] Ibid, [49].
[54] *Greenfield* (n 34).
[55] Ibid, per Lord Bingham at [19].

Given the relative low level of damages awarded by the Strasbourg court, it may therefore be advisable, if it is open to a claimant to pursue damages via a common-law route, to take that path rather than that provided by the HRA.

6.2 The Consequences of Any Decision

Section 8(3)(b) also obliges the court to take into account the consequences of any decision (of that or any other court) in respect of that act. It is unclear what is meant by 'consequences'. One possible interpretation is that when contemplating an award of damages, the court should take into account that it might be opening the 'floodgates'. The consequences of any decision in respect of that act may be that the same duty is imposed in a 'wide range of similar situations' with the result that the burden of liability on the class of defendant 'may be considered to be disproportionate to the conduct involved'.[56]

To make an award of damages in respect of that act may mean that hundreds, even thousands, of potential applicants will have a similar claim—representing a considerable strain on the public purse.[57] However, as in the law of tort, the floodgates argument should be approached with caution. As Lord Roskill warned in *Junior Books Ltd v Veitchi Ltd*, '[I]f it be just that the law should henceforth accord that remedy, that remedy should [not] be denied simply because it will, in consequence of this particular development, become available to many rather than to few.'[58]

Another possible interpretation, also related to the public purse, is that the consequences include the impact on public authorities generally and society as a whole. For example, in *Bernard*[59] the Administrative Court observed that:

> [On] a simplistic view of local authority accounting, the larger the award to the claimants under section 8 the less there will be for the London Borough of Enfield to spend on providing social service facilities for the many others in need of care within the borough.[60]

However, it was also noted that, to set against this public disbenefit, it was very much in the interests of society as a whole that public authorities should be encouraged to respect individual's rights under the Convention. 'A "restrained" or "moderate" approach to quantum will provide the necessary degree of encouragement whilst not unduly depleting the funds available to the defendant for the benefit of others in need of care.'[61]

---

[56] *Clerk & Lindsell on Torts* (London, Sweet & Maxwell, 1995, 17th edn), 229–32.

[57] See *M (A Minor) v Newham London Borough Council* [1995] 2 AC 633, per Staughton LJ at 674–75; *X v Bedfordshire County Council* [1995] 2 AC 633, per Lord Browne-Wilkinson at 749–51; *Stovin v Wise* [1996] AC 923 per Lord Hoffman at 958.

[58] *Junior Books Ltd v Veitchi Ltd* [1983] 1 AC 520, 539. See also *McLoughlin v O'Brian* [1983] 1 AC 410 and *Dulieu v White & Sons* [1901] 2 KB 669.

[59] *Bernard* (n 8).

[60] Ibid, [58].

[61] Ibid, [59]. See also *Anufrijeva* (n 2), [75].

6.3 Other Circumstances

In addition to the circumstances expressly set out in paragraphs (a) and (b) as discussed in the paragraphs above, other circumstances may be relevant. One circumstance may be any action the respondent public authority has taken following the finding of a violation. For example, if a court has found that a public authority has conducted a hearing in breach of Article 6, the public authority may then re-hear the matter in accordance with Article 6. Other examples may be where a minister rescinds a deportation order following a court decision that it is in violation of Article 3 or allows a public assembly to proceed following a court decision that banning it is in violation of Article 11. Satisfactory outcomes such as these suggest that the applicant should not be entitled to damages as he or she already has been afforded 'just satisfaction' and a just, appropriate and effective remedy. The matter has been re-heard, he or she has not been deported, the assembly has been allowed to proceed; in effect, the violations of the Convention have been corrected.[62] Also relevant may be the action of a public authority once the problem has been drawn to its attention. In *Bernard*[63] the Administrative Court held that it may reduce the level of damages awarded if the public authority acknowledged that something had gone wrong and provided an explanation, an apology and an assurance that steps had been taken to ensure that the same mistake would not happen again.[64]

Another relevant circumstance may be the question of fault. Should it make any difference to an award of damages if the unlawful act was intentional, negligent or innocent? For example, in *Wainwright*[65] the House of Lords observed that, although Article 8 guarantees a right of privacy, a remedy in damages for invasion of privacy is not guaranteed irrespective of whether the defendant acted intentionally, negligently or accidentally.

> Article 8 may justify a monetary remedy for an intentional invasion of privacy by a public authority, even if no damage is suffered other than distress for which damages are not ordinarily recoverable. It does not follow that a merely negligent act should, contrary to general principle, give rise to a claim in damages for distress because it affects privacy rather than some other interest like bodily safety.[66]

Judgments of the ECtHR offer little assistance in answering this question. However, the manner in which questions of fault are dealt with in EU law may hold some useful lessons for the award of damages under section 8 of the Act. There is a right to reparation in EU law where three conditions are met: the rule of law infringed must be intended to confer rights on individuals; the breach must be sufficiently serious; and there must be a direct causal link between the breach of the obligation resting on the state and the damage sustained by the injured parties.[67] Both the European Court of Justice and

---

[62] It was held in *Director General of Fair Trading v Proprietary Association of Great Britain* [2001] EWCA Civ 1217, [2002] 1 WLR 269, [34], in reliance upon *Kingsley v UK* (2001) 33 EHRR 288, that if a court has remedied a situation so that no violation of Art 6 will occur, those involved are not entitled to recover wasted legal costs as compensation.

[63] *Bernard* (n 8).

[64] Ibid, [39]. See also *W v Westminster City Council* [2005] EWHC (QB) 102.

[65] *Wainwright v Home Office* [2003] UKHL 53, [2004] 2 AC 406.

[66] Ibid, per Lord Hoffmann at [51].

[67] *Brasserie du Pecheur SA v Germany* and *R v Secretary of State for Transport ex parte Factortame* [1996] ECR I–1029, para 51. See also *Francovich and Bonifaci v Italy* [1991] ECR I–5357.

national courts have given guidance as to how sufficient seriousness is to be assessed. Factors taken into consideration include

> the clarity and precision of the rule breached, the measure of discretion left by that rule to the national or Community authorities, whether the infringement and the damage caused was intentional or involuntary, whether any error of law was excusable or inexcusable.[68]

A breach can be 'manifest and grave so as to make it sufficiently serious without it being intentional or negligent'. The 'lack of the intention to commit the breach or negligence or fault' are relevant circumstances, but their presence is not 'a condition precedent to a breach being sufficiently grave or manifest'.[69] Damages are therefore available even if the breach was innocent.[70]

7. The Principles Applied by the European Court of Human Rights

7.1 Introduction

The final constraint on the award of damages is contained in section 8(4), which provides that, in determining whether to award damages, or the amount of the award, the court must take into account the principles applied by the ECtHR in relation to the award of compensation under Article 41 of the Convention.[71] There are clear differences in wording between section 2(1) and section 8(4). 'The former requires the Court to take into account any judgment, decision etc. of the European Court; the latter requires the court to take into account "the principles applied" by the European Court.'[72] However, it has been observed that the significance of the difference is not obvious.

> The only possible significance ... is that Parliament may have wanted the UK court to have somewhat greater freedom in relation to decisions of the European Court on the amount of damages awarded in particular cases, quantum normally being a matter for the forum.[73]

Whilst there is nothing in the HRA or the jurisprudence of the European Court to prevent courts adjudicating on claims under the HRA from imposing more severe

---

[68] Paras 55–57. See also *R v HM Treasury ex parte British Telecommunications plc* [1996] ECR I–1631; *Denkavit Internationaal v Bundesamt fur Finanzen* [1996] ECR I–5063; *Dillenkofer and others v Federal Republic of Germany* [1996] ECR I–4845.

[69] *R v Secretary of State for Transport ex parte Factortame (No 5)* (1998) *The Times*, 28 April. See also *R v Secretary of State for the Home Department ex parte Gallagher* [1996] 2 CMLR 951; *Bowden v Secretary of State for the Environment and Others*, Divisional Court, 17 December 1997; *R v Ministry of Agriculture Fisheries and Food ex parte Lay*, Divisional Court, 15 May 1998.

[70] The lack of seriousness of the breach was a factor influencing the decision of the Court of Appeal in *Re P* [2007] EWCA Civ 2, [2007] 1 FLR 1957 not to award damages.

[71] For a discussion of the principles applied, see Law Commission, Report No 266 (n 42), Part III.

[72] *R (on the application of KB) v Mental Health Review Tribunal* [2003] EWHC (Admin) 193, [2004] QB 936 at [22].

[73] Ibid.

sanctions,[74] this has not been the path taken and in those cases where damages have been considered, relevant guidance from the European Court has been closely followed. However, that is not to say that this guidance has universally been regarded as useful and the observation is often made that the assistance to be derived from Strasbourg jurisprudence is limited.

> The remedy of damages generally plays a less prominent role in actions based on breaches of the articles of the ECtHR, than in actions based on breaches of private law obligations where, more often than not, the only remedy claimed is damages.[75]

Similarly, in *Rabone*[76] Lord Dyson noted that there were many ECtHR judgments in which the Court had awarded the victims of a breach of Article 2 compensation for non-pecuniary loss, but no decision was cited to the Court containing guidelines in which the range of compensation was specified and the relevant considerations articulated. In his view, it was therefore necessary for UK courts to do their best in the light of such guidance as could be gleaned from the Strasbourg decisions on the facts of the individual cases.[77] In *Faulkner*[78] Lord Reed observed that it was possible, over time, that the remedy would become 'naturalised':

> Reflecting the international origins of the remedy and its lack of any native roots, the primary source of the principles which are to guide the courts in its application is said to be the practice of the international court that is its native habitat. I would however observe that over time, and as the practice of the European court comes increasingly to be absorbed into our own case law through judgments such as this, the remedy should become naturalised. While it will remain necessary to ensure that our law does not fall short of Convention standards, we should have confidence in our own case law under section 8 once it has developed sufficiently, and not be perpetually looking to the case law of an international court as our primary source.[79]

Lord Reed also pointed out in his judgment in *Faulkner*[80] the important differences between an international court and domestic court. First, the ECtHR did not often articulate clear principles explaining when damages should be awarded or how they should be measured.[81] Second, the ECtHR did not normally undertake detailed fact-finding in relation to damages in the way in which a national court of first instance would do.[82] Domestic courts may be able to resolve disputed issues of fact in ways in which the ECtHR would not, and hence decisions in relation to the award of damages under section 8 may have a different factual basis from that which the ECtHR would have adopted.[83] Third, the awards made by the ECtHR reflect the relative value of money in the contracting states. Awards made to applicants from countries where the cost of living was relatively low tended to be low by comparison with awards to applicants from countries where the cost of living is much higher.[84] In his view, the

---

[74] *HM Advocate v R* [2002] UKPC D3, [2004] 1 AC 462, [58].
[75] *Anufrijeva* (n 2), [52].
[76] *Rabone v Pennine Care NHS Foundation Trust* [2012] UKSC 2, [2012] 2 AC 72.
[77] Ibid, [84].
[78] *R (Faulkner) v Secretary of State for Justice* [2013] UKSC 23, [2013] 2 WLR 1157.
[79] Ibid, [29].
[80] Ibid.
[81] Ibid, [34].
[82] Ibid, [37].
[83] Ibid, [37].
[84] Ibid, [38].

focus should be on awards made to applicants from the UK or from other countries with a comparable cost of living.[85]

It is clear that extracting the 'principles' applied by the ECtHR when awarding compensation under Article 41 is a difficult task.[86] The term 'principles' should be understood in a broad sense and the focus should be upon how the court applies Article 41, the factors which lead it to make an award of damages or to withhold such an award, and the practice in relation to the level of awards.[87] The Court treats its power as purely discretionary and the amount of compensation awarded, or whether compensation is awarded at all, depends very much on the circumstances of the case. Certain principles are clear. 'Just satisfaction' can only take the form of compensation[88] and the Court will not award damages, such as nominal damages and exemplary damages, which are not based strictly on compensation. The Court's awards for compensation are generally divided into an award for pecuniary damage and an award for non-pecuniary damage, although the Court does sometimes grant an aggregate sum where it is difficult to make a distinction.[89] Where a violation of the Convention is found, the Court may make an award for both types of damage, only one or neither, depending on its judgment of what is 'necessary' and what is 'just satisfaction'. Different considerations apply to the assessment of both types of damage and these are examined below.

Finally, it is important to note that the European Court routinely finds that a finding of a violation is, in itself, just satisfaction for the violation found. The House of Lords in *Greenfield*[90] noted that this reflected the fact that the focus of the Convention was on the protection of human rights and not the award of compensation. 'It is noteworthy that, in exercising its former jurisdiction under the original Art.32, the Committee of Ministers did not, before 1987, award compensation at all, even where a violation was found.'[91]

Similarly, in *Anufrijeva*[92] the Court of Appeal found that the concern will usually be to bring the infringement of an individual's human rights to an end and any question of compensation will be of secondary, if any, importance.[93]

7.2 Pecuniary Damage

In assessing compensation for pecuniary damage, the ECtHR endeavours to put the applicant as far as possible in a situation equivalent to the one in which he or she would have been if there had not been a breach of the Convention.[94] The principle of *restitutio in integrum* is also familiar to UK lawyers as the measure of damages in tort.[95]

---

[85] Ibid, [38].
[86] *Bernard* (n 8).
[87] *Faulkner* (n 78), [31].
[88] See eg *Vacher v France* (1997) 24 EHRR 482. The Court may also award costs and expenses and interest. But see V Colandrea, "On the Power of the European Court of Human Rights to Order Specific Non-monetary Measures" [2007] *Human Rights Law Review* 396.
[89] *Allenet de Ribemont v France* (1996) 22 EHRR 582.
[90] *Greenfield* (n 34).
[91] Ibid, per Lord Bingham at [9].
[92] *Anufrijeva* (n 2).
[93] Ibid, [53].
[94] *Papamichalopoulos v Greece* (1996) 21 EHRR 439, [38]. See also *Anufrijeva* (n 2), [59].
[95] *Livingstone v Rawyards Coal Co* (1880) 5 App Cas 25, per Lord Blackburn at 39. See L Loucaides, 'Reparation for Violations of Human Rights under the European Convention and Restitutio in Integrum' [2008] *European Human Rights Law Review* 182.

There must be a causal link between the violation complained of and the alleged pecuniary damage.[96] The need to show a causal link is demonstrated by many of the Article 6 (right to a fair trial) cases where the Court, in assessing compensation for pecuniary damage, has refused to speculate on what the outcome of the proceedings would have been if the proceedings had complied with Article 6.[97] For example, in *Saunders v UK*[98] the Court would not speculate on whether the outcome of the trial would have been different had the prosecution not used the transcripts. The Court found 'no causal connection ... between the losses claimed by the applicant and the Court's finding of a violation.'[99]

It is important for claims of pecuniary damage to be supported by evidence[100] and the burden is on the claimant to prove his or her damage. However, if there is no evidence but it is clear that pecuniary loss has occurred, the court will make a speculative assessment, assessing it as a whole and on an equitable basis.[101] It appears that there is no limit on the amount that may be awarded for this type of damage as long as the causal link is established.[102] Awards have been made for reduction in the value of property[103] and loss of past and future earnings.[104] The Court will also award compensation for pecuniary damage suffered through loss of opportunities. In *Weeks v UK* the Court awarded Mr Weeks compensation for the loss of opportunities he suffered by reason of the absence of proceedings to challenge the lawfulness of his re-detention in violation of Article 5(4). The award was made even though 'in the light of the recurrence of his behavioural problems the prospect of his realising them fully was questionable'.[105]

However, it appears the domestic courts have taken a harsher line. In *KB*[106] the Administrative Court stated that the jurisprudence of the European Court was replete with refusals to award damages for loss of a chance to obtain a favourable court or tribunal decision. 'The Court refuses to speculate on the prospects of success.'[107] It concluded that it would be contrary to these principles to award damages for loss of a

---

[96] *Vacher* (n 88); *Coyne v UK* Judgment of 24 September 1997. See also *R (on the application of Richards) v Secretary of State for the Home Department* [2004] EWHC (Admin) 93, [2004] ACD 69.

[97] *Vacher* (n 88); *Findlay v UK* (1997) 24 EHRR 221; *Schmautzer v Austria* (1996) 21 EHRR 511, [44].

[98] *Saunders v UK* (1997) 23 EHRR 313.

[99] Ibid, [86]. However, a sum may be awarded for pecuniary and non-pecuniary damage if it can be shown that detention resulted from the use of evidence that was incompatible with Art 6. See *Windisch v Austria* Judgment of 28 June 1993, [35]. See also *Teixeira de Castro v Portugal* Judgment of 9 June 1998, where the applicant was compensated for loss of earnings when he was deprived of his liberty and of opportunities when he came out of prison and also non-pecuniary damage.

[100] *Incal v Turkey* Judgment of 9 June 1998; *Pressos Compania Naviera SA v Belgium* Judgment of 3 July 1997.

[101] *Selçuk and Asker v Turkey* Judgment of 24 April 1998; *Akdivar v Turkey* Judgment of 1 April 1998; *Probstmeier v Germany* Judgment of 1 July 1997.

[102] One of the Court's highest awards for pecuniary damage was made in *Stan Greek Refineries and Stratis Andreadis v Greece* Judgment of 9 December 1994, where the Court awarded 116 million drachmas plus US$16 million plus 614,000 French francs plus interest. In *Pine Valley Developments v Ireland* (1993) 16 EHRR 379 the Court awarded IR£1,200,000 for pecuniary damage caused by a violation of Art 14 in conjunction with Art 1 of Protocol No 1.

[103] See eg *Pine Valley Developments*, Ibid.

[104] See eg *Young, James and Webster v UK* (1982) 4 EHRR 38.

[105] *Weeks v UK* (1988) 10 EHRR 293, para 13. See also *Probstmeier v Germany* Judgment of 1 July 1997; *Martins Moreira v Portugal* Judgment of 26 October 1988, [65]; *Silva Pontes v Portugal* (1994) Series A No 286-A, [46].

[106] *KB* (n 72).

[107] Ibid, [62].

chance of a favourable tribunal decision or for loss of opportunity as such. However, a claimant who seeks damages on the basis of an allegation that he would have had a favourable decision at an earlier date if his Convention right had been respected must prove his allegation on the balance of probabilities.[108] Similarly, in *Greenfield*[109] the House of Lords held that the key is to find a sufficient causal connection.

> [T]he Court will award monetary compensation under Art.41 only where it is satisfied that the loss or damage complained of was actually caused by the violation it has found, and it has repeatedly stressed that it will not speculate on what the outcome of the proceedings would have been but for the violation, it has on occasion been willing in appropriate cases to make an award if of the opinion that the applicant has been deprived of a real chance of a better outcome.[110]

Nevertheless, if pecuniary damage can be shown to the satisfaction of the court, there is no upper limit on the damages to be awarded. In *Infinis*[111] the Court of Appeal confirmed the decision of the High Court to award £94,393 for a breach of Article 1 of Protocol No 1. The Gas and Electricity Markets Authority had unlawfully refused accreditation to the claimant company, denying it a pecuniary benefit to which it was statutorily entitled.[112]

7.3 Non-pecuniary Damage

Whilst in many cases the Court has found that its judgment is sufficient reparation for non-pecuniary damage, on numerous occasions the Court has also found that the applicant has suffered non-pecuniary damage (also referred to as 'moral damage') as the result of a breach of the Convention, for which the mere finding of a violation does not constitute sufficient reparation. The Court may make an award of compensation for this type of damage even if it has not awarded compensation for pecuniary damage. Here it is also important for the applicant to show a causal link between the violation of the Convention and the non-pecuniary damage suffered. For example, in *Halford v UK* the Court concluded that there was no evidence to suggest that the stress Ms Halford suffered was directly attributable to the interception of her calls, rather than to her other conflicts with the Merseyside Police.[113] It has also been suggested under the HRA that the claimant must provide some evidence for this type of damage.[114]

The ECtHR has granted compensation for many types of non-pecuniary damage,

---

[108] Ibid, [64]. See also *Faulkner* (n 78).

[109] *Greenfield* (n 34).

[110] Ibid, per Lord Bingham at [14].

[111] *Gas & Electricity Markets Authority v Infinis plc* [2013] EWCA Civ 70, [2013] JPL 1037.

[112] See further T Tabori, 'Growth Industry: Article 1 of the First Protocol to the ECHR' [2013] *Judicial Review* 194.

[113] *Halford v UK* (1997) 24 EHRR 523, [76]. The Court did award Ms Halford £10,000 for non-pecuniary damage. Compensation for non-pecuniary damage may be awarded to surviving relatives. In *Kaya v Turkey* Judgment of 19 February 1998, the deceased's widow and children received £10,000 for violation of Arts 2 and 13.

[114] *Richards* (n 96), [128].

including distress and anxiety,[115] loss of reputation,[116] bouts of depression,[117] enduring psychological harm,[118] feelings of helplessness and frustration,[119] and feelings of injustice.[120] The fact that a claimant is particularly vulnerable may also be taken into account. For example, in *KB*[121] the Administrative Court took into account that the claimants had been detained on account of their mental health and were therefore in a vulnerable condition. 'Damages may be awarded to such persons under Article 5.5 although in analogous circumstances no award would be made to a healthy person, because they may suffer compensatable injury in circumstances where those of more robust health would not.'[122]

Such damage may have been caused by Convention violations such as inordinately lengthy proceedings,[123] the deprivation of property for a long period of time,[124] failure to provide a fair hearing,[125] ill treatment whilst in custody[126] and deprivation of liberty.[127] The Court assesses compensation on what it calls an 'equitable basis' and tends to be conservative, with the average award ranging from £5,000 to £15,000. However, on occasion, the Court makes larger awards. For example, in *Pine Valley Developments v Ireland*[128] Mr Healy was awarded IR£50,000 for non-pecuniary damage sustained through violation of Article 14 in conjunction with Article 1 of Protocol No 1. In *Leterme v France*[129] a violation of Article 6(1) was found in relation to the length of compensation proceedings brought by a haemophiliac who had been infected with HIV following blood transfusions. He awarded 200,000 French francs (approximately £20,000) for non-pecuniary damage. The applicant in *Aydin v Turkey*[130] was awarded £25,000 for the serious violation of Article 3 suffered while she was in custody and the enduring psychological harm she suffered on account of being raped.

In assessing the amount of compensation, the Court also appears to take into account notions such as mitigation and contributory fault. For example, in *Johnson v UK*[131] the Court decided to award £10,000 for non-pecuniary damage sustained by Mr Johnson when, no longer suffering from mental illness, he was detained in breach of Article 5(1).

> [T]he delay in his release cannot be attributed entirely to the authorities. In the first place, some period of deferment of release was inevitable having regard to the need to locate a hostel suited to the applicant's situation. ... Secondly, the applicant's negative attitude towards his

---

[115] *Incal* (n 100); *Cazenave de la Roche v France* Judgment of 9 June 1998; *Doustaly v France* Judgment of 23 April 1998.
[116] *Doustaly v France* Judgment of 23 April 1998.
[117] *Estima Jorge v Portugal* Judgment of 21 April 1998.
[118] *Aydin v Turkey* (1998) 25 EHRR 251.
[119] *Papamichalopoulos* (n 94).
[120] *Keegan v Ireland* (1994) 18 EHRR 342.
[121] *KB* (n 72).
[122] Ibid, [72]. Cf *Anufrijeva* (n 2).
[123] *Cazenave* (n 115).
[124] *Vasilescu v Romania* Judgment of 22 May 1998.
[125] *Papageorgiou v Greece* Judgment of 22 October 1997 [1998] HRCD 24.
[126] *Aydin* (n 118).
[127] *Tsirlis and Kouloumpas v Greece* (1998) 25 EHRR 198.
[128] *Pine Valley Developments* (n 102).
[129] Judgment of 29 April 1998; see also *Henra v France* Judgment of 29 April 1998.
[130] *Aydin* (n 118).
[131] *Johnson v UK* Judgment of 24 October 1997 [1998] HRCD 41.

rehabilitation did not facilitate their task and after October 1990 he refused to co-operate further with the authorities in finding a suitable hostel.[132]

Under the HRA in *Richards*,[133] in its assessment of non-pecuniary damages the Administrative Court took into account the fact that the claimant was responsible for some of the periods of delay.[134]

7.4 Exemplary Damages

The ECtHR has not awarded aggravated or punitive (exemplary) damages even for serious violations.[135] Exemplary damages are also not available under the HRA.[136] However, on occasion, the European Court does make an award for non-pecuniary damage 'bearing in mind the seriousness of the violations,'[137] suggesting that an element of aggravated damage has infiltrated the awards of the Court, although it is not labelled as such. For example, in *Aksoy v Turkey*[138] the Court held that

> in view of the extremely serious violations suffered by Mr Zeki Aksoy, and the anxiety and distress that these undoubtedly caused to his father, who has continued with the application after his son's death … the Court has decided to award the full amounts of compensation sought as regards pecuniary and non-pecuniary damage.[139]

The ability to award a form of aggravated damages has also been commented upon domestically. In *KB*[140] the Administrative Court stated that it was in general not the function of an award of damages to mark a court's disapproval of the conduct complained of or to reflect the importance of the right infringed, although the tendency of the European Court to award greater damages where it disapproved of the conduct of the state in question or where there had been repeated infringements was noted. Whilst this was not expressly reflected in any principle applied by the Court,

> it may be that it can be accommodated by the latitude (or 'margin of discretion') available to the court in awarding damages for non-pecuniary loss, or even, in an exceptional case of deliberate or persistent infringement, by an award of aggravated damages, which in principle are compensatory rather than penal.[141]

---

[132] Ibid, [77]. See also *A v Denmark* (1996) 22 EHRR 458; *McCann v UK* (1996) 21 EHRR 97.

[133] *Richards* (n 96).

[134] Ibid, [131].

[135] *Tekin v Turkey* Judgment of 9 June 1998, where, in violation of Art 3, the applicant had been held in a cold, dark cell, blindfolded and treated so as to leave wounds and bruises. See also *Selçuk and Asker v Turkey* Judgment of 24 April 1998.

[136] *Anufrijeva*, above n 2, at [55]; *KB*, above n 58, at [50].

[137] See eg *Selçuk and Asker* (n 135), where the Court found that the burning the applicants' property by the security forces involved violations of Arts 3, 8 and 13, and Art 1 of Protocol No 1. They were awarded £10,000 each for non-pecuniary damage 'bearing in mind the seriousness of the violations'. See also *Aydin* (n 118).

[138] *Aksoy v Turkey* (1997) 23 EHRR 553.

[139] Ibid, [113]. See also the comments in *Anufrijeva* (n 2), [67] and [68].

[140] *KB* (n 72).

[141] Ibid, [50].

8. The Level of Damages

The House of Lords has held that, when awarding damages under section 8, courts should not apply the domestic scale.[142] Three reasons were cited as to why this was not the approach to follow. First, in the view of their Lordships, the HRA was not a tort statute.

> Its objects are different and broader. Even in a case where a finding of violation is not judged to afford the applicant just satisfaction, such a finding will be an important part of his remedy and an important vindication of the right he has asserted. Damages need not ordinarily be awarded to encourage high standards of compliance by member states, since they are already bound in international law to perform their duties under the Convention in good faith, although it may be different if there is felt to be a need to encourage compliance by individual officials or classes of official.[143]

Similar views were expressed by Lord Brown in *Van Colle*[144] where he stated that civil claims were designed to compensate claimants for their losses whilst Convention claims were intended to 'uphold minimum human rights standards and to vindicate those rights'.

Secondly, their Lordships pointed out that the purpose of the HRA was not to give victims better remedies at home than they could recover in Strasbourg but to give them the same remedies without the delay and expense of resort to Strasbourg.[145] Finally, it was noted that section 8(4) requires a domestic court to take into account the principles applied by the European Court under Article 41. 'There could be no clearer indication that courts in this country should look to Strasbourg and not to domestic precedents.'[146] Furthermore, it was noted that the Court describes its awards as equitable, which was taken to mean that they are not precisely calculated but were judged by the Court to be fair in the individual case.

> Judges in England and Wales must also make a similar judgment in the case before them. They are not inflexibly bound by Strasbourg awards in what may be different cases. But they should not aim to be significantly more or less generous than the Court might be expected to be, in a case where it was willing to make an award at all.[147]

This conclusion of the House of Lords is slightly at odds with jurisprudence in the lower courts. For example, in *Anufrijeva*[148] the Court of Appeal held that the suggestion that damages under the HRA should be moderate and on the low side in comparison

---

[142] *Greenfield* (n 34). See J Varuhas, 'A Tort-based Approach to Damages under the Human Rights Act 1998' (2009) 72 *Modern Law Review* 750 where arguments in favour of a tort-based approach are presented.

[143] *Greenfield* (n 34), per Lord Bingham at [19].

[144] *Chief Constable of Hertfordshire v Van Colle* [2008] UKHL 50, [2009] 1 AC 225.

[145] *Greenfield* (n 34).

[146] Ibid.

[147] Ibid. See also the comments of Lord Hoffmann in *R (on the application of Wilkinson) v Inland Revenue Commissioners* [2005] UKHL 30, [2005] 1 WLR 1718, [25].

[148] *Anufrijeva* (n 2).

with those awarded for torts should in future be ignored.[149] In *Bernard*[150] the Administrative Court noted that there was no justification for the view that the quantum should be low by comparison with tortious awards. 'Bearing in mind the importance of securing compliance with the Convention, I see no justification for a further reduction, pushing damages under section 8 below the level of tortious awards.'[151] Also, in *KB*[152] the Administrative Court saw no justification for an award of damages being lower under the HRA than it would be for a comparable tort. It postulated that, if there was a breach of Article 5(1), there should be no difference between the measure of damages awarded for this and for the tort of false imprisonment.[153] This line of reasoning was continued in *Dennis*,[154] where substantial damages of £950,000 were awarded for the tort of nuisance. Also finding violations of Article 8 and Article 1 of Protocol No 1, the Divisional Court held that, had the common law of nuisance not provided a remedy in this case, compensation would have been awarded in the same sum under the HRA.[155] Nevertheless, the judgment of the House of Lords in *Greenfield*[156] is the latest and most authoritative word on this subject. Observations in *Anufrijeva*[157] that appropriate guidance could be obtained from the guidelines issued by the Judicial Studies Board, the levels of awards made by the Criminal Injuries Compensation Board, and by the Parliamentary Ombudsman and the Local Government Ombudsman[158] are now subject to doubt, the House of Lords having held that the only appropriate guidance was that emanating from the European Court of Human Rights.

As with other procedural features of the HRA, the best indication of the approach to section 8 is to study its application in practice. Cases where damages have been considered, and sometimes awarded, are considered in the following paragraphs.[159]

9. Application: Article 2

In addition to claims brought under the procedural limb of Article 2, claimants are increasingly bringing claims under the HRA concerning failures on the part of public

---

[149] Ibid, [73].
[150] *Bernard* (n 8).
[151] Ibid, [59].
[152] *KB* (n 72).
[153] Ibid, [53].
[154] *Dennis v Ministry of Defence* [2003] EWHC (QB) 793, [2003] 19 EG 118 (CS).
[155] Ibid, [92].
[156] *Greenfield* (n 34).
[157] *Anufrijeva* (n 2).
[158] Ibid, [74]. In *Bernard* (n 8) the Administrative Court held that assistance may be obtained from: damages for discomfort, inconvenience and injury to health arising out of breaches of repairing covenants in residential tenancies; recommendations by Local Commissioners for Administration (Local Government Ombudsman) that local authorities pay compensation when claimants have suffered as a result of maladministration; the JSB Guidelines for the Assessment of General Damages in Personal Injury Cases; W Norris et al, *Kemp and Kemp: Quantum of Damages* (London, Sweet & Maxwell, 1975); and the awards for pain and suffering in cases of minor personal injury.
[159] For an article-by-article analysis of the practice of the ECtHR, see Law Commission, Report No 266 (n 42), Part VI.

authorities to protect life pursuant to the Article 2 duty and in some instances damages have been awarded. For example, in *Savage*[160] the Divisional Court found that the defendant NHS Trust was in breach of its positive obligation under Article 2 when staff at one of its hospitals allowed a detained patient (the claimant's mother) to escape, resulting in her suicide shortly afterwards. Bearing in mind the claimant's statement that she had not brought the claim for financial reward, as well as the fact that there had been a full inquest which properly investigated the death, the court awarded £10,000 for non-pecuniary loss. It was observed as follows:

> The amount ... [granted] under this head ... can never compensate her for the loss of her mother and can only be a symbolic acknowledgement that the defendant ought properly to give her some compensation to reflect her loss.[161]

The positive duty to safeguard life was also at issue in *Rabone*[162] where Mr and Mrs Rabone, the parents of a young woman, brought a claim against an NHS hospital trust relating to the treatment of their daughter, a non-detained mental health patient. The hospital allowed her home leave and during this time she committed suicide. The Trust admitted negligence but did not admit liability for a breach of Article 2. As discussed in chapter 7, a breach of Article 2 was established before the Supreme Court which also considered the question of damages to be awarded under section 8 of the HRA. Mr and Mrs Rabone had already settled a negligence claim for £7,500. The Supreme Court held that this was not adequate redress in respect of their personal losses and noted the importance of compensation for non-pecuniary damage flowing from a breach of Article 2.[163] Unable to find clear guidance from Strasbourg, Lord Dyson considered the facts of individual cases cited to the court:

> What they show is that the sums awarded are fairly modest, but nevertheless within a con-siderable range. ... One would expect the court to have regard to the closeness of the family link between the victim and the deceased, the nature of the breach and the seriousness of the non-pecuniary damage that the victim has suffered. Factors which will tend to place the amount of the award towards the upper end of the range are the existence of a particularly close family tie between the victim and the deceased; the fact that the breach is especially egregious; and the fact that the circumstances of the death and the authority's response to it have been particularly distressing to the victims. Conversely, factors which will tend to place the award towards the lower end of the range are the weakness of the family ties, the fact that the breach is towards the lower end of the scale of gravity and the fact that the circumstances of the death have not caused the utmost distress to the victims.[164]

The Supreme Court was in no doubt that an award of £1,500 to each of her parents was too low. It found the family ties strong, and that the parents had expressed their anxiety to the hospital authorities about the dangers of home leave. It also found the fact that the risk which they warned the authorities about eventuated, 'must have made the death all the more distressing for them'.[165] Finding this was a bad case of breach of

---

[160] *Savage v South Essex Partnership NHS Foundation Trust* [2010] EWHC 865 (QB), [2010] HRLR 24.
[161] Ibid, [97].
[162] *Rabone* (n 76).
[163] Ibid, per Lord Dyson at [60].
[164] Ibid, [85].
[165] Ibid, [87].

the Article 2 positive duty, it merited an award well above the lower end of the range of awards and £5,000 was awarded to each parent.[166]

10. Application: Article 3

In B[167] the Administrative Court found that the decision by the Crown Prosecution Service to discontinue a prosecution for a serious assault was incompatible with Article 3. In relation to the claimant, this was found to be a serious breach:

> Looking at the proceedings as a whole, far from them serving the State's positive obligation to provide protection against serious assaults through the criminal justice system, the nature and manner of their abandonment increased the victim's sense of vulnerability and of being beyond the protection of the law.[168]

In relation to just satisfaction, it stated that the judgment would go some way towards providing just satisfaction but that there should also be some monetary compensation and the claimant was to be compensated for being deprived of the opportunity of proceedings running their proper course and the damage to his self-respect. An award of £8,000 was made in line with the customary 'modest' awards of the ECtHR in this area.[169]

An award of damages against police for failure to fulfil a positive obligation under Article 3 was also made in OOO.[170] The Divisional Court concluded that the police had failed in their duty to investigate under Article 3 as they had received a credible allegation that Articles 3, or 4, had been infringed. The claimants alleged that they had been brought to the UK from Nigeria illegally, subject to inhuman or degrading treatment, and held in slavery or servitude contrary to Articles 3 and 4. Each of the claimants sought compensation for non-pecuniary loss as they suffered distress and frustration on account of the failure to investigate. The court awarded £5,000 to each.

11. Application: Article 5

11.1 Section 9(3) Human Rights Act and Article 5(5)

Section 9(3) of the HRA provides that damages may not be awarded in respect of a

---

[166] Ibid, [89].
[167] R (B) v Director of Public Prosecutions [2009] EWHC 106 (Admin), [2009] 1 WLR 2072.
[168] Ibid, [70].
[169] Ibid, [71].
[170] OOO v Commissioner of Police of the Metropolis [2011] EWHC 1246 (QB), [2011] HRLR 29.

judicial act done in good faith otherwise than to compensate a person to the extent required by Article 5(5) of the Convention.[171] As originally drafted, without reference to Article 5(5), it was intended that this subsection would preserve the current position under section 2(5) of the Crown Proceedings Act 1947, which absolves the Crown of liability for the conduct of any person 'while discharging or purporting to discharge any responsibilities of a judicial nature vested in him'. However, following objections that this exemption was in breach of Article 5(5)[172] of the Convention, the government amended the section. The Lord Chancellor explained that where a complaint was made that Article 5 has been breached as a result of a judicial act or omission, it would be necessary first to establish whether the judicial act complained of was unlawful, then to rule on whether the aggrieved person was entitled to compensation under Article 5(5) and then to determine the amount of compensation.[173]

The importance of the change was evident in the case of *KB*,[174] where the Administrative Court held that the Mental Health Review Tribunal was a judicial body for these purposes and that none of the acts or omissions leading to violations of Article 5(4) were done other than in good faith. Article 5(5) was therefore central to the claims.[175]

11.2 Article 5(4): Delay

In *Faulkner*[176] the Supreme Court considered the circumstances in which a life or IPP (imprisonment for public protection) prisoner who had served his tariff period, and whose case had not been considered by the Parole Board within a reasonable period thereafter, should be awarded damages under the HRA and the quantum of such awards. It held that where it was established on the balance of probabilities that a violation of Article 5(4) had resulted in the detention of a prisoner beyond the date when he would otherwise have been released, damages should ordinarily be awarded as compensation for the resultant detention. The appropriate amount to be awarded in such circumstances was held to be a matter of judgment, reflecting the facts of the individual case and taking into account the guidance of the ECtHR and UK courts in comparable cases. It was clear that pecuniary losses proved to have been caused by the prolongation of detention should be compensated in full and it was not generally appropriate to take into account as a factor mitigating harm suffered, that the claimant was recalled to prison following release.

It was held that damages should not be awarded for merely the loss of a chance of earlier release and nor should damages be adjusted according to the degree of probability of release if the violation of Article 5(4) had not occurred. Where it was not established that an earlier hearing would have resulted in earlier release, there was nevertheless a strong presumption that delay in violation of Article 5(4) caused the prisoner to suffer feelings of frustration and anxiety. Where such feelings were presumed or

---

[171] Ibid, Appendix A.
[172] Art 5(5) of the Convention provides 'Everyone who has been the victim of arrest or detention in contravention of the provisions of this Article shall have an enforceable right to compensation.'
[173] HL Deb, Vol 585, col 289 (29 January 1998).
[174] *KB* (n 72).
[175] Ibid, [11].
[176] *Faulkner* (n 78).

shown to have been suffered, an award of damages should be made and such damages should be on a modest scale. It confirmed that no award should be made where the delay was such that any resultant frustration and anxiety were insufficiently severe to warrant such an award but this was unlikely to be the position where the delay was three months or more.[177] In the claims under consideration, £6,500 was awarded for a delay of ten months; £300 for a delay of six months.[178]

11.3 Article 5(4): Independence and Impartiality

In *Richards*[179] the claimant sought compensation in respect of his detention between the date on which the Parole Board recommended his release and his actual release, as he maintained that the Secretary of State's role in delaying his release was incompatible with Article 5(4). The court found that the Strasbourg decision in *Stafford*,[180] which made the detention unlawful, governed periods of detention that occurred both before and after the date of the decision.[181] This aspect of its decision has now been overruled[182] but its findings on the assessment of damages remain relevant. The court stated that the main issue was to determine what would have happened to the claimant between November 2001 and his release in August 2002 if the Parole Board's recommendation in November 2001 that he be released had taken effect.[183]

A number of factors were taken into account, including the claimant's disability, which made it difficult for him to find a hostel; his excessive use of alcohol; his wish to be released to a hostel where he could be visited by friends and family; and that any licence on which he would have been released would have been subject to a residence requirement. Taking these factors into account, the court noted that the appropriate starting period for assessing compensation was 5 January 2002. Also taken into account was the breach of licence on 3 January, resulting in his return to prison on 4 January following release on temporary licence. It concluded that the claimant would have been recalled to prison even if released and would have been detained until the end of May 2002. Furthermore, there were difficulties finding him a suitable hostel and he had indicated that he was prepared to wait in custody until a suitable location was found. The court concluded that there was no causal link between the interference with his Convention rights and his detention from 18 November 2001 until August 2002, and found that he would not have enjoyed greater freedom had the recommendation of the Parole Board taken effect as a direct order.

No award of compensation was needed to place the claimant in the same position as if his Convention rights had not been infringed.[184] Furthermore, no damages were awarded for frustration, anxiety and uncertainty because his prospects of release were low even if the Board's recommendation had taken effect as an order; he was respon-

---

[177] Ibid, [13] as summarised by Lord Reed with whom Lord Neuberger, Lord Mance and Lord Kerr agreed.
[178] See also *KB* (n 72).
[179] *Richards* (n 96).
[180] *Stafford v United Kingdom* (2002) 35 EHRR 1121.
[181] *Richards* (n 96), [81].
[182] *R (Wright) v Secretary of State for the Home Department* [2006] EWCA Civ 67, [2006] HRLR 23.
[183] *Richards* (n 96), [92].
[184] Ibid, [128].

sible for some of the periods of delay; and there was no evidence or allegation of frustration, uncertainty or anxiety on his part.[185] It concluded as follows.

> [T]he claim fails because no loss can be established. I consider that even if the Parole Board recommendation had taken effect as an instruction to release him, the claimant would still have been detained from the time of the Parole Board recommendation in November 2001 until his actual release on 12 August 2002. This was because of the claimant's severe disabilities, the consequential difficulties of finding accommodation for him, his previous misbehaviour and his unwillingness to move out of the area during some of this period.[186]

Whilst irrelevant in light of the conclusion above, the court also commented on the 'period of grace' issue, holding that the Secretary of State was entitled to a reasonable time to consider the implications of *Stafford*[187] and that this would not have expired prior to the time of his actual release.[188]

---

12. Application: Article 6

12.1 Article 6(1) Reasonable Time: Post Conviction

In *Mills*[189] the Privy Council considered the remedy for a breach of the reasonable time guarantee post-conviction. Lord Steyn noted that the remedies available could include 'an order for discontinuance of a prosecution, quashing of the conviction, reduction of the sentence, monetary compensation or a declaration. A finding of a violation of a guarantee may itself sometimes be a sufficient vindication of the right.'[190] Lord Hope held that the circumstances of the present case provided a clear example of a situation where the setting aside of the conviction would be regarded in domestic law as both unjustified and unnecessary.

> It would be regarded as unjustified because the appellant's appeal against his conviction was … wholly without merit. No grounds exist for regarding the conviction itself as unsound, nor is there any question of its having been affected in any way by the delay. And the setting aside of the conviction would be regarded as unnecessary, because the effects of the delay can be recognised perfectly well by a reduction in the appellant's sentence.[191]

It was concluded that a reduction in the sentence by nine months was a just disposal in the spirit of Article 6(1).[192]

---

[185] Ibid, [131].
[186] Ibid, [139].
[187] Ibid, [135].
[188] Ibid, [138].
[189] *Mills v HM Advocate* [2002] UKPC D2, [2004] 1 AC 441.
[190] Ibid, [16].
[191] Ibid, [53].
[192] Ibid, per Lord Steyn at [23]. See also *R v Galfetti* [2002] EWCA Crim 1916 concerning delay between conviction and eventual disposal by way of hospital order under s 37 of the Mental Health Act 1983.

12.2 Article 6(1) Reasonable Time: Pre Conviction

Under the HRA in England and Wales, a majority of the House of Lords held in *Attorney General's Reference No 2 of 2001*[193] that if, through the action or inaction of a public authority, a criminal charge was not determined at a hearing within a reasonable time, there must be afforded such remedy as may be just and appropriate.

> The appropriate remedy will depend on the nature of the breach and all the circumstances, including particularly the stage of the proceedings at which the breach is established. If the breach is established before the hearing, the appropriate remedy may be a public acknowledgement of the breach, action to expedite the hearing to the greatest extent practicable and perhaps, if the defendant is in custody, his release on bail. It will not be appropriate to stay or dismiss the proceedings unless (a) there can no longer be a fair hearing or (b) it would otherwise be unfair to try the defendant. The public interest in the final determination of criminal charges requires that such a charge should not be stayed or dismissed if any lesser remedy will be just and proportionate in all the circumstances.[194]

The majority confirmed that to hold a trial after the lapse of a reasonable time would not in itself be a breach of a Convention right and therefore would not in itself comprise unlawful conduct under section 6 of the HRA.[195] Lord Bingham appreciated that it was a powerful argument that, if a public authority caused or permitted such delay to occur that a criminal charge could not be heard against a defendant within a reasonable time, so breaching his right under Article 6(1), any further prosecution or trial of the charge must be unlawful within the meaning of the Article. But he cited four reasons which compelled its rejection. First, it would be anomalous if breach of the reasonable time requirement had an effect more far-reaching than breach of the defendant's other Article 6 rights when the breach did not taint the basic fairness of the hearing at all, and even more anomalous that the right to a hearing should be vindicated by ordering that there be no trial at all.[196] Secondly, he pointed out that a rule of automatic termination of proceedings on breach of the reasonable time requirement could not sensibly be applied in civil proceedings. '[T]ermination of the proceedings would defeat the claimant's right to a hearing altogether and seeking to make good his loss in compensation from the state could well prove a very unsatisfactory alternative.'[197]

Thirdly, a rule of automatic termination had been shown to have the effect in practice of emasculating the right which the guarantee was designed to protect. 'There is, however, a very real risk that if proof of a breach is held to require automatic termina-

---

[193] *Attorney General's Reference No 2 of 2001* (n 5).

[194] Ibid, [24] per Lord Bingham, with whom Lords Nicholls, Steyn, Hoffmann, Hobhouse and Scott agreed. Lord Bingham thought it unwise to attempt to describe the category of cases in which it may be unfair to try a defendant, but did cite as possible examples bad faith, unlawfulness, executive manipulation and extreme breach of prosecutor's professional duty. Lords Hope and Rodger agreed that the remedy must be that which was just and appropriate, but held that to hold the trial after a lapse of a reasonable time was itself a breach of Art 6. For application of this principle, see *R v Wheeler* [2004] EWCA Crim 572.

[195] *Attorney General's Reference No 2 of 2001* (n 5), per Lord Nicholls at [38]–[39]. Lords Hope and Rodger dissented on this point. The majority pointed out that if the very holding of the trial by the court would be unlawful, the trial must be stayed. Lord Bingham could not accept that it could ever be proper for a court, whose purpose was to uphold, vindicate and apply the law, to act in a manner which a statute declared to be unlawful. Ibid, [30].

[196] Ibid, [20].

[197] Ibid, [21].

tion of the proceedings the judicial response will be to set the threshold unacceptably high.'[198]

Fourthly, his Lordship found that the Strasbourg jurisprudence gave no support to the contention that there should be no hearing of a criminal charge once a reasonable time had passed.[199]

12.3 Article 6(1): Independence and Impartiality

The just and appropriate remedy for a breach of the guarantee of independence and impartiality was considered by the House of Lords in *Greenfield*,[200] where the appellant had also been denied legal representation in violation of Article 6(3)(c). Their Lordships pointed out that, whilst the rights contained in Article 6 were important rights, it did not follow from a finding that the trial process involved a breach of Article 6 that the outcome of the trial process was wrong or would have been otherwise had the breach not occurred. 'There is a risk of error if Strasbourg decisions given in relation to one article of the Convention are read across as applicable to another.'[201] It also pointed out that, in the great majority of cases in which the European Court had found a violation of Article 6, it had treated the finding of the violation as, in itself, just satisfaction under Article 41.[202] 'Where Art 6 is found to have been breached, the outcome will often be that a decision is quashed and a retrial ordered, which will vindicate the victim's Convention right.'[203]

Their Lordships did, however, find that the Court has been willing to depart from the practice of finding a violation of Article 6 to be, in itself, just satisfaction under Article 41, where it found a causal connection between the violation found and the loss for which an applicant claimed to be compensated. 'Such claim may be for specific heads of loss, such as loss of earnings or profits, said to be attributable to the violation.' However, it also pointed out that the court has been slow to award such compensation.[204] With respect to non-pecuniary damage, their Lordships pointed out that a

> claim under this head may be put on the straightforward basis that but for the Convention violation found the outcome of the proceedings would probably have been different and more favourable to the applicant, or on the more problematical basis that the violation deprived the applicant of an opportunity to achieve a different result which was not in all the circumstances of the case a valueless opportunity. While in the ordinary way the Court has not been easily persuaded on this last basis, it has in some cases accepted it.[205]

In the view of their Lordships, the key was to find a sufficient causal connection.

---

[198] Ibid, [22].
[199] Ibid, [23], citing *X v Germany* (1980) 25 DR 142; *Eckle v Germany* (1982) 5 EHRR 1; *Neuback v Germany* (1983) 41 DR 13; *Bunkate v Netherlands* (1995) 19 EHRR 477; *Beck v Norway* Judgment of 26 June 2001.
[200] *Greenfield* (n 34).
[201] Ibid, per Lord Bingham at [7].
[202] Ibid, [8].
[203] Ibid, [9].
[204] Ibid, [11].
[205] Ibid, [12] per Lord Bingham citing *Goddi v Italy* (1984) 6 EHRR 457; *Colozza v Italy* (1985) 7 EHRR 516; *Lechner and Hess v Austria* (1987) 9 EHRR 490; *Weeks v United Kingdom* (1988) 13 EHRR 435; *O v United Kingdom* (1988) 13 EHRR 578; *Delta v France* (1990) 16 EHRR 574.

[T]he Court will award monetary compensation under Art 41 only where it is satisfied that the loss or damage complained of was actually caused by the violation it has found, and it has repeatedly stressed that it will not speculate on what the outcome of the proceedings would have been but for the violation, it has on occasion been willing in appropriate cases to make an award if of opinion that the appellant has been deprived of a real chance of a better outcome.[206]

Their Lordships also discussed a second head of general or non-pecuniary damage which has been variously described in terms such as 'physical and mental suffering', 'prolonged uncertainty' and 'a certain feeling of frustration and helplessness'. Their Lordships noted that, in considering claims under this head and with its general approach, the Court has consistently only been willing to award compensation for anxiety and frustration attributable to the Article 6 violation.

It has recognised that for very many people involvement in legal proceedings is bound to cause anxiety irrespective of any Art 6 breach, and no award is made in such cases. In some cases the Court has found on the facts that the applicant had suffered attributable anxiety and frustration. ... In other cases the Court has found that the applicant 'must have' suffered such feelings ... or that it is reasonable to assume he did. ... To gain an award under this head it is not necessary for the applicant to show that but for the violation the outcome of the proceedings would, or would probably, or even might, have been different, and in cases of delay the outcome may not be significant at all. But the Court has been very sparing in making awards.[207]

Their Lordships concluded that whatever the practice in other classes of case, the ordinary practice was not to make an award in cases of structural bias.

Where, having found a violation of Art 6, the Court has made an award of monetary compensation under Art 41, under either of the heads of general damages considered in this opinion, whether for loss of procedural opportunity or anxiety and frustration, the sums awarded have been noteworthy for their modesty.[208]

In the present case, in the determination of a criminal charge there had been a denial of independence and impartiality and legal representation by the deputy controller of a private prison when determining whether the prisoner had committed drugs offence. Their Lordships concluded that this was pre-eminently a case in which the finding in the appellant's favour afforded just satisfaction and an award of damages was not necessary.[209] The claim for loss of opportunity to achieve a different result if he had been legally represented was also rejected their Lordships finding that the adjudication was conducted with exemplary conscientiousness, patience and regard for the appellant's interests.

The issue for Mr Parry was whether he believed the appellant and his witness. Clearly he did not. A legal representative might have persuaded Mr Parry or another tribunal to take a different view or he might not. It is inappropriate to speculate.[210]

---

[206] *Greenfield* (n 34), per Lord Bingham at [14].

[207] Ibid, [16].

[208] Ibid, [17].

[209] Ibid, [26].

[210] Ibid, [28]. Cf *R (on the application of Nunn) v First Secretary of State* [2005] EWCA Civ 101, [2005] 2 All ER 987, where the Court of Appeal held that, where the claimant had been deprived of her Art 6 rights to have her objections to the grant of planning permission heard and adjudicated upon, her only remedy would be a claim in damages.

The claim for damages for anxiety and frustration was also rejected.

> At the time, however, adjudication by a governor or deputy governor (or their private prison counterparts, also Crown servants) was the norm. The appellant had no expectation of any other procedure, and was treated no differently from anyone else. The conduct of the adjudication itself, as already noted, appears to have been exemplary. There is no special feature of this case which warrants an award of damages.[211]

---

13. Application: Article 8

13.1 Introduction

Whilst its comments were *obiter*, in *Anufrijeva*[212] the Court of Appeal observed that courts dealing with claims for damages for maladministration resulting in a breach of Article 8 should adopt a broad-brush approach.

> Where there is no pecuniary loss involved, the question whether the other remedies that have been granted to a successful complainant are sufficient to vindicate the right that has been infringed, taking into account the complainant's own responsibility for what has occurred, should be decided without a close examination of the authorities or an extensive and prolonged examination of the facts. In many cases the seriousness of the maladministration and whether there is a need for damages should be capable of being ascertained by an examination of the correspondence and the witness statements.[213]

It held that where a breach of Article 8 did arise from maladministration, the scale of such damages should be modest.

> The cost of supporting those in need falls on society as a whole. Resources are limited and payments of substantial damages will deplete the resources available for other needs of the public including primary care. If the impression is created that asylum seekers whether genuine or not are profiting from their status, this could bring the Human Rights Act into disrepute.[214]

It was also held that similar considerations applied to delay in processing asylum claims or the procedure for admitting the relatives of a refugee.[215]

---

[211] *Greenfield* (n 34), per Lord Bingham at [29].
[212] *Anufrijeva* (n 2).
[213] Ibid, [65].
[214] Ibid, [75].
[215] Ibid, [76]. The court also made a number of suggestions as to the procedure to be followed in future where damages were sought under the HRA for maladministration. This was in an effort to avoid the situation which it found arose in the present case where it would cost more to try the case than the amount of damages likely to be awarded. Ibid, [80]–[81].

13.2 Private Life—Breaches by Public Authorities

Despite these observations, damages have been awarded under the HRA for violations of Article 8. For example, in *Bernard*[216] the Administrative Court found serious violations of the claimant's private and family lives.

> The Council's failure to act on the September 2000 assessments showed a singular lack of respect for the claimants' private and family life. It condemned the claimants to living conditions which made it virtually impossible for them to have any meaningful private or family life for the purposes of Article 8 ... the defendant was not merely in breach of its statutory duty under the 1948 Act. Its failure to act on the September 2000 assessments over a period of 20 months was also incompatible with the claimants' rights under Article 8 of the Convention.[217]

Turning to the question of relief, the court was satisfied that an award of damages was necessary to give just satisfaction to the claimants.

> This was a serious breach of their rights under Article 8. The claimants and their family had to live in deplorable conditions, wholly inimical to any normal family life, and to the physical and psychological integrity of the second claimant for a considerable period of time.[218]

The fact that the defendant belatedly discharged its duties under the 1948 Act and Article 8 did not affect the decision to award damages, only quantum.[219] This was not a case where the defendant had taken all necessary steps, reasonably promptly, once the problem had been drawn to its attention.[220]

> [T]here has been no acknowledgment that the defendant was in error, no explanation, no apology and nothing to indicate that the defendant's procedures have been improved so that the same kind of mistake ... is less likely to occur in the future.[221]

The threat to evict the claimants, whilst withdrawn, was also taken into account.[222]

In determining the level of damages, the court found no comparable tort. There was no evidence of mental or physical injury caused by the conditions. The first claimant's back problems were aggravated but this cause him discomfort, distress and inconvenience rather than injury. The second claimant suffered discomfort, distress and frustration.[223] The court found that the Judicial Studies Board's *Guidelines for the Assessment of General Damages in Personal Injury Case* and the awards noted in Part K of Kemp and Kemp's *The Quantum of Damages*, dealing with minor injuries where there is a complete or almost complete recovery and where damages are principally for pain and suffering, might provide a useful comparison.[224] It also took into account the reports of the Local Government Ombudsman and the awards for pain and suffering in the case of minor personal injury.[225] It stated that the award should not be minimal as

---

[216] *Bernard* (n 8).
[217] Ibid, [34].
[218] Ibid, [36].
[219] Ibid, [38].
[220] Ibid, [40].
[221] Ibid, [41].
[222] Ibid.
[223] Ibid, [46].
[224] Ibid, [47].
[225] Ibid, [49].

that would undermine the policy underlying the Act that Convention rights should be respected by all public authorities, but it also noted that the consequences of awards for public authorities and society as a whole should not be ignored.[226]

The court concluded that the Local Government Ombudsman awards were the best comparables, finding that the case was, in essence, an extreme example of maladministration which deprived the second claimant of much needed social services care for a lengthy period.[227] The court also took into account that the ordeal was now over and the claimants had a home.

> That said, they had to endure deplorable conditions, wholly inimical to private and family life, for a long time. They have received no explanation or apology and do not have the comfort of knowing that their sufferings have not been in vain. There is no indication that this case has prompted the Council to introduce revised procedures. The claimants' problems have been compounded by the defendant's conduct.[228]

In total, £10,000 was awarded, comprising £2,000 to the first claimant and £8,000 to the second.

In W[229] the Divisional Court considered an award of damages for a violation of the right to respect for private life resulting from a disclosure of information. Taken into account was the fact that the defendant took steps reasonably promptly once the problem was drawn to its attention.

> He did acknowledge that something had gone wrong, provide an apology and an assurance that steps, in the form of the draft Correction, would be taken to ensure (so far as possible in an imperfect world) that the same mistake will not happen again.[230]

It concluded therefore that nothing more was required by way of monetary compensation to afford just satisfaction.[231] If damages were to be awarded, the court assessed these at £1,000. The violation was found to be not particularly grave, the publication was limited and there was an immediate agreement to investigate. The claimant received an apology and retraction. 'This is not a case which had to be brought in order to change procedures and prevent such an incident ever happening again.'[232] Whilst the claimant suffered frustration and distress, this did not result in him needing medical advice or assistance, nor was he shunned by anyone.[233] Whilst he was a particularly susceptible individual, the defendants were not responsible for that lack of understanding on his part.[234]

Damages were awarded against the police for a breach of private life in *Mohammed*[235] where it was found that police had breached Article 8 by administering a caution to the claimant even though he had not made an admission of guilt. The acceptance of the

---

[226] Ibid, [58]. Such an approach is now subject to doubt due to the conclusion of the House of Lords in *Greenfield* (n 34) that only the judgments of the ECtHR should be looked to in determining the level of damages.
[227] Ibid, [60].
[228] Ibid, [61].
[229] *W v Westminster City Council*, Divisional Court [2005] EWHC (QB) 102.
[230] Ibid, [247].
[231] Ibid.
[232] Ibid, [251].
[233] Ibid, [252].
[234] Ibid, [252].
[235] *R (Mohammed) v Chief Constable of West Midlands* [2010] EWHC 1228 (Admin).

caution by the Claimant made it mandatory for him to register as a sex offender. The Administrative Court was satisfied that the defendant knew of the risk of this type of interference when it administered the caution. The caution was quashed, the obligation to register as a sex offender ceased and the claimant was awarded damages of £500. In awarding damages, the court took into account the fact that the defendant admitted that the caution should not have been administered. Secondly, a caution for a sexual offence and obligation to register as a sex offender were very serious matters. The interference with the claimant's private life also continued for a significant period of time.

In *Waxman*[236] damages of £3,500 were awarded against the CPS for a breach of Article 8. The Administrative Court found that the CPS had failed in its positive duty under Article 8 to take action to protect the claimant's physical and psychological integrity in its decision not to proceed with a prosecution against a man who was harassing her. It stated as follows:

> [His] activities had been going on for several years and their effect on Ms Waxman was cumulative ... she was a vulnerable person whose psychological integrity the state had an obligation to protect from further action on his part ... the state owed her a duty to take proper measures to protect her and was in breach of its duty in failing to pursue the prosecution.[237]

13.3 Private Life—Breaches by the Private Sector

Damages for disclosure of private information was also at issue in *Mosley*[238] although this was not a claim against a public authority for a breach of a Convention right but against a private company. The cause of action was the tort of breach of confidence as modified by Article 8 and Article 10, and therefore this judgment is of limited relevance in determining the level of damages to be awarded under the HRA where the breach is on the part of a public authority. Nevertheless, it illustrates that breaches of private life can be taken seriously and this seriousness reflected in damages awards provided the respondent is the private, not the public sector.

The Divisional Court determined that it was not right to extend the application of exemplary damages to this field or to include an additional element specifically directed towards deterrence.[239] It held that the law here was concerned to protect such matters as personal dignity, autonomy and integrity,[240] and that damages for such an infringement may include distress, hurt feelings and loss of dignity. It also held that a legitimate consideration was that of vindication to mark the infringement of a right:

> It is simply to mark the fact that either the state or a relevant individual has taken away or undermined the right of another—in this case taken away a person's dignity and struck at the core of his personality ... the underlying policy is to ensure that an infringed right is met with an adequate remedy. If other factors mean that significant damages are to be awarded, in any event, the element of vindication does not need to be reflected in an even higher award.[241]

---

[236] *R (Waxman) v Crown Prosecution Service* [2012] EWHC 133 (Admin).
[237] Ibid, [24].
[238] *Mosley v News Group Newspapers* [2008] EWHC 1777 (QB), [2008] EMLR 20.
[239] Ibid, [235].
[240] Ibid, [214].
[241] Ibid, [216].

In the view of the court, if the objective was to provide an adequate remedy for the infringement of a right, it would not be served effectively if the court were merely to award nominal damages out of distaste for what the newspaper had revealed.[242] Taking Article 10 into account, it also held that the award had to be proportionate.[243] The defamation and personal injury scale was employed, aggravating conduct taken into account[244] as well as the claimant's own conduct.[245] The court also appreciated that an infringement of privacy could never be effectively compensated by a monetary award:

> [I]t has to be accepted that an infringement of privacy cannot ever be effectively compensated by a monetary award. Judges cannot achieve what is, in the nature of things, impossible. That unpalatable fact cannot be mitigated by simply adding a few noughts to the number first thought of. Accordingly, it seems to me that the only realistic course is to select a figure which marks the fact that an unlawful intrusion has taken place while affording some degree of *solatium* to the injured party. That is all that can be done in circumstances where the traditional object of *restitutio* is not available. At the same time, the figure selected should not be such that it could be interpreted as minimising the scale of the wrong done or the damage it has caused.[246]

It determined that £60,000 was an adequate financial remedy for the purpose of acknowledging the infringement and compensating, to some extent, 'for the injury to feelings, the embarrassment and distress caused'.[247]

13.4 Family Life

In *Re P*[248] the Court of Appeal considered an award of damages where a local authority had breached a young woman's right to respect for family life by abandoning a care plan for her rehabilitation with her only child without giving her an opportunity to participate in the decision-making process. The court rejected the contention that the claimant was entitled to compensation for loss of opportunity as this was a case of lawful removal[249] and took into account the fact that the breach was purely procedural. It found that there was no evidence that exclusion from the decision-making process was the 'cause of any independent or additional injury to the mother'.[250] It concluded that it was not necessary to award any just satisfaction other than a finding that her Convention right had been breached. Wilson LJ observed that on the 'spectrum of seriousness, the infringement of human rights perpetrated by the local authority in the present case' ranked near the low end.[251]

---

[242] Ibid, [217].
[243] Ibid, [218].
[244] Ibid, [222].
[245] Ibid, [225].
[246] Ibid, [231].
[247] Ibid, [235].
[248] *Re P* [2007] EWCA Civ 2, [2007] 1 FLR 1957.
[249] Ibid, [50].
[250] Ibid, [57].
[251] Ibid, [69].

14. Application: Article 14

In *Wilkinson*[252] their Lordships agreed that the general principle applied to affording just satisfaction was to put the applicant so far as possible in the position in which he would have been if the state had complied with its obligations under the HRA. However, this may not result in an award of damages in a discrimination case. As their Lordships pointed out, where

> the wrongful act is treating A better than B, this involves forming a view about whether the State should have complied by treating A worse or B better. Normally one would conclude that A's treatment represented the norm and that B should have been treated better. In some cases, however, it will be clear that A's treatment was an unjustifiable anomaly.[253]

An example given of such a case was *Van Raalte v Netherlands*,[254] where a breach of Article 14 with Article 1 of Protocol No 1 was found as the law exempted unmarried childless women over 45 from paying contributions under the General Child Benefits Act without exempting unmarried childless men. The European Court rejected a claim for repayment of the contributions from which the appellant would have been exempt if he had been a woman. In the view of their Lordships, the reason for the rejection of the claim was that if the state had complied with its Convention obligations, it would not in 1989 have exempted men or women. 'It follows that the applicant would have been no better off. He would still have had to pay. In the circumstances, the judgment itself was treated as being sufficient just satisfaction.'[255] Their Lordships concluded that the same principle applied in the present case.

> There was no justification whatever for extending the widows' allowance to men. If, therefore, Parliament had paid proper regard to article 14, it would have abolished the allowance for widows. Mr Wilkinson would not have received an allowance and no damages are therefore necessary to put him in the position in which he would have been if there had been compliance with his Convention rights.[256]

---

[252] *Wilkinson* (n 147).
[253] Ibid, [26] per Lord Hoffmann.
[254] *Van Raalte v Netherlands* (1997) 24 EHRR 503.
[255] Ibid, per Lord Hoffmann at [27].
[256] Ibid, per Lord Hoffmann at [28]. See also the comments of Lord Brown at [44]–[53].

PART II

THE CONVENTION RIGHTS

7

Article 2: The Right to Life

1. Introduction

The right to life is often described as the most fundamental of all human rights[1] and the fact that no derogation from Article 2 is permitted under Article 15 reinforces the importance of this right.[2] It has been held that compliance must rank among the highest priorities of a modern democratic state governed by the rule of law. 'Any violation or potential violation must be treated with great seriousness.'[3] But despite its fundamental nature, it is not expressed in the Convention in absolute terms. Article 2(1) preserves the death penalty whilst Article 2(2) permits the use of force, though no more than is absolutely necessary, in three instances.[4] The death penalty is also expressly preserved in Article 2(1) but it is important to note that the HRA has given further effect in UK law to Articles 1 and 2 of Protocol No 6 to the Convention. These Articles provide for the complete abolition of the death penalty except in respect of acts committed in time of war or of imminent threat of war.[5]

On its face, Article 2 provides that 'everyone's right to life shall be protected by law' and that no one 'shall be deprived of his life intentionally'. These words have been interpreted by the ECtHR and UK courts as including a duty not to take life, in some circumstances 'to take steps to prevent life being taken' and as part of that duty 'an obligation to investigate the circumstances surrounding the death'.[6]

Underpinned by the principle of the sanctity of human life,[7] Article 2 does not

---

[1] See eg *Re McKerr* [2004] UKHL 12, [2004] 1 WLR 807, per Lord Nicholls at [18]; *R (on the application of Bloggs 61) v Secretary of State for the Home Department* [2003] EWCA Civ 686, [2003] 1 WLR 2724, per Auld LJ at [63]; *R v Director of Public Prosecutions, ex p Manning* [2001] QB 330; *R (on the application of H) v Ashworth Hospital Authority* [2001] EWHC (Admin) 872, [2002] 1 FCR 206, [77].

[2] *Venables v News Group Newspapers* [2001] 2 WLR 1038.

[3] *R (on the application of Middleton) v HM Coroner for Western Somerset* [2004] UKHL 10 [2004] 2 AC 182, [5].

[4] In defence of any person from unlawful violence; in order to effect a lawful arrest or to prevent the escape of a person lawfully detained; and in action lawfully taken for the purpose of quelling a riot or insurrection.

[5] HC Deb, Vol 312, cols 987–1013 (20 May 1998).

[6] *R (on the application of Amin (Imtiaz) v Secretary of State for the Home Department* [2003] UKHL 51, [2004] 1 AC 653, per Lord Slynn at [40].

[7] Ibid, per Lord Bingham at [30].

extend beyond this and, in particular, does not confer a right to die or to enlist the aid of another in bringing about one's own death. In *Pretty*[8] the House of Lords confirmed that voluntary euthanasia, suicide, physician-assisted suicide and suicide assisted without the intervention of a physician do not derive protection from an article designed to protect the sanctity of life.[9]

Given the fundamental nature of the right to life and the importance with which it is regarded, deference is rarely shown by the courts to primary decision makers in Article 2 cases. In *Re A*[10] Ward LJ commented that deciding matters of disputed life and death was 'surely and pre-eminently a matter for a court of law to judge. That is what courts are here for.'[11] With respect to intentional deprivations of life and the procedural duty to investigate, there is in fact little room for the court to show any deference to the primary decision maker. Its essential role is to look at the facts and determine whether or not the allegation of breach of Article 2 is made out. Even when assessing whether or not there is a risk to life, the courts have given little margin to the primary decision maker. For example, *Wilkinson*[12] concerned a challenge to a decision to carry out medical treatment without consent. Article 2 was raised because of the risk of the claimant suffering a fatal heart attack if the treatment was administered. Articles 3 and 8 were also argued. Given the importance of the Convention rights involved, the Court of Appeal concluded that it was necessary for the court to reach its own view as to the relevant issues: '[W]hat would be required on a substantive challenge here would be a full merits review of the propriety of the treatment proposed and, for that purpose, cross-examination of the specialists.'[13]

Resources arguments have also been given short shrift in Article 2 jurisprudence. For example, in *Wright*[14] it was submitted by the Home Secretary that the costs and resources of setting up an inquiry should be taken into consideration. The Administrative Court held that, whilst it was conscious of the costs and resources which would be involved,

> [i]f this unsatisfactory situation is to be avoided in the future, steps should be taken to ensure that, in every case where Article 2 of the Convention may be engaged, the coroner's inquest complies with the procedural obligations arising under that article.[15]

There are limits to the role of a court interpreting and applying Article 2. Whilst the Article 2 argument was only a small part of the case, in *Pretty*[16] the claimant argued that she had a right to her husband's assistance in committing suicide and that section 2 of the Suicide Act 1961, so far as it made this a criminal offence requiring the Director of Public Prosecutions (DPP) to prosecute, was incompatible with various Convention

---

[8] *R v Director of Public Prosecutions, ex p Pretty* [2001] UKHL 61, [2001] 3 WLR 1598.

[9] Ibid, per Lord Bingham at [6].

[10] *Re A (Children) (Conjoined Twins: Surgical Separation)* [2001] Fam 147.

[11] See also the comments of Dame Butler-Sloss in *NHS Trust A v Mrs M* [2001] 2 WLR 942, [38] and *NHS Trust v P*, Family Division, 19 December 2000.

[12] *R (on the application of Wilkinson) v The Responsible Medical Officer Broadmoor Hospital* [2001] EWCA Civ 1545, [2002] 1 WLR 419.

[13] Ibid, per Simon Brown LJ at [36]; see also Hale LJ at [83].

[14] *R v Home Office, ex p Wright* [2001] EWHC (Admin) 520, [2002] HRLR 1.

[15] Ibid, [68]. See also *Manning* (n 1), [33] and *R (Khan) v Secretary of State for Health* [2003] EWCA Civ 1129, [2004] 1 WLR 971. Cf. *R (Haggerty) v St Helens Council* [2003] EWHC Admin 808, [2003] ACD 304.

[16] *Pretty* (n 8).

rights. Lord Bingham stated that the Judicial Committee of the House of Lords was not a legislative body, nor entitled or fitted to act as a moral or ethical arbiter.[17] Lord Steyn stated that any change in this area was a role for the legislature.[18] '[A]n interpretation requiring states to legalise euthanasia and assisted suicide would not only be enormously controversial but profoundly unacceptable to the people of many member states.'[19]

2. Scope

Article 2 provides that 'everyone's' right to life shall be protected by law, but there has been little discussion in the judgments as to the meaning of 'everyone'. Either end of the spectrum is clear. Life begins, it was established in pre-HRA case law, if, after birth, the child exists as a live child, 'that is to say, breathing and living by reason of its breathing through its own lungs alone, without deriving any of its living or power of living by or through any connection with its mother'.[20]

Post-HRA, in *Evans*[21] the Court of Appeal confirmed that a foetus, prior to the moment of birth, does not have independent rights or interests.[22] Life ends, it has also been established in pre-HRA case law, with brainstem death.[23]

Between the extremes of life and death, the courts have taken a broad approach. In *Pretty*[24] Lord Hope stated that the right to life is assumed to be inherent in the human condition which we all share.[25] It has been held that the terminally ill have a right to life,[26] as do patients diagnosed as in a permanent vegetative state within the guidelines of the Royal College of Physicians[27] and patients in a minimally conscious state.[28] Seriously disabled babies and children with very short life expectancies[29] have a right to life. In *Re A*,[30] a case concerning the separation of conjoined twins, the Court of Appeal unanimously held that Mary was alive even though she was not capable of separate survival from her sister Jodie, to whom she was joined at the lower abdomen.

---

[17] Ibid, [2].
[18] Ibid, [57].
[19] Ibid, [56].
[20] *Rance v Mid-Downs Health Authority* [1991] 1 QB 587, per Brooke J at 621. See also *R v Poulton* (1832) 5 C&P 329, per Littledale J at 330 and *R v Handley* (1874) 13 Cox CC 79, per Brett J at 81.
[21] *Evans v Amicus Healthcare Ltd* [2004] EWCA Civ 727, [2005] Fam 1.
[22] Ibid, per Thorpe and Sedley LJJ at [19] in reliance upon *Re F (in utero)* [1988] 2 All ER 193 and *Re MB (an adult: medical treatment)* [1997] 2 FCR 541. See also Arden LJ at [106]–[107]. The conclusion in *Evans* was confirmed by the ECtHR in *Evans v United Kingdom* (2008) 46 EHRR 34.
[23] *Re A (A Minor)* [1992] 3 Med L Rev 303. See also *Airedale NHS Trust v Bland* [1993] AC 789.
[24] *Pretty* (n 8).
[25] Ibid, [87].
[26] See eg *Pretty* (n 8).
[27] *NHS Trust A v Mrs M* (n 11), [17]. See also *Airedale NHS Trust v Bland* [1993] AC 789.
[28] *W v M* [2011] EWHC 2443 (Fam), [2012] 1 FCR 1.
[29] See eg *A National Health Service Trust v D* [2000] 2 FCR 577; *Re J (a minor) (wardship: medical treatment)* [1991] FCR 370.
[30] *Re A* (n 10).

She had her own brain, heart and lungs, other vital organs, and arms and legs. She was alive because of a common artery which enabled Jodie, who was stronger, to circulate oxygenated blood for both of them. Ward LJ commented that it would be contrary to common sense and to everyone's sensibilities to say that Mary was not alive or that there were not two separate persons.

---

3. Definition of 'Life'

Another question which arises from Article 2 is whether the 'life' everyone has a right to is merely a right to exist or whether it is a right to a life which meets certain qualitative benchmarks. Given the dangers inherent in making any assessment of someone's quality of life, understandably there has been little discussion of this question in the judgments given. In *Pretty*,[31] although the claimant suffered from motor neurone disease, a progressive degenerative illness from which she had no hope of recovery, had only a short time to live and faced the prospect of a humiliating and distressing death, the House of Lords resoundingly rejected the suggestion that it would be permissible under Article 2 for her husband to assist in her suicide and escape prosecution.[32]

Withholding or discontinuing treatment of the seriously disabled or those in a permanent vegetative state has been characterised as an omission rather than the intentional deprivation of the life of someone who has no quality of life. There is only a duty to treat a patient who does not have the capacity to accept or refuse treatment when treatment is in the patient's best interests.[33] However, if treatment is in a patient's best interests, any failure to treat will be in violation of Article 2:

> Article 2 therefore imposes a positive obligation to give life-sustaining treatment in circumstances where, according to responsible medical opinion, such treatment is in the best interests of the patient but does not impose an absolute obligation to treat if such treatment would be futile.[34]

Although kept from centre stage, it is clear that quality of life issues do play some part in the determination of what is in a patient's best interests. For example, in *NHS Trust A*,[35] a test case concerning the withdrawal of treatment from two patients in permanent vegetative states, Dame Butler-Sloss agreed that the quality of life may be relevant to the clinical assessment of whether it was in the patient's best interests for treatment to continue.[36] She later explained this decision as a conclusion to treat these patients with

---

[31] *Pretty* (n 8).

[32] Ibid, see the comments of Lord Steyn at [50] and [54].

[33] *NHS Trust A v Mrs M* (n 11), [37]. See also the pre-HRA case in which the same conclusion was reached: *Airedale NHS Trust v Bland* [1993] AC 789, per Lord Goff at 867 and Lord Brown Wilkinson at 884–85.

[34] *NHS Trust A v Mrs M* (n 11), [37]. See also *W v M* (n 28) which concerned a proposal to withdraw artificial nutrition and hydration to a patient in a minimally conscious state. See also *An NHS Trust v DJ* [2012] EWHC 3524 (COP).

[35] *NHS Trust A v Mrs M* (n 11).

[36] Ibid, [32].

respect and to allow them to 'die with dignity and in peace by withdrawing that which keeps them artificially alive'.[37]

In D[38] Cazalet J concluded that treatment of I which would include non-resuscitation in the event of a respiratory and/or cardiac failure and/or arrest with palliative care to ease his suffering and to permit his life to end peacefully with dignity was in I's best interests:

> Having regard to the minimal quality of life that I has in the short life span left to him through his irreversible and worsening lung condition, I weigh, from I's assumed standpoint, any possible very limited short-term extension to this that mechanical ventilation might give him against the increasing pain and suffering caused by the further mechanical ventilation. ... I consider that the thorough and careful analysis of the way ahead through full palliative treat-ment as advocated by the paediatricians in the declaration as sought is in the best interests of I.[39]

The issue presented itself slightly differently in *Re A*,[40] the case of the conjoined twins. Although the case was actually decided on common law principles, the Court of Appeal was unanimous in concluding that no different decision would have been made under Article 2. As discussed in the preceding paragraphs, Mary and Jodie were joined at the lower abdomen. If separated, Mary would die within minutes but Jodie would have some chance of a life 'which will be worthwhile'.[41] If they remained joined, doctors estimated they would both die within 3–6 months.

Ward and Brooke LJJ did not characterise the operation to separate the twins as being in Mary's best interests.[42] Ward LJ, with whom Brooke LJ agreed on this point, held that the sanctity of life doctrine compelled him to accept that each life had an equal inherent value and that life was worthwhile in itself whatever the diminution in one's capacity to enjoy it and however gravely impaired some of one's vital functions of speech, deliberation and choice may be.[43] Therefore, in his view, Mary's life, 'des-perate as it is', still had its 'own ineliminable value and dignity'. Whilst this seemed to indicate that he would conclude the operation could not go ahead, instead he placed in the scales the question of whether the treatment was worthwhile and held that this was a different exercise from the proscribed consideration of the worth of one life compared with another:

> In summary, the operation will give Jodie the prospects of a normal expectation of relatively normal life. The operation will shorten Mary's life but she remains doomed for death. Mary has a full claim to the dignity of independence which is her human entitlement. ... Mary is 'designated for death' because her capacity to live her life is fatally compromised. The pros-pect of a full life for Jodie is counterbalanced by an acceleration of certain death for Mary. That balance is heavily in Jodie's favour ... it is ... impossible not to put in the scales of each

---

[37] *Re G (adult incompetent: withdrawal of treatment)* [2002] 65 BMLR 6.

[38] *A National Health Service Trust v D* [2000] 2 FLR 677.

[39] See also the pre-HRA case of *Re J* (n 29) and *W v M* (n 28) which concerned a proposal to withdraw artificial nutrition and hydration to a patient in a minimally conscious state.

[40] *Re A* (n 10).

[41] Ibid, per Ward LJ.

[42] Robert Walker LJ held that the operation would be in Mary and Jodie's best interests 'since for the twins to remain alive and conjoined in the way they are would be to deprive them of the bodily integrity and human dignity which is the right of each of them'.

[43] Ward LJ quoted extensively from J Keown, 'Restoring Moral and Intellectual Shape to the Law after Bland' (1997) 113 *Law Quarterly Review* 481, 485–87.

child the manner in which they are individually able to exercise their right to life. Mary may have a right to life, but she has little right to be alive. She is alive because and only because, to put it bluntly, but none the less accurately, she sucks the lifeblood of Jodie and she sucks the lifeblood out of Jodie.

It is difficult to see how Ward LJ thought he was doing anything but balancing the worth of the one life compared with the other. As he himself concluded, what was proposed was an intentional deprivation of life, not a failure to treat, meaning that under existing law, questions as to whether or not treatment was in the patient's best interests did not arise. Once it was concluded that Mary was a life and had a right to life, a strict Article 2 interpretation would imply that under no circumstances could the operation go ahead unless it fell within one of the exceptions outlined in Article 2(2)—an unlikely prospect.[44] However, in the judgments given, whilst it was pointed out that no different conclusion would be reached under Article 2, it was not discussed in detail and all members of the Court of Appeal were careful to point out that their judgments were only authoritative in the particular unique circumstances which had given rise to the proceedings. In short, *Re A* is very unlikely to open the floodgates to 'quality of life'-based litigation.[45]

---

4. Intentional Deprivation of Life

Proceedings under the HRA concerning the intentional deprivation of someone's life by a public authority are rare. The bulk of litigation has concerned the positive duty to safeguard life and the procedural duty to investigate deaths. Those cases which have raised the question of intentional deprivation have mostly centred on one question: what actually constitutes an intentional deprivation of life? Although the case law is far from clear, brief definitions have been given. To fall within this limb of Article 2, it must be a deliberate act, as opposed to an omission, which results in death[46] and the purpose must be to cause death.[47] However, determining what is a deliberate act with the purpose of causing death is not as simple as it would first appear.

The Supreme Court confirmed in *Smith and Ellis*[48] that there was no intentional deprivation of life involved in deploying servicemen and women on active service overseas as part of an organised military force which is properly equipped and capable of defending itself, 'even though the risk of their being killed is inherent in what they are being asked to do'.[49] But it has been held that assisted suicide and voluntary

---

[44] As discussed in following paragraphs, Ward LJ suggested that Art 2 was subject to an implied limitation which justified balancing. Brooke LJ was reluctant to find that a right as fundamental as Art 2 could be subject to an implied limitation which destroyed its value.

[45] See generally S Michalowski, 'Sanctity of Life—Are Some Lives More Sacred Than Others?' (2002) 22 *Legal Studies* 377; R Huxtable, 'Separation of Conjoined Twins: Where Next for English Law?' [2002] *Commonwealth Law Reports* 459.

[46] *NHS Trust A v Mrs M* (n 11).

[47] *Re A* (n 10), per Robert Walker LJ.

[48] *Smith and Ellis v Ministry of Defence* [2013] UKSC 41, [2013] 3 WLR 69.

[49] Ibid, per Lord Hope at [62].

euthanasia do fall within the category of intentional deprivation.[50] If an NHS doctor were deliberately to bring about the death of a competent patient by withdrawing life-prolonging treatment contrary to that patient's wishes, Article 2 would be infringed.[51] In *Re A*,[52] the case of the conjoined twins discussed in preceding paragraphs, it was beyond doubt that separation would lead to the death of the weaker twin, Mary. In the Court of Appeal, Ward LJ and Brooke LJ held that the operation was not in Mary's best interests and would be an intentional deprivation of life. Ward LJ stated that it would be utterly fanciful to classify the invasive treatment as an omission in contradistinction to an act. Nor did he believe it could be classified as not continuing to provide treatment. Robert Walker LJ dissented on this point, holding that the word 'intentionally' in Article 2 must be given its natural and ordinary meaning and that it applied only to cases where the purpose of the prohibited action was to cause death. He concluded that Mary would die as a result of the operation 'not because she was intentionally killed, but because her own body cannot sustain her life'.

Difficult questions have also arisen concerning the treatment of seriously disabled children and those in a permanent vegetative state. To summarise, following on from the pre-HRA reasoning in the *Bland*[53] decisions on the part of NHS Trusts to withhold further treatment, or discontinue life support, have not been characterised by the courts as intentional deprivations of life under Article 2. The first so-called 'test case' was *NHS Trust A v Mrs M*,[54] which concerned two patients in a permanent vegetative state (PVS). In the Family Division of the High Court, Dame Butler-Sloss held that the first step was to confirm that the diagnosis of PVS fell within the guidelines of the Royal College of Physicians. Finding that this was so, she concluded that it would not be in the best interests of either patient to continue treatment. She then considered the question of whether or not an omission to provide a life-sustaining treatment constituted an intentional deprivation of life within the meaning of Article 2.

Pointing out that the question of discontinuing artificial nutrition and hydration to a patient in a PVS state had not yet arisen in the ECtHR, she held that guidance could be gleaned from decisions of that court dealing with entirely different situations.[55] She also relied upon the judgment of Robert Walker LJ in *Re A*. She concluded that there were limits to the extent of the negative obligation under Article 2(1). Here the purpose of the action was not to cause death:

> Although the intention in withdrawing artificial nutrition and hydration in PVS cases is to hasten death, in my judgment the phrase 'deprivation of life' must import a deliberate act, as opposed to an omission, by someone acting on behalf of the state, which results in death. A responsible decision by a medical team not to provide treatment at the initial stage could not amount to intentional deprivation by the state. Such a decision based on clinical judgment is an omission to act. The death of the patient is the result of the illness or injury from which he suffered and that cannot be described as a deprivation.[56]

---

[50] *Pretty* (n 8).
[51] *R (on the application of Burke) v The General Medical Council* [2005] EWCA Civ 1003, [39].
[52] *Re A* (n 10).
[53] *Airedale NHS Trust v Bland* [1993] AC 789.
[54] *NHS Trust A v Mrs M* (n 11).
[55] *Widmer v Switzerland* Application 20527/92 (1993); *Association X v United Kingdom* (1978) 14 D&R 31 were cited.
[56] *NHS Trust A v Mrs M* (n 11), [30].

She also concluded that there was no difference between this situation and a decision to discontinue treatment which was no longer in the best interests of the patient. She found the analysis of the House of Lords in *Bland*[57] to be entirely in accordance with Article 2.

The conclusion of Dame Butler-Sloss could be described as the only viable solution in the circumstances. If discontinuing treatment was to be characterised as an intentional deprivation, this would place hospitals in a difficult position. PVS patients would have to be kept alive indefinitely, and seriously disabled children would have to be resuscitated despite their pain and suffering and poor quality of life.[58] As Dame Butler-Sloss commented,

> in view of the absolute nature of the prohibition on intentional killing ... there would be a duty in every case to take steps to keep a terminally ill patient alive by all means possible, and to continue those steps indefinitely, until the patient's body could no longer sustain treatment, irrespective of the circumstances or the prognosis.[59]

In order to provide some way out in such circumstances, the courts may even have been tempted to embark down the dangerous road of defining who was to benefit from the right to life or whether life had to be of a certain quality. Classification as non-intentional has definitely resolved some problems, but, as discussed in the following paragraphs, it has also raised new ones given the positive obligation under Article 2 to take steps to safeguard life.

Finally, it is important to note that although the death penalty is no longer utilised as a punishment in the UK, national courts have considered the application of the HRA in those instances where an individual may face the death penalty if returned to another state. The test is whether or not there are substantial grounds for believing that the individual would face a real risk of execution. If the death penalty is a punishment available under the law of the destination state for the offence the individual is charged with, that is enough to give rise prima facie to a real risk of its being applied. The burden is on the Secretary of State to show that such a risk is not in fact made out.[60]

5. Positive Duty to Safeguard Life

5.1 Nature of the Duty

Although not apparent on its face, Article 2(1) also requires public authorities to take

---

[57] *Airedale NHS Trust v Bland* [1993] AC 789.
[58] See eg *National Health Service Trust v D* (n 29).
[59] *NHS Trust A v Mrs M* (n 11), [29].
[60] *R (Al-Saadoon) v Secretary of State for Defence* [2009] EWCA Civ 7, [2009] 3 WLR 957, [17]. See further B Malkani, 'The Obligation to Refrain from Assisting the Use of the Death Penalty' (2013) 62 *International & Comparative Law Quarterly* 523.

appropriate steps to safeguard the lives of those within its jurisdiction. The origin of this duty can be found in the judgment of the ECtHR in *Osman*:[61]

> The Court notes that the first sentence of Article 2(1) enjoins the State not only to refrain from the intentional and unlawful taking of life, but also to take appropriate steps to safeguard the lives of those within its jurisdiction. … Article 2 of the Convention may also imply in certain well-defined circumstances a positive obligation on the authorities to take preventive operational measures to protect an individual whose life is at risk from the criminal acts of another individual … where there is an allegation that the authorities have violated their positive obligation to protect the right to life in the context of their above-mentioned duty to prevent and suppress offences against the person, it must be established to its satisfaction that the authorities knew or ought to have known at the time of the existence of a real and immediate risk to the life of an identified individual or individuals from the criminal acts of a third party and that they failed to take measures within the scope of their powers which, judged reasonably, might have been expected to avoid that risk.[62]

Initially the *Osman* test was adopted wholesale by UK courts.[63] However, in *R (A) v Lord Saville of Newdigate*[64] and *Bloggs 61*,[65] the Court of Appeal lowered the threshold at which the positive duty arose. Subsequent confusion was put to rest by the judgment of the House of Lords in *Officer L*[66] where the *Osman* test was confirmed as the appropriate test under the HRA for this type of claim. Even where the threat to the life of an individual derives from the decision of a public authority, such as a decision to call a particular individual as a witness, a test lower than the ordinary *Osman* test, is not possible.[67] The *Osman* test is a constant and to be applied whatever the particular circumstances of the case.[68]

5.2 State Responsibility

Courts have now applied the *Osman* test to claims under the HRA in a variety of settings ranging from policing to health care. At the outset, often the concern is to establish that the state is actually responsible for the breach which has arisen. A distinction has been made in the jurisprudence between casual acts of negligence and a breach of operational duty. Whilst this has not been expressed in the language of 'state responsibility' it is clear that this is what the courts are trying to establish before applying the *Osman* test. For example, in *Rabone*[69] the Supreme Court approved its previous judgment in *Savage* that if the hospital authorities had performed their obligation to adopt appropriate general measures for the protection of the lives of patients in hospitals, casual acts of negligence by members of staff would not give rise to a breach

---

[61] *Osman v United Kingdom* (1997) 29 EHRR 245.
[62] Ibid, [115]–[116].
[63] See eg *Venables* (n 2); *H* (n 1).
[64] *R(A) v Lord Saville of Newdigate* [2001] EWCA Civ 2048, [2002] 1 WLR 1249.
[65] *Bloggs 61* (n 1).
[66] *Re Officer L* [2007] UKHL 36, [2007] 1 WLR 2135.
[67] *Chief Constable of the Hertfordshire Police v Van Colle* [2008] UKHL 50, [2009] 1 AC 225.
[68] Ibid.
[69] *Rabone v Pennine Care NHS Foundation Trust* [2012] UKSC 2, [2012] 2 AC 72.

of Article 2.[70] It was necessary to determine whether an operational duty had arisen and Article 2 was therefore engaged.

The Supreme Court held that an operational duty will exist (and the state will be responsible) where there has been an assumption of responsibility by the state for the individual's welfare and safety, including by the exercise of control. The paradigm example is where the state has detained an individual 'whether in prison, in a psychiatric hospital, in an immigration detention centre or otherwise'.[71] As noted by Lord Dyson, the operational obligations applied to all detainees but were particularly stringent in relation to those who were especially vulnerable by reason of their physical or mental condition.[72] In addition to the vulnerability of the victim, the nature of the risk, whether it is ordinary or exceptional, is also important.[73] Once an operational duty is established, the standard demanded for the performance of it is reasonableness.[74] Here the Supreme Court concluded that a health trust owed an operational duty to a woman to take reasonable steps to protect her from the real and immediate risk of suicide, even though she was not a detained patient.[75]

5.3 Justiciability

In some instances where the Article 2 positive duty could be engaged, courts have raised considerations of justiciability and questioned whether or not it is appropriate for a court to be involved. For example, in *Smith and Ellis*[76] some members of the Supreme Court were reluctant to apply the Article 2 duty where a risk to the life of members of the armed forces was at issue. Lord Hope, giving the judgment of the majority, noted that the fact that there were some issues relating to the conduct of armed hostilities which were non-justiciable was not really in doubt. However, he also stated as follows:

> [A] finding that in all circumstances deaths or injuries in combat that result from the conduct of operations by the armed forces are outside the scope of article 2 would not be sustainable. It would amount, in effect, to a derogation from the state's substantive obligations under that article. Such a fundamental departure from the broad reach of the Convention should not be undertaken without clear guidance from Strasbourg as to whether, and in what circumstances, this would be appropriate.[77]

5.4 Knew or Ought to Have Known

Once state responsibility is determined, and any concerns about justiciability resolved,

---

[70] Ibid, per Lord Dyson at [19].

[71] Ibid, [22].

[72] Ibid, [22].

[73] Ibid, [24].

[74] Ibid, [43].

[75] State responsibility was also important to the judgment of the Supreme Court in *R (Gentle) v The Prime Minister* [2008] UKHL 20, [2008] 1 AC 1356 although this concerned the Art 2 duty to investigate deaths.

[76] *Smith and Ellis* (n 48).

[77] Ibid, [58]. See also *Gentle* (n 75), where justiciability was discussed in the context of the Art 2 duty to investigate deaths and *R (Khan) v Secretary of State for Foreign & Commonwealth Affairs* [2012] EWHC 3728 (Admin).

the first element of the *Osman* test is knowledge. It must be established that that the authorities 'knew or ought to have known at the time of a real and immediate risk to life'. Lord Bingham in *Van Colle*[78] stated that this was a crucial part of the test since where a tragic killing has occurred 'it is all too easy to interpret the events which preceded it in the light of that knowledge and not as they appeared at the time'.[79] The application of the test does not just depend on what the authorities knew but also on what they ought to have known. In the view of Lord Bingham 'stupidity, lack of imagination and inertia' do not afford an excuse to a national authority which 'reasonably ought, in the light of what it knew or was told, to make further enquiries or investigations'.[80] He held that the court should endeavour to place itself in the chair of the police officer and 'assess events as they unfolded through his eyes'. In the present case, the House of Lords concluded that it could not reasonably be said that the police officer should have anticipated, from the information available to him at the time, that there was a real and immediate risk to life.[81]

5.5 Real and Immediate Risk to Life

The duty to take reasonable measures only arises where there is a real and immediate risk to life. The next step is to determine what actually qualifies as a real and immediate risk to life sufficient to engage Article 2. The threshold is high and not easily satisfied[82] and the 'standard is constant and not variable with the type of act in contemplation'.[83] It is clearly a more stringent test than the reasonably foreseeable negligence test.[84] In order for the risk to be real, it must be a substantial or significant risk, not a remote or fanciful one.[85] 'Present and continuing' captures the essence of the meaning of immediate and the idea is to 'focus on a risk which is present at the time of the alleged breach of duty and not a risk that will arise at some time in the future'.[86] It must also be a risk to the individual's life, not merely a risk of some harm.[87]

The existence of a subjective fear can indicate the presence of a real and immediate risk, but it is not a prerequisite to a finding of risk and of evidential value only as it must be established that the fear is objectively well-founded.[88] There must be reasonable grounds which show that the fears of a witness are objectively justified.[89] Although it has been held that the evidence supporting the case must demonstrate convincingly the risk to life, often there are no concrete facts or statistics as to future probability.[90] It might be that there is already a real and immediate risk to life, but that a further

---

[78] *Van Colle* (n 67).
[79] Ibid, [32].
[80] Ibid, per Lord Bingham at [32].
[81] See also *Mitchell v Glasgow City Council* [2009] UKHL 11, [2009] 1 AC 874, per Lord Hope at [33].
[82] In *Re Officer L* (n 66), [20]; Van Colle (n 67), per Lord Bingham at [30].
[83] *Re Officer L* (n 66), [20].
[84] *Rabone* (n 69), per Lord Dyson at [37].
[85] Ibid, [38].
[86] Ibid, [39].
[87] *R (AP) v HM Coroner for Worcestershire* [2011] EWHC 1453 (Admin), [2011] BLGR 952, [79].
[88] *Re Officer L* (n 66), [20].
[89] *R (on the application of Officer A) v HM Coroner for Inner South London* [2004] EWCA Civ 1439, [2005] UKHRR 44, per Gale LJ at [30], with whom the others agreed.
[90] See eg *Venables* (n 2).

act materially increases the risk. This increase in risk can also be considered under Article 2. For example, in *Officer L* the House of Lords identified the relevant question as whether or not giving evidence to an inquiry without anonymity would result in a materially increased risk to life of police officers who had served in the Royal Ulster Constabulary. Evidence had been given to support the view that all serving and former police officers were at some risk of death or injury from paramilitary attacks.[91] The House of Lords agreed with the view of the tribunal that there would be no material increase in risk; therefore Article 2 was not engaged and there was no need for the witnesses to be granted anonymity.[92]

The role that deference to the primary decision maker should play in any risk assessment exercise by the court is not clear. In *Bloggs 61*[93] the Court of Appeal held that any potential interference with the right to life required the most anxious scrutiny by the court since it was the most fundamental of human rights, but also held that this stopped short of merits review.[94] Despite the fundamental and unqualified nature of the right to life, the court held that it was still appropriate to show some deference to and/or to recognise the 'special competence of the Prison Service in making a decision going to the safety of an inmate's life'. However, it did hold that the degree of deference would be less and the intensity of the court's review would be greater—perhaps greatest—in an Article 2 case than for those human rights where the Convention required a balance to be struck.[95]

It is questionable whether this aspect of the judgment of the Court of Appeal is correct. It is not an approach which has been taken in any other case where the positive duty under Article 2 has been raised.[96] For example, in *H*[97] the Administrative Court held that, given the fundamental nature of the right to life, the court had to examine the factual evidence for itself to determine whether or not there was a risk to life.[98] And despite the comments concerning deference in *Bloggs 61*, it is clear that the court did not simply accept the Prison Service's word as to the safety of the prisoner. A police risk assessment had been carried out and the concerns of the Assistant Chief Probation Officer were taken into account. Whilst deference was urged, it appears that the facts justifying the conclusion of the court were apparent, Auld LJ stating that he would have reached the same conclusion as the Prison Service based on the reasons it gave.[99] Keene LJ, who agreed, pointed out that, even were it for the court to make the primary judgment, the court would have to attach considerable weight to the assessment of risk made by those with professional involvement in the areas with which the case was concerned. It may therefore in most cases make little difference whether one describes the court's approach as one of deference or simply as one of attaching weight to the judgment reached by such bodies: the end result would be the same.[100]

---

[91] *Re Officer L* (n 66), [23]–[24].

[92] Ibid, [24]–[25].

[93] *Bloggs 61* (n 1).

[94] Ibid, per Auld LJ at [63].

[95] Ibid, per Auld LJ at [65] in reliance upon *R v DPP ex p Kebilene* [2000] 2 AC 326, per Lord Hope at [80] and *R v BBC ex p Prolife Alliance* [2003] UKHL 23, [2004] 1 AC 185, per Lord Walker at [139].

[96] *Bloggs 61* was not even referred to in *Officer A* (n 89), a later Court of Appeal judgment.

[97] *H* (n 1).

[98] Ibid, [86]. See also *Wilkinson* (n 12).

[99] *Bloggs 61* (n 1), [70].

[100] Ibid, [82]. See also *R v Chief Constable of Norfolk Police, ex p F* [2002] EWHC 1738 (Admin), where the AC held that the risk assessment carried out by the Prison Service in relation to a request for admission to a protected witness unit was flawed and a new decision was required.

The court was not really affording deference but merely appreciating the expertise of those providing the evidence. Given the importance of the right to life, the appropriateness of deference in the true sense of the term at the stage of risk assessment is open to serious question.

5.6 Reasonable Measures

If a real and immediate risk to life has been found, the next stage is to determine what should be done to avoid it. In *Osman* such measures were described as 'reasonable measures', the ECtHR also holding that the obligation must be interpreted in a way which did not impose an impossible or disproportionate burden on the authorities.[101] In *Officer L* the House of Lords held that this was a reflection of the principle of proportionality, 'striking a fair balance between the general rights of the community and the personal rights of the individual'.[102] But rather than keeping to the language of proportionality, it went on to state the standard was based on reasonableness, which brought into consideration 'the circumstances of the case, the ease or difficulty of taking precautions and the resources available'.[103] In its view, the state was not expected to undertake an unduly burdensome obligation or satisfy an absolute standard 'requiring the risk to be averted, regardless of all other considerations'.[104]

The standard of proportionality has not been employed in other judgments. In *Van Colle*[105] Lord Bingham observed that in *Osman* the ECtHR had rejected the submission that the failure to perceive the risk to life in the circumstances known at the time, or to take preventative measures to avoid that risk, 'must be tantamount to gross negligence or wilful disregard of the duty to protect life'.[106] In his Lordship's view such a rigid standard would be 'incompatible with the obligation of member states to secure the practical and effective protection of the right laid down in article 2'.[107] He did not use the test of proportionality but held that what must be demonstrated is 'individual agents of the state have reprehensibly failed to exercise the powers available to them for the purpose of protecting life'.[108]

Given the balancing involved, it has been held that at this stage some degree of deference to the primary decision maker is appropriate. For example, in *H*[109] the Administrative Court held that there was a discretionary area of judgment to which a court should accord due weight to the views of the decision maker.[110] However, it is clear that the court only had a limited degree of deference in mind, stating that its task was to subject the contested policy to anxious scrutiny on an objective basis to 'satisfy itself that there is no other step which might reasonably have been required of

---

[101] *Osman* (n 61), [116].
[102] *Re Officer L* (n 66), [21].
[103] Ibid, [21].
[104] Ibid, [21].
[105] *Van Colle* (n 67).
[106] Ibid, [30]. This was also rejected as the test in *Reynolds v United Kingdom* (2012) 55 EHRR 35.
[107] Ibid, [30].
[108] Ibid, [31].
[109] *H* (n 1).
[110] Ibid, [111].

the defendant', giving 'proper weight to all the various factors, including the absolute nature of the right in issue'.[111]

5.7 Application

5.7.1 Protection of Those Whose Lives Are at Risk from the Acts of Another

Whilst the judgment of the ECtHR in *Osman* concerned the protection of a person at risk from the acts of another, there have actually been very few claims under the HRA concerning similar issues, particularly against the police. One example is *Van Colle*[112] which concerned witness protection by police. The parents of Giles Van Colle argued that the police failed to protect the life of their son who was murdered by his former employee. From September to December 1999 Giles Van Colle employed Brougham as a technician dispenser at his optical practice. After some weeks they had an argument and on Christmas Eve 1999 Brougham did not report for work, claiming to be unwell, and never returned. On 17 February 2000 DC Ridley of the Hertfordshire Police arrested Brougham on suspicion of theft and searched his garage where he found some items of optical equipment that Van Colle confirmed were his. Brougham was charged with theft and obtaining property by deception. He was bailed unconditionally. On 13 October Brougham telephoned Van Colle and threatened him. This was reported to DC Ridley. There were a number of other incidents concerning the alleged victims of Brougham's thefts. On 9 November Brougham telephoned Van Colle and threatened him again. Van Colle contacted DC Ridley who arranged to meet Van Colle on 23 November to take a full statement. At 7.25pm on 22 November, as Van Colle was leaving work, he was shot dead by Brougham, who was later convicted of murder.

Applying the *Osman* test, the House of Lords concluded that the murder was the action of a 'seriously disturbed and unpredictable individual'.[113] And that it could not reasonably be said that DC Ridley should have anticipated, from the information available to him at the time, that Brougham constituted a risk to Van Colle's life that was both real and imminent. Therefore, the *Osman* test was not met and there was no violation of the positive Article 2 duty.[114]

The protection of a person who provided information to a local authority about the tenant living next door to him was the subject of the Article 2 claim in *Mitchell*.[115] Mr Mitchell was attacked and killed by his next-door neighbour following a meeting with the Council. It was alleged that by failing to advise the deceased that a meeting was to take place with the tenant to discuss proceedings for recovery of possession, to alert police and to advise the deceased of what had happened at the meeting, the Council had breached its positive obligation to the deceased under Article 2. The House of Lords

---

[111] Ibid, [113]. See also *Haggerty* (n 15).

[112] *Van Colle* (n 67).

[113] Ibid, per Lord Hope at [68].

[114] This conclusion was confirmed by the ECtHR in *Van Colle v United Kingdom* (2013) 56 EHRR 23. See further G. Anthony, 'Positive Obligations and Policing in the House of Lords' [2009] *European Human Rights Law Review* 538.

[115] *Mitchell* (n 81).

concluded that there was no basis for saying that the Council ought to have known that there was a real and immediate risk to the deceased's life. Lord Rodger further found that there was nothing in the relationship between Mr Mitchell and the Council to give rise to a duty under Article 2:

> The public authority with the positive duty to protect Mr Mitchell from criminal assaults by Drummond was Strathclyde Police, not the Council. That position did not change just because the fatal assault occurred when, as landlords, the Council took steps towards exercising their statutory power to recover possession of Drummond's house.[116]

This does not take account of the fact that an element of the case against the Council was that they had failed to inform the police of the meeting.

The actions of a council were also at issue in *Selwood*,[117] an application for striking out. Here the claimant brought a claim in negligence and under Article 2 against the County Council, her employer, and two NHS Trusts with whom she collaborated in the course of her work. She alleged that as a result of their actions, she had been exposed to danger in the course of her work from a man who was mentally disturbed and had threatened to harm her. He eventually attacked her with a knife and caused serious injuries. The Court of Appeal held that the Article 2 claim should not be struck out, finding that it was arguable that an NHS Trust could be in a position analogous to that of the police who may be under an operational duty to warn a person whom they knew was at a real and immediate risk of being killed by a person with whom they had been involved.[118] Similarly in *Michael*[119] the Court of Appeal refused to strike out a claim under Article 2 against police where it was claimed that the mishandling of an emergency call from a woman at risk of attack from her former partner was a failure to protect her life in accordance with their Article 2 duty.

5.7.2 Protection of Witness Identity

In some instances the disclosure of a witness's identity can give rise to a risk to life. For example, *Officer A*[120] concerned a request for anonymity from two police officers due to give evidence to a coroner's inquest into the death of a man who had been shot by Officer A accompanied by Officer B. The two officers feared for their own safety and for that of their families. Taking the evidence as a whole, the Court of Appeal concluded that there were clear grounds which objectively justified the fears of the officers and Article 2 was therefore engaged.[121] It then considered countervailing considerations and concluded that there were none of sufficient weight to tip the balance in favour of an order for anonymity being refused. It was observed as follows:

> It is relevant to note that the respondents still have to give evidence before a jury. Their evidence will be given by video-link and will be subject to cross examination. This is not a case where the court is concerned with the trial of a defendant. It is a fact-finding exercise conducted by the coroner and the jury. The appellant's interest in the proceedings, although

---

[116] Ibid, [69].
[117] *Selwood v Durham County Council* [2012] EWCA Civ 979.
[118] Ibid, [57].
[119] *Michael v Chief Constable of South Wales* [2012] EWCA Civ 981, [2012] HRLR 30.
[120] *Officer A* (n 89).
[121] Ibid, [36].

very important and significant, is not in the same category as the interest of a defendant in a criminal trial.[122]

A different conclusion on anonymity for witnesses was reached by the House of Lords in *Officer L*.[123] It was proposed to call a number of police officers, who had served in the Royal Ulster Constabulary, to give evidence to the Robert Hamill Inquiry. The Inquiry was set up to inquire into the death of Robert Hamill in circumstances which had given rise to public controversy amid allegations that police had not prevented his death and had obstructed the subsequent investigation. Some of those police officers called made applications for anonymity, submitting that if they were not so protected, they would be exposed to an increased risk of terrorist attack. The House of Lords agreed with the assessment of the tribunal that there was no material increase in risk to life if the witnesses were to give evidence without anonymity. Therefore, Article 2 was not engaged and it was not necessary to consider whether or not the threshold of real and immediate risk was met.[124]

The protection of the identity of a witness can also be an issue outside of the context of giving evidence. In *Bloggs 61*[125] a serving prisoner challenged the Prison Service's decision to remove him from a protected witness unit to a mainstream prison regime. The Prison Service, relying on a police risk assessment containing a division of opinion, had determined that he be returned to mainstream prison conditions although there was a subsequent report revising his risk from high to medium. The Court of Appeal held that the Prison Service and police were better placed than the court to assess risk to life in such a context.[126] Subjective and objective tests were not explicitly applied, although the judgment in *R(A)* was referred to. Subjecting the decision of the Prison Service to the most anxious scrutiny, the court concluded that it was correct, stating that it was 'not just well within the bounds of what was reasonable',[127] and therefore Article 2 was not engaged.[128]

The actual location of proceedings can also give rise to a risk to the life of a witness. In *R(A)*[129] the Court of Appeal concluded that if soldier witnesses had to go to Londonderry to give evidence, many would be subjectively in fear for their lives.[130] Taking into consideration the evidence of the agencies concerned with security, the unique attractiveness of the soldiers as targets to some terrorists, and the scale of the security problem given that between 200 and 400 soldier witnesses were to be called to give evidence, this fear was found to be objectively justified.[131] But, before concluding that a change of venue was required, the court weighed the risk at the alternative venue, the risk to the likelihood of the tribunal getting at the truth and the impact on the families. The court was also concerned that a public authority should not be required

---

[122] Ibid, [37].

[123] *Re Officer L* (n 66).

[124] Ibid, [24]–[25]. It was further held that if Art2 was not engaged, common law principles of fairness may still require that a witness be granted anonymity. See [22].

[125] *Bloggs 61* (n 1).

[126] Ibid, per Auld LJ at [66].

[127] Ibid, [70].

[128] See also *F* (n 100). Applying the rest of real and immediate risk to life, the court concluded that the Prison Service had not carried out a proper risk assessment and a new decision was required as to whether or not the claimant should be admitted to the protected witness unit.

[129] *R(A)* (n 64).

[130] Ibid, [33].

[131] Ibid, [50]–[52].

to desist from a lawful and peaceful activity because of a terrorist threat. It stated as follows: 'The desirability of carrying on lawful activities in a democracy can constitute compelling justification for continuing to do so despite terrorist threats, leaving it to the security agencies to do their best to provide protection.'[132] However, it concluded that the risk posed in Londonderry to the soldier witnesses constituted a compelling reason why their evidence should be taken in a venue other than Londonderry. It did not agree that a change of venue for these witnesses would threaten the credibility of the tribunal or confidence in their inquiry.[133]

5.7.3 Protection of Identity Generally

Article 2 can also apply to protection of identity outside of the context of witness protection. In *Venables*[134] the claimants sought injunctions to restrain the publication of information relating to their identities and whereabouts. They had both been convicted of the murder of two-year-old James Bulger in 1993 when they were ten years old, a case which was widely publicised in the media. Although only three news groups were named as defendants, the injunction was sought *contra mundum*—against the world at large. Applying the *Osman* test, the Family Division of the High Court took into account evidence from the Home Secretary, press reports, evidence of risk reported by the press, evidence from defendant newspapers and judicial observations. It concluded that there was a real possibility that someone would seek them out and, if they were found, the media would be likely to reveal that information. 'If their new identities were discovered, I am satisfied that neither of them would have any chance of a normal life and that there is a real and strong possibility that their lives would be at risk.'[135]

Balancing Article 10 against Article 2, Dame Butler-Sloss concluded that the court had jurisdiction in exceptional cases to extend the protection of confidentiality of information where not to do so would be likely to lead to serious physical injury, or to the death, of the person seeking that confidentiality.[136] Taking into account the high risk of serious physical harm and the possibility that a claimant might be killed if identified, the injunctions protecting identity were granted.[137]

5.7.4 Protection of Those in the Care of the State

To date there have been very few cases where it has been argued that a facility, such as a secure hospital or prison, has failed in its positive duty under Article 2 to protect the life of a patient or prisoner who has committed suicide. Most cases of this type have been considered by the courts in the context of the Article 2 duty to investigate.

---

[132] Ibid, [17]. Reference was made to the judgment of the ECtHR in *Ergi v Turkey*, 28 July 1998.

[133] Ibid, [56]. See also *Deripaska v Cherney* [2012] EWCA Civ 1235, [2013] CP Rep 1 where the argument for witness protection on Art 2 grounds was not successful.

[134] *Venables* (n 2).

[135] Ibid, [102]. See also *Secretary of State for Defence v Times Newspapers Limited*, Divisional Court, 28 March 2001.

[136] Ibid, [105].

[137] See also *Times Newspapers Ltd v R* [2008] EWCA Crim 2559, [2009] Crim LR 114 and *R (M) v Parole Board* [2013] EWHC 1360 (Admin), [2013] EMLR 23.

One example is *Savage*[138] which concerned Mrs Savage, who, suffering from paranoid schizophrenia, absconded from Runwell Hospital where she was being treated as a detained patient in an open acute psychiatric ward. She walked two miles to a railway station and committed suicide by throwing herself in front of a train. Her daughter argued that the Trust had breached her Article 2 rights by allowing her to escape from the hospital and kill herself.

The House of Lords confirmed that *Osman* laid down the appropriate test which must be satisfied in this class of case and confirmed that health authorities were under an overarching obligation to protect the lives of patients in their hospitals. This required health authorities to ensure that the hospitals for which they were responsible employed competent staff and that they were trained to a high professional standard:

> In addition, the authorities must ensure that the hospitals adopt systems of work which will protect the lives of patients. ... If, for example, a health authority fails to ensure that a hospital puts in place a proper system for supervising mentally ill patients, and, as a result, a patient is able to commit suicide, the health authority will have violated the patient's right to life under article 2.[139]

The House of Lords also explained that if this duty was carried out by a health authority, and, on a particular occasion, a nurse negligently left his or her post and a patient took the opportunity to commit suicide, there would be no violation of any obligation under Article 2 since the health authority would have done all that was required of it.[140] However, it also made clear that a further operational obligation on health authorities arises if members of staff know or ought to know that a particular patient presents a real and immediate risk of suicide:

> In these circumstances article 2 requires them to do all that can reasonably be expected to prevent the patient from committing suicide. If they fail to do this, not only will they and the health authorities be liable in negligence, but there will also be a violation of the operational obligation under article 2 to protect the patient's life.[141]

The matter was remitted to the trial judge to apply the law to the facts. In the Divisional Court[142] it was concluded that the hospital, through its staff, had or ought to have had knowledge on the evidence available to it that there was a real and immediate risk that Mrs Savage would abscond and a similar risk of suicide.[143] It was also concluded that the defendant did not do all that it could reasonably have been expected to do. In the view of the court there was a real prospect or substantial chance that had she been made subject to 'level two' observations at 15- or even 30-minute intervals 'she would not have slipped away unnoticed'.[144] This raised level of observations was not seen by the court as an unreasonable or unduly onerous step to require of the defendant.[145]

This line of authority in relation to hospitals was continued by the Supreme Court in *Rabone*[146] where the patient was undergoing hospital treatment for a depressive dis-

---

[138] *Savage v South Essex Partnership NHS Foundation Trust* [2008] UKHL 74, [2009] 1 AC 681.
[139] Ibid, per Lord Rodger at [69].
[140] Ibid, [71].
[141] Ibid, [72].
[142] *Savage v South Essex Partnership Foundation* [2010] EWHC 865 (QB), [2010] HRLR 24.
[143] Ibid, [88].
[144] Ibid, [89].
[145] Ibid, [89].
[146] *Rabone* (n 69).

order as an informal patient, not detained under the Mental Health Act 1983. When on two days home leave from the hospital, she committed suicide. Her parents maintained that the hospital authorities should not have allowed her home leave and that they were responsible for her death. Making a distinction between an operational duty and casual acts of negligence, Lord Dyson stated that if the hospital authorities had performed their obligation to adopt appropriate general measures for the protection of the lives of patients in hospitals, 'for example by ensuring that competent staff are recruited, high professional standards are maintained and suitable systems of work are put in place',[147] casual acts of negligence by members of staff would not give rise to a breach of Article 2. Lord Dyson accepted that there were differences between detained and voluntary psychiatric patients, but stated that the difference between the two should not be exaggerated.[148] In the present case it was observed that the capacity of the patient to make a rational decision to end her life was impaired and she needed to be protected from the risk of death by those means.[149]

It was concluded that the trust owed the operational duty to her to take reasonable steps to protect her from the real and immediate risk of suicide.[150] In the view of the Supreme Court, she had been admitted to hospital because she was a real suicide risk. She was extremely vulnerable. 'The trust assumed responsibility for her. She was under its control.' Although she was not a detained patient, if she had insisted on leaving the hospital, the authorities could have exercised their powers to prevent her from doing so.[151] The Supreme Court concluded that there was a real and immediate risk of suicide when she was allowed home[152] and that the standard for the performance of the operational duty was reasonableness which had not been met in this case as no reasonable psychiatric practitioner would have allowed her two days home leave.[153] A breach of Article 2 was found and damages awarded.

Those in the care of the state may also be at risk from a change to their living arrangements. For example, in a number of cases it has been claimed that closure of a care home will result in a risk to the lives of the residents. In *Haggerty*[154] it was argued that the Council's decision not to enter into a more onerous arrangement with the private provider led to the provider deciding to close the home. Putting to one side chain of causation issues, the Administrative Court spent a considerable time assessing whether or not there was a risk to the claimant's lives by moving them. Not only measures proposed by the Council to facilitate the move but also reports from general practitioners and a consultant psychiatrist were taken into account. The court concluded that Article 2 was not engaged in the light of the precautions and steps to be taken by the Council.[155] Despite this conclusion, it did go on to consider reasonable measures and held that the courts accord a broad area of discretionary judgment to a public authority in deciding what is a fair balance between the interests of the individual and

---

[147] Ibid, [19].
[148] Ibid, [27].
[149] Ibid, [30].
[150] Ibid, [34].
[151] Ibid, per Lord Dyson at [34].
[152] Ibid, [41].
[153] Ibid, [43].
[154] *Haggerty* (n 15).
[155] See also *R (on the application of Dudley) v East Sussex County Council* [2003] EWHC (Admin) 1093, [2003] ACD 353; *McKellar v Mayor & Burgess of the London Borough of Hounslow* [2003] EWHC (QB) 3145.

that of the community.[156] It concluded that the Council had done all that was reasonable to prevent lives being put at risk. For example, it had liaised with relatives, sought alternative placements, attempted to preserve friendship groups and agreed to liaise with a consultant in geriatric psychiatry on the best way of moving the claimants. The court also considered the council's statutory obligation to take expense into account.[157]

Finally in relation to the application of Article 2 to those in the care of the state, it is important to consider the position of PVS patients. Although one set of problems was avoided by characterising the withdrawal of treatment from PVS patients as an omission rather than an intentional deprivation of life, another was created by holding that the positive obligation under Article 2 was engaged in these instances.[158] Applying *Osman*, the court held that reasonable measures had to be taken. However, it concluded that in a case where a responsible clinical decision is made to withhold treatment, on the grounds that it is not in the patient's best interests, and that clinical decision is made in accordance with a respectable body of medical opinion, the positive obligation under Article 2 was discharged.[159] It was also noted that assistance in determining the scope of the positive duty in such instances could be gained from the right to autonomy and self-determination as protected by Article 8.[160] The court summarised the position as follows:

> Article 2 therefore imposes a positive obligation to give life-sustaining treatment in circumstances where, according to responsible medical opinion, such treatment is in the best interests of the patient but does not impose an absolute obligation to treat if such treatment would be futile.[161]

Where a competent patient makes it clear that he does not wish to receive treatment which is, objectively, in his medical best interests, it is unlawful for doctors to administer that treatment. Personal autonomy or the right of self-determination prevails.[162] Furthermore, Article 2 does not entitle anyone to continue with life-prolonging treatment where to do so would expose the patient to inhuman or degrading treatment breaching Article 3.[163]

5.7.5 Protection of Members of the Armed Forces

Finally, and controversially, claims concerning the positive duty under Article 2 have also been made in relation to the protection of members of the armed forces. In *Smith*

---

[156] *Haggerty* (n 15), [49].

[157] Ibid. See also *R (Wilson) v Coventry City Council* [2008] EWHC 2300 (Admin).

[158] *NHS Trust A v Mrs M* (n 11) [35].

[159] Ibid, [35]. Reliance was placed on *Widmer* and *Association X* (n 55).

[160] Ibid, [41]. See also *National Health Service Trust v D* (n 29), where the court referred to Art 3 as protecting the right to die with dignity.

[161] Ibid, [37]. See also *NHS Trust v P* (n 11); *NHS Trust A v H* [2001] 2 FLR 501; *Trust A v H (An Adult Patient)* [2006] EWHC 1230, [2006] FLR 958.

[162] *Burke* (n 51), [30].

[163] Ibid, [39]. See further S McLean, 'Death, Decision-making and the Law' (2004) 3 *Judicial Review* 265. Art 2 has also been raised in relation to a hospital's no condoms policy. In *Ashworth Hospital Authority* (n 1) no breach of Art 2 was established. Arguments that Art 2 requires the state to fund certain types of treatment have not been successful to date. See eg *R (Rogers) v Swindon NHS Primary Care Trust* [2006] EWHC 171 (Admin), [2006] 88 BMLR 177 where the claimant later succeed in the Court of Appeal with an irrationality argument.

and Ellis[164] the Supreme Court considered an application to strike out a claim that the Ministry of Defence was in breach of its duty to take appropriate steps to protect life by providing suitable armoured equipment for use by soldiers on active service in Iraq and by causing or permitting a particular patrol to proceed, known as an operational decision. Adopting relevant ECtHR jurisprudence, it was confirmed that the deceased were within the Convention jurisdiction of the UK at the time.

It was accepted by the majority that there have been many cases where the death of service personnel indicated a systemic or operational failure on the part of the state,

> ranging from a failure to provide them with the equipment that was needed to protect life on the one hand to mistakes in the way they are deployed due to bad planning or inadequate appreciation of the risks that had to be faced on the other.[165]

The majority confirmed that failures of that kind ought not to be immune from scrutiny in pursuance of the procedural obligation under Article 2. In relation to the substantive obligation imposed by Article 2, it held the extent to which this was applicable to military operations would vary according to the context. Lord Hope stated as follows:

> There is a fundamental difference between manoeuvres conducted under controlled conditions in the training area which can be accurately planned for, and what happens when troops are deployed on active service in situations over which they do not have complete control. ... A court should be very slow indeed to question operational decisions made on the ground by commanders, whatever their rank or level of seniority.[166]

It was also held by the majority that the allocation of resources to the armed services and as between different branches of the services was also a question more appropriate for political resolution than it was by a court.[167] However, reviewing the ECtHR authorities, the majority held that the positive duty to safeguard life could extend to issues about training and the procurement of equipment before the forces are deployed on operations that will bring them into contact with the enemy.[168] It stated that servicemen and women should be given the same protection against the risk of death or injury by the provision of appropriate training and equipment as members of the police, fire and other emergency services. However, it was different when the serviceman or woman moved from recruitment and training to operations on active service: 'It is here that the national interest requires that the law should accord the widest measure of appreciation to commanders on the ground who have the responsibility of planning for and conducting operations there.'[169]

It concluded that the guidance from this jurisprudence was that the court must avoid imposing positive obligations on the state in connection with the planning for and conduct of military operations in situations of armed conflict which were unrealistic or disproportionate. 'But it must give effect to those obligations where it would be reasonable to expect the individual to be afforded the protection of the article.'[170] In the view of the majority, allegations were likely to be beyond the reach of Article 2

---

[164] *Smith and Ellis v Ministry of Defence* [2013] UKSC 41, [2013] 3 WLR 69.
[165] Ibid, per Lord Hope at [63] giving the judgment of the majority.
[166] Ibid, [64].
[167] Ibid, [65].
[168] Ibid, [68].
[169] Ibid, [71].
[170] Ibid, [76].

if the decisions that were or ought to have been taken about training, procurement or the conduct of operations were at a high level of command and closely linked to the exercise of political judgment and issues of policy.[171] This was also the case if the allegations related to things done or not done when those who might be thought to be responsible for avoiding the risk of death or injury to others were actively engaged in direct contact with the enemy. However, in relation to the middle ground, it held that there were no hard and fast rules and it would require the exercise of judgment and depend upon the facts of each case.[172]

The majority concluded that the claims under Article 2 should not be struck out and should proceed to trial. Whilst it had held that the procurement issues may give rise to questions that were essentially political in nature, it determined that it was not possible to decide without hearing the evidence. The allegations relating to operational decisions were also allowed to proceed as these could not be easily divorced from the allegations about procurement.[173] However, the claimants were put on notice that the trial judge would be expected to follow the guidance set out in this judgment as to the 'very wide measure of discretion which must be accorded' to those who were responsible 'on the ground for the planning and conduct of the operations during which these soldiers lost their lives' and also to the ways issues of procurement should be approached.[174] The minority dissenting judges were concerned that the majority judgment went too far and would be likely to lead to a court undertaking the trial of 'unimaginable issues'.[175] It was also thought that there was insufficient guidance from the ECtHR on the point.[176]

5.8 The Relationship between Article 2 and Common Law Negligence

The closeness of the relationship between the positive duty to safeguard life under Article 2 and common law negligence is becoming increasingly evident. In *Van Colle* Lord Bingham posed the question whether or not these two regimes should remain entirely separate 'or should the common law be developed to absorb Convention rights?'[177] He did not provide an answer but observed that the existence of a Convention right cannot call for instant manufacture of a corresponding common law right where none exists.[178] On the other hand, he also noted that it would be surprising if conduct which violated a fundamental right or freedom of the individual 'did not find a reflection in a body of law ordinarily as sensitive to human needs as the common law'.[179] Whilst not finally determining the question in the present case, he observed that there was a strong case for developing the common law action for negligence in the light of Convention rights.[180] In the view of Lord Hope, Lord Bingham did in fact

---

[171] Ibid, [76].
[172] Ibid, [76].
[173] Ibid, [80].
[174] Ibid, [81].
[175] Ibid, per Lord Mance at [148] with whom Lord Wilson agreed.
[176] See further R McGarry, G Mythen and S Walklate, 'The Soldier, Human Rights and the Military Covenant: A Permissible State of Exception?' (2012) 16 *International Journal of Human Rights* 1183.
[177] *Van Colle* [58].
[178] Ibid, [58].
[179] Ibid, [58].
[180] Ibid, [58].

utilise the Article 2 test in his dissenting judgment, formulating a new liability principle for common law negligence.[181]

By contrast to Lord Bingham, Lord Hope observed that the common law, with its own system of limitation periods and remedies, should be 'allowed to stand on its own feet side by side with the alternative remedy'.[182] His Lordship believed that one element to the case for preserving the separation was that if the common law was deficient, a remedy under the HRA might make up the shortfall.[183] Lord Phillips also stated that the circumstances where a positive duty arises under Article 2 are far from coextensive with the duty that the police would be under if the common law duty of care were applicable.[184] And Lord Brown agreed that the common law should not be developed to reflect Article 2 positive duty jurisprudence as civil actions were designed essentially to compensate claimants for their losses, and Convention claims were intended to uphold minimum human rights standards and to vindicate those rights.[185]

Whilst a majority in *Van Colle* were not willing to let the positive duty under Article 2 invade common law negligence in so far as it applied to policing, the question has to be asked whether policy reasons supporting the reluctance to impose a legal duty of care on police when combating and investigating crime[186] have invaded the application of Article 2. As the case law demonstrates, it is very difficult for a claimant to establish that police have breached the positive duty under Article 2. Often the reasons which have been put forward to prevent a common law duty of care arising are the same reasons given by a court finding that no breach of Article 2 has occurred. For example, in *Mitchell*, where both common law negligence and an Article 2 claim were advanced in relation to the same facts, Lord Hope stated, in relation to the common law claim, as follows:

> As in the case of the police, it is desirable too that social landlords, social workers and others who seek to address the many behavioural problems that arise in local authority housing estates and elsewhere, often in very difficult circumstances, should be safeguarded from legal proceedings arising from an alleged failure to warn those who might be at risk of a criminal attack in response to their activities. Such proceedings, whether meritorious or otherwise, would involve them in a great deal of time, trouble and expense which would be more usefully devoted to their primary functions in their respective capacities.[187]

From such a start, it is not surprising that their Lordships also found no violation of Article 2.[188] By contrast, in the area of health provision, there has been more of a convergence between the two regimes. It was pointed out by the House of Lords in *Savage* that it is actually more difficult to establish the *Osman* test in practice than it is to establish medical negligence. Baroness Hale observed that applying the *Osman* test in the context of a mental health facility should not persuade the professionals to 'behave any more cautiously or defensively than they are already persuaded to do by

---

[181] Ibid, [81].
[182] Ibid, [82].
[183] Ibid, [82].
[184] Ibid, [99].
[185] Ibid, [138].
[186] See *Hill v Chief Constable of West Yorkshire* [1989] AC 53.
[187] *Mitchell v Glasgow City Council* [2009] UKHL 11, [2009] 1 AC 874 at [28].
[188] However, in *Michael v Chief Constable of South Wales* [2012] EWCA Civ 981, [2012] HRLR 30 the Court of Appeal upheld the striking out of a claim in negligence against police whilst allowing the Art 2 claim to proceed to trial.

the ordinary law of negligence'.[189] This was put into effect in *Rabone*[190] which concerned a young woman who committed suicide while on a period of home leave whilst undergoing treatment for a depressive disorder. Her parents brought proceedings in negligence and under Article 2. The Trust admitted negligence and the Supreme Court found a breach of Article 2. However, as Baroness Hale noted, the ordinary law of tort did not recognise or compensate the anguish suffered by parents who were deprived of the life of their adult child. Whilst Lord Dyson noted that it was more difficult to establish a breach of Article 2 than mere negligence in this context, this was because in order to prove negligence, it was sufficient to show that the risk of damage was reasonably foreseeable. It was not necessary to show that the risk was real and immediate.[191] The Supreme Court unanimously found a breach of Article 2, perhaps encouraged by the fact that the Trust had already admitted negligence and the fact that it was decided that her parents would only be awarded £5,000 each.

Finally, in *Smith and Ellis*[192] common law negligence and Article 2 claims were also advanced in relation to the same facts. It was alleged that Ministry of Defence was negligent and in violation of the positive duty imposed by Article 2 in failing to provide appropriate equipment and training and in making certain operational decisions. A majority of the Supreme Court allowed both types of claim to proceed to trial, noting that its reservations about extending the Article 2 duty to this type of situation applied just as much to the common law claims.[193]

---

6. Duty to Investigate

6.1 Nature of the Duty

As with the positive duty to safeguard life, the duty to investigate has its origins in Strasbourg case law. It does not derive from the express terms of Article 2, but was implied to ensure that 'the substantive right was effective in practice'.[194] In *McCann*[195] the ECtHR held as follows:

> The obligation to protect the right to life under [Article 2(1)], read in conjunction with the State's general duty under Article 1 of the Convention to 'secure to everyone within their jurisdiction the rights and freedoms defined in [the] Convention,' requires by implication

---

[189] *Savage* (n 138), [100].

[190] Above n 69.

[191] Ibid, [37].

[192] Above n 164.

[193] Ibid, per Lord Hope at [99]. See also *Selwood v Durham CC* [2012] EWCA Civ 979, [2012] Med LR 531. See further C Mc Ivor, 'Getting Defensive about Police Negligence: The Hill Principle, the Human Rights Act 1998 and the House of Lords' (2010) 69 *Cambridge Law Journal* 133; M Burton, 'Failing to protect: victims' rights and police liability' (2009) 72 *Modern Law Review* 283.

[194] *Gentle* (n 75), per Lord Bingham at [5].

[195] *McCann v United Kingdom* (1996) 21 EHRR 97. See also *Yasa v Turkey* (1998) 28 EHRR 408, [98]; *Salman v Turkey* (2002) 34 EHRR 17, [104]; and *Jordan v United Kingdom* (2003) 37 EHRR 2, [105].

that there should be some form of effective official investigation when individuals have been killed as a result of the use of force by, *inter alios*, agents of the State.[196]

The essential purpose of the investigation is to secure the effective implementation of the domestic laws which protect the right to life and, in those cases involving state agents or bodies, to ensure their accountability for deaths occurring under their responsibility.[197] Lord Bingham expanded on this in *Amin*:[198]

> The purposes of such an investigation are clear: to ensure so far as possible that the full facts are brought to light; that culpable and discreditable conduct is exposed and brought to public notice; that suspicion of deliberate wrongdoing (if unjustified) is allayed; that dangerous practices and procedures are rectified; and that those who have lost their relative may at least have the satisfaction of knowing that lessons learned from his death may save the lives of others.[199]

The duty to investigate is secondary to the duties not to take life unlawfully and to protect life in the sense that it only arises where a death has occurred or life-threatening injuries have occurred. But 'in any case where a death has occurred in custody it is not a minor or unimportant duty'.[200] The duty is partly one owed to the next of kin of the deceased as representing the deceased and partly to others who may in similar circumstances be vulnerable and whose lives may need to be protected.[201] It is clear that it has had a major impact on the system for investigating deaths in England and Wales. For example, in *Clayton*[202] it was noted that a coroner's inquest has become a means by which the state fulfils its positive obligations under Article 2 to investigate effectively and publicly any death in the hands of the police or prison service. 'The time is past when coroners' courts could be regarded as an anachronism with practices and standards that would not be acceptable elsewhere in the system of justice.'[203]

6.2 When Does the Duty Arise?

6.2.1 Death or Life-threatening Injuries post 2 October 2000

The duty to investigate only arises where a death or life-threatening injuries have occurred.[204] A near suicide of a prisoner in custody that left the prisoner with the possibility of a serious long-term injury automatically triggered an obligation on the state under Article 2 to institute an enhanced investigation.[205] The prisoner's life was put at

---

[196] *McCann*, ibid, [161] as quoted in *Amin* (n 6), per Lord Bingham at [20] with whom the others agreed.
[197] *Jordan* (n 195), [105] as quoted in *Amin*, ibid, per Lord Bingham at [20].
[198] *Amin*, ibid.
[199] Ibid, [31]. See also *Middleton* (n 3), [9]–[15]. See also *R (JL) v Secretary of State for Justice* [2008] UKHL 68, [2009] 1 AC 588, per Lord Phillips at [29].
[200] *Amin* (n 6), per Lord Bingham at [31].
[201] Ibid, per Lord Slynn at [41].
[202] *Clayton v HM Coroner for South Yorkshire (East District)* [2005] EWHC (Admin) 1196.
[203] Ibid, [9].
[204] *Amin* (n 6), per Lord Bingham at [31] in reliance upon *Menson v United Kingdom* (2003) 37 EHRR CD 220. Where life-threatening injuries have occurred, it is possible that the duty to investigate may also arise under Art 3. In *R (on the application of Green) v Police Complaints Authority* [2004] UKHL 6, [2004] 1 WLR 725 only Lord Scott held that the allegation of the claimant that the police officer had driven the car at him deliberately in order to kill or seriously injury him engaged Art 2.
[205] *JL* (n 199), per Lord Phillips at [37].

risk, and, because of his injuries he could not take steps by himself to hold the authorities responsible for any failures on their part.[206] However, it has been held that the duty does not arise in cases of self-harming where the prisoner has not attempted suicide although it is possible in such instances that a duty might arise under Article 3.[207]

In *McKerr*[208] the House of Lords confirmed that the duty is consequential on the death. Therefore, if the death itself is not within the reach of the HRA because it occurred before 2 October 2000, when the HRA came into force, there is no duty to investigate.[209] It is not possible to characterise the failure to investigate as an ongoing failure to which the HRA would apply if the death had occurred prior to 2 October 2000. It is also not possible to characterise the issue as the application of section 3 to a provision of primary legislation. The argument that section 11(5)(b)(ii) of the Coroners Act 1988 had to be interpreted compatibly with Article 2, thereby requiring an inquest to determine in what circumstances the deceased met his death, even though the death had occurred prior to 2 October 2000, was dismissed by the House of Lords in *Hurst*.[210] However, if an inquest is commenced into a death that pre-dates the coming into force of the HRA, there is an obligation under the HRA to ensure that it complies with the requirements of Article 2.[211]

6.2.2 Link to the Substantive Obligations Imposed by Article 2

The duty to investigate is parasitic upon the existence of the substantive right, and cannot exist independently. An arguable case must be made that the substantive right arises on the facts.[212] Arguable has been held to be a low threshold which is 'anything more than fanciful'.[213] In *Smith*[214] the Supreme Court reformulated this holding that the duty to hold an Article 2 investigation arose where there were grounds for suspecting that a death may involve breach by the state of one of the substantive obligations imposed by Article 2.[215] It was appreciated that this raised the question of how the state was to identify that there were grounds for such suspicion. The answer was a staged system for investigating deaths where the first stage would take place automatically in relation to every death, whether or not there were grounds for suspecting that there was anything untoward about the death. Lord Phillips explained the system as follows:

> Where the first stage shows that the death has not, or may not have, resulted from natural causes, there will be a requirement for a further stage or stages of the investigation. The

---

[206] Ibid, [66]. See also *R (D) v Secretary of State for the Home Department* [2006] EWCA Civ 143, [2006] 3 All ER 946.

[207] *R (P) v Secretary of State for Justice* [2009] EWCA Civ 701, [2010] QB 317.

[208] *McKerr* (n 1).

[209] Ibid, per Lord Nicholls at [22]. See further C Bell and J Keenan, 'Lost on the Way Home? The Right to Life in Northern Ireland' (2005) 32 *Journal of Legal Studies* 68.

[210] *R (Hurst) v Commissioner of Police of the Metropolis* [2007] UKHL 13, [2007] 2 AC 189. See further M Requa and G Anthony, 'Coroners, Controversial Deaths and Northern Ireland's Past Conflict' [2008] *Public Law* 443.

[211] *In the matter of an application by Brigid McCaughey for Judicial Review* [2011] UKSC 20, [2011] 2 WLR 1279 in reliance upon *Šilih v Slovenia* (2009) 49 EHRR 996. See also *Keyu v Secretary of State for Foreign & Commonwealth Affairs* [2012] EWHC 2445 (Admin).

[212] *Gentle* (n 75), per Lord Bingham at [6].

[213] *R v Coroner for Worcestershire* (n 87), [60].

[214] *R (Smith) v Secretary of State for Defence* [2010] UKSC 29, [2011] 1 AC 1.

[215] Ibid, per Lord Phillips at [70].

requirement for an article 2 investigation will only arise if the preceding stage of the investigation discloses that there is a possibility that the State has not complied with a substantive article 2 obligation.[216]

In *Gentle* the House of Lords concluded that the duty to investigate did not arise in relation to two soldiers killed while serving in the British Army in Iraq as they could not show an arguable case that the substantive Article 2 right arose. One had been killed by a roadside bomb and one by 'friendly fire'. It was argued that there had been a breach of Article 2 and that breach was a failure to take proper steps to ascertain whether participation in the invasion of Iraq would comply with international law. Therefore, Article 2 required the government to establish an independent public inquiry into all the circumstances surrounding the invasion of Iraq by British forces in 2003, including the steps taken to obtain timely legal advice on the legality of the invasion.

The House of Lords did not agree that there was an arguable breach of Article 2, holding that Article 2 did not apply to the process of deciding on the lawfulness of a resort to arms despite the risk of fatalities that would inevitably arise. Lord Bingham explained that the lawfulness of military action had no immediate bearing on the risk of fatalities.[217] Lord Hope also held that the legality of the invasion in international law had nothing to do with the state's obligation under Article 2(1) to protect the servicemen and women within its jurisdiction.[218] And, as Baroness Hale stated, '[T]he lawfulness of a war has no direct link with the risk to the soldiers' lives. Soldiers are just as likely to die in a just cause as in an unjust one.'[219]

In the opinion of Lord Hope, Article 2 did not provide an 'absolute guarantee' that nobody will be exposed by the state to situations where there life is in danger, whatever the circumstances.[220] And furthermore, the extent of protection 'must take account of the characteristics of military life, the nature of the activities that they are required to perform and the risks that they give rise to'.[221] In his view, the guarantee in the first sentence of Article 2(1) was not violated simply by deploying servicemen and women on active service overseas as part of an organised military force which was properly equipped and capable of defending itself, 'even though the risk of being killed is inherent in what they are being asked to do'.[222] Lord Bingham also noted that the drafters of the ECHR could not 'have envisaged that it could provide a suitable framework or machinery for resolving questions about the resort to war'.[223]

In *Smith*[224] the Supreme Court also considered the application of Article 2 to the armed forces. It rejected the submission that the death of a serviceman on active service, assuming this was within the jurisdiction of the United Kingdom, automatically gave rise to an obligation to hold an Article 2 investigation. Lord Phillips observed as follows:

---

[216] Ibid, [70].
[217] *Gentle* (n 75), [8].
[218] Ibid, [22].
[219] Ibid, [57].
[220] Ibid, [18].
[221] Ibid, [18].
[222] Ibid, [19].
[223] Ibid, [8].
[224] *Smith* (n 214).

Troops on active service are at risk of being killed despite the exercise of due diligence by those responsible for doing their best to protect them. Death of a serviceman from illness no more raises an inference of breach of duty on the part of the State than the death of a civilian in hospital.[225]

However, it was accepted that where the death of service personnel indicated a systemic or operational failing on the part of the state, such as a failure to provide appropriate equipment or mistakes in deployment, the Article 2 duty to investigate did arise.[226]

Even it if cannot be established that state agents have failed to perform the substantive obligations imposed by Article 2, the duty to investigate may still arise. As Lord Rodger pointed out in *JL*, when a prisoner commits suicide it was at least possible that the prison authorities had failed either in their obligation to take general measures to diminish the opportunities for prisoners to harm themselves, or in their operational obligation to try to prevent the particular prisoner from committing suicide. 'Given the closed nature of the prison world, without an independent investigation you might never know.'[227]

The object of the investigation is not simply to ascertain whether or not state agents have been in breach of duty. The investigation is concerned to see what lessons can be learned for the future, whether or not there has been fault in the particular case.[228] In *JL* the House of Lords explained that there were two reasons why an internal investigation that did not disclose an arguable case of fault on the part of state authorities would not preclude the need for an enhanced investigation:

> [T]he object of the investigation goes beyond determination of whether or not the State authorities were at fault. ... The scope of an investigation into a near-suicide will normally be considerable. It will involve consideration of what was known, or should have been known, of the risk that the prisoner might commit suicide and an investigation of whether the prison procedures against suicide risk were appropriate and properly implemented.[229]

6.2.3 Justiciability

In *Gentle* the House of Lords raised a reluctance on the part of the courts to require an investigation where the tribunal of inquiry might be drawn into consideration of issues which 'judicial tribunals have traditionally been very reluctant to entertain because they recognise their limitations as suitable bodies to resolve them'.[230] Lord Bingham noted that in 'deciding whether a right exists it is relevant to consider what exercise of the right would entail'.[231] In this case the restraint traditionally shown by the courts in ruling on high policy militated against the existence of the right. Lord Bingham found it impossible to conceive that the 'proud sovereign states of Europe' could ever have

---

[225] Ibid, per Lord Phillips at [84], per Lord Hope at [97], per Lord Rodger at [126], per Lord Brown at [150].

[226] Ibid, per Lord Hope at [105], per Lord Mance at [218].

[227] *JL* (n 199), [59].

[228] Ibid, per Lord Phillips at [29].

[229] Ibid, per Lord Phillips at [42]. See also *D* (n 206) and *R (Allen) v HM Coroner for Inner North London* [2009] EWCA Civ 623.

[230] *Gentle* (n 75), per Lord Bingham at [8]. See also *R (Scholes) v Secretary of State for the Home Department* [2006] EWCA Civ 1343, [2006] HRLR 44.

[231] Ibid, [8].

contemplated 'binding themselves legally to establish an independent public enquiry into the process by which a decision might have been made to commit the state's armed forces to war'.[232] Baroness Hale also held that ruling upon the legality of the use of force against Iraq in international law was beyond the competence of the court, although she later contradicted herself by stating that if this was required by Article 2, 'domestic courts would have to do their best to decide if it had been broken'.[233] She also noted that if a Convention right required the court to examine and adjudicate upon matters which were previously regarded as non-justiciable, 'then adjudicate it must'.[234]

6.2.4 Intentional or Non-intentional Killing by an Agent of the State

It is beyond doubt that there should be some form of effective official investigation when individuals have been killed as a result of the use of force by agents of the state:

> Where agents of the state have used lethal force against an individual the facts relating to the killing and its motivation are likely to be largely, if not wholly, within the knowledge of the state, and it is essential both for the relatives and for public confidence in the administration of justice and in the state's adherence to the principles of the rule of law that a killing by the state be subject to some form of open and objective oversight.[235]

It is clear that the duty is not limited to deliberate killing and also arises where there has been a negligent failure to protect life.

> [W]hile any deliberate killing by state agents is bound to arouse very grave disquiet, such an event is likely to be rare and the state's main task is to establish the facts and prosecute the culprits; a systemic failure to protect the lives of persons detained may well call for even more anxious consideration and raise even more intractable problems.[236]

For example, the duty was found to arise in *Amin*,[237] where the deceased had been beaten to death by his cell-mate in Feltham Young Offenders Institution. The possibility of systemic failure on the part of the Prison Service was clear. It also arose in *Middleton*,[238] where the deceased prisoner had hanged himself in his cell;[239] in *Khan*,[240] where a little girl had died in hospital and there were allegations of gross negligence and concern that there may have been a medically orchestrated cover up;[241] and in *Medihani*,[242] where the parents of a young woman who was murdered alleged that police had failed to fulfil their Article 2 duty to protect her.

There is even more reason for an effective official investigation where an individual

---

[232] Ibid, [9].

[233] Ibid, [58].

[234] Ibid, [60].

[235] *McCann, Yasa, Salman* and *Jordan* (n 195), as quoted in *Amin* (n 6), per Lord Bingham at [20].

[236] *Amin*, ibid, at [21] per Lord Bingham in reliance upon *Edwards v United Kingdom* (2002) 35 EHRR 19. See also the comments of Lord Slynn at [41], Lord Steyn at [50] and Lord Hope at [62].

[237] *Amin* (n 6).

[238] *Middleton* (n 3).

[239] See also *R (on the application of Sacker) v HM Coroner for the County of West Yorkshire* [2004] UKHL 11, [2004] 1 WLR 796.

[240] *Khan* (n 15).

[241] See also *R (on the application of Davies) v Birmingham Deputy Coroner* [2003] EWCA Civ 1739, [2004] HRLR 13.

[242] *R (Medihani) v HM Coroner for Inner South District of Greater London* [2012] EWHC 1104 (Admin).

has died in custody. Persons in custody are in a vulnerable position and the authorities are under a duty to protect them. Consequently, where an individual is taken into police custody in good health and is found to be injured on release, it is incumbent on the state to provide a plausible explanation of how those injuries were caused. The obligation on the authorities to account for the treatment of an individual in custody is particularly stringent where that individual dies.[243] Similarly in *JL* the House of Lords noted that the positive duty on the state to protect life had particular application in relation to the risk of suicide by prisoners.[244]

6.2.5 Intentional or Non-intentional Killing by a Non-state Agent

The obligation to ensure that there is some form of effective official investigation when individuals have been killed as a result of the use of force is not confined to cases where it is apparent that the killing was caused by an agent of the state.[245] Although in *Challender*[246] the Administrative Court held that, as the death had occurred before 2 October 2000, it could not consider the application under Article 2, it did go on to consider whether the duty arose. The deceased was found dead in a friend's flat. His sister and partner applied for public funding to be legally represented at the inquest into his death. The Legal Services Commission argued that the Article 2 obligation did not arise as the state was not involved in the death. The Administrative Court disagreed and, relying on the admissibility decision in *Menson*,[247] held that there is an obligation to carry out an effective investigation where there is reason to believe an individual had died or sustained life-threatening injuries in suspicious circumstances.[248]

The duty may arise even where the state is not:

> directly involved in the death (whether through the acts of agents of the state or because the deceased was in the care of the state). The involvement of the state in the death gives rise to additional reasons why an effective investigation is needed, but the state's obligation to ensure the effective implementation of domestic laws protecting the right to life can be a sufficient basis for the need to carry out an effective investigation even in cases with no state involvement in the death.[249]

Here the court concluded that, as there was some evidence to suggest the deceased's death occurred in circumstances that amounted to unlawful killing, the investigative obligation was engaged.[250] This approach received the support of the House of Lords in its judgment in *JL* where Lord Phillips noted that the obligation to have an investigation in circumstances such as these is not so much a secondary procedural obligation but rather part of the positive obligation to have in place effective criminal law provisions

---

[243] *Salman* (n 195), [99] as quoted in *Amin* (n 6), per Lord Bingham at [20] and at [30]–[31]. See also *Middleton* (n 3), [5] and *R (on the application of Al-Skeini) v Secretary of State for Defence* [2004] EWHC (Admin) 2911, [2005] 2 WLR 1401, [323].

[244] *JL* (n 199), per Lord Phillips at [38].

[245] *Salman* (n 195), [105] as quoted in *Amin* (n 6), per Lord Bingham at [20].

[246] *R (on the application of Challender) v Legal Services Commission* [2004] EWHC (Admin) 925, [2004] ACD 57.

[247] *Menson v United Kingdom*, Admissibility Decision, 6 May 2003.

[248] *Challender* (n 246), [48].

[249] Ibid, [49].

[250] Ibid, [50].

to 'deter the commission of offences against the person, backed up by law enforcement machinery'.[251]

6.2.6 Exculpating Factors

The argument has been made that in some cases the full investigative duty under Article 2 should not apply if the contextual situation causes particular difficulties for the state. In *Al-Skeini*[252] the Divisional Court noted that the ECtHR had consistently rejected the idea that there was any displacement of the investigative duty by reason of a security situation.[253] In the present case, it had been argued that the application of the Convention to an Iraqi held in British custody during the period of the occupation of Iraq would create a raft of intractable legal issues. This was rejected by the court, which held that where a prisoner held in the custody of British forces had been tortured or killed, such difficulties shrank before the importance of state accountability.[254] However, in relation to the other deaths, where the deceased persons were shot at and killed by British troops—one in the course of an exchange of fire between British troops and Iraqi gunmen—assuming the HRA applied, the court held that the extremely difficult situation in which investigations had to be carried out were not to be discounted, and accepted that these must have amounted to grave impediments for anyone concerned to conduct investigations. However, it still concluded that the investigations held did not satisfy the Article 2 duty.[255]

6.3 Form of the Investigation

The form of investigation which will achieve the aims of securing the effective implementation of the domestic laws protecting the right to life and ensuring accountability will vary in different circumstances.[256] The ECtHR has not required that any particular procedure be adopted to examine the circumstances of a killing by state agents, nor is it necessary that there be a single unified procedure. 'But it is "indispensable" that there be proper procedures for ensuring the accountability of agents of the state so as to maintain public confidence and allay the legitimate concerns that arise from the use of lethal force.'[257]

The more serious the events that call for inquiry, the more intensive should be the process of public scrutiny.[258] There are limits, particularly where the issues raised

---

[251] *JL* (n 199), [26].

[252] *Al-Skeini* (n 243).

[253] Ibid, [324] in reliance upon *Kaya v Turkey* (1998) 28 EHRR 1; *Guleç v Turkey* (1998) 28 EHRR 121; *Ergi v Turkey* (2001) 32 EHRR 18; *Özkan v Turkey* Judgment of 6 April 2004.

[254] *Al-Skeini* (n 243), [335].

[255] *Al-Skeini* (n 243), [340]. At [341] the court noted that this conclusion did not mean that in other circumstances, it would ignore the strategic difficulties of the situation. '[T]here may come a point when that state's responsibility can only be measured against what is possible, and not against entirely objective standards.' The conclusions of the Divisional Court were not the subject of appeal to the House of Lords [2007] UKHL 26, [2008] 1 AC 153.

[256] *Jordan* (n 195), as quoted in *Amin* (n 6), per Lord Bingham at [20].

[257] *Amin*, ibid, per Lord Bingham at [20] in reliance on *Jordan*, ibid, at [143]–[144].

[258] *Khan* (n 15), at [62] per Brooke LJ giving the judgment of the court.

concern matters of high policy as was the position in *Gentle*. Lord Bingham noted that even if the appellants in that case were able to establish an arguable substantive right under Article 2, 'they would still fail to establish a right to a wide-ranging enquiry such as they seek'.[259]

Similarly in *JL* the House of Lords held that it was not possible to give definitive guidance that will apply to every case of near suicide in prison as much depended upon the circumstances of the case. Lord Phillips noted that '[d]ifferent circumstances will trigger the need for different types of investigation with different characteristics'.[260] Judges have also demonstrated that they are aware of the significant resources demanded by an effective investigation. It has been noted that an investigation need not have all the 'bells and whistles of the full-blown public inquiry' provided it is effective.[261] Certain minimum requirements have been specified where the Article 2 procedural duty is engaged.

6.3.1 Authorities Must Act of their Own Motion

The authorities must act of their own motion once the matter has come to their attention. They cannot leave it to the initiative of the next of kin either to lodge a formal complaint or to take responsibility for the conduct of any investigative procedures.[262] However, an assessment of the question whether the state has complied with the duty of reasonable promptitude depends upon the circumstances.[263]

6.3.2 Investigation Must Be Effective

The investigation must be effective in the sense that it is capable of leading to a determination of whether the force used was or was not justified in the circumstances, and to the identification and punishment of those responsible. 'This is not an obligation of result, but of means.'[264] The authorities must have taken the reasonable steps available to them to secure the evidence concerning the incident, and a requirement of promptness and reasonable expedition is implicit in this context.[265] The initial investigation must be prompt so that 'the facts are investigated while the evidence is still fresh and the material witnesses are readily available to be questioned'.[266] In *D*,[267] which concerned an attempted suicide in prison, the Court of Appeal held that there was no right to cross-examine witnesses but that the representatives of the severely injured prisoner are entitled to see written evidence, to be present during oral evidence and to make appropriate submissions including submissions as to what lines of enquiry should be

---

[259] *Gentle* (n 75), [9].

[260] *JL* (n 199), per Lord Phillips at [31]. See also *R (Humberstone) v Legal Services Commission* [2010] EWCA Civ 1479, [2011] 1 WLR 1460.

[261] *JL* (n 199), per Lord Rodger at [77]–[78].

[262] *Jordan* (n 195), [105] as quoted in *Amin* (n 6), per Lord Bingham at [20].

[263] *SP v Secretary of State for Justice* [2009] EWHC 13 (Admin), [2009] ACD 59, [100].

[264] *Jordan* (n 195), [107] as quoted in *Amin* (n 6), per Lord Bingham at [20]. See also *R (Pounder) v HM Coroner for the North & South Districts of Durham and Darlington* [2009] EWHC 76 (Admin).

[265] *Edwards* (n 236), [71]–[72] as quoted in *Amin* (n 6), per Lord Bingham at [22].

[266] *JL* (n 199), per Lord Phillips at [43].

[267] *D* (n 206).

adopted, what questions asked and, indeed, 'who should be permitted to ask witnesses questions about what'.[268] It may also be necessary to call particular witnesses in order for the investigation to be effective.[269] However, a coroner is not required by Article 2 to enquire into all possible issues. The coroner must focus the investigation and the inquisition on the central issue or issues in the case.[270]

Conducting an effective investigation compatibly with Article 2 can impact on the powers of an investigatory body. For example, in *Reynolds*,[271] which concerned a serious injury, possibly caused by the police, the Court of Appeal held that the Independent Police Complaints Commission (IPCC) had a power and a duty to independently investigate the cause of Mr Reynold's coma, even if that meant investigating events which occurred before he came into contact with the police.[272] The practices of the IPCC were also at issue in *Saunders*[273] where a challenge was made to the IPCC's investigations into the fatal shooting by police of two individuals. The claimants were particularly concerned that the IPCC took no steps to prevent the officers who were most centrally involved in the incidents from conferring and collaborating before giving their first accounts of what happened.

The Administrative Court held that in every case of killing by state agents there must be an effective investigation, and that in order to be effective, such an investigation must be independent and adequate. Furthermore, an investigation may be inadequate, and therefore ineffective, if appropriate steps are not taken to reduce the risk of collusion.[274] In each case, in the opinion of the court, it is necessary to consider the particular circumstances to judge whether the investigation was effective and/or adequate and what steps were appropriate. It concluded in the present cases that the failure of the IPCC to give directions requiring chief officers to take steps to prevent conferring and/ or collaboration was not incompatible with Article 2:

> [I]t was reasonable for the Commission to judge that the giving of directions that conflicted with the ACPO guidance would be more likely to hinder than to promote an effective investigation in these cases, because of the risk that it would encourage non-co-operation by officers.[275]

Furthermore, there were safeguards which diminished the risk that collaboration would lead to contamination of the officers' accounts.[276] However, the Administrative Court was careful to point out that the practice of permitting principal officers to collaborate generally in giving their first accounts was highly vulnerable to challenge under Article 2.[277]

---

[268] Ibid, [42].

[269] *R (Hair) v Her Majesty's Coroner for Staffordshire (South)* [2010] EWHC 2580 (Admin), [2010] Inquest LR 197; *R (Lepage) v HM Assistant Deputy Coroner for Inner South London* [2012] EWHC 1485 (Admin).

[270] *Lepage*, ibid, [53].

[271] *R (Reynolds) v Independent Police Complaints Commission* [2008] EWCA Civ 1160, [2009] 3 All ER 237.

[272] Ibid, [24].

[273] *Saunders v The Independent Police Complaints Commission* [2008] EWHC 2372 (Admin), [2009] 1 All ER 379.

[274] Ibid, [40] in reliance upon *Ramsahai v The Netherlands*, 15 May 2007, ECtHR.

[275] Ibid, [59].

[276] Ibid, [61].

[277] Ibid, [65].

6.3.3 Independence

For the investigation to be effective, it is generally regarded as necessary for the persons responsible for and carrying out the investigation to be independent from those implicated in the events. 'This means not only a lack of hierarchical or institutional connection but also a practical independence.'[278] In the case of death and serious injury in custody, the independence of the inquiry is essential.[279] The test is the common law test of apparent bias.[280] It must be asked whether the fair-minded and informed observer, having considered the facts, would conclude that there was a real possibility that the tribunal was biased.[281]

It is not necessary that the investigator should never have enjoyed an institutional connection with those implicated in the events. It has been held that it it that were so, no retired police officer could investigate a death in which a member of a force in which he had once served was implicated. No retired prison governor could investigate a near death in prison.[282] Current hierarchical or institutional connection by rank or responsibility will disqualify an investigator.[283] Also, past hierarchical or institutional connection between the investigator and someone implicated could well cause an objective lack of practical independence:

> That may arise because the investigator had once served with the person implicated in either a junior or senior capacity, whether or not they had personal contact when serving together. This would apply particularly where the nature of the issues arising in the investigation concerned not merely personal but also managerial and/or institutional accountability for the near-death incident.[284]

It has been held that it is crucial to identify the issues which are being investigated. If the issues raised concern a question whether national policy, such as Prison Service Orders, are adequate to meet the state's Article 2 obligations, then

> the fact that the investigator had spent his working life applying those Orders may ... deprive him of the practical independence necessary to perform his work effectively. The risk would be that his past experience might cause him uncritically to accept an institutional view which would not be accepted, except after thorough analysis and testing, by an investigator appointed from a discipline outside of the Prison Service.[285]

In *SP* the Administrative Court concluded that a retired prison governor was not sufficiently independent because when working as a prison governor he had applied and taken a role in formulation of the policy he was now asked to assess.[286] Whilst in some instances a fully independent second-stage investigator with the autonomy to override the first stage might rescue the independence of an investigation,[287] this does not work

---

[278] *Jordan* (n 195), [106] as quoted in *Amin* (n 6), per Lord Bingham at [20].
[279] *Reynolds v Police Complaints Commission* (n 271).
[280] *In re Medicaments and Related Classes of Goods (No 2)* [2001] 1 WLR 700; *Porter v Magill* [2002] 2 AC 357; *Lawal v Northern Spirit Ltd* [2003] ICR 856.
[281] *JL* (n 199).
[282] *SP* (n 263), [79].
[283] Ibid, [80].
[284] Ibid, [80].
[285] Ibid, [81].
[286] Ibid, [84].
[287] Ibid.

in the instances where there has been a death or near death in custody as the first stage calls for independence as well as the second. A key aspect of the House of Lords judgment in *JL* was whether or not the investigation of an incident where a prisoner attempted to commit suicide in prison, and caused himself serious injury in the attempt, had to be independent of the prison authorities from the outset. Their Lordships held that in such circumstances the Article 2 duty to investigate could not be discharged or removed by an internal investigation of the facts and an enhanced investigation was required, the level of which would depend upon the facts and circumstances.[288] However, if the investigation was to be and to be seen to be impartial, it was held to be essential that it should be carried out by a person who was independent of those involved.[289]

6.3.4 Public Scrutiny

While public scrutiny cannot be regarded as an automatic requirement under Article 2, there must be a sufficient element of public scrutiny of the investigation or its results to secure accountability in practice as well as in theory. The degree of public scrutiny required varies from case to case.[290] In *D*,[291] which concerned an attempted suicide in prison, the Court of Appeal concluded that there must be a public inquiry but this did not mean that the whole process had to be in public. What was necessary here was to make the evidence and any written submissions public and take oral evidence in public. Doubt was cast on this by a majority of the House of Lords in *JL*. In *SP* the Administrative Court held that the first stage of an investigation into a near death in custody may be in private, subject, in an appropriate case, to publication of the report.[292]

In *Scholes* the claimant unsuccessfully sought a public inquiry into the suicide of her son in a young offenders institution.[293] At the inquest the jury had returned a verdict of accidental death. Whilst the Court of Appeal found that the evidence at the inquest revealed a worrying situation with regard to the detention of young offenders, it found that investigation of the facts at an inquest would have little value as the jury could not be expected to give answers to questions of resources and policy which could provide reliable guides to an improvement in conditions.[294] It concluded that the investigations, assessment and debates in progress were such that it had not been established that the Secretary of State had breached Article 2 by failing to convene a public inquiry into this specific case. The court was not persuaded that setting up a public inquiry was the only way in which the obligation under Article 2 could be discharged, observing that questions of sentencing policy and allocation of resources were 'essentially for collegiate consideration and decisions by the Government'.[295]

---

[288] *JL* (n 199), per Lord Phillips at [37].
[289] Ibid, [42].
[290] *Jordan* (n 195), [121] and [109] as quoted in *Amin* (n 6), per Lord Bingham at [20].
[291] *D* (n 206).
[292] *JL* (n 199), *SP* (n 263), [89].
[293] *Scholes* (n 230).
[294] Ibid, [69].
[295] Ibid, [73].

6.3.5 Involvement of Next of Kin

In all cases, the next of kin of the victim must be involved in the procedure to the extent necessary to safeguard his or her legitimate interests.[296] Relatives may be able to provide information about an individual's state or mind or suggest lines of inquiry.[297] They need to be told that an investigation is under way, and given an opportunity to participate, but it is not necessary for them to be granted access to all aspects of a current investigation 'if this might prejudice private individuals or other investigations'.[298]

In certain circumstances financial support to family members to allow them to play a part may be required. There is no need to demonstrate that a case is exceptional before it can give rise to a need for representation.[299] For example, in *Khan*[300] the Court of Appeal held that the inquest would not be an effective one unless the family of the deceased could play a part in it—and they were in no fit state to play that part. Whilst making no final decision on the issue, it noted that it was seriously open to question whether a provision which required someone in the position of the father to fund the entire cost of his lawyer's appearance at the inquest into his daughter's death out of his own pocket in such a serious and complex case was compatible with Article 2: 'After all, the Convention imposes on states the obligation to conduct an effective investigation in a case like this, and without Mr Khan's participation the inquest cannot fulfil that role.'[301]

The court was unimpressed by the suggestion that economic exigencies might be called in aid by a state to whittle down its obligations in a case as serious as this.[302] A similar issue arose in *Challender*,[303] where the sister and partner of the deceased sought public funding to be legally represented at the coroner's inquest into the death. As the death occurred prior to 2 October 2000, the Administrative Court held that it could not consider the case. Nevertheless, it made observations on this point. It concluded that the Legal Services Commission's refusal of funding was correct as it had considered the question of whether, in the absence of legal representation, it would be possible for the family to have effective representation.[304] In the opinion of the court, the case was not of exceptional factual or legal complexity. It was within the competence of the coroner to carry out the necessary investigation without assistance from legal representatives for the family.

> An important additional consideration is that the claimants will be able to obtain advice and assistance under the Legal Help scheme, which will cover the making of written submissions to the coroner, and will enable them to attend the inquest themselves. All that they will be denied through lack of funding will be legal representation in the form of advocacy at the inquest. It does not seem to me that the circumstances are such as to place this case into

---

[296] *Jordan* (n 195), [109] as quoted in *Amin* (n 6), per Lord Bingham at [20].
[297] *JL* (n 199), per Lord Rodger at [76].
[298] Ibid.
[299] *Humberstone* (n 260), [78].
[300] *Khan* (n 15).
[301] Ibid, [98].
[302] Ibid, [99].
[303] *Challender* (n 246).
[304] Ibid, [67].

the exceptional category where legal representation is needed in order to ensure effective participation by the deceased's family and an effective investigation.[305]

The issue was considered again by the Court of Appeal in *Main*.[306] The Lord Chancellor refused legal aid funding for the claimant at the coroner's inquest following a railway accident in which five passengers, including the claimant's mother and sister, died. It concluded that the refusal was compatible with Article 2 as the coroner could reasonably be expected to carry out a proper investigation into the deaths, including the wider safety aspects, without full legal representation of the family. It observed as follows:

> An inquest is an inquisitorial and not an adversarial process. This is a case in which the actual facts appeal unlikely to be in dispute at all. It is not a case of suspected serious wrong-doing or dereliction by an agent or agents of the State.[307]

6.3.6 Outcome of the Investigation

The procedural duty under Article 2 may also extend to the outcome of the investigation. In *Middleton*[308] the House of Lords held that if an official investigation was to meet the state's procedural obligation under Article 2, the prescribed procedure had to work in practice and fulfil the purpose for which the investigation was established.[309] It concluded that the procedural obligation was unlikely to be met if it was

> plausibly alleged that agents of the state had used lethal force without justification, if an effectively unchallengeable decision has been taken not to prosecute and if the fact-finding body cannot express its conclusion on whether unjustifiable force has been used or not, so as to prompt reconsideration of the decision not to prosecute.

If an inquest was the instrument by which the state sought to discharge its investigative obligation, the House of Lords concluded that to comply with Article 2, an explicit statement, however, brief, of the jury's conclusion on the disputed factual issues at the heart of the case was required.[310] And in their Lordship's view, this applied in all categories of cases.[311]

In some instances the procedural obligation may be discharged by criminal proceedings. This is most likely where the defendant pleads not guilty and the trial involves a full exploration of the facts.[312] In other cases short inquest verdicts in the traditional form will enable the jury to express their conclusion on the central issue canvassed at the inquest, such as whether the deceased took his own life or was killed by another.[313] However, in order to ensure that the requirements of Article 2 are met, using section 3 of the HRA it is now necessary to read the Coroners Act 1988 and Rules 1984 as

---

[305] Ibid, [68]. See also *D* (n 206).
[306] *R (Main) v Minister for Legal Aid* [2007] EWCA Civ 1147, [2008] HRLR 8.
[307] Ibid, [50].
[308] *Middleton* (n 3).
[309] Ibid, [8].
[310] Ibid, [16] in reliance upon *McCann* (n 195); *Jordan* (n 195); *Keenan v United Kingdom* (2001) 33 EHRR 913; *Edwards* (n 236); *Mastromatteo v Italy*, 24 October 2002.
[311] *Middleton* (n 3), [17].
[312] Ibid, [30].
[313] Ibid, [31].

allowing the jury to express an opinion on by what means and in what circumstances the deceased came by his death.[314] It must be for the coroner

> to decide how best, in the particular case, to elicit the jury's conclusion on the central issue or issues. This may be done by inviting a form of verdict expanded beyond those suggested in ... the Rules. It may be done ... by inviting a narrative form of verdict in which the jury's factual conclusions are briefly summarised. It may be done by inviting the jury's answer to factual questions put by the coroner.[315]

If there is evidence in relation to equipment, training or effective procedures which need to be taken to prevent similar fatalities, this should be reported by the Coroner in accordance with Rule 43 of the Coroners Rules 1984 or a breach of Article 2 may result.[316] However, a coroner was not obliged to leave to the jury a fact or circumstance which could have caused or contributed to the death but cannot be shown probably to have done so.[317] If a coroner fails to explain to a jury that if they return a verdict of suicide or accident they may also append a narrative about the circumstances of the accident, this can result in a breach of Article 2 although this breach may be offset by the outcomes of other investigations, such as an ombudsman report, meaning there is therefore no need to order a new inquest.[318]

Article 2 has also had a limited impact on the decision of whether or not to prosecute. In *Manning*[319] the sisters of a man who had died in Blakehurst Prison challenged the decision taken by the DPP not to prosecute anyone for manslaughter as a result of the manner in which the deceased met his death. They argued that no adequate reasons were given for the decision. The High Court held that neither domestic law nor Strasbourg law imposed an absolute and unqualified obligation to give reasons for a decision not to prosecute. Relying on *McCann*,[320] the court held that, where an inquest culminated in a verdict of unlawful killing implicating a person who, although not named in the verdict, was clearly identified, who was living and whose whereabouts were known, 'the ordinary expectation would naturally be that a prosecution would follow.' It concluded that, in the absence of compelling grounds for not giving reasons,

> we would expect the Director to give reasons in such a case: to meet the reasonable expectation of interested parties that either a prosecution would follow or a reasonable explanation for not prosecuting be given, to vindicate the Director's decision by showing that solid grounds exist for what might otherwise appear to be a surprising or even inexplicable decision and to meet the European Court's expectation that if a prosecution is not to follow a plausible explanation will be given.[321]

---

[314] Ibid, [35].

[315] Ibid, [36]. See also [37]–[38]. See also *Sacker* (n 239); *Davies* (n 241). This has now been incorporated into the Coroners and Justice Act 2009.

[316] *R (Lewis) v HM Coroner for the Mid and North Division of the County of Shropshire* [2009] EWCA Civ 1403, [2010] 1 WLR 1836 [16].

[317] Ibid, [29].

[318] *R (P) v HM Coroner for the District of Avon* [2009] EWCA Civ 1367, [2010] 112 BMLR 77. See also *R (Pekkelo) v HM Coroner for Central & South East Kent* [2006] EWHC 1265 (Admin), [2006] Inquest LR 119; *R (Cash) v HM Coroner for the County of Northamptonshire* [2007] EWHC 1354 (Admin), [2007] 4 All ER 903.

[319] Above n 1.

[320] Above n 195.

[321] *Manning* (n 1), [33]. See also *R v Weaver* [2001] EWCA Crim 2768 where the Court of Appeal held that Art 2 provides no basis upon which to approach sentencing for homicide in the English courts and English criminal law provides its own machinery to punish those who take life unlawfully.

It was appreciated that review of the DPP was a power to be exercised sparingly.[322] Nevertheless, it was also appreciated that the standard of review should not be set too high since judicial review was the only means by which the citizen could seek redress against a decision not to prosecute.[323]

6.4 Application

Alongside the positive duty to protect life, this aspect of Article 2 has given rise to the most litigation under the HRA. Whilst the practice of inquiries into deaths was well established in the United Kingdom prior to the passage of the HRA, flaws in the system have become apparent.

6.4.1 Deaths in Custody

Deaths in custody have given rise to a number of Article 2 claims concerning deaths which have occurred in prison, young offenders institutions, police custody,[324] secure hospitals,[325] immigration detention[326] and secure training centres.[327] In *Amin*[328] the deceased, a young Asian man, was beaten to death by his cell-mate, Stewart, in Feltham Young Offenders Institution. Stewart was considered to be very dangerous, a threat to both staff and other inmates, and possibly violently racist. Stewart was convicted of the murder and the inquest into the death was adjourned, never to be resumed. A police investigation resulted in the advice of counsel that there was insufficient evidence to provide a realistic prospect of securing any convictions against Prison Service staff relating to the deceased. The Prison Service set up an internal inquiry but, whilst the family of the deceased were consulted about the terms of reference, they were not present at any stage of the investigation and did not avail themselves of the opportunity to meet the person conducting the inquiry. The report was made available to the family, police and Commission for Racial Equality (CRE), but was not published. The CRE conducted an investigation into racial discrimination in the Prison Service. The family were involved in the preparation of the terms of reference and expressed views on the procedures proposed, but the CRE declined their request to be allowed to participate in the inquiry and for its hearings to be in public.

The House of Lords concluded that the state's duty to investigate was undoubtedly engaged in this case and that, given that the death had occurred in custody, this duty was particularly important.[329] The House of Lords found a number of defects in

---

[322] Ibid (n 1), [23].

[323] Ibid. See also *R (da Silva) v The Director of Public Prosecutions* [2006] EWHC 3204 (Admin), [2006] Inquest LR 224.

[324] See for example *R (Cash) v HM Coroner for Northamptonshire* [2007] EWHC 1354 (Admin), [2007] 4 All ER 903.

[325] *R (Allen) v HM Coroner for Inner North London* [2009] EWCA Civ 623.

[326] *R (Pekkelo) v HM Coroner for Central & South East Kent* [2006] EWHC 1265 (Admin), [2006] Inquest LR 119.

[327] *R (Pounder) v HM Coroner for North & South Districts of Durham & Darlington* [2009] EWHC 76 (Admin), [2009] 3 All ER 150.

[328] Above n 6.

[329] Ibid, at [31] per Lord Bingham.

the procedure that had been followed. There was no inquest. The police investigation had been conducted in private without any participation by the family. The murder trial was directed solely at establishing Stewart's mental responsibility and there was little exploration of wider issues concerning the death. The man conducting the internal inquiry did not enjoy institutional or hierarchical independence. His investigation was conducted in private, his report was not published and the family were not able to play any effective part in the investigation. The CRE inquiry was confined to race-related issues and was conducted almost wholly in private. Again, the family were not able to play any effective part.[330] The House of Lords restored the order of the lower court that an independent public investigation be held.

In *Middleton*[331] the deceased had taken his own life by hanging himself in his cell. At the inquest the jury found the cause of death to be hanging and returned a verdict that the deceased had taken his own life when the balance of his mind was disturbed. It also gave the coroner a note which communicated its opinion that the Prison Service had failed in its duty of care for the deceased. The family asked that the note should be appended to the inquisition, but the coroner declined to do so. The sole issue before the House of Lords was whether the requirements of Article 2 had thereby been met. It concluded that they had not. In the view of their Lordships, the crux of the argument was whether the deceased should have been recognised as a suicide risk and whether appropriate precautions should have been taken to prevent him taking his own life. It held that the jury's verdict did not express its conclusions on these crucial facts which might have been done by a short and simple verdict such as 'the deceased took his own life, in part because the risk of his doing so was not recognised and appropriate precautions were not taken to prevent him doing so'.[332]

Although doubt was cast by the Court of Appeal on the Administrative Court's judgment in *Wright*,[333] it was expressly confirmed by the House of Lords in *Amin*.[334] This case also concerned a death in custody. Paul Wright died in prison as a result of a severe asthma attack. During the inquest the questions as to inadequate medical treatment were not addressed. Following a review of Strasbourg case law, Jackson J held that the inquest did not constitute an effective official investigation.[335] Mr Wright's cell mate on the evening he died was not called as a witness and the jury were directed to disregard his written statement. There was no consideration of the shortcomings in the medical treatment, and his mother and aunt were not represented. Jackson J also held that the civil action did not constitute an effective official investigation because liability was admitted at an early stage.[336] There was never a hearing at which evidence concerning the circumstances of the deceased's death was adduced or tested. He concluded that the proper remedy was an order that the Home Secretary set up an independent investigation into the circumstances of Mr Wright's death.[337]

A death in a British military prison in Iraq has also been examined for conformity

---

[330] Ibid, [33]–[37] per Lord Bingham.
[331] Above n 3.
[332] Ibid, at [45]. See also *Sacker* (n 239); *Davies* (n 241). See also *R (Lewis) v HM Coroner for the Mid and North Division of the County of Shropshire* [2009] EWCA Civ 1403, [2010] 1 WLR 1836.
[333] *Wright* (n 14).
[334] *Amin* (n 6).
[335] *Wright* (n 14), [60].
[336] Ibid, [61].
[337] Ibid, [67].

with the Article 2 procedural duty. In *Al-Skeini*[338] the Divisional Court found that the investigation had not been adequate.

> Even if an investigation solely in the hands of the SIB [Special Investigation Branch] might be said to be independent ... it is difficult to say that the investigation which has occurred has been timely, open or effective.[339]

More than a year had elapsed since the death. Other than in the early stages of the autopsy, the family was not involved and the outcome of the SIB report was not known. There were no conclusions and there had been no public accountability. 'All this in a case where the burden of explanation lies heavily on the United Kingdom authorities.'[340]

6.4.2 Near Deaths in Custody

In *JL*[341] the House of Lords considered the Article 2 duty to investigate where a prisoner in custody at Feltham Young Offenders Institution had made an attempt to commit suicide that nearly succeeded and which left him with serious injury. The London Area Manager of the Prison Service had initiated an investigation and instructed a retired prison governor to carry this out. He submitted a written report but no relative of JL or person representing his interests was involved in the investigation and the report was not published until more than two years later. JL's representatives claimed that Article 2 imposed a duty on the Secretary of State to carry out an independent investigation into his attempted suicide and the investigation which had taken place did not satisfy the requirements of Article 2.

The House of Lords concluded that a near-suicide of a prisoner in custody that left him with the possibility of a serious long-term injury automatically triggered an obligation on the state under Article 2 to institute an enhanced investigation. This obligation was not discharged or removed by an internal investigation of the facts. What was required to meet the requirements of Article 2 would depend upon the circumstances. Lord Phillips noted that in some circumstances an initial investigation will satisfy the requirements of Article 2. In others a further investigation will be necessary, which may well need to be a D-type public inquiry.[342] In the present case it was held that the investigation did not meet the requirements of Article 2 but this conclusion was of little practical importance as the Prison Service had already agreed to commission a further independent inquiry conducted as a D inquiry.[343] Whilst Lord Phillips stated that the Secretary of State was right to carry out a D-type investigation,[344] a majority of the House of Lords was not so convinced. Lord Rodger agreed with Lord Brown's statement that a D-type inquiry in such circumstances would be rare.[345] Lord Walker also observed that in the majority of cases some further investigation would be necessary

---

[338] *Al-Skeini* (n 243).
[339] Ibid, [331].
[340] Ibid, [332].
[341] *JL* (n 199).
[342] Ibid, [37].
[343] As established in *D* (n 206).
[344] *JL* (n 199), [50].
[345] Ibid, per Lord Brown at [107]–[108] and per Lord Rodger at [77].

'but that relatively few non-fatal incidents would call for a lengthy and expensive procedure involving taking oral evidence in public'.[346]

The observations of the majority cast considerable doubt on the judgment of the Court of Appeal in *D*,[347] which also concerned the near-suicide of a young man at HMP Pentonville. The Court of Appeal held that the investigation by a senior investigating officer in the prison service was not sufficient and that in the circumstances of the case what Article 2 required was that the inquiry be in public in the sense that the evidence and written submissions would be made public and oral evidence would be taken in public. D's representatives were also to be given reasonable access to all relevant evidence in advance and adequate funding for D's representatives made available. However, it was also held that Article 2 did not require that D's representatives have the right to cross-examine witnesses:

> They must in general be entitled to see the written evidence, to be present during oral evidence and to make appropriate submissions, including submissions as to what lines of enquiry should be adopted, what questions asked and, indeed, who should be permitted to ask witnesses questions about what.[348]

6.4.3 Deaths in Hospital

Khan[349] concerned the death of a little girl in hospital. The police conducted an extensive inquiry but no criminal proceedings were taken. The NHS Trust made its own investigations. The family were not involved in either investigation. The Court of Appeal concluded that it was the coroner's inquest which furnished the natural occasion for the effective judicial inquiry into the cause of death.

> The police investigation, in which the family played no part, and which culminated in a decision not to prosecute, could not act as a substitute. Nor could the investigations carried out privately by the Trust, in which again the family played no part, particularly as the Trust could not be regarded as having the requisite independence.[350]

It concluded that the inquest would not be effective unless the family could play a part in it, and they were in no fit state to play that part.[351] To discharge the obligation under Article 2 the Court of Appeal held that reasonable funding could be provided at the inquest to ensure the family was represented or to set up some other type of inquiry at which such funding would be possible.[352]

> With a wife and four other children to support it seems absurd, on the information at present available to the court, that he could reasonably be expected to fund the whole cost of his own representation himself in order to enable the state to perform the obligations that rest on it, and not on him.[353]

---

[346] Ibid, [95]. See also Lord Mance at [114]. See also *SP* (n 263); *R (JL) v Secretary of State for Justice* [2009] EWHC 2416 (Admin), [2010] HRLR 4.

[347] *D* (n 206).

[348] Ibid, [42]. Doubt was also case on the judgment in this case by the later decision of the Court of Appeal in *Scholes* (n 230).

[349] *Khan* (n 15).

[350] Ibid, [69].

[351] Ibid, [74].

[352] Ibid, [87].

[353] Ibid, [98].

However, no final judgment on the point was given, the hearing being adjourned to allow the state to make further representations as to the route to be followed.

In *Takoushis*[354] the Court of Appeal considered the suicide of Mr Takoushis, who was a long-term schizophrenic admitted to Chase Farm Hospital as a voluntary patient. Having obtained permission to leave the ward to visit the day hospital within the hospital grounds, he did not return. On attempting to commit suicide he was taken to St Thomas' Hospital but managed to leave and later that day committed suicide. The family asked for the coroner's inquest to be held with a jury; this was declined by the coroner. The Court of Appeal determined that where a person died as a result of what was arguably medical negligence in an NHS hospital, the state must have a system which provided for the practical and effective investigation of the facts and the determination of civil liability. It concluded that the system in operation in England met the requirements of Article 2:

> The system includes the possibility of civil process and … the inquest … an inquest of the traditional kind, without any reading down of the 1988 Act by giving a wider meaning to 'how' as envisaged in Middleton, and provided that it carries out the kind of full and fair investigation … satisfies the requirement that there will be a public investigation of the facts which will be both practical and effective … the family will be able to take full part.[355]

In *Humberstone*[356] it was the time taken for the ambulance to arrive which was at issue, the Court of Appeal concluding that this disclosed sufficient grounds for concern about the resources and operational systems of the Yorkshire Ambulance Service as to engage the Article 2 obligation proactively to undertake an enhanced investigation.[357]

6.4.4 Death Involving the Police

In *Medihani*[358] the family of a young girl who had been murdered argued that a Coroner's inquest should be resumed. The Administrative Court accepted that there was an arguable breach of Article 2 on the part of the police. It found that the risk to her life was real and immediate and the police could have taken measures within the scope of their powers which, judged reasonably, might have been expected to avoid the risk.

6.4.5 Death Involving the Armed Forces

Considerable litigation has taken place concerning the form of the investigations established by the Secretary of State for Defence to investigate claims of ill-treatment and killing by the British armed forces in Iraq, in particular, the structuring of the Iraq Historic Allegations Team. The Divisional Court has clarified a number of issues establishing that: there is no objection in principle to a service police force investigating service personnel of the service which they police, or another service police force; that the Royal Navy Police could investigate serious allegations relating to the involvement

---

[354] *R (Takoushis) v HM Coroner for Inner North London* [2005] EWCA Civ 1440, [2006] 1 WLR 461.
[355] Ibid, [106].
[356] *Humberstone* (n 260).
[357] Ibid, [70].
[358] *Medihani* (n 242).

of Royal Navy and Royal Marine personnel; that the Ministry of Defence and Royal Naval Command had no influence over prosecutorial decisions. Considerable guidance has also been given into the process the inquiry should adopt and measures to be taken to achieve an investigation in a timely, proportionate and cost-effective manner.[359]

6.4.6 Death of Member of the Armed Forces

In *Smith*[360] the Supreme Court considered the application of the Article 2 duty to investigate to a soldier who had died from heat stroke whilst serving with the armed forces in Iraq. Whilst there was considerable discussion in the judgment of the fact that he was serving with the armed forces at the time, it is possible to see the facts here as a death due to dangerous working conditions—an arguable operational or systemic failure on the part of the state which led to Smith's death. His body was brought back to the UK and an inquest into his death was held although his mother brought proceedings arguing that the coroner's inquest held should have satisfied the procedural requirements of Article 2. The Secretary of State conceded that a fresh inquest must be held satisfying the requirements of Article 2, but the Supreme Court still gave a judgment on the issue. It was held that the death of a serviceman on active service did not automatically give rise to an obligation to hold an Article 2 investigation.[361] However, in this case it was concluded that the evidence placed before the Coroner raised the possibility that there was a failure in the system that should have been in place to protect soldiers from the risk posed by the extreme temperatures in which they had to serve. Lord Phillips concluded it was arguable that there was a breach of the state's substantive obligations under Article 2 and that was enough to trigger the need to give a verdict that complied with the requirements of Article 2.[362] It was therefore necessary for the new inquest to satisfy the requirements of an Article 2 investigation.

6.4.7 Death of Vulnerable Adult

AP[363] concerned the death of a young man with Asperger's syndrome at the hands of another man. His grandparents argued that the Article 2 duty to investigate was engaged as there was an arguable case that the local authority and the police had failed to have in place adequate systems for the protection of vulnerable adults such as him and had failed to take reasonable steps to safeguard him against a real and immediate risk to his life. The Administrative Court did not agree, holding in relation to the Council that there was no evidence of systemic failure in the employment and training of staff[364] and that Article 2 did not require the Council to have a specific service for those with Asperger's syndrome.[365] In addition, there was no real and immediate risk to life of

---

[359] *R (Mousa) v Secretary of State for Defence* [2013] EWHC 1412 (Admin) [108]–[125], [213]–[225] and *R (Mousa) v Secretary of State for Defence No 2* [2013] EWHC 2941 (Admin).

[360] *Smith* (n 214).

[361] Ibid, per Lord Phillips at [84].

[362] Ibid, per Lord Hope at [87], [106], and per Lord Rodger at [119].

[363] *AP* (n 87).

[364] Ibid, [70].

[365] Ibid, [70].

which the Council ought to have been aware[366] and it did not owe a duty here as the deceased was not under its effective control: 'A local authority does not, simply by virtue of its community care service obligations, assume responsibility for the safety of those to whom it provides welfare services from criminal offences.'[367]

With respect to the police, it held that it was not the purpose of the general duty under Article 2 to address the specific needs of particular groups:

> Article 2 does not require systems that ensure that every police officer is trained to deal with every psychiatric and psychological condition; nor is it a requirement that there be specific police systems to deal with those suffering specifically from Asperger's Syndrome.[368]

Furthermore, it was concluded that there was no real and immediate risk to the individual's life of which the police ought to have been aware.[369] There was therefore no arguable breach of Article 2 and no obligation to hold an Article 2-compliant investigation into his death. The Administrative Court concluded that even if there was such an obligation, there was no matter outstanding that an inquest would or might address.[370]

---

7. Exceptions

The exceptions expressly set out in Article 2(2) have not yet been the subject of litigation under the HRA. As discussed in preceding paragraphs, in *Re A*,[371] the case of the conjoined twins, as a majority of the Court of Appeal had characterised the operation as an intentional deprivation of life, it was appreciated that it would therefore be necessary for it to be justified under Article 2(2). However, the reasoning was far from satisfactory. Relying on the opinion of the Commission in *Paton*,[372] Ward LJ held that Article 2 was subject to an implied limitation 'which would justify the balancing act we have undertaken'. Brooke LJ did not agree, stating that he would be reluctant to hold that a right as fundamental as the right to life could be subject to an implied limitation which destroyed its value and reached no firm conclusion on the point. Again, as the judgments given were confined to the unique facts of the case, Ward LJ's comments are unlikely to lead to the development of an implied exceptions jurisprudence.

---

[366] Ibid, [83].
[367] Ibid, [89].
[368] Ibid, [74].
[369] Ibid, [81].
[370] Ibid, [98]. See also *R (Kent County Council) v HM Coroner for Kent* [2012] EWHC 2768 (Admin) and *Worcestershire County Council v HM Coroner for Worcestershire* [2013] EWHC 1711 (QB).
[371] *Re A* (n 10).
[372] *Paton v United Kingdom* (1980) 3 EHRR 408.

8

Article 3: Prohibition of Torture and Inhuman or Degrading Treatment or Punishment

1. Introduction

Article 3, which proscribes torture and inhuman or degrading treatment or punishment, is considered to be one of the most fundamental and important of all the Convention rights.[1] It is expressed in absolute terms, permitting of no qualification or excuse, and derogation under Article 15 of the ECHR is not possible in any circumstances.[2] The importance with which Article 3 is regarded is reflected in the fact that deference to the primary decision maker is rarely mentioned by courts considering its application and interpretation. Often the underlying factual material is considered so as to enable the court to conclude for itself whether or not a violation of Article 3 is made out.[3] The courts have even admitted fresh evidence during appeal proceedings where Article 3 is possibly engaged.[4] For example in *Turgut*[5] the Court of Appeal held that the question of an illegal entrant being returned to Turkey to face treatment contrary to Article 3 was not an area in which the court would pay any especial deference to the Secretary

---

[1] See eg the comments of Lord Bingham in *R (Pretty) v Director of Public Prosecutions* [2001] UKHL 61, [2001] 3 WLR 1598 at [10] and [13].

[2] See further N Mavronicola, 'What Is an "absolute right"? Deciphering Absoluteness in the Context of Article 3 of the European Convention on Human Rights' (2012) 12 *Human Rights Law Review* 723.

[3] See eg *R v Secretary of State for the Home Department, ex p Turgut* [2001] 1 All ER 719; *R (on the application of Wilkinson) v The Responsible Medical Officer Broadmoor Hospital* [2001] EWCA Civ 1545, [2001] 1 WLR 419; *R (on the application of T) v Secretary of State for the Home Department* [2003] EWCA Civ 1285, [2003] UKHRR 1321; *R (on the application of B) v Responsible Medical Officer, Broadmoor Hospital* [2005] EWHC (Admin) 1936. But see *R (on the application of N) v M* [2002] EWCA Civ 1789, [2003] 1 WLR 562 and the comments of Carnwath LJ in *R (on the application of Limbuela) v Secretary of State for the Home Department* [2004] EWCA Civ 540, [2004] QB 1440, [129]–[130].

[4] See eg *A v Secretary of State for the Home Department* [2003] EWCA Civ 175, [20]; *Khan v Secretary of State for the Home Department* [2003] EWCA Civ 530. Cf *A v Secretary of State for the Home Department* [2004] EWCA Civ 255.

[5] *Turgut* (n 3).

of State's conclusion on the facts. Similarly, in X,[6] concerning a deportation allegedly in violation of Article 3, the court held that it had a duty to come to a decision itself on the material before it as to whether the proposed course of action by the executive would infringe the appellant's human rights.

Outside of the deportation context, this has also been the approach taken. For example, in T,[7] in considering whether the treatment of an asylum seeker was inhuman or degrading, the Court of Appeal commented that, once the facts were known, the question of whether they brought the applicant actually or imminently within the protection of Article 3 was one which could be answered by the court without deference to the initial decision maker.[8] Courts have also permitted cross-examination in judicial review proceedings so as to enable them to determine factual issues for themselves and it has been held that the duty of disclosure on a defendant to a claim for an infringement of Article 3 is acute.[9]

The majority of Article 3 HRA claims have arisen in the context of proposed deportations by the Home Secretary. This is because under the HRA it is not lawful to expel an individual within this jurisdiction to a destination state where there are strong grounds for believing that the person, if returned, faces a real risk of being subjected to torture or to inhuman or degrading treatment or punishment.[10] Outside of this context, there are no reported cases concerning torture and very few concerning punishment. Most claims have concerned inhuman or degrading treatment and generally the courts do not delineate between the two types of treatment and refer instead to the 'proscribed treatment' encompassing both.[11]

---

2. Severity of Ill-treatment

Whilst it is difficult to define all the human conditions that will engage Article 3,[12] it is clear that the standard of what constitutes inhuman or degrading treatment has been set at a high level. Only serious ill-treatment falls within the scope of the expression 'inhuman or degrading treatment or punishment'.[13] But although ill-treatment must obtain a minimum level of severity, this is an objective test and assessment of the minimum is relative as it all depends on the circumstances of the case.[14] Relevant factors are the nature and context of the treatment, the manner of its execution, its dura-

---

[6] $X v Secretary of State for the Home Department$ [2001] 1 WLR 740.

[7] T (n 3).

[8] Ibid, [19].

[9] R (Al-Sweady) v Secretary of State for Defence [2009] EWHC 2387 (Admin).

[10] $R v Special Adjudicator, ex p Ullah$ [2004] UKHL 26, [2004] 2 AC 323, per Lord Bingham at [24].

[11] See eg $R v Drew$ [2003] UKHL 25, [2003] 1 WLR 1213.

[12] R (on the application of Q) v Secretary of State for the Home Department [2003] EWCA Civ 364, [2004] QB 36, [60].

[13] $Pretty$ (n 1), per Lord Hope at [90]; Secretary of State for the Home Department v Z [2002] EWCA Civ 952.

[14] Ibid, per Lord Hope at [91]. See also the comments of Carnwath LJ in $Limbuela$ (n 3), [89]–[90] and $Grant v Ministry of Justice$ [2011] EWHC 3379 (QB).

tion, and its physical and mental effects, including, where relevant, its impact on the health of the person involved, both positive and negative.[15] In *Pretty v UK*[16] the ECtHR made some observations on the type of treatment which would fall within the scope of Article 3. Whilst not universally adopted by UK courts, many courts have found this to be a useful benchmark.[17] The Court held as follows:

> As regards the types of 'treatment' which fall within the scope of art 3 of the Convention, the court's case law refers to 'ill-treatment' that attains a minimum level of severity and involves actual bodily injury or intense physical or mental suffering. Where treatment humiliates or debases an individual showing lack of respect for, or diminishing, his or her human dignity or arouses feelings of fear, anguish or inferiority capable of breaking an individual's moral and physical resistance, it may be characterised as degrading and also fall within the prohibition of art 3. The suffering which flows from naturally occurring illness, physical or mental, may be covered by art 3, where it is, or risks being, exacerbated by treatment, whether flowing from conditions of detention, expulsion or other measures, for which the authorities can be held responsible.[18]

In *Limbuela*[19] having referred to the ECtHR *Pretty* test, Lord Bingham summarised that treatment was inhuman or degrading if to a seriously detrimental extent, it denied the most basic needs of any human being.[20] It has also been held that, with respect to degrading treatment, it is not enough for a victim to feel that he has suffered a loss of dignity. How he sees himself and how he is seen by others are matters which may be relevant, but they are not determinative.[21] It is relevant, but not requisite, that the purpose of the treatment is to debase or humiliate. What matters more is effect. Emotional distress of itself is not enough, but it is a factor.[22] Each case must be judged in relation to all the circumstances which are relevant to it.[23]

Unless a claimant can show, by direct or inferential evidence, that the ill-treatment in fact caused him or her serious suffering in terms of physical or psychiatric injury, or psychological harm or particularly serious evidenced distress, it will usually be difficult in practice to show that the objective test has been satisfied.[24] He or she may be able to

---

[15] *B* (n 3), [52].

[16] *Pretty v UK* Judgment of 29 April 2002.

[17] See eg *R (on the application of Q) v Secretary of State for the Home Department* [2003] EWCA Civ 364, [2004] QB 36, [62]–[63]; *R (Watts) v Beford Primary Care Trust* [2003] EWHC Admin 2401 [54]; *T* (n 3); *R (Limbuela) v Secretary of State for the Home Department* [2005] UKHL 66, [2006] 1 AC 396.

[18] *Pretty v UK* (n 16), [52].

[19] *Limbuela* (n 17).

[20] Ibid, [7].

[21] *T* (n 3), [12] in reliance upon *East African Asians v UK* (1973) 3 EHRR 76; *Lorsé v Netherlands* (2003) 37 EHRR 3.

[22] *T* (n 3).

[23] Ibid, [16]. The following have been held not to engage Art3: closure of a care home (*R (Haggerty) v St Helens Council* [2003] EWHC (Admin) 803, [2003] ACD 304); eviction of travellers from a site (*R (on the application of Fuller) v Chief Constable of Dorset Police* [2001] EWHC (Admin) 1057, [2003] QB 480); striking off from the Solicitors Roll (*Re a Solicitor No 11 of 2001* [2001] EWCA Civ 153801); the supply of heroin (*R (on the application of M) v Merseyside Police* [2003] EWHC (Admin) 1121); the denial of re-entry to a stateless Palestinian to the West Bank (*SH (Palestinian Territories) v Secretary of State for Home Department* [2008] EWCA Civ 1150, [2009] Imm AR 306); the use of handcuffs on a prisoner attending hospital appointments outside the prison (*R (Faizovas) v Secretary of State for Justice* [2009] EWCA Civ 373, [2009] UKHRR 1093); the denial of a particular drug to treat breast cancer (*R (Rogers) v Swindon NHS Primary Care Trust* [2006] EWHC 171 (Admin)); the withdrawal of tobacco (*R (Foster) v Governor of High Down Prison* [2010] EWHC 2224 (Admin)); shouting as an interrogation technique (*Hussein v Secretary of State for Defence* [2013] EWHC 95 (Admin)).

[24] *Grant* (n 14), [52].

do so if it can be inferred from the nature of the ill-treatment that anguish or distress of a sufficient level was suffered, or the individual 'suffered from a mental condition that meant that he could not fully appreciate his own suffering, or protect himself from it'.[25] It is important to take into account the status of the victim of ill-treatment when determining if the test is satisfied. For example, children have been held to be especially vulnerable and this is a factor in assessing whether the treatment to which they have been subjected reaches the minimum level of severity needed to attract the protection of Article 3:[26]

> The special vulnerability of children is a factor relevant to judging whether treatment to which they are subjected reach the minimum level of severity for Article 3 to apply. Exposing children, who are dependent on adults, to a terrifying experience which affects their emotional or psychological welfare may, depending on the circumstances, constitute a breach for them of Article 3. Separating young children from their parents may be an important consideration.[27]

Finally, in Article 3 claims under the HRA, where a claimant has the burden of proof, the standard is balance of probabilities:

> A finding that a state has contravened Article 3, which guarantees some of the most vital human rights, is of very substantial seriousness. Particularly given the high Article 3 threshold, a court is likely to require cogent evidence before making such a finding.[28]

---

3. Negative and Positive Duties

3.1 Distinguishing Negative from Positive

It is clear that Article 3 imposes both negative and positive duties on public authorities encompassing both acts and failures to act or, in the context of the article, treatments and failures to treat. The negative duty imposed by Article 3 is an absolute duty: '[N]o one shall be subjected to torture or to inhuman or degrading treatment or punishment.' However, the positive Article 3 duty is not absolute. It is therefore particularly important, when Article 3 is raised, to determine whether or not the activities of a public authority constitute treatment or a failure to treat. Although it has also been observed that it is not helpful to analyse obligations arising under Article 3 as negative or positive and the state's conduct as active or passive, 'The real issue in all these cases

---

[25] Ibid.

[26] *In re E (a child)* [2008] UKHL 66, [2009] 1 AC 536, per Baroness Hale at [8].

[27] *R (M) v Secretary of State for the Home Department* [2010] EWHC 3541 (Admin) [1]. In *Re A (A Child)* [2012] UKSC 60, [2012] 3 WLR 1484 the Supreme Court held that disclosure of information about sexual abuse did not meet the threshold of seriousness required by Art 3. However, in *ZH v Commissioner of Police of the Metropolis* [2013] EWCA Civ 69, [2013] 3 All ER 113 the Court of Appeal concluded that police treatment of a severely autistic young man was in violation of Art 3. See further A Lawson, 'Disability, Degradation and Dignity: the Role of Article 3 of the ECHR' (2005) 56 *Northern Ireland Legal Quarterly* 462.

[28] *Grant* (n 14), [78.1].

is whether the state is properly to be regarded as responsible for the harm inflicted (or threatened) upon the victim.'[29]

Distinguishing positive from negative duties is no simple task and caused considerable difficulty in the lower courts in the case of *Limbuela*.[30] The claim concerned the denial of support to asylum seekers who had not claimed asylum as soon as reasonably practicable on arrival in the United Kingdom. The House of Lords agreed with the majority of the Court of Appeal that whilst Article 3 did impose positive duties, the regime imposed on asylum seekers who were denied support engaged the negative duty and constituted treatment within the meaning of Article 3. The challenged legislation prohibited the Secretary of State from providing accommodation or support, but the asylum seeker was also prevented by law from working without permission. Furthermore, they could not lawfully be removed until their claim was determined.

Lord Bingham held that the duty under Article 3 to provide support arose when it appeared on a 'fair and objective assessment of all relevant facts and circumstances' that an individual applicant faced an 'imminent prospect of serious suffering caused or materially aggravated by denial of shelter, food or the most basic necessities of life'.[31] In keeping with Article 3 jurisprudence, he also noted that many factors may affect that judgment including age, gender, mental and physical health, the weather and time of year, and the period for which the applicant has already suffered or is likely to continue to suffer privation.[32]

As the Court of Appeal[33] had pointed out, the problem with characterising the issue as such was that some individuals who apply for asylum may already be in a condition which verges on the degree of severity capable of engaging Article 3. With others, their 'fate will be uncertain—charitable bodies or individuals may come to their assistance'.[34] But the court did not believe it was unlawful for the Secretary of State to decline to provide support unless it was clear that charitable support had not been provided and the individual was incapable of fending for himself—the 'wait and see' approach. Such an approach risked clogging the courts with hundreds of asylum seekers claiming to have fallen into a condition sufficient to engage Article 3. It was also contrary to the rationale behind the ECtHR's development of positive duties under Article 3, to ensure that individuals were not subjected to torture or inhuman or degrading treatment or punishment.[35]

A far simpler way to proceed would have been to adopt a risk test similar to that developed in Article 2 jurisprudence. There was a risk that a majority denied support would fall into conditions which would engage Article 3. The state obviously knowing what was occurring, the next question would be what reasonable or proportionate measures should be taken to avoid the risk. As asylum seekers could not lawfully be returned until their claims had been determined and as they were prohibited from working, it would seem that the reasonable response of the state in such circumstances would be to supply some minimum support until their claims were determined and, if resources were the major concern, speed up the decision-making process. It would also be pos-

---

[29] *Limbuela* (n 17), per Lord Brown at [92].
[30] Ibid.
[31] Ibid, [8]. Lord Hope at [62].
[32] Ibid, [8].
[33] *Limbuela* (n 3).
[34] Ibid, [62].
[35] *A v United Kingdom* (1998) 3 FCR 597, [22].

sible for the court to take into account the length of time before asylum was claimed and resources considerations. This would not open up the floodgates as asylum seekers are in a unique position.[36] Furthermore, Lord Bingham's test of 'imminent prospect of serious suffering' is very close to a positive duty test which does not contain the *Osman* 'reasonable measures' escape clause.

Given the difficulties in determining whether negative or positive duties are engaged, in *Gezer*,[37] Laws LJ, with whom the other members of the Court of Appeal agreed, stated that the utility of this distinction in the context of Article 3 was limited.[38] Repeating his judgment in the Court of Appeal in *Limbuela*,[39] he proposed the metaphor of a spectrum between the worst class of case—state-sponsored violence—and a decision made in the exercise of lawful policy which may expose the individual to a marked degree of suffering:

> The figure of a spectrum seems to imply the existence of a point upon the spectrum which marks the dividing line, in terms of State acts or omissions, between what violates Article 3 and what does not. There is such a point, but it does not, I fear, provide a brightline rule by which the court may readily determine whether any particular set of facts falls on this or that side of the line. The point is at the place between cases where government action is justified notwithstanding the individual's suffering, and cases where it is not. Various factors will determine where this place is to be found. They will include the severity of the threatened suffering, its origin in violence or otherwise, and the nature of the government's reasons or purpose in acting as it does.[40]

Such an approach has the potential to complicate matters unnecessarily and was also expressly disapproved of by Lord Hope in his judgment in *Limbuela* in the House of Lords where he observed that it had no foundation in ECtHR jurisprudence and it was 'hard to find a sound basis for it in the language of article 3'.[41] Exactly the same factors could be taken into account if the far simpler approach employed by the courts in relation to the positive duties under Article 2 were to be utilised. And the eventual conclusion reached would most likely remain the same. Despite earlier confusion, it appears that this is the path now being taken, and the distinction between negative and positive duties has been maintained.[42]

3.2 Positive Duty

3.2.1 When Does the Duty Arise?

The confusion as to whether or not the test for positive duty under Article 3 is the same

---

[36] For example, in *R (on the application of K) v Lambeth London BC* [2003] EWCA Civ 1150 it was held that the state owed no duty to support a foreign national who was in a position to return home.
[37] *Gezer v Secretary of State for the Home Department* [2004] EWCA Civ 1730, [2005] HRLR 7.
[38] Ibid, [28].
[39] *Limbuela* (n 3).
[40] *Gezer* (n 37), [71].
[41] *Limbuela* (n 17), [53]. See also the observations of Baroness Hale at [77].
[42] See further S Palmer, 'A Wrong Turning: Article 3 ECHR and Proportionality' (2006) 65 *Cambridge Law Journal* 438; S Fredman, 'Human Rights Transformed: Positive Duties and Positive Rights' [2006] *Public Law* 498.

as that for Article 2 set out in *Osman* has now been resolved. In *Munjaz*[43] the House of Lords held that it was the *Osman* test which was relevant to a claim of breach of positive duty under Article 3 and that such obligations must not 'impose a disproportionate or impossible burden on the authorities' and 'provide effective protection of vulnerable persons' including 'reasonable steps to prevent ill-treatment of which the authorities had or ought to have had knowledge'.[44] The question that must be asked first is whether there is a significant risk of ill-treatment of the kind that falls within the scope of Article 3.[45]

Further confirmation was provided by the House Lords in its judgment in *Re E*[46] which was a challenge to the policing of an ongoing demonstration by loyalists in Belfast. It was accepted that the positive obligation under Article 3 was similar to the *Osman* test imposed under Article 2 and was not absolute:

> The contracting states could sensibly bind themselves by an absolute and unqualified obligation not to take life and not to inflict inhuman or degrading treatment, matters which they themselves could control. They could not be expected to undertake a similarly absolute obligation to prevent other persons not under their direct control from taking such actions.[47]

It must therefore be shown that the authorities knew or ought to have known at the time of the existence of a real and immediate risk of a breach of Article 3 and that they failed to take measures, within the scope of their powers, which, judged reasonably, might have been expected to avoid that risk.[48]

3.2.2 Knew or Ought to Have Known

Whilst this aspect of the *Osman* test has not yet received detailed judicial consideration in an Article 3 case, it is important to remember that it was held in this case that it must also be shown that the authorities knew or ought to have known, at the time, of the existence of the risk.[49] Where the breach has occurred, and then recurred, over a lengthy period, as happened in *Re E*, this will not be difficult to demonstrate. Using this approach would have made the task of the Court of Appeal in *Gezer*[50] far simpler. Only Carnwath LJ agreed with the finding of the court below that the claimant had not established a particular and specific danger of ill-treatment within Article 3 directed against asylum seekers in the estate of which the public authority ought to have been aware.[51]

3.2.3 Reasonable Measures

When it arises, in contrast to the negative duty, it has been held that the positive

---

[43] *R (Munjaz) v Ashworth Hospital Authority* [2005] UKHL 58, [2006] 2 AC 148.

[44] Ibid, per Lord Hope at [78].

[45] Ibid, per Lord Hope at [80].

[46] *Re E* [2008] UKHL 66, [2009] 1 AC 536.

[47] Ibid, per Lord Carswell at [45].

[48] See also *R (on the application of Bagdanavicius) v Secretary of State for the Home Department* [2003] EWCA Civ 1605, [2004] 1 WLR 1207 upheld on appeal by the House of Lords [2005] UKHL 38, [2005] 2 WLR 1359; and *Gezer* (n 37).

[49] *Osman v UK* (1998) 29 EHRR 245, [116].

[50] *Gezer* (n 37).

[51] Ibid, [52].

obligation is not absolute and unqualified. In *Pretty*[52] Lord Bingham referred to the observations of the ECtHR in *Osman*,[53] where it had been held that a positive obligation to protect life must be interpreted in a way which did not impose an impossible or disproportionate burden on the authorities. He also referred to *Rees*,[54] where the ECtHR held that, in determining whether or not a positive obligation existed, regard had to be had to the fair balance that has to be struck between the general interests of the community and the interests of the individual. Lord Hope agreed that issues of proportionality would arise where a positive obligation was implied.[55] Both Carnwath LJ and Elias J in *Gezer* referred to reasonable steps[56] and reasonable protection.[57] In *Munjaz* Lord Hope expressed this in terms of whether or not the avoidance of the risk would impose a disproportionate burden.[58] It was concluded in this case that the state was not obliged to promulgate a code of conduct wherever there was a risk of Article 3 ill-treatment.

In *Re E* it was held that even though the police had available to them the means of stopping the protest and preventing the infliction of inhuman or degrading treatment, their obligation to use the measures at their disposal was not absolute and was not different in kind to that imposed by Article 2 as '[t]o hold otherwise would place an intolerable burden on the state'.[59] But rather than a test of reasonableness, the House of Lords held that the actions of the police here had to pass the test of proportionality[60] and that weight may be afforded to the primary decision maker in accordance with their knowledge and expertise.[61] The House of Lords held that the circumstances may also require other obligations to be taken into account in determining the proportionality of the actions of the public authority such as the UN Convention on the Rights of the Child and making the best interests of the child a primary consideration.[62] It concluded here that the actions of the police were not incompatible with their positive duty under Article 3.[63]

3.2.4 Application

To date there have been very few claims raising the positive duty on public authorities to prevent breaches of Article 3 from taking place. In *Al Rawi*[64] family members of those imprisoned by US authorities in Guantanamo Bay, UK residents with indefinite leave to remain, argued that the Foreign Secretary was under a duty to take such action as would alleviate their suffering and the Article 3 violations of their detained

---

[52] *Pretty* (n 1).
[53] *Osman* (n 49), [115]–[116].
[54] *Rees v United Kingdom* (1986) 9 EHRR 56, [37].
[55] *Pretty* (n 1), [90] and [93] See also Lord Steyn at [60].
[56] *Gezer* (n 37), [46].
[57] Ibid, [55]. See also the judgment of Carnwath LJ in *Limbuela* (n 3).
[58] *Munjaz* (n 43), [80].
[59] *Re E* (n 46), per Lord Carswell at [48].
[60] Ibid, [54].
[61] Ibid, [58].
[62] Ibid, [60].
[63] See further G Anthony, 'Positive Obligations and Policing in the House of Lords' (2009) *European Human Rights Law Review* 538.
[64] *R (Al Rawi) v Secretary of State for Foreign and Commonwealth Affairs* [2006] EWCA Civ 1279, [2007] 2 WLR 1219.

family members. This would take the form of representations to the United States. The positive duty under Article 3 was not mentioned in the judgment although was clearly relevant. Having reviewed ECtHR case law, the Court of Appeal concluded that the ECHR contained no requirement that a signatory state should take up the 'complaints of any individual within its territory touching the acts of another sovereign State.'[65] In the view of the court, this applied even where the allegations were of torture – a state was empowered but not obliged to intervene with another sovereign to insist on respect for the prohibition of torture.[66]

By contrast in *B*[67] it was held that Article 3 carried with it a positive obligation on the state to provide protection through its legal system against a person suffering Article 3 ill-treatment at the hands of others and that one aspect of this duty was the provision of a legal system for bringing to justice 'those who commit serious acts of violence against others'.[68] In the present case, where the victim had suffered a serious assault, the court concluded that the decision to terminate the prosecution on the eve of the trial was in breach of Article 3 and awarded just satisfaction of £8,000. The court stated as follows:

> Looking at the proceedings as a whole, far from them serving the State's positive obligation to provide protection against serious assaults through the criminal justice system, the nature and manner of their abandonment increased the victim's sense of vulnerability and of being beyond the protection of the law.[69]

In *AP*[70] the Supreme Court held that an anonymity order in control order proceedings should be upheld as there was force in the claimant's submission that if he were revealed to be someone who was formerly subject to a control order and was now subject to deportation proceedings for alleged matters relating to terrorism, 'he would be at real risk not only of racist and other extremist abuse but of physical violence'.[71]

---

4. Illness and Medical Treatment

Article 3 requires respect for physical and human integrity[72] and, in this respect, overlaps to some extent with the protection provided by Article 8 although there may be circumstances where only Article 8 affords protection if the treatment does not attain the level of severity required by Article 3.[73]

---

[65] Ibid, [98].
[66] Ibid, [102].
[67] *R (B) v Director of Public Prosecutions* [2009] EWHC 106 (Admin), [2009] 1 WLR 2072.
[68] Ibid, [65].
[69] Ibid, [70].
[70] *Secretary of State for the Home Department v AP* [2010] UKSC 26, [2010] 1 WLR 1652.
[71] Ibid, [14].
[72] *Pretty* (n 1), per Lord Bingham at [13].
[73] *Watts* (n 17).

4.1 State Responsibility

For Article 3 to be engaged, it is first necessary to show that the treatment, or failure to treat, by a public authority, is the cause of the suffering. Article 3 imposes positive obligations to take measures to ensure that the right is effectively protected[74] and such obligations may be imposed upon the authorities even where the underlying problem is the claimant's physical or mental illness.[75]

It is rare for a public authority to be found to have subjected someone to inhuman or degrading treatment in this area. For example, in *Pretty*[76] the claimant suffered from motor neurone disease, a progressive degenerative illness from which she had no hope of recovery. She faced the prospect of a humiliating and distressing death and wished to bring her life to her end. As she could not take her own life without help, her husband was willing to assist if the Director of Public Prosecutions (DPP) undertook not to prosecute him. The DPP refused to give such an undertaking. Ms Pretty argued that, in denying her the opportunity to bring her life to an end, the DPP was subjecting her to inhuman and degrading treatment. The House of Lords did not agree, holding that it could not plausibly be suggested that the Director or any other agent of the United Kingdom was inflicting the proscribed treatment on Mrs Pretty, 'whose suffering derives from her cruel disease'.[77] However, it did go on to consider the positive duty imposed by Article 3 as discussed below.

In *Altham*[78] it was argued as a defence to a criminal charge that Article 3 should permit the defence of medical necessity where the accused was utilising cannabis for pain relief. The Court of Appeal found that the state had done nothing to exacerbate his condition which arose from unrelated circumstances and it was not properly to be regarded as responsible for the harm inflicted upon him.[79]

4.2 The Right to Die and the Right to Die with Dignity

It is clear that Article 3 is not concerned with an individual's right to live or to choose not to live.[80] In *Pretty*,[81] although it concluded there was no 'treatment' by the DPP within the meaning of Article 3, the House of Lords went on to consider the positive obligation and whether the DPP's failure to give his consent meant that the claimant would go on suffering in a manner which engaged Article 3. Their Lordships were clear that this was not an absolute duty:

> [W]hile states may be absolutely forbidden to inflict the proscribed treatment on individuals
> within their jurisdiction, the steps appropriate or necessary to discharge a positive obligation

---

[74] Ibid, [45].

[75] Ibid, [46] in reliance upon *D v United Kingdom* (1997) 24 EHRR 423; *Bensaid v United Kingdom* (2001) 33 EHRR 205; and *Price v United Kingdom* (2001) 34 EHRR 128.

[76] *Pretty* (n 1).

[77] Ibid, per Lord Bingham at [13]. See also Lord Steyn at [60] and Lord Hope at [92]. The ECtHR also agreed with this conclusion. See *Pretty v UK* (n 16), [53].

[78] *R v Altham* [2006] EWCA Crim 7, [2006] 1 WLR 3287.

[79] Ibid, [27]

[80] *Pretty* (n 1), per Lord Bingham at [13] and per Lord Steyn at [60].

[81] Ibid.

will be more judgmental, more prone to variation from state to state, more dependent on the opinions and beliefs of the people and less susceptible to any universal jurisdiction.[82]

The House of Lords concluded that there was no positive obligation to ensure that a competent terminally ill person who wished but was unable to take his or her own life should be entitled to seek the assistance of another without that other being exposed to the risk of prosecution.[83] Lord Hope held as follows:

> [T]he object which s 2(1) was designed to achieve struck the right balance between the interests of the individual and the public interest which seeks to protect the weak and vulnerable ... although the effect of the Director's decision that he had no power to give the undertaking is likely to expose Mrs Pretty to acute distress as she succumbs to her illness, his act cannot be said to be unfair or arbitrary or to have impaired her Convention right more than is reasonably necessary.[84]

In *Pretty v UK* the ECtHR agreed, holding that Article 3 must be construed in harmony with Article 2, which was 'first and foremost a prohibition on the use of lethal force or other conduct which might lead to the death of a human being'. In the view of the ECtHR, Article 2 did not confer any claim on an individual to require a state to permit or facilitate his or her death.[85] However, whilst it does not extend to a right to die, it has been held that Article 3 does protect the right to die with dignity.[86] Article 2 does not entitle anyone to continue with life-prolonging treatment where to do so would expose the patient to inhuman or degrading treatment.[87]

4.3 Medical Treatment

Forcible medical treatment inflicted upon an incapacitated patient which is not a medical necessity may be inhuman or degrading. The same applies to forcible measures inflicted upon a capacitated patient.[88] However, it has been held that, as a general rule, treatment administered to a detained patient will not amount to a violation of Article 3 if the therapeutic or medical necessity for it has been convincingly shown.[89] The court itself must determine whether such necessity has been shown to the appropriate standard.[90] This cannot be expressed in terms of a standard of evidential proof but is a value judgment 'as to the future ... to be made by a court in reliance on medical evidence according to a standard of persuasion'.[91] The capacity of a patient is a relevant factor but is not determinative.[92] When considering the severity of the treatment, the

---

[82] Ibid, per Lord Bingham at [15].
[83] Ibid. See also [27]–[28].
[84] Ibid, [97]. See also Lord Steyn at [60] and the judgment of the ECtHR in *Pretty v UK* (n 16), [54]–[56].
[85] *Pretty v UK*, ibid, [54].
[86] *A National Health Service Trust v D* [2000] 2 FLR 677.
[87] *R (on the application of Burke) v The General Medical Council* [2005] EWCA Civ 1003, [39].
[88] *Wilkinson* (n 3), per Hale LJ at [79] in reliance upon *Herczegfalvy v Austria* (1992) 15 EHRR 437. See also *R (Wooder) v Feggetter* [2002] EWCA Civ 554, [2002] 3 WLR 591 in relation to the duty to give reasons in such circumstances.
[89] *B* (n 3), [55] in reliance upon *Herczegfalvy v Austria* (1993) 15 EHRR 432. See also *R (JB) v Haddock* [2006] EWCA Civ 961, [2006] HRLR 40.
[90] Ibid, [67].
[91] Ibid, [42].
[92] Ibid, [63].

fact that it was imposed by compulsion is more significant than the question of whether the patient had or had not capacity to consent to the treatment.[93] Classification of the particular form of mental disorder from which the appellant was suffering is irrelevant to the decision of whether the proposed treatment was necessary.[94]

A court reviewing a decision to treat a detained mentally ill patient without consent pursuant to section 58(3)(b) of the Mental Health Act 1983 must decide the matter for itself on the merits after a full consideration of the evidence.[95] As the court has no particular medical expertise, it is proper for the court to place particular weight on the evidence of the Responsible Medical Officer and Second Opinion Appointed Doctor.[96] Courts are careful to give consideration to the procedure to ensure that legal proceedings are not protracted and expensive requiring oral evidence from medical witnesses when there is no prima facie case.[97]

In *NHS Trust A v Mrs M*[98] it was held in relation to PVS patients that the continuation of futile treatment or the withdrawal of such treatment did not engage Article 3, which required the victim to be aware of the inhuman and degrading treatment which he or she was experiencing or at least to be in a state of physical or mental suffering. It was observed that an insensate patient suffering from PVS 'has no feelings and no comprehension of the treatment accorded to him or her'.[99]

In relation to other aspects of medical treatment, it has been held that hospital waiting times may give rise to an Article 3 claim. In *Watts*[100] the claimant, who needed urgent hip replacements and was unwilling to wait, had the operation in France, then sought to recover her costs from her NHS Trust. The Administrative Court confirmed that Article 3 imposed positive obligations to take measures to ensure that the right was effectively protected[101] and that such obligations may be thrown upon the authorities even where the underlying problem was the claimant's physical or mental illness.[102] However, no breach of the article was found here. First, the court was not satisfied that the ill-treatment had attained a minimum level of severity and involved actual bodily injury or intense physical or mental suffering. Even making every allowance for the constant pain and suffering that she was having to endure, it was not so 'severe or so humiliating as to engage Article 3.'[103] Secondly, given that the positive duty was not absolute, the court held that Article 3 was not designed for the circumstances of this sort where the challenge was to a health authority's allocation of finite funds between competing demands.[104]

[93] *R (B) v SS (Responsible Medical Officer)* [2006] EWCA Civ 28, [2006] 1 WLR 810, [50].
[94] Ibid, [53].
[95] *JB* (n 89), [13].
[96] Ibid, [68].
[97] *B* (n 93), [67].
[98] *NHS Trust A v Mrs M* [2001] 2 WLR 942.
[99] Ibid, [49].
[100] *Watts* (n 17).
[101] Ibid, [45].
[102] Ibid, [46] in reliance upon *D*, *Bensaid* and *Price* (n 75).
[103] Ibid, [54].
[104] Ibid, [50]–[53] in reliance upon *R v North West Lancashire Health Authority, ex p A* [2000] 1 WLR 977, 996A; *Matthews v Ministry of Defence* [2003] UKHL 4, [2003] 1 AC 1163 per Lord Hoffmann at [26].

5. Conditions of Detention

5.1 Conditions of Detention Generally

The conditions of detention in prisons, secure hospitals and other places of detention can undoubtedly engage Article 3. When considering whether the minimum level of severity is met by particular detention conditions, focus must be upon the conditions as a whole and their effect as a whole. This includes the intention or object of the treatment; the fact that the victim was in state detention; and the degree of suffering or humiliation caused to the victim by the treatment.[105] It has been held that where treatment or conditions in prison generated more humiliation, distress or other suffering than was inherent in a prison sentence, it was necessary for the claimant to show that in all of the circumstances, 'the treatment or conditions satisfy the minimum severity test'. Even if treatment would not be humiliating if endured outside prison, 'it may well be found to be humiliating and degrading if suffered in a prison context'.[106]

Many conditions of detention have been the subject of challenge under the HRA but often it is difficult for detainees to demonstrate that the treatment meets the Article 3 threshold. For example, *Mackenzie*[107] concerned the inspection of Category A prisoners during the course of the night at regular intervals to make sure that they were still in their cells and there had been no attempt at any escape. The Court held that this fell far below the threshold of Article 3 ill-treatment. Other aspects of detention are considered below.

5.2 Vulnerable Detainees

More is required of the authorities where vulnerable people have been deprived of their liberty.[108] This is particularly the case where the detainees are children. Convention jurisprudence requires Article 3, as it relates to children, to be interpreted in the light of international conventions, in particular the Convention on the Rights of the Child.[109] Distinctions have also been made between types of vulnerable people such as prisoners and compulsory psychiatric patients. The imprisonment of criminal offenders is an end in itself and it has been held that the necessary ingredients of imprisonment, provided that they meet the standards considered acceptable at the time, are unlikely to amount to inhuman or degrading treatment or punishment under Article 3. However, the detention of psychiatric patients is a means to an end, namely the assessment and treatment

---

[105] *Grant* (n 14), [39].
[106] Ibid, [46].
[107] *R (Mackenzie) v Governor of Wakefield Prison* [2006] EWHC 1746 (Admin).
[108] *R (on the application of R) v Shetty (Responsible Medical Officer)* [2003] EWHC (Admin) 3022, [23]. See also *R (C) v Secretary of State for Justice* [2008] EWCA Civ 882, [2009] QB 657.
[109] *C*, ibid, [60]

of their mental disorder. If the conditions of detention defeat rather than promote that end, these are more like to be amount to inhuman or degrading treatment.[110]

Detention of those who suffer from mental illness raises serious questions. The increase in suffering can reach the requisite level of severity and it is not necessary that the authorities had any intention to inflict suffering.[111] Where the detainee is severely mentally ill, he or she must be subject to effective monitoring and suitable expert advice as to how the detainee should be dealt with must be obtained.[112] In *S* the Administrative Court found a violation of Article 3, both the positive and negative duties, in the immigration detention of a mentally ill person:

> S was subjected to inhuman or degrading treatment both in the fact of his detention which was contrary to the undisputed psychiatric and medical advice and the continuation of his detention as his mental condition deteriorated rapidly without the effective addressing of the causes of his condition, notwithstanding the clearest warnings.[113]

5.3 Detention for Treatment of a Mental Disorder

The distinction between regular prison and detention where treatment for a mental disorder was received was made clear in *Shetty*.[114] Here the claimant argued that transfer back to prison from the psychiatric clinic where he was receiving treatment would violate Article 3. The Responsible Medical Officer of the clinic had concluded that the claimant no longer required treatment for mental disorder. The Administrative Court considered whether it was more likely than not that if the claimant was remitted to prison he would suffer treatment so damaging to him as to amount to inhuman and degrading treatment. It held that the claimant had to demonstrate that, following a transfer back to prison, he would relapse; that the treatment provided in response would be inadequate; and that as a consequence severe suffering would occur such that there would be a violation of Article 3.[115] The claimant failed to establish this to the satisfaction of the court, which held that it was open to the Home Secretary to conclude that remittal to prison would not violate Article 3.[116]

5.4 Prisoners with Medical Conditions

A prisoner may have a medical condition which requires treatment and it has been held that medical services in prison must seek to detect and treat physical or mental illnesses or defects from which prisoners suffer.[117] This also applies to those held in immigration

---

[110] See *Drew* (n 11).
[111] *R (S) v Secretary of State for the Home Department* [2011] EWHC 2120 (Admin), [198]–[199].
[112] Ibid, [202].
[113] Ibid, [211]. See also *R (EH) v Secretary of State for the Home Department* [2012] EWHC 2569 (Admin) and *R (D) v Secretary of State for the Home Department* [2012] EWHC 2501 (Admin).
[114] *Shetty* (n 108).
[115] Ibid, [87].
[116] Ibid, [77].
[117] *R v Qazi* [2010] EWCA Crim 2579, [2011] HRLR 4 [23].

detention.[118] In *Spinks*[119] the claimant, serving a life sentence for murder, had been diagnosed as suffering from terminal cancer of the colon with no prospect of recovery and a short life expectancy. His Article 3 complaint concerned a number of difficulties including: attending appointments at the hospital; handcuffing during treatment; the availability of colostomy bags; and problems with day attendance at a hospice. The relief sought was to quash the decision of the Secretary of State that he should not be released from prison on compassionate grounds. The Court of Appeal concluded that a breach of Article 3 had not been made out. It found that, for the moment, the claimant was fit and mobile, that there had been no recommendation that he should be treated full-time in a specialist clinic or removed to hospital and that there was no evidence of significant psychological harm.[120] With respect to the handcuffing, it found that this also did not constitute a violation of Article 3, and there had been a risk assessment carried out indicating a continuing significant degree of risk although the observation was made that such rigorous security may not be necessary in hospital.[121]

5.5 Handcuffing Outside of Prison

Particular aspects of prison conditions can also raise issues under Article 3 although it is often difficult for a claimant to establish that the ill-treatment is sufficiently serious. For example, in *Faizovas*[122] the claimant prisoner argued that it was contrary to Article 3 for him to be handcuffed whilst attending hospital appointments outside of the prison. There was no physical suffering but there was a sense of humiliation. The Court of Appeal confirmed that the wearing of handcuffs by a prisoner when he was outside the prison, when there was reason to believe that he would abscond or cause injury to others, did not in general amount to degrading treatment.[123] However, in light of the judgment of the ECtHR in *Uyan v Turkey*,[124] it held that it was also necessary to give separate consideration to the necessity for particular measures at the treatment stage. This required an assessment of the proportionality of the type of security measures in the light of the particular type of treatment.[125] In the opinion of the Court of Appeal, it was not the case that handcuffs could never be used during treatment.[126] In the present case, no violation of Article 3 was found as no evidence suggested that the nature of the treatment he had to undergo made the use of handcuffs an inappropriate security measure.[127]

---

[118] *R (MD (Angola)) v Secretary of State for the Home Department* [2011] EWCA Civ 1238.
[119] *R (on the application of Spinks) v Secretary of State for the Home Department* [2005] EWCA Civ 275.
[120] Ibid, [42] in reliance upon *Mouisel v France* (2004) 38 EHRR 34.
[121] Ibid, [47]. See also *FGP v Serco plc* [2012] EWHC 1804 (Admin) and *R (Hall) v University College Hospitals NHS Foundation Trust* [2013] EWHC 198 (Admin).
[122] *R (Faizovas) v Secretary of State for Justice* [2009] EWCA Civ 373, [2009] UKHRR 1093.
[123] Ibid, [3]
[124] *Uyan v Turkey* Application No 7496/03, 8 January 2009.
[125] *Faizovas* (n 122), [22].
[126] Ibid, [24].
[127] Ibid, [29].

5.6 Physical Restraint in Detention

New rules imposing new permissible uses of physical restraint in secure training centres were the subject of challenge in C^{128} where the Court of Appeal held that any system that involved physical intervention against another's will was degrading and an infringement of human dignity and that this was a fortiori the case when the person against whom that conduct was directed was a child who was in the custody of the state.[129] It concluded that the Code of Practice concerning physical restraint in the present case did not ensure no breach of Article 3 for a variety of reasons. These included the open-ended terms which left discretion in the hands of officers on the ground; the absence of a policy on what forms of physical restraint may be used in what circumstances and on what trainees; the history of secure training centres' disobedience of legal and contractual requirements; a report into one centre suggesting inappropriate and unauthorised behaviour on the part of staff; the fact that copies of the training manual were not available to staff; and the criticism by the Joint Committee on Human Rights of staff training. It concluded that the rules gave rise to a significant risk of Article 3 ill-treatment and the Rules were quashed on this ground.[130]

5.7 Seclusion and Segregation

Seclusion, or the removal from association with other prisoners for security, disciplinary or protective reasons, does not of itself amount to inhuman or degrading treatment or punishment. Regard must be had to the particular conditions, the stringency of the measure, its duration, the objective pursued and its effects on the person concerned.[131] In *Munjaz* the House of Lords agreed that seclusion gave rise to risks which were both physical and psychological. Therefore, regular medical reviews were necessary to ensure that the person's mental and physical health did not deteriorate. However, the positive duty to protect from the ill-effects of seclusion did not go so far as require the state to promulgate a code of practice so as to avert the risks.[132]

5.8 Slopping Out

There are still some prison facilities in the United Kingdom which do not have in-cell sanitation. A prisoner locked in his cell who needs the toilet may be unable to obtain prompt release to use the communal facilities and will have to use the bucket in his cell which he must later empty and clean – slopping out. This practice was the subject of challenge in *Grant*[133] where the Divisional Court concluded that in assessing whether

---

[128] *C* (n 108).

[129] Ibid, [64].

[130] In *R (Z) v Secretary of State for the Home Department* [2013] EWHC 498 (Admin) the Administrative Court held that the framework in place for the control and restraint of unlawful immigrants undergoing enforced removal from the UK by aircraft was compatible with Art 3.

[131] *Munjaz* (n 43), per Lord Hope at [79] in reliance upon *Van der Ven v The Netherlands* (50901/99) 4 February 2003. See also *R (AN) v Secretary of State for Justice* [2009] EWHC 1921 (Admin).

[132] See also *Hassan v Secretary of State for Justice* [2011] EWHC 1359 (Admin).

[133] *Grant* (n 14).

there had been a violation of Article 3, a court was required to consider all of the circumstances of the complainant's detention, including the circumstance of his use of the bucket.[134] It found that a requirement for a prisoner to urinate or defecate into a bucket was not, necessarily and of itself, degrading and a violation of Article 3.[135] Taking into account all the circumstances of the case, no violation of Article 3 was found here: 'The sanitation regime is not perfect, but it cannot be said that the Defendant has taken any step intended to lower the dignity of any prisoner.'[136]

---

6. Violence and Threatening Behaviour

Violence and serious racial abuse engage Article 3.[137] It is beyond doubt that public authorities must not engage in either. There is also a positive duty on the state, in certain circumstances, to protect individuals from such behaviour perpetrated by other private individuals. In *Gezer*, the claimant asylum seekers—Turkish nationals of Kurdish origin—had been provided with accommodation in the Toryglen council estate in Glasgow. Within days they were subjected to racial abuse and hostility, and their home was attacked by three men, one of whom tried to stab the youngest son. They were eventually returned to London.

Before the Court of Appeal there was no challenge to the finding in the court below that such behaviour undoubtedly engaged Article 3.[138] The question was whether or not the National Asylum Support Service (NASS), as the agency which conducted the dispersal, could be held responsible. Laws LJ employed his spectrum metaphor, first referred to in his judgment in *Limbuela*,[139] intended to demonstrate a sliding scale of instances in which Article 3 might be engaged, from those where the state enjoyed no power of discretion to those 'where the State might enjoy a considerable margin of discretion as to the adoption and exercise of policy'.[140] He concluded that in the present case the key question was what duty of enquiry was owed by NASS to obtain information as to the conditions prevailing on the estate before offering accommodation there.[141] Finding that it was open to the claimants to refuse the accommodation, he located the case at the lower end of the spectrum and NASS was not required to make special enquiries to save the claimant from harm.[142]

Carnwath LJ and Elias J reached the same conclusion via a far simpler process of reasoning. Carnwath LJ, whilst agreeing with Laws LJ, found that NASS did not know, nor ought to have known, about the risk to the claimants and that the steps taken, in

---

[134] Ibid, [67].
[135] Ibid, [68].
[136] Ibid, [223].
[137] *Gezer* (n 37).
[138] Ibid, per Laws LJ at [26].
[139] *Limbuela* (n 3).
[140] *Gezer* (n 37), [33].
[141] Ibid, [34].
[142] Ibid, [41].

light of the knowledge it had, were reasonable.[143] Elias J also agreed, but applied a real risk test.[144]

Violence and threatening and intimidating behaviour was also under consideration in *Re E*[145] which concerned a challenge on Article 3 grounds to the policing of a two-month demonstration by loyalists in Belfast which impacted on Catholic children being taken to school along the Ardoyne Road. Actions of the protesters included throwing missiles, making death threats and shouting sectarian verbal abuse, racist abuse and obscenities of a sexual nature. Applying the *Osman* test to the facts, the House of Lords concluded that the actions of the police were compatible with Article 3. It was not in dispute that the police had more than sufficient knowledge of the treatment to trigger their obligation to take preventative action. In determining whether the actions of the police passed the test of reasonableness, the House of Lords applied a test of proportionality, taking into account the knowledge and expertise of the police and the primary consideration of the best interests of the child as required by the UN Convention on the Rights of the Child. It was concluded that their actions were proportionate and therefore compatible with their positive duty under Article 3:

> The police had such responsibility and were uniquely placed through their experience and intelligence to make a judgment on the wisest course to take in all the circumstances. They had long and hard experience of the problems encountered in dealing with riotous situations in urban areas in Northern Ireland. ...The police had available to them sources of information about what was happening in the community and what was likely to happen if they took certain courses of action, which they were experienced in assessing.[146]

---

7. Sentencing

The question of inhuman or degrading punishment has arisen in relation to sentencing, specifically the automatic life sentence and the mandatory life sentence. For punishment to be inhuman or degrading, it has to attain a minimum level of severity.[147] However, punishment which is arbitrary or disproportionate can be regarded as inhuman.[148] It has been held that when assessing whether a sentence is disproportionate, factors other than simply the length of the sentence are important. These include 'the nature of the offence, the rationale for the sentencing framework, as well as the specific way in which the offence was committed, and the personal circumstances of the offender'.[149]

---

[143] Ibid, [52].

[144] Ibid, [55]. See also *R (F) v Secretary of State for Justice* [2012] EWHC 2689 (Admin) where it was held that the state was responsible for protecting one prison inmate from another.

[145] *Re E* (n 46).

[146] Ibid, [58].

[147] *R v Lichniak* [2002] UKHL 47, [2003] 1 AC 903, per Lord Hutton at [25] in reliance upon *Costello-Roberts v United Kingdom* (1993) 19 EHRR 112.

[148] Ibid, per Lord Hutton at [25] in reliance upon *Weeks v United Kingdom* (1987) 10 EHRR 293. See generally D van Zyl Smit and A Ashworth, 'Disproportionate Sentences as Human Rights Violations' (2004) 67 *Modern Law Review* 541.

[149] *R (Willcox) v Secretary of State for Justice* [2009] EWHC 1483 (Admin), [60].

However, if the sentence has been imposed by a state other than the UK, and the prisoner has been transferred back to the UK to serve the time in prison pursuant to treaty arrangements, it has been held that even if it is a disproportionate sentence, this does not breach Article 3. The fact of consensual transfer for humane purposes has been found to mean that it cannot constitute cruel, inhuman, or degrading treatment.[150]

7.1 Taking into Account Ill-health

When sentencing a prisoner with health issues, a court is entitled to take into account the fact that there are arrangements to ensure that prisoners with severe medical conditions in public prisons are treated in accordance with their Convention rights.[151] On this basis, a sentencing court need not be concerned in the allocation of a prisoner to a specific prison in the discharge of its duties under Article 3:

> [P]rovided that the arrangements … for the provision of health care under the overall responsibility of the Secretaries of State are maintained and work in practice, a sentencing court does not need to enquire into the facilities in prison for the treatment of a medical condition. The court can be satisfied that there is a proper system for allocation to a prison where health care can be provided … and that a sentence of imprisonment will not create a risk of a breach of Article 3.[152]

However, if the very fact of imprisonment itself might expose the individual to a real risk of an Article 3 breach, the court must enquire into whether sentencing a person to custody will mean a breach of Article 3. Such a claim must be supported by medical evidence.[153] Once a sentence of imprisonment has been imposed, the relevance of the medical condition relates solely to the assessment of the overall length of the sentence.[154]

7.2 Automatic Life Sentence

The automatic life sentence is imposed for a second serious offence where there are no exceptional circumstances.[155] In *Offen*[156] the Court of Appeal concluded that it was possible in some circumstances for the imposition of an automatic life sentence to be arbitrary and disproportionate. It gave the example of an unjustified push that

> can result in someone falling, hitting his head and suffering fatal injuries. The offence is manslaughter. The offender may have committed another serious offence when a young man. A life sentence in such circumstances may well be arbitrary and disproportionate and contravene art 5. It could also be a punishment which contravenes art 3.[157]

Using section 3 of the HRA, the court concluded that there would be no contravention

---

[150] Ibid, [71].
[151] *R v Qazi* [2010] EWCA Crim 2579, [2011] HRLR 4, [35].
[152] Ibid.
[153] Ibid.
[154] Ibid. See also *B v Secretary of State* [2011] EWCA Civ 828 and *R v Hall* [2013] EWCA Crim 82
[155] See s 109 Powers of Criminal Courts (Sentencing) Act 2000.
[156] *R v Offen* [2001] 1 WLR 253.
[157] Ibid, [95].

if the section was applied so that it did not result in offenders being sentenced to life imprisonment when they did not constitute a significant risk to the public.[158]

7.3 Mandatory Life Sentence

In *Lichniak*[159] it was argued that imposition of the mandatory life sentence[160] was incompatible with Article 3 because it required the same life sentence to be passed on all convicted murderers, whatever the facts of the case or the circumstances of the offender, and irrespective of whether they were thought to present a danger to the public or not. Relying on the judgment of the ECtHR in *V v United Kingdom*,[161] the House of Lords held that an indeterminate sentence, in its operation in practice, did not constitute an arbitrary or disproportionate punishment. In particular, their Lordships held that it was not arbitrary to postpone to the end of the tariff period the decision whether a person who has committed a murder would be a danger to the public if released, rather than decide this at the time of the trial. Whilst it was appreciated that this would cause uncertainty, it was not considered that such uncertainty could constitute treatment of such severity as to come within the ambit of inhuman punishment forbidden by Article 3 or can make the sentence of life imprisonment an arbitrary one.[162]

It also concluded that the fact that the imposition of a life sentence made the prisoner released on licence liable to recall to prison for the remainder of his life did not fall foul of Article 3.[163]

7.4 Whole Life Tariff

The imposition of a sentence of life imprisonment does not involve a violation of Article 3 if the sentence if reducible. However, an irreducible life sentence raises an issue under Article 3 in circumstances where it may result in an offender being detained beyond the term that is justified by the legitimate objects of imprisonment. The essential requirement is the possibility of a review that determines whether imprisonment remains justified.[164] In *Bieber* the Court of Appeal held that the legitimate objects of imprisonment were punishment, deterrence, rehabilitation and protection of the public. If a prisoner had served a sufficient term to meet the requirements of punishment, deterrence and rehabilitation but is to remain imprisoned for the rest of his life, the court

---

[158] Ibid, [97]. See also *R v Kelly* [2001] EWCA Crim 1030, [2002] 1 Cr Ap 11; *Drew* (n 11).

[159] *Lichniak* (n 147).

[160] Section 1(1) Murder (Abolition of Death Penalty) Act 1965.

[161] *V v United Kingdom* (1999) 30 EHRR 121.

[162] Ibid, per Lord Hutton at [35]. Lord Bingham reached a similar conclusion but also held that, if it had been the case that on imposition of a mandatory life sentence the convicted murderer forfeited his liberty to the state for the rest of his days, to remain in custody until (if ever) the Home Secretary concluded that the public interest would be better served by his release than by his continued detention, this would violate Art 3. See [8].

[163] Ibid, per Lord Hutton at [37] in reliance upon *V* (n 161). See also *R v Parchment* [2003] EWCA Crim 2428.

[164] *R v Bieber* [2008] EWCA Crim 1601, [2009] 1 WLR 223, [39] in reliance upon *Kafkaris v Cyprus*, Application No 21906/04, 12 February 2008.

held that it was at least arguable that was this inhuman treatment and an issue would arise in relation to Article 3.[165]

However, in the opinion of the Court of Appeal the imposition of an irreducible life sentence, (the imposition of a whole life term) did not itself constitute a violation of Article 3: 'Where a whole life term is specified this is because the judge considers that the offence is so serious that, for purposes of punishment and deterrence, the offender must remain in prison for the rest of his days.'[166]

The potential violation only occurs once the offender has been detained beyond the period that could be justified on the ground of punishment and deterrence.[167] Importantly, the Court of Appeal also observed that the whole life term imposed in the UK was not actually a sentence that was irreducible. The Secretary of State retains a limited power to release a life prisoner under section 30 of the Crimes (Sentences) Act 1997.[168] It therefore concluded that any Article 3 challenge where a whole life term has been imposed should be made not at the time of the imposition of the sentence but at the stage when the prisoner claimed that having regard to all the material circumstances, including the time that he has served and the progress made in prison, any further detention would constitute degrading or inhuman treatment.[169]

Irreducible life sentences have only been considered by the House of Lords in an extradition context. In *Wellington*[170] the House of Lords considered whether or not a sentence of life imprisonment, without eligibility for parole, was inhuman or degrading punishment. The appellant was wanted for two murders alleged to have been carried out in the state of Missouri and it was claimed that his extradition was incompatible with Article 3 as this was the penalty he would face if convicted. Drawing parallels with UK law, Lord Hoffmann held *obiter* that the imposition of a whole life sentence in the UK would not ipso facto infringe Article 3 given the existence of the Home Secretary's power of release.[171] However, it was also held that there may come a point where continued detention did infringe Article 3, but this was a question which had to be adjudicated upon when it arose. [172]

---

[165] Ibid, [40].
[166] Ibid, [45].
[167] Ibid, [43].
[168] Ibid, [49].
[169] Ibid, [49]. The conclusions in *Bieber* were approved of by the House of Lords in *R (Wellington) v Secretary of State for the Home Department* [2008] UKHL 72, [2009] 1 AC 335. See also *R v Bamber* [2009] EWCA Crime 962, [2010] 1 Prison LR 297 and *R v Oakes* [2012] EWCA Crim 2435. In *Vinter v United Kingdom* 34 BHRC 605 the ECtHR held that there had to be a review no later than 25 years after the imposition of a life sentence and further periodic reviews thereafter.
[170] *Wellington*, ibid.
[171] Ibid, per Lord Hoffmann at [19].
[172] See further S Kandelia, 'Life Meaning Life: Is there Any Hope of Release for Prisoners Serving Whole Life Orders?' (2011) 75 *Journal of Criminal Law* 70.

8. Criminal Law

The positive duty under Article 3 on the state to take action to prevent the subjection of individuals to the proscribed treatment impacts on the criminal law. However, the only aspect of the criminal law to come under scrutiny to date on this ground has been the defence of reasonable chastisement available to parents in relation to children. In *R v H*[173] a father who beat his son with a leather belt pleaded not guilty to the offence of actual bodily harm, his defence being that he was exercising his right as a parent to chastise his son who was not obeying a request to write his own name. Although the offence occurred before the HRA came into force, the Court of Appeal held it was appropriate for the trial judge to balance the rights of the child under Article 3 with the rights of a defendant under Articles 6 and 7. It held that the jury should be directed in detailed terms as to the factors relevant to whether the chastisement was reasonable and moderate.

> [T]hey must consider the nature and context of the defendant's behaviour, its duration, its physical and mental consequences in relation to the child, the age and personal characteristics of the child and the reasons given by the defendant for administering punishment.[174]

It concluded that it was a proper incremental development of the common law for such a direction to be given.[175]

9. State Support

In addition to the protection provided by Article 8, Article 3 can also have some impact on the provision, or non-provision, of state support. However, the case law in this area is far from clear. The failure to provide support may constitute a breach of the negative duty under Article 3 or the positive duty. In *Limbuela* the House of Lords found that the regime imposed on asylum seekers who were denied support engaged the negative duty and constituted treatment within the meaning of Article 3. The problems inherent in this approach have already been discussed. However, it is clear that the court's finding does not mean that the state is never under a positive obligation to provide support insofar as it is necessary to prevent persons reaching that condition of degradation which would infringe Article 3. It has been held that:

> [T]here is a stage at which the dictates of humanity require the State to intervene to prevent

---

[173] *R v H* [2001] EWCA Crim 1024, [2001] 2 FLR 431.
[174] Ibid, [31].
[175] Ibid, [35]. See further RKM Smith, 'Hands-off Parenting—Towards a Reform of the Defence of Reasonable Chastisement in the UK' (2004) 16 *Child and Family Law Quarterly* 261.

any person within its territory suffering dire consequences as a result of deprivation of suste-
nance. If support is necessary to prevent a person in this country reaching the point of Art 3
degradation, then that support should be provided.[176]

However, there has not yet been a reported case concerning the positive duty under
Article 3 and state support and given the observations of Lord Hope and Lord Scott
in *Limbuela*, such jurisprudence may be unlikely to develop. Lord Scott observed that
it was not the function of Article 3 to prescribe a minimum standard of social support
for those in need:

> That is a matter for the social legislation of each signatory state. If individuals find them-
> selves destitute to a degree apt to be described as degrading, the state's failure to give them
> the minimum support necessary to avoid that degradation may well be a shameful reproach
> to the humanity of the state and its institutions but ... does not without more engage article
> 3. Just as there is no ECHR right to be provided by the state with a home, so too there is no
> ECHR right to be provided by the state with a minimum standard of living.[177]

The judgment of the House of Lords in *Limbuela* provides an indication of how dire an
individual's circumstances must be before the duty under Article 3 to support them is
engaged. Lord Bingham held that the duty under Article 3 will arise when it appears on
a fair and objective assessment of all relevant facts and circumstances that an individual
faces 'an imminent prospect of serious suffering caused or materially aggravated by
denial of shelter, food or the most basic necessities of life'.[178] Many factors affect this
judgment, including:

> age, gender, mental and physical health and condition, any facilities or sources of support
> available to the applicant, the weather and time of year and the period for which the applicant
> has already suffered or is likely to continue to suffer privation.[179]

Whilst it was not possible to formulate a simple test applicable in all cases, Lord
Bingham held that if there were evidence that a person was obliged to sleep in the
street, save perhaps for a short and foreseeably finite period, or was seriously hungry,
or unable to satisfy the most basic requirements of hygiene, the threshold would be
crossed.[180] In the present case, the House of Lords agreed that each of the asylum
seeker claimants had crossed the threshold. The duty to provide support has also been
considered in a deportation context where it has been argued that deportation to a safe
EU country is incompatible with Article 3 due to the treatment of asylum seekers in
that state. In *S*[181] the Administrative Court held that *Limbuela* established that street
homelessness could meet the Article 3 threshold, but the risk of such ill-treatment must
be the responsibility of the state.[182]

---

[176] *Anufrijeva v Southwark LBC* [2003] EWCA Civ 1406, [2004] QB 1124, [35]. Cf *R (EW) v Secretary of State for the Home Department* [2009] EWHC 2957 (Admin).

[177] *Limbuela* (n 17), [66].

[178] Ibid, [8].

[179] Ibid, [8].

[180] Ibid, [9]. See also Lord Hope's observations at [59].

[181] *R (S) v Secretary of State for the Home Department* [2010] EWHC 705 (Admin)

[182] Ibid, [24]. See further J Kenny, 'European Convention on Human Rights and Social Welfare' [2010] *European Human Rights Law Review* 495.

10. Deportation and Extradition

10.1 The Nature of the Duty

10.1.1 Real Risk Test

Where there are strong grounds for believing that a person, if extradited or expelled, faces a real risk of being subjected to torture or to inhuman or degrading treatment or punishment in the destination state, it is unlawful to remove that person from the United Kingdom.[183] In *Soering v United Kingdom*,[184] which concerned extradition, the ECtHR explained the responsibility as follows:

> In sum, the decision by a Contracting State to extradite a fugitive may give rise to an issue under Article 3, and hence engage the responsibility of that State under the Convention, where substantial grounds have been shown for believing that the person concerned, if extradited, faces a real risk of being subjected to torture or to inhuman or degrading treatment or punishment in the requesting country. The establishment of such responsibility inevitably involves an assessment of conditions in the requesting country against the standards of Article 3 of the Convention. Nonetheless, there is no question of adjudicating on or establishing the responsibility of the receiving country, whether under general international law, under the Convention or otherwise. In so far as any liability under the Convention is or may be incurred, it is liability incurred by the extraditing Contracting State by reason of its having taken action which has as a direct consequence the exposure of an individual to proscribed ill-treatment.[185]

The risk might arise not only because of treatment in the destination state, but because there is a real risk the destination state may deport the individual on arrival to a state where he or she will suffer Article 3 ill-treatment.[186] En route risk may also be taken into account where the detail or the method of return is clearly or necessarily implicit within the immigration decision, and where the Secretary of State has committed herself to a detailed decision of this nature.[187]

The protection of Article 3 in these instances is not accompanied by a relaxation of its absolute nature,[188] and it applies however 'disgraceful, promiscuous or reprehensible' the claimant's conduct may have been.[189] Lord Hope observed in *RB*[190] as follows:

---

[183] *Ullah* (n 10), per Lord Bingham at [24] in reliance upon *Soering v United Kingdom* (1989) 11 EHRR 439, [91]; *Cruz Varas v Sweden* (1991) 14 EHRR 1, [69]; *Vilvarajah v United Kingdom* (1991) 14 EHRR 248, [103]. However, it is important to note that the crucial issue in this case was whether reliance could be placed on any other Article of the Convention. The House of Lords concluded that it could.

[184] *Soering* (n 183).

[185] Ibid, [91].

[186] *Khemiri v Court of Milan Italy* [2008] EWHC 1988 (Admin).

[187] *R (J) (Somalia) v Secretary of State for the Home Department* [2009] EWHC 1281 (Admin).

[188] *N v Secretary of State for the Home Department* [2005] UKHL 31, [2005] 2 AC 296, per Lord Hope at [28], [30] and [48].

[189] Ibid, [27].

[190] *RB (Algeria) v Secretary of State for the Home Department* [2009] UKHL 10, [2010] 2 AC 110.

The rights and fundamental freedoms that the Convention guarantees are not just for some people. They are for everyone. No one, however dangerous, however disgusting, however despicable, is excluded. Those who have no respect for the rule of law—even those who would seek to destroy it – are in the same position as everyone else.[191]

It is not clear whether the duty is negative or positive, and this is something that has not been addressed in the case law. As a UK public authority is not itself carrying out the torture or the inhuman or degrading treatment or punishment, it arguably falls within the category of positive obligation to protect. Given the real risk test is well established in this branch of Article 3 jurisprudence, it is questionable why it has not carried over to non-deportation/extradition cases. In N[192] Lord Brown did suggest, in the context of a deportation resisted on the ground of inadequate medical treatment in the receiving state, that it was actually a positive duty for which the claimant was contending:

> It is quite unreal to treat this article 3 complaint for all the world as if all that is required to safeguard the appellant's health is that the State refrain from deporting her. Realistically what she seeks is continuing treatment for her condition and is necessarily implicit in her case that the State is bound to provide it. There would simply be no point in not deporting her unless her treatment here were to continue.[193]

However, this line of reasoning was not fully developed, his Lordship stating that the Strasbourg case law did not indicate that there was an absolute right for seriously ill persons to remain in the host country to get treatment.[194]

10.1.2 Evidential Issues

What Article 13 of the ECHR requires in the context of deportation 'is independent scrutiny of the human rights claim, which need not be provided by a judicial authority'.[195] The burden of proof is on the claimant, and the standard of proof is that there must be substantial grounds for believing that he or she is at real risk of prohibited ill-treatment contrary to Article 3.[196] 'Substantial' means that there must be a proper evidential basis for concluding that there was such a real risk.[197] In MA[198] the Supreme Court inclined to the view, without finally determining the question, that there was no practical difference between the tests to determine whether a fear was well founded for the purposes of the Refugee Convention, a reasonable degree of likelihood that the applicant will be persecuted on return, and the Article 3 test.[199] It was also content to proceed on the basis that 'real possibility' was the correct test to apply to past and present facts both in Refugee Convention and Article 3 cases.[200]

---

[191] Ibid, [210].
[192] N (n 188).
[193] Ibid, [88].
[194] Ibid, [90].
[195] RB (n 190), per Lord Phillips at [87].
[196] McPherson v Secretary of State for the Home Department [2001] EWCA Civ 1955; I v Secretary of State for the Home Department [2005] EWCA Civ 886.
[197] AS (Libya) v Secretary of State for the Home Department [2008] EWCA Civ 289, [2008] HRLR 28, [24].
[198] MA (Somalia) v Secretary of State for the Home Department [2010] UKSC 49, [2011] 2 All ER 65.
[199] Ibid, [13].
[200] Ibid, [20].

If it is apparent that a claimant has lied, this will not usually finally determine his or her claim but the general evidence must be sufficiently strong to counteract the negative pull of the claimant's lies.[201] It is possible for the court, or reviewing authority, to have regard to closed material when assessing safety on return without breaching the procedural requirements of the Convention.[202] It is for the court itself to determine whether the claimant is at real risk rather than reviewing the assessment made by the Secretary of State.[203]

A claimant may be able to meet the test either by referring to evidence specific to his own circumstances or by evidence applicable to a class of which he or she is a member. In the latter category, the claimant will only be able to demonstrate substantial grounds for believing that there is such a real risk if he or she can point to a consistent pattern of gross and systemic violation of rights under Article 3.[204] Nevertheless, it has been held that great care needs to be taken with such epithets which are intended to elucidate the jurisprudential concept of real risk, not to replace it. It is important not to assimilate risk to probability.[205] With respect to past events, it has been held that these can only cast light, as a matter of evidence, on what would happen if the claimant were returned.

> Such past events cannot of themselves constitute some part of the apprehended breach, which by definition lies in the future. That is not to say that evidence of these events may not be of great importance. They may cast much light on what will happen if the applicant is returned. They may, in some cases, show that by reason of his history the applicant's health or mental state is especially vulnerable.[206]

10.1.3 Article 3 in an Extradition Context

In *Wellington*,[207] an Article 3 extradition case, a majority of the House of Lords held that in cases of extradition Article 3 did not apply as if the extraditing state were 'simply responsible for any punishment likely to be inflicted in the receiving state'. Lord Hoffmann stated that it applied 'only in a modified form which takes into account the desirability of arrangements for extradition'.[208]

Whilst it was held that it would not be compatible with the values of the Convention for a Contracting State knowingly to surrender a fugitive to another state if there were substantial grounds for believing that he or she was in danger of being subjected to torture, the position in relation to inhuman or degrading treatment was found to be more complicated. Lord Hoffmann stated that what amounts to such treatment depends on all the circumstances of the case.[209] In reliance upon the judgment in *Soering*, he concluded that the desirability of extradition was a factor to be taken into account in deciding whether the punishment likely to be imposed in the receiving state 'attains the minimum level of severity which would make it inhuman and degrading'. In his

---

[201] Ibid, [33].
[202] *RB* (n 190).
[203] *R (Evans) v Secretary of State for Defence* [2010] EWHC 1445 (Admin), [2011] ACD 11.
[204] *Batayav v The Secretary of State for the Home Department* [2003] EWCA Civ 1489, [7].
[205] Ibid, [37]–[40].
[206] *Strbac v Secretary of State for the Home Department* [2005] EWCA Civ 848, [43]. See further R Thomas, 'Risk, Legitimacy and Asylum Adjudication' (2007) 58 *Northern Ireland Legal Quarterly* 49.
[207] *Wellington* (n 169).
[208] Ibid, [22].
[209] Ibid, [23].

view, punishment which counted as inhuman and degrading in the domestic context would not necessarily be so regarded when the extradition factor had been taken into account.[210] A relativist approach to the scope of Article 3 was held to be essential if extradition was to continue to function.[211] The approach of the majority was followed in *Bary* where it was held that when considering whether the conditions in US 'supermax' prisons crossed the Article 3 threshold, it was relevant to take into account the 'importance of facilitating extradition, particularly where …the fugitive claimants would not be tried in this country or elsewhere'.[212]

In their judgments in *Wellington* Lords Brown and Scott dissented on this point, preferring an absolutist approach to what constitutes inhuman or degrading treatment. If the treatment or punishment likely to be faced by an individual if extradited to the requesting country would be inhuman or degrading for Article 3 purposes in the domestic context, this would also be considered inhuman or degrading in a foreign context. As Lord Scott observed, the right under Article 3 not to be subjected to torture or to inhuman or degrading treatment was an absolute right which cannot be balanced against other considerations.[213] Furthermore, he found no basis for distinguishing between torture and other forms of Article 3 ill-treatment and observed that Article 3 prescribed a minimum standard not a norm, believing '[i]t must be open to individual states to decide for themselves what, if any, higher standard they would set for themselves'.[214] It is also important to note that given that the majority concluded that there was no real risk of a breach of Article 3 on the facts of the case, its observations about the extradition context were *obiter*.[215]

10.1.4 Assurances from the Destination State

It is common for the Home Secretary to seek assurances from the governments of destination states as to the way in which those resisting deportation from the UK on Convention grounds will be treated. These assurances have been accepted by courts and other reviewing authorities, such as the Special Immigration Appeals Commission, as evidence that individuals will not face a real risk of Article 3 ill-treatment. Such assurances need not eliminate all risk of inhuman treatment before they can be relied upon:

> It is obvious that if a State seeks to rely on assurances that are given by a country with a record for disregarding fundamental human rights it will need to show that there is good reason to treat the assurances as providing a reliable guarantee that the deportee will not be subjected to such treatment. If, however, after consideration of all the relevant circumstances of which assurances form part, there are no substantial grounds for believing that a deportee will be at real risk of inhuman treatment, there will be no basis for holding that deportation will violate article 3.[216]

---

[210] Ibid, [24].

[211] Ibid, [27]. See also *R (McKinnon) v Secretary of State for the Home Department* [2009] EWHC 2021 (Admin), [2010] Crim LR 421.

[212] *R (Bary) v Secretary of State for the Home Department* [2009] EWHC 2068 (Admin), [60].

[213] *Wellington* (n 169), [40].

[214] Ibid, [42].

[215] See further N Mavronicola and F Messineo, 'Relatively Absolute? The Undermining of Article 3 ECHR in Ahmad v UK' (2013) 76 *Modern Law Review* 589.

[216] *RB* (n 190), per Lord Phillips at [114].

The question of whether assurances obviate the risk is a question of fact, to be decided in the light of all the evidence.[217] There is no rule that external monitoring of a destination state is required, but as Lord Hoffmann stated in *RB*, in the absence of some provision for external monitoring 'such assurances may be no more than empty words'.[218] It has been held by the Supreme Court that where an individual facing deportation or extradition wishes to adduce evidence from someone with inside knowledge of the position in the destination state, notwithstanding the government's official assurances, it is possible for the Special Immigration Appeals Commission to give an assurance to that witness that his identity and evidence will forever remain confidential to Commission and the parties to the appeal.[219]

10.1.5 Safe List of Countries

The United Kingdom also usually has in place a list of countries where it is deemed that a return is not incompatible with Article 3. Such a list was the subject of challenge in *Nasseri*.[220] The claimant, an Afghan national, had claimed asylum in Greece prior to his claim in the UK. Therefore, in accordance with EU law, Greece was responsible for determining his application. He argued his return to Greece was contrary to Article 3 as there was a real risk he would be returned to Afghanistan to face Article 3 ill-treatment. The Secretary of State's response was that Greece was on the safe list of destination states. Such lists are treated in a similar fashion to assurances and there still must be an inquiry by the court into whether there is a real risk of Article 3 ill-treatment. Also relevant is the fact that the state is a contracting party to the ECHR. The House of Lords concluded here that there was no real risk that a migrant returned to Greece would be sent to a country where he would suffer inhuman or degrading treatment. Where the list is contained in primary legislation, it was held that the situation must be kept under review:

> Parliament must have decided that the administrative convenience of having the list in primary legislation, to avoid administrative law challenges to the procedure for consideration of article 3 rights, or to the non-exercise of a discretionary power to remove a country from the list, outweighed the risk that there might be cases in which a court found that a listed country was in fact unsafe and made a declaration of incompatibility.[221]

It has also been argued that automatic return to such countries may result in Article 3 ill-treatment in the 'safe' country given that state's treatment of asylum seekers. Such an argument was unsuccessful in relation to Italy in *EW* where it was held that there

---

[217] Ibid, per Lord Hoffmann at [187].

[218] Ibid, [193]. See also *AS* (n 197); *MS (Algeria) v Secretary of State for the Home Department* [2011] EWCA Civ 306; *Ahmad v United States* [2006] EWHC 2927 (Admin), [2007] HRLR 8; *XX (Ethiopia) v Secretary of State for the Home Department* [2012] EWCA Civ 742, [2013] 2 WLR 178; and *J1 v Secretary of State for the Home Department* [2013] EWCA Civ 279.

[219] *W (Algeria) v Secretary of State for the Home Department* [2012] UKSC 8, [2012] 2 AC 115. See further J Middleton, 'Taking Rights Seriously in Expulsion Cases: A Case Study' [2013] *European Human Rights Law Review* 520; J Tooze, 'Deportation with Assurances: The Approach of the UK Courts' [2010] *Public Law* 362.

[220] *Secretary of State for the Home Department v Nasseri* [2009] UKHL 23, [2010] 1 AC 1.

[221] Ibid, [22]. See also *R (MD) v Secretary of State for the Home Department* [2011] EWCA Civ 121; *R (Elayathamby) v Secretary of State for the Home Department* [2011] EWHC 2182 (Admin); and *R (MV) v Secretary of State for the Home Department* [2013] EWHC 1017 (Admin).

was no right under the Convention to a minimum level of social support.[222] A similar argument has been made in relation to Greece in S[223] where it was held that there must be a close and direct link between destitution and the actions of the state and that this would hardly ever occur in this type of case as the link between the decision of a UK Secretary of State to return a person to a safe country and any destitution which occurred was too attenuated (remote).[224] It concluded that the failure by the Greek government to provide the means of subsistence did not amount to a breach of Article 3 by the Secretary of State in this type of expulsion case.[225]

10.1.6 Contracting States to the ECHR

Increasingly, where the destination state is a Contracting State to the ECHR, UK courts are deciding that it must be presumed the destination state will comply with their Article 3 obligations. The risk is taken to be 'eliminated or at least reduced below the level at that which it amounts to a real risk' by the rights which an individual appellant has in a Convention country and the 'real and practical obligations which that country owes to him'.[226] The presumption is that the destination state is able to, and will, fulfil its obligations under the ECHR. This presumption is not easily displaced but can be rebutted by clear and cogent evidence which establishes that deportation or extradition is not compatible with Convention rights. The burden of displacing the presumption is a heavy one but it does not mean that claimant must demonstrate exceptional circumstances.[227]

10.1.7 Member States of the European Union

Where the destination state is a Member State of the European Union, the claimant must establish that there are in that state 'systemic deficiencies in the asylum procedure' and in the reception conditions of asylum seekers which amount to 'substantial grounds' for believing that the asylum seeker would face a real risk of being subjected to inhuman or degrading treatment. In short, claimants will always be returned to EU states of first arrival unless the source of the risk is a systemic deficiency in asylum or reception procedures. 'Short of this, even powerful evidence of individual risk is of no avail.'[228]

---

[222] *EW* (n 176).

[223] *S* (n 181).

[224] Ibid, [24].

[225] Ibid, [137].

[226] *R (Klimas) v Lithuania* [2010] EWHC 2076 (Admin) at [12] in reliance upon *KRS v UK*, 2 December 2008.

[227] *Agius v the Court of Magistrates, Malta* [2011] EWHC 759 (Admin) in reliance upon *MSS v Belgium and Greece*, 21 January 2011. See further M Bossuyt, 'Belgium Condemned for Inhuman or Degrading Treatment Due to Violations by Greece of EU Asylum Law' [2011] *European Human Rights Law Review* 582.

[228] *EM (Eritrea) v Secretary of State for the Home Department* [2012] EWCA Civ 1336, [2013] HRLR 1, at [61]–[62] in reliance upon *NS v United Kingdom* [2011] EUECJ C-411/10 and C-493/10. See also *R (Al-Ali) v Secretary of State for the Home Department* [2012] EWHC 3638 (Admin). See further F Ippolito, 'The Contribution of the European Courts to the Common European Asylum System and its Ongoing Recast Process' (2013) 20 *Maastricht Journal of European and Comparative Law* 261.

10.2 Application

This particular Article 3 obligation has generated a very large number of claims. It is common practice now for those claiming asylum in the UK also to claim protection on Article 3 grounds, even though the two claims remain very different.[229] Given that an individual may be deported or extradited from the UK to anywhere in the world, British courts and tribunals have had to consider the engagement of Article 3 in circumstances which would be very unlikely to arise in the domestic context. A number of categories have developed, and these are examined in the paragraphs below.[230]

10.2.1 Exacerbation of Illness and Risk of Suicide

The act of deportation itself may exacerbate an existing mental or physical illness. This may occur when the claimant is informed that a final decision has been made to remove or when he or she is physically removed.[231] For example, in *Lamanovs*[232] the claimant was liable to epileptic attacks and asked for a stay of his removal to France on the ground that it would be in breach of Article 3. The Court of Appeal considered medical evidence and also undertakings by the Secretary of State that he would be medically examined prior to removal; that he would be accompanied by a medical escort; and that the Home Office would inform the French immigration authorities of his medical condition. It concluded that what was proposed for the applicant was not of sufficient severity to breach Article 3:

> One has to remember that epilepsy is not a condition which is new to this applicant or by any means an unusual one for him or his family to deal with. What is threatened is a journey to France which will take less than an hour in the aeroplane, following a medical examination and in the presence of a medical escort. A journey moreover to French authorities who will have been warned of this man's condition.[233]

Article 3 claims have also been made where a claimant alleges that he or she will commit suicide if removed, if it can be shown that there is a real risk of suicide.[234] The risk arises from the person's removal to a place where the condition was likely to worsen and from the direct impact on the person's mental health of the decision to remove.[235] A question of importance is whether the claimant's fear of ill-treatment in the receiving state upon which the risk of suicide is said to be based is objectively well-founded. If the fear is not well-founded, that will tend to weigh against there being a real risk that the removal will be in breach of Article 3.[236] However, what may be of equal importance is whether any genuine fear which the appellant may establish,

---

[229] *R (on the application of Borak) v Secretary of State for the Home Department* [2005] EWCA Civ 110.

[230] The determination is fact sensitive and in some instances the ECtHR has reached a different conclusion to the UK court. See eg *Aswat v United Kingdom* 34 BHRC 656; *Sufi and Elmi v United Kingdom* (2012) 54 EHRR 9; *SH v United Kingdom* (2012) 54 EHRR 4.

[231] *J v Secretary of State for the Home Department* [2005] EWCA Civ 629, [17].

[232] *R (Lamanovs) v Secretary of State for the Home Department* [2001] EWCA Civ 1239.

[233] Ibid, [16]. See also *X* (n 6).

[234] *J* (n 231), [29].

[235] *R (Tozlukaya) v Secretary of State for the Home Department* [2006] EWCA Civ 379, [2006] Imm AR 417, [62].

[236] Ibid, [30].

'albeit without an objective foundation, is such as to create a risk of suicide if there is an enforced return'.[237] It is important to take into account that individuals who are at serious risk of suicide if returned can be 'stabilised, using therapy and medication, and kept from self-harm so long as they feel safe here'.[238]

Where a risk of suicide is alleged, the role of expert witnesses in the proceedings becomes very important and it has been held that a fundamental aspect of their expertise is the evaluation of the individual's account of their symptoms: 'It is only if the tribunal has good and objective reason for discounting that evaluation that it can be modified or—even more radically—disregarded.'[239]

It is also relevant to consider whether the removing and/or the receiving state has effective mechanisms to reduce the risk of suicide. If there are effective mechanisms, that too will weigh heavily against a claim that removal will violate Article 3.[240] Such claims can also be considered under Article 8 private life although it has been held that it is very difficult for a suicide case which fails under Article 3 to succeed under Article 8.[241]

In *Y*[242] the Court of Appeal held that although some psychiatric care was available in Sri Lanka, the claimants were

> so traumatised by their experiences, and so subjectively terrified at the prospect of return to the scene of their torment, that they will not be capable of seeking the treatment they need … the chances of their finding a secure base from which to seek the palliative and therapeutic care that will keep them from taking their own lives are on any admissible view of the evidence remote.[243]

The claimant also succeeded in *Wrobel*[244] where the Administrative Court held that its task was to determine whether the risk that the fugitive would succeed in committing suicide, whatever steps are taken, was on the evidence sufficiently great to result in a finding of oppression, within the meaning of section 25 of the Extradition Act 2005.[245] Bearing in mind that there was a public interest in giving effect to treaty obligations; that it should be assumed the requesting state had facilities to cope with and treat mental illness; the high threshold to show oppression; and the need for independent and convincing evidence of a very high risk of suicide, it found a potential violation of Article 3 on the facts.[246] But it was later held that this was a truly exceptional case.[247]

---

[237] *Y (Sri Lanka) v Secretary of State for the Home Department* [2009] EWCA Civ 362, [2009] HRLR 22, [16].

[238] Ibid, [36].

[239] Ibid, [12].

[240] Ibid, [31]. See also *R (on the application of Kurtolli) v Secretary of State for the Home Department* [2003] EWHC (Admin) 2744.

[241] *AJ (Liberia) v Secretary of State for the Home Department* [2006] EWCA Civ 1736, [26].

[242] *Y* (n 237).

[243] Ibid, [61].

[244] *Wrobel v Poland* [2011] EWHC 374 (Admin).

[245] Ibid, [17].

[246] Ibid, [18].

[247] *Mazurkiewicz v Poland* [2011] EWHC 659 (Admin) [46]. See also *R (C) v Secretary of State for the Home Department* [2012] EWHC 801 (Admin); *Poland v Wolkowicz* [2013] EWHC 102 (Admin), [2013] 1 WLR 2402; *R (T) (Sri Lanka) v Secretary of State for the Home Department* [2013] EWHC 1093 (Admin); and *Tuba v Hungary* [2013] EWHC 1767 (Admin).

10.2.2 Medical Treatment in Destination State

It has also been claimed that the medical treatment and care available in the destination state is inadequate. However, it has been held that Article 3 does not require contracting states to undertake the obligation of providing aliens indefinitely with medical treatment lacking in their home countries. This is so even where, in the absence of medical treatment, the life of the would-be immigrant would be significantly shortened.[248] The question which must be asked in such cases is whether the present state of the claimant's health is such that, on humanitarian grounds, he or she ought not to be expelled unless it can be shown that the medical and social facilities needed are actually available to him or her in the receiving state.[249]

This principle was established and applied by the House of Lords in *N*,[250] where the appellant had arrived in the United Kingdom from Uganda in 1998 and was shortly after diagnosed as HIV positive, with an AIDS-defining illness. As a result of medication and medical treatment over a lengthy period, her condition improved. Her doctors advised that if such treatment continued, she would remain well for decades. Following the refusal of her asylum application, she argued that to return her to Uganda would be a breach of her rights under Article 3. Their Lordships unanimously concluded that her removal to Uganda would not violate Article 3.

> So long as she continues to take the treatment she will remain healthy and she will have several decades of good health to look forward to. Her present condition cannot be said to be critical. She is fit to travel, and will remain fit if and so long as she can obtain the treatment that she needs when she returns to Uganda. The evidence is that the treatment she needs is available there, albeit at considerable cost. She also still has relatives there, although her position is that none of them would be willing and able to accommodate and take care of her.[251]

The case law demonstrates that a claimant's situation must be exceptional before he or she can resist deportation in such instances. There are very few reported cases where a claimant has successfully resisted deportation on these grounds. In *ZT*[252] the Court of Appeal held that it might be an exceptional case where the particular treatment afforded to an AIDS sufferer on return, in terms of ostracism, humiliation or deprivation of basic rights was added to existing medical difficulties.[253] But this was not something that could be demonstrated by the claimant in the case under consideration. Similarly in *KH*[254] it was held that the claim must be exceptional and that the presence of mental illness among failed asylum seekers cannot really be regarded as exceptional. However in *Ibrahim*, where the claimant had limited cognitive ability, suffered from depression and had no resources open to her in Somalia that would ensure her protection there,

---

[248] *N* (n 188).

[249] Ibid. Their Lordships held that in *D v United Kingdom* (1997) 24 EHRR 425 it was the fact that the claimant was already terminally ill while still present in the territory of the receiving state that made his case exceptional; and in *BB v France*, 9 March 1998, Commission, it was the facts that the infection had already reached an advanced stage, necessitating repeated stays in hospital, and that the care facilities in the receiving country were precarious that made the case exceptional.

[250] Ibid.

[251] Ibid, per Lord Hope at [51]. The reasoning was approved by the ECtHR in *N v United Kingdom* (2008) 47 EHRR 39.

[252] *ZT v Secretary of State for the Home Department* [2005] EWCA Civ 1421, [2006] Imm AR 84.

[253] Ibid, [18].

[254] *KH (Afghanistan) v Secretary of State for the Home Department* [2009] EWCA Civ 1354.

the Court of Appeal found her case was an exceptional one as she would have had an almost total inability to fend for herself if returned to Somalia.[255]

10.2.3 Punishment and Sentencing

In *Wellington*, as discussed above, the House of Lords considered whether the extradition of an individual to Missouri where he faced the prospect of a mandatory life sentence for murder, without probation or parole, was compatible with Article 3. First it was necessary to determine whether or not the life sentence was reducible or irreducible as the ECtHR had held in *Kafkaris v Cyprus*[256] that it was an irreducible life sentence which potentially raised issues under Article 3. Lord Hoffmann held that in order to be considered irreducible, the national law must not afford a real possibility (de jure and de facto) of review with a view to commutation or release.[257] Lord Brown considered that this review could take place when the prisoner's whole life term was fixed and his individual circumstances taken into account.[258] Here, whilst there was a power of the Governor of Missouri to pardon, this had been used sparingly—the sentence was reducible de jure but not necessarily de facto. Nevertheless, it was concluded by a majority that the sentence was reducible and therefore the extradition was not in breach of Article 3.

Going on to consider *obiter* the position if the sentence actually was irreducible, Lord Hoffmann, with whom Baroness Hale and Lord Carswell agreed, concluded that extradition would only violate Article 3 if the sentence was likely, on the facts of the case, to be clearly disproportionate.[259] As discussed above, it also held that it was necessary to take into account the desirability of extradition. Here it was concluded that a sentence of life without parole would not be grossly disproportionate to the offence so as to meet the heightened standard for contravention of Article 3 in its application to extradition cases. Lord Hoffmann observed that, unlike *Soering*,

> there is no other jurisdiction in which the appellant can be tried. If he is not extradited to Missouri, he will be entitled to remain in this country as a fugitive from justice. The standard of what amounts to inhuman and degrading treatment for the purposes of article 3 must therefore be a high one.[260]

Agreeing with Lord Hoffmann, Baroness Hale and Lord Carswell found that an irreducible sentence in the present case would not breach Article 3. Whilst dissenting on the test to be applied, Lords Brown and Scott, also found that an irreducible sentence on the facts of the present case would not breach Article 3, but Lord Brown stated that there might come a point about which further detention would be incapable of justification.

---

[255] *Ibrahim v Secretary of State for the Home Department* [2005] EWCA Civ 1816. See also *FM (Zimbabwe) v Secretary of State for the Home Department* [2011] EWCA Civ 168 and *R (De Almeida) v Kensington & Chelsea Royal London Borough Council* [2012] EWHC 1082 (Admin).
[256] *Kafkaris v Cyprus* Application No 21906/04, 12 February 2008.
[257] *Wellington* (n 169), [12].
[258] Ibid, [69].
[259] Ibid, [35].
[260] Ibid, [36].

Summarising the present law in *Inzunza*, the Administrative Court held that there was a strong policy interest in an effective system of extradition[261] and that it was necessary to adopt a relativist view of the application of Article 3 in the extradition context.[262] Therefore, the test of whether a potential sentence in the receiving state was incompatible with Article 3 was set high and the potential sentence must be one which shocked the conscience or was likely on the facts of the case to be clearly dispropor-tionate.[263] Furthermore, it was not appropriate to impose English sentencing policy on other states[264] and it was also held that it was very unlikely that a determinate sentence or discretionary life sentence (whether irreducible or not) would satisfy the test.[265]

10.2.4 Conditions of Detention

If an individual subject to deportation is likely to be detained by the destination state on his or her return, the conditions of detention in the destination state may give rise to an Article 3 claim.[266] In reliance upon ECtHR case law, it has been held that the state must ensure that:

> a person is detained in conditions which are compatible with respect for his human dignity, that the manner and method of the execution of the measure do not subject him to distress or hardship of an intensity exceeding the unavoidable level of suffering inherent in detention and that, given the practical demands of imprisonment, his health and well-being are adequately secured.[267]

Once it is established that imprisonment is a real risk, conditions in which a prisoner is detained can be so unsatisfactory as to constitute inhuman or degrading treatment within the meaning of Article 3 even though there is no intention on the part of the authorities to humiliate or debase the victim.[268] It has been held that complete sensory isolation coupled with total social isolation would always be in breach of Article 3.[269] When assessing conditions of detention, account also has to be taken of the cumulative effect of these conditions.[270] However, it is important to note that in the extradition context, it has been held that punishment which would be regarded as inhuman or degrading in the domestic field will not necessarily be so regarded 'where the alternative to extradition is that the person sought to be extradited will escape justice altogether'.[271] In *Bary*, an extradition case, it was held that prison conditions at a US 'supermax' prison, combined with a whole life sentence and measures of special confinement, did not cross the Article 3 threshold.[272]

---

[261] *Inzunza v United States* [2011] EWHC 920 (Admin) [2011] ACD 68, [15].
[262] Ibid, [16].
[263] Ibid, [17].
[264] Ibid, [18].
[265] Ibid, [19].
[266] See eg *R (Evans) v Secretary of State for Defence* [2010] EWHC 1445 (Admin) where conditions of detention in Afghanistan were exhaustively considered.
[267] *Sorokins v Latvia* [2010] EWHC 1962 (Admin) at [8] in reliance upon *Caroll Vikius v Lithuania*, 7 April 2005.
[268] *Batayav* (n 204), [11] in reliance upon *Peers v Greece* (2001) 33 EHRR 1192.
[269] *R (Bary) v Secretary of State for the Home Department* [2009] EWHC 2068 (Admin).
[270] Ibid, [13] in reliance upon *Dougoz v Greece* (2001) 34 EHRR 1480, [45].
[271] Ibid, [69]. See also *Wellington* (n 169).
[272] Ibid.

Sometimes it is difficult for the claimant to satisfy the court that the law will be applied and imprisonment will result.[273] In *Mohammed Adam*[274] the Court of Appeal held that there must be a real risk that failure to do military service would be discovered on the claimant's return but also held that to place a burden on the claimant to show that there was a real risk of a fine and up to three years imprisonment was unfair. It held that the evidential burden had passed to the Home Office to produce the relevant evidence to show that there was no real risk that the penalties prescribed by law would be exacted.[275]

Conditions of detention in Russian prisons were at issue in *Batayav*.[276] It was necessary for the claimant to demonstrate substantial grounds for believing that there was a real risk of ill-treatment of the requisite degree of severity by pointing to a consistent pattern of gross and systemic violation of rights under Article 3.[277]

> To establish his case he does not need to refer to evidence specific to his own circumstances, but rather to the evidence bearing on the class of case of which he is a member; in other words ... to the evidence showing the conditions faced generally by persons incarcerated in the Russian prison system.[278]

The Court of Appeal took particular note of the judgment of the European Court in *Kalashnikov v Russia*,[279] where a violation of Article 3 had been found in relation to conditions of detention and the Russian Federation had admitted that such conditions applied to most detainees in Russia. It concluded that this established that any person held in a Russian prison at this time was at real risk of degrading treatment and that there was a consistent pattern of gross and systemic, even if not intentional, violations of human rights of those detained in Russian prisons.[280] Therefore, there was a real risk the claimant would be subjected to degrading treatment and his return to Russia was prima facie unlawful.[281] However, given the submission of fresh evidence concerning an improvement in conditions, the case was remitted to a freshly constituted tribunal. It found that conditions had improved to the extent that it was not necessarily a breach of Article 3 to return the claimant to the Russian Federation. This conclusion was upheld on appeal by the Court of Appeal.[282] Often it is the case that new evidence will be introduced to demonstrate that prison conditions in a particular destination state have improved.[283]

---

[273] See eg *Ngene v Secretary of State for the Home Department* [2002] EWCA Civ 185.

[274] *Mohammed Adam v Secretary of State for the Home Department* [2003] EWCA Civ 265.

[275] Ibid, [12] and [14].

[276] *Batayav* (n 204).

[277] Ibid, [7].

[278] Ibid, [23].

[279] *Kalashnikov v Russia* (2002) 36 EHRR 587.

[280] Ibid, [25].

[281] Ibid, [27]. See also *R (on the application of Bahrami) v Secretary of State for the Home Department*, Administrative Court, 22 June 2003; *R (on the application of Mbanjabahizi) v Immigration Appeal Tribunal*, Administrative Court, 10 June 2004.

[282] *Batayav* (n 204). Prison conditions in Thailand were assessed in *Aldhouse v Thailand* [2012] EWHC 3385 (Admin). See also *Achmant v Greece* [2012] EWHC 3470 (Admin) concerning conditions in Greek prisons; *Lutsyuk v Ukraine* [2013] 189 (Admin) concerning Ukraine prison conditions; and *Richards v Ghana* [2013] EWHC 1254 (Admin) concerning conditions in prisons in Ghana. The treatment of women in prison in Argentina were found to cross the Art 3 threshold in *Wright v Commissioner of the Metropolitan Police* [2012] EWHC 669 (QB); the conditions in a particular Lithuanian prison crossed the Art 3 threshold in *Lithuania v Campbell* [2013] NIQB 19.

[283] See eg *Pisarek v Regional Court in Elblag 11* [2010] EWHC 877 (Admin) and *Krolik v Poland* [2012] EWHC 2357 (Admin), [2012] 1 WLR 490 concerning Polish prison conditions.

10.2.5 Legal Restrictions on Homosexuality

Returning a homosexual to a country where homosexuality is illegal has been held not to engage Article 3. In Z[284] the Court of Appeal explained that it was possible that treatment aimed at a particular sexual group could engage Article 3 but the mere existence of a law prohibiting particular types of sexual conduct in private amongst adults did not.[285] Similarly, in S,[286] which concerned return to Kosovo, the Administrative Court held that Article 3 could not be invoked as a guarantee against the risk that prejudice would occur. 'Social consequences will only occur if the claimant's sexual orientation becomes public.'[287]

10.2.6 Ill-treatment by Non-state Actors: Sufficiency of State Protection

It is not necessary for the real risk of ill-treatment in the destination state to emanate from state actors.[288] However, where the risk emanates from non-state actors, any harm inflicted by such actors will not constitute Article 3 ill-treatment unless, in addition, the state has failed to provide reasonable protection.[289] Article 3 requires a state to provide machinery to deter a violation of that article which attains a satisfactory degree of effectiveness. The reasoning in *Osman*[290] applies equally in this context. This does not require a state to guarantee safety, but it is expected to take reasonable measures to make the necessary protection available.[291] The focus must not just be on willingness to provide protection but also on the state's ability to do so.

> [I]t is no answer that a state is doing its incompetent best if it nevertheless falls below the appropriate standard. One has to ask whether the state is failing to perform its basic function of protecting its citizens. Does the writ of law run or not?[292]

A state's obligation is to provide practical protection in the particular circumstances of an individual's case. The reach and content of the protection afforded to individuals will depend upon the circumstances 'touching the existence and character of the risk to which they have become exposed'.[293]

Such claims have been made in a variety of contexts. In *McPherson*[294] the claimant's Article 3 argument related to her fear of renewed and serious personal violence on the part of a man who had repeatedly assaulted her in earlier years. The Court of Appeal held that it was not enough for the claimant to show that the sanctions imposed for offences against the person under the criminal law of Jamaica were ineffective as in

---

[284] Z (n 13).
[285] Ibid, [16]. The Court of Appeal also considered Art 8.
[286] *R (on the application of S) v Secretary of State for the Home Department* [2003] EWHC (Admin) 352.
[287] Ibid, [22]. See also *Mudarikwa v Secretary of State for the Home Department* [2003] EWCA Civ 583; *Amare v Secretary of State for the Home Department* [2005] EWCA Civ 1600, [2006] Imm AR 217.
[288] *R (on the application of Bagdanavicius) v Secretary of State for the Home Department* [2005] UKHL 38, [2005] 2 WLR 1359.
[289] Ibid.
[290] *Osman* (n 49).
[291] *McPherson* (n 196), per Arden LJ at [36]–[39] in reliance upon *X and Y v Netherlands* (1985) EHRR 235, 241 and *A v United Kingdom* (1998) 27 EHRR 611, 629, [22].
[292] *Atkinson v Secretary of State for the Home Department* [2004] EWCA Civ 846, [2004] ACD 71.
[293] *R (Gedara) v Secretary of State for the Home Department* [2006] EWHC 1690 (Admin), [24].
[294] *McPherson* (n 196).

the context of domestic violence a state can provide effective measures of a different nature.[295] Arden LJ concluded as follows:

> Accordingly, to be 'effective', measures for the purposes of art 3 must be those which attain an adequate degree of efficacy in practice as well as exist in theory. If the appellant were able to show to the requisite standard of proof that the remedies provided under the law of Jamaica against domestic violence are unlikely to be an effective deterrent, in my judgment she would have shown that her removal from the United Kingdom to Jamaica would violate her rights under art 3.[296]

In *Bagdanavicius*[297] the claimants claimed persistent harassment in Lithuania due to the husband's Roma origin. They also claimed the police provided ineffective protection due to discrimination against Roma. The House of Lords unanimously found that, although the claimants were at real risk of serious injury by non-state agents, Lithuania provided a reasonable level of protection against violence of the sort threatened and there would be no violation of Article 3 if they were returned to Lithuania. Gang-related violence was the subject of two cases concerning proposed deportations to Jamaica. In *A*[298] the Court of Appeal concluded that return of the claimant, a suspected informer, would involve a real risk of Article 3 treatment regardless of her efforts to relocate and protect her identity. In *Britton*[299] the Court of Appeal remitted the case to the Immigration Appeals Tribunal but observed that the fact that law enforcement and security forces in Jamaica were overzealous did not mean that they exerted effective control, nor did the fact that they used armed response when apprehending criminal suspects.[300]

---

11. Duty to Investigate

11.1 The Nature of the Duty

The positive duty under Article 3 also encompasses a procedural duty to investigate where it is arguable that there has been a breach of the article.[301] It is important that

---

[295] Ibid, per Arden LJ at [32]–[35].

[296] Ibid, [38]. Sedley LJ agreed at [22], as did Aldous LJ at [41]. The appeal was allowed and the case remitted to another adjudicator. See also *P v Secretary of State for the Home Department* [2004] EWCA Civ 1640.

[297] *Bagdanavicius* (n 288).

[298] *A* (n 4).

[299] *Britton v Secretary of State for the Home Department* [2003] EWCA Civ 227.

[300] Ibid, [20]. See also *Atkinson* (n 292). As to other claims under this head, see *R (on the application of Tataw) v Immigration Appeal Tribunal* [2003] EWCA Civ 925 in which the claimant argued return to Cameroon to face female circumcision would engage Art 3; and *R (on the application of Bazdoaca) v Secretary of State for the Home Department* [2004] EWHC Admin 2054 in which the claimant argued the persecution he faced in Moldova as a homosexual engaged Art 3, and *McLean v Ireland* [2008] EWHC 547 (Admin) where the claimant submitted that he would not receive sufficient protection in prison.

[301] *R (on the application of Green) v Police Complaints Authority* [2004] UKHL 6, [2004] 1 WLR 725; *R (on the application of Wright) v Secretary of State for the Home Department* [2001] EWHC (Admin) 520, (2001) 62 BMR 16; *R (on the application of Al-Skeini) v Secretary of State for Defence* [2004] EWHC (Admin) 2911; *Spinks* (n 119).

it is established that there is an arguable breach and it has been held that there is no difference in substance between a credible assertion of a breach and an assertion on the evidence available that there was an arguable breach.[302] In *AM*[303] it was confirmed by a majority of the Court of Appeal that there is a duty to investigate, analogous to that under Article 2, where credible evidence suggests that one or more individuals has been subjected 'by or with the connivance of the state to treatment sufficiently grave to come within the article'.[304] The duty is triggered once the authorities knew or ought to have known that the alleged breaches of Article 3 had occurred.[305] The purpose is to 'inform the public and its government about what may have gone wrong in relation to an important civic and international obligation and about what can be done to stop it happening again'.[306]

It is important that the full facts are brought to light and lessons learned and implemented.[307] It is clear that the investigation may go well beyond the ascertainment of individual fault and reach questions of system, management and institutional culture.[308] However, it was also appreciated that a civil action for damages, or a properly conducted prosecution or disciplining of an offender, may satisfy Article 3.[309] An investigation ensures that accountability for a breach of Article 3 is established either in order that those who suffered thereby may be appropriately compensated, or in an attempt to ensure that such conduct does not reoccur.[310] The duty is similar, if not identical, to that under Article 2.[311] However, where the breach of Article 3 is continuing, the primary positive obligation of the state is to terminate the breach, the investigation to take place only when the breach has occurred and is over.[312]

11.2 The Content of the Duty to Investigate

In *AM* a majority of the Court of Appeal confirmed that the jurisprudence governing the investigative duty under Article 2 governed the same duty under Article 3.[313] However, Elias LJ held that the procedural requirement for an Article 3 investigation would often be less onerous than an Article 2 investigation.[314] A difference lies in the fact that usually the victim of an Article 3 breach is alive 'and knows of the acts and omissions said to infringe his Convention right'.[315] In *AM* it was agreed that the following was required:

---

[302] *R (P) v Secretary of State for Justice* [2009] EWCA Civ 701, [2010] QB 317, [48].
[303] *R (AM) v Secretary of State for the Home Department* [2009] EWCA Civ 219, [2009] Prison LR 133.
[304] Ibid, per Sedley LJ at [4]. Elias LJ, dissenting on this point, held that there must be specific allegations, not generalised statements.
[305] Ibid, per Elias LJ at [95].
[306] Ibid, per Sedley LJ at [57].
[307] Ibid, [59].
[308] Ibid, [60].
[309] Ibid, [61].
[310] *Spinks* (n 119) [31].
[311] *Green, Wright* and *Al-Skeini* (n 301); *Spinks* (n 119).
[312] *Spinks* (n 119), [30].
[313] *AM* (n 303), per Sedley LJ at [56].
[314] Ibid, [103].
[315] *P* (n 302).

- The investigation should be capable of leading to the identification and punishment of those responsible.
- It was necessary for the persons responsible for and carrying out the investigation to be independent from those implicated in the events. This meant not only a lack of hierarchical or institutional connection but also a practical independence.
- The investigation must be effective in the sense that it was capable of leading to a determination of whether the force used was or was not justified in the circumstances.
- The investigation must be thorough in that the authorities must make a serious attempt to find out what happened and should not rely on hasty or ill-founded conclusions to close their investigation or as the basis of their decisions. They must take all reasonable steps available to them to secure the evidence concerning the incident.
- The investigation must permit effective access for the complainant to the investigatory procedure.[316]

The exact nature of the inquiry depended on the circumstances:

> What will suffice for an isolated instance of inhuman or degrading treatment (which may be a prosecution or a civil action ...) will not necessarily suffice for systemic and multiple breaches of art 3 such as are alleged here.[317]

In the opinion of Sedley LJ, this was because what was at stake was not individual redress or culpability but the need to discover the reasons why the events engaging Article 3 occurred. In the present case Sedley LJ concluded that a further investigation was necessary in order to address issues raised about the culture and conduct of the detention centre management and staff. Elias LJ concluded that a further investigation was necessary to focus on the alleged ill-treatment and not the wider cultural or institutional difficulties which brought the problems to a head in the first place.[318]

The difference in approach between Sedley LJ and Elias LJ is reflected in later cases where concern about the resources implications of Article 3 investigations has been noted. In the case of P[319] the Court of Appeal held that where Article 3 was engaged, an inquiry was not mandatory but depended upon the circumstances of the case 'including the availability of other means of eliciting the relevant facts, such as civil proceedings and investigation by the prison ombudsman. ... Good reason for an Article 3 inquiry must be shown.'[320] Similarly in MM[321] the Court of Appeal held that claims for Article 3 inquiries had to be considered on their merits 'having regard to the nature, scale and consequences of the incident, the likelihood of recurrence' and also the existence of 'other investigations conducted or available'. Costs were also mentioned as a factor to be taken into consideration.[322]

---

[316] Ibid, per Sedley LJ at [32], per Elias LJ at [86].
[317] Ibid, per Sedley LJ at [33].
[318] Ibid, [115].
[319] P (n 302).
[320] Ibid, [58]. See also M (n 27).
[321] R (MM) v Secretary of State for the Home Department [2012] EWCA Civ 668.
[322] Ibid, [57].

11.3 The Duty to Investigate in Practice

11.3.1 Detention

As the duty to investigate under Article 2 also arises where life-threatening injuries have occurred,[323] the majority of claims have proceeded via the Article 2 route. For example, in *Wright*,[324] where a prisoner had died in his cell as a result of an asthma attack, the Administrative Court found Articles 2 and 3 engaged. With respect to Article 3, it found that the prisoner suffered from a serious asthmatic condition and that the medical treatment he had received was seriously deficient, and in the minutes leading up to his death he must have endured considerable pain and suffering. It was held that to leave a sick man locked in his cell and exposed to the risk of such pain and suffering might arguably be characterised as inhuman treatment.[325] The Secretary of State was ordered to set up an independent investigation into the circumstances of the death.[326]

In *AM* it was held by a majority of the Court of Appeal that the duty arose in relation to a disturbance which broke out at an immigration detention centre. Detainees not involved in the disturbance were kept in confinement while water from the sprinkler system entered their cells, ordered into the exercise yard in the cold, then locked in cells where they were affected by smoke from a fire started by inmates. Some were kept in these conditions for over 12 hours without food or water. By contrast in *MM*[327] the Court of Appeal held that Article 3 required no further investigation into an intervention at an immigration detention centre in response to a protest by detainees. Civil proceedings had been instituted by detainees and there had been an internal investigative report and a report from independent consultants.[328]

11.3.2 Policing

In *Green*,[329] which concerned the claimant's serious injury on being hit by an unmarked police car, only Lord Scott found that Article 2 was engaged. The majority proceeded on the assumption that Article 3 was engaged without exploring its precise ambit in this context or deciding whether Article 2 might also have been invoked. The House of Lords held that an effective investigation required proper procedures for ensuring accountability of agents of the state so as to maintain public confidence and allay the legitimate concerns that arose from the use of lethal force.[330] However, it found the degree of the involvement of the claimant in the investigation sufficient to safeguard his legitimate interests and meet the requirements of Article 3.[331]

---

[323] *R (on the application of Amin (Imtiaz) v Secretary of State for the Home Department* [2003] UKHL 51, [2004] 1 AC 653.

[324] *Wright* (n 301).

[325] Ibid, [56].

[326] Ibid, [67].

[327] *MM* (n 321).

[328] See also *R (NM) v Secretary of State for Justice* [2012] EWCA Civ 1182.

[329] *Green* (n 301).

[330] Ibid, per Lord Rodger at [59] in reliance upon *Amin* (n 323).

[331] Ibid, per Lord Rodger at [63].

Whether or not a duty to investigate had arisen under Article 4, not Article 3, was at issue in *OOO*[332] where the claimants alleged that they were held in slavery or servitude in London households for many years and that police had been asked to investigate, but had failed to do so. Whilst the claim was determined on the basis of Article 4, it was held that the duty under Article 3 was the same.[333] It concluded that a duty to investigate urgently would arise if the alleged victim was still in a harmful situation, otherwise the duty was to act promptly or with reasonable expedition.[334] Here, it was held that police were under a duty to carry out an effective investigation of an allegation of a breach of Article 4 once a credible account of an alleged infringement had been brought to its attention. The trigger for the duty 'would not depend upon an actual complaint from a victim or near relative of a victim'.[335] Furthermore, it was held that whilst the fact that no victim was identified made an effective investigation difficult to mount, the absence of a victim did not preclude the duty from arising.[336] It was accepted that the duty to investigate in a particular case may have to take account of priorities and resources and the duty must not impose an impossible or disproportionate burden upon the authorities. Furthermore, the police must respect due process and other guarantees including those contained in Articles 5 and 8.[337] Here it was concluded that a duty to investigate had arisen—officers had received credible complaints of serious breaches of Articles 3 and 4. Each claimant was awarded damages of £5,000.

11.3.3 Armed forces

In *Mousa*[338] it was claimed that the Secretary of State must order an immediate public inquiry into allegations that persons detained in Iraq at various times between 2003 and 2008 were ill-treated in breach of Article 3. Whilst the Secretary of State had already established investigatory procedures in relation to the allegations, it was argued that these measures were not sufficiently independent, effective or prompt. The Court of Appeal accepted in relation to independence that Articles 3 and 2 were similar and that public perception of unconscious bias was the key.[339] It was concluded here that existing arrangements were not sufficiently independent and therefore it was also not lawful under Article 3 for the Secretary of State to wait and see what conclusions were reached before determining whether or not to hold a public inquiry.

---

[332] *OOO v Commissioner of Police of the Metropolis* [2011] EWHC 1246 (QB), [2011] HRLR 29.
[333] Ibid, [162].
[334] Ibid, [153].
[335] Ibid, [154] in reliance upon *Rantsev v Cyprus and Russia* [2010] 51 EHRR 1.
[336] Ibid, [164].
[337] Ibid, [156].
[338] *R (Mousa) v Secretary of State for Defence* [2011] EWCA Civ 1334, [2012] HRLR 6.
[339] Ibid, [35].

9

Article 5: The Right to Liberty and Security

1. Introduction

Article 5 is primarily concerned that deprivation of liberty should be 'properly imposed', its lawfulness 'open to challenge so that a person unlawfully detained may be set free', and that the place of detention 'conforms to the purpose for which it is imposed'.[1] The rights protected by Article 5 also have a long history in English law. Lord Bingham has observed that the personal freedom of the individual is reflected in:

> the long libertarian tradition of English law, dating back to chapter 39 of Magna Carta 1215, given effect in the ancient remedy of habeas corpus, declared in the Petition of Right 1628, upheld in a series of landmark decisions down the centuries and embodied in the substance and procedure of the law to our own day.[2]

The importance of Article 5 is demonstrated by its absolute nature save only for the circumstances expressly provided for by Article 5(1).[3] Observations concerning the importance of personal freedom are often made; for example, in *A v Secretary of State for the Home Department* Lord Hope commented that it was impossible ever to over-state the importance of the right to liberty in a democracy.[4]

Deference to the primary decision maker is something that is rarely mentioned in

---

[1] *R (on the application of Munjaz) v Mersey Care NHS Trust* [2003] EWCA Civ 1036, [2004] QB 395, [70]. The appeal to the House of Lords, not concerning this observation, was successful [2005] UKHL 58, [2006] 2 AC 148. See also *P v Nottinghamshire Healthcare NHS Trust* [2003] EWHC (Admin) 1782, [2003] ACD 403.

[2] *A v Secretary of State for the Home Department* [2004] UKHL 56, [2005] 2 AC 68, per Lord Bingham at [36]. See also *R v East London and the City Mental Health NHS Trust, ex p von Brandenburg* [2003] UKHL 58, [2004] 2 AC 280, [6].

[3] See eg the comments of Lord Hope in *A*, ibid, [108].

[4] Ibid, [100]. See also Lord Nicholls at [74], Lord Hoffmann at [88] and Lord Bingham at [36].

Article 5 cases. This reflects the importance with which the right is regarded, its narrow construction and the fact that many of its protections are absolute. In *Lichniak*[5] brief mention was made of the fact that the mandatory life sentence for murder represented the settled will of a democratic assembly and a degree of deference was due to the judgment of a democratic assembly on how a particular social problem was best tackled.[6] Occasionally there are also references to resources constraints. For example, in *Cawser*[7] the Court of Appeal held that the Home Secretary could not be under an absolute duty to provide particular courses to all prisoners who wanted them in order to maximise chances of release. However, resources arguments are generally given short shrift, the Court of Appeal holding in *Noorkoiv*[8] that if further resources were necessary to avert a breach of Article 5(4), these must be provided.

Whilst very rare, it has been held that where there is a clash between a power or duty to detain exercisable on the express authority of the UN Security Council and Article 5 of the ECHR, the UN Security Council Resolution prevails:

> [T]he UK may lawfully, where it is necessary for imperative reasons of security, exercise the power to detain authorised by UNSCR 1546 and successive resolutions, but must ensure that the detainee's rights under article 5 are not infringed to any greater extent than is inherent in such detention.[9]

---

2. What Constitutes a Deprivation of Liberty?

It is usually clear whether or not there has been a deprivation of liberty to which Article 5 applies. Obvious examples include imprisonment following a conviction, arrest on reasonable suspicion of having committed an offence and detention in a secure hospital. However, sometimes it is difficult to discern on which side of the line facts fall.[10] The prohibition in Article 5 on depriving a person of his liberty has an autonomous meaning.[11] Relying on ECtHR authority, in *P*[12] the Court of Appeal held that there were three

---

[5] *R v Lichniak* [2002] UKHL 47, [2003] 1 AC 903.

[6] Ibid, per Lord Bingham at [14].

[7] *R (Cawser) v Secretary of State for the Home Department* [2003] EWHC Civ 1522, [2004] UKHRR 101.

[8] *R v Secretary of State for the Home Department, ex p Noorkoiv* [2002] EWCA Civ 770, [2002] 1 WLR 3284, [44].

[9] *R (Al-Jedda) v Secretary of State for Defence* [2007] UKHL 58, [2008] 1 AC 332, per Lord Bingham at [39]. In *Al-Jedda v United Kingdom* (2011) 53 EHRR 23 the ECtHR concluded that the UNSC Resolution did not explicitly or implicitly require the UK to place an individual into indefinite detention without charge. A violation of Art 5(1) was found. See further V Zambrano, 'State Responsibility for Human Rights Violations' (2013) *European Human Rights Law Review* 180.

[10] In *R (on the application of Saadi) v Secretary of State for the Home Department* [2002] UKHL 41, [2002] 1 WLR 3131 it was held that asylum seekers at Oakington Reception Centre were deprived of their liberty as they could not leave the centre and had to conform to rules as to mealtimes and being in their rooms at night.

[11] *Secretary of State for the Home Department v JJ* [2007] UKHL 45, [2008] 1 AC 385, per Lord Bingham at [13].

[12] *P and Q (by their litigation friend the Official Solicitor) v Surrey County Council* [2011] EWCA Civ 190, [2012] 2 WLR 1056.

elements to a deprivation of liberty: (a) the objective element of a person's confinement to a certain limited place for a not negligible length of time; (b) the additional subjective element that they have not validly consented to the confinement in question; and (c) the confinement was imputable to the state.[13]

In difficult cases where the question is whether or not the detention falls within Article 5, the burden of proof is on the claimant. And the task of a court is to assess the impact of the measures in question on a person in the situation of the person subject to them.[14] There is threshold that must be crossed and whether or not it has been crossed 'must be measured by the degree or intensity of the restriction'.[15] The decision is highly sensitive to the facts of each case.[16] It is important to assess the effect of the measures on the life the person would have been living otherwise.[17] Lord Bingham, relying upon ECtHR authority,[18] held as follows in *JJ*:

> [A]ccount should be taken of a whole range of factors such as the nature, duration, effects and manner of execution or implementation of the penalty or measure in question. ... There may be no deprivation of liberty if a single feature of an individual's situation is taken on its own but the combination of measures considered together may have that result[19]

In *Austin*[20] the House of Lords held that it was also important to take into account the purpose of the measure in question. 'If purpose is relevant, it must be to enable a balance to be struck between what the restriction seeks to achieve and the interests of the individual.'[21] The Court of Appeal later held that the word 'purpose' here was being used in the sense of the objective aim: '[B]ad faith, deception, improper motives or other forms of arbitrary behaviour may have the effect that what would otherwise not be a deprivation of liberty is in fact, and for that very reason, a deprivation.'[22] It held that it was legitimate in determining whether or not there was a deprivation of liberty to have regard both to the objective 'reason' why someone was placed and treated as they were and also to the objective 'purpose' (or 'aim') of the placement. In its opinion, good intentions were essentially neutral and could cancel out the existence of some improper motive or intention.[23]

Neither the presence nor the absence of a lock is determinative. A person can be deprived of his or her liberty even though departure is not prevented by a 'locked door or by any other physical barrier and even though he may be allowed extensive social and other contact with the outside world'.[24] It is also important to indentify what the court was comparing X's concrete situation with – what is the relevant comparator?[25] In

---

[13] Ibid, [17] in reliance upon *Storck v Germany* (2005) 43 EHRR 96.
[14] *JJ* (n 11), per Lord Bingham at [15].
[15] *Austin v Commissioner of Police of the Metropolis* [2009] UKHL 5, [2009] 1 AC 564, per Lord Hope at [18].
[16] Ibid, [26].
[17] Ibid, [18].
[18] *Guzzardi v Italy* (1980) 3 EHRR 333.
[19] *JJ* (n 11), [16].
[20] *Austin* (n 15).
[21] Ibid, per Lord Hope at [27].
[22] *Cheshire West v P* [2011] EWCA Civ 1257, [2012] 1 FLR 693, [71].
[23] Ibid, [76].
[24] Ibid, [37].
[25] Ibid, [39].

most cases this would be the 'ordinary adult enjoying liberty to do those things which in this country free men are entitle to do'.[26]

2.1 Restrictions on Liberty of Movement

It is clear that restrictions on liberty of movement fall within Article 2 of Protocol No 4 and do not engage Article 5.[27] The distinction is one of degree or intensity of restrictions, not of nature or substance. The court must start with the concrete or actual situation of the individual concerned and take account of a range of criteria such as type, duration, effects and manner of implementation of the measure in question. Account must also be taken of the cumulative effect of the various restrictions.[28] Finally, the purpose of any measures of restriction is a relevant consideration. If the measures are taken principally in the interests of the individual who is being restricted, they may well be regarded as not amounting to a deprivation of liberty.[29]

An example of the distinction was demonstrated in *PH*.[30] The Mental Health Review Tribunal had directed that PH be discharged subject to a number of conditions. The Secretary of State argued that the conditions imposed, in particular that he reside at specialist accommodation with security and not leave without an escort, were so restrictive as to deprive him of his liberty. The Court of Appeal held that the security measures and escorts were imposed to protect PH himself and it did not accept that the conditions inevitably meant that PH would be in a regime so restrictive that he would be deprived of his liberty.[31] By contrast, in *G*[32] the Administrative Court observed that any detention of a mentally ill person for treatment may be regarded as in his best interests, but that did not prevent such detention being a deprivation of liberty.[33] And in *Whiston*[34] the Court of Appeal was not satisfied that release on home detention curfew was properly to be viewed as the restoration of liberty sufficient to engage Article 5 if and when the prisoner was recalled to prison.[35]

2.2 Control Orders

Similar issues have been considered in the context of control orders where the facts of

---

[26] Ibid, [40]. See generally R Stone, 'Deprivation of Liberty: The Scope of Article 5 of the European Convention of Human Rights' (2012) *European Human Rights Law Review* 46.

[27] *Secretary of State for the Home Department v Mental Health Review Tribunal 'PH'* [2002] EWCA Civ 1868, [14] in reliance upon *Guzzardi* (n 18); *Ashingdane v United Kingdom* (1985) 7 EHRR 528; *HM v Switzerland* Judgment of 26 February 2002.

[28] *PH*, ibid, [15].

[29] Ibid, [16] in reliance upon *Nielsen v Denmark* (1988) EHRR 175; *HM v Switzerland* (n 27).

[30] Ibid.

[31] Ibid, [23]–[25]. See also *R (SR) v Mental Health Review Tribunal* [2005] EWHC 2923 (Admin)

[32] *R (on the application of G) v Mental Health Review Tribunal* [2004] EWHC (Admin) 2193.

[33] Ibid, [13] in reliance upon *Ashingdane* (n 27). See also *R (on the application of Secretary of State for the Home Department) v Mental Health Review Tribunal* [2004] EWHC (Admin) 2194. In *R (on the application of Davies) v South Devon Magistrates' Court*, Divisional Court, 21 December 2004, it was held that the condition of release on licence that the claimant reside at a bail hostel and only leave under escort or with express permission did not amount to a deprivation of liberty.

[34] *R (Whiston) v SS Justice* [2012] EWCA Civ 1374, [2013] 2 WLR 1080.

[35] Ibid, [31].

each case have influenced the conclusion of the court as to whether or not Article 5 was engaged. Control orders, made under the Prevention of Terrorism Act 2005, imposed a variety of obligations upon a controlled person with a view to protecting members of the public from a risk of terrorism. These included: a restriction on his association or communications with specified persons or with other persons generally; a prohibition on his being at a specified place or within a specified area at specified times or on specified days; and a prohibition or restriction on his movements to, from or within the United Kingdom. Contravention was an offence punishable by imprisonment for up to five years.[36]

In the early days of control orders considerable litigation took place as to whether or not a control order amounted to a deprivation of liberty within the meaning of Article 5. The House of Lords first considered the question in *JJ*.[37] Here the controlees were required to remain within their residences at all times save for a period of six hours between 10am and 4pm. Visitors had to be authorised by the Home Office. During the six hours when they were permitted to leave they were confined to restricted urban areas. They were prohibited from meeting anyone by pre-arrangement who had not been given Home Office clearance. A majority of the House of Lords concluded that the restrictions amounted to a deprivation of liberty. Lord Bingham observed as follows:

> The effect of the 18-hour curfew, coupled with the effective exclusion of social visitors, meant that the controlled persons were in practice in solitary confinement for this lengthy period every day for an indefinite duration, with very little opportunity for contact with the outside world. ... The area open to them during their six non-curfew hours was unobjectionable in size. ... But they were ... located in an unfamiliar area where they had no family, friends or contacts. ... Their lives were wholly regulated by the Home Office, as a prisoner's would be.[38]

The House of Lords considered the issue again in *E*[39] where the curfew was of 12 hours duration, from 7am until 7pm, and the residence was his own home in a part of London with which he was familiar, and he lived at home with his wife and family. There were no geographical restrictions during non-curfew hours and he was not prohibited from associating with named individuals. It was concluded that this did not amount to a deprivation of liberty within the meaning of Article 5.

In *AP*[40] the claimant placed a new twist on the question of whether or not Article 5 was engaged. The Supreme Court had to consider whether conditions which were proportionate restrictions on Article 8 rights could tip the balance in relation to Article 5. It also considered whether the judge could take into account subjective or person-specific factors, such as the particular difficulties of the subject's family in visiting him in a particular location, when considering whether or not a control order amounted to a deprivation of liberty. Here the claimant was subjected to a 16-hour curfew, electronic tagging and the other restrictions usually imposed. His order was later modified and he was required to move to a Midlands town 150 miles away. The Supreme Court concluded that an Article 8 restriction was capable of tipping the balance and that it was important for a judge to take into account subjective or person-specific factors when

---

[36] Section 1(4) Prevention of Terrorism Act 2005.
[37] *JJ* (n 11).
[38] Ibid, [24].
[39] *Secretary of State for the Home Department v E* [2007] UKHL 47, [2008] 1 AC 499.
[40] *Secretary of State for the Home Department v AP* [2010] UKSC 24, [2010] 3 WLR 51.

determining if there had been a deprivation of liberty. Lord Dyson noted that where the confinement was not sufficiently long of itself to amount to a deprivation of liberty, an assessment of the effect of the measures on the controlee may be decisive.[41]

2.3 Provision of Care

In P[42] it was argued that care arrangements made for sisters with substantial and permanent learning disabilities were a deprivation of their liberty within the meaning of Article 5. P attended a college where she resided for 38 weeks of the year and returned to live with her foster mother in the holidays. Q was resident in a non-secure supported living placement. The Court of Appeal held that a person's happiness was not relevant to whether she was deprived of her liberty. However, whether the person objected to confinement was relevant to the objective element[43] as was the use of medication to suppress liberty to express oneself,[44] the normality of the living arrangements,[45] and freedom to leave for purposes of recreation, education and social contact.[46] It concluded that P and Q had not been deprived of their liberty.

The issue was also considered by the Court of Appeal in *Cheshire West v P*[47] where the Court of Protection had determined that a care plan made for P was a deprivation of his liberty. P was born with cerebral palsy and Down's Syndrome and had significant physical and learning disabilities. The court confirmed that it was not appropriate to compare his situation with that of an ordinary adult. The relevant comparator here was an adult of similar age with the same capabilities and affected by the same condition or suffering the same inherent mental and physical disabilities and limitations.[48] It noted that there were many people required to live somewhere in the sense that they had nowhere to go other than the accommodation provided for them by another – but that this did not engage Article 5.[49] However, matters were different where a person had somewhere else to go and wanted to live there, but was prevented from doing so by a coercive exercise of public authority.[50] It stated that there would normally be no deprivation of liberty if someone was being cared for by their parents, friends or relatives in a family home, nor a foster placement or its adult equivalent, or small specialist sheltered accommodation.[51] It concluded that P was inherently restricted in the kind

---

[41] Ibid, [31]. See also *AH v Secretary of State for the Home Department* [2011] EWCA Civ 787 and *R (MA) v National Probation Service* [2011] EWHC 1332 (Admin) where the Administrative Court considered whether licence conditions imposed on a prisoner released on licence amounted to a deprivation of liberty. See further H Fenwick, 'Designing ETPIMs around ECHR Review or Normalisation of 'Preventive' Non-trial Based Executive Measures' (2013) 76 *Modern Law Review* 876; I Turner, 'The Prevention of Terrorism: In Support of Control Orders, and Beyond' (2011) 62 *Northern Ireland Legal Quarterly* 335; E Bates, 'Anti-terrorism Control Orders: Liberty and Security Still in the Balance' (2009) 29 *Legal Studies* 99; C Walker, 'Terrorism: Prevention of Terrorism Act 2005—Control Order' [2008] *Criminal Law Review* 486.
[42] *P and Q* (n 12).
[43] Ibid, [25].
[44] Ibid, [26].
[45] Ibid, [28].
[46] Ibid, [29].
[47] *Cheshire West* (n 22).
[48] Ibid, [86].
[49] Ibid, [54].
[50] Ibid, [58].
[51] Ibid, [103].

of life he could lead[52] and when he was at the accommodation, he was leading a life which was as normal as it could be for someone with his capabilities and there was no deprivation of liberty.[53]

By contrast in *Neary*,[54] where a local authority accepted a young man with autism and a severe learning disability into respite care for a few days at the request of his father, and then kept him there for a year, a deprivation of liberty was found. The Court of Protection stated that the key features were his objection to being at the support unit, the objection of his father and the total effective control of his 'every waking moment in an environment that was not his home'.[55]

2.4 Parents and Children

Commonly parents exercise restrictions upon the movement of their children and ordinary, acceptable parental restrictions do not engage Article 5.[56] By analogy with this principle, it was argued in *Re K*[57] that a secure accommodation order made in relation to a child under the Children Act 1989 did not engage Article 5. A majority of the Court of Appeal disagreed, holding that there was a point at which one had to stand back and ask whether or not this was within ordinary acceptable parental restrictions upon the movements of a child or whether it required justification.[58] It concluded that Article 5 was engaged, doubting whether the rights and responsibilities of a parent would cover such an exercise of parental authority for nearly two years.[59]

2.5 Crowd Control

Modern methods of policing, including 'kettling' demonstrators and 'stop and search', have also come under scrutiny. The appeal before the House of Lords in *Austin*[60] concerned police 'kettling' demonstrators as a means of controlling a demonstration organised in London on May Day 2001. The police stood in lines across the exits from Oxford Circus. From about 2.20pm people could leave only with the permission of the police, but many were prevented from leaving for a period of over seven hours. The claimants argued that this was a deprivation of liberty and that Article 5 was engaged.

The House of Lords saw the issue as determining the difference between a restriction of liberty and a deprivation of liberty. Lord Hope noted that if a deprivation of liberty were to be measured merely by the duration of the restriction, this would amount to a

---

[52] Ibid, [110].

[53] Ibid, [112].

[54] *Hillingdon London Borough Council v Neary* [2011] EWHC 1377 (Fam), [2011] 4 All ER 584.

[55] Ibid, [161].

[56] *Re K (a child) (secure accommodation order: right to liberty)* [2001] 2 All ER 719 in reliance upon *Nielsen v Denmark* (1988) 11 EHRR 175 and *Family T v Austria* (1990) 64 DR 176, 180.

[57] *Re K*, ibid.

[58] Ibid, per Dame Butler Sloss at [28].

[59] Ibid, [29]. See also the judgment of Judge LJ at [102]–[104]. Support for the conclusion was also found in *Koniarska v UK* 12 October 2000. Thorpe LJ at [61] dissented on this point, holding that the deprivation of liberty was a necessary consequence of an exercise of parental responsibility for the protection and promotion of his welfare.

[60] *Austin v Commissioner of Police of the Metropolis* [2009] UKHL 5, [2009] 1 AC 564.

deprivation. However, a whole range of factors had to be considered including nature, duration, effects and manner of execution.[61] Also important was the purpose of the restriction. Lord Hope, with whom the others agreed, stated as follows:

> [T]here is room, even in the case of fundamental rights as to whose application no restriction or limitation is permitted by the Convention, for a pragmatic approach to be taken which takes full account of all the circumstances ... the importance that must be attached in the context of article 5 to measures taken in the interests of public safety is indicated by article 2 of the Convention. ... This is a situation where a search for a fair balance is necessary if these competing fundamental rights are to be reconciled with each other ... any steps that are taken must be resorted to in good faith and must be proportionate to the situation which has made the measures necessary.[62]

The House of Lords held that if these requirements were met, it was proper to conclude that the measures of crowd control that were undertaken in the interests of the community would not infringe the Article 5 rights of individual members of the crowd whose freedom of movement was restricted by them.[63] In the view of Lord Hope, if kettling was to avoid being prohibited by the Convention:

> it must be by recognising that they are not within the ambit of article 5(1) at all ...measures of crowd control will fall outside the area of its application, so long as they are not arbitrary. This means that they must be resorted to in good faith, that they must be proportionate and that they are enforced for no longer than is reasonably necessary.[64]

2.6 Stop and Search

Whilst an arrest clearly triggers Article 5 protection, the exercise of police powers that fall short of arrest but nonetheless prevent an individual from doing what he or she likes, such as stop and search, fall into a grey area. Stop and search without reasonable suspicion under the Terrorism Act 2000 was the subject of challenge in *Gillan*.[65] At the time, there was no ECtHR authority on this particular question. The House of Lords held that there was no deprivation of liberty within the meaning of Article 5. Lord Bingham held as follows:

> [T]he procedure will ordinarily be relatively brief. The person stopped will not be arrested, handcuffed, confined or removed to any different place. I do not think, in the absence of special circumstances, such a person should be regarded as being detained in the sense of being confined or kept in custody, but more properly of being detained in the sense of kept from proceeding or kept waiting. There is no deprivation of liberty.[66]

---

[61] Ibid, per Lord Hope at [17].

[62] Ibid, [34].

[63] Ibid, [34].

[64] Ibid, [37]. Other members of the House of Lords agreed. In *Austin v United Kingdom* (2012) 55 EHRR 14 the ECtHR also found no deprivation of liberty. See further H Fenwick, 'Marginalising Human Rights: Breach of the Peace, "Kettling" the Human Rights Act and Public Protest' [2009] *Public Law* 737; D Mead, 'Of Kettles, Cordons and Crowd Control—Austin v Commissioner of Police and the Meaning of "Deprivation of Liberty"' [2009] *European Human Rights Law Review* 376.

[65] *R (Gillan) v Commissioner of Police for the Metropolis* [2006] UKHL 12, [2006] 2 AC 307.

[66] Ibid, [25]. See also *Laporte v Chief Constable of Gloucestershire* [2006] UKHL 55, [2007] 2 AC 105 where coaches containing demonstrators were stopped but the claimants only relied upon Arts 10 and 11.

The Administrative Court also considered the question in the later case of *Roberts*,[67] where the claimant had been searched by a police officer acting pursuant to an authorisation to search, without reasonable suspicion, pursuant to section 60 of the Criminal Justice and Public Order Act 1994. This time relying on ECtHR authority,[68] the Administrative Court held that there was no deprivation of liberty here:

> [T]he claimant was not confined, nor required to move to a police station, handcuffed or restrained. This claimant was only restrained when she sought to resist the exercise of the police power under s 60. ... Had the claimant not resisted, the search would probably only have been as short as three minutes.[69]

3. Article 5(1)

Article 5(1) guarantees liberty and security of person. The concepts of liberty and security are linked with the broad aim of protecting the person against an arrest or detention which is arbitrary.[70] Continued detention can be justified in a given case only if there are specific indications of a genuine requirement of public interest which, notwithstanding the presumption of innocence, outweighs the rule of respect for individual liberty.[71] To this end, Article 5(1) provides a right to liberty which is subject to six specified exceptions[72] and to two overriding requirements.[73] It has been held that it is revealing to note what is not included in paragraphs 1(a)–(f): 'Whatever their country's particular historical experiences, the framers of the Convention can hardly have forgotten the problem of public disorder or intended to deny the authorities the conventional means of coping with it.'[74]

The first overriding requirement of Article 5(1) is that any deprivation of liberty must be in accordance with a procedure prescribed by law. The second requirement is that it must be lawful.[75] If these requirements are met, Article 5(1) does not limit the period for which a person can be detained.[76]

In common with other Convention rights, extradition and deportation from the UK is not lawful if the claimant can establish a flagrant denial of his or her Article 5 rights in the destination state. In *Sullivan*[77] the claimant established that if he were to be extra-

---

[67] *R (Roberts) v Commissioner of Police of the Metropolis* [2012] EWHC 1977 (Admin), [2012] HRLR 28
[68] *Gillan v UK* (2010) 50 EHRR 45 and *Austin v UK* (n 64).
[69] *Roberts* (n 67), [15]. See further D Moeckli, 'Stop and Search under the Terrorism Act 2000' (2007) 70 Modern Law Review 659.
[70] *R v Crown Court at Leeds, ex p Wardle* [2001] UKHL 12, [2001] 2 WLR 865, per Lord Hope at [83] in reliance upon *Bozano v France* (1986) 9 EHRR 297, [54]; *Amuur v France* (1996) 22 EHRR 533, [50].
[71] Ibid.
[72] This is an exhaustive list. See *Re K* (n 56), per Dame Butler Sloss at [33] in reliance upon *Engel v Netherlands (No 1)* (1976) 1 EHRR 647, [57].
[73] Where the detention falls within Art 5, the burden of proof is on the claimant to bring the facts within one of the exceptions.
[74] *Cheshire West* (n 22), [26].
[75] Ibid, in reliance upon *R v Governor of Brockhill Prison, ex p Evans (No 2)* [2001] 2 AC 19.
[76] *Flynn v HM Advocate* [2004] UKPC D1, [2004] HRLR 17.
[77] *Sullivan v United States* [2012] EWHC 1680 (Admin).

dited to the United States there was a real risk he would be detained under a process known as civil commitment. Under this process a person may be committed indefinitely if he is found by a judge to be irresponsible for personal conduct with respect to sexual matters and thereby dangerous to other persons. The evidence suggested that no sex offender committed to indeterminate detention since the programme began had been released. The Administrative Court held that were an order of civil commitment to be made, it would be a flagrant denial of his rights under Article 5(1) as it fell outside the provisions of Article (1)(e).[78] Finding a risk that he would suffer such a flagrant denial of his rights, it gave the United States the opportunity to make an assurance.

3.1 Procedure Prescribed by Law

Any deprivation of liberty must be in accordance with a procedure prescribed by law. The notion underlying these words in Article 5(1) is one of fair and proper procedure, namely that any measure depriving a person of his liberty should issue from and be executed by an appropriate authority, and the procedure under which this is done should not be arbitrary.[79] This prevents reliance upon common law powers where there is already a statutory power to detain. So, for example, where mental health legislation provides an exhaustive code for compulsory hospital admissions, it is not possible also to resort to common law to justify a decision to detain.[80] Errors in what is said by counsel or a judge will not, of themselves, result in a procedure being unlawful. In contrast, defects such as a failure to give the individual an opportunity to be heard, or an opportunity properly to consider and to respond to the case or evidence against him, may lead to an infringement of Article 5(1).[81] Often this question is combined with the question of whether detention is lawful.

3.2 Lawful

Any deprivation of liberty under Article 5(1) must also be lawful. The first question is whether the detention is lawful under domestic law. Any detention which is unlawful in domestic law will automatically be unlawful under Article 5(1). The second question is whether, assuming that the detention is lawful under domestic law, it nevertheless complies with the general requirements of the Convention. These are based upon the principle that any restriction on human rights and fundamental freedoms must be prescribed by law. This principle includes the requirements that the domestic law must be sufficiently accessible to the individual and that it must be sufficiently precise to enable the individual to foresee the consequences of the restriction. The third question is whether, again assuming that the detention is lawful under domestic law, it is

---

[78] Ibid, [33].

[79] *Anderson v Scottish Ministers* [2001] UKPC D5, [2003] 2 AC 602, per Lord Hope at [25] in reliance upon *Winterwerp v The Netherlands* (1979) 2 EHRR 387, 405.

[80] *R (Sessay) v South London & Maudsley NHS Foundation Trust* [2011] EWHC 2617 (QB), [2012] 2 WLR 1071.

[81] *R (on the application of A) v Harrow Crown Court* [2003] EWHC (Admin) 2020, [16]. See also *Horgan v Horgan* [2002] EWCA Civ 1371; *Zakharov v White* [2003] EWHC (Ch) 2463.

nevertheless open to criticism on the ground that it is arbitrary because, for example, it was resorted to in bad faith or was not proportionate.[82]

3.2.1 Lawful under Domestic Law

Any detention which is unlawful in domestic law, will automatically be unlawful under Article 5(1).[83] However, detention does not automatically become unlawful in domestic law merely because the ECtHR has found a particular domestic practice contrary to the Convention.[84] In addition, if an individual is committed to detention by an ultra vires order, it has been held that the order is legally effective unless and until it is set aside and the detention consequential on that order is lawful as a matter of domestic law.[85] Breach of a public law duty on the part of the person authorising detention is capable of rendering that detention unlawful.[86] It may be that the Secretary of State has not given effect to a published policy related to the power to detain. A failure to adhere to such a policy without good reason is an error, which bears upon and is relevant to the decision to detain and is an abuse of power which renders the detention itself unlawful.[87]

3.2.2 Prescribed by Law

Even if detention is lawful under domestic law, the domestic law must be sufficiently accessible to the individual and sufficiently precise to enable the individual to forsee the consequences of the restriction.[88] It may only be necessary to point to the empowering statute rather than any policy or procedure which has been derived from it. In *Wardle*[89] it was argued that the substitution of a fresh custody time limit in relation to a new charge was not prescribed by law. A majority of the House of Lords disagreed holding that if a fresh custody time limit was to be substituted, the procedure under which this was to be done was laid down by statute and the regulation defined the length of the substituted time limit.[90] By contrast in *Nadarajah*[91] the policy of the immigration service was to not detain those to be imminently removed where proceedings challenging the right to remove had been instituted. However, it was also the policy to disregard information from those acting for asylum seekers that proceedings were about to be initiated. The latter aspect of the policy was not known or accessible, and the Court of Appeal therefore concluded that the detention was not lawful.[92]

---

[82] *Evans* (n 75), per Lord Hope in reliance upon *Sunday Times v United Kingdom* (1979–80) 2 EHRR 245; *Zamir v United Kingdom* (1985) 40 DR 42, [90]–[91]; *Engel* (n 72), [58]; *Tsirlis and Kouloumpas v Greece* [1997] 25 EHRR 198, [56]. See also *Anderson* (n 79), per Lord Hope at [22].

[83] *Evans*, ibid.

[84] *R (on the application of Middleton) v Secretary of State for the Home Department* [2003] EWHC (Admin) 315.

[85] *A* (n 2).

[86] *Walumba Lumba (Congo) v SSHD* [2011] UKSC 12.

[87] See *Lumba*, ibid, and *R (Kambadzi) v SSHD* [2011] 1 WLR 1299.

[88] *Evans* (n 75). See also *Nadarajah v Secretary of State for the Home Department* [2003] EWCA Civ 1768, [64]–[65].

[89] *Wardle* (n 70).

[90] Ibid, per Lord Hope at [88]. See also Lord Clyde at [107] and Lord Slynn at [34], and *Anderson* (n 79).

[91] *Nadarajah* (n 88).

[92] Ibid, [66]–[67].

3.2.3 Not Arbitrary

Finally, even if detention is lawful under domestic law, it is considered to be unlawful if it is arbitrary because, for example, it is resorted to in bad faith or is not proportionate.[93] In determining the arbitrariness of any detention, regard must be had to the legitimacy of the aim of detention and the proportionality of the detention in relation to that aim.[94] Detention does not become arbitrary simply because one cannot tell whether it will last longer than it would have done under the system that has been superseded.[95]

3.2.4 Extradition and Deportation

It is possible for the actions of a foreign court to be so flawed that there is no conviction of an offender for a crime and his detention in the UK therefore becomes unlawful. In *Willcox*[96] it was argued that the conviction of Willcox in Thailand was not the conviction of a competent court and a flagrant denial of justice. The Administrative Court did not find a flagrant denial here and this aspect of the Article 5 claim failed.

3.3 Article 5(1)(a): Conviction by a Competent Court

Article 5(1)(a) allows for the lawful detention of a person after conviction by a competent court.

3.3.1 Causal Link

There must be a causal link between the conviction and the subsequent detention. This has been of particular concern in relation to life sentences where the release date is not set by the sentencing court. Once the tariff period has expired, it is up to the Parole Board to decide whether or not the prisoner should be released. It has been held that the period of detention between the expiry of the tariff period and the decision of the Parole Board is not incompatible with Article 5(1)(a), although it must be subject to control through Article 5(4).[97]

In *James*[98] the House of Lords held that the situation does change once the prisoner has served the minimum term. The causal link required by Article 5(1)(a) might eventually be broken if a position were to be reached in which a decision not to release or to re-detain was based on grounds that were inconsistent with the objectives of the sentencing court:

---

[93] *Evans* (n 75).
[94] *Lichniak* (n 5), per Lord Bingham at [16].
[95] *Flynn* (n 76), per Lord Rodger at [87].
[96] *R (Willcox) v Secretary of State for Justice* [2009] EWHC 1483 (Admin), [2010] 2 Prison LR 179.
[97] *Noorkoiv* (n 8). See also *R (on the application of Smith) v Parole Board* [2005] UKHL 1, [2005] 1 WLR 350. See also *Secretary of State for Justice v James* [2009] UKHL 22, [2010] 1 AC 553 and *R v Pedley* [2009] EWCA Crim 840, [2009] 1 WLR 2517.
[98] *James*, ibid.

The objective that justifies continued detention at this stage is public protection. The sentencing judge makes no assessment of the extent to which, if at all, the prisoner will represent a danger to the public once he has served the minimum term.[99]

However, Lord Hope noted that it was hard to see how there could be an absence of causal connection in the case of a prisoner whose case has been referred to, and was still under consideration, by the Parole Board.[100] In his view, continued detention was not arbitrary until the Parole Board had determined detention was no longer necessary, but as soon as it made that assessment, the causal connection was broken.[101] Lord Brown also held that a decision not to release an indeterminate sentence public protection prisoner because the Parole Board remained unsatisfied of his safety for release could never be said to be inconsistent with the objectives of the sentencing court or to have no connection with the objectives of the legislature or the court.[102] Lord Hope did note that it was possible to conceive of circumstances where the system broke down with the result that the Parole Board was unable to perform its function: 'In that situation continued detention could be said to be arbitrary because there was no way in which it could be brought to an end in the manner that the original sentence contemplated.'[103] However, he did not see the delay in the present appeals as having created a breakdown in this instance and the causal link was not broken.[104]

The position is slightly more complicated where it is necessary for a prisoner to attend a treatment programme before the Parole Board will consider his or her release. For example, in *Cawser*[105] the prisoner complained that he had to wait a long time for his place on the Extended Sex Offender Treatment Programme and as a result his release date was substantially delayed because the Parole Board was precluded from directing a life prisoner's release unless it was satisfied that it was no longer necessary for the protection of the public that the prisoner should be confined. The Court of Appeal concluded that detention would not become unlawful under Article 5(1)(a) even if no provision were made for such courses.[106] The causal link was not broken by the delay in providing (or a failure to provide) treatment which itself may or may not thereafter have served to establish the absence of continuing dangerousness.[107]

The Secretary of State could hardly be under an absolute duty to devise and provide courses for all who want them, and, moreover, to do so early enough in the prisoner's sentence to maximise his hope of release on or very soon after his tariff expiry date.[108]

Laws LJ noted that there was a possibility that the Secretary of State might impose a condition so hard of fulfilment that continued detention for failure to meet the condition ought no longer to be regarded as justified by the original sentence, but this could

[99] Ibid, per Lord Hope at [12].
[100] Ibid, [14].
[101] Ibid, [14].
[102] Ibid, [49].
[103] Ibid, [15].
[104] See also Lord Brown at [51] and Lord Mance at [126]–[128]. In *James, Wells and Lee v United Kingdom* (2013) 56 EHRR 12 the ECtHR found that following the expiry of tariff periods and until steps were taken to progress them through the prison system with a view to providing them with access to approrpiate rehabilitative courses, their detention was arbitrary and therefore unlawful.
[105] *Cawser* (n 7).
[106] Ibid, per Simon Brown LJ at [31].
[107] Ibid, [32].
[108] Ibid, [34].

not arise by reference to any judicial perception as to scarce resources.[109] Arden LJ dissented on this point, holding that in an exceptional case the failure by the Secretary of State to provide a particular prisoner with an appropriate treatment course which in practice is a condition of release may, if sufficiently prolonged, break the causal link and render the detention unlawful.[110]

The sentence of a trial court has been held to satisfy Article 5(1) not only in relation to the initial term served by the prisoner but also in relation to a licence revocation since conditional release subject to recall forms an integral component of the composite sentence. However, a decision by the Parole Board to revoke a licence must comply with Article 5(4).[111] Provided the circumstances under which the original sentence was imposed are sufficiently reflected in those that pertain at the time when the recall order is made, the recall of a prisoner subject to a discretionary life sentence does not contravene Article 5(1)(a).[112] It is not necessary that there be some form of preliminary inquiry into the recall order immediately the recall takes place or that, in its absence, the statutory scheme is incompatible with Article 5.[113]

Release on home detention curfew is not viewed as the restoration of liberty sufficient to engage Article 5 if and when the prisoner is recalled to prison:[114]

> [R]elease on home detention curfew was much more closely integrated with the original sentence than is release as of right once the custodial period has been completed ... it is properly to be seen as a modified way of performing the original sentence imposed by the judge: the recall simply restores the primary way in which it was assumed that the sentence would be served.[115]

Detention is no longer lawful once the date for release has passed. In *Evans*[116] the respondent was entitled to a reduction in the actual period to be served in prison due to the time she spent in prison before trial. The governor calculated the date in accordance with what he thought the law to be, but the High Court subsequently held that this was not the law and her release date should have been earlier. The House of Lords concluded that her detention after the correct date was unlawful and contrary to Article 5(1)(a).

3.3.2 Disproportionate Period of Detention

It has also been argued that the imposition of a life sentence in certain circumstances is contrary to Article 5(1)(a) because it is disproportionate. For example, in *Lichniak*[117] it was argued that the mandatory life sentence for murder[118] was arbitrary and disproportionate as it required the same sentence to be passed on all convicted murderers

---

[109] Ibid, [44].

[110] Ibid, [45]–[54] in reliance upon *Van Droogenbroek v Belgium* (1982) 4 EHRR 443, [40].

[111] *R (West) v Parole Board* [2005] UKHL 1, [2005] 1 WLR 350. See also *Roberts v Secretary of State for the Home Department* [2005] EWCA Civ 1663, [2006] 1 WLR 843.

[112] *Hirst v Secretary of State for the Home Department* [2006] EWCA Civ 945, [2006] 1 WLR 3083. See also *Dunn v Parole Board* [2008] EWCA Civ 374, [2009] 1 WLR 728.

[113] *Hirst*, ibid, [21].

[114] *Whiston* (n 34), [31].

[115] Ibid.

[116] *Evans* (n 75).

[117] *Lichniak* (n 5).

[118] Imposed under s 1(1) Murder (Abolition of Death Penalty) Act 1965.

whatever the facts of the case or the circumstances of the offender, and irrespective of whether they were thought to present a danger to the public or not. The House of Lords held that if it was the case that, on imposition of a mandatory life sentence, the convicted murderer forfeited his liberty to the state for the rest of his days, this would violate Article 5 as being arbitrary and disproportionate.[119] However, it had been concluded in *Anderson*[120] that such was not the effect of the sentence. The punitive element of the sentence was represented by the tariff term, imposed as punishment for the serious crime. The preventative element was represented by the power to continue to detain until the Parole Board considered it safe to release him and also by the power to recall.[121]

Here, having regard to the legitimacy of the aim of the detention and the proportionality of the detention in relation to that aim, and viewing the complaints in the context of their treatment as a whole, the House of Lords concluded that the appellants were not sentenced to an arbitrary, rule-of-thumb term of imprisonment. Lord Bingham concluded as follows:

> Those responsible did their best to match the respective terms to the particular facts and circumstances of each case. ... There is, inevitably, a balance to be struck between the interest of the individual and the interest of society, and I do not think it objectionable, in the case of someone who has once taken life with the intent necessary for murder, to prefer the latter in case of doubt. ... But a prisoner recalled ... should be in no danger of recall in the absence of any resort to violence.[122]

A different conclusion was reached in relation to the automatic life sentence in *Offen*.[123] This sentence must be imposed for a second serious offence unless the court is of the opinion that there are exceptional circumstances relating to either of the offences or to the offender which justify its not doing so.[124] The Court of Appeal held that there have been and will be cases where the automatic life sentence has and will operate in a disproportionate manner. 'It is easy to find examples of situations where two offences could be committed which were categorised as serious by the section but where it would be wholly disproportionate to impose a life sentence to protect the public.'[125] However, using section 3 of the HRA, this problem was avoided, the Court of Appeal concluding that the Act should be applied so that it did not result in offenders being sentenced to life imprisonment when they did not constitute a significant risk to the public.[126]

---

[119] *Lichniak* (n 5), per Lord Bingham at [8].

[120] *R (on the application of Anderson) v Secretary of State for the Home Department* [2002] UKHL 46, [2003] 1 AC 837.

[121] *Lichniak* (n 5), per Lord Bingham at [8].

[122] Ibid, [16] in reliance upon *V v United Kingdom* (1999) 30 EHRR 121. See also *R v Parchment* [2003] EWCA Crim 2428.

[123] *R v Offen* [2001] 1 WLR 253.

[124] Section 2, Crime (Sentences) Act 1997.

[125] *Offen* (n 123), [95].

[126] Ibid, [97]. See also *R v Kelly* [2001] EWCA Crim 1751, [2001] Crim LR 836; *R v Drew* [2003] UKHL 25, [2003] 1 WLR 1213.

3.4 Article 5(1)(b): Non-compliance with the Lawful Order of a Court or to Secure the Fulfilment of any Obligation Prescribed by Law

Article 5(1)(b) permits the lawful arrest or detention of a person for non-compliance with the lawful order of a court or in order to secure the fulfilment of any obligation prescribed by law. It has been relied upon to justify: arrest under a default warrant for non-payment of a fine;[127] detention for contempt of court;[128] a condition of bail requiring the defendant during the hours of curfew to present himself at the door of his home if required to do so by a police officer;[129] the committal of an undischarged bankrupt to prison under the Insolvency Act 1986 for failure to co-operate with his trustee in bankruptcy;[130] and to remand a person for two weeks on the basis that he may be required to give evidence.[131] It has been held not to authorise a failure to comply with the conditions of the Court of Appeal's order granting bail.[132]

With respect to arbitrariness, it was held in *Chorley Justices*[133] that a condition of bail requiring the defendant during the hours of curfew to present himself at the door of his home if requested to do so by a police officer struck the appropriate balance in the interests of both the individual and society.

> [T]here was a real risk that the Defendant would be deprived of his liberty; in other words, the justices would have been entitled to have him remanded in custody. The ability of the justices, therefore, to impose conditions appropriate to avoid the risks to the public ... is one which is beneficial not only to the community, but also to the individual Defendant.[134]

3.5 Article 5(1)(c): Reasonable Suspicion of Having Committed an Offence

Article 5(1)(c) permits the lawful arrest or detention of a person effected for the purpose of bringing him before the competent legal authority on reasonable suspicion of having committed an offence, or when it is reasonably considered necessary to prevent his committing an offence or fleeing after having done so. In order to have a reasonable suspicion, there must be facts or information to support the suspicion which would satisfy an objective observer that the person concerned may have committed the offence.[135] 'Facts' must not be given a restrictive meaning, and clearly included is

---

[127] *Henderson v Chief Constable of Cleveland Constabulary* [2001] EWCA Civ 335. See generally D van Zyl Smit and A Ashworth, 'Disproportionate Sentences as Human Rights Violations' (2004) 67 *Modern Law Review* 541.

[128] *Horgan* (n 81).

[129] *R (on the application of the Crown Prosecution Service) v Chorley Justices* [2002] EWHC (Admin) 2163.

[130] *Hickling v Baker* [2007] EWCA Civ 287, [2007] 1 WLR 2386.

[131] *TH v Crown Court Wood Green* [2006] EWHC 2683 (Admin), [2007] 1 WLR 1670.

[132] *Stellato v Ministry of Justice* [2010] EWCA Civ 1435, [2011] 2 WLR 936, [31].

[133] *Chorley Justices* (n 129).

[134] Ibid, [33].

[135] *Cumming v Chief Constable of Northumbria Police* [2003] EWCA Civ 1844, [2004] ACD 42, [37] in reliance upon *Castorina v Chief Constable of Surrey* [1996] LG Rev Rep 241 and *Fox, Campbell and Hartley v United Kingdom* (1990) 13 EHRR 157.

information and information obtained from a third party.[136] Opportunity can amount to reasonable grounds for suspicion, and more than one person can be arrested even if the crime could only have been committed by one person.[137] A person can be arrested and detained in good faith for questioning in order to obtain evidence.[138]

In a crowd situation, it appears there is no need for individual consideration. It was held in *Hicks*[139] that the arrest and detention of the claimants to prevent them demonstrating and thereby causing a breach of the peace was within Article 5(1)(c). It confirmed that the two parts of Article 5(1)(c) 'for the purpose of bring him before the competent legal authority' and 'necessary to prevent his committing an offence' were separate bases for detention.[140]

At common law there is an additional requirement which must be satisfied even if there are reasonable grounds for suspicion. The officer must exercise his discretion in accordance with *Wednesbury* principles.[141] However, in *Cumming*[142] the Court of Appeal rephrased the test, holding that the court must consider whether or not the decision to arrest is one which no reasonable police officer, applying his mind to the matter, could reasonably take, bearing in mind the effect on the appellant's right to liberty.[143] The more substantial the interference with liberty, the narrower the otherwise generous *Wednesbury* ambit of reasonableness becomes.[144] It is possible that the test might approach one of necessity where the intrusion on a person's liberty is of an egregious or public nature and for a long period or accompanied by harsh treatment.[145]

3.6 Article 5(1)(d): Minors

Article 5(1)(d) permits the detention of a minor by lawful order for the purpose of educational supervision or his lawful detention for the purpose of bringing him before the competent legal authority. The meaning of educational supervision extends far beyond school.

> [I]t involves education in the broad sense, similar ... to the general development of the child's physical, intellectual, emotional, social and behavioural abilities, all of which have to be encouraged by responsible parents, as part of his upbringing and education, and for this purpose, an appropriate level of supervision of the child to enhance his development, where necessary, by restricting his liberty is permitted.[146]

Education need not be demonstrated to be the sole purpose of the detention; Article 5(1)(d) is satisfied if it is just one of the purposes of the detention. Only where there

---

[136] *Cumming*, ibid, [40].
[137] Ibid, at [41] in reliance upon *Hussein v Chong Fook Kam* [1970] AC 942.
[138] *Al Fayed v Commissioner of Police of the Metropolis* [2004] EWCA Civ 1579, at [88] in reliance upon *Brogan v United Kingdom* (1988) 11 EHRR 117 and *Murray v United Kingdom* (1994) 19 EHRR 193.
[139] *R (Hicks) v Commissioner of Police of the Metropolis* [2012] EWHC 1947 (Admin), [2012] ACD 102.
[140] Ibid, [184].
[141] *Castorina* (n 135), 249.
[142] *Cumming* (n 135).
[143] Ibid, [43].
[144] *Al Fayed*, (n 138), [83].
[145] Ibid, [82].
[146] See *Re K* (n 56), per Judge LJ at [107] in reliance upon *Bouamar v Belgium* (1989) 11 EHRR 1 and *Koniarska v United Kingdom* Judgment of 12 October 2000.

is no present or reasonably imminent educational provision does the Article 5(1)(d) defence fail.[147]

In K[148] it was argued that a secure accommodation order imposed under section 25 of the Children Act 1989 did not fall within Article 5(1)(d). The Court of Appeal disagreed, holding that K was receiving education which was carefully supervised and from which he was clearly benefiting. In the opinion of the court, it was not necessary for section 25 to refer to education since, by the provisions of the Education Act 1996, education was compulsory for any child under 16, as K was.[149] Judge LJ held that the purpose of the order, and its implementation by the local authority, was to provide the best available environment to enable K's education, both in the narrow and broad senses, under the degree of supervision and control necessary to avoid harm or injury to himself, and to improve his prospects of avoiding both in the long term as well as in the immediate future.[150]

3.7 Article 5(1)(e): Persons of Unsound Mind

Article 5(1)(e) permits the lawful detention of persons for the prevention of the spreading of infectious diseases, and of persons of unsound mind, alcoholics, drug addicts or vagrants. It is primarily in relation the detention of persons of unsound mind that cases have been brought under the HRA with one reported judgment concerning an incapacitated adult who was not mentally ill but had severe learning difficulties.[151]

3.7.1 Minimum Conditions

Three minimum conditions have to be satisfied for there to be lawful detention of persons of unsound mind within the meaning of Article 5(1)(e). These are commonly referred to as the 'Winterwerp criteria'.[152] The individual concerned must be reliably shown to be of unsound mind, that is to say, a true mental disorder must be established before a competent authority on the basis of objective medical expertise; the mental disorder must be of a kind or degree warranting compulsory confinement; and the validity of continued confinement depends upon the persistence of such a disorder.[153] It remains for domestic law to lay down the substantive and procedural rules which regulate the detention of persons of unsound mind.[154] In relation to an incapacitated adult, it has been held that expert evidence is usually provided by a psychologist or paediatrician.[155]

---

[147] Re K, ibid, per Thorpe LJ at [64] in reliance upon Bouamar, ibid.
[148] Re K, ibid.
[149] Ibid, per Dame Butler-Sloss at [35]–[36] in reliance upon Koniarsaka (n 146).
[150] Re K, ibid, [107].
[151] G v E (by his litigation friend the Official Solicitor) [2010] EWCA Civ 822, [2011] 3 WLR 652.
[152] Winterwerp (n 79).
[153] Anderson (n 79), per Lord Hope at [26] quoting from X v United Kingdom 4 EHRR 188, [40]. See also Luberti v Italy (1984) 6 EHRR 440, [27] and Johnson v UK (1997) 27 EHRR 296, [60].
[154] Anderson, ibid, per Lord Hope at [23] in reliance upon Winterwerp (n 79).
[155] G v E (n 151), [61].

(a) Burden of Proof

The same approach must be applied when considering whether to admit a patient as that which has to be applied when considering discharge. The burden of proof in both instances is on those seeking to detain and can never be imposed on the patient.[156] In H[157] the Court of Appeal concluded that sections 72 and 73 of the Mental Health Act 1983 were incompatible with Article 5(1)(e) because the burden of proof was effectively placed on the patient who wished to be discharged to prove that the criteria for admission were not satisfied.[158]

The standard of proof was the subject of debate in AN[159] where the standard applied when the claimant applied for discharge under section 73 of the Mental Health Act 1983 was the ordinary civil standard on the balance of probabilities. The Court of Appeal held that the civil standard was flexible in its application and enabled proper account to be taken of the seriousness of the allegations to be proved and the consequences of proving them.[160] '[T]he more serious the allegation or the more serious the consequences if the allegation is proved, the stronger must be the evidence before a court will find the allegation proved on the balance of probabilities.'[161]

In the view of the court, the practical application of the flexible approach meant that the criminal and civil standards were likely in certain contexts to produce the same or similar results.[162] In relation to sections 72 and 73 of the Mental Health Act 1983 it held that cogent evidence was in practice required in order to satisfy the tribunal, on the balance of probabilities, that the conditions for continuing detention were met.[163] 'The unwarranted detention of an individual on grounds of mental disorder is a very serious matter, but the unwarranted release from detention of an individual who is suffering from mental disorder is also a very serious matter.'[164]

The court confirmed that the application of a standard of proof on the balance of probabilities and a recognition that cogent evidence would in practice be required to meet the standard gave full effect to the *Winterwerp* test.[165] It also confirmed that the tribunal should apply the standard of proof on the balance of probabilities to all the issues it had to determine.[166]

(b) Discharge Subject to Supervision

Particular problems have arisen where a tribunal has ordered the discharge of a patient from detention subject to supervision in the community by a named social worker and named psychiatrist but no social worker or psychiatrist has been available. For

[156] R (on the application of H) v Mental Health Review Tribunal, North & East London Region [2001] EWCA Civ 415, [2002] QB 1.
[157] Ibid.
[158] The Mental Health Act 1983 (Remedial) Order 2001 came into force in 26 November 2001. Its effect is to reverse the burden of proof in ss 72 and 73 so that a tribunal is now obliged to direct the discharge of a patient unless satisfied that the relevant criteria for detention have been proved.
[159] R (AN) v Mental Health Review Tribunal [2005] EWCA Civ 1605, [2006] QB 468.
[160] Ibid, [59].
[161] Ibid, [62].
[162] Ibid, [69].
[163] Ibid, [72].
[164] Ibid, [73].
[165] Ibid, [80].
[166] Ibid, [104].

example, in *IH*[167] a mental health review tribunal had decided that the appellant could be discharged from detention at a secure hospital provided, inter alia, there was supervision of him by a named social worker and named psychiatrist. The health authority was unable to find a psychiatrist willing to supervise and his detention continued. Although more than two years later another mental health review tribunal decided that it was still appropriate for him to be detained, he contended that his detention between these dates was in breach of Article 5.

The House of Lords held that there was no time when the appellant was unlawfully detained and no breach of Article 5(1)(e).

> There was never a medical consensus, nor did the tribunal find, that the *Winterwerp* criteria were not satisfied. The tribunal considered that the appellant could be satisfactorily treated and supervised in the community if its conditions were met, as it expected, but the alternative, if these conditions proved impossible to meet, was not discharge, either absolutely or subject only to a condition of recall, but continued detention. The appellant was never detained when there were no grounds for detaining him.[168]

It concluded that the health authority only had to use its best endeavours to procure compliance with the conditions laid down by the tribunal and had no power to require any psychiatrist to act in a way which conflicted with the conscientious professional judgment of that psychiatrist.[169]

However, in *W*[170] the Court of Appeal held that if, although it has used its best endeavours, a health authority is unable to provide the necessary services, the tribunal must think again. 'If, as is likely in the circumstances, it concludes that it is necessary for the patient to remain detained in hospital in order to receive treatment it should record that decision.'[171]

(c) Unfit to be Tried

There is a genuine concern that those determined unfit to be tried pursuant to section 4(5) of the Criminal Procedure (Insanity) Act 1964 but who are then found to have committed the act charged and admitted to hospital under a restriction order have not met the *Winterwerp* criteria. This was raised in *Grant*,[172] where the defendant, charged with murder, had been found unfit to be tried. A second jury found that she had committed the act charged and the judge ordered that she be admitted to hospital. Once a person is found to be unfit to be tried there is no further consideration of his or her mental condition. No one is required specifically to address, prior to the person's detention, the question of whether he suffers from a mental disorder sufficiently serious to warrant detention. The Court of Appeal appreciated that the question was one of some difficulty and concluded that, in the circumstances of the present case, it was unnecessary for it to reach any conclusions on the issue since it was satisfied on the facts that the conditions for detention were in fact met.[173]

---

[167] *R v Secretary of State for the Home Department, ex p IH* [2003] UKHL 59, [2004] 2 AC 253.
[168] Ibid, per Lord Bingham at [28]. See also *H* (n 156).
[169] Ibid, per Lord Bingham at [29]. This answered the question raised by the Court of Appeal in *R (K) v Camden and Islington Health Authority* [2001] EWCA Civ 240, [2002] QB 198.
[170] *W v Doncaster Metropolitan Borough Council* [2004] EWCA Civ 378, [2004] LGR 743.
[171] Ibid, per Baker LJ at [50].
[172] *R v Grant* [2001] EWCA Crim 2611, [2002] 2 WLR 1409.
[173] Ibid, [54].

3.7.2 Public Safety

The Convention allows those within Article 5(1)(e) to be deprived of their liberty because they are a threat to public safety and their own interests may necessitate their detention. The need to protect the public from serious harm is in itself a legitimate reason for the detention of persons of unsound mind, provided always that the conditions set out above are satisfied. In this context, the fair balance which is inherent in the whole of the Convention between the demands of the general interest of the community and the requirements of the protection of the individual's fundamental rights favours the general interests of the community.[174] In *Grant*[175] the Court of Appeal concluded that it was not unreasonable for Parliament to have laid down a mandatory requirement of admission to hospital for a person who has been charged with murder, has been found to have done the act charged but was under a disability so as to be unfit to be tried, and detention in those circumstances was not arbitrary.[176]

In certain circumstances, the objective may not be general public safety but the safety of a section of the public. For example, in *Anderson*[177] one appellant argued that he was a criminal who simply wished to go back to prison rather than remain in a secure hospital. The Privy Council held that detention could also be justified on the ground of protecting a section of the public—here those he would come into contact with in prison, such as prison officers, other inmates and those who visit prisons for religious, educational, social work or other purposes. It concluded that his continued detention in the hospital was not disproportionate to the legitimate aim of protecting that section of the public from serious harm.[178]

3.7.3 Treatment

A mental patient's right to treatment appropriate to his condition cannot as such be derived from Article 5(1)(e). Although there must be some relationship between the ground of permitted deprivation of liberty relied and the place and conditions of detention, the Article is not in principle concerned with suitable treatment or conditions. The fact that a mental disorder is not susceptible to treatment does not mean that continued detention in a hospital is arbitrary or disproportionate.[179] In *Anderson*[180] the Privy Council concluded that it was not incompatible with Article 5(1)(e) for the Scottish Parliament to require the continued detention of restricted patients in a hospital where this was necessary on grounds of public safety, whether or not their mental disorder was treatable.[181]

---

[174] *Anderson* (n 79), per Lord Hope at [30] in reliance upon *Guzzardi* (n 18), [98]; *Witold Litwa v Poland* (2000) 33 EHRR 1267, [60].

[175] *Grant* (n 172).

[176] Ibid, [51].

[177] *Anderson* (n 79).

[178] Ibid, per Lord Hope at [37]–[38] and per Lord Clyde at [65].

[179] Ibid, per Lord Hope at [28]–[29] in reliance upon *Winterwerp* (n 79), [51] and *Ashingdane* (n 27), [44].

[180] *Anderson* (n 79).

[181] Ibid, per Lord Hope at [31] and per Lord Clyde at [60]–[64]. See also *von Brandenburg* (n 2).

3.8 Article 5(1)(f): Unauthorised Entry, Action Taken with a View to Deportation or Extradition

Article 5(1)(f) permits the lawful arrest or detention of a person to prevent his effecting an unauthorised entry into the country or of a person against whom action is being taken with a view to deportation or extradition. It does not permit immigration detention on security grounds.[182] It also does not permit detention with a view to compelling co-operation.[183] Deprivation of liberty under Article 5(1)(f) is justified only for so long as deportation proceedings are in progress, and detention ceases to be permissible if the proceedings are not pursued with due diligence.[184] It is clear that Article 5 affords those detained under this part no right to bail.[185]

Lawfulness, as discussed above, has a particular role to play in detention on these grounds and it is important to consider the lawfulness of detention and the circumstances of the individual. There are a number of immigration policies affecting particular categories of detainee and it is important that the Secretary of State adhere to these in order to comply with the requirement of lawfulness.[186] For example, a number of successful claims have been brought by claimants suffering from mental health problems who have been detained contrary to government policy.[187]

It has also been held that when considering lawfulness, Article 5 must be read in harmony with the general principles of international law including the UN Convention on the Rights of the Child.[188] Before the ECtHR, the immigration detention of a child has been held to contravene the UN Convention on the Rights of the Child (CRC) and amount to a breach of Article 5(1) because it failed to meet the requirements of the CRC even though the detention was otherwise lawful.[189] Following this jurisprudence, in *AAM*[190] the High Court found that the immigration detention of a child was in breach of Article 3 CRC as there was a failure to have regard to his best interests as a child. It was therefore in breach of Article 5(1) as it was unlawful.[191]

3.8.1 Unauthorised Entry: Detention of Asylum Seekers

Courts considering Article 5(1)(f) often refer to the principle of international law that sovereign states can regulate the entry of aliens into their territory.[192] It has been held that, until the state has authorised entry, the entry is unauthorised and the state has the power to detain without violating Article 5 until the application has been considered

---

[182] *HXA v Home Office* [2010] EWHC 1177 (QB).
[183] *R (Davies) v Secretary of State for the Home Department* [2010] EWHC 2656 (Admin).
[184] *R (Muqtaar) v SSHD* [2012] EWCA Civ 1270, [2013] 1 WLR 649 [75].
[185] *R v Secretary of State for the Home Department, ex p Sezek* [2001] EWCA Civ 795, [2002] 1 WLR 348.
[186] See *Lumba* (n 86) and *Kambadzi* (n 87). See also *R (S) v SSHD* [2011] EWHC 2120 (Admin).
[187] See eg *S v Secretary of State for the Home Department* [2012] EWHC 1939 (Admin).
[188] *AAM v Secretary of State for the Home Department* [2012] EWHC 2567 (QB). In *R (AA) v Secretary of State for the Home Department* [2013] UKSC 49 the Supreme Court held that this did not apply where an erroneous assessment of the age of a child had been made meaning he was not treated as a child.
[189] *AAM*, ibid, [137].
[190] Ibid.
[191] Ibid, [143]. See also *HXT v Secretary of State for the Home Department* [2013] 1962 (QB).
[192] See eg the comments of Lord Slynn in *Saadi* (n 10), [31].

and the entry is authorised.[193] In light of this view, in *Saadi*[194] the House of Lords concluded that the detention of asylum seekers at Oakington Reception Centre was compatible with Article 5(1)(f). This was detention for the purpose of inquiring whether the asylum seeker must or should be granted asylum, and it did not have to be shown that detention was necessary for that purpose.[195]

It must also be shown that detention in such instances is not arbitrary. In *Saadi*[196] it was argued that the detention was a disproportionate response to the reasonable requirements of immigration control. The House of Lords did not agree that the methods of selection of these cases (suitable for speedy decision), the objective (speedy decision) or the way in which people were held for short periods and in reasonable physical conditions, even if involving compulsory detention, could be said to be arbitrary or disproportionate.[197] Lord Slynn concluded as follows:

> It is regrettable that anyone should be deprived of his liberty other than pursuant to the order of a court but there are situations where such a course is justified. In a situation like the present with huge numbers and difficult decisions involved, with the risk of long delays to applicants seeking to come, a balancing exercise has to be performed. Getting a speedy decision is in the interests not only of the applicants but of those increasingly in the queue. Accepting as I do that the arrangements made at Oakington provide reasonable conditions, both for individuals and families and that the period taken is not in any sense excessive, I consider that the balance is in favour of recognising that detention under the Oakington procedure is proportionate and reasonable.[198]

3.8.2 Deportation: Detention of Deportees

Article 5(1)(f) also allows for the detention of those against whom action is being taken with a view to deportation. In *Nadarajah*[199] the Court of Appeal held that Article 5(1) (f) did not of itself import a test of proportionality so that it was necessary to balance the benefit of detention against the infringement of the right to personal liberty.[200] In the view of the court, it did not impose an obligation on states to give those whom they are in the process of removing a right to roam freely pending their removal whenever detention was not necessary to achieve ultimate removal.[201] This conclusion appears directly contrary to the approach taken in *Saadi*[202] and the fact that the prohibition of arbitrariness is an overarching requirement in relation to all Article 5(1) deprivations of liberty.[203]

---

[193] Ibid, per Lord Slynn at [35].

[194] Ibid.

[195] Ibid, per Lord Slynn at [35] in reliance upon *Chahal v UK* (1996) 1 BHRC 405; *Conka v Belgium* (2002) 11 BHRC 555.

[196] Ibid.

[197] Ibid, per Lord Slynn at [45]–[46].

[198] Ibid, [47]. In *Saadi v United Kingdom* (2008) 47 EHRR 17 the ECtHR found no violation of Art 5(1) but did find a violation of Art 5(2) in that the reasons for detention were not given sufficiently promptly.

[199] *Nadarajah* (n 88).

[200] Ibid, [50] in reliance upon *Chahal v UK* (1996) 23 EHRR 413.

[201] Ibid, [51].

[202] *Saadi* (n 10).

[203] See *Evans* (n 75), per Lord Hope in reliance upon *Sunday Times* (n 82); *Zamir* (n 82), [90]–[91]; *Engel* (n 72), [58]; *Tsirlis and Kouloumpas* (n 82), [56]. See also *Anderson* (n 79), per Lord Hope at [22].

The Court of Appeal also confused the question of lawfulness with arbitrariness, holding that the only question as to the policy on detention was whether it permitted arbitrary or irrational treatment.[204] It concluded that there was nothing arbitrary or irrational about a policy under which members of the immigration service would detain a person whom they were about to remove in circumstances where they had reason to doubt whether that person would provide the cooperation necessary for an orderly removal. It also found nothing arbitrary or irrational about a policy of not normally detaining an individual where removal was not imminent and the presumption that removal was not imminent if judicial proceedings had been commenced.[205] Although proportionality was not mentioned, it is likely that the Court of Appeal would have reached the same conclusion if the question of whether or not detention was a proportionate response to the reasonable requirements of immigration control had been asked. Nevertheless, the court eventually concluded that the detention was not lawful as it was not prescribed by law.[206]

3.8.3 Deportation: Length of Detention

With respect to the time an individual may be detained pending his or her removal or departure from the United Kingdom, Article 5 adds nothing to the common law.[207] The power of detention is limited to a period which is reasonably necessary for that purpose. The period which is reasonable will depend upon the circumstances of the particular case. Relevant considerations include:

> the length of the period of detention; the nature of the obstacles which stand in the path of the Secretary of State preventing a deportation; the diligence, speed and effectiveness of the steps taken by the Secretary of State to surmount such obstacles; the conditions in which the detained person is being kept; the effect of detention on him and his family; the risk that if he is released from detention he will abscond; and the danger that, if released, he will commit criminal offences.[208]

Non-cooperation by a person subject to removal or deportation is an important, possibly decisive factor in assessing the legality of continued detention.[209] Delays occasioned by an individual's refusal to return to his country of origin voluntarily may be relevant if a risk of absconding can be inferred from that refusal.[210] A reasonable period for the detention of an individual who does not co-operate in obtaining a travel document may be longer than in the case of an individual who co-operates.[211] However, the Secretary of State cannot detain a person pending deportation for more than a reasonable period even in the case of an individual who is deliberately seeking to sabotage efforts to deport.[212]

---

[204] *Nadarajah* (n 88), [61].
[205] Ibid.
[206] Ibid, at [64]–[67]. See also *Sezek* (n 185).
[207] *Re Hardial Singh* [1984] 1 All ER 983 expressly adopted in *R (on the application of I) v Secretary of State for the Home Department* [2002] EWCA Civ 888. See also *R (Lumba) v SSHD* [2011] 2 WLR 671
[208] *R (on the application of I)*, ibid, per Dyson LJ at [48].
[209] *Davies* (n 183), [19].
[210] *Lumba* (n 86), [128].
[211] *R (Sino) v SSHD* [2011] EWHC 2249 (Admin), [56].
[212] Ibid, [56].

A fact-sensitive approach must be adopted to delays occasioned by any legal proceedings an individual brings. If a hopeless or abusive legal challenge is pursued, and this is the only reason for not deporting, the period of detention involved should only be given minimal weight.[213] A prolonged period of detention pending the final resolution of an asylum claim is sometimes permissible, but a detained asylum seeker cannot invoke the delay necessarily occasioned by his own asylum claim to contend that his removal was not going to be possible within a reasonable time.[214] It has been held that detention does not become unreasonable on receipt of a rule 39 indication from the ECtHR as there remains a realistic prospect that the ECtHR proceedings concerning removal will be resolved within a reasonable period.[215]

If it is apparent to the Secretary of State that he is not going to be able to remove a person who it is intended to deport within a reasonable period, the Secretary of State cannot seek to exercise his power of detention. Furthermore, the Secretary of State must exercise all reasonable expedition to ensure that the steps are taken which will be necessary to ensure the removal of the individual within a reasonable time.[216] *I*[217] concerned an individual who had been in detention for nearly 16 months and there was no indication that enforced removal might become possible. Taking all the circumstances into account, a majority of the Court of Appeal held that he had been detained for a period that was longer than reasonable and ordered that he be released.[218]

3.8.4 Extradition: Meaning of Lawfulness

In relation to extradition, it is not necessary, in order for the detention to be lawful in Convention terms, to establish that the ultimate trial in another country will be fair or that the motives of the requesting party in bringing the prosecution abroad are beyond reproach.[219]

---

4. Article 5(2): Reasons for Arrest

Article 5(2) is the first of the procedural rights set out in Article 5 for persons who have been arrested or are being detained. Most, if not all, are reflected in other laws such as the Police and Criminal Evidence Act 1984 (PACE). Article 5(2) provides that everyone who is arrested shall be informed promptly, in a language which he understands, of the reasons for his arrest and of any charge against him. It has its counterpart in

---

[213] *Lumba* (n 86), [111]–[121].

[214] *I* (n 207), per Simon Brown LJ at [36] in reliance upon *Chahal* (n 200).

[215] *R (Muqtaar) v SSHD* [2012] EWCA Civ 1270, [2013] 1 WLR 649, [38]. A helpful summary of all relevant principles is contained in *R (Yakoub) v SSHD* [2012] EWHC 3109 (Admin), [104]–[105].

[216] *I* (n 207), [36].

[217] Ibid.

[218] See also *R (Murad) v SSHD* [2012] EWHC 1112 (Admin) for a recent application of the principles to facts.

[219] *R (Kashamu) v Governor of Brixton Prison* [2001] EWHC (Admin) 980, [2002] 2 WLR 907.

section 28(3) of PACE and it has been held that, although the wording is not the same, the principles expressed are,[220] and in the majority of cases it will be sufficient to apply Article 5(2).[221] The underlying rationale is that a person is entitled to know why he is being arrested so that he has the opportunity, for example, of giving an explanation of any misunderstanding or of calling attention to others for whom he might have been mistaken.[222] It is also a matter of respect for the dignity of the individual—if the state is taking away your liberty, you are entitled to know why.[223]

Any person arrested must be told, in simple, non-technical language that he can understand, the essential legal and factual grounds for his arrest, so as to be able, if he sees fit, to apply to a court to challenge its lawfulness in accordance with Article 5(4). The question of whether or not the information given is adequate has to be assessed objectively, having regard to the information which is reasonably available to the officer.[224] Whilst this information must be conveyed promptly, it need not be related in its entirety by the arresting officer at the very moment of the arrest. Whether the content and promptness of the information conveyed were sufficient is to be assessed in each case according to its special features.[225]

These principles were applied in *Taylor*,[226] which concerned the arrest of a ten-year-old boy at the site of one anti-vivisection protest for his activities at another. On his arrest, the officer informed him that he was arresting him on suspicion of violent disorder on 18 April 1998 at Hillgrove Farm. The Court of Appeal concluded that the reference to the farm and date gave clear information as to the event concerned.

> There can have been no reasonable doubt in his mind as to when and where the events occurred which led to his arrest. Despite the interval of time, there can have been no scope for confusion as to the incident to which WPC McKenzie was referring.

The court also pointed out that, even though he was only ten years old, his mother was present throughout.[227] It further held that there was no need to specify the precise way in which he was said to be taking part—violent disorder was a good enough description of what had happened on the occasion.[228] It concluded that Article 5(2) was satisfied.[229] Where an arrest was under section 364 of the Insolvency Act 1986, the Court of Appeal held that Article 5(2) only required that the order recite the basis on which the arrest was ordered under section 364(2).[230]

---

[220] *Taylor v Chief Constable of Thames Valley Police* [2004] EWCA Civ 858, [2004] 1 WLR 3155, [25].
[221] Ibid, [26].
[222] Ibid, [22].
[223] Ibid, per Sedley LJ at [58].
[224] Ibid, [30].
[225] *Fox v United Kingdom* (1991) 13 EHRR 157, [40], adopted in *Taylor*, ibid.
[226] Above n 220.
[227] Ibid, per Clarke LJ at [36].
[228] Ibid, [38] per Clarke LJ.
[229] Ibid, [40]. See also *Wilson v The Chief Constable of Lancashire Constabulary* [2001] 2 WLR 302.
[230] *Hickling* (n 130), [51].

5. Article 5(3)

Article 5(3) provides that everyone arrested or detained in accordance with Article 5(1)(c) shall be brought promptly before a judge or other officer authorised by law to exercise judicial power and shall be entitled to trial within a reasonable time or to release pending trial. Release may be conditioned by guarantees to appear for trial. Three distinct rights are evident. These are:

1. the right to be brought promptly before a judge or other officer authorised by law to exercise judicial power;
2. the right to be released on bail, except where continued detention can be justified; and
3. the right to be tried within a reasonable period.[231]

It has been held that the two key requirements imposed by Article 5(3) are, first, that the prosecution must bear the overall burden of justifying a remand in custody. It must advance good and sufficient public interest reasons outweighing the presumption of innocence and the general presumption in favour of liberty. Second, the judge must be entitled to take account of all relevant considerations pointing for and against grant of bail so as to exercise effective and meaningful judicial control over pre-trial detention.[232]

Whilst Article 5(3) only applies to arrests under Article 5(1)(c), it has been held that, by analogy, it also applies to an arrest under Article 5(1)(b), in this instance, the arrest of an undischarged bankrupt for non-cooperation. The Court of Appeal held that the order should itself require that, once arrested, the person in question be brought to court for a hearing at which the trustee in bankruptcy would also be represented.[233]

5.1 The Right to Be Released on Bail

The right to be released on bail is not absolute, but if bail is to be refused 'the refusal must be justified on the facts of each case to the satisfaction of the judge or other officer'.[234] Again, this aspect of Article 5 is already reflected in common law and statute such as the Bail Act 1976. However, the right to be released on bail has had some impact. For example, in *McKeown*[235] the Divisional Court concluded that if the Bail Act 1976 was interpreted so as to entitle a court to deny a defendant bail simply on the basis that he had been arrested for breaking conditions of bail, this may be incompatible with Article 5(3). It used section 3 of the HRA to hold that such an arrest should merely be

---

[231] *Wardle* (n 70), per Lord Hope at [84].
[232] *O v Harrow Crown Court* [2006] UKHL 42, [2007] 1 AC 249, per Lord Brown at [28].
[233] *Hickling* (n 130), [46].
[234] *O* (n 232), per Lord Hope at [85].
[235] *R (on the application of McKeown) v Wirral Borough Magistrates' Court* [2001] 1 WLR 805.

taken into account in determining whether or not any of the grounds for refusing bail existed; it was not to be determinative.[236]

Similarly section 3 of the HRA was used by the House of Lords in its judgment in O.[237] It was argued that section 25 of the Criminal Justice and Public Order Act 1994 was incompatible with Article 5(3) as it placed a burden on the defendant to establish the existence of exceptional circumstances required for bail to be granted. The House of Lords held that section 25 could be construed and applied in way which was compatible with Article 5(3). Furthermore, it found that section 25 had no substantive effect on bail applications as it served merely to remind courts of risks posed by those to whom section 25 applied. However, it concluded that section 25 should be read down, using section 3 of the HRA, to make plain that there was no burden on the section 25 defendant to rebut a presumption.[238]

5.2 The Right to Be Tried within a Reasonable Time

The purpose of the right to trial within a reasonable time under Article 5(3) is to ensure that no one spends too long in detention before trial. It therefore may be regarded as laying down a more exacting requirement than the Article 6(1) right to a hearing within a reasonable time.[239] However, usually the case law concerning both Articles is invoked and it is therefore important to consider the reasonable time provisions of Article 6 when considering this part of Article 5.[240]

The time span covered by Article 5(3) extends from the first remand into custody until the delivery of the judgment of the court.[241] What is a reasonable time depends on all the relevant circumstances of the case. It has been held that it is important to balance against the defendant's right to liberty the public interest in ensuring that those charged with serious offences are available to be tried, did not commit other offences whilst awaiting trial and did not interfere with witnesses.[242] Procedural time wasting on the part of the defendant and failure of the prosecution to show diligence can be taken into account.[243]

In Wardle[244] it was argued that allowing a fresh custody time limit to be applied in relation to each new charge was open to abuse and could result in detention for a time that was more than reasonable. Here, when the defendant appeared before the magistrates' court the prosecution offered no evidence on the murder charge but held that a new custody time limit should be applied to the manslaughter charge. A majority of the House of Lords held that the regulation which required that each offence charged attracted its own custody time limit had a legitimate purpose, which was to

---

[236] Ibid, [47]. See also R (on the application of Vickers) v West London Magistrates' Court [2003] EWHC (Admin) 1809, [2004] Crim LR 63, where it was held that breach of bail will be one factor as to whether or not the bailed person is admitted to bail again.

[237] O (n 232).

[238] Ibid, [35].

[239] Wardle (n 70), per Lord Hope at [85] in reliance upon Wemhoff v Germany (1968) 1 EHRR 55, [5] and Tagci and Sargin v Turkey (1995) 20 EHRR 505, [50].

[240] See eg Procurator Fiscal, Linlithgow v Watson [2002] UKPC D1, [2004] 1 AC 379.

[241] O (n 232), [34].

[242] Ibid.

[243] Ibid.

[244] Wardle (n 70).

give sufficient time to the prosecutor to prepare the evidence relating to each offence for examination by the justices, and any abuse was subject to judicial control. No incompatibility with Article 5(3) was found.[245]

It was argued in O[246] that once the statutory custody time limit had expired and had not been extended, there was a breach of Article 5(3) if the defendant was still held by virtue of the operation of section 25. This was dismissed by the House of Lords, with Lord Brown noting that even where the prosecution has been responsible for a lack of due diligence causative of delay, resulting in a refusal to extend the custody time limit, this did not necessarily mean that there was a violation of Article 5(3).[247]

6. Article 5(4)

6.1 Introduction

Article 5(4) provides that everyone who is deprived of his liberty by arrest or detention shall be entitled to take proceedings by which the lawfulness of his detention shall be decided speedily by a court and his release ordered if the detention is not lawful. It is this part of Article 5 which has generated the most litigation under the HRA. It reflects principles 'long cherished in this country by lawyers and the public' that no one shall be deprived of his liberty save on lawful authority; that anyone challenging the lawfulness of his detention shall have access to a court with power to decide whether his detention is lawful or not; and that if his detention is not held to be lawful his release shall be ordered.[248]

Article 5(4) does not guarantee a right to judicial control of the legality of all aspects or details of the detention.[249] '[D]etainees are entitled to a review hearing' upon the procedural and substantive conditions 'which are essential for the lawfulness of their deprivation of liberty'.[250] It is a free-standing right and a breach of Article 5(4) does not of itself make the detention unlawful.[251] Compliance with Article 5(4) can only be assessed in retrospect by reference to the specific facts of an actual case. It cannot be said in advance that a breach of Article 5(4) is inevitable.[252] Where the requirements of

---

[245] Ibid, per Lord Hope at [89], with whom Lord Clyde agreed. Lord Slynn reached the same conclusion. See also *R (on the application of Gibson) v Winchester Crown Court* [2004] EWHC (Admin) 361, [2004] 1 WLR 1623.

[246] *O* (n 232).

[247] Ibid, [63].

[248] *R (Giles) v Parole Board* [2003] UKHL 42, [2004] AC 1, per Lord Bingham at [3]. See also *R (on the application of Sim) v Parole Board* [2003] EWCA Civ 1845, [2004] QB 1288, [11].

[249] *James* (n 97), per Lord Hope at [17]. It does not permit a prisoner to challenge his prison category: *R (Munjaz) v Ashworth Hospital Authority* [2005] UKHL 58, [2006] 2 AC 148, per Lord Bingham at [30]. It does apply to bail proceedings: *R (Cart) v Upper Tribunal* [2009] EWHC 3052, [2010] 2 WLR 1012.

[250] *James* (n 97).

[251] *R (Guntrip) v Secretary of State for Justice* [2010] EWHC 3188 (Admin).

[252] *Roberts v Parole Board* [2005] UKHL 45, [2005] 3 WLR 152.

this part of Article 5 are clear, it is no answer that compliance would be burdensome, costly or difficult.[253]

6.2 Access to Court

The first requirement of Article 5(4) is that the detainee must have access to court to challenge the lawfulness of detention. It was argued in *MH*[254] that the present law under the Mental Health Act 1983 was incompatible with Article 5(4) in that it did not provide practical and effective rights of access to a court for a patient detained under section 2 who lacked the capacity to apply to a tribunal by herself. The House of Lords held that Article 5(4) does not require that every case be considered by a court. It requires that the person detained should have the right to take proceedings.[255] 'It leaves the person detained the choice of whether or not to put the matter before a court.'[256] The House of Lords held that every sensible effort should be made to enable the patient to exercise that right if there was reason to think that she would wish to do so. However, it found no ECtHR authority which implied into Article 5(4) the requirement of a judicial review in every case where the patient was unable to make her own application.[257] It also noted that even if the patient's nearest relative had no independent right of application, there was much that she, or other concerned members of the family, friends or professionals, could do to help put the patient's case before a judicial authority.[258]

Similarly in *Rayner*[259] the claim concerned the Mental Health Act 1983 which did not provide for a person in the position of the claimant, a restricted patient recalled to hospital, to make his own application to a tribunal after his recall. It was the duty of the Secretary of State to make a reference; the patient had a right after six months. The Court of Appeal detected in the ECtHR jurisprudence a shift of emphasis towards greater stress on the requirement that a detained person should be able to take the initiative himself to start proceedings to challenge the lawfulness of his detention.[260] However, it noted that in the UK the claimant could use judicial review to challenge the lawfulness of detention.[261] And although it was not possible for a judicial review challenge to result in an order for release, it was sufficient:

> [T]he combination of that statutory mechanism, the right of the patient to enforce the Secretary of State's statutory duty ... by way of judicial review, and the right of the patient to challenge the lawfulness of his detention directly in the courts on its substantive merits by judicial review and/or habeas corpus does suffice to comply with Article 5(4).[262]

---

[253] *R (on the application of P) v Secretary of State for the Home Department* [2003] EWHC (Admin) 2953, [14].

[254] *Secretary of State for the Department of Health v MH* [2005] UKHL 60, [2006] 1 AC 441.

[255] Ibid, [22].

[256] Ibid, [22].

[257] Ibid, [24].

[258] Ibid, [27]. In *MH v United Kingdom* 22 October 2013 the ECtHR found a violation of Art 5(4) in relation to her intitial detention as she did not have effective access to a mechanism enabling her to take proceedings.

[259] *Secretary of State for Justice v Rayner* [2008] EWCA Civ 176, [2009] 1 WLR 310.

[260] Ibid, [38].

[261] Ibid, [42].

[262] Ibid, [46]. A similar conclusion was reached by the Supreme Court in *R (Modaresi) v Secretary of State for Health* [2013] UKSC 53 concerning review of detention under the Mental Health Act 1983 ss 66 and 67.

6.3 Review of Lawfulness

6.3.1 Introduction

The review of lawfulness by a court as required by Article 5(4) must encompass lawfulness on Convention grounds as well as lawfulness under domestic law.[263] In some instances the appeal process will satisfy the requirements of Article 5(4).[264] It has also been held that the power of the court on judicial review is sufficient to meet the standards of Article 5(4).[265] It does not appear to matter which court reviews lawfulness, as long as lawfulness is reviewed.[266] In P[267] it was argued by a life sentence prisoner also subject to the Mental Health Act 1983 that he was entitled to have the lawfulness of his detention reviewed by a single tribunal exercising the functions of both a Mental Health Review Tribunal and a Discretionary Lifer Panel. The Administrative Court rejected the argument holding that there was no reason to require that the same court determine each head of detention.[268]

> If a person is detained under more than one head … and a court decides that his continued detention under one of those heads is lawful, his continued detention is lawful, irrespective of the lawfulness of his detention under the other head or heads.[269]

6.3.2 Unsound Mind

For those of unsound mind, there must be a review of the lawfulness of detention at reasonable intervals. The minimum for a judicial procedure is the right of the individual to present his own case and to challenge the medical and social evidence in support of his detention.[270] In Anderson[271] the appellants challenged new legislation which prevented their release on the ground of public safety. Medical knowledge had moved on and there was a strong body of opinion that their condition was not treatable. It was argued that, when applying the public safety test, the sheriff would not be conducting a review but exercising the function of primary decision maker. The Privy Council disagreed, holding that the exercise the sheriff was required to conduct was a review—a review of the patient's continued detention in the light of the new rules.[272]

6.3.3 Determinate Sentences

Where a prisoner has been lawfully detained within the meaning of Article 5(1)(a) following the imposition of a determinate sentence after his conviction by a competent

---

[263] Anderson (n 79), at [39] per Lord Hope in reliance upon Winterwerp (n 79), [55]. See also Smith (n 97), [37].

[264] Re Scriven, Court of Appeal, 22 April 2004.

[265] R v An Immigration Officer, ex p Xuereb [2000] 56 BMLR 180.

[266] See eg Kashamu (n 219).

[267] R (P) v Secretary of State for the Home Department [2003] EWHC 2953 (Admin).

[268] Ibid, [34].

[269] Ibid, [36].

[270] Anderson (n 79), per Lord Hope at [39].

[271] Ibid.

[272] Ibid, [42].

court, the review which Article 5(4) requires is incorporated in the original sentence passed by the sentencing court. Once the appeal process has been exhausted, there is no right to have the lawfulness of the detention under that sentence reviewed by another court. However, in *Black*[273] it was argued before the House of Lords that once a determinate prisoner's parole eligibility date arrived, he or she was entitled by virtue of Article 5(4) to a speedy judicial decision upon the lawfulness of any further period of detention. The Secretary of State maintained that in all determinate sentence cases, the requirements of Article 5(4) were satisfied once and for all when the original sentence was imposed following conviction and that there could be no right to any further Article 5(4) determination unless and until there arose new issues affecting the lawfulness of the detention.

Lord Brown, in the majority, observed that given the critical part played by the parole scheme in determining how long a determinate sentence prisoner would in fact remain in custody it was 'not difficult to suggest an equal need to operate that scheme judicially as to have a proper initial sentencing process'.[274] He also stated that it was not difficult to recognise the force of the suggested analogy between the position of lifers and that of long-term determinate sentence prisoners with regard to release on licence.[275] However, the majority concluded that to find Article 5(4) engaged would be to widen its reach beyond its proper limits: 'There is nothing intrinsically objectionable (certainly in Convention terms) in allowing the executive, subject to judicial review, to take the parole decision, notwithstanding that it involves rejecting another body's recommendation.'[276]

Lord Brown found that it was not the case that the fact that the UK had chosen to give the Parole Board a role and had chosen to fix the period in a determinate sentence when a prisoner was to be considered eligible for a parole that Article5(4) was necessarily engaged.[277] 'The administrative implementation of determinate sentences does not engage article 5(4); the decision when to release a prisoner subject to an indeterminate sentence does.'[278]

The same applies where a person sentenced to a determinate term is released early or conditionally. For example, in *Mason*[279] the High Court held that home detention curfew operated during the part of a sentence when custody was compulsory, before the point at which a prisoner would be released or become eligible for release on the recommendation of the Parole Board. Therefore, the review of the lawfulness of detention demanded by Article 5(4), at least up to that point, had already been conducted by the sentencing court.[280] This was the administrative implementation of the original sentence.

---

[273] *R (Black) v Secretary of State for Justice* [2009] UKHL 1, [2009] 1 AC 949.
[274] Ibid, [78].
[275] Ibid, [79].
[276] Ibid, per Lord Brown at [81].
[277] Ibid, [82].
[278] Ibid, [83]. See also *O'Connell v Parole Board* [2009] EWCA Civ 575, [2009] 1 WLR 2539 where it was held that the same principles applied to extended sentences, and *Mason v Ministry of Justice* [2008] EWHC 1787 (QB) where it was held that Art 5(4) had no application to home detention curfew.
[279] *Mason*, ibid.
[280] Ibid, [39].

6.3.4 Indeterminate Sentences

Where decisions as to the length of detention have passed from the court to the executive,[281] and there is a risk that the factors which informed the original decision will change with the passage of time, the review which Article 5(4) requires cannot be said to be incorporated into the original decision of the court. A further review in judicial proceedings is needed at reasonable intervals.[282] The underlying rationale is clear: a prisoner's danger to the public may diminish or disappear.[283]

Sometimes it is difficult to determine on which side of the line a sentence falls. For example, in *Giles*[284] the appellant argued that, once he had served the part of his determinate sentence imposed for punishment and was about to begin serving the balance of the sentence imposed for public protection, Article 5(4) applied. The House of Lords disagreed, holding that his detention was in accordance with a determinate sentence imposed by a court and was justified under Article 5(1)(a) without the need for any further reviews under Article 5(4). The review required by Article 5(4) was incorporated in the sentence passed by the judge.

> He was able to take this decision in the light of the information before him and, in the exercise of his ordinary powers of sentencing, to decide on the total length of the sentence which in all the circumstances was appropriate.[285]

It was also held by a majority of the House of Lords in *McClean*[286] that Article 5(4) did not apply to the accelerated programme for the release of prisoners convicted of offences scheduled under the Northern Ireland (Emergency Provisions) Acts 1973, 1978, 1991 or 1996 as, very broadly, offences motivated by political or sectarian considerations. In the opinion of the majority, the prisoner's human rights did not entitle him to an early release scheme.

> He has been convicted of serious offences and sentenced to lengthy terms of imprisonment. There are many years to go before he could, absent the 1998 Act scheme, have any expectation of release. His continued incarceration does not infringe his human rights. The 1998 Act and its Rules constitute a statutory scheme of which the respondent was, and still is, a potential beneficiary.[287]

A different issue arose in *Sim*,[288] where the respondent had been recalled to prison while on licence under an extended sentence passed under section 85 of the Powers of Criminal Courts (Sentencing) Act 2000. This enabled the court to impose in cases of a sexual or violent offence a sentence which consisted of a custodial term and an extension period during which the offender would be on licence beyond the normal licence period. Whilst the Court of Appeal found that the overall period of the extended

---

[281] As in the case of life sentences, although it is important to note that this function is no longer performed by the Home Secretary but by the Parole Board.

[282] *Giles* (n 248), per Lord Hope at [51] in reliance upon *De Wilde, Ooms and Versyp v Belgium (No 1)* (1971) 1 EHRR 373.

[283] Ibid, per Lord Bingham at [4].

[284] Ibid.

[285] Ibid, per Lord Hope at [52]. See also Lord Bingham at [9]–[11] and the speech of Lord Hutton.

[286] *In Re McClean* [2005] UKHL 46.

[287] Ibid, per Lord Scott at [51], with whom Lord Brown agreed. Lord Rodger agreed with Lord Brown.

[288] *Sim* (n 248).

sentence had been determined by the court, this did not conclude the issue.[289] It found that with an extended sentence under section 85, once the custodial term had passed, no court had sentenced him to imprisonment but had authorised him to be imprisoned if his licence was revoked.[290] It observed that the extension period was designed to provide greater protection for the public and this put it into the category of case where there may need to be further assessments of risk.[291] It therefore concluded that, where an offender is detained during the extension period of a section 85 sentence, such detention must be subject to review by a judicial body. '[I]t is the executive which decides upon an offender's recall during the extension period, and because that detention has not been ordered by a court it must be supervised by a judicial body.'[292] Here it was so supervised through the mechanism of the Parole Board.

6.4 Attributes of a Court

Article 5(4) specifies that the lawfulness of detention is to be decided by a court. It is not necessary for the decision-making body to actually be labelled a 'court' as such. However, it must possess the attributes of a court, such as complying with the principles of natural justice, as discussed in the following paragraphs. In addition, there are other attributes of a court such as being competent to take a legally binding decision leading to a person's release. In *IH*[293] it was argued that a mental health review tribunal lacked the attributes of a court as it lacked coercive power. The tribunal had ordered the discharge of the appellant provided there was supervision of him by a named social worker and psychiatrist. The health authority was unable to find a psychiatrist willing to supervise and his detention continued. The House of Lords did not agree, holding that the power to discharge conditionally was not incompatible with Article 5(4).[294]

It is also possible, where a mental health review tribunal has ordered the discharge of a patient, that the patient is readmitted shortly after. This raises questions as to the power of the tribunal to order release. In *H*[295] the claimant had been discharged from detention by the tribunal but seven days later an approved social worker made an application for his admission and detention, and since that date he had been detained for treatment. The Court of Appeal held that, in the absence of material circumstances of which the tribunal was not aware when it ordered discharge, it was not open to the professionals, until the tribunal's decision had been quashed by a court, to resection a patient. 'To countenance such a course as lawful would be to permit the professionals and their legal advisers to determine whether a decision by a court to discharge a detained patient should have effect.' In the opinion of the court, this would not be compatible with Article 5(4).[296] However, the court was willing to countenance a stay if there was strong evidence to justify it, the majority finding that this could even require

---

[289] Ibid, [28].
[290] Ibid, [33].
[291] Ibid, [35].
[292] Ibid, [36].
[293] *IH* (n 167).
[294] Ibid, [26]. This judgment answered questions raised in *K* (n 169).
[295] *R (on the application of H) v Ashworth Hospital Authority* [2002] EWCA Civ 923.
[296] Ibid, [56].

a forcible return to hospital.[297] In the present case it concluded that the principal ground on which the professionals relied in deciding to resection was one which had been rejected by the tribunal. Therefore, even if the tribunal's decision was unlawful, there were not sufficient reasons to resection.[298]

Whilst conditional discharge in *IH*[299] was found acceptable, another aspect of the decision in this case was found to be unacceptable. Once the tribunal had made its original order, it was not lawful for it to reconsider it. In the view of the House of Lords, this left the appellant in limbo for a period much longer than was compatible with Article 5(4).[300] It concluded that tribunals should no longer proceed on the basis that they cannot reconsider a decision to direct a conditional discharge on specified conditions where, after deferral and before directing discharge, there is a material change of circumstances.[301]

The fact that the Parole Board cannot require the Secretary of State for Justice and the Probation Service to produce relevant materials in their possession does not imply that it is not a court for the purposes of Article 5(4). It satisfies the structural requirements of being a court for the purposes of Article 5(4) even though it lacks the power to impose sanctions for breach of its procedural directions.[302]

6.5 Independence and Impartiality

The court reviewing the lawfulness of detention must be independent and impartial. Although it has not been confirmed, it is likely that the test for independence and impartiality is the same as that adopted under Article 6 and at common law.

6.5.1 Home Secretary

Particular problems have arisen in relation to the role of the Home Secretary, an office which does not embody the qualities of independence or impartiality.[303] Whilst many of the questions concerning the Home Secretary's role in sentencing have now been resolved,[304] some issues still remain. For example, *D*[305] concerned a discretionary life prisoner who was also the subject of a transfer and restriction direction under the Mental Health Act 1983. His detention was subject to two statutory regimes—mental health and penal. His case for discharge had to be considered by both the mental health tribunal and the Parole Board. However, if the tribunal decided he was no longer

---

[297] Ibid, per Dyson LJ at [57] and Mummery LJ at [94]. Simon Brown LJ took a stricter view at [105]–[106].

[298] Ibid, [64]. See also *von Brandenburg* (n 2); and *R (on the application of RA) v Secretary of State for the Home Department* [2002] EWHC (Admin) 1618, which concerned the Secretary of State's power to give or refuse his consent to community leave under the Mental Health Act 1983.

[299] *IH* (n 167).

[300] Ibid, [27].

[301] Ibid, [27]. See also *R (on the application of C) v Secretary of State for the Home Department* [2002] EWCA Civ 647.

[302] *R (Morales) v Parole Board* [2011] EWHC 28 (Admin), [2011] 1 WLR 1095.

[303] *Kashamu* (n 219).

[304] See eg *Anderson* (above n 120).

[305] *D v Secretary of State for the Home Department* [2002] EWHC Admin 2805, [2003] 1 WLR 1315.

detainable under the Mental Health Act, the intervention of the Home Secretary was required for his case to be referred to the Parole Board.

Although it was the Home Secretary's policy to always refer, the Administrative Court appreciated that there was no right to require the Home Secretary to refer.[306] It concluded that the present arrangement was not compatible with Article 5(4). 'The word "entitled" in Article 5(4) is not satisfied unless there is a legal right of access to a court that can determine the lawfulness of detention and direct the prisoner's release if his detention is not justified.'[307]

The existence of directions by the Home Secretary to the Parole Board in the discharge of its functions under section 28 of the Crime (Sentences) Act 1997 has also been the subject of challenge on independence grounds. In *Girling*[308] the Administrative Court observed that directions purporting to govern how the Board actually decided cases involved what would ordinarily be regarded as a trespass into the judicial sphere.

> Political accountability for the penal system is of great importance. It does not, however, entail that the Home Secretary should give directions as to judicial functions: on the contrary, when the Parole Board is exercising judicial functions the common law and recognised principles of political accountability both require that the Home Secretary and other members of the executive respect the judicial nature of those functions.[309]

However, it concluded that the problem could be resolved if section 32(6) of the Criminal Justice Act 1991, concerning directions which could be given by the Secretary of State, were read as inapplicable to the Parole Board's judicial functions, and in particular its functions under section 28 of the 1997 Act.[310] In the present case, it concluded that whilst there had been an inadvertent trespass on the Parole Board's independence, the content of the directions was innocuous and the trespass was not so substantial as to deprive the Parole Board of its true character as a judicial body. No breach of Article 5(4) was found.

Not all of the Home Secretary's functions run the risk of violating Article 5(4). In *Day*[311] the Administrative Court held that it was acceptable for the Secretary of State to fix the date for the next review by the Parole Board of the claimant's application for release under a mandatory life sentence licence.[312]

6.5.2 Medical Member, Mental Health Tribunal

Questions have been raised concerning the role of the medical member of mental health review tribunals. In *S*[313] the claimant challenged rule 11 of the tribunal rules, which required that he be seen by the medical member, before the hearing of his application. The Administrative Court held that care was required if rule 11 was not to result in

---

[306] Ibid, [18].
[307] Ibid, [24] in reliance upon *Benjamin and Wilson v United Kingdom* Judgment of 26 September 2002.
[308] *Girling v Parole Board* [2005] EWHC (Admin) 5469.
[309] Ibid, [70].
[310] Ibid, [78].
[311] *R (on the application of Day) v Secretary of State for the Home Department* [2004] EWHC (Admin) 1742, [2004] ACD 78.
[312] See also *Girling* (n 308).
[313] *R (on the application of S) v Mental Health Review Tribunal* [2002] EWHC (Admin) 2522.

unfairness.[314] However, it noted that the rule did not require the medical member to form an opinion as to the patient's mental condition, and therefore this would not give rise to unfairness.[315] It also held that there was normally no objection to members of a tribunal or court forming or discussing their provisional view of a case before the hearing. This would only be objectionable if the view formed was firm and concluded, in which case the hearing would be a charade.[316] Therefore, there was no objection to the expression of a provisional opinion by the medical member before the hearing provided other members were aware that this was only provisional and understood that they were free to disagree if the evidence and submissions led to a different conclusion.[317]

6.5.3 Parole Board

The independence and impartiality of the Parole Board itself has also been subject to challenge. The role of the Parole Board is to consider whether prisoners should be released before serving the full term of their sentences. The Secretary of State is required to give effect to decisions of the Board in relation to the release of prisoners and commonly gives the Board his own view. In *Brooke*[318] it was argued that the relationship between the Parole Board and the Department which sponsored it placed the Secretary of State in a position of apparent influence over the approach of the Parole Board to its curial duties.

The Court of Appeal held that the role of the Parole Board could not be compared too closely with that of a court.[319] However, a major part of the Board's duties was judicial in nature: 'The Board has to adjudicate, in respect of different types of sentence, on whether the continued detention of prisoners is lawful or whether they are entitled to be released under licence.'[320] It held that in relation to the exercise of risk assessment, both actual and perceived independence was required on the part of the Board.[321] The problem arose from the fact that the possibility existed that the Secretary of State may be anxious for the Board to apply a stricter or alternatively a more lenient test to releasing prisoners than that required by the law and it was not possible to equate the position of the Secretary of State to that of a party in an adversarial process.[322]

The Court of Appeal identified particular encroachments on the independence of the Board. The Secretary of State could give directions which were intended to go beyond mere guidance and to direct the Board as to how it should carry out its judicial function of determining applications for release.[323] The Secretary of State had sought to use his power of appointment of members of the Board in such a way as to affect the outcome

---

[314] Ibid, [15].
[315] Ibid, [21].
[316] Ibid, [22].
[317] Ibid, [23]. This was also found to be compatible with Convention jurisprudence in particular *DN v Switzerland* Judgment of 29 March 2001.
[318] *R (Brooke) v Parole Board* [2008] EWCA Civ 29, [2008] 1 WLR 1950.
[319] Ibid, [43].
[320] Ibid, [47].
[321] Ibid, [50].
[322] Ibid, [52].
[323] Ibid, [60].

of the Board's decisions.[324] Funding only allowed for interview of applicants for release in 10 per cent of cases.[325] The sponsorship relationship between the Board and Ministry of Justice also raised concerns as the extent to which the Board had to work with those administratively responsible for offender management including the Prison Service and Probation Service.[326]

The Court of Appeal concluded that the Board lacked both actual and apparent independence:

> The cause of the problem has been the change of function of the Parole Board from that of a body advising the Secretary of State in relation to an executive discretion to release prisoners whose penal sentences were part served to that of a judicial body assessing whether continued deprivation of a prisoner's liberty is justified because of the risk that he will re-offend if released.[327]

Areas specified where action was required included: transparency in the appointment process and stipulation of qualities of candidates;[328] establishment of a procedure that ensured that a member's appointment was not terminated without good cause and subject to fair process;[329] ensuring that the Board was so placed within the sponsorship responsibility of the Ministry of Justice that its independence was not open to question.[330]

6.6 Fairness

6.6.1 Introduction

Article 5(4) requires there to be in place a judicial procedure which not only meets the criterion of being in accordance with law, but which also provides the basic protection for a defendant inherent in the concept of judicial proceedings. In short, a person liable to detention is entitled to natural justice.[331] Although some of the general concepts of fairness in judicial proceedings have been borrowed from Article 6, this does not mean that the process required for conformity with Article 5 must also be in conformity with Article 6.

> That would conflate the convention's control over two separate sets of proceedings, which have different objects. Article 5, in the present context, is concerned to ensure that the detention of an accused person before trial is only justified by proper considerations relating to the risk of absconding, and of interfering with witnesses, or the commission of other crimes. Article 6 is concerned with the process of determining the guilt or otherwise of a person who if found guilty would be subject to criminal penalties.[332]

---

[324] Ibid, [61].
[325] Ibid, [66].
[326] Ibid, [73].
[327] Ibid, [78].
[328] Ibid, [84].
[329] Ibid, [88].
[330] Ibid, [99].
[331] *McKeown* (n 235), [27].
[332] Ibid, [35].

It is also important to note that Article 6 may not apply to some proceedings where guarantees of fairness may be important, such as proceedings before a Parole Board.[333]

As with Article 6, the constituent elements of fairness under Article 5(4) are not considered to be absolute. Fairness and its ingredients need to be judged in context. The formulation of hard-edged principles is eschewed. Qualifications are justified provided they are necessary and proportionate. In considering whether qualification to the right is proportionate, consideration must be given to ways of mitigating or counterbalancing the restriction so as to achieve substantial fairness. The extent to which qualification or flexibility is permitted depends upon the context. A greater degree of latitude is permitted in cases concerning civil rights than in criminal cases. In deciding what is necessary, it is legitimate to have regard to the interest of others, including the public if they are affected. The interaction of these interests is a matter of degree, to be judged on a case-by-case basis.

6.6.2 Burden of Proof and Evidence

The burden of justifying a person's detention lies on the person detaining.[334] In *Sim*[335] the Court of Appeal concluded that a conventional interpretation of section 44A(4) of the Criminal Justice Act 1991 would be incompatible with Article 5(4) as detention was to continue unless the Parole Board was satisfied that it was not necessary. However, using section 3 of the HRA, it construed the word 'necessary' in a flexible way so that the Board had to be positively satisfied that continued detention was necessary in the public interest.[336]

Question have been raised as to particular types of evidence affecting the fairness of Article 5(4) proceedings. It has been held that the court, when forming its opinion, must take proper account of the quality of the material upon which it is asked to adjudicate. 'This material is likely to range from mere assertion at the one end of the spectrum which may not have any probative effect, to documentary proof at the other end of the spectrum.'[337] The court must ensure that the defendant has a full and fair opportunity to comment on and answer that material.[338] There is no requirement that the underlying facts relevant to detention are to be proved to the criminal standard of proof.[339]

Hearsay evidence is not in principle inadmissible. However, the fact that it is hearsay should be borne in mind when determining the weight which is attached to it. If the evidence is fundamental to the decision, fairness may require that the offender is given the opportunity to test it by cross-examination before it is taken into account.[340] In *Sim*[341] the Court of Appeal concluded that the disputed matters were not the key factors in the decision and it did not accept that the admission of hearsay evidence about those

---

[333] See eg *Roberts* (n 252).
[334] *Sim* (n 248).
[335] Ibid.
[336] Ibid, [51]. See also *R (on the application of Jarvis) v The Parole Board* [2004] EWHC (Admin) 872; *H* (n 156); *Hirst v Parole Board*, Court of Appeal, 25 September 2002; and *McClean* (n 286).
[337] *McKeown* (n 235), [41].
[338] Ibid.
[339] Ibid, [39]–[40].
[340] *Sim* (n 248), [57].
[341] Ibid.

disputed matters rendered the proceedings unfair or in breach of Article 5(4).[342] Simi-larly, there is no rule against the admission of evidence from an anonymous witness. In *Eidarous*[343] the House of Lords concluded that it was no violation of Article 5(4) for the magistrate, when deciding a request for extradition, to take into account the affidavit of an anonymous witness. It observed that the principles of a fair trial require that, in appropriate cases, the interests of the defence are balanced against those of witnesses or victims called upon to testify. Here there were real grounds to fear for the safety of the witness.[344]

6.6.3 Oral Hearing

There is no duty under Article 5(4) to afford an oral hearing in every case. Article 5(4) is satisfied provided that the review is conducted in a manner which meets the require-ments of common law procedural fairness. In some instances, this may require an oral hearing. Even if important facts are not in dispute, they may be open to 'explanation or mitigation', or may lose some of their significance 'in the light of other new facts'.[345] There is a value to be placed upon the decision maker 'seeing and hearing both from the prisoner and from those who were responsible for the prisoner's management'. It allows the prisoner to address effectively any concerns the decision maker had. And it reflects the importance of what is at stake.[346]

It is for the court to decide what procedural fairness requires and it is not appropriate for the court to ask whether it was reasonably open to the Parole Board to conclude that procedural fairness did not require an oral hearing. However, in considering what procedural fairness requires, the court should give some, though not undue, weight to the decision of a specialist body such as the Board.[347] It would only be an exceptional case that procedural fairness would require an oral hearing on the basis of documents and information which the prisoner or his representatives could have put before the Board but did not do so.[348] It has been appreciated that the prospect of oral hearings on a significant scale in this context would raise very serious questions of resources and costs within the overall system for the administration of prisons and the management of prisons.[349]

In *Smith*[350] the House of Lords had to determine whether or not the procedure to be followed by the Parole Board should include an oral hearing when a determinate sentence prisoner released on licence sought to resist revocation of his licence. It stated that the Board may be assisted by exposure to the prisoner or those who had dealt with him. 'The prisoner should have the benefit of a procedure which fairly reflects, on the facts of his particular case, the importance of what is at stake for him, as for society.'[351]

---

[342] Ibid, [59].
[343] *R (Eidarous) v Governor of Brixton Prison* [2001] UKHL 69, [2002] 2 WLR 101.
[344] Ibid, per Lord Rodger at [166]. See also Lord Slynn at [44] and Lord Hutton at [85]–[88]. Reliance was placed on *Doorson v The Netherlands* (1996) 22 EHRR 330.
[345] *Smith* (n 97), per Lord Bingham at [35] and [37].
[346] *Roose v Parole Board* [2010] EWHC 1780 (Admin), [21].
[347] Ibid, [19].
[348] Ibid, [19].
[349] *R (Foster) v Secretary of State for Justice* [2013] EWHC 1951 (Admin), [34].
[350] Above n 97.
[351] Ibid, per Lord Bingham at [35].

Where there were issues of fact or explanations put forward to justify actions said to be in breach of licence conditions, or where the officer's assessment needed further probing, fairness may well require an oral hearing.[352] A breach of Article 5(4) was found in relation to each appellant, their Lordships concluding that their challenges could not be fairly resolved without an oral hearing.[353]

6.6.4 Equality of Arms

The principle of equality of arms also applies in Article 5(4) proceedings. Article 5(4) prohibits interference with the administration of justice designed to influence the judicial determination of a dispute other than on compelling grounds of the general public interest.[354] In *Anderson*[355] the Privy Council found that the purpose of the legislation was to protect the public and it was necessary for the Scottish Parliament to address the serious risk to public safety which would arise if others whose mental disorder was regarded as untreatable were to apply to the sheriff for their discharge. It concluded that this was a compelling ground of the public interest.[356]

In *Roberts*[357] a majority of the House of Lords held that the fact that information was withheld from a prisoner in Parole Board proceedings did not mean that there was automatically a breach of the prisoner's rights under Article 5(4).

> There can be an infinite variety of circumstances as to the degree of information that is withheld completely or partially without any significant unfairness being caused. The responsibility of the panel is to ensure that any unfairness is kept to a minimum while balancing the triumvirate of interests. ... There may need initially to be a total withholding of information, but at an early stage of the hearing the prisoner may be able to be informed of the gist of what is relied on against him. Documents can be edited. There has to be detailed management of the hearing to ensure that the prisoner has the widest information possible. In relation to this management the [specially appointed advocate] can have a critical role to play on the prisoner's behalf.[358]

The majority held that, in principle, to withhold material from the prisoner and his representatives and to disclose that material to the specially appointed advocate who would represent the prisoner in his absence at a closed hearing before the Board was not in violation of Article 5(4). However, it was also held that it was not possible to reach a final conclusion on Article 5(4) without examining the facts as a whole, including any appellate process.[359]

> To make rulings in advance of the actual hearing would be to introduce a rigidity that would make the task of the Board extraordinarily difficult. The position has to be looked at in the

---

[352] Ibid, per Lord Slynn at [50].

[353] See also *R (on the application of Williams) v Secretary of State for the Home Department* [2002] EWCA Civ 498, [2002] 1 WLR 2264 and *Hopkins v Parole Board* [2008] EWHC 2312 (Admin), [2009] Prison LR 223.

[354] *Anderson* (n 79), per Lord Hope at [43] in reliance upon *National and Provincial Building Society v United Kingdom* (1997) 25 EHRR 127, [112] and *Zielinski v France* (2001) 31 EHRR 532.

[355] *Anderson* (n 79).

[356] Ibid, [44].

[357] *Roberts* (n 252).

[358] Ibid, per Lord Woolf at [76].

[359] Ibid, per Lord Woolf at [77], per Lord Bingham at [19], per Lord Rodger [112] and per Lord Carswell at [144].

round examining the proceedings as a whole with hindsight and taking into account the task of the Board.[360]

Their Lordships also pointed out that the members of the public who could be affected by a decision of the Board have human rights as well as the prisoner.

If the Board releases a prisoner when it is unsafe to do so, the public's individual rights can be grievously affected. In addition in a situation where the Board has to consider whether to withhold evidence from a prisoner, for example to protect an individual whose life could be threatened if his identity were revealed, the Board is under a duty to protect this individual's interests. Not to do so could involve the breach of art 2 or 3 of the ECHR.[361]

In a later case the Administrative Court held that a person must be given sufficient information about the allegations against him to enable him to give effective instructions. If reliance can be placed upon a closed judgment or on findings based on closed material, with no further disclosure, there was no assurance that the minimum Article 5(4) standard had been met.[362] Finally, it has been held that it is not necessary for a defendant to be able to confront a witness. What matters is that the defence should have a proper opportunity to challenge and question the witness.[363]

6.7 Decided Speedily

6.7.1 Principles

The final guarantee contained in Article 5(4) is that the proceedings testing the lawfulness of detention are to be decided speedily. As with the reasonable time requirement in Article 6, there are no hard-and-fast rules about whether or not a period of time is speedy enough. However, there is a distinction between the articles. The fact that the state is dealing with people who are at least presumptively detained unlawfully, and the legality of whose detention is controlled by Article 5(4), imposes a more intense obligation than that entailed by the need for a prompt trial of people who are not in custody.[364] Delay may result in unjustified detention and prolongs the period of uncertainty, often causing distress and disappointment.[365]

To comply with Article 5(4), efforts must be made to see that the individual application is heard as soon as reasonably practicable having regard to the relevant circumstances of the case.[366] Such time must be allowed as is reasonably necessary to ensure that the tribunal is in a position, adequately and fairly, to adjudicate on the issues before it.[367] This may be affected by the nature and importance of the subject matter of

---

[360] Ibid, per Lord Woolf at [77].

[361] Ibid, per Lord Woolf at [80]. See also *McClean* (n 286).

[362] *R (BB) v Special Immigration Appeals Commission* [2011] EWC 336 (Admin), [2011] 3 WLR 958, [37].

[363] *R (Gardner) v Parole Board* [2006] EWCA Civ 1222, [2007] Prison LR 78.

[364] *Noorkoiv* (n 8).

[365] *R (on the application of K) v Mental Health Review Tribunal* [2002] EWHC (Admin) 639 at [8].

[366] *R (on the application of C) v The Mental Health Review Tribunal London and South West Region* [2001] EWCA Civ 1110, [2002] 1 WLR 176 at [66] in reliance upon *Winterwerp*, above n 110, *E v Norway* (1990) 17 EHRR 30 and *Sanchez-Reiss v Switzerland* (1986) 9 EHRR 71.

[367] *C*, ibid, at [52].

the case, the complexity of the issues, the preparation required before the hearing and the evidence considered. The fact that a case may be considered unmeritorious does not deprive the applicant of the right to a speedy hearing.[368] Automatically listing an application for hearing within a particular period of time without considering individual circumstances is not generally compatible with Article 5(4) unless this is the only practical way of ensuring that individual cases are determined as speedily as their individual circumstances reasonably permit.[369]

Considerations such as constraint of resources or administrative convenience are not relevant.[370] It is the obligation of the state to organise its legal system to enable it to comply with the Convention requirements. General faults in or underfunding of the system will provide no defence, but the practical realities of litigious life will.[371] There may be adjournments or cancelled hearings for a number of reasons, such as the illness of a judge, the unavailability of necessary witnesses, the overrunning of an earlier hearing or the need to accommodate an urgent case.[372] However, the excessive workload of the judge cannot be prayed in aid, nor can the fact that the judge is on holiday.[373] In *K*[374] the Administrative Court held that the correct approach was to consider first whether the delays in question were inconsistent with the requirement of a speedy hearing. If they were, the onus was on the state to excuse the delay.

> It may do so by establishing, for example, that the delay has been caused by a sudden and unpredictable increase in the workload of the tribunal, and that it has taken effective and sufficient measures to remedy the problem. But if the State fails to satisfy that onus, the Claimant will have established a breach of his right under Article 5(4).[375]

It is clear that it is for the state to ensure speedy hearings and it is irrelevant which government department or other public authority was at fault.[376]

6.7.2 Mental Health Detainees

The question of speediness of determination has arisen on a number of occasions in the context of mental health. In *C*[377] the claimant applied to the tribunal for discharge and in accordance with current practice, his case was listed for hearing eight weeks later. The Court of Appeal first noted that the practice of automatically listing an application for hearing eight weeks after the date of application was not compatible with Article 5(4) unless this was the only practical way of ensuring that individual cases were determined as speedily as their individual circumstances reasonably permitted.[378] It did not accept that it was impossible to tailor lead times inside the eight-week target to suit

---

[368] *K* (n 365), [31].
[369] *C* (n 366), [45].
[370] Ibid, [45] and [64] in reliance upon *Bezicheri v Italy* (1989) 12 EHRR 210.
[371] *Noorkoiv* (n 8), [25].
[372] *K* (n 365), [38] in reliance upon *Dyer v Watson* [2002] UKPC D1, [2002] 1 AC 379.
[373] *Noorkoiv* (n 8), [24] in reliance upon *Bezicheri* (n 370).
[374] *K* (n 365).
[375] Ibid, [47] in reliance upon *Koendjbiharie v The Netherlands* (1990) 13 EHRR 820; *Musial v Poland* (2001) 31 EHRR 29.
[376] *Noorkoiv* (n 8), [31]; *K* (n 365), [112].
[377] *C* (n 366).
[378] Ibid, [45].

particular cases[379] and concluded that the practice was bred of administrative convenience, not of administrative necessity. Whilst there was nothing wrong with having a
target date of eight weeks maximum, to comply with Article 5(4) efforts had to be made
to see that the individual application was heard as soon as reasonably practicable.[380]

In K[381] the issue was repeated adjournments rather than an inflexible policy. The
eight claimants had applied to the mental health review tribunal for a review of their
detention and it each case the hearing was repeatedly adjourned. The hearings took
place between nine weeks and over 22 weeks after the dates of their respective applications. The Administrative Court appreciated that it was not possible to have an effective
tribunal hearing immediately after a patient makes an application for the review of his
detention,[382] but held that the listing of cases must be considered on an individual basis
and that it should be practicable for the hearings to take place within eight weeks of
the application.[383]

In response to the argument that the state was doing all that could reasonably be
done to remedy the problem, the court held that the onus was on the state to excuse
the delay, which it may do by establishing that there was a sudden and unpredictable increase in workload but that it had taken effective and sufficient measures to
remedy the problem.[384] It found here that the state should have taken the likelihood
of continuing increases in applications, as well as the experience of actual increases,
into account in deciding on the allocation of resources to the tribunals.[385] It also found
that the lack of medical tribunal members that caused cancellations was due in part
to the previous inadequate rates of pay.[386] It was also not satisfied that the shortage of
appropriately qualified legal tribunal members had occurred without responsibility on
the part of the state.[387] In addition, to the extent that failures to provide speedy hearings
were due to shortages of staff, pressure of work on staff or the lack of suitably trained
staff, it was not satisfied that these were not due to matters that were the responsibility
of the state.[388]

The court concluded that the principal causes of cancellations and delays were the
shortage of tribunal members, particularly medical members, and shortage and lack of
training of staff. Inadequate IT provision was also a contributory factor.[389] A violation
of Article 5(4) was found in relation to all of the claimants.

In MH[390] it was argued that section 29(4) of the Mental Health Act 1983 was incompatible with Article 5(4). The House of Lords concluded that the system was capable of
being operated compatibly taking into account the availability of judicial review, habeas
corpus, county court proceedings or by a the Secretary of State's reference under section 67. '[T]he means exist of operating s.29(4) in a way which is compatible with the

---

[379] Ibid, [60].
[380] Ibid, [64]–[66].
[381] K (n 365).
[382] Ibid, [31].
[383] Ibid, [37].
[384] Ibid, [47] in reliance upon *Koendjbiharie* and *Musial* (n 375).
[385] Ibid, [56].
[386] Ibid, [74].
[387] Ibid, [79].
[388] Ibid, [83].
[389] Ibid, [87].
[390] MH (n 254).

patient's rights. It follows that the section itself cannot be incompatible, although the action or inaction of the authorities under it may be so.'[391]

In *Rayner*[392] the claimant challenged an alleged delay on the part of the Secretary of State in referring his case to a tribunal under section 75(1) of the Mental Health Act 1983. The Court of Appeal did not accept that the Secretary of State was generally entitled to take the statutory maximum of one month before making a reference.[393] However, it was not convinced immediate reference was correct either. It held that test was whether there was a failure to proceed with 'reasonable despatch, having regard to all the material circumstances'.[394] It stated that the reference should normally be within days, not weeks, of a return of the patient to hospital.[395] Here the Secretary of State was in breach.

6.7.3 Life Sentence Prisoners

In *Noorkoiv*[396] the claimant received an automatic life sentence in 1998. His tariff expired in April 2001 but his hearing before the Parole Board to determine whether he should continue to be detained was not held until June 2001. It was the policy of the Board to only schedule hearings for a date after the expiry of the tariff period and it was the position of the Secretary of State that a lack of resources prevented any improvement on the present procedures. The Court of Appeal held that there was no general principle that administrative necessity provided an excuse. It noted that here all cases were treated the same irrespective of preparation time and the authorities had the case under consideration for many months before expiry of the tariff. It could not therefore be suggested that delay after expiry of the tariff was necessary to give proper consideration to a difficult individual case.[397]

It concluded that the arrangements infringed Article 5(4) and that it was breached in the present case. The arrangements envisaged a delay of up to three months.[398] When the prisoner reached the end of his tariff period the authorities did not then start on consideration of his case with no prior knowledge of his situation. He was within the custody of and well known to the authorities.[399] The full penal regime was imposed on him and this was seen to be a strong reason for determining the lawful status of that treatment sooner rather than later.[400] Resources constraints did not offset what was objectively a breach on the part of the state.[401] The scheme treated every case alike and imposed delays for reasons that were unrelated to the nature or difficulty of the particular case.[402] The court found no support for the argument that the final decision

---

[391] Ibid, [32].
[392] *Secretary of State for Justice v Rayner* [2008] EWCA Civ 176, [2009] 1 WLR 310.
[393] Ibid, [21].
[394] Ibid, [24].
[395] Ibid, [24].
[396] *Noorkoiv* (n 8).
[397] Ibid, [26].
[398] Ibid, [33].
[399] Ibid, [34].
[400] Ibid, [36].
[401] Ibid, [36].
[402] Ibid, [37].

must be delayed to a date after the end of the tariff period.[403] It concluded that it was for the Secretary of State to consider in detail how to proceed, and if further resources were seen as necessary, these must be provided.[404]

> Given the imperative need to release from prison any post-tariff prisoner who no longer remains a danger (not least in these days of acute prison overcrowding), any system tending to delay such release (as the Board's present system does) requires the most compelling justification. Although by no means unsympathetic to the Board's difficulties, at the end of the day I am not persuade that any such compelling justification exists, or at any rate that it need continue to exist.[405]

Speediness is also an issue with respect to the period between reviews of the detention of those serving life sentences. In determining whether the interval complies with Article 5(4) on the facts of a particular case, the court asks itself whether the interval was reasonable.[406] For example, in *Spence*[407] the prisoner challenged the decision of the Secretary of State to extend the nine months recommended by the Parole Board, which should be passed in open prison conditions before the next review, to a period of 18 months. In light of the circumstances of the case, the Court of Appeal concluded that the interval was reasonable.[408] However, in *Murray*,[409] taking into account Strasbourg jurisprudence, the Court of Appeal held that an interval of up to a year has ordinarily to be shown to be in breach of Article 5(4) on some particular ground whilst an interval of more than a year has generally to be shown not to be in breach of it.[410] Here a delay of 15 months was not held to be excessive.[411] Failure to conduct a review in accordance with Article 5(4) does not make the detention unlawful but does constitute a breach of Article 5(4) entitling the prisoner to the appropriate remedy.[412]

6.7.4 Prisoners Serving Indeterminate Sentences

In *James*[413] the House of Lords considered the application of Article 5(4) where the Secretary of State had failed to provide the systems and resources that prisoners serving indeterminate sentences needed to demonstrate to the Parole Board by the time of the expiry of their tariff periods, or reasonably soon thereafter, that it was no longer necessary for the protection of the public that they should remain in detention. As Lord Brown explained, there were insufficient resources available to undertake required

---

[403] Ibid, [39]–[40].

[404] Ibid, [44].

[405] Ibid, per Simon Brown LJ at [58].

[406] *R (on the application of Spence) v Secretary of State for the Home Department* [2003] EWCA Civ 732; *Murray v Parole Board* [2003] EWCA Civ 1561; *D v Secretary of State for the Home Department* [2002] EWHC (Admin) 2805, [2003] 1 WLR 1315.

[407] *Spence*, ibid.

[408] Ibid, [30] in reliance upon *Oldham v UK* Judgment of 26 September 2000. See also *MacNeill v Parole Board* [2001] EWCA Civ 448 and *R (on the application of Clough) v Secretary of State for the Home Department* [2003] EWHC (Admin) 597.

[409] *Murray* (n 406).

[410] Ibid, [14] in reliance upon *Oldham v UK* (n 408) and *Hirst v United Kingdom* 24 October 2001.

[411] Ibid, [5]. See also *King v Secretary of State for the Home Department* [2003] EWHC (Admin) 2831, [2004] HRLR 9; *D* (n 406); *Day* (n 3110. See also *R (Loch) v Secretary of State for Justice* [2008] EWHC 2278 (Admin), [2009] Prison LR 212.

[412] *R (Parratt) v Secretary of State for Justice* [2013] EWHC 17 (Admin), [32].

[413] *Secretary of State for Justice v James* [2009] UKHL 22, [2010] 1 AC 553.

assessments, prepare sentence plans, provide necessary courses and generally enable prisoners to demonstrate their safety for release.

It was not possible for the Parole Board to conduct an effective review without the coursework which the prisoners needed to demonstrate they were no longer a risk to the public. The breach of Article 5(4) was accepted in relation to two of the prisoners but not the other. The House of Lords concluded that there was no breach. Lord Hope held that delays were apt to occur for all sorts of reasons:

> Continued detention will only become unlawful when the Board decides that it is no longer necessary for the protection of the public that the prisoner should be confined. Until that stage is reached each step that the Board takes in the review process confirms the lawfulness of the detention.[414]

In his view, it was open to the Board to determine how much information it needed, to conclude that the information it had was inadequate, and to set its own timetable:

> It is entitled to expect co-operation from those who are responsible for the management of the sentence in meeting its requirements. But a failure to meet them does not of itself mean that there will be a breach of article 5(4).[415]

In his opinion, it was only if the system broke down entirely because the Parole Board was denied the information it needed for such a long period that continued detention had become arbitrary that the guarantee of Article 5(4) would be violated and damages necessary.[416] Lord Mance also held that Article 5(4) was not directed to the operational inadequacies of a prison regime which may make it 'impossible for the prisoner to address his offending in the hope of or with a view to his reform and rehabilitation'.[417]

In *Faulkner*[418] the Supreme Court held that a prisoner whose detention was prolonged as the result of a delay in the consideration if his case by the Parole Board in violation of Article 5(4) was not the victim of false imprisonment. Nor was he the victim of a violation of Article 5(1) unless there were exceptional circumstances warranting the conclusion that the prisoner's continued detention had become arbitrary.[419] The assessment of damages in such instances is discussed in the following section.

6.7.5 Prisoners Serving Determinate Sentences

In *Johnson*[420] the Court of Appeal considered the application of speedy determination to a prisoner serving a determinate sentence who was entitled to be released on licence after he had served two-thirds of his sentence. There was a delay by the Parole Board and he ended up seeking judicial review nearly eight and a half months after his parole eligibility date. The Court of Appeal concluded that Article 5(4) applied, stating that if the prisoner could show that at an earlier consideration by the Parole Board he

---

[414] Ibid, per Lord Hope at [20].
[415] Ibid, [21].
[416] Ibid, [21]. See also the comments of Lord Brown at [60].
[417] Ibid, [132] The ECtHR found a breach of Art.5(1) in *James, Wells and Lee* (n 104).
[418] *R (Faulkner) v Secretary of State for Justice* [2013] UKSC 23, [2013] 2 WLR 1157.
[419] Ibid, [13].
[420] *R (Johnson) v Secretary of State for the Home Department* [2007] EWCA Civ 427, [2007] 1 WLR 1990.

would have been released, his detention for some period was arbitrary, unjustified and unlawful.[421]

---

7. Article 5(5): Enforceable Right to Compensation

Article 5(5) provides that everyone who has been the victim of arrest or detention in contravention of the provisions of Article 5 shall have an enforceable right to compensation. However, Article 5(5) does not create a right separate from the other Convention rights given effect by the HRA or create a separate, free-standing autonomous right capable of giving rise in itself to a cause of action under the HRA in the event of refusal to pay compensation. A right to compensation only arises if a breach of Article 5(1) or 5(4) can first be established.[422] The provisions of Article 5(5) are mandatory—if there has been a breach of Article 5, there is an enforceable right to compensation.[423] However, it is possible in some instances for no compensation to be awarded. For example, in *IH*[424] the House of Lords, although finding a violation of Article 5(4), did not consider that an award of compensation was required. This was because the violation had been publicly acknowledged and the appellant's right thereby vindicated; the law had been amended in a way which should prevent similar violations in future; and the appellant had not been the victim of unlawful detention, which Article 5 was intended to avoid.[425]

In *Faulkner*[426] the Supreme Court considered the circumstances in which a life or indeterminate sentence prisoner who had served his tariff period and whose case had not been considered by the Parole Board within a reasonable period thereafter should be awarded damages under the HRA and the quantum of such awards. It held that at the present stage of development of the remedy of damages under section 8 of the HRA, the courts should be guided by any clear and consistent practice of the ECtHR and the quantum of awards should broadly reflect the level of awards made by the ECtHR in comparable cases brought by applicants from the UK or other countries with a similar cost of living. It held that courts should resolve disputed issues of fact in the usual way even if the ECtHR in similar circumstances would not do so.[427]

Where it has been established on a balance of probabilities that a violation of Article 5(4) has resulted in the detention of a prisoner beyond the date when he would otherwise have been released, 'damages should ordinarily be awarded as compensation for the resultant detention'. The Supreme Court confirmed that the appropriate amount to be awarded was a matter of judgment 'reflecting the facts of the individual case' and taking into account such 'guidance as is available from awards made by the European

---

[421] Ibid, [29].
[422] *R (Wright) v Secretary of State for the Home Department* [2006] EWCA Civ 67, [2006] HRLR 23.
[423] *Evans* (n 75), per Lords Hope, Steyn and Hobhouse.
[424] *IH* (n 167).
[425] Ibid, [30].
[426] *Faulkner* (n 418).
[427] Ibid, [13].

Court', or by 'domestic courts under section 8 of the 1998 Act, in comparable cases'.[428] Detailed consideration was given to the type of loss to be compensated. It was held that pecuniary losses proved to have been caused by the prolongation of detention should be compensated in full. It was not appropriate, as a matter of course, to take into account as a factor mitigating harm that the claimant was recalled to prison following his eventual release. But, it noted, there may be circumstances in which the claimant's recall to prison is relevant to the assessment of damages.

The court held that damages should not be awarded merely for the loss of a chance of earlier release. 'Nor should damages be adjusted according to the degree of probability of release if the violation of article 5(4) had not occurred.' However, even if is not established that an earlier hearing would have resulted in earlier release, there is a strong but not irrebuttable presumption that delay in violation of Article 5(4) 'has caused the prisoner to suffer feelings of frustration and anxiety'. It held that where such feelings can be presumed or are shown to have been suffered, the finding of a violation will not ordinarily constitute sufficient just satisfaction and an award of damages should also be made although such damages should be on a modest scale. No award should be made where the delay was such that any resultant frustration and anxiety were insufficiently severe to warrant such an award. 'That is unlikely to be the position where the delay was of the order of three months or more.'[429]

In *KB*,[430] an earlier decision, the Administrative Court assessed the damages to be awarded to individuals whose rights under Article 5(4) were breached due to delays in the hearing of the applications by a mental health review tribunal. It held that a claimant who sought damages on the basis of an allegation that he would have had a favourable decision at an earlier date if his Convention rights had been respected had to prove this on the balance of probabilities.[431] The period to which any award of damages related was that from the time when the tribunal should have determined a patient's application to the date when it was actually determined. The court noted that the assessment of the period of delay was bound to be somewhat impressionistic.[432]

Whilst noting that every disappointment and feeling of distress did not constitute compensable damage, the court held that full account had to be taken of the fact that the claimants were patients detained on account of the state of their mental health and thus in a vulnerable mental condition. Damages could be awarded to such persons even though in analogous circumstances no award would be made to a healthy person. The frustration and distress must be significant, of such intensity that it would in itself justify an award of compensation for non-pecuniary damage. It noted that an important touchstone of that intensity in cases such as the present was that hospital staff considered it to be sufficiently relevant to the mental state of the patient to warrant its mention in clinical notes.[433] For some of the claimants the court held that a finding of violation was sufficient. For others, amounts ranging between £1,000 and £4,000 were awarded.

---

[428] Ibid, [13].

[429] Ibid, [13]. See also *R (Downing) v Parole Board* [2008] EWHC 3198 (Admin), [2009] Prison LR 327; Guntrip (n 251); *R (Hester) v Secretary of State for Justice* [2011] EWHC 3926 (Admin).

[430] *R (on the application of KB) v Mental Health Review Tribunal* [2003] EWHC (Admin) 193, [2004] QB 936.

[431] Ibid, [64].

[432] Ibid, [65].

[433] Ibid, [72]–[73].

10

Article 6: The Right to a Fair Trial

1. Introduction

The first sentence of Article 6(1) provides that in the determination of his civil rights and obligations, or of any criminal charge against him, everyone is entitled to a fair and public hearing within a reasonable time by an independent and impartial tribunal established by law. The Article also provides that judgment shall be pronounced publicly and in Articles 6(2) and 6(3), protects a range of other rights protecting those who have been charged with a criminal offence. The core right guaranteed is the right to a fair trial, and the focus of the Article is on achieving a result which is, and is seen to be, fair. Most of the other rights singled out for mention relate to the fairness and perceived fairness of the trial process.[1] However, each of the rights protected by Article 6 must be considered separately. A complaint that one of these rights was breached cannot be answered by showing that the other rights were not breached. Furthermore, the consequences of a breach are not necessarily the same for each right protected.[2]

The Article was conceived primarily as a 'bulwark to protect private citizens against the abuse of power by state and public authorities.'[3] The importance of the rights with which it deals is reflected in the fact that on its face the Article permits no restriction the only express qualification relating to the requirement of a public hearing. There is nothing to suggest that the fairness of the trial itself may be qualified, compromised or restricted in any way, 'whatever the circumstances and whatever the public interest in convicting the offender'.[4] However the rights protected by Article 6 can, in certain

---

[1] *Attorney General's Reference No 2 of 2001* [2003] UKHL 68, [2004] 2 AC 72, [10].
[2] *Porter v Magill* [2001] UKHL 67, [2002] 2 WLR 37, [87] and [108]. See also *Millar v Dickson* [2002] 1 WLR 1615; *Procurator Fiscal, Linlithgow v Watson* [2002] UKPC D1, [2004] 1 AC 379, [73]; *Mills v HM Advocate (No 2)* [2002] UKPC D2, [2004] 1 AC 441, [9]–[12]; *Attorney General's Reference No 2 of 2001*, ibid, [12].
[3] *R v Weir* [2001] 1 WLR 421.
[4] *Brown v Stott (Procurator Fiscal, Dunfermline)* [2001] 1 AC 681 per Lord Bingham. See also *Watson* (n 2), [73].

circumstances, be waived. For example, where parties have freely entered into an arbitration agreement, they are treated as having waived their rights under Article 6.[5]

In addition, Article 6 does not just protect those rights which appear on its face. A number of other rights have been implied by the ECtHR, including the right not to incriminate oneself, the right of access to a court and equality of arms. The purpose of these implied rights is to give effect in a practical way to the fundamental and absolute right to a fair trial.[6] These implied rights are not absolute and interference is possible if it has a legitimate aim in the public interest, and there is a reasonable relationship of proportionality between the means employed and the aim sought to be realised.[7]

Most of the rights protected by Article 6, both express and implied, are familiar to UK lawyers, and the observation is often made that the principles which are enshrined in Article 6 have long been a part of the common law.[8] However, it has also been recognised that some re-examination and revision of these principles in the light of the Article may be necessary.

> The scheme of the articles involves the application of different tests at each stage of the inquiry from those applied by the common law. It requires that a more structured approach be taken when the overriding test of fairness is applied to the facts.[9]

Article 6 has been considered in almost every context possible. However, it is rare for a court to refer to the principle of deference when adjudicating upon this Article. This is related to the absolute nature of many of the guarantees and the fact that UK courts are used to dealing with similar concepts at common law. An example of some deference being shown is the judgment of the House of Lords in *Kebilene*[10] where Lord Hope noted that in some circumstances it will be appropriate for the courts to recognise that there is an area of judgment within which the judiciary will defer, on democratic grounds, to the considered opinion of the elected body or person whose act or decision was said to be incompatible with the Convention:

> [E]ven where the right is stated in terms which are unqualified the courts will need to bear in mind the jurisprudence of the European Court which recognises that due account should be taken of the special nature of terrorist crime and the threat which it poses to a democratic society.[11]

In *McIntosh*[12] Lord Bingham noted that the statutory scheme regarding confiscation of the assets of those convicted of drug trafficking offences was one approved by a democratically elected Parliament and should not be at all readily rejected.[13] An appeal for deference was also made in *R v A*,[14] but was only considered by Lords Steyn and Hope. Lord Steyn noted that clearly the House must give weight to the decision of Parliament.

---

[5] *Stretford v Football Association Ltd* [2007] EWCA Civ 238, [2007] All ER (Comm) 1.
[6] *Brown* (n 4), per Lord Hope.
[7] Ibid.
[8] See eg the comments of Lord Hope in *R v A* [2001] UKHL 25, [2002] 1 AC 45, [51].
[9] *Brown* (n 4), per Lord Hope.
[10] *R v Director of Public Prosecutions, ex p Kebilene* [1999] 3 WLR 972.
[11] In reliance on *Murray v United Kingdom* (1994) 19 EHRR 193, [47].
[12] *McIntosh v Lord Advocate* [2001] 1 AC 1078.
[13] Ibid, [36].
[14] *R v A* (n 8).

On the other hand, when the question arises whether in the criminal statute in question Parliament adopted a legislative scheme which makes an excessive inroad into the right to a fair trial the court is qualified to make its own judgment and must do so.[15]

Lord Hope took the opposite position, noting that there were areas of law which lay within the discretionary area of judgment which the court ought to accord to the legislature.

[I]t is appropriate in some circumstances for the judiciary to defer, on democratic grounds, to the considered opinion of the elected body as to where the balance is to be struck between the rights of the individual and the needs of society.[16]

His Lordship saw the essential question as whether Parliament acted within its discretionary area of judgment when it was choosing the point of balance.[17] He continued:

The area is one where Parliament was better equipped than the judges are to decide where the balance lay. The judges are well able to assess the extent to which the restrictions will inhibit questioning or the leading of evidence. But it seems to me in this highly sensitive and carefully researched field an assessment of the prejudice to the wider interests of the community if the restrictions were not to take that form was more appropriate for Parliament. An important factor for Parliament to consider was the extent to which restrictions were needed in order to restore and maintain public confidence.[18]

Outside of the criminal justice context there is a little more scope for deference, particularly in the context of administrative decision making. For example, in *Alconbury*,[19] finding that the Secretary of State in his planning capacity was not independent and impartial but that this could be overcome by judicial review, all of their Lordships referred to the inappropriateness of allowing a court to substitute its decision for that of the administrative authority in questions of planning policy. Lord Slynn noted that the adoption of planning policy and its application to particular facts was quite different from the judicial function.

It is for elected Members of Parliament and ministers to decide what are the objectives of planning policy, objectives which may be of national, environmental, social or political significance and for these objectives to be set out in legislation, primary and secondary, in ministerial directions and planning policy guidelines.[20]

In Lord Nolan's view, to substitute for the Secretary of State an independent and impartial body with no central electoral accountability would not only be a recipe for chaos: it would be 'profoundly undemocratic'.[21] Lord Hoffmann also pointed out that the question of what the public interest requires for the purpose of property rights can and should be determined according to the democratic principle—by elected local or central bodies, or by ministers accountable to them subject to the rule of law.[22] '[P]olicy

---

[15] Ibid, [36].
[16] Ibid, [58].
[17] Ibid.
[18] Ibid, [99].
[19] *R v Secretary of State for the Environment, Transport and the Regions, ex p Alconbury Developments Ltd* [2001] UKHL 23, [2001] 2 WLR 1389.
[20] Ibid, [48].
[21] Ibid, [60].
[22] Ibid, [72]–[73].

decisions within the limits imposed by the principles of judicial review are a matter for democratically accountable institutions and not for the courts.'[23]

2. Deportation and Extradition

Prior to considering the meaning and application of each of rights protected by Article 6, it is important to note that an issue might exceptionally be raised under Article 6 by an extradition or deportation decision where the claimant has suffered or risks suffering a flagrant denial of Article 6 in the destination state.[24] The deficiency or deficiencies in the trial process must be such as to 'fundamentally to destroy the fairness of the prospective trial'.[25] Furthermore, the focus must be not simply on the unfairness of the trial process but on its potential consequences. An unfair trial is likely to lead to the violation of substantive human rights and the extent of that prospective violation must be an 'important factor in deciding whether deportation is precluded'.[26] For example, a conviction resulting from a flagrantly unfair trial cannot be relied upon under Article 5(1)(a) as justifying detention or justify the imposition and execution of the death penalty. Lord Phillips in *RB* summarised the position as follows:

> If an alien is to avoid deportation because he faces unfair legal process in the receiving state he must show that there are substantial grounds for believing that there is a real risk not merely that he will suffer a flagrant breach of his article 6 rights, but that the consequence will be a serious violation of a substantive right or rights.[27]

He noted that such a serious violation would include a sentence of death or a conviction and sentence of many years imprisonment.[28] In the present case it was held that life imprisonment and a sentence of 15 years imprisonment were sufficient to satisfy the second limb. However, in relation to the first limb of the test, the House of Lords found that the composition of the court was not a flagrant breach of Article 6. It also concluded that the United Kingdom was not required to retain a terrorist suspect unless it had a high degree of assurance that evidence obtained by torture would be adduced against him in the destination state (Jordan). It found no risk of a flagrant denial of justice from the use of torture evidence. Lord Hoffmann observed that there was no authority for a rule that in the context of the application of Article 6 to a foreign trial, the risk of the use of evidence obtained by torture necessarily amounted to a flagrant denial of justice.[29] In *Othman v United Kingdom*[30] the ECtHR concluded that there was a real risk that evidence obtained by torture of third persons would be admitted at the

---

[23] Ibid, [76]. See also the comments of Lord Clyde at [139] and [141]. See also *Begum (Runa) v Tower Hamlets London Borough Council* [2003] UKHL 5, [2003] 2 AC 430.

[24] *RB (Algeria) v Secretary of State for the Home Department* [2009] UKHL 10, [2010] 2 AC 110.

[25] Ibid, per Lord Phillips at [136].

[26] Ibid, [137].

[27] Ibid, [138].

[28] Ibid, [140].

[29] Ibid, [201].

[30] *Othman v United Kingdom* Judgment of 17 January 2012.

trial and that this was sufficient to demonstrate a real risk of a flagrant denial of justice. This finding was later given effect by the Special Immigration Appeals Commission,[31] and upheld by the Court of Appeal.[32]

By contrast in *Kapri*[33] the Supreme Court held that the extradition of the claimant to Albania to face a retrial could involve a flagrant denial of justice given the corruption in the judiciary in that country. It was observed that systemic corruption in a judicial system affected everyone who was subject to it and that no tribunal which operated within it could be relied upon to be independent and impartial.[34] The case was returned to the lower court so that it could reach a properly informed decision on the threshold test.[35]

---

3. Article 6(1) Application: Determination of Civil Rights and Obligations

The first sentence of Article 6(1) provides that a person is only entitled to the rights there protected 'in the determination of his civil rights and obligations or of any criminal charge against him'. The meaning of the phrase 'determination of civil rights and obligations' is autonomous[36] and has given rise to a number of claims from those seeking to bring themselves within the protection of Article 6(1). It has been held that a narrow view is inappropriate[37] and pragmatically, in *Beeson*,[38] the Court of Appeal held that it should lean towards finding that civil rights were engaged, given that, at common law, whether or not executive action touched the citizen's rights in private law was irrelevant to the availability of judicial review.[39] Nevertheless, a number of rules and restrictions apply.[40]

---

[31] Special Immigration Appeals Commission, 12 November 2012.

[32] *Othman v United Kingdom* [2013] EWCA Civ 277. See also *XX (Ethiopia) v Secretary of State for the Home Department* [2012] EWCA Civ 742, [2013] 2 WLR 178.

[33] *Kapri v Lord Advocate* [2013] UKSC 48, [2013] 1 WLR 2324.

[34] Ibid, per Lord Hope at [32].

[35] See also *Merchant International Co Ltd v Natsionalna Aktsionerna Kompaniia Naftogaz* [2012] EWCA Civ 196, [2012] 1 WLR 3036 where a Ukranian judgment was not recognised on the basis that it involved a flagrant breach of the principle of legal certainty.

[36] *Alconbury* (n 19), per Lord Clyde at [148] in reliance upon *König v Germany* (1978) 2 EHRR 170; *H v France* (1989) 12 EHRR 74.

[37] *Alconbury* (n 19), per Lord Clyde at [146] in reliance upon *X v United Kingdom* (1998) 28 D&R 177; *Ringeisen v Austria (No 1)* (1971) 1 EHRR 455; *Golder v United Kingdom* (1975) 1 EHRR 524; *Le Compte, Van Leuven and De Meyere v Belgium* (1981) 4 EHRR 1.

[38] *R (on the application of Beeson) v Secretary of State for Health* [2002] EWCA Civ 1812, [2003] HRLR 345.

[39] Ibid, [17] and [19].

[40] It is important to remember that even if Art 6 does not apply, the common law may provide a remedy. See eg *R (on the application of Smith) v Parole Board* [2005] UKHL 1, [2005] 1 WLR 350 and the comments of the Court of Appeal in *Beeson* (n 38), [17].

3.1 Civil Rights and Obligations

3.1.1 Generally

Civil rights and obligations are rights and obligations which can be said, at least on arguable grounds, to be recognised under domestic law.[41] It is not open to a court when applying Article 6 to create a substantive right which has no legal basis in the domestic system at all.[42] For example, in *Alconbury*,[43] which concerned the role of the Secretary of State in referring planning applications to himself and appointing inspectors to hold public planning inquiries, the House of Lords held that the rights with which the appeals were concerned were rights of property and clearly fell within the scope of civil rights. Similarly in *Lukaszewski*[44] the Supreme Court held that a British citizen enjoyed a common (or civil) law right to enter and remain in the United Kingdom as and when he pleased and that proceedings for extradition involved a determination of that civil right. By contrast, in *Kehoe*[45] a majority of the House of Lords held that, as the Child Support Act 1991 did not confer on the caring parent a right of recovering or enforcing a claim to child maintenance against an absent or non-resident parent, the caring parent had no civil right within the meaning of Article 6. In *Tom Hood School* the Court of Appeal held that there was no civil right to be educated at a particular school[46] and in *King*[47] that there was no civil right held by prisoners to associate with other prisoners.[48] Other examples of civil rights include: the right to practise a profession;[49] rights under family law;[50] rights under tort law;[51] and rights under employment law.[52] Due to the HRA, Convention rights are also considered to be civil rights within the meaning of Article 6(1). For example, in *Re S*[53] the House of Lords concluded that the making of a care order, which endowed a local authority with parental responsibility for a child, affected Article 8 rights of parents and children. Concluding that these were now civil rights, Article 6(1) was held to apply.[54] Similarly, in *McCann*[55] the House of Lords held that proceedings for an anti-social behaviour order under section 1 of the Crime and Disorder Act 1998 engaged rights under Articles 8, 10 and 11, and therefore Article 6(1) applied.[56]

---

[41] *Alconbury* (n 19), [148] in reliance upon *James v United Kingdom* (1986) 8 EHRR 123, [81].
[42] *R (on the application of Kehoe) v Secretary of State for Work and Pensions* [2005] UKHL 48, [2005] 3 WLR 252, per Lord Hope at [41].
[43] *Alconbury* (n 19).
[44] *Lukaszewski v Poland* [2012] UKSC 20, [2012] 1 WLR 1604.
[45] *Kehoe* (n 42).
[46] *R (V) v Independent Appeal Panel for Tom Hood School* [2010] EWCA Civ 142, [2010] HRLR 21.
[47] *R (King) v Secretary of State for Justice* [2012] EWCA Civ 376, [2012] 4 All ER 44.
[48] Ibid, [40].
[49] *Preiss v General Dental Council* [2001] UKPC 36, [2001] 1 WLR 1926; *R (Wright) v Secretary of State for Health* [2009] UKHL 3, [2009] 1 AC 739.
[50] *Re S* [2002] UKHL 10, [2002] 2 WLR 720.
[51] *Polanski v Condé Nast Publications* [2005] UKHL 10, [2005] 1 WLR 637.
[52] *Stansbury v Datapulse plc* [2003] EWCA Civ 1951, [2004] ICR 523.
[53] *Re S* (n 50).
[54] Ibid, [69]–[72]. See also *Principal Reporter v K* [2010] UKSC 56, [2011] 1 WLR 18.
[55] *R (on the application of McCann) v Crown Court at Manchester* [2002] UKHL 39, [2003] 1 AC 787.
[56] Ibid, per Lord Steyn at [29] and per Lord Hope at [80]. However in *King* (n 47) the Court of Appeal held that decisions on prisoner confinement and segregation did not engage Arts 3 or 8 to a sufficient extent to make these civil rights for the purposes of Art 6. Other examples include *R (on the application of Thompson) v Law Society* [2004] EWCA Civ 167, [2004] 1 WLR 2522, [107], where it was accepted by

3.1.2 Public Law Rights

Article 6(1) can also apply to administrative decisions on the ground that these can determine or affect rights in private law.[57] The ECtHR has gradually extended Article 6(1) to public law rights, such as entitlements to social security or welfare benefits under publicly funded statutory schemes, on the ground that they closely resemble rights in private law.[58] The position under the HRA is not yet clear and a case by case approach has been taken. In Begum,[59] whilst not finally deciding the issue, the House of Lords found the reasoning of Hale LJ in Adan[60] persuasive. Hale LJ had held that, once the local authority were satisfied that the statutory criteria for providing accommodation existed, they had no discretion and had to provide it irrespective of local conditions of demand and supply. She therefore concluded that this was more akin to a claim for social security benefits than a claim for social or other services where the authorities had a greater degree of discretion, and was therefore a determination of a civil right within the meaning of Article 6(1).[61] In Begum, the claimant was homeless and the Council owed her a duty under section 193 of the Housing Act 1993 to ensure that accommodation was available to her. Despite the comments on Adan, their Lordships noted that to apply Article 6(1) to the provision of benefits in kind, involving the amount of discretion which was inevitably needed in such cases, would be to go further than the ECtHR had gone.[62] However, they found no violation of the independence and impartiality guarantee without determining whether Article 6 actually applied to the decision.[63]

In A[64] the Supreme Court had to determine whether the decision whether or not to provide accommodation under section 20(1) of the Children Act 1989 was the determination of a civil right. Conclusions on other matters made it unnecessary to reach any firm conclusions on Article 6 but observations were made. Baroness Hale held that she was reluctant to accept, unless required by ECtHR authority to do so, that

the Court of Appeal that an order by the Office for Supervision of Solicitors that the claimant refund costs was a determination of civil rights and obligations as he was deprived of a possession; R (on the application of Q) v Secretary of State for the Home Department [2003] EWCA Civ 364, [2004] QB 36, [115]–[116], where, without finally determining the issue, the Court of Appeal proceeded on the basis that the decision concerning entitlement of an asylum seeker to support engaged civil rights because of the gravity of such a decision, in human rights terms, for the individual; S T and P v London Borough of Brent [2002] EWCA Civ 693, [2002] ACD 90, where the Court of Appeal held Art 6 was engaged by a school exclusion given its impact on the right to education. The opposite conclusion on this question was reached by the Court of Appeal in V (n 46).

[57] See eg Alconbury (n 19), and R (on the application of McLellan) v Bracknell Forest Borough Council [2002] 1 All ER 899.

[58] Begum (n 23), [30] in reliance upon Salesi v Italy (1993) 26 EHRR 187.

[59] Ibid.

[60] Adan v Newham London Borough Council [2001] EWCA Civ 1916, [2002] 1 WLR 2120.

[61] Ibid, [55].

[62] Begum (n 23), per Lord Hoffmann at [69], Lord Bingham at [6], Lord Millett at [94] and Lord Walker at [115].

[63] In Beeson (n 38) the Court of Appeal held that the decision of a County Council that an elderly man had deprived himself of certain property belonging to him in circumstances such that the value of the property fell to be taken into account in assessing his ability to pay for residential accommodation arranged for him by the Council engaged his civil rights. See generally P Craig, 'The Human Rights Act, Article 6 and Procedural Rights' [2003] Public Law 753; I Loveland, 'Does Homelessness Decision-making Engage Article 6(1) of the European Convention on Human Rights?' [2003] European Human Rights Law Review 176.

[64] R (A) v London Borough of Croydon [2009] UKSC 8, [2009] 1 WLR 2557.

Article 6 required the judicialisation of claims to welfare services of this kind. She was conscious of the impact on resources of doing so:

> If the officers making the decisions cannot be regarded as impartial, and the problem cannot be cured by the ordinary processes of judicial review based upon the usual criteria of legality, fairness and reasonableness or rationality, then tribunals will have to be set up to determine the merits of claims to children's services, adult social services, education services and many more. Resources which might be spent on the services themselves will be diverted to the decision-making process.[65]

She observed that if this was a civil right, it rested at the periphery of such rights and that the present decision-making process, coupled with judicial review on conventional grounds, was adequate to result in a fair determination within the meaning of Article 6.[66] Lord Hope, reaching a firmer conclusion, stated that it could now be asserted with reasonable confidence that the duty of the local authority under section 20(1) of the Act to provide accommodation for any child in need within their area who appeared to them to require accommodation as a result of the factors mentioned in the subsection did not give rise to a civil right within the meaning of Article 6(1).[67]

In its clearest judgment to date on this issue, the Supreme Court considered the jurisprudence once again in *Tomlinson*.[68] Here the question was whether a decision that a local housing authority took under section 193(5) of the Housing Act 1996, that it had discharged its duty to a homeless claimant, was a determination of civil rights within the meaning of Article 6(1). Lord Hope, with whom the others agreed, held that the scheme which Part VII of the Housing Act 1996 laid down provided a right to assistance if the relevant conditions were satisfied. But in his view, this was not a pecuniary right, nor was the benefit that was to be provided defined by the application of specific rules laid down by the statute.[69] He concluded that there was not a 'civil right' at issue here:

> [C]ases where the award of services or benefits in kind is not an individual right of which the applicant can consider himself the holder, but is dependent upon a series of evaluative judgments by the provider as to whether the statutory criteria are satisfied and how the need for it ought to be met, do not engage article 6(1) ... do not give rise to 'civil rights' within the autonomous meaning that is given to that expression for the purposes of that article.[70]

3.1.3 Public Sector Workers

It remains the position that the disputes of individuals in the public service sector who wield a portion of the state's sovereign power are outside the protection of Article 6(1).[71] For example, in *Mangera*[72] the Court of Appeal concluded that Article 6 had no

---

[65] Ibid, [44].
[66] Ibid, [45].
[67] Ibid, [65]; the other Lords agreed with Lady Hale and reached no firm conclusions on this point.
[68] *Tomlinson v Birmingham City Council* [2010] UKSC 8, [2010] 2 AC 39.
[69] Ibid, [27].
[70] Ibid, per Lord Hope at [49]. Lord Collins placed greater emphasis on an individual economic right in the applicant.
[71] *Heath v Commissioner of Police for the Metropolis* [2004] EWCA Civ 943, [2005] ICR 329 in reliance upon *Devlin v UK* (2002) EHRR 43. See further G Morris, 'Public Employment and the Human Rights Act 1998' [2001] *Public Law* 442.
[72] *Mangera v Ministry of Defence* [2003] EWCA Civ 801.

application to a case brought by a serving soldier under the Race Relations Act 1976.[73] However, the lower the grade of public servant, the more likely it is that Article 6(1) will apply. In *Heath*[74] the Court of Appeal held that a civilian police station reception officer was unlikely to meet the test of 'wielding a portion of the State's sovereign power' and therefore, whilst not finally determining the issue, held that it was likely Article 6(1) applied.[75]

3.2 Determination

For Article 6(1) to apply, it must also be shown that civil rights and obligations are being determined. In order for there to be a determination, there must be a dispute of a genuine and serious nature,[76] though it need not be a dispute in any formal sense.[77] The decision must directly affect civil rights and obligations by determining the existence of a right or the scope of manner in which it may be exercised.[78] For example, in *Alconbury*[79] the House of Lords found that the role of the Secretary of State in referring planning applications to himself, and appointing inspectors to hold public planning inquiries, fell within the meaning of determination of civil rights even though there was no issue about the existence of those rights and no determination of those rights in the strict sense. However, civil rights were directly affected and the dispute was of a genuine and serious nature.[80] In *Lukaszewski*[81] the Supreme Court held that extradition proceedings under the Extradition Act 2003 determined whether a British citizen may continue to enjoy his common law right to enter and remain in the United Kingdom. '[H]e is entitled to a fair determination as to his common law right to remain within the jurisdiction.'[82]

By contrast, in *Smith*[83] a majority of the House of Lords concluded that proceedings before the Parole Board, where a determinate sentence prisoner released on licence sought to resist subsequent revocation of his licence, did not constitute a determination of civil rights and obligations. In the opinion of the majority, what the Board was doing was giving effect, in the performance of functions given to it by statute, to the sentences which had previously been imposed by the judge when the appellants were convicted. None of the elements that were inherent in the sentence from the begin-

---

[73] In reliance upon *Pellegrin v France* (1999) 31 EHRR 651.

[74] *Heath* (n 71).

[75] Ibid, [60]–[61].

[76] *Alconbury* (n 19), [149]. See also *R v Lord Chancellor, ex p Lightfoot* [2000] QB 597.

[77] *Alconbury* (n 19), per Lord Clyde at [147] in reliance upon *Le Compte* (n 37), and *Moreira de Azevedo v Portugal* (1990) 13 EHRR 721.

[78] *Alconbury* (n 19) in reliance upon *Le Compte* (n 37); *Balmer-Schafroth v Switzerland* (1997) 25 EHRR 598.

[79] *Alconbury* (n 19).

[80] Ibid, per Lord Clyde at [150]. See also *R v Secretary of State for Health, ex p C* [2000] 1 FCR 471, where the Court of Appeal held that inclusion on the Department of Health's list of people about whom there were doubts about their suitability to work with children was not determinative of anything.

[81] *Lukaszewski* (n 44).

[82] Ibid, [32].

[83] *Smith* (n 40).

ning were being enlarged or altered.[84] Similarly, in *Harrison*[85] the Court of Appeal concluded that Article 6 did not apply because the legislation conferred no jurisdiction on the Secretary of State to determine in any authoritative way whether a person was a British citizen—this was something for the courts to decide.[86]

Interim orders are generally not considered to be determinations. For example, in *M*[87] the Court of Appeal held that, because an application for an interim anti-social behaviour order under the Crime and Disorder Act 1998 without notice could only be made when the justices' clerk was satisfied that it was necessary for the application to be made without notice, and because the order could only be made for a limited period, when the court considered that it is just to make it, and in circumstances where it could be reviewed or discharged, it was impossible to say that it determined civil rights.[88] Bail proceedings have also been held to be interlocutory measures relating to interim measures therefore Article 6 has no application.[89] It has also been held that disciplinary proceedings resulting in severe reprimand rather than the loss of the right to continue to practise a profession do not determine civil rights and obligations[90] and the decision by an employer to dismiss an employee does not determine the civil rights of the employee where the employee can continue to practise his or her profession.[91]

In some instances, interim measures can have consequences serious enough to amount to a determination of civil rights. For example, in *Jain*,[92] whilst the HRA did not apply as the facts had taken place prior to 2 October 2000, the House of Lords held that an interim measure resulting in the instant closure of a care home was a determination of the rights in question and constituted a determination of a civil right for the purposes of Article 6(1). Similarly in *Wright*[93] the House of Lords held that provisional listing on a list of people considered unsuitable to work with vulnerable adults was a determination of civil rights as the reality was that a listed person 'is most unlikely to be able to obtain such a job or keep it if she does not disclose that she has been listed'.[94]

Where there is a two-stage process, such as a first set of proceedings where civil rights and obligations are not being specifically determined, and a second set, where civil rights and obligations are being explicitly being determined, it has been considered whether Article 6 applies to both sets of proceedings. The Supreme Court held in *G*,[95] guided by ECtHR authority, that it was a sufficient condition for the application of Article 6 in the first proceedings that a decision in those proceedings would be truly

---

[84] Ibid, per Lord Hope at [81]. Lord Carswell agreed and Lord Slynn reached a similar conclusion. See also *St Brice v London Borough of Southwark* [2001] EWCA Civ 1138, [2002] 1 WLR 1537, where the Court of Appeal held that enforcement of a judgment did not involve a separate determination of civil rights and obligations.

[85] *Harrison v Secretary of State for the Home Department* [2003] EWCA Civ 432.

[86] Ibid, [31]–[32].

[87] *R (on the application of M) v Secretary of State for Constitutional Affairs and Lord Chancellor* [2004] EWCA Civ 312, [2004] 1 WLR 2298.

[88] Ibid, [39].

[89] *R (BB) v Special Immigration Appeals Commission* [2012] EWCA Civ 1499, [2013] 2 All ER 419.

[90] *Thompson* (n 56).

[91] *Mattu v University Hospitals of Coventry and Warwickshire NHS Trust* [2012] EWCA Civ 641, [2012] 4 All ER 359. Contrast the judgment in *Perry v Nursing & Midwifery Council* [2013] EWCA Civ 145, [2013] 1 WLR 3423.

[92] *Jain v Trent Strategic Health Authority* [2009] UKHL 4, [2009] 1 AC 853.

[93] *Wright* (n 49).

[94] Ibid, per Baroness Hale at [22].

[95] *R (G) v X School Governors* [2011] UKSC 30, [2011] 3 WLR 237.

dispositive of a civil right which was the subject of determination in the second set of proceedings.[96] A link that was merely more than tenuous or consequences that were merely more than remote was not sufficient.[97]

Lord Dyson observed that the ECtHR had adopted a pragmatic, context-sensitive approach to the problem and considered: whether the first proceedings were capable of being dispositive of the determination of civil rights in the second proceedings or at least 'causing irreversible prejudice, in effect, by partially determining the outcome of proceedings B';[98] how close the link was between the two sets of proceedings; whether the object of the two sets of proceedings was the same; and whether there were any policy reasons for deciding Article 6 did not apply to the first proceedings.[99] He held that the test to be applied was that applied by Laws LJ in the Court of Appeal: an applicant may by force of Article 6 enjoy appropriate procedural rights in relation to other sets of proceedings if the outcome of that other set of proceedings would have a substantial influence or effect on the determination of the civil right or obligation.[100] In the present case, a majority of the Supreme Court concluded that Article 6 did not apply to the disciplinary proceedings convened by a school. It was observed by Lord Dyson that the Independent Safeguarding Authority, which determined whether or not the claimant should be placed on the list of those prohibited from teaching or working with children, was required to exercise its own independent judgment both in relation to finding facts and making an assessment of their gravity and significance.[101]

> The school's disciplinary panel reaches its conclusions as part of an inquiry into a question which is different from that which is addressed by the ISA. More fundamentally, the case workers know that they are required to form their own opinion on the gravity and significance of the facts and on whether it is appropriate to include the referred person in the barred list. There is no reason to suppose that the ISA will be influenced profoundly (or at all) by the school's opinion of how the primary facts should be viewed.[102]

3.3 Administrative Decisions: The Two-stage Process

The higher judiciary is clearly not favourably disposed to the extension of Article 6(1) to administrative decision making.[103] For example, in *Alconbury*[104] Lord Hoffmann noted that, were it not for Strasbourg authority, he would have concluded that a decision as to what the public interest required in the planning context was not a determination of civil rights or obligations.[105] But whilst Article 6(1) may apply to the decision, this does not mean that the administrative decision maker must himself or herself comply with its requirements. In determining whether the requirements of Article 6(1) have been

---

[96] Ibid, per Lord Dyson at [64] with whom all agreed apart from Lord Kerr.
[97] Ibid, per Lord Dyson at [66].
[98] Ibid, [68].
[99] Ibid, [68].
[100] Ibid, [69].
[101] Ibid, [75].
[102] Ibid, [83].
[103] See *R (A) v London Borough of Croydon* [2009] UKSC 8, [2009] 1 WLR 2557.
[104] *Alconbury* (n 19).
[105] Ibid, [74].

met, regard must be had to all stages of the process.[106] In the case of administrative decisions, it is possible for a breach by the primary decision maker to be cured by the availability of judicial review. However, from ECtHR case law, it is not clear whether the reviewing court must exercise 'full jurisdiction' or 'full decision making power'. In *Alconbury*[107] the House of Lords concluded that full jurisdiction meant full jurisdiction in the context of the case, and that here a full merits review was not necessary and judicial review was sufficient.[108]

In determining the context of the case it is necessary to have regard to matters such as the subject matter of the decision, the manner in which that decision was arrived at and the content of the dispute, including the actual and desired grounds of appeal.[109] In the context of disciplinary proceedings, a more exhaustive remedy may be required to satisfy Article 6[110] and judicial review may not suffice for a decision on the factual question of whether or not there has been a breach of planning control.[111] Indeed, the more any given statutory scheme is likely to give rise to fact-laden issues, the more Article 6 will require independent adjudication on the facts.[112]

Whilst the Supreme Court had already concluded in *Tomlinson*[113] that the decision-making process under the Housing Act 1996 did not involve the determination of civil rights, observations were made about the Article 6 review required if it had applied. Lord Hope, with whom the others agreed, held that the question that had to be decided here was different to that in *Begum*. In his view, to separate out questions as to whether the formalities laid down by the subsection were complied with from those as to whether the accommodation was suitable would complicate a scheme which, 'in the interests of speed and economy, was designed to be simple to administer'.[114] He concluded that the absence of a full fact-finding jurisdiction in the court to which an appeal lay did not deprive it of what it needed to satisfy the requirements of Art.6(1).[115]

> [T]he narrower the interpretation given to 'civil rights', the greater the need to insist on a review by a tribunal exercising full powers. Conversely, the more elastic the interpretation given to that concept, the more elastic must be the approach to the independent and impartial review if the emasculation by over-judicialisation of administrative welfare schemes is to be avoided.[116]

Similarly in *Beeson*[117] the Court of Appeal held that the question of whether a person was in need of care and attention for the purposes of section 21 of the National Assis-

---

[106] Ibid, per Lord Slynn at [29] in reliance upon *Albert and Le Compte v Belgium* (1983) 5 EHRR 533; *Le Compte* (n 37); *Golder* (n 37); *Kaplan v United Kingdom* (1982) 4 EHRR 64; *ISKCON v United Kingdom*, 8 March 1994; *Bryan v United Kingdom* (1995) 21 EHRR 342; *Chapman v United Kingdom*, 18 January 2001; *Howard v United Kingdom*, 16 July 1987; *Varey v United Kingdom*, 27 October 1999.

[107] *Alconbury* (n 19).

[108] Ibid, per Lord Hoffmann at [87], per Lord Clyde at [154] and per Lord Hutton at [189].

[109] Ibid, per Lord Clyde at [154].

[110] Ibid, per Lord Clyde at [154].

[111] Ibid, per Lord Hoffmann at [100].

[112] *Beeson* (n 38), [23].

[113] *Tomlinson* (n 68).

[114] Ibid, [53].

[115] Ibid, [54].

[116] Ibid, [55]. See also *King* (n 47) where the Court of Appeal, on the assumption Art 6 applied, held that the decision-making process within the prison, role of the review board and safeguard of judicial review met the requirements of Art 6.

[117] *Beeson* (n 38).

tance Act 1948 was not a hard-edged issue of fact. It concluded that the scheme was exactly of the kind where the first decisions were properly confined within the public body having responsibility for the scheme's administration and, given the availability of judicial review, the requirements of Article 6 were met.[118] However, in *Re S*[119] the House of Lords held that judicial review would meet the demands of Article 6 in some instances but held that there were important decisions for which the Children Act 1989 made no provision. Cited as an example were questions for the local authority regarding a child's future, such as whether rehabilitation was a realistic possibility. Their Lordships were doubtful whether judicial review would meet the high degree of judicial control required in such circumstances.[120]

Wright[121] is an example where the House of Lords found that the requirements of Article 6 would not be met by a two-stage process. The appeal concerned placement on a list of people considered unsuitable to work with vulnerable adults. There was no opportunity for judicial hearing before being placed on the list. The scheme only provided for such an opportunity after a lengthy administrative process, during most of which the care worker was provisionally on the list. The House of Lords held that this could not be cured by judicial review or later access to the tribunal. This was a denial of one of the fundamental elements of the right to a fair determination of a person's civil rights, the right to be heard. And the detrimental effect of provisional listing was often irreversible and incurable.[122]

3.4 Examples: Determination of Civil Rights and Obligations

It has been held that there was a determination of civil rights and obligations in the following instances: a decision of a professional tribunal affecting the right to practise a profession;[123] proceedings conducted by an auditor under section 20 of the Local Government Finance Act 1982;[124] the making of a confiscation order as a result of convictions for certain types of offences;[125] the role of the Secretary of State in referring planning applications to himself and appointing inspectors to hold public planning inquiries;[126] the making of a care order which endows a local authority with parental responsibility for a child;[127] care proceedings under Part IV of the Children Act 1989;[128] proceedings for an anti-social behaviour order under section 1 of the Crime and Disorder Act 1998;[129] the making of a secure accommodation order;[130] a decision to forcibly treat

[118] Ibid, [33]–[34]. See also *R (on the application of Adlard) v Secretary of State for Environment, Transport & Regions* [2002] EWCA Civ 735, [2002] 1 WLR 2515; *Q* (n 56), [115]–[117]; *R (on the application of Whitmey) v The Commons Commissioners* [2004] EWCA Civ 951, [2005] QB 282. See generally, Craig (n 63).

[119] *Re S* (n 50).

[120] Ibid, [81].

[121] *Wright* (n 49).

[122] Ibid, per Baroness Hale at [25] approving the judgment of the Court of Appeal.

[123] *Preiss* (n 49). *Kulkarni v Milton Keynes Hospital NHS Trust* [2009] EWCA Civ 789, [2009] IRLR 829.

[124] *Porter* (n 2).

[125] *McIntosh* (n 12); *R v Rezvi* [2002] UKHL 1, [2003] 1 AC 1099.

[126] *Alconbury* (n 19).

[127] *Re S* (n 50).

[128] *Re V (a child) (care proceedings: human rights claims)* [2004] EWCA Civ 54, [2004] 1 All ER 997.

[129] *McCann* (n 55).

[130] *Re M (A child) (secure accommodation)* [2001] EWCA Civ 458, [2001] 1 FCR 692.

a patient detained under the Mental Health Act 1983;[131] a decision of the Disciplinary Appeals Tribunal of the Securities and Futures Authority finding an individual guilty of improper conduct as a trader in securities;[132] proceedings for possession;[133] an order for residential assessment under section 38(6) of the Children Act 1989;[134] proceedings of the Special Immigration Appeals Commission;[135] the obligation to pay VAT and penalties associated with its non-payment;[136] notification of a site as a site of special scientific interest under section 28 of the Wildlife and Countryside Act 1981;[137] placement on a list of people considered unsuitable to work with vulnerable adults;[138] proceedings for the extradition of UK citizens;[139] a decision of the Financial Ombudsman Service;[140] the making of a control order under the Prevention of Terrorism Act 2005[141].

It has been held that there had *not* been a determination of civil rights and obligations in the following instances: the procedure followed by the Parole Board when a determinate sentence prisoner, released on licence, sought to resist revocation of his licence;[142] a tax appeal claiming error or mistake relief as opposed to a private law claim against the Revenue based on unjust enrichment;[143] proceedings relating to the entry, stay or deportation of aliens;[144] proceedings for the extradition of aliens;[145] proceedings concerning a right to citizenship;[146] the assessment of refugee status;[147] the removal or exclusion of foreign nationals on national security grounds;[148] the detention of an individual pending deportation;[149] a decision by the Office for the Supervision of Solicitors to severely reprimand a solicitor;[150] a petitioner seeking a bankruptcy order under the Insolvency Act 1986 but unable to pay the deposit;[151] a school exclusion;[152] inclusion on a list of persons suspected of a connection with terrorism and freezing

---

[131] *R (on the application of Wilkinson) v The Responsible Medical Officer, Broadmoor Hospital* [2001] EWCA Civ 1545, [2002] 1 WLR 419.

[132] *R (on the application of Fleurose) v Securities and Futures Authority Ltd* [2002] EWCA Civ 2015, [2002] IRLR 297.

[133] *Sheffield City Council v Smart* [2002] EWCA Civ 4, [2002] ACD 56.

[134] *Re G (a child: residential assessment)* [2004] EWCA Civ 24, [2004] 1 FCR 317.

[135] *A v Secretary of State for the Home Department* [2002] EWCA Civ 1502, [2004] QB 335.

[136] *Begum v The Commissioners of Customs and Excise*, VADT, 30 May 2002.

[137] *R v English Nature ex p Aggregate Industries UK Ltd* [2002] EWHC (Admin) 908, [2003] Env LR 3.

[138] *Wright* (n 49).

[139] *Lukaszewski* (n 44).

[140] *R (Moor) v Financial Ombudsman Service* [2008] EWCA Civ 642.

[141] *Secretary of State for the Home Department v MB* [2007] UKHL 46, [2007] 3 WLR 681.

[142] *Smith* (n 40).

[143] *Eagerpath Ltd v Edwards (Inspector of Taxes)* [2001] STC 26.

[144] *R (on the application of Ullah) v Secretary of State for the Home Department* [2003] EWCA Civ 1366; *RB (Algeria) v Secretary of State for the Home Department* [2009] UKHL 10, [2010] 2 AC 110.

[145] *Lukaszewski* (n 44).

[146] *Harrison* (n 85).

[147] *HH (Iran) v Secretary of State for the Home Department* [2008] EWCA Civ 504; *R (MK (Iran)) v Secretary of State for the Home Department* [2010] EWCA Civ 115, [2010] 1 WLR 2059.

[148] *IR (Sri Lanka) v Secretary of State for the Home Department* [2011] EWCA Civ 704, [2011] 4 All ER 908 although it is important to note that procedural guarantees provided by Arts 5 and 8 may require a degree of fairness in such proceedings.

[149] *R (BB) v Special Immigration Appeals Commission* [2012] EWCA Civ 1499, [2013] 2 All ER 419.

[150] *Thompson* (n 56).

[151] *R v Lord Chancellor, ex p Lightfoot* [1999] 4 All ER 583.

[152] *V* (n 46).

of assets;[153] decisions to place or keep prisoners in confinement or segregation;[154] a disciplinary decision to dismiss an employee under a contract of employment.[155]

---

4. Article 6(1) Application: Determination of Any Criminal Charge

Establishing that there has been a determination of a criminal charge makes a significant difference to the range of protections available to an individual under Article 6. In addition to the protection of Article 6(1), Article 6(2) and (3) are also available and the ECtHR has consistently held that states have far greater latitude when dealing with civil cases than when dealing with criminal cases.[156] In *McCann*[157] the House of Lords confirmed that the concept of 'charged with a criminal offence' under Article 6(2) and (3) was coextensive with the concept of 'determination of any criminal charge'[158] and the case law concerning both definitions is considered in this section.

It may be the position that whilst there has not been a determination of a criminal charge, the facts are so serious that a high level of Article 6 protection nevertheless applies. For example, non-derogating control order proceedings have been held to not involve the determination of a criminal charge.[159]

> Parliament has gone to some lengths to avoid a procedure which crosses the criminal boundary: there is no assertion of criminal conduct, only a foundation of suspicion; no identification of any specific criminal offence is provided for; the order made is preventative in purpose, not punitive or retributive; and the obligations imposed must be no more restrictive than are judged necessary to achieve the preventative object of the order.[160]

However, it was accepted that the application of the civil limb of Article 6 entitled such persons to such measures of procedural protection as was commensurate with the gravity of the potential consequences.[161]

4.1 Determination

Before considering the meaning of 'criminal charge' it must first be established that

---

[153] *Secretary of State for the Foreign and Commonwealth Office v Maftah* [2011] EWCA Civ 350, [2012] 2 WLR 251.

[154] *King* (n 47).

[155] *Mattu v University Hospitals of Coventry & Warwickshire NHS Trust* [2012] EWCA Civ 641, [2012] 4 All ER 359.

[156] *McCann* (n 55), per Lord Steyn at [7] in reliance upon *Dombo Beheer v The Netherlands* (1993) 18 EHRR 213, [32].

[157] Ibid.

[158] Ibid, [28] in reliance upon *Lutz v Germany* (1987) 10 EHRR 182.

[159] *MB* (n 141), per Lord Bingham at [24].

[160] Ibid.

[161] Ibid.

there has been a determination to which Article 6 can apply. To be considered the 'determination of a criminal charge' the facts must expose the subject of the charge to the possibility of punishment, whether in the event punishment is imposed or not. A process which can only culminate in measures of a preventative, curative, rehabilitative or welfare-promoting kind will not ordinarily be the determination of a criminal charge.[162]

4.1.1 Pre-trial Decisions

The need for a 'determination' has caused difficulties with respect to decisions that have been made before a criminal trial has actually commenced. For example, in *Kebilene*[163] the claimants sought judicial review of the Director of Public Prosecution's consent to their prosecutions for offences under terrorism legislation as it was alleged that the legislation was incompatible with Article 6(2). The House of Lords held that it was rightly conceded that, once the HRA was fully in force, it would not be possible to apply for judicial review on the ground that a decision to prosecute was in breach of a Convention right and that the only available remedies would be in the trial process or on appeal.[164] Whilst it was not fully explained in the speeches given, it would appear this conclusion was reached because the DPP did not actually 'determine' the charge against the accused—that was a matter for the court.[165]

Due to the Scotland Act 1998, it may be that a different rule applies in Scotland. *Brown*[166] concerned Mrs Brown's challenge under the Scotland Act 1998 to the intention of the Procurator Fiscal to rely at trial on her admission obtained under the Road Traffic Act 1988 that she was driving her car when it was alleged that the driver of the car had committed certain specified offences. It was argued that use of this admission in evidence would infringe her right to a fair hearing. The Privy Council concluded that, under the Scotland Act 1998, the right of the accused to a fair trial was a responsibility of the Lord Advocate in the prosecution of offences as well as of the court. If this was not the case, the Privy Council saw much force in the argument that, as the determination during a criminal trial of the criminal charge in all its aspects was a matter for the court and not the prosecutor, the acts of the Lord Advocate lay outside the scope of the Article.[167]

It is possible for a criminal charge to be determined without the matter reaching trial. In *R (on the application of R) v Durham Constabulary*[168] the House of Lords considered the procedure for warning young offenders under sections 65 and 66 of the Crime and Disorder Act 1988. Although expressing considerable doubt, given the concession by

---

[162] *R (on the application of R) v Durham Constabulary* [2005] UKHL 21, [2005] 1 WLR 1184, per Lord Bingham at [12].

[163] *Kebilene* (n 10).

[164] Ibid, per Lord Steyn with whom Lords Slynn and Cooke agreed.

[165] See also *Lai v Commissioners of Customs & Excise*, VADT, 1 July 2002, where it was held that the steps leading up to the issue of assessment and a penalty notice were not the determination of a criminal charge.

[166] *Brown* (n 4).

[167] By contrast Lord Clyde held that even without the Scotland Act, Art 6 applied to activities occurring during the criminal trial which had a bearing on the fairness of the proceedings. See also *Montgomery v HM Advocate* [2003] 1 AC 641.

[168] *R* (n 162).

the Secretary of State, it assumed that the appellant faced a criminal charge once he had been formally notified by the police that allegations of criminal conduct against him were being investigated.[169] However, it concluded that the criminal charge ceased to exist when a firm decision was made not to prosecute.[170] This was despite the fact that the warning would be recorded on the Police National Computer and the Sex Offenders Register.

4.1.2 Sentencing

Sentencing is within the meaning of 'determination of a criminal charge' and therefore covered by Article 6 as it is part of the trial and the same procedural protections apply to the imposition of sentence as to the determination of guilt.[171] In *Anderson*[172] the House of Lords concluded that, in fixing a convicted murderer's tariff, the Home Secretary was assessing the term of imprisonment which the convicted murderer should serve as punishment for his crime.[173] Article 6(1) applied and the Home Secretary's role was declared incompatible with the guarantee of independence and impartiality.

4.2 Criminal Charge

The meaning of 'criminal charge' is autonomous. Under the HRA the courts have adopted the *Engel*[174] criteria formulated by the ECtHR. When determining whether there has been a determination of any criminal charge, the domestic classification, the nature of the offence and the severity of the potential penalty are taken into account.[175] These criteria are alternative and not cumulative. One criterion cannot be applied so as to divest an offence of a criminal character if that has been established under another criterion. However, a cumulative approach can be adopted if the separate analysis of each does not lead to a clear conclusion.[176]

4.2.1 Domestic Classification

The first test is the category into which the proceedings are placed by domestic law. Whilst this test is generally regarded as far from decisive, it is a starting point.[177] Regarding the test as such largely renders irrelevant the rationale underlying a national law which seeks to decriminalise conduct which would otherwise be treated, or gener-

---

[169] Ibid, per Lord Bingham at [11]–[12].
[170] Ibid, per Lord Bingham at [12] in reliance upon *X v United Kingdom* (1979) 17 DR 122 and *S v Miller* [2001] UKSC 977.
[171] *R v Secretary of State for the Home Department, ex p Anderson* [2002] UKHL 46, [2003] 1 AC 837, per Lord Bingham at [22], per Lord Steyn at [50]–[51] and per Lord Hutton at [67].
[172] Ibid.
[173] Ibid, per Lord Bingham at [13], [39], per Lord Steyn at [52] and per Lord Hutton at [75].
[174] *Engel v The Netherlands (No 1)* (1976) 1 EHRR 647, [82].
[175] See eg *McCann* (n 55).
[176] Ibid, per Lord Hope at [65] in reliance upon *Lauko v Slovakia* (1998) 33 EHRR 994, [57]; *Ozturk v Germany* 6 EHRR 409, [54].
[177] *McIntosh* (n 12), per Lord Bingham at [16].

ally regarded, as criminal in nature.[178] It is necessary to look at the substance of the matter rather than its form, and to look behind appearances and investigate the realities of the procedure.[179] Indications of classification as criminal may be: the involvement of the Crown Prosecution Service; a formal accusation of breach of the criminal law; the need to prove *mens rea*; and entry on the record as a conviction or a recordable offence for the purpose of taking fingerprints.[180] If the purpose of the proceedings is to punish rather than to protect or prevent, this is also an indication of classification as criminal.[181]

In *McCann*[182] the House of Lords had to determine whether the proceedings leading to the making of an anti-social behaviour order under the Crime and Disorder Act 1998 involved the determination of a criminal charge. Their Lordships were particularly influenced by Parliament's intention that the proceedings be civil and not attract the rigour of the hearsay rule.[183] Taking into account the facts that the Crown Prosecution Service was not involved, there was no formal accusation of a breach of the criminal law, *mens rea* did not need to be proved and that the purpose of the proceedings was preventative not to obtain a conviction, the House of Lords concluded that the proceedings were civil proceedings under domestic law.[184]

In *McIntosh*[185], a case brought under the Scotland Act 1998 concerning the application of Article 6(2) to confiscation proceedings under section 3(2) of the Proceedings of Crime (Scotland) Act 1995, the Privy Council concluded that the respondent would not be considered to be a person charged with a criminal offence as that expression was understood in these jurisdictions. The following considerations were taken into account:

> (1) The application is not initiated by complaint or indictment and is not governed by the ordinary rules of criminal procedure. (2) The application may only be made if the accused is convicted, and cannot be pursued if he is acquitted. (3) The application forms part of the sentencing procedure. (4) The accused is at no time accused of committing any crime other than that which permits the application to be made. (5) When, as is standard procedure in anything other than the simplest case, the prosecutor lodges a statement under section 9, that statement (usually supported by detailed schedules) is an accounting record and not an accusation. (6) The sum ordered to be confiscated need not be the profit made from the drug trafficking offence of which the accused has been convicted, or any other drug trafficking offence. (7) If the accused fails to pay the sum he is ordered to pay under the order, the term of imprisonment which he will be ordered to serve in default is imposed not for the commission of any drug trafficking offence but on his failure to pay the sum ordered and to procure compliance. (8) The transactions of which account is taken in the confiscation proceedings may be the subject of a later prosecution, which would be repugnant to the rule against double jeopardy

---

[178] *Customs and Excise Commissioners v Han* [2001] EWCA Civ 1040, [2001] 1 WLR 2253, [68].

[179] *Porter* (n 2), per Lord Hope at [84] in reliance upon *Deweer v Belgium* (1980) 2 EHRR 439.

[180] *McCann* (n 55), per Lord Steyn at [22].

[181] Ibid, [22]. See also *R v H* [2004] UKHL 3, [2004] 2 AC 134, where the House of Lords concluded that the procedure under s 4A of the Criminal Procedure (Insanity) Act 1964 which provided for a finding that the accused did the act which constituted the *actus reus* of the crime did not involve the determination of a criminal charge as the provision was designed to protect the public and not to punish the subject of the order.

[182] *McCann* (n 55).

[183] Ibid, per Lord Steyn at [18].

[184] Ibid, per Lord Steyn at [22]–[27], who placed reliance on *B v Chief Constable of Avon and Somerset Constabulary* [2001] 1 WLR 340 and *Gough v Chief Constable of the Derbyshire Constabulary* [2002] EWCA Civ 351, [2002] QB 459. See also Lord Hutton at [94]–[98].

[185] *McIntosh* (n 12).

if the accused were charged with a criminal offence in the confiscation proceedings. (9) The proceedings do not culminate in a verdict which would (in proceedings on indictment) be a matter for the jury if the accused were charged with a criminal offence.[186]

However, in *Briggs-Price*[187] the House of Lords held that if the prosecution adopted an approach to proving benefit from drug trafficking that involved charging the defendant with a criminal offence, this would bring the proceedings within Article 6(2) as the determination of a criminal charge.[188] In *Han*[189] a majority of the Court of Appeal was not convinced by the classification of the penalties for tax evasion as civil. In the opinion of the court, the levying and enforcement of the penalty concerned was designed to punish and deter members of the public at large in respect of dishonest conduct. It was also possible for the Commissioners to decide in the course of an investigation to switch from the civil regime to the criminal.[190]

4.2.2 Nature of the Offence

The second test is the nature of the offence, and again it is necessary to look behind appearances and investigate the reality of the procedure.[191] If the 'offence' applies to the public at large rather than a specific group it is likely to be regarded as criminal.[192] Proceedings which are punitive or disciplinary rather than compensatory, regulatory or preventative are likely to be considered more in the nature of a criminal charge. It has been held that the distinguishing feature of a criminal charge is that it may lead to punishment[193] even if the penalty is in the nature of a fine rather than imprisonment[194] and even if the fine is minor.[195] In *Porter*[196] it was argued that the proceedings under the Local Government Finance Act 1982 were in the nature of a criminal charge. The House of Lords disagreed, holding that these were compensatory and regulatory, not punitive. No fine was involved, nor was there provision for any penalty by way of imprisonment.[197]

In *McCann* it was noted that the person against whom an anti-social behaviour order was sought was not being charged with an offence and the conduct required to be demonstrated was not conduct which would be capable of being treated as criminal. Proceedings were preventative, not punitive or disciplinary. There was no power of arrest and proceedings could not result in the immediate imposition of a penalty.[198]

---

[186] Ibid, per Lord Bingham at [14].
[187] *R v Briggs-Price* [2009] UKHL 19, [2009] 1 AC 1026.
[188] Ibid, per Lord Phillips at [24].
[189] *Han* (n 178).
[190] Ibid, [75].
[191] *McCann* (n 55), [99] in reliance on *Deweer* (n 179).
[192] *Han* (n 178).
[193] *Smith* (n 40), per Lord Bingham at [40].
[194] *Han* (n 178), [66].
[195] *R (on the application of Mudie) v Kent Magistrates' Court* [2003] EWCA Civ 237, [2003] 2 WLR 1344.
[196] *Porter* (n 2).
[197] Ibid, per Lord Hope at [85].
[198] *McCann* (n 55), per Lord Hope at [71]–[74] in reliance upon *Lauko* (n 176); *Guzzardi v Italy* (1980) 3 EHRR 333; *Raimondo v Italy* (1994) 18 EHRR 237; *M v Italy* (1991) 70 DR 59; *Gough* (n 184). See also the speech of Lord Hutton at [102]–[108].

Similarly, in *R v H*[199] the House of Lords held that the procedure under the Criminal Procedure (Insanity) Act 1964 allowing for a finding that the accused committed the *actus reus* of the crime was not in the nature of a criminal charge as it could not result in conviction or punishment.[200] The absence of punishment was also the key to the House of Lords conclusion in *Smith*[201] that Parole Board proceedings determining whether or not a prisoner's licence should be revoked and he be recalled to prison did not constitute the determination of a criminal charge.[202] 'Recall of a prisoner on licence is not a punishment. It is primarily to protect the public against further offences.'[203]

4.2.3 Severity of the Potential Penalty

The final test is the severity of the potential penalty. Here the question is whether, by reason of its nature and degree of severity, the penalty or sanction amounts to a penalty in the sense of punishment.[204] Outside the context of disciplinary proceedings and, in particular, in the field of tax evasion, it appears that a substantial financial penalty which is imposed by way of punishment and deterrence may render the charges criminal in nature.[205] By contrast, the imposition of no penalty may indicate the opposite conclusion.[206]

In *McCann*[207] the House of Lords concluded that the anti-social behaviour order itself involved no penalty and that the proceedings were not in respect of a criminal charge.[208] In *R v H*[209] the House of Lords held that it was difficult, if not impossible, to conceive of a criminal proceeding which did not culminate in the imposition of any penalty.[210] Here there was no criminal charge as the statute merely sought to strike a fair balance between protecting a defendant who was unfit to plead and protecting the public from a defendant who had committed an injurious act.[211] However, in *Napier*[212] the Administrative Court concluded that it was the imposition of additional days to be served in prison that carried prison disciplinary proceedings over the line from civil to criminal.[213] This will never be the case with respect to life sentence prisoners as they cannot be subject to the punishment of additional days. In *Tagney*[214] the Court of

---

[199] *R v H* (n 181).

[200] Ibid, per Lord Bingham at [18]. See also *R v Grant* [2001] EWCA Crim 2611, [2002] 2 WLR 1409.

[201] Above n 40.

[202] Ibid, per Lord Bingham at [40] in reliance upon *Ganusaukas v Lithuania*, Application No 47922/99 and *Brown v United Kingdom*, Judgment of 26 October 2004.

[203] Ibid, per Lord Slynn at [56]. See also *Re M* (n 130).

[204] *Porter* (n 2), per Lord Hope at [84] in reliance upon *Engel* (n 174), [82]–[83]; *Lutz* (n 158), [54]; *Democoli v Malta* (1991) 14 EHRR 47, [34].

[205] *Han* (n 178), [67].

[206] *Mudie* (n 195).

[207] *McCann* (n 55).

[208] Ibid, per Lord Steyn at [30]. For a critique of this judgment see S Macdonald, 'The Nature of the Anti-Social Behaviour Order—R (McCann & Others) v Crown Court at Manchester' (2003) 66 *Modern Law Review* 630; A Ashworth, 'Social Control and "Anti-Social Behaviour": The Subversion of Human Rights?' (2004) 120 *Law Quarterly Review* 263.

[209] *R v H* (n 181).

[210] Ibid, [19].

[211] Ibid, per Lord Bingham at [20] in reliance upon *R v Antoine* [2000] 2 All ER 208, 221.

[212] *R (on the application of Napier) v Secretary of State for the Home Department* [2004] EWHC (Admin) 936, [2004] 1 WLR 3056.

[213] In reliance upon *Ezeh and Connors v United Kingdom*, Judgment of 15 July 2002.

[214] *Tangney v The Governor of HMP Elmley* [2005] EWCA Civ 1009.

Appeal held that in such instances it would be rare for the proceedings to constitute the determination of a criminal charge although it did not rule this out, suggesting that the Secretary of State may wish to consider amending the Prison Rules to give the governor the power to refer an adjudication to an independent adjudicator if, in the exceptional circumstances of the case, it was necessary to do so.[215]

4.3 Examples

It has been held that there was a determination of a criminal charge in the following instances: sentencing;[216] an application under the Debtors Act 1869;[217] the imposition of penalties for alleged dishonest evasion of pursuant to section 60(1) of the Value Added Tax Act 1994 and section 8(1) of the Finance Act 1994;[218] the regime under the Immigration and Asylum Act 1999 by which drivers and others bringing clandestine entrants into the United Kingdom in a vehicle are liable to a fixed penalty;[219] committal for breach of an order or for telling lies in the face of the court;[220] prison disciplinary proceedings where the sanction of additional days of imprisonment is imposed.[221]

It has also been held that there was *not* been a determination of a criminal charge in the following instances: proceedings for making an anti-social behaviour order;[222] confiscation proceedings;[223] proceedings conducted by an auditor under the Local Government Act 1982;[224] procedures under the Criminal Procedure (Insanity) Act 1964;[225] Parole Board proceedings determining whether or not a prisoner's licence should be revoked;[226] proceedings for making a secure accommodation order under section 25 of the Children Act 1989;[227] decisions of the Disciplinary Appeals Tribunal of the Securities and Futures Authority finding an individual guilty of improper conduct as a trader in securities;[228] proceedings leading to the making of banning orders under the Football Spectators Act 1989;[229] condemnation proceedings pursuant to schedule 3 and section 139 of the Customs and Excise Management Act 1979;[230] proceedings before the VAT and Duties Tribunal under the Customs and Excise Management Act 1979 and the Finance Act 1994 for restoration of condemned goods;[231] disqualification proceedings

---

[215] Ibid, [33].

[216] *Anderson* (n 171).

[217] *Murbarak v Murbarak* [2001] 1 FCR 193.

[218] *Han* (n 178).

[219] *International Transport Roth GmbH v Secretary of State for the Home Department* [2002] EWCA Civ 158, [2002] 3 WLR 344.

[220] *Berry Trade Ltd v Moussavi* [2002] WLR 1910. *Daltel Europe Ltd v Makki* [2006] EWCA Civ 94, [2006] 1 WLR 2704.

[221] *Napier* (n 212). But see *Tangney* (n 214), in relation to life sentence prisoners.

[222] *McCann* (n 55).

[223] *McIntosh* (n 12); *Briggs-Price* (n 187).

[224] *Porter* (n 2).

[225] *R v H* (n 181).

[226] *Smith* (n 40).

[227] *Re M* (n 130), although the Court of Appeal did conclude that at common law the child should be afforded the rights set out in Art 6(3).

[228] *Fleurose* (n 132).

[229] *Gough* (n 184).

[230] *Mudie* (n 195).

[231] *Gora v Customs and Excise Commissioners* [2003] EWCA Civ 525, [2004] QB 93.

under the Company Directors Disqualification Act 1986;[232] proceedings before the Special Immigration Appeals Commission;[233] the procedure for warning young offenders under sections 65 and 66 of the Crime and Disorder Act 1988;[234] the default surcharge VAT penalty and penalties for misdeclaration and late registration;[235] proceedings for extradition;[236] the making of a control order under the Prevention of Terrorism Act 2005.[237]

---

5. Access to Court

5.1 Generally

The first Article 6 right considered in this chapter is the implied right of access to court. This right has its roots in the notion that the 'first claim on the loyalty of the law' is that 'wrongs should be remedied'.[238] It requires the maintenance of fair and public judicial processes and forbids the state from denying individuals access to those processes for the determination of their civil rights.[239] However, it does not confer on the state adjudicative powers which it does not possess.[240] In particular, the right of access to court does not confer a right of appeal although, where such a right exists, Article 6 does apply to it.[241]

Essentially the question is whether an issue which ought to be decided by a court is being prevented from being so decided. The touchstone is the proper role of courts in a democratic society. 'A right of access to a court is one of the checks on the danger of arbitrary power.'[242] As this is an implied right, it is not absolute and may be made

---

[232] *Re Westminster Property Management Ltd* [2001] 1 WLR 2230.

[233] *A v Secretary of State for the Home Department* (n 135).

[234] *R* (n 162).

[235] *Ali and Begum v Customs & Excise Commissioners* V&DTr 30 May 2002.

[236] *Lukaszewski* (n 44).

[237] *MB* (n 141).

[238] *Holland v Lampen-Wolfe* [2000] 1 WLR 1573, per Lord Bingham quoting from *X v Bedfordshire County Council* [1995] 2 AC 633, 663. The right is also a common law constitutional right. See eg *R v Lord Chancellor, ex p Witham* [1997] 2 All ER 779 and *Lightfoot* (n 151). See also the common law application of this right in *HM Treasury v Ahmed* [2010] UKSC 2, [2010] 2 AC 534.

[239] Such a denial may arise, for example, from the compulsion of alternative dispute resolution. See *Halsey v Milton Keynes General NHS Trust* [2004] EWCA Civ 576, [2004] 1 WLR 3002.

[240] *Lampen-Wolfe* (n 238).

[241] *R (on the application of Aru) v Chief Constable of Merseyside* [2004] EWCA Civ 199, [2004] 1 WLR 1697; *BLCT (13096) Limited v J Sainsbury plc* [2003] EWCA Civ 884, [2004] 2 P&CR 32. See also *R v Dunn* [2010] EWCA Crim 1823, [2010] 2 Cr App R 30 where the Court of Appeal held that its role in certifying appeals to the Supreme Court was not incompatible with the right of access to court.

[242] *Wilson v Secretary of State for Trade and Industry* [2003] UKHL 40, [2003] 3 WLR 568, per Lord Nicholls at [35]. In *Sinclair Garden Investments (Kensington) Ltd v Lands Tribunal* [2005] EWCA Civ 1305, [2006] 3 All ER 650 the court held that the Lands Tribunal had the qualities of a court for the purposes of Art 6. Therefore, no special factors would justify a practice of entertaining claims for judicial review of refusals of leave to appeal by the Tribunal in the absence of special circumstances.

subject to procedural restrictions. However, these must not so restrict or reduce the litigant's right of access as to impair the essence of the right and must satisfy a test of proportionality.[243]

> It must pursue a legitimate aim, it must be necessary and suitable for the attainment of that aim and must not restrict the right of access to the court disproportionately in relation to the importance of the aim it pursues.[244]

The right of access to court is available to everyone, including serving prisoners conducting their own litigation[245] and illegal immigrants seeking access to the divorce courts.[246] In *Polanski*[247] a majority of the House of Lords held that a fugitive from justice, not willing to enter the United Kingdom to give evidence in his libel proceedings due to the risk of extradition to the United States, could give evidence by video link from France.

5.2 Substantive and Procedural Bars

The right of access to court for the determination of civil rights does not guarantee any particular content of those rights.[248] '[O]ne must take the domestic law as one finds it, and apply to it the autonomous Convention concept of civil rights.'[249] Therefore, if a restriction on access can be classified as a substantive element of national law, it is beyond the reach of Article 6. It is only if it can be classified as a procedural bar that it must satisfy the test of proportionality. The difficulty lies in distinguishing between substantive and procedural bars. Close to the borderline the distinction is difficult to make out,[250] and it has been held that ECtHR case law in this area remains uncertain.[251] In order to determine whether or not Article 6 is engaged, often the question is asked whether or not the legislature or executive has encroached on territory which ought properly to be the province of courts in a democratic society.[252]

The most common examples of purely procedural bars are those that have no connection with the substance of the would-be litigant's claim such as: security for

---

[243] *Matthews v Ministry of Defence* [2003] UKHL 4, [2003] 1 AC 1163 per Lord Walker at [121] in reliance upon *Golder* (n 37), [35]–[38]; *Stubbings v UK* (1996) 23 EHRR 213, [48].

[244] *Matthews*, ibid, [33].

[245] See eg *R (on the application of Ponting) v Governor of HMP Whitemoor* [2002] EWCA Civ 224.

[246] *Mark v Mark* [2005] UKHL 42, [2005] 3 WLR 111. The House of Lords upheld the conclusion that the wife had access to the English divorce court although not legally resident in the jurisdiction.

[247] *Polanski v Condé Nast Publications Limited* [2005] UKHL 10, [2005] 1 WLR 637.

[248] *Matthews* (n 243), per Lord Walker at [121] in reliance upon *James v UK* (1986) 8 EHRR 123, [81]; *Powell and Rayner v UK* (1990) 12 EHRR 355, [36]. See also *Wilson* (n 242), per Lord Nicholls at [32].

[249] *Matthews*, ibid, per Lord Bingham at [3].

[250] Ibid, per Lord Walker at [127], with whom all agreed apart from Lord Hoffmann. See also *Wilson* (n 242), per Lord Nicholls at [35].

[251] *Matthews*, ibid, per Lord Walker at [130]–[143]. The cases cited were *Ashingdane v United Kingdom* (1983) 6 EHRR 69; *Pinder v United Kingdom* (1984) 7 EHRR 464; *Powell and Rayner*, above n 187; *Fayed v United Kingdom* (1994) 18 EHRR 393; *Stubbings* (n 243); *Tinnelly & Sons Ltd v United Kingdom* (1998) 27 EHRR 249; *Osman v United Kingdom* (1998) 29 EHRR 245; *Waite and Kennedy v Germany* (1999) 30 EHRR 261; *Z v United Kingdom* (2002) 34 EHRR 3; *Fogarty v United Kingdom* (2002) 34 EHRR 13.

[252] See the comments of Lord Hoffmann in *Matthews*, ibid, at [29] and [39] and Lord Nicholls in *Wilson* (n 242), at [36]–[37].

costs;[253] a costs 'shield';[254] cause of action estoppel;[255] obtaining the court's permission to continue or commence proceedings; and statutes of limitation. State and diplomatic immunity[256] are substantive rules of law which, because they can be described as conferring immunity on a particular class of potential defendants may also be perceived as objectionable restrictions on a claimant's access to court, even though they cannot fairly be described as procedural bars.[257]

In *Matthews*[258] the House of Lords considered section 10 of the Crown Proceedings Act 1947 which provided, inter alia, that, on certification by the Secretary of State that a member of the armed forces was entitled to a pension by reason of suffering attributable to service in the armed forces, the Crown was not subject to liability in tort. Their Lordships unanimously characterised this as a substantive bar which substituted a no-fault system of compensation for a claim for damages.

> This was and is a matter of substantive law and the provision for an official certificate (in order to avoid or at least minimise the risk of inconsistent decisions on causation) does not alter that. Section 10(1)(b), taken on its own, is a provision for the protection of persons with claims against the Ministry.[259]

In *Wilson*[260] the question before their Lordships was whether section 127(3) of the Consumer Credit Act 1974 was a procedural or substantive bar. This section meant that the agreement between the pawnbroker and Ms Wilson was unenforceable as it did not contain all the prescribed terms. Their Lordships concluded it was a substantive bar as it did not bar access to court to decide whether the case was caught by the restriction but it did bar a court from exercising any discretion over whether to make an enforcement order. It was held that in taking that power away from a court the legislature was not 'encroaching on territory which ought properly to be the province of the courts' in a democratic society.[261] In the view of their Lordships, it no more offended the rule of law or the separation of powers than would be the case if Parliament had said that such an agreement was void.[262]

5.3 Limitation Periods

In order to be compatible with the right of access to court, limitation periods must

---

[253] See eg *Federal Bank of the Middle East v Hadkinson*, Court of Appeal, 5 November 1999.

[254] *Eastenders Cash & Carry plc v Revenue & Customs Commissioners* [2012] EWCA Civ 689, [2012] STC 2036.

[255] *Spicer v Tuli* [2012] EWCA Civ 845, [2012] 1 WLR 3088.

[256] Cited in *Matthews* (n 243), [128].

[257] Ibid, [129] citing *Osman* (n 251), as an example, although noting that the Court had withdrawn from this position in *Z* (n 251).

[258] Ibid.

[259] Ibid, per Lord Walker at [143]. See also per Lord Bingham at [15].

[260] *Wilson* (n 242).

[261] Ibid, per Lord Nicholls at [36].

[262] Ibid, at [37] per Lord Nicholls, per Lord Hope at [105] and per Lord Scott at [165]. However, even if Art 6 is not engaged, the law may deprive a person of his or her possessions, therefore Art 1 Protocol No 1 must also be considered. Other examples of substantive bars include *D'Souza v Lambeth London Borough* [2001] EWCA Civ 794, *Laws v Society of Lloyd's* [2003] EWCA Civ 1887 and *Pennycook v Shaws (EAL) Ltd* [2004] EWCA Civ 100, [2004] Ch 296. See further TR Hickman, 'The "Uncertain Shadow": Throwing Light on the Right to a Court under Article 6(1) ECHR', [2004] *Public Law* 122.

pursue a legitimate aim and be proportionate to the aim sought to be achieved.[263] It is in the interests of the state that there should be finality to litigation.[264] In *Anderton*[265] the Court of Appeal held that the fact that Civil Procedure Rule 6.7 concerning the calculation of a deemed day of service of a claim form sent by first-class post or by fax was not rebuttable by evidence proving the claim form had actually been received on an earlier day was compatible with the right of access to court.

> Procedural rules are necessary to achieve justice. Justice and proportionality require that there are firm procedural rules which should be observed, not that general rules should be construed to create exceptions and excuses whenever those, who could easily have complied with the rules, have slipped up and mistakenly failed to do so.[266]

By contrast, in *Goode v Martin*[267] the claimant sought to amend her statement of claim after the period of limitation had expired. Using section 3 of the HRA, the Court of Appeal interpreted Civil Procedure Rule 17.4(2) so as to allow her to do so, detecting no sound policy reason what she should not add to her claim the alternative plea she proposed. 'No new facts are being introduced: she merely wants to say that if the defendant succeeds in establishing his version of the facts, she will still win because those facts, too, show that he was negligent.'[268] In the view of the Court of Appeal, to prevent her from putting this case before the court would impose an impediment on her access to the court which would require justification.[269] Similarly in *Adesina*[270] the Court of Appeal held that the time limit within which a nurse or midwife must bring an appeal against a disciplinary decision of the Nursing and Midwifery Council to the High Court, 28 days without exception, was incompatible with Article 6. Utilising section 3 of the HRA, it held that a discretion must be applied in exceptional circumstances where the appellant had done all he or she could to bring the appeal timeously.

> The context, exclusion from a profession, is still one of great importance to an appellant. There is good reason for there to be time limits with a high degree of strictness. However ... without some margin for discretion, circumstances may cause absolute time limits to impair 'the very essence' of the right of appeal conferred by statute.[271]

In *Lukaszewski*[272] the Supreme Court held that the short time limits for appeal contained in the Extradition Act 2003, in some instances seven days, did not pursue a legitimate aim or involve a reasonable relationship of proportionality between the means employed and the aim sought to be achieved, resulting in the possibility of impairing the very essence of the right of appeal: 'Finality and certainty are important

---

[263] *Goode v Martin* [2001] EWCA 1899, [2002] 1 WLR 1828.

[264] *R (on the application of Blackett) v The Nursing and Midwifery Council* [2004] EWHC (Admin) 1494. *R v Ballinger* [2005] EWCA Crim 1060.

[265] *Anderton v Clwyd County Council* [2002] EWCA Civ 933, [2002] 1 WLR 3174.

[266] Ibid, [36]. In *Akram v Adam* [2005] 1 All ER 741 the Court of Appeal held that service by post to an individual's last known residence was compatible with the right of access to court. See also *Young v Western Power Distribution (South West) plc* [2003] EWCA Civ 1034; *Rowe v Kingtson-Upon-Hull City Council and Essex County Council* [2003] EWCA Civ 1281; *J & PM Dockeray (a firm) v Secretary of State for the Environment, Food & Rural Affairs* [2002] EWHC (Admin) 420, [2002] HLR 27.

[267] *Goode v Martin* (n 263).

[268] Ibid, [42].

[269] Ibid, [43].

[270] *R (Adesina) v Nursing & Midwifery Council* [2013] EWCA Civ 818, [2013] 1 WLR 3156.

[271] Ibid, [14].

[272] *Lukaszewski* (n 44).

legal values . . . neither finality nor certainty has been achieved to date . . . the statute will be capable of generating considerable unfairness in individual cases.'[273] Utilising section 3 of the HRA, the Supreme Court held that the statutory provisions concerning appeals can and should be read subject to the qualification that the court must have a discretion in exceptional circumstances to extend time for both filing and service where such statutory provisions would otherwise 'operate to prevent an appeal in a manner conflicting with the right of access to an appeal process'.[274]

5.4 Security for Costs

An order of security for costs can give rise to a breach of the right of access to court but this depends upon the circumstances of the case.[275] Closely analogous is the requirement under the Insolvency Act 1986, when petitioning for bankruptcy, to pay a deposit of £250 as security against the fees which the official receiver would incur. In *Lightfoot*,[276] although the Court of Appeal had concluded that Article 6 did not actually apply to such a situation, on the assumption that it did, it held that, insofar as the deposit precondition constituted a restriction upon the appellant's right to petition the court, it had a legitimate aim and by its nature was proportionate to that aim.

> Its legitimacy lies in an aspiring bankrupt's need to have the bankruptcy administered by a third party and the state's entitlement to require some payment at least in respect of the cost of that third party's service. The fee represents but a modest proportion of that cost and can hardly therefore be judged disproportionate.

5.5 Vexatious Litigants

Any court has an inherent jurisdiction to protect itself from abuse. Provided the very essence of a litigant's right of access to the court is not extinguished, a court has a right to regulate its processes as it thinks fit so long as its remedies are proportionate to the identified abuse.[277] There are two methods generally utilised by the courts to protect proceedings against abuse. The first is by the Attorney-General seeking an order under section 42 of the Supreme Court Act that a litigant be declared a vexatious litigant. It has been held that an order under this section is compatible with the right of access to court. It is made after a detailed inquiry. The individual is able to revisit the issue in the context of new facts and of new complaints that he wishes to make. Each step is the subject of a separate judicial decision. Furthermore, the procedures respect proportionality in the general access to public resources in that they seek to prevent the monopolisation of court services by a few litigants.[278]

---

[273] Ibid, [35].
[274] Ibid, [39].
[275] *Hadkinson* (n 253). See also *Nasser v United Bank of Kuwait* [2001] EWCA Civ 556, [2002] 1 WLR 1868, which concerned Art 14 and the right of access to court; and *Mahan Air v Blue Sky One Ltd* [2011] EWCA Civ 544.
[276] *Lightfoot* (above n 151).
[277] *Bhamjee v Forsdick (No 2)* [2003] EWCA Civ 1113.
[278] *Ebert v Official Receiver* [2001] EWCA Civ 340, [2002] 1 WLR 320, [9] in reliance upon *Golder* (n 37); *H v UK* (1985) 45 DR 281; *Ashingdane v UK* (1985) 7 EHRR 528. See also *Attorney General v Covey* [2001] EWCA Civ 254; *Attorney General v Wheen* [2001] IRLR 91.

The second means of protection is what is known as a *Grepe v Loam* order (civil restraint order) within the four corners of the particular proceedings. This requires a litigant, who has abused his or her rights, to obtain the permission of the court before any further applications are issued and served.[279] There is also the possibility of a general civil restraint order, which lasts for two years and restrains the litigant from commencing any action or making any application in that court without the prior permission of the court. Any application for permission must be made in writing and is dealt with in writing. It has been held that, if proportionate to the identified abuse, such orders are also compatible with the right of access to court.[280]

It has also been held that Article 6 permits the protection of those responsible for the care of mental patients from being harassed by litigation. In *Seal*[281] a majority of the House of Lords held that it was compatible with Article 6 for the Mental Health Act 1983 to impose a leave requirement upon those bringing civil proceedings. It concluded that the obtaining of leave was a jurisdictional condition such as to render null any proceedings brought without it.

5.6 Immunity from Suit

Any immunity from suit must pursue a legitimate aim and satisfy the test of proportionality.[282] For example, in *Heath*[283] the Court of Appeal held that judicial immunity extended to proceedings before a Police Disciplinary Board, thereby prohibiting claims of unlawful sex discrimination committed in the course of such proceedings. Its purpose was held to be legitimate and necessary and proportionate in the public interest for the protection of the integrity of the judicial system.[284] By contrast, in relation to witness immunity, the House of Lords held in *Darker*[285] that, although the absolute immunity from action given in the interests of the administration of justice to a party or witness, including a police witness, in respect of what he said or did in court extended to statements made for the purpose of court proceedings, and to prevent him from being sued for conspiracy to give false evidence, public policy did not require it to be extended to things done by the police during the investigative process which could not fairly be said to form part of their participation in the judicial process as witnesses. In particular, the immunity did not extend to cover the fabrication of false evidence.[286]

Such considerations do not apply to state immunity. An assertion by a foreign state

---

[279] *Parkins v Westminster City Council*, Court of Appeal, 20 March 2000.

[280] *Bhamjee* (n 277), [54]; *Mahajan v Department of Constitutional Affairs* [2004] EWCA Civ 946. There is also the possibility of an extended civil restraint order restraining all activity in the Court of Appeal, High Court and any county court for a period of two years unless permission is obtained following a written application.

[281] *Seal v Chief Constable of South Wales* [2007] UKHL 31, [2007] 1 WLR 1910.

[282] *Arthur J S Hall & Co (a firm) v Simons* [2000] 2 FCR 673, per Lord Hope at 718–19.

[283] *Heath v Commissioner of Police for the Metropolis* [2000] EWCA Civ 943, [2005] ICR 329.

[284] Ibid, at [70] Auld LJ commented that this particular immunity was more in the nature of a substantive than procedural bar although this is not in keeping with the judgment of the House of Lords in *Darker v Chief Constable of the West Midlands Police* [2000] 3 WLR 747.

[285] Ibid.

[286] Ibid, per Lord Hope at 752 and Lord Hutton at 773. See also *L v Reading Borough Council* [2001] 1 WLR 1575; *D v East Berkshire Community NHS Trust* [2003] EWCA Civ 1151, [2004] QB 558.

of immunity before the English courts does not infringe the right of access to court. In *Holland v Lampen-Wolfe*[287] the House of Lords described state immunity as a creature of customary international law, not a self-imposed restriction on the jurisdiction of its courts which the United Kingdom had chosen to adopt. 'The United Kingdom cannot, by its own act of acceding to the Convention and without the consent of the United States, obtain a power of adjudication over the United States which international law denies it.'[288]

However, in *Jones*[289] the House of Lords was required to determine whether an English court had jurisdiction to entertain proceedings brought in England by claimants against a foreign state and its officials at whose hands the claimants alleged that they suffered systematic torture in the territory of the foreign state. Lord Bingham observed that the issue turned on the relationship between two principles of international law:

> One principle is that one sovereign state will not, save in certain specified instances, assert its judicial authority over another. The second principle … is one that condemns and criminalises the official practice of torture, requires states to suppress the practice and provides for the trial and punishment of officials found to be guilty of it.[290]

The core of the claimant's case was that Part I of the State Immunity Act 1978 was incompatible with Article 6. Contrary to *Holland v Lampen-Wolfe* it was assumed by the House of Lords that this was a denial of access to court[291] and that therefore the claimants had to demonstrate that the restriction was not directed to a legitimate objective and was disproportionate. The House of Lords concluded that Part I was not disproportionate as inconsistent with a peremptory norm of international law, and its application did not infringe Article 6, assuming this to apply.[292]

5.7 Prisoners

Convicted prisoners have a right of access to court, although obstacles imposed primarily in the interests of security and safety considerations mean that this is generally not an unimpeded right. For example, in *Ponting*[293] the Court of Appeal considered whether limitations imposed on a dyslexic prisoner litigant's use of a computer and printer were legitimate and proportionate. It is important to note that the question of whether or not access to computers by prisoners was required in order to meet the obligation imposed by the right of access to court was not considered, the court proceeding on the basis that access to court in at least one of the four cases the prisoner was pursuing would be impaired if he did not have a computer. The conditions imposed restricted the use of the computer to the prisoner's cell, limited the times during which the computer could be in the prisoner's possession, prescribed conditions in which it

---

[287] *Holland v Lampen-Wolfe* (n 238).

[288] Cf the speeches of Lords Hope and Clyde. See further M Tomonori, 'One Immunity Has Gone … Another … Holland v Lampen-Wolfe' (2001) 64 *Modern Law Review* 472.

[289] *Jones v Saudi Arabia* [2006] UKHL 26, [2007] 1 AC 270.

[290] Ibid, [1].

[291] The House of Lords preferred the view that a state could not make available a jurisdiction which it did not possess.

[292] In reliance upon *Al-Adsani v United Kingdom* (2001) 34 EHRR 273.

[293] *Ponting* (n 245).

and all disks were to be stored, and made various provisions for the supervision of use and inspection of materials. They were imposed in the interests of safety and security. A majority of the court concluded that the conditions legitimate and proportionate, in particular the denial of 24-hour access to the computer.[294]

5.8 Absence of Legal Representation

Whilst the absence of legal representation in civil proceedings can also be considered in the context of the right to a fair hearing, it has been held that access to court must be effective access, and in some instances this may require legal representation.[295] However, a litigant who wishes to argue that without legal aid his right of effective access has been violated has a relatively high threshold to cross.[296]

> The test ... is whether a court is put in a position that it really cannot do justice in the case because it has no confidence in its ability to grasp the facts and principles of the matter on which it has to decide. In such a case it may well be said that a litigant is deprived of effective access; deprived of effective access because, although he can present his case in person, he cannot do so in a way which will enable the court to do its paramount and over-arching function of reaching a just decision.[297]

In *Perotti*,[298] given that the applications were for permission to appeal, the Court of Appeal held that the scope for advocacy was relatively limited and the absence of legal representation did not deprive the litigant of effective access to justice.[299]

5.9 Striking Out

Where the legal position is clear and an investigation of the facts would provide no assistance, a court may strike out the claim. It has been held that there is no question of any contravention of Article 6 in doing so as defendants as well as claimants are entitled to a fair trial and it is an important part of the case management function to bring proceedings to an end as expeditiously as possible.[300]

Issues have arisen concerning the striking out of claims in negligence. In *Osman v UK*[301] the ECtHR held that it was a breach of the right of access to court for the Court of Appeal to strike out a claim in negligence against the police in light of the clearly

---

[294] Clarke LJ dissented on this point, although his judgment was based more on equality of arms than access to court.

[295] *Perotti v Collyer-Bristow (a firm)* [2003] EWCA Civ 1521, [2004] 2 All ER 189 in reliance upon *Airey v Ireland* (1979) 2 EHRR 305.

[296] Ibid, [31].

[297] Ibid, [32].

[298] Ibid.

[299] Ibid, [37]. In *Alliss v Legal Services Commission* [2002] EWHC (Admin) 2079 the court found that the withdrawal of legal aid denied the claimant effective access to the court in breach of Art 6(1).

[300] *Kent v Griffiths* [2001] QB 36. See also *Outram v Academy Plastics* [2000] IRLR 499; *Terry v Hoyer (UK) Limited* [2001] EWCA Civ 678; *Rampal v Rampal (No 2)* [2001] EWCA Civ 989, [2001] 3 WLR 795.

[301] *Osman* (n 251).

established principle that the police owed no duty of care to individual citizens in relation to the vigour with which they carried out their duties.

> [T]he applicants must be taken to have had a right, derived from the law of negligence, to seek an adjudication on the admissibility and merits of an arguable claim that they were in a relationship of proximity to the police, that the harm caused was foreseeable and that in the circumstances it was fair, just and reasonable not to apply the exclusionary rule.[302]

This decision 'perplexed' common law judges and jurists[303] and led to a considerable reluctance on the part of English courts to use the striking out procedure in negligence proceedings.[304] However, in *Z v United Kingdom*[305] the ECtHR reversed the trend, holding that the inability of the applicants to sue the local authority in negligence flowed not from an immunity but from the applicable principles governing the substantive right of action in domestic law. There was no restriction on access to court.[306] If a court concludes that it is not fair, just and reasonable to impose a duty of care, striking out the claim is no longer considered with the same reluctance.[307]

6. Fair Hearing

The first right expressly protected by Article 6(1) is the right to a fair hearing which must be upheld in the determination of civil rights and criminal charges. The Article does not spell out in any detail what a fair hearing requires, and it has been held that this cannot be the subject of a single, unvarying rule or collection of rules: the facts and circumstances of the case must be taken into account.[308] Nevertheless, a number of subsidiary rights have emerged from the jurisprudence, such as the right to equality of arms, the presumption of innocence and the privilege against self-incrimination. Whilst the right to a fair hearing is an absolute right, irregularities or breaches of these subsidiary rights along the way are possible as long as, taking all the facts and circumstances into account, there has on the whole been a fair hearing. The fairness of the trial may not be qualified, compromised or restricted in any way whatever the circumstances and whatever the public interest in convicting the offender.[309]

The right to a fair hearing is a separate and distinct right. Therefore the consequences of a breach, or a threatened or prospective breach, need to be considered separately.[310] Difficult questions have arisen in relation to criminal proceedings. One breach of the right to a fair hearing along the way may not necessarily mean that a conviction is

---

[302] Ibid, [139].
[303] *D* (n 286), [14].
[304] See eg *Barrett v Enfield London Borough Council* [2001] 2 AC 550; *Griffiths* (n 300).
[305] *Z v United Kingdom* (2001) 34 EHRR 97.
[306] Ibid, [101]–[102]. See also *TP and KM v United Kingdom* (2001) 34 EHRR 42.
[307] See eg *D* (n 286). See generally J Wright, *Tort Law and Human Rights* (Oxford, Hart Publishing, 2001).
[308] *Brown* (n 4), per Lord Bingham.
[309] Ibid. See also *Watson* (n 2), per Lord Hope at [73].
[310] *Porter* (n 2); *Attorney General's Reference No 2 of 2001* (n 1).

unsafe.[311] However, if, on consideration of all the facts and the whole history of the proceedings, it is concluded that the right to fair trial has been infringed, a conviction must be held to be unsafe within the meaning of section 2 of the Criminal Appeal Act 1968.[312] For example, in *Lambert*[313] the House of Lords held that a breach of the right to be presumed innocent by a direction to the jury that the accused was under a persuasive rather than evidential burden would not necessarily lead to an unsafe conviction.

> There will be cases where a conviction cannot stand and must be quashed irrespective of the strength of the evidence against the defendant because the trial as a whole is judged to be unfair. But ... where the unfairness is claimed to arise from the transfer of the onus and it was open to the appellant to seek to rebut the presumption, and where there can be no doubt that the jury would have convicted if only an evidential burden had rested on the appellant, then the imposition of a persuasive burden as to knowledge resulted in no injustice and ... no breach of art 6(2).[314]

6.1 Equality of Arms

6.1.1 Generally

The first subsidiary right derived from the right to a fair hearing is the right to equality of arms. There must be a fair balance between the parties. In civil cases the claimant must be afforded an opportunity to present his case under conditions which do not place him at a substantial disadvantage as compared with the respondent. This may include a right to be heard.[315] In criminal cases the requirement that there be a fair balance is no less important. The purpose of Article 6 is not to make it impractical to bring those accused of crime to justice. The essential question is whether the alleged inequality of arms is such as to deprive the accused of his right to a fair trial.[316] What has to be demonstrated is that the prosecutor will enjoy some particular advantage that is not available to the defence or that would otherwise be unfair.[317] For example, it has been held that limited provision of computer facilities to a prisoner representing himself in proceedings could engage the principle of equality of arms.[318]

---

[311] The same applies where the ECHR has found a violation of Art 6. See *R v Lewis* [2005] EWCA Crim 859.

[312] *R v Forbes* [2001] UKHL 40, [2001] 3 WLR 428, endorsing the judgment of the Court of Appeal in *R v Togher* [2001] 3 All ER 463.

[313] *R v Lambert* [2001] UKHL 37, [2002] 2 AC 545.

[314] Ibid, [202]. See also Lord Clyde at [159], Lord Steyn at [43], Lord Hope at [117] and Lord Slynn at [18]. Also *R v Davis* [2001] 1 Cr App Rep 115, where the Court of Appeal held that the question to be asked was would a reasonable jury, after a proper summing up, convict the appellant on the rest of the evidence to which no objection could be taken.

[315] *R (Wright) v Secretary of State for Health* [2009] UKHL 3, [2009] 1 AC 739.

[316] *McLean v Procurator Fiscal* [2001] 1 WLR 2425, per Lord Hope at [39] in reliance upon *Dombo Beheer* (n 156), [33]; *De Haes and Gijsels v Belgium* (1997) 24 EHRR 1, [53]; *Montgomery* (n 167).

[317] *McLean*, ibid, [40]. Equality of arms does not apply to the role played by a clerk when giving legal advice to a justice in private as the clerk functions on the same side of the court as the justice. See *Clark (Procurator Fiscal) v Kelly* [2003] UKPC D1, [2004] 1 AC 681.

[318] *Ponting* (n 245).

6.1.2 Legal Representation

A number of claims have been made concerning legal representation and equality of arms. For example, in *McLean*[319] it was argued under the Scotland Act 1998 that regulations fixing payments to which solicitors were entitled was in breach of the principle of equality of arms. The Privy Council rejected the argument as it was not demonstrated that any inequality there may be was of such a character that the legal assistance provided would be ineffective and the trial unfair.[320] There was no reason to doubt that the solicitors would conduct the case for the defence according to the required standards.[321] In *Attorney General's Reference No 82a of 2000*[322] the appellants contended that, because the Crown had instructed leading counsel, it was in violation of the principle of equality of arms for them to be represented by junior counsel. The Court of Appeal disagreed, holding that a fair trial did not necessarily entail representation by a Queen's Counsel merely because the Crown were represented by Queen's Counsel. It held that what was important was to have an advocate, whether he be a barrister or a solicitor, 'who can ensure that a defendant's defence is properly and adequately placed before the court'.[323]

With respect to unrepresented litigants, it has been held that where there is an application made for the assistance of a McKenzie friend, there is a strong presumption in favour of granting such an application.[324] Where a party lacks litigation capacity, it may be necessary for the Official Solicitor to act.[325]

6.1.3 Disclosure

A breach of the right to equality of arms can arise from the failure of the prosecution to disclose to the defence a relevant piece of evidence.[326]

> [T]he prosecution is under a duty to disclose to the defence all material evidence in its possession for or against the accused. For this purpose any evidence which would tend to undermine the prosecution's case or to assist the case for the defence is to be taken as material. [But] the defence does not have an absolute right to the disclosure of all relevant evidence. There may be competing interests which it is in the public interest to protect. But decisions as to whether the withholding of relevant information is in the public interest cannot be left exclusively to the Crown. There must be sufficient judicial safeguards in place to ensure that information is not withheld on the grounds of public interest unless this is strictly necessary.[327]

It was argued in *McDonald*[328] that there was a breach of the duty of disclosure under Article 6(1) if there was a reasonable basis to apprehend that the Lord Advocate's duty

---

[319] *McLean* (n 316).
[320] Ibid, per Lord Hope at [41].
[321] Ibid, per Lord Hope at [43].
[322] *Attorney General's Reference No 82a of 2000* [2002] EWCA Crim 215.
[323] Ibid, [14].
[324] *Re O (children) (representation: McKenzie friend)* [2005] EWCA Civ 759.
[325] Guidance is given in *RP v Nottingham City Council* [2008] EWCA Civ 462, [2008] 2 FLR 1516. See also *In the Matter of M (A Child)* [2012] EWCA Civ 1905.
[326] *R v Bishop*, Court of Appeal, 10 November 2003.
[327] *Sinclair v HM Advocate* [2005] HRLR 26, per Lord Hope at [33].
[328] *McDonald v HM Advocate* [2008] UKPC 46, [2009] HRLR 3.

of disclosure had not been complied with. Lord Hope, with whom the other members of the Privy Council agreed, stated that an absolute guarantee cannot be given in any case that every single piece of information has been disclosed that ought to have been. The most that can be expected is that

> everything that can be done by way of instruction, organisation and training to eliminate the possibility of error has been done, and ... that an assurance is given in each particular case that to the best of the knowledge and belief of the Lord Advocate, or those acting for her, there has been full disclosure.[329]

He stated that it would be incompatible with the appellant's rights under Article 6 for the Lord Advocate to seek to support the conviction if the appellant was able to demonstrate that there was a reasonable possibility of unfairness as a result of the non-disclosure.[330]

In some instances there are questions over what exactly is material evidence which should be disclosed. For example, in *Sinclair*[331] the Privy Council held that it was incompatible with Article 6(1) for the Lord Advocate to bring proceedings and seek a conviction without having produced or disclosed the existence and contents of statements made to the police by a witness who was to corroborate the complainer's account of the incident. It was held that this was information that was plainly likely to be of material assistance to the defence. Their Lordships confirmed that the fact that the statements were not made available could not be attributed to any failure in duty on the part of the defence and the duty of disclosure was on the Crown.[332] It was also held that the police statements of all the witnesses who were to be called at the trial were to be regarded as containing material evidence either for or against the accused, and the Crown were therefore under an obligation in terms of Article 6(1) to disclose their statements to the defence.[333]

The prior convictions of witnesses are usually considered material evidence. For example, in *Holland*[334] the Privy Council held that it was in principle wrong that at trial the prosecutor should have official information about the witnesses' previous convictions which has been withheld from the defence.[335] Information about previous convictions of any witnesses to be led at the trial is likely to be of material assistance to the proper preparation or presentation of the accused's defence, and under Article 6(1) the accused's agents and counsel are accordingly entitled to have that information disclosed so that they can prepare his defence.[336] However, given that details of outstanding charges are more difficult to discover, there is no general duty to search for outstanding charges. 'If Crown officials are asked about a particular witness, they need only take such steps to search for any outstanding charges as are appropriate, having regard to any indications given in the defence request.'[337]

Previous convictions were also at issue before the Privy Council in *Murtagh*[338]

---

[329] Ibid, [33].
[330] Ibid, [37].
[331] *Sinclair* (n 327).
[332] Ibid, per Lord Hope at [34].
[333] Ibid, per Lord Rodger at [49].
[334] *Holland v HM Advocate* [2005] HRLR 25.
[335] Ibid, per Lord Rodger at [70].
[336] Ibid, per Lord Rodger at [72].
[337] Ibid, per Lord Rodger at [74].
[338] *HM Advocate v Murtagh* [2009] UKPC 36, [2010] 3 WLR 814.

where it considered whether the Crown was required to disclose to the accused all previous convictions and outstanding charges of Crown witnesses or whether it required the disclosure of only such previous convictions and outstanding charges as materially weakened the Crown's case or materially strengthened the case for the defence. Taking into account Article 8, respect for private life, it concluded that disclosure was required of such previous convictions and outstanding charges as materially weakened the Crown's case or materially strengthened the case for the defence. It was consistent with Article 6 for the Crown itself to take the initial decision as to whether or not such previous convictions and outstanding charges satisfied the test of materiality. Furthermore, it held that Article 6 required the disclosure of warnings or measures offered and accepted as an alternative to prosecution, but only where these materially weakened the case for the Crown or strengthened the case for the defence.[339]

In *McInnes*[340] the Supreme Court considered the consequences of violation of the duty of disclosure under Article 6. It held that a trial was not to be taken to have been unfair just because of the non-disclosure as the significance and consequences of the non-disclosure must be assessed.

> The question at the stage of an appeal was whether, given that there was a failure to disclose and having regard to what actually happened at the trial, the trial was nevertheless fair and ... as a consequence there was no miscarriage of justice.[341]

6.1.4 Public Interest Immunity

A claim of public interest immunity conflicts with the right to equality of arms, particularly in a criminal case where the prosecution seeks to withhold documents on this ground. Circumstances may arise in which material held by the prosecution and tending to undermine the prosecution or assist the defence cannot be disclosed to the defence fully, or even at all, without the risk of serious prejudice to an important public interest.[342] The public interest most regularly claimed is in the effective investigation and prosecution of serious crime. The courts have accepted that, in such circumstances, some derogation from the rule of disclosure may be justified, though such derogation must always be the minimum necessary to protect the public interest in question and must never imperil the overall fairness of the trial.[343]

In *R v H*[344] both of the appellants had been charged with conspiracy to supply a class A drug. The prosecution sought to withhold documents on the ground of public interest immunity. The appellants argued that it was incompatible with Article 6 for a judge to rule on a claim to public interest immunity in the absence of adversarial argument on behalf of the accused where the material which the prosecution was seeking to withhold was, or may be, relevant to a disputed issue of fact which the judge had to decide in order to rule on an application which would effectively determine the outcome of the proceedings. The House of Lords held that this would place the trial

---

[339] Ibid, per Lord Hope at [40] with whom the others agreed. See also *Allison v HM Advocate* [2010] UKSC 6, [2010] HRLR 16.
[340] *McInnes v HM Advocate* [2010] UKSC 7, [2010] HRLR 17.
[341] Ibid, per Lord Hope at [20]. See also *Fraser v HM Advocate* [2011] UKSC 24, [2011] HRLR 28.
[342] See eg *R v H* (n 181).
[343] See eg ibid, [18].
[344] Ibid.

judge in a straitjacket and the best approach was on a case-by-case basis, avoiding rigid or inflexible rules.[345] It concluded that, when any issue of derogation from the golden rule of full disclosure came before it, the court must address a series of questions, and if scrupulous attention was paid to these and the proper interests of the defendant, there should be no violation of Article 6.[346] The series of questions was as follows:

(1) What is the material which the prosecution seek to withhold? This must be considered by the court in detail. (2) Is the material such as may weaken the prosecution case or strengthen that of the defence? If, No, disclosure should not be ordered. If, Yes, full disclosure should (subject to (3), (4) and (5) below) be ordered. (3) Is there a real risk of serious prejudice to an important public interest (and, if so, what) if full disclosure of the material is ordered? If, No, full disclosure should be ordered. (4) If the answer to (2) and (3) is, Yes, can the defendant's interest be protected without disclosure or disclosure be ordered to an extent or in a way which will give adequate protection to the public interest in question and also afford adequate protection to the interests of the defence? This question requires the court to consider, with specific reference to the material which the prosecution seek to withhold and the facts of the case and the defence as disclosed, whether the prosecution should formally admit what the defence seek to establish or whether disclosure short of full disclosure may be ordered. This may be done in appropriate cases by the preparation of summaries or extracts of evidence, or the provision of documents in an edited or anonymised form, provided the documents supplied are in each instance approved by the judge. In appropriate cases the appointment of special counsel may be a necessary step to ensure that the contentions of the prosecution are tested and the interests of the defendant protected. ... In cases of exceptional difficulty the court may require the appointment of special counsel to ensure a correct answer to questions (2) and (3) as well as (4). (5) Do the measures proposed in answer to (4) represent the minimum derogation necessary to protect the public interest in question? If, No, the court should order such greater disclosure as will represent the minimum derogation from the golden rule of full disclosure. (6) If limited disclosure is ordered pursuant to (4) or (5), may the effect be to render the trial process, viewed as a whole, unfair to the defendant? If, Yes, then fuller disclosure should be ordered even if this leads or may lead the prosecution to discontinue the proceedings so as to avoid having to make disclosure. (7) If the answer to (6) when first given is, No, does that remain the correct answer as the trial unfolds, evidence is adduced and the defence advanced? It is important that the answer to (6) should not be treated as a final, once-and-for-all, answer but as a provisional answer which the court must keep under review.[347]

6.1.5 National Security: Control Order Cases

With the passage of the Prevention of Terrorism Act 2005, courts have had to consider difficult questions concerning the non-disclosure to potential controlees of sensitive evidence when making non-derogating control orders against them. In MB[348] the House of Lords held that such proceedings did not involve the determination of a criminal charge but were nevertheless under the civil limb of Article 6(1), and controlees were

[345] Ibid, [33].

[346] Ibid, [39].

[347] Ibid, [36]. See also *R v Smith* [2002] EWCA Crim 2561; *R v Brushett* [2001] Crim LR 471; *R v Botmeh* [2001] EWCA Crim 2226, [2002] 1 WLR 531; *Chief Constable of the Greater Manchester Police v McNally* [2002] EWCA Civ 14, [2002] Cr LR 832; *R v Templar* [2003] EWCA Crim 3186. As to the appointment of 'special advocates', see generally *Roberts v Parole Board* [2005] UKHL 45, [2005] 3 WLR 152.

[348] *MB* (n 141).

entitled to such measure of procedural protection as was commensurate with the gravity of the potential consequences.[349] Lord Bingham noted that the real problem arose where material was relied on in coming to a decision which the person at risk of an adverse ruling had no opportunity to challenge or rebut.[350] He acknowledged that the engagement of special advocates can help to enhance the procedural justice available to a controlled person. However, it was also appreciated that this can never be a panacea for the grave disadvantages of a person affected not being aware of the case against him.[351]

It was held that the task of the court was to decide, looking at the process as a whole, whether a procedure had been used which involved significant injustice to the controlled person.[352] In relation to the claimant MB, a majority of the House of Lords concluded that he was confronted by a bare, unsubstantiated assertion which he could no more than deny and the right to fair hearing was impaired.[353] In relation to the claimant AF the majority accepted that the case against him was in its essence entirely undisclosed to him and also in breach of Article 6.[354] It was agreed by a majority that section 3 of the HRA should be utilised to read down the relevant legislative provisions so that they would take effect only when it was consistent with fairness for them to do so.[355]

The House of Lords returned to the question in *AF*,[356] although took into account the judgment of the Grand Chamber of the ECtHR in *A v United Kingdom*.[357] Each of the appellants was subject to non-derogating control orders made under the Prevention of Terrorism Act 2005. Each argued that their right to a fair hearing was violated by reason of the reliance by the judge making the order upon material received in closed hearings, the nature of which was not disclosed to the appellant. Lord Phillips, with whom the others agreed, stated that the essence of the Grand Chamber's decision established that the controlee must be given sufficient information about the allegations against him to enable him to give effective instructions in relation to those allegations:

> Provided that this requirement is satisfied there can be a fair trial notwithstanding that the controlee is not provided with the detail or the sources of the evidence forming the basis of the allegations. Where, however, the open material consists purely of general assertions and the case against the controlee is based solely or to a decisive degree on closed materials the requirements of a fair trial will not be satisfied, however cogent the case based on the closed materials may be.[358]

Lord Phillips observed that the best way of producing a fair trial was to ensure that a party to it had the fullest information of both the allegations that were made against him and the evidence relied upon in support of those allegations. It was held that where the evidence was documentary, he should have access to the documents and where the evidence consisted of oral testimony, 'he should be entitled to cross-examine the wit-

---

[349] Ibid, per Lord Bingham at [24].
[350] Ibid, [33].
[351] Ibid, [35].
[352] Ibid, [35].
[353] Ibid, [41].
[354] Ibid, [43].
[355] Ibid, [44]. See also *AM v Secretary of State for the Home Department* [2011] EWCA Civ 710.
[356] *Secretary of State for the Home Department v AF* [2009] UKHL 28, [2009] 3 WLR 74.
[357] *A v United Kingdom* (2009) 49 EHRR 29.
[358] Ibid, [59].

nesses who give that testimony', whose identities should be disclosed.[359] It was decided that utilising section 3 of the HRA, the Act could be read down:

> [T]he judge will have to consider not merely the allegations that have to be disclosed in order to place in the open sufficient to satisfy the requirements laid down by the Grand Chamber, but whether there is any other matter whose disclosure is essential to the fairness of the trial.[360]

6.1.6 National Security—Other Types of Case

The issue was considered again by the Supreme Court in an employment law context in *Tariq*.[361] The claimant had argued that his security clearance as an immigration officer was withdrawn in circumstances involving direct or indirect discrimination on grounds of race and/or religion. The question before the Supreme Court was the compatibility with Article 6 of excluding the claimant and his representatives from certain aspects of the employment tribunal proceedings on grounds of national security. A special advocate had been appointed to represent his interests, in so far as possible, in relation to the aspects closed to him and his representatives.

The Supreme Court held that ECtHR jurisprudence established that the demands of national security may necessitate and justify a system for handling and determining complaints

> under which an applicant is, for reasons of national security, unable to know the secret material by reference to which his or her complaint is determined ... national security considerations may justify a closed material procedure, closed evidence (even without the use of a special advocate) and ...a blanket decision leaving the precise basis of determination unclear.[362]

There is a difference between the civil and criminal context. In the criminal context, it is considered better that the state should forego prosecution than that there should be any risk of an 'innocent person being found guilty through inability to respond to the full case against them'.[363] In a civil case, a 'balance may have to be struck between the interests of claimant and defendant'.[364] Lord Hope noted that an employment claim was different from a control order case as the individual was not faced with criminal proceedings against him or with severe restrictions on personal liberty.[365]

The Supreme Court concluded that a special advocate procedure was not, in principle, incompatible with Article 6. The majority held that there was no absolute requirement that the claimant personally, or his legal representatives, be provided with sufficient detail of the allegations made against him to enable him to give instructions

---

[359] Ibid, [64].

[360] Ibid, [68]. See also *BX v Secretary of State for the Home Department* [2010] EWCA Civ 481, [2010] 1 WLR 2463 concerning the modification of a control order. See also *Secretary of State for the Home Department v AHK* [2009] EWCA Civ 287, [2009] 1 WLR 2049 concerning refusal of application for British nationality where relevant material not disclosed on public interest grounds. See further A Kavanagh, 'Special Advocates, Control Orders and the Right to a Fair Trial' (2010) 73 *Modern Law Review* 836; J Ip, 'The Rise and Spread of the Special Advocate' [2008] *Public Law* 717.

[361] *Tariq v Home Office* [2011] UKSC 35, [2011] 3 WLR 322.

[362] Ibid, per Lord Mance at [36].

[363] Ibid, per Lord Mance at [40].

[364] Ibid, per Lord Mance at [40].

[365] Ibid, [81].

to his legal representatives on them.³⁶⁶ It was up to the Employment Tribunal, with the assistance of the special advocate, to keep under the review disclosure having regard to the nature of the allegations, and the significance of the allegations for the defence and the claimant.³⁶⁷

Ordering closed material procedures (where disclosure is made to special advocates) in civil claims has increased in recent years and the Supreme Court considered the compatibility of the practice with Article 6 again in *Al Rawi*.³⁶⁸ Here the claimants alleged that the Security Service, and other public authorities, had been complicit in the detention and ill-treatment of them by foreign authorities at various locations including Guantanamo Bay. The respondents claimed that they were in possession of material which they wished the court to consider, but that they would be obliged in the public interest to withhold from disclosure. They requested parallel open and closed proceedings and parallel open and closed judgments. Special advocates would represent the interests of the claimants in the closed hearings.

Lord Dyson, with whom the others agreed, held that at common law, a court could not exercise its power to regulate its own procedures in such a way as would deny parties their fundamental common law right to participate in the proceedings in accordance with the common law principles of natural justice and open justice.³⁶⁹ In his view, it was for Parliament to extend closed material procedures and the use of special advocates after full and proper consultation. Here, all that was available at present was the existing public interest immunity process.³⁷⁰

The compatibility of a closed material procedure with Article 6 was also considered by the Supreme Court in *Bank Mellat*,³⁷¹ which was an appeal against a financial restriction order made by the Treasury against Bank Mellat under the Financial Restrictions (Iran) Order 2009. The procedure was defined as follows:

> A closed material procedure involves the production of material which is so confidential and sensitive that it requires the court not only to sit in private, but to sit in a closed hearing (ie a hearing at which the court considers the material and hears submissions about it without one of the parties to the appeal seeing the material or being present), and to contemplate giving a partly closed judgment (ie a judgment part of which will not be seen by one of the parties).³⁷²

It was observed by the majority that the idea of a court hearing evidence or argument in private was contrary to the principle of open justice which was fundamental to the dispensation of justice in a modern, democratic society.³⁷³ However, it was also appreciated that, in rare cases, a court does have an inherent power to receive evidence and argument in a hearing from which the public and press are excluded, and that it

---

³⁶⁶ Lord Kerr held at [136] that the *AF* test was the appropriate test here and the claimant had to be provided with sufficient information about the allegations against him to allow him to give effective instructions to his legal representatives.

³⁶⁷ See further J Jackson, 'Justice, Security and the Right to a Fair Trial: Is the Use of Secret Evidence ever Fair?' [2013] *Public Law* 720; J Ip, "Al Rawi, Tariq and the Future of Closed Material Procedures and Special Advocates' (2012) 75 *Modern Law Review* 606.

³⁶⁸ *Al Rawi v Security Service* [2011] UKSC 34, [2011] 3 WLR 388.

³⁶⁹ Ibid, [22].

³⁷⁰ Lords Hope, Clarke, Brown, Phillips, Rodger and Kerr agreed.

³⁷¹ *Bank Mellat v HM Treasury* [2013] UKSC 38.

³⁷² Ibid, [1].

³⁷³ Ibid, [2].

can even give a judgment which is only available to the parties.[374] The majority also observed that even more fundamental to any justice system in a modern democratic society was the principle of natural justice, the most important aspect of which was that every party has a right to know the full case against him, and the 'right to test and challenge that case fully'.[375]

Summarising the ECtHR jurisprudence, the majority held that Article 6 was not infringed by a closed material procedure provided that appropriate conditions were met. These include:

> the court being satisfied that (i) for weighty reasons, such as national security, the material has to be kept secret from the excluded party as well as the public, (ii) a hearing to determine the issues between the parties could not fairly go ahead without the material being shown to the judge, (iii) a summary, which is both sufficiently informative and as full as the circumstances permit, of all the closed material has been made available to the excluded party, and (iv) an independent advocate, who has seen all the material, is able to challenge the need for the procedure, and, if there is a closed hearing, is present throughout to test the accuracy and relevance of the material and to make submissions about it.[376]

The majority also concluded that the Supreme Court could conduct a closed material procedure as section 40(2) of the Constitutional Reform Act 2005 gave it the power to do so.[377] It adopted a closed material procedure on appeal but concluded that there was really no point in doing so. It observed that appellate courts should be robust about acceding to applications to go into closed session or even to look at closed material. 'Given that the issues will have already been debated and adjudicated upon, there must be very few appeals where any sort of closed material procedure is likely to be necessary.'[378]

6.1.7 Child Witnesses

A child has a right to be heard in proceedings affecting him or her but a child has no right to give evidence.[379] A trial process must not expose a young defendant to avoidable intimidation, humiliation or distress. All possible steps must be taken to assist the young defendant to understand and participate in the proceedings.[380] For example, in D[381] it was argued that requiring the evidence of child witnesses to be given by video recording and/or video link, while not affording a similar facility to child defendants, was in breach of the principle of equality of arms. The House of Lords disagreed and also noted that the court had the power, in the exercise of its inherent jurisdiction, to make such an order in relation to a child defendant if necessary.[382]

The Supreme Court considered the principles which should guide the exercise of

---

[374] Ibid, [2].
[375] Ibid, [3].
[376] Ibid, [5].
[377] The minority held that it was not open to the Supreme Court to do this as it had not been expressly authorised by Parliament.
[378] Ibid, [74].
[379] *Re P-S (Children)* [2013] EWCA Civ 223, [2013] 2 FCR 299.
[380] *R v H* [2006] EWCA Crim 853, [33].
[381] *R v Camberwell Green Youth Court, ex p D* [2005] UKHL 4, [2005] 1 WLR 393.
[382] Ibid, per Lord Rodger at [16]–[17].

the court's discretion in deciding whether to order a child to attend to give evidence in family proceedings in *W*.[383] It held that the present law erected a presumption against a child giving evidence which had to be rebutted by anyone seeking to put questions to the child. It held that this could not be reconciled with the approach of the ECtHR, which always aimed to strike a fair balance between competing ECHR rights. Balancing Articles 6 and 8 in care proceedings, it observed that this may well mean that the child should not be called to give evidence in the great majority of cases; however, this was a result and not a presumption or a starting point.[384] Baroness Hale set out the test as follows:

> When the court is considering whether a particular child should be called as a witness, the court will have to weigh two considerations: the advantages that that will bring to the determination of the truth and the damage it may do to the welfare of this or any other child. A fair trial is a trial which is fair in the light of the issues which have to be decided.[385]

6.2 Self-incrimination

The right not to incriminate oneself is also a right which has been implied into Article 6 and is based on the presumption of innocence in Article 6(2) as well as the fair hearing guarantee in Article 6(1).[386] In keeping with other implied rights, it is not absolute and an interference with it may be justified if it pursues a legitimate aim and the scope of the interference is necessary and proportionate to the achievement of the aim.[387] The right is firmly anchored to the fairness of the trial and not concerned with extra-judicial inquiries.[388] For example, in *Green*[389] a company which was alleged to have unlawfully deposited waste refused to provide information about its activities on the ground that the answers may incriminate it. The House of Lords concluded that the right was not applicable as no answer had actually been tendered in evidence against the company.[390] As the right is primarily directed at respecting the will of an accused person to remain silent, it does not extend to the use in criminal proceedings of material which may be obtained from the accused through the use of compulsory powers, but which has an existence independent of the will of the subject, such as documents delivered under

---

[383] *Re W (Children)* [2010] UKSC 12, [2010] 1 WLR 701.

[384] Ibid, Baroness Hale at [22] per with whom the rest agreed. It was observed that the approach in private family proceedings between parents should be the same as the approach in care proceedings although there were specific risks to which the court must be alive [29].

[385] Ibid, [24]. See also *Re A (A Child: Disclosure of Third Party Information)* [2012] UKSC 60, [2012] 3 WLR 1484. See further A Keane, 'Towards a Principled Approach to the Cross-examination of Vulnerable Witnesses' [2012] *Criminal Law Review* 407; A Brammer and P Cooper, 'Still Waiting for a Meeting of Minds: Child Witnesses in the Criminal and Family Justice Systems' [2011] *Criminal Law Review* 925; M Hall, 'The Misfortune of Being Straightforward? The Impact of Re W on Children Giving Evidence in Care Proceedings' (2010) 22 *Child and Family Law Quarterly* 499.

[386] *R v Hertfordshire County Council, ex p Green Environmental Industries Ltd* [2000] 2 AC 483; *Brown* (n 4).

[387] *Brown*, ibid, per Lord Steyn.

[388] *Green* (n 386).

[389] Ibid.

[390] See also *R v Kearns* [2002] EWCA Crim 748, [2002] WLR 2815.

compulsion pursuant to the Insolvency Act 1986.[391] It is also not infringed by requiring an accused to be present at his or her trial where he may be identified by a witness.[392]

In claims under the HRA, interferences have been found in the context of compulsorily obtained admissions which are then sought to be relied upon at trial. For example, in *Brown*[393] Ms Brown had been required by police, exercising their powers under section 172(2)(a) of the Road Traffic Act 1988, to say who had been driving her car when she would have travelled in it to a store car park. She replied 'it was me' and the prosecution later sought to rely on this admission at her trial for driving a car after having consumed excessive alcohol. Her objection to the reliance on her admission was raised as a devolution issue under the Scotland Act 1998.The Privy Council concluded that section 172 was a proportionate response to a serious social problem and that reliance on her admission would not undermine her right to a fair trial. In particular, Lord Hope found that the system of regulation and the provisions which the legislation contained for the detection and prosecution of road traffic offences served a legitimate aim.

> The purpose which these offences are designed to serve would be at risk of being defeated if no means were available to enable the police to trace the driver of a vehicle who, as so often happens, had departed from the place where the offence was committed before he or she could be identified.

With respect to the question of proportionality, Lord Hope took into account the limited incursion presented by the section and the use made of the response. Under Scottish law at trial the admission had to be corroborated and there had to be other evidence to show beyond reasonable doubt that the driver committed the offence. All the usual protections against unreliable evidence, and evidence obtained by oppression or other improper means, remained in place.

Other objectives can also justify incursions into the right against self-incrimination. In *R v Allen*[394] the appellant's argument that the Revenue had breached the claimant's right against self-incrimination by compulsorily obtaining from him the schedule of assets upon which the prosecution case was based was dismissed by the House of Lords, which held that it was 'self-evident' that the payment of taxes, fixed by the legislature, was essential for the functioning of any democratic state. Furthermore, to ensure due payment of taxes, the House of Lords held that the state had to have the power to require its citizens to inform it of the amount of their annual income and to have sanctions available to enforce the provision of that information.[395] Such provisions could not constitute a violation of the right against self-incrimination.[396]

The right also extends to confession evidence, as obtaining a confession by oppression is a form of compulsion which constitutes a breach of the right of an accused

---

[391] *Attorney General's Reference No 7 of 2000* [2001] EWCA Crim 888, [2001] 1 WLR 1879. See also *R v Hundal; R v Dhaliwal* [2004] EWCA Crim 389.

[392] *Holland* (n 334).

[393] *Brown* (n 4).

[394] *R v Dimsey; R v Allen* [2001] UKHL 46, [2001] 3 WLR 843.

[395] Ibid, per Lord Hutton at [29].

[396] Ibid, per Lord Hutton at [30] in reliance upon *Brown* (n 4), and distinguishing *Saunders v UK* (1996) 23 EHRR 313. Their Lordships did note that the appellant's would have had a much stronger argument if, in response to the Hansard statement, he had given true and accurate information which disclosed that he had earlier cheated the Revenue and had then been prosecuted for that earlier dishonesty. See also *Westminster Property* (n 232); *Kearns* (n 390); and *R v K* [2009] EWCA Crim 1640, [2010] 2 WLR 905.

person not to incriminate himself.[397] In *Mushtaq*[398] the House of Lords held that the logic of section 76(2) of the Police and Criminal Evidence Act 1984 required that the jury should be directed that, if they consider that the confession was, or may have been, obtained by oppression, or in consequence of anything said or done which was likely to render it unreliable, they should disregard it.[399] It is incompatible with Article 6 for a judge to direct a jury that they are entitled to take into account a confession which he considered was, or might have been, obtained by oppression or any other improper means in violation of the defendant's right against self-incrimination.[400]

6.3 Right to Silence

The right to a fair hearing also encompasses a defendant's right to silence, although this is not an absolute right.[401] Considerable incursions on the right to silence are made by section 34 of the Criminal Justice and Public Order Act 1994 which, inter alia, allows the court or jury, in determining guilt, to draw such inferences as appear proper from the accused's failure to mention any fact relied on in his or her defence at the time of being charged which he or she could reasonably have been expected to mention. As the drawing of an adverse inference may infringe the right to a fair hearing, an appropriate balance must be struck between the accused's right to silence and the fair drawing of an adverse inference by the jury.[402] Provided the trial judge directs the jury in the required terms,[403] it has been held that section 34 is compatible with the right to a fair hearing under Article 6.[404]

Each case depends upon its own facts, and the failure to direct the jury in a particular way may in some circumstances amount to a breach of Article 6 whereas the same failure in other circumstances may not.[405] It does not necessarily follow from the fact that a direction which should have been given was not given that there has been a breach of Article 6 or that the convictions are unsafe.[406] For example, in *R v Chenia*[407] the Court of Appeal concluded that there was no breach in the fraud trial. The appellant did not refuse to answer questions in reliance upon a solicitor's advice.[408] The case against him was very strong, and the judge gave a clear and accurate direction under section 35 of the Criminal Justice and Public Order Act 1994 in relation to his failure to give evidence. This direction is almost in identical terms to the Judicial Studies Board section 34 direction. 'There was no realistic possibility that the jury drew an adverse

---

[397] *R v Mushtaq* [2005] UKHL 25, [2005] 1 WLR 1513, per Lord Carswell at [73].

[398] Ibid.

[399] Ibid, per Lord Rodger at [47].

[400] Ibid, [53].

[401] *R v Francom* [2001] 1 Cr App Rep 237, [42] in reliance upon *Murray v United Kingdom* (1996) 22 EHRR 29.

[402] *R v Betts; R v Hall* [2001] 2 Cr App R 257, [34] in reliance upon *Condron v UK* (2002) 31 EHRR 1.

[403] In accordance with the latest Judicial Studies Board Specimen Direction.

[404] *Francom* (n 401).

[405] *R v Chenia* [2002] EWCA Crim 2345, [2004] 1 All ER 543, [58] in reliance upon *Beckles v UK* (2002) 13 BHRC 522.

[406] Ibid, [59].

[407] Ibid.

[408] See further *R v Howell* [2003] EWCA Crim 01, [2005] 1 Cr App Rep 1, where the Court of Appeal held that it is not the case that if a suspect remains silent on legal advice he may systematically avoid adverse comment at his trial.

inference while at the same time thinking the appellant's statement of his reasons for silence might be true. The jury must have excluded both the reason for silence offered and the possibility of an innocent explanation before drawing any inference adverse to the appellant.'[409]

However, in the same case the court reached a different conclusion in relation to the appellant's drugs trial. The Court of Appeal found that the judge did not identify any of the facts relied upon at the trial which the prosecution said that the appellant could reasonably have been expected to mention.[410] It also found that the direction was insufficient because it may have given the impression that the jury might draw an adverse inference because the appellant was sheltering behind his solicitor's advice. It was only possible for the jury to draw such an inference if they were sure, not only that his failure to mention facts was the result of the advice, however adequate or inadequate that explanation might be, but also that the appellant had at that stage no explanation to offer or none that would stand up to questioning or investigation.[411] The Court concluded that the appellant did not receive a fair hearing and the convictions were unsafe notwithstanding the strength of the prosecution case.[412]

6.4 Presumption of Innocence

As well as being an express right under Article 6(2), the presumption of innocence is also an implied right as part of the fair hearing guarantee under Article 6(1).[413] The right is not absolute and may be subject to interferences which pursue a legitimate aim and are proportionate.[414] The fact that the presumption of innocence forms a part of the fair hearing guarantee is particularly important where Article 6(2) does not apply, such as in relation to the making of a confiscation order.

However, although the right applies, it has had little impact. For example, in *R v Rezvi*[415] the House of Lords noted that effective but fair powers of confiscating the proceeds of crime were essential as it was 'notorious fact that professional and habitual criminals frequently take steps to conceal their profits from crime'.[416] It concluded that the statutory measures, which allowed the court to assume that the property held by the defendant within the relevant period was received by him in connection with the commission of offences, was a proportionate response to the problem addressed.[417] Lord Steyn noted that Parliament had attempted to balance the interests of the defendant against that of the public in the following respects: it was only after conviction that the question of confiscation arose; the prosecution had the responsibility for initiating the confiscation proceedings unless the court regarded them as inappropriate; the court

---

[409] *Chenia* (n 405), [60]–[64].
[410] Ibid, [89].
[411] Ibid, [92].
[412] Ibid, [93]. See also *Francom* (n 401); *R v Betts* [2001] 2 Cr App R 257; *R v Robinson* [2003] EWCA Crim 2219. In relation to s 36 of the Criminal Justice and Public Order Act 1994, see *R v Compton* [2002] EWCA Crim 2835.
[413] *Rezvi* (n 125), in reliance upon *Phillips v United Kingdom*, 5 July 2001. See also *McIntosh* (n 12).
[414] *Rezvi*, ibid, per Lord Steyn at [11]; *McIntosh*, ibid.
[415] *Rezvi*, ibid.
[416] Ibid, per Lord Steyn at [14].
[417] Ibid, per Lord Steyn at [16].

must not make a confiscation order if there was a serious risk of injustice; and the role of the court on appeal was to ensure there was no unfairness.[418]

A different issue arose in *Briggs-Price*[419] where the House of Lords held that where the prosecution relied upon criminal offending to prove the existence of benefit in confiscation proceedings, they had to prove that offending and the defendant was presumed innocent until proved guilty. The Crown had to show that the convicted person benefited from drug trafficking and in the opinion of the majority the standard of proof was the criminal standard, ie proof beyond reasonable doubt.[420] However, in *Gale*[421] the Supreme Court held that if confiscation proceedings did not involve a criminal charge, but were subject to the civil standard of proof, there was no reason in principle why confiscation should not be based upon evidence that satisfied the civil standard.[422] The views on standard of proof in *Briggs-Price* were described as obiter.[423]

6.5 Representation

The absence of legal representation may have an adverse affect on the fairness of proceedings. However, there is no absolute right to legal representation. Provided that the court or tribunal is aware of and constantly reminds itself of the duty of fairness, it is very much a matter for the court or tribunal whether it is able to discharge the case fairly if the parties are not represented.[424] In *Pine*[425] the Court of Appeal held that the absence of legal representation before the Solicitors' Disciplinary Tribunal did not lead to unfairness. 'The procedure was not complex. The relevant facts were within the knowledge of Mr Pine. Mr Pine was a solicitor experienced in commercial litigation. Mr Pine had ample opportunity to indicate any defences he might wish to advance.'[426] In *Hammerton*,[427] however, the Court of Appeal found that an absence of legal representation in committal proceedings was in breach of Article 6. It held that a litigant in person who was liable to be sent to prison for contempt of court was entitled to legal representation, if necessary at public expense. 'Where the liberty of the subject is at stake, as it is in contempt proceedings, nobody should be sent to prison without having had the benefit of legal advice and representation.'[428] In addition to the absence of representation, it is possible for inadequate representation to also result in a denial of a fair hearing.[429]

---

[418] Ibid, [86]. See also *R v Benjafield* [2002] UKHL 2, [2003] 1 AC 1099 and *R v Barnham* [2005] EWCA Crim 1049.

[419] *Briggs-Price* (n 187).

[420] Ibid, per Lord Rodger at [77].

[421] *Gale v Serious Organised Crime Agency* [2011] UKSC 49, [2011] 1 WLR 2760.

[422] Ibid, per Lord Phillips at [44] with whom Lord Mance, Lord Judge, Lord Clarke and Lord Reed agreed

[423] Ibid, per Lord Phillips at [54]. See also *Crawford v Department of Agriculture and Rural Development* [2012] NICA 53.

[424] *Re B and T (care proceedings: legal representation)* [2001] 1 FCR 512.

[425] *Pine v Solicitors' Disciplinary Tribunal* [2001] EWCA Crim 1574, [2002] UKHRR 81.

[426] Ibid, [39]. See also *Perotti* (n 298), where the absence of legal representation was considered in the context of denial of access to court, and *Kulkarni v Milton Keynes Hospital NHS Trust* [2009] EWCA Civ 789, [2009] IRLR 829 concerning legal representation before the General Medical Council.

[427] *Hammerton v Hammerton* [2007] EWCA Civ 248, [2007] 2 FLR 1133.

[428] Ibid, [51].

[429] *R v Thakrar* [2001] EWCA Crim 1096.

6.6 Oral Hearing

In order to determine whether an oral hearing is required for a fair hearing in civil cases, the nature of the application must be examined. In *BLCT (13096) Limited*[430] the Court of Appeal held that Article 6 did not require an oral hearing of an application for leave to appeal. The question was a question of law, there was no question of any decision on the facts and there was no question as to a party's credibility.[431] Similarly, in criminal matters there is no absolute right to a oral hearing at every stage in the proceedings.[432]

> Account must be taken of the entirety of the proceedings of which they form part, including those at first instance. Account must also be taken of the role of the person or persons conducting the proceedings that are in question, the nature of the system within which they are being conducted and the scope of the powers that are being exercised. The overriding question, which is essentially a practical one as it depends on the facts of the case, is whether the issues that had to be dealt with at the stage could properly, as a matter of fair trial, be determined without hearing the applicant orally.[433]

Applying these principles in *Dudson*,[434] the House of Lords concluded that it was not obvious, given the comparatively limited nature of the exercise, that an oral hearing was needed to equip the Lord Chief Justice with the information that he needed for the proper conduct of setting the minimum term of the appellant, convicted of murder and sentenced to be detained at Her Majesty's pleasure. It was particularly important that it was not suggested by the appellant's solicitors that an oral hearing was required so that the appellant could appeal in person before the Lord Chief Justice and give evidence. The House of Lords held that all the signs were that an oral hearing would have been a formality as all relevant material was being disclosed and a sufficient opportunity was being given for representations to be made in writing.

It was also argued before the House of Lords in *Hammond*[435] that when setting the minimum term of a life sentence prisoner in accordance with new arrangements made following the reform of the Home Secretary's role, a judge must afford an oral hearing and that the legislative provision which prevented this was incompatible with Article 6. The House of Lords agreed that in this situation fairness would not, in many cases, require an oral hearing. However, in those cases where fairness did require an oral hearing, the legislation, by precluding the possibility of an oral hearing at first instance, was held to be incompatible with the ECHR.[436] Utilising section 3 of the HRA, it was held that the paragraph should be read subject to an implied condition that the judge had the discretion to order an oral hearing where it was required to comply with a prisoner's Article 6 rights.[437]

---

[430] *BLCT* (n 241).
[431] Ibid, [37]–[38].
[432] *R (on the application of Dudson) v Secretary of State for the Home Department* [2005] UKHL 52, per Lord Hope at [34].
[433] Ibid.
[434] Ibid.
[435] *R (Hammond) v Secretary of State for the Home Department* [2005] UKHL 69, [2006] 1 AC 603.
[436] Ibid, per Lord Bingham at [16].
[437] Ibid, per Lord Bingham [17].

6.7 Conducting a Proper Examination

The duty to afford a fair hearing requires the decision maker to conduct a proper examination of the submissions, arguments and evidence adduced by the parties without prejudice to its assessment of whether they are relevant to its decision.[438] Appearances are important, as is public confidence in the administration of justice. In *Stansbury*[439] the Court of Appeal found on the balance of probabilities that a lay member of an Employment Tribunal had consumed alcohol prior to, and fallen asleep during, an unfair dismissal hearing. It therefore concluded that the appellant could not have had the fair hearing to which he was entitled.

6.8 Evidence

6.8.1 Generally

The right to a fair hearing can have an impact on the rules of evidence. What Article 6 does is guarantee a fair trial and so, when the introduction of some form of evidence is said to have infringed the accused's Article 6 rights, the question always is whether admitting the evidence has resulted in the accused not having a fair trial in the circumstances of the particular case.[440] Under the HRA a number of claims have been made concerning different types of evidence, including evidence obtained by entrapment, hearsay evidence and illegally obtained evidence. These are examined in the following paragraphs.

6.8.2 Evidence Obtained by Entrapment

Entrapment occurs when an agent of the state[441] causes someone to commit an offence in order that he should be prosecuted. It is accepted that there are occasions when it is necessary for the police to resort to investigatory techniques in which the police themselves are the reporters and the witnesses of the commission of a crime. However, it is also appreciated that the use of evidence obtained by entrapment may deprive a defendant of the right to a fair trial. Although entrapment is not a substantive defence under English law, the court may stay the proceedings and exclude the evidence under section 78 of the Police and Criminal Evidence Act 1984. This gives the court the power to exclude evidence on which the prosecution proposes to rely if, having regard to all the circumstances, the court considers the admission of the evidence would have such an adverse effect on the fairness of the proceedings that the court ought not to admit it. The grant of a stay is normally regarded as the appropriate response. It has been held that this approach is compatible with Article 6.[442]

---

[438] *Stansbury* (n 52), [28] in reliance upon *Kraska v Switzerland* (1993) 18 EHRR 188.
[439] Ibid.
[440] *Holland* (n 334), per Lord Rodger at [39].
[441] Whilst generally such evidence is obtained by undercover police officers, an agent of the state may also be someone else such as an investigative journalist. See eg *R v Shannon* [2001] 1 WLR 51.
[442] *Attorney General's Reference No 3 of 2000* [2001] UKHL 53, [2001] 1 WLR 2060.

Whilst no two cases are the same, it has been held that a stay should be granted where there has been an abuse of executive power or an affront to public conscience, or where the court's participation in such proceedings would bring the administration of justice into disrepute.[443] The court must balance the competing requirements that those who commit crimes should be convicted and punished and that there should not be an abuse of process which would constitute an affront to public conscience. English courts have placed particular emphasis on

> the need to consider whether a person has been persuaded or pressurised by a law enforcement officer into committing a crime which he would not otherwise had committed, or whether the officer did not go beyond giving the person an opportunity to break the law, when he would have behaved in the same way if some other person had offered him the opportunity to commit a similar crime, and when he freely took advantage of the opportunity presented to him by the officer.[444]

In *R v Loosley*[445] the House of Lords held that the undercover officer and his superiors had reasonable cause to suspect that the defendant was a dealer and that the offer to purchase was in the course of a legitimate undercover purchase and not calculated to cause him to do anything which he would not have done in response to a similar request from any customer. The police did not have to take any steps to persuade him which might have taken them across the boundary between giving him the opportunity to commit the offence and causing him to do so, and the trial judge was right to reject the section 78 application.[446] However, in *Attorney General's Reference No 3 of 2000*, the House of Lords held that the trial judge was right to stay the proceedings. The defendant had never dealt in heroin.

> He was induced to procure heroin for the undercover officer by the prospect of a profitable trade in smuggled cigarettes. The judge was entitled to take the view that even if this was an authorised operation, the police had caused him to commit an offence which he would not otherwise have committed.[447]

6.8.3 *Illegally Obtained Evidence*

Section 78 of the Police and Criminal Evidence Act 1984 also applies to the admission of illegally obtained evidence and it has been confirmed that this approach is compatible with Article 6.[448] A defendant is not entitled to have the illegally obtained evidence excluded simply because it has been illegally obtained. What he is entitled to is an opportunity to challenge its use and admission, and a judicial assessment of the effect

---

[443] Ibid, per Lord Hoffmann at [47].
[444] Ibid, per Lord Hutton at [101].
[445] *R v Loosley* [2001] UKHL 53, [2001] 1 WLR 2060.
[446] Ibid, per Lord Hoffmann at [78].
[447] Ibid, per Lord Hoffmann at [81]. See also *Shannon* (n 441); *Lewis* (n 311). See further A Ashworth, 'Re-drawing the Boundaries of Entrapment' [2002] *Criminal Law Review* 161; S McKay, 'Entrapment: Competing Views on the Effect of the Human Rights Act on English Criminal Law' [2002] *European Human Rights Law Review* 764.
[448] *R v P* [2001] 2 WLR 463 in reliance upon *Schenk v Switzerland* (1988) 13 EHRR 242; *Teixeira de Castro v Portugal* (1998) 28 EHRR 101; *Khan v United Kingdom* (2000) 8 BHRC 310.

of its admission upon the fairness of the trial as provided for by section 78.[449] The same considerations apply to evidence obtained in violation of Article 8.[450]

6.8.4 Evidence Procured by Torture

In *A v Secretary of State for the Home Department*[451] the House of Lords determined on appeal whether the Special Immigration Appeals Commission, when hearing an appeal under the Anti-terrorism, Crime and Security Act 2001, could receive evidence which had been, or may have been, procured by torture inflicted, in order to obtain evidence, by officials of a foreign state without the complicity of British authorities. The House of Lords concluded that such evidence may not be lawfully admitted. Lord Bingham held that the principles of common law alone compelled the exclusion of third-party torture evidence as unreliable, unfair, offensive to ordinary standards of humanity and decency, and 'incompatible with the principles which should animate a tribunal seeking to administer justice'.[452] The same conclusion was reached by giving effect to the ECHR.

However, the House of Lords was divided on the question of standard of proof. The majority concluded that the detainee had to point to the fact that the information which was to be used against him may have come from a country that was alleged to practise torture. The onus then passed to the Special Immigration Appeals Commission which had to decide whether there were reasonable grounds to suspect that torture had been used. If it had such a suspicion, it had to investigate and refuse to admit the evidence if it concluded, on a balance of probabilities that the evidence was obtained by torture.[453]

6.8.5 Hearsay Evidence

Whilst Article 6(3)(d) effectively prohibits the admission of hearsay evidence in criminal proceedings, this does not affect its admission in civil proceedings. However, its admission is not automatic and must be proportionate in the circumstances.[454] In *McCann*[455] the House of Lords characterised the application for an anti-social behaviour order under the Crime and Disorder Act 1998 as determination of civil rights rather than a criminal charge, but held that, given the seriousness of the matters involved, the criminal standard of proof had to be applied. Nevertheless, this did not prevent the admission of hearsay evidence.

[T]he striking of a fair balance between the demands of the general interest of the community (the community in this case being represented by weak and vulnerable people who claim that they are the victims of anti-social behaviour which violates their rights) and the requirements

---

[449] See also *R v Bailey* [2001] EWCA Crim 733; *R v Everson* [2001] EWCA Crim 896.

[450] *R v P* (n 448); *R v Loveridge* [2001] 2 Cr App R 591; *R v Mason* [2002] 2 Cr App R 628; *R v Button* [2005] EWCA Crim 516; *R v Rosenberg* [2006] EWCA Crim 6, [2006] Crim LR 540.

[451] *A v Secretary of State for the Home Department* [2005] UKHL 71, [2006] 2 AC 221.

[452] Ibid, [52].

[453] Ibid, per Lord Hope at [117]–[118]. Lords Bingham, Nicholls and Hoffmann dissented on this point. Lord Bingham stated at [56] that if the SIAC was unable to conclude that there was not a real risk that the evidence had been obtained by torture, it should refuse to admit the evidence.

[454] *McCann* (n 55), [113].

[455] Ibid.

of the protection of the defendants' rights requires the scales to come down in favour of the protection of the community and of permitting the use of hearsay evidence in applications for anti-social behaviour orders.[456]

6.8.6 Dock Identification Evidence

The use of dock identification evidence is not always incompatible with the accused's right to a fair trial.[457] However, particular care must be taken where identification is likely to be a real issue in the case to ensure that the way the evidence is obtained and presented is compatible with Article 6(1).[458] The proper approach is to consider whether, having regard to all the elements of the proceedings, including the way in which the identification evidence was obtained, the accused had a fair trial in terms of Article 6.[459] It has been held that, where such evidence has been admitted, two factors which will weigh in favour of the conclusion that an accused did have a fair trial will be the fact that he was legally represented and that the rights of the defence were respected, with the accused's representative being able to challenge the admissibility of the evidence, to cross-examine the witness and then to address the jury on the weakness of the evidence.

> It will also be important to consider any directions which the judge gave to the jury about the identification evidence. The significance of the contested evidence in the context of the prosecution case as a whole will also be relevant. In particular, was it one of the principal planks in the case against the accused or was there a substantial body of other evidence pointing to his guilt?[460]

6.8.7 Exclusionary Rules

Anything which may prevent an accused person from putting forward evidence critical to his defence is likely to be incompatible with the right to a fair hearing. However, exclusionary rules are possible if these pursue a legitimate aim and are proportionate.[461] An example of the application of this principle is *R v A*[462] where the respondent was due to stand trial for rape. He alleged that, for approximately three weeks prior to the date of the alleged rape, he and the complainant had had a sexual relationship. His defence was that sexual intercourse took place with the complainant's consent or, alternatively, that he believed she consented. At a preparatory hearing, counsel for the respondent applied for leave to cross-examine the complainant about the alleged previous sexual relationship between the complainant and the respondent and to lead evidence about it. Relying on section 41 of the Youth Justice and Criminal Evidence Act 1999, the judge ruled that the complainant could not be cross-examined, nor could evidence be led,

---

[456] Ibid.
[457] *Holland* (n 334), per Lord Hope at [5].
[458] Ibid, per Lord Hope at [6].
[459] Ibid, per Lord Rodger at [41].
[460] Ibid, per Lord Rodger at [42].
[461] *R v A* (n 8).
[462] Ibid.

about her alleged sexual relationship with the defendant and that the prepared statement could not be put in evidence.

The House of Lords held that, on ordinary principles of construction, section 41 was prima facie capable of preventing an accused person from putting forward evidence critical to his defence and, thus construed, was incompatible with Article 6. In Lord Steyn's view, the question was whether, measured against the guarantee of a fair trial, the breadth of exclusionary provisions of section 41 in respect of sexual experience between a complainant and the defendant were justified and proportionate.[463] He concluded that whilst the statute pursued desirable goals, 'the methods adopted amounted to legislative overkill'.[464] A majority of the House of Lords agreed that a declaration of incompatibility could be avoided by applying the interpretative obligation under section 3 of the HRA. The test of admissibility under section 41(3)(c) was held to be whether the evidence (and questioning in relation to it) was nevertheless so relevant to the issue of consent that to exclude it would endanger the fairness of the trial under Article 6. If this test was satisfied, the evidence should not be excluded.[465]

Another example is *R v Connor*[466] where it was argued before the House of Lords that the common law rule which prevented evidence about the deliberations of a jury revealing a lack of impartiality from being admissible, however compelling the evidence, was incompatible with Article 6. A majority found the rule proportionate and consistent with Article 6, holding that the rationality of the rule was incontrovertible.

> The objects of the rule ... provide essential assistance for the jury to operate as a collective body independently of outside influences and be impartial. It helps them to reach a determination of the criminal charge within a reasonable time without the need for retrials every time a juror wanted to change his mind or express his or her dissatisfaction with the reasoning of the majority.[467]

6.8.8 Trial in Absentia

In criminal cases, whilst a defendant has, in general, a right to be present at his trial and a right to be legally represented, these rights can be waived, separately or together, wholly or in part, by the defendant himself. They may be wholly waived if, knowing, or having the means to know, when and where his trial is to take place, he deliberately and voluntarily absents himself and/or withdraws instructions from those representing him. They may be waived in part if, being present and represented at the outset, the defendant, during the course of the trial, behaves in such a way as to obstruct the proper course of the proceedings and/or withdraws his instructions from those representing

---

[463] Ibid, [35].

[464] Ibid, [43]. See also Lord Clyde at [122] and [137].

[465] See also *R v T; R v H* [2001] EWCA Crim 1877, [2001] 1 WLR 632; *R v Soroya* [2006] EWCA Crim 1884, [2007] Crim LR 181; *R v Hamadi* [2007] EWCA Crim 3048. In relation to the Scottish legislation, Sexual Offences (Procedure and Evidence) (Scotland) Act 2002, see *DS v HM Advocate* [2007] UKPC D1, [2007] HRLR 28. See further D Birch, 'Rethinking Sexual History Evidence: Proposals for Fairer Trials' [2002] *Criminal Law Review* 531; A Kavanagh, 'Unlocking the Human Rights Act: The "Radical" Approach to Section 3(1) Revisited' [2005] *European Human Rights Law Review* 259.

[466] *R v Connor; R v Mirza* [2004] UKHL 2, [2004] 1 AC 118.

[467] Ibid, per Lord Hobhouse at [145]–[147]. See also Lord Slynn at [50]–[51], Lord Hope at [129] and Lord Rodger at [168]. Lord Steyn dissented, holding at [4]–[5] and [20] in reliance upon *Remli v France* (1996) 22 EHRR 252 that there was a positive duty on judges to put things right where they had gone wrong.

him.[468] The trial judge has discretion as to whether a trial should take place or continue in the absence of a defendant and/or his legal representatives. That discretion must be exercised with great care, and it is only in rare and exceptional cases that it should be exercised in favour of a trial taking place or continuing, particularly if the defendant is unrepresented.[469] It is generally desirable that a defendant be represented even if he has voluntarily absconded.[470] In exercising that discretion, fairness to the defence is of prime importance but fairness to the prosecution must also be taken into account.[471]

The judge must have regard to all the circumstances of the case, including

- the nature and circumstances of the defendant's behaviour in absenting himself from the trial or disrupting it and whether, in so doing, his behaviour was deliberate, voluntary or as such that he plainly waived his right to appear;
- whether an adjournment might result in the defendant being caught or attending voluntarily and/or not disrupting the proceedings;
- the likely length of such an adjournment;
- whether the defendant, though absent, is, or wishes to be, legally represented at the trial or has, by his conduct, waived his right to representation;
- whether an absent defendant's legal representatives are able to receive instructions from him during the trial and the extent to which they are able to present his defence;
- the extent of the disadvantage to the defendant in not being able to give his account of events, having regard to the nature of the evidence against him;
- the risk of the jury reaching an improper conclusion about the absence of the defendant;
- the general public interest and the particular interest of victims and witnesses that a trial should take place within a reasonable time of the events to which it relates;
- the effect of delay on the memory of the witnesses;
- where there is more than one defendant and not all have absconded, the undesirability of separate trials, and the prospects of a fair trial for the defendants who are present.[472]

If the judge decides that a trial should take place or continue in the absence of an unrepresented defendant, he must ensure that the trial is as fair as the circumstances permit. In particular, he must take reasonable steps, both during the giving of evidence and in the summing up, to expose weaknesses in the prosecution case and to make such points on behalf of the defendant as the evidence permits. In summing up he must warn the jury that absence is not an admission of guilt and adds nothing to the prosecution's case.[473]

In civil cases a litigant whose presence is needed for the fair trial of a case, but who is unable to be present through no fault of his own, will usually have to be granted an adjournment, however inconvenient it may be to the tribunal or court and to the other parties.[474] However, the tribunal or court is entitled to be satisfied that the inability of

---

[468] *R v Hayward; R v Jones* [2001] EWCA Crim 168, [2001] 3 WLR 125, [22] as approved in *R v Jones* [2002] UKHL 5, [2002] 2 WLR 524. It is important to note that the question of waiver was not raised before the House of Lords. However, their Lordships did offer their views, the majority concluding that waiver was possible even if there was no direct evidence to show that the accused knew what the consequences of his absconding would be.

[469] Ibid.

[470] *Jones* (n 468), [15].

[471] *Hayward; Jones* (n 468), [22] as approved in *Jones*, ibid.

[472] Ibid.

[473] Ibid. See also *R v Singh* [2003] EWCA Crim 3712. See further PW Ferguson, 'Trial in Absence and Waiver of Human Rights' [2002] *Criminal Law Review* 554.

[474] *Teinaz v London Borough of Wandsworth* [2002] EWHC Civ 1040, [2002] ICR 1471.

the litigant to be present is genuine, and the onus is on the applicant for an adjournment to prove the need for such an adjournment.[475] In *FP*[476] the Court of Appeal held that immigration rules resulting in asylum appeals being heard in the absence of the claimants, with no further right of appeal, were incompatible with Article 6.

6.9 Reasons

Finally, the right to a fair hearing generally carries with it an obligation to give reasons, although a detailed answer to every argument is not required. The judgment must contain reasons that are sufficient to demonstrate that the essential issues that have been raised by the parties have been addressed by the court and how those issues have been resolved. It is not necessary to go further and explain why one contention, or piece of evidence, has been preferred to another.[477]

> Justice will not be done it if is not apparent to the parties why one has lost and the other has won. Fairness requires that the parties, especially the losing party, should be left in no doubt why they have won or lost.[478]

The extent to which the duty to give reasons applies varies according to the nature of the decision.[479] Where a judicial decision affects the substantive rights of the parties, the decision should be reasoned.[480] However, there are some judicial decisions where fairness does not demand reasons, such as interlocutory decisions in the course of case management. There are also some circumstances in which the reason for the decision will be implicit from the decision itself.[481] Where there are conflicts of expert evidence, the judge should explain why he accepted the evidence of one and rejected the evidence of the other.[482] Where the reason for an order as to costs is not obvious, the judge should explain why he or she has made the order. The explanation can usually be brief.[483]

It has been held that the reasoning of the ECtHR goes no further that that which is required under domestic law.[484] At common law, the adequacy of reasons depends on the nature of the case.[485] If the appellate process is to work satisfactorily, the judgment must enable the appellate court to understand why the judge reached his decision. '[T]he issues the resolution of which were vital to the judge's conclusion should be identified and the manner in which he resolved them explained.'[486]

---

[475] Ibid. See also *Andreou v Lord Chancellor's Department* [2002] EWCA Civ 1192, [2002] IRLR 728; *Re S (a child) (adoption: order made in father's absence)* [2001] 2 FCR 148; *Pine* (n 425); *Estate Acquisition and Development Ltd v Wiltshire* [2006] EWCA Civ 533; *Dhillon v Asiedu* [2012] EWCA Civ 1020.

[476] *FP (Iran) v Secretary of State for the Home Department* [2007] EWCA Civ 13, [2007] Imm AR 450

[477] *English v Emery Reimbold & Strick Ltd* [2002] EWCA Civ 605, [12] in reliance upon *Torija v Spain* (1994) 19 EHRR 553; *Van de Hurk v The Netherlands* (1994) 18 EHRR 481; *Helle v Finland* (1997) 26 EHRR 159.

[478] *Battista v Bassano* [2007] EWCA Civ 370, [28].

[479] *North Range Shipping Ltd v Seatrans Shipping Corporation* [2002] EWHC Civ 405, [2002] 1 WLR 2397, [20] in reliance upon *Hiro Balani v Spain* (1995) 19 EHRR 566, [27].

[480] See eg *Re K (Children)* [2010] EWCA Civ 1365, [2011] 1 FLR 1592 concerning a father's claim for contact with his children.

[481] *English* (n 477), [13].

[482] Ibid, [20].

[483] Ibid, [14].

[484] Ibid, [12].

[485] Ibid, [17].

[486] Ibid, [19].

In *North Range Shipping*[487] the Court of Appeal held that the practice of not giving reasons for granting or refusing leave to appeal from an arbitration award under the Arbitration Act 1996 was incompatible with Article 6. However, whilst it agreed that the judge should inform the unsuccessful applicant for leave about which of the statutory tests he failed, it did not think it necessary for the judge to go further and explain in every case why the relevant threshold test had been failed. Further reasons may be necessary where the issue is whether the tribunal's decision was wrong or not open to serious doubt. However, these need only be brief to show the losing party why he lost.[488]

---

7. Public Hearing and Public Pronouncement

In the determination of civil rights and obligations or a criminal charge, Article 6 requires a public hearing. Such a hearing is of benefit to the individual litigants and the wider public interest.[489] The public nature of the proceedings deters inappropriate behaviour on the part of the members of the court; maintains the public's confidence in the administration of justice by enabling the public to know that justice is being administered impartially; and can result in evidence becoming available which would not be available if the proceedings were conducted behind closed doors or with one or more of the parties' or witnesses' identity concealed.[490] Although it is possible to waive this right, waiver must not run counter to any important public interest.[491]

The right to a public hearing is not absolute. In Article 6 itself it is recognised that the press and public may be excluded in the interests of morals, public order or national security;[492] where the interest of juveniles or the protection of the private life of the parties so require;[493] or to the extent 'strictly necessary' in the opinion of the court in special circumstances where 'publicity would prejudice the interests of justice'. The latter has been held to apply to a situation where a witness refused to give evidence unless the public gallery was cleared.[494] Certain hearings, such as hearings before mental health review tribunals, are always held in private. In such circumstances, it is for the individual who desires a public hearing to demonstrate why the normal rules should not be followed. In *Mersey Care Trust*[495] the patient, Ian Brady, requested that his statutory review before the mental health tribunal be in public. The Divisional Court held that the tribunal had failed to take account of considerations of public order and

---

[487] *North Range Shipping* (n 479).

[488] Ibid, [27]. See also *Threlfall v General Optical Council* [2004] EWHC (Admin) 2683, [2005] Lloyd's Rep Med 250; *R (on the application of Luthra) v General Dental Council* [2004] EWHC (Admin) 458.

[489] *R (on the application of Mersey Care Trust) v Mental Health Review Tribunal* [2004] EWHC (Admin) 1749, [2005] 1 WLR 2469, [13].

[490] Ibid.

[491] Ibid.

[492] See eg *R (A) v B* [2009] UKSC 12, [2010] 2 AC 1.

[493] See eg *Arundel Corporation v Khokher* [2003] EWCA Civ 491.

[494] *R v Richards* [1999] Crim LR 764.

[495] *Mersey Care Trust* (n 489).

security and whether a public hearing would impose a disproportionate burden on the state.[496] It remitted the request to it for rehearing. Prison disciplinary proceedings are also held in private in the prison. In *Bannatyne*[497] the Administrative Court held that this practice was justified given the considerations of public order and the security problems that would be involved if the proceedings were conducted in public.[498]

Violations of the right to a public hearing are rare and have only been found where the judge has received some advice or information in private which has not been repeated in open court. For example, in *Kelly*[499] a majority of the Privy Council held that, in order to comply with Article 6, the advice of the clerk of the Scottish district court to the justice should be disclosed in open court and the parties given the opportunity to comment on it.[500]

Article 6(1) also provides that 'judgment shall be pronounced publicly', and it has been held that it is not possible for a court to simply apply by analogy the same restrictions as are available in relation to holding the trial in public.[501] However, if it is impossible to produce an anonymised or abridged version of the judgment, the interests of justice may permit pronouncement in private.[502]

8. Reasonable Time

8.1 Generally

Article 6 provides that the hearing determining civil rights and obligations or a criminal charge must be held within a reasonable time. This requirement is of benefit both to the individual and to the legal system. In criminal matters it is important that an accused person does not lie under a charge for too long in a state of uncertainty. Delays might jeopardise the effectiveness and credibility of the administration of justice.[503] For example, too long a delay may result in the loss of exculpatory evidence or a deterioration in the quality of evidence generally. The safety of a verdict reached a considerable time after the offence often becomes the subject of controversy and undermines public confidence in the criminal justice system.[504]

---

[496] Ibid, [64] in reliance on *Campbell and Fell v UK* (1985) 7 EHRR 165.

[497] *Bannatyne v Secretary of State for the Home Department* [2004] EWHC (Admin) 1912.

[498] Ibid, [52] in reliance on *Campbell and Fell* (n 496), and *Ezeh and Connors v United Kingdom* Judgment of 15 July 2002. Affirmed by Grand Chamber, 9 October 2003. See also *R (Moor) v Financial Ombudsman Service* [2008] EWCA Civ 642 concerning proceedings of the Financial Ombudsman Service.

[499] *Clark (Procurator Fiscal) v Kelly* [2003] UKPC D1, [2004] 1 AC 681.

[500] Ibid, per Lord Hope at [69] and per Lord Bingham at [7]. See also *The Bow Spring and the Manzanillo II* [2004] EWCA Civ 1007, [2005] 1 Lloyd's Rep 1.

[501] *In the Matter of the Trusts of the X Charity* [2003] EWHC (Ch) 1462, [2003] 1 WLR 2751. See also *Pelling v Bruce-Williams* [2004] EWCA Civ 845, [2004] Fam 155.

[502] *X Charity*, ibid.

[503] *Watson* (n 2), per Lord Bingham at [50] in reliance upon *Wemhoff v Federal Republic of Germany* (1968) 1 EHRR 55, [18]; *Stögmuller v Austria* (1969) 1 EHRR 155; *H v France* (n 26), [58]. See also *Mills* (n 2).

[504] *Mills* (n 2), [14]. See also *Attorney General's Reference No 2 of 2001* (n 1), [16].

The reasonable time requirement is a separate guarantee and is not to be seen as part of the overriding right to a fair trial. It does not require the person concerned to show that he has been prejudiced by the delay.[505] The right is not subject to any words of limitation, nor is it capable of modification on the ground of proportionality. The only question is whether, having regard to all the circumstances of the case, the time taken to determine the person's rights and obligations or criminal charge is unreasonable.[506] The question of remedy is complicated and is considered in detail at the end of this section. Article 5(3) also provides for trial within a reasonable time and the ECtHR case law concerning both Articles has often been considered together.[507]

8.2 Criminal Proceedings

8.2.1 Start of the Time Period

When considering the start of the relevant time period, regard must be had to the purpose of the reasonable time requirement—which is to ensure that criminal proceedings, once initiated, are prosecuted without undue delay so as to protect defendants from the trauma of awaiting trial for inordinate periods.[508] As a general rule, the relevant time period begins at the earliest time at which a person is officially alerted to the likelihood of criminal proceedings against him. Ordinarily this will be when a defendant is formally charged or served with a summons, but this rule is not inflexible.[509] Interviewing for the purposes of a regulatory inquiry in England and Wales will not meet this test.[510] Nor, ordinarily, will time begin to run until after the suspect has been interviewed under caution. Arrest will not ordinarily mark the beginning of the period, but an official indication that a person will be reported with a view to prosecution may do so.[511] The period ends when there is a determination of the charge and it includes the time taken by any appeal.[512]

In *Burns*[513] the appellant argued that the reasonable time started in February 2003 when he was arrested, interviewed and released on bail in England, rather than in December 2004 when he was indicted to stand trial on the same matter in Scotland. The Privy Council held that the time started in February 2003. Lord Rodger observed that it would be 'highly artificial' to treat the actions of the prosecuting authorities in Scotland as if they could be divorced from all that went before in England. 'This is particularly so when the prosecution relies on those actions.'[514] He also took into account wider considerations noting that the United Kingdom, rather than Scotland or England, was the party to the ECHR.

---

[505] *Porter* (n 2), [109].
[506] Ibid. See also *Watson* (n 2), per Lord Bingham at [50] and per Lord Hope at [73]; *Mills* (n 2), per Lord Steyn at [9].
[507] *Watson* (n 2), [30].
[508] *Attorney General's Reference No 2 of 2001* (n 1), per Lord Bingham at [27].
[509] Ibid.
[510] See eg *R v James* [2002] EWCA Crim 119.
[511] *Attorney General's Reference No 2 of 2001* (n 1), per Lord Bingham at [28].
[512] *HM Advocate v R* [2002] UKPC D3, [2004] 1 AC 462.
[513] *Burns v HM Advocate* [2008] UKPC 63, [2009] 1 AC 720.
[514] Ibid, [23].

[T]he way that the United Kingdom has chosen to distribute its criminal jurisdiction cannot impair or defeat an accused's right to be tried on a criminal charge within a reasonable time ... it is appropriate to look at the sum total of the actions of the competent English and Scottish authorities.[515]

8.2.2 Determining a Reasonable Time

It is not possible to identify from the case law a tariff by reference to which decisions may be taken as to whether a given period of delay is or is not acceptable. Each case must be judged according to its own facts and circumstances.[516] Whilst this right is important and should not be watered down or weakened, it has been held that the individual does not enjoy these rights in a vacuum. 'He is a member of society and other members of society also have interests deserving of respect.'[517] There is a public interest in the bringing to trial of those reasonably suspected of committing crimes and, if they are not convicted, in their being appropriately sentenced.[518]

The threshold of proving a breach of the reasonable time requirement is a high one, not easily crossed. The first step is to consider the period of time which has elapsed.

Unless that period is one which, on its face and without more, gives grounds for real concern it is almost certainly unnecessary to go further, since the convention is directed not to departures from the ideal but to infringements of basic human rights.[519]

Next it is necessary for the court to look into the detailed facts and circumstances of the particular case, and for the state to explain and justify any lapse of time which appears to be excessive.[520] In accordance with ECtHR case law, three areas call for particular inquiry. The first is the complexity of the case.

It is recognised, realistically enough, that the more complex a case, the greater the number of witnesses, the heavier the burden of documentation, the longer the time which must necessarily be taken to prepare it adequately for trial and for any appellate hearing. But with any case, however complex, there comes a time when the passage of time becomes excessive and unacceptable.[521]

The second matter is the conduct of the defendant.

In almost any fair and developed legal system it is possible for a recalcitrant defendant to cause delay by making spurious applications and challenges, changing legal advisers, absenting himself, exploiting procedural technicalities, and so on. A defendant cannot properly complain of delay of which he is the author. But procedural time-wasting on his part does not entitle the prosecuting authorities themselves to waste time unnecessarily and excessively.[522]

---

[515] Ibid, [27].

[516] *Watson* (n 2), per Lord Hope at [74] in reliance upon *Stögmuller* (n 503); *Obermeier v Austria* (1990) 13 EHRR 290.

[517] *Watson* (n 2), per Lord Bingham at [51] in reliance upon *Sporrong and Lönnroth v Sweden* (1982) 5 EHRR 35; *Soering v United Kingdom* (1989) 11 EHRR 439; *B v France* (1992) 16 EHRR 1; *Doorson v The Netherlands* (1996) 22 EHRR 330.

[518] *Watson* (n 2), per Lord Bingham at [51].

[519] Ibid, [52].

[520] Ibid, [52].

[521] Ibid, [53].

[522] Ibid, [54].

The third matter is the manner in which the case has been dealt with by the administrative and judicial authorities. It is generally incumbent on contracting states to organise their legal systems so as to ensure that the reasonable time requirement is honoured. But nothing in the convention jurisprudence requires courts to 'shut their eyes to the practical realities of litigious life even in a reasonably well-organised legal system.' However,

> a marked lack of expedition, if unjustified, will point towards a breach of the reasonable time requirement, and the authorities make clear that while, for the purposes of the reasonable time requirement, time runs from the date when the defendant is charged, the passage of any considerable period of time before charge may call for greater than normal expedition thereafter.[523]

8.2.3 Application

Given that each case is judged on its own facts and circumstances, what was a reasonable time in one case may not necessarily be reasonable in another. However, it is useful to consider some examples, such as the appeals determined by the Privy Council in *Watson*.[524] In the first case, police officers had been charged with perjury and 20 months had elapsed between charge and trial, although they were not in custody over this period. The Privy Council held that, although a shorter period would be desirable, this was not a period which caused real concern 'such as to suggest that a basic human right of the officers may have been infringed.'[525] It found a strong public interest in the integrity of the police and the interest of individual officers in vindicating their reputations, which required a careful and independent investigation. This inevitably took time and no violation was found.[526]

In the second case, 27 months had elapsed between the charge and the service of the indictment and 28 months would have elapsed had the trial proceeded as planned. During the period JK was not in custody, but he was a child at the time of the alleged offences. The Privy Council held that, when dealing with children, the reasonable time requirement had to be read in light of the UN Convention on the Rights of the Child, which required all due expedition.[527] In particular, delay may prejudice the fairness of the trial as a more mature accused may make a different impression and delay prolongs the stress to which a vulnerable accused is inevitably subject, and puts off the date at which his problems can be addressed and full counselling given.[528] The Privy Council found that this was not a complex case and it was not suggested that JK was responsible for the delay. There was no attempt to treat the case with the urgency which it deserved. A breach of the reasonable time requirement was found.[529]

---

[523] Ibid, [55]. See also Lord Hope at [76]–[77]. Lord Hope also noted at [83] that the reasonable time guarantee should not be seen as an impediment to maintaining high standards in the system of public prosecution.

[524] Ibid.

[525] Ibid, per Lord Bingham at [56].

[526] Ibid, [58].

[527] Ibid, [61].

[528] Ibid, [62].

[529] Ibid, [63]–[64]. See also *HM Advocate v R* (n 512), where the appellant was charged in 1995 and not indicted for trial until 2001. A breach of the reasonable time guarantee was assumed. See also *James* (n 510); *R v Coates* [2004] EWCA Crim 3049.

8.3 Civil Proceedings

8.3.1 Start of the Time Period

With respect to civil proceedings, time usually begins to run from the date when the proceedings in question are initiated.[530] In *Porter*[531] it was held that the time began to run from the date when the objections which gave rise to the investigation were received by the auditor.[532] What is of concern is procedural delay in the course of proceedings, not the delay between the commission of the allegedly wrongful actions and the commencement of proceedings.[533]

8.3.2 Determining a Reasonable Time

When determining the reasonableness of the duration of the proceedings, the same criteria as used in criminal proceedings apply.[534] Again, it all depends on the facts and circumstances of the case, but some examples are useful. In *Porter*[535] the House of Lords concluded that there was no basis for the suggestion that there was an unreasonable delay at the Divisional Court stage, having regard to the complexity of the issues and the volume of evidence that had to be prepared and presented.[536] Similarly, the 65 months which elapsed before the auditor issued his decision and certificates of surcharge was found to be reasonable. The House of Lords found that his investigation was vast and that he was constantly in action.[537]

In *Haikel*,[538] although no explanation was offered for the period of 22 months between the letter from the General Medical Council to the appellant and the commencement of the hearing, the Privy Council concluded it was reasonable.

> There was no evidence or suggestion by the Appellant that he had suffered any material prejudice in addition to the lapse of time. There was no complaint that witnesses were no longer available who would have been but for the delay. The records of the patients were available and full.[539]

8.4 Remedy

The reasonable time requirement is a separate guarantee which is not to be seen simply as part of the overriding right to a fair trial.[540] A violation may be found in the absence of any prejudice to the fairness of the defendant's trial.[541] Therefore, the consequences

---

[530] *Porter* (n 2), [107] in reliance upon *Ausiello v Italy* (1996) 24 EHRR 568 at [18].
[531] Ibid.
[532] Ibid, [107].
[533] *Haikel v The General Medical Council* [2002] UKPC 37, [2002] Lloyd's Rep 415, [14].
[534] *Porter* (n 2), per Lord Hope at [107] in reliance upon *König* (n 36), [99].
[535] Ibid.
[536] Ibid, [111].
[537] Ibid, [112]–[114].
[538] *Haikel* (n 533).
[539] Ibid, [14].
[540] *Porter*, *Watson* and *Mills* (n 2).
[541] *Watson* (n 2), per Lord Bingham at [50].

of any breach or threatened breach need to be considered separately. There has been little discussion in the jurisprudence of the appropriate remedy in civil proceedings.[542] However, the question of remedy in criminal proceedings has received detailed consideration.

8.4.1 Criminal Proceedings: Pre-conviction

A majority of the House of Lords held in *Attorney General's Reference No 2 of 2001*[543] that if, through the action or inaction of a public authority, a criminal charge was not determined at a hearing within a reasonable time, there must be afforded such remedy as may be just and appropriate:

> The appropriate remedy will depend on the nature of the breach and all the circumstances, including particularly the stage of the proceedings at which the breach is established. If the breach is established before the hearing, the appropriate remedy may be a public acknowledgement of the breach, action to expedite the hearing to the greatest extent practicable and perhaps, if the defendant is in custody, his release on bail. It will not be appropriate to stay or dismiss the proceedings unless (a) there can no longer be a fair hearing or (b) it would otherwise be unfair to try the defendant. The public interest in the final determination of criminal charges requires that such a charge should not be stayed or dismissed if any lesser remedy will be just and proportionate in all the circumstances.[544]

The majority confirmed that to hold a trial after the lapse of a reasonable time would not in itself be a breach of a Convention right and therefore it would not in itself comprise unlawful conduct under section 6 of the HRA.[545] Lord Bingham appreciated that it was a powerful argument that, if a public authority caused or permitted such delay to occur that a criminal charge could not be heard against a defendant within a reasonable time, so breaching his right under Article 6(1), any further prosecution or trial of the charge must be unlawful within the meaning of the Article. But he cited four reasons which compelled its rejection.

First, it would be anomalous if breach of the reasonable time requirement had an effect more far-reaching than breach of the defendant's other Article 6 rights when the breach did not taint the basic fairness of the hearing at all, and even more anomalous

---

[542] In *R v Gorman*, 2 April 2004, the Court of Appeal held that a delay of over seven years in granting leave to appeal against a confiscation order violated the reasonable time guarantee and resulted in the quashing of the order. See also *R v Goring* [2004] EWCA Crim 969 and *In the Matter of Saggar*, Court of Appeal [2005] EWCA Civ 174. In *Bangs v Connex South Eastern Ltd* [2005] EWCA Civ 14, [2005] 2 All ER 316, in the context of an Employment Tribunal's delay, the Court of Appeal held that the question was whether, due to the delay, there was a real risk of denial of a fair trial and whether it was unjust or unfair to allow the decision to stand.

[543] *Attorney General's Reference No 2 of 2001* (n 1).

[544] Ibid, per Lord Bingham at [24], with whom Lords Nicholls, Steyn, Hoffmann, Hobhouse and Scott agreed. Lord Bingham thought it unwise to attempt to describe the category of cases in which it may be unfair to try a defendant but did cite as possible examples bad faith, unlawfulness, executive manipulation or extreme breach of prosecutor's professional duty. Lords Hope and Rodger agreed that the remedy must be that which was just and appropriate, but held that to hold the trial after a lapse of a reasonable time was itself a breach of Art 6. For application of this principle, see *R v Wheeler* [2004] EWCA Crim 572.

[545] *Attorney General's Reference No 2 of 2001* (n 1), per Lord Nicholls at [38]–[39]. Lords Hope and Rodger dissented on this point. The majority pointed out that, if the very holding of the trial by the court would be unlawful, the trial must be stayed. Lord Bingham at [30] could not accept that it could ever be proper for a court, whose purpose was to uphold, vindicate and apply the law, to act in a manner which a statute declared to be unlawful.

that the right to a hearing should be vindicated by ordering that there be no trial at all.[546] Second, he pointed out that a rule of automatic termination of proceedings on breach of the reasonable time requirement could not sensibly be applied in civil proceedings. '[T]ermination of the proceedings would defeat the claimant's right to a hearing altogether and seeking to make good his loss in compensation from the state could well prove a very unsatisfactory alternative.'[547]

Third, a rule of automatic termination had been shown to have the effect in practice of emasculating the right which the guarantee was designed to protect. 'There is, however, a very real risk that if proof of a breach is held to require automatic termination of the proceedings the judicial response will be to set the threshold unacceptably high.'[548]

Fourthly, Lord Bingham found that the Strasbourg jurisprudence gave no support to the contention that there should be no hearing of a criminal charge once a reasonable time had passed.[549] Finally, his Lordship did not accept that 'compatible' bore a different meaning under the HRA to the Scotland Act, even though the statutory consequence was 'unlawfulness in the one instance' and 'lack of power in the other'. In each case the act was one that may not lawfully be done.[550] The Privy Council determined in *Spiers v Ruddy*[551] that the law was the same in Scotland and England and that the Lord Advocate did not act incompatibly with a person's Convention right by continuing to prosecute him after a breach of the reasonable time guarantee had occurred.

8.4.2 Criminal Proceedings: Post-conviction

Where there has been a breach of the reasonable time guarantee, setting aside a conviction is not a necessary consequence.[552] The appropriate remedy may be a public acknowledgement of the breach, a reduction in the penalty imposed on a convicted defendant or the payment of compensation to an acquitted defendant.[553] For example, in *Mills*[554] the appellant complained of a breach of the guarantee where there had been a delay in the hearing of his appeal of about 12 months for which the Crown was unable to give any explanation. The Privy Council found no precedent in domestic law for the setting aside of a conviction, which had been upheld on appeal as a sound conviction, on the ground that there was an unreasonable delay between the date of the conviction and the hearing of the appeal.[555] Taking into account the anxiety resulting from prolongation of the proceedings, and the fact that his life had changed during the period of the delay, the Privy Council concluded that the decision of the High Court

---

[546] Ibid, [20].
[547] Ibid, [21].
[548] Ibid, [22].
[549] Ibid, [23] citing *X v Germany* (1980) 25 DR 142; *Eckle v Germany* (1982) 5 EHRR 1; *Neuback v Germany* (1983) 41 DR 13; *Bunkate v Netherlands* (1995) 19 EHRR 477; *Beck v Norway*, Judgment of 26 June 2001.
[550] *Attorney General's Reference No 2 of 2001* (n 1), [30]. The majority held that *R v Lord Advocate* was wrongly decided. See further J Jackson and J Johnstone, 'The Reasonable Time Requirement: an Independent and Meaningful Right?' [2005] *Criminal Law Review* 3.
[551] *Spiers v Ruddy* [2007] UKPC D2, [2008] 1 AC 873.
[552] *Mills* (n 2), per Lord Hope at [41] in reliance upon *Bunkate* (n 549).
[553] *Attorney General's Reference No 2 of 2001* (n 1), per Lord Bingham at [24]. In *R v Shaw* [2011] EWCA Crim 98 the length of sentences imposed were reduced.
[554] *Mills* (n 2).
[555] Ibid, per Lord Hope at [52].

of Justiciary to reduce his sentence by nine months in order to compensate him for the effects of the delay was an appropriate and sufficient remedy.[556]

9. Independent and Impartial Tribunal

9. 1 Generally

When civil rights and obligations, or a criminal charge, are being determined, Article 6(1) provides that the hearing must be conducted by an independent and impartial tribunal.[557] Justice must not only be done, it must be seen to be done. The function of this right is not only to ensure that the tribunal is free from any actual or personal bias or prejudice; it also requires this matter to be viewed objectively so as to exclude any legitimate doubt as to the tribunal's independence and impartiality.[558] This part of Article 6(1) is not subject to any words of limitation and does not require or permit a balance to be struck between the right to an independent and impartial tribunal and other considerations, such as the public interest.[559] Independence and impartiality is an essential element if the trial is to satisfy the overriding requirement of fairness.[560] Nevertheless, it has been held that the rule of law lies at the heart of the Convention and it is not the purpose of Article 6 to make it impracticable to bring those who are accused of crime to justice.[561]

In common with the rights already examined, this right is separate and there is no room for the argument that the question of whether there was a breach could be tested after the event by asking whether the proceedings overall were fair.[562] To remedy a breach, a declaratory judgment and damages are possible. In criminal cases, if there has been a breach, a conviction must be quashed although it is possible to order a retrial.[563]

---

[556] Ibid, per Lord Hope at [55] in reliance upon *Bunkate* (n 549); *Eckle v Germany* (1983) 13 EHRR 556; *Beck v Norway*, Judgment of 26 June 2001. See also Lord Steyn at [16].

[557] This does not require the prosecutor to also be independent and impartial *R (Haase) v Independent Adjudicator* [2008] EWCA Civ 1089, [2009] QB 550.

[558] *Millar v Procurator Fiscal* [2001] 1 WLR 1615, per Lord Hope at [63] in reliance upon *McGonnell v United Kingdom* (2000) 30 EHRR 289; *Findlay v United Kingdom* (1997) 24 EHRR 221; *Rimmer v HM Advocate*, 23 May 2001.

[559] *Montgomery* (n 167); *Baragiola v Switzerland* (1993) 75 DR 76 distinguished.

[560] *Millar* (n 558), per Lord Hope at [52].

[561] *Montgomery* (n 167), per Lord Hope in reliance upon *Pullar v United Kingdom* (1996) 22 EHRR 391. See also *Preiss* (n 49), and the comments of Lord Hope in *Davidson v Scottish Ministers* [2004] UKHL 34, [2004] HRLR 34, [49].

[562] *Millar* (n 558), per Lord Hope at [66].

[563] *HM Advocate v R* (n 512), per Lord Steyn at [8]. See also *Attorney General's Reference No 2 of 2001* (n 1).

9.2 Test for Independence and Impartiality

There is a close relationship between the concept of independence and that of impartiality.

> In both cases the concept requires not only that the tribunal must be truly independent and free from actual bias, proof of which is likely to be very difficult, but also that it must not appear in the objective sense to lack these essential qualities.[564]

9.2.1 Subjective Test

The tribunal must actually be independent and impartial. Proof of actual lack of impartiality or independence is usually very difficult and such cases are unusual. Some examples would be if a judge has a personal interest, which is not negligible, in the outcome of the case; is a friend or relation of a party or a witness; or is disabled by personal experience from bringing an objective judgment to bear on the case in question. 'What disqualifies the judge is the presence of some factor which could prevent the bringing of an objective judgment to bear, which could distort the judge's judgment.'[565]

9.2.2 Objective Test

The objective test for independence and impartiality exists because the appearance of independence and impartiality is just as important as the question of whether those qualities exist in fact. Justice must not only be done, it must be seen to be done.[566] The common law test for bias originally formulated in *R v Gough*[567] has now been modified. Under Article 6, the court must ascertain all the circumstances which have a bearing on the suggestion that the judge was biased. It must then ask whether those circumstances would lead a fair-minded and informed observer to conclude that there was a real possibility that the tribunal was biased.[568] It is unnecessary to delve into the characteristics to be attributed to the observer. One is entitled to conclude that such an observer will adopt a balanced approach, neither complacent nor unduly sensitive or suspicious.[569] This test applies to both independence[570] and impartiality.[571]

When applying the test it is important that account is taken of all the circumstances. For example, in *Montgomery*[572] it was argued that there could not be a fair trial because of the impact pre-trial publicity would have on a jury. The Privy Council noted that the question was not confined to the residual effect of the publicity on the minds of each

---

[564] *Porter* (n 2), [88] in reliance on *Findlay* (n 558), [73].
[565] *Davidson* (n 561).
[566] *Millar* (n 558), per Lord Hope at [63], in reliance upon *McGonnell v United Kingdom*; *Findlay* (n 558); *Rimmer v HM Advocate*, 23 May 2001.
[567] *R v Gough* [1993] AC 646.
[568] *Porter* (n 2), per Lord Hope at [103]. See also *Director General of Fair Trading v The Proprietary Association of Great Britain* [2001] 1 WLR 700.
[569] *Lawal v Northern Spirit Ltd* [2003] UKHL 35, [2004] 1 All ER 187.
[570] *Boyd v The Army Prosecuting Authority* [2002] UKHL 31, [2003] 1 AC 734.
[571] *Porter* (n 2).
[572] *Montgomery* (n 167).

of the jurors. Account also had to be taken of the part the judge would play in order to ensure, so far as possible, that the defendants would receive a fair trial.[573]

9.2.3 Rehearing: Generally

The prospect of a complete rehearing of the case must also be taken into account. For example, in *Preiss*[574] the Privy Council, acting in the capacity of hearing appeals from decisions of the Professional Conduct Committee of the General Dental Council, held that the points taken under Article 6(1) could not succeed if the Privy Council was prepared to conduct a complete rehearing of the case, including a full reconsideration of the facts and of the question of whether the facts amounted to serious professional misconduct. Similarly, in *Porter*,[575] in relation to the multiplicity of roles performed by the auditor,[576] the House of Lords held that there was no breach of Article 6(1) if the proceedings were subject to subsequent control by a judicial body that had full jurisdiction and did provide the guarantees of Article 6(1).[577] Here the powers of the Divisional Court fully satisfied the requirements. It had the power to quash the decision taken by the auditor, to rehear the case and to take a fresh decision itself in the exercise of the powers given to the auditor.[578]

However, it is not clear whether a rehearing can cure a breach in criminal proceedings. To date the issue has only arisen in cases under the Scotland Act 1998. *Millar*[579] concerned four individuals who were the subject of criminal proceedings before temporary sheriffs, although the Scottish High Court had held that temporary sheriffs were not independent and impartial within the meaning of Article 6.[580] The Privy Council held that independence and impartiality of the tribunal in criminal cases was not a matter that could be cured by the existence of a right of appeal to a court which itself satisfied the requirements of Article 6(1).[581] The appearance that justice was being done was as important as the actual doing of justice. 'The independence of the judiciary is not an empty principle which can be forgotten simply because one thinks that a correct conclusion has been reached.'[582]

A different conclusion was reached in *Clark*,[583] which concerned the role of the clerk of the Scottish district court in criminal proceedings. It was alleged that, in trials in the district court, legal decisions were effectively taken by the clerk, who lacked the necessary independence for the purposes of Article 6(1). Finding that the clerk was a part of the court, the Privy Council held that, in order to determine whether the court lacked independence and impartiality due to the role of the clerk, it had to be looked

---

[573] Ibid, per Lord Hope in reliance upon *Pullar* (n 561).

[574] *Preiss* (n 49).

[575] *Porter* (n 2).

[576] He conducted the investigation, took the decision whether there was a case to answer, tried the case, assessed the loss and then appeared in the Divisional Court to defend his decision and his conduct.

[577] Ibid, [93] in reliance upon *Kingsley v United Kingdom*, 7 November 2000, [51] and [58]; *Bryan* (n 106), [44] and [46].

[578] *Porter* (n 2), per Lord Hope at [93].

[579] *Millar* (n 558).

[580] *Starrs v Ruxton* [2000] JC 208.

[581] *Millar* (n 558), per Lord Clyde at [81] in reliance upon *De Cubber v Belgium* (1984) 7 EHRR 236; *Findlay* (n 558).

[582] Ibid, [83].

[583] *Clark* (n 499).

at as a whole in the context of the procedures available for appeal and for the review of its decisions on the ground of alleged miscarriages of justice.[584] Even though the High Court did not have power to rehear the case, it had full power to re-examine all questions of law, practice and procedure, and to substitute its own decision on these matters for decisions taken by the justice on the advice of the clerk. The Privy Council held that this was sufficient to meet the requirements of Article 6(1).[585]

9.2.4 Rehearing: Administrative Decisions

Rehearing is particularly important in the context of administrative decision making, where it has been held that a breach of the guarantee of independence and impartiality can be overcome by the existence of a sufficient opportunity for appeal or review.[586] It has been held that such an approach takes into account democratic accountability, efficient administration and the sovereignty of Parliament.[587] What is required is sufficient judicial control to ensure a determination by an independent and impartial tribunal subsequently. This does not necessarily mean jurisdiction to re-examine the merits of the case but jurisdiction to deal with the case as the nature of the decision requires.[588]

In *Alconbury*,[589] although it had been found that the Secretary of State in his planning capacity was not an independent and impartial tribunal for the purposes of Article 6(1) due to the jurisdiction of the High Court to exercise judicial review, the House of Lords concluded that there was sufficient judicial control to ensure a subsequent determination by an independent and impartial tribunal.[590] Similarly in *Begum*,[591] the question was whether the provision of an appeal to the county court on a point of law from a review of a council housing decision conducted by the council's rehousing manager was sufficient. The House of Lords noted that the appeal against the enforcement notice was closely analogous to a criminal trial.[592] However, it also had regard to democratic accountability, efficient administration and the sovereignty of Parliament.[593] It noted that Parliament was entitled to take the view that it was not in the public interest that an excessive proportion of the funds available for a welfare scheme should be consumed in administration and legal disputes.[594] Nothing was found to recommend recourse to contracting out,[595] and the House of Lords concluded that, in the case of a Part VII Housing Act decision involving no human rights other than Article 6, a

---

[584] Ibid, per Lord Hope at [55].
[585] Ibid, per Lord Hope at [58] in reliance upon *Albert and Le Compte* (n 106), [29]; *Bryan v UK* (n 106).
[586] *Alconbury* (n 19).
[587] *Begum* (n 23), per Lord Hoffmann at [35].
[588] Ibid, per Lord Hoffmann at [33] and [35] and his Lordship's comments in *Alconbury* (n 19), [129].
[589] *Alconbury*, ibid.
[590] Whilst Lord Slynn agreed that the current scope of judicial review was sufficient to comply with Art 6(1), he also held that the time had come to recognise that the principle of proportionality was part of English administrative law and that the court also had jurisdiction to quash for a misunderstanding or ignorance of an established and relevant fact. See [51] and [53]. See also the comments of Lord Nolan at [61], Lord Hoffmann at [128] and Lord Clyde at [159].
[591] *Begum* (n 23).
[592] Ibid, per Lord Hoffmann at [42] in reliance upon *De Cubber* (n 581).
[593] Ibid, [43].
[594] Ibid, [44].
[595] Ibid, [46].

conventional judicial review was sufficient and the right of appeal to the county court was sufficient to satisfy Article 6.[596]

9.3 Separation of Powers

Beyond the objective and subjective tests for independence and impartiality, the principle of separation of powers has also found expression via Article 6. In *Anderson*,[597] in addition to the application of Article 6 to the facts, many references were also made to the separation of powers. Lord Bingham, commenting on the ECtHR's conclusion in *Stafford*, noted that it was right to describe the complete functional separation of the judiciary from the executive as fundamental 'since the rule of law depends on it'.[598] Lord Steyn observed that the principle of separation of powers was not something that arrived in our legal system at the same time as the HRA:

> [T]he separation of powers between the judiciary and the legislative and executive branches of government is a strong principle of our system of government. The House of Lords and Privy Council have so stated. … It is reinforced by constitutional principles of judicial independence, access to justice, and the rule of law.[599]

His Lordship pointed out that the decision to punish an offender by ordering him to serve a period of imprisonment was historically a decision which may only be made by the courts, and this idea was a principle feature of the rule of law on which the unwritten constitution was based. Although it had been overridden by Parliament, in his view the courts now had the ability to determine the compatibility of that statute with Article 6(1).[600] He also noted that in *Stafford* the ECtHR was rightly influenced by the strengthening of the principle of separation of powers between the executive and judiciary which underlies Article 6(1).[601]

However, it is not clear whether a court would find a violation of Article 6(1) if there were no legitimate doubt as to independence or impartiality but simply a violation of the separation of powers. In *Davidson*[602] Lord Hope stated that arguments based on the theory of the separation of powers alone would not suffice[603] and this is in keeping with Strasbourg authority. In *Kleyn v The Netherlands*[604] the ECtHR held that, although the notion of separation of powers had assumed growing importance in the Court's case law, neither Article 6 nor any other provision of the Convention required states to

---

[596] Ibid, [50] and [58]. See also Lord Bingham at [9]–[10]. In *Adan* (n 60), per Brooke LJ at [42], the Court of Appeal noted that if, on such a review, there was a dispute about the primary facts of a kind which had to be resolved because it was material to the decision-making process, there was a danger the proceedings as a whole would not be Convention compliant. See further *R (on the application of McLellan) v Bracknell Forest Borough Council* [2001] EWCA Civ 1510, [2002] QB 1129; *Beeson* (n 38).

[597] *Anderson* (n 171).

[598] Ibid, [27].

[599] Ibid, [39].

[600] Ibid, [51].

[601] Ibid, [54]; and per Lord Hutton at [76]. See also *Millar* (n 558).

[602] *Davidson* (n 561).

[603] Ibid, [53].

[604] *Kleyn v The Netherlands* Judgment of 6 May 2003.

comply with any theoretical constitutional concepts regarding the permissible limits of the powers' interaction.[605]

Regardless of whether or not the ECtHR continues to develop the principle of separation of powers, under the HRA British judges now have a far greater opportunity to uphold the principle than they have had in the past.[606] Recent reforms to the office of Lord Chancellor and the creation of the Supreme Court were clearly driven in part by Article 6.[607]

9.4 Waiver

It is possible to waive the entitlement to a determination by an independent and impartial tribunal.[608] Waiver results from a voluntary, informed and unequivocal election by a party not to claim a right or raise an objection which it is open to that party to claim or raise. The waiver must be voluntary, and it cannot be meaningfully said that a party has voluntarily elected not to claim a right or raise an objection if he was unaware that it was open to him to make the claim or raise the objection. For a waiver to be effective it must be unequivocal, which means clear and unqualified. Ignorance of the law does not suffice to found a plea of waiver.[609] Waiver was argued in *Millar*,[610] but the Privy Council held that it was impossible to accept that the qualification of temporary sheriffs was generally known to be open to serious question or that the representatives of the accused were subject to no misapprehension attributable to some established view of what the law was.[611] In *Ablyazov*[612] the Court of Appeal found that the appellant had waived his rights under Article 6(1) as he had failed to object to the judge, who had earlier found him guilty of contempt of court, as the judge in subsequent proceedings brought against him to freeze his assets.[613]

---

[605] Ibid, [193]. The applicants alleged that the Administrative Jurisdiction Division of the Netherlands Council of State was not independent and impartial in that the Council exercised both advisory and judicial functions. It was also alleged that the procedure for appointment to the Council of State meant that it had to be regarded as part of the legislature and executive. All Councillors are appointed by Royal Decree (Koninklijk Besluit) following nomination by the Minister of the Interior and Kingdom Relations in agreement with the Minister of Justice. The Court (Grand Chamber) held by 12 votes to 5 that there had been no violation of Art 6(1). See also *McGonnell v United Kingdom* (2000) 30 EHRR 289; *Pabla Ky v Finland*, 22 June 2004.

[606] The independence and impartiality of the judiciary has been upheld via the principles of natural justice. Separation-of-powers principles have influenced the conclusions of the court in several cases. See eg *Gouriet v Union of Post Office Workers* [1978] AC 435; *Duport Steels Ltd v Sirs* (1980) 1 WLR 142; *M v Home Office* [1994] 1 AC 377; *R v Secretary of State for the Home Department, ex p Fire Brigades Union* [1995] 2 AC 513.

[607] See N Barber, 'Prelude to the Separation of Powers' [2001] *Cambridge Law Journal* 59 and Lord Steyn, 'The Case for a Supreme Court' [2002] 118 *Law Quarterly Review* 382, 383. See also R Cornes, 'McGonnell v United Kingdom, the Lord Chancellor and the Law Lords' [2000] *Public Law* 166; and ME Amos, 'R v Secretary of State for the Home Department, ex p Anderson—Ending the Home Secretary's Sentencing Role' (2004) 67 *Modern Law Review* 108.

[608] *Millar* (n 558).

[609] Ibid, per Lord Bingham at [31] in reliance upon *Deweer* (n 179); *Pfeifer and Plankl v Austria* (1992) 14 EHRR 692. See also Lord Hope at [53]–[58] and Lord Clyde at [81].

[610] *Millar* (n 558).

[611] Ibid, per Lord Bingham at [38].

[612] *JSC BTA Bank v Ablyazov* [2012] EWCA Civ 1551, [2013] 1 WLR 1845.

[613] Ibid, [92].

9.5 Application

As with other Article 6 rights, whether or not the rights to independence and impartiality are satisfied depends very much on the circumstances of the case. Precedent can be helpful in focusing the mind on the relevant issues and producing consistency of approach. However, it is important to remember that the search is for the reaction of the fair-minded and informed observer.

> The court has to apply an objective assessment as to how such a person would react to the material facts. There is a danger when applying such a test that citation of authorities may cloud rather than clarify perception. The court must be careful when looking at case precedent not to permit it to drive common sense out of the window.[614]

The following selected examples illustrate the impact of this part of Article 6 in a number of key areas.

9.5.1 Judiciary

The independence of the judiciary is viewed with particular seriousness and is often said to be of fundamental constitutional importance. 'We are fortunate in this country that for a very considerable length of time this principle has never been lost, although through the annals of history there may have been times when its light burned less brightly.'[615]

(a) Part-time and Temporary Judges

In *Starrs v Ruxton*[616] the High Court in Scotland held that temporary sheriffs were not an independent and impartial tribunal. They were appointed for one year only and were subject to recall during that period at the instance of the Lord Advocate. In *Millar*[617] the Privy Council considered the argument that the Lord Advocate and procurators fiscal who conducted the prosecutions were acting incompatibly with Article 6 by prosecuting before temporary sheriffs. Whilst there was nothing to suggest that the outcome would have been any different had the prosecution been before a permanent sheriff, the Privy Council concluded that the right could not be compromised or eroded.[618] It found that the Lord Advocate had infringed the right of the accused to have the criminal charges against them determined by an independent and impartial tribunal contrary to section 57(2) of the Scotland Act 1998.[619]

The Scottish position was considered again in *Kearney*[620] by the Privy Council. The judge had been appointed as a temporary judge for three years. The appointment was made by the Lord President and the Privy Council found nothing incompatible with Article 6 in this. He was not removable from office, at the behest of the Scottish

---

[614] *R (on the application of PD) v West Midlands and North West Mental Health Review Tribunal* [2004] EWCA Civ 311.
[615] *Millar* (n 558), per Lord Clyde at [80].
[616] *Starrs v Ruxton* 2000 JC 208.
[617] *Millar* (n 558).
[618] Ibid, per Lord Bingham at [16].
[619] Ibid, per Lord Bingham at [27].
[620] *Kearney v HM Advocate* [2006] UKPC D 1, [2006] HRLR 15.

Ministers, at any time and without good cause and Article 6 was not infringed by the possibility of removing a judge shown to be unfit to hold office. Furthermore, it was held that the fair minded and informed observer would not suspect that the judge would seek to commend himself to the prosecuting authority in order to obtain a permanent appointment or renewal of his existing temporary appointment.[621] Furthermore, a temporary judge seeking reappointment would wish to impress his judicial superiors, but would have no incentive to commend himself to the Lord Advocate.[622] Lord Hope observed as follows:

> The security of tenure which he enjoyed during the period of his appointment, together with the fact that issues as to the work that he was to be employed to do and as to his reappointment at the expiry of that period were in the hands not of the Lord Advocate but of the Lord President, provided the guarantees that were needed to meet the requirements of independence and impartiality guaranteed by article 6(1) of the Convention.[623]

In *Lawal*[624] the question before the House of Lords was whether, in circumstances in which a Queen's Counsel appearing on an appeal before the Employment Appeal Tribunal (EAT) had sat as a part-time judge in the EAT with one or both of the lay members ('wing members') hearing that appeal, the hearing before the EAT was compatible with Article 6. The House of Lords considered that the observer was likely to approach the matter on the basis that the lay members look to the judge for guidance on the law, and can be expected to develop a fairly close relationship of trust and confidence with the judge. Furthermore, the observer was credited with knowledge that a Recorder, who in a criminal case had sat with jurors, may not subsequently appear in a case in which one or more of those jurors serve and the knowledge that part-time judges in the Employment Tribunal are forbidden from appearing as counsel before an Employment Tribunal which includes lay members with whom they had previously sat.[625] Their Lordships concluded that the present practice undermined public confidence in the system and there should be a restriction on part-time judges appearing as counsel before a panel of the EAT consisting of one or two lay members with whom they had previously sat.[626]

(b) Extra-judicial Activities

All members of the judiciary have a past and in some instances, their past can raise concerns about their independence and impartiality. For example, *Davidson*[627] concerned Lord Hardie, who had previously held the office of Lord Advocate. In this role he piloted the Scotland Bill through the House of Lords and advised the House of Lords on the effect of section 21 of the Crown Proceedings Act 1947 on the remedies which

---

[621] Ibid, per Lord Bingham at [8].
[622] Ibid.
[623] Ibid, [53].
[624] *Lawal* (n 569).
[625] Ibid, [21].
[626] Ibid, [23]. See also *PD* (n 614), where it was held not to be incompatible with Art 6 for a consultant psychiatrist, employed by an NHS Trust party to the proceedings, to sit on the Mental Health Review Tribunal. In *Scanfuture UK Ltd v Secretary of State for Trade and Industry* [2001] IRLR 416 the Employment Appeal Tribunal held that it was incompatible with Art 6(1) for lay members to sit on cases where the Secretary of State was a party.
[627] *Davidson* (n 561).

might be available to the courts in Scotland against the Scottish Ministers. In particular, he advised that the effect of section 21 was to preclude the grant of any coercive order against the Scottish Ministers. He later became a judge in the Scottish Court of Session. In this role he refused leave to appeal to Mr Davidson. Part of Mr Davidson's claim was for an order requiring the Scottish Ministers to secure his transfer to prison conditions which would comply with Article 3. The lower court had refused the order, relying, inter alia, on section 21.

On becoming aware of Lord Hardie's role in the House of Lords, Mr Davidson argued that the refusal of leave was vitiated for want of independence and impartiality. Applying the objective test, the House of Lords noted that rarely, if ever, in the absence of injudicious or intemperate behaviour, can a judge's previous activity as such give rise to an appearance of bias. Adherence to an opinion expressed judicially in an earlier case does not of itself denote a lack of open-mindedness. However, their Lordships also recognised that problems are liable to arise where the exercise of judicial functions is preceded by the exercise of legislative functions.[628] Here it concluded that the fair-minded and informed observer, having considered the facts, would conclude that there was a real possibility that Lord Hardie, sitting judicially, would subconsciously strive to avoid reaching a conclusion which would undermine the very clear assurances he had given to Parliament.[629] In reaching this conclusion the judicial oath was not overlooked, their Lordships holding that the observer would regard it as important protection but not as a sufficient guarantee to exclude all legitimate doubt.[630] It was also noted that a failure to disclose prior activities in a case which calls for it must inevitably colour the thinking of the observer.[631]

(c) Earlier Involvement with a Claimant

In some instances the activity raising concerns with judicial independence and impartiality may be an earlier involvement with the claimant. For example, in *Ablyazov*[632] a judge refused to recuse himself as the nominated judge of a trial in circumstances where he had to hear, prior to the trial, an application to commit one of the parties for contempt of court and had found a number of contempts proven. The Court of Appeal confirmed that the principles of apparent bias were well established and the application

---

[628] Ibid, per Lord Bingham at [10].
[629] Ibid, [17].
[630] Ibid, [18].
[631] Ibid, [20]. See also the speech of Lord Hope and *R v Secretary of State for the Home Department, ex p Al-Hasan* [2005] UKHL 13, [2005] 1 WLR 688. Other examples include *Taylor v Lawrence* [2001] EWCA Civ 119 (affirmed on a reopened appeal at [2002] EWCA Civ 90, [2003] QB 528), where no violation of Art 6 was found and where the deputy judge was a client of the claimant's solicitors. In *Wilkinson v S* [2003] EWCA Civ 95, [2003] 1 WLR 1254 no violation of Art 6 was found where the judge who found the appellant guilty of contempt had witnessed the contempt herself. In *Birmingham City Council v Yardley* [2004] EWCA Civ 1756 no violation of Art 6 was found where the Recorder and counsel for one of the parties were members of the same chambers. Considerable guidance is also contained in *Locabail (UK) Ltd v Bayfield Properties Ltd* [2000] 1 All ER 65, although it is important to note the pre-HRA 'real danger' test applied in this judgment is not compliant with Art 6. See also *R v Dunn* [2010] EWCA Crim 1823, [2010] 2 Cr App R 30 where the Court of Appeal rejected the argument that the Court of Appeal was not sufficiently independent or impartial to certify appeals to the Supreme Court and *CD (Democratic Republic of Congo) v Secretary of State for the Home Department* [2011] EWCA Civ 1425 where the Court of Appeal held it was compatible with Art 6 for an immigration judge to decide a case he had expressed an earlier view upon.
[632] *Ablyazov* (n 612).

of these was fact sensitive.[633] It held that it was necessary to consider, through the eyes of the fair minded and informed observer, that there was not only convenience but also 'justice to be found in the efficient conduct of complex civil claims' with the help of the designated judge.[634] It found that a case for recusal may arise where a judge has expressed himself in 'vituperative or intemperate terms' but this was not alleged here.[635] It stated as follows:

> The critical consideration is that what the first judge does he does as part and parcel of his judicial assessment of the litigation before him: he is not 'pre-judging' by reference to extraneous matters or predilections or preferences. He is not even bringing to this litigation matters from another case. ... He is judging the matter before him, as he is required by his office to do. If he does so fairly and judicially, I do not see that the fair-minded and informed observer would consider that there was any possibility of bias.[636]

(d) Clerks of the Court

In *Clark*[637] the Privy Council agreed that the clerk of the Scottish district court in criminal proceedings was part of the court but lacked the necessary independence for the purposes of Article 6. However, in the context of the procedures available for appeal and review on the ground of alleged miscarriage of justice, it concluded that there was sufficient protection to satisfy Article 6 even though the High Court did not have the power to rehear the case.[638]

9.5.2 Juries

In *Montgomery*[639] it was argued that there could not be a fair trial of the two defendants for the murder of a young Asian man because of the publicity which the case and facts had already received. Applying the objective test and considering the part the judge would play, the Privy Council concluded that the acts of the Lord Advocate in bringing the prosecution were not incompatible with Article 6(1) as the careful direction which the judge may be expected to give the jury in the course of the trial would be sufficient to remove any legitimate doubt that may exist about the objective impartiality of the tribunal.[640]

9.5.3 Courts Martial

A number of aspects of the court martial procedure were considered by the House of Lords in *Boyd*.[641] At the outset, the House of Lords confirmed that Article 6 did not

---

[633] Ibid, [65].
[634] Ibid, [65].
[635] Ibid, [65].
[636] Ibid, [70].
[637] *Clark* (n 499).
[638] Ibid, per Lord Hope at [55] and [58] in reliance upon *Albert and Le Compte* (n 106), [29]; *Bryan* (n 585).
[639] *Montgomery* (n 167).
[640] See also *R v Thoron* [2001] EWCA Crim 1797 and *R v Smith (No 2)* [2005] UKHL 12, [2005] 1 WLR 704. See further K Quinn, 'Jury Bias and the ECHR: A Well Kept Secret?' [2004] *Criminal Law Review* 998.
[641] *Boyd* (n 570).

require that the members of the tribunal should not share the values of the military community to which they belong.[642] With respect to the position of permanent presidents, it was held that the absence of a formal recognition of irremovability did not in itself imply a lack of independence provided that it was recognised in fact and that other necessary guarantees were present.[643] However, it was noted that the practice of the Air Force of preparing reports on officers who were serving as permanent presidents was undesirable and unnecessary, and it would be better if it were discontinued.[644]

The position of other officers in courts martial was a little more complicated, as in *Morris*[645] the ECtHR had found a violation of Article 6 in relation to the two serving officers who sat on the applicant's court martial, primarily due to the insufficiency of safeguards against outside pressures. The House of Lords found that the ECtHR had been given less information about the safeguards than the House of Lords. These included selection of officers ad hoc; the oath taken by members; the directions of the judge advocate; the fact that officers were always taken from another unit; the briefing notes; and the list of witnesses. The House of Lords found it hard to see how anyone, either in the court or outside it, could improperly influence the members' decision. It saw no reason to think that, when duly directed by the judge advocate, officers sitting on a court martial could not properly assess the evidence and return a true verdict based on it.[646]

With respect to sentencing, it was argued that, as the members would have regard to such issues as the impact of the offence on Service morale and discipline, and would be more aware of these effects than a civil judge, the sentences may therefore not coincide exactly with the sentences which a civil judge would pass. The House of Lords held that this did not call the decisions of the courts martial into question. The judge advocate advised on sentencing, and the sentence imposed was subject to review and appeal.[647] The House of Lords also dispensed with remaining arguments. It found that the absence of legal training did not undermine independence and impartiality.[648] The fact that the officers were subject to Army discipline and reports did not mean that they were under the command of any higher authority in their function as members of the courts martial and did not compromise their independence and impartiality.[649]

9.5.4 Government Ministers

As part of the executive, government ministers do not satisfy the test of independence. In *Anderson*[650] the House of Lords confirmed that it was incompatible with Article 6

---

[642] Ibid, per Lord Rodger at [57] in reliance upon *Morris v United Kingdom* (2002) 34 EHRR 1253, [58].
[643] Ibid, per Lord Rodger at [69] in reliance on *Morris*, ibid, [68]–[69].
[644] Ibid, per Lord Rodger at [62].
[645] *Morris* (n 642).
[646] Ibid, per Lord Rodger at [85].
[647] Ibid, [86].
[648] Ibid, [88].
[649] Ibid, [89]–[90] per Lord Rodger. The House of Lords also found that the role played by the reviewing authority was not incompatible with Art 6—also contrary to the conclusion of the ECtHR in *Morris* (n 642). See per Lord Rodger at [94] and per Lord Bingham at [13]. See also *R v Skuse* [2002] EWCA Crim 991 concerning the independence of the judge advocate at a naval court martial; *R v Dundon* [2004] EWCA Crim 621, [2004] UKHRR 717; *R v Dudley* [2005] EWCA Crim 719; and *R v Stow* [2005] EWCA Crim 1157.
[650] *Anderson* (n 171).

for the Secretary of State for the Home Department to exercise the judicial function of fixing the tariff of a convicted murderer. However, in *Smith*[651] the House of Lords held that this constraint only applied to the setting of the minimum term and where the term of imprisonment was to be increased by executive decision. It did not apply to a reduction in sentence as this was a 'well-recognised exercise of executive clemency'.[652] In the civil context, in *Alconbury*[653] the House of Lords concluded that the Secretary of State for the Environment, Transport and the Regions, when exercising his planning powers, was not an independent and impartial tribunal. The Secretary of State himself had accepted that he made policy and applied that policy in particular cases and that was sufficient to prevent him from being either independent or impartial for the purposes of Article 6.[654]

9.5.5 Local Authorities

Using a member of staff of a local authority to conduct review of particular decisions will sometimes involve a breach of Article 6, although this breach may be cured by the availability of judicial review or appeal to a court on a point of law. For example, in *Begum*[655] the House of Lords held that the council's rehousing manager, who had conducted a review of the council's decision to offer particular accommodation to Ms Begum under the Housing Act 1996, was not an independent tribunal as she was an administrator and could not be described as part of the judicial branch of government[656]:

> One of the purposes of Art.6, in requiring that disputes over civil rights should be decided by or subject to the control of a judicial body, is to uphold the rule of law and the separation of powers. ... If an administrator is regarded as being an independent and impartial tribunal on the ground that he is enlightened, impartial and has no personal interest in the matter, it follows there need not be any possibility of judicial review of his decision. He is above the law. That is a position contrary to basic English constitutional principles. It is also something which the Strasbourg court has been unable to accept.[657]

9.5.6 Professional Bodies

Finally, professional bodies also have the potential to fall foul of the requirements of independence and impartiality. For example, in *Preiss*[658] the appellant objected to the role of the President in the disciplinary system of the General Dental Council. As Preliminary Screener, he had the function of setting in train proceedings before

---

[651] *R (on the application of Smith) v Secretary of State for the Home Department* [2005] UKHL 51.
[652] Ibid, per Lord Bingham at [13].
[653] *Alconbury* (n 19).
[654] Ibid, per Lord Slynn at [45] and per Lord Hoffmann at [124]. It is important to note that this breach was cured by the availability of judicial review.
[655] *Begum* (n 23).
[656] Ibid, [27].
[657] Ibid, in reliance upon *Golder* (n 37), and *Alconbury* (n 19). See also *McLellan* (n 57); *Adan* (n 60); *Beeson* (n 38). In *Heald v Brent London Borough Council* [2009] EWCA Civ 930, [2010] 1 WLR 990 the Court of Appeal held that it was compatible with Art 6 for reviews under the Housing Act 1996 to be contracted out to a third party.
[658] *Preiss* (n 49).

the Preliminary Proceedings Committee (PPC) unless he considered that the matter need not proceed further. It was the function of the PPC to decide whether the case should be referred to the Professional Conduct Committee (PCC). The Privy Council concluded that, when the participation of the President both as Preliminary Screener and as Chairman of the PCC was seen in conjunction with the predominance of Council members in both the PPC and the PCC, and in conjunction moreover with the fact that the disciplinary charge was brought on behalf of the the council, the cumulative result was a real danger that the PCC lacked the necessary independence and impartiality.[659]

---

10. Tribunal Established by Law

The final right protected by Article 6(1) in relation the determination of civil rights and obligations or any criminal charge is the right to a tribunal established by law. There is very little jurisprudence concerning this part of Article 6, either under the HRA or before the ECtHR. In criminal trials it has been confirmed that it is appropriate to treat the court made up of both judge and jury as the tribunal for the purposes of Article 6—it is not possible to regard the jury as a separate entity.[660]

This Article 6 guarantee was considered by the Court of Appeal in *Coppard*,[661] where it was discovered following judgment that the judge was not actually authorised to sit as a judge of the High Court. As the judge did not know, nor ought to have known, that he was not so authorised, the court found that at common law he was a judge-in-fact of the High Court and his judgment therefore was a judgment of the High Court.[662] But this did not get around the problem presented by the right to a tribunal established by law. The Court of Appeal held that at common law, a person who was believed and believed himself to have the necessary judicial authority, would be regarded in law as possessing such authority and the judge in fact was a tribunal whose authority was established by the common law.[663] The next question was whether this met the Article 6 standard. The court noted that the purpose of this right was to ensure that justice was administered by, and only by, the prescribed exercise of the judicial power of the state, not by ad hoc 'people's courts' and the like. 'Such a principle must be fundamental to any concept of the rule of law. Implicit in it is that the composition and authority of a court must not be arbitrary.'[664]

---

[659] The breach was cured by the availability of appeal to the Privy Council. See also *R (on the application of Mahfouz) v Professional Conduct Committee of the General Medical Council* [2004] EWCA Civ 233, [2004] Lloyd's Rep Med 389; *R (on the application of Panjawani) v Royal Pharmaceutical Society of Great Britain* [2002] EWHC (Admin) 1127; *P, a barrister v The General Council of the Bar* [2005] 1 WLR 3019; *Shrimpton v The General Council of the Bar*, The Visitors to the Inns of Court, 6 May 2005; *Pine* (n 425); *Holder v Law Society* [2000] EWHC (Admin) 2023; *Holmes v Royal College of Veterinary Surgeons* [2011] UKPC 48.

[660] *Mushtaq* (n 397).

[661] *Coppard v HM Customs and Excise* [2003] EWCA Civ 511, [2003] QB 1428.

[662] Ibid, [24].

[663] Ibid, [32].

[664] Ibid, [34].

A problem was presented by the word 'established', which, it was argued, required a tribunal to have been established by the time the individual's civil rights and obligations came before it.[665] However, the court reminded itself that it should be less concerned with close analysis of the language of the Convention than with the principles which animate it. It concluded that

> [p]rovided the United Kingdom's legal response … is not such as to ratify the acts of usurpers or to operate arbitrarily and is limited, in effect, to the correction of mistakes of form rather than of substance—and in our judgment it meets all these tests—we do not consider that the Convention requires the disqualification of a judge purely because his authority was not formally established before he sat.[666]

11. Article 6(2): Presumption of Innocence

11.1 Generally

Starting with Article 6(2), the remaining rights set out in Article 6 only apply to those who have been charged with a criminal offence. The meaning of 'charged with a criminal offence' is coextensive with the meaning of 'determination of any criminal charge' in Article 6(1).[667] With respect to the application of these rights, it is therefore important to consider that section of this chapter.

Article 6(2) provides that everyone charged with a criminal offence shall be presumed innocent until proved guilty according to law. It is often noted by the courts that this Article reflects a fundamental common law principle, the 'golden thread' that it is the duty of the prosecution to prove the prisoner's guilt.[668]

> [I]t is repugnant to ordinary notions of fairness for a prosecutor to accuse a defendant of a crime and for the defendant to then be required to disprove the accusation on pain of conviction and punishment if he fails to do so.[669]

However, Article 6(2) is not an absolute right and is subject to modifications or limitations which pursue a legitimate aim and satisfy the principle of proportionality.[670] Furthermore, a breach of Article 6(2) does not necessarily mean a conviction is unsafe, particularly if a jury would have reached the same conclusion notwithstanding the breach.[671] It has been held that Art.6(2) must be read in the context of Art.6(1) and that

---

[665] Ibid, [37].

[666] Ibid, [39].

[667] *McCann* (n 55).

[668] *Woolmington v Director of Public Prosecutions* [1935] AC 462, per Viscount Sankey LC at 481 as quoted by Lord Hope in *Kebilene* (n 10). See also the comments of Lord Steyn in *Lambert* (n 313), [32].

[669] *Attorney General's Reference No 4 of 2002* [2004] UKHL 43, [2005] 1 AC 264, per Lord Bingham at [9]. See further L Campbell, 'Criminal Labels, the European Convention on Human Rights and the Presumption of Innocence' (2013) 76 *Modern Law Review* 681.

[670] *Lambert* (n 313), per Lord Hope at [88] in reliance upon *Ashingdane* (n 278), and *Brown* (n 4). See also *Kebilene* (n 10) and *McIntosh* (n 12).

[671] *Lambert* (n 313).

the article as a whole is concerned essentially with procedural guarantees to ensure that there is a fair trial, not with the substantive elements of the offence with which the person has been charged.

> So when article 6(2) uses the words 'innocent' and 'guilty' it is dealing with the burden of proof regarding the elements of the offence and any defences to it. It is not dealing with what those elements are or what defences to the offence ought to be available.[672]

Consequently, the House of Lords concluded in *R v G*[673] that offences of strict liability may subject a defendant to conviction in circumstances where he has done nothing blameworthy but such legislation does not render the trial under which it is enforced unfair or infringe the presumption of innocence.[674]

11.2 Burden of Proof

In claims under the HRA, Article 6(2) has mainly been considered in relation to the burden of proof and in his judgment in *Kebilene*[675] Lord Hope gave detailed considera-tion to the question. In his Lordship's view the first step is to identify the nature of the provision which is said to transfer the burden of proof from the prosecution to the accused. This involves distinguishing between the evidential burden—the burden of introducing evidence in support of a case—and the persuasive or legal burden—the burden of persuading the jury as to guilt or innocence. A persuasive burden of proof requires the accused to prove, on a balance of probabilities, a fact which is essential to the determination of his guilt or innocence. It reverses the burden of proof by removing it from the prosecution and transferring it to the accused. An evidential burden requires only that the accused must adduce sufficient evidence to raise an issue before it has to be determined as one of the facts in the case. The prosecution does not need to lead any evidence about it, so the accused needs to do this if he wishes to put the point in issue. But if it is put in issue, the burden of proof remains with the prosecution. The accused need only raise a reasonable doubt about his guilt.[676]

Lord Hope stated that statutory presumptions which place an evidential burden on the accused, requiring the accused to do no more than raise a reasonable doubt on the matter with which they deal, do not breach the presumption of innocence and are not incompatible with Article 6(2). However, statutory presumptions which transfer the persuasive burden to the accused require further examination. In his Lordship's view, there were three categories. First, the mandatory presumption of guilt as to an essen-tial element of the offence. This was inconsistent with the presumption of innocence. Second was the presumption of guilt as to an essential element which was discre-tionary—the tribunal of fact may or may not rely on the presumption, depending upon its view as to the cogency or weight of the evidence. If a presumption was of this kind, it may be necessary for the facts of the case to be considered before a conclusion could

---

[672] *R v G* [2008] UKHL 37, [2009] 1 AC 92, per Lord Hope at [27].
[673] Ibid.
[674] See also *R v Deyemi* [2007] EWCA Crim 2060, [2008] Crim LR 327.
[675] *Kebilene* (n 10). Lord Hope's comments were *obiter* as their Lordships had concluded that the DPP's consent to a prosecution was not amenable to judicial review.
[676] See also *Attorney General's Reference No 4 of 2002* (n 669), per Lord Bingham at [1].

be reached as to whether the presumption of innocence had been breached. The third category was provisions which related to an exemption or proviso which the accused must establish if he wished to avoid conviction but which were not an essential element of the offence. These may or may not violate the presumption of innocence, depending on the circumstances.[677]

In relation to this last category, Lord Hope was careful to note that this was not an exact science and that the provisions varied widely in their detail as to what the prosecutor must prove before the onus shifts—and these matters may not be capable of being fully assessed until after the trial. More importantly, his Lordship stated that, even if the conclusion was reached that prima facie the provision breached the presumption of innocence, this would not lead inevitably to the conclusion that the provision was incompatible with Article 6(2). As stated above, although Article 6(2) is in absolute terms, it is not regarded as imposing an absolute prohibition on reverse onus clauses, whether they be evidential (presumptions of fact) or persuasive (presumptions of law).

In striking the balance, his Lordship adopted the questions posed by counsel: (1) what does the prosecution have to prove in order to transfer the onus to the defence? (2) What is the burden on the accused—does it relate to something which is likely to be difficult for him to prove, or does it relate to something which is likely to be within his knowledge or to which he readily has access? (3) What is the nature of the threat faced by society which the provision is designed to combat? [678]

Later judgments have expanded on this. In *R v Johnstone*[679] the House of Lords held that the more serious the punishment which may flow from conviction, the more compelling must be the reasons.

> The extent and nature of the factual matters required to be proved by the accused, and their importance relative to the matters required to be proved by the prosecution, have to be taken into account. So also does the extent to which the burden on the accused relates to facts which, if they exist, are readily provable by him as matters within his own knowledge or to which he has ready access.[680]

Furthermore, it was held that the court would reach a different conclusion from the legislature only when it was apparent that the legislature had attached insufficient importance to the fundamental right of an individual to be presumed innocent until proved guilty.[681] In *Attorney General's Reference No 4 of 2002*[682] the House of Lords held that relevant to any judgment on reasonableness or proportionality

> will be the opportunity given to the defendant to rebut the presumption, maintenance of the rights of the defence, flexibility in application of the presumption, retention by the court of a power to assess the evidence, the importance of what is at stake and the difficulty which the prosecutor may face in the absence of a presumption.[683]

---

[677] See also the comments of Lord Steyn in *Lambert* (n 313), [37].

[678] In *McIntosh* (n 12), Lord Hope stated that the questions he posed in this judgment were not presented as a set of rules. 'They were no more than an indication of an approach which it might be useful to adopt when the interest of the individual are being balanced against those of society. Each case will vary, and they may be more helpful in some cases than others.'

[679] *R v Johnstone* [2003] UKHL 28, [2003] 1 WLR 1736.

[680] Ibid, per Lord Nicholls at [50].

[681] Ibid, [51].

[682] *Attorney General's Reference No 4 of 2002* (n 669).

[683] Ibid, per Lord Bingham at [21]. See generally P Roberts, 'The Presumption of Innocence Brought Home? Kebilene Deconstructed' (2002) 118 *Law Quarterly Rewview* 41; V Tadros and S Tierney, 'The Presumption of Innocence and the Human Rights Act' (2004) 67 *Modern Law Review* 402.

11.3 Application

The justifiability of any infringement of the presumption of innocence cannot be resolved by any 'rule of thumb, but on examination of all the facts and circumstances of the particular provision as applied in the particular case'.[684] It is therefore instructive to consider the application of Article 6(2) in a number of key areas.[685]

11.3.1 Confiscation Orders

Although in *McIntosh*[686] the Privy Council concluded that Article 6(2) did not apply to a confiscation order, it did consider its application to section 3 of the Proceeds of Crime (Scotland) Act 1995. Section 3 provided, inter alia, that, in making an assessment of the value of the proceeds of the person's drug trafficking, the court may assume that any property appearing to the court to have been held by him at any time since his conviction, or to have been transferred to him at any time since a date six years before his being indicted or being served with the complaint, was received by him as a payment or reward in connection with drug trafficking carried on by him. The court had a discretion whether to make the statutory assumptions or not; the assumptions were rebuttable by the accused on a balance of probabilities; the proceedings in question related to drug trafficking and not the commission of drug-trafficking offences; and the assumptions related to property which appeared to the court to meet the conditions specified and to expenditure of the accused during the relevant period.[687]

Concluding that reliance on the assumption permitted under section 3 struck the appropriate balance between conflicting interests and would not violate Article 6(2), even if it did apply, the Privy Council identified the nature of the public threat to which the legislation was directed as the punishment and deterrent from drug trafficking given that the unlawful consumption of drugs was a very 'grave, far-reaching and destructive social evil.'[688] It also found it significant that the United Nations Convention against Illicit Traffic in Narcotic Drugs and Psychotropic Substances 1998,[689] ratified by the UK in 1991, provided that state parties may consider a reverse onus of proof regarding

---

[684] *Attorney General's Reference No 4 of 2002* (n 669), per Lord Bingham at [21].

[685] Other examples include: *Davies v Health and Safety Executive* [2002] EWCA Crim 2949 where the court concluded that the legal burden imposed by s 40 of the Health and Safety at Work Act 1974 was justified, necessary and proportionate. In *R v Matthews* [2003] EWCA Crim 813, [2004] QB 690 the court concluded that ss 139(4) and 139(5) of the Criminal Justice Act 1988 were proportionate. See also *Attorney General's Reference No 1 of 2004* [2004] EWCA Crim 1025, where the Court of Appeal considered s 352 Insolvency Act 1986, s 1(2) Protection from Eviction Act 1977, s 4(2) Homicide Act 1957 and s 51(7) Criminal Justice and Public Order Act 1994. The House of Lords held in *Attorney General's Reference No 4 of 2002* (n 669) that the conclusions of the Court of Appeal were correct in each case. Other examples are: *R v Navabi* [2005] EWCA Crim 2865 (conviction for entering the UK without an immigration document); *Khan v Revenue & Customs* [2006] EWCA Civ 89, [2006] STC 1167 (VAT evasion); *R v Keogh* [2007] EWCA Crim 528, [2007] 1 WLR 1500 (ss 2 and 3 Official Secrets Act 1989); *R v Clarke* [2008] EWCA Crim 893 (providing immigration services when not qualified to do so); *R v Webster* [2010] EWCA Crim 2819, [2011] 1 Cr App R 16 (conviction under the Public Bodies Corrupt Practices Act 1889); *R v Williams* [2012] EWCA Crim 2162, [2013] 1 WLR 1200 (possession of a prohibited weapon contrary to the Firearms Act 1968);

[686] *McIntosh* (n 12).

[687] Ibid, [8].

[688] Ibid, per Lord Bingham at [4].

[689] (1992) Cm 1927.

the lawful origin of alleged proceeds or other property liable to confiscation.[690] It took into account the fact that the confiscation order procedure could only be initiated if the accused was convicted of a drug-trafficking offence. It was then incumbent on the prosecutor to prove the amount of property held by the accused and his expenditure. It was only if a significant discrepancy was shown between the property and expenditure of the accused on the one hand and his known sources of income on the other that the court would think it right to make the section 3 assumptions.[691]

11.3.2 Drugs Offences

A majority of the House of Lords in *Lambert*[692] held that the HRA had no application to the appeal as the trial had taken place before the HRA came into force but their Lordships still commented on section 28(3) of the Misuse of Drugs Act 1971. The appellant had been convicted of possession of a controlled drug contrary to the Act. He relied upon section 28(3)(b)(i) of the Act, asserting that he did not believe or suspect, or have reason to suspect, that the bag which he carried contained a controlled drug. The trial judge directed the jury that the prosecution only had to prove that he had and knew that he had the bag in his possession and that the bag contained a controlled drug. To establish the defence under section 28(3) he had to prove on the balance of probabilities that he did not know that the bag contained a controlled drug. This was the legal rather than the evidential burden.

Their Lordships found that the defence put forward by the appellant under section 28 was an ingredient of the offence. Therefore, section 28 derogated from the presumption of innocence.[693] With respect to the question of justification, it was held that there was an objective justification for some interference with the burden of proof in prosecutions under the Act.

> The basis of this justification is that sophisticated drug smugglers, dealers and couriers typically secrete drugs in some container, thereby enabling the person in possession of the container to say that he was unaware of the contents. Such defences are commonplace and they pose real difficulties for the police and prosecuting authorities.[694]

On the question of proportionality, it was noted that a guilty verdict may be returned in respect of an offence punishable by life imprisonment even though the jury may consider that it was reasonably possible that the accused had been duped.[695] Taking into account domestic, Canadian and South African authorities, and also the fact that a number of factors have now significantly reduced the difficulties of the prosecution in

---

[690] Art 5(7), [32]. The PC also referred to a 1991 report of the Irish Law Reform Commission, *The Confiscation of the Proceeds of Crime* LRC 35 (1991), in which the Commission recommended the adoption of such a presumption.

[691] *McIntosh* (n 12), per Lord Bingham at [35]–[36]. See also *Hughes v Customs and Excise Commissioners* [2002] EWCA Civ 670, [2002] 4 All ER 633, where the Court of Appeal held that it was compatible with Art 6(2) for a receiver appointed by a court pursuant to the Criminal Justice Act 1988 or Drug Trafficking Act 1994 to use the defendant's assets under his control to meet the costs of the receivership whether or not the defendant had been convicted or a confiscation order made against him. See also *R v Goodenough* [2004] EWCA Crim 2260, [2005] 1 Cr App R (S) 88.

[692] *Lambert* (n 313).

[693] Ibid, per Lord Steyn at [35].

[694] Ibid, [36].

[695] Ibid, [38].

drugs cases, it was concluded that a reverse legal burden was a disproportionate means of addressing the legislative goal of easing the task of the prosecution. However, using section 3 of the HRA, their Lordships read the sections to create an evidential burden only.[696]

11.3.3 Road Traffic Offences

In *Director of Public Prosecutions v Sheldrake*[697] the appellant challenged section 5(2) of the Road Traffic Act 1988, which provided that it was a defence to prove that, at the time he was alleged to have committed the offence, the circumstances were such that there was no likelihood of his driving the vehicle whilst the proportion of alcohol in his breath, blood or urine remained likely to exceed the prescribed limit. Assuming that section 5(2) infringed the presumption of innocence, the House of Lords held that the provision was directed to a legitimate object: the prevention of death, injury and damage caused by unfit drivers. Furthermore, it found that the burden was not beyond reasonable limits or arbitrary.

> The defendant has full opportunity to show that there was no likelihood of his driving, a matter so closely conditioned by his own knowledge and state of mind at the material time as to make it much more appropriate for him to prove on the balance of probabilities that he would not have been likely to drive than for the prosecutor to prove, beyond reasonable doubt, that he would.[698]

11.3.4 Trade Marks Offences

Section 92 of the Trade Marks Act 1994 was considered by the House of Lords in *R v Johnstone*.[699] The defendant had been convicted of possessing some 500 bootleg recordings to which had been applied a sign identical to, or likely to be mistaken for, a registered trade mark. Section 92(5) provided a defence if the accused could show that he believed on reasonable grounds that the use of the sign in the manner in which it was used was not an infringement of the registered trade mark. The House of Lords accepted that this subsection imposed a legal burden on the defendant and prima facie derogated from the presumption of innocence.[700] However, it concluded that there were compelling reasons for the imposition of the legal burden, including international pressure in the interests of consumers and traders to restrain fraudulent trading in counterfeit goods, the framing of section 92 offences as offences of near absolute liability and the dependence of the subsection (5) defence on facts within the defendant's own knowledge.[701] Also taken into consideration was the fact that those who trade in brand

---

[696] Ibid, [41]–[42]. See also Lord Slynn at [17], Lord Hope at [87]–[91] and Lord Clyde at [133], [150] and [153]–[157]. Lord Hutton, at [190]–[197], whilst agreeing that a persuasive burden was imposed, did not find this incompatible with Art 6(2).

[697] *DPP v Sheldrake* [2004] UKHL 43, [2005] 1 AC 264.

[698] Ibid, per Lord Bingham at [41]. In *R v Drummond* [2002] EWCA Crim 527, [2002] 2 Cr Ap R 25, the court held that the persuasive burden imposed by s 15 of the Road Traffic Offenders Act 1988 was justified and necessary. See also *Director of Public Prosecutions v Ellery*, Divisional Court, 14 July 2005.

[699] *R v Johnstone* [2003] UKHL 28, [2003] 1 WLR 1736.

[700] Ibid, per Lord Nicholls at [47].

[701] Ibid, [52].

products are aware of the need to be on guard against counterfeit goods, the need to deal with reputable suppliers and the risks they take if they do not; and the fact that those who supply traders are unlikely to be cooperative. If the prosecution had to prove that a trader acted dishonestly, fewer prosecutions would take place.[702]

11.3.5 Terrorism Offences

In *Kebilene*,[703] although the House of Lords concluded that the Director of Public Prosecution's consent to a prosecution was not amenable to judicial review, Lord Hope commented on section 16A of the Prevention of Terrorism (Temporary Provisions) Act 1989. Section 16A provided that a person was guilty of an offence if he had any article in his possession in circumstances giving rise to a reasonable suspicion that the article was in his possession for a purpose connected with the commission, preparation or instigation of acts of terrorism. Under section 16A(3) it was a defence for a person charged under the section to prove that at the time of the alleged offence the article was not in his possession for such a purpose. Lord Hope characterised this section as imposing a persuasive burden of proof on the accused. If that burden was not discharged, subsection (1) contained a mandatory presumption that the article was in his possession for a purpose connected with terrorism which was applied if the prosecutor proved that it was in his possession in circumstances giving rise to a reasonable suspicion that it was in his possession for that purpose. Subsection (4) also imposed a persuasive burden on the accused that he did not know that the article was in the premises or, if he did, that he had no control over it. If that burden was not discharged, or the accused elected not to undertake it, the subsection contained a discretionary presumption that he was in possession of the article.

His Lordship noted that the legislative problem which these provisions sought to address was how to curb a grave evil which postulated a guilty mind or mental element on the part of the offender when proof of that guilty mind or mental element was likely to be a matter of inherent difficulty. He concluded that the discretionary presumption in subsection (4) could not be objected to at this stage. With respect to subsections (1) and (3), he found good reasons for thinking that they might not be as damaging to the presumption of innocence as might at first sight appear, and stated that account may legitimately be taken of the problems which the legislation was designed to address, noting that society has a strong interest in preventing acts of terrorism before they are perpetrated. He concluded that a sound judgment on this question was unlikely to be possible until the facts were known, but it was not immediately obvious to him that

> it would be imposing an unreasonable burden on an accused who was in possession of articles from which an inference of involvement in terrorism could be drawn to provide an explanation for his possession of them which would displace that inference.

In *Attorney General's Reference No 4 of 2002*[704] the House of Lords considered section

---

[702] Ibid, [53]. In *Attorney General's Reference No 4 of 2002* (n 669), the House of Lords answered the comment that there was significant difference between the approach in *Lambert* and *Johnstone*, stating that the justifiability and fairness of the respective exoneration provisions had to be judged in the particular context of each case; see per Lord Bingham at [30].

[703] *Kebilene* (n 10).

[704] *Attorney General's Reference No 4 of 2002* (n 669).

11(2) of the Terrorism Act 2000. Section 11(1) made it an offence to belong or profess to belong to a proscribed organisation. Section 11(2) provided a defence if the accused could prove that the organisation was not proscribed on the last (or only) occasion on which he became a member or began to profess to be a member and that he had not taken part in the activities of the organisation at any time while it was proscribed. Their Lordships concluded that section 11(2) imposed a legal burden on the accused in breach of the presumption of innocence[705] but that this was directed to a legitimate end: deterring people from becoming members and taking part in the activities of proscribed terrorist organisations.[706] However, a majority of their Lordships concluded that imposition of a legal burden in this particular situation was not a proportionate and justifiable legislative response to an undoubted problem.[707]

A number of factors led to this conclusion. A person who was innocent of any blameworthy or properly criminal conduct could fall within section 11(1), and there would be clear breach of the presumption of innocence and a real risk of unfair conviction if such persons could exonerate themselves only by establishing the defence provided on the balance of probabilities; it might be impossible for a defendant to show that he had not taken part in the activities of the organisation at any time while it was proscribed; the subsection provided no flexibility and there was no room for the exercise of discretion; the potential consequences were severe, with the possibility of imprisonment for up to ten years; security considerations do not absolve states from their duty to ensure that basic standards of fairness are observed; and little significance could be attached to the fact that the requirement that the Director of Public Prosecutions give his consent to a prosecution.[708] Section 3 of the HRA was employed to read down the subsection so that it only imposed an evidential burden.

---

12. Article 6(3)(a): Informed of the Nature and Cause of the Accusation

Article 6(3) sets out minimum rights for everyone charged with a criminal offence. The first of these contained in Article 6(3)(a) is the right to be informed promptly, in a language which the accused understands and in detail, of the nature and cause of the accusation against him.[709]

---

[705] Ibid, per Lord Bingham at [50].
[706] Ibid.
[707] Ibid.
[708] Ibid, per Lord Bingham at [51]. Lords Rodger and Carswell dissented on this point.
[709] See *Newman v Modern Bookbinders Ltd* [2000] 2 All ER 814.

13. Article 6(3)(b): Adequate Time and Facilities for Preparation of Defence

Article 6(3)(b) provides for the right to have adequate time and facilities for the preparation of a defence. 'Facilities' is not satisfied simply by the provision of money; the paragraph is

> principally directed to the securing for an accused person the opportunity and the services necessary for the preparation of his defence. It strikes at the imposition of restraints on his freedom to organise the preparation of his defence. A refusal of access to his lawyer while he is detained pending trial would be an obvious example.[710]

Another example may be failure to grant an adjournment so as to allow an accused to obtain expert reports[711] or call witnesses.[712] In *McLean*[713] the Privy Council held that a fixed fee system was not incompatible with this right, although Lord Clyde commented that, whilst the provision of funding was not immediately a facility for the preparation of the defence, it may be the means of providing those facilities.[714]

14. Article 6(3)(c): Legal Assistance

Article 6(3)(c) provides that everyone charged with a criminal offence has the right to defend himself in person or through legal assistance of his own choosing, or, if he has not sufficient means to pay for legal assistance, to be given it free when the interests of justice so require. This forms an important part of the guarantee of 'equality of arms' and identifies three distinct rights for the accused: to defend himself in person,[715] to defend himself through legal assistance of his own choosing[716] and, under certain conditions, to be given free legal assistance. The three rights are not alternatives;[717] therefore the accused cannot be forced to defend himself.[718] The paragraph guarantees the right to an adequate defence either in person or through a lawyer, the right being

---

[710] *McLean v Procurator Fiscal Fort William* [2001] 1 WLR 2425, per Lord Clyde at [56].
[711] See eg *R v Porter* [2001] EWCA Crim 2699.
[712] *R v Haslam* [2003] EWCA Crim 3444. See also *R v Harrison* [2006] EWCA Crim 18.
[713] Ibid.
[714] Ibid.
[715] See eg *Raja v van Hoogstraten* [2004] EWCA Civ 968, [2004] 4 All ER 793.
[716] See *Berry Trade Ltd v Moussavi*, Court of Appeal, 21 March 2002 and *R (on the application of Van Hoogstraten) v Governor of Belmarsh Prison* [2002] EWHC (Admin) 1965, [2003] 4 All ER 309.
[717] *McLean* (n 710), per Lord Clyde, with whom Lords Nicholls and Millet agreed, in reliance on *Pakelli v Germany* (1983) 6 EHRR 1.
[718] Ibid, per Lord Clyde at [59].

reinforced by an obligation on the part of the state to provide free legal assistance in certain cases.[719]

14.1 Waiver of the Right

Lord Rodger indicated in his judgment in *Cadder* that it was possible for an accused to have waived his right to consult a lawyer so no violation of Art 6 would arise.[720] This was given more detailed consideration by the Supreme Court in *Jude*[721] where it was claimed that the accused had waived his right of access to a lawyer when he made his unsolicited statement following his police interview. The Supreme Court held that there was no absolute rule that the accused must have been given legal advice on the question of whether or not he should exercise his right of access to a lawyer before he can be held to have waived it.[722]

Waiver was considered again by the Supreme Court in *McGowan*.[723] Again the question was whether the accused could be taken to have validly waived his right of access to a lawyer without having received advice from a lawyer on this point. The majority held that there was no rule in the domestic case law that said a detainee cannot ever waive his right to legal advice when he was being questioned by the police when he had not had access to legal advice on the question whether or not he should waive that right.[724] It also found no clear and constant jurisprudence from the ECtHR that legal advice was, as a rule, a necessary safeguard in order to ensure that any waiver was valid.[725] However, it did find a theme running through the ECtHR jurisprudence which indicated that access to a lawyer may well be a necessary prerequisite of a valid waiver in some cases. Lord Hope held that the court must be alive to the possibility that the words of the caution, and advice that the detainee has the right to a private consultation with a solicitor before any questioning begins and at any other time during such questioning 'may not be fully understood by everyone.'[726] However, the majority was not in favour of an absolute rule to ensure the accused had a clear understanding. Lord Hope was of the view that the ECtHR had provided a guiding principle as to what was needed for there to be an effective waiver and its application in determining whether there will be, or has been, a fair trial, would depend on the facts of each case.[727]

---

[719] Ibid.

[720] *Cadder v HM Advocate* [2010] UKSC 43,[96].

[721] *Jude v HM Advocate* [2011] UKSC 55, [2012] HRLR 8.

[722] Ibid, per Lord Hope at [28]. Lord Kerr dissented on this point, holding that it had not been established that there had been an effective waiver of the right to legal consultation.

[723] *McGowan (Procurator Fiscal) v B* [2011] UKSC 54, [2011] 1 WLR 3121.

[724] Ibid, per Lord Hope at [12].

[725] Ibid, [46].

[726] Ibid, [47].

[727] Ibid, [50]. Lord Kerr at [127] dissented on this point, holding that the waiver should not be regarded as effective unless it was shown that the suspect had a proper insight into the significance of the decision to waive his right.

14.2 Process of Investigation

The right to legal assistance applies to the process of investigation, although it does not impose a blanket requirement that each time a person is detained legal advice must be obtained for him before he can do or say anything. Evidence obtained in breach of this right may be excluded at any subsequent trial pursuant to section 78 of the Police and Criminal Evidence Act 1984. Police interviews of suspects in detention were considered by the Supreme Court in *Cadder*.[728] Here the claimants had been interviewed by police while they were being detained and made admissions which the Crown intended to rely upon at trial or did rely upon and obtained a conviction. They did not have access to legal advice which in detention nor was a solicitor present while they were being interviewed.

Taking account of the decision of the Grand Chamber of the ECtHR in *Salduz v Turkey*[729] the Supreme Court concluded that this had to be followed holding that it was incompatible with Arts 6(1) and 6(3)(c) for the Lord Advocate to lead evidence of answers to questions elicited by the police when the accused had no right to legal advice and had not had legal advice.[730] Lord Hope quoted from the Grand Chamber's judgment:

> Against this background, the Court finds that in order for the right to a fair trial to remain sufficiently 'practical and effective' article 6(1) requires that, as a rule, access to a lawyer should be provided as from the first interrogation of a suspect by the police, unless it is demonstrated in the light of the particular circumstances of each case that there are compelling reasons to restrict this right. Even where compelling reasons may exceptionally justify denial of access to a lawyer, such restriction—whatever its justification—must not unduly prejudice the rights of the accused under article 6. The rights of the defence will in principle be irretrievably prejudiced when incriminating statements made during police interrogation without access to a lawyer are used for a conviction.[731]

As stated above the right to legal assistance at the stage when a suspect is being questioned is not an absolute right, but is only subject to exceptions where there are compelling reasons to restrict it[732]—it is not a proportionality test.

In *P*[733] the Supreme Court considered whether the principle in *Salduz* extended to lines of enquiry derived from answers the accused gave to questions while being detained in the police station. Incriminating answers were given to questions put by police when the accused did not have access to legal advice. It held that there was no absolute rule that the fruits of questioning an accused without access to a lawyer must always be a violation of rights under Arts 6(1) and 6(3)(c) of the Convention:

> It is one thing if the impugned evidence was created by answers given in reply to such impermissible questioning. ... It is another thing if the evidence existed independently of those answers, so that those answers do not have to be relied upon to show how it bears upon the question whether the accused is guilty of the offence with which he has been charged.[734]

---

[728] Cadder (n 720).
[729] *Salduz v Turkey* (2008) 49 EHRR 421.
[730] Ibid, per Lord Rodger at [106].
[731] Ibid, ECtHR at [55], Lord Hope at [35].
[732] *Cadder* (n 720), per Lord Rodger at [95]. See further J Chalmers and F Leverick, 'Substantial and Radical Change—A New Dawn for Scottish Criminal Procedure' (2012) 75 *Modern Law Review* 837.
[733] *HM Advocate v P* [2011] UKSC 44, [2011] 1 WLR 2497.
[734] Ibid, [27].

The Supreme Court concluded that the question of whether evidence of this kind should be admitted had to be tested by considering whether the accused's right to a fair trial would be violated by the leading of the evidence.[735]

In *Ambrose*[736] the Supreme Court considered the more complex question of whether the principle in *Salduz* applied where the evidence that was objected to was obtained by the police otherwise than by questioning at a police station following detention. Lord Hope, with whom all agreed apart from Lord Kerr, held that it was the task of the Supreme Court to clearly identify where ECtHR stood on the issue and not to expand the scope of Article 6 further than the Strasbourg court justified.[737] Considering *Salduz*, he observed that the language used and the international materials referred to suggested that the Grand Chamber had in mind the need for protection of the accused against abusive coercion while he was in custody.[738] It was held that the starting point was to identify the moment from which a person was charged for the purposes of Article 6(1). This would be satisfied when the individual was detained and taken into custody, also when he was subject to the initial stages of police interrogation: 'The moment at which article 6 is engaged when the individual is questioned by the police requires very sensitive handling if protection is to be given to the right not to incriminate oneself.'[739] He stated that a good guide was the moment at which the individual was no longer a potential witness but had become a suspect.

It was observed that the ECtHR had not held that a person who had become a suspect and was not in custody must, as a rule, have access to a lawyer while being questioned. 'If it was practicable for access to legal advice to be offered, this will be one of the circumstances that should be taken into account in the assessment as to whether the accused was deprived of a fair hearing.'[740] In such an instance, the fact that the incriminating statements were made without access to a lawyer does not of itself mean that the rights of the defence were irretrievably prejudiced.[741]

14.3 Effective Representation

The representation to which an accused is entitled must be an effective representation. 'The right to an effective representation should be satisfied by the services of a lawyer actually exercising the ordinary professional skill and care in the interests of the defence of his client.'[742] The principle of equality of arms provides another way of formulating the breach of Article 6 which can occur through the absence of a competent and effective representation.[743]

---

[735] Ibid, per Lord Hope at [27], with whom the others agreed.
[736] *Ambrose v Harris* [2011] UKSC 43, [2011] 1 WLR 2435.
[737] Ibid, [20].
[738] Ibid, [32].
[739] Ibid, [63].
[740] Ibid, [64].
[741] Ibid, [64]. See further R White and P Ferguson, 'Sins of the Father? The Sons of Cadder' [2012] *Criminal Law Review* 357.
[742] *McLean* (n 710), per Lord Clyde at [60] in reliance on *Artico v Italy* (1980) 3 EHRR 1; *Goddi v Italy* (1984) 6 EHRR 457.
[743] Ibid, per Lord Clyde at [61].

It is not necessary for a contravention of Article 6(3)(c) that the accused should have suffered injury as a result of the contravention:

> He need not show that with an effective representative the trial would have gone differently or that the outcome would have been different. Where in a serious case an accused has no effective representation that fact may be enough to constitute a contravention. ... The appearance of fairness may be a relevant consideration in this context. That justice should not only be done but should be seen to be done is a principle often referred to in relation to cases of bias or partiality, but it may also be applied to an absence of effective representation.[744]

Where an accused represents himself, it has been held that he cannot pray in aid the ordinary and anticipated disadvantages of his choice in support of the argument that there was inequality of arms which renders his conviction unsafe.[745] Where no defence is put forward at a trial in consequence of the defendant's deliberate decision not to be present, there is no violation of the right as the defendant has chosen not to exercise it.[746]

14.4 Legal assistance

The right to legal assistance is not absolute and in the context of civil proceedings, there may be reasonable grounds for refusing legal aid.[747] In criminal proceedings consideration of the cost-effective use of funds has been recognised by the European Commission of Human Rights as an appropriate consideration in determining the work for which payments may be made. 'But in such proceedings, particularly where there is a risk of a loss of liberty, it would be far more difficult to find examples where legal aid might be refused, particularly at first instance.'[748]

Even in relation to an appeal the interests of justice may require the state to grant legal assistance in the light of such considerations as the severity of the sentence, the need for professional skill in handling the case and the complexity of the issues.[749] In some instances, proceedings may change from civil to criminal, such as where, in disobedience of an order of the Family Court, an individual faces committal proceedings for contempt of court.[750] At least in the context of legal aid, the accused may not be absolutely entitled to a representative of his own choice.[751]

The Privy Council considered both effective representation and legal assistance in its

---

[744] Ibid, per Lord Clyde at [62] in reliance on *S v Switzerland* (1991) 14 EHRR 670; *Artico* (n 742); *Boner v United Kingdom* (1994) 19 EHRR 246.

[745] *R v Brown* [2001] EWCA Crim 1771.

[746] Ibid, per Lord Hutton at [36]. *Jones* (n 468).

[747] *McLean* (n 710), per Lord Clyde at [63] in reliance on *Thaw v UK* (1996) 22 EHRR CD 100; *S & M v UK* (1993) 18 EHRR CD 172.

[748] See eg *Newman* (n 709).

[749] *McLean* (n 710), per Lord Clyde at [63] in reliance on *M v UK* (1983) 6 EHRR 345; *Monnell & Morris v UK* (1987) 10 EHRR 205; *Pakelli* (n 717); *Granger v UK* (1990) 12 EHRR 469. In *R v Oates*, Court of Appeal, 25 April 2002 the court, in reliance on *Monnell*, ibid, held that representation was not required on an application for leave to appeal.

[750] *In the Matter of K (children)* [2002] EWCA Crim 1071, [2002] 1 WLR 2833. See also *In the Matter of G (a child)* [2003] EWCA Civ 489, [2003] 1 WLR 2051 and *Begum v Anam* [2004] EWCA Civ 578.

[751] *McLean* (n 710), per Lord Clyde at [64] in reliance on *Croissant v Germany* (1992) 16 EHRR 135 at [29].

judgment in *McLean*.[752] In April 1999 the appellants were charged with racially aggravated assault and breach of the peace. They were granted criminal legal aid pursuant to section 24 of the Legal Aid (Scotland) Act 1986. They instructed two Glasgow firms of solicitors to conduct their defence. The payments to which the solicitors were entitled for conducting the proceedings were set out in the Criminal Legal Aid (Fixed Payments) (Scotland) Regulations 1999. In July 1999 the solicitors lodged pleas in bar of trial on the appellants' behalf raising two devolution issues. The first issue was whether the act of the Lord Advocate in continuing to prosecute the appellants was incompatible with Article 6. The second issue was whether the failure of the Scottish Executive to repeal or amend the Criminal Legal Aid (Fixed Payments) (Scotland) Regulations 1999 was incompatible with Article 6.

The Privy Council unanimously held that what must be shown was that some form of actual or inevitable prejudice would result so that the Sheriff could not be expected to reach a fair verdict in all the circumstances.[753] The principle that there must be equality of arms on both sides required that there must be a fair balance between the parties. However, the purpose of Article 6 was not to make it impractical to bring those accused of crime to justice. The essential question was whether the alleged inequality of arms was such as to deprive the accused of his right to a fair trial. The majority concluded that in the present case it was not shown that the fixed fee regime would give rise to any actual or inevitable prejudice at the appellants' trial. It was wrong to assume that the solicitors who were instructed would reduce their standards of preparation simply because they considered that they would not receive adequate remuneration for their work when they were paid the fixed fee. In the absence of any contrary evidence, the assumption was that they would conduct the defence according to the standards which are expected of their profession as they were required to do by the codes.[754]

However, it was pointed out that different considerations would arise were the solicitors to withdraw and the appellants were unable to find replacement solicitors because of the inflexibility of the Regulations. Lord Clyde in particular held that there was a real likelihood that in another case a serious risk of a contravention of Article 6 may arise. If the result of the Regulations was that no legal representative was available for an accused in a case where the ECHR requires that he should be represented, a breach would occur.[755]

---

15. Article 6(3)(d): Witnesses

Article 6(3)(d) provides that everyone charged with a criminal offence has the right to examine or have examined witnesses against him and to obtain the attendance and

---

[752] Ibid.

[753] Ibid, per Lord Hope at [37], with whom Lords Nicholls and Millet agreed.

[754] Ibid, per Lord Hope at [38]–[43].

[755] Ibid, [32]. Lord Hobhouse at [75]–[81] did not accept that the regulations as they stood were fully compatible with Art 6.

examination of witnesses on his behalf under the same conditions as witnesses against him. It has been held that this guarantee does not add anything of significance to the requirements of English law for witnesses to give their evidence in the presence of the accused.[756] No conviction should be based solely or to a decisive extent upon the statements or testimony of anonymous witnesses. 'The reason is that such a conviction results from a trial which cannot be regarded as fair.' This is the view traditionally taken by the common law of England.[757]

This right does not guarantee the accused a right to be in the same room as the witness giving evidence[758] and does not prevent evidence being given by live television link or video recording as long as the defence has an adequate and proper opportunity to challenge and question a witness on his statement at some stage.[759] It is not necessarily incompatible with this article for depositions to be read even if there has been no opportunity to question the witness at any stage of the proceedings. However, the trial must be fair, and the quality of the evidence and its inherent reliability plus the degree of caution exercised in relation to reliance on it will be relevant to this question.[760] Where that witness provides the sole or determinative evidence against the accused, permitting the statement to be read may risk infringing this right.[761] Much depends on whether or not the witness has been intimidated by the defendant. It has been held that, where the court is sure that the sole witness has been kept away by the defendant or persons acting for him, there would be no breach of the article if

> care has been taken to see that the quality of the evidence was compelling, if firm steps were taken to draw the jury's attention to aspects of that witnesses' credibility and if a clear direction was given to the jury to exercise caution.[762]

More difficulty arises where it is not quite so clear-cut, but it has also been held that where there is a high probability of witness intimidation on behalf of the defence, and where the court is sure to the criminal standard of proof that witnesses cannot be traced or brought before the court, there is no absolute rule that, where compelling evidence is the sole or decisive evidence, admission of a statement would infringe the article.[763]

The House of Lords considered the issue of witness intimidation in *R v Davis*[764] where seven witnesses claimed to be in fear for their lives if it became known they had given evidence against the appellant. Various measures were taken including giving evidence under pseudonym, withholding addresses and personal details, mechanically distorting voices, and giving evidence from behind a screen. It was held that it was necessary to consider the impact of the protective measures on the conduct of the defence. The House of Lords concluded that the protective measures imposed here hampered the conduct of the defence in a manner and to an extent which was unlawful and rendered the trial unfair.[765] In essence, the ability of counsel for the appellant to

---

[756] *R v Davis* [2008] UKHL 36, [2008] 1 AC 1128.

[757] Ibid, per Lord Bingham at [25].

[758] *R v Camberwell Green Youth Court ex p D* [2005] UKHL 4, [2005] 1 WLR 393, per Lord Rodger at [15].

[759] Ibid, per Lord Rodger at [12]. See also *R v Radak* [1999] 1 Cr App Rep 187.

[760] *R v Sellick* [2005] EWCA Crim 651, [50]. See also *R v Denton* [2001] 1 Cr App Rep 227; *R v Abiodun* [2003] EWCA Crim 2167.

[761] *R v Arnold* [2004] EWCA Crim 1293.

[762] *Sellick* (n 760), [52].

[763] Ibid, [53].

[764] *Davis* (n 756).

[765] Ibid, per Lord Bingham at [35].

cross-examine the decisive witnesses against him was gravely compromised.[766] Lord Carswell held as follows:

> An important consideration is the relative importance of the witness's testimony in the prosecution case. If it constitutes the sole or decisive evidence against the defendant, anonymising which prevents or unduly hinders the defendant and his advisers from taking steps to undermine the credit of the witness is most likely to operate unfairly. It is a question of fact in any given case what, if any, measures would be compatible with sufficient fairness of the trial. Courts trying criminal cases should not be over-ready to resort to such measures[767]

The Supreme Court considered the issue again in *Horncastle*.[768] Here the appeals of the appellants were based upon the ground that each did not receive a fair trial, contrary to Article 6 as there was placed before the jury the statement of a witness who was not called to give evidence pursuant to exceptions to the hearsay rule contained in the Criminal Evidence (Witness Anonymity) Act 2008, which had been enacted in response to the judgment in *Davis*. The exceptions were not subject to the sole and decisive rule as the Act contained safeguards, including a code, to ensure that hearsay evidence was only admitted when it was fair that it should be.

In each case the witness was the victim of the alleged offence. The principal issue raised by the appeals was whether a conviction based solely or to a decisive extent on the statement of a witness whom the defendant had no chance of cross examining necessarily infringed the defendant's right to a fair trial under Articles 6(1) and 6(3) (d). The appellants relied upon the judgment of the ECtHR in *Al-Khawaja and Tahery v United Kingdom*.[769] However, unusually the Supreme Court held that it was open to it to decline to follow this decision, giving reasons for adopting this course, thereby giving the ECtHR the opportunity to reconsider.[770]

In a joint judgment, the Supreme Court held that the ECtHR had recognised that exceptions to Article 6(3)(d) were required in the interests of justice. However, it noted that the manner in which it had developed these exceptions had resulted in a jurisprudence that lacked clarity. It held that the sole or decisive rule would create severe practical difficulties if applied here and that *Al-Khawaja* did not establish that it was necessary to apply the sole or decisive rule in this jurisdiction.[771] It concluded that the provisions of the Criminal Justice Act 2003 struck the right balance between the imperative that a trial must be fair and the interests of victims in particular and society in general that a criminal should not be immune from conviction where a witness, who had given critical evidence in a statement that could be shown to be reliable, died or could not be called to give evidence for some other reason.[772] In its view, the regime enacted by Parliament creating exceptions to the hearsay rule contained safeguards that rendered the sole or decisive rule unnecessary.[773]

---

[766] Ibid, per Lord Rodger at [44].

[767] Ibid, per Lord Carswell at [59].

[768] *Horncastle* [2009] UKSC 14, [2010] 2 AC 373.

[769] *Al-Khawaja and Tahery v United Kingdom* (2009) 49 EHRR 1.

[770] Ibid, [11].

[771] Ibid, [14].

[772] Ibid, [108].

[773] Ibid, [14]. See also *R v Al-Khawaja* [2005] EWCA Crim 2697, [2006] 1 WLR 1078; *R v Ibrahim* [2012] EWCA Crim 837, [2012] 4 All ER 225. See further M Redmayne, 'Hearsay and Human Rights: Al Khawaja in the Grand Chamber' (2012) 75 *Modern Law Review* 865.

16. Article 6(3)(e): Interpreter

Finally, Article 6(3)(3) protects the right to have the free assistance of an interpreter if the accused cannot understand or speak the language used in court. Provided that the interpreter is competent, the right is not infringed.[774] If an interpreter is required to be present during an interview between a solicitor and his client, the interpreter is subject to exactly the same duties in relation to confidentiality as the solicitor who is giving the advice.[775]

---

[774] *R v Ungvari* [2003] EWCA Crim 2346.
[775] *R (on the application of Bozkurt) v South Thames Magistrates Court* [2001] EWHC (Admin) 400.

11

Article 8: The Right to Respect for Private Life

1. Introduction

Article 8(1) provides that everyone has the right to respect for his private and family life, his home and his correspondence. In essence, the nature of this right is the right to live one's personal life without unjustified interference and to have the right to personal integrity.[1] These are not absolute rights: Article 8(2) provides that the rights contained in Article 8(1) may be subject to interference provided the interference is in accordance with law and necessary in one of the interests set out. This is the first of the Convention rights drafted in this manner, the others being Article 9 (freedom of thought, conscience and religion), Article 10 (freedom of expression) and Article 11 (freedom of assembly and association).

Except for the right to respect for correspondence, the rights protected by Article 8(1) have generated a number of claims under the HRA and are therefore considered separately in this and the following two chapters. But despite considerable judicial attention, in contrast to other Convention rights, the importance of the right to respect for private life is rarely commented on. It has been recognised that a proper degree of privacy is essential for the 'well-being and development of an individual' and that restraints imposed on government to 'pry into the lives of citizens go to the essence of a democratic state'.[2] Much can be explained by the fact that prior to the HRA the right to respect for private life was relatively underdeveloped in national law. At common law, the courts have been unwilling, or unable, to formulate a tort of invasion of privacy although there are a number of common law and statutory remedies which do provides some private life protection.[3] These include the torts of trespass, nuisance,

---

[1] *Anufrijeva v Southwark LBC* [2003] EWCA Civ 1406, [2004] QB 1124.
[2] *Campbell v MGN Ltd House of Lords* [2004] UKHL 22, [2004] 2 AC 457, per Lord Nicholls at [12].
[3] *Wainwright v Home Office* [2003] UKHL 53, [2004] 2 AC 406, per Lord Hoffmann at [18].

defamation and malicious falsehood, breach of confidence and the statutory remedies under the Protection from Harassment Act 1997[4] and the Data Protection Act 1998.[5]

---

2. Private Life

2.1 Generally

It is necessary for a court first to determine whether or not the issue raised is within the scope of Article 8 as if it is not within its scope, the question of a possible breach of it does not arise at all.[6] Private life is a broad term and there has been no real attempt to define it comprehensively.[7] It has been held that the content of the right is elusive and that it 'does not lend itself to exhaustive definition'.[8] It has also been observed that an interference with privacy is 'not even like the elephant, of which it can be said it is at least easy to recognise if not to define'.[9] The definition is flexible and capable of development 'as thinking within the Council of Europe also grows and develops'.[10] In difficult or borderline cases, there is much to be said for taking a broad view of the scope of the right and requiring the state to justify its interference.[11]

At a very general level private life covers all aspects of a person's physical identity and thus freedom to live life as he or she chooses.[12] Others have attempted more comprehensive definitions.

> [T]he privacy of a human being denotes at the same time the personal 'space' in which the individual is free to be itself, and also the carapace, or shell, or umbrella, or whatever other metaphor is preferred, which protects that space from intrusion. An infringement of privacy is an affront to the personality, which is damaged both by the violation and by the demonstration that the personal space is not inviolate.[13]

A number of definitions were offered by members of the House of Lords in the *Countryside Alliance* case. Lord Bingham held that the purpose of Article 8 was to protect the individual against intrusion by agents of the state, unless for good reason, into the private sphere within which individuals expect to be left alone to conduct their personal

---

[4] In *KD v Chief Constable of Hampshire* [2005] EWHC 2550 (QB) [2005] Po LR 253, the High Court held that the Protection from Harassment Act 1997 had to be interpreted compatibly with Art 8 [144].
[5] Ibid.
[6] *R (L) v Commissioner of Police of the Metropolis* [2009] UKSC 3, [2010] 1 AC 410, per Lord Hope at [23].
[7] *R (on the application of Razgar) v Secretary of State for the Home Department* [2004] UKHL 27, [2004] 2 AC 368, per Lord Bingham at [9].
[8] *R (Countryside Alliance) v Attorney General* [2007] UKHL 52, [2007] 3 WLR 922, per Lord Bingham at [10].
[9] *R v Broadcasting Standards Commission ex p BBC* [2001] QB 885, per Lord Woolf MR at [14].
[10] *Countryside Alliance* (n 8), per Baroness Hale at [121].
[11] Ibid.
[12] *Orejudos v Royal Borough of Kensington and Chelsea* [2003] EWCA Civ 1967, [20].
[13] *BBC* (n 9), per Mustill LJ at [48].

affairs and live their personal lives as they choose.[14] Baroness Hale stated that Article 8 reflected two separate but related fundamental values:

> One is the inviolability of the home and personal communications from official snooping, entry and interference without a very good reason. It protects a private space, whether in a building, or through the post, the telephone lines, the airwaves or the ether, within which people can both be themselves and communicate privately with one another. The other is the inviolability of a different kind of space, the personal and psychological space within which each individual develops his or her own sense of self and relationships with other people. ... Article 8 protects the private space, both physical and psychological, within which individuals can develop and relate to other around them. But that falls some way short of protecting everything they might want to do even in that private space; and it certainly does not protect things that they can only do by leaving it and engaging in a very public gathering and activity.[15]

The claim here concerned a challenge to the Hunting Act 2004 and there were two broad groups of claimants: those professionally involved in hunting and dependent upon the sport for their occupation; and those who permitted hunting across their land. Lord Bingham observed that common to some members of both groups was a strong psychological and social commitment to hunting as a traditional rural activity involving the individual, the family and the community more deeply than any ordinary recreation. It was for most of these individuals a core part of their lives.[16] Nevertheless, the House of Lords unanimously held that hunting wild mammals with dogs did not come within the scope of Article 8. Lord Bingham, and the other members of the House of Lords, was not persuaded as fox-hunting was a very public activity carried out in daylight with considerable colour and noise, often attracting the attention of onlookers attracted by the spectacle.[17] Furthermore, the hunting fraternity was not seen as analogous to a distinctive group, with a traditional culture and lifestyle 'so fundamental as to form part of its identity'.[18]

This conclusion was clearly difficult for some of their Lordships. For example, Lord Rodger argued that Article 8 protected those features of a person's life which were integral to his or her identity.[19] He would have found the hunting ban was within the scope of private life but for the fact that it was not a private activity.[20] Lord Brown also found the conclusion difficult and although he agreed with Lord Bingham's findings as to the scope of Article 8, he strongly wished it were otherwise, asking why Article 8 'should not encompass a broad philosophy of live and let live'.[21]

> Article 8's protection is recognised to extend to a right to identity and to personal development and ... the notion of personal autonomy. It encompasses almost any aspect of a person's sexuality and a good deal else that is clearly personal. But why should respect for private life not encompass also wider concepts of self-fulfilment? ... Many people in a real sense live for some particular activity, whether their profession or their recreation. In a real sense it

---

[14] *Countryside Alliance* (n 8), [11].
[15] Ibid, [116].
[16] Ibid, [9].
[17] Ibid, [15].
[18] Ibid, [15].
[19] Ibid, [101].
[20] Ibid, [108].
[21] Ibid, [139].

defines them. Often if provides them with their feelings of identity, self-esteem and position in the community.[22]

As this jurisprudence indicates, often there is no simple answer as to whether or not private life is engaged. In some instances, such as the hunting example, a conclusion can only be reached by consideration of a variety of factors. Similarly difficulties were present in N[23] where a challenge was brought to a ban on smoking at a secure hospital. A majority of the Court of Appeal held that a combination of factors had to be considered to determine if the activity was within the scope of Article 8, including whether smoking was integral to identity, an aspect of social interaction, or whether the hospital was to be regarded as a patient's home.[24] It was appreciated that the hospital was not the same as a private home.[25] As the nature of the place was not compatible with a strong Article 8 right, the appellants had to rely upon the proximity of the activity to personal identity or physical and moral integrity. The majority concluded that whilst it was difficult to judge the importance of smoking to the integrity of a person's identity, it was not sufficiently close to be protected by Article 8 and was not to be equated with development of personality.[26] Also rejected was the argument that the right to smoke was an aspect of the right to establish and develop relationships with other human beings and the outside world.[27] The majority concluded that Article 8 did not protect a right to smoke in a secure hospital.[28]

Some matters are clearly not within the scope of respect for private life. For example, in Orejudos[29] the Court of Appeal held that the terms on which a homeless person was provided with accommodation by a public authority were not within his private sphere. A majority of the House of Lords in R v G[30] held that prosecution policy and sentencing did not fall under Article 8. Lord Hoffmann observed that if the prosecution had been unduly heavy handed, that may be unfair and unjust, but not an infringement of human rights.[31] Dissenting on this point, Lord Hope held that the prosecutor had acted incompatibly with Article 8 in that he continued the prosecution under a much harsher law when the offence fell within the ambit of another law.[32]

Other matters, such as information, identity, physical and psychological integrity and autonomy, are undoubtedly included within the concept of private life and are examined in more detail in the following paragraphs. Issues such as sexual behaviour

---

[22] Ibid, [139]. He gave at [140] as examples music, dance, chess, bridge, polo, golf, climbing, and canoeing. See also *Friend v Lord Advocate* [2007] UKHL 53, [2008] HRLR 11 where the claim against the Protection of Wild Mammals (Scotland) Act 2002 was considered and similar reasons given for the non-application of Art 8.

[23] *R (N) v Secretary of State for Health* [2009] EWCA Civ 795, [2009] HRLR 31.

[24] Ibid, [37].

[25] Ibid, [40] and [44].

[26] Ibid, [49].

[27] Ibid, [50].

[28] Ibid, [51]. See also *R (Foster) v Governor of High Down Prison* [2010] EWHC 2224 (Admin).

[29] *Orejudos* (n 12).

[30] *R v G* [2008] UKHL 37, [2009] 1 AC 92.

[31] Ibid, [10]. See also *SXH v Crown Prosecution Service* [2013] EWHC 71 (QB).

[32] Lord Carswell agreed. See also *MacMahon* [2012] NIQB 93 where the NI High Court held that prosecutorial decisions came within the broad range of interests protected by Art 8. See further B Malkani, 'Article 8 of the European Convention on Human Rights and the Decision to Prosecute' [2011] *Criminal Law Review* 943.

and private space, which have generated a number of applications before the ECtHR have given rise to very few claims under the HRA but still form a part of private life.[33]

2.2 Information

2.2.1 Generally

Private information concerning an individual is within the protection of Article 8. The holding, disclosure and refusal to allow access to such information may all constitute interferences with this right.[34] Liability is not dependent on carelessness or bad faith and a breach may be committed unwittingly.[35] Photographs also convey information and are similarly protected if the activity photographed is private.[36] Filming a private activity may also constitute a violation of Article 8(1)[37] and if photography or filming takes place without consent, this may also constitute an interference with autonomy.[38] It has been held that the truth or falsity of the information is an irrelevant inquiry in deciding whether the information is entitled to be protected, although a defamation action is open where the information is false.[39]

2.2.2 Is the Information Private?

It must be determined that the information or activity is private and not public. Article 8 is engaged if the person publishing the information knows or ought to know that there is a reasonable expectation that the information in question will be kept confidential[40] (or private).[41] This is an objective question and the reasonable expectation is that of the person who is affected by the publicity. The question is what a reasonable person of ordinary sensibilities would feel if he or she was placed in the same position as the claimant and faced with the same publicity.[42] In *Murray* the Court of Appeal expanded upon this:

> [T]he question whether there is a reasonable expectation of privacy is a broad one, which takes account of all the circumstances of the case. They include the attributes of the claimant, the nature of the activity in which the claimant was engaged, the place at which it was hap-

---

[33] On the definition of private life, see further K Hughes, 'A Behavioural Understanding of Privacy and its Implications for Privacy Law' (2012) 75 *Modern Law Review* 806.

[34] *Baker v Secretary of State for the Home Department* [2001] UKHRR 1275.

[35] *W v Westminster City Council* [2005] EWHC (QB) 102, [2005] 4 All ER 96.

[36] *Campbell* (n 2), per Baroness Hale at [154]. Baroness Hale commented that, in this case, the photographs by themselves were not objectionable but became so with the accompanying text. It is clear that photographs taken without consent do not amount to an interference with private life per se.

[37] See eg *Jones v University of Warwick* [2003] EWCA Civ 151, [2003] 1 WLR 954.

[38] *Douglas v Hello! Ltd* [2001] QB 967, per Sedley LJ at [139] and Keene LJ at [165]. See also *BKM Ltd v British Broadcasting Corporation* [2009] EWHC 3151 (Ch).

[39] *Ash v McKennitt* [2006] EWCA Civ 1714, [2007] 3 WLR 194.

[40] In *Campbell* (n 2) Lord Nicholls commented that the essence of the tort was now better encapsulated as misuse of private information.

[41] Ibid, per Lord Nicholls at [21], Lord Hope at [85] and Baroness Hale at [134]. Doubt was cast on the test proposed by Gleeson CJ in *Australian Broadcasting Corporation v Lenah Game Meats Pty Ltd* (2001) 185 ALR 1, [42].

[42] Ibid, per Lord Hope at [99].

pening , the nature and purpose of the intrusion, the absence of consent and whether it was known or could be inferred, the effect on the claimant and the circumstances in which and the purposes for which the information came into the hands of the publisher.[43]

Where information is generally accessible, it is not private. However, the fact that it is known to a limited number of members of the public does not prevent it having and retaining the character of privacy, or even that it has previously been widely available.[44] It may also be necessary to take into account the use to which the information will be put. For example, in *Robertson*[45] the Divisional Court held that the sale of the Electoral Register to commercial organisations engaged Article 8.[46]

Certain types of information are obviously private. These include information about a person's health and treatment for ill-health;[47] private conversations[48] and private telephone conversations;[49] the information contained in a DNA sample;[50] documents subject to legal professional privilege;[51] a private consultation with a lawyer;[52] information given to a police officer about sexual activities for the purposes of criminal proceedings;[53] a taxpayer's financial and fiscal affairs;[54] and information stored on a person's mobile phone.[55] In other instances, the courts proceed on a case-by-case basis.[56] For example, in *Campbell*[57] the House of Lords concluded that Ms Campbell would have had a reasonable expectation of privacy in relation to: the fact that she was receiving treatment at Narcotics Anonymous; the details of the treatment; and the photograph (visual portrayal) of her leaving a specific meeting with other addicts. '[I]t related to an important aspect of Miss Campbell's physical and mental health and the treatment she was receiving for it. It had also been received from an insider in breach of confidence.'[58]

In *Douglas*[59] the Court of Appeal held that the wedding was not private, attended by a few members of family and friends.[60] Furthermore, the appellants had sold their

---

[43] *Murray v Big Pictures (UK) Ltd* [2008] EWCA Civ 446, [2008] 3 WLR 1360, [36].

[44] *Mills v News Group Newspapers Ltd* [2001] EMLR 41, [25]. See also *Trimingham v Associated Newspapers Ltd* [2012] EWHC 1296 (QB), [2012] 4 All ER 717. In *R (on the application of Pearson) v Driving & Vehicle Licensing Agency* [2002] EWHC (Admin) 2482, [2003] Crim LR 199 the court held that the endorsement of driving licences with road traffic offences was not an interference.

[45] *R (Robertson) v Wakefield Metropolitan District Council* [2001] EWHC (Admin) 915, [2002] 2 WLR 889.

[46] Ibid, [34]. However, in *Farrer v Secretary of State* [2002] EWHC (Admin) 1917 the court held that the supply by the DVLA of vehicle registration details to detective agencies and others was a moderate interference and proportionate to the legitimate aim of the enforcement of fines.

[47] *Robertson* (n 45); *Campbell* (n 2), per Baroness Hale at [145]. See also *R (on the application of S) v Plymouth City Council* [2002] EWCA Civ 388, [2002] 1 WLR 2583; *H (A Healthcare Worker) v Associated Newspapers Ltd* [2002] EWCA Civ 195, [2002] EMLR 23.

[48] *R v Mason* [2002] EWCA Crim 385, [2002] 2 Cr App R 38.

[49] *R v P* [2001] 2 WLR 463; *R (N) v Ashworth Special Hospital Authority* [2001] EWHC (Admin) 339, [2001] 1 WLR 25.

[50] *Attorney General's Reference No 3 of 1999* [2001] 2 AC 91.

[51] *R (on the application of Morgan Grenfell & Co Ltd) v Special Commissioners of Income Tax* [2002] UKHL 21, [2003] 1 AC 563.

[52] *Re McE* [2009] UKHL 15, [2009] 1 AC 908.

[53] *KD v Chief Constable of Hampshire* [2005] 2550 (QB), [2005] Po LR 253.

[54] *Revenue and Customs Commissioners v Banerjee* [2009] EWHC 1229 (Ch), [2009] 3 All ER 930.

[55] *AMP v Persons Unknown* [2011] EWHC 3454.

[56] *X and Y v Persons Unknown* [2006] EWHC 2783 (QB), [2007] EMLR 10 [48].

[57] *Campbell* (n 2).

[58] Ibid, at [147] per Baroness Hale. See also Lord Hope at [95] and Lord Carswell at [165].

[59] Above n 26.

[60] Ibid, per Brooke LJ at [95] and per Keene LJ at [168]–[169].

privacy to the magazine *OK!* for a handsome sum.[61] The only aspect of private life which remained was not information but autonomy, in particular, their right of veto over publication of the photographs in order to maintain the kind of image professionally and personally important to them. Prince Charles's private journal describing his participation in events which marked the handing over of Hong Kong was held to be private although it had been sent to approximately 75 people.[62] It was held in *Mosley*[63] that anyone indulging in sexual activity was entitled to a degree of privacy[64] and that the clandestine recording of sexual activity on private property engaged Article 8. However, arrest for misconduct which took place at home, and the public removal of an individual from the scene by the police, have been held not to be private matters[65] and abusive activity or sexual harassment is not private.[66] It has also been held that the author of a blog has no reasonable expectation of privacy in respect of his or her identity.[67]

A difficult question arose in *Attorney General's Reference No 3 of 1999*[68] where it was held that the fact that a person was acquitted of rape was not private. However, in a television programme the BBC wished to draw attention to the fact that a DNA profile obtained from a saliva sample that was taken from him when he was arrested for an offence of burglary matched the DNA profile obtained from swabs taken from the rape victim. Referring to the conclusion of the ECtHR in *S and Marper v United Kingdom*,[69] Lord Hope explained that as the indiscriminate retention of samples of a person's DNA was incompatible with Article 8, publication of the fact that his retained DNA had been used to link him to the commission of a crime of which he had been acquitted also engaged Article 8 and he had a reasonable expectation of privacy in relation to this information.

> The link that his DNA samples provides to the commission of the rape is personal information. The giving of publicity to the link will inevitably suggest that he is guilty of the offence. ... His reputation, his personality, the umbrella that protects his personal space from intrusion, will just as inevitably be damaged by it.[70]

2.2.3 Public Figures and Private Life

It is possible for public figures to retain a private life. It has been held that an individual who is photographed and described in print, and about whom information or speculation is published regarding his or her private life, has not forfeited or waived their entitlement to privacy with regard to 'intimate personal relationships or the conduct of a private life generally'.[71] However, close attention may need to be paid to how much information came into the public domain and its limits as some public figures take the

---

[61] Ibid, per Sedley LJ at [140].

[62] *HRH Prince of Wales v Associated Newspapers Ltd* [2006] EWCA Civ 1776, [2007] 3 WLR 222.

[63] *Mosley v News Group Newspapers Ltd* [2008] EWHC 1777 (QB).

[64] Ibid, [98].

[65] *H v Tomlinson* [2008] EWCA Civ 1258, [2009] ELR 14.

[66] *BUQ v HRE* [2012] EWHC 774 (QB), [2012] IRLR 653.

[67] *Author of a Blog v Times Newspapers Ltd* [2009] EWHC 1358 (QB), [2009] EMLR 22.

[68] *Attorney General's Reference No 3 of 1999* [2009] UKHL 34, [2010] 1 AC 145.

[69] *S and Marper v United Kingdom* (2009) 48 EHRR 50.

[70] Above n 68, [22].

[71] *X and Y v Persons Unknown* [2006] EWHC 2783 (QB), [2007] EMLR 10 [28].

view that any publicity is good publicity, 'being prepared to reveal any titbit to attract attention to themselves or to make money'.[72] It has been appreciated by the courts that a bland answer in response to enquiries as to how things are going in their lives does not constitute a waiver of Convention rights.[73] For example, in *X and Y* the court held that the circumstances of marital breakdown or tension were likely to be individual and specific to the people concerned.[74]

Even if something has already been published, further coverage can infringe private life. Where a claimant has chosen to put personal information into the public domain, the media is not free to publish other details relating to the same subject matter as individuals have some degree of control over how much information is released.[75] For example, in *Mosley*[76] the High Court held that video footage of the claimant on a newspaper's website had been seen by thousands of people around the world and was so widely accessible that an order for an injunction would make little practical difference. It held that this was either because the claimant no longer had a reasonable expectation of privacy in relation to it or because it had entered the public domain to the extent that in practical terms there was no longer anything for the law to protect.[77]

If a public figure has made untrue pronouncements about the information which has been revealed, this does not make the information any less private[78] but will ultimately affect the balance struck between private life and freedom of expression. Where a public figure makes untrue pronouncements about his or her private life, the press is normally entitled to put the record straight.[79]

2.2.4 Relationships

In *McKennitt*[80] the Court of Appeal held that it was important to have regard to the relationship between the parties and the expectation of confidence which this created.[81] This will further strengthen a private life claim such as here where it found that a person's health was a private matter and 'doubly private' when information about it was imparted in the context of a relationship of confidence.[82] Furthermore, it is not possible to undermine the privacy of particular information by arguing that the fact it was disclosed in a relationship made it less private as the relationship gave the person disclosing access to the information in the first place.[83]

In *B&C v A*[84] the Court of Appeal held that there is a difference between the confidentiality which attaches to permanent relationships and that which attaches to affairs.[85]

---

[72] Ibid, [28].
[73] Ibid, [37].
[74] Ibid, [38].
[75] Ibid, [65].
[76] *Mosley v News Group Newspapers Ltd* [2008] EWHC 687 (QB).
[77] Ibid, [36].
[78] *Campbell* (n 2), per Baroness Hale at [147].
[79] Ibid, per Lord Hope at [82].
[80] *Ash v McKennitt* [2006] EWCA Civ 1714, [2007] 3 WLR 194.
[81] Ibid, [16].
[82] Ibid, [23].
[83] Ibid, [32]. Where there is a duty of confidence it is possible that reference to Art 8 is not really necessary as the tort of breach of confidence will suffice to provide protection. See *HRH Prince of Wales* (n 62).
[84] *B & C v A* [2002] EWCA Civ 337, [2002] 3 WLR 542.
[85] Ibid, [43](ii).

Nevertheless, there was still a modest degree of confidentiality (or privacy) concerning these relationships to which the claimant was entitled.[86] There is no general rule that an adulterer can never obtain an injunction to restrain the publication of matters relating to his or her adulterous relationship. Even an adulterous relationship may attract in certain respects a legitimate expectation of privacy.[87] For example, in *ETK*[88] the Court of Appeal held that a sexual relationship was a private matter and the fact that it became known to work colleagues did not put the information in the public domain.[89] Where it is sought to publish information about an affair, the claimant's family members and their Article 8 rights must also be taken into account.[90] However, there has been a slight retreat from this in the decision of the High Court in *Goodwin*[91] which concerned an injunction prohibiting the disclosure of information concerning a sexual relationship between Fred Goodwin and a colleague of his at the Royal Bank of Scotland.

The High Court held that the fact that the parties were in a sexual relationship may, in principle, be a fact in respect of which they had a reasonable expectation of privacy.[92] However, it also held that the fact that details of a sexual relationship were private did not necessarily mean that the bare fact of a sexual relationship was private.[93] The question depended upon the particular circumstances of each case. The bare fact of a relationship may need to be kept private where an abusive family will not allow a couple to be together, or where details of a relationship have already been disclosed so that if a name is published, it will be linked to details already known.[94] In the present case it concluded that there was no reasonable expectation of privacy in respect of the bare fact of the relationship.[95] However, the privacy of the female's name and work position were considered separately, the court concluding that on balance against Article 10 her name should not be published but her job description should be.[96]

2.2.5 Photographs in Public Places

It has been argued by a number of respondents that where a photograph is taken in a public place, this can never constitute an interference with private life. One example is *Murray*[97] where a photograph was taken of the child of famous parents in a public street, without their knowledge or consent, and subsequently published. The Court of Appeal found that the child may have a reasonable expectation of privacy in circumstances in which his famous mother might not.[98] It held that whether or not Article

---

[86] Ibid, [44]. See also *Theakston v MGN Limited* [2002] EWHC (QB) 137, [2002] EMLR 22; *R (on the application of Ford) v The Press Complaints Commission* [2001] EWHC (Admin) 683, [2002] EMLR 5.
[87] *CC v AB* [2006] EWHC 3083 (QB), [2007] EMLR 11 [30].
[88] *ETK v News Group Newspapers Ltd* [2011] EWCA Civ 439, [2011] 1 WLR 1827.
[89] Ibid, [11].
[90] *CTB v News Group Newspapers Ltd* [2011] EWHC 1232 (QB), [3].
[91] *Goodwin v NGN Ltd* [2011] EWHC 1437 (QB).
[92] Ibid, [69].
[93] Ibid, [90].
[94] Ibid, [96].
[95] Ibid, [100].
[96] See also *LNS v Persons Unknown* [2010] EWHC 119 (QB), [2010] EMLR 16; *Ferdinand v MGN Ltd* [2011] EWHC 2454 (QB); *SKA v Persons Unknown* [2012] EWHC 766 (QB).
[97] *Murray (by his litigation friends) v Big Pictures (UK) Ltd* [2008] EWCA Civ 446, [2008] 3 WLR 1360.
[98] Ibid, [14].

8 was engaged when a photographs was taken in a public place depended upon the circumstances:

> This was not the taking of a single photograph of David in the street. On the claimant's case ... it was the clandestine taking and subsequent publication of the Photograph in the context of a series of photographs which were taken for the purposes of their sale for publication, in circumstances in which BPL did not ask David's parents for their consent to the taking and publication of his photograph.[99]

The Court of Appeal also noted that the case of a child was different from that of an adult.[100] In its view, if the parents of a child had courted publicity by procuring the publication of photographs of the child in order to promote their own interests, the position would be different.[101] Here it was concluded that it was at least arguable that the child had a reasonable expectation of privacy.[102]

In *Wood*[103] the claim also concerned a photograph taken in a public place, although here the photograph was taken by police and was of an adult, the claimant, who had attended the annual general meeting of a company concerned in the organisation of trade fairs for the arms industry. The claimant was also asked by the police for his identity and when he refused they tried to obtain his identity from his travel document with the assistance of railway staff. The photograph was retained although subject to some controls. In contrast to *Murray*, the Court of Appeal here focused more on personal autonomy, another aspect of private life as discussed below. Laws LJ, with whom the other justices agreed on this point, held that the notion of the personal autonomy of every individual 'marches with the presumption of liberty enjoyed in a free polity'.[104] In Laws LJ's view, an individual's personal autonomy made him master of all those facts about his own identity,

> such as his name, health, sexuality, ethnicity, his own image ... and also of the zone of interaction ... between himself and others. He is the presumed owner of these aspects of his own self; his control of them can only be loosened, abrogated, if the State shows an objective justification for doing so.[105]

However, he also cautioned against this right being read too widely. He held that there were three safeguards: the alleged threat to personal autonomy must attain a certain level of seriousness; the claimant must enjoy a reasonable expectation of privacy; and the breadth of Article 8(1) may be curtailed by the scope of the justifications available under Article 8(2).[106] In the present case, it was acknowledged that there were circumstances in which a photograph taken in a public place may turn the event into one where Article 8 was not merely engaged but grossly violated.[107] Here it was concluded that the bare act of taking pictures in a public place was not capable of engaging Article 8(1) unless there were aggravating circumstances.[108] However, the police operation was

---

[99] Ibid, [17].
[100] Ibid, [37].
[101] Ibid, [38].
[102] Ibid, [45].
[103] *Wood v Commissioner of Police of the Metropolis* [2009] EWCA Civ 414, [2010] 1 WLR 123.
[104] Ibid, [21].
[105] Ibid, per Laws LJ at [21].
[106] Ibid, [22].
[107] Ibid, [34].
[108] Ibid, [36].

judged as a whole from the taking of the pictures to their actual and intended retention and use.[109] The Court of Appeal concluded that Article 8 was engaged:

> On the particular facts the police action, unexplained at the time it happened and carrying as it did the implication that the images would be kept and used, is a sufficient intrusion by the State into the individual's own space, his integrity, as to amount to a prima facie violation of Article 8(1). It attains a sufficient level of seriousness and in the circumstances the appellant enjoyed a reasonable expectation that his privacy would not thus be invaded.[110]

2.2.6 Filming in Public Places

Despite the prevalence of closed-circuit television (CCTV) in the modern world, there has been very little judicial consideration of how this engages Article 8. In *Kinloch*,[111] a devolution case, the Supreme Court held similarly to the judgments above that there was a zone of interaction with others, even in a public context, which may fall within the scope of private life, but did not extend this to CCTV monitoring in public places:

> But measures effective in a public place outside the person's home or private premises will not, without more, be regarded as interfering with his right to respect for his private life. Occasions when a person knowingly or intentionally involves himself in activities which may be recorded or reported in public, in circumstances where he does not have a reasonable expectation of privacy, will fall into that category. ... A person who walks down a street has to expect that he will be visible to any member of the public who happens also to be present. So too if he crosses a pavement and gets into a motor car. He can also expect to be the subject of monitoring on closed circuit television in public areas where he may go, as it is a familiar feature in places that the public frequent. The exposure of a person to measures of that kind will not amount to a breach of his rights under article 8.[112]

2.2.7 Convictions and Other Information Retained by Police

Information about a person's convictions, which is collected and stored in central records, can fall within the scope of private life.

> It is, in one sense, public information because the convictions took place in public. But the systematic storing of this information in central records means that it is available for disclosure under Part V of the 1997 Act long after the event when everyone other than the person concerned is likely to have forgotten about it. As it recedes into the past, it becomes a part of the person's private life which must be respected.[113]

The information contained in an enhanced criminal record certificate (ECRC) issued under section 115 of the Police Act 1997 has also been held to be private. The certificate contains information in addition to that which is recorded in central records. It

---

[109] Ibid, [39].
[110] Ibid, [46]. See also *R (RMC) v Commissioner of Police of the Metropolis* [2012] EWHC 1681 (Admin), [2012] 4 All ER 510 where the Administrative Court held that police retention of custody photographs engaged Art 8.
[111] *Kinloch v HM Advocate* [2012] UKSC 62, [2013] 2 WLR 141.
[112] Ibid, per Lord Hope at [19] with whom the others agreed.
[113] *L* (n 6). See also *HM Advocate v Murtagh* [2009] UKPC 36, [2010] 3 WLR 814.

may concern offences of which the person is suspected of committing even though his responsibility has not been and cannot be proved.[114] In L[115] the ECRC disclosed that the claimant's son had been put on the child protection register and that he was removed after he had been found guilty of robbery and received a custodial sentence.

> His conviction could be seen as public information because his trial was held in public. But the fact that the appellant was the mother of the person who had been convicted and sentenced to detention was private information. So too was information about the proceedings in which it was alleged that she failed to exercise the required degree of care and supervision of her son and that she had refused to co-operate with the social services.[116]

It has also been held that prior convictions, spent for the purposes of the Rehabilitation of Offenders Act 1974, are private information,[117] as are unspent convictions.[118] The conclusion in X v Y[119] that a caution received by an individual for committing a sex offence with another man in a transport café lavatory, to which the public had access, was not private as in committing the offence the individual would not have had a reasonable expectation of privacy does not sit easily with this line of authority. The better view would be that the caution needs to be considered apart from the details of the offence. And the caution itself is private information.

In $Catt$[120] the Court of Appeal concluded that information about a man which police had obtained and entered on a database, including his name, age, appearance and history of attending political demonstrations, was private but reached this conclusion on the basis of autonomy and control over information rather than the test of reasonable expectation of privacy.[121]

2.2.8 Corporate Information

Privacy of information is also important in the corporate world. In *Banque Internationale à Luxembourg*[122] it was accepted without question by the High Court that notices issued by the Commissioners of the Inland Revenue to the bank requiring specific classes of documents in relation to named taxpayers as part of an investigation into a large-scale corporate tax avoidance scheme impinged on the confidentiality and rights of privacy of the bank and the targets.[123] In *Newman*[124] it was accepted by the Lands Tribunal that sale price information contained in Particulars Delivered Forms (provided to the Inland

---

[114] *R (on the application of X) v Chief Constable of West Midlands Police* [2004] EWCA Civ 1068, [2005] 1 WLR 65. See also *Woolgar v Chief Constable of Sussex Police* [2000] 1 WLR 25, and *R v A Local Authority in the Midlands, ex p LM* [2000] 1 FCR 736 and *R (L) v Commissioner of Police of the Metropolis* [2009] UKSC 3.

[115] *L* (n 6).

[116] Ibid, per Lord Hope at [28].

[117] *N v Governor of HM Prison Dartmoor*, Administrative Court, 13 February 2001. But see *Pearson* (n 44).

[118] *R (Ellis) v Chief Constable of Essex Police* [2003] EWHC (Admin) 1321, [2003] 2 FLR 566; *R (on the application of A) v National Probation Service* [2003] EWHC (Admin) 2910.

[119] *X v Y* [2004] EWCA Civ 662, [2004] ICR 1634.

[120] *R (Catt) v Association of Chief Police Officers* [2013] EWCA Civ 192, [2013] 3 All ER 583.

[121] Ibid, [31].

[122] *R v Inland Revenue Commissioners, ex p Banque Internationale à Luxembourg SA* [2000] STC 708.

[123] See also *Guyer v Walton (Inspector of Taxes)* [2001] STC (SCD) 75.

[124] *Newman (Inspector of Taxes) v Hatt* [2002] 04 EG 175.

Revenue for stamp duty purposes) were private.[125] The fact that correspondence is of a business character does not exclude the protection of Article 8 in respect of both private life and correspondence.[126]

2.3 Identity

The right to respect for private life also protects a person's identity—how they see themselves and how others see them. Respect for this aspect of private life requires that everyone should be able to establish details of their identity as individual human beings. This includes their origins and the opportunity to understand them.[127] In *Rose*[128] the Administrative Court considered the application of individuals born as a result of artificial insemination by donor (AID) who wished to obtain identifying and non-identifying information about the donor. It concluded that Article 8 was engaged, stating that '[a] human being is a human being whatever the circumstances of his conception and an AID child is entitled to establish a picture of his identity as much as anyone else'.[129]

Claims under the HRA have been brought concerning the failure of United Kingdom law to recognise a transsexual's change in sex from their sex at birth. In *Bellinger*[130] the appellant, a male to female transsexual, argued that her marriage to a man was a valid marriage under the Matrimonial Causes Act 1973 although this Act provided that the marriage would be void if the parties were not male and female. The House of Lords was not prepared to recognise the appellant as a female for the purposes of the Matrimonial Causes Act, holding that the issues were ill-suited for determination by the courts and pre-eminently a matter for Parliament. This was particularly so given the government's intention to bring forward legislation on the subject.[131] However, their Lordships did declare that, in so far as section 11(c) of the Matrimonial Causes Act 1973 made no provision for the recognition of gender reassignment, it was incompatible with Articles 8 and 12.[132]

The position is different when the individual is not a transsexual but is of indeterminate sex or 'physical inter-sex'. In *W v W*[133] the Family Court held that, as the person was not a transsexual, the purely biological test did not apply. It concluded that, when determining whether such an individual was male or female for the purposes of marriage, it was necessary to take into account chromosomal factors, gonadal factors, genital factors, psychological factors, hormonal factors and secondary sexual charac-

---

[125] See also *Igroup Ltd v Ocwen* [2003] EWHC (Ch) 2431, [2004] 1 WLR 451; *Financial Services Authority v Amro International* [2010] EWCA Civ 123, [2010] 3 All ER 723; *Veolia ES Nottinghamshire Limited v Nottinghamshire County Council* [2010] EWCA Civ 1214, [2011] Eu LR 172.

[126] *R (Hafner) v Westminster Magistrates Court* [2008] EWHC 524 (Admin) [2009] Bus LR 489 [22].

[127] *R (on the application of Rose) v Secretary of State for Health* [2002] EWHC (Admin) 1593, [2002] 3 FCR 731, [45]. See also *Re T (a child) (DNA tests: paternity)* [2001] 3 FCR 577.

[128] *Rose*, ibid.

[129] Ibid, [47]. See also *C (A Child) v XYZ County Council* [2007] EWCA Civ 1206, [2008] 3 WLR 445.

[130] *Bellinger v Bellinger* [2003] UKHL 21, [2003] 2 AC 467.

[131] Ibid, per Lord Nicholls at [37].

[132] Ibid, per Lord Nicholls at [53] in reliance upon *Goodwin v United Kingdom* (2002) 35 EHRR 18. See also Lord Hope at [70] and Lord Hobhouse at [79]. See further S Cowan, 'That Woman Is a Woman! The Case of Bellinger v Bellinger and the Mysterious (Dis)appearance of Sex' (2004) 12 *Feminist Legal Studies* 79. See also *Chief Constable of West Yorkshire Police v A* [2004] UKHL 21, [2005] 1 AC 51, but note that this judgment turned on rights under the Equal Treatment Directive 1976, not Art 8.

[133] *W v W* [2001] 2 WLR 674.

teristics. Furthermore, the decision could be made with the benefit of hindsight looking back from the date of the marriage. Whilst not explicitly mentioned, it is clear that identity played a part in the conclusion reached.[134]

The subject matter of the claim in *Bellinger* has now been resolved by the Gender Recognition Act 2004 which provides legal recognition to those who have undergone gender reassignment. However, difficulties still arise. In *AB*[135] a preoperative transgender woman claimed that the decision of the Secretary of State to keep her in a male prison was incompatible with Article 8. The High Court agreed that the essence of the claim was the interference with the claimant's ability to progress to full gender reassignment by continued detention in a male prison.[136] It concluded that the interference with her autonomy was a significant and personal one and went to the heart of her identity.[137]

A person's reputation also forms a part of his or her identity and psychological integrity. The Supreme Court concluded that publication of the fact that an individual was subject to an order under the Terrorism (United Nations Measures) Order 2006 for facilitating the commission of acts of terrorism would affect his reputation as a member of the community in which he lived and affect his relationship with other members of that community and seriously affect his private life.[138] In *Morrison*[139] the High Court held that the extent to which attacks on reputation engaged Article 8 depended on the nature of the attack and the circumstances. It was accepted that where a professional person was accused of lying in a CV and of other serious professional misconduct, the right was clearly engaged.[140]

2.4 Physical and Psychological Integrity

2.4.1 Generally

Private life includes the physical and psychological integrity of a person[141] and extends to those features which are integral to a person's identity or ability to function socially as a person.[142] However, to qualify as an interference with psychological integrity, the interference must be serious. For example, Article 8 is not engaged every time a public body informs someone that it has decided to take some formal step which is the pre-cursor to some active and potentially unpleasant means of enforcement.[143]

---

[134] See also *E v DPP* [2005] EWHC 147 (Admin).
[135] *R (AB) v Secretary of State for Justice* [2009] EWHC 2220 (Admin) [2010] 2 All ER 151.
[136] Ibid, [50].
[137] Ibid, [53].
[138] *In the Matter of Guardian News and Media* [2010] UKSC 1, [2010] 2 AC 697, [42].
[139] *Morrison v Buckinghamshire CC* [2011] EWHC 3444 (QB). See also *Clift v Slough Borough Council* [2010] EWCA Civ 1484, [2011] 1 WLR 1774.
[140] Ibid, [51].
[141] *Razgar* (n 7), per Lord Bingham at [9] in reliance upon *Pretty v United Kingdom* (2002) 35 EHRR 1, [61]. See also *NHS Trust A v Mrs M* [2001] 2 WLR 942, [41].
[142] Ibid.
[143] *R (on the application of Denson) v Child Support Agency* [2002] EWHC (Admin) 154, [2002] 1 FCR 460, [43]. See also *Brumfitt v Ministry of Defence* [2005] IRLR 4.

2.4.2 Medical Treatment

Any medical treatment, including the taking of samples, without consent is an interference with the right to respect for physical integrity.[144] An adult of full capacity has an absolute right to choose whether to consent to medical treatment; this applies to every aspect of treatment and every occasion of treatment.[145] It does not matter if the patient is capacitated or incapacitated, although it has been held that the degree of interference is greater where there is a capacitated refusal because not only is privacy being invaded but also the ability to make decisions, though not impaired, is being overridden. In such instances there is also an interference with autonomy.[146]

The treatment of patients in a permanent vegetative state which is not in their best interests is an intrusion into bodily integrity which has to be justified under Article 8(2).[147] It has also been held that a decision by a court, having proper regard to the patient's personal autonomy and the expressed wishes and feelings of the patient and her family, that it would be in her best interests to withhold or withdraw treatment, does not give rise to a breach of Article 8.[148]

To become infected with a sexually transmissible disease such as hepatitis C is a violation of physical integrity which the state has a positive obligation to prevent.[149] However, Article 8 imposes no positive obligation to provide medical treatment.[150]

2.4.3 Policing

The taking of fingerprints and DNA samples undoubtedly involves an interference with private life[151] and, following the judgment of the ECtHR in *Marper*,[152] it has been confirmed by the Supreme Court that the retention of fingerprints, cellular samples and DNA profiles also engages Article 8.[153] It is still not clear whether or not stop and search engages Article 8.[154] In *Roberts*[155] the Administrative Court, relying on the judg-

---

[144] *Whitefield v General Medical Council* [2002] UKPC 62, [2003] HRLR 243, [31]; *R (Wooder) v Feggetter* [2002] EWCA Civ 554, [2003] QB 219; *R (on the application of Wilkinson) v The Responsible Medical Officer Broadmoor Hospital* [2001] EWCA Civ 1545, [2002] 1 WLR 419, [14]; *R (on the application of Burke) v The General Medical Council* [2005] EWCA Civ 1003, [30].

[145] *R (H) v Mental Health Review Tribunal* [2007] EWHC 884 (Admin) [35].

[146] *R (on the application of B) v Responsible Medical Officer, Broadmoor Hospital* [2005] EWHC (Admin) 1936, [75]. Whether an interference with Art 8(1) in such circumstances may be justified turns on the orthodox test under Art 8(2)—see [82]. This conclusion was approved by the Court of Appeal [2006] EWCA Civ 28, [2006] 1 WLR 810.

[147] *Mrs M* (n 141) [28] and [41].

[148] *W v M* [2011] EWHC 2443 (Fam). Here the patient was in a minimally conscious state.

[149] *R (on the application of H) v Ashworth Hospital Authority* [2001] EWHC (Admin) 872, [2002] 1 FCR 206, [124] in reliance upon *Guerra v Italy* (1998) 4 BHRC 63; *Lopez Ostra v Spain* (1994) 20 EHRR 277.

[150] *R (on the application of A) v North West Lancashire Health Authority* [2000] 1 WLR 977; *R (on the application of Watts) v Bedford Primary Care Trust* [2003] EWHC (Admin) 2228, [2004] Lloyd's Rep Med 113.

[151] *R (on the application of S) v Chief Constable of South Yorkshire Police* [2004] UKHL 39, [2004] 1 WLR 2196; *Attorney General's Reference No 3 of 1999* (n 50); *R (R) v Chief Constable* [2013] EWHC 2864 (Admin).

[152] *S and Marper v United Kingdom* (n 69).

[153] *R (GC) v Commissioner of Police of the Metropolis* [2011] UKSC 21, [2011] 1 WLR 1230.

[154] *Howarth v Commissioner of Police of the Metropolis* [2011] EWHC 2818 (Admin) in reliance upon *Gillan v Commissioner of Police of the Metropolis* [2006] 2 AC 307.

[155] *R (Roberts) v Commissioner of Police of the Metropolis* [2012] EWHC 1977 (Admin), [2012] ACD 104.

ment of the judgment of the ECtHR in *Gillan v UK*, held that the search in the instant case, which involved an element of humiliation and embarrassment and included a search of the claimant's handbag, should be regarded as engaging Article 8.[156]

2.4.4 Prison and Prison Conditions

Imprisonment engages Article 8 particularly where it is alleged that imprisonment is accompanied by ill-treatment.[157] However in a prison context, it can be more difficult to establish an interference with Article 8. For example in *Mackenzie*[158] the Administrative Court concluded that night inspections of prisoners to make sure they were still in their cells did not impact on Article 8 rights as the instructions were to ensure no noise, or as little noise as possible. The flap of the cell door was opened and no more light than was necessary was used.

The practice of slopping out, where there is no in-cell sanitation, has also been the subject of challenge. In *Grant* the High Court held that a prison sanitation regime was capable of interference with privacy or dignity so that there was an adverse effect on physical, psychiatric or psychological well-being.[159] However, in the present case it concluded that the sanitation system did not substantially interfere with the dignity or privacy of the prisoners.[160]

Seclusion of prisoners, improperly used, may violate Article 8[161] although the Court of Appeal has thrown doubt on whether or not Article 8 is engaged by seclusion per se. In *Malcolm*[162] it held that enjoyment of exercise in the open air was capable in principle of constituting an interest protected by Article 8 and may have particular significance in the context of prison life and 'all the more so in the context of solitary confinement in a segregation unit'.[163] However, in the present case it concluded that Article 8 was not engaged by the exercise regime in the segregation unit for a variety of reasons including the fact that the claimant got around 30 minutes exercise in the open air each day.[164] Furthermore, it was the prisoner's choice to remain in the segregation unit and hence the loss of the full hour was the result of his own deliberate decision.[165]

---

[156] Ibid, [18]. *Gillan v UK* (2010) 50 EHRR 45.

[157] *R (Al Rawi) v Secretary of State for Foreign & Commonwealth Affairs* [2006] EWCA Civ 1279, [2007] 2 WLR 1219.

[158] *R (Mackenzie) v Governor of Wakefield Prison* [2006] EWHC 1746 (Admin), [2006] ACD 100.

[159] *Grant v Ministry of Justice* [2011] EWHC 3379 (QB).

[160] Ibid, [234].

[161] *R (on the application of Munjaz) v Mersey Care NHS Trust* [2005] UKHL 58, [2006] 2 AC 148. See also *R (on the application of P) v Secretary of State for the Home Department* [2003] EWHC (Admin) 1963 and *R (AN) v Secretary of State for Justice* [2009] EWHC 1921 (Admin).

[162] *Malcolm v Ministry of Justice* [2011] EWCA Civ 1538.

[163] Ibid, [26].

[164] Ibid, [28].

[165] Ibid, [29]. See also *R (Dowsett) v Secretary of State for Justice* [2013] EWHC 687 (Admin) concerning the policy in respect of rub-down searches of prisoners; *R (T) v Secretary of State for Justice* [2013] EWHC 1119 (Admin); and *R (HC) v Secretary of State for the Home Department* [2013] EWHC 982 (Admin), [2013] Crim LR 918 where it was held that it was inconsistent with Art 8 to treat 17 year olds as adults when in detention.

2.4.5 State Support

The denial of welfare support may impact on a person's autonomy and physical and psychological integrity to such an extent as to amount to an interference under Article 8.[166] However, as discussed in the chapter on Article 3 and in the following paragraphs, failure to provide support is usually more appropriately considered as a failure to fulfil a positive obligation rather than a negative duty.

2.4.6 Environmental Pollution

Environmental pollution can constitute an interference with physical integrity. In *Furness*[167] it was argued that the conditions of authorisation granted by the Environment Agency for the incineration of municipal waste were insufficient to protect the claimant's right to information. The Divisional Court held that, since the threat to health and property was not of a substantial kind, there was no necessity for the information to be made available before it was placed in the register.[168] However, in *Andrews*[169] the court held that the increase in road and traffic noise on the road in which the claimant lived constituted a violation of his rights under Article 8.

2.4.7 Deportation and Extradition

In the immigration context, the rights protected by Article 8 can be engaged by the foreseeable consequences for health of removal from the United Kingdom pursuant to an immigration decision, even where removal does not violate Article 3, if the facts relied upon by the applicant are sufficiently strong.[170] It has been held, for example, that to remove an AIDS sufferer from free care and treatment in one of the best health services in the world, which had 'rescued her from what would otherwise have been a terminal condition', was a clear interference with her physical and psychological integrity and thus an invasion of her private life.[171]

In *Razgar*[172] the main emphasis was not on the severance of family and social ties but on the consequences for the applicant's mental health of removal to the receiving country. A majority of the House of Lords concluded that a decision which, if implemented, might lead to Mr Razgar taking his own life could not be dismissed as of insufficient gravity.[173] In some instances, where a family is being deported, it may

---

[166] *R (on the application of Q) v Secretary of State for the Home Department* [2003] EWCA Civ 364, [2004] QB 36; *R (on the application of Bernard) v London Borough of Enfield* [2002] EWHC (Admin) 2282, [2003] HRLR 4.

[167] *Furness v Environment Agency* [2002] Env LR 26.

[168] Ibid, [26]. *Guerra v Italy* (1998) 26 EHRR 357 was distinguished.

[169] *Andrews v Reading Borough Council* [2005] EWHC (QB) 256.

[170] *Razgar* (n 7), per Lord Bingham at [10] in reliance upon *Bensaid v United Kingdom* (2001) 33 EHRR 205.

[171] *DM (Zambia) v Secretary of State for the Home Department* [2009] EWCA Civ 474.

[172] *Razgar* (n 7).

[173] Ibid, per Lord Bingham at [23], with whom Lords Steyn and Carswell agreed. See also *Djali v Immigration Appeal Tribunal* [2003] EWCA Civ 1371; *R (on the application of Kastrati) v Special Adjudicator* [2002] EWHC (Admin) 415; *R (on the application of Bardiqi) v Secretary of State for the Home Department* [2003] EWHC (Admin) 1788; *R (on the application of Mehmeti) v Secretary of State*

be necessary to look at the family as a whole. The mental health or condition of one member may have relevance to that of another.[174] Prior to removal, the possibility of the 'dispersal' of an asylum seeker impacting on his/her psychological integrity has also been considered.[175]

2.5 Autonomy (Self-determination)

Article 8(1) also protects personal autonomy or self-determination, the scope of which is an evolving concept. For example, it was held by the House of Lords in *Pretty* that this aspect of Article 8 could only be taken so far and did not, for example, incorporate an individual's choice to live no longer.[176] The ECtHR disagreed, finding that the applicant had been prevented by law[177] from exercising her choice to avoid what she considered would be an undignified and distressing end to her life. It was not prepared to exclude that this constituted an interference with her right to respect for private life.[178] Following the judgment of the ECtHR, in *Purdy*[179] the House of Lords held that the right to respect for private life was engaged. The claimant wished to travel to a country where assisted suicide was lawful and end her life while she was still physically able to do so. Her husband would assist her in this journey but she sought clarification from the Director of Public Prosecutions as to his risk of prosecution under section 2(1) of the Suicide Act 1961 for assisting her to commit suicide. Lord Hope quoted from the ECtHR judgment:

> The very essence of the Convention is respect for human dignity and human freedom. Without in any way negating the principle of sanctity of life protected under the Convention, the Court considers that it is under article 8 that notions of the quality of life take on significance. In an era of growing medical sophistication combined with longer life expectancies, many people are concerned that they should not be forced to linger on in old age or in states of advanced physical or mental decrepitude which conflict with strongly held ideas of self and personal identity.[180]

To film or photograph a person without his or her consent is also an interference with private life because it interferes with personal autonomy and the control every person

---

for the Home Department [2004] EWHC (Admin) 2999; *R (on the application of Ali) v Secretary of State for the Home Department*, Administrative Court, 21 January 2005. *KR (Iraq) v Secretary of State for the Home Department* [2007] EWCA Civ 514, [2007] INLR 373; *Savage v United States* [2012] EWHC 3317 (Admin).

[174] *R (on the application of Ahmadi) v Secretary of State for the Home Department* [2002] EWHC (Admin) 1897, [52].

[175] See eg *R (on the application of Blackwood) v Secretary of State for the Home Department* [2003] EWHC (Admin) 98, [2003] HLR 638; *R (on the application of Muwangusi) v Secretary of State for the Home Department* [2003] EWHC (Admin) 813.

[176] *R v Director of Public Prosecutions, ex p Pretty* [2001] UKHL 61, [2001]3 WLR 1598, per Lord Bingham at [26], per Lord Steyn at [61], per Lord Hobhouse at [112] and per Lord Scott at [124]. Lord Hope at[100] held that the way Ms Pretty chose to pass the closing moments of her life was part of the act of living and she had a right to ask that this be respected. See further A Pedain, 'The Human Rights Dimension of the Diane Pretty Case' (2003) 62 *Cambridge Law Journal* 181.

[177] The Suicide Act 1961.

[178] *Pretty v United Kingdom* (2002) 35 EHRR 1, [67].

[179] *R (Purdy) v Director of Public Prosecutions* [2009] UKHL 45, [2009] 3 WLR 403.

[180] Ibid, ECtHR [65], per Lord Hope at [36]. See further A Jackson, 'Thou Shalt Not Kill' (2013) 77 *Journal of Criminal Law* 468.

has over his own identity.[181] In *R v Loveridge*[182] the police had arranged for the appellants to be filmed by video camera, without their knowledge, while they were at a magistrates' court. The Court of Appeal held that secret filming was objectionable in terms of Article 8(1) per se.[183] Similarly, in *Douglas*[184] Sedley LJ perceived the unauthorised photographs of the wedding as an interference with the fundamental value of personal autonomy.[185] In *Catt*[186] the Court of Appeal concluded that police retention of personal information about a man on the National Domestic Extremism Database engaged Article 8. Its reasoning, rather than based on reasonable expectation of privacy, was based on personal autonomy and retaining control over his personal information.[187]

In *Roddy*[188] the Family Division held that the personal autonomy protected by Article 8 embraced the right to decide who was to be within the inner circle—the right to decide whether that which was private should remain private or whether it should be shared with others.

> Article 8 thus embraces both the right to maintain one's privacy and, if this is what one prefers, not merely the right to waive that privacy but also the right to share what would otherwise be private with others or, indeed, with the world at large.[189]

If the person is a child, the older the child, it has been held, the greater the weight the court should give to his or her wishes.[190] In *Roddy* the court concluded that a 17-year-old woman who had a baby when she was aged 13 was of an age and of sufficient understanding and maturity to decide for herself whether that which was private, personal and intimate should remain private or whether it should be shared with the whole world.[191]

2.6 Social Life and Working Life

The capacity to enter into social relationships with others is included within the scope of private life. There is a right to establish and develop relationships with other human

---

[181] *BBC* (n 9), although it is important to note that in this case the Court of Appeal was considering a complaint under the Broadcasting Act 1996 where 'privacy' is not expressed identically to Art 8.

[182] *R v Loveridge* [2001] EWCA Crim 1034, [2001] 2 Cr App R 29.

[183] Ibid, [30]. See also *BKM* (n 38).

[184] *Douglas* (n 38).

[185] Ibid, [126]. See also *Ford* (n 86); *BBC* (n 9). Other examples of interferences with autonomy include *R (M) v Secretary of State for Health* [2003] EWHC (Admin) 1094, [2003] ACD 389 (changing nearest relative under Mental Health Act 1983); *Evans v Amicus Healthcare Ltd* [2004] EWCA Civ 727, [2004] 3 WLR 681 (refusal of fertility clinic to continue treatment with frozen embryos); *L v Human Fertilisation & Embryology Authority* [2008] EWHC 2149 (Fam), [2008] 2 FLR 1999 (storage of sperm taken from a deceased man).

[186] *R (Catt) v Association of Chief Police Officers* [2013] EWCA Civ 192, [2013] 3 All ER 583.

[187] Ibid, [31]. See also *R (RMC) v Commissioner of Police of the Metropolis* [2012] EWHC 1681 (Admin), [2012] 4 All ER 510 concerning the retention of custody photographs and Wood (n 103).

[188] *Re Roddy (a child) (identification: restriction on publication)* [2003] EWHC (Fam) 2927, [2004] FCR 481.

[189] Ibid, [36].

[190] Ibid, [55].

[191] Ibid, [56]. However in *E v Director of Public Prosecutions* [2005] EWHC (Admin) 147 the court concluded that to proscribe sexual intercourse between 15 year olds did not interfere with private life having regard to the tender age of those involved. See also *E (by her litigation friend the Official Solicitor) v Channel Four* [2005] EWHC (Fam) 1144, [2005] EMLR 30 concerning the consent of a woman with a learning disability to the broadcast of a documentary about her.

beings, and the fact that there is no existing relationship does not prevent the engage-ment of Article 8.[192] The ability to take employment is also an aspect of private life and it has been held that the right to work generally is a human right set forth in the Universal Declaration of Human Rights and the European Social Charter and that the scope of private life should be developed taking into account these 'related require-ments of international requirement or commitment'.[193] Employment enables individuals to develop social relations with others as well as the ability to develop an ordinary life when one was in possession of the 'means of living to permit travel and other means of communication with other human beings'.[194]

However, claimants have found it difficult to establish an interference with this aspect of Article 8. For example, in *Atapattu*[195] the Administrative Court held that being prevented from gaining further qualifications or from obtaining a particular employ-ment within a career path did not substantially hinder a person's ability to find work generally or to develop personal relationships within the work environment. There-fore, it concluded that the delay in granting a visa was not a sufficiently substantial interference with the claimant's right to personal development so as to engage Article 8.[196] In *Friend*[197] the House of Lords appreciated that Article 8 could protect activities which allowed a person to establish and develop relationships with others. However, as hunting was carried on in public, and had many social aspects to it which involved the wider community, it was outside the private sphere of a person's existence which was protected by Article 8.[198] And in *Whitefield*[199] the Privy Council was not satisfied that the ban on the consumption of alcohol imposed by the General Medical Council on the appellant in order to retain his registration was an interference. In its view, he was not prevented from going to his local public house or engaging in his social life while drinking non-alcoholic drinks.[200]

By contrast, it was successfully argued in *Gunn*[201] that licence conditions imposed on an individual released from prison, restricting where he could live and whom he could visit, constituted an interference with private life. And it was also successfully argued in *KB*[202] that in a prison context that if contact or social integration with other inmates was removed, Article 8 was engaged. It was held in *L*[203] that excluding a person from employment in her chosen field, due to information disclosed in an enhanced criminal record certificate, was liable to affect her ability to develop relationships with others, and the problems that this creates as regards the possibility of 'earning a living can

---

[192] *Rose* (n 127), [45]. See also *R (on the application of J) v Southend Borough Council*, Administrative Court, 5 August 2005 concerning the right to maintain relationships.

[193] *Tekle v Secretary of State for the Home Department* [2008] EWHC 3064 (Admin) [2009] 2 All ER 193; *Turner v East Midlands Trains Ltd* [2012] EWCA Civ 1470, [2013] 3 All ER 375.

[194] *Tekle*, ibid; cf *R (Atapattu) v Secretary of State for the Home Department* [2011] EWHC 1388 (Admin). See further R O'Connell, 'The Right to Work in the ECHR' [2012] *European Human Rights Law Review* 176.

[195] *R (Atapattu) v Secretary of State for the Home Department* [2011] EWHC 1388 (Admin).

[196] Ibid, [158]–[159].

[197] *Friend* (n 22).

[198] Ibid, per Lord Hope at [22].

[199] *Whitefield* (n 144).

[200] Ibid, [27].

[201] *R (Gunn) v Secretary of State for Justice* [2009] EWHC 1812 (Admin).

[202] *R (KB) v Secretary of State for Justice* [2010] EWHC 15 (Admin).

[203] *L* (n 6).

have serious repercussions on the enjoyment of her private life'.[204] It was further noted that she was also entitled to have her good name and reputation protected: the fact that a person has been excluded from employment is 'likely to get about and, if it does, the stigma will be considerable'.[205]

Successful arguments have also been made in the immigration context, particularly where a claimant has been living in the UK for a number of years, formed relationships, pursued employment,[206] opened a business[207] or undertaken a programme of study.[208] It has been confirmed in a number of claims that delay on the part of the authorities in determining an immigration claim does not of itself give rise to an Article 8 claim. However, it does increase the ability of an individual to demonstrate private life and thus bring himself within Article 8.[209]

> [U]ndue delay that is the responsibility of the Home Office's inefficiency both increases the right to respect for private life that is carried on of necessity during the period of delay, and can be said to diminish the strength of immigration control factors that would otherwise support refusal of permission to work.[210]

It has also been held that the claimant's contribution to the community, and his or her success in the UK, is also not determinative but may support the fact that an individual does have a private life in the UK.[211]

It was held in *Tekle*[212] that in relation to asylum seekers, the positive prohibition on being able to take up employment, self-employment or establish a business, when placed alongside the inability to have recourse to cash benefits, restricted the ability of the claimant 'to form relations either in the work place and outside it'.[213] The Administrative Court concluded that when such a requirement was imposed on someone who could not be removed from the UK and was maintained against someone who had been resident in the UK for more than four years, the restriction was an interference with private life.[214]

2.7 Correspondence

Finally, whilst correspondence is protected separately under Article 8(1), it is examined in this chapter as it is often considered by the courts within the context of 'private life' rather than correspondence. Correspondence includes legal correspondence between a

---

[204] Ibid, per Lord Hope at [24].
[205] Ibid.
[206] See eg *Jasarevic v Secretary of State for the Home Department* [2005] EWCA Civ 1784 and *R (S) v Secretary of State for the Home Department* [2007] EWCA Civ 546.
[207] *RU (Sri Lanka) v Secretary of State for the Home Department* [2008] EWCA Civ 753.
[208] *OA (Nigeria) v Secretary of State for the Home Department* [2008] EWCA Civ 82, [2008] HRLR 24.
[209] *RU* (n 207), [36].
[210] *Tekle* (n 193).
[211] *RU* (n 207), [40]. See also *Birmingham City Council v Clue* [2010] EWCA Civ 460, [2011] 1 WLR 99
[212] *Tekle* (n 193).
[213] Ibid, [36].
[214] Ibid, [36]. This was distinguished in *R (Negassi) v Secretary of State for the Home Department* [2013] EWCA Civ 151 and *R (Rostami) v Secretary of State for the Home Department* [2013] EWHC 1494 (Admin) where it was held that it was lawful to restrict access of asylum seekers to jobs on the shortage of occupations list.

prisoner and legal advisor. A custodial order does not wholly deprive a prisoner of all the rights enjoyed by other citizens.[215]

3. Positive Duties

3.1 Generally

The state must itself refrain from interference with private life, but in addition it must provide for an effective respect for private life.[216] In certain circumstances, Article 8(1) may also impose a positive duty to act. However, this has proved difficult for claimants to establish. It has been held by the Court of Appeal that there is no universal yardstick for determining the scope of a state's positive obligations under Article 8.[217]

> The Strasbourg Court has been particularly wary of attempts to establish a positive obligation under article 8 in the provision of state benefits, because questions about how much money should be allocated by the state on competing areas of public expenditure, and how the sums allocated to each area should be applied, are essentially matters which lie in the political domain. Such decisions are characteristically made either by politicians who are answerable to the electorate or by bodies appointed by government to make such decisions.[218]

The Court of Appeal pointed out that although the ECtHR has recognised that in principle Article 8 may be relied on to impose a positive obligation on a state to take measures to provide support for an individual, including medical support, there was no reported case in which the court had upheld such a claim by an individual complaining of the state's non-provision of medical treatment.[219] Nevertheless, there are some examples at the UK level of the positive application of Article 8. The House of Lord's declaration in *Bellinger*[220] that section 11(c) of the Matrimonial Causes Act 1973, which made no provision for the recognition of gender reassignment, was incompatible with Articles 8 and 12 was obviously based on a failure of the state to act in this area with respect to private life. In *Wooder*[221] Sedley LJ suggested that the interference with private life involved in medical treatment for a psychiatric condition against a patient's will was such that Article 8 may require written and adequate reasons to be given.[222] However, the principle of autonomy, or self-determination, does not entitle a patient to insist on receiving a particular medical treatment regardless of the nature

---

[215] *R (on the application of Daly) v Secretary of State for the Home Department* [2001] UKHL 26, [2001] 2 AC 532. See also *R (on the application of Ponting) v Governor of HMP Prison Whitemoor* [2002] EWCA Civ 224; *R (on the application of Szuluk) v The Governor of HMP Full Sutton* [2004] EWCA Civ 1426.

[216] *Hadiova v Secretary of State for the Home Department* [2003] EWCA Civ 701.

[217] *R (Condliff) v North Staffordshire Primary Care Trust* [2011] EWCA Civ 910, [2012] 1 All ER 689.

[218] Ibid, [40].

[219] Ibid, [41].

[220] *Bellinger* (n 130).

[221] *Wooder* (n 144). See also *R (on the application of B) v Haddock* [2005] EWHC (Admin) 921.

[222] *Wooder*, ibid, [48]–[49]. See also *Rose* (n 127).

of the treatment.[223] In an application for an anonymity order in civil proceedings, the Supreme Court described its role as fulfilling its positive obligation under Article 8 to secure that other individuals respect someone's private and family life.[224]

3.2 The Test to Establish a Breach of the Positive Duty

It has been suggested that the test to be applied to an allegation that the state has failed to respect private life is in principle the same test as that to be applied to an allegation that the state has failed to protect life in breach of Article 2. If there is a risk to respect for private life of which a public authority knows or ought to know, it must take reasonable measures within the scope of its powers to obviate that risk.[225] However, the courts have not consistently applied this test. For example, in *Al Rawi*[226] the claimant UK residents had been imprisoned by US authorities in Guantanamo Bay. They and their relatives sought an order compelling the Foreign Secretary to make a formal request of the US authorities for their release. The Court of Appeal accepted that Article 8 was engaged but did not apply the *Osman* test to the actions of the Foreign Secretary.

Considering Strasbourg jurisprudence, it concluded that the ECHR contained no requirement that a signatory state should take up the complaints of any individual within its territory 'touching the acts of another sovereign State'.[227] Furthermore, referring to *Botta v Italy*,[228] it held that a positive obligation would only be imposed in the Article 8 context where there was a direct and immediate link between the measures sought by an applicant and his or her private life. In the opinion of the Court of Appeal the difficulties which, on the evidence, would confront any diplomatic initiative on the detainee claimants' behalf put the case well outside such a category.[229] It also found that a wide discretionary area of judgment should be afforded to the Foreign Secretary here.[230]

3.3 State Support

Difficult questions have arisen in the context of state support. It has been recognised that there are some circumstances in which a public authority will be required to devote resources to make it possible for individuals to enjoy the rights that they are entitled to respect for under Article 8.[231] However, this has proved hard for claimants to establish.

---

[223] *Burke* (n 144), [31].

[224] *In the Matter of Guardian News and Media* [2010] UKSC 1, [2010] 2 AC 697, [29]. See further on positive duties, E Palmer, 'Beyond Arbitrary Interference: The Right to a Home?' (2010) 61 *Northern Ireland Legal Quarterly* 225.

[225] *H* (n 149). See also *Anufrijeva* (n 1) and the *obiter* comments made in *Bedford v Bedfordshire County Council* [2013] EWHC 1717 (QB), [2013] HRLR 33.

[226] *Al Rawi* (n 157).

[227] Ibid, [98].

[228] *Botta v Italy* (1998) 26 EHRR 341.

[229] Ibid, [111].

[230] Ibid, [112].

[231] *Anufrijeva* (n 1), [28] and [33]. See also *R (McDonald) v Kensington & Chelsea Royal London Borough Council* [2011] UKSC 33, [2011] 4 All ER 881.

While it is possible to identify a degree of degradation which demands welfare support, it is much more difficult to identify some other basic standard of private and family life which Art.8 requires the State to maintain by the provision of support.[232]

Often it is noted that it is hard to conceive of a situation in which the predicament of an individual will be such that Article 8 requires him or her to be provided with welfare support but will not be sufficiently severe to engage Article 3.[233] In so far as Article 8 does impose positive obligations, it has been held that these are not absolute. Before inaction can amount to a lack of respect for private and family life, there must be some ground for criticising the failure to act. It is often held that the actions of a public authority in allocating resources do not involve a lack of respect for private life. For example, in O[234] the Court of Appeal stated that where a local authority simply chose one way of meeting a child's needs rather than another, it could not be said to have interfered with the exercise by the child or the parents of their right to respect for their private or family life.[235]

Where the complaint is one of delay, there is no infringement unless substantial prejudice has been caused to the applicant. 'There is a need to have regard to resources', and the demands on resources would be significantly increased if states were to be faced with claims for breaches of Article 8 'simply on the ground of administrative delays'.[236] Maladministration will only infringe Article 8 where the consequence is serious. The more glaring the deficiency in the behaviour of the public authority, the easier it will be to establish the necessary want of respect. Isolated acts of even significant carelessness are unlikely to suffice.[237]

Applying these principles to two appeals, the Court of Appeal concluded in *Anufrijeva*[238] that the accommodation provided was not ideal but fell far short of placing the family in the type of conditions that would impose a positive obligation under Article 8 to install them in superior accommodation.[239] In *N* it concluded that the maladministration in determining his asylum claim did not breach Article 8 simply because it led a particularly susceptible individual to suffer harm in circumstances where this was not reasonably to be anticipated.[240]

The Supreme Court considered the duty *McDonald*[241] where the claimant had argued that the continuation of her night-time care by a local authority, rather than her having to use incontinence pads, was required by Article 8. A majority, referring to the wide margin of appreciation enjoyed by states in striking the fair balance between the competing interests of the individual and community, concluded that her claim was hopeless. Furthermore, in the opinion of the majority, the local authority had respected her private life by going to great lengths to consult her and try to reach agreement. 'In

---

[232] Ibid, [37].

[233] Ibid, [43]. See also *R (Chen) v Secretary of State for the Home Department* [2012] EWHC 2531 (Admin), [2012] HRLR 33.

[234] *R (O) v Hammersmith & Fulham London Borough Council* [2011] EWCA Civ 925, [2012] 1 WLR 1057.

[235] Ibid, [43].

[236] *Anufrijeva* (n 1), [46] and [47].

[237] Ibid, [48].

[238] *Anufrijeva* (n 1).

[239] Ibid, [115].

[240] Ibid, [143]. See also *R (on the application of Khan) v Oxfordshire County Council* [2004] EWCA Civ 309, [2004] BLGR 257.

[241] *McDonald* (n 231).

doing so they sought to respect as far as possible her personal feelings and desires, at the same time taking account of her safety, her independence and their own responsibilities towards all their other clients.'[242]

Even assuming that she had established an interference, the majority held that it would be justified on the grounds that it was necessary for the economic well-being of the respondents and the interests of their other service-users and was a proportionate response to the appellant's needs because it afforded her the 'maximum protection from injury, greater privacy and independence and resulted in substantial costs saving'.[243]

Provision of state health care was considered in *Condliff*[244] where the claimant argued that Article 8 made it unlawful for a Primary Care Trust to adopt a policy whereby social and non-clinical factors were excluded from individual funding requests. The claimant was morbidly obese and had been refused funding for gastric by-pass surgery. Whilst the Court of Appeal recognised that his state of health had a serious affect on his private and family life, it concluded that the application of the policy did not involve a lack of respect for his private and family life. In the view of the Court, it was the function of the Trust to use the limited resources provided to it for the purposes of the provision of health care and to allocate these in accordance with medical need, ensuring preferential treatment on non-medical grounds was not given.[245] It concluded that Article 8 could not be relied upon as giving rise to a positive duty to take into account welfare considerations wider than the comparative medical conditions and medical needs of different patients.[246] It also held that on the assumption Article 8 was engaged, there were legitimate equality reasons for the Trust to adopt the policy that it did and its decision was well within the area of discretion open to it.[247] Similarly in *Rogers*[248] the High Court held that Article 8 did not confer on a breast cancer patient a right to a particular type of drug to treat it.

By contrast in *Clue*[249] it was argued by the local authority that it had a limited social services budget and could not afford to support an individual whose application for leave to remain was outstanding. The Court of Appeal held that if Article 8 was engaged, the financial situation of the local authority was irrelevant. It stated as follows:

> [L]ocal authorities may not invoke article 8(2) by reference to budgetary considerations and the rights of others if the effect of so doing will be to require an applicant to return to his country of origin and thereby forfeit his claim for indefinite leave to remain.[250]

3.4 Policing and Criminal Justice

In *Bryant* it was argued,[251] in the context of phone hacking, that police were under a duty to notify the claimants that they may have been the victim of an attempt to

---

[242] Ibid, per Lord Brown at [19].
[243] Ibid. See also *Clue* (n 211).
[244] *Condliff* (n 217).
[245] Ibid, [36].
[246] Ibid, [44].
[247] Ibid, [52].
[248] *R (Rogers) v Swindon NHS Primary Care Trust* [2006] EWHC 171 (Admin).
[249] *Clue* (n 211).
[250] Ibid, [75].
[251] *R (Bryant) v Commissioner of Police of the Metropolis* [2011] EWHC 1314 (Admin).

intercept their communications. Granting permission to bring the claim, the court held that point was arguable reasoning by analogy that if police had come into possession of information that suggested elderly residents were likely to be the target of a team of confidence tricksters and that these tricksters were hacking 'into their phones, this would raise an arguable case under Article 8 that police owed a positive obligation to take steps.[252]

The Crown Prosecution Service was the subject of the claim in *Waxman*[253] where it was argued that they had breached their positive duty under Article 8 in deciding not to prosecute a man for harassment of the claimant. The Administrative Court agreed that Article 8 imposed on the state a positive obligation to take effective action to protect a person's private and family life, including his physical and psychological integrity.[254] It concluded there was a breach of the duty here as the claimant was a vulnerable person whose psychological integrity the state had an obligation to protect from further action on his part. It also noted that there may be a breach of the state's positive duty under Article 8 'without there being a fundamental failure of the system'. It concluded that in light of the history of the matter, and the serious effects of the man's behaviour, 'the state owed her a duty to take proper measures to protect her and was in breach of its duty in failing to pursue the prosecution'.[255] Damages of £3,500 were awarded.

4. Who Has a Private Life?

Article 8(1) provides that 'everyone' has the right to respect for his private life. Whilst this extends to all persons, it is sometimes questioned whether 'everyone' includes legal persons such as companies. In relation to the meaning of privacy under the Broadcasting Act 1996, the Court of Appeal has held that a company could make a complaint about infringement of its privacy.[256]

> [A] company does have activities of a private nature which need protection from unwarranted intrusion. It would be a departure from proper standards if, for example, the BBC without any justification attempted to listen clandestinely to the activities of a board meeting. ... The company has correspondence which it could justifiably regard as private.[257]

A similar view has been reached in HRA Article 8 cases, although no discussion of the issue has arisen.[258] A company's privacy may not extend as far as an individual's. For example, it has been held that the reading and copying of personal diaries, letters to relatives or lovers, poems and so on is especially objectionable 'because of the insult

---

[252] Ibid, [57].
[253] *R (Waxman) v Crown Prosecution Service* [2012] EWHC 133 (Admin).
[254] Ibid, [21].
[255] Ibid, [24].
[256] *BBC* (n 9).
[257] Ibid, per Lord Woolf MR at [33] and per Hale LJ at [42] and [44]. Cf Mustill LJ at [45]–[50].
[258] See eg *Banque Internationale à Luxembourg* (n 122).

done to the person as a person'.[259] It is likely that no such complaint would be feasible when made by a company.

[A]n intrusion into such matters has an extra dimension, in the shape of the damage done to the sensibilities of a human being by exposing to strangers the inner workings of his or her inward feelings, emotions, fears and beliefs, a damage which an artificial 'person', having no sensibilities, cannot be made to suffer.[260]

5. Who Must Respect Private Life?

Even though the HRA does not apply directly to private bodies, courts, as public authorities, must act compatibly with Convention rights when adjudicating on existing remedies such as the tort of breach of confidence. Modification of this tort in the light of Articles 8 and 10 has had a considerable impact on some parts of the private sector, in particular media companies. It has been held that the values embodied in Arts 8 and 10 are as much applicable in disputes between 'individuals or between an individual and a non-governmental body such as a newspaper as they are in disputes between individuals and a public authority'.[261] There is no logical ground for saying that a person should have less protection against a private individual than he would have against the state for the publication of personal information for which there is no justification.[262]

As discussed earlier in this chapter, for private bodies, a duty of confidence arises whenever the party subject to the duty is in a situation where he knows or ought to know that the other person can reasonably expect his privacy to be protected.[263] An intrusion in such a situation will be capable of giving rise to liability in an action for breach of confidence unless the intrusion can be justified.[264] In addition, Article 8 has also had an impact on the inherent jurisdiction of the High Court to protect the children for whom it is responsible.[265]

However, the judicial creation of a general 'privacy tort' appears a long way off. As the HRA did not apply to the facts of the case, it was argued before the House of Lords in *Wainwright*[266] that there was, and always has been, a tort of invasion of privacy. The House of Lords disagreed, holding that the courts have so far refused to formulate a

---

[259] *BBC* (n 9), per Mustill LJ at [49].

[260] Ibid.

[261] *Campbell* (n 2), per Lord Nicholls at [17].

[262] Ibid, per Lord Hoffmann at [50].

[263] Ibid, per Lord Hope at [85]. See also *Douglas* (n 38); *Theakston* (n 86); *B & C v A* (n 84); *Douglas v Hello! Ltd (No 3)* [2003] EWHC (Ch) 786, [2003] 3 All ER 996; *Archer v Williams* [2003] EWHC (QB) 1670, [2003] EMLR 38.

[264] *B & C v A*, ibid, [11(ix)]—[11(x)]. See generally G Phillipson, 'Transforming Breach of Confidence? Towards a Common Law Right of Privacy under the Human Rights Act' (2003) 66 *Modern Law Review* 726; J Morgan, 'Privacy, Confidence and Horizontal Effect: "Hello" Trouble' (2003) 62 *Cambridge Law Journal* 444; A Sims, 'A Shift in the Centre of Gravity: the Dangers of Protecting Privacy through Breach of Confidence' (2005) *Intellectual Property Quarterly* 27.

[265] See eg *Re S (A Child)* [2004] UKHL 47, [2004] 1 AC 593, at per Lord Steyn [22]–[23]; *Roddy* (n 188).

[266] *Wainwright* (n 3).

general principle of invasion of privacy[267] and finding no suggestion that they should do so.[268] It found a great difference between identifying privacy as a value which underlay the existence of a rule of law and privacy as a principle of law in itself.[269] Furthermore, it saw nothing in the jurisprudence of the European Court of Human Rights which suggested that the adoption of some high-level principle of privacy was necessary to comply with Article 8.[270] It concluded that this was an area which required a detailed approach that could be achieved only by legislation rather than the 'broad brush of the common law principle'.[271] Finally, it noted that the coming into force of the HRA weakened the argument even further. The creation of a general tort would preempt the controversial question of the extent, if any, to which the Convention required states to provide remedies for invasions of privacy by persons who were not public authorities.[272]

6. Permitted Interferences

The right to respect for private life is not an absolute right. Article 8(2) provides that interferences are permissible if they are in accordance with the law and necessary in a democratic society in the interests of national security, public safety or the economic well-being of the country, for the prevention of disorder or crime, for the protection of health or morals, or for the protection of the rights and freedoms of others.

6.1 In Accordance with the Law

Increasingly claimants are making successful arguments based on the fact that an interference with private life is not in accordance with the law. The principle of legality is considered fully in Chapter 4. One example is *Purdy*[273] where the House of Lords concluded that the Director of Public Prosecutions' Code offered almost no guidance at all to those who may face prosecution for assisting in a suicide of a person who was

> terminally ill or severely and incurably disabled, who wishes to be helped to travel to a country where assisted suicide is lawful and who, having the capacity to take such a decision, does so freely and with a full understanding of the consequences.[274]

---

[267] Ibid, per Lord Hoffmann at [19].
[268] Ibid, [26].
[269] Ibid, [32].
[270] Ibid, in reliance upon *Earl Spencer v UK* (1998) 25 EHRR CD 105; *Peck v UK* (2003) 13 BHRC 669.
[271] Ibid, [33].
[272] Ibid, [34]. See also *Theakston* (n 86), [27] and *B & C v A* (n 84), [11(vi)]. See generally NW Barber, 'A Right to Privacy?' [2003] *Public Law* 602.
[273] *Purdy* (n 179).
[274] Ibid, per Lord Hope at [54]. See also *Malcolm v Ministry of Justice* [2011] EWCA Civ 1538; *R (Ali) v Minister for the Cabinet Office* [2012] EWHC 1943 (Admin); *J Council v GU* [2012] EWHC 3531 (COP); and *R (Nicklinson) v Ministry of Justice* [2013] EWCA Civ 961, (2013) 16 CCL Rep 413 where it was held that the policy was still not sufficiently clear to satisfy the requirements of Art 8(2) in relation to healthcare professionals. See further, J. Rogers, 'Prosecutorial Policies, Prosecutorial Systems and the Purdy Litigation' [2010] *Criminal Law Review* 543.

The absence of lawful authority was at issue in *Mengesha*[275] where the Administrative Court found a breach of Article 8 as it was not lawful for police to require those contained, or 'kettled' at a demonstration to give their names, addresses and dates of birth and to be filmed.

6.2 General Factors Affecting the Proportionality Analysis

Just as a freedom of expression claim is affected by the subject matter of the expression, so too there are strong and weak claims to respect for private life. As Baroness Hale stated in *Countryside Alliance*:

> What may be 'necessary in a democratic society' has to take account the comparative importance of the right infringed in the scale of rights protected. What may be a proportionate interference with a less important right might be a disproportionate interference with a more important right.[276]

The strength or otherwise of such a claim will have a considerable impact on the balancing processes carried out by a court when determining whether or not an interference is justified. When determining the strength of claims, the first factor taken into account is the level of harm which the interference will cause. The more harm caused, the stronger the private life claim. For example, in *Campbell*,[277] picking up on the comments of Keene LJ in *Douglas v Hello! Ltd*,[278] Lord Hope held that there are different degrees of privacy and, in the present context, the potential for disclosure of the information to cause harm was an important factor to be taken into account in the assessment of the extent of the restriction that was needed to protect Ms Campbell's right to privacy.[279] Here he found that the publication of the details of her treatment at Narcotics Anonymous had the potential to cause harm to her, so he attached a 'good deal of weight to this factor'.[280] He commented that for someone in her position there were few areas of the life of an individual that were more in need of protection on the grounds of privacy than the combating of addiction to drugs or to alcohol.[281] Furthermore, in his view it was 'hard to break the habit which has led to the addiction' and even more so if 'efforts to do so are exposed to public scrutiny'.[282]

Baroness Hale reached a similar conclusion to Lord Hope, although she also noted that the interests involved in *Re S*, which concerned the private life of a child whose mother was being tried for the murder of his brother, were far more serious than those of a 'prima donna celebrity against a celebrity-exploiting tabloid newspaper'.[283] However, in *Re S* the House of Lords concluded that the interference with the Article 8 rights of the boy were not of the same order when compared with cases of juveniles

---

[275] *Mengesha v Commissioner of Police of the Metropolis* [2013] EWHC 1695 (Admin), [2013] ACD 120.
[276] *Countryside Alliance* (n 8), [124].
[277] *Campbell* (n 2).
[278] *Douglas* (n 38), [168].
[279] Ibid, [118].
[280] Ibid, [119].
[281] Ibid, [81].
[282] Ibid. See also the comments of Baroness Hale at [157].
[283] Ibid, [143].

who were directly involved in criminal trials.[284] A particularly strong interference with private life was also at issue in *Mosley*[285] where the claim related to the recording on private property of sexual activity.

The harm caused may be ameliorated by measures taken to conceal the identity of the person such as pixellation. Where the BBC had conducted secret filming at a care home, the court noted that there was little invasion of privacy if the resident merely sitting in the lounge was shown heavily pixellated.[286]

Secondly, where different pieces of information are published together, or where there are a number of interferences, considering them as a whole may significantly bolster the strength of a private life claim. For example, in *Campbell*[287] Lord Hope commented that, were it not for the photographs, he would have regarded the balance between private life and freedom of expression as even.[288] Similarly, as Baroness Hale remarked:

> A picture is 'worth a thousand words' because it adds to the impact of what the words convey; but it also adds to the information given in those words ... it also added to the potential harm, by making her think that she was being followed or betrayed, and deterring her from going back to the same place again.[289]

It has been held that the degree of intrusion into a person's private life which was caused by internet publications was different from the degree of intrusion caused by print and broadcast media. This is because once a person's name appears in a newspaper or other media archive, it may remain there indefinitely. 'Names mentioned on social networking sites are less likely to be permanent.'[290]

Finally, it is possible that the strength of a claim to privacy can be affected by the fact that a person, in particular a public figure, has previously lied about the information sought to be kept private, or the public's interest in knowing about certain traits of his or her personality and certain aspects of his or her private life. The better view is that this only affects the freedom of expression side of the equation. For example, where a public figure has lied, it may be a matter of public interest that the record is set straight.[291] This is examined in more detail in the chapter concerning freedom of expression.

6.3 Deference to the Primary Decision Maker

Affording deference to the primary decision maker is not uncommon in private life claims under the HRA. Given that the right is subject to exceptions, the nature of the subject matter raised by many private life claims and that UK courts were not used

---

[284] Re S [2004] UKHL 47, [2005] 1 AC 593, per Lord Steyn at [27]. See also *Theakston* (n 86); *B & C v A* (n 84); *X (a woman formerly known as Mary Bell) v O'Brien* [2003] EWHC (QB) 1101, [2003] 2 FCR 686.

[285] *Mosley v News Group Newspapers* [2008] EWHC 1777 (QB), [2008] EMLR 20.

[286] *BKM* (n 38), [32].

[287] *Campbell* (n 2).

[288] Ibid, [121] and [123].

[289] Ibid, [155]. See also *Theakston* (n 86); *B & C v A* (n 84). See further NA Moreham, 'Privacy in the Common Law: A Doctrinal and Theoretical Analysis' (2005) 121 *Law Quarterly Review* 628.

[290] *Goodwin* (n 91), [125].

[291] This was the view adopted by Baroness Hale in *Campbell* (n 2). See also *Theakston* (n 86) and *B & C v A* (n 84).

to dealing with a right to respect for private life at common law pre-HRA, this is not surprising. Particular deference has been shown to the legislature. In some instances courts have also taken into account that the UK may have a margin of appreciation before the ECtHR in the particular subject area, meaning that it should not attempt to second guess the conclusion which Parliament has reached.[292] However, Lord Brown, in *Countryside Alliance*, warned against too much deference to the legislature, stating that the democratic process is a necessary but not a sufficient condition for the protection and vindication of human rights. 'Sometimes the majority misuses its powers. Not least this may occur when what are perceived as moral issues are involved.'[293]

An example is *Bellinger*[294] where the House of Lords was not prepared to recognise the appellant as a female for the purposes of the Matrimonial Causes Act, holding that the issues were ill-suited for determination by the courts and pre-eminently a matter for Parliament. This was particularly so given the government's intention to bring forward legislation on the subject.[295] Similarly, in *Evans*[296] the Court of Appeal was not prepared to dispense with a biological father's consent under the Human Fertilisation and Embryology Act 1990. In *Pretty*[297] Lord Steyn pointed out that that such a fundamental change could not be brought about by judicial creativity. 'Essentially, it must be a matter for democratic debate and decision making by legislatures.'[298] In *S*[299] the House of Lords virtually gave Parliament free rein to utilise new technologies in the pursuit of the guilty. And in *Friend*[300] the House of Lords held that the social impacts of the proposed hunting ban were for the legislature to judge.

> The 2002 Act is to be seen as one more step on a long legislative sequence in which animal welfare has been promoted by the legislature in relation to contemporary needs and problems. The question whether the measures proposed were now necessary in a democratic society was pre-eminently one for Parliament.[301]

Similar deference was shown in the *Countryside Alliance* case where Lord Bingham observed that the present claim was 'pre-eminently one in which respect should be shown to what the House of Commons decided'.[302]

Deference to primary decision makers is also common. For example, in *Woolgar*[303] the Court of Appeal held that the primary decision as to disclosure should be made by the police, not the court. In *N*[304] the Administrative Court held that the secure hospital was entitled to a margin of appreciation in recording and listening to the incoming and outgoing phone calls of patients. In *E*[305] the Administrative Court held that the starting

---

[292] *Countryside Alliance* (n 8), per Baroness Hale at [126].
[293] [158].
[294] *Bellinger* (n 130).
[295] Ibid, per Lord Nicholls at [37].
[296] *Evans* (n 185).
[297] *Pretty* (n 176).
[298] Ibid, [58].
[299] *S* (n 151).
[300] *Friend* (n 22).
[301] Ibid, per Lord Hope at [31].
[302] *Countryside Alliance* (n 8), [45].
[303] *Woolgar* (n 114).
[304] *R (on the application of N)* (n 49).
[305] *R (on the application of E) v Ashworth Hospital Authority* [2001] EWHC (Admin) 1089, [2002] ACD 149.

point for determining whether a particular interference was necessary was the view taken by those responsible for the claimant in the hospital.

However, it cannot be concluded that the courts have abdicated their responsibility under Article 8. Even where deference has been afforded, the courts have gone on to balance the interference against the justification and in many instances have found a breach of Article 8. The process engaged in by the courts in claims raising the permitted justifications for interference under Article 8 are examined the following paragraphs.

7. National Security

Interferences with private life in accordance with the law may be permitted if necessary in the interests of national security. This was the justification pleaded by the Secretary of State in *Baker*,[306] where, under the Data Protection Act 1998, the claimant, a serving Member of Parliament, contended that the Security Service held or had held personal information about him. He required them to say whether or not that was correct and to disclose the data to him. The Secretary of State signed a certificate purporting to exempt the Service from complying with Part II of the Act. Reading the Act in a manner which protected Article 8,[307] the Information Tribunal, whilst affording considerable deference, concluded that the Secretary of State did not have reasonable grounds for providing the Service with a blanket exemption. The blanket exemption was wider than necessary to protect national security; some personal data relating to individuals could be released to them without endangering national security; there was no reason to suppose that the burden of dealing with claimants individually would be unduly onerous; and evidence as to practice in other countries did not show an identical unchallengeable provision. It concluded that the proportionate and reasonable response was to consider each request on its merits.[308]

8. Economic Well-being of the Country

Interferences with private life in accordance with the law are permitted if necessary in the interests of the economic well-being of the country. A variety of interferences have sought to be justified on this basis. It is clear that, whilst not all deportations will be justified on the ground of economic well-being, the majority are sought to be justified as such. Deportations are therefore considered in this section.

---

[306] *Baker* (n 34).
[307] Ibid, [57].
[308] Ibid, [113].

8.1 Deportation and Extradition: Foreign cases

8.1.1 Generally

The right to respect for private life can be engaged by the deportation or extradition of an individual. In a domestic case, the contracting state is directly responsible, because of its own act or omissions, for the breach of Convention rights and these cases are considered below. In foreign cases the contracting state is not directly responsible. Its responsibility is engaged because of the real risk that its conduct in expelling the person will lead to a gross invasion of his most fundamental rights.[309] With respect to these cases, to successfully resist deportation or extradition it must be shown that Article 8(1) rights will be subject to flagrant denial or gross violation in the destination country. In short, it must be shown that the right will be completely denied or nullified.[310] As it was only finally determined in June 2004 that Article 8 applied to these types of cases,[311] many of the earlier cases are now of dubious authority and are only examined in the paragraphs below if the test applied was the same as the test now established. Once a claimant has established flagrant denial or gross violation in the destination state, it is then necessary for the court to consider proportionality under Article 8(2).[312] As the following examples demonstrate, it is very difficult to establish flagrant denial or gross violation. There is also a rebuttable presumption that signatory states to the ECHR will adhere to their obligations.[313]

8.1.2 Medical Treatment

In *Razgar*[314] Lord Bingham commented *obiter* that, under Article 8, removal cannot be resisted merely on the ground that medical treatment or facilities are better or more accessible in the removing country than in that to which the applicant is to be removed.

> It would indeed frustrate the proper and necessary object of immigration control in the more advanced member states of the Council of Europe if illegal entrants requiring medical treatment could not, save in exceptional cases, be removed to the less developed countries of the world where comparable medical facilities were not available.[315]

He also commented that the Convention is directed to the protection of fundamental human rights, not the conferment of individual advantages or benefits.[316] He applied this to welfare, noting that an applicant could never hope to resist an expulsion decision without showing something very much more extreme than relative disadvantage as compared with the expelling state.[317] This has been followed by the lower courts and it

---

[309] *Razgar* (n 7), per Baroness Hale at [41].
[310] *R (on the application of Ullah) v Special Adjudicator* [2004] UKHL 26, [2004] 2 AC 323, per Lord Bingham at [24].
[311] Ibid.
[312] *ZT v Secretary of State for the Home Department* [2005] EWCA Civ 1421, [2006] Imm AR 84; *SN v Secretary of State for the Home Department* [2005] EWCA Civ 1683, [2006] INLR 273.
[313] *Lendvai v Veszprem City Court of Hungary* [2009] EWHC 3431 (Admin), [1.48].
[314] *Razgar* (n 7).
[315] Ibid, [4]. Lords Steyn, Walker and Carswell agreed. See also Baroness Hale at [59].
[316] Ibid.
[317] Ibid, [10].

is very difficult for a claimant to argue that their claim falls within the small minority of exceptional cases. For example, in ZT[318] the claimant was HIV positive and argued that if she was returned to Zimbabwe, treatment for her illness would be difficult or impossible to obtain. The Court of Appeal held that whilst medical treatment was not free, it was available and it could not be said that on return she would face a flagrant or fundamental breach of her rights under Article 8 amounting to a complete denial of those rights.[319]

8.1.3 Homosexuality

It has been argued that deportation is unlawful on the ground that homosexuality is illegal in the destination state. In Z[320] the Court of Appeal held that the tribunal's view that laws against sodomy, even if not enforced, were a breach of the right to respect for private life was too wide. It held that it was necessary for the tribunal to go further and examine whether there would be any possibility of a prosecution.[321] Furthermore, the court held it should also have examined whether, and in what circumstances, any criminal investigation short of prosecution might be embarked upon.[322]

8.2 Deportation and Extradition: 'Domestic' Cases

The right to respect for private life can be engaged by the deportation or extradition of an individual. In a domestic case, the contracting state is directly responsible, because of its own act or omissions, for the breach of Convention rights. In a domestic case where removal is resisted in reliance on Article 8, questions which are likely to be important are as follows:

(1) Will the proposed removal be an interference by a public authority with the exercise of the applicant's right to respect for private or (as the case may be) family life?
(2) If so, will such interference have consequences of such gravity as potentially to engage the operation of Article 8?[323]
(3) If so, is such interference in accordance with the law?
(4) If so, is such interference necessary in a democratic society in the interests of national security, public safety or the economic well-being of the country, for the prevention of disorder or crime, for the protection of health or morals, or for the protection of the rights and freedoms of others?

---

[318] *ZT v Secretary of State for the Home Department* [2005] EWCA Civ 1421, [2006] Imm AR 84.
[319] Ibid, [28]. See also *MM (Zimbabwe) v Secretary of State for the Home Department* [2012] EWCA Civ 279.
[320] *Secretary of State for the Home Department v Z* [2002] EWCA Civ 952, [2002] Imm AR 560.
[321] Ibid, [29].
[322] Ibid, [30]. See also *Hadiova* (n 216); *Z v The Secretary of State for the Home Department* [2004] EWCA Civ 1578; *R (on the application of S) v Secretary of State for the Home Department* [2003] EWHC (Admin) 352; *R (on the application of M) v Immigration Appeal Tribunal* [2005] EWHC (Admin) 251.
[323] It is important to note that domestic cases are not governed by a flagrancy threshold. See *Huang v Secretary of State for the Home Department* [2007] UKHL 11, [2007] 2 AC 167.

(5) If so, is such interference proportionate to the legitimate public end sought to be achieved?[324]

It has been held that interferences are always likely to be in accordance with law and, where removal is proposed in pursuance of lawful immigration policy, question (4) will almost always fall to be answered affirmatively.

> This is because the right of sovereign states, subject to treaty obligations, to regulate the entry and expulsion of aliens is recognised in the Strasbourg jurisprudence ... and implementation of a firm and orderly immigration policy is an important function of government in a modern democratic state. In the absence of bad faith, ulterior motive or deliberate abuse of power it is hard to imagine an adjudicator answering this question other than affirmatively.[325]

Question (5) involves the striking of a fair balance between the rights of the individual and the interests of the community. The Secretary of State must exercise his judgment in the first instance. On appeal the adjudicator must exercise his or her own judgment.[326] A reviewing court must assess the judgment which would or might be made by an adjudicator on appeal. 'Decisions taken pursuant to the lawful operation of immigration control will be proportionate in all save a small minority of exceptional cases, identifiable only on a case by case basis.'[327]

In these types of cases it has been held that the court or adjudicator is not called upon to judge policy, and therefore no question of deference arises.[328] Their duty is to see to the protection of individual fundamental rights, which is the particular territory of the courts.[329] Furthermore, it is not necessary for a claimant to demonstrate an exceptionally grave interference with private life. Tribunals and courts must take the language of Article 8 'at face value and, wherever an interference of the kind the article envisages is established, consider whether it is justified under art 8(2)'.[330]

Relevant to a proportionality analysis may be the contribution a particular individual has made to the community.[331] Detailed consideration was given to the proportionality analysis required in such cases by the Court of Appeal in UE[332] where it held as follows:

> [A] public interest in the retention in this country of someone who is of considerable value to the community can properly be seen as relevant to the exercise of immigration control. It goes to the weight to be attached to that side of the scales in the proportionality exercise. The weight to be attached to the public interest in removal of the person in question is not some fixed immutable amount. It may vary from case to case, and where someone is of great value to the community in this country, there exists a factor which reduces the importance of maintaining firm immigration control in his individual case. The weight to be given to that aim is correspondingly less.[333]

---

[324] *Razgar* (n 7), per Lord Bingham at [17].
[325] Ibid, per Lord Bingham at [19].
[326] The adjudicator must decide for himself or herself, on the merits, whether the removal would be proportionate or not. See *Huang* (n 323).
[327] *Razgar* (n 7), [20].
[328] *Huang* (n 323).
[329] Ibid.
[330] *KR* (n 173).
[331] *RU* (n 207).
[332] *UE (Nigeria) v Secretary of State for the Home Department* [2010] EWCA Civ 975, [2011] 2 All ER 352.
[333] Ibid, [18].

In *Razgar*[334] a majority of the House of Lords found that there was a threat to the private life of the applicant in that, if the decision was implemented, it might lead him to take his own life. As the Secretary of State had not considered the proportionality of the interference, the majority concluded that he could not certify the claim as manifestly unfounded.[335] In *Ay*,[336] decided before *Razgar*, the Court of Appeal considered the claim that to remove four children to Germany would have a significant impact on their physical and psychological development. It held that it was possible to take into account the message that would be sent if the court decided against the Secretary of State. Considering the medical evidence that the impact would only be for a confined period, it held the Secretary of State was entitled to certify the case that the family's appeal to the adjudicator was bound to fail.[337] However, the claimant in *DM* who had been diagnosed with HIV/AIDS did not succeed in her argument that deportation was disproportionate. The Court of Appeal agreed with the tribunal's assessment that she would have appropriate support or treatment in Zambia.[338]

8.3 Other

Also justified on the ground of economic well-being are interferences in the area of taxation. For example, in *Banque Internationale à Luxembourg*[339] the High Court held that, although notices issued by the Inland Revenue requiring specific classes of documents did impinge on private life, there was ample justification '[f]or the notices were issued according to law, in pursuit of a legitimate aim and necessary in a democratic society for protecting the taxation system and revenue'.[340]

The argument in *Robertson*[341] that the supply of the electoral register to commercial interests who utilise it for marketing purposes was justified as the benefits reflect on the economy was ultimately unsuccessful, the court holding that the sale of the register, absent an individual right of objection, was disproportionate.[342]

In *Tekle*[343] the High Court considered the justification for the ban on asylum seekers taking employment, having already found that this constituted an interference with private life. It concluded that none of the reasons relied upon for justification of the blanket policy sufficed. It concluded that there were

> other ways to address abuse by ill deserved claims, and there comes a point when the delay is such that any general deterrent effect that may remain in the interests of immigration control is so weakened in comparison with the requirement to put the life on hold without any indication of when it will be started again, that the generic reliance on policy will not do.[344]

---

[334] *Razgar* (n 7).
[335] Ibid, per Lord Bingham at [24]. See also *KR* (n 173).
[336] *R (on the application of Ay) v Secretary of State for the Home Department* [2003] EWCA Civ 1012.
[337] See also *Djali* and *Mehmeti* (n 173). Cf *R (Tozlukaya) v Secretary of State for the Home Department* [2006] EWCA Civ 379, [2006] Imm AR 417, [6].
[338] *DM* (n 171).
[339] See eg *Banque Internationale à Luxembourg* (n 122).
[340] Ibid, [17] in reliance upon *Funke v France* (1993) 16 EHRR 297 and *Chappell v United Kingdom* (1989) 12 EHRR 1. See also *Guyer* (n 123); *Morgan Grenfell* (n 51), [39].
[341] *Robertson* (n 45).
[342] Ibid, [36]–[39].
[343] *Tekle* (n 193).
[344] Ibid, [51].

However, it found that the question of precisely when and in what circumstances the maintenance of the prohibition on employment ceased to be justifiable depended upon a policy judgment that it was not open to the court to make.[345] Nevertheless, it did declare the present policy to be unlawfully overbroad and unjustifiably detrimental to anyone who had to wait as long as the claimant had.[346]

Resource considerations were at issue in *AB*[347] where a preoperative male-to-female transgender woman sought transfer from a male to a female prison. Given the need for segregation in the women's prison, the Secretary of State justified the refusal to transfer on economic grounds. The justification was dismissed by the High Court, who found a breach of Article 8 and stated as follows:

> When issues so close to the identity of the prisoner as here, so intimately concerned with her personal autonomy, the deployment of resources as a justification for the infringement of such rights must be clear and weighty in order to be proportionate. Here they are neither.[348]

---

9. Prevention of Disorder or Crime

Interferences with the right to respect for private life which are in accordance with law and necessary in a democratic society are also possible for the prevention of disorder or crime.

9.1 Evidence Obtained by Secret Filming or Recording

It is not uncommon for evidence to be obtained for criminal and civil trials by secret filming. For example, in *Jones*,[349] a personal injury claim, the claimant was filmed in her home without her knowledge after the person taking the film obtained access to her home by deception. The Court of Appeal found that there is usually no question of justification in such cases and a breach of Article 8 was found.[350] However, as discussed in the preceding chapter, this does not necessarily mean the evidence will be excluded from the trial.

In criminal proceedings, the court considers whether such evidence adversely affects the fairness of the proceedings and, if it does, may exclude it under section 78 of the Police and Criminal Evidence Act 1984.[351] In civil cases, the breach of Article 8 is a relevant circumstance for the court to weigh in the balance when coming to a decision as to how it should properly exercise its discretion in making orders as to the manage-

---

[345] Ibid, [52].
[346] Ibid, [53].
[347] *R (AB) v Secretary of State for Justice* [2009] EWHC 2220 (Admin).
[348] Ibid, [77].
[349] *Jones* (n 37).
[350] Ibid.
[351] *R v P* (n 49); *R v Loveridge* [2001] 2 Cr App R 591; *R v Mason* [2002] 2 Cr App R 628. See also *R v E* [2004] EWCA Crim 1234, [2004] 1 WLR 3279; *R v Allsopp* [2005] EWCA Crim 703.

ment of proceedings.[352] The significance of the evidence will differ according to the facts of the particular case, as will the gravity of the breach of Article 8. The decision will depend on all the circumstances. In *Jones*[353] the Court of Appeal concluded that the conduct was not so outrageous that the defence should be struck out.[354] However, it did note that its disapproval of the conduct of the insurers could be reflected in the orders for costs.[355]

In *Re McE*[356] the evidence against a solicitor, charged with incitement to murder, was obtained via covert electronic surveillance carried out by the police of conversations between himself and his clients at a police station. The issue was whether the interference was prescribed by law—in particular, whether the Regulation of Investigatory Powers Act 2000 (RIPA) detracted from statutory rights to consult lawyers privately. A majority of the House of Lords held that RIPA was intended to override or qualify a detainee's right to a private consultation with a solicitor at common law and under statute. Lord Hope observed that neither Article 6 nor Article 8 imposed an absolute prohibition on covert surveillance of legal consultations, provided it is authorised by law and is proportionate.[357] Nevertheless, as Baroness Hale observed, it did not follow that because an act of covert surveillance was lawful it could never result in a contravention of Convention rights.[358]

9.2 Fingerprints, DNA Samples and Other Personal Information— Taking and Retention

It has been held that the taking of fingerprints and DNA samples from persons suspected of having committed relevant offences is a reasonable and proportionate response to the scourge of serious crime.[359] In *S* the House of Lords held that on the assumption that the retention of fingerprints and samples engaged Article 8, indefinite retention was a proportionate interference.[360] However, the ECtHR reached the opposite conclusion[361] and its reasoning was adopted by the Supreme Court in *GC*,[362] where it was confirmed that the indefinite retention of the claimant's data was an interference with their rights

---

[352] *Jones* (n 37), [25].

[353] Ibid.

[354] Ibid, [28].

[355] Ibid, [30]. See also *McGowan v Scottish Water* [2005] IRLR 167 concerning evidence covertly obtained for the purpose of disciplinary proceedings against an employee. See further D Ormerod, 'ECHR and the Exclusion of Evidence: Trial Remedies for Article 8 Breaches?' [2003] *Criminal Law Review* 61.

[356] *Re McE* [2009] UKHL 15, [2009] 1 AC 908.

[357] Ibid, [62].

[358] Ibid, [71].

[359] *S* (n 151), per Lord Steyn at [3]. See also *R (R) v A Chief Constable* [2013] EWHC 2864 (Admin).

[360] *S*, ibid, per Lord Steyn at [40]. See further A Roberts and N Taylor, 'Privacy and the DNA Database' [2005] *European Human Rights Law Review* 373. See also *Attorney General's Reference No 3 of 1999* (n 50), which concerned a sample which should have been destroyed but eventually resulted in the conviction of the defendant for a serious crime. The House of Lords found no violation of Art 8 and, even assuming there was, held that the evidence was admissible under s 78 of the Police and Criminal Evidence Act 1984.

[361] *S and Marper v UK* (n 69).

[362] *GC* (n 153).

to respect for private life which was not justified under Article 8(2).[363] The ECtHR observed as follows:

> [T]he blanket and indiscriminate nature of the powers of retention of the fingerprints, cellular samples and DNA profiles of persons suspected but not convicted of offences ... fails to strike a fair balance between the competing public and private interests.[364]

In *GC* a majority of the Supreme Court found the present guidelines on retention of data to be unlawful but declined to make a declaration of incompatibility. Lord Judge observed that it was possible for ACPO to reconsider and amend the guidelines in the light of the decision of the ECtHR and that of the Supreme Court.[365]

In *Catt*[366] the Court of Appeal considered similar claims relating to the powers of police to collect and retain information of a personal nature, including photographs and allegations made to police, and retain it on a database. The Court of Appeal held as follows:

> In order to justify the collection, processing and retention of personal information the state must be able to satisfy the court that each of those steps is governed by clear rules of law or police which are both accessible and intelligible and do not give the authorities an excessively broad discretion over the manner of their implementation. In such cases it is therefore necessary for the court to pay careful attention to the nature of the information in question, the circumstances under which it can be obtained, the ways in which it can be processed and by whom, the period for which it can be retained (together with any arrangements for interim review) and the arrangements for its destruction.[367]

In relation to the first claimant it found that the retention of name, attendance at demonstrations and other information on the National Domestic Extremism Database was disproportionate:

> The systematic collection, processing and retention on a searchable database of personal information, even of a relatively routine kind, involves a significant interference with the right to respect for private life. It can be justified by showing that it serves the public interest in a sufficiently important way, but in this case the respondent has not in our view shown that the value of the information is sufficient to justify its continued retention.[368]

9.3 Police Photography

Increasingly police are taking photographs of individuals and retaining these for use in policing. One aspect of the practice was challenged in *Wood*.[369] The Court of Appeal

---

[363] Ibid, per Lord Dyson at [15].

[364] *S and Marper v UK* (n 69), [125]

[365] Ibid, [81]. In *Gaughran* [2012] NIQB 88, the NI Divisional Court held that indefinite retention of the fingerprints, photographs, DNA samples and DNA profiles of those convicted was proportionate. In *R (TD) v Commissioner of the Police of the Metropolis* [2013] EWHC 2231 (Admin) it was held that it was proportionate to retain police records relating to an unfounded allegation of sexual assault. See further L Campbell, 'A Rights-based Analysis of DNA Retention' [2010] *Criminal Law Review* 889.

[366] *R (Catt) v Association of Chief Police Officers* [2013] EWCA Civ 192, [2013] 3 All ER 583.

[367] Ibid, [24].

[368] Ibid, [44]. It also concluded that police retention of a warning letter sent to the second claimant was disproportionate. See also *Mengesha v Commissioner of Police of the Metropolis* [2013] EWHC 1695 (Admin).

[369] *Wood* (n 103).

concluded unanimously that Article 8 was engaged by police photographing and retaining the image of a man who had just left the annual general meeting of a company involved in organising arms trade fairs. However, Laws LJ dissented with respect to the proportionality of the interference. Dyson LJ, in the majority on this point, held that the taking and retention of the photos were in pursuit of the legitimate aim of the prevention of disorder or crime, or for the protection of the rights and freedoms of others.[370] He noted that the court was required to carry out a careful exercise of weighing the legitimate aim to be pursued, the importance of the right which is the subject of the interference and the extent of the interference.[371] In his view, 'an interference whose object is to protect the community from the danger of terrorism' is more readily justified as proportionate than an interference whose object is to protect the community from the risk of low level crime and disorder.[372] Whilst he accepted that the retention of the photos was not an interference of the utmost gravity, it should not be dismissed as of little consequence. 'The retention by the police of photographs taken of persons who have not committed an offence, and who are not even suspected of having committed an offence, is always a serious matter.'[373] Here it was thought that the justification had to be compelling as the interference was in pursuit of the protection of the community from the risk of public disorder or low level crime (disruption at the annual general meeting or in the area).[374] The majority concluded that there was no justification for retaining the photos for any more than a few days after the annual general meeting and that the interference was disproportionate.[375]

9.4 Stop and Search

It remains unclear as to whether or not stop and search constitutes an interference with private life. In *Gillan*[376] Lord Bingham stated that he was doubtful whether or not an ordinary superficial search of a person could be said to show a lack of respect for private life.[377] The ECtHR did not agree and in *Gillan v UK*[378] held as follows:

> Irrespective of whether in any particular case correspondence or diaries or other private documents are discovered and read or other intimate items are revealed in the search … the use of coercive powers conferred by the legislation to require an individual to submit to a detailed search of his person, his clothing and his personal belongings amounts to a clear interference with the right to respect for private life.[379]

Nevertheless, the judgment of the House of Lords was followed in *Howarth*,[380] the

---

[370] Ibid, [79].
[371] Ibid, [84].
[372] Ibid, [84].
[373] Ibid, [85].
[374] Ibid, [86].
[375] See also *R (RMC) v Commissioner of Police of the Metropolis* [2012] EWHC 1681 (Admin), [2012] 4 All ER 510 where the Administrative Court concluded that the blanket retention of all custody photographs was disproportionate.
[376] *Gillan* (n 154).
[377] Ibid, [28].
[378] *Gillan and Quinton v UK* (n 156).
[379] Ibid, [63]
[380] *Howarth* (n 154).

Administrative Court concluding that Article 8 was not engaged when a man travelling to a demonstration was searched by police. On the assumption that Article 8 was engaged, the search was found to be proportionate given the reasonable suspicion of significant damage in the past and actual intelligence of similar intentions. '[I]t was a sensible reaction to the problem to try to prevent trouble before it happened by a moderate search of those suspected of being possible offenders. It was a manner of ensuring, rather than preventing peaceful protest.'[381]

The court concluded with the observation that minimal intrusions into privacy are the 'price today of participation in numerous lawful activities conducted in large groups of people'.[382] In *Roberts*[383] the Administrative Court found that Article 8 was engaged by what it described as a search involving some humiliation and embarrassment, but concluded that it was in accordance with the law and proportionate. This was despite the fact that the authorisation granted police authority to search without reasonable suspicion for offensive weapons or dangerous instruments. Here it was used to search the claimant, a 38-year-old woman of good character, for a form of identification when she had insufficient funds to pay her bus fare.[384]

9.5 Disclosure of Police Information

9.5.1 Enhanced Criminal Record Certificates

Enhanced criminal record certificates (ECRCs) issued under section 115 of the Police Act 1997 raise particular issues. These contain information about offences of which the person is suspected of committing, even though responsibility has not been proved. The Chief Constable must be of the opinion that the information might be relevant to a position which involves regularly caring for, training, supervising or being in sole charge of persons under 18 or vulnerable persons aged 18 or over. The information can be highly prejudicial and could 'blight an individual's opportunity to obtain employment in his chosen field'.[385]

The Court of Appeal held in *X*[386] that the legislation itself did not contravene Article 8.[387] However, it also considered proportionality in relation to the individual claimant. Here the certificate contained allegations of indecent exposure. The claimant had applied for a job which would involve work with those under 18. The court stated that, as long as the Chief Constable was entitled to form the opinion that the information disclosed might be relevant, absent any untoward circumstance, it was difficult to see that there could be any reason why the information that might be relevant ought not

---

[381] Ibid, [38].

[382] Ibid, [41].

[383] *R (Roberts) v Commissioner of Police of the Metropolis* [2012] EWHC 1977 (Admin), [2012] HRLR 28.

[384] See also *Beghal v Director of Public Prosecutions* [2013] EWHC 2573 (Admin) where it was held that the power under the Terrorism Act 2000 to stop, question and detain persons at a port or in a border area was lawful. See further G Lennon, 'Suspicionless Stop and Search—Lessons from the Netherlands" (2013) 12 *Criminal Law Review* 978.

[385] *X* (n 114).

[386] Ibid.

[387] Ibid, [20].

to be included in the certificate. But it did accept that it might be disproportionate to include information as to some trifling matter or information which evidence made unlikely to be correct.[388] It also stated that responsibility for forming an opinion was on the Chief Constable, and if that opinion was formed properly it was not for the courts to interfere.[389] It concluded that disclosure was proportionate, holding that if 'the claimant was guilty of the conduct alleged, then that conduct would be highly relevant to the question of his employment with children or vulnerable adults. It was information of which the prospective employer should be aware'.[390]

This approach was the subject of challenge in the Supreme Court in L[391] where it was argued that it involved a disproportionate interference with Article 8 rights bearing in mind the damaging effects to the applicant that the disclosure of such information might give rise to.[392] Here it was argued that the disclosure would lead to loss of employment and to long-term inability to work in any form of employment involving care for or contact with children or vulnerable adults. The ECRC disclosed that the claimant's son had been put on the child protection register and that he was removed from it after he had been found guilty of robbery and received a custodial sentence.

The Supreme Court agreed that the legislation itself did not contravene Article 8 and that the issue was one of applying it in a way which was proportionate.[393] It concluded that the approach of the Court of Appeal in X was to tilt the balance against the claimant too far as it had 'encouraged the idea that priority must be given to the social need to protect the vulnerable as against the right to respect for private life of the applicant'.[394] It was held that the words 'ought to be included' in the legislation must be read and given effect in a way that was compatible with the applicant's Convention right and that of any third party who may be affected by the disclosure.[395] In relation to the guidance on disclosure, it was held that it should indicate that careful consideration was required in all cases where the disruption to the private life of anyone was 'judged to be as great, or more so, as the risk of non-disclosure to the vulnerable group'. It was no longer to be assumed that the presumption was for disclosure unless there was a good reason for not doing so.[396] Where there was doubt, it was held that Chief Constables should offer claimants an opportunity to make representations before the information was released.[397] In the present case it concluded that the disclosure was proportionate as the information bore directly on the question whether she was a person who could safely be entrusted with the job of supervising children in a school canteen or in the playground.[398]

---

[388] Ibid, [41].
[389] Ibid, [47].
[390] Ibid, [43]. See also *Maddock v Devon County Council*, Divisional Court, 13 August 2003.
[391] L (n 6).
[392] Ibid, per Lord Hope at [3].
[393] Ibid, [41].
[394] Ibid, [44].
[395] Ibid, [44].
[396] Ibid, [45].
[397] Ibid, [46].
[398] Ibid, [48]. See also *R (W) v Chief Constable of Warwickshire* [2012] EWHC 406 (Admin); *R (J) v Chief Constable of Devon & Cornwall* [2012] EWHC 2996 (Admin); *R (A) v Chief Constable of Kent* [2013] EWHC 424 (Admin); and *R (L) v Chief Constable of Cumbria Constabulary* [2013] EWHC 869 (Admin).

9.5.2 Convictions and Cautions

In T[399] the Court of Appeal considered three claims that the disclosure of police warnings, cautions and convictions were disproportionate. The Court of Appeal concluded that the statutory regime requiring the disclosure of all convictions and cautions relating to recordable offences was disproportionate to the general aim of protecting employers, children and vulnerable adults and to the particular aim of enabling employers to make an assessment of whether an individual was suitable for a particular kind of work.[400] It held as follows:

> The fundamental objection to the scheme is that it does not seek to control the disclosure of information by reference to whether it is relevant to the purpose of enabling employers to assess the suitability of an individual for a particular kind of work. Relevance must depend on a number of factors including the seriousness of the offence; the age of the offender at the time of the offence; the sentence imposed or other manner of disposal; the time that has elapsed since the offence was committed; whether the individual has subsequently re-offended; and the nature of the work that the individual wishes to do.[401]

9.5.3 Notification and Licence Requirements

Closely related are notification requirements such as those contained in the Sexual Offences Act 2003 which imposed on all who were sentenced to 30 months imprisonment or more for a sexual offence the duty to keep the police notified of where they were living and of travel abroad. This duty persisted until the day they died. There was no right to a review of the notification requirements and this aspect of the scheme was the subject of challenge in F.[402] The Supreme Court accepted the importance of the legislative objective, Lord Phillips stating that the prevention of sexual offending was of great social value.[403] However, the debate was as to the necessity and utility of imposing notification requirements for life without any review.

The Supreme Court found that the notification requirements were a serious interference with private life. Lord Phillips observed that giving information to the police in relation to address and movements, coupled with the explanation that this is necessary because one is on the Sexual Offences Register, will necessarily carry the risk that the information may be conveyed to third parties in circumstances where this is not appropriate.[404] It concluded that the notification requirements were a disproportionate interference with Article 8 rights because no provision was made for individual review:

> If some of those who are subject to lifetime notification requirements no longer pose any significant risk of committing further sexual offences and it is possible for them to demonstrate that this is the case, there is no point in subjecting them to supervision or management or to

---

[399] R (T) v Chief Constable of Greater Manchester [2013] EWCA Civ 25, [2013] 2 All ER 813.
[400] Ibid, [37].
[401] Ibid, [38].
[402] R (F) v Secretary of State for the Home Department [2010] UKSC 17, [2010] 2 WLR 992.
[403] Ibid, [18].
[404] Ibid, [42].

the interference with their article 8 rights involved in visits to their local police stations in order to provide information about their places of residence and their travel plans.[405]

The fact that notification requirements are imposed automatically, without any discretion on the trial judge to not apply them, has also been the subject of challenge. However, this challenged failed, the Court of Appeal finding that the automatic notification requirements 'contribute to the protection of children everywhere', as well as the detection of offenders minded to exploit them, or to involve themselves in the exploitation of children by others.[406]

Claims made under the HRA concerning licence conditions which are imposed on release from prison, restricting matters such as where an individual may reside, or who may visit, have not been successful. Whilst proportionality will depend upon the facts of the case, it is difficult for a claimant to establish that the effect of the conditions is disproportionate.[407] For example, a condition of a licence that a former prisoner attend regular polygraph sessions to detect whether or not he was lying about his activities has also been the subject of an unsuccessful challenge.[408] However, the procedural rights implicit in Article 8 require the decision-making process to be fair and afford due respect to the interests safeguarded by Article 8. This may afford a prisoner due to be released the right to make representations about additional licence conditions.[409]

9.6 Offender Naming Schemes

Whilst not finally determining the lawfulness or otherwise of the scheme, in *Ellis*[410] the Divisional Court considered an offender naming scheme devised by Essex Police. The scheme involved displaying posters at train stations and other travel locations where it was thought they would have the greatest effect on the itinerant criminal. The first poster would have a picture of an individual who was not recognisable and was not an offender. Above the photograph would appear the words 'If you commit a crime in Brentwood' and below 'Your name and image will be on this poster'. The other poster would contain a photograph of the face of a selected offender and above the photograph would appear the name of the offender, the nature of his offence and the sentence he was serving. Below the picture would appear the words 'If you come to Brentwood to commit crime, expect to do the time'. Offenders selected would be given seven days to register a legal objection to their inclusion, and selection would only follow a risk assessment.

Taking into account the rights of the offender and the public, the court pointed out that the lawfulness or otherwise of the scheme would depend on the circumstances of the offender selected. It had in mind that it should not declare unlawful a genuine

---

[405] Ibid, per Lord Phillips at [51]. In *R (Irfan) v Secretary of State for the Home Department* [2012] EWCA Civ 1471, [2013] 2 WLR 1340 the Court of Appeal concluded that a ten-year notification requirement imposed under the Counter-Terrorism Act 2008 was proportionate.

[406] *F* (n 402), [19]. See also *R v H* [2007] EWCA Crim 2622 and *R (Prothero) v Secretary of State for the Home Department* [2013] EWHC 2830 (Admin).

[407] *R (Gunn) v Secretary of State for Justice* [2009] EWHC 1812 (Admin).

[408] *R (C) v Ministry of Justice* [2009] EWHC 2671 (Admin).

[409] *R (Tabbakh) v Staffordshire & West Midlands Probation Trust* [2013] EWHC 2492 (Admin).

[410] *Ellis* (n 118).

initiative on the part of the police to reduce crime.[411] However, it noted that there was a real question about whether it would ever be appropriate to select a father of young children;[412] further, there was a need for appraisal and monitoring, and a need for a structured assessment of the risks involved.[413] The court was not prepared to declare that the scheme could not be operated lawfully during the trial period.[414]

Similarly, in *Stanley*[415] it was argued that for the police to distribute leaflets and publicise other material carrying the claimants' images, names and ages, and details of anti-social behaviour orders issued against them, was a breach of Article 8. Although noting that those considering post-order publicity in future should have in mind the Convention rights of those against whom orders were made, the court concluded here that the interference was proportionate.

> [W]hether publicity is intended to inform, to reassure, to assist in enforcing the existing orders by policing, to inhibit the behaviour of those against whom the orders have been made, or to deter others, it is unlikely to be effective unless it includes photographs, names and at least partial addresses. Not only do the readers need to know against whom orders have been made, but those responsible for publicity must leave no room for misidentification.[416]

A comparable scheme was challenged in *Clift*[417] where the claimant had been placed on the Council's Violent Persons Register following an argumentative interaction with a council worker. The Court of Appeal held that the protection of the safety of all council employees and employees of partner organisations was a legitimate aim. However, here it concluded that publication to those not likely to be directly approached by the claimant was disproportionate as they were not at risk of harm from her. It stated as follows:

> Ill-considered and indiscriminate disclosure is bound to be disproportionate and no plea of administrative difficulty in verifying the information and limiting publication to those who truly have the need to know or those reasonably thought to be at risk can outweigh the substantial interference with the right to protect reputations.[418]

9.7 Prisoners

Article 8 does not render unlawful that interference with private life which inevitably follows from a lawfully imposed custodial sentence.[419] However, a custodial order does not wholly deprive a prisoner of all rights enjoyed by other citizens.[420]

In *Daly*[421] the House of Lords held that a blanket policy which required the absence

---

[411] Ibid, [32].
[412] Ibid, [35].
[413] Ibid, [37].
[414] Ibid, [39].
[415] *R (on the application of Stanley, Marshall and Kelly) v Metropolitan Police Commissioner* [2004] EWHC (Admin) 2229, [2005] EMLR 3.
[416] Ibid, [40].
[417] *Clift v Slough Borough Council* [2010] EWCA Civ 1484, [2011] 1 WLR 1774.
[418] Ibid, [35].
[419] *R (on the application of Morley) v Nottinghamshire Health Care NHS Trust* [2002] EWCA Civ 1728, [2003] 1 All ER 784.
[420] *Daly* (n 215), per Lord Bingham at [5].
[421] Ibid.

of prisoners when their legally privileged correspondence was opened interfered with Article 8 rights to a much greater extent than necessity required. However, it was possible for a rule to provide for the exclusion of a prisoner while the examination took place if there was reasonably believed to be good cause for excluding him to safeguard the efficacy of the search.[422] In *Ponting*[423] the Court of Appeal held that it was proportionate to require a prisoner not to password-protect the files on his computer and to only print documents in the presence of an appointed member of staff.[424] In *Szuluk*[425] the Court of Appeal held that it was proportionate for the prison medical officer to read the correspondence between a prisoner and his NHS consultant. The need for order and prevention of crime in prisons and secure hospitals also has been held to permit the random recording of and subsequent listening to the outgoing and incoming telephone calls of patients and inmates.[426]

Whilst seclusion of prisoners, or detained patients, engages Article 8, it has been held that it may be the only means of protecting others from violence or intimidation.[427] 'Properly used, the seclusion will not be disproportionate because it will match the necessity giving rise to it.'[428] Here it was argued that the seclusion was unlawful because it was not prescribed by a binding general law. A majority of the House of Lords did not agree, finding that requirement that hospitals have clear written guidelines was sufficient. 'The procedure adopted by the Trust does not permit arbitrary or random decision-making. The rules are accessible, foreseeable and predictable.'[429]

9.8 Control orders

Surprisingly the imposition of control orders has given rise to very few Article 8 claims and most control orders have been challenged under Articles 5 and 6. In *CD*[430] the Administrative Court considered under Article 8 a control order which included relocation, electronic tagging, a home curfew, an obligation to report to a police station, restrictions on meeting people and restrictions on leaving a confined area. It was confirmed that the obligations amounted to a very considerable interference with private and family life, and the discussion therefore centred on proportionality.

It was held that in a case involving an individual suspected of involvement in terrorist activities, an interference with Convention rights may more easily be justified as proportionate because its object is to protect the public from the risk of terrorism.[431] With considerable deference to the Secretary of State, the court concluded that each of the obligations was a necessary and proportionate measure for the protection of the

---

[422] Ibid, [22].
[423] *Ponting* (n 215).
[424] Ibid, [38] and [40].
[425] *Szuluk* (n 215).
[426] *N* (n 49). In *R (on the application of Taylor) v The Governor of Her Majesty's Prison Risley*, Administrative Court, 20 October 2004, the court found a call enabling system, requiring the prisoner to makes calls through the use of a PIN number and the prior notification of outside numbers desired to be called, to be compatible with Art 8.
[427] *Munjaz* (n 161), per Lord Bingham at [32].
[428] Ibid, per Lord Bingham at [33] and per Lord Hope at [89]–[90].
[429] Ibid, per Lord Bingham at [34], per Lord Hope at [90]–[94] and per Lord Scott at [103].
[430] *Secretary of State for the Home Department v CD* [2011] EWHC 2087 (Admin).
[431] Ibid, [51].

public.[432] In a later case the Administrative Court held that whilst a degree of deference should normally be paid to the decisions taken by the Secretary of State in this area, the court remained under an obligation to subject 'to intense scrutiny the necessity for each of the obligations imposed on an individual under a control order'.[433]

10. Protection of Health

Interference with the private lives of those working in the health sector in the interests of health is common and usually proportionate. For example, in *Whitefield*[434] the Privy Council found that the conditions imposed by the General Medical Council on the appellant general practitioner, in order for him to keep his registration, were necessary and proportionate. The conditions included a complete ban on the consumption of alcohol; blood and urine testing; and attendance at Alcoholic Anonymous meetings. In *Woolgar*[435] the court held that it was proportionate for the police to disclose to the UK Central Council for Nursing, Midwifery and Health Visiting the contents of an interview between the claimant and the police. Allegations had been made, including an allegation of overadministration of diamorphine, about the claimant, following the death of a patient in her care.[436] Article 8 also permits the disclosure of communicable illnesses such as the fact that a healthcare worker is infected with hepatitis B.[437]

In *N*[438] although the Court of Appeal had determined a smoking ban in a secure hospital did not engage Article 8, it went on to consider whether the interference, assuming there was one, was justified. It concluded that the ban was justified for a number of reasons including: the evidence of the dangers of smoking both to smokers and to those subject to second hand smoke; the substantial health benefits from the ban; security requirements; and the deference afforded to the regulations following an extensive consultation exercise.[439]

It has also been held that the disclosure of patient records, here dental records, was proportionate where it was necessary for a professional disciplinary body to perform its function effectively and ensure public confidence in the dental profession was maintained.[440] Safeguards must be in place to guard against the risk of further disclosure.

---

[432] Ibid, [58].
[433] *Secretary of State for the Home Department v CE* [2011] EWHC 3159 (Admin). See also *Birmingham City Council v James* [2013] EWCA Civ 552 concerning restrictions on private life imposed by an injunction to restrain gang violence (IRGV).
[434] *Whitefield* (n 144).
[435] *Woolgar v Chief Constable of Sussex Police* [1999] 3 All ER 604.
[436] See also *A Health Authority v X* [2001] EWCA Civ 2014, [2002] 2 All ER 780.
[437] *Saha v General Medical Council* [2009] EWHC 1907 (Admin).
[438] *R (N) v Secretary of State for Health* [2009] EWCA Civ 795, [2009] HRLR 31.
[439] Ibid, [71].
[440] *In the Matter of General Dental Council* [2011] EWHC 3011 (Admin).

11. Protection of Morals

This justification rarely arises in claims under the HRA but was at issue in *Friend*[441] where it was accepted by the House of Lords that the hunting ban was justified by prevention of cruelty to animals. Baroness Hale observed that when it comes to the protection of morals

> the Convention also has to take account of the very different importance attached to certain moral values in different member states. The British have long attached importance to protecting animals from harm and the hunting ban is simply the latest in a long line of legislation to that end.[442]

It was also the justification put forward in the *Countryside Alliance* case[443] where Lord Bingham concluded that the aim of the Hunting Act 2004 was the protection of morals and this did not fall outside of the aims permitted under Article 8(2).[444] Affording considerable defence to the legislature, on the assumption that the claim was within the scope of Article 8, a majority of their Lordships concluded that the Act was proportionate to the end it sought to achieve. Lord Brown did not find the ban justified, stating that were the Article 8 rights engaged, he would not have found the ethical objection of the majority as a sufficient basis for holding the ban to be 'necessary'.[445] He appreciated that the UK had a long and proud tradition of animal welfare legislation but had difficulty in seeing this ban as 'just another step in that process, just another development of social policy'.[446]

12. Protection of Rights and Freedoms of Others

As with other similarly drafted Convention rights, the 'rights and freedoms of others' is fairly open ended. Nevertheless, the majority of claims have fallen within the purview of another Convention right. These are examined in the following paragraphs.

---

[441] *Friend* (n 22).
[442] Ibid, [40].
[443] *Countryside Alliance* (n 8).
[444] Ibid, [44].
[445] Ibid, [159].
[446] Ibid, [160].

12.1 Fair Trial and Open Justice

12.1.1 Generally

Where the necessity for a fair trial is at issue, this will usually justify interferences with Article 8(1) by requiring, for example, the disclosure of medical records,[447] the disclosure of allegations or requiring a particular witness to give evidence.[448] This is particularly so in relation to Children Act 1989 proceedings.[449] The interests of a fair trial may also require one of the parties to submit to a medical examination, particularly where what is at issue is compensation for physical or psychological injury.[450] However, in *A Mother*[451] the Court of Appeal held that certain evidence referable to a mother in care proceedings should not be disclosed to her husband as this could have serious adverse consequences for her. Where a conviction and sentence are already a matter of public record, it has been held that publication of a claimant's name in further proceedings does not breach Article 8.[452] However, it has been held that it is not compatible with Article 8 for the entire criminal history of a witness to be disclosed and that the right to a fair trial did not require information to be disclosed unless it was material:

> It is open to the criticism that the release of such information without regard to its materiality to the case in hand would be arbitrary, as no legitimate purpose would be served by the release of information that was not material. It would go beyond what was necessary for the protection of the accused's right to a fair trial, so it would not be justifiable under article 8(2).[453]

12.1.2 Access to Court

In certain circumstances, an interference with private life may be necessary in order to provide access to court pursuant to Article 6. For example, in *S*[454] the Court of Appeal concluded that a mother should have access to confidential information concerning her son, who was in the local social services authority's guardianship under the Mental Health Act 1983. As his nearest relative she wished to have access to enough information about him to exercise her statutory functions under the Act.

> Proper access to the court therefore requires that she have proper access to legal advice before she sets that process in motion. Proper access to legal advice requires that she have access to the information which will be relevant to the court's decision.[455]

---

[447] See eg *B R & C (Children)* [2002] EWCA Civ 1825; *A v X* [2004] EWHC (QB) 447.
[448] *Re A (A Child: Disclosure of Third Party Information)* [2012] UKSC 60, [2012] 3 WLR 1484. See also *In the Matter of FI Call Ltd* [2013] EWCA Civ 819, [2013] 1 WLR 2993. See further M Hall, 'The Misfortune of Being Straightforward? The Impact of Re W on Children Giving Evidence in Care Proceedings' (2010) 22 *Child and Family Law Quarterly* 499.
[449] *A*, ibid. See also *A Health Authority v X* [2001] EWCA Civ 2014, [2002] 2 All ER 780.
[450] See eg *De Keyser Ltd v Wilson* [2001] IRLR 324. With respect to a fair trial generally and the right to respect for private life, see *Newman* (n 124).
[451] *A Mother v A Father* [2009] EWCA Civ 1057, [2010] 2 FLR 1757.
[452] *R (Minter) v Chief Constable of Hampshire* [2011] EWHC 1610 (Admin).
[453] *Murtagh* (n 113).
[454] *S* (n 47).
[455] Ibid, [41].

12.1.3 Applications for Anonymity

Increasingly courts are considering applications from claimants for anonymity. It has been held that open justice is of cardinal importance. However, even as protected by Article 6, the open justice rule is not absolute.

> [W]here the court concludes that it is right to grant an injunction … restraining the publication of private information, the court may then have to consider how far it is necessary to impose restrictions on the reporting of the proceedings in order not to deprive the injunction of its effect.[456]

The general rule is that the names of parties are included in orders and judgments of the court and there are no general exceptions where private matters were in issue. As an order for anonymity is a derogation from the principle of open justice and Article 10, the court must closely scrutinise the application and consider whether a degree of restraint on publication is necessary and whether there is a less restrictive alternative. Where a court is asked to restrain publication of the names of parties or subject matter of claim under Article 8, the question is whether there is sufficient general, public interest in publishing a report of the proceedings which identifies a party and/or the normally reportable details to justify any resulting curtailment of his right and his family's right to respect for their private and family life. There is to be no special treatment for public figures or celebrities and an order is not to be made simply because the parties consented.[457]

Control order proceedings raise additional issues and it has been accepted by the courts that Article 8 rights can be engaged as a consequence of publicity being given to the Secretary of State's suspicion that an individual is involved in terrorism but that this must be balanced against freedom of expression and open justice.[458] It has been held that proceedings in the Court of Protection are private and Article 8 is engaged although it has also been recognised that on occasions there may be a public interest in the individual case which may outweigh the privacy considerations.[459]

12.2 Right to Life

In *Pretty*[460] it was argued that Article 8 conferred a right to self-determination, and the refusal of the Director of Public Prosecutions to undertake that he would not, under section 2(4) of the Suicide Act 1961, consent to the prosecution of Mr Pretty under section 2(1) if he were to assist his wife to commit suicide was incompatible with this right. The House of Lords doubted that Mrs Pretty's rights under Article 8 were

---

[456] *JIH v News Group Newspapers Ltd* [2011] EWCA Civ 42, [2011] 2 All ER 324.

[457] Ibid, [21]. See also *Revenue & Customs Commissioners v Banerjee* [2009] EWHC 1229 (Ch), [2009] 3 All ER 930; *Gray v UVW* [2010] EWHC 2367 (QB); and *CVB v MGN Ltd* [2012] EWHC 1148 (QB). In relation to anonymity in the EAT, see *F v G* UKEAT/0042/11/DA 21 September 2011. See further A Zuckerman, 'Common Law Repelling Super injunctions, Limiting Anonymity and Banning Trial by Stealth' (2011) 30 *Criminal Justice Quarterly* 223; C McGlynn, 'Rape, Defendant Anonymity and Human Rights: Adopting a "Wider Perspective"' [2011] *Criminal Law Review* 199.

[458] *Times Newspapers Ltd v Secretary of State for the Home Department* [2008] EWHC 2455 (Admin); *Secretary of State for the Home Department v AP* [2010] UKSC 26, [2010] 1 WLR 1652.

[459] *A v Independent News & Media Ltd* [2010] EWCA Civ 343, [2010] 1 WLR 2262.

[460] *Pretty* (n 176).

engaged at all.[461] The ECtHR later reached the opposite conclusion, finding that her rights were engaged.[462] Nevertheless, assuming there was an infringement, the House of Lords went on to consider whether the infringement was justifiable under Article 8(2) and concluded that it was.[463] The basis of the justification was the protection of the vulnerable.

> It is not hard to imagine that an elderly person, in the absence of any pressure, might opt for a premature end to life if that were available, not from a desire to die or a willingness to stop living, but from a desire to stop being a burden to others.[464]

The ECtHR also found the blanket ban proportionate. In the later case of *Purdy*[465] Lord Brown held that it was implicit in the Court's reasoning that in certain cases, not merely would it be appropriate not to prosecute, but a prosecution under section 2(1) would actually be inappropriate.

> If in practice the ban were to operate on a blanket basis, the only relaxation in its impact being by way of merciful sentences on some occasions when it is disobeyed, that would hardly give sufficient weight to the article 8 rights with which the ban, if obeyed, is acknowledged to interfere.[466]

12.3 Private Life

In certain circumstances, it may be necessary to balance the private life of one individual against that of another. For example, in *Evans*,[467] affording considerable deference to Parliament, the Court of Appeal held that the refusal of a fertility clinic, in accordance with the Human Fertilisation and Embryology Act 1990, to treat a woman following the withdrawal of her former partner's consent to the storage and use of the frozen embryos was proportionate.

> The need, as perceived by Parliament, is for bilateral consent to implantation, not simply to the taking and storage of genetic material, and that need cannot be met if one half of the consent is no longer effective. To dilute this requirement in the interests of proportionality, in order to meet Ms Evans' otherwise intractable biological handicap, by making the withdrawal of the man's consent relevant but inconclusive, would create new and even more intractable difficulties or arbitrariness and inconsistency.[468]

---

[461] Ibid, per Lord Bingham at [26].

[462] *Pretty* (n 141).

[463] *Pretty* (n 176), per Lord Bingham at [30], per Lord Steyn at [62], per Lord Hope at [102], per Lord Hobhouse at [112] and per Lord Scott at [112].

[464] Ibid, per Lord Bingham at [29] and per Lord Steyn at [50]. See further D Morris, 'Assisted Suicide under the European Convention on Human Rights: a Critique' [2003] *European Human Rights Law Review* 65.

[465] *Purdy* (n 179).

[466] Ibid, [74].

[467] *Evans* (n 185).

[468] Ibid, [69]. See also *Roddy* (n 188), where the right to autonomy of one individual was balanced against the rights of others to keep their identities secret.

12.4 Freedom of Expression

Where respect for private life is asserted via the tort of breach of confidence against a media organisation, the right to freedom of expression is the opposing right placed in the balance.

> [T]he right to privacy which lies at the heart of an action for breach of confidence has to be balanced against the right of the media to impart information to the public. And the right of the media to impart information to the public has to be balanced in its turn against the respect that must be given to private life.[469]

The same applies where an injunction is sought under the inherent jurisdiction of the High Court to protect identity.[470] Freedom of expression is considered fully in Chapter 15, including the factors which contribute to a strong claim and consideration of a number of examples.

One Convention right has no priority over another even taking into account section 12(4) of the HRA.[471]

> Any restriction of the right to freedom of expression must be subjected to very close scrutiny. But so too must any restriction of the right to respect for private life. Neither Art 8 nor Art 10 has any pre-eminence over the other in the conduct of this exercise. As Resolution 1165 of the Parliamentary Assembly of the Council of Europe (1998), para 11, pointed out, they are neither absolute nor in any hierarchical order, since they are of equal value in a democratic society.[472]

Both Articles 8 and 10 are qualified, and the proportionality of interfering with one has to be balanced against the proportionality of restricting the other. 'As each is a fundamental right, there is evidently a "pressing social need" to protect it.'[473] A basic approach is first to examine the comparative importance of the actual rights being claimed in the individual case; then look at the justifications for interfering with or restricting each of those rights; and then apply the proportionality test to each.[474] The means chosen to limit the Article 10 right must be rational, fair and not arbitrary, and impair the right as minimally as is reasonably possible.[475] It is clear that weighing and balancing these factors is a process which may well lead different people to different conclusions.[476]

If the invasion of private life is held to be a matter of legitimate public interest because, for example, a public figure has previously lied about the matter, the claim to freedom of expression will be particularly strong and will often defeat the strongest privacy claim.[477] '[W]here a public figure chooses to make untrue pronouncements about his or her private life, the press will normally be entitled to put the record straight.'[478]

---

[469] *Campbell* (n 2), per Lord Hope at [105].

[470] See eg *Re S* (n 265).

[471] *Campbell* (n 2), per Lord Hope at [106] and [111].

[472] Ibid, per Lord Hope at [113]. See also Lord Nicholls at [12]. Also *Re S* (n 265), per Lord Steyn at [17].

[473] *Campbell*, ibid, per Baroness Hale at [140].

[474] Ibid, per Baroness Hale at [141]. This test was employed by the House of Lords in *Re S* (n 265), per Lord Steyn at [17].

[475] *Campbell*, ibid, per Lord Hope at [115] with whom Lord Carswell agreed at [167].

[476] Ibid, per Lord Carswell at [168].

[477] See eg ibid, where the House of Lords unanimously held that Ms Campbell could not seek a remedy in relation to the disclosure of the fact of her drug addiction and the fact that she was receiving treatment as she had previously lied about both.

[478] Ibid, per Lord Hope at [82].

For example, in *Campbell*[479] the House of Lords concluded unanimously that Ms Campbell had no claim in relation to the fact of her drug addiction or to the fact that she was receiving treatment as she had lied about these facts and also sought to benefit from this by comparing herself with others in the fashion business who were addicted. However, in relation to the fact that she was receiving treatment at Narcotics Anonymous, the details of the treatment and the visual portrayal (photograph) of her leaving a specific meeting, the majority concluded that the balance was in favour of respect for her private life and the invasion of that right entitled her to damages.[480]

Whilst a public figure was not seeking protection in *Re S*,[481] the House of Lords was required to balance the freedom of the press to report on everything that took place in a criminal court against the right to respect for private life of an eight-year-old boy whose mother was being tried for the murder of his older brother. An order had been granted to prohibit publication of any information which might lead to his identification or that of the mother or deceased child. The House of Lords held that the Article 8 right was not of the same order when compared with the cases of juveniles who were directly involved in criminal trials.[482] Balanced against the importance of the press to report the progress of a criminal trial without restraint, it concluded that injunction should not be granted.

The following five reasons were given. First, adult non-parties to a criminal trial would be added to the prospective pool of applicants who could apply for such injunctions confronting newspapers with an ever wider spectrum of potentially costly proceedings.[483] Secondly, further exceptions to the principle of open justice would be encouraged and would gain in momentum.[484] Thirdly, a report of a sensational trial without revealing the identity of the defendant would be a disembodied trial and informed debate about criminal justice would suffer.[485] Fourthly, it was costly for newspapers to contest an application for an injunction.[486] Finally, local newspapers threatened with the prospect of an injunction were likely to be silenced and this would seriously impoverish public discussion of criminal justice.[487]

In *Clayton*[488] a father challenged an injunction imposed to prevent him from dis-

---

[479] Ibid.

[480] See also *Douglas* (n 38); *Theakston* (n 86); *B & C v A* (n 84); *X v O'Brien* (n 284); *AAA v Associated Newspapers Ltd* [2013] EWCA Civ 554; *LNS v Persons Unknown* [2010] EWHC 119 (QB), [2010] 2 FLR 1306; *Ferdinand* (n 96); *Trimingham* (n 44); *AAA v Associated Newspapers Ltd* [2012] EWHC 2103 (QB), [2012] HRLR 31; *McClaren v News Group Newspapers Ltd* [2012] EWHC 2466 (QB); *Rocknroll v News Group Newspapers Ltd* [2013] EWHC 24 (Ch). See further discussion of this issue in the chapter concerning freedom of expression.

[481] *Re S* (n 265).

[482] Ibid, per Lord Steyn at [27].

[483] Ibid, [32].

[484] Ibid, [33].

[485] Ibid, [34].

[486] Ibid, [35].

[487] Ibid, [36]. See also *R v Teeside Crown Court, ex p Gazette Media Co Ltd* [2005] EWCA Crim 1983; *E v Channel Four* (n 191); *Re X & Y (Children)* [2012] EWCA Civ 1500, [2013] 2 FLR 628; and *R (A) v Lowestoft Magistrates' Court* [2013] EWHC 659 (Admin). In *Pelling v Bruce-Williams* [2004] EWCA Civ 845, [2004] Fam 155 the Court of Appeal held that, in Children Act 1989 cases, the time had come for the court to consider in each case whether a proper balance of competing rights required the anonymisation of any report of the proceedings and judgment following a hearing that was conducted in public. See further H Fenwick, 'Clashing Rights, the Welfare of the Child and the Human Rights Act' (2004) 67 *Modern Law Review* 889. See also *R (Trinity Mirror Plc) v Croydon Crown Court* [2008] EWCA Crim 50, [2008] QB 770

[488] *Clayton v Clayton* [2006] EWCA Civ 878, [2006] 3 WLR 599.

closing details of the custody dispute concerning his daughter. He wished to be at liberty to discuss the case to demonstrate what he perceived as flaws in the family justice system. The Court of Appeal held that where an injunction was imposed under the Children Act 1989, it was necessary for the court to consider the right of the child to privacy in relation to the proceedings and confidentiality of his or her personal data; the right of the parent under Article 10 to tell his or her story to the world; and in the case of an application by media interests, their wish to publish or broadcast the story or comment on the issues.[489] Here it was concluded that the injunction was too wide, bearing in mind the position of the father as an active campaigner for improvement in the family justice system.[490]

12.5 Children and Vulnerable Adults

Finally, a number of Article 8 claims have been brought concerning disclosure of information private to an individual concerning allegations of sexual abuse of children. In some cases, the allegation has been investigated and then no further action taken. In others, criminal charges have been brought and the defendant later acquitted. Local authorities have been found to have a power to disclose such information arising by implication from their responsibilities for the welfare and protection of children.[491] Nevertheless, such disclosure must still meet the requirements of Article 8. The necessity for disclosure has been considered under a variety of interests listed in Article 8(2), including public safety and prevention of crime. The majority, however, have been considered as an aspect of the protection of the rights of the child.

In *LM*[492] the High Court held that a blanket approach was impermissible and disclosure should only be made if there was a pressing need. 'Disclosure should be the exception, and not the rule. That is because the consequences of disclosure of such information for the subject of the allegations can be very damaging indeed.'[493]

The court stated that it was important to take into account its own belief as to the truth of the allegation. At one end of the spectrum is the person who has actually been convicted. At the other is the situation where the allegation has been investigated but it has been concluded that there is no substance to it. The interest of the third party in obtaining the information must also be considered.

> The more intense the legitimacy of the interest in the third party in having the information, the more pressing the need to disclose is likely to be. Thus, at one extreme are local authorities with a statutory responsibility for the protection of children. At the other are members of the public whose sole interest is to expose those whom they consider to be child sex abusers.[494]

The degree of risk posed by the person if disclosure is not made should also be taken into account.

---

[489] Ibid, [59].
[490] Ibid, [72]. Other examples include *In the Matter of Guardian News & Media Ltd* [2010] UKSC 1, [2010] 2 AC 697 and *In re British Broadcasting Corporation* [2009] UKHL 34, [2009] 3 WLR 142.
[491] See *R (on the application of A) v Hertfordshire CC* [2001] EWHC (Admin) 211, [2001] ACD 469.
[492] *LM* (n 114).
[493] In reliance upon *R v Chief Constable of North Wales, ex p AB* [1998] 3 FCR 371.
[494] Ibid, 746.

In the present case, the court concluded that a pressing need for disclosure had not been demonstrated. In particular, LM had no criminal record. There had been an internal investigation into the allegations of the first child at the end of which the evidence was destroyed. The allegation of his daughter was not proved. He had worked on a school bus run for the past 12 years and it had never been alleged that he used his position as a school bus driver to indecently assault a child. Similarly he had been involved in teaching children archery for the past 18 years and no allegations had been made.[495]

By contrast, *N v Governor of HM Prison Dartmoor*[496] concerned an actual prior conviction for gross indecency with a child. N challenged the decision of the prison governor to notify local authority social services departments and the probation service that a prisoner who had been in the past convicted of an offence against a child had been received into custody notwithstanding that this conviction was spent for the purposes of the Rehabilitation of Offenders Act 1974. The court concluded that the governor was entitled to communicate this information to the appropriate department of social services.

> [C]hildren are accorded a special place in terms of international Conventions (both UN and ECHR). It is their human rights which have a high need of domestic protection. Against that is the impact of the Governor's decision which would not necessarily lead to any adverse effect on the prisoner's rights. If there is then aggregated with those internationally recognised rights, the state's obligation to afford children every protection, the balance is ineluctably in terms of necessity on the side of the Governor's decision.[497]

The rights of the victims of child abuse may also, in certain circumstances, outweigh any Article 8 right asserted against disclosure of information. For example, in *X*[498] leave was sought to disclose two documents—the transcript of the judgment given by the judge and the local authority's statement of the threshold criteria in respect of X, who had been accused of child abuse by the local authority, and M, his wife. It was sought to disclose the material to the victims of X's abuse and a limited class of people standing in a close and confidential relationship with them. It was recognised by the court that there would be no further dissemination and no breach of the curtain of privacy, and the disclosure would be for the positive benefit of the children.[499] Particular emphasis was placed on the fact of limited disclosure.[500]

The court accepted that X's rights under Article 8 were implicated; however, these rights were subject to the rights of the victims of his abuse. In particular, the court noted the child's right to obtain from public records information necessary to know and understand their childhood and early development.[501] It concluded that, in a case such as the present, the Article 8 rights of the child victims of sexual and other abuse outweighed the conflicting Article 8 rights of the perpetrator.

---

[495] See also *Re S* [2001] EWHC (Admin) 334, [2001] FLR 776.

[496] *N v Governor of HM Prison Dartmoor* Administrative Court, 16 February 2001.

[497] Ibid, [26]. See also *R v Smethurst* [2001] EWCA Crim 772, [2002] 1 Cr App R 6. See also *H v A City Council* [2011] EWCA Civ 403, [2011] UKHRR 599 where it was held that disclosure was not proportionate as the claimant did not work with children.

[498] *In the Matter of X*, Family Division, 21 February 2001.

[499] Ibid, [20].

[500] Ibid, [26].

[501] Ibid, [34] relying on *Gaskin v United Kingdom* (1989) 12 EHRR 36.

> There are … clear and compelling reasons why these children, the victims of X's abuse, should, by being afforded the disclosure which is sought, be placed in a position where they will be better able to know and to understand their childhood, development and history.[502]

Finally, in *Wright*[503] the House of Lords considered the list maintained of those considered unsuitable to work with vulnerable adults. The process of listing was found to be incompatible with Article 6. In relation to Article 8 it was held that in some instances Article 8 could be breached by listing and the low threshold for provisional listing added to the risk of arbitrary and unjustified interferences and thus contributed to the 'overall unfairness of the scheme'.[504]

---

[502] Ibid. See also *Maddock v Devon County Council*, Divisional Court, 13 August 2003.
[503] *R (Wright) v Secretary of State for Health* [2009] UKHL 3, [2009] 1 AC 739.
[504] Ibid, per Baroness Hale at [37]. See also *X (South Yorkshire) v Secretary of State for the Home Department* [2012] EWHC 2954 (Admin), [2013] 1 WLR 2638 where the Administrative Court held that following the Child Sex Offender Disclosure Scheme Guidance Document could, in some instances, result in a breach of Article 8.

12

Article 8: The Right to Respect for Family Life

1. Introduction

The second right protected by Article 8 is the right to respect for family life. As with the right to respect for private life, this is not an absolute right and may be subject to interferences in accordance with law and necessary in one of the interests listed in Article 8(2). Prior to the HRA although there was an array of laws relating to children and families, there was no overriding legal principle of respect for family life or a duty to ensure that decisions impacting on family life were proportionate. Now that the principle of respect for family life is actually part of UK law, it is questionable what impact it has actually had. It is often held by courts that the right to respect for family life has made no difference at all to the approach they take in relation to children and families.[1] Nevertheless, this right has had significant impact in other areas, in particular immigration and prisoners' rights, and has the potential for impact in even more, including state support. As the meaning of 'family' develops, so too will the reach of this part of Article 8.[2]

2. Family Life

2.1 Definition

Such is the diversity of forms that the family takes in contemporary society that it is

---

[1] See eg *Payne v Payne* [2001] EWCA Civ 166, [2001] 2 WLR 1826.
[2] See further S Choudhry and J Herring, *European Human Rights and Family Law* (Oxford, Hart Publishing, 2010).

impossible to define what it meant by family life.[3] It has been observed that families differ widely in their composition and in the mutual relations which exist between the members and 'marked changes are likely to occur over time within the same family'. There is no 'pre-determined model of family or family life to which Article 8 must be applied'.[4] In determining whether or not family life exists, it is important to appreciate that there have been profound changes in family life in recent decades: '[M]any adults and children, whether through choice or circumstance, live in families more or less removed from what until comparatively recently would have been recognised as the typical nuclear family.'[5]

Article 8 requires respect to be shown for the right to such family life as is or may be enjoyed by those asserting the right bearing in mind the 'participation of other members who share in the life of that family'.[6] There must be a proper appreciation of the basic proposition that a person's family or extended family is the ground on which many people most heavily depend socially, emotionally and often financially.[7]

The existence of family life is a question of fact, depending upon whether there is a close personal relationship, one which has sufficient constancy and substance to create de facto family ties.[8] The meaning of family life is not confined to families based on marriage and may encompass other relationships, such as those between: grandparents and grandchildren;[9] uncle and nephew;[10] siblings;[11] cousins;[12] and married spouses.[13] Family life can be found to exist even where a husband and wife in a genuine subsisting marriage have not cohabited.[14] In relation to elderly relatives it has been held that the issue must be how dependent the older relative is on the younger ones and does that dependency create something more than the normal emotional ties?[15]

2.2 Parents and Children

Close personal ties are usually presumed to exist between children and their natural parents, although exceptionally this presumption may be displaced[16] and does not

---

[3] *Singh v Entry Clearance Officer New Delhi* [2004] EWCA Civ 1075, [2005] QB 608, per Munby J at [72].

[4] *EM (Lebanon) v Secretary of State for the Home Department* [2008] UKHL 64, [2008] 3 WLR 931, per Lord Bingham at [37].

[5] *Singh* (n 3), per Munby J at [63].

[6] *EM* (n 4), per Lord Bingham at [37].

[7] *ZB (Pakistan) v Secretary of State for the Home Department* [2009] EWCA Civ 834, [2010] INLR 195, [41].

[8] *Singh* (n 3), per Munby J at [79].

[9] Ibid, per Dyson LJ in reliance upon *Marckx v Belgium* (1979) 2 EHRR 330. See also Munby J at [58]–[62]. Grandparents have been held to automatically have a family life with a child even if the child has never lived with them. See *C (A Child) v XYZ County Council* [2007] EWCA Civ 1206, [2008] 3 WLR 445.

[10] See eg *R (on the application of L) v Secretary of State for Health* [2001] 1 FLR 406.

[11] See eg *Senthuran v Secretary of State for the Home Department* [2004] EWCA Civ 950, [2004] 4 All ER 365.

[12] *Singh* (n 3), per Munby J at [58] in reliance upon *Abdulaziz v UK* (1985) 7 EHRR 471; *Berrehab v Netherlands* (1988) 11 EHRR 322; *Marckx* (n 9); *Boyle v UK* [1994] 2 FCR 822.

[13] *Quila v Secretary of State for the Home Department* [2011] UKSC 45, [2012] 1 AC 621. Baroness Hale observed at [67] that family life arises virtually automatically upon a genuine marriage.

[14] *A (Afghanistan) v Secretary of State for the Home Department* [2009] EWCA Civ 825, [38].

[15] *ZB* (n 7), [42].

[16] *Singh* (n 3), per Dyson LJ at [21].

usually apply when the child reaches adulthood.[17] Further elements of dependency, involving more than the normal emotional ties, are required if the relationship between the adult child and his parents is to acquire protection under Article 8.[18] A mere time gap in contact between child and parent is not in itself sufficient to indicate that the normal family tie has been broken.[19]

The natural connection between mother and child at birth has been held to amount to family life which subsequent events can only break in exceptional circumstances.[20] Fathers will normally have family life with their children if they are married to or living with the mother and child. However, cohabitation is not essential: family life 'will depend upon the relationship established and the degree of commitment shown'.[21] In *Principal Reporter v K* the Supreme Court held that the father did enjoy family life with his child. He was living with her mother when she was born, they registered the birth together and lived as one household after the child's birth. He had regular contact with her after the separation.[22]

Claims have been brought concerning the family life rights of biological fathers who have no relationship with their child. For example, in *Re J*[23] the Family Division found that D, the biological father of J, of whom he was not aware, did not have a right to respect for his family life with J. His relationship with J's mother was not one of cohabitation and there were no exceptional facts to show that their relationship had sufficient constancy to create de facto family ties.[24] Similarly, in *Leeds Teaching Hospital*,[25] where, following a mix up, Mrs A's eggs had been fertilised with Mr B's sperm rather than that of Mr A her husband, the Divisional Court concluded that Mr B had no right to respect for family life. He was the biological father of the twins but had had no opportunity to forge any relationship with them.[26] By contrast, Mr A had rights under Article 8 as he was in the position of father and had established a close relationship with the twins.[27] In *C*[28] the Court of Appeal held that family life between a father and child born out of wedlock was not automatic.[29]

The position is different where a biological father does have a relationship with the child, even if that relationship is not particularly strong. For example, in *Re H*[30] the question was whether or not the natural fathers should be joined as respondents to the

---

[17] *Kugathas v Secretary of State for the Home Department* [2003] EWCA Civ 31. In *Evans v Amicus Healthcare Ltd* [2004] EWCA Civ 727, [2005] Fam 1 it was held that a potential mother could not assert a right to family life with a future child whose embryo had not yet been transferred to her.

[18] *JB (India) v Entry Clearance Officer* [2009] EWCA Civ 234 [11]. See also *Patel v Entry Clearance Officer, Mumbai* [2010] EWCA Civ 17 and *R (Gurung) v Secretary of State for the Home Department* [2013] EWCA Civ 8.

[19] *R (on the application of Doka) v Immigration Appeal Tribunal* [2004] EWHC (Admin) 3072, [2005] 1 FCR 180.

[20] *Principal Reporter v K* [2010] UKSC 56, [2011] 1 WLR 18, [36].

[21] Ibid.

[22] Ibid, [39]

[23] *Re J (Adoption: Contacting Father)* [2003] EWHC (Fam) 199, [2003] 1 FLR 933.

[24] Ibid, [23].

[25] *Leeds Teaching Hospital NHS Trust v A* [2003] EWHC (QB) 259.

[26] Ibid, [48] in reliance upon *M v Netherlands* (1993) 74 D&R 120.

[27] Ibid, at [49]. See also *Re R (a child)* [2003] EWCA Civ 182, [2003] Fam 129, where the court concluded that a man who was neither biological father nor had a relationship with the child but had participated as the mother's partner during IVF treatment had no right to respect for family life.

[28] *C (A Child) v XYZ County Council* [2007] EWCA Civ 1206, [2008] 3 WLR 445.

[29] Ibid, [31].

[30] *Re H; Re G (adoption: consultation of unmarried fathers)* [2001] 1 FLR 646.

adoption proceedings. In each case the mother was unmarried and did not wish to disclose the identity of the father. The Family Division held that not every natural father had a right to respect for family life with regard to every child of whom he may be the father and the application of Article 8 would depend upon the facts of each case.[31]With respect to *H*, the court found that the parents had a relationship, including cohabitation, that lasted for several years. It broke down before the birth of S but was resumed with a view to reconciliation. The reconciliation failed and the relationship came to an end. The mother of H said that the father was a good dad to S, but a part-time dad, and had no wish to take on a more involved role. However, the father had shown a continuing commitment to S and the fact of the attempted reconciliation underlined to the court that there had also been a genuine commitment to each other, even though the attempt failed. The father had two children by the mother and was in regular contact with one of them. The decision of the mother to bring up S herself and to involve the father in the life of S demonstrated a continuing relationship between them for the benefit of S and was an important factor in illuminating the question of whether there were family ties. The court was satisfied that H was part of a family unit with her father, with the consequence that it gave the father a right under Art 8(1).[32] However, in the joined case of *Re G*, the court concluded that the facts were far less strong—the parents had never cohabited and, their relationship having faded and died, they had lost touch—and there were no exceptional factors to show that the relationship had sufficient constancy to create de facto family ties.[33]

Family members, other than biological parents may also enjoy family life with a child.[34]

2.3 Adoptive Relationships

The relationship between adoptive parent and child can also give rise to family life within the meaning of Article 8,[35] although Article 8 does not guarantee a right to adopt a child.[36] These issues where considered in *Singh*[37] which concerned a six-year-old Indian boy who had been adopted by a couple in the United Kingdom. The adoption was valid according the law of India but was not recognised by the United Kingdom. He was therefore refused entry clearance to join his adoptive parents. The adoptive father and natural father were cousins. His natural parents and the sponsors agreed that the appellant should be adopted by the sponsors. The sponsors travelled to India and a religious ceremony took place, as a result of which he was adopted according to the religious laws and practices of the Sikh faith. The arrangement for the transfer

---

[31] Ibid, per Butler-Sloss P at [38] in reliance upon *B v UK* [2000] 1 FLR 1; *McMichael v UK* (1995) 20 EHRR 205; *K v UK* (1987) 50 D&R 199; *Keegan v Ireland* (1994) 18 EHRR 342; *Kroon v The Netherlands* (1994) 17 EHRR 263.

[32] *Re H; Re G*, ibid, [44].

[33] Ibid, [51]. See also *Re T (a child) (DNA tests: paternity)* [2001] 2 FLR 1190; *Re M (adoption: rights of natural father)* [2001] 1 FLR 745.

[34] *Principal Reporter* (n 20).

[35] See eg *Gunn-Russo v Nugent Care Society* [2001] EWHC (Admin) 566, [2002] 1 FLR 1.

[36] *R (on the application of Thomson) v Secretary of State for Education and Skills* [2005] EWHC (Admin) 1378.

[37] *Singh* (n 3).

of parental responsibility was made at the appellant's birth because the sponsors were unable to have any more children.

It was a genuine transfer of responsibility in the sense that it was not an arrangement of convenience to facilitate the appellant's entry into the United Kingdom. There was a genuine change in the appellant's status following his adoption, so that, for example, he had no right to inherit his natural parents' estate. He was cared for by the sponsors when they were in India. They had made all the major decisions about his care and future, including the decision to send him to boarding school when he was five. Since his birth, one or other or both of them have visited India two or three times each year in order to see him. The sponsors communicated with the appellant frequently by telephone, and supported him financially. The appellant was unaware of the adoption and called his natural parents 'uncle' and 'aunt', and was brought up to regard the sponsors as his real parents.[38]

The Court of Appeal unanimously held that family life was established between the child and his adoptive parents in the United Kingdom. Whilst the failure to satisfy the requirements of international instruments was taken into account, it was not decisive. However, it was noted that, if the departure was one of substance rather than procedure and went to the heart of the safeguards the instrument was intended to promote, it may be appropriate to give the adoption order little weight.[39]

2.4 Same-sex Relationships

Whether the Convention meaning of family life includes same-sex couples has been determined in the context of Article 14 but not yet finally determined in the context of Article 8. In *Secretary of State for Work and Pensions v M*[40] Lord Nicholls held that at common law a same-sex couple were as much capable of constituting a family as a heterosexual couple.[41] However, in the present case he held that the context was the proper interpretation of Article 8 in the ECHR and that the concept of family life had to have the same meaning in all contracting states. 'According to the established Strasbourg jurisprudence that meaning does not embrace same sex partners. Under the Strasbourg case law same sex partners still do not fall within the scope of family life.'[42]

In Lord Nicholls's view, this meant that the law of the UK was not subject to scrutiny by the ECtHR in so far as its Convention compatibility was challenged on the basis that the relationship between a same-sex couple constituted family life within Article 8.[43] He held that it was highly undesirable for the courts of the UK, when giving effect to the Convention rights, to be out of step with the Strasbourg interpretation of the relevant Convention article.[44] Lord Mance also held that the concept of family life under Article 8 could not be regarded as including same-sex relationships during the

[38] Ibid, [40].
[39] Ibid, per Dyson LJ at [33]. See also *MN (India) v Secretary of State for the Home Department* [2008] EWCA Civ 38, [2008] 2 FLR 87.
[40] *Secretary of State for Work and Pensions v M* [2006] UKHL 11, [2006] 2 AC 91.
[41] Ibid, [23].
[42] Ibid, [24] in reliance upon *Estevez v Spain* 10 May 2001.
[43] Ibid, [27].
[44] Ibid, [29].

relevant period from 13 August 2001 to 18 February 2002.[45] However, he did note that great change had taken place across Europe during the last five years 'of which any Court considering the current scope of article 8(1) would take most careful account'.[46]

Lord Walker, with whom Lord Bingham agreed, also considered the scope of Article 8 but not the question of whether the relationship just between same-sex partners constituted family life. He was content to assume that the unit consisting of the claimant and her new same-sex partner, and their children by their former marriages, should be regarded as a family for Article 8 purposes.[47] However, he found that the interference only had a tenuous link with family life and was not within the ambit of Article 8 for this reason. Baroness Hale also saw the issue as one involving children holding that what was at stake was the mother's right to respect for her family life with her children.[48] Here she observed that this mother and her partner were enjoying their right to respect for family life which they had with their children while those children were with them.[49]

Whether or not the relationship between same-sex partners constitutes family life within the meaning of Article 8 therefore remains unresolved, although where there are children involved it is clear that the unit of partners and children will constitute 'family life'. Despite the views of the House of Lords, in G[50] the Family Court held that it was now established beyond doubt that the relationship between a same-sex couple constituted family life for the purposes of Article 8 although the judgment was in relation to partners and children[51] and it is unlikely that the court meant that the relationship simply between the couple was to be included within the concept.[52]

3. Interference

Considering that respect for family life entails members of a family being able to share family life together,[53] an interference with this right can arise in a variety of ways including: the imposition of a custodial sentence;[54] a refusal to transfer supervision to a different probation board;[55] placement of an incapacitated adult in supported living

---

[45] Ibid, [151].
[46] Ibid, [152].
[47] Ibid, [87].
[48] Ibid, [108].
[49] Ibid, [112].
[50] *In the Matter of G (A Child) v D* [2013] EWHC 134 (Fam), [2013] 1 FLR 1334.
[51] Ibid, [113].
[52] See further F Hamilton, 'Why the Margin of Appreciation is Not the Answer to the Gay Marriage Debate' [2013] *European Human Rights Law Review* 47; N Bamforth, 'Families but Not (Yet) Marriages? Same Sex Partners and the Developing European Convention "Margin of Appreciation"' (2011) 23 *Child and Family Law Quarterly* 128.
[53] *Anufrijeva v Southwark LBC* [2003] EWCA Civ 1406, [2004] QB 1124, per Lord Woolf CJ at [12].
[54] *R (on the application of P & Q) v Secretary of State for the Home Department* [2001] EWCA Civ 1151; *R (on the application of Stokes) v Gwent Magistrates' Court* [2001] EWHC (Admin) 569.
[55] *R (Francis) v West Midlands Probation Board* [2010] EWCA Civ 1470.

accommodation;[56] the allocation of public housing;[57] and the imposition of a control order under the Prevention of Terrorism Act 2005.[58]

Public authorities are under a negative duty not to interfere with the right as well as a positive duty to ensure that family life is respected. The right also carries with it procedural rights and proceedings engaging the right must be conducted fairly to ensure due respect to the interests protected by Article 8.[59] From the case law, the areas where interferences commonly arise can be identified. These are examined in the following paragraphs.

3.1 Children

3.1.1 Generally

Any court order which regulates or restricts the mutual enjoyment of company between a parent and child will amount to an interference.[60] Such orders include: a court order placing a child in care;[61] an order giving permission to a local authority to refuse contact between parents and children taken into care;[62] adoption orders;[63] dispensing with parental consent to an adoption order;[64] dispensing with a natural father's consent to an adoption order;[65] an order allowing one parent to remove a child permanently from the jurisdiction;[66] an order to pay child support if it impacts on family relationships with others;[67] a parental order under the Human Fertilisation and Embryology Act 2008;[68] an emergency protection order removing children into the care of foster parents;[69] and the removal of an adult child from her family home into residential care.[70] Policies and procedures can also impact on family life involving children. For example, prohibiting babies from remaining with their mothers in prison after they have reached the age of 18 months may also impact on family life. It has been held that this is not a right which

---

[56] *K v LBX* [2012] EWCA Civ 79, [2012] 1 FCR 441; *Hillingdon London Borough Council v Neary* [2011] EWHC 1377 (Fam), [2011] 4 All ER 584.

[57] *Yumsak v London Borough of Enfield* [2002] EWHC (Admin) 280.

[58] *BX v Secretary of State for the Home Department* [2010] EWHC 990 (Admin).

[59] *Re S* [2002] UKHL 10, [2002] 2 WLR 720.

[60] *Principal Reporter* (n 20).

[61] *Lancashire County Council v Barlow* [2002] 2 AC 147; *Re S* (n 59). In *Re B (A Child)* [2013] UKSC 33, [2013] 1 WLR 1911 the Supreme Court held that the interference occurred when the care order was made, not when it was concluded that the threshold in s 31(2) of the Children Act 1989 was crossed.

[62] *Re C and B (children) (care order: future harm)* [2002] 2 FCR 614.

[63] *Re B (a child) (sole adoption by unmarried father)* [2001] UKHL 70, [2002] 1 WLR 258.

[64] *ML v ANS* [2012] UKSC 30, [2012] HRLR 27.

[65] *Re B (a child) (adoption order)* [2001] EWCA Civ 347, [2001] 2 FCR 89. But see *Re J* (n 23).

[66] *Re A (permission to remove child from jurisdiction: human rights)* [2000] 2 FLR 225; *Payne v Payne* (n 1).

[67] *R (on the application of Denson) v Child Support Agency* [2002] 1 FLR 938; *R (on the application of Plumb) v Secretary of State for Work and Pensions* [2002] EWHC (Admin) 1125. See also *Brookes v Secretary of State for Work and Pensions* [2010] EWCA Civ 420, [2010] 1 WLR 2448.

[68] *A v P* [2011] EWHC 1738 (Fam), [2012] 3 WLR 369.

[69] *Langley v Liverpool City Council* [2005] EWCA Civ 1173.

[70] *Gunter v South Western Staffordshire Primary Care Trust* [2005] EWHC 1894 (Admin), (2006) 9 CCL Rep 121.

a prisoner should necessarily lose by reason of his or her incarceration.[71] Finally, the manner in which a local authority discharges its parental responsibilities to a child in its care may also violate the rights of the child or its parents.[72]

3.1.2 Procedural Rights

In *Principal Reporter v K*[73] the Supreme Court confirmed that there are positive procedural rights inherent in the right to respect for family life: 'Parents must be enabled to play a proper part in the decision-making process before the authorities interfere in their family life with their children.'[74]

Article 8 also affords children procedural rights in relation to decision-making processes which fundamentally affect their family life. If the child has sufficient understanding, and direct participation in such proceedings would not pose an obvious risk of harm, separate representation may be required.[75] Local authorities must conduct their decision-making processes in relation to children in care fairly and so as to afford due respect to the interests protected by Article 8. Parents must be involved to a degree which is sufficient to provide adequate protection for their interests.[76] The requirements of fairness apply to the other persons and agencies involved in child protection work just as they apply to the local authority.[77] It is also important to remember that Article 6 applies to such proceedings and that many of these rights are absolute, unlike Article 8.[78]

These principles have been applied in many cases. For example, it has been held that, if the parents are to have a fair and adequate opportunity to make representations to the court on whether a care order should be made, the care plan must be appropriately specific.[79] Detailed guidance in relation to care proceedings was given in *Re C*.[80] The Family Division held that social workers should, as soon as practicable, notify parents of criticisms of their parenting and advise them how to improve. All professionals involved should keep clear and accurate notes of conversations and meetings. The local authority should make a full and frank disclosure of all key documents at an early stage in the proceedings. Where it was proposed that social workers and/or guardian should meet with expert witnesses, clear written notice of the meeting must be given. The parent must be given the opportunity to make representations, and should be able to attend or be represented at the meeting.[81]

---

[71] *P & Q* (n 54). See also *L* (n 10), which concerned restrictions on visits by children to patients in high-security hospitals; and *R v Secretary of State for the Home Department, ex p Mellor* [2001] EWCA Civ 472, [2002] QB 13 where the court held that in exceptional circumstances denial of access to a life sentence prisoner of facilities for artificial insemination may constitute a breach.

[72] *Re S* (n 59), [54].

[73] *Principal Reporter* (n 20).

[74] Ibid, [41]

[75] *Mabon v Mabon* [2005] EWCA Civ 634, [2004] 3 WLR 460.

[76] *Re S* (n 59), [55] in reliance upon *W v United Kingdom* (1987) 10 EHRR 29. See also *P & Q* (n 54); *R (on the application of S) v Plymouth City Council* [2002] EWCA Civ 388, [2002] 1 WLR 2583.

[77] *Re C (care proceedings: disclosure of local authority's decision making process)* [2002] EWHC (Fam) 1379, [2002] 2 FCR 673, [88]–[90].

[78] Ibid, [113].

[79] Ibid, [99]. In *Re D (Children) (care order)* [2003] EWCA Civ 1592 it was held that the irregularities in the proceedings did not justify the unravelling of the care order. See also *Claire F v Secretary of State for the Home Department* [2004] EWHC (Fam) 111, [2004] 2 FLR 517.

[80] *Re C* (n 77).

[81] Ibid, [154]. In *C v Bury Metropolitan Borough Council* [2002] EWHC (Fam) 1438, [2003] 2 FLR 868, whilst the Family Division found procedural irregularities, it granted no remedy in relation to the finding

The claim in *Principal Reporter v K* concerned the rights of unmarried fathers to take part in children's hearings under Part II of the Children (Scotland) Act 1995. It had been decided, following allegations of wrongdoing, to deny all contact between father and child yet he had been given no opportunity to be heard to refute the allegations. The Supreme Court held that it was necessary to ask whether the interference with the procedural rights of father and child was necessary in a democratic society and to keep this separate from the justifications for excluding the father from the decision-making process at a crucial stage. It held that such justification as there was would fall within the overall aim of protecting health or morals or the rights and freedoms of others. The justification advanced here for excluding the father was that these were meant to be informal round-table discussions with only the people present who could make a meaningful contribution to the debate. The Supreme Court found it difficult to see how excluding the father could possibly be proportionate to this aim.[82]

> [W]hen the alleged grounds for referring the child for compulsory measures of intervention consist almost entirely of allegations against the father, it cannot possibly be legitimate to exclude him for the purpose of restricting the numbers. He has to be there so that the grounds for interfering in the child's life, let alone his, can be properly established. If they are established, he has to be there so that sensible and proportionate measures can be taken to protect the child.[83]

It also confirmed that the child herself had the right and the duty to attend the hearing.[84] It concluded that the present system of children's hearings violated the Article 8 rights of the father, child and risked violating the rights of others in the same situation.[85] Utilising section 3 of the HRA, the relevant legislation was interpreted so as to ensure compatibility.[86]

3.1.3 Positive Duties

Failures on the part of public authorities to act may constitute interferences with the right to respect for family life. For example, failure on the part of a court to join the natural father as a respondent to adoption proceedings, even if he has played no part in the child's care or upbringing, may constitute an interference.[87] Similar considerations may apply in relation to other biological relatives. In *R*[88] the Family Division held that it would constitute an interference to fail to contact the biological relatives of a small

---

that, even if the mother had been informed and involved, the local authority would have reached the same conclusion. In *RP v Nottingham City Council* [2008] EWCA Civ 462, [2008] 2 FLR 1516 the Court of Appeal gave guidance on the role of the official solicitor and in *R (R) v Child & Family Court Advisory & Support Service* [2012] EWCA Civ 853, [2012] 2 FLR 1432 guidance was given on when a children's guardian should be appointed in care proceedings.

[82] *Principal Reporter* (n 20), [45].

[83] Ibid, [45].

[84] Ibid, [46].

[85] Ibid, [48].

[86] These principles also apply in other areas where children are affected such as mental health. In *Re S* (n 59) a mother required access to information about her son to exercise powers under the Mental Health Act 1983. See also *Re A (A Child)* [2013] EWCA Civ 1104, [2013] 3 FCR 257 where procedural failings in relation to contact orders over a period of many years were found, as a whole, to be in breach of Art 8.

[87] *Re S (a child) (adoption proceedings: joinder of father)* [2001] 1 FCR 158. See also *Re P (care proceedings: father's application to be joined as a party)* [2001] FLR 781; *Re H* (n 30); *Re M* (n 33).

[88] *Z County Council v R* [2001] 1 FLR 365.

child who did not know of his existence and see if they could offer him a suitable home prior to him being freed for adoption. However in C[89] the Court of Appeal held that when a decision had to be made about the long-term care of a child, whom a mother wished to be adopted, there was no duty to make enquiries which it was not in the interests of the child to make. Such enquiries must 'genuinely further the prospect of finding a long-term carer for the child without delay'.[90] It has also been held that failure on the part of the court to order blood and DNA tests to show who is the father of a child may constitute an interference with the right to respect for family life of the child.[91]

Claims directed at specific deficiencies in the system of child protection and family law have utilised the positive duty under Article 8. For example, in Re S[92] it was argued that the Children Act 1989 did not contain an adequate remedy if the local authority failed to discharge its parental responsibilities properly by, for example, failing to implement a care plan, and therefore the rights of the child or parents under Article 8 were violated. The House of Lords did not agree, holding that the possibility that something may go wrong with the local authority's discharge of its parental responsibilities or its decision-making processes and that this would be a violation of Article 8 so far as the child or parent was concerned did not mean that the legislation itself was incompatible or inconsistent with Article 8.[93]

However, the House of Lords did find that if a local authority fails to discharge its parental responsibilities properly, and in consequence the rights of parents under Article 8 are violated, 'the parents may, as a longstop, bring proceedings against the authority under section 7 [of the HRA]'.[94] It also drew attention to the case where there is no parent able and willing to become involved. 'In this type of case the Article 8 rights of a young child may be violated by a local authority without anyone outside the local authority becoming aware of the violation. In practice, such a child may not always have an effective remedy.'[95] But, in the opinion of their Lordships, this did not mean that the Children Act was incompatible with Article 8.[96]

In relation to contact orders, a concerted effort was made in F v M[97] to use Article 8 to bolster the right of a father to contact with his daughter and also her right to contact with him. The Family Division recognised the positive obligation of the court in protecting those rights and noted that the positive obligations extended in principle to the taking of coercive measures not merely against the recalcitrant parent but even against

---

[89] C (A Child) v XYZ County Council [2007] EWCA Civ 1206, [2008] 3 WLR 445. See also M v F [2011] EWCA Civ 273, [2011] 2 FLR 123.

[90] C, ibid, [3].

[91] Re T (n 33). In Leeds Teaching Hospital (n 25), it was held that the presumption in the Human Fertilisation and Embryology Act that Mr A was not the father of the twins (his wife had been inseminated with Mr B's semen by mistake) was an interference with his right to respect for family life but his position was safeguarded by the remedies of residence order and adoption. See also R (on the application of Rose) v Secretary of State for Health [2002] EWHC (Admin) 1593, [2002] 3 FCR 731, which concerned children conceived by artificial insemination seeking information about donors. The Administrative Court saw the issue as one of identity and private life rather than strictly family life.

[92] Re S (n 59).

[93] Ibid, [56].

[94] Ibid, [62]–[63].

[95] Ibid, [63] and [113].

[96] Ibid, [64]. See further J Herring, 'The Human Rights of Children in Care' [2002] 118 Law Quarterly Review 534.

[97] F v M [2004] EWHC (Fam) 727.

the children.[98] It was also held that the national authorities could not shelter behind the applicant's lack of action[99] and that there was no room for complacency about the way in which the courts handle these cases.[100] Although no findings of breach were made, it was observed that the two great vices of the present system were the fact that the system was still almost exclusively court based and that the court's procedures were not working—or not working as speedily and efficiently as they could, and therefore should, be.[101] Another example is *B v G*[102] where proceedings for variation of a contact order took over five years. The Supreme Court noted that the duty to avoid undue delay in the determination of disputes of this nature, in order to comply with the obligations imposed by Article 8 of the ECHR, had been made clear many times by the ECtHR.[103] It was also noted that the cost of proceedings in this instance was wholly disproportionate to the complexity of the issues which had to be resolved.[104]

It has been held that the common law, notwithstanding the important interest of both parent and child in their family life as reflected in Article 8, should not be developed to recognise that public authorities, responsible for the protection of children from abuse, owe a duty of care to parents when investigating or taking steps in protection considered to be at risk.[105] In *Lawrence*[106] the Court of Appeal held that there was an important difference between Article 8 and a common law duty of care.

> Article 8 is not concerned with the establishment of any such duty, but of a threshold of interference by a public authority with family life. It is not based on a breach of duty of care by such authority, which, once surmounted, is for the authority to justify. It is the justification, not the infringement, with which the Strasbourg court was primarily concerned.[107]

It was concluded that the common law, as it stood, was compatible with Article 8(2) in its treatment of parents.[108]

3.2 State Support

The right to respect for family life can impose upon the state a positive obligation to provide support. For example, where the welfare of children is at stake, Article 8 may require the provision of state support in a manner which enables family life to continue.[109] The impact on family life must be sufficiently serious and foreseeable.[110]

---

[98] Ibid, [30].

[99] Ibid, [33].

[100] Ibid, [35].

[101] Ibid, [36].

[102] *B v G* [2012] UKSC 21, [2012] Fam LR 56.

[103] Ibid, [22].

[104] Ibid, [23].

[105] *JD v East Berkshire Community Health NHS Trust* [2005] 2 AC 373. See also *Lawrence v Pembrokeshire County Council* [2007] EWCA Civ 446, [2007] 2 FLR 705.

[106] *Lawrence*, ibid.

[107] Ibid, [32].

[108] Ibid, [39]. See also *R (Axon) v Secretary of State for Health* [2006] EWHC 37 (Admin), [2006] QB 539 where it was held that parents had no positive right under Article 8 to information relating to the advice or treatment of their child on sexual matters.

[109] *Anufrijeva* (n 53), [43] in reliance upon *J v London Borough of Enfield* [2002] EWHC (Admin) 735, [2002] 2 FLR 1; and *Bernard v London Borough of Enfield* [2002] EWHC (Admin) 2282, [2003] HRLR 4.

[110] *Anufrijeva*, ibid.

Where the complaint is one of delay, an infringement will not be found unless substantial prejudice has been caused to the claimant.[111] Insofar as any obligation is imposed, it is not absolute.

> Before inaction can amount to a lack of respect for private and family life, there must be some ground for criticising the failure to act. There must be an element of culpability. At the very least there must be knowledge that the claimant's private and family life were at risk.[112]

Resources must also be taken into consideration.[113] And, the more glaring the deficiency in the behaviour of a public authority, the easier it will be to establish the necessary want of respect. 'Isolated acts of even significant carelessness are unlikely to suffice.'[114]

A glaring deficiency was found by the Administrative Court in the case of *Bernard*.[115] The court held that, following assessments, the defendant local authority was under an obligation to take positive steps, including the provision of suitably adapted accommodation, to enable the claimants and their children to lead as normal a family life as possible, bearing in mind the second claimant's severe disabilities.

> Suitably adapted accommodation would not merely have facilitated the normal incidents of family life, for example the second claimant would have been able to move around her home to some extent and would have been able to play some part, together with the first claimant, in looking after their children. It would also have secured her 'physical and psychological integrity'. She would no longer have been housebound, confined to a shower chair for most of the day, lacking in privacy in the most undignified of circumstances, but would have been able to operate again as part of her family and as a person in her own right, rather than being a burden, wholly dependent upon the rest of her family. In short, it would have restored her dignity as a human being.[116]

In *J*[117] the Divisional Court accepted that, whilst Article 8 did not require the provision of accommodation for a family, if the failure to provide support resulted in a child being taking away from her mother and put into care this would violate Article 8. It concluded that, if all other possible routes to providing accommodation or financial support were inapplicable, the local authority would not be able to justify taking the child into care, thereby separating mother and child, because of difficulties in acquiring accommodation. 'Typically it will be cheaper to provide accommodation (or the finance to acquire it) for the family than to take the child into care, and moreover that step will keep the family together.'[118]

3.3 Deportation and Extradition

Removal or exclusion of one family member from a state where other members of the family are lawfully resident will not necessarily infringe Article 8 provided that

---

[111] Ibid, [46].
[112] Ibid, [45] in reliance upon *Osman v UK* (1998) 29 EHRR 245.
[113] Ibid, [47].
[114] Ibid, [48]. See also *R (on the application of Q) v Secretary of State for the Home Department* [2003] EWCA Civ 364, [2004] QB 36, [64]; *Greenfield v Irwin* [2001] EWCA Civ 113, [2001] 1 WLR 1279.
[115] *Bernard* (n 109).
[116] Ibid, [33]. See also *R (MK) v Secretary of State for the Home Department* [2010] EWHC 1002 (Admin)
[117] *J* (n 23).
[118] Ibid, [48].

there are no insurmountable obstacles to the family living together in the country of origin of the family member excluded, even where this involves a degree of hardship for some or all members of the family.[119] However, Article 8 is likely to be violated by the expulsion of a member of a family that has been long established in a state if the circumstances are such that it is not reasonable to expect the other members of the family to follow that member expelled.[120] Where deportation is proposed, it has been held that the authorities must take into account the impact of the proposed removal on the Article 8 rights of the individual being removed, as well as upon all those sharing family life with him.[121] With regard to married couples, Article 8 does not impose any general obligation on a state to respect their choice of residence. Knowledge on the part of one spouse at the time of marriage that the rights or residence of the other were precarious militates against a finding that an order excluding the latter spouse violates Article 8.[122]

3.4 Deportation and Extradition—Foreign Cases

As discussed in other chapters, in accordance with the principles established in *Ullah*,[123] it is also possible that a claimant may establish that removal from the UK would result in a real risk of a flagrant denial of the right to family life in the destination state. For example, in *EM*[124] the claimant argued that if she and her son were returned to Lebanon, shari'a law would pass custody to his father or another male member of his family and she would have no legal right to custody of him. Lord Hope observed that ECtHR authority indicated that except in wholly exceptional circumstances the return of a woman with her child who was in the UK to escape from the system of family law of her own country would not violate Article 8 with Article 14: '[T]he Contracting States cannot be expected to return aliens only to a country whose family law is compatible with the principle of non-discrimination assumed by the Convention.'[125] Lord Hope further observed that the key to identifying those cases where the breach of Article 8, with Article 14, would be flagrant lay in an assessment of the effects on both mother and child of destroying or nullifying the family life that they have shared together and that the cases where that 'assessment shows that the violation will be flagrant will be very exceptional'.[126] However, where the humanitarian grounds against their removal were compelling, he held there was an obligation not to remove.[127]

In the present case Lord Hope found the case on humanitarian grounds compelling

---

[119] *R v Secretary of State for the Home Department, ex p Mahmood* [2001] 1 WLR 840, per Lord Phillips MR at [55]. See also *R v Secretary of State for the Home Department, ex p Isiko* [2001] 1 FLR 930; *R (on the application of Samaroo) v Secretary of State for the Home Department* [2001] EWCA Civ 1139; *R (on the application of L) v Secretary of State for the Home Department* [2003] EWCA Civ 25, [2003] 1 All ER 1062; *R (Sandhu) v Secretary of State for the Home Department* [2003] EWHC (Admin) 2152; *Norris v United States* [2010] UKSC 9, [2010] 2 AC 487 concerning extradition.

[120] *Mahmood*, ibid, [55].

[121] *Beoku-Betts v Secretary of State for the Home Department* [2008] UKHL 39, [2009] 1 AC 115.

[122] Ibid.

[123] *R (Ullah) v Special Adjudicator* [2004] UKHL 26, [2004] 2 AC 323.

[124] *EM* (n 4).

[125] Ibid, [15].

[126] Ibid, [17].

[127] Ibid, [17].

and concluded that there was a real risk of a flagrant denial of the mother and son's Article 8 rights (not considering Article 14) if they were returned to Lebanon.[128] In Lord Bingham's view, the effect of return on the mother and son's right to respect for family life would be not only flagrantly violated but completely denied and nullified.[129] He observed that the claim under Article 14 was difficult given Lebanon was not a party to the ECHR and that the UK had no mandate to impose its own values on other countries who did not share them. However, it was sufficient for the claimants to rely simply upon Article 8.[130] Lord Carswell also found a real risk of flagrant violation based only on Article 8.[131] Baroness Hale observed as follows:

> [T]he only family life which this child has ever known is with his mother. If he were obliged to return to a country where he would inevitably be removed from her care, with only the possibility of supervised visits, then the very essence of his right to respect for his family life would be destroyed. And it would be destroyed for reasons which could never be justified under article 8(2) because they are purely arbitrary and pay no regard to his interests. The violation of his right is in my view of greater weight than the violation of his mother's right.[132]

3.5 Entry Clearance and Visas

Initially it was not clear whether or not the right to respect for family life applied to entry clearance, although in a number of judgments this was assumed to be the case—it was often characterised as a positive obligation to permit family reunion.[133] It is now established that the right to respect for family life does, in most instances, apply to entry clearance. In *AS*[134] the House of Lords held that there may be entry clearance cases which engage the applicant's right to respect for his or her family life under Article 8.[135] However, this did not require a state to permit a claimant seeking to enter for family reasons to be permitted to enter, or to remain in the state on public support pending resolution of a disputed claim.[136] And the House of Lords held in *C*[137] that a procedural requirement requiring a person to leave the UK and make an application for entry clearance from outside the UK was a disproportionate interference with family life in the instant case.[138]

A considerable delay in the process of family reunion will not necessarily lead to a breach of Article 8. For example, in *M*[139] the claimant arrived in the United Kingdom from Angola in May 1996 and claimed asylum. His claim was allowed on appeal in

---

[128] Ibid, [18].
[129] Ibid, [41].
[130] Ibid, [42].
[131] Ibid, [58]. See also Lord Brown at [60].
[132] Ibid, [46].
[133] See eg *Singh* (n 3); *R (Suresh) v Secretary of State for the Home Department* [2001] EWHC (Admin) 1028; *Sayania v Immigration Appeal Tribunal*, Administrative Court, 5 April 2001; *R (on the application of Singh) v Immigration Appeal Tribunal* [2002] EWHC (Admin) 2096.
[134] *AS (Somalia) v Secretary of State for the Home Department* [2009] UKHL 32, [2009] 1 WLR 1385.
[135] Ibid, per Lord Hope at [16].
[136] *R (on the application of K) v Lambeth London Borough Council* [2003] EWCA Civ 1150, [2004] 1 WLR 272.
[137] *C (Zimbabwe) v Secretary of State for the Home Department* [2008] UKHL 40, [2008] 1 WLR 1420.
[138] See also *Secretary of State for the Home Department v Hayat* [2012] EWCA Civ 1054, [2013] Imm AR 15.
[139] One of the three appeals considered by the Court of Appeal in *Anufrijeva* (n 53).

January 2001. M then wished to start proceedings for family reunion; however, the letter confirming his grant of refugee status was not received until August 2001. The issue of visas for his family, who were then in Kinshasa, did not take place until November 2002. The Court of Appeal held that, although there were enormous administrative failings, what had happened did not entail a lack of respect for the claimant's family life.[140]

There is no positive duty under Article 8 to permit entry of a parent to join an adult son or daughter. However, there is a positive duty on states to admit children of settled immigrants who are minors unless there are sufficiently strong countervailing reasons to make it proportionate to refuse entry.[141] A requirement that an entrant should be maintained without recourse to public funds has been held to be a fair and necessary limitation on what would otherwise become an overwhelming burden. 'It is an unfortunate reality of life that states … cannot undertake to allow all members of a family to join together here, even those members who can show emotional and financial dependency, without creating unsupportable burdens.'[142]

The requirement to pay a fee for an immigration application for those seeking entry clearance based on compelling compassionate circumstances can amount to an interference with family life.

[A] requirement to pay a fee before an Article 8 claim could be advanced, could prevent people from entering this country in order that the could exercise the rights protected by Article 8 and thus, could potentially interfere with those Article 8 rights.[143]

It was also held by the Court of Appeal in *Bibi*[144] that a change to the immigration rules, requiring the foreign spouse or partner of a British citizen or person settled in the UK to produce a test certificate of knowledge of the English language to a prescribed standard before entering the UK was an interference with Article 8 rights.

Finally, *Quila*[145] concerned a challenge to rules by which the Secretary of State for the Home Department determined an application for a visa to enter or remain the UK made by the spouse of a person settled and present in the UK, ie a marriage visa. The rule, designed to prevent forced marriage, provided that in the absence of exceptional compassionate circumstances, a marriage visa was not to be granted until both the sponsor and applicant had attained the age of 21. Having taken account of the decision of the ECtHR in *Abdulaziz v United Kingdom*,[146] the Supreme Court declined to follow it and found an interference with Article 8. Lord Wilson explained that it was an old decision, there was dissent from it at the time and more recent decisions were inconsistent with it. He continued:

[T]he refusal of the Secretary of State in the present case to allow the foreign spouses to reside in the UK with the British citizens with whom they had so recently entered into a

---

[140] Ibid, [165]. See also *R (on the application of A) v National Asylum Support Service* [2003] EWCA Civ 1473, [2004] 1 WLR 752, [82]–[83]. In *R (on the application of Montana) v Secretary of State for the Home Department* [2001] 1 WLR 552 it was held that the refusal of British citizenship could not in itself be an interference with family life.

[141] *Muse v Entry Clearance Officer* [2012] EWCA Civ 10, [2012] Imm AR 476, [21].

[142] *Odawey v Entry Clearance Officer* [2011] EWCA Civ 840, [49].

[143] *QB v Secretary of State for the Home Department* [2010] EWHC 483 (Admin), [30].

[144] *R (Bibi) v Secretary of State for the Home Department* [2013] EWCA Civ 322.

[145] *Quila* (n 13).

[146] *Abdulaziz v United Kingdom* (1985) 7 EHRR 471.

consensual marriage must a fortiori represent such an interference. The only sensible enquiry can be into whether the refusals were justified.[147]

4. Permitted Interferences

The right to respect for family life is not an absolute right and, under Article 8(2), interferences by a public authority with the exercise of the right are possible if in accordance with the law and necessary in a democratic society in the interests of: national security; public safety; the economic well-being of the country; for the prevention of disorder or crime; for the protection of health or morals; or for the protection of the rights and freedoms of others. Not all of these justifications have been examined in claims brought under the HRA. Those which have been considered are discussed in the following paragraphs.

In common with other non-absolute Convention rights, interferences with Article 8 must be in accordance with the law. The principle of legality here is the same as it is in relation to other Convention rights.[148] In *ML*[149] the Supreme Court recognised that in some instances, particularly in the context of family law, considerable discretion is left to the judge. However, it was held that this reflected the nature of the subject-matter and it was impossible to spell out exhaustively the particular circumstances in which an 'order dispensing with parental consent may be necessary'.[150] It concluded that the use of general language in such a context is not inconsistent with the Convention rights.[151]

5. Economic Well-being of the Country

5.1 Deportation and Removal

5.1.1 Generally

In order for a deportation or removal to take place lawfully, it must be shown that the interference is in accordance with the law, necessary in one of the interests set out in Article 8(2) and proportionate to the legitimate public end sought to be achieved.[152]

---

[147] Ibid, [43].
[148] *AS* (n 134), per Lord Hope at [17].
[149] *ML* (n 64).
[150] Ibid, [47].
[151] Ibid, [48].
[152] *R (on the application of Razgar) v Secretary of State for the Home Department* [2004] UKHL 27, [2004] 2 AC 368, per Lord Bingham at [17].

In such claims the interest pursued under Article 8(2) is not usually made clear. The argument most often made is that removal is in the interests of maintaining firm immigration control. In *Isiko*[153] the Court of Appeal held that the mere fact that the presence of an individual and his family in this country did not in itself constitute a threat to one of the interests enumerated in Article 8(2) did not prevent a decision to enforce a lawful immigration policy from being lawful.[154] Nevertheless, in this chapter, deportation is examined under the heading of economic well-being of the country as, in a few judgments, this has been the justification given.[155] It is also possible, where a deportee has committed a crime, that deportation is for the prevention of disorder or crime, as discussed below.

Interferences are always likely to be in accordance with law and where removal is proposed in pursuance of lawful immigration policy and necessary in one of the interests set out in Article 8(2).

> This is because the right of sovereign states, subject to treaty obligations, to regulate the entry and expulsion of aliens is recognised in the Strasbourg jurisprudence ... and implementation of a firm and orderly immigration policy is an important function of government in a modern democratic state. In the absence of bad faith, ulterior motive or deliberate abuse of power it is hard to imagine an adjudicator answering this question other than affirmatively.[156]

However, it has also been held that human beings are social animals and depend on others:

> Their family, or extended family, is the group on which many people most heavily depend, socially, emotionally and often financially. There comes a point at which, for some, prolonged and unavoidable separation from this group seriously inhibits their ability to live full and fulfilling lives.[157]

If there are insurmountable obstacles to a family living together in the country of origin of the family member excluded, or it is not reasonable to expect the other members of the family to follow the family member expelled,[158] the right to respect for family life will be engaged. The material question in gauging the proportionality of a removal or deportation which will or may break up a family unless the family itself decamps is whether it is reasonable to expect the family to leave with the claimant.[159] Concentration on whether family members can reasonably be expected to relocate with the applicant ensures that the seriousness of the difficulties which they are likely to encounter in the destination state are properly assessed as a whole and taken duly into account, together with all other relevant matters, in determining the proportionality of the deportation. The matter must be looked at as a whole.[160] Even if it is unreasonable to expect family

---

[153] *Isiko* (n 119).

[154] Ibid, [36].

[155] See eg *Samaroo* (n 119), where it was held that the maintenance of a firm but fair immigration policy was necessary for the economic well-being of the UK and for the prevention of disorder and crime.

[156] *Razgar* (n 152), per Lord Bingham at [19].

[157] *Huang v Secretary of State for the Home Department* [2007] UKHL 11, [2007] 2 AC 167, [18].

[158] *Mahmood* (n 119), [55].

[159] *VW (Uganda) v Secretary of State for the Home Department* [2009] EWCA Civ 5, [2009] Imm AR 436, [24].

[160] *JO (Uganda) v Secretary of State for the Home Department* [2010] EWCA Civ 10, [26]

members to join the applicant in the destination state, that will not necessarily be a decisive feature in the overall assessment of proportionality.[161]

Attempts to legislate so as to reduce this type of claim under the HRA have generally not been successful. It has been held that it is not possible for immigration rules to provide in detail in advance for every nuance in the application of Article 8 in individual cases:

> By reason of the sheer variety of human life and family associations and the wide application of the immigration regime and Article 8—which carries with it the need for a degree of flexibility to make suitable accommodation for individual cases reflecting that variety—there will always be the possibility in principle for particular factors in individual cases to be of especially compelling force in favour of a grant of leave to remain even though not fully reflected in the new rules.[162]

5.1.2 Assessing Proportionality—The Task of an Appellate Immigration Authority

In *Huang*[163] the House of Lords held that pursuant to section 65 of the Immigration and Asylum Act 1999, the task of the appellate immigration authority, on an appeal on a Convention ground against a decision of the primary official decision-maker refusing leave to enter or remain in this country, was to decide whether the challenged decision was unlawful as incompatible with a Convention right or compatible and so lawful.

> It is not a secondary, reviewing, function depending on establishing that the primary decision-maker misdirected himself or acted irrationally or was guilty of procedural impropriety. The appellate immigration authority must decide for itself whether the impugned decision is lawful and, if not, but only if not, reverse it.[164]

The House of Lords clarified that the appellate immigration authority, deciding an appeal under section 65, was not reviewing the decision of another decision maker. It was deciding whether or not it was unlawful to refuse leave to enter or remain, and it was doing so on the basis of up-to-date facts.[165] The House of Lords held that the appellate immigration authority would wish to consider and weigh all that told in favour of the refusal of leave which was challenged, with particular reference to justification under Article 8(2).

> There will, in almost any case, be certain general considerations to bear in mind: the general administrative desirability of applying known rules if a system of immigration control is to be workable, predictable, consistent and fair as between one applicant and another; the damage to good administration and effective control if a system is perceived by applicants internationally to be unduly porous, unpredictable or perfunctory; the need to discourage non-nationals admitted to be country temporarily from believing that they can commit serious crimes and

---

[161] Ibid, [27]. See further B Hale, 'Families and the Law: The Forgotten International Dimension' (2009) *Child and Family Law Quarterly* 413.

[162] *R (Nagre) v Secretary of State for the Home Department* [2013] EWHC 720 (Admin), [26]. See also *R (SM) v Secretary of State for the Home Department* [2013] EWHC 1144 (Admin).

[163] *Huang* (n 157).

[164] Ibid, [11].

[165] Ibid, [13]. The facts must be those at the time the appeal is heard. See *MS* [2007] EWCA Civ 133, [2007] Im AR 538.

yet be allowed to remain; the need to discourage fraud, deception and deliberate breaches of the law.[166]

Where particular reasons for refusal were relied upon by the Secretary of State, such as deterring drug traffickers[167] or threats to community relations,[168] the House of Lords held that giving weight to these factors was not deference but performance of the 'ordinary judicial task' of weighing up the competing considerations on each side and according 'appropriate weight to the judgment of a person with responsibility for a given subject matter and access to special sources of knowledge and advice'.[169] It held that proportionality was the key question and whether or not deportation was proportionate would depend on a variety of things:

> Matters such the age, health and vulnerability of the applicant, the closeness and previous history of the family, the applicant's dependence on the financial and emotional support of the family, the prevailing cultural tradition and conditions in the country of origin and many other factors may all be relevant.[170]

It confirmed that a test of exceptionality was not appropriate and that the appellate immigration authority had to ask whether the refusal of leave to enter or remain, in circumstances where the life of the family could not reasonably be expected to be enjoyed elsewhere, taking full account of all considerations weighing in favour of the refusal, prejudiced the family life of the claimant in a manner sufficiently serious to amount to a breach of the fundamental right protected by Article 8.[171]

Judgments pre-dating this decision are now of dubious authority. The principles established have been applied by the lower courts in numerous cases but there is still sometimes confusion. For example in *MT*[172] the Court of Appeal held that to speak of exceptional or rare cases did nothing to explain what principle should be applied in identifying such cases.[173] However, it went on to confirm that its role was to consider whether the adjudicator's approach placed insufficient weight on the importance of immigration control or too much weight on family life.[174] In *AG*[175] the Court of Appeal confirmed that there was no test of exceptionality.

> The fact that in the great majority of cases the demands of immigration control are likely to make removal proportionate and so compatible with art 8 is a consequence, not a precondition, of the statutory exercise ... to treat exceptionality as the yardstick of success is to confuse effect with cause.[176]

---

[166] *Huang*, ibid, [16].

[167] *Samaroo* (n 119).

[168] *R (Farrakhan) v Secretary of State for the Home Department* [2002] EWCA Civ 606.

[169] *Huang* (n 157), [16].

[170] Ibid, [18].

[171] Ibid, [20]. See further S Singh, 'Immigration and Article 8 Family Life' (2010) *Judicial Review* 377; M Amos, 'Separating human Rights Adjudication from Judicial Review' (2007) *European Human Rights Law Review* 679.

[172] *MT (Zimbabwe) v Secretary of State for the Home Department* [2007] EWCA Civ 455.

[173] Ibid, [22].

[174] Ibid, [25].

[175] *AG (Eritrea) v Secretary of State for the Home Department* [2007] EWCA Civ 801, [2008] 2 All ER 28.

[176] Ibid, [31].

5.1.3 Impact on Other Family Members

Where deportation is proposed, it has been held that the authorities must take into account the impact of the proposed removal on the Article 8 rights of the individual being removed, as well as upon all those sharing family life with him or her.[177] There is only one family life and assuming the proposed removal would be disproportionate, each affected family member is to be regarded as a victim.[178] Similarly, in *EM*[179] Baroness Hale observed that it was of great importance to consider the case from the child's point of view. However, she noted that separate consideration and separate representation were two different things. In her view, in most immigration situations the interests of different family members were unlikely to be in conflict with one another and separate legal representation would rarely be necessary.[180]

5.1.4 Children

In some deportations it is important to take into consideration the weight to be given to the best interests of children who are affected by the decision to remove or deport one of their parents. In *ZH*[181] the question was in what circumstances it was permissible to remove or deport a non-citizen parent where the effect would be that a child who was a UK citizen would have to leave. Baroness Hale, with whom Lord Brown and Lord Mance agreed, noted that if a non-citizen parent was compulsorily removed and agreed to take his or her children with her, the effect was that the children had little or no choice in the matter as there was no machinery for consulting them or giving independent consideration to their views.[182] She held that it was of particular importance whether a spouse or child could reasonably be expected to follow the removed parent to the country of removal.[183]

Baroness Hale observed that the ECtHR had become more sensitive to the welfare of the children who were innocent victims of their parents' choices by taking into account international law protecting the rights of the child.[184] She held that in the UK, the most relevant national and international obligation was Article 3 of the UN Convention on the Rights of the Child, which provided that the best interests of the child should be a primary consideration in all actions concerning children.[185] She also noted that section 55 of the Borders, Citizenship and Immigration Act 2009 provided that in relation to immigration, asylum or nationality, the Secretary of State had to ensure that functions were discharged having regard to the need to safeguard and promote the welfare of children who were in the UK.[186] It was held that decisions taken without having regard to this would not be in accordance with the law for the purposes of Article 8(2).

---

[177] *Beoku-Betts* (n 121).
[178] Ibid, per Lord Brown at [43].
[179] *EM* (n 4).
[180] Ibid, [49].
[181] *ZH (Tanzania) v Secretary of State for the Home Department* [2011] UKSC 4, [2011] 2 WLR 148.
[182] Ibid, [1].
[183] Ibid, [15].
[184] Ibid, [21]. See further U Kilkelly, 'Protecting Children's Rights under the ECHR: The Role of Positive Obligations' (2010) 61 *Northern Ireland Legal Quarterly*, 245.
[185] *ZH*, ibid, [23].
[186] Ibid, [23].

A 'primary consideration' is not the same as 'the paramount consideration'.[187] The important thing, in Baroness Hale's view, was to consider best interests first.[188] In this context, it was held that the best interests of the child broadly meant the well-being of the child. This involved asking whether it was reasonable to expect the child to live in another country.[189] A number of factors are relevant:

> Relevant to this will be the level of the child's integration in this country and the length of absence from the other country; where and with whom the child is to live and the arrangements for looking after the child in the other country; and the length of the child's relationships with parents or other family members which will be severed if the child has to move away.[190]

The importance of citizenship was also not to be played down.

> As citizens these children have rights which they will not be able to exercise if they move to another country. They will lose the advantages of growing up and being educated in their own country, their own culture and their own language. They will have lost all this when they come back as adults.[191]

Therefore, it was held that in making the proportionality assessment under Article 8 the best interests of the child must be a primary consideration and must be considered first. However, a child's best interests can be outweighed by the cumulative effect of other considerations.[192]

5.1.5 Delay

Finally, it has been recognised by the courts that a period of delay in the immigration decision-making process may affect a claim under Article 8. The House of Lords held in *EB*[193] that delay can be relevant in any one of three ways. First, it may allow the claimant to develop closer personal and social ties and establish deeper roots in the community.[194] Second, it may indicate that a relationship which has been entered into is genuine.[195] Third, it may reduce the weight otherwise to be accorded to the requirements of firm and fair immigration control if the delay is shown to be the result of a 'dysfunctional system which yields unpredictable, inconsistent and unfair outcomes'.[196] However, it remains difficult to establish that delay, unless serious, means that a family life claim will be successful. In *A*[197] the Court of Appeal held that a delay of 23 months

---

[187] Ibid, [25].
[188] Ibid, [26].
[189] Ibid, [29].
[190] Ibid, [29].
[191] Ibid, [32].
[192] Ibid, [33]. To discover the best interests of the child it was suggested at [36]–[37] that immigration authorities must be prepared to consider hearing directly from a child. For an application of the test, see *R (BN) v Secretary of State for the Home Department* [2011] EWHC 2367 (Admin); *SS (Nigeria) v Secretary of State for the Home Department* [2013] EWCA Civ 550; and *CW (Jamaica) v Secretary of State for the Home Department* [2013] EWCA Civ 915. See further G Ifezue and M Rajabali, 'Protecting the Interests of the Child' [2013] *Cambridge Journal of International and Comparative Law* 77.
[193] *EB (Kosovo) v Secretary of State for the Home Department* [2008] UKHL 41, [2008] 3 WLR 178.
[194] Ibid, per Lord Bingham at [14] with whom the others agreed.
[195] Ibid, per Lord Bingham at [15] with whom the others agreed.
[196] Ibid, per Lord Bingham at [16] with whom the others agreed. Lord Brown did not agree on this point
[197] *R (A) v Secretary of State for the Home Department* [2007] EWCA Civ 655, [2007] Imm AR 817.

was not an extreme case of delay sufficient to strengthen the claimant's Article 8 right. It was not a point of national disgrace or evidence of the system having broken down so that it would inequitable to enforce the procedural rules.

5.2 Entry Clearance and Visas

5.2.1 Leaving the UK to Apply for Entry Clearance

The House of Lords held in C[198] that a procedural requirement requiring a person to leave the UK and make an application for entry clearance from outside the UK was a disproportionate interference with family life in the instant case. Here the claimant, from Zimbabwe, had married a man with refugee status in the UK and had had a child. They were settled in the UK and would eventually have permission to live in the UK together. Lord Brown, with whom the others agreed, held that effective immigration control did not require the claimant and her child to travel back to Zimbabwe to obtain entry clearance before returning to the UK to resume her family life.[199] It was subsequently held by the Administrative Court that the application of a blanket requirement to leave the county imposed by immigration rules relating to entry clearance was unsustainable.[200]

5.2.2 Fees and Other Barriers

In AS[201] Lord Hope observed that legislation which gave rise to delay and expense in entry clearance could give rise to a violation in future. The law here provided that the tribunal hearing appeals against the refusal of entry clearance could only take into account the circumstances as they were at the time of the refusal and not matters arising afterwards.[202]

In relation to fees, a reasonable relationship between the application fee and the burden involved on the state and the benefit potentially to be gained by an applicant for entry to the UK has been found to be proportionate. It is seen as a form of contribution or tax levied on those who sought to make use of the immigration system to secure entry to the UK 'imposed in the interest of securing the overall quality of the system for them and others'.[203] A request for waiver of the fee has been characterised as an imposition of positive duties under Article 8.

> The question under Article 8 is whether, by insisting on payment of a fee, the state has failed properly to accord respect to family life where there may (or may not) be a good claim under Article 8 to enter the United Kingdom to deepen such family life as already exists.[204]

---

[198] C (Zimbabwe) v Secretary of State for the Home Department [2008] UKHL 40, [2008] 1 WLR 1420. See also Secretary of State for the Home Department v Hayat [2012] EWCA Civ 1054, [2013] Imm AR 15.
[199] C, ibid, [46].
[200] R (Zhang) v Secretary of State for the Home Department [2013] EWHC 891 (Admin).
[201] AS (n 134).
[202] Ibid, [21]. See also R (Mohamed) v Secretary of State for the Home Department [2010] EWHC 1227 (Admin).
[203] R (Sheikh) v Secretary of State for the Home Department [2011] EWHC 3390 (Admin), [74].
[204] Ibid, [74].

It was held in *Sheikh* that a court would be reluctant to impose upon the state significant additional expenditure.[205] It concluded that where the claimant could show no ability to pay the fee, it would be necessary to assess in broad terms the strength and force of the underlying claim. If there was a strong claim under Article 8 to enter the UK, the Administrative Court held that an obligation may arise under Article 8 on the Secretary of State to waive the fee.

It was argued in *Bibi*[206] that a rule which required a foreign spouse or partner of a British citizen or person settled in the UK to produce a test certificate of knowledge of the English language prior to entering the UK was a disproportionate interference with family life. A majority of the Court of Appeal, affording the Secretary of State a wide margin of appreciation, did not agree and found the rule proportionate.

> The Secretary of State identified a social problem ... she considered an ameliorating solution; she assessed the implications of introducing it; she provided for exempt and exceptional cases; and, in the event, the effect on applications and grants was not numerically significant.[207]

However, in *MM*[208] the Administrative Court concluded that an immigration rule raising the minimum income level of a UK sponsor and other onerous requirements was a disproportionate interference with genuine spousal relationships.

5.2.3 Historic Injustice

It has been held that where the proportionality balancing exercise is carried out, historic injustice to a particular group can be taken into account. This has been important in the claims concerning entry clearance brought by the dependent adult children of veterans of the Gurkha Brigade who have settled in the UK. The Court of Appeal has held that if a Gurkha can show that but for the historic injustice he would have settled in the UK at a time when his dependant, now adult, child would have been able to accompany him, that is a strong reason for holding that it is proportionate to permit the adult child to join his family now.[209]

5.3 Dispersal of Asylum Seekers

In *Yumsak*[210] the Administrative Court was not satisfied that the decision of the local authority to place the claimant and her children in temporary accommodation in Birmingham was a proportionate response to the interference with her family life that this would entail. There was no evidence that the only way of meeting the statutory obligation was to send the claimant and her children to Birmingham, 100 miles away.

---

[205] Ibid.
[206] *Bibi* (n 144).
[207] Ibid, [32].
[208] *MM (Lebanon) v Secretary of State for the Home Department* [2013] EWHC 1900 (Admin).
[209] *Gurung* (n 8), [42].
[210] *Yumsak* (n 57).

6. Prevention of Disorder or Crime

6.1 Deportation and Removal

As noted above, a distinction has been made between deportation cases where the legitimate aim is the prevention of crime or disorder, and removal cases where it is the maintenance of effective immigration controls.[211] The Court of Appeal has held that the public interest in deportation of those who commit serious crimes goes well beyond depriving the offender in question from the chance to reoffend in the UK: it extends to deterring and preventing serious crime generally and to upholding public abhorrence of such offending.[212] A decision to remove may pursue a double of aim of prevention of disorder or crime as well as the maintenance of effective immigration control. Care must be taken in articulating the reason:

> Where the prevention of disorder or crime is an aim, the person's criminal offending can weigh positively in favour of removal, in the same way as in a deportation case. But if reliance is placed only on effective immigration control, it is difficult to see how the person's criminal offending would relate to that aim or, therefore, count as a factor positively favouring removal ... it might still have a significant effect ... where a person has spent long periods in detention, his family ties and social ties are likely to be fewer or weaker[213]

Deportation can also be on national security grounds where similar considerations apply. However, importantly for claimants, an element of procedural fairness is implied by the procedural obligations under Article 8. Where family life is at stake, there must be some form of adversarial proceedings before an independent body competent to review the reasons for the decision and relevant evidence 'if need be with appropriate procedural limitations on the use of classified information'.[214]

6.2 Extradition

6.2.1 Generally

A number of international conventions have been concluded imposing on states an obligation to extradite or prosecute in respect of certain offences or which limit the grounds upon which a state can refuse to extradite. 'These reflect increasing international cooperation in the fight against crime.'[215] The critical issue in most extradition

---

[211] *SS (India) v Secretary of State for the Home Department* [2010] EWCA Civ 388, [53].
[212] *DS (India) v Secretary of State for the Home Department* [2009] EWCA Civ 544, [2010] Imm AR 81, [37].
[213] *JO* (n 160), [30]. See also *RU (Bangladesh) v Secretary of State for the Home Department* [2011] EWCA Civ 651, [2011] Imm AR 662.
[214] *IR (Sri Lanka) v Secretary of State for the Home Department* [2011] EWCA Civ 704, [2011] 4 All ER 908 at [11] in reliance upon *Al-Nashif v Bulgaria* (2003) 36 EHRR 37.
[215] *Norris* (n 119), [5].

cases is whether the interference with family life is necessary for the prevention of disorder or crime. In *Norris* the Supreme Court held as follows:

> This is a domestic case. The family rights that are in issue are rights enjoyed in this country. The issue of proportionality involves weighing the interference with those rights against the relevant public interest. The public interest in extraditing a person to be tried for an alleged crime is of a different order from the public interest in deporting or removing from this country an alien who has been convicted of a crime and who has served his sentence for it, or whose presence here is for some other reason not acceptable.[216]

There is no rule that every interference with Article 8 rights as a consequence of extradition is proportionate. However, the public interest in extradition weighs very heavily and it is not right to equate extradition with expulsion or deportation in this context.[217]

> It is of critical importance in the prevention of disorder and crime that those reasonably suspected of crime are prosecuted and, if found guilty, duly sentenced. Extradition is part of the process for ensuring that this occurs, on a basis of international reciprocity.[218]

The Supreme Court held in *Norris* that the interference with human rights would have to be extremely serious if the public interest was to be outweighed.[219] 'The reality is that only if some quite exceptionally compelling feature, or combination of features, is present that interference with family life consequent upon extradition will be other than proportionate to the objective that extradition serves.'[220]

The gravity of the crime in respect of which extradition was sought is capable of being a material factor.[221] The concern is not solely with the family rights of the applicant to the exclusion of those of other members of the family including children.[222] And the possibility of trying a defendant in a forum where his fundamental rights would not be at risk can also be a material factor.[223] Here the Supreme Court held that it was not inappropriate for the District Judge to have explained his rejection of the Article 8 challenge by remarking that there was nothing out of the ordinary or exceptional in the consequences that extradition would have for the family life of the person resisting extradition.[224] However, it noted that it was more accurate and helpful to say that the consequences of interference with Article 8 rights must be 'exceptionally serious before this can outweigh the importance of extradition'.[225]

6.2.2 Impact on Children

Where children are affected by the proposed extradition of a claimant, more is required

---

[216] Ibid, [15].
[217] Ibid, [51].
[218] Ibid, [52].
[219] Ibid, [55].
[220] Ibid, [56].
[221] Ibid, [32].
[222] Ibid, [32].
[223] Ibid, [32].
[224] Ibid, [56].
[225] Ibid, [56]. The claimant in *Potocky v Slovakia* [2013] EWHC 2052 (Admin) established that his extradition to Slovakia was disproportionate as did the claimant in *United States v Shlesinger* [2013] EWHC 2671 (Admin).

to justify the interference with family life. In *HH v Italy*[226] those resisting extradition on Article 8 grounds were the parents of young children. In the first appeal, an Italian court had issued a European Arrest Warrant (EAW) in respect of both parents of three children aged 11, 8 and 3. In the second appeal, a Polish court had issued EAW's in respect of the mother of five children aged 21, 17, 13, 8 and 3. There was no dispute as to the impact on the younger children of the removal of their primary carers and attachment figures. The issue was the relevance of their interests in the proceedings.

Baroness Hale, with whom Lords Hope, Brown and Kerr agreed on the law but not the application to the facts, held that *Norris* determined that in extradition cases the court had to examine carefully the way in which it would interfere with family life.[227] In her view, there were no grounds for treating extradition cases as falling into a special category which diminished the need to examine carefully the way the process will interfere with the individual's right to respect for his family life.[228] She also confirmed, and the Supreme Court was unanimous in agreement, that exceptionality was a prediction, and not a test.[229] In relation to the impact on children, taking into account *ZH*,[230] she held as follows:

> [I]n considering article 8 in any case in which the rights of a child are involved, the best interests of the child must be a primary consideration. They may be outweighed by countervailing factors, but they are of primary importance. The importance of the child's best interests is not to be devalued by something for which she is in no way responsible, such as the suspicion that she may have been deliberately conceived in order to strengthen the parents' case.[231]

Baroness Hale held that depriving a child of her family life was more serious than depriving an adult of hers. Careful attention must be paid to what will happen to the child if her sole or primary carer is extradited.[232] Unlike other forms of expulsion, it was unlikely that the child would be able to accompany the extraditee. She also found a strong public interest in ensuring that children were properly brought up. She concluded that as the effect upon a child's interests was always likely to be more severe than the effect upon an adult's, the court may have to consider whether there was any way in which the public interest in extradition could be met without doing such harm to the child.[233]

In relation to procedure, it was held that if the children's interest were to be properly taken into account by the extraditing court, it would need to have some information about them:

> The court will need to know whether there are dependent children, whether the parent's removal will be harmful to their interests and what steps can be taken to mitigate this. ... The cases likely to require further investigation are those where the extradition of both parents, or of the sole or primary carer, is sought.[234]

It was important that everyone, the parties and their representatives, but also the court,

---

[226] *HH v Italy* [2012] UKSC 25, [2012] 3 WLR 90.
[227] Ibid, [8].
[228] Ibid, [31].
[229] Ibid, [32].
[230] *ZH* (n 181).
[231] *HH* (n 226), [15].
[232] Ibid, [33].
[233] Ibid, [33].
[234] Ibid, [82]–[83].

was 'alive to the need to obtain the information necessary' in order to have regard to the best interests of the children as a primary consideration 'and to take steps accordingly'.[235]

The Supreme Court considered the interests of children again in *BH v Lord Advocate*.[236] Here the issue was whether the appellant and his wife should be extradited to the United States to face trial in Arizona. Lord Hope, with whom the other members of the court agreed, observed that the crimes of which they were accused were very serious and the public interest in honouring extradition arrangements compelling but they had children.

> It is obvious that the children's interests will be interfered with to at least some degree by the extradition of either parent. If both parents are to be extradited the effect on the family life of the children will be huge. The weight to be given to their best interests lies at the heart of the issue whether the extradition of both parents, or either of them, would be proportionate.[237]

Mrs H was the mother of six children of whom the eldest was aged 14 and the youngest one year old. Mr H was the father of the four younger children. Here it was concluded that the best interests of the children were to continue to live with their mother. Therefore, it was important to examine alternatives to extradition and to bring these into the balance to see if they carried any weight.[238] It was concluded that it would not be appropriate for them to be tried in the UK and the best interests of the children, even when weighed together with their mother's Article 8 right, were not strong enough to overcome the overwhelming public interest in giving effect to the extradition request.[239]

6.3 Prisoners

The right to respect for family life is not a right necessarily lost by reason of incarceration. However, the rights of prisoners to see members of their families are inevitably and seriously curtailed simply by virtue of them being deprived of their liberty.[240] The desire to avoid disorder in prisons, or the perpetration of crime, usually means that most interferences with the right to respect for family life of prisoners are justified, although there are some exceptions. For example, *P & Q*[241] concerned two mothers, both serving substantial prison sentences, who claimed that the policy of the Prison Service which prohibited babies from remaining with their mothers in prison after they had reached the age of 18 months, was incompatible with Article 8.

The Court of Appeal found that the intervention with the right to respect for family life here was serious and required a compelling justification.[242] A number of interests had to be balanced: those of the state in the proper management of prisons; of the mothers in their family life; and of the children in the protection, not only of their

---

[235] Ibid, [86].
[236] *BH v Lord Advocate* [2012] UKSC 24, [2012] 3 WLR 151.
[237] Ibid, per Lord Hope at [1].
[238] Ibid, [65].
[239] Ibid, [71]. The principles were applied in *A v Hungary* [2013] EWHC 3132 (Admin).
[240] *R (Shaheen) v Secretary of State for Justice* [2008] EWHC 1195 (Admin), [2009] Prison LR 91.
[241] *P & Q* (n 54).
[242] Ibid, [78].

family life but also of their best interests.[243] It concluded that the Prison Service was entitled to have a policy.[244] However, it was not entitled to operate its policy in a rigid fashion and the policy needed to be flexible to meet its own aims of promoting the welfare of the child and striking a fair balance in accordance with Article 8(2).[245] The court noted that in the great majority of cases the mother and child should be separated at or before the age of 18 months. But it also pointed out that there would be rare exceptions where the interests of the mother and child outweighed other considerations.[246] In the case of P it concluded that the harm done to P's child by separation would not outweigh all the other relevant considerations. In the case of Q it found that this might be such an exceptional case as to justify a departure from the policy.[247]

In *MP*[248] Childcare Resettlement Leave (CRL) was challenged on Article 8 grounds. This is a type of temporary licence available to prisoners who have sole caring responsibility for a child under the age of 16. It enables prisoners to spend up to three days at home, including nights, provided certain conditions are met. It was argued that it was in breach of Article 8 to restrict CRL to female prisoners who were within two years of their earliest release date. The Administrative Court accepted that Article 8 was engaged. Taking into account Article 3(1) of the UN Convention on the Rights of the Child (CRC), it held that the best interests of the child were a primary consideration[249] and also that it was important to give the views of the child due weight in accordance with the age and maturity of the child.[250] It concluded that little consideration was given to Article 8 of the ECHR or to Article 3 of the UN CRC when the policy was reviewed or when individual decisions were made. It held that where Article 8 was engaged, the policy must be sufficiently flexible to enable the decision maker to strike a fair balance and determine whether the interference was proportionate.[251] It concluded that inflexible application of policy without regard to merits was disproportionate and unlawful.

A completely different issue arose in *Mellor*.[252] Here the appellant was serving a life sentence for murder. He was married and wished to found a family, but the Secretary of State denied his request to have access to facilities for artificial insemination. The Court of Appeal held that the qualifications on the right to respect for family life recognised in Article 8(2) applied equally to the right under Article 12 to found a family. Whilst imprisonment was incompatible with the exercise of conjugal rights and involved an interference with family life and the right to found a family, this was found to be ordinarily justifiable under Article 8(2) taking into account the consequences of imprisonment, public concern and the disadvantage of single parent families. It did appreciate that in exceptional circumstances it may be necessary to relax the imposition of detention in order to avoid a disproportionate interference with a human right. However, it found that a prisoner was not entitled to assert the right to found a family

---

[243] Ibid, [88].
[244] Ibid, [99].
[245] Ibid, [101]–[102].
[246] Ibid, [106].
[247] Ibid, [115]. See also *Claire F* (n 79) and *Re L (A Child)* [2013] EWCA Civ 489, [2013] 3 FCR 90.
[248] *R (MP) v Secretary of State for Justice* [2012] EWHC 214 (Admin).
[249] Ibid, [170].
[250] Ibid, [172].
[251] Ibid, [183].
[252] *Mellor* (n 71).

by the provision of semen for the purpose of artificially inseminating his wife.[253] Here, as there were no exceptional circumstances, the court concluded that the prison authorities were not in breach of Articles 8 or 12 by failing to provide assistance with artificial insemination.[254]

6.4 Parenting Orders

In making a parenting order under section 8 of the Crime and Disorder Act 1998, a magistrate must be satisfied that the order is desirable in the interests of preventing any further offence by a child. An order requires the parent in respect of whom it is made to comply with requirements specified in the order and attend counselling and guidance services specified. It is designed to prevent repetition of behaviour in the child, which led to a safety order, anti-social behaviour order or sex offender order being made. Such orders have been held to constitute an interference with family life.[255] However, in M^{256} the Divisional Court held that such orders were achieving the aim of cutting youth crime and were necessary.[257] In considering proportionality, the court held that deference had to be shown to Parliament as parenting orders were designed to balance the community's right to protection of life, limb and property against the parent's rights to respect for private and family life. It concluded that sections 8–10 of the Act were compatible with Article 8[258] but found the making of the order in the present case to be irrational, not disproportionate.[259]

6.5 Compellable Witnesses

Only the wife or husband of a person charged is prevented from being a compellable witness under section 80(1) of the Police and Criminal Evidence Act 1984. In *Pearce*[260] it was accepted that to compel the defendant's cohabitee to give evidence against him was an interference with family life but necessary for the prevention of crime.[261] The argument in relation to his daughter was found to be even weaker.[262]

---

[253] Ibid, [39] in reliance upon *X v Switzerland* (1978) 13 D&R 241; *Hamer v UK* (1979) 4 EHRR 139; *Draper v UK* (1980) 24 DR 72; *ELH v UK* (1997) 91A DR 61.

[254] See also *L* (n 10), which concerned a challenge to the guidance for visits by children to patients in high-security hospitals; and *R (on the application of Kpandang) v Secretary of State for the Home Department* [2004] EWHC (Admin) 2130, which concerned detention in order to process an asylum claim; and *Francis* (n 55) concerning choice of probation board.

[255] *R (M) v Inner London Crown Court* [2003] EWHC (Admin) 301, [2003] 1 FLR 994.

[256] Ibid.

[257] Ibid, [22] and [61].

[258] Ibid, [67].

[259] Ibid, [74].

[260] *R v Pearce* [2001] EWCA Crim 2834, [2002] 1 WLR 1553.

[261] Ibid, [12].

[262] Ibid, [13].

7. Protection of the Rights and Freedoms of Others

The final interest which may justify an interference with the right to respect for family life is the protection of the rights and freedoms of others. In common with other Convention rights, the 'rights' of others is not limited to Convention rights,[263] and it has been held that too close a definition of the rights and freedoms of others may be too difficult and too restrictive of the variety and development of human interests.[264] The 'rights' of others have been held to include the right of a crime victim's family to go about their business with a minimum of anxiety, and without undue restriction on their own movements.[265] However, the most common justification put forward within this category is the rights of children, in particular, their right to protection from harm. In addition to the rights of the child protected under Article 8(2), when determining cases where children are involved a court must also have in mind section 1(1) of the Children Act 1989, which provides that, when a court determines any question with respect to the upbringing of a child, the child's welfare shall be the court's paramount consideration. Where this principle is in conflict with a parent it is overriding.[266]

7.1 Children: Care Orders

Provisions of the Children Act 1989 generally and Part IV (care and supervision orders) have been held to be compatible with Article 8.[267] It has also been held that Article 8 is to a lesser or greater extent engaged in each and every application issued by a local authority under Part IV of the Act. In every case where the threshold criteria under section 31 of the 1989 Act are established, the court, in deciding what (if any) order to make, is required to apply the welfare checklist under section 1(3) of the 1989 Act; to balance the competing Article 8 rights to respect for family life of the parties and the child; and to achieve a result which is both proportionate and in the best interests of the child.[268] Furthermore, every court hearing proceedings under Part IV has a duty under section 3 of the HRA to give effect to the provisions of the 1989 Act in a way which is compatible with Convention rights.[269] Article 8 also applies to other decisions made by the local authority.[270] Any allegation made in care proceedings that a local authority has acted in a way which is incompatible with a Convention right can and should be dealt with in the care proceedings by the court hearing those proceedings under section

---

[263] *R (on the application of Craven) v Secretary of State for the Home Department* [2001] EWHC (Admin) 813.

[264] Ibid, [35].

[265] Ibid, [43].

[266] *Payne v Payne* (n 1), at per Butler-Sloss P [82] in reliance upon *Johansen v Norway* (1996) 23 EHRR 33. See also *Re S (a child) (contact)* [2004] EWCA Civ 18, [2004] 1 FLR 1279, [15].

[267] *Re V (a child) (care proceedings: human rights claims)* [2004] EWCA Civ 54, [2004] 1 WLR 1433.

[268] Ibid, [8].

[269] Ibid.

[270] *R (H) v Kingston Upon Hull City Council* [2013] EWHC 388 (Admin), [2013] Fam Law 804, [54].

7(1)(b) of the HRA. It has been held that it is neither necessary nor desirable to transfer proceedings to a superior level of court merely because a breach of Convention rights is alleged,[271] although it has been recognised that post-care order challenges under the HRA are different.[272]

Cutting off all contact and relationship between a child and his or her family is rarely justified. The local authority must work to support and eventually to reunite the family unless the risks are so high that the child's welfare requires alternative family care.[273] For example, in Re C and B[274] the Court of Appeal found that care orders in relation to two of the children were disproportionate as the local authority could not justify the early removal and complete severance of all ties between the children and their parents. The court accepted that there were cases where the local authority was not bound to wait until the inevitable harm happened but could intervene to protect a child long before that, but the cases where it was appropriate to do so were likely to involve long-standing problems which interfered with the capacity to provide even 'good enough' parenting in a serious way, such as serious mental illness, a serious personality disorder, intractable substance abuse, evidence of past chronic neglect or abuse, or evidence of serious ill-treatment and physical harm.[275] The court also held that it did not follow that every case where there was a significant risk of harm to a young child should result in a care order in which the care plan was adoption.[276]

When there is a choice between making a care order and the less draconian supervision order supported by the agreement of all the parties, the court should, so far as is consistent with the paramountcy of the child's welfare, favour the making of a supervision order. This has been held to be the 'sufficient and proportionate response' to any risk presented to the child, in preference to the protection afforded by a care order, given the potentially greater inroad into the parents' (and indeed the child's) rights to respect for their family and private life.[277] Furthermore, it has been held by the Court of Appeal that in a case where the care plan leads to adoption, the full expression of the terms of Article 8 must be explicit in the judgment because 'ultimately, there can be no greater interference with family life ... any judge must show how his decision is both necessary and proportionate'.[278]

A local authority's intervention in the life of a child, although justified at the outset when the care order was made, may cease to be justifiable under Article 8(2).[279] For example, a care order which keeps a child away from his family for purposes which, as time goes by, are not being realised will sooner or later become a disproportionate interference with the child's primary Article 8 rights.[280]

---

[271] Ibid.

[272] Ibid, [107] in reliance upon Re L (care proceedings: human rights claims) [2003] EWHC (Fam) 665, [2004] 1 FCR 289.

[273] Re C and B (n 62).

[274] Ibid.

[275] Ibid, [30]. See also Re H (a child) (interim care order) [2002] EWCA Civ 1932, [2003] 1 FLR 350. In Barlow (n 61), the House of Lords held that, where a court was not able to identify whether the parents or the childminder was responsible for the child suffering harm, it was still proportionate to make the care order given the need for caution and restraint.

[276] Re C and B, ibid, [30].

[277] Ibid, [48].

[278] Re A (Children) v X London Borough Council [2010] EWCA Civ 344, [2010] 2 FLR 661, [64].

[279] Re S (n 59), [54].

[280] Ibid. Art 8 also applies to Emergency Protection Orders made under the Children Act 1989 although such orders call for compelling justification. See Langley v Liverpool City Council [2005] EWCA Civ 1173.

7.2 Children: Contact Orders

When considering a contact order, the court must take into account the rights of each parent and of the child under Article 8. Contact is a fundamental element of family life and is almost always in the interests of the child. There is a positive obligation on the state and therefore the court, to take measures to maintain and to reconstitute the relationship between parent and child.[281] The key question is whether the judge has taken all necessary steps to facilitate contact as could reasonably be demanded in the circumstances of the particular case.

> Contact between parent and child is to be terminated only in exceptional circumstances, where there are cogent reasons for doing so and when there is no alternative. Contact is to be terminated only if it will be detrimental to the child's welfare.[282]

The welfare of the child is paramount and the child's interest must have precedence over any other consideration.[283] The court must have the greatest flexibility in deciding on the type and amount of contact allowed according to the circumstances of each individual case.[284] Cutting off all contact and relationship between a child and his or her family is only justified by the overriding necessity of the interests of the child. The aim should be to reunite the family when the circumstances enable it, and the effort should be devoted towards that end.[285] Whilst permission to refuse contact was granted in relation to two of the children in *Re C and B*,[286] the Court of Appeal noted that the local authority would still have a duty to try to promote contact unless this was not reasonably practicable or consistent with the welfare of the children.[287]

In *G*[288] the Family Division considered the application of two men for leave to apply for orders under section 8 of the Children Act 1989. In each case the application concerned a child conceived using sperm provided by the man and born to a woman in a civil partnership with another woman. Legal parenthood of the children was vested in the mothers and their respective civil partners to the exclusion of biological fathers who had no right to apply for orders in respect of the children without the leave of the court. The court found that the policy underpinning the law was to put lesbian couples and their children in the same legal position as other types of parents and children. In the present case, the biological fathers were not strangers to the children and it was held to be arguable that the relationships, which they had been allowed to establish with the children, amounted to family life. A refusal to allow the applicants at least permission to apply for orders under section 8 of the Children Act would be to a breach of their rights under Articles 6 and 8.[289] Leave was granted to make an application for contact.

---

[281] *In the Matter of C (A Child)* [2011] EWCA Civ 521, [2011] 2 FLR 912, [47].
[282] Ibid. See further *Re A (A Child)* [2013] EWCA Civ 1104, [2013] 3 FCR 257 and *M (Children)* [2013] EWCA Civ 1147 concerning contact where there was a history of domestic violence.
[283] *In the Matter of C* (n 281), [47].
[284] *Re S* (n 266), [27].
[285] *Re C and B* (n 62), [34].
[286] Ibid.
[287] Ibid, [39].
[288] *In the Matter of G (A Child) v D* [2013] EWHC 134 (Fam), [2013] 1 FLR 1334.
[289] Ibid, [120].

7.3 Children: Adoption

7.3.1 Generally

Adoption orders engage the Article 8 rights of the child and his or her parents. The adoption order must meet a pressing social need and be a proportionate response to that need. It has been held that the balancing exercise required by Article 8 does not differ in substance from that undertaken by a court when deciding whether adoption would be in the best interests of the child.[290] A high degree of justification is required when it is determined that a child should be adopted or placed in care with a view to adoption.[291] It has been held that a child's best interests include being brought up by the natural family, unless overriding requirements of the child's welfare make that impossible. A court must consider all options before coming to a decision, and any assessment of the parents' ability to discharge their responsibilities towards the child must take into account the assistance and support the authorities would offer.[292]

When an appellate court is reviewing the proportionality of a care order made with a view to adoption, a majority of the Supreme Court held in *Re B*[293] that it was not required to address the issues with any particular degree of intensity or rehear all the evidence relevant to the Convention issue.[294] The majority held that the appellate court should not interfere with the trial judge's conclusion on proportionality in such a case, unless it decides that conclusion was wrong.[295]

7.3.2 Adoption without Consent

The making of an adoption order against the wishes of a parent is a very serious intervention by the state in family relationships and the courts will not lightly authorise such intervention.[296] The Supreme Court has held that legislation authorising the severing of family ties between parents and their children will not readily be construed as setting anything less than a test of necessity.[297]

> There must ... be an overriding requirement that the adoption proceed for the sake of the child's welfare, which remains the paramount consideration. The court must be satisfied that the interference with the rights of the parents is proportionate: in other words, that nothing less than adoption will suffice. If the child's welfare can be equally well secured by a less drastic intervention, then it cannot be said that the child's welfare 'requires' that consent to adoption should be dispensed with.[298]

---

[290] *Re B (sole adoption)* (n 63), [31]. See also *Re B (adoption order)* (n 65); and *Re M (a child) (adoption)* [2003] EWCA Civ 1874, [2004] 1 FCR 157.

[291] *Re B* (n 61).

[292] *Re B-S (Children)* [2013] EWCA Civ 1146, [26]–[28]. See further S Harris-Short, 'Making and Breaking Family Life: Adoption, the State, and Human Rights' [2008] *Journal of Law and Society* 28.

[293] *Re B* (n 61).

[294] Ibid, per Lord Wilson at [36].

[295] Ibid, per Lord Neuberger at [90]. The test was applied by the Court of Appeal in *Re G (A Child)* [2013] EWCA Civ 965, [2013] 3 FCR 293.

[296] *ML* (n 64), [33].

[297] Ibid, [34].

[298] Ibid, [34].

Here the Supreme Court held that the legislation was to be construed in accordance with the presumption that it was not intended to place the UK in breach of its international obligations, including the ECHR. Therefore, the test had to be interpreted as one which called for an overriding requirement of necessity and proportionality.[299] It held that the observation of the ECtHR that family ties may only be severed in very exceptional circumstances was not a legal test but an observation about the rarity of circumstances in which the compulsory severing of family ties would be in accordance with Article 8.[300]

7.3.3 Adoption with Consent

In Re B[301] the natural father sought an adoption order with the consent of the mother. Since birth the mother had never met the child nor, save at a distance, seen her. The father had been looking after the child since she was two months old. He sought an adoption order primarily because he was anxious to secure the child's future in his sole care and he would feel more secure knowing that the mother's parental responsibility had been removed. This could only be achieved by an adoption order, and an adoption order would mean that the child was treated in law as if she were not the child of her mother.

The House of Lords held that there must be some reason justifying the exclusion of the other natural parent. 'The reason must be sufficient to outweigh the adverse consequences such an order may have by reason of the exclusion of one parent from the child's life.'[302] It pointed out that the circumstances in which it would be in the best interests of a child to make an adoption order in favour of one natural parent alone, thereby taking away one half of the child's legal family, are likely to be exceptional.[303] It upheld the decision of the judge of first instance to make the order as it was in the child's best interests and therefore could not infringe the child's rights under Article 8.

7.3.4 Contacting Relatives Prior to Adoption

Although in R[304] the Family Division held that it would be an interference with family life to fail to contact the biological relatives of a small child who did not know of his existence and see if they could offer him a suitable home prior to him being freed for adoption, the court held that, as his mother did not want them informed, failing to inform them was necessary and proportionate in the present case for the protection of the child, who could gain nothing from them being informed and who could lose the longer term cooperation and involvement of the mother. Furthermore, the court pointed out that the mother has her own right to respect for her private life and it would be a grave interference to impart this information to people from whom she wanted to keep it secret.

Similarly, in Re M[305] the Family Division held that there was no need to inform the

---

[299] Ibid, [37].
[300] Ibid, [44]. See also Re P [2008] EWCA Civ 535, [2008] 2 FLR 625.
[301] Re B (n 61).
[302] Ibid, [22].
[303] Ibid, [27].
[304] Z County Council v R [2001] 1 FLR 365.
[305] Re M [2001] FLR 745.

natural father regarding the child's adoption. He had no knowledge of the existence of the child and had a history of violence towards the mother. However, in *Re H*[306] the Family Division held that, balancing the rights of all the parties, the father should be made aware of the proceedings and given an opportunity to take part.[307]

7.3.5 Time Limits

Tight time limits in adoption proceedings are not necessarily incompatible with Article 8. In *Re F*[308] the Court of Appeal held that the fact that the law did not prohibit the placement of a child when a natural father had applied for leave to apply for revocation of the adoption order was not incompatible with Article 8.

> If the automatic consequence of the mere issue of their applications for leave were to be a prohibition against placement without leave, they would be able to arrest, at any rate tempo-rarily, a long-arranged placement for which the children had been fully prepared and which should in their interests proceed without hitch.[309]

7.4 Children: Removing a Child from the Jurisdiction

Article 8 has not necessitated a revision of the fundamental approach which remains to apply child welfare as the paramount consideration.[310] Where one parent seeks to remove a child from the jurisdiction, the right to respect for family life of the child and the other parent are engaged, as is often the right to respect for private life of the parent wishing to move. For example, in *Re A*[311] a mother sought the permission of the court to permanently remove the child from the jurisdiction in order to take up a life in New York as she had been offered work there. The Court of Appeal stated that, whilst the child and father had a right to family life, Article 8 also gave the mother a right to her private life.[312] It concluded permission had been correctly granted by the lower court.

In *Payne v Payne*[313] Butler-Sloss P suggested that the following considerations should be in the forefront of the mind of a judge in this type of case:

> (a) The welfare of the child is always paramount. (b) There is no presumption created by s 13(1)(b) in favour of the applicant parent. (c) The reasonable proposals of the parent with a residence order wishing to live abroad carry great weight. (d) Consequently the proposals have to be scrutinised with care and the court needs to be satisfied that there is a genuine motivation for the move and not the intention to bring contact between the child and the other parent to an end. (e) The effect upon the applicant parent and the new family of the child of a refusal of leave is very important. (f) The effect upon the child of the denial of contact

---

[306] *Re H* (n 30).

[307] Ibid, [48]. See further J Marshall, 'Concealed Births, Adoption and Human Rights Law: Being Wary of Seeking to Open Windows into People's Souls' (2012) 71 *Cambridge Law Journal* 325.

[308] *Re F (A Child) v East Sussex CC* [2008] EWCA Civ 439, [2008] 2 FLR 550.

[309] Ibid, [113].

[310] *Payne* (n 1), [37] in reliance upon *Johansen v Norway* (1996) 23 EHRR 33; *L v Finland* [2000] 3 FCR 219; *Scott v UK* [2000] 2 FCR 560.

[311] *Re A (permission to remove child from jurisdiction: human rights)* [2001] 1 FCR 43.

[312] Ibid, [5].

[313] *Payne* (n 1).

with the other parent and in some cases his family is very important. (g) The opportunity for continuing contact between the child and the parent left behind may be very significant.[314]

7.5 Children: Abduction

The removal of a child to another jurisdiction without permission is regulated by international law, specifically the Hague Convention on the Civil Aspects of International Child Abduction 1980. In *Re E*[315] the Supreme Court considered the impact in the UK of this Convention as interpreted by the ECtHR in *Neulinger and Shuruk v Switzerland*[316] where it was held that to return a child to Israel in accordance with the Hague Convention would be incompatible with the private and family lives of the mother and child. Baroness Hale, giving the judgment of the court, held that the fact that the best interests of the child were not expressly made a primary consideration in Hague Convention proceedings did not mean that they were not at the forefront of the whole exercise.[317] The Supreme Court concluded that the Hague Convention and the Brussels II revised Regulation had been devised with the best interests of children generally, and of the individual children involved in such proceedings, as a primary consideration.[318] It was held that the child's interests comprised two limbs: maintaining family ties and ensuring his or her development within a sound environment, not such as would harm his health and development.[319] The impact of ECtHR case law was summarised as follows:

> The guarantees in article 8 have to be interpreted and applied in the light of both the Hague Convention and the UNCRC; that all are designed with the best interests of the child as a primary consideration; that in every Hague Convention case where the question is raised, the national court does not order return automatically and mechanically but examines the particular circumstances of this particular child in order to ascertain whether a return would be in accordance with the Convention; and that is not the same as a full blown examination of the child's future; and that it is, to say the least, unlikely that if the Hague Convention is properly applied, with whatever outcome, there will be a violation of the article 8 rights of the child or either of the parents.[320]

Further clarification was provided by the Supreme Court in *S*[321] which concerned a mother who had appealed against an order of the Court of Appeal that she return her son to Australia pursuant to Article 12 of the Convention on the Civil Aspects of International Child Abduction. The Supreme Court confirmed, with the greatest respect to the ECtHR, that neither the Hague Convention, nor Article 8, required a court which determined an application under the Hague Convention, to conduct an in-depth examination of the entire family situation.[322]

---

[314] Ibid, [85]. See also *Re S (a child) (residence order: condition) (No 2)* [2002] EWCA Civ 1795, [2003] 1 FCR 138, where the Court of Appeal held that the exceptional circumstances justified the imposition of a condition on a residence order prohibiting the mother from moving the daughter to live in Cornwall. See also *S v B (a child) (abduction: objections to return)* [2005] EWHC 733.

[315] *Re E (Children)* [2011] UKSC 27, [2011] 2 WLR 1326.

[316] *Neulinger and Shuruk v Switzerland* [2011] 1 FLR 122.

[317] *Re E* (n 315), [14].

[318] Ibid, [18].

[319] Ibid, [21].

[320] Ibid, [26].

[321] *In the Matter of S (A Child)* [2012] UKSC 10, [2012] 2 AC 257.

[322] Ibid, [38]. See further K Beevers, 'Child Abduction: Inchoate Rights and the Unmarried Father' (2006)

7.6 Children and Parents: Paternity

Whilst the right to respect for family life of a child may extend to him or her discovering his or her true paternity, this must be balanced against the rights of others—particularly rights to respect for private life. For example, in *Re T*[323] the Family Division held that failure on the part of the court to order blood and DNA tests to establish who was the father of the child could constitute an interference with the right to respect for family life of the child. However, it also appreciated that the mother and her husband had a right to respect for their private and family life. Balancing the rights, it held that weightiest was that of the child, namely that he should have the possibility of knowing his true roots and identity.

> [A]ny such interference as would occur to the right to respect for family/private life of the mother and her husband, to be proportionate to the legitimate aim of providing T with the possibility of certainty as to his real paternity, a knowledge which would accompany him throughout his life.

A slightly different issue arose in *Leeds Teaching Hospital*.[324] The Divisional Court found that the presumption in the Human Fertilisation and Embryology Act that Mr A was not the father of the twins (Mrs A had been inseminated with Mr B's semen by mistake) was an interference with his right to respect for family life.[325] However, it concluded that within the domestic family legislation there were remedies which could underpin and protect the position of Mr A with respect to the twins,[326] namely a residence order to give him parental responsibility[327] and adoption.[328] The court found this remedy to be proportionate to the aim of providing necessary protection to the twins whose rights and welfare must predominate.[329] Although they lost the immediate certainty of the irrebuttable presumption that Mr A was their legal father, they remained within a stable and secure home and retained the great advantage of preserving the reality of their paternal identity.[330]

7.7 Children and Parents: Health

In *Axon*[331] the Administrative Court considered the compatibility with Article 8 of guidance issued by the Department of Health which provided that a medical professional could provide advice and treatment on sexual matters for young people under the age of 16, without the knowledge or consent of their parents, provided the young person

---

18 *Child and Family Law Quarterly* 499; J Herring and R Taylor, 'Relocating Relocation' (2006) 18 *Child and Family Law Quarterly* 517.

[323] *Re T* (n 33).
[324] *Leeds Teaching Hospital* (n 25).
[325] Ibid, [49].
[326] Ibid, [51].
[327] Ibid.
[328] Ibid, [52].
[329] Ibid, [54].
[330] Ibid, [56]–[57]. See further J Fortin, 'Children's Right to Know their Origins—Too Far, Too Fast?' (2009) 21 *Child and Family Law Quarterly* 336.
[331] *Axon* (n 108).

was 'Gillick' competent.[332] This meant that the person had sufficient maturity and intelligence to understand the nature and implications of the proposed treatment and that certain conditions were satisfied. The Court had already concluded that the guidance was not an interference with the Article 8 rights of parents, but went on to consider proportionality. The Court noted the clear evidence that an assurance to young people of medical confidentiality increased the use of contraceptive and abortion services by those aged under 16. It also referred to the disturbing consequences of young people being deterred from obtaining advice and treatment, and stated that the child's Article 8 rights overrode those of the parent. It concluded that the guidance was proportionate.[333]

7.8 Vulnerable People: Entry Clearance

The justification given for the interference with family life in *Quila*[334] did not concern the rights of children but the rights of those possibly vulnerable to a forced marriage. Here the immigration rule provided that in the absence of exceptional compassionate circumstances a marriage visa should not be granted until both the sponsor and the applicant had attained the age of 21. It was submitted by the Secretary of State that the rule was to prevent forced marriages and thereby protect the rights and freedoms of others. Lord Wilson observed that the rule was a blunt instrument and had a drastic effect on thousands of young adults who had entered into bona fide marriages.[335] He observed that the rule was rationally connected to the objective of deterring forced marriages but the number of forced marriages which it deterred was 'highly debatable'.[336] In his view, what seemed clear was that the number of unforced marriages which it obstructed from their intended development for up to three years vastly exceeded the number of forced marriages which it deterred.[337] He held that the Secretary of State had failed to establish that the rule was no more than was necessary to accomplish her objective and that it struck a fair balance between the rights of the parties to unforced marriages and the interests of the community in preventing forced marriages.

> On any view it is a sledge-hammer but she has not attempted to identify to size of the nut. At all events she fails to establish that the interference with the rights of the respondents under article 8 is justified.[338]

A breach of the Article 8 rights of the claimants was established.[339]

---

[332] *Gillick v West Norfolk and Wisbech Area Health Authority* [1986] 1 AC 112.
[333] See further R Taylor, 'Reversing the Retreat from Gillick?' (2007) 19 *Child and Family Law Quarterly* 81.
[334] *Quila* (n 13).
[335] Ibid, [54].
[336] Ibid, [58].
[337] Ibid, [58].
[338] Ibid, [58].
[339] Other members of the Supreme Court agreed apart from Lord Brown who dissented and found the interference with Art 8 rights justified.

13

Article 8: The Right to Respect for Home

1. Introduction

The final right protected by Article 8 considered in this book is the right to respect for home. In common with other Article 8 rights, this is not an absolute right and can be subject to interference such as in accordance with the law and necessary in one of the interests set out in Article 8(2). It has been held that 'few things are more central to the enjoyment of human life than having somewhere to live'.[1] It has also been held that the essence of the right lies in the concept of respect for the home as one among various things that affect a person's right to privacy:

> The emphasis is on the person's home as a place where he is entitled to be free from arbitrary interference by the public authorities. Article 8(1) does not concern itself with the person's right to the peaceful enjoyment of his home as a possession or as a property right.[2]

As examined in Chapter 17, property rights are protected separately by Article 1 of Protocol No 1 to the ECHR but this right is often raised in conjunction with the right to respect for home.

By contrast to the other parts of Article 8, when interpreting and applying the right to respect for home, the courts have directed particular attention to the word 'respect'. A right to respect for home has been held to be an entirely different concept to a right to a home.[3] The comment has also been made that, at the time of the drafting of the Convention, the intention was to enshrine fundamental rights and freedoms, not to 'engage in social engineering in the housing field'.[4]

---

[1] *Harrow London Borough Council v Qazi* [2003] UKHL 43, [2004] AC 983, per Lord Bingham at [8].
[2] Ibid, per Lord Hope at [50] in reliance upon *Marckx v Belgium* (1979) 2 EHRR 330.
[3] See eg the comments of Lord Home in *Qazi*, ibid, [69].
[4] *Qazi*, ibid, per Lord Scott at [123]. See also the comments of Lord Millett at [100].

2. Home

The meaning of 'home' is autonomous. What is required is a 'down-to-earth, pragmatic consideration' of whether the place in question is that where a 'person lives and to which he returns and which forms the centre of his existence'. A simple, 'factual and untechnical test' must be applied, taking full account of the factual circumstances and 'very little of the legal niceties'.[5] The meaning of home is not defined by the particular building which a person owns or occupies. As stated above, a person's home is the place where he and his family are entitled to be left in peace free from interference by the state or agents of the state: 'It is an important aspect of his dignity as a human being, and is protected as such and not as an item of property.'[6]

In order for premises to be a home, it is not necessary for a person to have a proprietary interest in them. A person may make his home where he has no right to be; and a person may choose not to make his home where he does have a right to live.[7] In *Qazi*[8] the House of Lords held that that the premises were the claimant's home, even though his former wife, a joint tenant, had served a notice to quit on the landlord, thereby terminating the tenancy. He had lived at the premises for eight years. The house had been his home and he had no other.

> The expiry of his wife's notice to quit brought his right to occupy the house as a tenant to an end, but it did not bring his occupation to an end. The house continued to be the place where he lived and so his home.[9]

In *Malik*[10] it was common ground before the Court of Appeal that the squatters had established their home on a particular plot of land and therefore the prospect of eviction engaged Article 8.[11] A home includes a caravan occupied by a gypsy regardless of whether or not the gypsy is living in the caravan on a site in breach of planning control.[12] It also includes the site occupied by travelling show-people and travellers;[13] an NHS facility for the long-term disabled;[14] a care home;[15] accommodation provided

---

[5] Ibid, per Lord Bingham at [8]–[10] in reliance upon *Gillow v UK* (1986) 11 EHRR 335 and *Buckley v UK* (1996) 23 EHRR 101.

[6] *Qazi*, ibid, per Lord Millett at [89].

[7] Ibid, per Lord Millett at [97]. See also *Royal Borough of Kensington and Chelsea v O'Sullivan* [2003] EWCA Civ 371, [2003] 2 FLR 459.

[8] *Qazi*, ibid.

[9] Ibid, per Lord Bingham at [11]. See also per Lord Steyn at [29] and per Lord Hope at [68]. Contrast the judgment of the Court of Appeal in *Sims v Dacorum Borough Council* [2013] EWCA Civ 12, [2013] HLR 14. See also *Hounslow London Borough Council v Powell* [2011] UKSC 8, [2011] 2 WLR 287 where the Supreme Court held that premises occupied by an introductory tenant constituted his home.

[10] *Malik v Fassenfelt* [2013] EWCA Civ 798.

[11] Ibid, [9].

[12] *South Bucks District Council v Porter* [2003] UKHL 26, [2003] 2 AC 558. See also *Chief Constable of Wiltshire v McDonagh* [2008] EWHC 654 (QB), [24].

[13] *Davis v Tonbridge & Malling Borough Council* [2004] EWCA Civ 194; *R (Fuller) v Chief Constable of the Dorset Police* [2001] EWHC (Admin) 1057, [2003] QB 480.

[14] *R v North and East Devon Health Authority, ex p Coughlan* [2001] QB 213. See also *R (on the application of Phillips) v Walsall Metropolitan Borough Council* [2001] EWHC (Admin) 789.

[15] *Johnson v Havering London Borough Council* [2007] UKHL 27, [2008] 1 AC 95.

by a health authority;[16] and a hotel room where someone was continuing their private life away from their normal residence.[17] Business premises may also come within the meaning of home. It was accepted with no argument in *Miller Gardner*[18] that Article 8 was engaged by a search of the solicitor's premises for material relating to a particular client.[19]

The meaning of 'home' does not include land over which the owner permits or causes sport to be conducted and which would never, in any ordinary usage, be described as 'home'.[20] However, a garden can be part of a home and the felling of a tree in the garden can be an interference with it.[21] It is possible for premises to cease being a home. In *Le Roi*[22] the appellant had erected two buildings on agricultural land, adapted these to residential purposes and from time to time lived there. The Court of Appeal pointed out that, at the time of the enforcement action under planning legislation, he was not actually living on the premises and 'therefore the effect of having to demolish will not in fact be that he is deprived of accommodation, even though he may be forced to live in less agreeable circumstances than he otherwise would'.[23]

---

3. Interference

An interference with the right to respect for home can arise in a variety of ways. The main categories into which interferences fall are examined in the following paragraphs.

3.1 Planning

Planning decisions have the potential to interfere with the right to respect for home. For example, enforcement action by the local planning authority to secure the removal of a gypsy from a site involves an interference with the gypsy's right to respect for home.[24] A measure which prevents a traveller from residing in his vehicle on identified land, also interferes with the right.[25] It has been held to be as much a lack of respect not to allow them to move onto the site that they own as it is to make them move off:

---

[16] *R (on the application of C) v Brent, Kensinton, Chelsea and Westminster Mental Health NHS Trust* [2002] EWHC (Admin) 181, [2002] Lloyd's Med Rep 321.

[17] *R v Hardy* [2003] EWCA Crim 3092.

[18] *R (on the application of Miller Gardner Solicitors) v Minshull Street Crown Court* [2002] EWHC (Admin) 3077.

[19] See also *Office of Fair Trading v X* [2003] EWHC (Comm) 1042, [2004] ICR 105.

[20] *R (Countryside Alliance) v Attorney General* [2007] UKHL 52, [2007] 3 WLR 922, per Lord Bingham at [15].

[21] *Lane v Kensington & Chelsea Royal London Borough* [2013] EWHC 1320 (QB), [13].

[22] *Salisbury District Council v Le Roi* [2001] EWCA Civ 1490.

[23] Ibid, per Buxton LJ at [31].

[24] *Porter* (n 12), in reliance upon *Buckley* (n 5), and *Chapman v UK* (2001) 33 EHRR 399.

[25] *Fuller* (n 13).

The effect in either instance is to deny them a stable base. Their home is their caravan and that is where they carry on their private life. That is the right that is being infringed by not allowing them to put it on their land.[26]

However, the loss in value of a home as a result of a planning decision has been held not to constitute an interference.[27] In *Lough*[28] a group of residents complained that the development of a site in the Bankside area would lead to a loss of privacy, a loss of light, a loss of a view and interference with television reception. The Court of Appeal held that, whilst Article 8 required respect for the home and protection for the environment of the home, it created no absolute right to amenities currently enjoyed. 'Its role though important, must be seen in the context of competing rights, including rights of other landowners and of the community as a whole.'[29]

It further held that the contents of Article 8(2) threw light on the extent of the right in Article 8(1) and concluded that the degree of seriousness required to trigger a lack of respect for the home depended on the circumstances but had to be substantial.[30] '[T]he reasonableness and appropriateness of measures taken by the public authority are relevant in considering whether the respect required by Article 8(1) has been accorded.'[31] In the present case it found no interference with the right to respect for home.[32]

3.2 Proceedings for Possession

Difficult issues have arisen in relation to the question of whether or not Article 8(1) is engaged by proceedings to recover possession of a home. In *Qazi*[33] a majority of the House of Lords concluded that any attempt to evict a person, whether directly, indirectly or by process of law, from his or her home was 'a derogation from the respect to which the home is prima facie entitled'[34] and therefore Article 8 was engaged.[35] However, as discussed later in this chapter, a different majority[36] determined that it was not necessary for a court to consider whether the making of an order for possession would be proportionate.[37] This has now been overruled as discussed later in this chapter.

---

[26] *Rafferty v Secretary of State for Communities & Local Government* [2009] EWCA Civ 809, [2010] JPL 485, [28]. A compulsory purchase order also amounts to an interference: see *R (Mortell) v Secretary of State for Communities & Local Government* [2009] EWCA Civ 1274.
[27] *Lough v First Secretary of State* [2004] EWCA Civ 905, [2004] 1 WLR 2557, [51].
[28] Ibid.
[29] Ibid, [41].
[30] Ibid, [43].
[31] Ibid.
[32] Ibid, [46]. Other planning decisions include *Vallen International Limited v Secretary of State for Transport, Local Government and the Regions* [2002] EWHC (Admin) 1107, [2002] 21 EG 145 (CS); *R (on the application of Morgan) v Secretary of State for Transport, Local Government and the Regions* [2002] EWHC (Admin) 2652; *Massingham v Secretary of State for Transport, Local Government and the Regions* [2002] EWHC (Admin) 1578; *Cranage Parish Council v First Secretary of State* [2004] EWHC (Admin) 2949.
[33] *Qazi* (n 1).
[34] Ibid, per Lord Hope at [70].
[35] Ibid, per Lord Hope at [71], per Lord Millett at [103], per Lord Bingham at [23] and per Lord Steyn at [27].
[36] Lords Hope, Millett and Scott.
[37] See also *Mayor and Burgesses of the London Borough of Lambeth v Howard* [2001] EWCA Civ 468; *Poplar Housing and Regeneration Community Association v Donoghue* [2001] EWCA Civ 595, [2001] QB 48; *Sheffield City Council v Hopkins* [2001] EWCA Civ 1023, [2001] 26 EG 163 (CS); *St Brice v London*

The process of dispossession involves a variety of stages and Article 8 is applicable at each stage:

The court's task is to subject the process of dispossession by the public authority to a proportionality review. That is a process which may typically involve a number of stages, beginning in the present case with a notice to quit, followed by the issue of possession proceedings, the obtaining of judgment after a hearing, and the enforcement of an order for possession by the obtaining and execution of a writ of possession.[38]

The Court of Appeal held in *JL*[39] that in the overwhelming majority of cases Article 8 rights will be sufficiently respected by provision of a proportionality review during possession proceedings themselves.[40] However, it appreciated that there may be exceptional cases where the raising of Article 8 rights at the enforcement stage would not be an abuse of process.[41] In the present case, during possession proceedings as the law stood, the defendant was not able to raise Article 8 as a defence. The law subsequently changed as a result of the judgment in *Pinnock* and she was able to raise the defence at the enforcement stage.

3.3 Care Homes

A number of claims have been brought concerning respect for home and the proposed closure of care homes. Prior to the coming into force of the HRA, it was held in *Coughlan*[42] that the closure of an NHS facility for the long-term disabled constituted an interference with the right to respect for home. However, in *Phillips*[43] the Administrative Court held that, whilst it was ready to assume that in the present context Article 8 required the council permanently to provide a home for the applicants, this did not mean that the council could not substitute one home for another and this would not constitute an interference.[44] This reasoning was doubted in *C*,[45] where it was held by the Administrative Court in relation to the closure of a hospital for the mentally ill that it was plain that a health authority having the responsibility for the long-term care of mental patients and their placement in appropriate accommodation was required to act compatibly with Article 8.[46] Similarly, in *Madden*,[47] which concerned a challenge to the proposed closure of two residential homes, the Administrative Court held that Article 8 was engaged.[48]

Even though a local authority has contracted out its obligations to a private company, in certain circumstances its actions can still be construed as involving a lack of respect

---

Borough of Southwark [2001] EWCA Civ 1138, [2002] 1 WLR 1537; *R (McLellan) v Bracknell Forest Borough Council* [2001] EWCA Civ 1510, [2002] QB 1129.

[38] *R (JL) v Secretary of State for Defence* [2013] EWCA Civ 449.
[39] Ibid.
[40] Ibid, [39].
[41] Ibid, [41].
[42] *Coughlan* (n 14).
[43] *Phillips* (n 14).
[44] Ibid, per Lightman J at [11].
[45] *C* (n 16).
[46] Ibid, per Newman J at [38].
[47] *R (on the application of Madden) v Bury Metropolitan Borough Council* [2002] EWHC (Admin) 1882.
[48] Ibid, per Richards J at [68].

for the right to home. For example, in *Haggerty*[49] proceedings were brought against a council in relation to its decision not to enter into a new contract with a private company which operated a private nursing home. It was argued that this decision had led to the private company deciding to close the home. However, the Administrative Court was not satisfied that Article 8 was engaged, holding that there was no cogent evidence of disruption.[50] A great deal had been done to ensure the move was as undisruptive as possible.

> [T]he individual assessments of all residents have been carried out ... the Council has agreed to liase with the claimants' expert consultant psychiatrist on the best ways of moving the claimants so as to reduce any risk to them.[51]

In *Johnson*[52] a majority of the House of Lords concluded that in providing care and accommodation to a resident pursuant to arrangements made with a local authority under the National Assistance Act 1948, a care home was not performing functions of a public nature for the purposes of section 6(3)(b) of the Human Rights Act 1998. Therefore, it was not obliged to act compatibly with Article 8.

3.4 Environmental Pollution

Whilst there have been very few claims decided on this basis under the HRA, environmental pollution can also constitute an interference with respect for home. For example, in *Dennis*[53] it was held that the effect of noise from Harrier jet fighters on the claimant's estate constituted an interference with Article 8 rights.[54] However, the argument in *Westminster City Council*[55] by a group of residents that the congestion charge would result in an increase in traffic in their area with consequential noise and air pollution and constitute a violation of Article 8 was not successful. The Administrative Court held that evidence of such effects had to be reasonable and convincing, and here it was not.[56]

A unique claim was made in *Harrow Community Support Ltd*[57] concerning the decision of the Secretary of State for Defence to locate a ground-based air defence system and military personnel on the roof of a residential tower block in Leytonstone for the duration of the 2012 London Olympics. It was held that it was necessary for the claimant to show a serious breach of the right to the physical area or quiet enjoyment of his or her home. The Administrative Court found that the facts of this case were a

---

[49] *R (on the application of Haggerty) v St Helens Council* [2003] EWHC (Admin) 803.

[50] Ibid, per Silber J at [58].

[51] Ibid, [59]. See also *McKellar v Mayor & Burgesses of the London Borough of Hounslow* [2003] EWHC (QB) 3145.

[52] *Johnson* (n 15).

[53] *Dennis v Ministry of Defence* [2003] EWHC (QB) 793, [2003] 19 EG 118 (CS).

[54] Ibid, [61].

[55] *R (on the application of Westminster City Council) v Mayor of London* [2002] EWHC (Admin) 2440.

[56] Ibid, per Maurice Kay at [115]. See also *Andrews v Reading Borough Council* [2005] EWHC (QB) 256, where it was held that an increase in road and traffic noise constituted an interference with the right to respect for private life; and *Arscott v The Coal Authority* [2004] EWCA Civ 892, [2005] Env LR 6, where it was held that developing land so that floodwater damaged someone else's property constituted an interference.

[57] *R (Harrow Community Support Ltd) v Secretary of State for Defence* [2012] EWHC 1921 (Admin).

far cry from cases of long-term sustained noise pollution as the deployment would be unobtrusive and have no impact on the ability of residents to use their properties. It was also limited in time.[58] No interference was found, the court concluding that the detriment complained of was negligible. On the assumption that there was an interference, the proportionality of the deployment was held to be overwhelming.[59]

3.5 Criminal Justice

Interferences may also arise from the operation of the criminal justice system. For example, a police search of premises constituting a home undoubtedly engages Article 8(1).[60] A confiscation order may also result in an interference if it results in the sale of a home. For example, in *Re A*[61] it was held that the sale of a home to satisfy a criminal confiscation order made against her husband was an interference with the wife's Article 8 rights.[62] It was held in *McDonagh*[63] that the seizure and taking away of a caravan under section 8 of the Police and Criminal Evidence Act 1984, in relation to the investigation of an offence, was an interference with the right to respect for home.[64] Other interferences have been found from: a closure order of premises used in connection with class A drugs;[65] a condition of bail requiring an accused person to present himself at the door of his home if required to by a police officer;[66] and a licence condition preventing an individual access to his home.[67]

---

4. Positive Duties

The right to respect for home does not just entail refraining from interference; in certain circumstances a positive duty of respect may arise—although there are limits. For example, there is no positive right to require the state to provide a home,[68] nor is the

---

[58] Ibid, [45].
[59] Ibid, [50].
[60] *R (on the application of Rottman) v Commissioner of Police of the Metropolis* [2002] UKHL 20, [2002] 2 WLR 1315.
[61] *Re A* [2002] EWHC (Admin/Fam) 611, [2002] 2 FCR 481.
[62] See also *R v Goodenough* [2004] EWCA Crim 2260, [2005] 1 Cr App R (S) 88; and *R v Ahmed* [2004] EWCA Crim 2599, [2005] 1 WLR 122.
[63] *McDonagh* (n 12).
[64] Ibid, [24].
[65] *R (Leary) v Chief Constable of West Midlands* [2012] EWHC 639 (Admin), [2012] ACD 67.
[66] *R (on the application of CPS) v Chorley Justices* [2002] EWHC (Admin) 2162.
[67] *R (on the application of Davies) v Secretary of State for the Home Department* [2004] EWHC (Admin) 1512.
[68] *Wandsworth LBC v Michalak* [2002] EWCA Civ 271, [2003] 1 WLR 617, [18]; *R (on the application of W) v Lambeth London Borough Council* [2002] EWCA Civ 613, [2002] 2 All ER 901, [85]; *O'Sullivan* (n 7), [46]; *R (on the application of J) v Enfield London Borough Council* [2002] EWHC (Admin) 432, [2002] 2 FLR 1.

state required to provide housing benefit.[69] It has also been held that Article 8 imposes no duty on a council to exercise its powers so as to provide an adequate number of gypsy sites.[70] Lord Bingham held in *Kay*[71] that Article 8 did not guarantee a right to a home or the right to have one's housing problems solved by the authorities.[72]

Nevertheless, there are some positive duties. A failure to grant planning permission may amount to an interference with the right to respect for home,[73] as may failures to act resulting in pollution and damage to a home. In *Marcic*[74] it was held by the House of Lords that the failure to construct new sewers with a greater capacity, leading to serious and repeated external flooding of a person's home, constituted an interference. The courts are wary of 'judicial creativity' in the field of social housing responsibilities. Nevertheless, it has been held that local authority landlords are obliged to take steps to ensure that the condition of houses let for social housing are such that Article 8 rights are not infringed.[75]

Where local authorities have contracted out functions to a private company, positive obligations under Article 8 may require them to ensure the ongoing protection of the right to respect for home. In *Heather*[76] the Court of Appeal held that, if the local authority had made the arrangements with the private company after the HRA had come into force, it would arguably have been possible for a resident to require the local authority to enter into a contract with its provider which fully protected the resident's Article 8 rights.[77] Finally, it is important to remember that, as Article 8 protects both substantive and procedural rights, an interference can also arise from a failure to consult.[78]

5. Permitted Interferences

In common with the other rights protected by Article 8, it is possible to interfere with the exercise of the right to respect for home if such interference is in accordance with the law and necessary in a democratic society in the interest of national security, public safety or the economic well-being of the country, for the prevention of disorder or crime, for the protection of health or morals, or for the protection of the rights and

---

[69] *R (on the application of Painter) v Carmarthenshire County Council Housing Benefit Review Board* [2001] EWHC (Admin) 308.

[70] *Chichester District Council v The First Secretary of State*, Administrative Court, 29 July 2003, [36]; *Codona v Mid-Bedfordshire District Council* [2004] EWCA Civ 925, [2005] HLR 1.

[71] *Kay v Lambeth London Borough Council* [2006] UKHL 10, [2006] 2 AC 465.

[72] Ibid, [28].

[73] See eg *Chichester District Council v The First Secretary of State* [2004] EWCA Civ 1248, [2005] 1 WLR 279.

[74] *Marcic v Thames Water Utilities Ltd* [2003] UKHL 66, [2004] 2 AC 42.

[75] *Lee v Leeds City Council* [2002] EWCA Civ 6, [2002] 1 WLR 1488.

[76] *R (on the application of Heather) v Leonard Cheshire* [2002] EWCA Civ 366, [2002] HLR 893.

[77] Ibid, [34].

[78] See eg *C* (n 16).

freedoms of others. The justifications that have been put forward under the HRA for interferences with respect for home are examined in the following paragraphs.

6. For the Prevention of Disorder or Crime

Searches of a home by police following arrest are generally sought to be justified on the ground of prevention of crime. In *Rottman*[79] a majority of the House of Lords concluded that the common law power of police to search for and seize any goods or documents following an arrest under section 8 of the Extradition Act 1989 had the legitimate aim in a democratic society of preventing crime, and was necessary in order to prevent the disappearance of material evidence after the arrest of a suspect.

> The power is proportionate to that aim because it is subject to the safeguards that it can only be exercised after a warrant of arrest has been issued by a magistrate or a justice of the peace in respect of an extradition crime and where the evidence placed before him would, in his opinion, justify the issue of a warrant for the arrest of a person accused of a similar domestic offence.[80]

Confiscation orders have raised issues in relation to a number of Convention rights, including Article 6 and Article 1 of Protocol No 1 and where it is necessary to sell a home to satisfy a criminal confiscation order, Article 8 rights may also be involved. In *Re A*[81] it was argued that it was a disproportionate interference with a wife's Article 8 rights to sell the matrimonial home to satisfy a criminal confiscation order made against her husband. The court held that had to exercise its powers in a way which was compatible with the Convention and having regard to a number of potentially conflicting rights and interests: the wife's right to respect for her private life and her home under Article 8; the husband's right to liberty under Article 5 and his right under Article 1 of Protocol No 1 to use his assets to discharge his liabilities; and the interests of the prosecutor, representing the public's interest in the prevention of crime, the protection of health and the protection of the rights and freedoms of potential victims of drug traffickers.[82] It concluded that there was a compelling case for making an order that would allow the wife to go on living in the house.[83]

The justification of crime prevention has been raised in other contexts. Where a closure order was made in relation to someone's home under the Anti-social Behaviour Act 2003, as it had been used in connection with class A drugs, it was held that there was no obligation on the authorities to demonstrate that they had tried less draconian measures. It was observed that the misuse of premises for class A drugs may have a grievous effect on other people.[84] A bail condition which required the accused to present

---

[79] *Rottman* (n 60).
[80] Ibid, per Lord Hutton at [80]. See also *Miller Gardner* (n 18).
[81] *Re A* (n 61).
[82] Ibid, [171].
[83] Ibid, [221].
[84] *Leary* (n 65).

himself at the door of his accommodation, if required to do so by a police officer, was held to be necessary for the prevention of crime.[85] However, in *McDonagh*[86] the seizure and taking away of a caravan under section 8 of the Police and Criminal Evidence Act 1984, in relation to the investigation of an offence, was held to be disproportionate given the caravan formed the home of a woman in the advanced stages of pregnancy.

---

7. Economic Well-being of the Country

7.1 Care Home Closures

Resources arguments are an important feature of HRA claims concerning care home closures. Usually such arguments are successful, although in *Coughlan*,[87] a pre-HRA case, such arguments did not prevail. In this case, the Court of Appeal concluded that the price of the saving was to be

> not only the breach of a plain promise made to Miss Coughlan but, perhaps more importantly, the loss of her only home and of a purpose-built environment which had come to mean even more to her than a home does to most people.[88]

Post-HRA, this outcome was unusual. For example, in *C*,[89] which concerned the closure of a hospital for the mentally ill, it was appreciated that the NHS Trust, in accordance with the principle of proportionality, had to strike a fair balance between the interference with the claimants' Convention rights and the requirements of other patients for whom the Trust was responsible, and to involve the claimants in the process of making the decision so that it was sensitive to the needs of the claimants.[90] No breach of Article 8 was found. Similarly, in *Haggerty*,[91] when considering Article 8(2), the Administrative Court pointed out that the financial resources of the council were an important element to be considered in the balancing exercise and justified the decision here not to enter into a new contractual arrangement with the private company. The court noted that a local authority was obliged by statute and entitled to take into consideration resources when deciding how to meet individual needs.[92] It also found that the council was entitled to a substantial degree of deference relating to the way in which it allocated its resources and provided services. 'These are matters very much within the expertise of a local authority and with which a court should only interfere where the evidence is very clear.'[93]

---

[85] *CPS* (n 66), [32].
[86] *McDonagh* (n 12).
[87] *Coughlan* (n 14).
[88] Ibid, [92].
[89] eg *C* (n 16).
[90] Ibid, [39].
[91] *Haggerty* (n 49).
[92] Ibid, [60].
[93] Ibid, [61]. See also *Phillips* (n 14); *R (on the application of Cowl) v Plymouth City Council* [2001] EWCA Civ 1935, [2002] 1 WLR 803; *Madden* (n 47); *R (on the application of Dudley) v East Sussex County Council* [2003] EWHC (Admin) 1093; *McKellar* (n 51).

7.2 Standards of Public Housing

Whilst it has been held that a local authority landlord is under a positive obligation to keep houses which it has let for social housing in such a condition that Article 8 rights are not infringed, resources considerations are still important. In *Lee*[94] the Court of Appeal held that the steps which a public authority will be required to take in order to ensure compliance with Article 8 must be determined, in each case, by 'having due regard to the needs and resources of the community and of individuals'.[95] The allocation of resources to meet the needs of social housing was seen as very much a matter for democratically determined priorities. The court found no support in domestic or Strasbourg jurisprudence for the proposition that Article 8 imposed some general and unqualified obligation on local authorities in relation to the condition of their housing stock.[96] However, the court was careful to point out that this did not mean that there would never be cases where a local authority, as the landlord of a dwelling house let for the purpose of social housing which was unfit for human habitation or in a state prejudicial to health, would be in breach of the positive duty. But it had not been shown that there had been a breach in the present cases.[97]

7.3 Management of Sewage and Drainage

Whilst flooding arising from overloaded sewers can interfere with respect for home, resources considerations play a considerable role in determining whether or not such interference is justified. For example, in *Marcic*[98] the House of Lords accepted that the repeated and serious external sewer flooding arising from overloaded sewers endured by Mr Marcic was prima facie a violation of Article 8. However, it saw the issue as whether or not the statutory scheme as a whole was Convention compliant. In its view, the role of the domestic policy maker should be given special weight and a fair balance struck between the interests of the individual and those of the community as a whole. In the present case

> the interests Parliament had to balance included, on the one hand, the interests of customers of a company whose properties are prone to sewer flooding and, on the other hand, all the other customers of the company whose properties are drained through the company's sewers. The interests of the first group conflict with the interest of the company's customers as a whole in that only a minority of customers suffer sewer flooding but the company's customers as a whole meet the cost of building more sewers.[99]

Their Lordships concluded that the scheme whereby a general drainage obligation was imposed on a sewerage undertaker but enforcement of this obligation was entrusted to

---

[94] *Lee* (n 75).
[95] Ibid, [49].
[96] Ibid.
[97] Ibid, [50]. See also *Fuller* (n 13), where the court held that the eviction of travellers from a site was necessary in the interests of the economic well-being of the country as the council wished to have a contract for the conversion of compost carried out there.
[98] *Marcic* (n 74).
[99] Ibid, [42].

an independent regulator and decisions of the Director General of Water Services were subject to judicial review struck a reasonable balance.[100]

> [T]he malfunctioning of the statutory scheme on this occasion does not cast doubt on its overall fairness as a scheme. A complaint by an individual about his particular case can, and should, be pursued with the Director pursuant to the statutory scheme, with the long stop availability of judicial review. That remedial avenue was not taken in this case.[101]

There was some concern about the uncertain position regarding payment of compensation to those who suffer flooding while waiting for flood alleviation works to be carried out.

> [I]n principle, if it is not practicable for reasons of expense to carry out remedial works for the time being, those who enjoy the benefit of effective drainage should bear the cost of paying some compensation to those whose properties are situated lower down in the catchment area and, in consequence, have to endure intolerable sewer flooding, whether internal or external . . . the flooding is the consequence of the benefit provided to those making use of the system . . . The minority who suffer damage and disturbance as a consequence of the inadequacy of the sewerage system ought not to be required to bear an unreasonable burden.[102]

However, not finding a violation, their Lordships merely stated that this was a matter for the Director and others to reconsider in the light of the facts of the present case.[103]

---

8. Protection of the Rights and Freedoms of Others

8.1 Generally

As with the interpretation of other Convention rights, the interpretation of the 'rights and freedoms of others' in relation to respect for home is wide. The 'rights of the community' generally and the 'public interest' are frequently cited as justifications for interference. For example, in *Dennis*[104] it was held that the noise of Harrier jets flying over the claimant's estate was justifiable in the public interest but that a fair balance could not be struck without the payment of compensation to the claimants.[105] In *Lough*[106] it was argued that the development of a site in the Bankside area would interfere with the Article 8 rights of residents. Although holding that there was no interference, the Court of Appeal went on to consider questions of proportionality, noting that Article 8

---

[100] Ibid, [43].

[101] Ibid.

[102] Ibid, [45].

[103] Ibid. In *Arscott* (n 56) the Court of Appeal held that the common enemy rule, which in this case prevented an action in nuisance being brought where land had been developed so that floodwater flooded someone else's property, was compatible with Art 8 as it struck the correct balance between the interests of persons whose homes and property were affected.

[104] *Dennis* (n 53).

[105] Ibid, [63].

[106] *Lough* (n 27).

had to be seen in the context of competing rights, including rights of other landowners and the community as a whole.[107] It also noted that a certain margin of appreciation was to be granted to the public authority.[108] Here the court found that the correct balance had been struck by the Inspector, taking into consideration such matters as the removal of an unsightly building, the provision of affordable housing and the contribution to the regeneration of this area of London.[109] More specific 'rights of others' justifications are considered in the following paragraphs.

8.2 Bankruptcy—The Rights of Creditors

It has been held that the sale of a home as the result of a bankruptcy order under section 335 of the Insolvency Act 1986 provided the necessary balance between the rights of creditors and the respect for privacy and home of the debtor and served the legitimate aim of protecting the rights and freedoms of others.[110]

8.3 Public Interest in Preserving the Environment

The enforcement of planning laws often involves interfering with the right to respect for someone's home. When determining whether or not such interferences are justified, usually it is argued that the interference is proportionate to the public interest in preserving the environment. For example, in *Porter*[111] the House of Lords considered the grant of injunctions against gypsies on the application of local planning authorities under section 187B of the Town and Country Planning Act 1990 ordering the removal of mobile homes occupied on sites in breach of planning permission. The House of Lords concluded that, when asked to grant injunctive relief under section 187B, the court must consider whether, on the facts of the case, such relief was proportionate in the Convention sense and grant relief only if it judges it to be so.[112]

> Proportionality requires not only that the injunction be appropriate and necessary for the attainment of the public interest objective sought—here the safeguarding of the environment—but also that it does not impose an excessive burden on the individual whose private interests—here the gipsy's private life and home and the retention of his ethnic identity—are at stake.[113]

In striking the balance, the House of Lords held that a number of factors were present

---

[107] Ibid, [41].

[108] Ibid, [43].

[109] Ibid, [47]. See also *Mountney v Treharne* [2002] 2 FLR 406 and *Barca v Mears* [2004] EWHC (Ch) 2170, [2005] 2 FLR 1, where it was held the rights of others included the rights of a bankrupt's creditors; *Westminster City Council* (n 55), concerning the legitimate aim of reducing congestion in central London; and *Davies* (n 67), where it was held that the rights of the victims of a perpetrator of sexual abuse justified a licence condition excluding him from his own home on his release.

[110] *Ford v Alexander* [2012] EWHC 266 (Ch), [49].

[111] *Porter* (n 12).

[112] Ibid, per Lord Bingham at [37] and per Lord Steyn at [53].

[113] Ibid, quoting from the judgment of the Court of Appeal [2001] EWCA Civ 1549, [2002] 1 WLR 1359, [41].

and again endorsed the approach of the Court of Appeal.[114] The Court of Appeal had held that the judge should not grant injunctive relief unless he would be prepared, if necessary, to contemplate committing the defendant to prison for breach of the order, and that he would not be of this mind unless he had considered for himself all questions of hardship for the defendant and his family if required to move, including the availability of alternative sites, the family's health and education. Countervailing considerations were also important, such as the need to enforce planning control in the general interest, the planning history of the site, the degree and flagrancy of the postulated breach of planning control, considerations of health and safety, and previous planning decisions.[115] The Court of Appeal also highlighted the relevance of the local authority's decision to seek injunctive relief. 'They, after all, are the democratically-elected and accountable body principally responsible for planning control in their area.'[116]

A similar approach in relation to travelling show-people was taken by the Court of Appeal in *Davis*,[117] the court confirming that this was a two-stage process. First, the court must look at the planning merits of the matter and accord respect to the local planning authority's conclusions. And secondly, it should consider for itself, in the light of the planning merits and any other circumstances, whether to grant injunctive relief.[118] Here the court held that the lower court was entitled to reach the conclusion that the combination of the seriousness of the environmental damage caused by the planning violation in respect of this highly sensitive site and the appellant's deliberately unlawful conduct in commencing and persisting in it for some three years outweighed the hardship that they would suffer in having to leave it.[119] In *Webb*[120] the Divisional Court held that a court was unlikely to grant an injunction unless it had considered such questions as hardship to the defendants and family members if required to move home, as well as questions of health and education.[121] It was also necessary to consider whether there was a real prospect that a fresh application for planning permission would succeed, notwithstanding adverse decisions in relation to earlier similar applications: '[C]ircumstances may have changed, government policy and guidance may have changed, and evidence may have crystallised as to relevant matters, such as the availability of alternative sites.'[122] It is important for courts to also consider the impact on children and the best interests of the child should be the primary consideration.[123]

---

[114] *Porter* (n 12), [38]–[42].

[115] Ibid, [38]. See also *Clarke v Secretary of State for Transport, Local Government and the Regions* [2002] EWCA Civ 819.

[116] Ibid, [39]. Applications of these principles are very fact specific and there are a number of examples. See *Coates v South Bucks DC* [2004] EWCA Civ 1378, [2005] BLGR 626; *South Somerset District Council v Hughes* [2009] EWCA Civ 1245 and *Broadland District Council v Brightwell* [2010] EWCA Civ 1516; *South Cambridgeshire District Council v Flynn* [2006] EWHC 1320 (QB), [2007] JPL 440; *Bath & North East Somerset Council v Connors* [2006] EWHC 1595 (QB); *Tewkesbury Borough Council v Brown* [2006] EWHC 2697 (QB); *Dacorum Borough Council v Purcell* [2009] EWHC 742 (QB); *Medhurst v Secretary of State for Communities & Local Government* [2011] EWHC 3576 (Admin); *AZ v Secretary of State for Communities & Local Government* [2012] EWHC 3660 (Admin).

[117] *Davis* (n 13).

[118] Ibid, [37].

[119] Ibid, [64]. See also *South Buckinghamshire District Council v Cooper* [2004] EWHC (QB) 155; *Brazil v Secretary of State for Transport, Local Government and the Regions* [2001] EWHC (Admin) 991; and *Lee v Secretary of State for Local Government, Transport and the Regions*, Administrative Court, 13 March 2003, regarding Art 8 considerations at the stage of grant of planning permission.

[120] *Chiltern District Council v Webb* [2007] EWHC 1686 (QB), [2008] JPL 1323.

[121] Ibid, [38].

[122] Ibid, [41]. See also *South Cambridgeshire District Council v Price* [2008] EWHC 1234 (Admin), [5].

[123] *Doncaster Metropolitan Borough Council v AC* [2013] EWHC 45 (QB), [69].

This approach applies not only where injunctive relief is sought, but also at the stage of planning permission. For example, in *Chichester District Council*[124] the claimant gypsies sought planning permission to use land they owned as a private gypsy site with mobile homes and associated outbuildings. A majority of the Court of Appeal held that the inspector was entitled to take account of the limited environmental harm caused by the presence of the caravan sites in this location, and to balance that limited harm against the factors that weighed in the gypsies' favour.

> The latter properly included the fact that the council had, on the inspector's findings, failed to fulfil its role as local planning authority for Chichester, in pursing the national planning objective of seeking to meet the accommodation needs of gypsies.[125]

8.4 Compulsory Purchase

In *Mortell*[126] it was accepted that a compulsory purchase order was an interference with the right to respect for home. The Court of Appeal stated that the fact that a property had been in a family's ownership for generations, that an elderly person had lived all his life there and that relatives and friends lived nearby were all examples of matters that were capable of being relevant for the purposes of considering whether in any particular case a compulsory purchase order, even with financial compensation, was proportionate.[127] Such orders may sought to be justified in the interests of the rights of others or for the economic well-being of the country.[128] A decision to confirm a compulsory purchase order may be proportionate even though it does not amount to the least intrusive interference of the land owner's rights under Article 8.[129] It has also been held that a test of a compelling need in the public interest is apt to protect the human rights of those whose property is acquired compulsorily.[130]

A variety of litigation took place in relation to compulsory purchase orders made to enable development for the 2012 London Olympics to take place. It was held in *Sole*[131] that whilst the court was sympathetic to those losing their homes the importance of the Olympics and Legacy project, its 'benefits and the urgency of its timing, make the case for compulsory purchase overwhelming'.[132] Where a compulsory purchase order is made, it has been held that there is no duty to investigate:

> It is for the objectors to establish the facts which show that their human rights have been or would be interfered with and the degree of interference which that entails, such that the public authority then has to show justification sufficient to outweigh the interference demonstrated.[133]

---

[124] *Chichester District Council* (n 73).
[125] Ibid, [91]. See also *R (on the application of Evans) v First Secretary of State* [2005] EWHC (Admin) 149.
[126] *R (Mortell) v Secretary of State for Community & Local Government* [2009] EWCA Civ 1274.
[127] Ibid, [31]. See also *R (IA) v Secretary of State for Communities & Local Government* [2011] EWCA Civ 1253, [2012] JPL 579.
[128] *Pascoe v First Secretary of State* [2006] EWHC 2356 (Admin), [2007] 1 WLR 885.
[129] *Smith v Secretary of State for Trade & Industry* [2007] EWHC 1013 (Admin), [2008] 1 WLR 394, [42].
[130] *Maley v Secretary of State for Communities & Local Government* [2008] EWHC 2652 (Admin), [75]. See also *Braithwaite v Secretary of State for Communities & Local Government* [2012] EWHC 2835 (Admin), [2013] JPL 312.
[131] *Sole v Secretary of State for Trade & Industry* [2007] EWHC 1527 (Admin), [33].
[132] Ibid, [68].
[133] *Maley v Secretary of State for Communities & Local Government* [2008] EWHC 2652 (Admin).

8.5 Proceedings for Possession

8.5.1 Generally—Conflicting Jurisprudence

As discussed, it has been established that any attempt to evict a person, whether directly, indirectly or by process of law, from his or her home is an interference with the right to respect for home.[134] However, until recently, the correct approach to the application of Article 8(2) in such cases was not clear. In *Qazi*[135] a majority of the House of Lords concluded that Article 8(2) was met where the law afforded an unqualified right to possession on proof that the tenancy had been terminated. It found that such interference with the right to respect for home which came from the application of the law enabling the public authority landlord to recover possession did not violate the essence of the right to respect for the home.[136] Both Lords Bingham and Steyn dissented on this point, holding that the domestic law procedures should be subjected to scrutiny for conformity with the Article 8(2) standards and the issue of justification remitted to the county court. Mr Qazi's application to the ECtHR was declared inadmissible. However, in *Connors v United Kingdom*[137] the issue returned to the ECtHR, and in *Kay*[138] the House of Lords reconsidered the jurisprudence accordingly. Once again, the House of Lords was divided on the correct approach. Lord Hope, in the majority,[139] accepted that the reasoning in *Qazi* had to be modified slightly in the light of *Connors*.[140] In his view, where an order for possession was made in accordance with domestic property law, the essence of Article 8(1) would not be violated and Article 8(2) did not have to be considered by the county court as the law itself provided the answer to that question: 'The only matter which the court needs to consider is whether the requirements of the law and the procedural safeguards which it lays down for the protection of the occupier have been satisfied.'[141]

However, there was allowance made for special cases where special consideration of Article 8 interests may be required. In the majority's view, a defence which did not challenge the law under which the possession order was sought as being incompatible with Article 8 should be struck out.[142] Lord Bingham, in the minority,[143] held that Strasbourg jurisprudence provided that Article 8(2) prohibited interference by a public authority with Article 8(1) rights unless the excepting conditions were satisfied.

> Compliance with domestic property law is a necessary excepting condition but not a sufficient one, since the other conditions must also be met, notably that the interference must answer a pressing social need and be proportionate to the legitimate aim which it is sought to achieve.[144]

However, he was careful to point out that nothing in his opinion must be taken as

---

[134] *Qazi* (n 1).
[135] Ibid.
[136] Ibid, [83].
[137] *Connors v United Kingdom* (2005) 40 EHRR 9.
[138] *Kay v Lambeth London Borough Council* [2006] UKHL 10, [2006] 2 AC 465.
[139] Lord Hope, Lord Scott, Baroness Hale, Lord Brown.
[140] Ibid, [64].
[141] Ibid, [72].
[142] Ibid, [110].
[143] Including Lord Bingham, Lord Nicholls and Lord Walker.
[144] Ibid, [28].

applying to any landlord or owner who was not a public authority.[145] He held that it necessarily followed that where a public authority sought to evict a person from premises which he occupied as a home, that person must be given a 'fair opportunity to contend that the excepting conditions in article 8(2) have not been met on the facts of his case'.[146] He held that if the occupier wished to raise an Article 8 defence to prevent or defer the making of a possession order, it was for him to do so and the public authority must rebut the claim if called upon to do so. 'In the overwhelming majority of cases this will be in no way burdensome. In rare and exceptional cases, it will not be futile.'[147] In the view of the minority, an order for possession could be resisted on one of two grounds: the law which required the court to make a possession order was incompatible with Article 8; or having regard to the occupier's personal circumstances, the local authority's exercise of its power to seek a possession order was an unlawful act within the meaning of section 6.[148]

The House of Lords considered the issue once again in *Doherty*.[149] Here the local authority sought to obtain a summary order for possession against an occupier of a site that it owned which had been used for many years as a gipsy and travellers' caravan site. This occupier's licence had come to an end and he had no enforceable right to remain there under English property law but claimed his removal would violate his rights under Article 8. *Kay* and *Connors* were once again considered as well as a new judgment of the ECtHR in *McCann v United Kingdom*[150] where it held that, as in *Connors*, the procedural safeguards required by Article 8 for the assessment of the proportionality of the interference were not met by the possibility for the applicant to apply for judicial review.[151] It did not accept that the grant of the right to the occupier to raise an issue under Article 8 would have serious consequences for the functioning of the system or for the domestic law or landlord and tenant.[152]

The House of Lords declined the opportunity to abandon the reasoning of the majority in *Kay* in favour of the reasoning of the minority. Lord Hope observed that the judgment of the ECtHR could be given effect by developing the reasoning of the majority in *Kay*.[153] In his view, the ECtHR in *McCann* had not appreciated the real problems that may be caused by departing from the majority view in *Kay* in favour of the minority.[154] 'Unless parameters or guidelines are set down, the judgment in each case will be a subjective one.'[155] Furthermore, his view remained that acts authorised by primary legislation, could only be dealt with under section 6(2) of the HRA. 'Incompatible primary legislation remains fully effective unless and until it has been repealed or modified.'[156] He confirmed the basic rule remained that such interference with the right to respect for home as may flow from the application of the law which enabled a public

---

[145] Ibid, [28].
[146] Ibid, [29].
[147] Ibid, [29].
[148] Ibid, [39].
[149] *Doherty v Birmingham City Council* [2008] UKHL 57, [2008] 3 WLR 636.
[150] *McCann v United Kingdom* (2008) 47 EHRR 40.
[151] Ibid, [53].
[152] Ibid, [54].
[153] Ibid, [19].
[154] Ibid, [20].
[155] Ibid, [20].
[156] Ibid, [21].

authority to exercise its unqualified right to possession did not violate the essence of the Convention right. He continued:

> Unless the legislation itself can be attacked, this is conclusion which can be applied to all cases of this type generally. It is not open to the court, once it has decided in any individual case that the effect of the legislation is that the public authority's right to possession is unqualified, to hold that the exercise of that right should be denied because of the occupier's personal circumstances.[157]

To modify the conclusion of the majority in *Kay*, he held that special consideration to the needs of gipsies and their different lifestyle required provision for a defence to a claim for possession that the decision to evict was justified by a pressing social need and was proportionate.[158] He would have made a declaration of incompatibility here but the law was already to be amended. He repeated his view in *Kay* that a defence to a possession order which did not challenge the law under which it was sought but was based only on the personal circumstances of the occupier should be struck out. If the law was challenged, the question was then whether the incompatibility can be removed through exercise of powers under the HRA utilising either sections 3 or 4.[159] If this was not possible, in his view judicial review might be sought.[160] In lengthy judgments, the other members of the House of Lords reached similar conclusions.

8.5.2 The Current Approach to Proceedings for Possession: Pinnock and Powell

Once again, the issue was considered by the Supreme Court in *Pinnock*,[161] although to add some much needed clarity on this occasion the members of the Supreme Court all contributed to a joint unanimous judgment. The question in this appeal was whether Article 8 required a court, asked to make an order for possession under section 143D(2) of the Housing Act 1996 against a person occupying premises under a demoted tenancy, to have the power to consider whether the order would be necessary in a democratic society and, if so, whether section 143D(2) was compatible with Article 8 of the ECHR. The Supreme Court answered both questions in the affirmative although it was made clear that nothing in the judgment was intended to bear on cases where the person seeking the order for possession was a private landowner.[162] In the appeal the Council had sought possession from secure tenants on the ground of serious anti-social behaviour in breach of the covenants in the tenancy.

By contrast to previous authority, the Supreme Court concluded that the jurisprudence of the ECtHR[163] required that before making an order for possession of property which consisted of a person's home, pursuant to a claim made by a local authority, or other public authority, a domestic court should be able to consider the proportionality

---

[157] Ibid, [22].
[158] Ibid, [33].
[159] Ibid, [42]–[43].
[160] Ibid, [52].
[161] *Manchester City Council v Pinnock* [2010] UKSC 45, [2010] 3 WLR 1441.
[162] Ibid, [4].
[163] *Connors v UK* (2004) 40 EHRR 189; *Blečić v Croatia* (2004) 41 EHRR 185; *McCann v UK* (2008) 47 EHRR 913; *Ćosić v Croatia* 15 January 2009; *Zehentner v Austria* 16 July 2009; *Paulić v Croatia* 22 October 2009; *Kay v United Kingdom* (2012) 54 EHRR 30.

of evicting that person from his home under Article 8 and, in the process of doing so, resolve any relevant factual disputes between the parties.[164] The Supreme Court held that from the jurisprudence of the ECtHR it was established that any person at risk of being dispossessed of his home at the suit of a local authority should in principle have the right to raise the question of the proportionality of the measure, 'and to have it determined by an independent tribunal in the light of article 8, even if his right of occupation under domestic law has come to an end'.[165]

It also held that the case law indicated that a judicial procedure limited to addressing the proportionality of the measure through traditional judicial review was inadequate as it was not appropriate for resolving sensitive factual issues.[166] Where the measure included proceedings involving more than one stage, the proceedings as a whole had to be considered to see if Article 8 had been complied with. The Supreme Court also concluded that the ECtHR jurisprudence indicated that if a court found that it would be disproportionate to evict a person from his home notwithstanding the fact that he had no domestic right to remain there, it was unlawful to evict him so long as the conclusion remained.[167] It also stated that whilst it was not a point of principle, ECtHR jurisprudence 'indicated that it was only in exceptional cases that Art.8 would give a right to continued possession'.[168]

Taking into account the ECtHR jurisprudence, the Supreme Court held that it should be followed given that it was a clear and constant line of decisions whose effect was 'not inconsistent with some fundamental substantive or procedural aspect of our law, and whose reasoning does not appeal to overlook or misunderstand some argument or point of principle'.[169]

The judgments in *Qazi*, *Kay* and *Doherty* were overruled, the Supreme Court holding that the minority view in *Kay* should now be the view applied.[170]

[I]f our law is to be compatible with article 8, where a court is asked to make an order for possession of a person's home at the suit of a local authority, the court must have the power to assess the proportionality of making the order, and, in making that assessment, to resolve any relevant dispute of fact.[171]

The Supreme Court also held that it was unsafe and unhelpful to invoke exceptionality as a guide as exceptionality was an outcome and there may be more cases than the ECtHR or Lord Bingham supposed 'where article 8 could reasonably be invoked by a residential tenant'.[172] It preferred to express the position slightly differently:

The question is always whether the eviction is a proportionate means of achieving a legitimate aim. Where a person has no right in domestic law to remain in occupation of his home, the proportionality of making an order for possession at the suit of the local authority will be supported not merely by the fact that it would serve to vindicate the authority's ownership rights. It will also, at least normally, be supported by the fact that it would enable the authority to

---

[164] *Pinnock* (n 161), [21].
[165] Ibid, [45].
[166] Ibid, [45].
[167] Ibid, [45].
[168] Ibid, [45].
[169] Ibid, [48].
[170] Ibid, [49].
[171] Ibid, [49].
[172] Ibid, [51].

comply with its duties in relation to the distribution and management of its housing stock. ... Furthermore, in many cases ... other cogent reasons, such as the need to remove a source of nuisance to neighbours, may support the proportionality of dispossessing the occupiers.[173]

It appreciated that to require the local authority routinely to plead that the possession order sought was justified would in the majority of cases be burdensome and futile. It stated that the fact the local authority was entitled to possession would be a strong factor in support of proportionality.[174] It found that requiring the court to decide on proportionality of an order for possession presented no difficulties of principle or practice in relation to secure tenancies as there was already a requirement of reasonableness.[175] However, it appreciated that problems may arise where there was no requirement of reasonableness and an unqualified right to an order for possession. It noted that the implications of this would have to be worked out by judges in the county court.[176] This may justify an extended period for possession or may require certain statutory and procedural provisions to be revisited.[177] It also noted that proportionality was more likely to be a relevant issue in respect of occupants who were vulnerable.[178]

The present appeal concerned application of the principles to an order possession made against a demoted tenant. Construing section 143D of the Housing Act 1996, it found that section 3 of the HRA should be utilised to read the section as not excluding the power of a court to consider proportionality under Article 8.[179] It concluded that once it was open to a demoted tenant to seek judicial review of a landlord's decision, it was open to a tenant to challenge that decision on the ground that it would be disproportionate. The court considering such a challenge had to have power to make its own assessment of the relevant facts.[180] '[S]ection 143D(2) should be read as allowing the court to exercise the powers which are necessary to consider and, where appropriate, to give effect to, any article 8 defence which the defendant raises in the possession proceedings.[181]

It held that section 7(1)(b) conferred the necessary jurisdiction on County Court judges when it was necessary for them to deal with a defence which relied on Article 8.[182] It stated that the tenant should be entitled to raise that contention in the possession proceedings themselves, even if they are in the County Court.[183] It also found that section 6(2) of the HRA had no application to the decision of a local authority to bring or continue possession proceedings against a demoted tenant.[184] It concluded here that the order for possession was proportionate given the history of crime, nuisance and harassment on the part of those living a the property.[185]

The most recent consideration by the Supreme Court of these issues was in *Powell*.[186]

---

[173] Ibid, [52].
[174] Ibid, [53].
[175] Ibid, [55].
[176] Ibid, [57].
[177] Ibid, [62]–[63].
[178] Ibid, [64].
[179] Ibid, [70].
[180] Ibid, [73].
[181] Ibid, [79].
[182] Ibid, [80].
[183] Ibid, [81].
[184] Ibid, [101].
[185] Ibid, [126].
[186] *Hounslow London Borough Council v Powell* [2011] UKSC 8, [2011] 2 WLR 287.

The appeals concerned possession proceedings brought where the occupier was not a secure tenant. Two were introductory tenancies, one was a person granted a licence under the homelessness regime. Common to all appeals was the claim that the property the subject of proceedings of possession was their home, and that to avoid a breach of Article 8 the interference had to be justified under Article 8(2). The Supreme Court confirmed that the principles established in *Pinnock* applied to all cases where a local authority sought possession in respect of a property that constituted a person's home— including introductory tenancies and those granted under the homelessness regime.

The Supreme Court reiterated that the first question in each case was whether the property constituted the defendant's home for the purposes of Article 8.[187] It also stated that in the great majority of cases, the local authority need not plead the precise reasons why it sought possession but if an Article 8 defence was raised, it may wish to plead a more precise case in reply.[188] It confirmed that where domestic law imposed no requirement of reasonableness, and gave an unqualified right to an order for possession, there was a requirement for an independent determination by a court of the issue of proportionality.[189] It also held that the threshold for raising an arguable case on proportionality was a high one which would succeed only in a small proportion of cases.[190] Proportionality of making the order will be supported by the local authority's ownership rights and enable the authority to comply with its public duties in relation to the allocation and management of its housing stock.[191]

> [T]here will be no need, in the overwhelming majority of cases, for the local authority to explain and justify its reasons for seeking a possession order. ... The court need be concerned only with the occupier's personal circumstances and any factual objections she may raise and, in the light only of what view it takes of them, with the question whether making the order for possession would be lawful and proportionate.[192]

It also confirmed that the defence must be seriously arguable before a judge should adjourn a case for further consideration of lawfulness and proportionality.[193] In relation to introductory tenancies, the Supreme Court found that section 127(2) of the Housing Act 1996 afforded a court no discretion as to making an order for possession. However, utilising section 3 of the HRA, it was possible to read the section to permit the tenant to raise his Article 8 rights.[194] This was not necessary in relation to section 89 of the Housing Act 1980 as it was concluded that the time limit set was not incompatible with Article 8.[195]

---

[187] Ibid, per Lord Hope at [33].
[188] Ibid, [34].
[189] Ibid, [34].
[190] Ibid, [35].
[191] Ibid, [36].
[192] Ibid, [37].
[193] Ibid, [41].
[194] Ibid, [56].
[195] Ibid, [64]. See further: S Nield, ;Article 8 Respect for Home: A Human Property Right?' (2013) 24 *King's Law Journal* 147; D Cowan and C Hunter, 'Yeah But, No But – Pinnock and Powell in the Supreme Court' (2012) 75 *Modern Law Review* 78; A Latham, 'Taking Without Speaking, Hearing Without Listening? Evictions, the Law Lords and the European Court of Human Rights' [2011] *Public Law* 730.

8.5.3 *Lower Courts post* Pinnock

Any lower court authority pre-dating *Pinnock*, decided on 3 November 2010, is now of dubious authority and no longer discussed in this chapter. However, there are now a number of judgments interpreting and applying the principles confirmed by the Supreme Court where the lower courts are applying the principles established in *Pinnock* in a variety of contexts.

In *Scott*[196] the Court of Appeal applied the principles where a council sought proceedings for possession against an introductory tenant (sections 124–30 Housing Act 1996) for rent arrears and to a housing association seeking possession from an assured shorthold tenant (sections 19A–21 Housing Act 1988) following allegations of nuisance. It noted that in both instances the tenant would rarely have a domestic law defence against a possession claim. It held that the effect of *Pinnock* was that it would only be in very highly exceptional cases that it would be appropriate for the court to consider a proportionality argument although 'exceptionality is an outcome and not a guide'.[197] In the present appeals it held that the facts concerning the introductory tenant got nowhere near justifying the contention that it would be disproportionate for the council to obtain possession.[198] In relation to the shorthold tenant, it also held that the appellant had not established a strong enough case to justify a hearing on proportionality.[199] It warned against giving general guidance on the facts of any one case, but held that in such cases, judges should be rigorous in ensuring that only relevant matters are taken into account on the proportionality issue, and should not let sympathy for a particular tenant lower the threshold identified by Lord Hope in *Powell*. In its view, the facts needed to be exceptional before an Article 8 case could have a real prospect of success.[200] It held that it was desirable for a judge to consider at an early stage whether the tenant had an arguable case on Article 8 proportionality: 'If it is a case which cannot succeed, then it should not be allowed to take up further court time and expense to the parties, and should not be allowed to delay the landlord's right to possession.'[201]

In *Lloyd*[202] the Court of Appeal also held that based on *Pinnock* it was only in highly exceptional circumstances that a court should consider a proportionality argument in relation to introductory tenants. And that this was even more true in the case of someone who had entered the property as a trespasser and remained a trespasser.[203] Here the defendant was not merely a trespasser but had never had any right to occupy the premises. It was accepted that it was wrong to say that it could never be right for the court to permit a person, who had never been more than a trespasser, to invoke Article 8 as a defence. But such a person seeking to raise an Article 8 argument would 'face a very uphill task' and would require the 'most extraordinarily exceptional circumstances'.[204] It found here that the defendant was well short of being able to cross the high threshold which an occupier with no domestic legal right to occupy his home

---

[196] *Corby Borough Council v Scott* [2012] EWCA Civ 276, [2012] HLR 23.
[197] Ibid, [18].
[198] Ibid, [24].
[199] Ibid, [33].
[200] Ibid, [35].
[201] Ibid, [39]. See also *Telchadder v Wickland (Holdings) Ltd* [2012] EWCA Civ 635, [2012] HLR 35.
[202] *Birmingham City Council v Lloyd* [2012] EWCA Civ 969, [2012] HLR 44.
[203] Ibid, [12].
[204] Ibid, [18].

had to cross in order to invoke Article 8.[205] Procedurally it held that where an Article 8 defence is raised, the judge should identify the grounds on which it was said to be based, so it could assess whether there was a real prospect of success.[206] In its view it was not appropriate to list for a one-day hearing without seeing the defence.

In West[207] the Court of Appeal explained that the reason why the threshold was so high lay in the public policy and public benefit inherent in the functions of the housing authority in dealing with its housing stock 'a precious and limited resource'.[208] It held that local authorities held their housing stock for the benefit of the whole community and they were best equipped to make management decisions about the way such stock should be administered.[209] Procedurally it also held that the court must at the earliest opportunity consider whether the Article 8 defence, as pleaded, and on the assumption that the pleaded facts are correct, reaches the threshold of seriously arguable. If it does not, it must be dismissed or struck out.[210] It also found it difficult to imagine circumstances in which the defendant, with no legal right to remain, could obtain an unlimited and unconditional right to remain from Article 8.[211] It observed as follows:

> Otherwise, the effect of the Article 8 defence would be that the Court would have assumed the local authority's function of allocating its housing stock, preferring the right of the defendant to remain, without any tenancy or contract, over all the other people entitled to rely on the local authority's statutory housing duties and without the benefit of any knowledge of who those people are and their circumstances and of other relevant matters which would properly guide the local authority in housing management decisions.[212]

In the present case where the defendant and his family had stayed on in a flat following his grandmother's death (a secure tenant), it found no exceptional circumstances.[213]

Finally, in CN[214] the Court of Appeal held that the issue of proportionality need only be considered by the court if it was raised in the proceedings by or on behalf of the occupier. It confirmed that a court considering a judicial review challenge in this field had the power to assess the proportionality of the measure and could make its own assessment of any relevant facts which were in dispute.[215] It also held that regard had to be had to the decision-making process as a whole[216] and that states had a wide margin of appreciation in implementing social and economic policies in matters concerning housing.[217] In the present case it held that possession proceedings were not required before eviction in all cases where temporary accommodation had been provided. In its view, the result would be to impose on local authorities and other landlords the burden of instituting legal proceedings in a very large number of cases, the vast majority of which would involve no Article 8 issue.[218]

---

[205] Ibid, [25].
[206] Ibid, [26].
[207] *Thurrock Borough Council v West* [2012] EWCA Civ 1435, [2013] HLR 5.
[208] Ibid, [25].
[209] Ibid, [25].
[210] Ibid, [30].
[211] Ibid, [31]
[212] Ibid, [31].
[213] See also *Fareham Borough Council v Miller* [2013] EWCA Civ 159, [2013] HLR 22.
[214] *R (CN) v Lewisham LBC* [2013] EWCA Civ 804.
[215] Ibid, [65].
[216] Ibid, [66].
[217] Ibid, [68].
[218] Ibid, [70].

[T]he pressure on social housing is immense. The relief sought in these cases would therefore have a real and serious impact on homeless families … the relief sought would seriously impact upon the ability of authorities to provide accommodation to those who appear to need it most.[219]

It concluded that Article 8 did not require possession proceedings before a person may be evicted from temporary accommodation occupied under licence pursuant to sections 188 or 190(2) of the Housing Act 1996.

The lower courts have considered the principles in relation to a non-secure tenant assisted as a homeless person under Part VII of the Housing Act 1996;[220] an introductory tenant under Part 5 of Chapter 1 of the Housing Act 1996 accused of anti-social behaviour;[221] a daughter who remained in occupation and argued that she should have succeeded to a public sector tenancy on the death of her mother;[222] and the claim made by a private landowner against a trespasser.[223]

---

[219] Ibid, [71].
[220] *Holmes v Westminster City Council* [2011] EWHC 2857 (QB).
[221] *Southend-On-Sea Borough Council v Armour* [2012] EWHC 3361 (QB).
[222] *Birmingham City Council v Beech* [2013] EWHC 518 (QB).
[223] *Malik v Fassenfelt* [2013] EWCA Civ 798.

14

Article 9: Freedom of Thought, Conscience and Religion

1. Introduction

Article 9 of the ECHR, which protects freedom of thought, conscience and religion, was not included in the first edition of this book as there was very little case law despite the interest in this right generated during the parliamentary debates on the Human Rights Bill. In comparison to other Convention rights, there is still not as much jurisprudence. Most claims which concern discrimination on the grounds of religion or belief are brought under the Employment Equality (Religion or Belief) Regulations 2003.[1] It has been held that the approach under the Regulations is more stringent than that which is currently applied when considering Article 9 of the ECHR and that Article 9 adds nothing to such claims.[2] However, those Article 9 claims which have been determined under the HRA have attracted considerable interest. A discussion of Article 9 jurisprudence under the HRA has therefore been included in this edition.

The importance of this Convention right should not be underestimated. As Mummery LJ has observed:

> It is probably only a matter of time … before the fundamental and pervasive character of Article 9 will be more fully revealed. If the Article means what it says, it has the potential to be far reaching in its legal, social, economic and political effects. Its subject matter (strongly held beliefs affecting what we live for and how we live) is a unique force in both uniting and dividing human beings in society.[3]

Other judges have also commented on the importance of the rights protected by Article 9. For example, in *Williamson*[4] Lord Nicholls observed:

> Religious and other beliefs and convictions are part of the humanity of every individual. They are an integral part of his personality and individuality. In a civilised society individuals

---

[1] See eg *Ladele v Islington London Borough Council* [2009] EWCA Civ 1357, [2010] 1 WLR 955.
[2] *C MBA v London Borough of Merton* EAT 13/12/2012, [2013] Eq LR 209.
[3] *Copsey v WWB Devon Clays Ltd* [2005] EWCA Civ 932, [2005] HRLR 32, [3].
[4] *R (Williamson) v Secretary of State for Education and Employment* [2005] UKHL 15, [2005] 2 AC 246.

respect each other's beliefs. This enables them to live in harmony. This is one of the hall-marks of a civilised society.[5]

Slightly more strongly worded, Pill LJ in *Stewart*[6] stated that freedom of religion was 'one of the foundations of a democratic society'. In his view, it was a 'vital element in a believer's conception of life', also implying a freedom to manifest one's religion.[7] In the same case Arden LJ held that protection of this freedom was 'essential for the continued existence of a plural and democratic society governed by the rule of law' and could be exercised 'alone or in common with others' and therefore could be claimed by a religious organisation on behalf of its adherents.[8] It is true that this is a unique aspect of Article 9 given the restrictions placed on the victim status of groups by section 7 of the HRA although it has not yet been fully tested in the courts.[9]

The task of a court adjudicating on an Article 9 claim is not simple, as Munby LJ explained in *Johns*:[10]

> Although historically this country is part of the Christian west, and although it has an estab-lished church which is Christian, there have been enormous changes in the social and reli-gious life of our country over the last century. Our society is now pluralistic and largely secular. But one aspect of its pluralism is that we also now live in a multicultural community of many faiths. One of the paradoxes of our lives is that we live in a society which has at one and the same time become both increasingly secular but also increasingly diverse in religious affiliation.[11]

Consciously or unconsciously, judges often give the impression that if the application and interpretation of Article 9 can be avoided, it will be, often by applying common law principles instead. For example, the Administrative Court declared the practice of saying public prayers at full meetings of Bideford Town Council unlawful through the application of the common law rather than the application of Article 9. The saying of prayers as part of the formal meeting of a council was not lawful under section 111 of the Local Government Act 1972 and there was no statutory power permitting the practice to continue.[12]

Finally, by way of introduction it is important to note that Article 9 is one of the two Convention rights singled out for special mention in the HRA. Section 13(1) of the HRA provides:

> If a court's determination of any question arising under this Act might affect the exercise by a religious organisation (itself or its members collectively) of the Convention right to freedom of thought, conscience and religion, it must have particular regard to the importance of that right.

---

[5] Ibid, [15].
[6] *New Testament Church of God v Stewart* [2007] EWCA Civ 1004, [2008] HRLR 2.
[7] Ibid, [43].
[8] Ibid, [58].
[9] *New Testament Church of God* concerned a group with beliefs concerning legal relations and contracts of employment.
[10] *R (Johns) v Derby City Council* [2011] EWHC 375 (Admin), [2011] 1 FLR 2094.
[11] Ibid, [38].
[12] *R (National Secular Society) v Bideford Town Council* [2012] EWHC 175 (Admin), [2012] 2 All ER 1175. See also *R (Ghai) v Newcastle City Council* [2010] EWCA Civ 59, [2010] 3 WLR 737 where the Court of Appeal determined that a Hindu could be lawfully cremated on a funeral pyre within the existing law, without resort to Art 9.

However, in common with section 12 of the HRA, section 13 has received very little judicial consideration and it is doubtful that its application by a court would make any real difference to the outcome of an Article 9 claim.

---

2. The Right to Believe

Two rights are protected by Article 9: the right to freedom of thought, conscience and religion; and the right to manifest religion or belief in worship, teaching, practice and observance. The first of these rights is absolute. The second may be subject to restriction provided this is in accordance with the limitations set out in Article 9(2). In accordance with Article 9, individuals have an absolute right to think and believe whatever they like. It has been held that it does not matter whether a belief is categorised as religious or not. 'The atheist, the agnostic, and the sceptic are as much entitled to freedom to hold and manifest their beliefs as the theist.'[13] Courts are reluctant to pass judgment on the validity or otherwise or an individual's views or beliefs. Lord Nicholls explained the position of a court in an Article 9 claim in *Williamson*:[14]

> When the genuineness of a claimant's professed belief is an issue in the proceedings the court will inquire into and decide this issue as a question of fact. This is a limited inquiry. The court is concerned to ensure an assertion of religious belief is made in good faith … neither fictitious, nor capricious, and that it is not an artifice … it is not for the court to embark on an inquiry into the asserted belief and judge its 'validity' by some objective standard such as the source material upon which the claimant founds his belief or the orthodox teaching of the religion in question or the extent to which the claimant's belief conforms to or differs from the views of others professing the same religion. Freedom of religion protects the subjective belief of an individual … religious belief is intensely personal and can easily vary from one individual to another. Each individual is at liberty to hold his own religious beliefs, however irrational or inconsistent they may seem to some, however surprising.[15]

In the same case Lord Walker stated that it was not right for a court to impose an evaluative filter at the first stage. 'For the Court to adjudicate on the seriousness, cogency and coherence of theological beliefs is …to take the Court beyond its legitimate role.'[16] For example, in *Pretty*[17] it was accepted by the House of Lords that Mrs Pretty, who suffered from motor neurone disease, a progressive degenerative illness from which she had no hope of recovery, had a sincere belief in the virtue of assisted suicide and it was agreed, as Lord Bingham observed, that she was 'free to hold and express that belief'.[18] Other examples from the case law include pacifism, vegetarianism and total abstinence

---

[13] Ibid, [24].
[14] *Williamson* (n 4).
[15] Ibid, [22].
[16] Ibid, [57]. See further P Edge, 'Determining Religion in English Courts' (2012) 1 *Oxford Journal of Law and Religion* 402.
[17] *R v Director of Public Prosecutions ex p Pretty* [2001] UKHL 61, [2002] 1 AC 800.
[18] Ibid, [31].

from alcohol.[19] Utilising Article 9 jurisprudence for the purpose of determining the scope of 'belief' in the Employment Equality (Religion or Belief) Regulations 2003, the Employment Appeals Tribunal held that a belief in man-made climate change, and the alleged resulting moral imperatives, was capable, if genuinely held, of being a philosophical belief for the purpose of the Regulations. However, in *Friend*[20] the House of Lords, without finally determining the question, was doubtful that a belief in hunting with hounds would cross the threshold required by Article 9:

> The current jurisprudence does not support the proposition that a person's belief in his right to engage in an activity which he carries on for pleasure or recreation, however fervent or passionate, can be equated with beliefs of the kind that are protected by art 9.[21]

---

3. The Right to Manifest

3.1 Recognising a Manifestation of Belief

Manifestations of religion or belief 'in worship, teaching, practice and observance' are also protected by Article 9. As Lord Nicholls has observed:

> [w]ithout this, freedom of religion would be emasculated. Invariably religious faiths call for more than belief. To a greater or lesser extent adherents are required or encouraged to act in certain ways, most obviously and directly in forms of communal or personal worship, supplication and meditation.[22]

The identification of manifestations of belief is a fact-finding function of the court and all relevant matters must be considered carefully and conscientiously.[23] The manifestation must be motivated or inspired by religion or belief but it need not be obligatory to be protected.[24] It has been held that if the act in question is sufficiently intimately linked to the applicant's religion or belief to amount to a manifestation of it, then the court should be slow to make a judgment of the importance or significance of that manifestation.[25] Familiar examples of manifestation of belief include the days and times when worship is prescribed or encouraged, the need to abstain from work on certain days, forms of dress, rituals connected with the preparation of food or drink, and the need for abstinence from all of some types of food at certain times.[26] Manifestations

---

[19] *Williamson* (n 4), per Lord Walker at [55].
[20] *Friend v Lord Advocate* [2007] UKHL 53, [2007] SLT 1209.
[21] Ibid, per Lord Bingham at [18].
[22] *Williamson* (n 4), [16].
[23] *New Testament Church of God* (n 6), per Arden LJ at [62].
[24] *R (Bashir) v Independent Adjudicator* [2011] EWHC 1108 (Admin), [2011] HRLR 30, [21].
[25] *Black v Wilkinson* [2013] EWCA Civ 820, [2013] 1 WLR 2490, [53]. See also *R v D*, Crown Court, 16/9/2013, at [15]–[17].
[26] *Williamson* (n 4), per Lord Nicholls at [17]. A form of religious dress was the subject matter of the claim in *R (Begum) v Denbigh High School* [2006] UKHL 15, [2007] 1 AC 100 although its status as a manifestation was not contested.

of belief are not as readily protected as the right to hold a belief. Laws LJ observed in *McFarlane*[27] as follows:

> The common law and ECHR Article 9 offer vigorous protection of the Christian's right (and every other person's right) to hold and express his or her beliefs. And so they should. By contrast they do not, and should not, offer any protection whatever of the substance or content of those beliefs on the ground only that they are based on religious precepts. These are twin conditions of a free society.[28]

It is clear that Article 9 does not protect 'every act motivated or inspired by a religion or belief'.[29] First it is necessary for a court to identify the nature and scope of the belief. If the belief takes the form of a perceived obligation to act in a specific way, then, 'in principle, doing that act pursuant to that belief is itself a manifestation of that belief in practice'.[30] This is so whether the perceived obligation is of a religious, ethical or social character.[31] Whilst the courts are prepared to accept almost anything as a belief, religion or matter of conscience protected by Article 9, some limits have been placed on what is accepted to be a protected manifestation of belief. Lord Walker, in *Williamson*, described this as the first necessary filter 'in order to prevent article 9 becoming unmanageably diffuse and unpredictable in its operation'.[32] As Lord Nicholls noted in the same case, when questions of manifestation arise, 'a belief must satisfy some modest, objective minimum requirements'.[33] His Lordship held that this was implicit in Article 9 and comparable guarantees in other human rights instruments. Lord Nicholls set out these minimum requirements as follows:

> The belief must be consistent with basic standards of human dignity or integrity. Manifestation of a religious belief, for instance, which involved subjecting others to torture or inhuman punishment would not qualify for protection. The belief must relate to matters more than merely trivial. It must possess an adequate degree of seriousness and importance ... it must be a belief on a fundamental problem. With religious belief this requisite is readily satisfied. The belief must also be coherent in the sense of being intelligible and capable of being understood ... too much should not be demanded in this regard. Typically, religion involves belief in the supernatural. It is not always susceptible to lucid exposition or, still less, rational justification.[34]

No priority is afforded to any particular religion—in particular, the Christian religion. As Laws LJ has observed:

> The general law may of course protect a particular social or moral position which is espoused by Christianity, not because of its religious imprimatur, but on the footing that in reason its merits commend themselves. ... But the conferment of any legal protection or preference upon a particular substantive moral position on the ground only that it is espoused by the adherents of a particular faith, however long its tradition, however rich its culture, is deeply unprincipled. It imposes compulsory law, not to advance the general good on objective grounds, but to give effect to the force of subjective opinion. This must be so, since in the eye

---

[27] *McFarlane v Relate Avon Ltd* [2010] EWCA Civ 880, [2010] IRLR 872.
[28] Ibid, [22].
[29] *Williamson* (n 4), [30].
[30] *Williamson* (n 4), per Lord Nicholls at [32].
[31] Ibid.
[32] Ibid, [62].
[33] Ibid, [23].
[34] Ibid, [23].

of everyone save the believer, religious faith is necessarily subjective, being incommunicable by any kind or proof or evidence.[35]

In Laws LJ's view, the precepts of any one religion, could not, 'by force of their religious origins, sound any louder in the general law than the precepts of any other'. In his view if this occurred, 'those out in the cold would be less than citizens; and our constitution would be on the way to a theocracy, which is of necessity autocratic'.[36] This view has been supported in other judgments. In *Newcastle City Council v Z*[37] the Family Court held as follows:

> A secular judge must be wary of straying across the well recognised divide between church and state. It is not for a judge to weigh one religion against another. The court recognises no religious distinctions and generally speaking passes no judgment on religious beliefs or on the tenets, doctrines or rules of any particular section of society. All are entitled to equal respect, whether in times of peace or, as at present, amidst the clash of arms.[38]

It does not matter if the belief is religious or non religious. Both must satisfy the minimum requirements. For the manifestation of a non-religious belief to be protected by Article 9, it must relate to an aspect of human life or behaviour 'of comparable importance to that normally found with religious beliefs'.[39]

3.2 Manifestations within the Protection of Article 9

Claims under the HRA have raised a variety of practices which have been accepted, with little discussion, as coming within the scope of a manifestation of belief. These have included: running a hotel along Christian principles;[40] running a bed and breakfast in way which reflects religious and moral values;[41] orthodox Jewish relatives seeking the exhumation and reburial of a relative in a Jewish cemetery in accordance with Jewish law;[42] a widow seeking the exhumation of her husband from consecrated ground as both he and she were humanists;[43] the sending of photographs to pharmacists of aborted foetuses by a Roman Catholic (this claim was mostly considered as an Article 10 freedom of expression claim);[44] a female Muslim pupil's decision to wear at school the niqab, a veil that covered her entire face and head save for her eyes;[45] a female Muslim pupil's decision to wear at school a jilbab, a long coat-like garment;[46] and a Muslim prisoner's fasting prior to a Court of Appeal appearance as part of his religious preparation for that hearing.[47] In *Ghai*[48] the Administrative Court accepted that the

---

[35] *McFarlane* (n 27), [23].
[36] Ibid, [24].
[37] *Newcastle City Council v Z* [2005] EWHC 1490 (Fam), [2007] 1 FLR 861.
[38] Ibid, [53].
[39] *Williamson* (n 4), per Lord Nicholls at [24].
[40] *Bull v Hall* [2012] EWCA Civ 83, [2012] 2 All ER 1017.
[41] *Black* (n 25).
[42] *In Re Durrington Cemetery* [2000] 3 WLR 1322.
[43] *In Re Crawley Green Road Cemetery, Luton* [2001] 2 WLR 1175.
[44] *Connolly v Director of Public Prosecutions* [2007] EWHC 237 (Admin), [2007] 2 All ER 1012.
[45] *R (X) v Headteachers and Governors of Y School* [2007] EWHC 298 (Admin), [2008] 1 All ER 249.
[46] *R (Begum) v Governors of Denbigh High School* [2005] 2 WLR 3372.
[47] *Bashir* (n 24).
[48] *Ghai v Newcastle City Council* [2009] EWHC 978 (Admin).

Hindu claimant's genuine belief that he must be cremated on an open-air funeral pyre was within the protection of Article 9. However, on appeal, the Court of Appeal did not consider Article 9 as it found there was nothing in existing legislation preventing the cremation of the claimant in accordance with his wishes.[49]

Controversially, in *Re Christian Institute*[50] it was accepted by the High Court, with little discussion, that the orthodox Christian belief that the practice of homosexuality was sinful, manifested by teaching, practice and observance 'to maintain the choice not to accept, endorse or encourage homosexuality', was not a belief unworthy of recognition and Article 9 was engaged.[51] In other judgments the question of manifestation has given rise to considerable discussion. One example was the opposition to the slaughter of their temple bullock, to prevent bovine tuberculosis, by the Community of the Many Names of God.[52] The Community was committed to the preservation of life and regarded the slaughter of the bullock as a sacrilege and a desecration of their temple.[53] The manifestation eventually recognised for protection by Article 9 was keeping the bullock as the Community's temple bull and doing all that they could to ensure that it lived on to a natural death.[54] Another example is *Stewart*[55] where the Court of Appeal accepted that in determining whether or not a minister of religion was an employee, Article 9 required a different approach from that in a context in which religious practices and observances were not present. Here the manifestation was one of a religious organisation rather than an individual but, nevertheless, a religious organisation was also able enjoy the protection of Article 9 and be 'allowed to function peacefully and free from arbitrary state intervention'.[56] This required that respect be given to the faith and doctrine of the particular church, 'which may run counter to there being a relationship enforceable at law between the priest, curate or minister and the church'.[57] In the view of the Court of Appeal, the religious beliefs of a community may be such that their manifestation does not involve the creation of a relationship enforceable at law between members of the religious community and one of their number appointed to minister to the others:

> The law should not readily impose a legal relationship on members of a religious community which would be contrary to their religious beliefs. These beliefs and practices may be such, in the context of a particular church, that no intention to create legal relations is present.[58]

In determining the content of the manifestation, it was held that the contents of a church's book of rules was relevant to the question of whether there was an intention to create legal relations and throw light on whether the relationship is 'capable of formulation in terms of a contract between identifiable parties'.[59] Nevertheless, in the

---

[49] *R (Ghai) v Newcastle City Council* [2010] EWCA Civ 59, [2010] 3 WLR 737.
[50] *Re Christian Institute* [2007] NIQB 66, [2008] NI 86.
[51] Ibid, [50].
[52] *R (Suryananda) v Welsh Ministers* [2007] EWCA Civ 893.
[53] Ibid, [83].
[54] Ibid, [84].
[55] *New Testament Church of God* (n 6).
[56] Ibid, [60].
[57] Ibid, [46].
[58] Ibid, [47].
[59] Ibid, [49].

present case it concluded that there was an intention to create legal relations and that the contract was a contract of employment.[60]

One of the most difficult questions to date concerning manifestation arose in *Williamson*[61] where the claimants claimed to speak on behalf of a large body of the Christian community in the UK whose fundamental beliefs included a belief that part of the duty of education in the Christian context was that teachers should be able to stand in the place of parents and administer physical punishment to children who were guilty of indiscipline. They rejected the general standards of state education available as not fitting their religious and moral beliefs. Their beliefs were based on their interpretation of certain passages in the Bible. The House of Lords held that it was difficult to see how all corporal punishment of children, however mildly administered, was of its nature so contrary to a child's integrity that a belief in its infliction is necessarily excluded from the protection of Article 9. Lord Nicholls observed as follows:

> It is difficult to see how corporal punishment, administered in circumstances and in a way which does not violate articles 3 or 8, can at the same time be so contrary to personal integrity that belief in its administration is ipso facto excluded from the scope of article 9.[62]

He held that where the act of inflicting corporal punishment was pursuant to a deeply held conviction that this form of punishment was divinely ordained as being in the best interests of the child 'the act of administering corporal punishment on a child is, for that person, an expression of his conviction in practice'.[63] In the present case he concluded that when parents administered corporal punishment to their children in accordance with their beliefs, or when they authorised the school to administer corporal punishment, they were manifesting their beliefs and Article 9 was engaged.[64] With respect to teachers, it was held that their beliefs were ancillary to those of the parents so their beliefs did not call for separate consideration from those of the parents.[65]

3.3 Manifestations Outside of the Protection of Article 9

Whilst it is rare, on occasion a court will find a particular manifestation does not come within the scope of Article 9. For example, in *Pretty*[66] although it was accepted that Mrs Pretty was free to hold and express her belief in assisted suicide, this could not found a requirement that her husband should be absolved from the consequences of conduct which, although it would be consistent with her belief, was proscribed by the criminal law.[67] Lord Steyn observed that Article 9 was 'never intended to give individuals a right to perform any acts in pursuance of whatever beliefs they may hold'.[68]

---

[60] Ibid, [50]. See also *President of the Methodist Conference v Preston* [2011] EWCA Civ 1581, [2012] 2 All ER 934.

[61] *Williamson* (n 4).

[62] Ibid, [27].

[63] Ibid, [34].

[64] Ibid, [35]. It was held that Art 2 of Protocol No 1 to the ECHR was also engaged.

[65] Ibid, per Lord Nicholls at [37].

[66] *Pretty* (n 17).

[67] Ibid, per Lord Bingham at [31]. The ECtHR agreed with this conclusion in *Pretty v UK* (2002) 35 EHRR 1.

[68] *Pretty* (n 17), [63]. See also *R (Playfoot) v Millais School Governing Body* [2007] EWHC 1698 (Admin), [2007] HRLR 34 where the Administrative Court held that the claimant was not manifesting her belief in sexual abstinence before marriage by wearing a ring.

3.4 Conscientious Objection

The House of Lords has held that Article 9 does not entail a right of conscientious objection to refuse military service.[69] Nevertheless, in a later case the Court of Appeal considered the issue at length. Whilst it recognised that, intuitively, a matter of conscience lay well within the ambit of Article 9, difficulties with this interpretation were caused by Article 4 of the ECHR which makes explicit mention of conscientious objection and that conscientious objectors may be required to perform civilian service in substitution for compulsory military service.[70] Considering Strasbourg jurisprudence, in particular *Thlimmenos v Greece*,[71] it stated as follows:

> We fear to trespass on this ground, but, while fully agreeing that there has been no decision that conscientious objection has led to a breach of article 9, we would diffidently suggest that the whole of the Commission, and not merely the minority report, reasoned that the state's reaction to conscientious objection both could and had in that case led to an interference with the applicant's right to manifest his religion.[72]

However, it was not willing to overrule the judgment of the House of Lords[73] and concluded that Article 9 could not provide a defence to the appellant's charge of being absent without leave.[74] Nevertheless, it did make some observation on the questions of manifestation and interference. With respect to manifestation of belief, it held that a conscientious objector had not manifested his belief until he expressed it in some way to his service. Whilst in some circumstances it held that the mere act of absence or desertion could be such an expression, where the background was one of volunteer service, and the call-out was on the basis that there may be an exception on compassionate grounds, there was no manifestation of belief until the individual had informed his service of it, and done so in a formal way.[75] This also affected the question of interference, the court finding that there was no material interference until he had formally applied for discharge as a conscientious objector.[76]

It found that the appellant's right to invoke a claim to conscientious objection was prescribed by law.[77] It also found that any interference which may have arisen was justified:

> [T]here could be no breach under article 9 arising from the fact that the appellant was arrested, prosecuted, convicted and (very mildly) punished for being absent without leave before any indication whatsoever of any conscientious objection, despite every opportunity of making his concerns known, and where, despite raising the issue in conversations during his absence, he never formally applied to be treated as a conscientious objector prior to his arrest, prosecution or at any relevant time.[78]

This analysis by the Court of Appeal is now particularly useful as the ECtHR has held that Article 9 does encompass a right to conscientious objection. In *Bayatyan*

---

[69] *Sepet v Secretary of State for the Home Department* [2003] UKHL 15, [2003] 1 WLR 856.
[70] *Khan v Royal Air Force Summary Appeal Court* [2004] EWHC 2230 (Admin), [2004] HRLR 40, [68].
[71] *Thlimmenos v Greece* (2001) 31 EHRR 15.
[72] *Khan* (n 70), [88].
[73] Ibid, [89].
[74] Ibid, [92].
[75] Ibid, [64].
[76] Ibid, [65].
[77] Ibid, [53].
[78] Ibid, [60].

v Armenia[79] the Grand Chamber of the ECtHR held that Article 9 could afford a foundation for a refusal to accept conscription into the armed forces on grounds of conscientious objection:

> [O]pposition to military service, where it is motivated by a serious and insurmountable conflict between the obligation to serve in the army and a person's conscience or his deeply and genuinely held religious or other beliefs, constitutes a conviction or belief of sufficient cogency, seriousness, cohesion and importance to attract the guarantees of Article 9[80]

This judgment was adopted by the Court Martial Appeal Court in *Lyons*[81] where it was confirmed that Article 9 would apply to a person who had engaged in military service as a volunteer but had subsequently had a change of mind on grounds of conscience. It held that the fact that a person has volunteered for military service, and so voluntarily accepted the responsibilities which go with such service, may be highly material when considering the balance to be struck between the 'individual's conscience and the interest of public safety, the protection of public order and the protection of the rights of others'.[82] It concluded that the present procedures for dealing with claims of conscientious objection were prescribed by law and necessary in the interests of public safety, the protection of public order and the protection of others. It stated as follows:

> A person who voluntarily enters military service undertakes serious responsibilities potentially involving the lives and safety of others. If he seeks to be discharged from further service on the ground of conscientious objection, it is right that there should be a proper process for deciding whether his claim is well-founded. Until that has been established it is necessary and just that he should continue to be subject to the requirements of military service and military discipline.[83]

In the present case it concluded that it was compatible with Article 9 for the appellant to be convicted of intentionally disobeying a lawful command when he applied for discharge from the Royal Navy on grounds that he was a conscientious objector rather than be deployed to Afghanistan.

---

4. Interference with Manifestation of Belief

4.1 Difficulties in Establishing an Interference with Manifestation of Belief

To date an interference with belief has not been considered in a claim under the HRA. However, the concept of interference with manifestation of belief has been the subject

---

[79] *Bayatyan v Armenia* (2012) 54 EHRR 15.
[80] Ibid, [110]. See further P Munzy, 'Bayatyan v Armenia: The Grand Chamber Renders a Grand Judgment' (2012) *Human Rights Law Review* 135.
[81] *R v Lyons* [2011] EWCA Crim 2808.
[82] Ibid, [28].
[83] Ibid, [31].

of extensive judicial, and academic, analysis.[84] It is clear that an infringement of manifestation of belief is not established where the alleged interference merely renders the manifestation of belief less easy or convenient[85] or does not really interfere with it at all. For example in *Friend*[86] the House of Lords held that assuming the claimant's belief in hunting was protected, his freedom to hold and impart information about the views that he held about hunting and to manifest his beliefs by the wearing of traditional hunting dress in public was not really an issue:

> The Act does not compel him to act contrary to his conscience or to refrain from holding and giving visible expression to his beliefs about the practice of hunting in the way he dresses. The activities which he is permitted to carry on have been limited to those permitted by the Act. But this does not interfere with the holding or expression of beliefs about the practice of hunting, nor is the wearing of the dress that is traditionally associated with it prohibited.[87]

But beyond the 'less easy or convenient' threshold, claimants clearly unable to manifest their beliefs without considerable difficulties have found it almost impossible to persuade the courts to accept that there has been an interference with their manifestation of belief within the meaning of Article 9. It has been consistently held that what constitutes interference depends on all the circumstances of the case, 'including the extent to which in the circumstances an individual can reasonably expect to be at liberty to manifest his beliefs in practice'.[88] In exercising the freedom to manifest his beliefs, it has been held that an individual may need to take his or her specific situation into account.[89] Where an individual has a choice, the courts are almost always unwilling to find that there has been an interference with their right to manifest. As Lord Bingham stated in *Begum*:[90]

> The Strasbourg institutions have not been at all ready to find an interference with the right to manifest religious belief in practice or observance where a person has voluntarily accepted an employment or role which does not accommodate that practice or observance and there are other means open to the person to practise or observe his or her religion without undue hardship or inconvenience.[91]

It may be that a person has chosen a particular job, sent a child to a particular school or pursued their studies at a particular university. Lord Bingham, part of the majority of the House of Lords in *Begum* on this issue, held that even if the Strasbourg authority is considered too strict, there remains a 'coherent and remarkably consistent body of authority which our domestic courts must take into account and which shows that interference is not easily established'.[92] In the present case, he concluded that there was no interference with the claimant's Article 9 right to manifest her religious beliefs when the school excluded her for wearing a particular form of Islamic dress. A number of

---

[84] See eg: T Lock 'Religious Freedom and Belief Discrimination in Germany and the United Kingdom: Towards a Common European standard?' (2013) 38 *European Law Review* 655; N Gibson, 'Faith in the Courts: Religious Dress and Human Rights' (2007) *Cambridge Law Journal* 657; M Hill and R Sandberg, 'Is Nothing Sacred? Clashing Symbols in a Secular World' [2007] *Public Law* 488.

[85] *R (R) v Leeds City Council* [2005] EWHC 2495 (Admin), [40].

[86] *Friend* (n 20).

[87] Ibid, [19].

[88] *Williamson* (n 4), [38].

[89] Ibid, [38].

[90] *Begum* (n 26).

[91] Ibid, [23].

[92] Ibid, [24].

factors influenced his judgment: her family had chosen a school outside their own catchment area; her parents were informed of the uniform policy; the required uniform had been worn by the claimant's sister throughout her time at the school and by the claimant for her first two years; and there were three schools in the area which permitted the form of dress adopted by the claimant and there was no real difficulty in her attending one of these schools. Lord Hoffmann also found that there was nothing to stop her from going to a school where this particular form of dress was permitted. He stated that Article 9 did not require that she should be allowed to manifest her religion 'at any time and place of one's own choosing. Common civility also has a place in the religious life.'[93] Lord Scott stated as follows:

> [A] rule of a particular public institution that requires, or prohibits, certain behaviour on the part of those who avail themselves of its services does not constitute an infringement of the right of an individual to manifest his or her religion merely because the rule in question does not conform to the religious beliefs of that individual. And in particular this is so where the individual has a choice whether or not to avail himself or herself of the services of that institution, and where other public institutions offering similar services, and whose rules do not include the objectionable rule in question, are available.[94]

However, this stance on interference is by no means universally accepted and two members of the House of Lords, Baroness Hale and Lord Nicholls, held that the restriction on the religious dress this particular pupil wished to adopt was an interference with her right to manifest her beliefs. Lord Nicholls held that the assumptions listed by Lord Bingham above may over-estimate the ease with which the claimant could move to another, more suitable school and 'under-estimate the disruption this would be likely to cause to her education'.[95] Baroness Hale was also uneasy about the majority's conclusion that there was no interference, pointing out that the choice of secondary school was usually made by parents not the child. '[S]he has not yet reached the critical stage in her development where this particular choice may matter to her.'[96] In her opinion, it could not be assumed that the choices were the product of a fully developed individual autonomy and she held that there was an interference here with the claimant's right to manifest her religious beliefs.[97]

4.2 Examples of No Interference with Manifestation of Belief

A similar issue to that in *Begum* arose in the later case of *R (X) v Headteachers and Governors of Y School*[98] where a school refused to allow a Muslim female pupil to wear at school a niqab, a veil that covered her entire face and head save for her eyes. However, as the High Court pointed out, an important difference was that the claimant believed that it was permissible for her to wear the niqab at school and there was no established policy regarding the wearing of the niqab and her three older sisters had attended the school and worn the niqab. Silber J held that his task was to ascertain

---

[93] Ibid, [50].
[94] Ibid, [87].
[95] Ibid, [41].
[96] Ibid, [92].
[97] Ibid, [93].
[98] *R (X)* (n 45).

whether there was an interference with an Article 9 right where there was an alternative school available and where there had not been a well-known practice at the school of prohibiting wearing the niqab.[99] Somewhat confusingly, he then stated that the issue could be refined to being a question of

> whether a person's article 9 rights are infringed if a person is prohibited from wearing the article of clothing connected with his or her religion at their present school but that person is permitted to wear the article in another available suitable alternative school.[100]

He concluded that the claimant's Article 9 rights had not been infringed by the school's decision not to allow her to wear the niqab for four reasons: she had a choice whether or not to attend this particular school; Article 9 did not require that one should be allowed to manifest one's religion at any time and place of one's own choosing; Strasbourg jurisprudence should be followed by the English courts; and there was no decision of the ECtHR or an English court in which it was held that there was an infringement of Article 9 rights when a claimant 'could without excessive difficulty manifest or practice their religion as they wished in another place or in another way'.[101] The High Court concluded that there was no interference with her rights as she could have accepted an offer at another school 'which achieved good academic results and which is easy for her to get to and most significantly where she could wear her niqab'.[102]

This approach to Article 9 has also caused difficulties for claimants in the context of employment. In the Court of Appeal judgment in *Copsey*,[103] pre-dating *Begum*, the judges were also divided on the approach they should take to interference. This claim was slightly different to *Begum* in that there did not appear to be a choice for this particular claimant. The claim was brought by a Christian employee who sought to manifest his religious beliefs by observing Sunday as a day of rest. He was dismissed by his employer when he refused to accept their requirement that he should agree to work on Sundays, if needed. It is important to note that the claim was not made under the HRA as it was against a private-sector employer. It was a dispute about the possible legal limitations placed by Article 9 on the right of an employer to set the working hours of employees and dismiss an employee who did not keep to the agreed working hours or agree to reasonable changes in them. A contractual variation to his working hours was proposed by his employer so as to provide that he should work a seven-day shift, including Sunday, if needed.

Disregarding authority, Mummery LJ found that the link between the claimant's dismissal and his wish to manifest his religious belief was sufficiently material to bring circumstances of the dismissal within the ambit of Article 9.[104] However, he then took into account Strasbourg authority and stated as follows:

> There is, however, a clear line of decisions by the Commission to the effect that Article 9 is not engaged where an employee asserts Article 9 rights against his employer in relation to his hours working. The reason given is that if the employer's working practices and the

---

[99] Ibid, [29].
[100] Ibid, [30].
[101] Ibid, [31]–[38].
[102] Ibid, [39]. See also *R (Playfoot) v Millais School Governing Body* [2007] EWHC 1698 (Admin), [2007] HRLR 34, [32].
[103] *Copsey* (n 3).
[104] Ibid, [30].

employee's religious convictions are incompatible, the employee is free to resign in order to manifest his religious beliefs.[105]

Nevertheless, Mummery LJ made a number of critical observations concerning this line of authority, including the following:

> The rulings are difficult to square with the supposed fundamental character of the rights. It hardly seems compatible with the fundamental character of Article 9 that a person can be told that his right has not been interfered with because he is free to move on, for example, to another employer, who will not interfere with his fundamental right, or even to a condition of unemployment in order to manifest the fundamental right.[106]

He compared the judgment of the ECtHR in *Smith v UK*[107] which did not concern Article 9 but where no argument was advanced that the application fell outside the ambit of Article 8 as the applicants were free to resign from the armed forces and thereby avoid the application to them of the Ministry of Defence policy on sexual orientation. But, finding that he was bound by the Commission rulings, he concluded that the qualified Article 9 right of a citizen in an employment relationship to manifest his belief was not engaged when the employer required an employee to work hours which interfered with the manifestation of his religion or dismissed him for not working or agreeing to work those hours 'because he wishes to practise religious observances during normal working hours'.[108] He found no interference with the claimant's Article 9 rights but observed that this was not satisfactory:

> [I]n some sections of the community this is a controversial question which will not go away … its resolution requires a political solution following full consultation between government, leaders of employers and the trade unions, and religious leaders. Courts do not have access to the same range of expertise or to the same consultative procedures as legislation. Neither judges nor lawyers have relevant knowledge or experience. The adversarial trial processes in the courts and tribunals are not suited to deciding questions of this kind.[109]

By contrast, Rix LJ took a different view of Commission jurisprudence and stated that he was unable to understand how it could be said that the applicant was not prevented from manifesting his religion by asking him to choose between his employment and his observance of the sabbath.[110] He disapproved of the Commission decision in *Stedman v UK*[111] and held that it was not necessary to follow this decision as it was not the clear and constant jurisprudence of Strasbourg.[112] Limiting himself to the facts of the case, he held that where an employer sought to change the working hours and terms of his contract of employment with his employee in 'such a way as to interfere materially with the employee's right to manifest his religion', then Article 9(1) of the Convention was potentially engaged.[113] However, he did point out that if a reasonable solution was

---

[105] Ibid, [31].
[106] Ibid, [35].
[107] *Smith v UK* (1999) 29 EHRR 493.
[108] *Copsey* (n 3), [36].
[109] Ibid, [39].
[110] Ibid, [60].
[111] *Stedman v UK* (1997) 23 EHRR CD 168.
[112] *Copsey* (n 3), [66].
[113] Ibid, [69].

offered to the employee and not accepted by him, it remained possible to say that there was no material interference.[114]

Those pursuing alternative legal remedies for similar treatment have had far more success. For example, in *Singh*[115] a school girl challenged the decision of her school to refuse to allow her to wear a kara (the steel bangle worn by Sikhs as an indication of their faith) as indirect unjustified race and religious discrimination contrary to the Race Relations Act 1976. The Administrative Court found that there was unlawful indirect discrimination on the grounds of race and religion committed by the school when it refused to allow her to attend wearing a kara. It did note that there were two unusual features of the case which may not be met by other pupils: the honest belief of the claimant that the wearing of a kara was of exceptional importance to her for racial or religious reasons; and the unobtrusive nature of a kara:

> The fear of the school that permitting the claimant to return to school wearing her Kara will lead to an end of its uniform policy with many other girls wearing items to show their nationality, political or religious beliefs is totally unjustified.[116]

4.3 Examples of Interferences with Manifestation of Belief

It is rarely that a claim concerning protection of manifestation of belief is made under Article 9 where a claimant can demonstrate that he or she did not have a choice. The House of Lords has held that it is not necessary to demonstrate that the situation is impossible to get around as that 'would be inconsistent with the bedrock principle that human rights conventions are intended to afford practical and effective protection to human rights'.[117] Therefore, there is scope for some claimants to be able to demonstrate an interference and a few have succeeded. In *Williamson*[118] it was held that there was no choice for the claimant parents and an interference was established. Until the Education Act 1996 was amended in 1998, parents were at liberty to manifest their belief in corporal punishment and corporal punishment by parents and teachers in private schools was lawful. The House of Lords held that there was no real alternative and that the ban on corporal punishment contained in the Education Act 1996 did interfere materially with the claimant parents' rights under Article 9.

Similarly, in *Re Christian Institute*,[119] where the claimants brought a claim against the making of the Equality Act (Sexual Orientation) Regulations (Northern Ireland) 2006 which prohibited discrimination and harassment on grounds of sexual orientation, the High Court also found an interference. The claimants opposed the regulations on the ground that they offended orthodox Christian beliefs and would prohibit teaching, practice and observance to maintain the choice not to accept, endorse or encourage

---

[114] Neuberger LJ reached no decision on this point but did state at [91] that the decisions of the Commission on this topic were surprising and the reasoning hard to follow. See further S Leader, 'Freedom of Futures: Personal Priorities, Institutional Demands and Freedom of Religion' (2007) 70 *Modern Law Review* 713; H Collins, 'The Protection of Civil Liberties in the Workplace' (2006) *Modern Law Review* 619.

[115] *R (Singh) v Aberdare Girls' High School Governors* [2008] EWHC 1865 (Admin), [2008] 3 FCR 203.

[116] Ibid, [162].

[117] *Williamson* (n 4), per Lord Nicholls [39].

[118] Ibid.

[119] *Re Christian Institute* (n 50).

homosexuality.[120] Prisoners can also usually demonstrate that they have not voluntarily accepted an interference with their Article 9 rights. Although it was argued in *Bashir*[121] that a prisoner had voluntarily accepted the restrictions implicit in a prison environment by committing the offences for which he had been convicted, this was rejected by the Administrative Court. The court held that as the Muslim prisoner was fasting, to require him to provide a sample of urine which he was not able to provide without breaking his fast was an interference with his Article 9 rights.[122]

4.4 A Change in Approach

Following the judgment of the ECtHR in *Eweida v UK*[123] it is clear that the current approach of UK courts to interference under Article 9 is starting to change. Crucially in this judgment, the ECtHR held as follows:

> Given the importance in a democratic society of freedom of religion, the Court considers that, where an individual complains of a restriction on freedom of religion in the workplace, rather than holding that the possibility of changing job would negate any interference with the right, the better approach would be to weigh that possibility in the overall balance when considering whether or not the restriction was proportionate.[124]

In *Black*[125] the Court of Appeal, following this judgment, held that rather than holding that the possibility of circumventing the limitation would negate any interference with the right, the better approach is to weigh that possibility in the overall balance when considering whether or not the restriction is proportionate.[126] It is likely that judgments in Article 9 claims under the HRA will continue to evolve in this direction although there is still no Supreme Court authority on the point.[127]

4.5 Deportation and Extradition

Finally, where an individual can demonstrate that his or her Article 9 rights will be subject to flagrant denial or gross violation in the destination state, removal of that individual from the United Kingdom is not lawful. It must be shown that the right will be completely denied or nullified in the destination country.[128] In *Ullah* Lord Steyn, in reference to Article 9, held that it was necessary to establish 'at least a real risk of a flagrant violation of the very essence of the right before other articles could become engaged'.[129] The claimants in the appeal did not meet this threshold and many of their

---

[120] Ibid, [69].
[121] *Bashir* (n 24).
[122] Ibid, [23].
[123] *Eweida v UK* [2013] IRLR 231.
[124] Ibid, [83].
[125] *Black* (n 25).
[126] Ibid, [38].
[127] See further M Pearson, 'Article 9 at a Crossroads: Interference Before and After Eweida' (2013) 13 *Human Rights Law Review* 580; M Hill, 'Religious Symbolism and Conscientious Objection in the Workplace: An Evaluation of Strasbourg's Judgment in Eweida' (2013) 15 *Ecclesiastical Law Journal* 191.
[128] *R (Ullah) v Special Adjudicator* [2004] UKHL 26, [2004] 2 AC 323.
[129] Ibid, [50].

Lordships noted that it was difficult to envisage a case meeting this test which did not also come within Article 3.[130]

5. Permitted Interference with the Right to Manifest

If a claimant can establish that there has been an interference with his or her manifestation of belief, the next step is justification as the right to manifest religion or belief is not absolute. 'This is to be expected, because the way a belief is expressed in practice may impact on others.'[131] And, as Munby LJ has explained, reliance upon religious belief, 'however conscientious the belief and however ancient and respectable the religion, can never of itself immunise the believer from the reach of the secular law'. It is clear that invocation of religious belief does not necessarily provide a defence to what is otherwise a valid claim.[132]

Article 9(2) provides that freedom to manifest religion and belief shall be subject only to such limitations as are prescribed by law and are necessary in a democratic society in the interests of public safety, for the protection of public order, health or morals, or for the protection of the rights and freedoms of others.[133] Often the justification relied upon to balance against the manifestation of belief is obvious and the court spends little time discussing why the interference is proportionate. There have been no reported judgments concerning public safety or public order and very few concerning health or morals. Justifications mainly focus upon the rights and freedoms of others, and in common with other Convention rights, this type of justification is often very open ended as demonstrated in the following paragraphs.

5.1 Health or Morals

In *Taylor*[134] the Court of Appeal considered a trial judge's ruling that criminal charges in relation to cannabis possessed but destined for use in connection with Rastafarian religious purposes engaged Article 9. It upheld the conclusion of the trial judge that the Misuse of Drugs Act 1971 fulfilled the UK's obligations under international conventions and these provided powerful evidence of an 'international consensus that an unqualified ban on the possession of cannabis, with intent to supply, is necessary to combat public health and public safety dangers arising from such drugs'.[135] Furthermore, it was not necessary to read the Act so that it incorporated a Rastafarian religious defence. It did not overturn the conviction but it did reduce the length of the sentence

---

[130] See also *SS (Malaysia) v Secretary of State for the Home Department* [2013] EWCA Civ 888.
[131] *Williamson* (n 4), per Lord Nicholls at [17].
[132] *Johns* (n 10), [43].
[133] Detailed explanation of each requirement was given by the Crown Court in *R v D* (n 25).
[134] *R v Taylor* [2001] EWCA Crim 2263, [2002] 1 Cr App R 37.
[135] Ibid, [14].

imposed as it was conceded by the prosecution that the contemplated supply was for religious purposes and there was a lack of evidence that he was engaged in supply for commercial benefit rather than for a religious purpose.[136]

Public health was at issue in *Suryananda*[137] where the government sought to slaughter a temple bullock in order to eradicate or control bovine tuberculosis. The Court of Appeal held that the Minister was entitled to conclude that it was necessary for the protection of public health, which included animal health, to interfere with the manifestation of the Community's beliefs.

5.2 Protection of the Rights and Freedoms of Others

5.2.1 Respect for the Homosexual Community

There have been a number of claims, and defences, made under Article 9 where it is sought to justify acts on the ground that homosexuality is contrary to religious, usually Christian beliefs. These have not been successful. In *Ladele*[138] the Court of Appeal held that the claimant registrar's belief that same-sex unions were contrary to God's instructions, and that she would not register civil partnerships, did not override the local authority's concern 'to ensure that all its registrars manifest equal respect for the homosexual community as for the heterosexual community'.[139] In *Bull*[140] it was held that the extent to which the Equality Act (Sexual Orientation) Regulations 2007 limited the manifestation of the appellants' religious beliefs was necessary in a democratic society for the protection of the rights and freedoms of others.[141] Here the appellants sought to set aside a declaration that they had acted contrary to the Regulations by refusing to honour a same-sex couple's booking at their hotel in accordance with their religious beliefs that only double-bedded rooms would be offered to married couples. Similarly in *Black*[142] the balance came down in favour of the claimants, the Court of Appeal finding that the defendant unlawfully discriminated against them in the provision of bed and breakfast facilities on the ground of their sexual orientation contrary to the 2007 Regulations. First, it held that it was right to give considerable weight to the balance struck by the Regulations themselves.[143] Second, there was no evidence as to what the defendant could or would be likely to do in order to make up for the loss that she would suffer if she withdrew from the bed and breakfast business or ran it at a lower level of profitability.[144]

---

[136] Ibid, [34].
[137] *Suryananda* (n 52).
[138] *Ladele v Islington London Borough Council* [2009] EWCA Civ 1357, [2010] 1 WLR 955.
[139] Ibid, [55].
[140] *Bull v Hall* [2012] EWCA Civ 83, [2012] 2 All ER 1017.
[141] Ibid, [51].
[142] *Black* (n 25).
[143] Ibid, [54].
[144] Ibid, [57].

5.2.2 Vulnerable People

Although in *Pretty*[145] the House of Lords concluded that Article 9 did not protect a manifestation of belief in assisted suicide which extended to absolving Mrs Pretty's husband from the consequences of conduct inconsistent with the criminal law, it was also observed that if an interference with Article 9 was established, the justification shown by the state in relation to Article 8 would defeat it.[146] The concern was that such a change to the law would be open to abuse and put the lives of the weak and vulnerable at risk. Lord Steyn stated that the law criminalising assisted suicide was a 'legitimate, rational and proportionate response to the wider problem of vulnerable people who would otherwise feel compelled to commit suicide'.[147] Lord Bingham observed as follows:

> It is not hard to imagine that an elderly person, in the absence of any pressure, might opt for a premature end to life if that were available, not from a desire to die or a willingness to stop living, but from a desire to stop being a burden to others.[148]

5.2.3 Children

The rights of children were the justification put forward in *Williamson*[149] where the House of Lords considered the justification for the ban on corporal punishment having determined that this was an interference with the right to manifest a belief as protected by Article 9(2). Deciding that the ban was proportionate, Lord Nicholls observed as follows:

> [C]hildren are vulnerable, and the aim of the legislation is to protect them and promote their wellbeing. Corporal punishment involves deliberately inflicting physical violence. The legislation is intended to protect children against the distress, pain and other harmful effects this infliction of physical violence may cause. That corporal punishment may have these harmful effects is self-evident ... the legislature was entitled to take the view that, overall and balancing the conflicting considerations, all corporal punishment of children at school is undesirable and unnecessary and that other, non-violent means of discipline are available and preferable.[150]

Particular deference was shown to Parliament on this issue as it was one of broad social policy and pre-eminently well suited for decision by Parliament. Lord Nicholls observed:

> The legislature is to be accorded a considerable degree of latitude in deciding which course should be selected as the best course in the interests of school children as a whole. The subject has been investigated and considered by several committees ... the issue was fully debated in Parliament.[151]

---

[145] *Pretty* (n 17).
[146] Ibid, [31].
[147] Ibid, [63].
[148] Ibid, [29].
[149] *Williamson* (n 4).
[150] Ibid, [50].
[151] Ibid, [51].

The proposed adoption of a child was at issue in *Newcastle City Council v Z*[152] where the Family Court held that a parental view based on religious belief, however profound, could never be determinative when it came to considering what was to be done in relation to a child. Here the mother of a child opposed his adoption as she considered adoption to be against Islamic law. It was held that the mother's rights were qualified by the child's rights such as his right to family life, albeit with a substitute family.[153]

> [T]he question is whether, having regard to the evidence and applying the current values of our society, the advantages of adoption for the welfare of S are sufficiently strong to justify overriding the religious and other views and interests of the mother.[154]

Although a majority of the House of Lords in *Begum*[155] found there was no interference with the right to manifest flowing from a school's uniform policy, the majority did consider the question of justification on the assumption that such an interference had been demonstrated. Affording considerable deference to the way in which the school went about formulating its uniform policy, Lord Bingham, and all other members of the House of Lords, concluded that any interference was justified. The main justification put forward was the rights and freedoms of other pupils; as Lord Bingham explained, it was felt by the school that adherence to the school uniform policy 'was necessary to promote inclusion and social cohesion, fearing that new variants would encourage the formation of groups or cliques identified by their clothing'.[156] Lord Hoffmann also noted that it was the school's wish to avoid clothes which were perceived by some as signifying adherence to an extremist version of the Muslim religion and to protect girls against external pressures.[157] Baroness Hale gave the fullest consideration to this question, stating as follows:

> A uniform dress code can play its role in smoothing over ethnic, religious and social divisions … this is a society committed, in principle and in law, to equal freedom for men and women to choose how they will lead their lives within the law. Young girls from ethnic, cultural or religious minorities growing up here face particularly difficult choices: how far to adopt or to distance themselves from the dominant culture. A good school will enable and support them.[158]

Similarly in *R (X)*,[159] where a female Muslim school pupil was prevented from wearing a niqab, the High Court found no interference with manifestation of religion, given she could attend a different school, but still went on to consider the question of proportionality. Finding the assumed interference proportionate, a number of factors were noted, including the fact that the decision of the head teacher was arrived at as a result of many thoughtful and sensible inquiries. The justifications were as follows: educational factors resulting from a teacher being unable to see the face of the girl; the importance of a uniform policy as promoting uniformity and an ethos of equality and cohesion; security; and avoiding applying pressure on girls to wear a niqab.[160] In the opinion

---

[152] *Newcastle City Council v Z* (n 37).
[153] Ibid, [54].
[154] Ibid, [61].
[155] *Begum* (n 26).
[156] Ibid, [18].
[157] Ibid, [65].
[158] Ibid, [97].
[159] *R (X)* (n 45).
[160] Ibid, [64].

of the High Court, the school had taken account of the relevant interests at stake and balanced them.[161]

5.2.4 Employers

Whilst a majority of the Court of Appeal held that there was no need to consider the question of justification under Article 9 in *Copsey*[162], given they had found no interference with Article 9 rights, the question of justification was considered by some members of the Court of Appeal. The claim had been brought by a Christian employee who had been dismissed by his employer when he refused to accept their requirement that he should agree to work on Sundays, if needed. Mummery LJ found that there were compelling economic reasons which made it necessary to change the working practices of the workforce to a seven-day shift and no sensible alternative to dismissal could be found. He concluded that the dismissal was justified.[163] Rix LJ also considered the question of justification, having found an interference with Article 9 rights. In the present case he found that the rights of others would include the rights of the employer, who has a business or other form of undertaking to run, the rights of fellow-employees, and the 'rights of the public in general, mediated through parliament, who have an interest in fair but efficient employment laws'.[164] Here he held that in the case of a private employee, the state's interest and obligation was in ensuring that employment laws allowed room for an individual's Convention-protected rights to be capable of being vindicated.[165]

Rix LJ concluded that an employer who sought to change an employee's working hours so as to prevent that employee from practising his sincere adherence to the requirements of his religion may be acting unfairly if he made no attempt to accommodate his employee's needs.[166] However, in his view, an employer who sought to find a reasonable accommodation for his employee would have nothing to fear.[167] Here as the employer had acted reasonably, the claim for unfair dismissal under statute, or Article 9, failed.

5.2.5 Prisons and Prisoners

The Administrative Court held in *Bashir*[168] that is was disproportionate to find a Muslim prisoner who was undertaking a personal fast guilty of failing to obey a lawful order by failing to provide a urine sample that he could not physically provide without breaking his fast. It noted that care needs to be taken before a court 'accepts at face value assertions of an un-particularised sort that making reasonable adjustments would be too administratively inconvenient or too expensive to be contemplated'.[169] It was observed

---

[161] Ibid, [67]. See also *Playfoot* (n 102), which concerned a school uniform policy banning jewellery.
[162] *Copsey* (n 3).
[163] Ibid, [41].
[164] Ibid, [69].
[165] Ibid, [69].
[166] Ibid, [71].
[167] Ibid, [71].
[168] *Bashir* (n 24).
[169] Ibid, [29].

that the quality of the evidence indicated that the Prison Service had not 'attempted seriously to assess the impact of making adjustments for Muslims undertaking personal fasting'.[170]

5.2.6 Fair Administration of Justice

In *R v D*[171] the Crown Court determined the extent to which a defendant in criminal proceedings was entitled to wear a niqab. It held that the question was whether her right to manifest her religion or belief under Article 9 outweighed the public interest in the courts conducting criminal proceedings in accordance with the rule of law, open justice and the adversarial trial process. It held that the protection of the rights and freedoms of others included the rights and freedoms of persons who come before the court as complainants, witnesses and jurors and 'the public interest insofar as the public has an interest in the fair administration of criminal justice by the Crown Court'.[172] It concluded that the basis in law for any restriction on the wearing of a niqab came from the judicial Equal Treatment Bench Book.[173] It also held that the fair and effective operation of the criminal courts was a legitimate aim[174] and that some restriction on the right of the defendant to wear a niqab during proceedings against her in the Crown Court was necessary in a democratic society. In its view, no tradition or practice, whether religious or otherwise, could 'claim to occupy such as privileged position that the rule of law, open justice, and the adversarial trial process are sacrificed to accommodate it'.[175] However, considering proportionality, it was concluded that the Court's aim could be achieved by an approach other than removing the niqab at all times.[176] It specified that the niqab should be removed for purposes of identification and when giving evidence. She was also to be permitted to give evidence from behind a screen shielding her from public view.

---

[170] Ibid, [30].
[171] *R v D* (n 25).
[172] Ibid, [39].
[173] Ibid, [76].
[174] Ibid, [77].
[175] Ibid, [78].
[176] Ibid, [79].

15

Article 10: The Right to Freedom of Expression

1. Introduction

Article 10 provides that everyone has the right to freedom of expression. This right includes freedom to hold opinions and to receive and impart information and ideas without interference by public authority and regardless of frontiers. Furthermore, Article 10 does not prevent states from requiring the licensing of broadcasting, television or cinema enterprises. Corporate bodies, as well as individuals, have been held to have a right to freedom of expression within the scope of Article 10.[1] The right to freedom of expression is not an absolute right and, under Article 10(2), it may be subject to such formalities, conditions, restrictions or penalties as are prescribed by law and are necessary in a democratic society in one of the interests there set out.

Before the Human Rights Act 1998 came into force, the right to freedom of expression enjoyed considerable protection in the context of particular torts and statutory wrongs and via the common law. In early cases, freedom of expression or freedom of speech was referred to exclusively as a liberty or freedom, and although the term 'right' was used, it was clear that it was actually 'liberty' that was meant.[2] In the late 1970s there was a change in terminology and judges began referring to the 'right' to freedom of expression, sometimes the 'constitutional right' to freedom of expression.[3] In many cases, Article 10 was also mentioned.[4] Now that the HRA is in force, it is widely thought that Article 10 reinforces and gives greater weight to the principles already

---

[1] *Core Issues Trust v Transport for London* [2013] EWHC 651 (Admin), [2013] HRLR 22, [72].

[2] See eg *R v Secretary of State for Home Affairs, ex p O'Brien* [1923] 2 KB 361; *Silkin v Beaverbrook Newspapers Ltd* [1958] 2 All ER 516; *Webb v Times Publishing Co Ltd* [1960] 2 QB 535.

[3] See eg *Cassell & Co v Broome* [1972] 2 WLR 645, per Lord Kilbrandon at 726; *Harman v Secretary of State for the Home Department* [1982] 2 WLR 338, per Lord Scarman at 351; *Secretary of State for Defence v Guardian Newspapers Ltd* [1984] 3 WLR 986, per Lord Fraser at 1001.

[4] See eg *R v Lemon* [1979] 2 WLR 281, per Lord Scarman at 315; *Associated Newspapers Group Ltd v Wade* [1979] 1 WLR 697, per Lord Denning at 708–09; *A-G v BBC* [1980] 3 WLR 109, per Lord Scarman at 130; *Schering Chemicals Ltd v Falkman Ltd* [1981] 2 WLR 848, per Lord Denning at 862 and 864. It is possible that this development was driven by the finding of a violation of Art 10 by the ECtHR in *Sunday Times v UK* (1979) 2 EHRR 245.

established in the common law.[5] Therefore, unlike most other Convention rights, when considering Article 10 it is important to remember the common law protection which operates alongside the HRA. In accordance with section 11 of the HRA a person's reliance on a Convention right does not restrict any other right or freedom conferred on him. Where freedom of expression is threatened, as Lord Steyn noted in *Reynolds*,[6] there are now actually three routes to protection: first is the principle of liberty—that individuals are free to do whatever is not specifically forbidden by law[7]; secondly, there is a constitutional right to freedom of expression[8]; and thirdly, there is Article 10, which is given further effect in domestic law by the HRA. In this chapter the focus will be predominantly on the interpretation of Article 10.

Finally, by way of introduction it is also essential to note the importance with which the right to freedom of expression is regarded by the courts. It is widely recognised that there is a public interest per se in freedom of expression and freedom of the press.[9] Judicial observations are often made as to why the right is fundamental. One example is the comments of Lord Bingham in *R v Shayler*:[10]

> Modern democratic government means government of the people by the people for the people. But there can be no government by the people if they are ignorant of the issues to be resolved, the arguments for and against different solutions and the facts underlying those arguments.

In a later case his Lordship observed that freedom to publish free of unjustifiable restraint was 'a distinguishing feature of the sort of society which the Convention seeks to promote'.[11] Where freedom of expression is at issue, deference to the primary decision maker is rarely shown. This may be a result of the fact that cases concerning freedom of expression generally do not involve difficult moral questions or difficult political questions such as immigration[12] or the allocation of resources. Furthermore, given the pre-HRA protection afforded to freedom of expression, it is possible that judges are simply more comfortable with upholding this right despite the views of the primary decision maker. However, where moral questions must be considered, there is evidence that some deference is shown. For example, in a case concerning the licensing of a sex shop, the House of Lords held that a broad power of judgment should be entrusted to the local authority.[13] And where difficult political issues arise, particularly where Parliament has already considered the implications for freedom of expression, deference is also afforded.[14]

---

[5] *Venables v News Group Newspapers Ltd* [2001] WLR 1038, at [36]. See also *R (Calver) v Adjudication Panel for Wales* [2012] EWHC 1172 (Admin), [41].

[6] *Reynolds v Times Newspapers Ltd* [1999] 4 All ER 609.

[7] See eg *R v Secretary of State for the Home Department, ex p Simms* [2000] 2 AC 115 and *Redmond-Bate v Director of Public Prosecutions* [2000] HRLR 249.

[8] See eg *Simms*, ibid.

[9] See eg *Ashdown v Telegraph Group Ltd* [2001] EWCA Civ 1142, [2001] 3 WLR 1368.

[10] *R v Shayler* [2002] UKHL 11, [2002] 2 WLR 754, [21].

[11] *Jameel v Wall Street Journal Europe SPRL* [2006] UKHL 44, [2006] 3 WLR 642.

[12] Except in *R v Secretary of State for the Home Department, ex p Farrakhan* [2002] EWCA Civ 606, [2002] 3 WLR 481. See also *R (Lord Carlile of Berriew) v Secretary of State for the Home Department* [2013] EWCA Civ 199.

[13] *Belfast City Council v Miss Behavin' Ltd* [2007] UKHL 19, [2007] 1 WLR 1420, per Lord Hoffmann at [16].

[14] *R (Animal Defenders International) v Secretary of State for Culture Media & Sport* [2008] UKHL 15, [2008] 2 WLR 781, per Lord Bingham at [33].

2. Expression

The term 'expression' includes a wide range of material and actions, such as the written word, spoken word, web pages,[15] photographs,[16] archived material[17], a parade[18] and advertisements.[19] Also included is behaviour. For example, in *Percy*[20] the Divisional Court confirmed that it was protected expression for the appellant, whilst protesting at an American airbase, to deface the American flag with the words 'Stop Star Wars' and stand on it.[21] Behaviour may take the form of a performance. In *Pay*[22] it was held that the claimant's hobby of a circus-related fire act was protected expression within Article 10. The House of Lords has also assumed, without finally deciding, that freedom of expression includes the right to use particular premises to distribute pornographic books, videos and other articles although it was noted that this was not the most important aspect of the right.[23]

In order to be protected, the expression does not have to pass a test of quality or truth[24] and the protection of freedom of speech has been 'accorded to the unpopular, tasteless or offensive, as well as to the popular, moderate or reasoned'.[25] There is no need for there to be an identifiable special public interest in any particular material being published, and it is not for the courts to act as censors or arbiters of taste.[26] Article 10 protects in substance and in form a right to freedom of expression which others may find insulting,[27] abusive,[28] shocking or disturbing.[29] For example, in *O'Shea*[30] the Divisional Court held that a pornographic advertisement, which may have been regarded by many as squalid and degrading to women and distasteful, was a form of protected expression. In *Perrin*[31] the Court of Appeal held that a web page showing

---

[15] *R v Perrin* [2002] EWCA Crim 747.

[16] *Douglas v Hello! Ltd* [2001] QB 967.

[17] *Loutchansky v Times Newspapers Ltd (No 2)* [2001] EWCA Civ 1805, [2002] 2 WLR 640.

[18] *Tweed v Parades Commission for Northern Ireland* [2006] UKHL 53, [2007] 1 AC 650.

[19] *Smithkline Beecham plc v Advertising Standards Authority* [2001] EWHC (Admin) 6, [2001] EMLR 23; *R (on the application of British American Tobacco UK Ltd) v The Secretary of State for Health* [2004] EWHC (Admin) 2493; *Animal Defenders International* (n 14); *Core Issues Trust* (n 1).

[20] *Percy v DPP* [2001] EWHC (Admin) 1125, [2002] Crim LR 835.

[21] See also *R (on the application of Brehony) v Chief Constable of Greater Manchester Police* [2005] EWHC (Admin) 640. In relation to protest see also *R (Singh) v Chief Constable of West Midlands* [2006] EWCA Civ 1118, [2006] 1 WLR 3374.

[22] *Pay v Lancashire Probation Service* [2004] ICR 187.

[23] *Belfast City Council* (n 13), per Lord Hoffmann at [16].

[24] *Reynolds* (n 6).

[25] *R (Green) v City of Westminster Magistrates' Court* [2007] EWHC 2785 (Admin), [2008] HRLR 12 [17].

[26] *B & C v A* [2002] EWCA Civ 337, [2002] 3 WLR 542, [11].

[27] *Percy* (n 20), [27]. See also *R (Gaunt) v Office of Communications* [2011] EWCA Civ 692, [2011] 1 WLR 2355 and *In the Matter of Kirk Session of Sandown Free Presbyterian Church's Application* [2011] NIQB 26.

[28] *Livingstone v Adjudication Panel for England* [2006] EWHC 2533 (Admin), [2006] HRLR 45.

[29] *Connolly v DPP* [2007] EWHC 237 (Admin), [2007] 2 All ER 1012.

[30] *O'Shea v MGN Ltd* [2001] EMLR 40, [37].

[31] *Perrin* (n 15). For the purposes of s 1(3) of the Obscene Publications Act 1959 the court held at [18] that a person publishes an article who transmits data: '[T]here is publication for the purposes of section 1(3) both when images are uploaded and when they are downloaded'.

people covered in faeces, coprophilia or coprophagia and men involved in fellatio was protected expression. In *Norwood*[32] the Divisional Court held that a poster containing the words 'Islam out of Britain' with a photograph of the World Trade Centre in flames was protected expression.[33]

It is rare for a court to find that expression is not protected under Article 10 but this is possible. In *Thomas*[34] the Court of Appeal considered whether or not to strike out the particulars of a claim under the Protection from Harassment Act 1997 on the ground that the course of conduct did not constitute harassment within the meaning of the Act. The parties agreed that the publication of press articles calculated to incite racial hatred of an individual provided an example of conduct which was capable of amounting to harassment under the Act.[35] It was also agreed that the right to freedom of expression did not extend to protect remarks directly against the Convention's underlying values.[36] Whilst the court did not comment on this the discussion indicated its approval particularly its observation that such publications constitute an abuse of the freedom of the press.[37]

A similar conclusion was reached by the Administrative Court in *Woolas*[38] where it was held that dishonest statements aimed at the destruction of the rights of the public to free elections and the right of each candidate to his reputation were not protected by Article 10. The court stated as follows:

> The right of freedom of expression does not extend to the publishing, before or during an election for the purpose of affecting the return of any candidate at an election, of a statement that is made dishonestly, that is to say when the publisher knows that statement to be false or does not believe it to be true.[39]

A claim to freedom of expression may also be weakened where someone is seeking entry clearance to the United Kingdom to express their views. In *Farrakhan*[40] the Court of Appeal held that, whilst Article 10 required the authorities of a state to permit those within its boundaries freely to express their views, even if these are deeply offensive to the majority of the community, it did not believe that it followed that those authorities should be obliged to allow into the state a person bent on giving its citizens such offence.[41]

Some activities have been held to be clearly not expression. For example, the House of Lords has held that hunting with dogs is not within the scope of Article 10 as neither

---

[32] *Norwood v Director of Public Prosecutions* [2003] EWHC (Admin) 1564, [2003] Crim LR 888.

[33] See also *Re Roddy (a child) (identification: restriction on publication)* [2003] EWHC (Fam) 2927, [2004] 2 FLR 949; *Hammond v Director of Public Prosecutions* [2004] EWHC (Admin) 69. See generally A Geddis, 'Free Speech Martyrs or Unreasonable Threats to Social Peace?—Insulting Expression and Section 5 of the Public Order Act 1986' [2004] *Public Law* 853.

[34] *Thomas v News Group Newspapers* [2001] EWCA Civ 1233, [2002] EMLR 4.

[35] Ibid, [37].

[36] Ibid.

[37] Ibid, [50]. The court referred to *Jersild v Denmark* (1994) 19 EHRR 1, [35] and *Lehideux and Isorni v France* (1998) 5 BHRC 540. It found little assistance in First Amendment jurisprudence from the United States. It is possible for other forms of harassment under the Act to constitute protected expression. See eg *Silverton v Gravett*, Divisional Court, 19 October 2001 and *Emerson Developments Ltd v Avery* [2004] EWHC (QB) 194.

[38] *R (Woolas) v Parliamentary Election Court* [2010] EWHC 3169 (Admin), [2011] 2 WLR 1362.

[39] Ibid, [106]. See further H Cannie and D Voorhoof, 'The Abuse Clause and Freedom of Expression in the European Human Rights Convention' [2011] NQHR 54.

[40] *Farrakhan* (n 12).

[41] Ibid, [33].

Article 11 nor Article 10 guaranteed a right to assemble for purely social purposes as this falls 'well short of the kind of assembly whose protection is fundamental to the proper functioning of a modern democracy'.[42] However, Lord Bingham cast doubt on this conclusion in the *Countryside Alliance* case where he held that he was not content to treat Article 11 as inapplicable, stating that a right to 'assemble and protest is of little value if one is free to assemble but not, having done so, to protest'. In his view, if people only assemble to act in a certain way and that activity is prohibited, the effect in reality is to restrict their right to assemble.[43] By contrast, Lord Hope held that neither Articles 11 nor 10 were applicable as these were merely people who wished to assemble for sporting or recreational purposes and this fell well short of the 'kind of assembly whose protection is fundamental to the proper functioning of a modern democracy'.[44] Baroness Hale took the middle approach, finding that the right of the hunt and its followers to gather together publicly to demonstrate in favour of their sport and against the ban, even by riding over the countryside to demonstrate what they do, was protected by Article 11, but the right to chase and kill the fox was not.[45] She did later note that she was inclined to the view that the ban on hunting did not engage Article11 at all.[46]

---

3. Medium, Manner and Timing of Communication

Also protected by Article 10 are the medium, manner and timing of communication. It has been recognised by the courts that television and radio advertising has greater immediacy and impact than the press, cinema and all other media of communication.[47] In *Hirst*[48] the Home Secretary had denied a serving prisoner's request that he be entitled, in certain circumstances, to speak to the media by telephone on matters of legitimate public interest relating to prisons and prisoners. In the Home Secretary's view, he could exercise his right to freedom of expression by expressing his views in writing. The Administrative Court disagreed and found the blanket ban to be a disproportionate interference.[49]

A similar approach was applied by the High Court in *BBC v Secretary of State for Justice*.[50] The BBC and one of its correspondents had applied to the Secretary of State for permission to conduct, for the purposes of broadcast, a face-to-face interview with Babar Ahmad who was detained in a UK prison and whose extradition was sought by the United States. Permission was refused. Making reference to the Secretary of

---

[42] *Friend v Lord Advocate* [2007] UKHL 53, [2008] HRLR 11, per Lord Hope at [26].
[43] *R (Countryside Alliance) v Attorney General* [2007] UKHL 52, [2007] 3 WLR 922, [18].
[44] Ibid, [58].
[45] Ibid, [118].
[46] Ibid, [119]. See also the observations of Lord Brown at [143].
[47] *Animal Defenders International* (n 14), per Lord Bingham at [30].
[48] *Hirst v Secretary of State for the Home Department* [2002] EWHC (Admin) 602, [2002] 1 WLR 2929.
[49] Ibid, [88].
[50] *BBC v Secretary of State for Justice* [2012] EWHC 13 (Admin), [2012] 2 All ER 1089.

State's own policy that in some instances face-to-face interviews with prisoners were permitted, the court concluded that the refusal here was disproportionate. It rejected various reasons put forward by the Secretary of State, including that refusal was necessary to protect victims of terrorism from distress and that a broadcast interview would undermine public confidence in the criminal justice system.

By contrast in *Farrakhan*,[51] when concluding that Mr Farrkhan's exclusion from the United Kingdom was proportionate, the Court of Appeal took into account the very limited extent to which his right to freedom of expression was restricted as he remained free to disseminate information and opinions within the United Kingdom by any means of communication other than his presence in the country.[52] In *Naik*,[53] which also concerned the exclusion from the UK of a high-profile Muslim speaker, the Court of Appeal pointed out that this worked both ways and asked why his words were more likely to have adverse consequences delivered in person given that there was no evidence of potential public disorder.[54] Nevertheless, it accepted that his presence may have symbolic significance transcending purely practical considerations.[55]

With respect to the manner of communication, in *Percy*[56] the Divisional Court noted that the appellant could have demonstrated her message in a way which did not involve the use of a national flag of symbolic significance to her target audience. Nevertheless, this was only one factor and was not decisive.[57] The manner and form of a particular protest can be crucial, as Laws LJ has observed; it depends on the facts: '[T]he supposed distinction between the essence of a protest and the manner and form of its exercise has to be treated with considerable care. In some cases it will be real, in others insubstantial.'[58]

In the claim before the court, the women could continue to protest; they were only being stopped from camping in particular areas. Laws LJ recognised that this manner and form may constitute the actual nature and quality of the protest: '[I]t may have acquired a symbolic force inseparable from the protesters' message; it may be the very witness of their beliefs.'[59] He concluded that this was the case as the camp had been established for approximately 23 years. In his view, the camp had:

> borne consistent, long-standing, and peaceful witness to the convictions of the women who have belonged to it . . . to them, and . . . to many who support them, and indeed to others who disapprove and oppose them, the 'manner and form' is the protest itself.[60]

It was concluded that a byelaw removing the right to camp in the area was disproportionate. A similar approach was taken by the Court of Appeal in *Hall*[61] which was a challenge to efforts to disband a protest camp located in Parliament Square Gardens. Lord Neuberger observed as follows:

---

[51] *Farrakhan* (n 12).

[52] Ibid, [77].

[53] *R (Naik) v Secretary of State for the Home Department* [2011] EWCA Civ 1546, [2012] Imm AR 381.

[54] Ibid, [66].

[55] Ibid, [67].

[56] *Percy* (n 20).

[57] Ibid, [31]. See also *Hutchinson v Newbury Magistrates Court*, Divisional Court, 9 October 2000; *Re Roddy* (n 33).

[58] *Tabernacle v Secretary of State for Defence* [2009] EWCA Civ 23.

[59] Ibid, [37].

[60] Ibid, [37].

[61] *Hall v Mayor of London* [2010] EWCA Civ 817.

The right to express views publicly, particularly on the important issues about which the defendants feel so strongly, and the right of the defendants to assemble for the purpose of expressing and discussing those views, extends to the manner in which the defendants wish to express their views and to the location where they wish to express and exchange their views. If it were otherwise, these fundamental human rights would be at risk of emasculation.[62]

Finally, the perishable nature of news is often referred to in the context of protecting the timing of a communication. It has been held that an important aspect of freedom of speech is that one should be able to publish what one wishes but also to do so when one wishes.[63] 'News is a perishable commodity. Public and media interest in topical issues fades.'[64]

---

4. Freedom to Receive and Impart Information and Ideas

Expressly included in the right to freedom of expression set out in Article 10(1) is the freedom to receive and impart information and ideas. However, this aspect of Article 10 has been the subject of little litigation under the HRA. In *Ashdown*[65] the court made clear that the freedom to convey information and ideas extended to the freedom to convey ideas and information using the form of words devised by someone else.[66] However, in *Marmont*[67] the Divisional Court was not convinced that the compulsory television licence fee was an interference with the right to receive commercial programmes although it did consider the question of justification, assuming that the licence was at least a 'condition' attached to the exercise of Article 10 freedoms which needed justification. The right to receive information was also briefly considered by the Court of Appeal in *Farrakhan*,[68] the court recognising that, if it upheld the Home Secretary's exclusion order, it would impinge on the freedom of those who wished to hear Mr Farrakhan speak to receive his views and information face to face.[69]

This aspect of Article 10 has received the most attention in relation to the holding of public inquires, and conflicting High Court decisions have resulted. In *Persey*[70] the claimants challenged the government's decision to set up three separate private inquiries into the 2001 foot and mouth outbreak rather than a full-scale open public inquiry. By contrast to the judgment of the Divisional Court in *Wagstaff*,[71] the Divisional Court here

---

[62] Ibid, [37]. See also *R (Gallastegui) v Westminster City Council* [2013] EWCA Civ 28, [2013] HRLR 15 [24].

[63] *R v Sherwood, ex p The Telegraph Group plc* [2001] EWCA Crim 1075, [2001] 1 WLR 1983, [16].

[64] *Attorney General v Punch Ltd* [2002] UKHL 50, [2003] 1 AC 1046, [31].

[65] *Ashdown* (n 9).

[66] Ibid, [31].

[67] *Marmont v Secretary of State for Culture, Media and Sport* [2003] EWHC (QB) 2300.

[68] *Farrakhan* (n 12).

[69] Ibid, [77]. See also *Naik* (n 53).

[70] *Persey v Secretary of State for Environment, Food and Rural Affairs* [2002] EWHC (Admin) 371, [2003] QB 794.

[71] *R (on the application of Wagstaff) v Secretary of State for Health* [2001] 1 WLR 292.

concluded that Article 10 was simply not engaged by a decision to hold a closed public inquiry and that it did not confer the right of access to information.[72]

> It is not a corollary of the right to freedom of expression that public authorities can be required to put in place additional opportunities for its exercise. Article 10 imposes no positive obligation on government to provide, in addition to existing means of communication, an open forum to achieve the yet wider dissemination of views.[73]

The Supreme Court considered the impact of Article 10 upon access to information in *Sugar*[74] where it was argued that a particular provision of the Freedom of Information Act 2000 should be construed in light of an Article 10 right of access to information so as to enable the claimant to have access to a particular report held by the BBC. Lord Brown, giving the judgment of the Court on this issue, having taken into account relevant ECtHR jurisprudence, observed as follows:

> [T]hese three cases fall far short of establishing that an individual's article 10(1) freedom to receive information is interfered with whenever, as in the present case, a public authority, acting consistently with the domestic legislation governing the nature and extent of its obligations to disclose information, refuses access to documents . . . article 10 creates no general right to freedom of information and where, as here, the legislation expressly limits such right to information held otherwise than for the purposes of journalism, it is not interfered with when access is refused to documents which are held for journalistic purposes.[75]

Whilst Lord Brown firmly concluded that the claimant here had no right of access to information, he went on to consider the position if there was an interference with the right to receive information. He concluded that the interference would be justified observing that it was open to the state to legislate a blanket exclusion of any requirement to disclose information held (whether predominantly or not) for the purposes of journalism.[76] The Court of Appeal in *Kennedy*[77] confirmed that the judgment in *Sugar* established that Article 10 was not engaged and that it was irrelevant to the Article 10 issue whether or not the individual seeking the information was acting as a social watchdog or was a member of the press.[78]

---

[72] Ibid, [50] and [52] in reliance upon *Leander v Sweden* (1987) 9 EHRR 433; *Gaskin v United Kingdom* (1990) 12 EHRR 36; *Taylor v United Kingdom* (1994) 18 EHRR CD 215; *Guerra v Italy* (1998) 26 EHRR 357.

[73] *Wagstaff* ibid, [53]. The court added that, even if it had found Art 10(1) engaged, it would have concluded that the interference was justified. In *R (on the application of Howard) v Secretary of State for Health* [2002] EWHC (Admin), [2003] QB 830 the court distinguished *Wagstaff* on the ground that in the present case the claimants were entitled to be present and the media were not parties. Nevertheless, it was also stated that the judgment in *Wagstaff* was wrong as it was not supported by jurisprudence of the ECtHR.

[74] *Sugar (deceased) v BBC* [2012] UKSC 4, [2012] 1 WLR 439.

[75] Ibid, [94].

[76] Ibid, [98].

[77] *Kennedy v Charity Commission* [2012] EWCA Civ 317, [2012] EMLR 20.

[78] Ibid, [55]. See further CJS Knight, 'Article 10 and a Right of Access to Information' [2013] *Public Law* 468; M McDonagh, 'The Right to Information in International Human Rights Law' (2013) 13 *Human Rights Law Review* 25.

5. Interference

An interference with the right to freedom of expression may arise in any number of ways. However, hypothetical interferences are not sufficient. For example, in *Rusbridger*[79] it was held that the mere existence of section 3 of the Treason Act 1848 was not an interference.[80] An injunction restraining publication or further publication is obviously an interference.[81] Awards of damages and costs against newspapers can generally impinge upon and have a chilling effect upon freedom of expression.[82] A blanket exemption from orders for costs for charitable donors to a litigant running a defamation case has been held to constitute an interference,[83] as has a requirement that a newspaper editor seek confirmation from the Attorney General or court that the facts are not confidential prior to publication.[84] Proceedings for defamation;[85] an order that the identity of parties to an action not be disclosed;[86] an order requiring a journalist to disclose his or her source;[87] a production order of journalistic material under the Terrorism Act 2000;[88] reporting restrictions;[89] proceedings for contempt of court;[90] advertising restrictions;[91] trading licence restrictions;[92] and a finding by the Office of Communications (Ofcom) that the broadcasting of an interview was in breach of the Broadcasting Code[93] can all interfere with freedom of expression.

An interference may also arise from a conviction under the: Public Order Act 1986;[94] Official Secrets Act 1989;[95] Obscene Publications Act 1959;[96] Protection of Children Act 1978;[97] Contempt of Court Act 1981;[98] Terrorism Act 2000 which penalises the profession of membership of a proscribed organisation;[99] section 75 of the Representation of the People Act 1983 for incurring unauthorised election expenses;[100] section

---

[79] *R (on the application of Rusbridger) v Attorney General* [2003] UKHL 38, [2004] 1 AC 357.
[80] Ibid.
[81] See eg *Douglas* (n 16).
[82] See eg *Ashdown* (n 9), [52].
[83] *Hamilton v Al Fayed* [2002] EWCA Civ 665, [2003] QB 1175.
[84] *Attorney General v Times Newspapers Ltd* [2001] EWCA Civ 97, [2001] 1 WLR 885.
[85] *Reynolds* (n 6).
[86] *H (A Healthcare Worker) v Associated Newspapers Ltd* [2002] EWCA Civ 195, [2002] EMLR 23.
[87] *Ashworth Hospital Authority v MGN Ltd* [2002] UKHL 29, [2002] 1 WLR 2033.
[88] *Malik v Manchester Crown Court* [2008] EWHC 1362 (Admin), [2008] 4 All ER 403.
[89] See eg *Briffet v DPP* [2001] EWHC (Admin) 841, [2002] EMLR 12; *McKerry v Teesdale & Wear Valley Justices* [2001] EMLR 5.
[90] *Punch* (n 64).
[91] *British American Tobacco* (n 19); *Animal Defenders International* (n 14).
[92] *Belfast City Council* (n 13).
[93] *Gaunt* (n 27).
[94] *Percy* (n 20).
[95] *Shayler* (n 10).
[96] *Perrin* (n 15).
[97] *R v Smethurst* [2001] EWCA Crim 772, [2002] 1 Cr App R 6. See also *R v DM* [2011] EWCA Crim 2752.
[98] *Attorney General v Scotcher* [2005] UKHL 36, [2005] 1 WLR 1867.
[99] *Attorney General's Reference No 4 of 2002* [2004] UKHL 43, [2005] 1 AC 264, [54].
[100] *R v Holding* [2005] EWCA Crim 3185, [2006] 1 WLR 1040.

106 of the Representation of the People Act 1983 for making false statements;[101] and a conviction for displaying an advertisement on a property without consent.[102]

Some interferences have a particular impact on protesters such as: a restraining order under the Protection from Harassment Act 1997;[103] the dispersal of protestors pursuant the Anti-social Behaviour Act 2003;[104] a ban on camping in a particular area which affected the Aldermaston Women's Peace Camp protesting against nuclear weapons;[105] stopping coaches carrying protesters to a demonstration and turning the coaches around;[106] and a conviction common law offence of causing a public nuisance.[107]

Sometimes the interference is not obvious. For example, it was found that an interference arose from dismissing a probation officer from his employment because his hobby was a circus-related fire act which he performed in hedonist and fetish clubs.[108] It has also been held that requiring journalists' interviews with Category A prisoners to be conducted within earshot of officials and tape recorded constituted a interference.[109] In relation to the laws of copyright, it has been argued that these do not constitute an interference with freedom of expression as the information can still be conveyed. This argument was dismissed by the Court of Appeal in *Ashdown*,[110] the court finding that copyright was antithetical to freedom of expression as it prevented all, save the owner of the copyright, from expressing information in the form of the literary work protected by the copyright.[111] However, as copyright does not normally prevent the publication of the information, the court concluded that it would not normally constitute a significant encroachment.[112]

Difficult questions have arisen in relation to entry clearance. In *Farrakhan*,[113] relying on Strasbourg authorities, the Court of Appeal held that, where the authorities of a state refuse entry to or expel an alien from their territory solely for the purpose of preventing the alien from exercising a Convention right within the territory, or by way of sanction for the exercise of a Convention right, the Convention would be directly engaged.[114] Therefore, where the authorities refused entry to an alien solely to prevent his expressing opinions within its territory, Article 10 would be engaged.[115] However, in the case of Mr Farrakhan the court observed that the reason for his exclusion was the

---

[101] *Watkins v Woolas* [2010] EWHC 2702 (QB).

[102] *Butler v Derby City* Council [2005] EWHC 2835 (Admin), [2006] 1 WLR 1346.

[103] *R v Debnath* [2005] EWCA Crim 3472, [2006] Crim LR 451.

[104] *R (Singh) v Chief Constable of West Midlands* [2006] EWCA Civ 1118, [2006] 1 WLR 3374.

[105] *Tabernacle v Secretary of State for Defence* [2009] EWCA Civ 23.

[106] *R (Laporte) v Chief Constable of Gloucestershire* [2006] UKHL 55, [2007] 2 AC 105.

[107] *R v Goldstein* [2003] EWCA Crim 3450, [2004] WLR 2878.

[108] *Pay* (n 22).

[109] *R (on the application of A) v Secretary of State for the Home Department* [2003] EWHC (Admin) 2846, [2004] HRLR 12.

[110] *Ashdown* (n 9).

[111] Ibid, [30].

[112] Ibid, [31]. See also *Imutran Ltd v Uncaged Campaigns Ltd* [2001] 2 All ER 385 and *Levi Strauss & Co v Tesco Stores Ltd* [2002] EWHC (Ch) 1556, [2003] RPC 18 concerning trade marks.

[113] *Farrakhan* (n 12).

[114] *Agee v United Kingdom* (1976) 7 D&R 164; *Piermont v France* (1995) 20 EHRR 301; *Swami Omkarananda and the Divine Light Zentrum v Switzerland* (1997) 25 D&R 105; *Adams and Benn v United Kingdom* (1997) 88A D&R 137.

[115] *Farrakhan* (n 12), [55]–[56].

risk that his presence in this country might prove a catalyst for disorder.[116] Therefore, preventing Mr Farrakhan from expressing his views was not the primary object of his exclusion. However, in contrast to the Strasbourg authorities reviewed, the Court concluded that it was clear that one object of his exclusion was to prevent him from exercising the right of freedom of expression in this country, and therefore Article 10 was in play.[117] A similar issue arose in *Naik*[118] where a Muslim speaker of international reputation was excluded from the United Kingdom by the Home Secretary and his visa revoked. Without finally determining the question, and instead relying on the Article 10 rights of his supporters in the UK, the Court of Appeal stated the modern jurisprudence supported the approach in *Farrakhan*.[119]

6. Positive Duties

Positive duties under Article 10 before are not yet well developed and there have been a number of observations made in HRA judgments that Article 10 does not actually impose positive duties. For example, in *Smeaton*[120] the Administrative Court held that Article 10 does not require the public subsidy of campaigning free speech. In *Persey*[121] the Divisional Court held that Article 10 prohibited interference with expression, rather than requiring its facilitation.[122] Similarly, it was held by a majority of the House of Lords in *Prolife Alliance*[123] that Article 10 did not entitle the Prolife Alliance or anyone else to make free television broadcasts.[124] Nevertheless, it concluded that the principle underlying Article 10 required that access to an important public medium of communication should not be refused on discriminatory, arbitrary or unreasonable grounds. Nor should access be granted subject to discriminatory, arbitrary or unreasonable conditions. 'A restriction on the content of a programme, produced by a political party to promote its stated aims, must be justified. Otherwise it will not be acceptable.'[125]

---

[116] Ibid, [58].

[117] Ibid, [62].

[118] *Naik* (n 53).

[119] Ibid, [31]. See also *R (Lord Carlile of Berriew) v Secretary of State for the Home Department* [2013] EWCA Civ 199.

[120] *R (on the application of Smeaton on behalf of the Society for the Protection of Unborn Children) v The Secretary of State for Health* [2002] EWHC (Admin) 886, [2002] 2 FLR 146.

[121] *Persey* (n 70).

[122] Ibid, [53].

[123] *R (on the application of Prolife Alliance) v British Broadcasting Corporation* [2003] UKHL 23, [2004] 1 AC 185.

[124] Ibid, per Lord Nicholls at [8] and per Lord Hoffmann at [56].

[125] Ibid, per Lord Nicholls at [8] and per Lord Hoffmann at [58].

7. Permitted Interferences

The right to freedom of expression is not an absolute right. Article 10(2) provides that the exercise of these freedoms:

> since it carries with it duties and responsibilities, may be subject to such formalities, conditions, restrictions or penalties as are prescribed by law and are necessary in a democratic society, in the interests of national security, territorial integrity or public safety, for the prevention of disorder or crime, for the protection of health or morals, for the protection of the reputation or rights of others, for preventing the disclosure of information received in confidence, or for maintaining the authority and impartiality of the judiciary.

The notion of a right carrying with it 'duties and responsibilities' is not found in any other Convention right, but it has played little part in Article 10 case law to date. In *Shayler*[126] Lord Hutton put particular emphasis on the special conditions attached to life in the security service and the special duties and responsibilities incumbent on the defendant whereby he was prohibited by statute from disclosing information about his work. Moreover, these duties and responsibilities were specifically acknowledged and accepted.[127] Also in *Gaunt*[128] the Court of Appeal placed emphasis upon the responsibilities carried with freedom of expression 'which themselves reflect the power of words, whether spoken or written'.[129]

The question of whether or not an interference is prescribed by law also rarely arises in Article 10 claims although it is important not to overlook this requirement. In *Laporte*[130] the House of Lords determined that the actions of police in stopping a coach of protesters proceeding to a demonstration was not prescribed by law and was therefore incompatible with Article 10. In *Core Issues Trust*[131] the Administrative Court accepted that an advertising policy adopted by a public body in the exercise of its statutory powers had a basis in domestic law. It was accessible, on the internet, and would have been available for the claimant to check before placing its advertisement.[132]

However, as an aspect of necessity, the most important question in the freedom of expression cases brought under the HRA has been whether or not the interference is proportionate to the legitimate aim pursued. The important differences between this principle and traditional grounds of review were outlined in *Daly*.[133] The reviewing court may be required to assess the balance which the decision maker has struck. Secondly, the proportionality test may go further than the traditional grounds of review inasmuch as it may require attention to be directed to the relative weight accorded to

---

[126] *Shayler* (n 10).
[127] Ibid, [95].
[128] *Gaunt* (n 27).
[129] Ibid, [23].
[130] *R (Laporte) v Chief Constable of Gloucestershire* [2006] UKHL 55, [2007] 2 AC 105.
[131] *Core Issues Trust* (n 1).
[132] Ibid, [86].
[133] *R v Secretary of State for the Home Department, ex p Daly* [2001] UKHL 26, [2001] 2 AC 532, per Lord Steyn. See further I Leigh, 'Taking Rights Proportionately: Judicial Review, the Human Rights Act and Strasbourg' [2002] *Public Law* 265.

interests and considerations. When this process is carried out in a freedom of expression case, it appears that, in addition to the considerations peculiar to each objective or interest listed in Article 10(2), certain general principles affect the balancing process. Although alone it is difficult for any one principle to tip the scales too far, when combined these represent a formidable argument against countervailing interests. These general principles are examined in the following paragraphs.

---

8. General Principles

8.1 Section 12 HRA

The first general principle is section 12 of the HRA. Section 12 was inserted during the parliamentary debates on the Bill in response to press fears that the HRA, in particular the right to respect for private life, would lead to untrammelled restrictions on freedom of expression and the freedom of the press. It was the wish of the government:

> [s]o far as we are able, in a manner consistent with the convention and its jurisprudence . . . [to say] to the courts that whenever there is a clash between article 8 rights and article 10 rights, they must pay particular attention to the article 10 rights.[134]

The section applies if a court is considering whether to grant any relief which, if granted, might affect the exercise of the Convention right to freedom of expression. Section 12(2) relates to unrepresented defendants,[135] section 12(3) to prior restraints and section 12(4) to the importance of freedom of expression.

Section 12 adds very little to existing UK or ECtHR jurisprudence. In *Ashdown*, the Court of Appeal held that section 12 does no more

> than underline the need to have regard to contexts in which . . . [Strasbourg] jurisprudence has given particular weight to freedom of expression, while at the same time drawing attention to considerations which none the less justify restricting that right.[136]

It does not give Article 10 presumptive priority.[137] Nevertheless, some small changes have occurred.

Section 12(3) imposes a threshold test which has to be satisfied before a court may grant interlocutory injunctive relief. It provides that no such relief (which might affect the exercise of the Convention right to freedom of expression) is to be granted so as to restrain publication before trial unless the court is satisfied that the applicant is *likely* to establish that publication should not be allowed. There has been considerable litigation as to the meaning of 'likely' in this context. In *Cream Holdings Ltd* [138] the

---

[134] HC Deb, vol 315, col 543 (2 July 1998), Secretary of State for the Home Department, Mr Jack Straw.
[135] See eg *AMP v Persons Unknown* [2011] EWHC 3454 (TCC).
[136] *Ashdown* (n 9), [27]. See also *Imutran* (n 112), [18]–[19].
[137] *Douglas* (n 16), per Sedley LJ at [135] and per Keene LJ at [150].
[138] *Cream Holdings Ltd v Banerjee* [2004] UKHL 44, [2005] 1 AC 253.

House of Lords held that it did not mean 'more likely than not' or 'probably'.[139] In the opinion of their Lordships, that, as a test of universal application, would set the degree of likelihood too high and some flexibility was essential.[140] It concluded that the effect of section 12(3) was that the court was not to make an interim restraint order unless satisfied that the applicant's prospects of success at the trial were sufficiently favourable to justify such an order being made in the particular circumstances of the case.[141] As to what degree of likelihood made the prospects of success sufficiently favourable, it held that the general approach should be that courts will be exceedingly slow to make interim restraint orders where the applicant has not satisfied the court that he will probably (more likely than not) succeed at the trial. However, it appreciated that there would be cases where it would be necessary for a court to depart from this general approach and where a lesser degree of likelihood would suffice. This may apply where the potential adverse consequences of the disclosure are particularly grave or where a short-lived injunction was needed to enable the court to hear and give proper consideration to an application for interim relief pending the trial or any relevant appeal.[142]

Finally, section 12(4) elevates the Press Complaints Commission (PCC) Code of Practice to a position it did not previously occupy. This is of particular relevance in private life cases where it has been held that, where the Code has been flouted and no public interest claim is asserted, a claim to freedom of expression is likely to be trumped by Article 10(2).[143]

8.2 Importance of Freedom of Expression

Although section 12 has proved largely irrelevant, other threshold principles established at common law and by the ECtHR are also utilised by the courts. The first is the importance of freedom of expression. As already noted, of all the Convention rights given further effect by the HRA, freedom of expression was the most developed in UK law prior to the HRA coming into force. UK courts have generally given great respect to freedom of expression. In *Douglas*, Brooke LJ stated that, although the 'right to freedom of expression is not in every case the ace of trumps, it is a powerful card to which the courts of this country must always pay appropriate respect'.[144]

It is widely recognised that there is a public interest per se in freedom of expression.[145] By contrast to other Convention rights, frequent judicial explanations are given

---

[139] Ibid, [16].
[140] Ibid, [20].
[141] Ibid, [22].
[142] Ibid. This proviso was held not to apply in *Ntuli v Donald* [2010] EWCA Civ 1276, [2011] 1 WLR 294. Section 12(3) does not apply to defamation cases, where the rule remains that claimants will be unable to obtain an interim injunction to restrain the publication of an allegedly defamatory statement unless it is plain that the plea of justification is bound to fail. See *Greene v Associated Newspapers Ltd* [2004] EWCA Civ 1462, [2005] 3 WLR 281.
[143] *Douglas* (n 16), per Brooke LJ at [94]; *Theakston v MGN Ltd* [2002] EWHC (QB) 137, [2002] EMLR 22, [26]; *Campbell v Mirror Group Newspapers Ltd* [2004] UKHL 22, [2004] 2 AC 457; and *X (a woman formerly known as Mary Bell) v O'Brien* [2003] EWHC (QB) 1101, [2003] 2 FCR 686.
[144] *Douglas*, ibid, [49].
[145] *Ashdown* (n 9), [66].

as to why it is important to protect freedom of expression.[146] For example, in *Animal Defenders International*[147] Lord Bingham stated as follows:

> Freedom of thought and expression is an essential condition of an intellectually healthy society. The free communication of information, opinions and argument about the laws which a state should enact and the policies its government at all levels should pursue is an essential condition of truly democratic government. These are the values which article 10 exists to protect, and their importance gives it a central role in the Convention regime, protecting free speech in general and free political speech in particular.[148]

8.3 Importance of Freedom of the Press

It is generally recognised by the courts that the media have a positive duty to act as a watchdog or as the eyes and ears of the general public and to inform their readers about matters of public interest.[149] It has been held that the existence of a free press is in itself desirable and in the public interest[150] irrespective of whether a particular publication is in the public interest.[151] The possibility that some sectors of the press may abuse their freedom to report has been held to be an insufficient reason for curtailing that freedom for all members of the press.[152] It has also been held that the press are entitled to a reasonable margin of appreciation in taking decisions as to what details need to be included in an article to give it credibility as this is an essential part of the journalistic exercise.[153] '[J]ournalists need to be permitted a degree of exaggeration even in the context of factual assertions not only when making comments or voicing their opinions.'[154]

As discussed below, the Court of Appeal has emphasised that to restrict publication to save the blushes of the famous:

> could have the wholly undesirable chilling effect on the necessary ability of publishers to sell their newspapers. We have to enable sales if we want to keep our newspapers. Unduly to fetter their freedom to report as editors judge to be responsible is to undermine the pre-eminence of the deserved place of the press as a powerful pillar of democracy.[155]

Whilst freedom of the press was recognised in the House of Lords' pre-HRA decision in *Reynolds*, it was not held to be outweigh other interests where a claim of qualified privilege was made and had to be balanced against protection of reputation. Incursions into press freedom in order to ensure responsible journalism were held to be neces-

---

[146] See eg *R v Secretary of State for the Home Department, ex p Simms* [1999] 3 WLR 328, per Lord Steyn at 337.

[147] *Animal Defenders International* (n 14).

[148] Ibid, [27]. See also *Gaunt* (n 27), [22].

[149] *Sherwood* (n 63), [17]–[18]. See also *Re S (A Child) (Identification: Restriction on Publication)* [2004] UKHL 47, [2005] 1 AC 593 concerning the freedom of the press to report a criminal trial and *ETK v News Group Newspapers Ltd* [2011] EWCA Civ 439; [2011] 1 WLR 1827, [13].

[150] *Ashdown* (n 9), [66]. *Financial Times v Interbrew* [2002] EWCA Civ 274, [2002] EMLR 446, per Sedley LJ at [52].

[151] *B & C v A* (n 26), [11(iv)].

[152] Ibid, [72].

[153] *Campbell* (n 143), per Lord Hope at [112] and per Baroness Hale at [143]. See also *Re Attorney General's Reference No 3 of 1999* [2009] UKHL 34, [2010] 1 AC 145, per Lord Hope at [25].

[154] *Turcu v News Group Newspapers Ltd* [2005] EWHC (QB) 799, [108].

[155] *ETK* (n 149), [13].

sary.[156] Post-HRA the message remains that freedom of a *responsible* press is what is important. This is reflected in the approach taken by the courts to disclosure of journalists' sources. Although the *Norwich Pharmacal*[157] jurisdiction to order disclosure has now expanded,[158] any order made must still conform to section 10 of the Contempt of Court Act 1981 and Article 10 of the ECHR. In both the *Ashworth*[159] and *Interbrew*[160] cases the importance of the protection of sources to press freedom was recognised, as was the importance of freedom of the press. Nevertheless, in both cases disclosure was found to be proportionate—in *Ashworth* because the confidentiality of psychiatric medical records was at issue and in *Interbrew* because the expression was of low value, designed to wreck legitimate commercial activity. The public interest in protecting the source of information was found in both cases to be very low, insufficient to outweigh countervailing considerations.[161]

8.4 The Public Interest

It has been held that there is a public interest in freedom of expression and freedom of the press per se. In addition, it may be in the public interest for particular material to be published. Of all the general considerations taken into account by a court considering the application of Article 10, the public interest in publication is the most important. It has been held by the High Court that the extent to which the content is of public interest or contributes to a debate of general interest is the decisive factor in deciding where the balance falls between Articles 8 and 10.[162] However, it remains impossible to state with certainty that where there is a public interest in publication, this will outweigh other interests and publication will be allowed: '[T]here can never be any "trump card" defence called either "public interest"' or "Article 10". The issue is always going to turn on how the law provides for resolving the conflict between (at least) two competing public interests.'[163]

Much still depends on countervailing public interests, such as the protection of reputation,[164] maintenance of national security[165] and protection of property interests,[166] and also the category of public interest the information falls into from political information to information about public figures.

To rely on a public interest defence, it is not necessary that the defendant be aware at the time of publication of the matters and actually communicate these to the public.[167] It is for the court to decide whether or not a particular publication is in the public

---

[156] *Reynolds* (n 6), per Lord Nicholls.
[157] *Norwich Pharmacal Co v Customs and Excise Commissioners* [1973] 2 All ER 943.
[158] See *Ashworth* (n 87); *Interbrew* (n 150).
[159] *Ashworth*, ibid.
[160] *Interbrew* (n 150).
[161] See further P Wragg, 'Free Speech Is Not Valued if Only Valued Speech Is Free' (2009) 15 *European Public Law* 111; L Blom-Cooper, 'Press Freedom: Constitutional Right or Cultural Assumption?' [2008] *Public Law* 260.
[162] *Ferdinand v MGN Ltd* [2011] EWHC 2454 (QB), [62].
[163] *Hunt v Times Newspapers Ltd* [2012] EWHC 110 (QB), [4].
[164] *Reynolds* (n 6).
[165] *Shayler* (n 10).
[166] *Ashdown* (n 9).
[167] *Mosley v News Group Newspapers* [2008] EWHC 1777 (QB), [2008] EMLR 20, [112].

interest.[168] In *Mosley*, the High Court held that a decision on public interest must be capable of being tested by objectively recognised criteria. But held that it could be argued as a matter of policy that 'allowance should be made for a decision reached which falls within a range of reasonably possible conclusions'.[169] It was also suggested that there may be scope for paying regard to the concept of responsible journalism.[170] This would involve a judge enquiring whether the relevant journalist's decision prior to publication was reached as a result of carrying out enquiries and checks consistent with responsible journalism.[171]

8.4.1 Defining the Public Interest

The question of whether it is in the public interest for material to be published is a difficult one. In *B&C v A* the Court of Appeal stated that in the majority of situations, whether the public interest is involved or not will be obvious.[172] Furthermore, it held that it was impossible to define the public interest as the circumstances in any particular case under consideration 'can vary so much that a judgment in one case is unlikely to be decisive in another case'.[173] Despite these protestations, the Court of Appeal went on to define the public interest essentially as what the public is interested in: 'The courts must not ignore the fact that if newspapers do not publish information which the public are interested in, there will be fewer newspapers published, which will not be in the public interest.'[174]

Such a perspective is at odds with other UK jurisprudence, ECtHR jurisprudence,[175] and the Press Complaints Commission Code of Practice. It is also at odds with the eventual conclusion of the Court of Appeal in the case that there was a public interest in the material not because it would sell newspapers but because the footballer concerned was a role model for young people and it was important his undesirable behaviour and unfortunate example be exposed.[176] Nevertheless, this particular viewpoint surfaced again in 2011 in another Court of Appeal judgment where the court stated:

> [F]or sections of the media, developments in privacy law impinging on their ability to publish such matters, may not only give rise to issues of principle as to freedom of expression in the individual case but also to real commercial concerns—which at least to the extent of the general public interest in having a thriving and vigorous newspaper industry, representing all legitimate opinions, may also be argued to give rise to a relevant factor for the court to take into account.[177]

By contrast, in a later judgment the High Court stated that:

> [W]hat is of interest to the public is not the same as what it is in the public interest to publish.

---

[168] Ibid, [135].
[169] Ibid, [138].
[170] Ibid, [140].
[171] Ibid, [141].
[172] *B & C v A* (n 26), [11(viii)].
[173] Ibid.
[174] Ibid, [11(xii)].
[175] See further S Tierney, 'Press Freedom and the Public Interest: The Developing Jurisprudence of the European Court of Human Rights' [1998] 4 *European Human Rights Law Review* 419.
[176] *B & C v A* (n 26), [43(vi)].
[177] *Hutcheson v News Group Newspapers Ltd* [2011] EWCA Civ 808, [34].

Newspaper editors have the final decision on what is of interest to the public: judges have the final decision what is in the public interest to publish.[178]

To define the public interest a far better and more logical starting point is the PCC Editor's Code of Practice. Here, the public interest is defined to include: detecting or exposing crime[179] or serious impropriety; protecting public health and safety; and preventing the public from being misled by an action or statement of an individual or organisation.[180]

8.4.2 Political Information

The next step is to examine the case law. At one end of the spectrum is 'political information', where a public interest in publication is generally always found to exist. It has been held that freedom of political speech 'is a freedom of the very highest importance in any country which lays claim to being a democracy. Restrictions on this freedom need to be examined rigorously by all concerned, not least the courts'.[181]

In *Campbell*[182] Baroness Hale stated that political speech included information and ideas on matters relevant to the organisation of the economic, social and political life of the country, which included information about public figures, especially those in elective office, that would otherwise be private but was relevant to their participation in public life. An example is *Ashdown*, where it was held that information about a meeting between the Prime Minister and an opposition party leader to discuss possible close cooperation between those parties was very likely to be of legitimate and continuing public interest.[183] Another is *Rusbridger*,[184] where the House of Lords held that a press campaign advocating the peaceful and constitutional replacement of the monarchy by a republican form of government would be considered political speech. A political advertisement is also a form of political speech. This was confirmed by the House of Lords in *Animal Defenders International*[185] where the claimants had been prevented by the Communications Act 2003 from placing an advertisement on television with the object of directing public attention towards the use of primates by humans, and the threat presented by such use to the survival of primates.

Sometimes political speech must be separated from what is merely insulting speech. For example, in *Calver*[186] a councillor challenged the Adjudication Panel's determination that he had breached the Council's Code of Conduct with blogs and comments on his personal website. The Administrative Court held that many of the comments were

---

[178] *Goodwin v NGN Ltd* [2011] EWHC 1437 (QB), [2011] EMLR 27, [2].
[179] It was held in *Mosley* (n 167), [111] and [118] that it is not an automatic defence to intrusive journalism to argue that a crime was being committed in someone's home and that those who have committed serious crimes do not lose their right to respect for private life.
[180] www.pcc.org.uk/cop/practice.html
[181] *Prolife Alliance* (n 123), per Lord Nicholls at [6].
[182] *Campbell* (n 143).
[183] *Ashdown* (n 9), [64]. See further I Hare, 'Is the Privileged Position of Political Expression Justified?' in J Beatson and Cripps (eds), *Freedom of Expression and Freedom of Information* (Oxford, Oxford University Press, 2000).
[184] *R (on the application of Rusbridger) v Attorney General* [2003] UKHL 38, [2004] 1 AC 357.
[185] *Animal Defenders International* (n 14).
[186] *R (Calver) v Adjudication Panel for Wales* [2012] EWHC 1172 (Admin).

political expression and that it was necessary for politicians to have 'thicker skins' than others:

> The comments were in no sense 'high' manifestations of political expression. But they (or many of them) were comments about the inadequate performance of Councillors in their public duties . . . fall within the term 'political expression' in the broader sense.[187]

Also at the high end of the spectrum is information concerning activities in the public sector. In *Shayler* Lord Hope suggested that Shayler might have had good grounds for his claim that it was in the public interest for him to disclose what he perceived to be the unlawfulness, irregularity, incompetence, misbehaviour and waste of resources in the security service.[188] In *H (A Healthcare Worker)* the Court of Appeal held that the story that Associated Newspapers wished to publish had a number of features of considerable public interest. These included whether N, the health authority, should have reacted swiftly and forcefully when faced with a healthcare worker who was challenging the Department of Health Guidelines with regard to the fact that there were no guidelines in place covering notification to patients that a healthcare worker with a particular speciality who is or was treating them is HIV-positive.[189] In *London Regional Transport* the decision to allow publication of a redacted version of a report concerning the public–private partnership for London Underground was influenced by the strong public interest in publication.[190]

It was held in *Attorney General's Reference No 3 of 1999*[191] that a programme the BBC wished to broadcast, inspired by removal of the double-jeopardy rule, was a matter of legitimate public interest. It has also been held that publication of the identity of a person subject to an order under the Terrorism (United Nations Measures) Order 2006 was a matter of public interest[192] and that the public had a right to receive information about the treatment of a prisoner who has been in detention for a very long time without charge; and the extradition arrangements applied in his case.[193] Also held to be of public interest are the workings of the family justice system[194] and the standards in care homes and the ability of a regulator to maintain them.[195]

8.4.3 Public Figures

Further down the spectrum is information concerning public figures. These are defined in Resolution 1165 of the Parliamentary Assembly of the Council of Europe (1998)

---

[187] Ibid, [80].
[188] *Shayler* (n 10), [51].
[189] *H* (n 86), [24].
[190] *London Regional Transport v The Mayor of London*, Divisional Court, 31 July 2001, [40]. The conclusion of the High Court was later upheld on appeal; see *London Regional Transport v The Mayor of London* [2001] EWCA Civ 1491, [2003] EMLR 4. See also *Re X* [2001] 1 FCR 541; *Medway Council v BBC* [2002] 1 FLR 104; and *Ackroyd v Mersey Care NHS Trust* [2003] EWCA Civ 663, [2003] EMLR 36.
[191] *Attorney General's Reference No 3 of 1999* [2009] UKHL 34, [2010] 1 AC 145.
[192] *In the Matter of Guardian News and Media* [2010] UKSC 1, [2010] 2 AC 697, [52].
[193] *R (BBC) v Secretary of State for Justice* [2012] EWHC 13 (Admin) [2012] 2 All ER 1089.
[194] *Re Webster* [2006] EWHC 2733, [2007] 1 FLR 1146.
[195] *BKM Ltd v British Broadcasting Corporation* [2009] EWHC 3151. See also *Stone v South East Coast Strategic Health Authority* [2006] EWHC 1668 (Admin) concerning the care treatment and supervision of a convicted murderer. The question of public interest also frequently arises in defamation claims where the defence of qualified privilege is pleaded.

as 'persons holding public office and/or using public resources and, more broadly speaking, all those who play a role in public life, whether in politics, the economy, the arts, the social sphere, sport or in any other domain'.[196]

The courts have been considered a variety of claims concerning respect for private life from public figures working in the arts and sport. Generally the claim of respect for private life is lessened by the individual's status as a public figure. However, the situation is made slightly worse for the individual by the tendency of the courts to find the Article 10 claim strengthened by a public interest in exposing the perceived duplicity of public figures. The duplicity is 'perceived' as, in the majority of cases, the individual concerned has not given any firm indication that they do not participate in the undesirable behaviour at issue. As role models for young people, they are expected by the courts not to visit brothels[197] or have extra-marital affairs,[198] and it has been held to be in the public interest for them to be exposed.

However, in its judgment in *Campbell* a majority of the House of Lords adopted a more moderate approach, holding that the public had a need to know that Naomi Campbell had been misleading them by her denials of drug addiction and that she was receiving therapy for her drug addiction. However, other confidential details she had chosen not to put in the public domain were off limits, including the fact that she was receiving treatment at Narcotics Anonymous, the details of the treatment and the visual portrayal of her leaving a specific meeting with other addicts.[199] Baroness Hale commented that it might be questioned why 'if a role model has adopted a stance which all would agree is beneficial rather than detrimental to society, it is so important to reveal that she has feet of clay'.[200] However, in the present case she concluded that the possession and use of illegal drugs was a criminal offence and a matter of serious public concern.[201]

Following the decision of the majority in *Campbell*, the courts took a more generous approach to public figures seeking some protection for their private lives.[202] The High Court held that whilst a judge may hold personal moral views about the issues of the day, it was important not to let them intrude when interpreting and applying the law:

> With such a wide range of different views in society, perhaps more than for many generations, one must guard against allowing legal judgments to be coloured by personal attitudes. Even among judges, there is no doubt a wide range of opinion. It is all the more important, therefore, that the outcome of a particular case should not be determined by the judge's personal views.[203]

In the light of this observation it concluded that there was no general rule than an adulterer could never obtain an injunction to restrain the publication of matters relating

---

[196] In *Archer v Williams* [2003] EWHC (QB) 1670, [2003] EMLR 38 the court held that Mary Archer was not a public figure and there was therefore no public interest in the matters she sought to keep confidential.

[197] *Theakston* (n 143).

[198] *B & C v A* (n 26).

[199] *Campbell* (n 143). See generally R Singh and J Strachan, 'The Right to Privacy in English Law' [2002] 2 *European Human Rights Law Review* 129.

[200] Ibid, [151].

[201] Ibid.

[202] See eg *Ash v McKennitt* [2006] EWCA Civ 1714, [2007] 3 WLR 194 and *ETK* (n 149) and *CTB v News Group Newspapers Ltd* [2011] EWHC 1232 (QB).

[203] *CC v AB* [2006] EWHC 3083, [2007] 2 FLR 301.

to his adulterous relationship.[204] It was also held that sexual relationships of those who were in the public eye were generally likely to be interesting to the public but this did not necessarily make them of public interest.[205] Similarly, the argument in *Mosley* that the nature of the sexual activities of the claimant was such that the public had a right to know that the claimant engaged in them was not successful.[206] However, the High Court did hold that if it had been proved there was a Nazi theme to the sexual activity, there could have been a public interest in revealing this to at least those in the Fédération Internationale de l'Automobile (FIA) to whom the claimant was, as President of the FIA, responsible. It stated as follows:

> He has to deal with many people of all races and religions, and has spoken out against racism in sport. If he were really behaving in the way I have just described, that would, for many people, call seriously into question his suitability for his FIA role. It would be information which people arguably should have the opportunity to know and evaluate.[207]

On the facts it found that there was no public interest in the sexual activity stating that it was not for the state or for the media to expose sexual conduct which did not involve any significant breach of the criminal law:

> It is not for journalists to undermine human rights, or for judges to refuse to enforce them, mere on grounds of taste or moral disapproval. Everyone is entitled to espouse moral or religious beliefs to the effect that certain types of sexual behaviour are wrong or demeaning to those participating. That does not mean that they are entitled to hound those who practise them or to detract from their right to live life as they choose.[208]

It also stated that the fact 'that a particular relationship happens to be adulterous, or that someone's tastes are unconventional or "perverted", does not give the media carte blanche'.[209] Furthermore, it was held that even if there was wrongdoing, it did not necessarily follow that photographs of every single detail must be published in order to achieve the public interest objective.[210] Nor would it automatically justify clandestine recording, whether visual or audio.[211]

In more recent times, protection may be swinging away from public figures once again as the courts become willing to find a public interest in exposing perceived duplicity. In *LNS* the claimant footballer sought to restrain publication of information about a relationship. Without reaching a final conclusion on the issue, the High Court stated that the claimant's position in life, both professional and personal, could form the basis for a submission that publication of at least the fact of the relationship would be in the public interest.[212] In *Ferdinand*[213] it was held that in a plural society there will be a 'range of views as to what matters or is of significance in particular in terms of a person's suitability for a high profile position'.[214] It stated that one facet of the public

---

[204] Ibid, [30].
[205] Ibid, [37].
[206] *Mosley* (n 167), [25].
[207] Ibid, [122].
[208] Ibid, [127].
[209] Ibid, [128].
[210] Ibid, [16].
[211] Ibid, [16]. See also *HRH Prince of Wales v Associated Newspapers* [2006] EWCA Civ 1776, [2008] Ch 57, [70].
[212] *LNS v Persons Unknown* [2010] EWHC 119 (QB), [2010] EMLR 16, [8].
[213] *Ferdinand* (n 162).
[214] Ibid, [64].

interest could be 'correcting a false image'.[215] Here it concluded that articles concerning a footballer's affair were in the public interest given he had portrayed himself in the media as a reformed character and his appointment as captain of the England football team[216] was a 'job that carried with it an expectation of high standards'.[217]

Similarly in *Goodwin*[218] the High Court held that it was in the public interest that there should be a public discussion of the circumstances in which it is proper for a chief executive (or other person holding public office or exercising official functions) 'should be able to carry on a sexual relationship with an employee in the same organisation'.[219] It stated:

> It is in the public interest that newspapers should be able to report upon cases which raise a question as to what should or should not be a standard in public life. The law, and standards in public life, must develop to meet changing needs. The public interest cannot be confined to exposing matters which are improper only by existing standards and laws, and not by standards as they ought to be, or which people can reasonably contend that they ought to be.[220]

However, it did confirm that the press was not free to interfere with a person's private life and family life by exposing confidential information, and then seek to justify that by speculating the information may have distracted him or her from doing his or her job.[221]

8.4.4 Commercial Expression

Even further down the scale of protected expression is commercial expression such as advertising, which has traditionally been treated as of less significance than freedom of political or artistic expression.[222] There are also indications that the right to sell pornographic literature and images is considered low-value expression, and may not even qualify for protection under Article 10 at all.[223]

---

9. National Security

The first of the permitted interferences as set out in Article 10(2) is national security. Interference with freedom of expression on this ground has not often arisen in HRA claims but, when it has, it has been taken very seriously notwithstanding the

---

[215] Ibid, [65].
[216] Ibid, [84]–[89].
[217] Ibid, [89].
[218] *Goodwin* (n 178).
[219] Ibid, [133].
[220] Ibid, [133].
[221] Ibid, [137].
[222] *British American Tobacco* (n 19), [28].
[223] *Belfast City Council* (n 13). See further J. Rowbottom, 'To Rant, Vent and Converse: Protecting Low Level Digital Speech' (2012) 71 *Cambridge Law Journal* 355.

comment has also been made that the security services are not entitled to immunity from criticism.[224] The key case concerning the balance between freedom of expression and national security is *Shayler*.[225] This claim concerned a former member of the security services who had been indicted on three counts of unlawful disclosure contrary to sections 1(1)(a), 4(1) and 4(3)(a) of the Official Secrets Act 1989. At a preparatory hearing, the questions were whether the sections under which the defendant was charged afforded him a public interest defence and, if not, whether those sections were compatible with Article 10. The defendant argued that he believed it to be in the public interest to disclose what he perceived to be unlawfulness, irregularity, incompetence, misbehaviour and waste of resources in the security service.

The House of Lords concluded that a defendant prosecuted under sections 1(1)(a), 4(1) and 4(3)(a) of the Act was not entitled to be acquitted if he demonstrated that it was or that he believed it was in the public or national interest to make the disclosure.[226] It then considered whether or not this was in breach of Article 10. The need to preserve the secrecy of information was recognised, the real question in the opinion of the House of Lords was whether the 'interference with the individual's convention right prescribed by national law is greater than is required to meet the legitimate object which the state seeks to achieve'.[227]

In reaching its conclusion that the interference was proportionate, the House of Lords was particularly influenced by the fact that the ban was not an absolute ban—it was a ban on disclosure 'without lawful authority'.[228] Under section 7(3)(a) a former member may make disclosure to a Crown servant for the purposes of his functions as such. It is also open to a former member to seek official authorisation to make a disclosure to a wider audience.[229] If such authority is refused, in the opinion of the House of Lords, a former member is entitled to seek judicial review of the decision to refuse and, as freedom of expression is at issue, 'the court will now conduct a much more rigorous and intrusive review than was once thought to be permissible'.[230] Furthermore, a fair hearing would require disclosure to a qualified lawyer from whom the former member wished to seek advice. If the material was too sensitive, 'arrangements could be made'.[231]

Taking into account these safeguards, and the further safeguard that section 9(1) of the Official Secrets Act 1989 required the consent of the Attorney General before any prosecution, the House of Lords concluded that there were sufficient and effective safeguards and sections 1(1), 4(1) and 4(3) were found to be compatible with Article 10.[232]

---

[224] *Punch* (n 64), [29].
[225] *Shayler* (n 10).
[226] Ibid, per Lord Bingham at [20].
[227] Ibid, per Lord Bingham at [26].
[228] Ibid, per Lord Bingham at [27] and per Lord Hope at [70]–[71].
[229] Ibid, per Lord Bingham at [29].
[230] Ibid, per Lord Bingham at [33], per Lord Hope at [72], [75], [77]–[78] and per Lord Hutton at [107].
[231] Ibid, per Lord Bingham at [34], per Lord Hope at [73]–[74] and per Lord Hutton at [111]–[114].
[232] Ibid, Lord Bingham at [36] per and per Lord Hope at [83]–[85]. See also *Secretary of State for Defence v Times Newspapers Ltd*, Divisional Court, 28 March 2001; *A* (n 109) and *Naik* (n 53). See further ATH Smith, 'Assessing the Public Interest in Cases Affecting the Media—The Prosecution Guidelines' [2013] *Criminal Law Review* 449.

10. Prevention of Disorder or Crime

Expression has the potential to provoke disorder, although, again, consideration of interferences with freedom of expression on this ground under the HRA has been rare. In *Farrakhan*[233] the Home Secretary argued that his decision to exclude Mr Farrakhan from the United Kingdom turned on his evaluation of the risk that, because of his notorious opinions, a visit by him might provoke disorder. In evaluating the risk, the Home Secretary had regard to tensions in the Middle East current at the time of his decision, the 'fruits of widespread consultation' and sources of information available to him not available to the court. He chose not to describe his sources of information or the purport of that information.[234] Nevertheless, the Court of Appeal held that this was sufficient explanation, although commenting 'it would have been better had he been less diffident about explaining the nature of the information and the advice that he had received'.[235]

As a result of this decision, the level of proof required to show that disorder would result from the exercise of the right to freedom of expression appears very low. It is not clear whether the absence of proof will apply only in cases where the decision of the executive are an issue or generally to all decisions, such as decisions of police under the Public Order Act in relation to marches and assemblies. There was no conclusive evidence in *Farrakhan* that disorder would result from his visit. In fact, in his decision letter of 20 November 2000 the Home Secretary noted that, apart from one incident, there was no record of violent disorder associated with the group in the United Kingdom, that Farrakhan was not excluded from any other country, that nothing objectionable occurred during his visits to Israel, Australia and Canada, that he has signed assurances as to his behaviour and that his current message was one of reconciliation. Nevertheless, the Home Secretary remained satisfied that Mr Farrakhan has expressed anti-semitic and racially divisive views. Therefore, a visit would pose a threat to public order and stir up racial hatred contrary to the Public Order Act 1986.

The potential for disorder, along with administrative difficulties, was also the justification put forward in *Hirst*[236] to limit the prisoner's telephone contact with the media. The Administrative Court found that the limitation on telephone contact with the media was not part of the sentence of imprisonment itself and therefore Article 10(2) had to be considered. It concluded that the administrative difficulties presented and the alleged potential for prison disorder did not justify what was effectively a blanket ban on media interviews, particularly as the conditions proposed on the exercise of the right went a considerable way towards meeting the concerns of the prison authorities.[237] Along with national security, this justification was also employed in *A*,[238] where, affording considerable deference, the Divisional Court held that it was proportionate for the Secretary of

---

[233] *Farrakhan* (n 12).
[234] Ibid, [78].
[235] Ibid.
[236] *Hirst* (n 48).
[237] Ibid, [78]–[84].
[238] *A* (n 109).

State's to permit Category A prisoners detained under section 21 of the Anti-Terrorism Crime and Security Act 2001 only to be interviewed by journalists if the interviews were conducted within the earshot of officials and tape recorded.

A different issue was at the heart of the claim in *British Sky Broadcasting*[239] where Essex Police sought production orders requiring news broadcasters to produce footage recorded by them of the Dale Farm evictions carried out by police in October 2011. Police argued that for the prevention of similar disorder in future it was necessary for them to identify as many as possible of those committing offences. The High Court held that the police had to demonstrate that the interference with Article 10 rights was proportionate because of the substantial value of the material in the context of the investigation. It found nothing to justify such a conclusion here.[240] Eady J observed as follows:

> There is no doubt that the statutory provisions governing disclosure orders can be of great value in tracing those responsible for public order and other offences and thus in serving the public interest. The importance of establishing the access conditions, however, should never be underestimated. There is a burden to be discharged and disclosure orders against the media, intrusive as they are, can never be granted as a formality. There must at least be cogent evidence as to (i) what the footage sought is likely to reveal, (ii) how important such evidence would be to carrying out the investigation and (iii) why it is necessary and proportionate to order the intrusion by reference to other potential sources of information.[241]

---

11. Protection of Health or Morals

Legislation such as the Obscene Publications Act 1959 does constitute a significant interference with the right to freedom of expression. Nevertheless, in the interests of the protection of morals, the courts are usually willing to grant the legislature and primary decision maker a wide margin of discretion. In *Perrin*,[242] dismissing an appeal against a conviction under the Act, the Court of Appeal commented that there was no public interest to be served by permitting a business for profit to supply material which most people would regard as pornographic or obscene and further, that there was 'no reason why a responsible government should abandon that protection in favour of other limited remedies'.[243]

Whilst the House of Lords did not finally determine the question of whether or not Article 10 was wide enough to cover the use of premises to sell pornographic books, in *Belfast City Council*[244] it proceeded on the basis that in an appropriate case it may be

---

[239] *R (British Sky Broadcasting) v Chelmsford Crown Court* [2012] EWHC 1295 (Admin), [2012] 2 Cr App R 33.

[240] Ibid, [24].

[241] Ibid, [31].

[242] *Perrin* (n 15).

[243] Ibid, [49] in reliance upon *Muller v Switzerland* (1991) 13 EHRR 212 and *Wingrove v United Kingdom* (1997) 24 EHRR 1.

[244] *Belfast City Council* (n 13).

necessary for a council to restrict the use of premises via licensing in order to protect health or morals, and a measure of deference was to be afforded to the council's decision in such matters. Baroness Hale observed, that the the local authority was much better placed than the court to 'decide whether the right of sex shop owners to sell pornographic literature and images should be restricted'.[245] However, in the present case the views of the local authority carried little weight as it had made no attempt to address that question.

Similarly, where the protection of health is put forward as the justification, the courts appear willing to grant the decision maker considerable latitude. In *British American Tobacco*[246] six corporations in the tobacco industry challenged the lawfulness of new advertising regulations which provided for a total ban on the advertising of tobacco products with limited exceptions relating to the display of products at points of sale. The Administrative Court held that the protection of public health was a very important counterbalance to unrestricted commercial expression[247] and it was principally for the decision maker to resolve how best the aim of protecting health could be achieved by restricting promotion of extremely harmful but lawful products.[248] It concluded that the regulations were proportionate, noting that, given

> the enormous health risks and economic costs to society caused by smoking tobacco and a substantial weight of expert opinion as to the effects of advertising . . . upon the levels of consumption, I believe it to have been a responsible and proportionate step to have regulated as the Minister has now done.[249]

---

12. Protection of the Reputation of Others

The law of defamation is an undoubted interference with the right to freedom of expression, although in many instances its application to particular facts is justified in the interests of the protection of the reputation of others. Prior to the HRA coming into force, the common law constitutional right to freedom of expression had already had some impact on the law of defamation, and the comment is often made that no different conclusion would have been reached had Article 10 been applied.[250] Under the HRA, Article 10 has continued to shape the law of defamation, ensuring in particular that the interference posed by this law is proportionate to the aim of protecting reputation.[251] Protection of reputation now also engages the right to respect for private life, as pro-

---

[245] Ibid, [37].
[246] *British American Tobacco* (n 19).
[247] Ibid, [32].
[248] Ibid, [37].
[249] Ibid, [52].
[250] See eg *Derbyshire County Council v Times Newspapers Ltd* [1993] AC 534.
[251] The only case to arise under this ground outside of the defamation context has been *Pay* (n 22), where the Employment Appeal Tribunal decided that the dismissal of the claimant because of his hobby of a circus-related fire act which he performed in fetish and hedonist clubs was not disproportionate to protecting the reputation of the Probation Service.

tected by Article 8,[252] and therefore in a defamation claim courts must balance not only protection of reputation against Article 10 but also the Article 8 rights of the claimant.

12.1 Qualified Privilege

The right to freedom of expression has had a significant impact on the defamation defence of qualified privilege. The key case is *Reynolds*,[253] which concerned an article published in the British mainland edition of the *Sunday Times* about the resignation of Mr Reynolds as Prime Minister of Ireland. Mr Reynolds alleged that the sting of the article was that he had deliberately and dishonestly misled the Dáil and his cabinet colleagues.

The *Sunday Times* argued that the defence of qualified privilege applied to the article. In particular, relying on the right to freedom of expression, the *Sunday Times* sought the incremental development of the common law by the creation of a new category of occasion when privilege derived from the subject matter alone: political information. The House of Lords rejected this development. Although the importance of the role discharged by the media 'in the expression and communication of information and comment on political matters'[254] was recognised, the public interest that the 'reputation of public figures should not be debased falsely'[255] was also taken into account. With respect to defamatory imputations of fact, as was at issue here, it was concluded that the established common law approach was essentially sound. Where publication is to the world at large, the publication will be privileged if the public is entitled to know the particular information. However, all the circumstances must be taken into account in determining whether the test is satisfied.

> The duty–interest test, or the right to know test, cannot be carried out in isolation from these factors and without regard to them. A claim to privilege stands or falls according to whether the claim passes or fails this test.[256]

By way of illustration, Lord Nicholls listed ten matters which may be taken into account, depending on the circumstances:

> (1) The seriousness of the allegation. The more serious the charge, the more the public is misinformed and the individual harmed, if the allegation is not true. (2) The nature of the information, and the extent to which the subject matter is a matter of public concern. (3) The source of the information. Some informants have no direct knowledge of the events. Some have their own axes to grind, or are being paid for their stories. (4) The steps taken to verify the information. (5) The status of the information. The allegation may have already been the subject of investigation which commands respect. (6) The urgency of the matter. News is often a perishable commodity. (7) Whether comment was sought from the plaintiff. He may have information others do not possess or have not disclosed. An approach to the plaintiff will not always be necessary. (8) Whether the article contained the gist of the plaintiff's side of the story. (9) The tone of the article. A newspaper can raise queries or call for an investigation.

---

[252] *In the Matter of Guardian News and Media* [2010] UKSC 1, [2010] 2 AC 697.
[253] *Reynolds* (n 6). Although this judgment actually pre-dated the coming into force of the HRA, their Lordships indicated that no different conclusion would have been reached under the HRA.
[254] Ibid, per Lord Nicholls.
[255] Ibid, per Lord Nicholls.
[256] Ibid, per Lord Nicholls.

It need not adopt allegations as statements of fact. (10) The circumstances of the publication, including the timing.

A majority concluded that, given the article made no mention of Reynolds's explanation, this was not information the public had a right to know and was not protected by privilege.[257]

12.1.1 The Nature of Reynolds Privilege

As the Court of Appeal pointed out in its judgment in *Loutchansky*,[258] the modifications made by the judgment in *Reynolds* to the defence of qualified privilege were significant. First, it was established that privilege attaches to the publication itself rather than the occasion of the publication. Secondly, once it attaches, there is little scope for any subsequent finding of malice.[259] As was later confirmed in *Flood*:

> Reynolds privilege arises because of the subject matter of the publication itself . . . it arises only where the test of responsible journalism is satisfied, and this requirement leaves little or no room for separate consideration of malice.[260]

In later judgments further explanation has been given. In *Jameel*[261] Lord Bingham confirmed that the precondition of reliance upon qualified privilege was that the matter published should be one of public interest.[262] Referring to Lord Nicholls statement he summarised that there was no duty to publish and the public had no interest in reading material:

> which the publisher has not taken reasonable steps to verify . . But the publisher is protected if he has taken such steps as a responsible journalist would take to try and ensure that what is published is accurate and fit for publication.[263]

Considerable discussion of the defence once again took place in the Supreme Court judgment in *Flood*.[264] Lord Phillips, simplifying matters still further, stated that *Reynolds* privilege protects publication of defamatory matter to the world at large where (i) it was in the public interest that the information should be published and (ii) the publisher has acted responsibly in publishing the information.[265] Later he stated that the importance of the public interest in receiving the relevant information had to be weighed against the public interest in preventing the dissemination of defamatory allegations.[266]

Summarising the principles to date, the key questions when qualified privilege is

---

[257] See further K Williams, 'Defaming Politicians: The Not So Common Law' (2000) 63 *Modern Law Review* 748; I Loveland, 'Freedom of Political Expression: Who Needs the Human Rights Act?' [2001] *Public Law* 233.

[258] *Loutchansky* (n 17).

[259] Ibid, [33].

[260] *Times Newspapers Ltd v Flood* [2012] UKSC 11, [2012] 2 WLR 760, per Lord Phillips at [38].

[261] *Jameel* (n 11).

[262] Ibid, [31].

[263] Ibid, [32].

[264] *Flood* (n 260).

[265] Ibid, [2].

[266] Ibid, [44].

claimed are whether responsible journalism has been exercised and whether the subject matter of the publication is such that it is in the public interest that it be published.

12.1.2 Public Interest

In *Jameel* Lord Bingham noted that where a complaint related to one particular ingredient of a composite story, consideration should be given to the thrust of the article:

> If the thrust of the article is true, and the public interest condition is satisfied, the inclusion of an inaccurate fact may not have the same appearance of irresponsibility as it might if the whole thrust of the article is untrue.[267]

Lord Hoffmann also held that when determining whether the subject matter of the article was a matter of public interest, the article as a whole had to be considered.[268] He stated that in matters of public interest, there was a professional duty on the part of journalists to impart the information and an interest in the public in receiving it and this was a proposition of law which did not need to be decided each time as a question of fact.[269] He also observed that allowance had to be made for editorial judgment.[270]

In *Flood* the Supreme Court considered the application of the defence where it was stated in a newspaper article that allegations had been made against a police officer that had led police to investigate whether he was guilty of corruption in the extradition of a Russian oligarch to Russia. The investigation had ended with a finding that he was not guilty of corruption. Here it was necessary to consider whether, and in what circumstances, it was in the public interest to refer to the fact that accusations had been made, and in particular that 'accusations have been made to the police, that a named person has committed a criminal offence'.[271] It was also asked whether it was in the public interest that the details of the supporting facts should be published and whether it was in the public interest that the police officer should be named.[272] It was concluded that subject to the issue of verification, it was in the public interest that both the accusation and most of the facts supporting it should be published: 'The story, if true, was of high public interest. That interest lay not merely in the fact of police corruption, but in the nature of that corruption.'[273] It was also concluded that naming the individual was not contrary to responsible journalism or the public interest as it was not possible to publish the details without identifying him.[274]

12.1.3 Responsible Journalism

In *Jameel* Lord Bingham noted that Lord Nicholls's list of *Reynolds* factors were pointers, which might be more or less indicative, and not a series of hurdles. He stated that weight should ordinarily be given to the professional judgment of an editor or jour-

---

[267] *Jameel* (n 11), [34].
[268] Ibid, [48]; see also Lord Hope at [108].
[269] Ibid, [50].
[270] Ibid, [51].
[271] *Flood* (n 260), [24].
[272] Ibid, [54].
[273] Ibid, per Lord Phillips at [68].
[274] Ibid, per Lord Phillips at [74].

nalist 'in the absence of some indication that it was made in a casual, cavalier, slipshod or careless manner'.[275] Lord Hoffmann also stated that these were not ten hurdles but should be applied in a practical and flexible manner having regard to practical realities.[276] Similarly Lord Phillips in *Flood* held that not all of the items in Lord Nicholls' list were intended to be requirements of responsible journalism in every case. 'It may be on the facts of the case, the requirements of responsible journalism did not include a duty of verification.'[277] However, the responsible journalist should have regard to the 'full range of meanings that a reasonable reader might attribute to the publication'.[278]

In *Flood* the Supreme Court held that where the publication alleged that accusations had been made of misconduct on the part of the claimant, or there were grounds to suspect him of misconduct, the question was what verification was required on the part of the responsible journalist.[279] Where the allegations of another are simply reported, there is no need for verification. This has been described as 'reportage', as Lord Phillips explained:

> It is an example of circumstances in which the public interest justifies publication of facts that carry defamatory inferences without imposing on the journalist any obligation to attempt to verify the truth of those inferences. Those circumstances may include the fact that the police are investigating the conduct of an individual, or that he has been arrested, or that he has been charged with an offence.[280]

But reportage is just the starting point as Lord Mance explained. At one end of the spectrum was pure reportage 'where the mere fact of a statement is itself of, and is reported as being of, public interest'.[281] But, as he stated, higher up was a case such as the present were a greater or lesser degree of suspicion was reported and the 'press could not disclaim all responsibility for checking their sources'. He concluded that provided the report was of 'real and unmistakeably public interest and is fairly presented', the press need not be in a position to produce primary evidence of the information given by such sources.[282] Where a journalist alleged that there were grounds for suspecting that a person had been guilty of misconduct, the responsible journalist should satisfy himself that such grounds exist but this did not necessarily require that he should know what those grounds are. 'Their existence can be based on information from reliable sources, or inferred from the fact of a police investigation in circumstances where such inference is reasonable.'[283] Here the Supreme Court concluded that responsible journalism required that the journalists should be reasonably satisfied that the supporting facts were true and there was a serious possibility he was guilty.[284] This was satisfied on the facts of the case and the defence was made out.[285]

In *Jameel* the House of Lords also found that the publication fell within the defence of qualified privilege. The subject matter was that the Saudi Arabian Monetary Authority

---

[275] *Jameel* (n 11), [33].
[276] Ibid, [56].
[277] *Flood* (n 260), [75].
[278] Ibid, [51].
[279] Ibid, [25].
[280] Ibid, [35].
[281] Ibid, [158].
[282] Ibid, [158].
[283] Ibid, per Lord Phillips [81].
[284] Ibid, [81].
[285] Ibid, [99].

was, at the request of US law enforcement agencies, monitoring bank accounts associated with some of the country's most prominent businessmen in a bid to prevent them from being used for the direction of funds to terrorist organisations. Lord Bingham explained the application of the *Reynolds* factors as follows:

> The subject matter was of great public interest, in the strictest sense. The article was written by an experienced specialist reporter and approved by senior staff on the newspaper and The Wall Street Journal who themselves sought to verify its contents. The article was unsensational in tone and (apparently) factual in content. The respondent's response was sought, although at a late stage, and the newspaper's inability to obtain a comment recorded. It is very unlikely that a comment, if obtained, would have been revealing since even if the respondents' accounts were being monitored it was unlikely that they would know.[286]

12.2 The Impact of Article 10 on Other Aspects of Defamation Law

Although the greatest impact has been on qualified privilege, Article 10 has also been applied in HRA claims and defences to other aspects of the law of defamation. It has also impacted on the defence of qualified privilege as claimed by those who are not journalists. For example, in *Culnane v Morris*[287] the High Court held that section 10 of the Defamation Act 1952 did not prevent a claim of qualified privilege in relation to defamatory statements published by or on behalf of a candidate in any election to local government or Parliament.

However, it is important to note that many attempts to modify aspects of defamation law considered to be disproportionate interferences with freedom of expression have not been successful. It has been held that the rule that each individual publication of libel gives rise to a separate cause of action is compatible with Article 10,[288] as is requiring a defendant who relies on the defence of justification to justify the essence or sting of an assault on reputation rather than a diminished version of it.[289] It has also been held that a defence of justification based upon reasonable grounds for suspicion, which focuses on some conduct of the individual claimant that itself gives rise to the suspicion, is compatible with Article 10.[290] In *Baturina*[291] it was argued that the law relating to innuendo should be modified. The Court of Appeal declined to do so holding that the development of Reynolds defence was sufficient acknowledgement by the courts of the need for protection of the press over and above the defence of honest comment.[292]

Most controversially it has been held that it is compatible with Article 10 for a trading corporation to be entitled to sue in respect of defamatory matters which could be seen as having a tendency to damage it in the way of its business. Although *obiter*, this was

---

[286] *Jameel* (n 11), [35]. See also *Galloway v Telegraph Group Ltd* [2006] EWCA Civ 17, [2006] HRLR 13 and *Bento v Chief Constable of Bedfordshire* [2012] EWHC 1525 (QB). See further A Mullis and A Scott, 'The Swing of the Pendulum: Reputation, Expression and the Re-centring of English Libel Law' (2012) 63 *Northern Ireland Legal Quarterly* 27.

[287] *Culnane v Morris* [2005] EWHC 2438 (QB), [2006] 1 WLR 2880.

[288] *Loutchansky* (n 17).

[289] *Berezovsky v Forbes* [2001] EWCA Civ 1251, [2001] EMLR 45.

[290] *Chase v Newsgroup Newspapers Ltd* [2002] EWCA Civ 1772, [2003] EMLR 11.

[291] *Baturina v Times Newspapers Ltd* [2011] EWCA Civ 308, [2011] 1 WLR 1526.

[292] Ibid, [28].

confirmed by a majority the House of Lords in *Jameel*,[293] where it was pointed out that the national rule had been accepted by the ECtHR and was within the UK's margin of appreciation.[294] It also dismissed the argument made by the newspaper on the chilling effect of the rule.[295] Lord Bingham observed as follows:

> The good name of a company, as that of an individual, is a thing of value. A damaging libel may lower its standing in the eyes of the public and even its own staff, make people less ready to deal with it, less willing or less proud to work for it.[296]

The majority concluded that Article 10 did not require it to disqualify corporations from bringing libel actions unless able to allege and prove actual damage caused by the libel.[297] In the minority, Baroness Hale observed that the power wielded by the major multinational corporations was enormous and growing: 'The freedom to criticise them may be at least as important in a democratic society as the freedom to criticise the government.'[298]

Other claims have had more success. In *O'Shea*[299] the Divisional Court concluded that the strict liability principle which applied to cases of 'look alike' defamation, making the intention of the publisher irrelevant, was a disproportionate interference with freedom of expression. The court reasoned that it would impose an impossible burden on a publisher if he were required to check if the true picture of someone resembled someone else who because of the context of the picture was defamed.[300] And in *Badu* the High Court struck out a claim of defamation against the BBC in respect of three articles contained on the web in the BBC's archive. It noted, inter alia, that when balancing the proportionality of allowing the claim to proceed it was important to consider that it related to archived internet material and the claim was taking place many years after the original publication.[301]

---

13. Protection of the Rights of Others

The 'rights of others' has the potential to justify a wide range of interferences with freedom of expression. However, most interferences on this basis have sought to be justified by reference to another Convention right, in particular Article 8.

---

[293] *Jameel* (n 11).
[294] Ibid, per Lord Bingham at [20].
[295] Ibid, [21].
[296] Ibid, [26].
[297] Ibid, per Lord Scott at [125].
[298] Ibid, [158].
[299] *O'Shea* (n 30).
[300] Ibid, [43]–[45].
[301] *Badu v BBC* [2010] EWHC 616 (QB) [118].

13.1 Articles 2 and 3

In certain circumstances, the publication of information may lead to someone being killed or seriously injured. In such circumstances the right to life and the right to freedom from torture or inhuman or degrading treatment or punishment must be considered. For example, in *Venables*[302] the claimants sought injunctions to restrain the publication of information relating to their identities and whereabouts. They had both been convicted of the murder of two-year-old James Bulger in 1993 when they were ten years old, a case which was widely publicised in the media. Although only three news groups were named as defendants, the injunction was sought *contra mundum*—against the world at large.

The Family Division found that it had the jurisdiction, in exceptional cases, to extend the protection of confidentiality of information where not to do so would be likely to lead to serious physical injury, or to the death, of the person seeking that confidentiality.[303] Here the court was satisfied that, if the claimant's identities were discovered, neither of them would have the chance of a normal life and there was a real and strong possibility that their lives would be at risk.[304] It concluded that the extension of the tort here was proportionate to the legitimate aim of protecting the claimants from serious and possibly irreparable harm.[305]

In *AP* the Supreme Court held that the anonymity order made at the outset of control order proceedings should be upheld, partly on Article 8 grounds but it was also accepted that there was force in the individual's submission that if he was revealed to be someone formerly subject to a control order and was now subject to deportation proceedings for alleged matters relating to terrorism, 'he would be at real risk not only of racist and other extremist abuse but of physical violence'.[306]

13.2 Article 8

Restrictions on freedom of expression justified on the basis of respect for private life are common. In recent years these types of claim have grown and now protect a variety of privacy-based interests. These are examined in the following paragraphs.

13.2.1 Private Lives of Public Figures

Freedom of expression and the right to respect for private life are commonly balanced against each other where the media seeks to publish details of the private life of a public figure. Article 10 rights may also be claimed by a party to a relationship with a public figure who seeks to tell his or her own story.[307] The values enshrined in these rights are now part of the cause of action for breach of confidence[308] and are 'as much

---

[302] *Venables* (n 5), [80].
[303] Ibid, [81].
[304] Ibid, [94].
[305] Ibid, [86]. See also *R (M) v Parole Board* [2013] EWHC 1360 (Admin), [2013] EMLR 23.
[306] *Secretary of State for the Home Department v AP* [2010] UKSC 26, [2010] 1 WLR 1652, [14].
[307] See eg *Ash* (n 202).
[308] *Campbell* (n 143).

applicable in disputes between individuals or between an individual and a non-governmental body such as a newspaper as they are in disputes between individuals and a public authority'.[309] It is often stated that both are vitally important rights and neither has precedence over the other.[310]

> [W]here the values under the two articles are in conflict, an intense focus on the comparative importance of the specific rights being claimed in the individual case is necessary … the justifications for interfering with or restricting each right must be taken into account. Finally, the proportionality test must be applied to each.[311]

As discussed at the start of this section, various factors affect the balancing process, in particular the question of whether or not the information is of public interest, the importance of freedom of expression and the importance of freedom of the press. In these types of cases, these factors have a tendency to skew the result of the balancing exercise in favour of freedom of expression. For example, in *Campbell*[312] it was accepted by the claimant and not commented upon by the House of Lords that, as she had lied about the fact of her drug addiction and the fact that she was receiving treatment, this gave the press the right to put the record straight[313] as this was a matter of legitimate public comment.[314] '[W]here a public figure chooses to make untrue pronouncements about his or her private life, the press will normally be entitled to put the record straight.'[315] However, this did not affect three other pieces of information: the fact that she was receiving treatment at Narcotics Anonymous; the details of the treatment; and the visual portrayal of her leaving a specific meeting. The majority concluded that the protection of Ms Campbell's rights under Article 8 was sufficiently important to justify limiting the fundamental right to freedom of expression which the press asserted on behalf of the public.[316]

> [T]he right of the public to receive information about the details of her treatment was of a much lower order than the undoubted right to know that she was misleading the public when she said that she did not take drugs.[317]

Furthermore, it was noted that the political and social life of the community, and the intellectual, artistic or personal development of individuals, were not obviously assisted by poring over the intimate details of a fashion model's private life.[318]

Following *Campbell*, courts have not been as willing to find an almost unfettered right to publish private information concerning public figures. Strong public interest, as discussed above, must be demonstrated and other matters, such as confidentiality in employment relationships, are given great weight.[319] The approach of the courts in

---

[309] Ibid, per Lord Nicholls at [17]. See also *Re S* (n 149), concerning the inherent jurisdiction of the court.
[310] See eg the comments of Lord Nicholls in *Campbell* (n 143), at [12], Lord Hoffmann at [55], Lord Hope at [111], [113], Baroness Hale at [138].
[311] *Re S* (n 149), [17]. See also *Mosley* (n 167), [131].
[312] *Campbell* (n 143).
[313] Ibid, per Lord Nicholls at [24].
[314] Ibid, per Lord Hope at [82].
[315] Ibid.
[316] Ibid, per Lord Hope at [115].
[317] Ibid, per Lord Hope at [117].
[318] Ibid, per Baroness Hale at [149]. See also *Douglas* (n 16) and the judgment on liability, *Douglas v Hello! Ltd* [2005] EWCA Civ 595; *B & C v A* (n 26); *Theakston* (n 143). In *MGN Limited v United Kingdom* (2011) 53 EHRR 5 the ECtHR found no violation of Art 10 in the conclusion of the House of Lords.
[319] See eg *HRH Prince of Wales* (n 211); *Murray v Big Pictures (UK) Ltd* [2008] EWCA Civ 446, [2008]

recent years is best illustrated in the claim of *Mosley*.[320] The claimant had been the President of the Fédération Internationale de l'Automobile (FIA) since 1993 and his claim concerned an article published in the *News of the World* in 2008 describing an event attended by the claimant sub-headed 'Son of Hitler-loving Fascist in Sex Shame' which was described as an 'orgy'. He also complained about accompanying photographs, images and information on the website.

The High Court confirmed that generalisations were not determinative and in every case it depended upon an intense focus on the individual circumstances.[321] It also noted that the judge would often have to ask whether the intrusion, or perhaps the degree of the intrusion, into the claimant's privacy was 'proportionate to the public interest supposedly being served by it'. It found that clandestine recordings of sexual activity on private property engaged Article 8 and that there was no countervailing public interest to justify the intrusion. In particular, it found that there was no public interest in discovering his adultery and it was recognised that there was now a 'greater willingness ... to accord respect to an individual's right to conduct his or her personal life without state interference or condemnation'.[322]

In particular, it was recognised that the fact that a particular relationship was adulterous, or an individual's tastes were unconventional, did not give the media carte blanche.[323] It concluded that none of the visual images or the information conveyed in the verbal images could be justified in the public interest. Damages of £60,000 were awarded to the claimant.[324]

A slightly different tone was adopted by the High Court in the later case of *LNS* where the claimant sought an injunction to prevent publication of information concerning a relationship. The injunction was declined on the ground that the claimant was unlikely to establish that publication should not be allowed. The court was not satisfied that it would not be in the public interest for there to be a publication. It stated that: 'Freedom to live as one chooses is one of the most valuable freedoms. But so is the freedom to criticise ... the conduct of other members of society as being socially harmful, or wrong.'[325]

Furthermore, in the present case, the information was already widely available and the court assumed that it was likely the real concern of the claimant was the effect of publication on sponsorship--something for which damages would be an adequate remedy if he did succeed at trial.[326]

13.2.2 Anonymity Orders in Legal Proceedings

Increasingly, anonymity orders are being sought in legal proceedings by both public

---

3 WLR 1360; *Hutcheson v News Group Newspapers Ltd* [2011] EWCA Civ 808, [2012] EMLR 2; *X and Y v Persons Unknown* [2006] EWHC 2783 (QB), [2007] HRLR 4; *CC v AB* [2006] EWHC 3083 (QB), [2007] 2 FLR 301.

[320] *Mosley* (n 167).
[321] Ibid, [12].
[322] Ibid, [125].
[323] Ibid, [128].
[324] See also *CTB v News Group Newspapers Limited* [2011] EWHC 1232 (QB).
[325] *LNS* (n 212), [104].
[326] Ibid, [130]–[131]. See also *Goodwin* (n 178) and *Ferdinand* (n 162). See further P Wragg, 'The Benefits of Privacy-invading Expression' (2013) 64 *Northern Ireland Legal Quarterly* 187.

and private figures. As Lord Rodger stated, the first term docket of the Supreme Court read like 'alphabet soup'.[327] The importance of the right of the media to publish the names of defendants in criminal trials has been recognised. In *Re S*[328] the House of Lords considered whether the right to freedom of expression outweighed the request for an injunction protecting his identity of a boy whose mother was to be tried for the murder of his older brother. Their Lordships held that the interference with Article 8 rights was not of the same order when compared with cases of juveniles who were directly involved in criminal trials.[329] Furthermore, it found the freedom of the press to report the progress of a criminal trial to be of considerable importance.[330] It concluded that the rights under Article 8 were not sufficient to outweigh those under Article 10. A number of factors led to this conclusion. First, it would seriously inhibit the freedom of the press to report criminal trials. Secondly, it would be a further exception to the principle of open justice. Thirdly, informed debate about criminal justice would suffer. Fourthly, it was a costly process for newspapers to contest an application for an injunction and often it would be too late. Finally, it was thought that such injunctions would have a particularly chilling effect on local newspapers.[331]

Anonymity was also sought in proceedings challenging the designation of three individuals under the Terrorism (United Nations Measures) Order 2006 as facilitating the commission of acts of terrorism.[332] The Supreme Court appreciated that even if the press were aware of the names of the individuals concerned from other sources, this could not be used. Therefore, if the orders were made, the court would interfere with the Article 10 right of the press to impart information which would normally be available to them.[333] It also held that it would interfere with freedom to report proceedings as they would wish.[334] It appreciated that stories about particular individuals were more attractive to readers than stories about unidentified people and that editors knew best about how to present material in a way that will 'interest the readers of their particular publication and so help them to absorb the information'. It held as follows:

> A requirement to report it in some austere, abstract form, devoid of much of its human interest, could well mean that the report would not be read and the information would not be passed on. Ultimately, such an approach could threaten the viability of newspapers and magazines, which can only inform the public if they attract enough readers and make enough money to survive.[335]

---

[327] *Application by Guardian News and Media Ltd in Her Majesty's Treasury v Ahmed* [2010] UKSC 1, [2010] 2 AC 697.

[328] *Re S* (n 149).

[329] Ibid, [27].

[330] Ibid, [31].

[331] Ibid, [36]. See also *Pelling v Bruce-Williams* [2004] EWCA Civ 845, [2004] Fam 155; *A Local Authority v A Health Authority* [2003] EWHC (Fam) 2746, [2004] Fam 96; *Blunkett v Quinn* [2004] EWHC (Fam) 2816, [2005] 1 FLR 648; *R v Teeside Crown Court, ex p Gazette Media Co. Ltd* [2005] EWCA Crim 1983. See also *O'Riordan v Director of Public Prosecutions* [2005] EWHC (Admin) 1240, where the court held that the statutory prohibition on a child's name imposed by the Sexual Offences (Amendment) Act 1982 was compatible with Art 10. See further H Fenwick, 'Clashing Rights, the Welfare of the Child and the Human Rights Act' (2004) 67 *Modern Law Review* 889.

[332] *In the Matter of Guardian News & Media Ltd* [2010] UKSC 1, [2010] 2 AC 697.

[333] Ibid, [34].

[334] Ibid, [35].

[335] Ibid, [63].

In the present case it held that a report of proceedings challenging freezing orders which did not reveal the identities of the appellants would be disembodied. Readers would be less interested and, realising that, 'editors would tend to give the report a lower priority. In that way informed debate about freezing orders would suffer.'[336] It was thought that if newspapers could identify the people concerned, they may be able to give a more 'vivid and compelling account' which will stimulate discussion about the use of freezing orders and their 'impact on the communities in which the individuals live'.[337] Furthermore, it was held that irrespective of the outcome, the public had a legitimate interest in not being kept in the dark about who was challenging such orders.[338] The fact that some members of the press would abuse their freedom to report was held not to be a sufficient reason for curtailing freedom for all members of the press.[339] The Supreme Court concluded that there was a powerful public interest in identifying the individual in any report of the proceedings and that justified curtailment of his and his family's Article 8 rights.[340] The anonymity order was set aside.[341]

With respect to public figures, the Court of Appeal gave guidance in *JIH*[342] as to when an anonymity order in proceedings to protect private life should be granted. It held that the question was whether there was sufficient general public interest in publishing a report of the proceedings which identifies a party and/or the normally reportable details to justify any resulting curtailment of his right and his family's right to respect for their private and family life.[343] It held that no special treatment should be accorded to public figures or celebrities as, in principle, they were entitled to the same protection as others.[344]

13.2.3 Super-injunctions

A by-product of the ability of public figures to now seek some protection for disclosure of details of their private lives is the 'super-injunction', which restrains disclosure of the existence of legal proceedings, preventing, for example, the media reporting that a well-known musician had obtained an injunction prohibiting the publication of lurid personal details. Combined with an anonymity order, discussed above, this prevents publication of the name of the parties, and the fact that legal proceedings are in progress. It has been explained that if the media could publish the name of the claimant and the substance of the information which he is seeking to exclude from the public domain 'then the whole purpose of the injunction would be undermined, and the claimant's private life may be unlawfully exposed'.[345] The Court of Appeal has also stated:

---

[336] Ibid, [64].
[337] Ibid, [65].
[338] Ibid, [68].
[339] Ibid, [72].
[340] Ibid, [76].
[341] See also *Secretary of State for the Home Department v AP* [2010] UKSC 26, [2010] 1 WLR 1652 where an anonymity order in control order proceedings was upheld. See also *Re LM* [2007] EWHC 1902 (Fam), [2008] 1 FLR 1360 which concerned anonymity in inquest proceedings.
[342] *JIH v News Group Newspapers Ltd* [2011] EWCA Civ 42, [2011] 2 All ER 324.
[343] Ibid, [21].
[344] Ibid, [21]. See also *AMM v HXW* [2010] EWHC 2457 (QB). See further C McGlynn, 'Rape, Defendant Anonymity and Human Rights: Adopting a Wider Perspective' [2011] *Criminal Law Review* 199.4
[345] *JIH* (n 342), [23].

It would be wrong to permit unrestrained reporting in the normal way, as that would involve publishing the name of the claimant and the details of the information whose publication he seeks to prevent, thereby rendering the court's order pointless. On the other hand, public coverage of court proceedings is a fundamental aspect of freedom of expression, with particular importance: the ability of the press freely to observe and report on proceedings in the courts is an essential ingredient of the rule of law.[346]

Super-injunctions have been controversial and in recent years the courts have appeared far less willing to grant them.[347]

13.2.4 Protection of Identity

The right to respect for private life can, in some instances, require the protection of identity and this must also be balanced against freedom of expression. For example, in *X (a woman formerly known as Mary Bell)* the claimant and her daughter sought lifetime anonymity from the intrusions of the media and any disclosures of their identities, their addresses or any details about their lives which might identify them. The Family Division found that, whilst neither had courted publicity, Mary Bell remained a legitimate subject of public interest.[348] However, it concluded that there were special features of the case which required the balance between Articles 8 and 10 to be resolved in favour of recognising the confidentiality of some information to protect them. Injunctions *contra mundum* were granted to protect their anonymity.[349] However, a police officer's attempt to secure continuing anonymity for himself as the author of an anonymous blog about policing failed, the High Court finding no Article 8 right engaged and concluding that, even if there was, this would be outweighed by the countervailing public interest in revealing that a particular police officer had been making these communications.[350]

In *Attorney General's Reference No 3 of 1999*[351] the individual had been acquitted of rape in 1999 and an anonymity order was made in 2000. The BBC applied for the order to be discharged as it wished to include details of the case in a proposed television programme suggesting he was wrongly acquitted and identifying him as the perpetrator. Having concluded that to broadcast this information would engage the individual's right to respect for private life, as he would have a reasonable expectation of privacy in relation to this information, the House of Lords turned to the freedom of expression point. Here it took into account the freedom of the media to exercise its own judgment in the presentation of journalistic material,[352] the fact that the subject matter was of public interest and the fact the publication of the individual's name would give added

---

[346] Ibid, [4].
[347] See, for example, *Ntuli v Donald* [2010] EWCA Civ 1276, [2011] 1 WLR 294 where a super-injunction and anonymity were denied and *JIH* (n 342) where anonymity was upheld.
[348] *Mary Bell* (n 143), [30].
[349] Ibid, [60]. See also *Carr v News Group Newspapers*, Divisional Court, 24 February 2005; *Archer v Williams* (n 196); *Re Roddy* (n 33); *E (by her litigation friend the Official Solicitor) v Channel Four* [2005] EWHC (Fam) 1144, [2005] EMLR 30 and *R (Y) v Ayelsbury Crown Court* [2012] EWHC 1140 (Admin), [2012] Crim LR 893. In *Chancellor, Masters and Scholars of the University of Oxford v Broughton* [2004] EWHC (QB) 2543, balancing Art 8 rights of employees against Art 10 rights of animal rights protesters, the court granted an injunction under the Protection from Harassment Act 1997.
[350] *Author of a Blog v Times Newspapers Ltd* [2009] EWHC 1358 (QB), [33].
[351] *Attorney General's Reference No 3 of 1999* [2009] UKHL 34, [2010] 1 AC 145.
[352] Ibid, per Lord Hope at [25].

credibility to the account they wished to present.[353] It concluded that the interference with the individual's Article 8 right would be significant but that it was proportionate when account was taken of the weight that must be given to the 'competing right to freedom of expression that the BBC wish to assert'.[354]

13.2.5 Restrictions on Reporting Legal Proceedings

It has been recognised that the media plays a vital role in 'ensuring the proper functioning of our democracy, as also in furthering the rule of law and the administration of justice. The role of the court reporter is that of public watchdog over the administration of justice.'[355]

It has also been recognised that in the investigation of possible miscarriages of justice and in righting judicially inflicted wrongs, campaigning and investigative journalists and the media in general have an absolutely vital role to play.[356] The Family Division of the High Court has held that the statutory prohibition on publication must be dispensed with when Article 10 required it.[357] Webster[358] concerned care proceedings where the parents wished to tell their story. The Family Division concluded that the reporting restriction was too wide and was disproportionate. The claim involved a miscarriage of justice, the parents wanted publicity, there had already been extensive publicity and there was a need for the full facts to emerge in a way that commanded public confidence.[359] It was seen as particularly important for the workings of the family justice system to be openly debated in the media and important for parents who felt aggrieved to be able to express their views publicly about what they perceived to be failings.[360] Here a miscarriage of justice had been suggested:

> In these circumstances there is a pressing need for public confidence to be restored—either by the public and convincing demonstration that there has not been a miscarriage of justice or, as the case may be, by public acknowledgment that there has been ... as few as obstacles as possible should be placed in the way of the media doing their job. For in the proper exercise by the media of their investigative and other functions there exists perhaps the best chance of the truth, whatever it may be, emerging at the end of the day.[361]

A number of cases have also related to the jurisdiction of a court under section 1(1) of the Children Act 1989 to restrain publication of material relating to a child's upbringing where the child's welfare would be affected. For example, Re X[362] concerned the policy

---

[353] Ibid, [26].

[354] Ibid, [28]. See also T v British Broadcasting Corporation [2007] EWHC 1683 (QB), [2008] 1 FLR 281.

[355] Re Webster (A Child) v Webster [2006] EWHC 2733 (Fam), [2007] 1 FLR 1146, [29].

[356] Ibid, [34].

[357] Ibid, [59].

[358] Ibid.

[359] Ibid, [99].

[360] Ibid, [100].

[361] Ibid, [104] See also A v Independent News & Media Ltd [2010] EWCA Civ 343 where the decision of the Court of Protection not to allow the media to attend a particular hearing was upheld. Contrast the decision of the Court of Protection itself in Hillingdon London Borough Council v Neary [2011] EWHC 413 (Fam); [2011] CP Rep 32. Also Crawford v Crown Prosecution Service [2008] EWHC 854 (Admin) where an order prohibiting reporting of proceedings in the magistrates' court and Crown Court was lifted.

[362] Re X (n 190).

of a local authority in relation to transracial placements of foster children. The Family Division held that it was important to respect private life but that the public importance of the story and the freedom of the press necessitated a modification of the injunction.[363]

13.2.6 Private Lives of Private Figures

It is also possible for an exercise of freedom of expression to interfere with the private life of a private figure. For example, in *Stone*[364] the High Court had to determine whether or not a report of an inquiry into the care, treatment and supervision of a man convicted of two murders should be published in full. It was concluded that the public interest required publication of the report in full and that the decision to publish was justified and proportionate and did not constitute an unwarranted interference with Article 8 of the ECHR. It may also be the case that whilst one party to the claim is a public figure, others affected by disclosure of private information are private figures, or children. Here courts are reluctant to find freedom of expression outweighs public interest.[365]

13.3 Article 9

Those seeking to justify an interference with freedom of expression based on Article 9 have had little success. In *Green*,[366] which concerned an attempt to have the producers of *Jerry Springer the Opera* charged with blasphemous libel, the Administrative Court held that insulting a man's religious beliefs would not normally amount to an infringement of Article 9 since his right to hold to and practise his religion was generally unaffected by such insults.[367] If there was a justification, the court found it was better based in the risk of disorder or damage to the community generally.

13.4 Article 1 Protocol No 1

As copyright constitutes a possession within the scope of Article 1 Protocol No 1, where courts are considering the remedy for infringement of copyright, it has been held that Article 10 must be balanced against Article 1 Protocol No 1.[368] In *Ashdown*[369] the Court of Appeal considered itself bound to apply the Copyright, Designs and Pat-

---

[363] See also *Clayton v Clayton* [2006] EWCA Civ 878, [2006] Fam 83; *R v ITN News* [2013] EWCA Crim 773, [2013] EMLR 22 concerning reporting restrictions ordered under the Youth Justice and Criminal Evidence Act 1999; *Z v News Group Newspapers* [2013] EWHC 1371 (Fam).

[364] *Stone v South East Coast Strategic Health Authority* [2006] EWHC 1668 (Admin), [2006] MHLR 288.

[365] See for example, *ETK* (n 149) and *OPQ v BJM* [2011] EWHC 1059 (QB), [2011] EMLR 23 and *AMP v Persons Unknown* [2011] EWHC 3454 (TCC). Contrast *Spelman v Express Newspapers* [2012] EWHC 355 (QB).

[366] *R (Green) v City of Westminster Magistrates' Court* [2007] EWHC 2785 (Admin), [2008] HRLR 12.

[367] Ibid, [17].

[368] *Ashdown* (n 9). See also *Twentieth Century Fox Film Corp v British Telecommunications plc* [2011] EWHC 1981 (Ch), [2012] 1 All ER 806.

[369] *Ashdown*, ibid.

ents Act 1988 in a manner that accommodated the right of freedom of expression.[370] Applying the Act in this way, it declined the discretionary relief of an injunction but required the newspaper to indemnify the author for any loss caused or alternatively account to him for any profit.[371]

It also considered the defence of public interest preserved by section 171(3) of the Act. The courts have an inherent jurisdiction to refuse to allow their process to be used in certain circumstances—here, to refuse to enforce copyright.[372] Following a review of the authorities, the court concluded that the circumstances in which public interest may override copyright are not capable of precise categorisation or definition.[373]

> Now that the Human Rights Act 1998 is in force, there is the clearest public interest in giving effect to the right of freedom of expression in those rare cases where this right trumps the rights conferred by the 1988 Act. In such circumstances, we consider that section 171(3) of the Act permits the defence of public interest to be raised.[374]

In the opinion of the court, this would not lead to a flood of cases where freedom of expression was invoked as a defence to a claim for breach of copyright as it would be very rare for the public interest to justify the copying of the form of a work to which copyright attaches.[375] The court then considered section 30(2), the defence of fair dealing for the purpose of reporting current events. Interpreting the expression 'reporting current events' liberally, and without articulated resort to the HRA, the court concluded that information about a meeting between the Prime Minister and an opposition party leader during the then current Parliament to discuss possible close co-operation between the parties was likely to be of legitimate and continuing public interest. Noting that the section was 'clearly intended to protect the role of the media in informing the public about matters of current concern',[376] it concluded that the publication was arguably for the purpose of reporting current events.[377] This was despite the fact that the meeting took place in October 1997 but the report did not appear in the *Sunday Telegraph* until November 1999.

It was then for the court to determine whether what had occurred was in fact 'fair dealing'. It noted that, where part of a work is copied in the course of a report on current events, this defence will normally afford the court all the scope that it needs properly to reflect the public interest in freedom of expression and freedom of the press. There was no need to give separate consideration to the section 171 public interest defence.[378] Relying on pre-HRA authorities, the court concluded that there was no realistic prospect that a defence of fair dealing would be made out.[379] Furthermore, the facts of the case post-HRA were not such that the importance of freedom of expression outweighed

---

[370] Ibid, [45].
[371] Ibid, [46].
[372] Ibid, [44].
[373] Thereby overruling the interpretation of *Lion Laboratories* [1985] QB 526, adopted by the Court of Appeal in *Hyde Park Residence Ltd v Yelland* [2001] Ch 143.
[374] Ibid, [58].
[375] Ibid, [59].
[376] Ibid, [64].
[377] Ibid, [65].
[378] Ibid, [66].
[379] Ibid, [77].

the conventional considerations so as to afford a defence of fair dealing. There was no justification found for the extent of reproduction of Mr Ashdown's own words.[380]

In *Twentieth Century Fox*[381] the High Court concluded that it was proportionate to grant an order to film production companies and studios against BT, an internet service provider. In essence, it was sought to block or at least impede access by BT's subscribers to a website which infringed the studio's copyright. It was accepted that the proposed order engaged the Article 10 rights of BT's subscribers and that it was proportionate to interfere with those rights having regard to the studio's rights as protected by Article 1 Protocol 1. The High Court held as follows:

> It is necessary and appropriate to protect the Article 1 First Protocol rights of the Studios and other copyright owners. Those interests clearly outweigh the Article 10 rights of the users of Newzbin2, and even more clearly outweigh the Article 10 rights of the operators of Newzbin2. They also outweigh BT's own Article 10 rights to the extent that they are engaged.[382]

13.5 Right Not to Be Insulted and Distressed

Also considered to be within the category of 'rights of others' is the right not to be insulted and distressed, although this is clearly not a Convention right.[383] Often this right, or interest, arises in the context of protest and the actions of protesters. Whilst this type of claim would seem to make more sense under Article 11, Article 11 features rarely in HRA claims and usually the claim is considered under Article 10, although Article 11 may be added with the comment that the result under this Convention right would be the same. It is important to note that whilst protest raises issues concerning insult and distress, it can also engage the prevention of disorder and crime and restrictions are often sought to be justified under either category.

13.5.1 Protest

The rights of protesters are rarely considered by the highest courts with the exception of *Laporte*.[384] Here the House of Lords concluded that the actions of police in stopping a coach of protesters attending a demonstration was not prescribed by law and was disproportionate. In relation the claimant, Lord Bingham observed that it was wholly disproportionate to restrict her exercise of her rights under Articles 10 and 11 because she 'was in the company of others some of whom might, at some time in the future, breach the peace'.[385]

---

[380] Ibid, [82]. Also raising issues under Art 1 Protocol No 1 are breach of contract cases, eg *Psychology Press Limited v Flanagan* [2002] EWHC (QB) 1205, and trade mark cases, eg *Levi Strauss v Tesco* (n 112) and *Boehringer Ingelheim Ltd v Vetplus Ltd* [2007] EWCA Civ 583, [2007] HRLR 33.

[381] *Twentieth Century Fox* (n 368).

[382] Ibid, [200]. See also *Dramatico Entertainment Ltd v British Sky Broadcasting Ltd* [2012] EWHC 1152 (Ch). In *Olympic Delivery Authority* [2012] EWHC 1012 (Ch) an injunction was granted to stop protesters obstructing access to a building site on Art 1 Protocol No 1 grounds.

[383] See further A Khan, 'A "Right Not to Be Offended" under Article 10(2) of the ECHR? Concerns in the Construction of the Rights of Others' [2012] *European Human Rights Law Review* 191.

[384] *R (Laporte) v Chief Constable of Gloucestershire* [2006] UKHL 55, [2007] 2 AC 105.

[385] Ibid, [55].

Claims and defences have concerned the specific actions of particular protestors. In *Percy*[386] the Divisional Court considered whether the conviction of a protester under section 5 of the Public Order Act 1986 for defacing then standing on the American flag at an American airbase struck the appropriate balance between freedom of expression and the right not to be insulted and distressed. The court found that

> [s]ome people will be more robust than others. What one person finds insulting and distressing may be water of a duck's back to another. A civilised society must strike an appropriate balance between the competing rights of those who may be insulted by a particular course of conduct and those who wish to register their protest on an important matter of public interest.[387]

Taking into consideration the fact that the appellant could have demonstrated her message in a way which did not involve use of the national flag and the fact that her actions were deliberate with consequences of which she was well aware, the court nevertheless concluded that the conviction was disproportionate.[388] By contrast, in *Abdul*[389] the Divisional Court concluded that prosecutions and convictions under section 5 of the Public Order Act 1986 were proportionate. Here the protestors disrupted a parade in Luton to celebrate the homecoming of the local regiment from duties in Afghanistan and Iraq. They were heard to shout 'British soldiers murderers' and 'British soldiers go to hell'. It was noted that context was important and that there as a difference between expressing the view that the wars were illegal or immoral and that British forces should not be engaged in them and the 'abusive and insulting chants of the Appellants'.[390]

This type of restriction on freedom of expression can also extend to poster campaigns. In *Butler*[391] the High Court accepted that restrictions on advertising on property could be justified as a restriction on one particular means of imparting information which had the potential to have adverse effects upon amenity.[392] The High Court asked as follows:

> [W]hy should a person who feels strongly about a political issue have an absolute right to impart his views in a particular manner that may be highly damaging to the amenities of his fellow citizens[?] There is no absolute right to impart one's views, political or otherwise, in such a way as to amount, for example, to a noise nuisance. Visual intrusion may, in certain circumstances, be no less harmful to the rights of others.[393]

In the present case, given consent for the advertisement could be obtained, the interference was determined to be proportionate. It was also held that the requirement to apply for consent was not a disproportionate interference with freedom of expression.

Claims and defences under the HRA have also concerned the location of protests such as *Tabernacle*[394] where the Secretary of State for Defence sought to prohibit, via byelaw, the Aldermaston Women's Peace Camp from camping in the vicinity of the Atomic Weapons Establishment at Aldermaston. Their actions were not distressing, as

---

[386] *Percy* (n 20).
[387] Ibid, [28].
[388] See also *Norwood* (n 32); *Hammond* (n 33).
[389] *Abdul v Director of Public Prosecutions* [2011] EWHC 247 (Admin), [2011] Crim LR 553.
[390] Ibid, [52].
[391] *Butler v Derby City Council* [2005] EWHC 2835 (Admin), [2006] 1 WLR 1346.
[392] Ibid, [37].
[393] Ibid, [38].
[394] *Tabernacle v Secretary of State for Defence* [2009] EWCA Civ 23.

the Court of Appeal found; the camp was seen by the Secretary of State as more akin to a nuisance.[395] In relation to the value of this form of expression, Laws LJ stated as follows:

> Rights worth having are unruly things. Demonstrations and protests are liable to be a nuisance. They are liable to be inconvenient and tiresome, or at least perceived as such by others who are out of sympathy with them. Sometimes they are wrong-headed and misconceived. Sometimes they betray a kind of arrogance: an arrogance which assumes that spreading the word is always more important than the mess which, often literally, the exercise leaves behind.[396]

In the present case he found no factor of the latter kind and the Court of Appeal held that the byelaw preventing the camp was incompatible with Articles 10 and 11.

A protest camp in Parliament Square Gardens, to protest about a variety of issues including the war in Afghanistan, genocide and war crimes, was the subject of proceedings in *Hall*[397] where protesters challenged the Mayor of London's claim for possession and injunction. The Court of Appeal recognised the importance of their right:

> The importance of having an unrestricted right to express publicly and strongly a controversial view on a political, or any other, topic cannot be doubted: it is of the essence of a free democratic society and should be vigilantly protected by the legislature, the executive and the judiciary.[398]

It concluded that the protesters' desire to express their views, on the basis of relatively long-term occupation with tents and placards were within the scope of Articles 10 and 11 and the manner and location were also protected.[399] However, it was also pointed out that the greater the extent of the right claimed under Article 10 or Article 11, the greater the potential for the exercise of the claimed right interfering with the rights of others and the greater risk of it being curtailed or rejected by virtue of Articles 10(2) and 11(2).[400] Taking into account the limited ability of others to demonstrate in the Gardens, the prevention of crime and protection of health, it was found that the actions to remove the protesters were proportionate, with the exception of one protester, Mr Haw, mounting a separate demonstration in the same area. His case was remitted to the High Court.[401]

The high-profile Occupy Movement protest met a similar fate.[402] The camp had been located in the St Paul's Cathedral churchyard in London for over five months. It was confirmed by the Court of Appeal that Articles 10 and 11 were engaged[403] particularly given the Occupy Movement's objective to educate and engage in dialogue and through the 'activities, leaflets, books, newspapers and speeches at the Camp, reinforced by its attendant publicity'.[404] The Court of Appeal found the various orders to remove the camp proportionate. Factors taken into consideration were: the Movement could protest

---

[395] Ibid, [42].
[396] Ibid, [43].
[397] *Hall v Mayor of London* [2010] EWCA Civ 817, [2011] 1 WLR 504.
[398] Ibid, [17].
[399] Ibid, [37].
[400] Ibid, [38].
[401] See further *Mayor of London (On behalf of the Greater London Authority) v Haw* [2011] EWHC 585 (QB). See also *R (Gallastegui) v Westminster City Council* [2013] EWCA Civ 28, [2013] HRLR 15.
[402] *City of London v Samede* [2012] EWCA Civ 160, [2012] 2 All ER 1039.
[403] Ibid, [24].
[404] Ibid, [28].

elsewhere; there were many rights the camp interfered with adversely; interference with the public right of way and the rights of those who wished to worship; breach of planning control; strain on public health facilities; damage to local business.[405]

13.5.2 Extreme Protest

Actions of particular protesters may be so extreme that severe restrictions on their ability to protest have been upheld by the courts as compatible with Articles 10 and 11. It has been held that human rights cannot be used as a charter for law breaking and that protestors are not entitled to commit the tort of harassment or to commit criminal acts in the course of exercising their rights to freedom of expression and freedom of assembly.[406] One example is *Avery*[407] where anti-social behaviour orders were imposed on the claimant animal rights activists, indefinitely preventing them from knowingly participating in, organising or controlling any demonstration, meeting, gathering or website protesting against animal experimentation. The Court of Appeal accepted that this was a severe matter, but also held that the circumstances were exceptional and in this instance the restrictions were proportionate except in the case on one claimant.[408]

In *Singh*[409] whilst the Court of Appeal was conscious of the impact of a particular play on some members of the Sikh community, and held that they were entitled to protest lawfully against the play, it also held that with those rights came duties and responsibilities, primarily the duty to respect other's rights:

> However deeply someone may feel about his religion or a particular cause, if he wishes to protest, he must do so peacefully and lawfully. He should not seek to intimidate others and impose upon them his way of thinking by unlawful means.[410]

In the opinion of the Court of Appeal, it was important to take into account the rights of those who wrote and staged and wished to see this particular play as they also had the right to freedom of expression, just as others at or near the theatre had the 'right to go about their business' without being subjected to scenes which were 'unnecessarily frightening, intimidating and distressing'.[411] It concluded that it was proportionate for the group of protestors to be dispersed utilising powers contained in the Anti-social Behaviour Act 2003.[412]

13.5.3 Pre-emptive Policing and Protest

Increasingly police are using powers to arrest and detain known protestors prior to

---

[405] Ibid, [44]. See also *Islington Borough Council v Jones* [2012] EWHC 1537 (QB). See further S Turenne, 'The Compatibility of Criminal Liability with Freedom of Expression' [2007] *Criminal Law Review* 866.

[406] *Harlan Laboratories UK Ltd v Stop Huntingdon Animal Cruelty* [2012] EWHC 3408 (QB), [69].

[407] *R v Avery* [2009] EWCA Crim 2670, [2010] 2 Cr App R (S) 33.

[408] See also *Novartis Pharmaceuticals UK Ltd v Stop Huntingdon Animal Cruelty* [2009] EWHC 2716 (QB), [2010] HRLR 8 and *Wife and Children of Othman v English National Resistance* QBD Admin 25/2/2013.

[409] *R (Singh) v Chief Constable of West Midlands* [2006] EWCA Civ 1118, [2006] 1 WLR 3375.

[410] Ibid, [74].

[411] Ibid, [75].

[412] See also *Heathrow Airport Ltd v Garman* [2007] EWHC 1957 (QB).

a demonstration actually taking place. For example, in *Hicks*[413] the High Court considered claims concerning the lawfulness of policing immediately prior to the Royal Wedding on 29 April 2011. It was argued that police equated intention to protest with intention to cause unlawful disruption and adopted an impermissibly low threshold of tolerance for public protest resulting in the arrest of persons viewed as being likely to express anti-monarchist views. The High Court concluded that all the arrests were lawful and proportionate

13.5.4 Taste Decency and Causing Offence

Questions of taste and decency also raise issues in relation to the right not to be insulted and distressed. In some instances, it has been held that those insulted or distressed, such as politicians, may be assumed to have thicker skins than others.[414] Offensive language was at issue in *Gaunt*[415] where Ofcom had found that the broadcasting of a radio interview breached the Broadcasting Code. In summary, the interviewer had been found to treat the interviewee as if it were a personal attack, and treated him in an oppressive and intimidating fashion calling him a 'Nazi' and an 'ignorant pig'.[416] The Court of Appeal held that the interview had to be considered as a whole and in context.[417] It concluded that when one combined the extremely aggressive tone of the interview, the constant interruptions, the insults, 'the ranting, the consequent lack of any substantive content, and the time which the interview was allowed to run on' there was a clear breach of the Code.[418] The Court had due regard to the judgment of Ofcom as the statutory regulator.[419] It also found the sanction, publication of the finding, to be proportionate.

Offensive language was also at issue in *Livingstone*[420] where the Mayor of London was suspended for a period of four weeks for failing to comply with the Code of Conduct of the Greater London Authority. Following a reception, he had compared a Jewish reporter to a concentration camp guard. The Administrative Court concluded that the sanction was disproportionate stating as follows:

> However offensive and undeserving of protection the appellant's outburst may have appeared to some, it is important that any individual knows that he can say what he likes, provided it is not unlawful, unless there are clear and satisfactory reasons within the terms of Article 10(2) to render him liable to sanctions.[421]

In *Connolly*[422] where the appellant had been convicted under the Malicious Communications Act 1988 for sending photographs of aborted foetuses to pharmacists selling the 'morning after' pill, it was held that the position of a doctor who routinely performed such abortions may well be materially different to that of employees in a pharmacy

---

[413] *R (Hicks) v Commissioner of Police of the Metropolis* [2012] EWHC 1947 (Admin), [2012] ACD 102.
[414] *Calver* (n 5), [81].
[415] *Gaunt* (n 27).
[416] Ibid, [13].
[417] Ibid, [39].
[418] Ibid, [46].
[419] Ibid, [47].
[420] *Livingstone v Adjudication Panel for England* [2006] EWHC 2533 (Admin), [2006] HRLR 45.
[421] Ibid, [39]. See also *Calver* (n 5).
[422] *Connolly v Director of Public Prosecutions* [2007] EWHC 237 (Admin), [2007] 2 All ER 1012.

selling the 'morning after' pill, the doctor less likely to find the photographs offen-sive.[423] The court concluded that the conviction here was necessary as her right to express her views about abortion did not justify the distress and anxiety she intended to cause. It was noted that even if the three pharmacies were persuaded to stop selling the pill, 'it is difficult to see what contribution this would make to any public debate about abortion generally and how that would increase the likelihood that abortion would be prohibited'.[424]

Advertising may also be considered offensive and the Advertising Standards Authority administers the British Code of Advertising Practice. In *Kirk Session of San-down*[425] judicial review was sought of its adjudication finding an advertisement placed by a Church group implying that homosexual people were perverted and an abomina-tion would be likely to cause, and had caused, serious offence in breach of the Code. The Divisional Court found the adjudication to be a disproportionate interference with freedom of expression. It noted that the context of the advertisement was important, observing that it was placed by people who were seeking to stand up for their beliefs and to encourage others. It stated that Article 10 protected expression which shocked and disturbed and protected also the means of dissemination. In the view of the court, the advertisement 'did not condone and was not likely to provoke violence, contained no exhortation to other improper or illegal activity, constituted a genuine attempt to stand up for their religious beliefs and to encourage others to similarly bear witness'.[426]

By contrast in *Core Issues Trust*[427] where Transport for London had rejected an anti-homosexuality advertisement placed by the Trust to appear on the outside of its busses, the Administrative Court was satisfied that the advertisement would cause grave offence to a significant section of those who would view it and that the decision was justified and proportionate.[428]

13.6 Democratic Rights

The final category of rights of others recognised in the case law as providing some jus-tification for interferences with freedom of expression is democratic rights. In *Animal Defenders International*[429] it was accepted by the House of Lords that the ban on polit-ical advertising contained in sections 319 and 321 of the Communications Act 2003 was prescribed by law and had the legitimate aim of protecting the rights of others, namely their democratic rights. It was held that the only issue in the case was whether the restriction was necessary. In the present case, it was held that the standard of jus-tification required was high, particularly as political speech was in issue. The House of Lords concluded that the interference was proportionate. Lord Bingham explained that the fundamental rationale of the democratic process was that if competing views,

[423] Ibid, [28].
[424] Ibid, [32].
[425] *In the Matter of Kirk Session of Sandown Free Presbyterian Church's Application* [2011] NIQB 26.
[426] Ibid, [73].
[427] *Core Issues Trust* (n 1).
[428] See also *Prolife Alliance* (n 123).
[429] *Animal Defenders International* (n 14).

opinions and policies were publicly debated and exposed to public scrutiny, the good would, over time, drive out the bad and the true prevail over the false. He continued:

> It must be assumed that, given time, the public will make a sound choice when, in the course of the democratic process, it has the right to choose. But it is highly desirable that the playing field of debate should be so far as practicable level. This is achieved where, in public discussion, differing views are expressed, contradicted, answered and debated. It is the duty of broadcasters to achieve this object in an impartial way by presenting balanced programmes in which all lawful views may be ventilated. It is not achieved if political parties can, in proportion to their resources, buy unlimited opportunities to advertise in the most effective media, so that elections become little more than an auction. Nor is it achieved if well-endowed interests which are not political parties are able to use the power of the purse to give enhanced prominence to views which may be true or false, attractive to progressive minds or unattractive, beneficial or injurious. The risk is that objects which are essentially political may come to be accepted by the public not because they are shown in public debate to be right but because, by dint of constant repetition, the public has been conditioned to accept them. The rights of others which a restriction on the exercise of the right to free expression may properly be designed to protect must, in my judgment, include a right to be protected against the potential mischief of partial political advertising.[430]

Whilst in the present case Lord Bingham held that the proposed advertisement was wholly inoffensive and it was possible to be sympathetic to the aims, he raised hypothetical examples which the ban covered which would be far more controversial such as adverts by 'well-endowed multi-national companies seeking to thwart or delay action on climate change; adverts by wealthy groups seeking to ban abortion'.[431] Also taken into consideration was the fact that television and radio advertising is of greater immediacy and impact.[432] His Lordship also found it difficult to see how any alternative system such as rationing or capping could work[433] and considered that other alternatives were open to the claimant such as newspapers, direct mail shots, billboards, public meetings and marches.[434]

It is important to note that the House of Lords was also particularly influenced in its conclusion in this case by the fact that Parliament had resolved when passing the Act that it might infringe Article 10 but nonetheless resolved to proceed under section 19(1)(b) of the HRA. Lord Bingham stated that a general rule means that a line must be drawn and it was for Parliament to decide where.[435] By contrast to other members of the House of Lords, in Lord Scott's opinion, the width of the statutory ban was remarkable and there could be a possible future claim against sections 319 and 321 of the Communications Act 2003 on Article 10 grounds.[436]

It has also been held that the present limits on expenses with a view to promoting or procuring the election of a candidate contained in section 75 of the Representation of the People Act 1983 are compatible with Article 10.[437] Similarly, it has been held that

---

[430] Ibid, [28].
[431] Ibid, [29].
[432] Ibid, per Lord Bingham at [30].
[433] Ibid, [31].
[434] Ibid, [32].
[435] Ibid, [33].
[436] Ibid, [41]. See also *R (London Christian Radio) v Radio Advertising Clearance Centre* [2012] EWHC 1043 (Admin), [2012] HRLR 19. In *Animal Defenders International v United Kingdom* (2013) 57 EHRR 21 the ECtHR by nine votes to eight found no violation of Art 10.
[437] *R v Holding* [2005] EWCA Crim 3185, [2006] 1 WLR 1040.

section 106 of the Representation of the People Act 1983, which prohibits false state-ments, is directed at protecting the reputation and rights of others, as well as the right of the electorate to express its choice at an election, a right also protected by Article 3 Protocol No 1.[438] 'False statements which relate to a candidate's personal character or conduct distort, or may distort, the electorate's choice and hence the democratic process.'[439]

14. Preventing the Disclosure of Information Received in Confidence

14.1 Generally

Interferences with the right to freedom of expression may also be justified on the ground of preventing the disclosure of information received in confidence. Where the tort of breach of confidence is at issue, it is important to take into account the modifications made by Article 8, the right to respect for private life. As discussed in the preceding paragraphs, where 'modified breach of confidence' constitutes the interference, the court will most likely consider whether the interference is justified by balancing Article 8 against Article 10 rather than considering this part of Article 10(2).[440]

However, where the right to respect for private life is not at issue, there is some scope for the application of this part of Article 10(2). For example, in *London Regional Transport v The Mayor of London*[441] the Divisional Court considered a report by Deloitte & Touche which criticised the value for money calculations that had been undertaken by London Underground Limited as part of the public–private partnership appraisal process. London Underground had obtained an interim injunction restraining the Mayor of London and Transport for London from releasing the report on the basis that it contained confidential information. It was proposed to publish a redacted version of the report, omitting detailed information which might be of assistance to bidders.

In deciding whether to lift the injunction, the court held that it had a discretion and would carry out a balancing exercise having regard to the public interest.[442] It confirmed that it was impossible to assert, in the face of Article 10, that confidentiality must be regarded as an absolute requirement and that the court had no discretion but to enforce a confidentiality agreement. Nevertheless, the court decided that, in the circumstances of the case, the defendants had to show an exceptional case to justify publication.[443]

---

[438] *Watkins v Woolas* [2010] EWHC 2702 (QB).
[439] Ibid, [45]. See also *R (Woolas) v Parliamentary Election Court* [2010] EWHC 3160 (Admin), [2011] 2 WLR 1362. See further J Rowbottom, 'Lies, Manipulation and Elections—Controlling False Campaign Statements' (2012) 32 *Oxford Journal of Legal Studies* 507.
[440] See eg *Campbell* (n 143).
[441] *London Regional Transport v The Mayor of London*, Divisional Court, 31 July 2001.
[442] Ibid, [11].
[443] Ibid, [39].

Finding it genuinely in the public interest that the material be made available, and that London Regional Transport had failed to put forward a very persuasive case of harm, publication of the redacted report was permitted.[444]

Although in *H*[445] the right to respect for private life could have been put forward as a justification, the matter was considered on the basis of protection of confidentiality. The claim concerned an HIV-positive healthcare worker's attempts to maintain his anonymity whilst he challenged the legality of the health authority's actions in response to his disclosure. The Court of Appeal recognised that this was an issue of confidentiality as H had disclosed the fact that he was HIV-positive in confidence.[446] The court found a public interest in preserving the 'confidentiality of victims of the AIDS epidemic' and, in particular, of 'healthcare workers who report the fact that they are HIV-positive'.[447] Furthermore, it was accepted that the health authority had a legitimate interest in striving to protect the information, which they had obtained in confidence, that one of their healthcare workers was HIV-positive.[448] However, the court did not accept that it was possible to grant an injunction restraining freedom of expression merely on the ground that the release of the information would give rise to 'administrative problems and a drain on resources'.[449] Weighing these considerations against freedom of expression, freedom of the press and the public interest, the court concluded that the order that the health authority and health worker only be identified by initials was appropriate.[450] However, it was not acceptable to restrain the disclosure of the health worker's speciality or to restrain the newspaper from soliciting information which may lead to the disclosure of the identity of the health worker or his patients.[451]

14.2 Disclosure of a Journalist's Source

It has been held that an order for a journalist to disclose his or her source has a chilling effect on freedom of the press[452] and that there is a public interest not only in the freedom of the press per se but also in the confidentiality of their sources.[453] However, in accordance with the principle in *Norwich Pharmacal*,[454] it is possible for a court to order that a source be disclosed. Essentially, where a person, albeit innocently and without incurring any personal liability, becomes involved in a wrongful act of another, that person thereby comes under a duty to assist the person injured by those acts by giving him any information which he is able to give by way of discovery that discloses

---

[444] An appeal against this order was dismissed by the Court of Appeal on 24 August 2001. See also *Imutran* (n 112), where disclosure of confidential documents on public interest grounds was not permitted; *Tillery Valley Foods v Channel Four Television* [2004] EWHC (Ch) 1075; *Volkswagen Aktiengesellschaft v Garcia* [2013] EWHC 1832 (Ch); and *Barclays Bank v Guardian* [2009] EWHC 591 (QB).

[445] *H* (n 86).
[446] Ibid, [26].
[447] Ibid, [27].
[448] Ibid, [32].
[449] Ibid, [41].
[450] Ibid, [58].
[451] Ibid, [61].
[452] *Ashworth* (n 87), [61].
[453] *Interbrew* (n 150), [54].
[454] *Norwich Pharmacal* (n 157).

the identity of the wrongdoer.[455] The principle is not confined to cases in tort and is of general application.[456]

However, any order must still conform to section 10 of the Contempt of Court Act 1981 and Article 10, which have a 'common purpose in seeking to enhance the freedom of the press by protecting journalistic sources'.[457] Section 10 provides:

> [N]o court may require a person to disclose, nor is any person guilty of contempt of court for refusing to disclose, the source of information contained in a publication for which he is responsible, unless it be established to the satisfaction of the court that disclosure is necessary in the interests of justice or national security or for the prevention of disorder or crime.

The 'interests of justice' exception is not limited to cases where disclosure is required for existing or intended proceedings[458] and may also encompass disclosure to facilitate the detection of crime.[459]

These principles were applied by the House of Lords in *Ashworth Hospital Authority v MGN Ltd*.[460] In 1999 MGN had published in the *Daily Mirror* an article written by a journalist about Ian Brady. The article included a series of verbatim extracts from information held on a database maintained by staff of Ashworth Hospital Authority. The journalist had received these extracts from one of his regular sources (the intermediary), who had in turn received the information from a member of staff at Ashworth (the source). Ashworth wished the identity of the intermediary to be disclosed as a means of identifying the source.

The House of Lords concluded that, given the probability that the source was a member of staff, they were undoubtedly wrongdoers as they were acting in breach of their contract of employment or in breach of confidence.[461] Furthermore, it did not matter if the wrongdoing was tortious or in breach of contract: all that mattered was that there was involvement or participation on the part of the journalist and/or newspaper. This requirement was undoubtedly satisfied in the view of the House of Lords as the information wrongfully obtained was published.[462] Furthermore, the jurisdiction applied whether or not the victim intended to pursue action in the courts against the wrongdoer.[463] Taking into consideration the importance of maintaining confidentiality in medical records, particularly in the case of the class of patients that the authority is responsible for caring for at Ashworth, the House of Lords concluded that the situation was exceptional and orders to disclose were necessary and justified.[464]

In *Interbrew*[465] a Norwich Pharmacal order had been made against five media companies requiring them to preserve and deliver up to the claimant their original copies of a leaked and partially forged document concerning a contemplated takeover by the

---

[455] *Ashworth* (n 87), [61].
[456] Ibid.
[457] Ibid, [38].
[458] Ibid, [39].
[459] Ibid, [53], expressly disagreeing with the conclusion of the Court of Appeal in *Interbrew* (n 150).
[460] Ibid.
[461] Ibid, [31]–[32].
[462] Ibid, [34].
[463] Ibid, [49] in reliance on *British Steel Corp v Granada Television Ltd* [1981] AC 1096.
[464] Ibid, [63] and [66] taking into account *Goodwin v United Kingdom* (1996) 22 EHRR 123 and *Z v Finland* (1998) 25 EHRR 371. It was also noted that the fact that Ian Brady had himself disclosed his medical history did not detract from the need to prevent staff from revealing medical records of patients. His conduct did not damage the integrity of Ashworth's patients' records; see [66]. See also *Ackroyd* (n 190).
[465] *Interbrew* (n 150).

claimant, a major brewer, of another brewery company. Entitlement to delivery up was established by the existence of a breach of confidence.[466] The Court of Appeal then considered whether the public interest in doing justice was sufficient to make disclosure necessary drawing particular attention to the purpose of the leak. 'If it is to bring wrongdoing to public notice it will deserve a high degree of protection. ... If the purpose is to wreck legitimate commercial activity ... it will be less deserving of protection.'[467] If the falsehood of the nub of the story has been established, this is an additional reason for overriding the protection accorded to the source.[468] In the present case, it concluded that the order for disclosure was rightly made against all the defendants.[469]

These two judgments have caused particular disquiet in media circles. Prior to the HRA coming into force, there was some expectation on the part of the media that it would lead to greater protection for journalists' sources. However, in both cases, Article 10 was applied with considerable regard to the public interest in the freedom of the press and also in the confidentiality of their sources.[470] It has also been recognised that any disclosure of a journalist's source does have a chilling effect on the freedom of the press.[471] Although the jurisdiction is now easier to invoke, it will still not be exercised unless in conformity with Article 10. The decision in both cases came down to whether or not the disclosure was necessary. The circumstances in both were exceptional: in *Ashworth* the confidentiality of psychiatric medical records was at issue, whilst in *Interbrew* the key factor was that the expression was of low value, designed to 'wreck' legitimate commercial activity. The public interest in protecting the source of such information was found in both cases to be very low, insufficient to outweigh countervailing considerations. Although not stated as such, it is clear that the courts were continuing the 'responsible journalism' line of reasoning of *Reynolds*.[472] Responsible journalism concerning matters in the public interest is generally protected whilst irresponsible journalism concerning matters not in the public interest is not.

In further developments, MGN's compliance with the order did not actually reveal the name of the source, only the name of Mr Ackroyd and as he declined to reveal his source, proceedings were issued against him. Holding that the position in 2006 was different from that in 2000, the Court of Appeal upheld the trial judge's finding that Mr Ackroyd did not have to reveal his source:

> He was ... entitled to hold that an order for disclosure would not be proportionate to the pursuit of the hospital's legitimate aim to seek redress against the source, given the vital public interest in the protection of a journalist's source.[473]

Nevertheless, the Court of Appeal stated that nothing in its judgment was intended to lead to the conclusion that medical records were less private or confidential, or less deserving of protection.[474]

---

[466] Ibid, [28].

[467] Ibid, [42] and [55].

[468] Ibid, at [57].

[469] Ibid, [49]. In *Financial Times v United Kingdom* (2010) 50 EHRR 46 the ECtHR found a violation of Art 10 as a result of the order to disclose.

[470] *Interbrew* (n 150), [54].

[471] *Ashworth* (n 87), [61].

[472] *Reynolds* (n 6).

[473] *Mersey Care NHS Trust v Ackroyd* [2007] EWCA Civ 101, [2007] HRLR 19, [80].

[474] Ibid, [81]. See also *Assistant Deputy Coroner for Inner West London v Channel 4 Television Corporation*

The disclosure of a journalist's source may also come about by other means, such as an order for production under the Terrorism Act 2000. In *Malik*[475] police sought a production order of journalistic material from a freelance journalist writing a book about the experiences of a British jihadist. The Administrative Court referred to the weight of justification required for an interference that compelled a journalist to reveal confidential material about or provided by a source.[476] However, it concluded here that the order for production was proportionate having in mind the 'gravity of the activities that are the subject of the investigation', the 'benefit likely to accrue' to the investigation and the 'weight to be accorded to the need to protect the sources'.[477] It stated as follows:

> Parliament has decided that the public interest in the security of the state must be taken into account. A balance has to be struck between the protection of the confidential material of journalists and the interest of us all in facilitating effective terrorist investigations. It is for the court to strike that balance applying the carefully calibrated mechanism enacted by Parliament in schedule 5 of the 2000 Act.[478]

Nevertheless, it also held that the terms of the order were too wide and that some redaction of material to protect sources should be allowed.

---

15. Maintaining the Authority and Impartiality of the Judiciary

Finally, an interference with freedom of expression may be justified in the interests of maintaining the authority and impartiality of the judiciary. Under the HRA this justification has been invoked only in relation to the laws of contempt of court. It has been held that the Contempt of Court Act 1981 requires proof to the criminal standard that the publications in question have created a substantial risk of serious impediment or prejudice to the course of justice and that this fell comfortably within the limitations acknowledged in Article 10.[479]

Third-party contempt, applied by the House of Lords in the 'Spycatcher' case[480] but rarely invoked since, remains a part of the common law and was invoked by the Attorney General in *Attorney General v Punch Ltd*[481] in relation to an article by David Shayler, formerly an officer in the security service. It is a contempt of court for a third party, with the intention of impeding or prejudicing the administration of justice by the court in an action between two other parties, to do the acts which the injunction

---

[2007] EWHC 2513 (QB), [2008] 1 WLR 945. See further R Costigan, 'Protection of Journalists' Sources' [2007] Public Law 464.

[475] *Malik v Manchester Crown Court* [2008] EWHC 1362 (Admin), [2008] 4 All ER 403.
[476] Ibid, [50].
[477] Ibid, [56].
[478] Ibid, [110].
[479] *Attorney General v MGN Ltd* [2011] EWHC 2074 (Admin), [2012] 1 Cr App R 1.
[480] *A-G v Times Newspapers Ltd* [1992] 1 AC 191.
[481] *Punch* (n 64).

restrains the defendant in that action from committing if the acts done have some significant and adverse affect on the administration of justice in that action.[482] In short, it must be proved that the individual did the relevant act (*actus reus*) with the necessary intent (*mens rea*).[483]

In 1997 an order had been made against Mr Shayler and Associated Newspapers restraining disclosure or publication of information obtained by Mr Shayler in the course of or by virtue of his employment in and position as a member of the security service. In 1998, Mr Shayler started writing a regular column in *Punch*. In July 2000 *Punch* notified the Treasury Solicitor that it intended to publish an article by Mr Shayler relating to the Bishopsgate bombing. The article was published, amended from the draft version, but did not reflect all of the amendments which had been notified to *Punch* by the Treasury Solicitor. The Attorney-General brought proceedings for contempt at common law.

Actus reus was admitted and the House of Lords found that there was no doubt with respect to *mens rea*, holding that the editor must have appreciated that by publishing the article he was doing precisely what the order was intended to prevent, 'namely, pre-empting the court's decision on these confidentiality issues'. This was held to be knowing interference with the administration of justice.[484] Little comment was made in the speeches given as to the impact of Article 10. Lord Hope held that in the present context, when determining proportionality, three requirements had to be met: first, that there was a genuine dispute as to whether the information was confidential because its publication might be a threat to national security; secondly, that there were reasonable grounds for thinking that publication of the information before trial would impede or interfere with the administration of justice; and thirdly, that the interference with the right of free speech was no greater than was necessary.[485]

It was observed that the proviso in the original order that those seeking to publish should seek the consent of the Attorney General was acceptable as it set out a 'simple, expeditious and inexpensive procedure' which avoids the necessity of an application to the court whose outcome would not be in dispute.[486] Nevertheless, it was also observed that this type of proviso should make plain that it was also possible to apply to the court for a variation in the terms of the order.[487] A warning was also given about overly wide interlocutory injunctions which, although not disproportionate in the present case, had the potential to have a chilling effect on the press and the media generally, and were better avoided.[488]

Orders made under the Contempt of Court Act 1981 postponing the reporting of court cases also raise issues under Article 10. In *ex p The Telegraph Group plc*[489] the Court of Appeal determined an appeal against an order made under section 4(2) of the Act postponing any reporting of a case until after the conclusion of another trial arising out of the same or closely related facts. It was held that the phrase 'authority and impartiality of the judiciary' should be given a broad interpretation and was 'certainly

---

[482] Ibid, [4].
[483] Ibid, [20].
[484] Ibid, [52].
[485] Ibid, [114].
[486] Ibid, [59].
[487] Ibid, [60].
[488] Ibid, [62]–[63].
[489] *Sherwood* (n 63).

wide enough to embrace the concept of a fair trial.'[490] Orders under section 4(2) were found to fulfil the criteria of prescribed by law and necessary in a democratic society but it was held should only be made if the court is persuaded that it is necessary in the interests of justice.[491] The court noted that 'necessary' is used in two senses in this context. First, the statute requires the court to address the question of whether a ban is necessary to avoid prejudice. Secondly, the order must be necessary in the sense contemplated by Article 10(2). At this stage, 'wider considerations of public policy will come into play'.[492] It must be considered whether there is a way to overcome the risk of prejudice to the administration of justice by less restrictive means. It may be that the degree of risk is tolerable in the sense of being the 'lesser of two evils'.[493] It was concluded in the present case that the evidence in the two trials was going to be inextricably linked and the problems were incapable of being overcome by judicial directions to the second jury. The order was upheld as unavoidable 'in order to ensure that the three defendants in the second trial have a fair hearing in accordance with the rights guaranteed under article 6 of the Convention'.[494]

The freedom of expression of members of a jury is also affected by the law of contempt of court. Scotcher[495] concerned a disclosure by a juror of what was said or done by the jury during the course of their deliberations. The House of Lords emphasised that the secrecy of jury deliberations was a crucial and legitimate feature of English trial law and the objective of section 8 of the Contempt of Court Act 1981 in punishing disclosures by jurors was sufficiently important to justify limiting freedom of expression.[496] 'The provision is rationally connected to its aim and the means adopted are no more than is reasonably necessary, since the restriction does not apply to bona fide disclosures to the court authorities.'[497]

---

[490] Ibid, [13].
[491] Ibid, [18].
[492] Ibid, [20].
[493] Ibid, [22].
[494] Ibid, [34].
[495] Scotcher (n 98).
[496] Ibid, [29] in reliance upon Gregory v United Kingdom (1997) 25 EHRR 577.
[497] Ibid, [29]. See also Archer v Williams (n 196). See also HRH Prince of Wales (n 211).

16

Article 14: Prohibition of Discrimination

1. Introduction

Article 14 provides that the enjoyment of the rights and freedoms set forth in the Convention shall be secured without discrimination on any ground. Unlike Article 1 of Protocol No 12 to the ECHR, Article 14 does not confer a free-standing right of non-discrimination but precludes discrimination in the enjoyment of Convention rights. For Article 14 to be applicable, the facts must fall within the ambit of one or more of the Convention rights.[1] It is important to note that where Article 14 claims have been made under the HRA, there is often overlap with anti-discrimination law, both domestic and EU. It has also been held that the common law principle of equal treatment covers much of the same ground.[2]

Judges often observe that Article 14 is very important. For example, in *Ghaidan* Lord Nicholls commented that discrimination was an insidious practice and that:

> [d]iscriminatory law undermines the rule of law because it is the antithesis of fairness. It brings the law into disrepute. It breeds resentment. It fosters an inequality of outlook which is demeaning alike to those unfairly benefited and those unfairly prejudiced.[3]

In the same case, Baroness Hale noted:

> Treating some as automatically having less value than others not only causes pain and distress to that person but also violates his or her dignity as a human being ... such treatment is damaging to society as a whole. Wrongly to assume that some people have talent and others do not is a huge waste of human resources, it also damages social cohesion, creating not only an under-class, but an under-class with a rational grievance ... it is the reverse of the rational behaviour we now expect of the government and the state. ... Finally, it is a purpose

---

[1] *Ghaidan v Godin-Mendoza* [2004] UKHL 30, [2004] 2 AC 557, [10].
[2] *R (Limbu) v Secretary of State for the Home Department* [2008] EWHC 2261 (Admin), [2008] HRLR 48, [50].
[3] *Ghaidan* (n 1), [9].

of all human rights instruments to secure the protection of the essential rights of members of minority groups, even when they are unpopular with the majority.[4]

Lord Hope has held that cases about discrimination in areas of social policy 'will always be appropriate for judicial scrutiny' and that the constitutional responsibility in this area of law resides with the courts:

> The more contentious the issue is, the greater the risk is that some people will be discriminated against in ways that engage their Convention rights. It is for the courts to see that this does not happen. It is with them that the ultimate safeguard against discrimination rests.[5]

Although it is expressed shortly and simply, applying Article 14 to a factual situation is complex. To simplify matters, in a series of judgments the Court of Appeal adopted what it called the 'structured approach' and posed a series of questions to be answered. The most well known is the list formulated by Brooke LJ in *Michalak*,[6] later modified by the Court of Appeal in *Carson*.[7] The questions formulated were as follows:

> (1) Do the facts fall within the ambit of one or more of the Convention rights? (2) Was there a difference in treatment in respect of that right between the complainant and others put forward for comparison? (3) If so, was the difference in treatment on one or more of the proscribed grounds under article 14? (4) Were those others in an analogous situation? (5) Was the difference in treatment objectively justifiable in the sense that it had a legitimate aim and bore a reasonable relationship of proportionality to that aim?[8]

However, this approach is not to be employed without caution. In *Ghaidan*[9] Baroness Hale noted that there was a considerable overlap between the questions, 'in particular between whether the situations to be compared were truly analogous, whether the difference in treatment was based on a proscribed ground and whether it had an objective justification'. In her view, a rigid formulaic approach was to be avoided.[10] Nevertheless, noting this caveat, in its judgment shortly after in *S*[11] the House of Lords followed the five questions without comment, as did their Lordships in *A v Secretary of State*.[12] It was not until its judgment in *Carson*[13] that the House of Lords suggested avoiding the structured approach altogether, Lord Nicholls stating that the issues in Article 14 cases should be kept as simple and non-technical as possible[14] and Lord Hoffmann noting that the questions were not always helpful as a framework of reasoning,[15] in particular

---

[4] Ibid, [132]. See also the comments of Lord Bingham in *A v Secretary of State for the Home Department* [2004] UKHL 56, [2005] 2 AC 68, [46] and Baroness Hale at [237]; and the comments of Lord Walker in *R (on the application of Carson) v Secretary of State for Work and Pensions* [2005] UKHL 37, [2005] 2 WLR 1369, [49].

[5] *Re P* [2008] UKHL 38, [2008] 3 WLR 76, [48].

[6] *Wandsworth London Borough Council v Michalak* [2002] EWCA Civ 271, [2003] 1 WLR 617. These questions were actually first formulated in *St Brice v London Borough of Southwark* [2001] EWCA Civ 1138, [2002] 1 WLR 1537.

[7] *R (on the application of Carson) v Secretary of State for Work and Pensions* [2003] EWCA Civ 797, [2003] 3 All ER 577.

[8] As set out by Lord Steyn in *R (on the application of S) v Chief Constable of South Yorkshire* [2004] UKHL 39, [2004] 1 WLR 2196, [42].

[9] *Ghaidan* (n 1).

[10] Ibid, [134].

[11] *S* (n 8).

[12] *A v Secretary of State* (n 4), per Lord Bingham at [50].

[13] *Carson* (n 4).

[14] Ibid, [3].

[15] Ibid, [29].

because of the overlap between analogous situation and justification.[16] However, whilst their Lordships did not use the framework, it is clear that by doing so they would have reached exactly the same conclusion.[17]

Rather than abandoning the structured approach altogether, it may be best to follow the advice of Baroness Hale in *Ghaidan*. The questions are a useful tool for analysis but should not be applied rigidly. The advice of Lord Nicholls in *Carson* is also helpful. Once ambit, difference in treatment and ground are established, the question for the court is whether the alleged discrimination can withstand scrutiny.

> Sometimes the answer to this question will be plain. There may be such an obvious, relevant difference between the claimant and those with whom he seeks to compare himself that their situations cannot be regarded as analogous. Sometimes, where the position is not so clear, a different approach is called for. Then the court's scrutiny may best be directed at considering whether the differentiation has a legitimate aim and whether the means chosen to achieve the aim is appropriate and not disproportionate in its adverse impact.[18]

Despite the doubts expressed by the House of Lords in *Carson*, the structured approach is followed in this chapter, subject to the caveats set out in the paragraph above. It has been held that, in practice, both approaches will usually reach the same result.[19]

2. Application: No Independent Existence

2.1 Within the Ambit of One or More Convention Rights

For Article 14 to be applicable, the facts at issue must fall within the ambit of one or more of the Convention rights but it is not necessary for that other Convention right to be breached:

> Article 14 comes into play whenever the subject matter of the disadvantage 'constitutes one of the modalities' of the exercise of a right guaranteed or whenever the measures complained of are 'linked' to the exercise of a right guaranteed.[20]

The meaning of 'ambit' is not clear and it has been interpreted widely and narrowly. Lord Nicholls in *Secretary of State for Work and Pensions v M*[21] held that the approach of the ECtHR was flexible but its jurisprudence did not support the suggestion that any link, however tenuous, would suffice:

---

[16] See also the doubts expressed by Simon Brown LJ in *R (on the application of Purja) v Ministry of Defence* [2003] EWCA Civ 1345, [2004] 1 WLR 289, [44]–[47].

[17] See also the comments of Lord Walker in *Carson* (n 4), at [61]–[70].

[18] Ibid, [3].

[19] *R (British Gurkha Welfare Society) v Ministry of Defence* [2010] EWCA Civ 1098 and *R (Harrison) v Secretary of State for Health* [2009] EWHC 574 (Admin). See further R O'Connell, 'Cinderella Comes to the Ball: Art 14 and the Right to Non-discrimination in the ECHR' (2009) 29 *Legal Studies* 211.

[20] *Ghaidan* (n 1), per Lord Nicholls at [10] in reliance upon *Petrovic v Austria* (2001) 33 EHRR 307. See further A Baker, 'The Enjoyment of Rights and Freedoms: A New Conception of the "Ambit" under Article 14 ECHR" (2006) 69 *Modern Law Review* 714.

[21] *Secretary of State for Work and Pensions v M* [2006] UKHL 11, [2006] 2 AC 91.

Rather, the approach to be distilled from the Strasbourg jurisprudence is that they more seriously and directly the discriminatory provision or conduct impinges upon the values underlying the particular substantive article, the more readily will it be regarded as within the ambit
of that article; and vice versa.[22]

In his view, the ECtHR made in each case a value judgment.[23] Lord Bingham observed
in *Secretary of State for Work and Pensions v M*[24] as follows:

[T]he further a situation is removed from one infringing those core values, the weaker the
connection becomes, until a point is reached when there is no meaningful connection at all.
At the inner extremity, a situation may properly be said to be within the ambit or scope of
the right, nebulous those expressions necessarily are. At the outer extremity, it may not. There
is no sharp line of demarcation between the two. An exercise of judgment is called for. ... I
cannot accept that even a tenuous link is enough. That would be a recipe for artificiality and
legalistic ingenuity of an unacceptable kind.[25]

Where legislation is the subject of the claim, it is necessary to look at both the purpose
and the effect of the legislation. It does not have to be enacted for the purpose of
promoting a Convention right, but it must have as its purpose the furthering of a right
which is in fact guaranteed by the Convention.[26] Furthermore, whilst a particular Convention right may not require the state to act so as to secure that right, if it does do so,
it must do so without discrimination.[27] In *Secretary of State for Work and Pensions v M*,
Lord Nicholls gave the example of a state choosing to grant a parental leave allowance
and thereby demonstrating respect for family life. The allowance would come within
the scope of Article 8, and Article 14 read with Article 8 was engaged.[28] In *Friend*[29] the
House of Lords concluded that the Protection of Wild Mammals (Scotland) Act 2002
was not directed at anything which the state itself had provided or sought to provide.[30]
Decisions on ambit are very fact sensitive. Some examples are examined in the following paragraphs.[31]

2.2 Article 3

In *Re E*[32] it was accepted by the House of Lords that the claim that the policing of a
protest targeted at parents and children was within the ambit of Article 3.

---

[22] Ibid, [14]. See also Lord Walker at [58].

[23] Ibid.

[24] Ibid.

[25] Ibid, [4]. See also his observations in *R (Clift) v Secretary of State for the Home Department* [2006]
UKHL 54, [2007] 2 WLR 24, [13]. See further J Scherpe, 'Family and Private Life, Ambits and Pieces—M
v Secretary of State for Work and Pensions' (2007) 19 *Child and Family Law Quarterly* 390.

[26] *R (on the application of Erskine) v London Borough of Lambeth* [2003] EWHC (Admin) 2479, [33]–
[34].

[27] *Nasser v United Bank of Kuwait* [2001] EWCA Civ 1454, [51].

[28] *M* (n 21), [16].

[29] *Friend v Lord Advocate* [2007] UKHL 53, [2008] HRLR 11.

[30] Ibid, per Lord Hope at [30].

[31] In *R (on the application of Hooper) v Secretary of State for Work and Pensions* [2005] UKHL 29, [2005]
1 WLR 1681 the House of Lords found that the willingness of the government to reach a friendly settlement
with those who petitioned the ECtHR before the HRA came into force, but not those who petitioned after,
did not come close to the ambit of any Convention right.

[32] *Re E* [2008] UKHL 66, [2009] 1 AC 536.

2.3 Article 5

In *A v Secretary of State*[33] it was held that the facts fell within the ambit of Article 5. The appellants were being detained without charge or trial under the Anti-Terrorism, Crime and Security Act 2001. In *Clift*[34] the House of Lords held that the right of a prisoner to seek early release, where domestic law provided for such a right, was clearly within the ambit of Article 5.[35]

2.4 Article 8: Private Life

Alleged discrimination in the provision of welfare benefits has been argued in some instances to come within the ambit of the right to respect for private life but such claims have not been successful. For example, in *T*[36] the claimant asylum seeker, who was HIV-positive, with a daughter born HIV-negative, sought two additional benefits, including the entitlement for a child under the age of one year to receive a given weekly quantity of dried milk or liquid milk. The court accepted that a mother who was HIV-positive should not breastfeed her baby for fear of passing on her condition to it but held that her claim did not come within the ambit of Article 2 (right to life) or Article 8 (private life).[37] In *Harrison*[38] the Administrative Court concluded that the difference to the private lives of disabled claimants receiving healthcare services of a cash payment allowing them to make their own arrangements was not so substantial as to constitute a very close connection with Article 8 so as to come within its ambit for the purposes of Article 14.[39]

Claims concerning discrimination in immigration law and policy have had more success. In *AL*[40] it was accepted by the House of Lords that it was within the ambit of Article 8 (private life) where claims for asylum were treated differently as the claimants had arrived in the UK as children without families from those who arrived as children with families. And in *Limbu*[41] it was accepted by the Administrative Court that a policy on indefinite leave to remain on the grounds of close links with the UK was a policy designed in part to promote the private and family life of those eligible for admission and was sufficiently within the ambit of Article 8 to allow consideration of Article 14.[42]

Other private life claims have included *S*[43] where the House of Lords held that the retention of fingerprints and samples did not fall within the ambit of Article 8, and

---

[33] *A v Secretary of State* (n 4). See also *R (on the application of Clift) v Secretary of State for the Home Department* [2006] UKHL 54, [2007] 1 AC 484 concerning the role of the Secretary of State in determining when prisoners should be released from prison on licence.

[34] *Clift*, ibid.

[35] Ibid, per Lord Bingham at [18]. See also *R (Primrose) v Secretary of State for Justice* [2008] EWHC 1625 (Admin), [2009] Prison LR 165 and *R (Serrano) v Secretary of State for Justice* [2012] EWHC 3216 (Admin).

[36] *R (on the application of T) v Secretary of State for Health*, Court of Appeal, 29 July 2002.

[37] See also *X v Y* [2004] EWCA Civ 662, [2004] IRLR 625.

[38] *Harrison* (n 19).

[39] Ibid, [89].

[40] *AL (Serbia) v Secretary of State for the Home Department* [2008] UKHL 42, [2008] 1 WLR 1434.

[41] *Limbu* (n 2).

[42] Ibid, [47]. See also *R (A) v Secretary of State for the Home Department* [2008] EWHC 2844 (Admin), [2009] 1 FLR 531.

[43] *S* (n 8).

the conclusion of the Court of Appeal that smoking did not come within the ambit of Article 8 (private life) and therefore it was not possible to make a claim about discrimination against smokers under Article 14.[44]

2.5 Article 8: Family Life

Claimants have had more success with allegations that the discriminatory provision of welfare benefits comes within the ambit of family life. As the Court of Appeal has held, such benefits can provide a final safety net to prevent families from being split up or on the streets, and are often intended to promote family life.[45] A wide variety of benefits have been subject to challenge. It has been held that maternity grant is within the ambit of Article 8 (family life),[46] as is additional asylum support for dependants[47] and housing benefit.[48] In *Morris*[49] the Court of Appeal held that the effect of the Housing Act 1996 which was to deny a parent priority for accommodation as her dependent child was subject to immigration control, was within the ambit of Article 8 as this was a modality of the state's manifestation of respect for family life.[50] 'It sets out to give effect to a legislative policy of preserving family life for the homeless.'[51] Similarly in *Esfandiari*[52] the Court of Appeal held that a funeral benefit funding UK funerals for those otherwise unable to afford it fell within the ambit of Article 8 (family life):

> The need for a decent funeral is a basic requirement of human dignity, whether from the point of view of the individual or from that of the family. ... By offering it, the state demonstrates its respect for this important aspect of family life.[53]

However, in *Secretary of State for Work and Pensions v M*[54] a majority of the House of Lords concluded that it was not within the ambit of either Article 8 (family life) or Article 1 Protocol No 1 for a non-resident parent with a same-sex partner to have to make a greater contribution for child support than she would have to if she was living with a heterosexual partner. It was not considered that the enhanced contribution impaired in any material way

> her family life with her children and former husband, or her family life with her children and her current partner, or her private life ... this does not impair the love, trust, confidence, mutual dependence and unconstrained social intercourse which are the essence of family life, nor does it invade the sphere of personal and sexual autonomy which are the essence of private life.[55]

---

[44] *R (N) v Secretary of State for Health* [2009] EWCA Civ 795, [2009] HRLR 31.

[45] *R (Morris) v Westminster City Council* [2004] EWHC Admin 2191, [2005] 1 WLR 865, [14].

[46] *Francis v Secretary of State for Work and Pensions* [2005] EWCA Civ 1303, [2006] 1 WLR 3202.

[47] *R (Chen) v Secretary of State for the Home Department* [2012] EWHC 2531 (Admin), [2012] HRLR 33.

[48] *R (MA) v Secretary of State for Work & Pensions* [2013] EWHC 2213 (QB), [2013] Eq LR 972.

[49] *Westminster City Council v Morris* [2005] EWCA Civ 1184, [2006] 1 WLR 505.

[50] Ibid, per Sedley LJ at [23].

[51] Ibid, [25].

[52] *Esfandiari v Secretary of State for Work and Pensions* [2006] EWCA Civ 282, [2006] HRLR 26.

[53] Ibid, [23].

[54] *Secretary of State for Work and Pensions v M* (n 21).

[55] Ibid, per Lord Bingham at [5]. See also Lord Nicholls at [30] and [32]. Contrast the judgment of the House of Lords in *In Re P* (n 5).

In Lord Walker's view Article 8 was concerned with the failure to accord respect.[56] He concluded that the claimant's complaint had nothing to do with respect for her relationship with her children.[57] However, by contrast to Lord Nicholls and Lord Mance, he held that the unit consisting of the claimant, her new partner and their children should be regarded as a family for Article 8 purposes and that the legislation was intended to be a positive measure promoting family life. However, in his view this was no more than a tenuous link and did not bring it within the ambit of respect for family life or private life under Article 8.[58] He also found the statutory scheme was not within the ambit of Article 1 Protocol No 1 as child support was neither a tax nor a form of expropriation.[59]

Lord Mance held that if the claimant's relationship with her same-sex partner fell to be regarded as having involved family life within the meaning of Article 8, the regime fell within the ambit. However, he concluded that as the ECtHR had held that homosexual relations did not fall within the scope of family life as protected by Article 8, the concept of family life under Article 8 could not be regarded as having included same-sex relationships during the relevant period.[60] He also rejected the claim that the child support regime interfered with the claimant's private life[61] or Article 1 Protocol No 1.[62] Baroness Hale did not agree with the conclusion of the majority. She held that the operation of the child support scheme fell within the ambit of the mother's right to respect for her family life with her children.[63] 'It is one aspect, among many others, of the state's support for family life.'[64]

Other discriminatory impacts upon family life have also been accepted as falling within the ambit of Article 8 by the courts. In *Re P* it was held that the prohibition on unmarried couples adopting children was within the ambit of the right to respect for family life guaranteed by Article 8.[65] In *Al-Rawi*[66] the Court of Appeal accepted that the alleged discriminatory treatment in the failure of the Foreign Secretary to make a formal request for release of UK residents from the Guantanamo Bay detention facility was within the ambit of family life.[67] Immigration decisions affecting those seeking to enter the UK can also come within the ambit of Article 8 (family life).[68]

2.6 Article 8: Respect for Home

A number of applications have concerned the right to respect for home protected under

---

[56] Ibid, [83].
[57] Ibid, [85].
[58] Ibid, [87]–[88].
[59] Ibid, [89].
[60] Ibid, [151]. Lord Nicholls reached the same conclusion at [30] and [32]. Lord Bingham did not comment.
[61] Ibid, [157].
[62] Ibid, [159].
[63] Ibid, [108].
[64] Ibid, [108]. The ECtHR in *JM v United Kingdom* (2011) 53 EHRR 6 found that the scheme fell within the ambit of Article 1 Protocol No 1 and did not consider the ambit of Art 8.
[65] *Re P* (n 5).
[66] *R (Al-Rawi) v Secretary of State for Foreign & Commonwealth Affairs* [2006] EWCA Civ 1279, [2007] 2 WLR 1219.
[67] Ibid, [84].
[68] *AM (Somalia) v Entry Clearance Officer* [2009] EWCA Civ 634, [2009] UKHRR 1073.

Article 8 which is often argued together with the right to protection of property protected by Article 1 Protocol No 1. For example, in *Ghaidan*[69] it was concluded that paragraph 2 of Schedule 1 to the Rent Act 1977, which enabled the survivor of a heterosexual couple, but not the survivor of a homosexual couple, to become a statutory tenant by succession, fell within the ambit of the right to respect for home guaranteed by Article 8.[70] In *Michalak*[71] the claimant sought to overcome an order for possession of the council flat he occupied by arguing that he was a member of the deceased former tenant's family. The Court of Appeal was satisfied that the complaint was within the ambit of the right to respect for home.[72] Similarly, in *O'Sullivan*,[73] seeking an order for possession against a wife who carried on living in the premises following her husband's determination of the tenancy without disclosing to the local authority that she was still living in the premises engaged Article 8. However, Arden LJ pointed out that Article 8 was not engaged when the tenancy was granted to her husband in 1970 as Article 8 did not confer a right to be provided with a home.[74]

Not all claims concerning housing engage Article 8. In *Erskine*[75] the Administrative Court held that the legislation subject to challenge must have as its purpose the furthering of a right which was in fact guaranteed by the Convention. Here it concluded that the purpose of section 189 of the Housing Act 1985 was to protect and promote public health and to improve the condition of low-cost housing stock. Therefore, the differences in the enforcement regime applicable to different categories of tenant did not fall within Article 14.[76]

2.7 Article 9

In *Gallagher*[77] it was held by the House of Lords that the alleged discrimination was not within the ambit of Article 9 as the liability to tax did not prevent the members of a group from manifesting their religion. '[T]heir religion prevents them from providing the public benefit necessary to secure a tax advantage.'[78] Lord Scott was uneasy about this conclusion, holding that the levying of taxation on a place of religious worship, or on those who enter the premises for that purpose, would be capable in particular circumstances of constituting a breach of Article 9; therefore, in his opinion, this was within the ambit of Article 9 and the question of justification should be considered.[79]

---

[69] *Ghaidan* (n 1).

[70] Ibid, per Lord Nicholls at [12].

[71] *Michalak* (n 6).

[72] See also *Sheffield City Council v Personal Representative of Wall* [2010] EWCA Civ 922, [2010] HRLR 35.

[73] *Royal Borough of Kensington and Chelsea v O'Sullivan* [2003] EWCA Civ 371, [2003] 2 FLR 459.

[74] Ibid, [48]. Other claims concerning the right to respect for home and Art 14 include *Clarke v Secretary of State for Transport, Local Government and the Regions* [2002] EWCA Civ 819; *Waite v London Borough of Hammersmith & Fulham* [2002] EWCA Civ 482; *St Brice* (n 6); *Tucker v Secretary of State for Social Security* [2001] EWCA Civ 1646.

[75] *Erskine* (n 26).

[76] Ibid, [43]–[44].

[77] *Gallagher v Church of Jesus Christ of Latter-Day Saints* [2008] UKHL 56, [2008] 1 WLR 1852.

[78] Ibid, [13].

[79] Ibid, [49].

2.8 Article 1 Protocol No 1

It has been held that widow's bereavement allowance by way of deduction from liability for income tax which was not available for widowers comes within the ambit of Article 1 Protocol No 1,[80] as does widow's payment, widowed mother's allowance and widow's pension,[81] a war pension,[82] housing benefit[83] and entitlement to child tax credit.[84] Not paying annual increases to pensioners ordinarily resident abroad also comes within the ambit of Article 1 Protocol No 1.[85] In *RJM*[86] the question before the House of Lords was whether non-payment of the disability premium to income support to those who were homeless was in violation of Article 14. In reliance upon the judgment of the ECtHR in *Stec*,[87] the House of Lords held that the claim was within the ambit of Article 1 Protocol No 1[88] However, ex gratia payments, unenforceable by action under domestic law, have been held to be outside the scope of the Article.[89]

2.9 Article 2 Protocol 1: Education

It was held in *McDougal*[90] that the closure of a particular school did not come within the ambit of Article 2 Protocol No 1 as education was available at other schools nearby. In *Douglas*[91] the claimant was denied a student loan because he was over the age of 55 on the first day of the course. The Court of Appeal concluded that the loan arrangements could be described as a facilitator of education but were one stage removed from the education itself: 'The absence of funding arrangements may make it difficult for a student to avail himself of his Article 2 Protocol No 1 rights but they are not so closely related as to prevent him from doing so.'[92]

---

[80] *R (on the application of Wilkinson) v Inland Revenue Commissioners* [2005] UKHL 30, [2005] 1 WLR 1718.

[81] *Hooper* (n 31).

[82] *Ratcliffe v Secretary of State for Defence* [2009] EWCA Civ 39, [2009] ICR 762.

[83] *Burnip v Birmingham City Council* [2012] EWCA Civ 629.

[84] *Humphreys v Revenue & Customs Commissioners* [2012] UKSC 18, [2012] 1 WLR 1545. See also *R (RD) v Secretary of State for Work and Pensions* [2010] EWCA Civ 18, [2010] HRLR 19.

[85] *Carson* (n 4), per Lord Hoffmann at [12]. See also *Purja* (n 16).

[86] *R (RJM) v Secretary of State for Work & Pensions* [2008] UKHL 63, [2009] 1 AC 311.

[87] *Stec v United Kingdom* (2005) 41 EHRR SE295.

[88] *RJM* (n 86), per Lord Neuberger at [34].

[89] *Association of British Civilian Internees—Far East Region, v Secretary of State for Defence* [2003] EWCA Civ 473, [2003] QB 1397. Other claims concerning Art 1 Protocol No 1 include: *Lloyds UDT Finance Ltd v Chartered Finance Trust Holdings plc* [2002] EWCA Civ 806, [2002] STC 956; *Waite* (n 74); and *R (on the application of Middlebrook Mushrooms Ltd) v The Agricultural Wages Board of England & Wales* [2004] EWHC (Admin) 1447, where it was held that legislation fixing minimum wages came within the ambit of Art 1 Protocol No 1.

[90] *R (McDougal) v Liverpool City Council* [2009] EWHC 1821 (Admin).

[91] *R (on the application of Douglas) v North Tyneside Metropolitan Borough Council* [2003] EWCA Civ 1847.

[92] Ibid, [57]. Other claims concerning Art 2 Protocol No 1 and Art 14 include *R (on the application of Hounslow London Borough Council) v Schools Admissions Appeal Panel for Hounslow* [2002] EWCA Civ 900.

3. Without Discrimination

Article 14 provides that the enjoyment of the Convention rights and freedoms must be secured without discrimination. The meaning of discrimination under Article 14 encompasses both direct and indirect discrimination. Direct discrimination occurs where there is a failure to 'treat like cases alike'. Indirect discrimination occurs when there is a failure to treat differently persons whose situations are significantly different.[93]

The concept of discrimination involves less favourable treatment,[94] and it is not possible to argue that someone has been discriminated against directly or indirectly unless he or she has been subjected to less favourable treatment. For example, in *Re E*[95] the House of Lords found no evidence to support the claim that police had been biased against Catholic parents and children in their handling of a protest.[96] In *St Brice*[97] the claimant argued that he was discriminated against on the ground of status in that he was a defendant in the County Court rather than the High Court, where he would have had notice of an application for a warrant of possession. The Court of Appeal concluded that in fact he was not treated less favourably than a defendant in the High Court. He had an equal opportunity to require the court to hear him before eviction.[98]

Sometimes the fact of less favourable treatment may not be clear. In *Clift*[99] the House of Lords concluded that the differential treatment of one prisoner as compared with another, otherwise than on the merits of their respective cases, gave rise to a potential complaint under Article 14.[100] Lord Bingham observed that the ECtHR had consistently recognised the possibility of a claim under Article 14 in relation to Article 5, where a parole scheme was operated in an objectionably discriminatory manner.[101]

3.1 Difference in Treatment: Direct Discrimination

In order to determine whether or not there has been a difference in treatment, or a failure to treat like cases alike, there must be a comparator person or group. Usually this is easy to identify. For example, in *Ghaidan*[102] it was clear that there was a difference in treatment in respect of the right to respect for home between survivors of heterosexual relationships and survivors of homosexual relationships. Under the Rent Act 1977, only the former could become a statutory tenant by succession.[103] In *A v*

---

[93] *Carson* (n 4), per Lord Hoffmann at [14].
[94] *St Brice* (n 6).
[95] *Re E* (n 32).
[96] Ibid, [66].
[97] *St Brice* (n 6).
[98] See also *O'Sullivan* (n 73), [64] and *Esfandiari* (n 52).
[99] *Clift* (n 33).
[100] Ibid, per Lord Bingham at [18].
[101] Ibid, [19].
[102] *Ghaidan* (n 1), [10].
[103] See also *Secretary of State for Work and Pensions v M* (n 21), concerning the calculation of child support liability for those living in same-sex relationships.

Secretary of State[104] the comparison was between suspected international terrorists who were not UK nationals and suspected international terrorists who were UK nationals. However, in *S*[105] it was not so straightforward. The appellants complained that, by retaining their fingerprints and DNA samples, the police were discriminating against them as compared with the general body of persons who had not had fingerprints and samples taken by the police in the course of a criminal investigation.[106]

3.2 No Difference in Treatment: Indirect Discrimination

Indirect discrimination is rarely considered in HRA claims although Elias LJ gave a thorough explanation of the concept in *AM (Somalia)*.[107] He stated that in its traditional form, indirect discrimination recognises 'that a rule, policy or practice' might in practice 'adversely affect a particular group notwithstanding that it is neutral in form'.[108] He observed that this was not the same as treating different cases differently. Here the complaint was that even if the rule could be justified in its application to others, it ought not to be applied to the claimant because his or her situation was materially different, and that difference ought to be recognised by the adoption of a 'different rule, which may take the form of an exemption from the general rule'. The complaint is not that the single rule adopted is inappropriate because discriminatory and unjustified; it is that the 'circumstances require that there should be more than one rule'.[109] Furthermore, in his view, where there is one rule applied to a range of cases and the question is whether different cases should be treated differently, the issue was whether the failure or refusal to draw the distinction could be justified.[110] As Laws LJ explained in *MA*,[111] where discrimination is direct, it is the rule itself which has to be justified. Where the discrimination is indirect, it is the disparate impact which has to be justified.[112]

Examples where courts have considered claims raising indirect discrimination are considered in the following paragraphs.

3.2.1 Gypsies and Travellers

Whilst not appreciated as such, in *Clarke*[113] the Court of Appeal essentially determined a question of indirect discrimination by holding that, in certain circumstances, it could amount to a breach of Article 8 with Article 14 to weigh in the balance and hold against a gypsy applying for planning permission or resisting eviction that he or she had refused conventional housing accommodation as being contrary to his or her culture.[114]

---

[104] *A v Secretary of State* (n 4).
[105] *S* (n 8).
[106] Ibid, per Lord Steyn at [45].
[107] *AM* (n 68).
[108] Ibid, [41].
[109] Ibid, [44].
[110] Ibid, [51].
[111] *MA* (n 48).
[112] Ibid, [38].
[113] *Clarke* (n 74).
[114] Ibid, [9]. See also *Codona v Mid-Bedfordshire District Council* [2004] EWCA Civ 925, [2005] HLR 1.

In the later claim of *Wilson*[115] it was argued that planning control legislation, making an exception for dwelling houses but not for residential caravans, discriminated against Romany gypsies and Irish travellers. It was conceded by the Secretary of State that a higher proportion of gypsies and travellers than any other group would be likely to be affected by this aspect of planning control. Therefore, it was indirectly discriminatory and there was an onus on the state to justify it.[116]

The Court of Appeal held that as this was indirect discrimination, less justification was called for as the measure was not targeting gypsies and travellers.[117]

> Thus, although the indirect discriminatory impact on gypsies and travellers makes it appropriate to apply the intense or severe scrutiny referred to in *Ghaidan* and *Carson*, the case does not fall within the scope of the very strict reasoning applied in *Timishev* to direct discrimination on grounds of race or ethnic origin.[118]

Gypsies and travellers were also claimants in *Knowles*[119] where it was argued that the present housing benefit scheme treated gypsies and travellers on private sites and non-gysies and travellers on private sites the same in circumstances where they were in different situations. It was submitted that gypsies and travellers have greater accommodation costs, which imposes a positive obligation on the state to make provision to cater for the difference. This was rejected the Administrative Court which held that these costs fell outside the scope of the housing benefit scheme and that the additional costs were not significant.

3.2.2 Nationality

In *Esfandiari*[120] the Court of Appeal held that the claim concerning funeral benefit for those to be buried in the UK could be characterised as indirect discrimination in that recent migrants to the UK may prefer their relatives buried abroad. However, it was not convinced that the limitation of the benefit to UK burials involved less favourable treatment, or that the effects of the condition were 'disproportionately prejudicial' to the group as a whole.[121]

3.2.3 Disability

In *Burnip*[122] the Court of Appeal advocated a non-technical approach, finding that where a group recognised as being in need of protection against discrimination, the severely disabled, was significantly disadvantaged by the application of ostensibly neutral criteria, here housing benefit, discrimination was established, subject to justification.[123]

---

[115] *R (Wilson) v Wychavon District Council* [2007] EWCA Civ 52, [2007] 2 WLR 798.
[116] Ibid, [27].
[117] Ibid, [55].
[118] Ibid, [55].
[119] *R (Knowles) v Secretary of State for Work & Pensions* [2013] EWHC 19 (Admin).
[120] *Esfandiari* (n 52).
[121] Ibid, [18].
[122] *Burnip* (n 83).
[123] Ibid, [13]. A similar approach was taken in *MA* (n 48).

The claim in *MA*[124] also concerned changes to housing benefit, which reduced entitlement where there was an excess bedroom. Laws LJ found that there was no precise class of persons which could be identified in practical and objective terms and sufficiently differentiated from other groups equally in need of extra space. However, he still found that Article 14 applied as the policy had markedly disparate effects between groups of persons, even if the groups had no sharp edges. Article 14 obliged the Secretary of State to see that the means chosen were appropriate and not disproportionate in its adverse impact.[125]

In *AM*[126] it was argued that in entry clearance decisions, the UK had, without an objective and reasonable justification, failed to treat differently persons whose situations were significantly different. Here it was disability on the part of the UK citizen sponsor, who wished her husband to join her in the UK. The Court of Appeal accepted that the disabled as a group were adversely affected by the entry requirement to be self-sufficient.

3.2.4 Sex

The Supreme Court characterised the discrimination at issue in *Humphreys*[127] as indirect. Child tax credit was payable to one person only in respect of each child even where the care of the child was shared between separated parents. It was accepted that the rule discriminated indirectly against fathers 'because experience shows' that they are far more likely than mothers to be 'looking after the child for the smaller number of days in the week'.[128] Indirect discrimination based on sex was also claimed in in *S*[129] which concerned the imposition of deductions from earnings by prisoners working for private employers on release schemes outside prison to raise funds for Victim Support. The argument that the scheme had a disproportionate impact on women was not accepted by the Administrative Court which found that female prisoners were not in a significantly different position from male prisoners in light of the objectives of the deductions scheme:

> [T]here are no significant grounds for regarding the application of a single set of rules to them all as prima facie questionable or such as to call for the state to make out a case of objective justification in relation to it.[130]

It found no statistical evidence to show that there was in practice a greater detrimental impact on female prisoners as a group arising from the application of the deduction rules than on male prisoners.[131]

---

[124] *MA* (n 48).
[125] Ibid, [53].
[126] *AM* (n 68).
[127] *Humphreys* (n 84).
[128] Ibid, per Baroness Hale [1].
[129] *R (S) v Secretary of State for Justice* [2012] EWHC 1810 (Admin), [2013] 1 All ER 66.
[130] Ibid, [86].
[131] Ibid, [88]. See also *Stewart v Secretary of State for Work and Pensions* [2011] EWCA Civ 907 where it was accepted that denying funeral payment to the family of a prisoner who had died was indirectly discriminatory against prisoners.

4. Positive Duty

The question of whether or not Article 14 imposes a positive duty on the state to act so as to avoid discrimination is not yet well developed in HRA case law. The strength of any argument concerning positive duties and Article 14 is linked closely to whether or not the Article it is taken in conjunction with imposes a positive duty on the facts. One example is *O'Sullivan*[132] where it was argued that the respondent local authority had an obligation to offer to make the female claimant a joint tenant, given that it had granted a sole tenancy to her husband in 1970 as at that time it was common practice to grant tenancies to husbands alone. Arden LJ stated that the question of whether the positive obligation arose entailed an inquiry into whether the imposition of such an obligation on the respondent would fairly balance the parties' respective interests:

> It must be accepted in answering this question (a) that as a matter of law the consent of the tenant would be necessary; (b) that the positive obligation could not be limited to female spouses: it would have to extend to male spouses and also analogous relationships, whether heterosexual or not; and (c) that it would not be enough simply to write a few letters: other inquiries would have to be made. The appellant, on the other hand, could have initiated the process herself and she would receive a measure of protection on the alternative basis of being treated as the remaining joint tenant for the purpose of the Housing Allocation Scheme policy.[133]

Arden LJ concluded that such a positive obligation would impose an excessive burden on the respondent in practice which would result in the balance being swung unfairly in the appellant's direction. Therefore, she concluded that no such obligation was imposed.[134]

5. Grounds

5.1 Introduction

Various grounds of prohibited discrimination are set out in Article 14. These are sex, race, colour, language, religion, political or other opinion, national or social origin, association with a national minority, property, birth and 'other status'. Whilst the list

---

[132] *O'Sullivan* (n 73).

[133] Ibid, [60].

[134] Ibid, [61]. See also *R (on the application of L) v Manchester City Council* [2001] EWHC (Admin) 707, [2002] FLR 43, and *Campbell v South Northamptonshire District Council* [2004] EWCA Civ 409, [2004] 3 All ER 387.

of grounds is not exhaustive, it is limited, and the limit depends upon the meaning of 'other status'.[135]

5.2 'Other Status'

Despite some earlier conflicting authority in the Court of Appeal,[136] it was held by the House of Lords in S[137] that 'other status' means a personal characteristic[138] analogous to the grounds expressed in the Article itself.[139] '[I]t has to do with who people are, not with what their problem is.'[140] In Clift[141] Lord Hope held that the grounds of discrimination listed in Article 14 existed independently of the treatment of which complaint was made.

> In that sense they are personal to the complainant. They can be an acquired characteristic, such as the person's religion or political opinion. They can also, like a person's race or birth, be a characteristic over which he has no control.[142]

He observed that a generous meaning should be given and that the protection of Article 14 should not be denied because the distinguishing feature enabling the discriminator to persons or groups of persons differently had not been previously recognised.[143] By contrast, in RJM[144] Lord Walker stated that he found the expression 'personal characteristics imprecise'. He stated that in his view 'personal characteristics' were more like a series of concentric circles:

> The most personal characteristics are those which are innate, largely immutable, and closely connected with an individual's personality: gender, sexual orientation, pigmentation of skin, hair and eyes, congenital disabilities. Nationality, language, religion and politics may be almost innate ... or may be acquired ... but all are regarded as important to the development of an individual's personality. ... Other acquired characteristics are further out in the concentric circles; they are more concerned with what people do, or with what happens to them, than with who they are; but they may still come within article 14.[145]

5.3 Included within 'Other Status'

It has been accepted by UK courts determining claims under the HRA that Article 14

---

[135] S (n 8), per Lord Steyn at [48]. See further J Gerards, 'The Discrimination Grounds of Article 14 of the European Convention on Human Rights' [2013] Human Rights Law Review 99.

[136] Michalak (n 6); Waite (n 74).

[137] S (n 8).

[138] Ibid, per Lord Steyn at [48].

[139] Ibid, [51].

[140] C v Secretary of State for the Home Department [2004] EWCA Civ 234, [36]. See also the comments of Lord Neuberger in RJM (n 86), [45].

[141] Clift (n 25).

[142] Ibid, [45]

[143] Ibid, [48]. See also the observations of Lord Bingham at [27]–[28] and R (Minter) v Chief Constable of Hampshire [2013] EWCA Civ 697 but note that in Clift v United Kingdom 13 July 2010 the ECtHR determined that the grounds of discrimination did fall within Art 14.

[144] RJM (n 86).

[145] Ibid, [5]. Lord Neuberger and the others agreed.

precludes discrimination on the grounds of: sexual orientation;[146] nationality;[147] national origin;[148] sex;[149] residence;[150] age;[151] physical or mental capacity;[152] residence;[153] distance of family relationship;[154] ethnicity;[155] family relationship;[156] status as an asylum seeker;[157] being married or unmarried;[158] not being part of a family unit;[159] homelessness;[160] majority and minority shared carer of child;[161] a person with parental responsibility for a child by reason of a residence order rather than adoption;[162] disability;[163] patients who are prisoners and those who are not;[164] status as a foster child;[165] status as a foster-carer related to a foster children;[166] status as a prisoner;[167] residence in Scotland;[168] status as a disabled person in receipt of healthcare services;[169] status as the tenant of a private landlord;[170] status as a prisoner in a mental health unit not in prison;[171] status as a grower of a particular type of crop.[172]

In *Morris*[173] a majority of the Court of Appeal held that identifying one single ground may not be possible and it may be sufficient to determine that various grounds have operated in combination resulting in less favourable treatment.[174]

5.4 Not Included within 'Other Status'

In *S* the House of Lords concluded that the difference in treatment between those who had to provide fingerprints and DNA samples pursuant to a criminal investigation as compared with the rest of the public, who had not, was not on the grounds of status.

---

[146] *Ghaidan* (n 1), and *Secretary of State for Work and Pensions v M* (n 21).

[147] *A v Secretary of State* (n 4); see also *Clift* (n 25).

[148] *Westminster City Council v Morris* [2005] EWCA Civ 1184, [2006] 1 WLR 505 although no final decision was reached on this point.

[149] *Wilkinson* (n 80); *Hooper* (n 31).

[150] *Carson* (n 4), per Lord Hoffmann at [13].

[151] *R (on the application of Reynolds) v Secretary of State for Work and Pensions* [2005] UKHL 37, [2005] 2 WLR 1369; *Douglas* (n 91).

[152] *R (on the application of Pretty) v Director of Public Prosecutions* [2001] UKHL 61, [2001] 3 WLR 1598, [105]; *B v Secretary of State for Work and Pensions* [2005] EWCA Civ 929.

[153] *Nasser* (n 27).

[154] *Michalak* (n 6).

[155] *Clarke* (n 74).

[156] *L* (n 134).

[157] *R (on the application of G) v Immigration Appeal Tribunal* [2004] EWCA Civ 173, [2005] 1 WLR 1445.

[158] *Re P* (n 5); *Principal Reporter v K* [2010] UKSC 56, [2011] 1 WLR 18.

[159] *AL* (n 40). See also *R (A)* (n 42).

[160] *RJM* (n 86).

[161] *Humphreys* (n 84).

[162] *Francis* (n 46).

[163] *AM* (n 68); *Burnip* (n 83).

[164] *RD* (n 84).

[165] *Wall* (n 72).

[166] *R (X) v Tower Hamlets* [2013] EWHC 480 (Admin).

[167] *Stewart* (n 131).

[168] *R (Primrose) v Secretary of State for Justice* [2008] EWHC 1625 (Admin), [2009] Prison LR 165.

[169] *Harrison* (n 19), [95].

[170] *Knowles* (n 119).

[171] *N* (n 44).

[172] *Middlebrook Mushrooms* (n 89).

[173] *Morris* (n 148).

[174] Ibid, per Sedley LJ at [50].

The fact that the police are now in possession of fingerprints and samples which were previously lawfully acquired as a result of a criminal investigation does not give rise to a 'status' within the meaning of article 14. The appellants, and other individuals in their position, are as fully entitled to the presumption of innocence as the general body of citizens.[175]

Similarly, in *Hooper*[176] the House of Lords held that being a person who had started legal proceedings did not qualify as a status.[177] In *Clift*[178] it was argued that the other status leading to the distinctions between prisoners was the length of their sentence. Lord Bingham, and other members of the House of Lords, with some hesitation, held that this was not a status within the meaning of Article 14.[179] Nevertheless he went on to consider the question of justification. Lord Hope similarly found that it was possible to regard what the claimant had done, rather than who or what he was, as the true reason for the difference in treatment and that Article 14 did not apply.[180] However, in *Clift v UK* the ECtHR reached the opposite conclusion and it was held that the claimant did enjoy other status for the purposes of Article 14.[181]

In *Friend*[182] the House of Lords concluded that the Scottish hunting legislation was not directed at the claimant—it was the activity of hunting with hounds for sport that had been singled out for differential treatment. 'The real reason for it lies in the nature of the activity, not any personal characteristics of his or of any of the many other people of all kinds and social backgrounds who participate in hunting.'[183]

5.5 Suspect Grounds of Discrimination

Certain grounds of discrimination are regarded more seriously by the courts, requiring more intense scrutiny and more cogent reasons if differential treatment is to be justified. In *Carson*[184] Lord Hoffmann made a distinction between two categories of grounds. In the first, which he labelled 'values', he included race, caste, noble birth, membership of a political party and gender, and stated that such characteristics are seldom, if ever, acceptable grounds for differences in treatment. Furthermore, in his view, discrimination on such grounds could not be justified merely on utilitarian grounds and would be

---

[175] *S* (n 8).

[176] *Hooper* (n 31).

[177] Ibid, per Lord Hoffmann at [65]. See also *St Brice* (n 6), where the Court of Appeal held that the landlord's choice of forum for a possession action was not based on any personal characteristic of the tenant; and *Lancashire County Council v Taylor* [2005] EWCA Civ 284, [2005] HRLR 17. It is doubtful whether the conclusions in *Michalak* (n 6), concerning public sector tenants and private sector tenants and *Waite* (n 74) concerning the appellant's status as an HMP detainee would be decided in the same way post the judgments of the House of Lords in these cases.

[178] *Clift* (n 33).

[179] Ibid, [28]. The ECtHR reached the opposite conclusion in *Clift v United Kingdom* (n 143). See also *Minter* (n 143).

[180] *Clift* (n 33), [49]. See also per Baroness Hale at [63] and *R (Countryside Alliance) v Attorney General* [2007] UKHL 52, [2007] 3 WLR 922.

[181] In *R (Foley) v Parole Board for England & Wales* [2012] EWHC 2184 (Admin) the Administrative Court held that it was bound by the judgment of the House of Lords rather than that of the ECtHR on this question.

[182] *Friend* (n 29).

[183] Ibid, per Lord Hope at [30]. See also *Chen* (n 47) where it was held that a difference in treatment based on length of cohabitation was not an 'other status' within the meaning of Art 14.

[184] *Carson* (n 7).

carefully examined by the courts. In *AM*[185] the Court of Appeal held that disability discrimination may fall within the suspect group because of its recognition not only in UK law but also in numerous international instruments.[186] However, it decided that this may only apply in instances of direct discrimination rather than indirect discrimination.[187]

In Lord Hoffmann's second category, which he labelled 'questions of rationality', he included grounds such as ability, education, wealth and occupation. He stated that differences in treatment here usually depended upon considerations of the general public interest and that decisions which underpinned differences in treatment in this category were very much a matter for the elected branches of government.[188] He also noted that there may be borderline cases in which it is not easy to allocate a ground to one category or the other and, citing sexual orientation discrimination, that there may be shifts in the values of society in these matters.[189]

In her judgment in *AL*, Baroness Hale was not convinced by Lord Hoffmann's distinction, pointing out that it was drawn from US jurisprudence and that there were important differences between the 14th Amendment and Article 14 'which mean that it cannot simply be transplanted to the European situation'.[190] She stated:

> The Strasbourg grounds, largely focussing on the personal characteristics of the individual which he cannot or should not be asked to change, are more likely to require more than just a rational explanation. Nor has Strasbourg ever substituted a simple 'rational explanation' test for the proportionality test which has been its 'clear and constant jurisprudence' since first articulated in the Belgian Linguistics case.[191]

She held that, in certain circumstances, a difference in treatment between children who did or did not have parents to look after them, unless designed to correct the factual inequalities between them, would require particularly careful scrutiny. In her view:

> To deny a benefit to a child whose parents were dead, had disappeared, or were incapable of looking after him, which was available to a child who had parents available to look after him, might be very hard indeed to justify.[192]

In her view, had the policy here discriminated between the children while they were children it would have been particularly hard to justify. However, the policy here discriminated between young adults and she observed that their status as being without parents or family did not require particularly weighty reasons to justify.[193]

Whilst the identification of suspect grounds requiring more weighty justification may be subject to doubt, in some judgments more intense scrutiny has been applied to differences in treatment based on race, sex, sexual orientation,[194] nationality or national origin,[195] but not age[196] or status as a prisoner.[197]

---

[185] *AM* (n 68).
[186] [15].
[187] [16].
[188] *Carson* (n 7), [15]–[16].
[189] Ibid, [17]. See also the comments of Lord Walker at [55]–[60].
[190] *AL* (n 40), [31].
[191] Ibid, [31].
[192] Ibid, [34].
[193] Ibid, [35].
[194] *Ghaidan* (n 1), per Lord Nicholls at [19]. See also *Catholic Care (Diocese of Leeds) v Charity Commission for England & Wales* [2010] EWHC 520 (Ch), [2010] 4 All ER 1041.
[195] *Morris* (n 148).
[196] *Carson* (n 4), per Lord Walker at [59]–[60].
[197] *Stewart* (n 131).

6. Analogous Position

6.1 Determining Analogous Situations

There may be such an obvious, relevant difference between the claimant and those with whom he seeks to compare himself that their situations cannot be regarded as analogous[198] and Article 14 does not apply. However, it is important to note that in recent years this aspect of Article 14 has tended to merge with the question of justification.

When determining whether the claimant and those put forward for comparison are in an analogous position, Laws LJ suggested in his judgment in *Carson*[199] in the Court of Appeal that the question should be whether the circumstances of X and Y are so similar as to call (in the mind of a rational and fair-minded person) for a positive justification for the less favourable treatment of Y in comparison with X.[200] This was adopted by Lord Bingham in *A v Secretary of State*,[201] his Lordship finding that suspected international terrorists who were UK nationals were in a situation analogous with the appellants (suspected international terrorists who were non-UK nationals) because they shared the most relevant characteristics of the appellants.

In the House of Lords' judgment in *Carson*[202] doubt was cast on this approach, Lord Hoffmann suggesting a single question: '[I]s there enough of a relevant difference between X and Y to justify different treatment?'[203] Whatever way the question is approached, it appears that there is the potential for overlap between this question and the question of justification. In *AL (Serbia)*[204] Baroness Hale observed that unless there were very obvious relevant differences between the two situations, it was better to concentrate on the reasons for the difference in treatment and whether these amounted to an objective and reasonable justification.[205]

However, as the judgments of the House of Lords in *A v Secretary of State for the Home Department* and *Ghaidan* show, where the questions are applied correctly, there is room for both. It was clear in *Ghaidan*[206] that the survivors of unmarried heterosexual couples and homosexual couples were in an analogous situation. Homosexual relationships can have exactly the same 'qualities of intimacy, stability and inter-dependence that heterosexual relationships do'.[207] Furthermore, the capacity to have children was irrelevant, as it was the long-standing social and economic interdependence which qualified for the protection of the Rent Act 1977.[208] '[A] homosexual couple whose

---

[198] *Carson* (n 4), per Lord Nicholls at [3].
[199] [2003] EWCA Civ 797, [2003] 3 All ER 577, [61].
[200] See also *Purja* (n 16).
[201] *A v Secretary of State* (n 4), [53].
[202] *Carson* (n 4).
[203] Ibid, [31].
[204] *AL* (n 40).
[205] Ibid, [25].
[206] *Ghaidan* (n 1).
[207] Ibid, per Baroness Hale at [139].
[208] Ibid, [141].

relationship is marriage-like in the same ways that an unmarried heterosexual couple's relationship is marriage-like are indeed in an analogous situation.'[209]

Their Lordships then went on to consider whether the aim of preserving the traditional family unit was legitimate, and justified this difference in treatment as discussed in the following paragraphs. Questions of analogous situation did not enter this discussion. Similarly, in *A v Secretary of State*, once it had been determined that the two groups were in an analogous situation, the question of justification centred on whether the legitimate aim of the prevention of terrorist acts justified the difference in treatment. The issue in *Carson* could have been resolved simply by their Lordships finding that UK resident pensioners and UK non-resident pensioners were not in an analogous position.[210] If it had been necessary to consider justification, the legitimate aim would most likely have been the economic well-being of the United Kingdom.

6.2 Examples of Analogous Situations

As with other aspects of Article 14, determining whether or not those put forward are in an analogous situation to the claimant is fact-sensitive and the case law cannot be easily categorised. In some instances it is obvious that an analogy can be drawn. In *Wilkinson*[211] and *Hooper*[212] the House of Lords confirmed that widows and widowers were in an analogous position in relation to bereavement allowance by way of deduction from liability for income tax and in relation to widow's pension, widow's payment and widowed mother's allowance. In *Nasser*[213] the Court of Appeal concluded that claimants and appellants before English courts not resident in a contracting state to the Brussels or Lugano Conventions were in an analogous position to all other personal claimants or appellants before the English courts when it came to awarding security for costs.[214] In *Middlebrook Mushrooms*[215] the Administrative Court held that mushroom growers and harvesters were in an analogous position to growers and harvesters of other crops when it came to the determination of minimum wages.

In *Francis*[216] the Court of Appeal had to determine whether those who had adopted children were in an analogous position to those caring for children via a residence order for the purposes of receiving a maternity grant. It held that both mothers faced the costs associated with a new baby and that they were in an analogous or relatively similar situation.[217] In *Ratcliffe*[218] the Court of Appeal held that the married and unmarried partners of a member of the armed forces who died before 2005 and after 2005 were in an analogous position.[219]

---

[209] Ibid, [143].
[210] *Carson* (n 4).
[211] *Wilkinson* (n 80).
[212] *Hooper* (n 31).
[213] *Nasser* (n 27).
[214] Ibid, [58].
[215] *Middlebrook Mushrooms* (n 89).
[216] *Francis* (n 46).
[217] Ibid, [19].
[218] *Ratcliffe* (n 82).
[219] Ibid, [72].

6.3 Examples of Non-analogous Situations

In S^{220} the House of Lords found no analogous position to exist between individuals who have had their fingerprints and DNA samples lawfully taken in consequence of being charged with a recordable offence and those who had not.[221] In *Michalak*[222] the Court of Appeal found too many differences between the regimes for private sector tenants and public sector tenants to conclude that the two groups were in an analogous situation with respect to successor tenancies. However, it did find in favour of the claimant on his alternative argument that distant relatives were in a relevantly similar situation to close relatives entitled to succeed to a tenancy under section 113 of the Housing Act 1985. In *Waite*[223] the Court of Appeal held that the positions of the HMP detainee and remand prisoner were not sufficiently analogous to make an Article 14 case in the light of the differential treatment of those two classes for the purposes of housing benefit. 'The HMP detainee has been convicted of murder. The remand prisoner has not been convicted of anything. He enjoys the presumption of innocence.'[224]

In *Al-Rawi*[225] the Court of Appeal held that UK residents and UK citizens were not in analogous positions.

> A person who is not a British National is not entitled to the protection of a State to State claim. ... That is not an attribute of the non-British national. It is not a function of how he is likely to behave. It is ... simply a legal fact.[226]

In the view of the Court of Appeal, the non-nationals imprisoned in Guantanamo Bay were treated differently by the Foreign Secretary from the nationals not because of their race or nationality but because one group was entitled to diplomatic protection and the other was not.[227]

In many claims it is not obvious on which side of the line a situation falls. For example, *Purja*[228] concerned allegations of the Gurkha Brigade of the British Army that terms as to pension rights, pay whilst on long leave in Nepal and accompanied service discriminated against Gurkhas on the ground of their nationality. With respect to pension rights and pay whilst on long leave, looking at the basis and circumstances of the Gurkhas' recruitment, service and discharge, the court unanimously held that the Gurkhas were not in an analogous position to British soldiers. Gurkhas leave the UK and return to Nepal, where their pensions will be paid and where conditions are

---

[220] *S* (n 8).

[221] Ibid, per Lord Steyn at [53].

[222] *Michalak* (n 6).

[223] *Waite* (n 74).

[224] Ibid, [30]. See also *R (on the application of Montana) v Secretary of State for the Home Department* [2001] 1 WLR 552, where the Court of Appeal concluded that those who acquired citizenship under s 2 of the British Nationality Act 1981 as of right at birth were not true comparators with those who may apply for it under s 3; *R v Kirk* [2002] EWCA Crim 1580, [2002] Crim LR 756, where the Court of Appeal held that a woman who had sexual intercourse with a boy aged under 16 years was not in an analogous position with a man who had sexual intercourse with a girl aged under 16 years; and *G* (n 157), where the Court of Appeal held that asylum seekers were not in an analogous position to others seeking to appeal from decisions of tribunals.

[225] *Al-Rawi* (n 66).

[226] Ibid, [78].

[227] Ibid, [78].

[228] *Purja* (n 16).

markedly different from those in the UK. Pensions are also payable to Gurkhas from a much earlier age.[229]

The question of accompanied service was more difficult. The majority took into account the fact that Gurkhas could return to Nepal for five months' long leave every third year, which made it more tolerable for them to be separated from their families.[230] Also considered were the need to maintain linkages with Nepal and the fact that they tended to marry at a younger age and therefore the provision of considerably more married quarters would have a tangible impact on effectiveness and deployability.[231] Although the majority concluded that the Gurkha and British soldiers were not in an analogous position with regard to accompanied service, this was not without reservations, Chadwick LJ commenting that the decision of the court should not be taken to suggest that Gurkha soldiers do not have a legitimate grievance about the limited provision of married accommodation.[232]

---

7. Objective and Reasonable Justification

7.1 Determining Justification

Article 14 is not an absolute right. Differences in treatment can be justified if these pursue a legitimate aim and there is a reasonable relationship of proportionality between the means employed and the aim sought to be realised.[233] In common with Article 1 Protocol No 1, no legitimate objectives are set out in Article 14. However, there has been much more consideration of justification in claims concerning Article 1 Protocol No 1 than there has in claims concerning Article 14. It is therefore helpful to examine how justificatory arguments are approached in Article 1 Protocol No 1 claims.

As discussed in the following chapter, in relation to Article 1 Protocol No 1 there is a three-stage test: first to consider the lawfulness of the interference; second, the legitimate aim; and finally proportionality. In the same way that Article 1 Protocol No 1 has been interpreted, legitimate aims should be accepted by the court unless manifestly without reasonable foundation. If a legitimate aim is accepted on this basis, it remains necessary to consider the question of proportionality. However, in its judgment in *Hum-*

---

[229] Ibid, per Simon Brown LJ at [60].

[230] Ibid, [62].

[231] Ibid, [66].

[232] Ibid, [90]. See also *British Gurkha Welfare Society* (n 19); *R (Gurung) v Ministry of Defence* [2008] EWHC 1496 (Admin); and *Limbu* (n 2). Other claims concluding non- analogous position include: *Primrose* (n 168) (Scottish prisoners and English prisoners eligible for early release); *R (Brooke) v Secretary of State for Justice* [2009] EWHC 1396 (Admin) (serious offenders who were foreign nationals and serious offenders who were not); *R (Massey) v Secretary of State for Justice* [2013] EWHC 1950 (Admin) (those sentenced under different sentencing regimes); *Chen* (n 47) (those who have cohabitated for less than two years and those who have not); *R (Bibi) v Secretary of State for the Home Department* [2013] EWCA Civ 322, [2013] 3 All ER 778 (those who have knowledge of the English language to a prescribed standard and those who do not).

[233] *Ghaidan* (n 1), per Lord Nicholls at [18].

phreys[234] the Supreme Court did not follow this approach. Baroness Hale suggested that the normally strict test of justification for sex discrimination gave way to the manifestly without reasonable foundation test in the context of state benefits.[235] This is not correct and is not in keeping with ECtHR authority. In *Stec*[236] the ECtHR stated as follows:

> A difference of treatment is, however, discriminatory if it has no objective and reasonable justification; in other words, if it does not pursue a legitimate aim or if there is not a reasonable relationship of proportionality between the means employed and the aim sought to be realised.[237]

References to manifestly without reasonable foundation in the judgment of the ECtHR concerned the contracting states' margin of appreciation, an international law concept, not intended to be applied by a national court. The Supreme Court has also failed to follow the decision in *RJM*.[238] Here every member of the House of Lords referred to the test of proportionality which was to be applied to justify discrimination in the availability of benefits to those who were homeless.[239] It is suggested that the correct approach is first to consider whether the objective is manifestly without reasonable foundation. If not, the next step is to consider the proportionality of the interference. This has also been the approach taken in judgments after *Humphreys* in the Court of Appeal.[240]

Justification must be assessed by reference to the position when the issue to be determined arises, not when the legislation was enacted. It is possible that legislation may be justified when introduced but may cease to be so by the time the differential treatment is applied to the claimant.[241] It is possible that less justification is required in instances of indirect discrimination than direct discrimination.[242] As noted above, it is often stated that some grounds of discrimination call for more justification than others. If it is determined that a ground does not call for strict scrutiny, and it is a matter of general public interest, often a court affords considerable deference to the primary decision maker.[243]

It has also been held that the less restrictive alternative test is not an integral part of the analysis of proportionality under Article 14.[244] However, in *Wilson* the Court of Appeal contradicted itself, stating that the existence of a less restrictive alternative could, in an appropriate case, be considered as one of the tools of analysis in examining the cogency of the reasons put forward in justification.[245] And in *AM (Somalia)*[246] the Court of Appeal held that the lack of proportionality may be found in the failure to introduce appropriate exceptions to the general policy or measure.[247]

---

[234] *Humphreys* (n 84).
[235] Ibid, [19].
[236] *Stec* (n 87).
[237] Ibid, [51].
[238] *RJM* (n 86).
[239] Ibid, per Lord Mance at [14]–[15] and per Lord Neuberger at [48]. The approach of the Supreme Court in *Humphreys* was applied in *MA* (n 48).
[240] See eg *Swift v Secretary of State for Justice* [2013] EWCA Civ 193.
[241] *Wilson* (n 115), [40]–[41].
[242] Ibid, [55].
[243] See eg *N* (n 44), [78].
[244] *Wilson* (n 115), [61].
[245] Ibid, [62].
[246] *AM* (n 68).
[247] Ibid, [20].

7.2 Reasonable Time for Change

As society changes, it is often the case that discrimination which was previously accepted is no longer justified.[248] It has been held that, where this is the case, a period of consultation, drafting and debate must be included in the time which the legislature may reasonably consider appropriate for making a change. Up to the point at which that time is exceeded, there is no violation of a Convention right.[249] Lord Bingham observed in *Secretary of State for Work and Pensions v M*[250] that the claimant's argument about discrimination in arrangements for child support against those in same-sex relationships was anachronistic and that she was applying the standards of today to criticise a regime which when it was established represented the accepted values of society.[251] The Civil Partnerships Act 2004 had removed the feature of which she complained and in his Lordship's view it was unrealistic to 'stigmatise as unjustifiably discriminatory' a regime which, given the size of the 'overall task and the need to recruit the support of the public, could scarcely have been reformed sooner'.[252]

However, in her dissenting judgment, Baroness Hale rejected this justification:

> It is hugely to the credit of the United Kingdom Government and Parliament that they have recognised this. They are ahead of much of Europe, although parts of Europe are ahead of them. But can this be an objective justification for not having recognised it sooner? I do not see how it can be. Race discrimination was always wrong, long before the world woke up to that fact. Sex discrimination was always wrong, long before the world woke up to that fact.[253]

In her view whilst it was acceptable to use historical disadvantage and exclusion to justify some compensatory treatment for the excluded group which was denied to others, it was not acceptable to use historical disadvantage and exclusion to justify continued disadvantage and exclusion of the excluded group.[254]

The issue of affording a reasonable time for change, before finding a violation of Article 14, was also important to the Court of Appeal's judgment in *Ratcliffe*.[255] Here the claimant claimed it was incompatible with Article 14 to deny her a war pension as her partner, to whom she was not married, had died before 6 April 2005. If he had died after this date she would have been eligible for a war pension. The Court of Appeal held that the case fell within the principle that if discrimination in the field of pensions were not based on suspect grounds, 'courts will be very reluctant to find that the discrimination is not justified'. In its view, the decision as from what point in time unmarried partners were put in an analogous position to spouses in the field of pensions was a decision for government with which the courts would not ordinarily interfere.[256]

---

[248] See eg the comments made concerning discrimination on the ground of sexual orientation on *Ghaidain* (n 1).

[249] *Hooper* (n 31), per Lord Hoffmann at [62].

[250] *Secretary of State for Work and Pensions v M* (n 21).

[251] Ibid, [6].

[252] Ibid, [6]. See per Lord Walker at [96] and per Lord Mance at [155].

[253] Ibid, [114].

[254] Ibid, [115].

[255] *Ratcliffe* (n 82).

[256] Ibid, [89].

7.3 Social and Economic Factors

7.3.1 Generally

Where social or economic factors are raised as a justification for different treatment, the courts are more willing to defer to judgment of the primary decision maker although this may not be the case if the discrimination is regarded as particularly invidious. For example, in *Ghaidan*[257] it was stated by their Lordships that national housing policy was a field where the court would be less ready to intervene, but as the alleged violation comprised differential treatment based on the ground of sexual orientation, it scrutinised with intensity the reasons said to constitute justification.[258] It concluded that the distinction here fell outside the discretionary area of judgment.[259]

However, in *Michalak*[260] the Court of Appeal held that determining who should succeed to a secure tenancy was pre-eminently a matter for Parliament, which has to determine the 'manner in which public resources should be allocated for local authority housing on preferential terms'.[261] Similarly in *MA*,[262] which concerned a change to housing benefit, Laws LJ held that the Secretary of State had a wide margin of discretion.[263] Finding the exclusion of some disabled persons from the new scheme, and not others, was justified, he observed as follows:

> Much of our modern law, judge-made and statutory, makes increasing demands on public decision-makers in the name of liberal values: the protection of minorities, equality of treatment, nondiscrimination, and the *quietus* of old prejudices. The law has been enriched accordingly. But it is not generally for the courts to resolve the controversies which this insistence involves. That is for elected government. The cause of constitutional rights is not best served by an ambitious expansion of judicial territory, for the courts are not the proper arbiters of political controversy.[264]

7.3.2 Welfare Benefits

A number of claims have been made concerning the provision of welfare benefits. Usually the justification put forward for paying one group but not another, or paying different rates to different groups, includes social and economic factors. These types of claims have proved very difficult for claimants to win. For example, in *Hooper*[265] it was argued that the preservation of widow's pension for widows bereaved before 9 April 2001 discriminated against widowers contrary to Article 14 taken together with Article 1 Protocol No 1. The House of Lords appreciated that the pension was not means tested but paid upon the perception that older widows as a class were likely to be needier than older widowers as a class or younger widows as a class.[266] Furthermore,

---

[257] *Ghaidan* (n 1).
[258] Ibid, per Lord Nicholls at [19].
[259] Ibid, [23].
[260] *Michalak* (n 6).
[261] Ibid, [41].
[262] *MA* (n 48).
[263] Ibid, [61].
[264] Ibid, [74].
[265] *Hooper* (n 31).
[266] Ibid, per Lord Hoffmann at [16].

in the social conditions which prevailed for most of the last century, it was unusual for married women to work and ... it was unreasonable to expect them to be equipped to earn their own living if they were widowed in middle age. This argument self-evidently did not apply to men.[267]

Noting that the question of the precise moment at which special treatment was no longer justified was a social and political question within the competence of Parliament,[268] their Lordships concluded that the preservation of the widow's pension for widows bereaved before 9 April 2001 was objectively justified.[269]

Social and economic factors were also at issue in *Carson*.[270] Mrs Carson had been denied the annual increase payable to pensioners living in the UK because she lived in South Africa. Whilst the House of Lords did not find the formulaic approach to Article 14 helpful, its conclusion in short was that the discrimination was justified. In its view, discrimination on the ground of residence did not require intensive scrutiny on the part of the court, unlike discrimination on the ground of race, sex or sexual orientation.[271] Furthermore, it was found that she moved to South Africa voluntarily and thereby placed herself outside of the UK social security system[272] and that she was not in the same position as a UK resident.[273] Furthermore, it was found that this was very much a case in which Parliament was entitled to decide whether the differences justify a difference in treatment. 'And in deciding what expatriate pensions should be paid, Parliament must be entitled to take into account competing claims on public funds.'[274]

Similarly, in *Reynolds*[275] the House of Lords concluded that it was justified to pay those under the age of 25 income support at a reduced rate.

[O]nce it is accepted that the necessary expenses of young people, as a class, are lower than those of older people, they can properly be treated differently for the purpose of social security payments. No doubt there are different ways of giving effect to the distinction, but that is a matter for Parliament to chose.[276]

Furthermore, although the 25th birthday was accepted to be a very arbitrary line, their Lordships held that the justification was also the need for legal certainty and a workable rule.[277]

The question in *RJM*[278] concerned the provision of disability premium to income support which was not payable to those without accommodation, ie the homeless. The key question was justification. The Secretary of State had argued that the objectives

---

[267] Ibid, [17].
[268] Ibid, [32].
[269] Ibid, [40]. See also *R (Cockburn) v Secretary of State for Health* [2011] EWHC 2095 (Admin).
[270] *Carson* (n 4).
[271] Ibid, per Lord Hoffmann at [18].
[272] Ibid, [18].
[273] Ibid, [25].
[274] Ibid, [25]. The ECtHR found no violation of Art 14 in *Carson v United Kingdom* (2010) 51 EHRR 13
[275] *Reynolds* (n 151).
[276] Ibid, per Lord Hoffmann at [40].
[277] Ibid, [41]. Social and economic justifications were also successful in *Tucker* (n 74), which concerned a challenge to the regulation preventing a tenant, who was responsible for a child of the landlord, from being paid housing benefit; *Michalak* (n 6), concerning the justification for only allowing close relatives to succeed to a secure tenancy under the Housing Act 1985; and *Douglas* (n 91), concerning an age bar in relation to the provision of student loans. However, in *L* (n 134) the Administrative Court held that paying short-term foster carers who were friends or relatives of the child at a different rate to other foster carers was not justified.
[278] *RJM* (n 86).

were to encourage the disabled homeless to seek shelter and that those without accom-modation were actually less likely to need a supplement. The House of Lords concluded that the discrimination was justified in the sense that the government was entitled to adopt and apply the policy at issue: 'This is an area where the court should be very slow to substitute its view for that of the executive, especially as the discrimination is not on one of the express, or primary, grounds.'[279]

There are very few reported cases where a successful Article 14 claim has been made against a change to welfare provision.[280] One example is *Burnip*[281] where the Court of Appeal considered alleged discrimination against the severely disabled inherent in the award of housing benefit. Because of the claimants' severe disabilities, they were assessed as needing the presence of carers throughout the night in rented flats in which they lived and for this reason they needed two-bedroom flats. They were only given housing benefit at the one-bedroom rate. As this was indirect discrimination, particularly weighty reasons were not required.[282] However, the Court of Appeal concluded that the discrimination was not justified. It found that the benefit was in order to allow indi-viduals to meet their basic human need for accommodation of an acceptable standard. The exception was sought for only a limited category of claimants and these would be few in number. Therefore, the cost and human resource implications would be modest. The extra assistance available was seen as not sufficient and, furthermore, it was taken into account that Parliament had actually legislated to alleviate the most severe impacts the Court of Appeal, stating that to do so at a time of economic hardship recognised the justice of such claims and proportionate cost and nature of the remedy.[283]

7.3.3 Taxation

Tax arrangements are also an area where it has been determined by the courts that the state should be granted considerable deference. In *Gallagher*[284] a majority of the House of Lords concluded that the inability of Mormons to secure a particular tax advantage was not within the ambit of Article 9. Nevertheless, the question of justification was also considered. It was held that Parliament must have a wide discretion in deciding what should be regarded as a sufficient public benefit to justify exemption from taxa-tion and 'it was entitled to take the view that public access to religious services was such a benefit'.[285] Lord Scott, who by contrast to the majority had determined that the taxation was within the ambit of Article 9, considered the law justified:

---

[279] Ibid, per Lord Neuberger at [56]. Other unsuccessful welfare challenges include: Stewart (n 131) (non-payment of funeral benefits for prisoners); *Swift* (n 240) (exclusion of those cohabitating for less than two years from a claim under the Fatal Accidents Act 1976); *R (RD) v Secretary of State for Work and Pensions* [2010] EWCA Civ 18, [2010] 1 WLR 1782 (non-payment of welfare benefits to convicted prisoners serving part of their sentences in psychiatric hospital); *Esfandiari* (n 52) (limitation of funeral expenses to UK burials); *Wall* (n 72) (foster child unable to succeed to secure tenancy).

[280] Successful Art 14 claims include: *R (X) v Tower Hamlets* [2013] EWHC 480 (Admin) (lower payment to foster parents related to child); *In the Matter of an Application by Brewster for Judicial Review* [2012] NIQB 85 (different treatment of cohabitating partner in relation to survivors pension); *Francis* (n 46) (non-payment of maternity grant to those with a residence order).

[281] *Burnip* (n 83).

[282] Ibid, [28].

[283] Ibid, [64]. Contrast the decision in *MA* (n 48). See also Knowles (n 119).

[284] *Gallagher* (n 77).

[285] Ibid, per Lord Hoffmann at [15].

I can see every reason why a state should adopt a general policy under which fiscal relief for premises used for religious worship is available where the premises are open to the general public and is withheld where they are not.[286]

Discrimination on the ground of childcare responsibilities was at issue in *Humphreys*.[287] Here the claimant father challenged child tax credit which was payable to one person in respect of each child even where care of the child was shared between separated parents. It was accepted that this was indirect discrimination against fathers and that the question was one of justification of sex discrimination, although Baroness Hale also stated that this was discrimination based on childcare division which could affect a father or mother depending on where a child spent most of his or her time.[288] As discussed above, the Supreme Court confused the questions of legitimate aim and proportionality. The test applied was not proportionality but the less strict test of whether the justification was manifestly without reasonable foundation. It was accepted that the discrimination was justified on the basis that by targeting one household, support for children would be delivered in the most effective manner and also it was simpler and less expensive to administer, thus maximising the amount available.[289]

7.3.4 Immigration Control

Economic and social reasons are the primary justification put forward for discrimination in immigration measures and these are usually accepted with little question by the courts. For example, in *AM (Somalia)*[290] the claimant had married a UK citizen who was disabled, but was refused entry clearance as he had no offer of employment prior to entry and there were doubts about support from personal resources. The Court of Appeal held that there was nothing disproportionate in a general rule or policy which made self-sufficiency a requirement of entry.

> [I]t is reasonable and proportionate to have a criterion of self-sufficiency without a general exemption for the disabled. It will produce cases of hardship but that in itself does not render it disproportionate, particularly where provision is made for exceptional compassionate circumstances.[291]

Elias LJ rejected the submission that weighty reasons were required for justification in this instance given this was indirect discrimination in circumstances where there was equality of treatment:

> The range of characteristics linked to one of the identified forms of status is potentially very wide indeed, and it would severely inhibit a state's power to legislate if it had to provide weighty reasons for adopting policies which adversely impacted on groups not by reason of status alone, but for reasons connected to it. Furthermore, the need for weighty reasons is in any even less prominent where questions of social policy are in issue.[292]

---

[286] Ibid, [51].
[287] *Humphreys* (n 84).
[288] Ibid, [20].
[289] Ibid, per Baroness Hale at [29].
[290] *AM* (n 68).
[291] Ibid, [29].
[292] Ibid, [61] and [65]–[71].

In *AL*[293] the claimants, who had arrived in the UK as children without families, challenged the policy which, as a one-off exercise, granted indefinite leave to remain to those who arrived in the UK as children with their families. It was recognised by the House of Lords that the objective of the policy was to save public funds by clearing the ground to promote greater efficiency in the future. 'It was directed to improving the system of asylum control in the general public interest.'[294] Their Lordships concluded that the policy was proportionate. It was held to be devised as a solution to pressing administrative and financial problems and how best to deal with the problems was 'primarily a matter for the exercise of judgment by the executive'.[295] Weighty reasons were not required to justify treatment on the ground of adult status and there was nothing to indicate that they were being targeted for unfavourable treatment.[296]

Baroness Hale found it relevant that this was a policy aimed at benefiting family groups and was not targeted against the claimants. In addition, she noted that the favourable treatment given to the family groups was an aspect of the respect accorded by the state to family life.[297]

> The family life of the family groups who are here is undoubtedly in play, whereas it is only the private life of the appellants which may be in play ... we are not therefore looking at differential treatment in relation to exactly the same Convention right.[298]

She concluded that the policy could withstand scrutiny. By contrast, the Administrative Court concluded in *A*[299] that applying a general presumption that indefinite leave to remain would be granted to relevant children when they live with a parent who also required leave but not applying it to those who did not live with such a parent (none of whom were to be removed) had no justification.

> The difference in treatment of the relevant children appears to be simply arbitrary when regard is had to the aim of that policy which is to protect the interests of those children who have established their private life in this country, who should normally not be uprooted from it as a result and who should accordingly normally be regarded as settled here.[300]

A different issue arose in *Morris*[301] where it was necessary for the Secretary of State to justify the distinction made in the Housing Act 1996 which meant that the claimant could not be treated as in priority need for housing as her dependent daughter was subject to immigration control. A majority of the Court of Appeal accepted that reducing the incentive for people to come to the UK for the purpose of claiming benefits or services was a perfectly legitimate policy objective. However, it found that its application to an adult who was here as of right and who had her child with her was far from obvious:

> There was no good reason to regard Mrs Morris' application for emergency housing assistance with her daughter as in any sense benefit tourism rather than as a reaction to a crisis

---

[293] *AL* (n 40).
[294] Ibid, per Lord Hope at [6].
[295] Ibid, per Lord Hope at [8].
[296] Ibid, per Lord Hope at [9]–[10].
[297] Ibid, [48].
[298] Ibid, [48].
[299] *R (A)* (n 42).
[300] Ibid, [61].
[301] *Morris* (n 148).

which had overtaken them while she was lawfully here and her daughter, who was subject to immigration control, was with her.[302]

The majority concluded that the rule was not a proportionate response to the perceived problem and that this was not within the discretionary area of judgment of the legislature or of the executive.[303]

7.4 Protection of the Environment

The justification put forward by the state in *Wilson*[304] for the disproportionate impact of planning control on gypsies and travellers, as opposed to dwelling houses, was primarily protection of the environment. The Court of Appeal also held that as this was indirect discrimination, less justification was called for as the measure was not targeting gypsies and travellers.[305]

> Thus, although the indirect discriminatory impact on gypsies and travellers makes it appropriate to apply the intense or severe scrutiny referred to in *Ghaidan* and *Carson*, the case does not fall within the scope of the very strict reasoning applied in *Timishev* to direct discrimination on grounds of race or ethnic origin.[306]

The Court of Appeal found that the provision was not automatically open to challenge on the basis that a less restrictive solution would have been possible. It concluded that the complete absence of an exemption for residential caravans was justified and fell within the legislature's discretionary area of judgment essentially because a change in use of a building to a dwelling would cause less immediate environmental damage than the stationing of a residential caravan.[307] Moses LJ observed that the fact that the removal of the exemption did not entail an abandonment of the obligation properly to consider the special situation of gypsies and travellers under Article 8 when issuing a stop notice was a powerful factor in considering the proportionality of the measure.[308]

7.5 Health

Distinctions in the smoking policy between prisoners in mental health units and those who were not was the subject matter of the claim in *N*.[309] Although it had been held that smoking was not within the ambit of Article 8, the question of justification was considered. The Court of Appeal concluded that this was not a ground of discrimination calling for severe scrutiny. It had also been the subject of a recent and considered judgment by the legislature after extensive consultation. It found that there was a legitimate basis for distinguishing between those in mental health units and those in prison.

---

[302] Ibid, per Sedley LJ at [40].
[303] Ibid, [49]. See further H Wray, 'Greater than the Sum of their Parts: UK Supreme Court Decisions on Family Migration' [2013] *Public Law* 838.
[304] *Wilson* (n 115).
[305] Ibid, [55].
[306] Ibid, [55].
[307] Ibid, [89].
[308] Ibid, [102].
[309] *N* (n 44).

The best possible healthcare was the justification put forward in *Harrison*[310] as the reason why the law did not permit the making of direct cash payments to individuals receiving healthcare services under the NHS which would enable recipients to make their own arrangements for medical care. The Administrative Court accepted the justifications for the refusal of cash payments: health treatment was to be given free at the point of delivery; patients would receive healthcare appropriate to their needs and of suitable quality; patients would not become subject to contractual obligations; and limited NHS resources would be used in a way which best met the needs of all patients.[311]

7.6 Protection of the Traditional Family Unit

Justifications for discrimination based upon the protection of the traditional family unit have not been successful. For example, in *Ghaidan*[312] it was argued that the difference in treatment between heterosexual and same-sex partnerships was to provide protection for the traditional family as same-sex partners were unable to have children with each other and there was a reduced likelihood of children being part of such a household. This was rejected by the House of Lords; no reason was found for believing these factual differences had any bearing on why succession rights had been conferred on heterosexual couples but not on homosexual couples.

> Protection of the traditional family unit may well be an important and legitimate aim in certain contexts. ... Marriage is not now a prerequisite to protection. ... Nor is parenthood, or the presence of children in the home. ... Nor is procreative potential a prerequisite.[313]

Furthermore, it was noted that a homosexual couple, as much as a heterosexual couple, share each other's life and make their home together.[314] Here no legitimate aim was found, and their Lordships used section 3 of the HRA to read the legislation in such a way that cohabiting heterosexual couples and cohabiting homosexual couples would be treated alike for the purposes of succession as a statutory tenant.[315]

In *Re P*[316] the claimants challenged a Northern Ireland Order which excluded unmarried couples from consideration as the adoptive parents of a child. In defence of the order it was argued that married couples tend to have more stable relationships and this would secure the stability needed by an adopted child. Lord Hoffmann stated that the rule was irrational and contradicted the principle that the court was obliged to consider whether adoption was in the best interests of the child.[317] He continued:

> It is one thing to say that, in general terms, married couples are more likely to be suitable adoptive parents than unmarried ones. It is altogether another to say that one may ration-

---

[310] *Harrison* (n 19).
[311] Ibid, [106].
[312] *Ghaidan* (n 1).
[313] Ibid, per Lord Nicholls at [16].
[314] Ibid, [17]. See also the comments of Baroness Hale at [143].
[315] Ibid, [35]. See further P Johnson, 'An Essentially Private Manifestation of Human Personality: *Constructions* of Homosexuality in the European Court of Human Rights' (2010) 10 *Human Rights Law Review* 67.
[316] *Re P* (n 5).
[317] Ibid, [16].

ally assume that no unmarried couple can be suitable adoptive parents. Such an irrebuttable presumption defies everyday experience.[318]

Utilising the appropriate language of proportionality, Lord Hope held that to allow considerations favouring marriage to prevail over the best interests of the child was neither objectively justified nor proportionate.[319]

Marital status was also at issue before the Supreme Court in *Principal Reporter v K*[320] which concerned the rights of unmarried fathers to take part in children's hearings under Part II of the Children (Scotland) Act 1995. The case was determined by the application of the right to respect for family life, but the Supreme Court observed that it was likely to find, if it had to, that the automatic imposition of a burdensome procedural hurdle before some unmarried fathers could become involved in vital decisions about their children's lives was in breach of Article 14.

> [I]f an unmarried father has in fact established family life with his child, it is no more justifiable to interfere in that relationship without proper procedural safeguards that it is justifiable to interfere in the relationship between a married father and his child.[321]

7.7 Crime and Sentencing

Although the House of Lords found in *S*[322] that the Article 14 claim failed for a number of other reasons, it went on to consider whether the retention of the fingerprints and DNA samples of those who had had these taken lawfully in the consequence of being charged with a recordable offence was justified. It concluded that it was as it promoted the public interest by the detection and prosecution of serious crime and by exculpating the innocent, and was proportionate to this aim, affording due deference to Parliament in the fight against serious crime.[323]

Discrimination has also been claimed in relation to the role of the Secretary of State in determining when prisoners should be released from prison on licence. The Home Secretary still has jurisdiction, together with the Parole Board, in relation to those serving a determinate sentence of 15 years or more. In *Clift*[324] it was argued that the early release provisions to which each of the prisoners was subject were not justified under Article 14. In relation to a prisoner sentenced to more than 15 years, it was concluded that there was no justification for denying him the assessment of the Parole Board, rather than the Secretary of State. Lord Bingham observed that it was a task

---

[318] Ibid, [18].

[319] Ibid, [54]. See also *In the Matter of Northern Ireland Human Rights Commission's Application for Judicial Review* [2012] NIQB 77. See further A Kavanagh, 'Strasbourg, the House of Lords or Elected Politicians: Who Decides about Rights after Re P?' (2009) 72 *Modern Law Review* 828.

[320] *Principal Reporter* (n 158).

[321] Ibid, [53]. See further R Auchmuty, 'What's So Special about Marriage? The Impact of Wilkinson v Kitzinger' (2008) 20 *Child and Family Law Quarterly* 475.

[322] *S* (n 8).

[323] Ibid, per Lord Steyn at [55].

[324] *Clift* (n 33). See also *R v Witchell* [2005] EWCA Crim 2900 concerning the fact that a suspended sentence was not available for a young offender.

with no political content and one to which the Secretary of State could not bring any superior expertise.[325]

Similarly, no justification was found for the different treatment, based on national origin, of the two indeterminate sentence prisoners subject to removal (deportation on release). Lord Bingham observed that this was not a political decision and remained an indefensible anomaly, and such prisoners should be able to have their cases reviewed by the Parole Board in the same manner as other long-term prisoners.[326] However, the House of Lords did not grant a remedy under Article 14 given that it had already concluded, contrary to the later conclusion of the ECtHR, that there was no protected status within the meaning of Article 14.

In *Foley*[327] the Administrative Court also considered justifications for the difference in approach to early release between long-term determinate and indeterminate prisoners, having earlier concluded, on the basis of the House of Lords judgment in *Clift*, that the status was not protected. It concluded that there was no justification although, as was the position in the House of Lords, it did not find a breach of Article 14 given its earlier conclusion about status:

> [T]he two classes of case are sufficiently analogous in the context of early release provisions to justify comparison. When in each case what is under consideration at the early release stage relates to the risk of future offending I can see no basis upon which the present situation which exposes those subject to determinate sentences to a stiffer release test than those who must be taken to represent a greater risk to the safety of others can be objectively justified.[328]

7.8 Protection against Terrorist Acts

Finally, the legitimate aim put forward to justify the detention of suspected international terrorists who were not UK nationals in *A v Secretary of State*[329] was protection against terrorist acts. Their Lordships did not find this sufficient justification as the threat was also presented by UK nationals, who were not so detained.

> The comparison contended for by the Attorney General might be reasonable and justified in an immigration context, but cannot in my opinion be so in a security context, since the threat presented by suspected international terrorists did not depend on their nationality or immigration status.[330]

Their Lordships declared section 23 of the Anti-Terrorism Crime and Security Act 2001 incompatible with Article 14.[331]

---

[325] *Clift*, ibid, [33] His appeal did not succeed however as it had already been determined his status was not a status protected from discrimination by Art 14.

[326] Ibid, [40].

[327] Foley (n 181).

[328] Ibid, [76].

[329] *A v Secretary of State* (n 4).

[330] Ibid, per Lord Hoffmann at [54].

[331] See further D Campbell, 'The Threat of Terror and the Plausibility of Positivism' [2009] Public Law 501.

8. Remedy for Breach

In addition to the usual constraints regarding remedies under the Human Rights Act, particular considerations apply to any remedy for breach of Article 14. A general principle applied to affording just satisfaction is to put the applicant so far as possible in the position in which he would have been if the state had complied with its obligations under the Act.

> In a discrimination case, in which the wrongful act is treating A better than B, this involves forming a view about whether the State should have complied by treating A worse or B better. Normally one would conclude that A's treatment represented the norm and that B should have been treated better. In some cases, however, it will be clear that A's treatment was an unjustifiable anomaly.[332]

Although the House of Lords found the respondent protected by section 6(2)(a) of the HRA in *Wilkinson*,[333] their Lordships went on to indicate what remedy they would have awarded if the claimant did have a cause of action. Mr Wilkinson, a widower, claimed that, if he had been a widow, he would have been entitled to a widow's bereavement allowance by way of deduction from his liability for income tax. Their Lordships held that there was no justification for extending the widow's allowance to men.

> If, therefore, Parliament had paid proper regard to Article 14, it would have abolished the allowance for widows. Mr Wilkinson would not have received an allowance and no damages are therefore necessary to put him in the position in which he would have been if there had been compliance with his Convention rights.[334]

In the case of *Re P*, a majority of the House of Lords held that the solution to the violation of Article 14 would be to treat unmarried couples as married couples for the purposes of adoption. Lord Hope did not see this as giving rise to practical difficulties such as to make the intervention of the courts inappropriate.[335]

---

[332] *Wilkinson* (n 80), per Lord Hoffmann at [26]. See also the comments of Lord Brown at [47]–[52].
[333] Ibid.
[334] Ibid, per Lord Hoffmann at [28]. See also *Langley v Bradford Metropolitan District Council* [2004] EWCA Civ 1343, [2005] 2 WLR 740.
[335] Ibid, [55].

17

Article 1 Protocol No 1: Protection of Property

1. Introduction

The Human Rights Act also gives further effect to the rights contained in Protocol No 1 to the European Convention on Human Rights. The rights protected by Protocol No 1 are the right to education (Article 2), the right to free elections (Article 3) and the subject of this chapter, Article 1, the right to peaceful enjoyment of possessions. Article 1 is the only Protocol No 1 right examined in this book as it has generated a considerable number of claims under the HRA.[1]

Article 1 contains three distinct rules:

> The first rule is set out in the first sentence, which is of a general nature and enunciates the principle of the peaceful enjoyment of property. It then deals with two forms of interference with a person's possessions by the state: deprivation of possessions which it subjects to certain conditions, and control of the use of property in accordance with the general interest. In each case a balance must be struck between the rights of the individual and the public interest to determine whether the interference was justified. These rules are not unconnected as, before considering whether the first rule has been complied with, the court must first determine whether the last two rules are applicable ... the second and third rules are concerned with particular instances of interference with the right to peaceful enjoyment of property. They should be construed in the light of the general principle enunciated in the first rule.[2]

Often the subject matter of Article 1 claims also raises a point of EU law. For example, in *Collis Ltd*,[3] a challenge to the ban on selling tobacco from automatic vending machines, the Master of the Rolls pointed out that freedom to pursue a trade, like the

---

[1] The right to peaceful enjoyment of property is also a right recognised at common law: *Entick v Carrington* (1765) 19 Howell's State Trials 1029.

[2] *Aston Cantlow and Wilmcote with Billesley Parochial Church Council v Wallbank* [2003] UKHL 37, [2004] 1 AC 546, per Lord Hope at [67] in reliance upon *Sporrong and Lonnroth v Sweden* (1982) 5 EHRR 35 and *James v United Kingdom* (1986) 8 EHRR 123. See also *R v Secretary of State for Health, ex p Eastside Cheese Co* [1999] 3 CMLR 12 and *Axa General Insurance Ltd v Lord Advocate* [2011] UKSC 46, [2012] 1 AC 868, per Lord Hope at [21].

[3] *R (Collis Ltd) v Secretary of State for Health* [2011] EWCA Civ 437.

right to property, was one of the general principles of Community law. Any restriction had to be proportionate 'which is very much the same test as is raised (in addition to domestic lawfulness) by A1P1(2)'.[4]

2. Possessions

2.1 Generally

The meaning of 'possessions' is autonomous and wide,[5] and a variety of things have been held to come within the scope of Article 1. The Court of Appeal has observed as follows:

> [P]ossessions may be tangible or intangible ... the reach of human rights goes beyond economic protection. In the case of tangible objects, such as land or goods, and also in the case of certain intangible assets, an individual's right to enjoy them as possessions may not be, or not just be, of an economic nature. Something may have value to a person though it may have no value in the market. One cannot comprehensively define a possession for this purpose by reference to a person's ability or wish to sell it.[6]

The general principles applicable when determining the existence of a possession are difficult to identify, although it has been held that only existing possessions are protected and the Article does not guarantee the right to acquire possessions.[7] For example, in *Re A*[8] the court held that Article 1 only protected the wife's existing interest in the house and not anything she might hope to acquire from her husband in the future pursuant to her claim under the Matrimonial Causes Act 1973.[9] Therefore, when a confiscation order was made against her husband under the Drug Trafficking Act 1994, she had no right to protection from the prosecutor's claim to the husband's interest in the house.[10]

It is difficult to describe anything as a 'possession' where the decision maker has a discretion as to whether or not to make the claimed possession available. For example, *Association of British Civilian Internees*[11] concerned the British government's decision to make an ex gratia payment of £10,000 to those who had been interned by the

---

[4] Ibid, [193]. In this case although there were issues under Art 1 Protocol No 1 and EU law, it was decided to address the issue by reference to Arts 34 and 36 of the TFEU. See also *R (Shiner) v Revenue & Customs Commissioners* [2011] EWCA Civ 892, [2011] STC 1878 concerning Art 56 of the EC Treaty and *R (Petsafe Ltd) v Welsh Ministers* [2010] EWHC 2908 (Admin), [2011] EuLR 270 concerning Art 34 of the TFEU; and *Revenue & Customs Commissioners v Total Technology (Engineering) Ltd* [2012] UKUT 418 (TCC) which concerned EC Council Directive 2006/112 (the VAT Directive).

[5] *Davies v Crawley Borough Council* [2001] EWHC (Admin) 854.

[6] *R (Malik) v Waltham Forest NHS Primary Care Trust* [2007] EWCA Civ 265, [2007] 1 WLR 2092.

[7] See eg *R (on the application of the National Farmers Union) v Secretary of State for the Environment, Food and Rural Affairs*, Administrative Court, 6 March 2003, [65].

[8] *Re A* [2002] 2 FCR 481.

[9] Ibid, [164].

[10] See also *Ram v Ram* [2004] EWCA Civ 1452, [2004] 3 FCR 425.

[11] *Association of British Civilian Internees—Far East Region v Secretary of State for Defence* [2003] EWCA Civ 473, [2003] QB 1397.

Japanese during the Second World War who were born in the United Kingdom or had a parent or grandparent born there. The claimant association represented a number of British citizens interned during the war and their surviving spouses who did not meet these criteria and had therefore been refused an ex gratia payment. The Court of Appeal held that claims which had been held to be without foundation could not be possessions within the meaning of Article 1. There was no right to judicial review of the scheme to vindicate their public law rights to receive compensation.[12] It has also been held that a visa not yet granted is not a possession.[13]

The only way a future possession may become a possession within the meaning of Article 1 is if the claimant has a legitimate expectation in relation to it. In *Rowland*[14] it was confirmed by the Court of Appeal that a legitimate expectation, even if arising from ultra vires acts by a public authority, can constitute a possession for the purposes of Article 1.[15] In *National Farmers Union*[16] the issue was a legitimate expectation not as to payment but as to a particular level of payment. It had been argued that merely having made an application to enter the scheme for compensation for the slaughter of livestock as a result of the outbreak of foot and mouth prior to 30 April did not confer any right to payment at the originally agreed higher rates. However, it was held to be arguable that there was a legitimate expectation as to payment at the rates prevailing at the time and this was considered to be possession within the meaning of Article 1.[17]

The term 'possessions' also includes rights to property:

> There is protection for familiar property interests in physical things of significant economic value. There is also protection for rights in judgments, awards and recognised property claims under domestic law, such as a claim to payment of state compensation or a claim to repayment of VAT paid under mistake.[18]

In *Infinis*[19] the Court of Appeal found that the company's legitimate expectation was founded on a legal provision—the right to accreditation for renewals obligation certificates under a statutory scheme. This sufficed as a possession without the addition of a legitimate expectation:

> It is not necessary to establish a legitimate expectation for the purpose of article 1 that there should be both a legal provision giving the applicant an entitlement to some pecuniary benefit and a legal act such as a judicial decision confirming that entitlement. A legal provision or a legal act such as a judicial decision will suffice.[20]

---

[12] Ibid, [82]. See also *R (on the application of Toovey) v The Law Society* [2002] EWHC (Admin) 391, where the court held that an application for a discretionary discount was not capable of being a possession; and *Shaw (Inspector of Taxes) v Vicky Construction Ltd* [2002] EWHC (Ch) 5659, [2002] STC 1544, where the court held that the refusal to grant a fresh certificate to a taxpayer under s 561 of the Income and Corporation Taxes Act 1988 was not an interference with the peaceful enjoyment of a possession.

[13] *R (Atapattu) v Secretary of State for the Home Department* [2011] EWHC 1388 (Admin), [175].

[14] *Rowland v Environment Agency* [2003] EWCA Civ 1885, [2005] Ch 1.

[15] See ibid, [66]–[68], for an explanation of the circumstances in which a legitimate expectation may arise.

[16] *National Farmers Union* (n 7).

[17] See also *PW & Co v Milton Gate Investments Ltd* [2003] EWHC (Ch) 1994, [2004] Ch 142; *Re an application to vary the undertakings of A* [2005] STC (SCD) 103; and *Re West Norwood Cemetery* [2005] 1 WLR 2176.

[18] *R (Huitson) v Revenue & Customs Commissioners* [2011] EWCA Civ 893, [2012] 2 WLR 490, [5].

[19] *Gas & Electricity Markets Authority v Infinis plc* [2013] EWCA Civ 70.

[20] Ibid, [25].

Finally, it has been held that a contract for personal services, such as medical treatment, is not a possession within the meaning of Article 1.[21]

> They are intangible; they are not assignable; they are not even transmissible; they are not realisable and they have no present economic value. They cannot realistically be described as an 'asset'. That is the touchstone of whether something counts as a possession for the purposes of A1 P1.[22]

2.2 Personal Possessions

A range of personal possessions have been held to be within the scope of Article 1, including: money;[23] a home;[24] land;[25] copyright;[26] shares;[27] the rights to a retirement annuity and associated benefits under an annuity contract or personal pension arrangement;[28] an unregistered interest in land even if not in possession;[29] a share in the equity of redemption of a property subject to a mortgage;[30] a judgment on liability for negligence damages to be assessed;[31] money earned by a prisoner while on release from prison;[32] and a claim for tax relief.[33]

Contributory benefits, such as the state pension, have generally been considered in the context of Article 14 of the ECHR, where it has been held that such benefits are within the ambit of Article 1.[34] It has also been held that non-contributory rights under a pension scheme may be considered possessions if they are part of a package of remuneration which, unlike a non-contributory social security benefit, the individual has earned by service.[35] However, Article 1 does not guarantee a right to a pension of

---

[21] *Murungaru v Secretary of State for the Home Department* [2008] EWCA Civ 1015, [2009] INLR 180, [30].

[22] Ibid, per Lewison J at [58].

[23] *R v Dimsey; R v Allen* [2001] UKHL 46, [2001] 3 WLR 843; *R v Benjafield* [2002] UKHL 2, [2003] 1 AC 1099; *R (on the application of Denson) v Child Support Agency* [2002] EWHC (Admin) 154, [2002] 1 FLR 938.

[24] *Marcic v Thames Water Utilities Ltd* [2003] UKHL 66, [2004] 2 AC 42.

[25] *Beaulane Properties Limited v Palmer* [2005] HRLR 19.

[26] *Ashdown v Telegraph Group Ltd* [2001] EWCA Civ 1142, [2001] 3 WLR 1368.

[27] *Weir v Secretary of State for Transport* [2005] EWHC 2192 (Ch). However, here the court held that the alleged violation of the company's rights leading to a diminution in the value of the shares would only give a shareholder cause for complaint if there was a factual or legal impossibility preventing the company suing for the loss. See also *SRM Global Master Fund LP v Treasury Commissioners* [2009] EWCA Civ 788, [2009] UKHRR 1219.

[28] *Krasner v Dennison* [2000] 3 WLR 720.

[29] *Kingsalton Ltd v Thames Water Developments Ltd* [2001] EWCA Civ 20.

[30] *Horsham Properties Group Ltd v Clark* [2008] EWHC 2327 (Ch); [2009] 1 WLR 1255, [25].

[31] *Summers v Fairclough Homes Ltd* [2012] UKSC 26, [2012] 1 WLR 2004, [47].

[32] *R (S) v Secretary of State for Justice* [2012] EWHC 1810 (Admin), [2013] 1 All ER 66.

[33] *Huitson* (n 18): not having to pay UK income tax on the profits of an Isle of Man partnership trade paid to the UK taxpayer through and under a Manx trust.

[34] *R (on the application of Hooper) v Secretary of State for Work and Pensions* [2005] UKHL 29, [2005] 1 WLR 1681; *R (on the application of Carson) v Secretary of State for Work and Pensions* [2005] UKHL 37, [2005] 2 WLR 1369. In relation to non-contributory benefits, see *Campbell v South Northamptonshire District Council* [2004] EWCA Civ 409, [2004] 3 All ER 387. It was held in *B v Secretary of State for Work and Pensions* [2005] EWCA Civ 929 that overpaid non-contributory benefits were outwith the scope of Art 1 Protocol No 1.

[35] *R (Smith) v Secretary of State for Defence and Secretary of State for Work and Pensions* [2004] EWHC (Admin) 1797, [2005] 1 FLR 97, [27].

a particular amount or payment of it at a particular time.[36] It has been held that rights under an earlier version of a pension scheme, prior to its amendment, were possessions for the purposes of Article 1. These were held to be substantive expectations enforceable in domestic public law.

[I]individual civil servants had an administrative expectation that the Old Scheme would be operated to the full extent of its terms and a statutory right to expect that the scheme would not be changed to his/her detriment without the consent of his/her trade union.[37]

The right to be employed or not to have a contract of employment terminated have been held to be outside the scope of Article 1.[38] An individual's economic interest in making a living from employment or self-employment is not a possession within the meaning of Article 1 because an expectation of future income is not a possession. A passport, which is not marketable and has no monetary value, but confers an entitlement to do certain things, is not a possession.[39] Finally, it has also been held that overpaid welfare benefit is not a possession protected by Article 1 Protocol No 1.[40]

2.3 Business Possessions

Many claims under Article 1 have concerned the possessions necessary to run a business. It has been held that the following come within the definition of possessions: the business itself;[41] licences such as a telecommunications licence[42] or an operator's licence for goods vehicles;[43] a contractual right to receive payment as well as the money paid when received;[44] a trade mark;[45] a claim for repayment of VAT paid in error;[46] valuable commercial information;[47] and a fixed fishing quota allocation.[48] Lord Reed confirmed in *Axa General Insurance*[49] that the ECtHR had interpreted possessions as including a wide range of economic interests and assets 'but one paradigm example of a possession is a person's financial resources'.[50] In the case of an insurance company,

---

[36] Ibid. See also *Head v Social Security Commissioner* [2009] EWHC 950 (Admin), [2009] Pens LR 207.

[37] *Public & Commercial Services Union v Minister for the Civil Service* [2011] EWHC 2041 (Admin), [2012] 1 All ER 985, [37].

[38] *A v Hounslow London Borough Council*, Employment Appeal Tribunal, 11 July 2001.

[39] *Atapattu* (n 13), [164]–[165].

[40] *McGrath v Secretary of State for Work & Pensions* [2012] EWHC 1042 (Admin).

[41] *R (on the application of Kelsall) v Secretary of State for the Environment, Food and Rural Affairs* [2003] EWHC (Admin) 459, [62].

[42] *R (on the application of Orange Personal Communications Ltd) v Secretary of State for Trade and Industry*, Administrative Court, 25 October 2000; *R (Data Broadcasting International Ltd) v Office of Communications* [2010] EWHC 1243 (Admin), [2010] ACD 77.

[43] *Crompton v Department of Transport North Western Area* [2003] EWCA Civ 64.

[44] *Vicky Construction* (n 12).

[45] *Levi Strauss and Co v Tesco Stores Ltd* [2002] EWHC (Ch) 1556.

[46] *Local Authorities Mutual Investment Trust v Customs and Excise Commissioners* [2003] EWHC (Ch) 2766, [2004] STC 246.

[47] *Veolia ES Nottinghamshire Ltd v Nottinghamshire CC* [2010] EWCA Civ 1214, [2010] UKHRR 1317, [121].

[48] *UK Association of Fish Producer Organisations v Secretary of State for Environment, Food & Rural Affairs* [2013] EWHC 1959.

[49] *Axa General Insurance* (n 2).

[50] Ibid, [114].

the Supreme Court confirmed that the fund out of which it met claims constituted a possession within the meaning of Article 1 Protocol No 1.

It is not clear whether planning permission to run a particular type of business can be considered a possession. In *Davies*[51] the claimants each owned a mobile catering van. One had obtained planning permission for her van, the other had obtained a certificate of lawful use. In 2001 the streets where the vans were located were designated as prohibited and both were offered a site on a 'consent street' for £5,000 per year. It was argued that the claimants had an economic interest in their vans and that the planning permission was a component of that. The Administrative Court held that it was doubtful that the definition of possessions was as wide as contended but it did not finally decide the issue, proceeding on the assumption that their possessions had been subject to interference.[52]

State regulatory approval for a product can clearly have an effect on the ability of a company to sell the product; however, it is not clear whether such approval can be considered to be a possession. *Amvac Chemicals UK Ltd*[53] concerned a decision to suspend regulatory approvals for dichlorvos, a chemical used in pesticides. The claimant manufactured dichlorvos for non-agricultural uses and supplied it to the distributors of such products. The Administrative Court noted that such approvals may have an economic value to a person or company and that the withdrawal of such approval may have serious economic effects. Without finally deciding, it was inclined to the view that regulatory approval could not be a possession.[54] However, in the present case, where only provisional approval had been granted, it concluded that this was definitely not a possession.[55] By contrast in the later case of *Petsafe Ltd*, the High Court held that the ability lawfully to sell a particular product was an economic interest in the nature of goodwill which constituted a possession.[56] And in *Jain*[57] the House of Lords held that the benefit of registration under Part II of the Registered Homes Act 1984, enabling the claimants to use the property as a nursing home, qualified as a possession.[58]

2.4 Licences

Licences raise difficult issues and are not always considered to be possessions within the protection of Article 1. The question was first considered in detail by the Administrative Court in *Nicholds*[59] where the claimants argued that the licensing criteria for door supervisors were unlawful. Whilst they had previously worked as door supervisors, none qualified under the new licensing criteria as each had a conviction for a relevant criminal offence. The Administrative Court confirmed that the goodwill of a business may constitute a possession but that an expectation of future income was not

---

[51] *Davies* (n 5).

[52] Ibid, [129].

[53] *R (on the application of Amvac Chemicals UK Ltd) v Secretary of State for the Environment, Food and Rural Affairs* [2001] EWHC (Admin) 1011, [2002] ACD 219.

[54] Ibid, [94].

[55] Ibid, [95]–[96]. See also *Petsafe Ltd* (n 4).

[56] *Petsafe*, ibid, [77].

[57] *Jain v Trent Strategic Health Authority* [2009] UKHL 4, [2009] 1 AC 853.

[58] Ibid, per Lord Scott at [12]. However, it was not possible for the claimants to pursue this argument as the facts took place prior to the HRA coming into force.

[59] *Nicholds v Security Industry Authority* [2006] EWHC 1792 (Admin), [2007] 1 WLR 2067.

a possession.[60] It also held that Article 1 protects only goodwill as a form of asset with monetary value and does not protect an expected stream of future income which cannot be capitalised.[61]

Some licences and permissions are assets and have a monetary value and can be marketed such as milk quotas or spectrum licenses.[62] However, in the opinion of the Administrative Court, other licenses or permissions are not marketable or obtained at market price. Such a license was held to have value to the holder but were not assets having monetary value in the sense required by Article 1 Protocol No 1 as such licences do not as such represent a 'distinct asset having a monetary value'.[63] The court held that to treat such licences as possessions would risk introducing unjustified distinctions into what was already a fairly complex area of law.[64] In the present case it concluded that the permissions were not marketable and were not obtained at market price. They were not therefore assets although valuable to the claimants, and were not possessions protected by Article 1[65] although questions of interference and proportionality were considered on the assumption that the licenses were possessions.

The Court of Appeal applied these principles in the later case of *Malik*.[66] Here the facts concerned inclusion on the medical performers lists maintained by the NHS to provide general practitioner services. The Court of Appeal held that where the possessory right claimed was to some intangible entitlement conferred by a licence or other form of permission, an additional factor was necessary to render it a possessory entitlement as distinct from the broader concept of a legal right to do so: 'In many or most cases, such identification is likely to depend on the existence of some present economic value of the entitlement to the individual claiming it conferred by a licence or other form of permission.'[67] Here it held that an individual's monetary loss, in the sense of loss of future livelihood, unless based on loss of some professional or business goodwill or other present legal entitlement, did not constitute a possession attracting the protection of Article 1.[68] In the opinion of the Court of Appeal, there was a line to be drawn between presently vested possessions and the prospect of future income or livelihood.[69] Therefore, it concluded that the personal right of Dr Malik to practise in the NHS flowing from his inclusion in the performers list was not a possession within Article 1.[70] There was no evidence to support a loss of remuneration or actual or prospective loss of patients.[71] An NHS doctor's goodwill had no economic value and could not be regarded as an asset or a possession for the purposes of Article 1 Protocol No 1. 'It is neither a physical thing (land or chattels) nor a right or other chose in action, not an asset of any kind.'[72] Inclusion on the performers list was not seen as a licence in itself but a condition precedent to a doctor being able to perform services himself in the

---

[60] Ibid, [71].
[61] Ibid, [73].
[62] Ibid, [74].
[63] Ibid, [75].
[64] Ibid, [76].
[65] Ibid, [77].
[66] *Malik* (n 6).
[67] Ibid, [38].
[68] Ibid, [45].
[69] Ibid, [54].
[70] Ibid, [48].
[71] Ibid, [50].
[72] Ibid, [66].

NHS. Here his suspension from the list did not prevent his contract continuing, only his personal performance as a sole practitioner under it.[73]

Similarly, in *New London College Ltd*[74] the Court of Appeal considered the status, as a possession protected by Article 1, of a student sponsor licence held by a college. The licence enabled it to issue a visa letter or a confirmation of acceptance of studies to non-EEA students who wished to study in the United Kingdom. It concluded that a sponsor licence was not itself a possession within Article 1 as a sponsor licence was not marketable or even transferable, nor was it obtained at a market price.[75] It held that the relevant possession was the goodwill of the business and that the suspension or withdrawal of a licence would not amount to an interference with the right to peaceful enjoyment of possessions within Article 1 unless it had an adverse effect on that goodwill.[76] Here there was no concrete evidential basis on which to found a conclusion that the goodwill of the business had been or would be adversely affected by suspension or withdrawal of the licence.[77] It found that it was not clear that the expected income stream from EEA students could be

> capitalised as part of the value of the business, in particular because it depends on a licence that is non-transferable and has no market value in itself: in order to maintain the income stream, a purchaser of the business would have to obtain a licence of its own.[78]

---

3. Interferences with the Peaceful Enjoyment of Possessions

3.1 Generally

When determining whether or not there has been an interference with the peaceful enjoyment of possessions, it is important to look behind appearances and investigate the realities of the situation complained of.[79] The most common interferences with peaceful enjoyment arise from deprivation or control of possessions, although it is possible for an interference to not constitute either. Lord Reed in *Axa General Insurance*[80] held that given that the second and third rules are only 'particular instances of

---

[73] Ibid, [72]. The ECtHR agreed in *Malik v United Kingdom* 13 March 2012.
[74] *R (New London College Ltd) v Secretary of State for the Home Department* [2012] EWCA Civ 51, [2012] Imm AR 563.
[75] Ibid, [94].
[76] Ibid, [95].
[77] Ibid, [96].
[78] Ibid, [97]. By contrast in *Belfast City Council v Miss Behavin' Limited* [2007] UKHL 19, [2007] 1 WLR 1420 the House of Lords assumed that Art 1 was engaged by a council refusing a licence for a sex shop although the question was not finally decided. See also *R (Warnborough College Ltd) v Secretary of State for the Home Department* [2013] EWHC 1510 (Admin).
[79] *Eastside Cheese* (n 2), in reliance upon *Sporrong and Lonnroth* (n 2), [63].
[80] *Axa General Insurance* (n 2).

interference' with the right guaranteed by the first rule the 'importance of classification should not be exaggerated'.[81]

It may be that the particular interference amounts to neither deprivation nor control, but is still considered to be an interference which must be justified. This was the position in *Khaled*[82] where the claim concerned financial restrictions imposed under the Counter Terrorism Act 2008 where the claimant's expenditure was monitored, but not restricted. As the Administrative Court observed: 'There is no free use of property if one has to account for it.'[83] Similarly in *Public & Commercial Services Union*[84] it was held that a change in a pension scheme to the detriment of members was an interference, without specifying whether this was a deprivation or control.

3.2 Deprivation

In many instances, the fact that a deprivation of a possession has occurred is clear. For example: a transfer in ownership;[85] the imposition of taxes and duties;[86] a compulsory purchase order;[87] the vesting in the trustee in bankruptcy of the bankrupt's rights to a retirement annuity or personal pension;[88] a confiscation order under the Drug Trafficking Act 1994;[89] a post-conviction confiscation under the Proceeds of Crime Act 2002;[90] an infringement of copyright;[91] striking out a claim for damages where a judgment has already been obtained;[92] an order of the court declining rectification of the Land Registry if the order fails to give effect to the substantive property rights of a party.[93]

Nationalisation of a formerly privately run building society, Northern Rock plc, by transfer of the entire share capital of the company to the Treasury Solicitor as a nominee of the Treasury, was held by the Court of Appeal to amount to a deprivation of the shareholders' shares.[94] It is also possible that a legal requirement to pay a minimum wage constitutes a deprivation, although this has only been considered in the context of Article 14.[95] Whilst a fixed fishing quota allocation has been held to be a possession,

---

[81] Ibid, [108].

[82] *R (K) v HM Treasury* [2009] EWHC 1643 (Admin).

[83] Ibid, [52].

[84] *Public & Commercial Services Union* (n 37).

[85] *Eastside Cheese* (n 2).

[86] *Lydiashourne Ltd v The Commissioners of Customs & Excise*, Court of Appeal, 1 November 2000; *Dimsey; Allen* (n 23); *Lindsay v Customs and Excise Commissioners* [2002] EWCA Civ 267, [2002] 1 WLR 1766. A failure to process within a reasonable time an application for tax relief is not an interference with possessions. See *Neil Martin Ltd v Revenue & Customs Commissioners* [2007] EWCA Civ 1041.

[87] *R (on the application of Aina) v London Borough of Hackney*, Court of Appeal, 24 November 2000; *London Borough of Bexley v Secretary of State for the Environment, Transport and the Regions* [2001] EWHC (Admin) 323; *R (on the application of Peart) v The Secretary of State for Transport, Local Government and the Regions* [2002] EWHC (Admin) 2964.

[88] *Krasner* (n 28).

[89] *Benjafield* (n 23), [17].

[90] *R v Waya* [2012] UKSC 51, [2012] 3 WLR 1188.

[91] *Ashdown* (n 26), [28].

[92] *Summers* (n 31), [47].

[93] *Kingsalton* (n 29), [45].

[94] *SRM Global Master Fund LP v Treasury Commissioners* [2009] EWCA Civ 788, [2009] UKHRR 1219

[95] *R (on the application of Middlebrook Mushrooms Ltd) v The Agricultural Wages Board of England and Wales* [2004] EWHC (Admin) 1447.

where the quota has been unused there is no deprivation when the unused quota is reallocated to others.[96]

A reduction in market value also amounts to a deprivation. In *Dennis v Ministry of Defence*[97] it was held that the noise from Harrier jets flying over the claimant's estate significantly reduced its market value and thus constituted an interference with Article 1 rights. In *Marcic*[98] the House of Lords held that serious flooding of a person's home was an interference with his Article 1 rights.[99] However, claimants have a high threshold to surmount when a claim is based on environmental impact and a reduction in property values.[100] It has been held that a loss of a quiet and pleasant environment, without evidence of loss of value, is not enough to engage Article 1. In *Thomas*[101] where the claimants alleged depreciation in the value of their houses attributable to noise and other nuisance from a new relief road, the Court of Appeal held that rather than deprivation, an interference with peaceful enjoyment could be shown by interference with peaceful enjoyment, combined with evidence of loss of value.[102]

3.2.1 Incident of Ownership

It is possible for there to be no deprivation if the interference is held to be simply an incident of ownership of the possession. The House of Lords has considered this issue in two cases, but its observations have been *obiter* and the issue is still waiting to be conclusively determined. In the first case of *Wallbank*[103] the respondents were freeholders of a farm which included rectorial property, constituting them as lay rectors and subjecting them to the liability of paying for all and necessary repairs to the chancel of St John the Baptist church, the parish church of Aston Cantlow. When the Parochial Church Council served notices on the respondents requiring them to put the chancel in proper repair, they disputed their liability. The House of Lords did not need to deal with the question of Article 1 as it had decided that the Parochial Church Council was not a public authority and, not exercising a public function, was therefore not bound by the HRA. However, Lords Hope, Scott and Hobhouse did consider the application of Article 1 to the facts.

Their Lordships concluded that the respondents were not being deprived of their possessions or being controlled in the use of their property. The liability was simply an incident of the ownership of the land which gave rise to it. The peaceful enjoyment of the land involved the discharge of burdens which were attached to it as well as the enjoyment of its rights and privileges.

---

[96] *UK Association of Fish Producer Organisations v Secretary of State for Environment, Food & Rural Affairs* [2013] EWHC 1959.

[97] *Dennis v Ministry of Defence* [2003] EWHC (QB) 793, [2003] 19 EG 118 (CS).

[98] *Marcic* (n 24).

[99] Ibid, per Lord Nicholls at [37].

[100] *R (on the application of Westminster City Council) v Mayor of London* [2002] EWHC (Admin) 2440 in reliance upon *S v France* (1990) 65 D&R 250. See also *Lough v First Secretary of State* [2004] EWCA Civ 905, [2004] 1 WLR 2557; *R (on the application of Trailer & Marina (Leven) Ltd) v Secretary of State for the Environment, Food & Rural Affairs* [2004] EWCA Civ 1580, [2005] 1 WLR 1267.

[101] *Thomas v Bridgend County Borough Council* [2011] EWCA Civ 862, [2012] 2 WLR 624.

[102] Ibid, [48].

[103] *Wallbank* (n 2).

This is a burden on the land, just like any other burden that runs with the land. It is, and has been at all times, within the scope of the property right which she acquired and among the various factors to be taken into account in determining its value. She could have divested herself of it at any time by disposing of the land to which it was attached. The enforcement of the liability under the general law is an incident of the property right. ... It is not ... an outside intervention by way of a form of taxation.[104]

A similar issue arose in *Wilson*[105] concerning a loan agreement regulated by the Consumer Credit Act 1974. However, the reasoning of their Lordships on the issue was not clear. Mrs Wilson argued that, as the agreement did not contain all the prescribed terms, by reason of section 127(3) of the Act the court would not be able to make an enforcement order. As the case was determined on the issue of retrospective effect, there was actually no need for their Lordships to comment on the Article 1 issue. However, all apart from Lord Rodger did. Lord Nicholls and Lord Hobhouse found that the relevant provisions of the Consumer Credit Act constituted a statutory deprivation of the lender's rights of property. In their opinion, the lender's rights were extinguished in favour of the borrower by legislation for which the state was responsible. This was a deprivation of possessions within the meaning of Article 1.[106] By contrast Lord Hope and Lord Scott, taking a similar line to that in *Wallbank*, did not find Article 1 engaged. Lord Hope pointed out that the agreement which was entered into was improperly executed from the outset, so it was always subject to the restrictions on its execution in the Act. In their view, the lender never had an 'absolute and unqualified right' to enforce this agreement or to enforce the rights arising from the delivery of the motor car.[107]

The issue was also relevant to the claim in *Jain*[108] where the House of Lords considered the impact of Article 1 on the cancellation of registration to run a nursing home. Lord Scott found that the benefit of registration was a possession[109] and proceeded on the assumption that the cancellation was a deprivation, stating that limitations imposed in the public interest on rights to the enjoyment of possessions must be reasonable and proportionate to the purpose sought to be achieved.[110]

In the lower courts, both approaches have been utilised. For example, in *Beaulane Properties*[111] the Chancery Division held that Article 1 was engaged where a property right was acquired which was subject to a law with the potential for depriving the owner of it, if and when this subsequently happened.[112] It held that, in *Wilson*, the reason why there was a delimitation of rights and not a deprivation was that the

---

[104] Ibid, per Lord Hope at [71]. See also Lord Hobhouse at [91] and Lord Scott at [92] and [133].

[105] *Wilson v First County Trust* [2003] UKHL 40, [2003] 3 WLR 568.

[106] Ibid, per Lord Nicholls at [44] in reliance upon *James* (n 2), [38]. See also Lord Hobhouse at [136].

[107] Ibid, [108]. See also Lord Scott at [168]. On this issue see also *Mills v MI Developments (UK) Ltd* [2002] EWCA Civ 1576 concerning the creation of an easement over a property; *Local Authorities Mutual Investment Trust* (n 46) concerning a limitation period within which to reclaim VAT paid in error; *Pennycook v Shaws (EAL) Ltd* [2004] EWCA Civ 100, [2004] Ch 296 concerning the statutory right to renew a business tenancy under the Landlord and Tenant Act 1954; *Kay v London Borough of Lambeth* [2004] EWCA Civ 926, [2004] 3 WLR 1396 concerning secure tenancies under Part IV. of the Housing Act 1985; and *Soteriou v Ultrachem Ltd* [2004] EWHC (QB) 983, [2004] IRLR 870 concerning a contract unenforceable for illegality.

[108] *Jain* (n 57).

[109] Ibid, [12].

[110] Ibid, [13] obiter as the HRA claim was not possible given the act the subject of challenge occurred prior to the HRA coming into force.

[111] *Beaulane Properties* (n 25).

[112] Ibid, [146].

legislation did not bite subsequently but at the moment the transaction took effect. Therefore the lender never had a right of which he could be deprived. In the present case it concluded that the effect of section 17 of the Limitation Act 1980 and section 75 of the Land Registration Act 1925 was to deprive the owner of the land of all his rights to it and of any means, whether by taking direct action or by going to the law, of recovering possession of it, and thus to transfer the right to possession and title to the trespasser—a deprivation of possessions within the meaning of Article 1.[113]

By contrast in *Hughes v Paxman*[114] the Court of Appeal held that ordering licences under a patent on the application of one co-proprietor was not a deprivation as this was a part of the nature of the property right concerned.[115] Similarly in *Loomba*[116] the Divisional Court held that legal aid payments to solicitors on account did not become their property in an unqualified way.

> As items of property they were subject to the limitation that they were paid on account of an ultimate assessment of entitlement. The defendants only had the right to keep them where they complied with the conditions under which they had been received.[117]

It may be that whilst a variation to a broadcasting licence results in loss in revenue, if it has been varied within the terms of the statutory scheme or licence, it has been held that this does not amount to a deprivation: 'Article 1 does not protect any expectation of being able to continue activities where the licence itself contains provisions for its variation, if the licence is varied in accordance with those provisions.'[118]

3.2.2 Future Deprivation

Whilst there was little discussion of the point, in *Axa General Insurance*[119] the Supreme Court proceeded on the assumption that a change in the law meaning that insurance claims would fall upon the claimant insurance companies amounted to a deprivation of possessions although it had not yet taken place. Most of the discussion which did take place concerned whether or not the claimants had victim status. Lord Hope held that the fact that the interference was not present or immediate and may not occur until some time in the future did not exclude the person from being a victim.

Lord Brown observed as follows:

> [T]heir liability to claimants under the 2009 Act will only arise once all the elements of the relevant damages claims against the insured employers have been established and, true too, the appellants have expressly reserved their position as to whether liability under their various policies of insurance will actually be engaged. But nobody doubts that a very large number of claims will be established against employers and the clear underlying intention of the 2009 Act was that the cost of these claims should indeed fall on the insurers.[120]

---

[113] Ibid, [136].
[114] *Hughes v Paxman* [2006] EWCA Civ 818, [2007] RPC 2.
[115] Ibid, [28].
[116] *Legal Services Commission v Loomba* [2012] EWHC 29 (QB), [2012] 2 All ER 977.
[117] Ibid, [82].
[118] *R (Data Broadcasting International Ltd) v Office of Communications* [2010] EWHC 1243 (Admin) [96]. See also *Sims v Dacorum Borough Council* [2013] EWCA Civ 12, [2013] HLR 14 and *Horsham Properties Group Ltd v Clark* [2008] EWHC 2327 (Ch), [2009] 1 WLR 1255.
[119] *Axa General Insurance* (n 2).
[120] Ibid, [73].

Lord Reed confirmed that legislation which had the object and effect of establishing a new category of claims and which in consequence diminished the fund out of which an insurance company met claims, could be regarded as an interference with possessions.[121] However, his Lordship was not clear whether this was an interference with peaceful enjoyment, a deprivation or control. Nevertheless, as he had already stated, the same general rule was to be applied to each type of interference.[122]

3.3 Control

If there is no transfer of ownership and therefore no deprivation, there may still be an interference with peaceful enjoyment if control is exercised over possessions. Control can take many forms and examples include: planning laws;[123] housing laws;[124] the powers retained by public authorities to enter land for the purpose of carrying out land drainage works;[125] laws preventing trade and business vehicles being driven in certain areas;[126] the conditions imposed by a professional body;[127] notification of a site as being of special scientific interest under the Wildlife and Countryside Act 1981;[128] a requirement to pay child support;[129] a ban on the sale of tobacco from automatic vending machines;[130] the right to detain property pending payment;[131] the licensing of businesses by councils;[132] the law of adverse possession;[133] restrictions effectively amounting to exclusion from the UK financial market;[134] a restriction on a landlord's right to terminate a tenant's lease;[135] and removing access to the highway from a property.[136]

In *Eastside Cheese*[137] an emergency control order under section 13 of the Food Safety Act 1990 was made in relation to cheese following a boy becoming seriously ill with *E. coli*. The effect of the order was to prohibit the carrying out of any commercial operation in relation to cheese originating from a particular company. It paralysed

---

[121] Ibid, [114].

[122] Ibid, [115].

[123] *Waltham Forest London Borough Council v Secretary of State for Transport, Local Government and the Regions* [2002] EWCA Civ 330, [2002] 13 EG 99 (CS). See also *R (on the application of Fuller) v Chief Constable of Dorset Police* [2001] EWHC Admin 1057, [2003] QB 480, in which it was held that a direction to travellers to leave land under s 61 of the Criminal Justice and Public Order Act 1994 was a control on property.

[124] *Stanley v London Borough of Ealing*, Court of Appeal, 16 April 2003.

[125] *R (on the application of MWH & H Ward Estates Ltd) v Monmouthshire CC* [2002] EWCA Civ 1915, [2003] ACD 115.

[126] *Phillips v DPP* [2002] EWHC (Admin) 2903, [2003] RTR 8.

[127] *Whitefield v General Medical Council* [2002] UKPC 62, [2003] HRLR 243.

[128] *R (on the application of Fisher) v English Nature* [2004] EWCA Civ 663, [2005] 1 WLR 147. See also *Leven* (n 100).

[129] *Denson* (n 23). See also *Secretary of State for Work and Pensions v M* [2004] EWCA Civ 1343, [2005] 2 WLR 740, in which a majority of the Court of Appeal held that the requirement to pay child support was within the ambit of Art 1 for the purposes of a claim under Art 14.

[130] *R (Sinclair Collis Ltd) v Secretary of State for Health* [2011] EWCA Civ 437, [2012] 2 WLR 304.

[131] *Global Knafaim Leasing Ltd v Civil Aviation Authority* [2010] EWHC 1348 (Admin), [2011] 1 Lloyd's Rep 324.

[132] *Belfast City Council* (n 78).

[133] *Ofulue v Bossert* [2008] EWCA Civ 7, [2008] 3 WLR 1253.

[134] *Bank Mellat v HM Treasury* [2011] EWCA Civ 1, [2011] 3 WLR 714.

[135] *Salvesen v Riddell & Lord Advocate* [2013] UKSC 22, [2013] HRLR 23.

[136] *Cusack v Harrow London Borough Council* [2013] UKSC 40, [2013] 1 WLR 2022.

[137] *Eastside Cheese* (n 2).

that company's cheese-making business and also paralysed the business of cheese processers and maturers to the extent that they depended on supplies from this company. Rather than a deprivation of possessions, the Court of Appeal concluded that the order was an instance where the state had deemed it necessary to control the use of possessions in accordance with the general interest.[138] Similarly, the Administrative Court concluded in *Davies*[139] that the council's new street trading scheme, which required the claimant owners of mobile catering vans to pay £5,000 per year for a new site, was not a deprivation of possessions but a measure of control of the use of property.[140] In the *Countryside Alliance case*[141] the House of Lords concluded that the Hunting Act 2004, which prohibited the hunting of wild mammals with dogs and hare coursing, was a control on the use of property. As Lord Bingham stated:

> [T]here are … landowners who cannot hunt over their own land or permit others to do so, those who cannot use their horses and hounds to hunt, the farrier who cannot use his equipment to shoe horses to be used for hunting, owners of businesses which have lost their marketable goodwill, a shareholder whose shares have lost their value.[142]

4. Justifying Interferences

4.1 Generally

The right to the peaceful enjoyment of possessions is not an absolute right. However, the process of justifying interferences with the peaceful enjoyment of possessions is complicated by the drafting of Article 1. The Article provides that 'no one shall be deprived of his possessions except in the public interest and subject to the conditions provided for by law and by the general principles of international law'.

In relation to control, Article 1 provides that the right to the peaceful enjoyment of possessions shall not 'in any way impair the right of a State to enforce such laws as it deems necessary to control the use of property in accordance with the general interest'.

But despite the different wording in relation to deprivation and control, it has been established in the case law that any interference with the peaceful enjoyment of possessions, whether by deprivation or control, must achieve a fair balance between the demands of the general interest of the community and the requirements of the protection of the individual's fundamental rights. There must therefore be a reasonable relationship of proportionality between the means employed and the aim pursued.[143]

---

[138] See also *Collis Ltd* (n 3), although here the Court of Appeal assessed the lawfulness of the control by reference to EU law rather than Art 1 Protocol No 1.

[139] *Davies* (n 5).

[140] Ibid, [135].

[141] *R (Countryside Alliance) v Attorney General* [2007] UKHL 52, [2007] 3 WLR 922. See also Baroness Hale at [129].

[142] Ibid, [20].

[143] *Dimsey; Allen* (n 23) in reliance upon *Gasus Dosier-und Fordertecknik GmbH v The Netherlands* (1995) 20 EHRR 403, [62]; *Marcic* (n 24). See also *Eastside Cheese* (n 2). See also *Belfast City Council* (n 78).

It has been held that the point at which the line is drawn is quite different from that established in proportionality decisions under Articles 8(2), 9(2), 10(2) and 11(2).

> These articles place on the court the obligation to decide whether an interference with the primary right has been 'necessary in a democratic society', and a sophisticated jurisprudence … now exists in this regard. When, however, the court speaks of proportionality under art 1 of the First Protocol, its starting point is an extant judgment by the state signatory as to what is necessary in the public interest. The court's duty is to gauge whether the state has nevertheless gone beyond what the article will tolerate.[144]

But this view is not universal. In *Clays Lane Housing*[145] the Court of Appeal held that there was no real difference in the test to be applied between the jurisprudence of the European Court of Human Rights[146] and the conclusion of the House of Lords in *Daly*.[147] They both allow 'necessary', where appropriate, to mean 'reasonably', rather than 'strictly' or 'absolutely' necessary. 'Everything then depends on the context.'[148] In *Belfast City Council*[149] the House of Lords applied a test of proportionality to the alleged interference with the peaceful enjoyment of possessions by the refusal of the Council to grant a licence to run a sex shop. However, it was noted that in relation to control on use, of which it was held licensing forms a part, Member States were accorded a wide margin of appreciation when striking the balance between the 'general interests of the community and the requirement of the protection on an individual's rights under the Article'.[150]

Where the claim concerned a control on the use of property in the *Countryside Alliance* case, the House of Lords indicated that whether or not this was necessary in accordance with the general interest was in the first instance for Parliament to decide.[151] However, it had already given consideration to the proportionality of the interference under Articles 8 and 11 and indicated that the conclusion under Article 1 Protocol No 1 was no different on the questions of lawfulness, objective and necessity (pressing social need and proportionality).[152] Lord Bingham concluded as follows:

> It is, in the first instance, for Parliament to decide what laws are necessary in accordance with what it judges to be the general interest. It has decided that the 2004 Act is necessary in accordance with the general interest. As already pointed out, Parliament's judgment is not immune from challenge. The national courts, in the first instance, and ultimately the Strasbourg court, have a power and a duty to measure national legislation against Convention standards. But for reasons already given, respect should be paid to the recent and closely-considered judgment of a democratic assembly, and no ground is shown for disturbing that judgment in this instance.[153]

---

[144] *R (on the application of Hamilton) v United Kingdom Central Council for Nursing, Midwifery and Health Visiting* [2003] EWCA Civ 1600, [2004] 79 BMLR 30, per Sedley LJ at [33]. See also the comments of Baroness Hale in *Jain* (n 57) at [44].

[145] *R (on the application of Clays Lane Housing Co-Operative Limited) v The Housing Corporation* [2004] EWCA Civ 1658, [2005] 1 WLR 2229.

[146] *James* (n 2).

[147] *R (on the application of Daly) v Secretary of State for the Home Department* [2001] UKHL 26, [2001] 2 AC 532.

[148] *Clays Lane* (n 145), [23].

[149] *Belfast City Council* (n 78).

[150] Ibid, per Lord Neuberger at [99].

[151] *Countryside Alliance* (n 141), per Lord Bingham at [47].

[152] Ibid, [43]–[45]. Lord Hope at [65].

[153] Ibid, per Lord Bingham at [47].

Lord Hope also applied a proportionality test and also held that it was not for the House of Lords to say whether the ban on hunting 'was or was not in the public interest or the general interest' as this was a question for the 'democratically elected members of the House of Commons to decide'.[154] In his view, the question for the House of Lords was whether it was open to the House of Commons to take that view and whether the prohibitions that were enacted were proportionate.[155] Finding this to be a matter of social policy, he also held that there was an area of discretionary judgment for the legislature:

> Whether there was a pressing social need to give effect to those views involved a question of balance between competing interests. This raises the familiar question as to where the margin lies between the area of discretionary judgment that the court will accord to a democratically elected assembly in matters of social policy and those areas where the court can legitimately intervene on the ground that it is especially well placed to assess whether an interference is needed and is proportionate.[156]

The better view, in keeping with the jurisprudence of the ECtHR, is that any interference must be proportionate but given the circumstances in which interferences with possessions occur, often deference to the judgment of the primary decision maker tilts the balance in favour of its judgment.

Further confirmation that it is correct to utilise the same approach in relation to each type of interference (peaceful enjoyment, deprivation and control) has been provided by the Supreme Court in *Axa*.[157] Here Lord Hope held that the three rules contained in Article 1 were not distinct in the sense of being unconnected. In his view, the second and third rules (deprivation and control) were concerned with particular instances of interference with the right to peaceful enjoyment of property and should therefore be 'construed in the light of the general principle set out in the first rule'.[158] In his view, it was not necessary for the Supreme Court to concern itself with whether the question raised in the claim was directed to deprivation rather than the general principle referred to in the first sentence: 'Whichever it is, the interference must comply with the principle of lawfulness, and it must pursue a legitimate aim by means that are reasonably proportionate to the aim sought to be realised.'[159]

Lord Reed also held that although where an interference is categorised as falling under the second or third rule, the ECtHR will usually consider the question of justification by reference to the language of the specific provisions of Article 1, the test was in substance the same however the interference was classified:

> If an interference has been established, it is then necessary to consider whether it constitutes a violation. It must be shown that the interference complies with the principle of lawfulness and pursues a legitimate aim by means that are reasonably proportionate to the aim sought to be achieved. This final question focuses upon the question whether a fair balance has been struck between the demands of the general interest of the community and the requirements of

---

[154] Ibid, [75].
[155] Ibid, [75].
[156] Ibid, [76]. Baroness Hale at [129]. Lord Brown seemed only to look for a sufficient public interest justification without mentioning proportionality [155].
[157] *Axa General Insurance* (n 2).
[158] Ibid, [22].
[159] Ibid, [22].

the protection of the individual's fundamental rights. ... In that regard, the Strasbourg court accepts that a margin of appreciation must be left to the national authorities.[160]

In accordance with the approach of the Supreme Court in *Axa*, the correct method for considering justifications for interferences with the peaceful enjoyment of possessions is first to consider whether or not there has been an interference with the peaceful enjoyment of possessions whether by deprivation, control or something else. The second step is to consider the lawfulness of the interference, third, legitimate aim and finally, proportionality.

4.2 Lawfulness of Interference

Although it is specified in Article 1 that a deprivation must be subject to the conditions provided for by law, there has been little mention in the case law of legality forming part of the test for a justified interference[161] although this is generally assumed.[162] In *Axa* Lord Reed stated that the ECtHR had often held that the first and most important requirement of Article 1 Protocol No 1 was that any interference by a public authority with the peaceful enjoyment of possessions should be lawful: 'In this context, as elsewhere in the Convention, the concept of "law" does not merely require the existence of some domestic law, but requires it to be compatible with the rule of law.'[163]

In *Axa*[164] the claimants argued that the challenged legislation was incompatible with the rule of law by reason of its retroactive effects, which challenged legal certainty. Lord Reed held that the ECtHR had interpreted conformity to the rule of law as requiring, amongst other things, that the relevant domestic law must be adequately accessible and sufficiently precise to be foreseeable in its effects, and that it should not operate in an arbitrary manner.[165] However, he pointed out that the criteria of accessibility and foreseeability were not absolute nor was the 'prohibition of arbitrariness incompatible with the exercise of discretion'.[166] He stated that whilst there was only limited scope for retroactive legislation in the criminal sphere, the position was different in the civil sphere.[167] 'Changes in the law, even if resulting from prospective legislation or judicial decisions, will frequently and properly affect legal relationships which were established before the changes occurred.'[168]

In Lord Reed's view, it was possible to draw a distinction between laws which altered prospectively the rights and obligations arising from pre-existing legal relationships, and laws which altered such rights and obligations retrospectively. To the extent that laws of the latter kind may 'undermine legal certainty more severely, they may

---

[160] Ibid, [108].
[161] Two exceptions are *Krasner* (n 28), and *Al-Kishtaini v Shanshal* [2001] EWCA Civ 264, [2001] 2 All ER (Comm) 601. See also *Countryside Alliance* (n 141).
[162] See eg *Axa General Insurance* (n 2) and *Gibson v Revenue & Customs Prosecution Office* [2008] EWCA Civ 645, [2009] 2 WLR 471 and *Crown Prosecution Service v Eastenders Group* [2012] EWCA Crim 2436, [2013] 1 Cr App R 24.
[163] *Axa General Insurance* (n 2), [116]. See also the comments of Lord Hope at [21].
[164] Ibid.
[165] Ibid, [119].
[166] Ibid, [119].
[167] Ibid, [120].
[168] Ibid, [120].

be more difficult to justify', but in his view, there was no doubt that justification for such laws sometimes exists.[169] This may be where legislation has a remedial purpose: 'In such circumstances, retrospective legislation which restores the position to what it was previously understood to be may not be incompatible with legal certainty or the rule of law.'[170]

Lord Reed observed that the ECtHR usually considered retroactive effects in its assessment of proportionality rather than when considering the lawfulness of the interference. In his opinion, the ECtHR only found such effects to be objectionable where an individual or excessive burden was imposed upon the claimant.[171] In the present case he concluded the fact that the legislation may alter the continuing effect of insurance contracts entered into in the past did not offend against the rule of law as reflected in Article 1 Protocol No 1.

4.3 Legitimate Aim

In common with Article 14, legitimate aims are not set out in Article 1. As the judgment of the Supreme Court in *Axa*[172] indicates, the notion of a legitimate aim under Article 1 is very wide and the notion of 'public interest' is extensive. Quoting from *Draon v France*,[173] Lord Hope held that it is very much up to the legislature to determine a legitimate aim in the public interest, unless that judgment is manifestly without reasonable foundation.[174] When considering whether or not a matter of public interest is at stake, Lord Hope held that respect on democratic grounds should be afforded to the considered opinion of the elected body which has made the choices.[175] Lord Reed also held that domestic courts must be circumspect when determining whether an objective is within the public or general interest, 'since social and economic policies are properly a responsibility of the legislature, and policy-making of this nature is amenable to judicial scrutiny only to a limited degree'.[176]

In the present case the Supreme Court concluded that the Scottish Parliament was entitled to regard the predicament of those diagnosed as having developed pleural plaques as a social injustice. Its judgment that this was a matter of public interest on which it should legislate was not without reasonable foundation or manifestly unreasonable.[177] Making reference to *James v UK*,[178] Lord Hope held that eliminating what are judged to be social injustices was an example of the function of the modern legislature.[179]

Other categories of legitimate aim can be identified from the case law including:

---

[169] Ibid, [121].
[170] Ibid, [121].
[171] Ibid, [122].
[172] Ibid.
[173] *Draon v France* (2005) 42 EHRR 807.
[174] *Axa General Insurance* (n 2), [31]. See also the observations made by the Court of Appeal in *SRM Global* (n 94) and *Salvesen* (n 135).
[175] *Axa General Insurance* (n 2), [32].
[176] Ibid, [124].
[177] Ibid, [33].
[178] *James v UK* (1986) 8 EHRR 123.
[179] *Axa General Insurance* (n 2), [29].

consumer protection;[180] public health;[181] prevention of crime;[182] and the economic well-being of the country.[183] These are examined below.

4.4 Proportionality

4.4.1 Generally

In *Axa* Lord Reed held as follows:

> [T]here must be a reasonable relationship of proportionality between the means employed and the aim sought to be realised. This involves an assessment of whether a fair balance has been struck between the demands of the general interest of the community and the requirements of the protection of the individual's fundamental rights: the individual should not be required to bear an individual and excessive burden.[184]

The proportionality of an interference may be affected by a variety of factors including deference, the absence of compensation and the absence of procedural safeguards as discussed in the following paragraphs. Where an interference is retrospective in its application, this may also affect the fair balance struck.[185]

4.4.2 Deference

Given the subject matter of claims engaging Article 1, the question of deference to the primary decision maker, usually the legislature, often arises. In *Axa*[186] given the subject matter of the claim concerned a matter of social or economic policy, Lord Reed held as follows:

> [T]he courts also recognise that, in certain circumstances, and to a certain extent, other public authorities are better placed to determine how those interests should be balanced. Although the courts must decide whether, in their judgment, the requirement of proportionality is satisfied, there is at the same time nothing in the Convention, or in the domestic legislation giving effect to Convention rights, which requires the courts to substitute their own views for those of other public authorities on all matters of policy, judgment and discretion.[187]

In addition to the legislature, sometimes the judgment of primary decision makers, such as a regulatory authority, is also deferred to.[188]

---

[180] See eg *Wilson* (n 105).
[181] See eg *Eastside Cheese* (n 2); *Amvac Chemicals* (n 53); and *Stanley* (n 124). See also *Collis Ltd* (n 3).
[182] See eg *Benjafield* (n 23).
[183] Ibid, [126]. See eg *Lindsay* (n 86).
[184] Ibid, [126]. See also the observations of Lord Hope at [34].
[185] In *Axa General Insurance* (n 2) this was considered in the assessment of the lawfulness of the interference and in the assessment of proportionality. See also *Salvesen* (n 135).
[186] *Axa General Insurance* (n 2).
[187] Ibid, [131]. See also *Public & Commercial Services Union* (n 37).
[188] *Nicholds* (n 59); *S* (n 32).

4.4.3 Compensation

Where there has been a deprivation of possessions without compensation of an amount reasonably related to the value of the possessions, this will normally constitute a disproportionate interference. There is no need to compensate the owner at full value; the touchstone is to find a fair balance.[189] A total lack of compensation is justifiable under Article 1 only in exceptional circumstances.[190]

> [S]ome public interest is necessary to justify the taking of private property for the benefit of the state and ... when the public interest does so require, the loss should not fall upon the individual whose property has been taken but should be borne by the public as a whole.[191]

Often the court will have to assess the proportionality of a statutory compensation scheme. The court must treat the compensation rights created as part of the fair balance necessary. Where a class of potential claimants is excluded from those rights, the court is entitled to enquire into the reasons for the exclusion and ask whether it serves any 'legitimate purpose', or leads to results 'so anomalous as to render the legislation unacceptable'.[192] In *SRM Global*, concerning compensation to former shareholders following the nationalisation of Northern Rock, the Court of Appeal held as follows:

> The paradigm case of a reasonable relationship between compensation and the property's value arises ... where full market value is paid ... where for example a single property is taken to achieve a specific and limited local objective ... proportionality is likely to require market value or something close to it, and the margin of appreciation may offer little or no scope to justify the deprivation of property for less. But there will be other cases in which the objective of the deprivation is much broader. ... In such instances the policy aim of the measure in question may be diminished or undermined or even contradicted by a requirement of full market value. The measure's intention may be to re-distribute wealth, or to achieve a necessary social reform, goals which are or may be perceived to be inconsistent with full compensation payable to the previous owner. In these cases, the margin of appreciation allows a flexible approach to the right protected by [Article 1 Protocol No 1] which may give place to those aspects of the policy which override the case for payment of full value.[193]

The question of compensation arose in *Kelsall*,[194] which concerned a challenge by ten mink farmers to the compensation scheme designed to compensate them for the effects of the Fur Farming Prohibition Act 2000. The Secretary of State accepted that their businesses were possessions and that they were deprived of these possessions by the Act. The Administrative Court held that the compensation should be reasonably related to the value of the property taken[195] and that the provisions for compensation must not be so inflexible that they fail to take account of substantially different situations.[196] Here it concluded that the scheme did not comply with the requirements of Article 1:

---

[189] *SRM Global* (n 94), [48].

[190] *Eastside Cheese* (n 2), in reliance upon *Holy Monasteries v Greece* (1994) 20 EHRR 1, [71]. See also *Kingsalton* (n 29); *MWH & H Ward* (n 125); *Corton Caravans and Chalets Limited v Anglian Water Services Limited* [2003] RVR 323.

[191] *Davies* (n 5), quoting from *Grape Bay Ltd v AG of Bermuda* [2000] 1 WLR 574, per Lord Hoffmann at 583.

[192] *Thomas* (n 101).

[193] *SRM Global* (n 94), per Laws LJ at [56].

[194] *Kelsall* (n 41).

[195] Ibid, [62] in reliance upon *Lithgow v UK* (1986) EHRR 329.

[196] Ibid, [62] in reliance upon *Papachelas v Greece* Judgment, 25 March 1999.

The provisions of the Order as to compensation ... fail on every count ... they operate unfairly as between different farmers and generally; they fail to take account of the different values of premium breeds ... and they produce arbitrary effects. Reasons have been put forward to justify provisions of the order that do not bear scrutiny and are irrational. The consequences of the defects in the Order are too great to be contained within a permissible margin for workability or approximation.[197]

The question of compensation also arose in *Dennis*,[198] which concerned the effect of noise from Harrier jet fighters on the market value of an estate. The Divisional Court concluded that a fair balance could not be struck in the absence of compensation. '[C]ommon fairness demands that where the interests of a minority, let alone an individual, are seriously interfered with because of an overriding public interest, the minority should be compensated.'[199] It held that damages were to be considered under three heads: past and future loss of amenity; past and future loss of use; loss of capital value. The overall figure arrived at was £950,000. Whilst this was an assessment of damages for nuisance at common law, the court made it clear that, if nuisance had not provided a remedy, the claim would have succeeded under Article 1 and compensation in the same sum would have been awarded to enable a fair balance to be struck.[200]

Where there is a control on the use of possessions, the payment of compensation is not normally required for the interference to be justifiable. This is so even if the legislation in general terms affects some people more than others.[201]

4.4.4 Procedural Rights

Finally, where there has been deprivation or control, it may not be possible for a fair balance to be struck unless certain procedural rights have been afforded. The claimant must have a reasonable opportunity of putting his or her case to the responsible authorities for the purpose of effectively challenging the measures interfering with the rights guaranteed.[202] There is a considerable overlap between this aspect of Article 1 and Article 6. Where both apply, it is likely that a finding of breach of Article 6 will also entail a breach of the procedural guarantees of Article 1.[203]

Procedural rights were important in *Jain*[204] where the House of Lords considered the proportionality of the cancellation of registration to run a nursing home although the comments were *obiter* given that the act the subject of challenge took place prior to the HRA coming into force. Lord Scott held that the interference involved in cancelling the registration had to be reasonable and proportionate to the purpose sought to

---

[197] Ibid, [63].
[198] *Dennis* (n 97).
[199] Ibid, [63] in reliance upon *S v France* (n 100).
[200] Ibid, [88]–[92]. See also *Marcic* (n 24), where it was held that those who enjoyed the benefit of effective drainage should bear the cost of paying compensation to those whose properties are situated lower down in the catchment area and who, in consequence, have to endure intolerable sewer flooding; *R (on the application of London and Continental Stations and Property Ltd) v Rail Regulator* [2003] EWHC (Admin) 2607, concerning compensation for the deprivation of property resultant from the redevelopment of St Pancras Station; and *Beaulane Properties* (n 25), which concerned the acquisition of land by adverse title.
[201] *Leven* (n 100), [58]. See also *Cusack* (n 136).
[202] *Bank Mellat* (n 134), [65] in reliance upon *Jokelala v Finland* (2003) 37 EHRR 26.
[203] See eg *Bank Mellat*, ibid.
[204] *Jain* (n 57).

be achieved, striking a fair balance between the demands of the general interest of the community and the requirements of the protection of the individual's rights. However, when striking this fair balance, he held that the requirements of Article 6 had to be borne in mind:

> The right under Article 6 to a 'fair and public hearing' becomes very relevant when a judicial or quasi-judicial order has deprived an individual of his possessions, has been made at a hearing of which he was given no notice, is an order that he has no opportunity of resisting until it is too late, and has been made in response to an application by the State or agents of the State that ought not to have been made.[205]

In the present case he held that an application to a court or tribunal without prior notice to a respondent whose economic interests would be prejudiced by that order had an inherent potential for injustice and could be accepted and compatible with Article 6 and Article 1 Protocol No 1 only if 'hedged around with precautions and procedures designed to limit the injustice so far as practicable'.[206] In the view of the House of Lords, the procedures under the Registered Homes Act 1984 for applications for the cancellation of registration were not compliant with Article 6 or made in the public interest for Article 1 purposes where it was established that the application ought never to have been made:

> How could it be compatible with their Convention rights to deprive them by judicial order of the benefit of registration of their Ash Lea Court nursing home without according them the opportunity of showing the application to be insubstantial and based on insufficient grounds and without there being any circumstances of urgency arguably sufficient to justify depriving them of that opportunity?[207]

---

5. Consumer Protection

An objective often put forward to justify an interference with the peaceful enjoyment of possessions is consumer protection. Although in *Wilson*[208] the outcome was determined by the issue of retrospective effect, four of their Lordships considered the application of Article 1 to the facts. As discussed earlier, the lender could not enforce a loan agreement as the agreement did not contain all the prescribed terms required by the Consumer

---

[205] Ibid, [13].
[206] Ibid, [14].
[207] Ibid, [18]. No HRA remedy was available to the claimants as the act the subject of challenge took place prior to the HRA coming into force. See also *R (on the application of Orange Personal Communications Ltd) v Secretary of State for Trade and Industry*, Administrative Court, 25 October 2000 and *Bank Mellat* (n 134) where the majority held that procedural protections encompassing a closed hearing and special advocates satisfied the requirements of Art 1 Protocol No 1 and Art 6. The procedural requirement can be met by the availability of judicial review, *SRM Global* (n 94), [84]. Art 1 does not extend to setting up an inquiry: *Persey v Secretary of State for Environment, Food and Rural Affairs* [2002] EWHC (Admin) 371, [2003] QB 794.
[208] *Wilson* (n 105).

Credit Act 1974. Assuming this did amount to a deprivation of the lender's possessions, Lord Nicholls held that the Act pursued a legitimate aim in that it protected persons wishing to borrow money from exploitation.[209] Furthermore, in his view, Parliament was charged with the primary responsibility for deciding whether the means chosen to deal with a social problem were both necessary and appropriate.[210] He concluded that the response of Parliament was proportionate. Lords Hope,[211] Hobhouse[212] and Scott[213] reached a similar conclusion.

The protection of the consumer is also the objective of laws regulating competition. *Interbrew SA v Competition Commission*[214] concerned a challenge to the Competition Commission's recommendation that Interbrew should be ordered to divest itself of the entire UK beer business of Bass Brewers which it had recently acquired. The Administrative Court concluded that the divestment of Bass was strictly necessary and there was no other effective remedy available to restore effective competition to the market.[215]

A number of professions are also regulated to protect the consumers using the services provided. Claims under Article 1 have been made concerning interventions by the Law Society into solicitors' practices. In *Wright*[216] the Chancery Division held that the public interest required a balance to be struck between the draconian effect of intervention and the protection of clients, other solicitors, and the general reputation of the profession.[217] In the view of the court, it was not possible to devise a different and less draconian remedy, and the balance came down in favour of protecting the public.[218] In *Nicholds*,[219] on the assumption that a door supervisor's licence was a possession, the High Court held that the criteria drawn up by the Security Industry Authority for recognising persons as fit and proper to be door supervisors were proportionate. 'The Authority had good grounds for concluding that a fundamental aim of the Act, to eliminate criminality in door supervision, could only be achieved by imposing an absolute automatic bar if the applicant committed certain very serious offences.'[220]

---

[209] Ibid, [68].
[210] Ibid, [70].
[211] Ibid, [109].
[212] Ibid, [138].
[213] Ibid, [169].
[214] *Interbrew SA v Competition Commission* [2001] EWHC (Admin) 367.
[215] Nevertheless the decision was struck down as unfair as Interbrew was not given a proper opportunity to deal with a particular issue. See also *R (on the application of Pow Trust) v The Chief Executive and Registrar of Companies* [2002] EWHC (Admin) 2783, [2004] BCC 268, in which the court held that penalties under the Companies Act 1985 for non-compliance with requirements for delivery of accounts and reports were proportionate.
[216] *Wright v Law Society*, Chancery Division, 4 September 2002.
[217] Ibid, [61].
[218] Ibid. See also *Holder v Law Society* [2003] EWCA Civ 39, [2003] 1 WLR 1059; *Law Society v Sritharan* [2005] EWCA Civ 476; *Keazor v Law Society* [2009] EWHC 267 (Admin); and *Hamilton* (n 144), which concerned the suspension of the appellant from practice as a state-registered nurse and midwife.
[219] *Nicholds* (n 59).
[220] Ibid, [90].

6. Planning and the Environment

Planning and environmental rules and regulations often interfere with the peaceful enjoyment of possessions. However, given the beneficial consequences of these measures, such interferences are generally found to be justified.[221] For example, in *Davies*[222] the Administrative Court stated that Article 1 bestowed a very wide margin of appreciation. It concluded that the Council's adoption of a street trading scheme, meaning that certain streets, including those where the claimants traded, were prohibited and charging £5,000 per year for a consent site, was proportionate and struck a fair balance.[223]

> All that happened was that in the public good, and in common with others, they were required to move to a different position in the same general location. A system of appeals was set up. A fee, payable by instalments, was reasonably decided upon. The fact that Mrs Atkins ceased to trade does not, I am afraid, make the use of the Act disproportionate.[224]

Similarly, in *Phillips*[225] the Divisional Court held that the Royal Parks and Other Open Spaces Regulations 1997, which made it an offence to drive or ride any trade or business vehicle in specified areas, were proportionate.

> The areas covered by the Regulations are areas of particular historical and patrimonial significance and also of natural beauty. It seems clear that the Secretary of State has considered it appropriate to proscribe, so far as is possible, trade activities within these areas, no doubt with a view to preserving their status ... for the benefit of society as a whole.[226]

Compulsory purchase orders also raise issues under Article 1. In *London Borough of Bexley*[227] the Administrative Court considered a compulsory purchase order under section 226(1) of the Town and Country Planning Act 1990 which had been confirmed by the Secretary of State. The court noted that the right to peaceful enjoyment of possessions was a qualified rather than an absolute right and involved a balancing exercise between the 'public interest and the individual's right whereby any interference with the individual's right must be necessary and proportionate'.[228] The court was not persuaded that there was anything materially different between those principles and the principles applied by the Secretary of State under Circular 14/94 whereby a compulsory purchase order was not to be made unless there was a compelling case in the public interest as such an approach 'necessarily involves weighing the individuals rights against the

---

[221] *Cusack* (n 136), [44].
[222] *Davies* (n 5).
[223] Ibid, [100]–[105].
[224] Ibid, [139].
[225] *Phillips* (n 126).
[226] Ibid, [20]. See also: *Kingsalton* (n 29); *Waltham Forest* (n 123); *Rowland* (n 14); *Fisher* (n 128); *Leven* (n 100); and *Young v First Secretary of State* [2004] EWHC (Admin) 2167. It is also possible for a tax or levy to have an environmental rationale. See eg *R (on the application of British Aggregates Associates) v Her Majesty's Treasury* [2002] EWHC (Admin) 926. Variations of restrictive covenants must be carried out compatibly with Art 1 Protocol No 1: see *Lawntown Ltd v Camenzuli* [2007] EWCA Civ 949.
[227] *London Borough of Bexley* (n 87).
[228] Ibid, [46].

public interest'.[229] The court concluded that there was a compelling case in the public interest and that a fair balance had been struck between the rights of the individual and the public interest.[230]

As noted above, where there has been a compulsory purchase order, the level of compensation will affect whether or not the interference with Article 1 rights is proportionate. However, it was decided by the Lands Tribunal in *Kerr*[231] that this did not require the state to discharge the claimant's mortgage debt, even though his compensation at market rates would result in him still having a mortgage given the devaluation in his property since his purchase.

Article 1 may also apply where residents are affected by road building or the opening of a new relief road. In *Thomas*[232] the claimants owned houses close to a new relief road and had claimed compensation under a statutory scheme for the alleged depreciation in the value of their houses attributable to noise and nuisance from the road. The Court of Appeal held that the compensation rights created had to strike a fair balance[233] and that the three-year limit here did not strike a fair balance. 'The fairness of the balance between public and private interests was destroyed by the opportunity so given to the authorities to evade the responsibility otherwise imposed on them.'[234] A violation of Article 1 Protocol No 1 was established. The Court of Appeal used section 3 of the HRA to interpret the Act so that the claimants were entitled to compensation.

7. The Rights of Others

7.1 Freedom of Expression

The Convention rights of others have been utilised to justify an interference with the peaceful enjoyment of possessions. In *Ashdown*[235] the Court of Appeal considered an infringement of the copyright held by the former leader of the Liberal Democrats, Paddy Ashdown, by the *Sunday Telegraph*. A major part of the defence was the right to freedom of expression. However, the court concluded that it was not arguable that Article 10 required the Telegraph Group should be able to profit from this use of Mr Ashdown's copyright without paying compensation.[236]

---

[229] Ibid.
[230] Ibid, [48]. See also *Clays Lane* (n 145), concerning the compulsory transfer of land under s 27 of the Housing Act 1996 following mismanagement on the part of a registered social landlord; and *Alliance Spring Co Ltd v First Secretary of State* [2005] EWHC (Admin) 18, *Hall v First Secretary of State* [2007] EWCA Civ 612 and *R (Argos Ltd) v Birmingham City Council* [2011] EWHC 2639 (Admin).
[231] *Kerr v Northern Ireland Housing Executive Lands* Tr NI 10/1/2013.
[232] *Thomas* (n 101).
[233] Ibid, [53].
[234] Ibid, [57].
[235] *Ashdown* (n 26).
[236] Ibid, [82].

7.2 Article 1 Protocol 1

7.2.1 Generally

In some HRA claims, one person's Article 1 rights have to be balanced against the Article 1 rights of another. For example, in *Levi Strauss*[237] the court recognised that there were competing property rights: Tesco's interest in the jeans which it had acquired from outside the EEA; and Levi's interest in the trade marks. It found that the balance which the EU legislature and the domestic legislature had decided to hold between them prohibited parallel importation from outside the EEA of trade-marked goods. Noting that the scope of discretion conferred on the legislature was wide, it concluded that the prohibition was proportionate.[238]

The Article 1 rights of creditors must be considered where a bankruptcy order is made. It was argued in *Krasner*[239] that it was incompatible with a bankrupt's rights for rights to a retirement annuity, and pension benefits, to vest in the trustee in bankruptcy in circumstances which excluded the power of the court to make an income payment order under section 310 of the Insolvency Act 1986. The Court of Appeal noted that a wide margin of appreciation was available to the legislature here. It concluded that it was not a violation of Article 1 for annuity and pension benefits to be used in this way.

> Clearly Parliament has been responding to a perception of what the public interest requires in this field. It has done so against a background of judicial decisions, over very many years, that that public interest requires, generally, that a bankrupt's property should be available to answer the claims of his creditors.[240]

Whilst it was not entirely clear from the judgments given, it could also be argued that in *Marcic*[241] the House of Lords was essentially balancing the property rights of one group against those of another. As Lord Nicholls expressed it, the balance was between the interests of customers of a company whose properties are prone to sewer flooding and, on the other hand, all the other customers of the company whose properties were drained through the company's sewers. The interests of the first group conflicted with the interests of the company's customers as a whole in that only a minority of customers suffered sewer flooding but the company's customers as a whole met the cost of building more sewers.[242]

Affording a broad discretion to Parliament, the House of Lords concluded that the balance struck by the statutory scheme to impose a general drainage obligation on a sewerage undertaker but to entrust enforcement of this obligation to an independent regulator who had regard to all the different interests involved struck a reasonable balance and that Parliament had acted well within its bounds as policy maker.[243] The

---

[237] *Levi Strauss* (n 45).
[238] Ibid, [40]. See also *MWH & H Ward* (n 125), which concerned an interference with property in order to alleviate a long-standing flooding problem relating to other properties.
[239] *Krasner* (n 28).
[240] Ibid, [74]. See also *Fuller* (n 123), which concerned a direction under s 61 of the Criminal Justice and Public Order Act 1994 requiring travellers to leave land.
[241] *Marcic* (n 24).
[242] Ibid, [42].
[243] Ibid, per Lord Nicholls at [43], per Lord Hoffmann at [71] and per Lord Hope at [87].

claimant here had not taken this remedial avenue and that is why his claim failed. Nevertheless, their Lordships did point to one item of concern with the present scheme concerning the payment of compensation to those suffering external sewer flooding. It recommended that, if it was not practicable to carry out remedial works, those who enjoy the benefit of effective drainage should bear the cost of paying some compensation. 'The minority who suffer damage and disturbance as a consequence of the inadequacy of the sewerage system ought not to be required to bear an unreasonable burden.'[244]

In the context of a mortgage the High Court has held that any deprivation of possessions constituted by the exercise by a mortgagee of its powers under section 101 of the Law of Property Act 1925 after a default by the mortgagor was justified in the public interest:

> [I]t reflects the bargain habitually drawn between mortgagors and mortgagees for nearly 200 years, in which the ability of a mortgagee to sell the property offered as a security without having to go to court has been identified as a central and essential aspect of the security necessarily to be provided if substantial property based secured lending is to be available at affordable rates of interest.[245]

Again, whilst not articulated as such, it was clear in *Summers*[246] that the Supreme Court was balancing the Article 1 Protocol No 1 rights of a successful claimant in a negligence action against the Article 1 Protocol No 1 rights of the defendant who argued that the claim was fraudulent and had evidence to establish this. It was accepted by the Supreme Court that it was in the public interest that there should be a power to strike out a statement of case for abuse of process. However, it was also held that

> in deciding whether or not to exercise the power the court must examine the circumstances of the case scrupulously in order to ensure that to strike out the claim is a proportionate means of achieving the aim of controlling the process of the court and deciding cases justly.[247]

It was noted that the draconian step of striking a claim out was always a last resort 'where to do so would deprive the claimant of a substantive right to which the court had held that he was entitled after a fair trial'. In the view of the Supreme Court, it was difficult to think of circumstances in which such a conclusion would be proportionate.[248] It suggested that such circumstances might include a case where there had been a massive attempt to deceive the court but the award of damages would be very small.[249]

Whilst the Supreme Court accepted that it was important to deter fraudulent claims, it held that there was a balance to be struck. To date this had been struck by assessing both liability and quantum and, provided this could be done fairly, to give judgment in the ordinary way.[250] It noted that there were many ways in which dishonest claimants could be deterred including 'ensuring that the dishonesty does not increase the award of damages, making orders for costs, reducing interest, proceedings for contempt and

---

[244] Ibid, per Lord Nicholls at [45]. See also *Arscott v The Coal Authority* [2004] EWCA Civ 892, [2005] Env LR 6.

[245] *Horsham Properties* (n 30), [44]

[246] *Summers* (n 31).

[247] Ibid, [48].

[248] Ibid, [49].

[249] Ibid, [49].

[250] Ibid, [50].

criminal proceedings'.[251] In the present case, it concluded that it was not proportionate to strike the action out instead of giving judgment for the claimant:

> [T]he court has power under the CPR and under its inherent jurisdiction to strike out a statement of case at any stage of the proceedings, even where it has already determined that the claimant is in principle entitled to damages in an ascertained sum, we have concluded that that power should in principle only be exercised where it is just and proportionate to do so, which is likely to be only in very exceptional circumstances ... this is not such a case.[252]

7.2.2 Adverse Possession

Pursuant to section 17 of the Limitation Act 1980 and section 75 of the Land Registration Act 1925, adverse title to land can be obtained after the expiration of 12 years of adverse possession. In *JA Pye (Oxford) Ltd v United Kingdom*[253] the ECtHR held that that the law of adverse possession engaged Article 1, but that the Article was not breached. The impact of this decision was considered by the Court of Appeal in *Ofulue v Bossert*[254] which determined that the decision of the ECtHR should be followed. The ECtHR had held that the law on adverse possession was designed to regulate questions of title and limitation periods in the context of the ownership and use of land as between individuals. In its view, the limitation period of 12 years for actions for the recovery of land pursued a legitimate aim in the general interest. In striking this balance, the ECtHR held that the UK enjoyed a wide margin of appreciation.

The Court of Appeal held that as the UK had a margin of appreciation in this area, it was up to the national authorities to determine the content of the rules concerning extinction of title:

> Since the period of limitation is fixed by statute in the United Kingdom, the question of the length of time for which adverse possession must take place is one which Parliament is entitled to decide, provided that the period so fixed serves a legitimate aim and is proportionate.[255]

However, it concluded that it was not possible to disregard the decision in *Pye* by distinguishing this case on its facts. For the doctrine of the margin of appreciation to be inapplicable, 'the results would have to be so anomalous as to render the legislation unacceptable'.[256] It found that it was not possible to apply the test of legitimate aim and proportionality to each different case of adverse possession which arose. Arden LJ observed as follows:

> The Strasbourg court considered the compatibility with the Convention of the limitation period in the case of adverse possession with art 1 of Protocol No 1 and assessed its legitimate aim and proportionality as a general rule and not simply in the context of the specific facts of the Pye case. It would not therefore be appropriate for this court to proceed to examine the questions of legitimate aim and proportionality simply from the perspective of the facts of this case and the relationship between them and the policy considerations in the Law Commission's Consultation Paper.[257]

---

[251] Ibid, [51].
[252] Ibid, [65].
[253] *JA Pye (Oxford) Ltd v United Kingdom* (2008) 46 EHRR 45.
[254] *Ofulue v Bossert* [2008] EWCA Civ 7, [2008] 3 WLR 1253.
[255] Ibid, [50].
[256] Ibid, [52].
[257] Ibid, [53].

In her view, there were no special circumstances shown to justify departing from the decision of the ECtHR.[258]

7.3 Vulnerable People

Whilst for reasons of retrospective effect the House of Lords was unable to determine for the claimants their HRA claim in *Jain*,[259] it was observed that the state was entitled in the public interest to impose limitations for the purpose of safeguarding vulnerable people, such as elderly and infirm residents in nursing homes.[260] Here the claim concerned cancellation of registration as a nursing home under Part II of the Registered Homes Act 1984.

---

8. Social Justice

In *Axa* the Supreme Court considered the proportionality of an interference by the Scottish Parliament with the possessions of insurance companies. The legislation subject to challenge had been passed to reverse a decision of the House of Lords and made it possible for those suffering from certain asbestos-related conditions to bring actions in damages for personal injury. The insurance companies claimed that reversing the court decision by this law, would expose them to claims under their indemnity insurance policies amounting to millions of pounds annually and perhaps several billion pounds in total. The Supreme Court accepted that the legitimate aim was rectifying a social injustice: '[T]he Scottish Parliament were entitled to regard their predicament as a social injustice ... its judgment that asbestos-related pleural plaques should be actionable cannot be dismissed as unreasonable.'[261]

The insurance companies argued that the insurance industry was being called upon to bear a disproportionate and excessive burden compounded by the fact that the new law had retroactive effect. The Supreme Court did not agree, concluding that the balance struck was proportionate. Lord Hope held that two important factors were taken into account. First, claims would only succeed if it was shown that exposure to asbestos was caused by the employer's negligence.[262] Second, it was held that the business in which insurers were engaged was a commercial venture 'inextricably associated with risk'.[263] In the opinion of Lord Hope, these were long-term policies and there was inevitably a

---

[258] Ibid, [55]. See also *R (Newhaven Port & Properties Ltd) v Secretary of State for the Environment* [2013] EWCA Civ 673, [2013] 3 All ER 719 where the Court of Appeal held that s 15(4) of the Commons Act 2006, which enables land used for sports and pastimes for 20 years or more to be registered as a village green, was compatible with Art 1 Protocol 1. See further, L Fox O'Mahony and N Cobb, 'Taxonomies of Squatting: Unlawful Occupation in a New Legal Order' (2008) 71 *Modern Law Review* 878.

[259] *Jain* (n 57).

[260] Ibid, Lord Scott at [12].

[261] *Axa* (n 2), per Lord Hope at [33].

[262] Ibid, [37].

[263] Ibid, [38].

risk that circumstances, unseen at the date when they were written, might occur which would increase the burden of liability.[264] He stated that the 'nature, number and value of claims were therefore always liable to develop in ways that were unpredictable'.[265]

Lord Brown, also finding the interference proportionate, was more influenced by the fact that the legislation was not actually an extreme departure from the previous common law position.[266] Lord Reed took a variety of factors into account in concluding that the legislation was proportionate. These included the fact that when the insurers entered into the contracts, it could not be predicted with confidence that the conditions affected by the legislation would be actionable or not. Furthermore, the legislation was not a dramatic change to the position prior to the judgment of the House of Lords which it reversed. He also noted that it was necessary to afford deference to the legislature given this was a matter of policy, judgment and discretion in the field of social or economic policy.[267] Although the legislation was retrospective in effect, he cited examples of decisions of the ECtHR where retrospective legislation designed to remedy a social problem was held to be proportionate.[268]

Social justice was also essentially the justification at issue in S.[269] Here the claimants argued that making deductions from their earnings paid by private employers to raise funds for Victim Support was disproportionate. The Administrative Court held that there was a wide margin of appreciation given the social and economic judgment involved. It observed that the deductions proposed were closely analogous to a tax to be levied on them[270] and that the imposition of a special tax upon prisoners in receipt of enhanced earnings for the purpose of supporting victims of crime was well within the UK's margin of appreciation. It concluded that a fair balance was struck between the general interests of the community and the requirement of the protection of the individual prisoner's rights—they were not bearing an individual and excessive burden.[271]

---

9. Protection of Morals

Protection of morals was assumed to be the justification for the control by licensing of individuals opening sex shops in *Belfast City Council*.[272] Lord Hoffmann stated that this was an area where the ECtHR had always afforded a wide margin of appreciation which in terms of the domestic constitution translated into a 'broad power of judgment

---

[264] Ibid, [38].
[265] Ibid, [39].
[266] Ibid, per Lord Brown at [83].
[267] Ibid, [131].
[268] Ibid, [132].
[269] S (n 32).
[270] Ibid, [45].
[271] Ibid, [47]. See also *Salvesen* (n 135) where the legislation designed to deal with landlords serving notice before a particular date in order to avoid being adversely affected by new legislation was held to be disproportionate.
[272] *Belfast City Council* (n 78).

entrusted to local authorities by the legislature'.[273] Baroness Hale reached a similar con-clusion, noting that there were good reasons for refusing to licence a sex shop on this particular street and even better ones for refusing this particular company a licence.[274] And Lord Neuberger held that as the claimant had not succeeded in his Article 10 claim, it was difficult to conceive of circumstances in which a disappointed applicant for a sex establishment licence could succeed on an Article 1 claim concerning the same facts.[275]

Protection of morals was also the justification put forward for the control on posses-sions considered by the House of Lords to be imposed by the Hunting Act 2004, which prohibited hunting wild mammals with dogs and hare coursing. Lord Bingham, quoting from Scottish case law which was quoting from the Scottish Parliament, confirmed that the enactment of the statute was the making of a moral judgment concerning the prevention of cruelty to animals and animal welfare.[276] His Lordship held as follows:

> [T]his Act was based upon a moral principle, whether one agrees with that principle or not, and I do not think that doubt can be thrown on the rationale of the Act, as expressed by the courts below, by showing that the underlying principle, if carried to its logical extremes, would have justified a much more far-reaching measure.[277]

Given the subject matter of the claim, Lord Hope indicated that an area of discretionary judgment was due to the legislature. It had been argued for the respondents that the jus-tification for the ban was to be found in the objectives of reducing suffering, reducing instances of disorder associated with hunting and dealing with criminality associated with hare coursing. Lord Hope held that it was open to the legislature to focus on the nature of the activities banned without comparing these to others, bearing in mind that they were being engaged in for sport and recreation. He concluded as follows:

> It was open for them to form their own judgment as to whether they caused a sufficient degree of suffering in that context for legislative action to be taken to deal with them. Having decided that there was a sufficient degree of suffering in that context, it was open to them too to decide that prohibiting these activities in the manner laid down by the 2004 Act was proportionate.[278]

10. Prevention of Crime and Illegality

10.1 Confiscation Orders

A nine-member panel of the Supreme Court considered the compatibility of confisca-

---

[273] Ibid, [16].
[274] Ibid, [38].
[275] Ibid, [100].
[276] *Countryside Alliance* (n 141), [36].
[277] Ibid, [41].
[278] Ibid, [78]. See also *Petsafe Ltd* (n 4) where the High Court held that the prohibition on the use on cats and dogs of an electronic collar designed to administer an electric shock was proportionate to the objective of animal welfare.

tion orders with Article 1 in *Waya*.[279] Here it was common ground that there had to be a reasonable relationship of proportionality between the means employed by the state in, inter alia, the deprivation of property as a form of penalty, and the legitimate aim which was sought to be realised by the deprivation.[280] It was confirmed that section 3 of the HRA required the court to interpret the Proceeds of Crime Act 2002 so that violations of Article 1 were avoided. More specifically, it was confirmed by the majority that section 6(5)(b) of the Act, setting out the final stage of the process of assessment of a confiscation order, should be read subject to the qualification that an order should be made 'except insofar as such an order would be disproportionate and thus a breach of Article 1, Protocol 1'.[281] Therefore, in the view of the majority, a judge should, if confronted by an application for an order which would be disproportionate, refuse to make it but 'accede only to an application for such as sums as would be proportionate'.[282]

The majority held that the Crown had an important preliminary function in ensuring that a disproportionate order was not sought. But it confirmed that the safeguard must not depend upon prosecutorial discretion and that control must be in the person of the Crown Court judge subject to the reviewing jurisdiction of the Court of Appeal on appeal.[283] The majority found that the essence, and frequently declared purpose of the legislation, was to remove from criminals the pecuniary proceeds of their crime. It concluded that a confiscation order must therefore bear a proportionate relationship to this purpose.[284] It confirmed that a legitimate and proportionate confiscation order may have one or more of three effects: require the defendant to pay the whole of a sum which he has obtained jointly with others; require several defendants each to pay a sum which has been obtained, successively, by each of them; or require a defendant to pay the whole of a sum which he has obtained by crime without enabling him to set off expenses of the crime.[285] It stated as follows:

> Although these propositions involve the possibility of removing from the defendant by way of confiscation order a sum larger than may in fact represent his net proceeds of crime, they are consistent with the statute's objective and represent proportionate means of achieving it.[286]

The majority further held that it would be disproportionate to make a confiscation order when the subject of the order has restored to the loser any proceeds of crime which he had ever had. It would not achieve the statutory objective of removing his proceeds of crime 'but would simply be an additional financial penalty'.[287]

The present case concerned money lent because of fraud, but subsequently repaid in full and always fully secured. However, as this was mortgage fraud, a substantial benefit was gained from the fraud in the form of a large increase in the value of the flat which the fraud enabled the offender to buy. The majority held as follows:

> In general, where the mortgage loan has been repaid or is bound to be repaid because it is amply secured, and absent other property obtained, a proportionate confiscation order is likely

---

[279] *R v Waya* [2012] UKSC 51, [2012] 3 WLR 1188.
[280] Ibid, [12].
[281] Ibid, [16].
[282] Ibid, [16].
[283] Ibid, [19].
[284] Ibid, [22].
[285] Ibid, [26].
[286] Ibid, [26].
[287] Ibid, [28] and [32]. See also *R v Jawad* [2013] EWCA Crim 644, [2013] Crim LR 698, [21].

to be the benefit that the defendant has derived from his use of the loan, namely the increase in the value of the property attributable to the loan.[288]

It later confirmed that depriving him of that prospective capital gain, or a proportionate part of it,

> would therefore be the appropriate way of making the confiscation order fit the crime. Moreover that is the way in which the provisions of [the Proceeds of Crime Act 2002] apply in this case, on a fair and purposive construction that takes account of section 3 of HRA and the need for proportionality under [Article 1 Protocol No 1].[289]

The minority disagreed on this point holding that to base the confiscation order on the increase in value of the flat would be disproportionate. '[T]he judge should have applied [Article 1 Protocol No 1] and reduced the confiscation order to reflect the modest benefit that Mr Waya may have enjoyed of obtaining the mortgage on better terms.'[290]

In *Benjafield*[291] the House of Lords considered the proportionality of a confiscation under section 72AA of the Criminal Justice Act 1988 and section 4 of the Drug Trafficking Act 1994. It concluded that the legislation was a precise, fair and proportionate response to the important need to protect the public.[292] Similarly, in *Hughes*[293] the Court of Appeal stated that there was a significant public interest in ensuring that criminals do not profit from their crimes and that the proceeds of crime are confiscated in the event of conviction.[294] In *AP*[295] the Court of Appeal concluded that section 41(4) of the Proceeds of Crime Act 2002 was proportionate. This section provided that no exception was to be made to a restraint order making provision for legal expenses in proceedings relating to the relevant offences. It stated as follows:

> To permit ... monies which could well be the proceeds of crime being used to pay lawyers for the benefit of a defendant who is either suspected or being, or has been found to be, a criminal raises a clear social issue. Parliament, it seems to us, is entitled to take the view that funds which may have criminal origins should not be so used. Parliament had to take into account the consequences, namely that other means would have to be provided to enable defendants to have legal representation during restraint and confiscation proceedings. The course adopted was to provide state aid.[296]

It further held that any problem of not attracting counsel of the requisite seniority would have to be addressed when proceedings were heard in the light of Article 6.[297]

---

[288] Ibid, [35].

[289] Ibid, [42]. These principles were applied in *R v Hursthouse* [2013] EWCA Crim 517; *R v Jawad* [2013] EWCA Crim 644, [2013] Crim LR 698; *R v Harvey* [2013] EWCA Crim 1104; *R v Morgan* [2013] EWCA Crim 1307; *Ahmed v Revenue & Customs Commissioners* [2013] EWHC 2241 (Admin).

[290] Ibid, [124]. See also *R v Axworthy* [2012] EWCA Crim 2889. See further D Thomas, 'R v Waya' [2013] *Criminal Law Review* 256; P Alldridge, 'The Limits of Confiscation' [2011] *Criminal Law Review*; J Ulph, 'Confiscation Orders, Human Rights and Penal Measures' (2010) 126 *Law Quarterly Review* 251.

[291] *Benjafield* (n 23).

[292] Ibid, [17] in reliance upon *Phillips v UK* [2001] Crim LR 817.

[293] *Hughes v Customs and Excise Commissioners* [2002] EWCA Civ 670.

[294] Ibid, [52] in reliance upon *Raimondo v Italy* (1994) 18 EHRR 237. See also *R v Goodenough* [2004] EWCA Crim 2260; *In the Matter of D (Interim Receiver Order: Proceeds of Crime Act 2002)*, Administrative Court, 7 December 2004; and *R v May* [2005] EWCA Crim 97, [2005] 1 WLR 2902; *Sinclair v Glatt* [2009] EWCA Civ 176, [2009] 1 WLR 1845; *R v Shabir* [2008] EWCA Crim 1809, [2009] 1 Cr App R (S) 84.

[295] *AP v Crown Prosecution Service* [2007] EWCA Crim 3128.

[296] Ibid, [20].

[297] See also *Eastenders* (n 162) where it was held to be disproportionate to allow a receiver appointed under the Proceeds of Crime Act 2002 to recover his costs and expenses where his appointment was later quashed.

10.2 Anti-terror Measures

In *Khaled*[298] the High Court held that financial monitoring of expenditure under the Counter Terrorism Act 2008 was proportionate.

10.3 Illegality

Al-Kishtaini[299] concerned a claimant prevented from recovering damages for breach of contract as, in order to prove his rights under the contract, he had to rely on his own illegal act. The Court of Appeal found that the public interest reflected by the doctrine of illegality weighed particularly heavily in the scales. It was also influenced by two further factors. First, the secondary legislation which resulted in the illegality on which the claim was based originated in the resolutions of the UN Security Council in an international emergency—implementation of the UN sanctions against Iraq following the invasion and occupation of Kuwait.[300]

Secondly, the prohibition was not an absolute one. It was open to the claimant to obtain advance clearance from the Treasury, so that he could find out precisely where he stood before entering into and carrying out a potentially illegal transaction. 'In such a case it does not offend the principle of proportionality invoked by the claimant to apply to its full extent the high public policy applicable to this case, so as to prevent the enforcement of his claim.'[301]

---

11. Economic Well-being of the Country

The final justification considered is the economic well-being of the country. Whilst a number of interests come under this category, the most important is the payment of taxes and duties.

11.1 Taxes

It is expressly stated in Article 1 that the right to peaceful enjoyment of possessions shall not impair the right of a state to enforce such laws as it deems necessary to secure the payment of taxes or other contributions or penalties. As for other interferences with peaceful enjoyment, taxes and duties must meet the fair-balance test. However, as the

---

[298] *R (K) v HM Treasury* [2009] EWHC 1643 (Admin).
[299] *Al-Kishtaini* (n 161).
[300] Ibid, per Mummery LJ at [58].
[301] Ibid, Mummery LJ at [59] per. Holman J at [68] and Rix LJ at [96] expressly stated that the 'fair balance' test was met. See also *Soteriou* (n 107).

Court of Appeal noted in *Lydiashourne Ltd*,[302] attempts to challenge fiscal measures in the ECtHR have failed almost without exception. This is an area where considerable deference is afforded and a claim that tax laws infringe Article 1 is a very steep hill to climb.[303]

In *Dimsey*[304] the House of Lords considered sections 739–46 of the Income and Corporations Taxes Act 1988, which concerned provisions designed to counter tax avoidance by the transfer of assets abroad. The appellant argued that to use section 739(2) to deem the income of the offshore companies to be the income of an individual for tax purposes and also for it to remain for tax purposes the income of the companies was inconsistent with Article 1 as it amounted to double taxation. The House of Lords made clear that it regarded the section as a penal one intended to be an effective deterrent which would put a stop to practices considered to be against the public interest.[305] It concluded that the section was well within the margin of appreciation allowed to Member States in respect of tax legislation. 'The public interest requires that legislation designed to combat tax avoidance should be effective. That public interest outweighs, in my opinion, the objections, mainly theoretical.'[306]

The claim also failed in *Huitson*[307] where it was alleged that it was in breach of Article 1 for HMRC to rely on retrospective amendments to legislation to deny the claimant, retrospectively, tax relief previously available on income received by him from a trust in the Isle of Man. The Court of Appeal concluded that the retrospective measures achieved a fair balance between community interests and individual rights and did not place an unreasonable burden on the claimant.[308]

> [T]he retrospective amendments were enacted pursuant to a justified fiscal policy that was within the State's area of appreciation and discretionary judgment in economic and social matters. The legislation achieves a fair balance between the interests of the general body of taxpayers and the right of the claimant to enjoyment of his possessions, without imposing an unreasonable economic burden on him. This outcome accords with the reasonable expectations of the taxation of residents in the State on the profits of their trade or profession. The legislation prevents the [Double Taxation Agreement] tax relief provisions from being misused for a purpose different from their originally intended use.[309]

A similar approach was taken by the Court of Appeal in *Federation of Tour Operators v HM Treasury*.[310] Here a challenge was brought by the Federation of Tour Operators to the doubling of Air Passenger Duty. Package tour operators were largely precluded from passing on the increase to passengers who had already booked their holidays and the effect was to impose the burden of tax upon them. The Court of Appeal agreed that it was possible to scrutinise tax measures under Article 1 and that the question was

---

[302] *Lydiashourne Ltd* (n 86).
[303] Ibid, [21]. See also *Vicky Construction* (n 12). See also *Revenue & Customs v Smith* [2007] EWHC 488 (Ch), [2008] STC 1941 and *Bysermaw Properties Ltd v Revenue & Customs Commissioners* [2008] STC (SCD) 322 where it was held proportionate for the state to impose a fixed penalty to secure compliance by taxpayers with their obligations to file returns.
[304] *Dimsey* (n 23).
[305] Ibid, [66].
[306] Ibid, [71]. See also *Greengate Furniture Ltd v The Commissioners of Customs and Excise*, VAT and Duties Tribunals, 11 August 2003; *Re A* (n 8).
[307] *Huitson* (n 18).
[308] Ibid, [57].
[309] Ibid, [95].
[310] *Federation of Tour Operators v HM Treasury* [2008] EWCA Civ 752, [2008] STC 2524.

whether or not the decision not to exempt passengers who had pre-booked through tour operators placed an individual and excessive burden upon tour operators such as to render the decision devoid of reasonable foundation.[311] This was later modified to a question of whether or not the tax was proportionate.[312] The Court of Appeal concluded that the imposition was proportionate. A postponement for tour operators alone would have been difficult to justify to airline operators. It would have involved a substantial loss in revenue and the tour operators were held to be not uniquely disadvantaged.[313]

Penalties for the non-payment or late payment of taxes, or duties, must be proportionate to the aims pursued. It is possible for the penalty regime to be unobjectionable but which may nevertheless lead occasionally to the imposition of a penalty so high as to be disproportionate.[314] The question of infringement must be addressed at the level of the individual.[315] Where the penalty is for late submission of a return, it has been held that ensuring submission by the due date is the objective rather than payment of tax by the due date.[316] In *Total Technology*[317] it was held that the VAT default surcharge scheme for penalising late returns was proportionate although there was the prospect that in a particular case the penalty could be assessed as disproportionate.

11.2 Duties

With respect to duties, a number of claims have been brought under the HRA, particularly in relation to forfeiture provisions. *Lindsay v Customs and Excise Commissioners*[318] concerned the alleged importation of excise goods without paying duty. Section 49 of the Customs and Excise Management Act 1979 provided that goods imported without payment of duty chargeable on them were subject to forfeiture. Section 141 provided that, where anything became liable to forfeiture, any vehicle which had been used for its carriage also became liable to forfeiture. Mr Lindsay had been stopped by British Customs just as he was about to drive onto the Shuttle in Calais to return to England. The officer found that he was carrying a substantial quantity of cigarettes and tobacco. He said that he had purchased some of this for members of his family with money provided by them. The officer informed him that he should have paid duty on the goods and proceeded to forfeit both the dutiable goods and his car in which those goods were being carried. This was in accordance with the Commissioners' policy that any car used for smuggling would be seized and not restored.

The Court of Appeal agreed that the decision of the Commissioners had to comply with Article 1.[319] The court understood the issue before it to be whether the current policy of the Commissioners so fettered their discretion when reviewing decisions taken to forfeit vehicles of those who evaded duty on cigarettes tobacco and alcohol as to prevent them from considering proportionality and thus to render their decisions

---

[311] Ibid, [27].
[312] Ibid, [28].
[313] Ibid, [31].
[314] *Total Technology* (n 4), [73].
[315] Ibid, [75].
[316] Ibid, [82].
[317] Ibid.
[318] *Lindsay* (n 86).
[319] Ibid, [40].

unlawful.[320] It noted that the prevention of the evasion of excise duty that was imposed in accordance with EU law was a legitimate aim. The question was whether the policy was liable to result in the imposition of a penalty in the individual case that was disproportionate with regard to that aim.[321] The court noted that the policy did not suggest that any regard should be paid to the value of the car. And it did not suggest that it was relevant to consider whether the goods were being imported to be distributed between family and friends or whether the importation was pursuant to a commercial venture under which the goods were to be sold at a profit.[322] The court quoted from the comments of the ECtHR in *Allgemeine Gold-und Silverscheideanstalt v UK*[323] that, when striking a fair balance, the behaviour of the owner of the property had to be taken into account.[324] It also held that it was appropriate to consider the scale of evil against which the policy was directed: 'the trade that is carried on in smuggled cigarettes is massive';[325] the fact that free movement of persons within the internal market greatly facilitated illicit importation; and the fact that notice was given that smuggling could lead to forfeiture of vessels.[326]

The court concluded that the policy was disproportionate as it did not draw a distinction between the commercial smuggler and the driver importing goods for social distribution to family or friends in circumstances where there was no attempt to make a profit:

> But where the importation is not for the purpose of making a profit, I consider that the principle of proportionality requires that each case should be considered on its particular facts, which will include the scale of importation, whether it is a 'first offence', whether there was an attempt at concealment or dissimulation, the value of the vehicle and the degree of hardship that will be caused by forfeiture. There is open to the commissioners a wide range of lesser sanctions that will enable them to impose a sanction that is proportionate where forfeiture of the vehicle is not justified.[327]

As the Customs officers had drawn no distinction between the true commercial smuggler and the driver importing goods for family and friends, the court concluded that the decision could not stand.[328]

It is clear that the judgment of the Court of Appeal in *Lindsay* opened up a new route for those who wished to challenge the application of the forfeiture provisions to them. In *Fox*[329] the Administrative Court held that, in order to establish that the goods owned by Fox were liable to forfeiture, it was necessary to prove that the goods owned by Everett (part of the share load) were liable to forfeiture rather than simply deeming these as such. In *Newbury*[330] the Divisional Court confirmed that the court consid-

---

[320] Ibid, [45].
[321] Ibid, [55].
[322] Ibid, [57].
[323] *Allgemeine Gold-und Silverscheideanstalt v UK* (1986) 9 EHRR 1, [54].
[324] *Lindsay* (n 86), [58].
[325] Ibid, [60].
[326] Ibid, [61]–[62].
[327] Ibid, [64].
[328] Ibid, [67]. See also *R (Hoverspeed Ltd) v Customs and Excise Commissioners* [2002] EWCA Civ 1804, [2003] QB 1041.
[329] *Fox v HM Customs and Excise* [2002] EWHC (Admin) 1244, [2003] 1 WLR 1331.
[330] *Customs and Excise Commissioners v Newbury* [2003] EWHC (Admin) 702, [2003] 2 All ER 964.

ering whether goods were liable to forfeiture was under a duty to consider Convention rights.[331]

> The right to peaceful enjoyment is engaged from the moment of seizure and continues thereafter. The initial act of seizure may not be disproportionate because the Commissioners are entitled to investigate. But the interference should cease once an opportunity is available properly to consider whether it complies with Convention rights. The court should not be asked or expected to make an order which is not only in breach of those rights in itself but also legitimates continuing breach by the Commissioners unless and until the review process takes place.[332]

11.3 Penalties—Clandestine Entrants

Harsh penalties are imposed on those who intentionally or negligently allow clandestine entrants into the United Kingdom. In *International Transport Roth*[333] a challenge was brought to Part II of the Immigration and Asylum Act 1999 which created a new penalty regime. Those responsible, generally the owner, hirer or driver, were liable for each such entrant to a fixed penalty of £2,000 unless they could establish that they were acting under duress or that they had neither actual nor constructive knowledge of the clandestine entrant and there was an effective system for preventing the carriage of clandestine entrants which was operated properly on the occasion in question. Once the Secretary of State had issued a penalty notice, the vehicle could be detained if it was considered that there was a serious risk that the penalty would not be paid. The penalty imposed was fixed and cumulative; no flexibility was allowed for degrees of blameworthiness or mitigating circumstances. Even if a carrier was determined not to be liable, his vehicle may have been detained and he would receive no compensation for this unless the Secretary of State acted unreasonably in issuing the penalty notice.

A majority of the Court of Appeal held that there was a wide discretion in the Secretary of State in his task of devising a suitable scheme and a high degree of deference due by the court to Parliament when it came to determining its legality.[334] However, it was also held that it was the court's role under the HRA to be the guardian of human rights. 'It cannot abdicate this responsibility. If ultimately it judges the scheme to be quite simply unfair, then the features that make it so must inevitably breach the Convention.'[335]

It concluded that the scale and inflexibility of the penalty, taken in conjunction with the other features of the scheme, imposed an excessive burden on the carriers in breach of Article 1.

---

[331] Ibid, [21].

[332] Ibid, [23]. Cf *Helman v Commissioners of Customs and Excise*, Administrative Court, 18 October 2002; *Crilly v the Commissioners of Customs and Excise*, VADT 28 July 2003; *Harding v The Commissioners of Customs and Excise*, VADT, 4 August 2003. See also *Gascoyne v HM Customs and Excise* [2004] EWCA Civ 1162, [2005] Ch 215; *Golobiewska v The Commissioners of Customs and Excise* [2005] EWCA Civ 607 and *Revenue & Customs Commissioners v Berriman* [2007] EWHC 1183 (Admin), [2007] 4 All ER 925; See further A Lidbetter, 'Customs, Cars and Article 1 of the First Protocol' [2004] *European Human Rights Law Review* 272.

[333] *International Transport Roth* [2002] EWCA Civ 158, [2003] QB 728.

[334] Ibid, [26] and [139].

[335] Ibid, [27] and [139].

Even acknowledging, as I do, the great importance of the social goal which the scheme seeks to promote, there are nevertheless limits to how far the state is entitled to go in imposing obligations of vigilance on drivers (and vicarious liability on employers and hirers) to achieve it and in penalising any breach.[336]

It was declared to be incompatible with Article 1 and Article 6.

11.4 Child Support

Whilst the payment of child support has a number of legitimate aims, it is considered in this section as it has been held that one of the aims of recovering maintenance from absent parents is to reduce the burden on the taxpayer of the single parent.[337] In *Denson*[338] the claimant argued that the Child Support Agency's attempts to make him pay maintenance in accordance with the Child Support Act 1991 were in breach of Article 1. The Administrative Court held that it was 'in the interests of the general community that the state should be able, by recovering maintenance from absent parents, to reduce the burden on the tax-payer of single parent families'.[339]

It concluded that the statutory scheme, and the Child Support Agency's administration of it, struck a fair and reasonable balance between, on the one hand, the absent parent's responsibilities for his or her children and, on the other hand, the need for a system that (i) produces fair and consistent results, (ii) preserves the parents' incentive to work, (iii) reduces the dependency of parents with care on income support and (iv) provides consequent savings to taxpayers.[340]

11.5 Nationalisation in the Public Interest

It was common ground in the Court of Appeal in the appeal concerning the challenge by shareholders to the nationalisation of Northern Rock that the nationalisation was lawful and in the public interest. The former shareholders argued that the statutory scheme for their compensation was in breach of Article 1 Protocol No 1 as they would get nothing or virtually nothing for their shares. As noted above, the Court of Appeal held that in this instance, proportionality did not necessarily require that full market value be paid in compensation.[341] It determined that the nationalisation was not to confer a benefit on the shareholders of Northern Rock but it was a service to the national economy to prevent damage or further damage to the banking system as a whole.[342] It concluded that the assumptions which the valuer of the shares was required to make pursuant to statute, meaning that the claimants would be deprived of their shares for nothing, or a derisory amount, was proportionate.[343]

---

[336] Ibid, [53] and [183], [187] and [188].
[337] *Denson* (n 23).
[338] Ibid.
[339] *SRM* (n 27), [31].
[340] Ibid, [32]. See also *R (on the application of Qazi) v Secretary of State for Work and Pensions* [2004] EWHC (Admin) 1331.
[341] [56].
[342] [66].
[343] [78].

11.6 Reduction of the National Budget Deficit

In *Public & Commercial Services Union*[344] the High Court accepted that the objective of a new and less generous Civil Service pension scheme was the reduction of the national budget deficit. It held that the state had a wide margin of appreciation in this area as it was economic and social policy. 'It would be utterly impossible for the court to embark upon a strictly arithmetical analysis of the processes by which central government might properly reduce compensation payments to meet the objectives of government spending policy.'[345]

It held that the test was to determine whether the claimants had been required to endure what went beyond a reasonable and commensurate reduction in entitlements.[346] The court was reluctant fully to engage with the claimants' arguments, stating that the submissions tended to draw the court into areas of 'impermissible scrutiny'.[347] It stated as follows:

> It is impossible for the court to 'second guess' the government's assessment of what is affordable. Nor can it be for the court to interfere with the government's assessment of spending priorities, requiring government to take money from one spending area and to allot it to this one. The only question is whether the Defendant has shown that the interference with scheme members' rights was a proportionate one within the limits of what can be afforded.[348]

It concluded that the interference with Article 1 Protocol No 1 rights did not go beyond what was reasonably necessary to achieve the legitimate aim recognised on both sides of the case.[349]

11.7 Recovery of Overpaid Welfare Benefit

Finally, in *McGrath*[350] on the assumption that Article 1 was engaged, which the court doubted, it held that where benefit had been mistakenly overpaid by the state, the decision to recover it from the claimant by way of deduction from current payments to her of employment and support allowance was proportionate.

---

[344] *Public & Commercial Services Union* (n 37).
[345] Ibid, [51].
[346] Ibid, [52].
[347] Ibid, [59].
[348] Ibid, [60].
[349] Ibid, [62].
[350] *McGrath* (n 40).

Index

Introductory Note

References such as '178–9' indicate (not necessarily continuous) discussion of a topic across a range of pages. Wherever possible in the case of topics with many references, these have either been divided into sub-topics or only the most significant discussions of the topic are listed. Because the entire work is about 'human rights law', the use of this term (and certain others which occur constantly throughout the book) as an entry points has been minimised. Information will be found under the corresponding detailed topics.

abortion 27, 594–5
absconding 198, 241, 292, 306, 369
absolute obligations 184, 200, 233
absolute rights 14, 83, 227, 409, 649
absolute rules 401–2, 406
abuse
    racial 243–4
    sexual 230, 462, 515
abuse of power 116, 279, 319
access to court
    deprivation of liberty 298
    fair trial 340–8
    and immunity from suit 345–6
    and interference with private life 457
    and legal representation 347
    and limitation periods 342–4
    prisoners 346–7
    right of 340–7
    and security for costs 344
    and striking out 347–8
    substantive and procedural bars 341–2
    vexatious litigants 344–5
accidents 46, 105, 218
accommodation 46–8, 51–2, 243, 325–6, 476, 504–5, 630–1
    provision of 48, 50–2, 231, 325, 476
    secure accommodation orders 275, 286, 331, 339
    temporary 487, 525–6
accountability 205, 211, 264
    of agents 211, 266
    democratic 41, 46, 94, 382
    political 304
accusations 26, 336, 392, 399, 577–8
    formal 336
actio popularis 37–9
active service overseas 186, 207
acts of non-UK actors 72–3

acts of public authorities 10, 18, 59, 73
acts to which HRA applies 59–82
adjournments 311, 369–70, 400
adjudicators 45, 93, 96, 99, 263, 443–4, 481
    independent 339, 379, 530
administration of justice 127, 209, 309, 364–5, 371–2, 587, 601–3
administrative convenience 254, 311–12
administrative decisions 69, 321, 325, 329–30
    rehearing 382–3
    two-stage process 329–31
administrative necessity 312–13
admissibility 106, 125, 143, 210, 348, 367–8
    test of 106, 125, 368
admissions 37, 52, 175, 302, 334, 359, 369
adoption 467–9, 474, 495, 497–9, 501, 546, 635
    with consent 498
    contacting of relatives prior to 498–9
    orders 469, 471, 497–9
    time limits 499
    without consent 497–8
adoptive parents 22, 35, 468–9, 635–6
adoptive relationships 468–9
adult children 204, 467, 471, 487
adulterous relationships 417, 568–9
adults
    vulnerable 140, 224, 328, 331–2, 450–1, 462, 464
    young 502, 622
adverse possession 666–7
advertisements 551, 553, 558, 560, 574, 591, 595–6
Afghanistan 38, 254, 258, 260, 466, 536, 591–2
age 109, 248–9, 426–7, 451, 453, 491–2, 501–2
agents
    accountability 211, 266
    diplomatic and consular 75–6
    non-state 210, 263
    of the state 75, 77, 205, 208–11, 213, 217, 364

authority and control 74–5, 78
  intentional or non-intentional killing by 209–10
alcohol 168, 397, 428, 437, 455, 530, 674
  excessive 105, 359
Algeria 72, 95, 150, 250, 254, 322, 332
aliens 35, 290, 322, 332, 489, 558
  expulsion 443, 481
alleged sexual relationships 81, 106, 125, 368
allocation of resources 201, 215, 312, 432, 513, 550
allowances 115, 178, 238, 518, 565, 608, 638
  widowed mother's 116, 613, 624
analogous position 623–6, 628
anguish 204, 229–30
animal welfare 439, 456, 669
anonymity 192, 195–6, 584–6, 598
  applications for 458
  orders 235, 431, 581, 583–6
anonymous witnesses 308, 406
anti-social behaviour orders 15, 324, 331, 336–9, 366–7, 453, 493
anti-terrorism measures
  and property 672
  and s 3 HRA 126–7
anxiety 37, 161–2, 165, 167–9, 172–3, 317, 378
anxious scrutiny 192–3, 196
apologies 155, 174–5
appeal 61–5, 93, 96–7, 343–4, 356–7, 377–8, 386–91
  right of 102, 340, 343, 370, 381, 383
appellate immigration authorities 93–6, 482–3
appropriate balance 284, 360, 395, 591
arbitrariness 88, 90, 280, 284, 291–2, 459, 655
arbitrary interference 89, 431, 503
Argentina 261
arguable case 206–8, 224, 434, 523–4
armed forces 77–8, 94, 96, 190, 207, 211, 342
  death involving 223–4
  death of members 224
  duty to investigate 267
  and extra-territorial effect 77–8
  protection of members 200–2
  service personnel 186, 201, 207–8, 223–4
arrest 270, 276–7, 284–5, 293–5, 297, 511, 593–4
  lawful 181, 284, 290
  reasons for 293–4
  victims of 167, 316
artificial insemination 100, 421, 472, 474, 492–3
artificial nutrition 184–5, 187
Asperger's Syndrome 224–5
assessment
  of damages 168, 315, 317, 659
  judicial 365, 388
  objective 231, 249, 385
  of proportionality 87, 92, 98, 100, 482, 485, 656–7
  risk, see risk assessment
assets 320, 333, 359, 642–3, 645, 673, 677
assurances 155, 175, 253–4, 278, 310, 322, 351

assurances from destination states 253–4
asylum 76, 231–2, 254–5, 478, 484, 609
  seekers 85, 228, 231–3, 248–9, 254–5, 429, 620
    detention 290–1
    dispersal 487
auditors 331, 339, 376, 381
Australia 77, 500, 572
Austria 89, 159, 171, 237, 372, 374, 384
automatic life sentences 43, 127, 244–5, 283, 313
automatic termination of proceedings 170, 378
autonomy 176, 412–13, 415, 420, 422–3, 426–7, 430
  personal 200, 411, 418, 423, 425–7, 445

bad faith 18, 84, 170, 279–80, 377, 413, 443
bail 148, 170, 284, 290, 295–6, 373, 377
  conditions 284, 509, 511
  proceedings 297, 328
  right to be released on 295–6
balance 27, 273–4, 321, 459–61, 542–4, 653–4, 663–6
  appropriate 284, 360, 395, 591
  correct 514–15
  fair, see fair balance
  of probabilities 287, 316–17, 364, 366, 393, 395–7, 399
  reasonable 514, 664, 677
balancing exercises 291, 487, 497, 512, 582, 597, 662
bankruptcy 284, 295, 344, 647, 664
  creditor rights 515
  orders 332, 515, 664
Belgium 74, 282, 285, 291, 323, 330, 336
beliefs 6, 527–38, 540–1, 543, 545, 548, 554
  manifestation of 530, 532, 535–7, 541, 543, 545
  religious 529, 531–3, 537–41, 543–4, 546, 588, 595
benefit and burden of Human Rights Act 31–57
benefit of Convention rights 31–9
bereavement allowance, widows 115, 613, 638
best interests 184–8, 200, 423, 484–5, 490–2, 497–8, 500
  of children 484, 500
bias 71, 214, 380, 387–8, 404
  common law test for 71, 214, 380
  unconscious 267
biological relatives 467–8, 473, 496, 498; see also natural fathers; natural parents
biometric data 119
blameworthiness 393, 399, 676
blanket bans 100, 459, 553, 572
blanket exemptions 131, 440, 557
blasphemous libel 588
bodily integrity 185, 423
breach of confidence 57, 414, 416, 435, 460, 597, 599–600
  modified 597
British citizens 70, 73, 324, 327–8, 479, 484, 487
British forces, see armed forces

British Overseas Territories 79
broadcasting 427, 549, 553, 557, 567, 586, 594
budget deficit reduction 678
burden
    disproportionate 193, 234, 267, 372
    evidential 125–6, 261, 349, 393, 396–7, 399
    of proof 61, 125, 287, 307
        persuasive 393, 398
        and presumption of innocence 393–4
        reverse 394–5
burden of Convention rights 39–40
business possessions 643–4

camping 554, 558, 591
cannabis 236, 543
capacity 32, 104, 184–5, 199, 237–8, 427, 436
caravan sites 517, 519
caravans 504, 506, 509, 512
care 51–3, 129, 199–200, 258, 348, 471–2, 474–6
    duty of 57, 203, 220, 348, 475
    health, see healthcare
    homes 47–8, 51–2, 504, 507–8, 644, 649, 667
    orders 33, 43, 324, 331, 471–2, 495, 497
        children 494–5
    plans 33, 128, 177, 274, 472, 474, 495
    proceedings 331, 358, 362, 457, 472–3, 494–5,
        587
    social 47, 51
care homes 507–8, 512
care standards and s 4 HRA 140
carelessness 413
    isolated acts of even significant 432, 476
case-by-case basis 133, 307, 353, 414
caste 109, 621
casual acts of negligence 189, 199
causal connection/link 159–60, 168, 171, 280–2
cautions 175–6, 373, 401, 420, 451
celebrities 458, 585; see also public figures
cells 3, 96, 209, 239, 242, 266, 424
cellular samples 423, 447
certainty 24, 87, 124, 130, 343–4, 501, 655–6
certiorari 152–3
Channel Islands 78
charges, criminal 170–2, 333–9, 366, 368, 371–4,
    377–9, 391–2
charities 48, 51–4, 372
child protection register 420, 450
child support 131, 471, 610–11, 628, 651, 677
Child Support Agency 44, 422, 471, 642, 677
child tax credits 613, 617, 632
child welfare 494–7, 499, 587
child witnesses 357–8
children 357–8, 461–3, 466–78, 484–7, 490,
    492–501, 630–3
    abduction 500
    adoption, see adoption
    adult 204, 467, 471, 487
    care orders 494–5
    contact orders 473–5, 496

corporal punishment 534, 545
    and deportation 484–5
    and extradition 489–91
    family life 466–8, 471–5, 494–502
    health 501–2
    and manifestation of belief 545–7
    paternity 421, 468, 501
    positive duties/obligations 473–5
    private life 462–4
    procedural rights 472–3
    protection 452, 462, 475
    removal from jurisdiction 499–500
    rights 494, 498, 502, 545–6
    welfare 475, 484
    young 43, 474, 495
chilling effect 557, 563, 580, 584, 598, 600, 602
church 44–5, 49, 114, 532–3, 612
citizens 6–7, 9, 18, 34, 39, 532, 540
    British 70, 73, 324, 327–8, 479, 487, 641
civil partnerships 496, 544
civil procedure 130
civil procedure and s 3 HRA 130
civil proceedings 64–5, 151–2, 265–6, 336, 345,
    347, 376–8
    reasonable time 376
    retrospective effect 64–5
    satellite litigation 81–2
civil restraint orders 345
civil rights 319, 323–8, 330–2, 340–1, 371, 379,
    390–2
    administrative decisions, see administrative
        decisions
    determination of civil rights and obligations 80,
        323, 325–32, 341, 348, 366, 371
        definition 327–9
        examples 331–3
    fair trial 323–33
    public law rights 325–6
civilised society 527–8, 591
clandestine entrant penalties 676–7
clandestine entrants 141, 339, 676
clandestine recordings 415, 569, 583
clear and constant jurisprudence, see constant
        jurisprudence
clerks 328, 349, 372, 381–2, 388
clinical judgment 44, 187
closed hearings 309, 354, 356–7, 660
closed judgments 310, 356
closed material procedures 150, 355–7
closed materials 252, 310, 354, 357
closeness of relationships/links 50, 165, 202, 483
coercive powers 51, 302, 448
cogency 393, 529, 627
cogent evidence 230, 255, 287, 508, 573
cohabitation 467–8, 621
commercial expression 570, 574
commitment 428, 467–8
    civil 278
common law 3–4, 56–7, 71, 87–8, 202–3, 320, 391

claims 203–4
negligence 202–4
powers 88, 116, 118, 278, 511
principles 3, 185, 196, 356, 366, 436, 605
and sufficiently accessible and precise
principle 87–9
common law test for bias 71, 214, 380
companies 49, 51, 53, 434–5, 644, 652, 664
insurance 111, 643, 651, 667
private 46, 51, 53, 176, 507–8, 510, 512
comparators 271, 274, 614, 625
compassionate grounds 241, 479, 535
compatibility, statements of 114, 144–5
compellable witnesses 493
compelling justification 197, 314, 491, 495
compensation 36–7, 153, 155–62, 164–8, 316–17,
657–9, 663
awards of 37, 156, 158, 160, 168, 316–17
deprivation of liberty 316–17
monetary 166, 169, 172, 175
payment of 151–2, 378, 514, 659, 665
property 658–9
competing interests 98, 100, 350, 432, 654
competing rights 358, 664
complexity 139, 311, 374, 376, 404, 475
compulsion 238, 340, 359
compulsory purchase orders 506, 517, 647, 662–3
computers 346–7, 349, 454
concessions 35, 115, 334
conditions
of bail 284, 509, 511
of detention 229, 239–43, 289
deportation and extradition 260–2
handcuffing outside of prison 241
physical restraint in detention 242
prisoners with medical conditions 240–1
seclusion and segregation 242
slopping out 242–3, 424
for treatment of a mental disorder 240
vulnerable detainees 239–40
of release 272, 282
confessions 359–60
confidence, breach of, *see* breach of confidence
confidentiality 197, 417, 420, 581–2, 586, 597–8,
600
protection 197, 581, 598
psychiatric medical records 564, 600
confinement 266, 271, 274, 286, 333
solitary 273, 424
confiscation 320, 361–2, 396, 671
orders 26, 361–2, 395–6, 509, 511, 640, 669–71
and presumption of innocence 395–6
post-conviction 126, 647
proceedings 26, 336–7, 339, 361–2, 671
confusion 33, 91, 94, 102, 114, 189, 232
conjoined twins 102, 182–3, 185–7, 225
conscience 83, 111, 260, 409, 527–9, 531, 535–7
public 365
conscientious objection 89, 535–6, 542

consent 80–1, 125, 238, 413–14, 417–18, 423,
458–9
adoption with 498
adoption without 497–8
parental 439, 471, 480
conspiracy 345, 352
constant jurisprudence 19–22, 401, 540, 622
constitutional rights 27, 549, 564, 629
construction 17, 66, 120, 123, 590
narrow 24, 103, 270
ordinary principles of 125, 368
purposive 17, 40, 63, 671
constructive knowledge 676
consultation
legal 401, 446
period of 135, 628
private 401, 414, 446
consumer protection 103, 657, 660
and property 660–1
contact orders 473–5, 496
contempt of court 284, 362, 384, 387, 404, 599,
601–3
contra mundum injunctions 197, 581
contracts 46, 48–9, 510, 513, 525, 533–4, 672
of employment 333, 534, 540, 599, 643
contributory fault 161
control 74–6, 78–9, 426–7, 646–7, 651–5, 659,
668–70
crowds 22, 275–6
effective 74–8, 94, 225, 263, 275, 482
immigration, *see* immigration control
judicial 295, 297, 331, 382
orders 15, 99, 272–4, 332, 340, 353–5, 454–5
as deprivations of liberty 272–4
and prevention of disorder or crime 454–5
over possessions 651–2
planning 42, 330, 504, 516, 593, 616, 634
control order proceedings 127, 235, 333, 458, 581,
585
controlled drugs 61, 125, 396
convenience 388, 469
administrative 254, 311–12
Convention rights
Art 2, *see* rights, to life
benefit of 31–9
burden of 39–40
given further effect 11–17
impact of other international conventions 12–13
nature and scope 11–12
non-absolute nature of majority 14–15
conversations 85, 446, 472, 535
private 414
telephone 9, 414
convicted murderers 139, 246, 282–3, 335, 390, 567
convicted prisoners 346, 631
voting 100
convictions 61–4, 169, 280, 348–9, 351–2, 378–9,
392–5
prior 351, 420, 463

copyright 558, 588–9, 642, 647, 663
core public authorities 40–5
    application 44–5
    as category of victim 33
    courts and tribunals 42
    definition 40–1
    determination of responsible authority 43–4
    Parliament 42–3
coroners 69, 71, 128, 206, 212–13, 216–20, 223–5
    inquests, see inquests
corporal punishment 534, 541, 545
corporate information 420–1
correspondence 83, 173, 409, 421, 429–30, 434, 454
    legal 429
    privileged 454
corruption 323, 577
costs 157–8, 173, 342, 344, 616, 624, 664–5
councillors 384, 566–7
counsel 68, 81, 125, 143, 350–1, 386–7, 394
counterfeit goods 397–8
courts martial 21, 388–9
covenants 132, 164, 520
covert surveillance 85, 446
creativity, judicial 439, 510
credibility 197, 363, 372, 406, 563, 587
criminal charges 170–2, 333–9, 366, 368, 371–4,
        377–9, 391–2
    definition 335–9
    domestic classification 335–7
    fair trial 333–40
        determination 333–4
        examples 339–40
        pre-trial decisions 334–5
        sentencing 335
    nature of offence test 337–8
    severity of potential penalty test 338–9
criminal justice
    deference 104–7
    and respect for home 509
    and s 3 HRA 125–6
    and s 4 HRA 139
criminal justice system 18, 80–1, 166, 235, 372,
        509, 554
criminal offences 333, 336–7, 392, 399–400, 405,
        568, 577
criminal procedure 11, 288, 336, 338–9, 402
criminal proceedings 217, 355, 358, 373, 376–8,
        381, 548
    reasonable time 373–5, 377–9
    retrospective effect 61–4
    satellite litigation 80–1
criminal trials 18, 21, 101, 108, 334, 461, 584
cross-examination 182, 228, 307, 358
crowd control 22, 275–6
Crown Prosecution Service 166, 176, 284, 336, 412,
        434, 587
cruelty to animals 53, 111, 456, 669
    deference 111
culture 7–9, 12, 21, 112, 144–5, 265, 485

cumulative effect 260, 272, 485
curfews 273, 284
    home detention 272, 282, 300, 454
custodial orders 430, 453
custodial sentences 420, 450, 453, 470
custody 210–11, 214–15, 219–21, 245–6, 295–6,
        375, 403
    photographs 419, 427, 448
customers 51, 365, 513, 664
    interests of 513, 664
Cyprus 246, 259, 267

D-type investigations 221
damages 32, 147, 150–68, 172–8, 315–17, 434–5,
        665–7
    assessment 168, 315, 317, 659
    exemplary 158, 162, 176
    general 164, 172, 174
    level of 163–4
    nominal 158, 177
    power to award 150–1
        court must have 152
    quantum of 154, 156, 164, 167, 174, 316, 665
    significant 176, 449
data
    biometric 119
    personal 4, 440, 462
databases 420, 447, 599
daughters 106, 462–3, 474, 479, 493, 500, 633–4;
        see also children
de facto family ties 466–8
death 69–71, 77–8, 181–3, 185–7, 195–7, 205–11,
        214–22
    in custody 219–21
    in hospital 222–3
    involving the armed forces 223–4
    involving the police 223
    of member of the armed forces 224
    penalty 107, 181, 188, 246, 282, 322
    risk of 192, 199, 201–2
    of vulnerable adults 224–5
decency 86, 366, 594
deception 95, 194, 271, 445, 483
decision-makers 69–71, 92, 100, 308, 482, 492, 574
declarations of incompatibility 66, 68, 99, 113–14,
        126–7, 132–41, 150–1
    problems with 137–8
declaratory judgments 147, 379
defamation 177, 410, 557, 574, 579–80
    look alike 580
defamatory statements 562, 579
defences 114–18, 349–53, 367–9, 396–400, 402–6,
        507–8, 522–5
    fair dealing 589–90
    justification 579
    qualified privilege 563, 567, 575–6, 578–9
    trump card 564
deference 182, 192–3, 320–1, 438–40, 454–5, 550,
        657

criminal justice 104–7
cruelty to animals 111
definition 96–8
degree of 107, 192–3, 270, 455, 512
and determination of incompatibility 96–112
expertise rather than democratic
        credentials 98–102
family law 110–11
housing 110
national security 107–8
pensions 109–10
policing 106–7
political decisions 112
in practice 104–12
prevention of terrorism 104–5
to primary decision maker
    in private life claims 438–40
    in property claims 657
rape complainant's prior sexual history 106
road traffic offences 105
sentencing 107
social and economic policy 109–11
social justice 111
state support 109
when appropriate 102–4
degrading treatment, see inhuman or degrading
        treatment or punishment
delay 167–70, 172–3, 292–3, 310–15, 317, 372–9,
        485–6
    deportation/removal 485–6
    remedies 167–8
    undue 373, 429, 475
    unreasonable 376, 378
democracy 5, 7, 98–9, 103, 112, 563, 566
democratic accountability 41, 46, 94, 382
democratic assemblies 107, 111, 270, 653
democratic credentials 98–100
democratic grounds 97, 320–1, 656
democratic process 111, 439, 595–7
democratic rights 595–7
democratic societies 105, 108, 340–2, 436–7, 444–5,
        542–4, 548–9
demonstrations 437, 447, 449, 558, 560, 590, 592–4
denial of access to court 346, 362
denial of shelter, food or the most basic
        necessities 231, 249
Denmark 77, 162, 272, 275, 552
dental profession 455
dental records 455
dependencies 72, 78–9
deportation 249–51, 253–5, 290–3, 440–2, 480–1,
        483–4, 488–9
    application 256–63
    assurances from destination states 253–4
    and children 484–5
    conditions of detention 260–2
    contracting states to ECHR 255
    delay 485–6
    detention of deportees 291–2

EU member states 255
evidential issues 251–2
exacerbation of illness and risk of suicide 256–7
fair trial 322–3
and family life 476–8, 480–6, 488
homosexuality 262, 442
ill-treatment by non-state actors 262–3
impact on other family members 484
inhuman or degrading treatment or
        punishment 250–63
length of detention 292–3
and manifestation of belief 542–3
medical treatment 441–2
    in destination state 258–9
nature of duty 250–5
and physical and psychological integrity 425–6
prevention of disorder or crime 488
proceedings 235, 290, 581
proportionality 482–3
real risk test 250–1
safe list of countries 254–5
unlawful 148
deprivation
    future 650–1
    of liberty 23, 161, 269–78, 289–90, 297
        access to court 298
        Art 5(4) 297–317
        attributes of a court 302–3
        control orders 272–4
        conviction by competent court 280–3
            causal link 280–2
        disproportionate period of detention 282–3
        crowd control 275–6
        definition 270–7
        detention of deportees 291–3
        enforceable right to compensation 316–17
        equality of arms 309–10
        extradition 293
        fairness 306–10
        independence and impartiality of court 303–6
        lawfulness 278–80
            not arbitrary 280
            extradition and deportation 280
            prescribed by law 279
            under domestic law 279
        lawfulness review 299–302
        minors 285–6
        non-compliance with the lawful order of a
                court or to secure the fulfilment of
                any obligation prescribed by law 284
        parents and children 275
        persons of unsound mind 286–9
            minimum conditions 286–8
            public safety 289
            treatment 289
        procedure prescribed by law 278
        proceedings decided speedily 310–16
        provision of care 274–5

reasonable suspicion of having committed an
offence 284–5
reasons for arrest 293–4
restrictions on liberty of movement 272
right to be released on bail 295–6
right to be tried within a reasonable
time 296–7
stop and search 276–7
unauthorised entry 290–1
of life, intentional 182, 184, 186–8, 200, 225
of possessions 647–51
of possessions/property 161, 639, 649–50, 652,
658–9, 665, 670
derogations 15–16, 181, 190, 227, 352–3, 458, 506
designated 11, 15–16
destination states/countries 250, 253–5, 258, 260,
322, 441–2, 481–2
assurances from 253–4
detained patients 44, 165, 190, 198–9, 237, 302, 454
speediness of determination 311–13
detainees 239–40, 266, 290, 298, 401, 621, 625
vulnerable 239
detection 105, 359, 452, 599, 636
detention 167–8, 239–42, 269–72, 277–85, 287–93,
295–307, 314–16; see also confinement;
deprivation, of liberty; imprisonment
asylum seekers 290–1
conditions of, see conditions, of detention
of deportees 291–3
duty to investigate 266
immigration 190, 219, 240, 266, 290
indefinite 16–17, 270
indeterminate 278
lawful 280, 285–6
lawfulness of 290, 298–300, 302–4, 310
period of 280, 292–3, 300
physical restraint in 242
prolongation of 167, 317
for treatment of a mental disorder, conditions of
detention 240
unlawful 316
determinate sentence prisoners 300, 308, 327, 332
determinate sentences 260, 299–301, 315, 636–7
lawfulness review 299–300
speediness of determination 315–16
determination of civil rights and obligations 80, 323,
325–32, 341, 348, 366, 371
deterrence 176, 246–7, 338, 438, 488, 502
devolution claims, judgments in 26
dialogue 21, 24, 98, 592
diaries 434, 448
differential treatment 614, 621, 625, 627, 629, 633
dignity 176, 185, 229–30, 236–7, 242–3, 424, 426
loss of 176, 229
right to die with 200, 236–7
diligence 292, 296
due 208, 290, 297
diplomatic and consular agents 75–6
and extra-territorial effect 76–7

direct discrimination 614–16, 622, 627, 634
disabilities 86, 169, 230, 289, 476, 617, 620
indirect discrimination 616–17
learning 274–5, 427
disability premium 613, 630
disciplinary proceedings 68, 328–30, 338, 446
prison 71, 339, 372
discipline 389, 536, 545
disclosure 92, 350–3, 355–6, 450–1, 462–4, 571,
598–603
duty of 228, 350–2
and equality of arms 350–2
full 351, 353
of information received in confidence 83, 560,
597–601
limited 353, 463
of police information 449–52
discomfort 164, 174
discretion 107–8, 115, 117–18, 325, 342–4, 369, 664
margin of 108, 162, 243
prosecutorial 18, 670
discretionary area of judgment 94, 96, 321, 634,
654, 669, 673
discretionary life prisoners 141, 303
discretionary life sentences 260, 282
discretionary powers 3, 148, 254
discrimination 22, 83, 109–10, 131, 134, 263,
605–38
analogous position 623–6, 628
application of prohibition 607–13
Art 3 608
Art 5 609
crime and sentencing 636–7
direct 614, 616, 622, 627, 634
education 613
environmental protection 634
family life 610–11
grounds 618–22
health 634–5
home 611–12
indirect 355, 541, 614–17, 622, 627, 631–2, 634
manifestation of belief 612
objective and reasonable justification 617, 623,
626–37
other status 618–21
positive duties 618
private life 609–10
protection against terrorist acts 637
protection of traditional family unit 635–6
Protocol No 1, Art 1 613
racial 28, 219, 628
reasonable time for change 628
remedies for breach 638
sex, see sex discrimination
social and economic factors 629–34
suspect grounds 621–2
within ambit of one or more Convention
rights 607–8
without 614–17

dismissal 539, 547, 574
    unfair 56, 364, 547
disorder, prevention of 436, 442, 445, 448, 480–1,
    488–9, 590
disproportionate burden 193, 234, 267, 372
disproportionate interference 93, 97, 450–1, 486–7,
    492, 495, 579–80
disqualification 214, 339, 380, 392
disruption 448, 450, 508, 538
    unlawful 594
distress 155, 161–2, 165, 174–7, 317, 590, 595
distributive justice 14
disturbance 266, 514, 665
DNA
    profiles 415, 423, 447
    samples 414–15, 423, 446–7, 615, 620, 625, 636
    tests 421, 468, 474, 501
dock identification evidence 367
doctors 46, 185, 200, 258, 594–5
dogs 53, 411, 552, 652, 669
domestic law 5–6, 9, 11–12, 84–5, 88, 278–80, 521
domestic violence 263, 496
double-jeopardy rule 567
dress 89, 530, 537–8
    Islamic 537
    religious 530, 537–8
drug addiction 286, 460–1, 568, 582
drug trafficking 320, 336–7, 362, 395–6, 511
drugs 352, 395, 433, 437, 509, 511, 543
    controlled 61, 125, 396
due diligence 208, 290, 297
duty of care 57, 203, 220, 348, 475
duty to investigate 204–25, 263–7
    armed forces 267
    circumstances triggering 205–11
    content 264–5
    death or life-threatening injuries post 2 October
        2000 205–6
    detention 266
    form of investigation 211–19
    inhuman or degrading treatment or
        punishment 263–7
    intentional or non-intentional killing by agent of
        the state 209–10
    intentional or non-intentional killing by non-state
        agent 210–11
    justiciability 208–9
    link to substantive obligations imposed by Art
        2 206–8
    nature 204–5, 263–4
    policing 266–7
duty–interest test 575

early release 139, 167, 317, 609, 626, 636–7
earnings 159, 171, 428, 617, 668
    enhanced 111, 668
economic interests 643–4, 660
economic policy 103, 108–9, 525, 656–7, 668

economic well-being 440, 442, 444, 480–1, 510,
    512–13, 672
    of the country
        and family life 480–7
        and home 512–14
        and private life 440–5
        and property 672–8
ECRCs, see enhanced criminal record certificates
ECtHR, see European Court of Human Rights
education 285–6, 516, 527, 534, 538, 613, 622
    discrimination 613
effective access 265, 298, 347
effective control 74–8, 94, 225, 263, 275, 482
effective drainage 514, 659, 665
effective implementation 205, 210–11
effective instructions 310, 354, 356
effective investigations 205, 209–10, 212–13,
    216–17, 220, 223, 266–7
effective protection 104, 193, 233, 541
effective remedies 18, 62, 70, 131, 138, 149–50, 155
effectiveness 23, 138, 262, 292, 372, 626
elected bodies 97, 111, 320–1, 656
elected branches of government 109, 622
elections 100, 384, 552, 579, 596–7
    free 100, 552, 639
electoral register 414, 444
electronic tagging 273, 454
embarrassment 107, 177, 424, 449
emergency protection orders 471, 495
employees 328, 333, 446, 453, 533, 539–41, 547
employers 87, 195, 328, 451, 539–40, 650, 677
    and manifestation of belief 547
    private 56, 539, 617, 668
employment 87, 428–9, 445, 449–50, 527–8, 537,
    539–40
    contracts 333, 534, 540, 599, 643
    law 324, 355, 547
    tribunals 56, 355–6, 364, 386
enforcement 49, 70, 73, 119, 133, 513, 515
    orders 342, 649
enhanced criminal record certificates (ECRCs) 132,
    419–20, 428, 449–50
enhanced earnings 111, 668
enhanced investigations 205, 208, 215, 221, 223
enquiries 101, 191, 212, 222, 243, 402, 474
entrapment, evidence obtained by 364–5
entry clearance 35, 468, 478–9, 486–7, 502, 552,
    558; see also visas
    and extra-territorial effect 76
    and family life 478–80, 486–7
    fees and other barriers 486–7
    historic injustice 487
    vulnerable people 502
environment 512, 515, 634, 640, 643–4, 647–8, 662
    public interest in preserving 515–17
environmental pollution 425, 508
    and physical integrity 425
    and respect for home 508–9
envrionment, and property 662–3

equality 99, 546, 629, 632
  of arms 13, 309, 320, 347–58, 400, 403, 405
    and child witnesses 357–8
    control order cases 353–5
    deprivation of liberty 309–10
    and disclosure 350–2
    and legal representation 350
    and national security 353–7
    and public interest, immunity 352–3
equipment 194, 201, 204, 208, 218, 652
error 156, 171, 174, 278–9, 332, 643, 649
ethnicity 418, 515, 616, 620, 634
European Court of Human Rights 12–14, 37, 73–6,
    150–1, 518–21, 653–6, 666–8
  principles applied in relation to remedies 156–62
  relationship between UK courts and 19–25
European Union (EU) 3–4, 255, 605
  law 4, 41, 90, 153, 155, 254, 639–40
euthanasia 182–3, 187
eviction 174, 504, 506, 518–21, 525, 614–15
  of travellers 229, 513
evidence 195–8, 252–5, 353–60, 362–4, 366–72,
    405–7, 445–6; see also burden, of proof
  cogent 230, 255, 287, 508, 573
  confession, see admissions; confessions
  dock identification 367
  exclusionary rules 367–8
  expert 286, 370
  and fair hearing 364–70
  fresh 227, 261
  hearsay 15, 307, 364, 366–7, 407
  illegally obtained 364–6
  material 87–8, 350–1, 511
  medical 237, 245, 256, 444
  obtained by entrapment 364–5
  oral 212, 215, 222, 238, 354
  procured by torture 322, 366
  torture 322, 366
  trial in absentia 368–70
evidential burden 125–6, 261, 349, 393, 396–7, 399
ex gratia payments 151, 613, 640–1
exacerbation of illness 256
exceptional circumstances 18, 127, 343–4, 492–3,
    496, 498, 524–5
exceptionality 483, 490, 521, 524
  test of 95, 483
exceptions 14, 20–2, 25, 61, 72, 277, 407
  interests of justice 599
  right to life 225
excessive alcohol 105, 359
excise duties and property 674–6
exclusions 35, 496, 498, 554, 558–9, 628–9, 631
executive manipulation 170, 377
exemplary damages 158, 162, 176
exemptions 167, 394, 615, 631, 634
  blanket 131, 440, 557
exercise of judgment 202, 608, 633
expectations 73, 173, 301, 416, 570, 643–4, 650
  legitimate 18, 73, 417, 641

reasonable 218, 413, 419, 673
expenses 147, 151, 158, 163, 200, 203, 670–1
expert evidence 286, 370
expertise 19, 38, 98–100, 102–4, 106, 234, 244
expression 460–1, 549–54, 556–66, 570–5, 579–82,
    586–9, 591–3
  definition 551–3
  freedom of, see freedoms, of expression
  political 566–7, 576
  protected 551–2, 570, 595
expulsion 72, 229, 441, 443, 477, 481, 489–90
extended sentences 300
extra-judicial activities 386–7
extra-territorial effect 59, 72–9
  acts of non-UK actors 72–3
  acts of UK public authorities 73–6
  and armed forces 77–8
  and British diplomatic and consular agents 76–7
  British Overseas Territories 79
  Channel Islands and Isle of Man 78
  effective control over an area 75–6
  and entry clearance 76
  exceptions to territorial jurisdiction 74–5
  jurisdiction as defined by European Court of
      Human Rights 74
  in practice 76–8
  state agent authority and control 75
extra-territorial jurisdiction 74–5
extradition 290, 322–4, 332, 340–1, 441–2, 476–7,
    488–91
  application 256–63
  Art 3 252–3
  assurances from destination states 253–4
  and children 489–91
  conditions of detention 260–2
  contracting states to ECHR 255
  crimes 87–8, 511
  EU member states 255
  evidential issues 251–2
  exacerbation of illness and risk of suicide 256–7
  fair trial 322–3
  and family life 476–8, 480–6, 488
  homosexuality 262, 442
  ill-treatment by non-state actors 262–3
  inhuman or degrading treatment or
      punishment 250–63
  lawfulness 293
  and manifestation of belief 542–3
  medical treatment 441–2
    in destination state 258–9
  nature of duty 250–5
  and physical and psychological integrity 425–6
  prevention of disorder or crime 488–91
  punishment and sentencing 259–60
  real risk test 250–1
  safe list of countries 254–5
extreme protest 593

failure to act 42, 59, 79–80, 118, 135, 174, 432

failure to legislate 42, 135–6
fair administration of justice 548
fair balance 90–1, 349, 492, 512–14, 657–60,
    662–3, 673
  test 672
fair dealing defence 589–90
fair determination 326–7, 331
fair hearing 161, 170, 334, 347–71, 377, 403, 571
  equality of arms, see equality, of arms
  and evidence 364–70
  giving of reasons 370–1
  independent and impartial tribunal, see
        independence and impartiality, tribunal
  and legal representation 362
  and oral hearings 363
  and presumption of innocence 361–2
  proper examination 364
  and right to silence 360–1
  and self-incrimination 358–60
fair-minded and informed observers 71, 214, 380,
    385, 387–8
fair trial 13, 102, 106, 159, 308, 319–408, 457
  access to court 340–8
  adequate time and facilities for preparation of
        defence 400
  criminal charges 333–40
  deportation and extradition 322–3
  determination of civil rights and
        obligations 323–33
  fair hearing, see fair hearing
  and interpreters 408
  and legal assistance, see legal assistance
  presumption of innocence, see presumptions, of
        innocence
  protection of rights and freedoms of
        others 457–8
  public hearing and public pronouncement 371–2
  public law rights 325–6
  and reasonable time, see reasonable time, and
        fair trial
  and right to be informed of nature and cause of
        accusation 399
  tribunal established by law 391–2
  and witnesses 405–7
fairness 125–7, 306–7, 319–20, 354–5, 362–4,
    368–70, 377–9
  and deprivation of liberty 306–10
  procedural 308, 488
false imprisonment 153, 164, 315
families 219–23, 465–6, 476–7, 481–3, 491–2,
    495–6, 609–11
  single parent 492, 677
family law 87, 324, 465, 474, 477, 480
  deference 110–11
  and s 3 HRA 128–9
family life 93–5, 174–5, 177, 431–4, 465–502,
    608–11, 636
  adoptive relationships 468–9
  children 466–8, 471–5, 494–502

compellable witnesses 493
  definition 465–6
  and deportation/extradition/removal 476–8, 480–
        6, 488
  discrimination 610–11
  dispersal of asylum seekers 487
  and economic well-being of the country 480–7
  and entry clearance/visas 478–80, 486–7
  interference 470–80
  parenting orders 493
  parents and children 466–8
  permitted interferences 480
  prevention of disorder or crime, see prevention
        of disorder or crime
  prisoners 491–3
  remedies 177
  same-sex relationships 469–70
  and state support 475–6
family members 216, 234–5, 414, 468, 476–7, 481,
    484–5
family ties 165, 467–8, 488, 497–8
  de facto 466–8
fathers 275, 461–2, 467–8, 473–4, 498–9, 501, 632;
    see also parents
  adoptive 468
  biological, see fathers, natural
  natural 467–8, 473, 496, 498–9
  unmarried 129, 467, 471, 500, 636
fault 44, 155–6, 208, 311, 369
  contributory 161
fees 51, 132, 344, 479, 486–7, 662
fertility clinics 427, 459
filming 413
  in public places 419
finality 343–4
fingerprints 423, 446–7, 615, 620–1, 625, 636
  retention 119, 423, 446, 609
fixed fees 400, 405
fixed penalties 141, 339, 673, 676
flagrant denial
  of justice 280, 322–3
  of rights 72–3, 277–8, 322, 441, 477–8, 542
floodgates argument 154, 186, 232
flooding, sewer 513–14, 659, 664–5
food 231, 249, 266, 530
forced marriages 479, 502
forcible medical treatment 237
foreign nationals 101, 108, 332, 626
foreign spouses 479, 487
foreseeability 86, 89, 655
forfeiture 674–6
formalities 83, 330, 363, 549, 560, 573
France 34–5, 158, 256, 258, 277, 372, 656
fraud 95, 360, 483, 670
free elections 100, 552, 639
free legal assistance 400–1
free speech, see freedoms, of speech
freedoms 5–11, 527–9, 548–57, 560–4, 572–5,
    580–9, 597–600

of assembly 83, 409, 593
of expression 5, 83–4, 120, 438, 458, 460–1,
     549–603
  and Art 9 588
  and authority and impartiality of
       judiciary 601–3
  democratic rights 595–7
  and disclosure of information received in
       confidence 597–601
  freedom to receive and impart information
       and ideas 555–6
  general principles 561–70
  importance 561–3, 582, 589
  interference 557–9
  medium, manner and timing of
       communication 553–5
  and national security 570–1
  permitted interferences 560–1
  positive duties 559
  prevention of disorder or crime 572–3
  and property 663
  protection of health or morals 573–4
  protection of rights of others 580–97
  protection of the reputation of others, see
       protection, of reputation of others
  and Protocol No 1, Art 1 588–90
  and public interest 564–70
  and respect for private life 460–2
  right not to be insulted and distressed 590–5
  s 12 HRA 561–2
fundamental 251, 278
of others 456, 514
of the press 550, 552, 561, 563–4, 584, 588–9,
     598–600
  importance 563–4
  to receive and impart information and
       ideas 555–6
of religion 528–30, 542
of speech 549, 551, 555, 559, 564, 602
of thought, conscience and religion 83, 409,
     527–48
  right to believe 529–30
fresh evidence 227, 261
frozen embryos 427, 459
frustration 37, 161, 166–9, 172–4, 317
fugitives 73, 250, 252–3, 257, 259, 341
full disclosure 351, 353
full market value 658, 677
functional public authorities 41, 50, 54
fundamental freedoms 251, 278
funding 52, 216, 222, 306, 400
  public 38, 41, 46–7, 51–2, 210, 630, 633
funeral benefits 616, 631
funeral pyres 528, 533
future deprivation 650–1

gardens 505
gender 14, 109, 231, 249, 619, 621
  reassignment 139, 421–2, 430

and s 4 HRA 139
general damages 164, 172, 174
general interest 90–1, 289, 652–4, 656–7, 660, 666,
     668
general principles 78, 155, 178, 561, 638–40, 652,
     654
general public interest 46, 109, 309, 369, 622, 627,
     633
Germany 171, 333, 335, 341, 378–9, 400, 404
Ghana 261
girls 209, 222, 541, 546, 625
golden thread 392
good faith 57, 163, 167, 276, 285, 529
goods 87, 214, 511, 640, 674–6
  branded 36
  condemned 339
  counterfeit 397–8
goodwill 644–6, 652
government departments 43–4, 142, 311
government ministers 29, 44, 137, 143, 389
  independence and impartiality 389–90
government policy 6, 50, 99, 143, 290, 516
governmental functions 45–6, 50–1
grandparents 224, 466, 641
gravity 325, 329, 333, 435, 442, 446, 448
Greece 41, 158–9, 161, 254–5, 260–1, 535, 658
gross negligence 193, 209
guarantee of independence and impartiality 97, 171,
     335, 382
guardians 33, 128, 472, 676
guidance 86, 138, 157, 386–7, 472–3, 493, 501–2
  clear 165, 190
guilty mind 398
Gurkhas 487, 625–6
gypsies 504–5, 510, 515, 517, 519–20, 615–16, 634;
     see also travellers

habeas corpus 269, 298, 312
hacking, phone 433–4
handcuffing 229, 241
Hansard 92, 359
  use in compatibility cases 141–3
harassment 415, 434, 522, 541, 552, 593
hardship 260, 477, 516, 632, 675
  economic 631
hare coursing 652, 669
harm 437–8, 453, 456, 471–2, 490, 492, 494–5
  physical 197, 495
  psychological 161, 229, 241
health 135–6, 323–4, 425, 455, 500–1, 543, 609–10
  children 501–2
  discrimination 634–5
  mental, see mental health
  physical 231, 242, 249
  protection of 83, 101, 112, 436, 442, 480, 510–
       11
  public 543–4, 566, 574, 612, 657
health authorities 51–2, 198, 288, 455, 457, 505,
     598

healthcare 189, 245, 433, 635
    workers 86, 414, 436, 455, 557, 567, 598
hearsay evidence 15, 307, 364, 366–7, 407
helplessness 161, 172
heroin 229, 365; *see also* drugs
heterosexual couples 129, 469, 612, 623, 635
high standards 163, 375, 570
HIV/AIDS 24, 161, 258, 442, 444
hobbies 551, 558, 574
holidays 274, 311, 673
home 7–9, 110, 165, 199, 273, 503–26, 611–12
    care homes 507–8, 512
    and criminal justice 509
    discrimination 611–12
    and economic well-being of the country 512–14
    and environmental pollution 508–9
    interference 505–9
    permitted interferences 510–11
    planning decisions 505–6
    possession proceedings 506–7, 518–26
    prevention of disorder or crime 511–12
    protection of rights and freedoms of others 514–26
    public housing standards 513
    sewage and drainage management 513–14
home detention curfews 272, 282, 300
Home Secretary 9, 139, 240, 246–7, 253, 553, 572
    independence and impartiality 303–4
    role 303, 335, 363
homelessness 325–6, 523, 526, 610, 613, 627, 630
homosexual couples 56, 129, 612, 623, 635
homosexuality 442, 533, 542, 635
    deportation/extradition 262, 442
    and manifestation of belief 544
hospitals 52–3, 165, 188–9, 198–200, 208–9, 241, 288–9
    death in 222–3
    secure 89, 112, 197, 219, 288–9, 412, 454–5
hotels 47, 532, 544
housing 91, 110, 129–30, 515, 525, 612, 633; *see also* accommodation; accommodation, and s 3 HRA
    associations 45, 50, 52, 524
    authorities 47, 326, 525
    benefit 510, 610, 613, 616–17, 625, 629–31
    deference 110
    social 50, 110, 510, 513, 526
    stock 50, 513, 522–3, 525, 612
human dignity, *see* dignity
human rights, *see Introductory Note and detailed entries*
Human Rights Bill 5–8, 133, 527
humanitarian grounds 258, 477
humanity 248–9, 366, 527
humiliation 184, 229, 236, 238–9, 241, 258, 260
hunting 411, 456, 537, 552–3, 621, 652, 654
husbands 466–7, 501, 509, 511, 532, 617–18, 640;
    see also spouses
hybrid public authorities 33, 40, 45–54

application 49–54
approval of minority buy-outs 54
definition 45–8
denial of application to participate in a farmers' market 53
enforcement of chancel repairs 49
ensuring HRA protection when contracting out 48–9
provision of care and accommodation 51–3
regulation of membership 53–4
seeking possession of a property 50
hydration 184–5, 187

identification 41, 57, 107, 212, 367, 548, 552
identity 196–7, 411–12, 418, 421–2, 460–1, 584–6, 598–9
    protection of, *see* protection, of identity
    witnesses 194–7
ignorance 382, 384
ill-health 414
    and sentencing 245
ill-treatment 228–30, 233–5, 238–9, 241–2, 249–51, 253–4, 262
    real risk of 261–2
    serious 228, 495
    severity of 228–30
illegally obtained evidence 364–6
illness 187, 208, 229, 235–8, 256, 311, 442
    mental 161, 236, 238, 240, 257–8, 495
    physical 256
    progressive degenerative 184, 236, 529
    right to die and right to die with dignity 236–7
    state responsibility 236
images 101, 415, 418–19, 448, 452–3, 570, 574
immediate risk 189, 191, 193, 195–6, 198, 224–5, 233
immediate risk of suicide 190, 198–9
immigration 104, 240, 483–5, 550
    appellate authorities 93–6, 482–3
    control 141, 441, 443–4, 481, 483, 610, 632–4
        effective 486, 488
        fair 485
        reasonable requirements of 291–2
    detention 190, 219, 240, 266, 290
    entry clearance 35, 76, 468, 478–9, 486–7, 552, 558
    lawful immigration policy 443, 481
    officers 76, 299, 355
    rules 95–6, 98, 370, 479, 482, 486, 502
    and s 4 HRA 141
imminent threat of war 181
immunity 345–6, 348, 571
    and access to court 345–6
    public interest 352, 356
    state 131, 345–6
impartial tribunals 14, 80, 139, 379, 382, 384–5, 390
impartiality 168, 171–2, 303, 305, 379–87, 389–91, 601–3; *see also* independence and impartiality

implementation 88, 271–2, 286, 443, 447, 481, 672
   effective 205, 210–11
implied repeal 119
impossible or disproportionate burden 193, 234, 267
imprisonment 239, 245–6, 260–1, 301–2, 322,
   335–7, 491–2; *see also* confinement;
   detention
   false 153, 164, 315
   life 65, 127, 246–7, 283, 322, 396
in-cell sanitation 242, 424
inaction 73, 170, 313, 377, 432, 476
incarceration, *see* imprisonment
incentives 126, 386, 633, 677
incidents of ownership 648–50
income 396, 643–5, 673; *see also* earnings
   support 109–10, 613, 630, 677
   tax 115, 414, 613, 624, 638
incompatibility 66, 113–14, 119–20, 123, 126–7,
   132–42, 150–1
   declarations of 66, 68, 99, 113–14, 126–7, 132–
      41, 150–1
   determination of 17, 83–112
      and deference 96–112
      necessary 90
      prescribed by law 84–90
      proportionality 90–6
      statements of compatibility 114, 144–5
      use of Hansard and other materials 141–3
inconsistency 103, 459; *see also* consistency
inconvenience 164, 174, 537
incorporation 5–7, 12, 53
   debate 4–6
indefinite detention 16–17, 270
independence 171–2, 214–15, 303, 305–6, 379–87,
   389–90, 433
   investigations 208, 214–15, 220–1, 266, 375
independence and impartiality
   application 385–91
   clerks of court 388
   courts martial 388–9
   deprivation of liberty 303–6
   government ministers 389–90
   guarantee of 97, 171, 335, 382
   Home Secretary 303–4
   judiciary 385–8
      earlier involvement with claimant 387–8
      extra-judicial activities 386–7
   juries 388
   local authorities 390–1
   Medical Member, Mental Health Tribunal 304–5
   Parole Board 305–6
   part-time and temporary judges 385–6
   remedies 168–9, 171–3
   and separation of powers 383–4
   test for 380–3
      objective 380–1
      rehearing 381–3
      subjective 380
   tribunal 379–91

and waiver 384
independent adjudicators 330, 339, 379, 530
independent investigation 208, 220–1, 266, 375
independent investigations 208, 220–1, 266, 375
indeterminate sentences 246, 281, 300, 314, 316
   lawfulness review 301–2
   speediness of determination 314–15
indictment 336–7, 375
indirect discrimination 355, 541, 614–17, 622, 627,
   631–2, 634
indirect victims 34
inequality 350, 404, 605; *see also* equality, of arms
inferences 208, 360–1, 398, 578
inflexibility 312, 353, 405, 492, 676
information received in confidence, disclosure 83,
   560, 597, 599
inhuman or degrading treatment or punishment 9,
   106, 166, 200, 227–67, 551, 581
   conditions of detention, *see* conditions, of
      detention
   deportation and extradition, *see* deportation;
      extradition
   duty to investigate, *see* duty to investigate
   illness, *see* illness
   medical treatment 237–8
   negative and positive duties distinguished 230–2
   positive duty 232–5
   sentencing 244–7
   severity of ill-treatment 228–30
   state support 248–9
   violence and threatening behaviour 243–4
injunctions 197, 416–17, 458, 460–2, 515–17,
   583–6, 588–90
   contra mundum 197, 581
   interim 562, 597
   super-injunctions 585–6
injunctive relief, *see* injunctions
injury 174, 177, 187, 190, 192, 201–2, 205–6
   life-threatening injuries 205, 210, 266
   personal 111, 164, 174, 177, 445, 667
   physical 174, 197, 581
   serious 77, 105, 195, 213–15, 221, 263, 266
injustice 161, 349, 362, 660
   social 656, 667
inmates, *see* prisoners
innocence 361, 392–4
   presumption of 90, 348, 358, 361, 392–9, 621,
      625
inquests 67, 69, 71, 205–6, 210, 215–20, 222–5
   and s 3HRA 128
inquiries 196–7, 214, 216, 219, 221–2, 265, 618
   internal 219–20
   public 19, 82, 207, 212, 215, 221, 267
   public planning 324, 327, 331
inquisition 213, 217, 220
insemination, artificial 100, 421, 472, 474, 492–3
instructions 79, 169, 351, 355, 368–9, 424, 544
   effective 310, 354, 356
   supplementary 95, 98

insults 434, 588, 590, 594
insurers 446, 650, 667–8
integrity
    bodily 185, 423
    personal 409, 534
    physical 423, 425
    psychological 174, 176, 412, 422, 425–6, 434,
        476
    territorial 83, 560
intention 62, 65, 135, 137, 239–40, 271, 533–4
    of Parliament 62, 116, 118, 127, 144, 336
intentional deprivation of life 182, 184, 186–8, 200,
    225
interests 307–9, 480–1, 490–3, 513–14, 545–9,
        563–6, 664–5
    best 184–8, 200, 423, 484–5, 490–2, 497–8, 500
    competing 98, 100, 350, 432, 654
    economic 643–4, 660
    general 90–1, 289, 652–4, 656–7, 660, 666, 668
    of justice 372, 400, 404, 407, 599, 603
    legitimate 216, 266, 585, 598
    of national security 83, 436, 440, 442, 560
    personal 34, 39, 380, 390
    private 447, 515, 663
    of public safety 276, 536, 543
interference 422–30, 442–6, 448, 501–15, 535–43,
        555–8, 644–57
    arbitrary 89, 431, 503
    disproportionate 93, 97, 450–1, 486–7, 492, 495,
        579–80
    with family life 470–80
    freedom of expression 557–9
    manifestation of belief 536–43
        change of approach 542
        deportation/extradition 542–3
        difficulties in establishing 536–8
        examples of interference 541–2
        examples of no interference 538–41
    permitted, see permitted interferences
    proportionate 437, 443, 446, 546, 668
    with respect for home 505–9
interferences with peaceful enjoyment of
        possessions 646–52
interim injunctions 562, 597
interlocutory measures 328
internal inquiries 219–20
internal investigations 208, 215, 221, 463
international law 11–13, 15–16, 23, 28, 63–4, 207,
    209
international obligations 3, 23, 28, 63, 71, 119, 264
interpretation 3–4, 12, 17–20, 24–6, 65, 119–22,
    128–9
    case law and instruments from other
        jurisdictions 27–8
    judgments in devolution claims 26
    principles of 17–19
    reports of Joint Committee on Human
        Rights 28–9
    s 4 HRA 132–4

interpretative obligations 120, 139, 368
interpretative process 139, 141
interpretative supremacy 112, 145
interpreters 408
intervention 32, 120, 182, 266, 491, 497, 661
interviews 148, 306, 408, 455, 553–4, 557–8, 594
intimidation 105, 244, 357, 406, 454
introductory tenants 504, 523–4, 526
intrusion 410, 414–15, 423, 435, 573, 583, 586
    degree of 438
inuman or degrading treatment or punishment,
        criminal law 248
invasion of privacy 155, 409, 435–6
investigations 69–70, 205–8, 210–24, 264–6, 376,
        573, 575; see also duty to investigate
    authorities must act of own motion 212
    effective 205, 209–10, 212–13, 216–17, 220,
        223, 266–7
    enhanced 205, 208, 215, 221, 223
    form 211–19
    independence 208, 214–15, 220–1, 266, 375
    internal 208, 215, 221, 463
    involvement of next of kin 216–17
    outcome 217–19
    police 219–20, 222, 578
    public scrutiny 215
investigative journalists 364, 587
investigative obligation 210, 217
Iran 332, 356, 370
Iraq 12, 19, 77–8, 201, 207, 209, 211
Ireland 16, 159, 161, 263, 347, 468
irrationality argument 94, 200
irrebuttable presumptions 111, 317, 501, 636
Islamic dress 537
Isle of Man 78, 673
isolated acts of even significant carelessness 432,
        476
Israel 38–9, 500, 572
Italy 171, 337, 403, 423, 425, 431, 490

Joint Committee on Human Rights 28–9, 45, 112,
        133, 138, 144
journalism 556
    intrusive 566
    responsible 563, 565, 576–8, 600
journalistic material 557, 586, 601
journalists 29, 34, 564, 569, 573, 577–9, 598–601
    investigative 364, 587
    sources 131, 598–601
judgment
    exercise of 202, 608, 633
    political 16, 108, 111, 202
    professional 288, 577
judicial assessment 365, 388
judicial bodies 103, 167, 302, 304, 306, 381, 390
judicial control 295, 297, 331, 382
judicial creativity 439, 510
judicial deference, see deference
judicial functions 304–5, 321, 384, 387, 390

judicial review 32, 38–9, 41, 92–3, 298–300, 330–1, 519–22
  proceedings 18, 67, 152, 228
juries 215, 217–18, 220, 360–1, 367–9, 391–3, 396
  independence and impartiality 388
  second 288, 603
jurisdiction 26–7, 62, 73–8, 327–8, 346, 382, 499–500
  extra-territorial 74–5
  full 330, 381
  territorial 35, 72–4
  universal 237
just satisfaction 147, 151–6, 158, 166, 171–2, 174–5, 177–8
  any other relief or remedy granted 153–4
  consequences of any decision 154
justice
  administration of 127, 209, 309, 364–5, 371–2, 587, 601–3
  distributive 14
  flagrant denial of 280, 322–3
  interests of 372, 400, 404, 407, 599, 603
  miscarriages of 352, 382, 388, 587
  natural 302, 306, 356–7, 384
  open 356, 457–8, 461, 548, 584
  procedural 126, 354
justiciability 92
  duty to investigate 208–9
  duty to safeguard life 190
justification 444–5, 473, 543, 545–7, 623–4, 626–38, 668–9
  defence of 579
  objective 396, 418, 606, 617
  objective and reasonable 617, 623, 626–37

kettling 275–6
knew or ought to have known principle 190–1, 233
knowledge 191, 233–4, 244, 386, 394, 397, 501
  constructive 676
  medical 299
  special sources of 95, 97–8, 483

land 504–6, 514, 640, 642, 648–52, 663–4, 666–7
landlords 55, 130, 132, 504, 513, 519, 524–5
landowners 506, 515, 652
lawful arrest 181, 284, 290
lawful authority 297, 437
  without 571
lawful detention 280, 285–6
lawful immigration policy 443, 481
lawful orders 284–5, 547
lawfulness 207, 290, 292–4, 297–300, 452, 652–3, 655–7
  deprivation of liberty 278–80, 299–302
  of detention 290, 298–300, 302–4, 310
  determinate sentences 299–300
  extradition 293
  indeterminate sentences 301–2
  requirement 84–5, 87, 290, 654

learning disabilities 274–5, 427
Lebanon 466, 477–8, 487
legal advice 148, 360, 362, 401–3, 457
  timely 207
legal assistance 350, 400–5
  and effective representation 403–4
  free 400–1
  and investigation process 402–3
  waiver of right 401
legal basis in domestic law 85
legal consultations 401, 446
legal proceedings 10, 31–2, 45, 60–1, 70, 583, 585
  anonymity orders in 583
legal representation 171–2, 216–17, 347, 350, 362, 671
  and access to court 347
  and equality of arms 350
  and fair hearing 362
legal representatives 216, 355–6, 369
Legal Services Commission 44, 210, 212, 216, 347, 650
legality 17, 69, 86, 207, 209, 292, 297
  principle 84, 436, 480
legislative overkill 106, 368
legislatures 105–8, 110–11, 439, 634, 656–7, 664, 668–9
legitimacy 98, 252, 280, 283, 344, 462
legitimate aims 90, 343–5, 358–9, 624, 626–7, 654–6, 666–7
legitimate expectations 18, 73, 417, 641
legitimate interests 216, 266, 585, 598
legitimate purposes 296, 457, 658
lenders 649–50, 660
lethal force 209, 211, 217, 237, 266
liability 70, 115, 117, 165, 250, 612–13, 648–50
  absolute 397
libel 579–80
  blasphemous 588
liberty 159, 161, 239, 246, 537, 541, 549–50; *see also* rights, to liberty and security
  personal 291, 355
  restoration of 272, 282
licences 168, 300–2, 308, 327, 332, 643–6, 650
  conditions/requirements 274, 309, 428, 451–2, 509, 515
life imprisonment 65, 127, 246–7, 283, 322, 396
life prisoners 247, 281
  discretionary 141, 303
life sentences 127, 241, 245–7, 259–60, 280, 282–3, 301; *see also* life imprisonment
  automatic 43, 127, 244–5, 283, 313
  discretionary 260, 282
  mandatory 107, 244, 246, 259, 270, 282–3, 304
  whole life tariff 246–7
life-sustaining treatment 184, 187, 200
life-threatening injuries 205, 210, 266
limitation periods 59–60, 203, 342–3, 649, 666
  and access to court 342–4

limitations 150, 152, 274, 342–3, 542–3, 649–50, 666–7
limited disclosure 353, 463
listing 311–12, 464
    provisional 328, 331, 464
Lithuania 255, 260–1, 263, 338
living instrument, Convention as 13–14, 17, 25
local authorities 47–9, 51–3, 128–9, 432–3, 471–4, 494–6, 519–23
    independence and impartiality 390–1
Local Government Ombudsman 164, 174–5
local planning authorities 42, 505, 515–17
look alike defamation 580
loss 159–61, 165, 169–72, 506, 645, 648, 658–9
    non-pecuniary 151, 157, 162, 165–6
    pecuniary 159, 167, 173, 317

magistrates 255, 296, 308, 427, 493, 511, 587
maladministration 164, 173, 175, 432
malice 84, 576
mandatory presumptions 393, 398
manifestation of belief
    and children 545–7
    conscientious objection 89, 535–6, 542
    discrimination 612
    and fair administration of justice 548
    health or morals 543–4
    and homosexuality 544
    identification 530–2
    interference 536–43
    outside protection of Art 9 534
    permitted interferences 543–8
    prisons and prisoners 547–8
    protected by Art 9 532–4
    protection of rights and freedoms of others 544–8
    and vulnerable people 545
manslaughter 218, 245, 296
margin of appreciation 97, 470
margin of discretion 108, 162, 243
market value 646, 648, 658–9
    full 658, 677
markets 53, 640, 661
    commercial 51
    financial 651
marriage 64, 68, 421–2, 466, 470, 477, 635–6
    consensual 480, 502
    forced 479, 502
married couples 131, 477, 544, 635, 638
material evidence 87–8, 350–1, 511
materiality 352, 457
maternity grants 610, 624, 631
maturity 427, 492, 502
measure of damages 158, 164
media 197, 553, 555–6, 569–73, 575, 581, 584–7
medical evidence 237, 245, 256, 444
medical examination 256, 457
medical knowledge 299

Medical Member, Mental Health Tribunal, independence and impartiality 304–5
medical necessity 236–7
medical negligence 203, 223
medical officers, responsible 44, 93, 103, 182, 227, 238–40, 423
medical records 455, 457, 599–600
medical treatment 182–3, 235, 238, 258, 423, 430, 441–2
    and deportation and extradition 441–2
    forcible 237
    inadequate 220, 251
    inhuman or degrading treatment or punishment 237–8
    and physical and psychological integrity 423
medication 257–8, 274
mental condition 190, 230, 240, 288, 305, 317
mental disorder 44, 52, 238, 240, 286–9, 309
mental health 161, 256, 303, 311, 317, 414, 425–6
    and s 4 HRA 140–1
    tribunals 303–4, 371
mental health detainees, see detained patients
mental illness 161, 236, 238, 240, 257–8, 495
mental patients 199, 239, 289, 345, 507
merits review 93–6
midwives 343, 661
military action 75, 207
military service 261, 535–6
minimum level of severity 228–30, 238–9, 244, 252
minimum term 280–1, 363, 390
minimum wages 613, 624, 647
ministers, government 29, 44, 137, 143, 389
minorities 442–3, 514, 518–19, 521, 659, 665, 671
minors 479; see also children
    deprivation of liberty 285–6
miscarriages of justice 352, 382, 388, 587
misconduct 415, 578
    serious professional 68, 381, 422
mitigation 161, 308
mobile homes 515, 517
modified breach of confidence 597
monetary compensation 166, 169, 172, 175
monetary value 643, 645
moral values 456, 532
morals 436, 442, 473, 480, 543, 573–4, 668–9
    protection of 456, 573, 668–9
morning after pill 594–5
mortgages 642, 663, 665, 670–1
most basic necessities 231, 249
mothers 457, 467–8, 470–1, 473–4, 476–8, 490–2, 498–501; see also parents
motivations 7, 209, 271, 293, 499
motor neurone disease 184, 236, 529
murder 107, 194, 197, 246–7, 282–3, 288–9, 581
    trials 57, 220
murderers, convicted 139, 246, 282–3, 335, 390, 567
Muslim prisoners 532, 542, 547

narrow construction 24, 103, 270

national authorities 22, 90, 104, 149–50, 191, 475, 655

national budget deficit 678

national flag 554, 591

national origin 620, 622, 637

national security 355, 357, 440, 564, 570–2, 599, 602
  control order cases 353–5
  deference 107–8
  and equality of arms 353–7
  and freedom of expression 570–1
  interests of 83, 436, 440, 442, 560
  and private life 440

nationalisation 647, 658
  in the public interest 677

nationality 140, 484, 541, 619–20, 622, 625, 637
  indirect discrimination 616

natural fathers 467–8, 473, 498–9

natural justice 302, 306, 356–7, 384

natural parents 466, 468–9, 498

near deaths in custody 221–2

near-suicides 208, 221–2

necessity 237, 241, 451, 454–5, 457, 462–3, 496–8
  administrative 312–13
  medical 236–7

negative duties 187, 230–1, 233, 240, 248, 425, 471

negligence 37, 153, 156, 195, 198, 202–4, 347–8
  casual acts of 189, 199
  claims 36–7, 165
  common law 202–4
  gross 193, 209
  medical 203, 223

Netherlands 178, 277–8, 308, 311, 333, 335, 466–8

newspapers 57, 461, 563, 565, 579–80, 584–5, 598–9

NGOs, see non-governmental organisations

niqab 532, 538–9, 546, 548

no-fault system 342

noise 132, 411, 508, 514, 648, 659, 663
  traffic 425, 508

nominal damages 158, 177

non-disclosure 351–3, 450

non-governmental bodies 46, 57, 435, 582

non-governmental organisations (NGOs) 5, 32, 40–1

non-intentional killing 209–10

non-nationals 34, 94–5, 98, 108, 482, 625

non-pecuniary damage 37, 158–62, 165, 171–2, 317

non-pecuniary loss 151, 157, 162, 165–6

non-resident parents 324, 610

non-state agents 263
  intentional or non-intentional killing by 210–11

normal life 185, 197, 581

Northern Ireland 69–70, 107, 133, 206, 244, 301, 541

Norway 171, 310, 378–9, 494, 499

notification 79, 332, 567, 651
  requirements 139, 451–2

nuisance 57, 164, 522, 524, 592, 659, 663

nurses 198, 343

nursing homes, see care, homes

nutrition, artificial 184–5, 187

objective and reasonable justification 617, 623, 626–37

objective assessment 231, 249, 385

objective justification 396, 418, 606, 617, 628

objective tests 196, 228–9, 380, 387–8

obligations 48–9, 69–70, 204–8, 210, 221–5, 323–5, 327–9
  operational 190, 198, 208
  positive 165–6, 188–90, 200–5, 230–8, 430–4, 473–5, 618
  procedural 37, 69–70, 77, 182, 201, 210, 217
  substantive 69, 190, 201, 206, 208, 224
  unqualified 218, 233, 513

observers, fair-minded and informed 71, 214, 380, 385, 387–8

occupiers 98, 518–20, 522–5

offender naming schemes 452–3

omissions 68, 76, 117, 167, 184, 186–7, 441–2

onus of proof, see burden, of proof

open justice 356, 461, 548, 584
  protection of rights and freedoms of others 457–8

operational decisions 201–2, 204

operational duty 189–90, 195, 199

operational obligations 190, 198, 208

oppression 257, 359–60

oral evidence 212, 215, 222, 238, 354

oral hearings 132, 308–9
  and fair hearing 363

Osman test 189, 191, 194, 197, 203, 233, 244

other status 618–21

overkill, legislative 106, 368

ownership 29, 49, 87, 647–8, 651, 666
  incidents of 648–50

pain 101, 164, 174, 188, 266, 392, 545

parental authority 275

parental consent 439, 471, 480

parental responsibilities 324, 331, 469, 472, 474, 498, 501

parenting orders 493

parents 466–8, 471–2, 474–5, 490–1, 493–502, 534, 622; see also family life; fathers; mothers
  adoptive 22, 35, 468–9, 635–6
  natural 466, 468–9, 498
  non-resident 324, 610
  separated 617, 632

Parliament
  as core public authority 42–3
  intention of 62, 116, 118, 127, 144, 336

Parliamentary Ombudsman 164

Parliamentary sovereignty 4, 113–15, 119, 121, 133, 138, 382

parochial church councils 27, 32, 44–5, 49, 118, 639, 648

parole 139, 247, 259, 300

eligibility dates 300, 315
  scheme 300, 614
Parole Board 43–4, 167–8, 280–3, 297, 300–10,
    313–17, 636–7
  independence and impartiality 305–6
  and s 3 HRA 127
part-time and temporary judges 385–6
paternity 421, 468, 501
patients 140–1, 183–9, 197–200, 287–8, 298–9, 302,
    423
  detained 44, 165, 190, 198–9, 237, 302, 454
  mental 199, 239, 289, 345, 507
  restricted 289, 298
payments 116, 118, 404–5, 641, 643, 674, 677–8
  ex gratia 151, 613, 640–1
  extra-statutory 116
  widow's 116, 613, 624
PCC, see Professional Conduct Committee
peaceful enjoyment 639, 641, 646, 648, 651–5,
    662–3, 672
  interferences with 646–52
pecuniary damage 158–60
pecuniary losses 159, 167, 173, 317
penalties 332, 334, 337–40, 661, 670, 672, 674–6
  financial 338, 670
pensions 342, 608, 625–6, 628–9, 642–3, 647
  deference 109–10
  widows 109, 613, 624, 629–30
permanent vegetative state, see PVS
permission 130, 345, 347, 496, 499–500, 553, 645
  planning 172, 515–17, 615, 644
permitted interferences 570
  family life 480
  freedom of expression 560–1
  home 510–11
  manifestation of belief 543–8
  private life 436–40
    in accordance with the law 436–7
    deference to primary decision maker 438–40
    general factors affecting proportionality
      analysis 437–8
personal autonomy 200, 411, 418, 423, 425–7, 445
personal characteristics 248, 619, 621–2
personal circumstances 42, 244, 519–20, 523
personal data 4, 440, 462
personal information 57, 415–16, 427, 435, 440,
    446–7
personal injury 111, 164, 174, 177, 445, 667
personal integrity 409, 534
personal interests 34, 39, 380, 390
personal possessions 642–3
personality 176, 410, 412, 415, 438, 527, 619
persuasive burden of proof 393, 398
phone hacking 433–4
photographs 413–15, 417–18, 426, 447–8, 452–3,
    461, 551–2
  in public places 417–19
  unauthorised 88, 427

physical and psychological integrity 174, 176, 412,
    422–6, 434, 476
  and deportation and extradition 425–6
  and environmental pollution 425
  and medical treatment 423
  and policing 423–4
  and prison 424–5
physical harm 197, 495
physical health 231, 242, 249
physical injury 174, 197, 581
physical integrity, see physical and psychological
    integrity
physical violence 235, 545, 581
planning 201–2, 505, 662
  control 42, 330, 504, 516, 593, 616, 634
  permission 172, 515–17, 615, 644
  and property 662–3
Poland 130, 257, 261, 289, 311, 324
police 84–6, 194–6, 222–5, 275–7, 401–3, 418–20,
    446–9
  actions 106, 419, 560, 590
  convictions and other information retained
    by 419–20
  officers 87–9, 191–2, 195–6, 277, 509, 512, 577
  photography 447–8
  powers 276–7, 447
  risk assessment 192, 196
  stations 85, 277, 402–3, 446, 454
  warnings 139, 451
police interrogation 402–3
police investigations 219–20, 222, 578
policing 189, 194, 233–4, 447, 453, 586, 594
  deference 106–7
  duty to investigate 266–7
  and physical and psychological integrity 423–4
  pre-emptive 593–4
  and private life 433–4; see also private
    information
political decisions 637
  deference 112
political expression 566–7, 576
political information 564, 566, 575
  and public interest 566–7
political judgment 16, 108, 111, 202
political parties 109, 559, 596, 621
political speech 563, 566, 595
pornographic literature 101, 570, 574
positive duties/obligations 79–80, 165–6, 188–90,
    200–5, 230–8, 248–9, 430–4, 618
  children 473–5
  discrimination 618
  freedom of expression 559
  inhuman or degrading treatment or
    punishment 232–5
    application 234–5
    circumstances triggering duty 232–3
    knew or ought to have known 233
    reasonable measures 233–4
  respect for home 509–10

respect for private life 430–4
  policing and criminal justice 433–4
  state support 431–3
  test to establish breach 431
to safeguard life 188–204
  application 194–202
  Art 2 and common law negligence 202–4
  justiciability 190
  knew or ought to have known principle 190–
    1, 233
  nature of duty 188–9
  protection of identity generally 197
  protection of members of the armed
    forces 200–2
  protection of those in the care of the
    State 197–200
  protection of those whose lives are at risk
    from the acts of another 194–5
  protection of witness identity 194–7
  real and immediate risk to life 191–3, 196,
    224
  reasonable measures 193–4
  state responsibility 189–90
possession
  adverse 666–7
  orders 518–20, 522–3
  proceedings 68, 132, 332, 506–7, 518–26
    lower courts post Pinnock 524–6
    Pinnock and Powell 520–3
possessions 640–6
  business 643–4
  control over 651–2
  deprivation of, see deprivation, of possessions/
    property
  peaceful enjoyment of 639, 646, 652–3, 655,
    660, 662–3, 672
    interferences with 646–52
  personal 642–3
post-conviction confiscation 126, 647
potential victims 32, 34, 48, 511
powers 86–90, 113–15, 117–19, 132–3, 381–4,
    519–22, 664–6
  common law 88, 116, 118, 278, 511
  discretionary 3, 148, 254
  general 117, 133, 137
  police 276–7, 447
  separation of 109, 342, 383–4, 390
  statutory 41, 51, 53, 195, 278, 528, 560
pre-emptive policing and protest 593–4
pre-trial decisions, criminal charges 334–5
premises 504–5, 509, 511, 519, 573–4, 612, 632
preparatory hearings 81, 125, 367, 571
prescribed by law principle 84–90
  applied in a way which is not arbitrary 89–90
  legal basis in domestic law 85
  sufficiently accessible and precise 85–9
press, freedom of the 550, 552, 561, 563–4, 584,
    588–9, 598–600
presumptions 255, 292, 296, 358, 361, 498–9, 501

of innocence 90, 277, 295, 348, 358, 621, 625
  application 395–9
  and burden of proof 393–4
  and confiscation orders 395–6
  and drugs offences 396–7
  and fair hearing 361–2
  and fair trial 392–9
  and road traffic offences 397
  and terrorism offences 398–9
  and trade marks offences 397–8
  irrebuttable 111, 317, 501, 636
  mandatory 393, 398
  rebuttable 441
  strong 167, 350
prevention of disorder or crime 83, 101
  control orders 454–5
  deportation/extradition/removal 488–91
  disclosure of police information 449–52
  evidence obtained by secret filming or
    recording 445–6
  freedom of expression 572–3
  interferences with respect for family life 488–93
  interferences with respect for home 511–12
  interferences with respect for private life 445–55
  offender naming schemes 452–3
  police photography 447–8
  prisoners 453–4
  stop and search 448–9
  taking and retention of fingerprints,
    DNA samples and other personal
    information 446–7
prevention of terrorism 80, 104, 274, 398
  deference 104–5
  and s 4 HRA 140
primary decision makers 94, 96–100, 102–4, 182,
    192–3, 438–9, 550
primary legislation 9–10, 18, 20, 55, 91–2, 150–1,
    254
  defence of 113–45
    s 3 HRA 119–32
    s 4 HRA 132–41
    s 6(2) HRA 114–19
principles of interpretation 17–19
prior convictions 351, 420, 463
prison 167–8, 214–15, 239–41, 245–7, 282, 289,
    491
  authorities 208, 215, 493, 572
  cells 3, 96, 209, 239, 242, 266, 424
  conditions of detention, see conditions, of
    detention
  disciplinary proceedings 71, 339, 372
  governors 214, 221, 463
  in-cell sanitation 242, 424
  and manifestation of belief 547–8
  and physical and psychological integrity 424–5
  slopping out 242, 424
  young offenders institutions 209, 215, 219, 221
Prison Service 192, 196, 205, 209, 214, 219–22,
    491–2

prisoners 239–43, 245–7, 280–3, 308–10, 313–17, 452–4, 620–2
  access to court 346–7
  conditions of detention, *see* conditions, of detention
  determinate sentence 300, 308, 327, 332
  family life 491–3
  female 492, 617
  life sentence 299, 338–9, 363, 472
    speediness of determination 313–14
  manifestation of belief 547–8
  prevention of disorder or crime 453–4
  release, *see* release
  remand 625
  rights 132, 309, 463, 668
privacy 55, 155, 409–10, 413–17, 427, 433–8, 462–3
  invasion of 155, 409, 435–6
  reasonable expectation of 413–20, 427, 586
private bodies 40, 47, 54–7, 435
  development of common law 56–7
  interpretation of primary legislation in accordance with s 3 HRA 55–6
private companies 46, 51, 53, 176, 507–8, 510, 512
private consultation 401, 414, 446
private employers 56, 539, 617, 668
private figures 584, 588
  private lives of 588
private functions 33, 40, 45, 47, 50
private information 176, 413, 420, 458, 582, 588
  convictions and other information retained by police 419–20
  corporate information 420–1
  filming in public places 419
  photographs in public places 417–19
  private character 413–15
  public figures and private life 415–16, 581
  relationships between parties 416–17
private interests 447, 515, 663
private life 175–6, 409–65, 498–9, 581–2, 585–6, 597–8, 608–11
  and access to court 457
  applications for anonymity 458
  autonomy 426–7
  to be respected by whom 435–6
  children and vulnerable adults 462–4
  correspondence 429–30
  and deportation and extradition 441–4
  discrimination 609–10
  and economic well-being of the country 440–5
  and freedom of expression 460–2
  identity 421–2
  information, *see* private information
  meaning of everyone 434–5
  and national security 440
  permitted interferences 436–40
  physical and psychological integrity, *see* physical and psychological integrity

positive duties, *see* positive duties/obligations, respect for private life
prevention of disorder or crime, *see* prevention of disorder or crime
  and protection of health 455–6
protection of rights and freedoms of others, *see* protection, of rights and freedoms of others
  and public figures 415–16
  remedies
    breaches by private sector 176–7
    breaches by public authorities 174–6
  and right to life 458–9
  scope 411, 419, 427–8
  self-determination 426–7
  social life and working life 427–9
private property 415, 438, 583, 658
privilege 348, 575–6, 648
  professional 85, 414
  qualified 563, 567, 575–9
privileged correspondence 454
probabilities 167, 287, 316–17, 364, 366, 393, 395–7
  balance of 287, 316–17, 364, 366, 393, 395–7, 399
procedural duties 69, 182, 186, 212, 217, 221, 263
procedural fairness 308, 488
procedural justice 126, 354
procedural obligations 37, 69–70, 77, 182, 201, 210, 217
procedural protections/safeguards 333, 335, 354, 518–19, 636, 657, 660
procedural requirements 69, 224, 252, 264, 478, 486, 660
procedural rights 293, 325, 329, 452, 471–3, 510, 659
  children 472–3
  property 659–60
Professional Conduct Committee (PCC) 67–8, 70, 381, 391, 562
professional judgment 288, 577
professional privilege 85, 414
professions 324, 328, 331, 343, 405, 411, 661
profit 48, 51, 53, 663, 671, 673, 675
progressive degenerative illness 184, 236, 529
prohibition of discrimination, *see* discrimination
promptness 212, 294
proof 125–6, 287, 362, 366, 380, 393, 395–6; *see also* evidence
  burden of 61, 125, 287, 307, 393
proper examination 364
property 161–2, 324–5, 395–6, 513–14, 517, 522–4, 639–78
  and adverse possession 666–7
  and anti-terrorism measures 672
  and budget deficit reduction 678
  and child support 677
  and clandestine entrant penalties 676–7
  compensation 658–9

and consumer protection 660–1
deference to primary decision maker 657
deprivation of, *see* deprivation, of possessions/
    property
and economic well-being of the country 672–8
and excise duties 674–6
and freedom of expression 663
interferences with peaceful enjoyment of
    possessions 646–52
justification of interferences 652–60
lawfulness of interference 655–6
legitimate aims 656–7
and nationalisation in the public interest 677
peaceful enjoyment of 639, 654
planning and environment rules 662–3
possessions, *see* possessions
prevention of crime and illegality 669–72
private 415, 438, 583, 658
procedural rights 659–60
proportionality 657–60
and protection of morals 668–9
and Protocol No 1, Art 1 664–7
and recovery of overpaid welfare benefit 678
rights of others 663–7
and social justice 667–8
and taxation/taxes 672–4
and vulnerable people 667
proportionality 97–102, 110–12, 519–25, 626–7,
    653–5, 657–9, 666–7
assessment of 87, 92, 98, 100, 482, 485, 656–7
definition 90–1
deportation/removal 482–3
and determination of incompatibility 90–6
merits review 93–6
property 657–60
reasonable relationship of 83, 320, 343, 606,
    626–7, 652, 657
shift from *Wednesbury* 92–3
test 83, 92, 341, 345, 622, 627, 653–4
proportionate interference 437, 443, 446, 546, 668
proportionate response 292, 359, 361, 433, 487,
    495, 497
prosecuting authorities 21, 61–3, 68, 373–4, 380,
    386, 396
prosecution 80–1, 295–7, 350, 352–3, 361–2, 392–4,
    396–9
prosecutorial discretion 18, 670
prosecutors 349, 351, 377, 379, 392, 394, 396–8
protected expression 551–2, 570, 595
protection
    of children 452, 462, 475
    of confidentiality 197, 581, 598
    effective 104, 193, 233, 541
    of health 83, 101, 112, 436, 442, 510–11, 573–4
        and respect for private life 455–6
    of human rights 3–4, 24, 45, 92, 158
    of identity 197, 586–7
        witnesses 194–7
    of members of the armed forces 200–2

of morals 456, 573, 668–9
procedural 518–19, 636, 657
of property, *see* property
public 167, 281, 301
of public order 536, 543
of reputation 563–4
    of others 574–80
of rights and freedoms of others
    fair trial and open justice 457–8
    family life 494–502
    freedom of expression 580–97
    home 514–26
    manifestation of belief 544–8
    private life 456–64
    property 663–7
    witnesses 194, 197
protest 106, 234, 551, 553–4, 590–4, 608, 614
    camps 554, 592
    extreme 593
    and pre-emptive policing 593–4
    and right not to be insulted or distressed 590–4
protesters 244, 554, 558, 560, 586, 590–3
psychiatric patients, *see* mental patients
psychiatrists 43, 53, 287–8, 302
psychological harm 161, 229, 241
psychological integrity 174, 176, 412, 422, 425–6,
    434, 476
public acknowledgement of breach 148, 170, 377–8,
    587
public authorities 9–10, 39–51, 54–7, 59–68,
    113–18, 149–55, 517–20
    burden of Convention rights 39–40
    core 40–5
    hybrid 33, 40, 45–54
public authority landlords 98, 518
public benefit 50, 525, 612, 631
public conscience 365
public domain 415–17, 568, 585
public duties 47, 523, 567
public emergency 16, 101, 103, 108
public figures 415–16, 438, 458, 460–1, 566–9,
    581–2, 585
    and private life 415–16, 581–3
    and public interest 567–70
public functions 39–40, 45–8, 50–4, 648
public funding 38, 41, 46–7, 51–2, 210, 630, 633
public health 543–4, 566, 574, 612, 657
public hearings 80, 319, 371–2
public inquiries 19, 82, 207, 212, 215, 221, 267
    closed 556
public interest 488–91, 563–71, 575–9, 582–3,
    588–9, 600–1, 658–65
    defence 564, 571, 589
    definition 565–6
    and freedom of expression 564–70
    general 46, 109, 309, 369, 622, 627, 633
    immunity 352, 356
        and equality of arms 352–3
    legitimate 460, 553, 567

nationalisation in the 677
and political information 566–7
in preserving the environment 515–17
and public figures 567–70
and qualified privilege 577
strong/important 352–3, 371, 375, 490, 567, 582
public law rights, fair trial 325–6
public life 566, 568, 570
public order 371–2, 543, 572–3
public places
    filming in 419
    photographs in 417–19
public planning inquiries 324, 327, 331
public policy 345, 525, 603, 672
public protection 167, 281, 301
public resources 344, 568, 629
public safety 289, 299, 309, 436, 442, 536, 543
    interests of 276, 536, 543
    and persons of unsound mind 289
public scrutiny 211, 215, 437, 596
    investigations 215
public sector tenants 526, 621, 625
public sector workers 326–7
publication 417–18, 457–8, 557–8, 561–9, 575–8,
    583, 585–7
publicity 371, 380, 388, 413, 415–16, 453, 587
publishers 414, 552, 563, 576, 580
punishment 227–8, 230–1, 244–8, 250–3, 334–5,
    337–8, 394–5
    corporal 534, 541, 545
    inhuman or degrading 244, 246–7, 531
purpose of Human Rights Act 1998 8–10
purposive construction 17, 40, 63, 671
PVS (permanent vegetative state) 183–4, 187, 238,
    423

qualified privilege defence 563, 567, 575–9
    nature 576–7
    and public interest 577
quality of life 184, 186, 188, 426
quantum of damages 154, 156, 164, 167, 174, 316,
    665
quiet enjoyment, see peaceful enjoyment

race 109, 616, 618, 622, 625, 630, 634
racial abuse 243–4
racial discrimination 28, 219, 628
racism 27, 219, 235, 569, 581
rape 125, 367, 415, 458, 585–6
    deference 106
rational explanation test 622
rationality 94, 326, 368, 622
real and immediate risk to life 191–3, 196, 224
real risk 188, 245, 250–6, 260–1, 263, 322–3, 477–8
    test 244, 250–1
reasonable balance 514, 664, 677
reasonable expectations 218, 413, 419, 673
    of privacy 413–20, 427, 586
reasonable expedition 212, 267, 293

reasonable foundation, without 111, 626–7, 632,
    656, 674
reasonable measures 80, 191, 199–200, 232, 262,
    431
    inhuman or degrading treatment or
        punishment 233–4
    to safeguard life 193–4
reasonable period 167, 292–3, 295, 316
    for amendment of domestic law 134
reasonable suspicion 89, 270, 276–7, 284, 398, 449
reasonable time 33, 169–71, 293, 295–6, 368–9,
    372–5, 377–8
    application 375
    civil proceedings 376
    criminal proceedings 373–5, 377–9
    determination 374–6
    and fair trial 372–9
    guarantee/requirement 26, 148, 169–70, 310,
        373–8
    post conviction 169
    pre conviction 170–1, 377
    remedies 376–9
    right to be tried within a 296–7
    start of time period 373–4, 376
reasonableness 80, 190, 193, 199, 234, 244, 522–3
rebuttable presumptions 441
reconciliation 468, 572
recordable offences 336, 451, 625, 636
records
    dental 455
    medical 455, 457, 599–600
recreation 274, 411, 530, 553, 669
redress 7, 25, 40, 63, 219, 600
    adequate 36–7, 165
    individual 265
reform of Human Rights Act 29
refugee status 332, 479, 486
rehearing 372, 381–2, 388, 497
    administrative decisions 382–3
relatives 173, 200, 209, 216, 258, 431, 434
    biological 473, 498
    close 34, 73, 625, 630
release 168–70, 246–7, 280–3, 295, 297–301,
    304–6, 314–15
    early 139, 167, 317, 609, 626, 636–7
reliance 277–9, 282–6, 308–12, 323–7, 335–8,
    359–61, 378–82
religion 527–33, 535, 537–41, 543, 546–8, 588,
    618–19
religious beliefs 529, 531–3, 537–41, 543–4, 546,
    588, 595
religious dress 530, 537–8
religious life 528, 538
religious organisations 44, 528, 533
religious worship 612, 632
remand prisoners 625
remedial orders 10, 28, 42, 79, 133, 135
remedies 33–4, 130, 136–8, 147–78, 311–12, 376–7,
    637–8

Art 2 164–6
Art 3 166
Art 5 166–9
Art 6 169–73
Art 8 173–7
Art 14 178
damages, *see* damages
delay 167–8
discrimination 638
effective 18, 62, 70, 131, 138, 149–50, 155
family life 177
independence and impartiality 168–9
just and appropriate principle 148
just satisfaction, *see* just satisfaction
principles applied by European Court of Human
    Rights 156–62
private life
    breaches by private sector 176–7
    breaches by public authorities 174–6
reasonable time 376–9
    post conviction 169, 378–9
    pre conviction 170–1, 377–8
s 9(3) HRA and Art 5(5) 166–7
removal 256–8, 291–3, 425–6, 441–3, 476–7,
    480–1, 484; *see also* deportation
enforced 242, 293
reporting of legal proceedings 587–8
representation, legal 171–2, 216–17, 347, 350, 362,
    671
representative bodies as victims 35–6
representatives 212, 222, 308–9, 355, 384, 490
    legal 216, 355–6, 369
reputation 415, 422, 429, 560, 563–4, 574–5, 579
    protection of, *see* protection, of reputation
reservations 11, 15–16, 204, 626
residence 273, 452, 477, 620, 630
    orders 474, 499–501, 620, 624, 631
residential care 49, 471
resources 173, 182, 313–14, 326, 431–2, 445,
    512–13
    allocation 201, 215, 312, 432, 513, 550
    arguments 80, 182, 270, 512
    financial 512, 643
    public 344, 568, 629
respect
    for family life, *see* family life
    for home, *see* home
    for private life, *see* private life
respect for home, positive duties 509–10
responsibilities 7–9, 43–8, 97–8, 244–5, 249–50,
    312, 560
responsible journalism 563, 565, 576–8, 600
responsible medical officers (RMOs) 44, 93, 103,
    182, 227, 238–40, 423
restoration of liberty 272, 282
retention, fingerprints, DNA samples and other
    personal information 119, 423, 446–7, 609
retirement annuities 642, 647, 664
retroactive effects 87, 655–6, 667

retrospective effect 17, 59–71, 87, 149, 649, 660,
    667
    acts not yet complete 70
    application of ss 3 and 4 HRA 65–7
    civil proceedings 64–5
    criminal proceedings 61–4
    and investigations into deaths occurring before 2
        October 2000 69–70
    modified common law 71
    and ongoing violation of Convention rights 68–9
    s 22(4) HRA 67–8
    and sufficiently accessible and precise
        principle 87
    utilisation of pre-HRA position 70–1
retrospective legislation 87, 656, 668
reverse onus 394–5
review, judicial, *see* judicial review
Reynolds privilege, *see* qualified privilege defence
right to know test 575
rights
    absolute 14, 83, 227, 409, 649
    of access to court 340–7
    of appeal 102, 340, 343, 370, 381, 383
    to be released on bail 295–6
    to be tried within a reasonable time 296–7
    to believe 529–30
    children 494, 498, 502, 545–6
    civil, *see* civil rights
    competing 358, 664
    constitutional 27, 549, 564, 629
    democratic 595–7
    to die 182, 200, 236–7
    to die with dignity 200, 236–7
    to a fair trial, *see* fair trial
    to freedom of expression, *see* freedoms, of
        expression
    to liberty and security 269–317
        Art 5(1) 277–93
        depivation of liberty, *see* deprivation, of
            liberty
    to life 80, 102, 105, 107, 181–225, 581, 609
        application 219–25
        deaths in custody 219–21
        deaths in hospital 222–3
        deaths involving the armed forces 223–4
        deaths involving the police 223
        deaths of members of the armed forces 224
        deaths of vulnerable adults 224–5
        definition of life 184–6
        duty to investigate, *see* duty to investigate
        exceptions 225
        intentional deprivation of life 182, 184, 186–
            8, 200, 225
        near deaths in custody 221–2
        positive duty to safeguard life, *see* positive
            duties/obligations, to safeguard life
        and respect for private life 458–9
        scope 183–4
    to manifest, *see* manifestation of belief

prisoners 132, 309, 463, 668
procedural 293, 325, 329, 452, 471–3, 510, 659
property 321, 324, 503, 647, 664
to respect for family life, *see* family life
to respect for home, *see* home
to respect for private life, *see* private life
to silence 360–1
not to be insulted and distressed 590–5
not to be insulted or distressed
   and extreme protest 593
   pre-emptive policing and protest 593–4
   and protest 590–3
   taste, decency and causing offence 594–5
unmarried fathers 473, 636
risk
  assessment 192–3, 241, 305, 452
    police 192, 196
    proper 196
  of death 192, 199, 201–2
  immediate 189, 191, 193, 195–6, 198, 224–5, 233
  significant 65, 127, 191, 233, 242, 246, 283
  of suicide 208, 210, 220, 256–7
road traffic offences 359, 414
  deference 105
  and presumption of innocence 397
role models 565, 568
Russia 261, 267, 577

safeguards, procedural 333, 335, 354, 518–19, 636, 657, 660
safety 190, 192, 195, 217, 225, 308, 315
  public, *see* public safety
same-sex relationships 55, 131, 544, 610–11, 614, 628, 635
  and family life 469–70
samples 415, 423, 446–7, 609, 615, 621
sanctity of life 181–2, 185, 426
satellite litigation 18, 59, 80–2
  civil proceedings 81–2
  criminal proceedings 80–1
Saudi Arabia 20, 28, 73, 346, 578
schools 89, 100–1, 328–9, 532, 537–9, 541, 545–7
scrutiny 8, 19, 23, 124, 616, 622, 634
  anxious 192–3, 196
  public 211, 215, 437, 596
search
  rub-down 424
  stop and 86, 89–90, 275–7, 423, 448–9
  warrants 88
seclusion 89, 242, 454
secret filming 427, 438, 445
secure accommodation orders 275, 286, 331, 339
secure hospitals 89, 112, 197, 219, 288–9, 412, 454–5
secure tenants 520, 523, 525
security 241–2, 332, 339, 341, 344, 346–7, 665; *see also* rights, to liberty and security
  national, *see* national security

service 3, 131, 356, 560, 567, 571, 601–2
security for costs 344
segregation 242, 324, 333, 424, 445
seizure 62, 88, 509, 512, 676
self-determination 200, 426–7, 430, 458
self-employment 429, 643
self-incrimination 13, 27, 105, 320, 348, 358–60, 403
  and fair hearing 358–60
semen 474, 493, 501
sentences 244–7, 259, 282–3, 300–2, 304–5, 322, 389–90
  custodial 420, 450, 453, 470
  determinate 260, 299–301, 315, 636–7
  indeterminate 246, 281, 300–1, 314, 316
  life, *see* life sentences
  tariff periods 43, 167, 246, 280–1, 283, 313–14, 316
sentencing 244–5, 301, 303, 335, 339, 389, 412
  automatic life sentences 43, 127, 244–5, 283, 313
  deference 107
  discrimination 636–7
  extradition 259–60
  fair trial 335
  inhuman or degrading treatment or punishment 244–7
  mandatory life sentences 107, 244, 246, 259, 270, 282–3, 304
  and s 3 HRA 127
  taking into account ill-health 245
  whole life tariff 246–7
separated parents 617, 632
separation 183, 187, 203, 384, 467, 492
separation of powers 109, 342, 383–4, 390
  and independence and impartiality 383–4
serious crimes 245, 283, 296, 301, 446, 482, 636
serious injury 77, 105, 195, 213–15, 221, 263, 266
serious professional misconduct 68, 381, 422
service personnel 78, 186, 196, 201–2, 207–8, 223–4
severity 232, 235, 237, 240, 246, 335, 338
  minimum level of 228–30, 238–9, 244, 252
sewage and drainage management 513–14
sewer flooding 513–14, 659, 664–5
sex discrimination 345, 627–8, 632
  indirect 617
sexual abuse 230, 462, 515
sexual activity 125, 414–15, 438, 569, 583
sexual intercourse 125, 367, 427, 625
sexual offences 176, 368, 451, 584
sexual orientation 262, 540–1, 544, 619–20, 622, 628–30
sexual relationships 81, 125, 367, 417, 569–70
  alleged 81, 106, 125, 368
shareholders 32, 647, 652, 658, 677
sheriffs, temporary 381, 384–5
shorthold tenants 50, 524
significant risk 65, 127, 191, 233, 242, 246, 283

Sikhs 468, 541, 593
silence, right to 360; *see also* self-incrimination
single parent families 492, 677
sisters 183, 210, 216–18, 274, 538
slavery 166, 267
slopping out 242–3, 424
smoking 112, 412, 455, 610, 634
social care 47, 51
social housing 50, 110, 510, 513, 526
social injustice 656, 667
social justice 668
    deference 111
    and property 667–8
social life 427–9, 582
social policy 110, 129, 456, 545, 606, 632, 654
social security 65, 110, 325, 612, 630, 642
social services 52, 326, 420, 463
social ties 425, 485, 488
social workers 203, 287–8, 302, 472
soldiers, *see* service personnel
solicitors 332, 350, 401–2, 405, 408, 446, 661
solitary confinement 273, 424
Somalia 250–1, 258–9, 478, 611, 615, 627, 632
sons 35, 37, 69, 71, 248, 420, 477–9; *see also*
    children
sources 23, 117, 119, 564, 575, 578, 598–601
    journalists 131, 598–601
South Africa 27, 630
sovereign power 103, 326–7
sovereignty, Parliamentary 4, 113–15, 119, 121, 133,
    138, 382
special sources of knowledge 95, 97–8, 483
special treatment 109, 458, 585, 630
spectrum metaphor 243
speedy hearings 44, 311–12
sponsor licences 646
spouses 129, 477, 479, 484, 628; *see also* husbands;
    wives
    foreign 479, 487
    surviving 55–6, 129, 131, 641
Sri Lanka 257, 332, 429, 488
standards 11, 205, 239, 405, 518, 567, 570
    basic 399, 531
    high 163, 375, 570
state agents, *see* agents, of the state
state immunity 131, 345–6
state responsibility 13, 46, 51, 71
    duty to safeguard life 189–90
    illness and medical treatment 236
state support 425, 465, 475
    deference 109
    and family life 475–6
    inhuman or degrading treatment or
        punishment 248–9
    and private life 431–3
statements
    of compatibility 114, 144–5
    defamatory 562, 579
statutory powers 41, 51, 53, 195, 278, 528, 560

statutory tenants 55, 129, 612, 614, 635
stop and search 86, 89–90, 276–7, 423, 448–9
striking out 195, 203, 347–8, 647
    and access to court 347–8
structure of Human Rights Act 1998 10–11
student loans 613, 630
subordinate legislation 89, 113, 119, 132
substantive obligations 69, 190, 201, 206, 208, 224
suicide 86, 182–4, 197–9, 208, 223, 256–7, 545
    immediate risk of 190, 198–9
    risk of 208, 210, 220, 256–7
super-injunctions 585–6
supermax prisons 253, 260
supervision 89, 285–8, 302, 325, 347, 420, 451
    discharge subject to 287–8
    orders 494–5
supplementary instructions 95, 98
support 231–2, 248–9, 429–30, 432–3, 475–6, 522,
    632
    state 109, 248–9, 425, 431, 465, 475
    welfare 80, 425, 432
supremacy, interpretative 112, 145
surveillance, covert 85, 446
surviving spouses 55–6, 129, 131, 641
survivors 56, 129, 612, 614, 623
suspected international terrorists 16, 140, 615, 623,
    637
suspicion 89, 194, 205–6, 284–5, 294, 333, 578–9
    reasonable 89, 270, 276–7, 284, 398, 449
Switzerland 35, 41, 86, 272, 364–5, 493, 500

tagging, electronic 273, 454
tariff periods 43, 167, 246, 280–1, 283, 313–14, 316
taste 86, 551, 569, 583, 594
tax, income 115, 414, 613, 624, 638
tax evasion 337–8
tax relief 642, 647, 673
taxation/taxes 420, 611–12, 631–2, 641, 647, 649,
    662
    and property 672–4
taxpayers 414, 420, 641, 673, 677
telephone conversations 9, 414
television 112, 145, 549, 553, 566, 596, 598
    closed circuit 419
    programmes 415, 586
temporary accommodation 487, 525–6
temporary sheriffs 381, 384–5
tenants 50, 194, 519, 522–4, 526, 618, 620–1
    introductory 504, 524, 526
    public sector 526, 621, 625
    secure 520, 523, 525
    shorthold 50, 524
    statutory 55, 129, 612, 614, 635
termination of proceedings, automatic 170, 378
territorial integrity 83, 560
territorial jurisdiction 35, 72–4
territoriality, principle of 77
terrorism 102, 104–5, 273–4, 398, 422, 581, 584
    and presumption of innocence 398–9

testimony, *see* evidence
Thailand 261, 280
time of war 16, 181
tobacco 229, 574, 639, 651, 674
tort 11, 151, 153–4, 164, 174, 176, 435
torture 131, 227–8, 230–1, 235, 250–3, 322, 346;
    see also inhuman or degrading treatment or
    punishment
    evidence 322, 366
trade unions 35, 540, 643
trafficking, drugs 320, 336–7, 362, 395–6, 511
training 15, 201–2, 204, 218, 224, 242, 312
travellers 504–5, 519, 615–16, 634, 651, 664; *see*
    also gypsies
travelling show-people 504, 516
treaty obligations 43, 257, 443, 481
trial in absentia 368–70
trial process 18, 81, 171, 319, 322, 353, 357
trustees in bankruptcy 284, 295, 647, 664
Turkey 75, 159–62, 197, 204, 211, 227, 402
twins 185, 467, 474, 501
    conjoined 102, 182–3, 185–7, 225

Uganda 24, 258, 481
UK citizens, *see* British citizens
Ukraine 261
ultra vires acts 279, 641
unconscious bias 267
undue delay 373, 429, 475
unfair dismissal 56, 364, 547
unfairness 65, 305, 309, 344, 349, 351, 362
unfit to be tried determination 288–9
United Nations 13, 28, 43
United States 27, 277–8, 341, 346, 489, 491, 552–3
unlawfulness 107, 151, 170, 377–8, 567, 571; *see*
    also lawfulness
unmarried couples 110, 131, 611, 635–6, 638
unmarried fathers 129, 467, 471, 500, 636
    rights 473, 636
unqualified obligation 218, 233, 513
unreasonable delay 376, 378
unrepresented defendants 369, 561
unsound mind 286–9, 299
    lawfulness review 299
urine 397, 455, 542
    samples 542, 547

validity 9–10, 113, 119, 133, 137, 139, 529
values 443, 580–2, 640, 645–6, 648–9, 658–9,
    670–1
VAT 332, 641, 643, 649, 674
vexatious litigants 344–5
victim status 32, 34, 36, 38, 528, 650
    loss of 36–7
victims 31–4, 36–7, 153, 165, 238–9, 267, 463–4
    categories of 33–6
    core public authorities 33
    indirect 34
    loss of victim status 36–7

    non-nationals and persons living outside
        UK 34–5
    potential 32, 34, 48, 511
    representative bodies 35–6
video links 341, 357
video recordings 357, 406
violence 105, 121, 126, 232, 235, 243–4, 262–3
    domestic 263, 496
    physical 235, 545, 581
visas 428, 486, 559, 641; *see also* entry clearance
    and family life 478–80, 486–7
    fees and other barriers 486–7
    historic injustice 487
visual portrayals 57, 414, 461, 568, 582; *see also*
    photographs
voting, convicted prisoners 100
vulnerability 166, 190, 235, 483
vulnerable adults 140, 328, 331–2, 450–1
    deaths of 224–5
    private life 462–4
vulnerable detainees 239–40
vulnerable people 140, 176, 233, 239, 366, 434, 449
    entry clearance 502
    and manifestation of belief 545
    and property 667

wages, minimum 613, 624, 647
waiver 369, 371, 384, 416, 486
    and independence and impartiality 384
    of right to legal assistance 401
war 16, 19, 181, 207, 209, 591–2, 641
    pensions 613, 628
    time of 16, 181
warrants 87, 89, 168, 284, 317, 511, 614
wasted legal costs 155
websites 416, 551, 566, 583, 590, 593
Wednesbury, shift from 92–3
welfare 73, 461–2, 484, 492, 496, 499, 501
    animal 439, 669
    benefits 103, 109, 325, 609–10, 629–31
    children 494–7, 499, 587
    support 80, 425, 432
well-being, economic 440, 442, 444, 480–1, 510,
    512–13, 672
whole life tariff 246–7
widowers 68, 115–16, 118, 613, 624, 629, 638
widows 109, 115–16, 118, 178, 624, 629–30, 638
    bereavement allowance 115, 613, 638
    pensions 109, 613, 624, 629–30
withdrawal of treatment 184–5, 187, 200
witnesses 191–2, 196–7, 308, 310, 351, 369, 406–7
    anonymous 308, 406
    expert 257, 472
    and fair trial 405–7
    identity 194–7
    protection of identity 194–7
women 89, 178, 201, 207, 421, 496, 554
    young 36, 165, 177, 204, 209
working hours 539–40, 547

working life 427–9
workloads 63, 311–12
worship 529–30, 593, 612, 632

young children 43, 230, 453, 474, 490, 495
young offenders institutions 209, 215, 219, 221

Zimbabwe 259, 442, 478, 483, 486
zone of interaction 418–19